T0310577

SQL Server Database Programming with C#

Databases have become an integral part of modern-day life. We live in an information-driven society and database technology has a direct impact on our daily lives. Decisions are routinely made by organizations based on the information collected and stored in the databases. Because databases play such an important role in business and society, database programming is a key skill.

SQL Server Database Programming with C#: Desktop and Web Applications is for college students and software programmers who want to develop practical and commercial skills in database programming with C# or Visual C#.NET 2022 as well as the relational database Microsoft SQL Server 2019. The book explains the practical considerations and applications in database programming with Visual C# 2022 and provides realistic examples and detailed explanations. A direct writing style is combined with real-world examples to provide readers with a clear picture of how to handle database programming issues in the Visual C#.NET 2022 environment.

Highlights include:

- A complete sample database **CSE_DEPT**, built with Microsoft SQL Server 2019 Express, is provided and used for the entire book. Step-by-step, detailed illustrations and descriptions show how to design and build a practical relational database.
- Both fundamental and advanced database-programming techniques are covered to benefit beginning students and experienced programmers.
- An advanced database query technique, LINQ API, which includes LINQ to Objects, LINQ to DataSet, LINQ to SQL, LINQ to Entities and LINQ to XML, is discussed, analyzed, and implemented in actual projects with line-by-line explanations.
- Homework and class projects are provided for each chapter to strengthen and improve students' abilities to learn and understand the topics they studied.
- PowerPoint teaching slides and selected homework solutions help instructors to teach and organize their classes easily and effectively.

Useful and practical, this textbook is an intuitive guide on how to develop and build professional and practical database applications.

SQL Server Database Programming with C#

Desktop and Web Applications

Ying Bai
Johnson C. Smith University,
Charlotte, NC, US

CRC Press is an imprint of the
Taylor & Francis Group, an **informa** business
AN AUERBACH BOOK

Cover Image Credit: Shutterstock.com

First edition published 2024
by CRC Press
2385 NW Executive Center Drive, Suite 320, Boca Raton, FL 33431

and by CRC Press
4 Park Square, Milton Park, Abingdon, Oxon, OX14 4RN

CRC Press is an imprint of Taylor & Francis Group, LLC

ISBN: 978-1-032-33477-6 (hbk)
ISBN: 978-1-032-33487-5 (pbk)
ISBN: 978-1-003-31983-2 (ebk)

DOI: 10.1201/9781003319832

Typeset in Times
by SPi Technologies India Pvt Ltd (Straive)

Access the Support Materials: https://www.routledge.com/9781032334776

This book is dedicated to my wife, Yan Wang,
and my daughter, Xue Bai Cunningham.

Contents

Copyrights and Trademarks

Preface

Databases have become an integral part of our modern-day lives. We are an information-driven society and database technology has a direct impact on our daily lives. Decisions are routinely made by organizations based on the information collected and stored in the databases. For example, a record company may decide to market certain albums in selected regions based on the music preference of teenagers. Similarly, grocery stores display more popular items at eye level and reorders are based on the inventories taken at regular intervals. Other examples include patients' records in hospitals, customers' account information in banks, book orders by the libraries, club memberships, auto parts orders, winter cloth stock by department stores and many others.

In addition to database management systems, in order to effectively apply and implement databases in real industrial or commercial systems, a good Graphic User Interface (GUI) is needed to enable users to access and manipulate their records or data in databases. Visual C#.NET is an ideal candidate to be selected to provide this GUI functionality. Unlike other programming languages, Visual C#.NET is a language that has a number of advantages, such as being easy to learn and easy to understand with relatively shallow learning curves. Beginning with Visual Studio.NET 2003, Microsoft integrated a number of programming languages, such as Visual C++, Visual Basic, C# and Visual J#, into a dynamic model called .NET Framework which makes Internet and Web programming easy and simple .Any language integrated in this model can be used to develop professional and efficient Web applications that can be used to communicate with others via the Internet. ADO.NET and ASP.NET are two of the most important sub-models of .NET Framework. The former provides all components, including the Data Providers, DataSet and DataTable, to access and manipulate data against different databases. The latter provides support to develop Web applications and Web Services in the ASP.NET environment to assistant users to exchange information between clients and servers easily and conveniently.

This book is mainly designed for college students and software programmers who want to develop practical and commercial database programming with C# or Visual C#.NET 2022 and some relational databases, such as Microsoft SQL Server 2019. The book provides a detailed description about the practical considerations and applications in database programming with Visual C# 2022 with authentic examples and detailed explanations. More importantly, a different writing style is developed and implemented in this book, combined with real examples, to provide readers with a clear picture about how to handle the database programming issues in the Visual C#.NET 2022 environment.

The outstanding features of this book include, but are not limited to:

1) A different writing style, which is adopted to try to attract students' or beginning programmers' interesting in learning and developing practical database programs, and to avoid the headache caused by using huge blocks of codes present in the traditional database programming books.
2) A real completed sample database, **CSE_DEPT**, which is built using Microsoft SQL Server 2019 Express is provided and used throughout the entire book. Step-by-step, detailed illustrations and descriptions about how to design and build a practical relational database are provided.
3) Coverage of both fundamental and advanced database-programming techniques to appeal to both beginning students and experienced programmers.
4) An advanced database query technique, LINQ API, which includes LINQ to Objects, LINQ to DataSet, LINQ to SQL, LINQ to Entities and LINQ to XML, is discussed, analyzed and implemented in actual projects with line-by-line explanations.

5) More than 40 real sample database programming projects are covered in the book, with detailed illustrations and explanations to help students to understand key techniques and programming technologies.
6) A popular database system, Microsoft SQL Server 2019Express, is adopted and implemented in the book.
7) Various actual data providers are introduced and discussed in the book. A popular database system, Microsoft SQL Server 2019 Express, is involved in all sample or class projects.
8) Homework and class projects are provided for each chapter to strengthen and improve students' abilities of learning and understanding for topics they studied.
9) PowerPoint teaching slides and selected homework solutions are also provided to help instructors to teach and organize their classes easily and effectively.
10) This volume is a good textbook for college students, and an invaluable reference book for programmers, software engineers and academic researchers.

I sincerely hope that this book will be a useful and practical guide to all of its readers or users. I will be extremely satisfied to know that all of you will be able to develop and build professional and practical database applications with the help of this book.

Acknowledgements

The first and most special thanks to my wife, Yan Wang. I could not have finished this book without her sincere encouragement and support.

Special thanks to Dr. Satish Bhalla, who made great contributions to Chapter 2. Dr. Bhalla is a specialist in database programming and management, especially in SQL Server, Oracle and DB2. Dr. Bhalla spent a lot of time preparing materials for the first part of Chapter 2 and I offer him a great debt of thanks.

Many thanks should also be given to the Acquisition Editor, Mr. John Wyzalek, who has made this book available to the public. This book would not be available to you without John's deep perspective and hard work. The same thanks are extended to the editorial team of this book. Without this team's contributions, the publication of this book would not have been possible.

Last but not least, I would like to express my thanks to all those people, too numerous to mention, who have supported me in the finishing of this book.

About the Author

Dr. Ying Bai is a Professor in the Department of Computer Science and Engineering at Johnson C. Smith University located at Charlotte, North Carolina. His special interests include: artificial intelligence, soft computing, database programming, fuzzy logic controls, automatic and robots controls, as well as robot calibrations. His industrial experience includes positions as software and senior software engineers at companies such as Motorola MMS, Schlumberger ATE Technology, Immix TeleCom, and Lam Research. Since 2003, Dr. Bai has published 19 books with publishers such as Prentice-Hall, CRC Press, Springer, Cambridge University Press and Wiley IEEE Press. He has also published more than 65 academic research papers in IEEE Trans. journals and international conferences. The majority of his books focus on the micro-controller control and programming, fuzzy logic implementations, classical and modern controls, cross-language interface programming, and database programming and applications.

1 Introduction

For many years during my teaching of database programming and Visual C#.NET programming courses at my college, I found that it was not easy to find a good textbook for this topic, meaning that I had to combine a few different professional books together as references to teach those courses. Most of those books are specially designed for programmers or software engineers, and cover a lot of programming strategies and huge blocks of codes. This can be a terrible headache to the college students or to programmers who are new to the C# and database programming. I had to prepare my class presentations and figure out all homework and exercises for my students. I dreamt that one day I would find a good textbook that is suitable for the college students or beginning programmers and helps them to learn and master the database programming with C# both easily and conveniently. Finally, I decided that I needed to do something about this myself.

Another reason for me to have this idea is the job market. As you know, most industrial and commercial companies in the US belong to database applications businesses such as manufactures, banks, hospitals and retails. The majority of these require professional people to develop and build database-related applications, but not database management and design systems. To enable our students to become good candidates for those companies, we need to create a good textbook such as this one.

Unlike most of the database programming books in the current market, which discuss and present the database programming techniques with huge blocks of programming codes from the first page to the last page, this book tries to adopt a different writing style to show readers, especially college students, how to develop professional and practical database programs in C# through the use of Visual Studio.NET Design Tools and Wizards related to ADO.NET 4.5, and to apply codes that are auto-generated by various Wizards. By using this new style, the headache caused by using those huge blocks of programming codes can be removed; instead, a simple and easy way to create database programs using the Design Tools can be taken to attract students' learning interest, and furthermore to enable students to build professional and practical database programming in more efficient and interesting ways.

There are so many different database-programming books available on the market, but rarely can you find a book such as this, which has implemented a novel writing style to attract the students' learning interests in this topic. To meet the needs of some experienced or advanced students or software engineers, the book contains two programming methods: the interesting and easy-to-learn fundamental database programming method – Visual Studio.NET Design Tools and Wizards; and the advanced database programming method – runtime object method. In the second method, all database-related objects are created and applied during or when your project is running by utilizing quite a few of blocks of codes.

1.1 OUTSTANDING FEATURES ABOUT THIS BOOK

1) All programming projects can be run in Microsoft Visual Studio.NET 2022, which is the latest version released by Microsoft Inc.
2) A new writing style has been adopted to try to attract students' or beginning programmers' interests in learning and developing practical database programs, and to avoid the difficulties caused by using huge blocks of codes in the traditional database programming books.
3) Updated database programming tools and components are covered in the book, such as.NET Framework 4.6, LINQ, ADO.NET 4.5 and ASP.NET 4.7, to enable readers to

DOI: 10.1201/9781003319832-1

easily and quickly learn and master advanced techniques in database programming and develop professional and practical database applications.
4) A real completed sample database **CSE_DEPT** with the Microsoft SQL Server 2018 database engine is provided and used throughout the entire book. Step by step, a detailed illustration and description about how to design and build a practical relational database is provided.
5) The book covers both fundamental and advanced database-programming techniques to convenience both beginning students and experienced programmers.
6) Various actual data providers are discussed and implemented, such as OleDb, ODBC and SQL Server data providers. Instead of using the OleDb to access the SQL Server, the real SQL Server data provider is utilized to connect to the Visual C#.NET 2022 directly in order to perform data operations.
7) The book provides additional learning and teaching materials, and those materials enable students to gain a better understanding of what they have learned by doing something themselves. It also allows instructors to organize and prepare their courses easily and rapidly.
8) The volume should be a good textbook for college students, and a good reference book for programmers, software engineers and academic researchers.

1.2 WHO THIS BOOK IS FOR

This book is designed for college students and software programmers who want to develop practical and commercial database programming with C# or Visual C#.NET and relational databases such as Microsoft SQL Server 2019. A fundamental knowledge and understanding of C# and Visual Studio. NET IDE is assumed.

1.3 WHAT THIS BOOK COVERS

Nine chapters are included in this book. The contents of each chapter can be summarized as below:

- Chapter 1 provides an introduction and summary of the whole book.
- Chapter 2 provides a detailed discussion and analysis of the structure and components about relational databases. Some key technologies in developing and designing databases are also given and discussed. The procedure and components used to develop a practical relational database with SQL Server 2019 is analyzed in detail with some real data tables in our sample database **CSE_DEPT**.
- Chapter 3 provides an introduction to the ADO.NET, which includes the architectures, organizations and components of the ADO.NET. Detailed discussions and descriptions are provided in this chapter to give readers both fundamental and practical ideas and pictures about how to use components in ADO.NET to develop professional data-driven applications. Two ADO.NET architectures are discussed to enable users to follow the directions to design and build their preferred projects based on the different organizations of the ADO. NET. Four popular data providers, OleDb, ODBC, SQL Server and Oracle, are also discussed in detail. The basic ideas and implementation examples of DataTable and DataSet are also analyzed and described with some real coding examples.
- Chapter 4 provides a detailed discussion and analysis about the Language-Integrated Query (LINQ), which includes LINQ to Objects, LINQ to DataSet, LINQ to SQL, LINQ to Entities and LINQ to XML. An introduction to LINQ general programming guide is provided in the first part of this chapter. Some popular interfaces widely used in LINQ, such as IEnumerable, IEnumerable(Of T), IQueryable and IQueryable(Of T), and Standard Query Operators (SQO) including the deferred and non-deferred SQO, are discussed in that part. An introduction to LINQ Query is given in the second section of the chapter. Following

this introduction, a detailed discussion and analysis about the LINQ queries that is implemented for different data sources is provided in detail.

- Starting from Chapter 5, the real database programming techniques with Visual C#.NET such as data selection queries are provided and discussed. Two parts are covered in this chapter: Part I contains the detailed descriptions of how to develop professional data-driven applications with the help of the Visual Studio.NET design tools and wizards with some real projects, and this part contains a number of hidden codes that are created by Visual C#.NET automatically when using those design tools and wizards. Therefore, the coding for this part is very simple and easy. Part II of the chapter covers an advanced technique, the runtime object method, which is employed in developing and building professional data-driven applications. Detailed discussions and descriptions about how to build professional and practical database applications using this runtime method are provided and are then combined with some real projects.
- Chapter 6 provides detailed discussions and analyses about three popular data insertion methods with Microsoft SQL Server 2019 database:

  1. Using TableAdapter's DBDirect methods **TableAdapter.Insert()** method
  2. Using the TableAdapter's **Update()** method to insert new records that have already been added into the DataTable in the DataSet
  3. Using the Command object's **ExecuteNonQuery()** method

  This chapter is also divided into two parts: Methods 1 and 2 are related to Visual Studio. NET design tools and wizards and therefore are covered in Part I. The third method relates to the runtime object and it is therefore covered in Part II. Three real projects are used to illustrate how to perform the data insertion into the Microsoft SQL Server 2019 database. Some professional and practical data validation methods are also discussed in this chapter to confirm the data insertion actions.
- Chapter 7 provides discussions and analyses on three popular data updating and deleting methods with four real-world examples:

  1. Using TableAdapter DBDirect methods such as **TableAdapter.Update()** and **Table Adapter.Delete()** to update and delete data directly again the databases.
  2. Using **TableAdapter.Update()** method to update and execute the associated Table Adapter's properties such as UpdateCommand or DeleteCommand to save changes made for the table in the DataSet to the table in the database.
  3. Using the run time object method to develop and execute the Command's method **ExecuteNonQuery()** to update or delete data again the database directly.

  This chapter is also divided into two parts: Methods 1 and 2 are related to Visual Studio. NET design tools and wizards and therefore are covered in Part I. The third method is related to runtime object and it is covered in Part II. Four real projects are used to illustrate how to perform the data updating and deleting against the database Microsoft SQL Server 2019. Some professional and practical data validation methods are also discussed in this chapter to confirm the data updating and deleting actions. The key points in performing the data updating and deleting actions against a relational database, such as the order to execute data updating and deleting between the parent and child tables, are also discussed and analyzed.
- Chapter 8 provides introductions and discussions about the developments and implementations of ASP.NET Web applications in Visual Studio.NET 2022 environment. At the beginning of Chapter 8, a detailed and complete description about the ASP.NET and the .NET Framework is provided, and this part is especially useful and important to students or programmers who do not have any knowledge or background in the Web application developments and implementations. Following the introduction section, a detailed discussion on how to install and configure the environment to develop the ASP.NET Web applications is

provided. Some essential tools such as the Web server and IIS, as well as the installation process of these tools are introduced and discussed in detail. Starting from Section 8.3, the detailed development and building process of ASP.NET Web applications to access databases are discussed with six real Web application projects. The popular database SQL Server 2019 is utilized as the target databases for those development and building processes.

- Chapter 9 provides introductions and discussions about the developments and implementations of ASP.NET Web services in the Visual Studio.NET 2022 environment. A detailed discussion and analysis about the structure and components of the Web services is provided at the beginning of this chapter. One of the most popular databases, Microsoft SQL Server 2019, is discussed and used for three kinds of example Web service projects, which include:

  1. **WebServiceSelect**
  2. **WebServiceInsert**
  3. **WebServiceUpDt**

  Each Web service contains different Web methods that can be used to access different databases and perform the desired data actions such as Select, Insert, Update and Delete via the Internet. To consume those Web services, different Web service client projects are also developed in this chapter. Both Windows-based and Web-based client projects are discussed and built for each kind of Web service listed above. A total of nine projects, including the Web services and the associated Web service clients, are developed in this chapter. All projects have been debugged and tested and can be run in any Windows-compatible operating systems such as Windows 7/8, and Windows 10/11.

1.4 HOW THIS BOOK IS ORGANIZED AND HOW TO USE THIS BOOK

This book is designed for both college students who are new to database programming with C# and professional database programmers who have professional experience on this topic.

Chapters 2–4 provide the fundamentals on database structures and components, ADO.NET and LINQ components. Starting from Chapter 5, and also including Chapters 6 and 7, each chapter is divided into two parts: the fundamental part and the advanced part. The data-driven applications developed with design tools and wizards provided by Visual Studio.NET, which can be considered as the fundamental part, have lower coding loads and therefore they are more suitable to students or programmers who are new to the database programming with Visual C#.NET. Part II contains the runtime object method and it covers a lot of coding developments to perform the different data actions against the database; this method is more flexible and convenient to experienced programmers event a lot of coding jobs is concerned.

Chapters 8 and 9 give a full discussion and analysis about the developments and implementations of ASP.NET Web applications and Web services. These technologies are necessary for students and programmers who want to develop and build Web applications and Web services to access and manipulate data via Internet.

Based on the organization of this book we described above, this book can be used as two categories such as Level I and Level II, which is shown in Figure 1.1.

For undergraduate college students or beginning software programmers, it is highly recommended to learn and understand the contents of Chapters 2, 3 and 4, and Parts I of Chapters 5, 6 and 7 since those are fundamental knowledge and techniques in database programming with Visual C#.NET 2022. Both Chapters 8 and 9 are optional for instructors and their use depends on the time and schedule.

In the case of experienced college students or software programmers who already have some knowledge and techniques in database programming, it is recommended to learn and understand the contents of Part II of Chapters 5, 6 and 7 as well as Chapters 8 and 9 since the runtime data objects

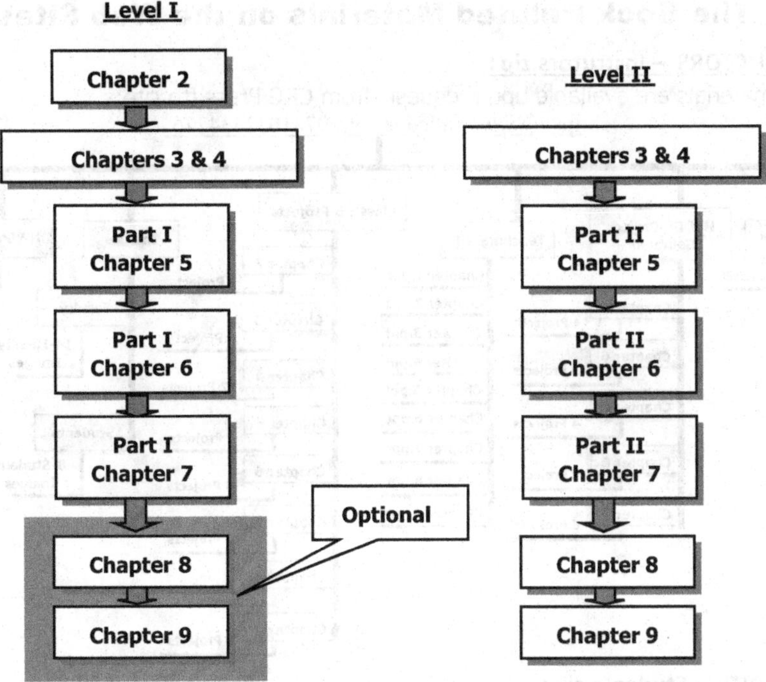

FIGURE 1.1 Two study levels in the book.

method and some sophisticated database programming techniques such as joined-table query and nested stored procedures are discussed and illustrated in those chapters with the use of real examples. In addition, the ASP.NET Web applications and ASP.NET Web services are discussed and analyzed with many real database program examples for SQL Server 2019 database.

1.5 HOW TO USE SOURCE CODES AND SAMPLE DATABASE

All source codes in each project developed in this book are available, and all projects are categorized into the associated chapters that are located at the folder **Class DB Projects** that is under the **Students** folder located on the CRC Press ftp site: https://www.routledge.com/9781032334776. You can copy or download those codes into your computer and run each project as you like. To successfully run those projects, the following conditions must be met:

- Visual Studio.NET 2022 or higher must be installed on your computer.
- The database management system, Microsoft SQL Server 2018 Management Studio 18, must be installed on your computer.
- The sample database, **CSE_DEPT.mdf**, must be installed on your computer in the appropriate folders.
- To run the projects developed in Chapters 8 and 9, in addition to the conditions listed above, an Internet Information Services (IIS), such as FrontPage Server Extension 2000 or 2002, must be installed in your computer. This works as a pseudo server for those projects.

All related teaching and learning materials, including the sample databases, example projects, homework solutions, faculty and student images as well as sample Windows forms and Web pages, can be found from the associated folders, **Instructors** or **Students**, located on the CRC Press ftp site, as shown in Figure 1.2.

The Book Related Materials on the Web Sites

FOR INSTRUCTORS – Instrutors.zip:

Teaching materials are available upon request from CRC Press ftp site:

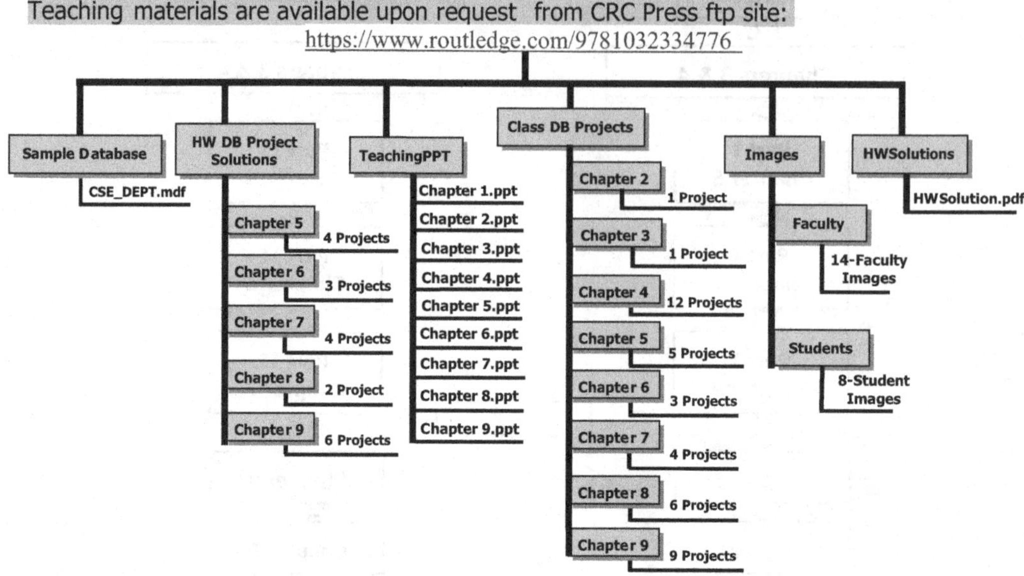

FOR STUDENTS – Students.zip:

Learning materials are free to access via the CRC Press ftp site:

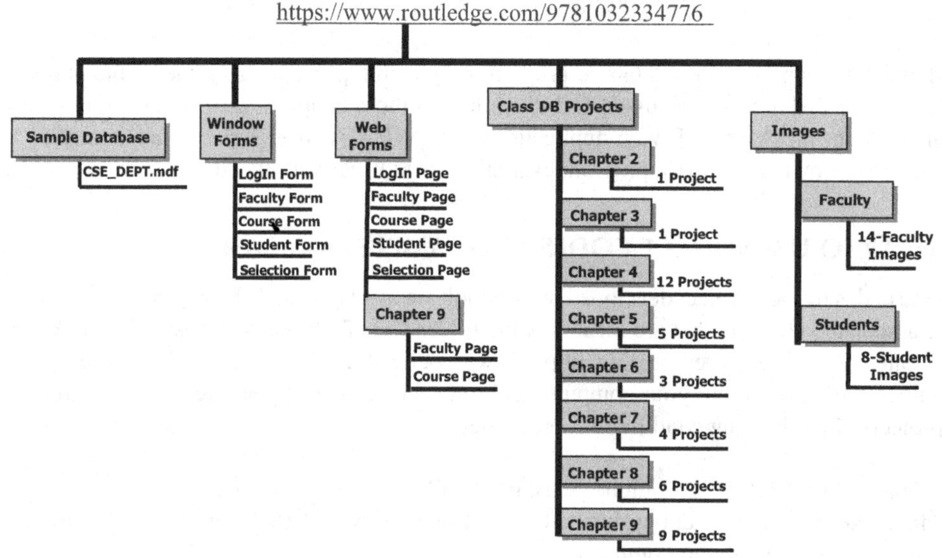

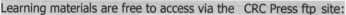

FIGURE 1.2 Book related materials on web site.

These materials are categorized and stored in different folders based on the teaching purpose (for instructors) and learning purpose (for students):

1. **Sample Database** Folder: Contains our sample database, **CSE_DEPT.mdf** (SQL Server 2019). Refer to **Appendix D** on the CRC Press ftp site to get details in how to use this database for your applications or sample projects.

2. **Class DB Projects** Folder: Contains all class projects developed in the book. Projects are categorized and stored in the different Chapter subfolder based on the book chapter sequence. Readers can directly use the codes and GUIs of those projects by downloading them from the **Class DB Projects** folder on the CRC Press ftp site.
3. **Images** Folder: Two subfolders are under that folder: **Images\Faculty** and **Images\Students**. Each of these contains all sample faculty and student image files used in all sample projects in the book. Readers can copy and paste those image files to their projects to use them.
4. **Window Forms** Folder: Contains all sampled Windows-based Forms developed and implemented in all class projects in the book. Readers can use those Forms by copying and pasting them into their real projects.
5. **Web Forms** Folder: Contains all sampled Web-based Pages developed and implemented in all class projects in the book. Two modified pages, **Faculty** and **Course**, are located in the **Chapter 9** subfolder. Readers can use those pages by adding them into their real projects.
6. **TeachingPPT** Folder: Contains all MS-PPT teaching slides for all chapters.
7. **HWSolutions** Folder: Contains selected solutions for the homework exercises developed and used in the book. The solutions are categorized and stored at the different Chapter subfolder based on the book chapter sequence.
8. **HW DB Project Solutions** Folder: Contains all exercises solutions and is stored based on the book chapter sequence.

Folders 1–5 belong to learning materials for students, and therefore they are located at the sub-folder **Students** on the CRC Press ftp site. Folders 1–3 and 6–8 belong to teaching materials for instructors, they are located at the sub-folder **Instructors** at the same site (password-protected) and available upon requests by instructors.

1.6 INSTRUCTORS' AND CUSTOMERS' SUPPORT

The teaching materials for all chapters have been extracted and represented by a sequence of Microsoft Power Point files, one file for one chapter. The interested instructors can find them from the folder **TeachingPPT**, which is located in a sub-folder **Instructors** at the CRC Press ftp site (https://www.routledge.com/9781032334776) and those instructor materials are available upon request from the book's listing on that site (password protected).

A selected homework solution is also available upon request from the site. E-mail support is available to readers of this book. When you send e-mail to us, please provide the following information:

- The detailed description about your problems, including the error message and debug message as well as the error or debug number if it is provided.
- Your name and company name.
- Please send all questions to the e-mail address: ybai@jcsu.edu.

Detailed structure and distribution of all book-related materials is on the CRC Press ftp site, including the teaching and learning materials, are shown in Figure 1.2.

2 Introduction to Databases

Databases have become an integral part of our modern-day life. Today we are an information-driven society. Large amounts of data are generated, analyzed and converted into different information at each moment. One recent example of biological data generation is the Human Genome project, which was jointly sponsored by the Department of Energy (DOE) and the National Institute of Health (NIH). Many countries participated in this venture, which took place over a period of more than ten years. The project was a tremendous success. It was completed in 2003 and resulted in the generation of a huge amount of genome data, which is currently stored in databases around the world. The scientists will be analyzing this data continuously in the years to come.

Database technology has a direct impact on our daily lives. Decisions are routinely made by organizations based on the information collected and stored in the databases. A record company, for example, may decide to market certain albums in selected regions based on the music preference of teenagers. Grocery stores display more popular items at eye level and reorders are based on the inventories taken at regular intervals. Other examples include book orders by the libraries, club memberships, auto part orders, winter cloth stock by department stores and many others.

Database management programs have been in existence since the 1960s. However, it was not until the 1970s when E. F. Codd proposed the then revolutionary Relational Data Model that database technology really took off. In the early 1980s it received a further boost with the arrival of personal computers and microcomputer-based data management programs like dBase II (later followed by dBase III, and IV). Today we have a plethora of vastly improved programs for PCs and mainframe computers, including Microsoft Access, SQL Server, IBM DB2, Oracle, Sequel Server, MySQL and others.

This chapter covers the basic concepts of database design followed by implementation of a specific relational database to illustrate the concepts discussed here. The sample database, **CSE_DEPT**, is used as a running example. The database creation is shown in detail by using Microsoft Access and Microsoft SQL Server. The topics discussed in this chapter include:

- What are databases and database programs?
    - File Processing System
    - Integrated Databases
- Various approaches to developing a Database
- Relational Data Model (RDM) and Entity-Relationship Model (ER)
- Identifying Keys
    - Primary Keys, Foreign Keys and Referential Integrity
- Defining Relationships
- Normalizing the Data
- Implementing the Relational Sample Database
    - Create Microsoft SQL Server 2019 Express Sample Database

2.1 WHAT ARE DATABASES AND DATABASE PROGRAMS?

A modern-day database is a structured collection of data which is stored in a computer. The term structured implies that each record in the database is stored in a certain format. For example, all entries in a phone book are arranged in a similar fashion: Each entry contains a name, an address, and a telephone number of a subscriber. This information can be queried and manipulated by database programs. The

DOI: 10.1201/9781003319832-2

data retrieved in answer to queries become information that can be used to make decisions. The databases may consist of a single table or related multiple tables. The computer programs used to create, manage and query databases are known as a DataBase Management Systems (DBMS). Just as is the case with databases the DBMS's vary in complexity. Depending on the need of a user one can use either a simple application or a robust program. Some examples of these programs were given earlier.

2.1.1 File Processing System

File Processing System (FPS) is a precursor of the integrated database approach. The records for a particular application are stored in a file. An application program is needed to retrieve or manipulate data in this file. Thus, various departments in an organization will have their own file processing systems with their individual programs to store and retrieve data. The data in various files may be duplicated and unavailable to other applications. This causes redundancy and may lead to inconsistency, meaning that various files that supposedly contain the same information may actually contain different data values. Thus, the duplication of data creates problems with data integrity. Moreover, it is difficult to provide access to multiple users with the file processing systems without granting them access to the respective application programs, which manipulate the data in those files.

The FPS may be advantageous under certain circumstances. For example, if data is static and a simple application will solve the problem, a more expensive DBMS is not needed. For example, in a small business environment you want to keep track of the inventory of the office equipment purchased only once or twice a year. The data can be kept in an Excel spreadsheet and manipulated with ease from time to time. This avoids the need to purchase an expensive database program, and to hire a knowledgeable database administrator. Before the DBMS's became popular, the data was kept in files and application programs were developed to delete, insert or modify records in the files since specific application programs were developed for specific data. These programs lasted for months or years before modifications were necessitated by business needs.

2.1.2 Integrated Databases

A better alternative to a file processing system is an integrated database approach. In this environment all data belonging to an organization is stored in a single database. The database is not a mere collection of files; there is a relation between the files. Integration implies a logical relationship, usually provided through a common column in the tables. The relationships are also stored within the database. A set of sophisticated programs known as a Database Management System (DBMS) is used to store, access and manipulate the data in the database. The details of data storage and maintenance are hidden from the user. The user interacts with the database through the DBMS. A user may interact either directly with the DBMS or via a program written in a programming language such as Visual C++, Java, Visual Basic or Visual C#. Only the DBMS can access the database. Large organizations employ Database Administrators (DBA's) to design and maintain large databases.

There are many advantages to using an integrated database approach rather than a file processing approach:

1) **Data sharing:** The data in the database is available to a large numbers of users who can access the data simultaneously and create reports, manipulate the data given proper authorization and rights.
2) **Minimizing data redundancy:** Since all the related data exists in a single database, there is a minimal need of data duplication. The duplication is needed to maintain relationship between various data items.
3) **Data consistency and data integrity:** Reducing data redundancy will lead to data consistency. Since data is stored in a single database, enforcing data integrity becomes much easier. Furthermore, the inherent functions of the DBMS can be used to enforce the integrity with minimum programming.

4) **Enforcing standards:** DBAs are charged with enforcing standards in an organization. DBA takes into account the needs of various departments and balances it against the overall need of the organization. DBA defines various rules such as documentation standards, naming conventions, update and recovery procedures etc. It is relatively easy to enforce these rules in a Database System, since it is a single set of programs which is always interacting with the data files.
5) **Improving security:** Security is achieved through various means such as controlling access to the database through passwords, providing various levels of authorizations, data encryption, providing access to restricted views of the database etc.
6) **Data independence:** Providing data independence is a major objective for any database system. Data independence implies that even if the physical structure of a database changes the applications are allowed to access the database as before the changes were implemented. In other words the applications are immune to the changes in the physical representation and access techniques.

The downsides of using an integrated database approach are mainly concerned with the exorbitant costs associated with it. The hardware, the software, and maintenance are expensive. Providing security, concurrency, integrity, and recovery may add further to this cost. Furthermore, since DBMS consists of a complex set of programs, trained personnel are needed to maintain it.

2.2 DEVELOP A DATABASE

Database development process may follow a classical Systems Development Life Cycle.

1) **Problem Identification** – Interview the user, identify user requirements. Perform a preliminary analysis of user needs.
2) **Project Planning** – Identify alternative approaches to solving the problem. Does the project need a database? If so, define the problem. Establish the scope of the project.
3) **Problem Analysis** – Identify specifications for the problem. Confirm the feasibility of the project. Specify detailed requirements.
4) **Logical Design** – Delineate detailed functional specifications. Determine screen designs, report layout designs, data models etc.
5) **Physical Design** – Develop physical data structures.
6) **Implementation** – Select DBMS. Convert data to conform to DBMS requirements. Code programs; perform testing.
7) **Maintenance** – Continue program modification until desired results are achieved.

An alternative approach to developing a database is through a phased process which will include designing a conceptual model of the system that will imitate the real-world operation. It should be flexible and alter when the information in the database changes. Furthermore, it should not be dependent upon the physical implementation. This process consists of the following phases:

1) **Planning and Analysis** – This phase is roughly equivalent to the first three steps mentioned above in the Systems Development Life Cycle. This includes requirement specifications, evaluating alternatives, determining input, output, and reports to be generated.
2) **Conceptual Design** – Choose a data model and develop a conceptual schema based on the requirement specification that was laid out in the planning and analysis phase. This conceptual design focuses on how the data will be organized without having to worry about the specifics of the tables, keys and attributes. Identify the entities that will represent tables in the database; identify attributes that will represent fields in a table; and identify each entity attribute relationship. Entity-relationship diagrams provide a good representation of the conceptual design.

3) **Logical Design** – Conceptual design is transformed into a logical design by creating a roadmap of how the database will look before actually creating the database. The data model is identified; usually, it is the relational model. Define the tables (entities) and fields (attributes). Identify primary and foreign key for each table. Define relationships between the tables.
4) **Physical Design** – Develop physical data structures; specify file organization, and data storage etc. Take into consideration the availability of various resources, including hardware and software. This phase overlaps with the implementation phase. It involves the programming of the database taking into account the limitations of the DBMS used.
5) **Implementation** – Choose the DBMS that will fulfill the user needs. Implement the physical design. Perform testing. Modify if necessary or until the database functions satisfactorily.

2.3 SAMPLE DATABASE

We will use a sample database CSE_DEPT to illustrate some essential database concepts. Figures 2.1–2.5 show sample data tables stored in this database.

user_name	pass_word	faculty_id	student_id
abrown	america	B66750	
ajade	tryagain		A97850
awoods	smart		A78835
banderson	birthday	A52990	
bvalley	see		B92996
dangles	tomorrow	A77587	
hsmith	try		H10210
terica	excellent		T77896
jhenry	test	H99118	
jking	goodman	K69880	
dbhalla	india	B86590	
sjohnson	jermany	J33486	
ybai	come	B78880	

FIGURE 2.1 LogIn table.

faculty_id	faculty_name	title	office	phone	college	email	fimage
A52990	Black Anderson	Professor	MTC-218	750-378-9987	Virginia Tech	banderson@college.edu	NULL
A77587	Debby Angles	Associate Professor	MTC-320	750-330-2276	University of Chicago	dangles@college.edu	NULL
B66750	Alice Brown	Assistant Professor	MTC-257	750-330-6650	University of Florida	abrown@college.edu	NULL
B78880	Ying Bai	Associate Professor	MTC-211	750-378-1148	Florida Atlantic University	ybai@college.edu	NULL
B86590	Davis Bhalla	Associate Professor	MTC-214	750-378-1061	University of Notre Dame	dbhalla@college.edu	NULL
H99118	Jeff Henry	Associate Professor	MTC-336	750-330-8650	Ohio State University	jhenry@college.edu	NULL
J33486	Steve Johnson	Distinguished Professor	MTC-118	750-330-1116	Harvard University	sjohnson@college.edu	NULL
K69880	Jenney King	Professor	MTC-324	750-378-1230	East Florida University	jking@college.edu	NULL

FIGURE 2.2 Faculty table.

course_id	course	credit	classroom	schedule	enrollment	faculty_id
CSC-131A	Computers in Society	3	MTC-109	M-W-F: 9:00-9:55 AM	28	A52990
CSC-131B	Computers in Society	3	MTC-114	M-W-F: 9:00-9:55 AM	20	B66750
CSC-131C	Computers in Society	3	MTC-109	T-H: 11:00-12:25 PM	25	A52990
CSC-131D	Computers in Society	3	MTC-109	M-W-F: 9:00-9:55 AM	30	B86590
CSC-131E	Computers in Society	3	MTC-301	M-W-F: 1:00-1:55 PM	25	B66750
CSC-131I	Computers in Society	3	MTC-109	T-H: 1:00-2:25 PM	32	A52990
CSC-132A	Introduction to Programming	3	MTC-303	M-W-F: 9:00-9:55 AM	21	J33486
CSC-132B	Introduction to Programming	3	MTC-302	T-H: 1:00-2:25 PM	21	B78880
CSC-230	Algorithms & Structures	3	MTC-301	M-W-F: 1:00-1:55 PM	20	A77587
CSC-232A	Programming I	3	MTC-305	T-H: 11:00-12:25 PM	28	B66750
CSC-232B	Programming I	3	MTC-303	T-H: 11:00-12:25 PM	17	A77587
CSC-233A	Introduction to Algorithms	3	MTC-302	M-W-F: 9:00-9:55 AM	18	H99118
CSC-233B	Introduction to Algorithms	3	MTC-302	M-W-F: 11:00-11:55 AM	19	K69880
CSC-234A	Data Structure & Algorithms	3	MTC-302	M-W-F: 9:00-9:55 AM	25	B78880
CSC-234B	Data Structure & Algorithms	3	MTC-114	T-H: 11:00-12:25 PM	15	J33486
CSC-242	Programming II	3	MTC-303	T-H: 1:00-2:25 PM	18	A52990
CSC-320	Object Oriented Programming	3	MTC-301	T-H: 1:00-2:25 PM	22	B66750
CSC-331	Applications Programming	3	MTC-109	T-H: 11:00-12:25 PM	28	H99118
CSC-333A	Computer Arch & Algorithms	3	MTC-301	M-W-F: 10:00-10:55 AM	22	A77587
CSC-333B	Comp Arch & Algorithms	3	MTC-302	T-H: 11:00-12:25 PM	15	A77587
CSC-335	Internet Programming	3	MTC-303	M-W-F: 1:00-1:55PM	25	B66750
CSC-432	Discrete Algorithms	3	MTC-206	T-H: 11:00-12:25 PM	20	B86590
CSC-439	Database Systems	3	MTC-206	M-W-F: 1:00-1:55 PM	18	B86590
CSE-138A	Introduction to CSE	3	MTC-301	T-H: 1:00-2:25 PM	15	A52990
CSE-138B	Introduction to CSE	3	MTC-109	T-H: 1:00-2:25 PM	35	J33486
CSE-330	Digital Logic Circuits	3	MTC-305	M-W-F: 9:00-9:55 AM	26	K69880
CSE-332	Foundation of Semiconductor	3	MTC-305	T-H: 1:00-2:25 PM	24	K69880
CSE-334	Elec. Measurement & Design	3	MTC-212	T-H: 11:00-12:25 PM	25	H99118
CSE-430	Bioinformatics in Computer	3	MTC-206	Thu: 9:30-11:00 AM	16	B86590
CSE-432	Analog Circuits Design	3	MTC-309	M-W-F: 2:00-2:55 PM	18	K69880
CSE-433	Digital Signal Processing	3	MTC-206	T-H: 2:00-3:25 PM	18	H99118
CSE-434	Advanced Electronic Systems	3	MTC-213	M-W-F: 1:00-1:55 PM	26	B78880
CSE-436	Automatic Control & Design	3	MTC-305	M-W-F: 10:00-10:55 AM	29	J33486
CSE-437	Operating Systems	3	MTC-303	T-H: 1:00-2:25 PM	17	A77587
CSE-438	Adv Logic & Microprocessor	3	MTC-213	M-W-F: 11:00-11:55 AM	35	B78880
CSE-439	Special Topics in CSE	3	MTC-206	M-W-F: 10:00-10:55 AM	22	J33486

FIGURE 2.3 Course table.

student_id	student_name	gpa	credits	major	schoolYear	email	simage
A78835	Andrew Woods	3.26	108	Computer Science	Senior	awoods@college.edu	NULL
A97850	Ashly Jade	3.57	116	Info System Engineering	Junior	ajade@college.edu	NULL
B92996	Blue Valley	3.52	102	Computer Science	Senior	bvalley@college.edu	NULL
H10210	Holes Smith	3.87	78	Computer Engineering	Sophomore	hsmith@college.edu	NULL
T77896	Tom Erica	3.95	127	Computer Science	Senior	terica@college.edu	NULL

FIGURE 2.4 Student table.

s_course_id	student_id	course_id	credit	major
1000	H10210	CSC-131D	3	CE
1001	B92996	CSC-132A	3	CS/IS
1002	T77896	CSC-335	3	CS/IS
1003	A78835	CSC-331	3	CE
1004	H10210	CSC-234B	3	CE
1005	T77896	CSC-234A	3	CS/IS
1006	B92996	CSC-233A	3	CS/IS
1007	A78835	CSC-132A	3	CE
1008	A78835	CSE-432	3	CE
1009	A78835	CSE-434	3	CE
1010	T77896	CSC-439	3	CS/IS
1011	H10210	CSC-132A	3	CE
1012	H10210	CSC-331	2	CE
1013	A78835	CSC-335	3	CE
1014	A78835	CSE-438	3	CE
1015	T77896	CSC-432	3	CS/IS
1016	A97850	CSC-132B	3	ISE
1017	A97850	CSC-234A	3	ISE
1018	A97850	CSC-331	3	ISE
1019	A97850	CSC-335	3	ISE
1020	T77896	CSE-439	3	CS/IS
1021	B92996	CSC-230	3	CS/IS
1022	A78835	CSE-332	3	CE
1023	B92996	CSE-430	3	CE
1024	T77896	CSC-333A	3	CS/IS
1025	H10210	CSE-433	3	CE
1026	H10210	CSE-334	3	CE
1027	B92996	CSC-131C	3	CS/IS
1028	B92996	CSC-439	3	CS/IS

FIGURE 2.5 StudentCourse table.

The data in CSE_DEPT database is stored in five tables – LogIn, Faculty, Course, Student, and StudentCourse. A table consists of row and columns (Figure 2.6). A row represents a record and the column represents a field. A row is called a tuple and a column is called an attribute. For example, Student table has seven columns or fields – student_id, name, gpa, major, schoolYear, and email. It has five records or rows.

2.3.1 Relational Data Model

A data model is like a blueprint for developing a database. It describes the structure of the database and various data relationships and constraints on the data. This information is used in building tables, keys and defining relationships. The relational model implies that a user perceives the database as made up of relations, a database jargon for tables. It is imperative that all data elements in the tables are represented correctly. In order to achieve these goals, designers use a range of tools. The most commonly used tool is the Entity-Relationship Model (ER). A well-planned model will give consistent results and will allow changes if needed later on. The following section elaborates further on the ER Model.

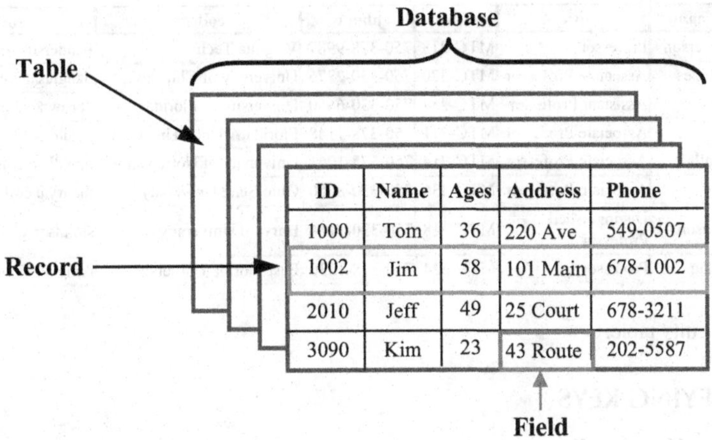

FIGURE 2.6 Records and fields in a table.

2.3.2 Entity-Relationship Model (ER)

The Entity-Relationship (ER) model was first proposed and developed by Peter Chen in 1976. Since then Charles Bachman and James Martin have added some refinements. The model was designed to communicate the database design in the form of a conceptual schema. It is based on the perception that the real world is made up of entities, their attributes, and relationships. The ER model is graphically depicted in terms of Entity-Relationship diagrams (ERD). ERDs are a major modeling tool; they graphically describe the logical structure of the database. They can be used with ease to construct the relational tables and are a good vehicle for communicating the database design to either the end user or a developer. The three major components of ERD are entities, relationships, and attributes.

Entities: An entity is a data object, either real or abstract, about which we want to collect information. For example, we may want to collect information about a person, a place, or a thing. An entity in an ER diagram translates into a table. It should preferably be referred to as an entity set. Some common examples are departments, courses, students. A single occurrence of an entity is an instance. There are four entities in the CSE_Dept database: LogIn, Faculty, Course, and Student. Each entity is translated into a table with the same name. For example, an instance of the Faculty entity will be Alice Brown and her attributes.

Relationships: A database is made up of related entities. There is a natural association between the entities; these are referred to as relationships. For example,

- Students take courses
- Departments offer certain courses
- Employees are assigned to departments

The number of occurrences of one entity associated with single occurrence of a related entity is referred to as **cardinality**.

Attributes: Each entity has properties or values called attributes associated with it. The attributes of an entity map into fields in a table. *Database Processing* is one attribute of an entity called *Courses*. The domain of an attribute is a set of all possible values from which an attribute can derive its value.

faculty_id	faculty_name	title	office	phone	college	email	fimage
A52990	Black Anderson	Professor	MTC-218	750-378-9987	Virginia Tech	banderson@college.edu	NULL
A77587	Debby Angles	Associate Professor	MTC-320	750-330-2276	University of Chicago	dangles@college.edu	NULL
B66750	Alice Brown	Assistant Professor	MTC-257	750-330-6650	University of Florida	abrown@college.edu	NULL
B78880	Ying Bai	Associate Professor	MTC-211	750-378-1148	Florida Atlantic University	ybai@college.edu	NULL
B86590	Davis Bhalla	Associate Professor	MTC-214	750-378-1061	University of Notre Dame	dbhalla@college.edu	NULL
H99118	Jeff Henry	Associate Professor	MTC-336	750-330-8650	Ohio State University	jhenry@college.edu	NULL
J33486	Steve Johnson	Distinguished Professor	MTC-118	750-330-1116	Harvard University	sjohnson@college.edu	NULL
K69880	Jenney King	Professor	MTC-324	750-378-1230	East Florida University	jking@college.edu	NULL

FIGURE 2.7 Faculty table.

2.4 IDENTIFYING KEYS

2.4.1 Primary Key and Entity Integrity

An attribute that uniquely identifies one and only one instance of an entity is called a primary key. Sometimes a primary key consists of a combination of attributes. It is referred to as a *composite key*. The *entity integrity rule* states that no attribute that is a member of the primary (composite) key may accept a null value.

A **faculty_id** may serve as a primary key for the Faculty entity, assuming that all faculty members have been assigned a unique FacultyID. However, caution must be exercised when picking an attribute as a primary key. Last Name may not make a good primary key because a department is likely to have more than one person with the same last name. Primary keys for the CSE_DEPT database are shown in Figure 2.7.

Primary keys provide a tuple-level addressing mechanism in the relational databases. Once you define an attribute as a primary key for an entity, the DBMS will enforce the uniqueness of the primary key. Inserting a duplicate value for a primary key field will fail.

2.4.2 Candidate Key

There can be more than one attribute which uniquely identifies an instance of an entity. These are referred to as *candidate keys*. Any one of them can serve as a primary key. For example, ID Number as well as Social Security Number may make a suitable primary key. Candidate keys that are not used as primary key are called *alternate keys*.

2.4.3 Foreign Keys and Referential Integrity

Foreign keys are used to create relationships between tables. A foreign key is an attribute in one table whose values are required to match those of primary key in another table. Foreign keys are created to enforce ***referential integrity***, which states that you may not add a record to a table containing a foreign key unless there is a corresponding record in the related table to which it is logically linked. Furthermore, the referential integrity rule also implies that every value of a foreign key in a table must either match the primary key of a related table or be null. MS Access also makes provision for cascade update and cascade delete, which implies that changes made in one of the related tables will be reflected in the other table.

Consider two tables, Course and Faculty, in the sample database, CSE_DEPT. The Course table has a foreign key entitled faculty_id, which is primary key in the Faculty table. The two tables are thus logically related through the **faculty_id** link. Referential integrity rules imply that we may not add a record to the Course table with a faculty_id which is not listed in the Faculty table. In other words, there must be a logical link between the two related tables. Secondly, if we change or delete a **faculty_id** in the Faculty table this must be reflected in the Course table, meaning that all records in the Course table must be modified using a cascade update or cascade delete (Figure 2.8).

course_id	course	faculty_id
CSC-132A	Introduction to Programming	J33486
CSC-132B	Introduction to Programming	B78880
CSC-230	Algorithms & Structures	A77587
CSC-232A	Programming I	B66750
CSC-232B	Programming I	A77587
CSC-233A	Introduction to Algorithms	H99118
CSC-233B	Introduction to Algorithms	K69880
CSC-234A	Data Structure & Algorithms	B78880

faculty_id	faculty_name	office
A52990	Black Anderson	MTC-218
A77587	Debby Angles	MTC-320
B66750	Alice Brown	MTC-257
B78880	Ying Bai	MTC-211
B86590	Davis Bhalla	MTC-214
H99118	Jeff Henry	MTC-336
J33486	Steve Johnson	MTC-118
K69880	Jenney King	MTC-324

FIGURE 2.8 Course (partial data shown) Faculty (partial data shown).

2.5 DEFINE RELATIONSHIPS

2.5.1 Connectivity

Connectivity refers to the types of relationships that entities can have. Basically, this can be *one-to-one, one-to-many, and many-to-many*. In ER diagrams these are indicated by placing 1, M or N at one of the two ends of the relationship diagram. Figures 2.9–2.12 illustrates the use of this notation.

- A ***one-to-one*** **(1:1)** relationship occurs when one instance of entity A is related to only one instance of entity B. For example, **user_name** in the LogIn table and **user_name** in the Student table (Figure 2.9).
- A ***one-to-many*** **(1:M)** relationship occurs when one instance of entity A is associated with zero, one, or many instances of entity B. However, entity B is associated with only one instance of entity A. For example, one department can have many faculty members; each faculty member is assigned to only one department. In the CSE_DEPT database, a one-to-many relationship is represented by **faculty_id** in the Faculty table and **faculty_id** in the Course table, **student_id** in the Student table and **student_id** in the StudentCourse table, **course_id** in the Course table and **course_id** in the StudentCourse table (Figure 2.10).
- A ***many-to-many*** **(M:N)** relationship occurs when one instance of entity A is associated with zero, one, or many instances of entity B. And also when one instance of entity B is associated with zero, one, or many instance of entity A. For example, a student may take many courses and one course may be taken by more than one student, as shown in Figure 2.11.

In CSE_DEPT database, a many-to-many relationship can be realized by using the third table. For example, in this case, the StudentCourse that works as the third table, set a many-to-many relationship between the Student and the Course tables.

LogIn

user_name	pass_word
ajade	tryagain
awoods	smart
bvalley	see
hsmith	try
terica	excellent

Student

user_name	gpa	credits	student_id
ajade	3.26	108	A97850
awoods	3.57	116	A78835
bvalley	3.52	102	B92996
hsmith	3.87	78	H10210
terica	3.95	127	J77896

FIGURE 2.9 One-to-one relationship in the LogIn and Student tables.

Faculty

faculty_id	faculty_name	office
A52990	Black Anderson	MTC-218
A77587	Debby Angles	MTC-320
B66750	Alice Brown	MTC-257
B78880	Ying Bai	MTC-211
B86590	Davis Bhalla	MTC-214
H99118	Jeff Henry	MTC-336
J33486	Steve Johnson	MTC-118
K69880	Jenney King	MTC-324

Course

course_id	course	faculty_id
CSC-132A	Introduction to Programming	J33486
CSC-132B	Introduction to Programming	B78880
CSC-230	Algorithms & Structures	A77587
CSC-232A	Programming I	B66750
CSC-232B	Programming I	A77587
CSC-233A	Introduction to Algorithms	H99118
CSC-233B	Introduction to Algorithms	K69880
CSC-234A	Data Structure & Algorithms	B78880

FIGURE 2.10 One-to-many relationship between faculty and course tables.

Student

student_id	student_name	gpa	credits
A78835	Andrew Woods	3.26	108
A97850	Ashly Jade	3.57	116
B92996	Blue Valley	3.52	102
H10210	Holes Smith	3.87	78
T77896	Tom Erica	3.95	127

Course

course_id	course	faculty_id
CSC-132A	Introduction to Programming	J33486
CSC-132B	Introduction to Programming	B78880
CSC-230	Algorithms & Structures	A77587
CSC-232A	Programming I	B66750
CSC-232B	Programming I	A77587
CSC-233A	Introduction to Algorithms	H99118

StudentCourse

s_course_id	student_id	course_id	credit	major
1000	H10210	CSC-131D	3	CE
1001	B92996	CSC-132A	3	CS/IS
1002	T77896	CSC-335	3	CS/IS
1003	A78835	CSC-331	3	CE
1004	H10210	CSC-234B	3	CE
1005	T77896	CSC-234A	3	CS/IS
1006	B92996	CSC-233A	3	CS/IS

FIGURE 2.11 Many-to-Many relationship between student and course tables.

This database design assumes that the course table only contains courses taught by all faculty members in this department for one semester. Therefore, each course can only be taught by a unique faculty. If one wants to develop a Course table that contains courses taught by all faculty in more than one semester, the third table, say FacultyCourse table, should be created to set up a many-to-many relationship between the Faculty and the Course table since one course may be taught by the different faculty for the different semester.

The relationships in CSE_DEPT database are summarized in Figure 2.12.

Database name: **CSE_DEPT**

The five entities are:

- LogIn
- Faculty
- Course
- Student
- StudentCourse

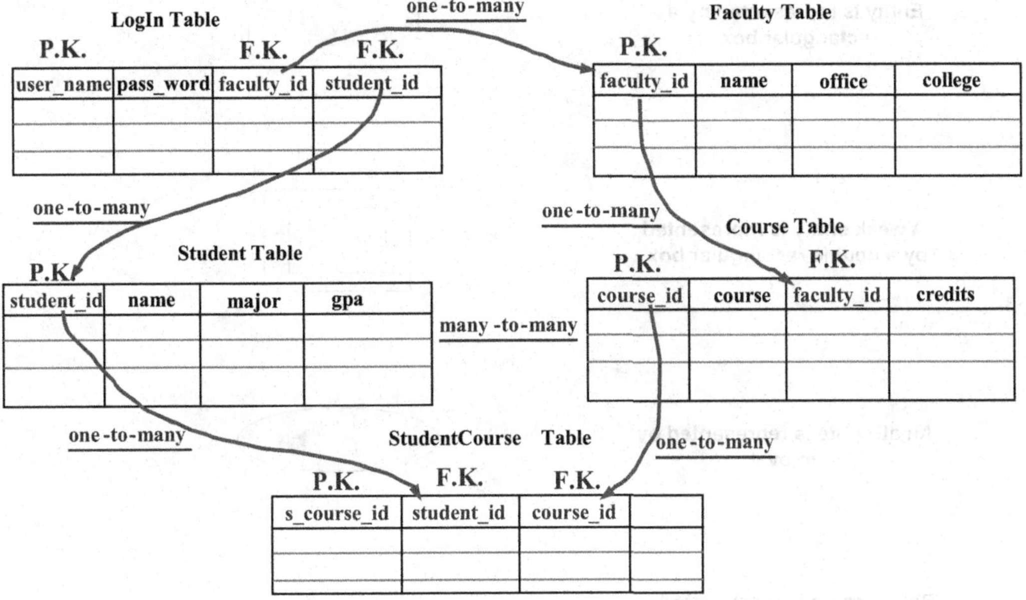

FIGURE 2.12 Relationships in CSE_DEPT database.

The relationships between these entities are shown below. **P.K.** and **F.K** represent the primary key and the foreign key, respectively.

Figure 2.13 displays the Microsoft Access relationships diagram among various tables in CSE_Dept database. One-to-many relationships is indicated by placing 1 at one end of the link and ∞ at the other. The many-to-many relationship between the Student and the Course table was broken down to two one-to-many relationships by creating a new StudentCourse table.

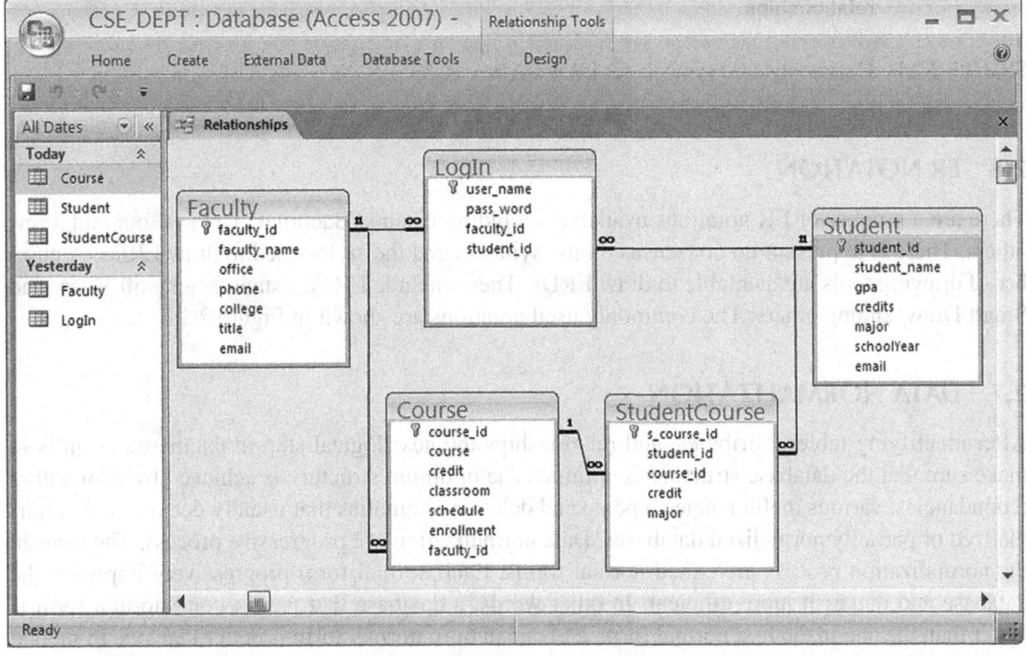

FIGURE 2.13 Relationships are illustrated using MS Access in the CSE_DEPT database.

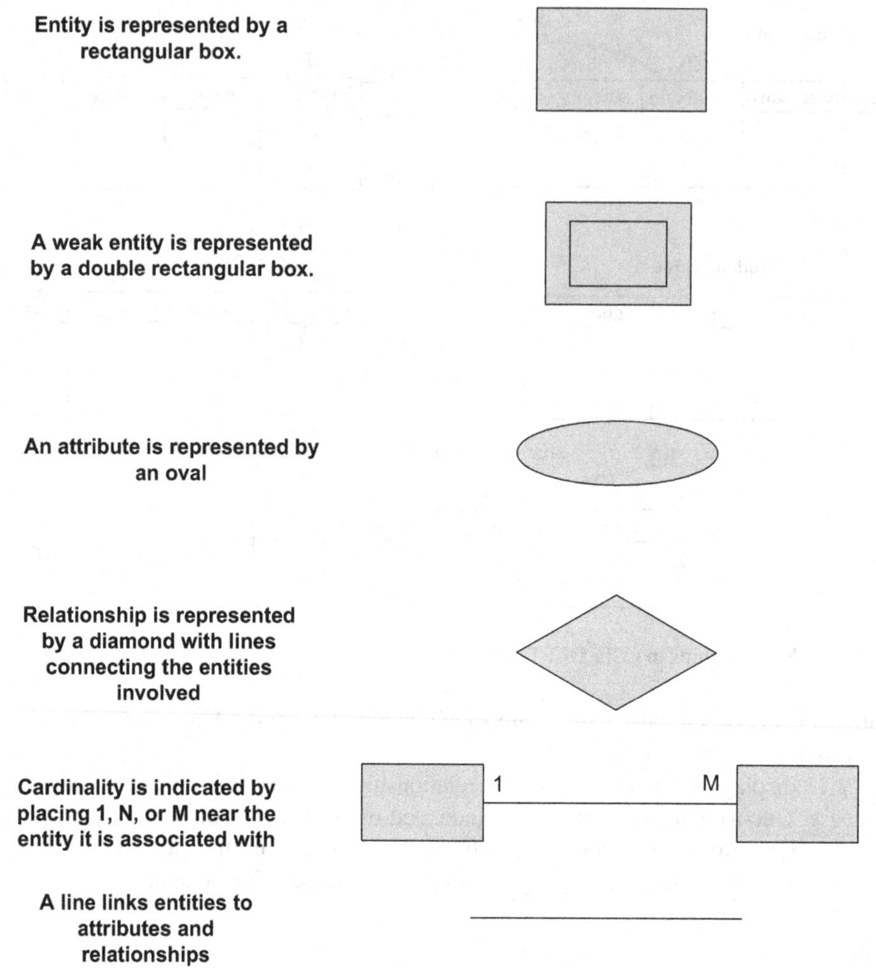

Entity is represented by a rectangular box.
A weak entity is represented by a double rectangular box.
An attribute is represented by an oval
Relationship is represented by a diamond with lines connecting the entities involved
Cardinality is indicated by placing 1, N, or M near the entity it is associated with
1
M
A line links entities to attributes and relationships

FIGURE 2.14 Commonly used symbols for ER notation.

2.6 ER NOTATION

There are a number of ER notations available, including Chen's, Bachman, Crow's foot and a few others. There is at present no consensus on the symbols and the styles used to draw ERDs. A number of drawing tools are available to draw ERDs. These include ER Assistant, Microsoft Visio, and Smart Draw, among others. The commonly used notations are shown in Figure 2.14.

2.7 DATA NORMALIZATION

After identifying tables, attributes, and relationships the next logical step in database design is to make sure that the database structure is optimal. The optimum structure is achieved by eliminating redundancies, various inefficiencies, update and deletion anomalies that usually occur in the unnormalized or partially normalized databases. Data normalization is a progressive process. The steps in the normalization process are called normal forms. Each normal form progressively improves the database and makes it more efficient. In other words, a database that is in second normal form is better than the one in the first normal form, and one in third normal form is better than one in second normal form. To be in the third normal form a database has to be in both the first and second normal

faculty_id	faculty_name	office	phone
A52990	Black Anderson	MTC-218, SHB-205	750-378-9987, 555-255-8897
A77587	Debby Angles	MTC-320	750-330-2276
B66750	Alice Brown	MTC-257	750-330-6650
B78880	Ying Bai	MTC-211, SHB-105	750-378-1148, 555-246-4582
B86590	Davis Bhalla	MTC-214	750-378-1061
H99118	Jeff Henry	MTC-336	750-330-8650
J33486	Steve Johnson	MTC-118	750-330-1116
K69880	Jenney King	MTC-324	750-378-1230

FIGURE 2.15 Unnormalized faculty table with repeating groups.

faculty_id	faculty_name	office	phone
A52990	Black Anderson	MTC-218	750-378-9987
A52990	Black Anderson	SHB-205	555-255-8897
A77587	Debby Angles	MTC-320	750-330-2276
B66750	Alice Brown	MTC-257	750-330-6650
B78880	Ying Bai	MTC-211	750-378-1148
B78880	Ying Bai	SHB-105	555-246-4582
B86590	Davis Bhalla	MTC-214	750-378-1061
H99118	Jeff Henry	MTC-336	750-330-8650
J33486	Steve Johnson	MTC-118	750-330-1116
K69880	Jenney King	MTC-324	750-378-1230

FIGURE 2.16 Normalized faculty table.

forms. There are also fourth and fifth normal forms, but for most practical purposes a database meeting the criteria of the third normal form is considered to be of good design.

2.7.1 First Normal Form (1NF)

A table is in first normal form if the values in each column are atomic; that is, there are no repeating groups of data.

The Faculty table in Figure 2.15 is not normalized. Some faculty members have more than one telephone number listed in the phone column. These are called repeating groups.

In order to convert this table to the First Normal Form (1NF), the data must be atomic. In other words, the repeating rows must be broken into two or more atomic rows. Figure 2.16 illustrates the Faculty table in 1NF where repeating groups have been removed. Now it is in 1NF.

2.7.2 Second Normal Form (2NF)

A table is in second normal form (2NF) if it is already in 1NF and every non-key column is fully dependent upon the primary key.

This implies that if the primary key consists of a single column then the table in 1NF is automatically in 2NF. The second part of the definition implies that if the key is composite then none of the non-key columns will depend upon just one of the columns that participate in the composite key.

The Faculty table in Figure 2.16 is in first normal form. However, it has a composite primary key, made up of faculty_id and office. The phone number depends on a part of the primary key, the office and not on the whole primary key. This can lead to update and deletion anomalies, such as those mentioned above.

Old Faculty table in 1NF

faculty_id	faculty_name	office	phone
A52990	Black Anderson	MTC-218	750-378-9987
A52990	Black Anderson	SHB-205	555-255-8897
A77587	Debby Angles	MTC-320	750-330-2276
B66750	Alice Brown	MTC-257	750-330-6650
B78880	Ying Bai	MTC-211	750-378-1148
B78880	Ying Bai	SHB-105	555-246-4582
B86590	Davis Bhalla	MTC-214	750-378-1061
H99118	Jeff Henry	MTC-336	750-330-8650
J33486	Steve Johnson	MTC-118	750-330-1116
K69880	Jenney King	MTC-324	2750-378-1230

New Faculty table

faculty_id	faculty_name
A52990	Black Anderson
A52990	Black Anderson
A77587	Debby Angles
B66750	Alice Brown
B78880	Ying Bai
B78880	Ying Bai
B86590	Davis Bhalla
H99118	Jeff Henry
J33486	Steve Johnson
K69880	Jenney King

New Office table

office	phone	faculty_id
MTC-218	750-378-9987	A52990
SHB-205	555-255-8897	A52990
MTC-320	750-330-2276	A77587
MTC-257	750-330-6650	B66750
MTC-211	750-378-1148	B78880
SHB-105	555-246-4582	B78880
MTC-214	750-378-1061	B86590
MTC-336	750-330-8650	H99118
MTC-118	750-330-1116	J33486
MTC-324	750-378-1230	K69880

FIGURE 2.17 Converting faulty table into 2NF by decomposing the old table in two, faculty and office.

By splitting the old Faculty table (Figure 2.17) into two new tables, Faculty and Office, we can remove the dependencies mentioned earlier. Now the faculty table has a primary key, faculty_id and the Office table has a primary key, office. The non-key columns in both tables now depend only on the primary keys only.

2.7.3 Third Normal Form (3NF)

A table is in third normal form if it is already in 2NF and every non-key column is non-transitively dependent upon the primary key. In other words, in this situation all non-key columns are mutually independent, but at the same time they are fully dependent upon the primary key only.

Another way of stating this is that in order to achieve 3NF no column should depend upon any non-key column. If column B depends on column A, then A is said to functionally determine column B; hence the term determinant. Another definition of 3NF says that the table should be in 2NF and the only determinants it contains are candidate keys.

For the Course table in Figure 2.18, all non-key columns depend on the primary key – course_id. In addition, name and phone columns also depend on faculty_id. This table is in second normal form but it suffers from update, addition, and deletion anomalies because of transitive dependencies. In order to conform to the third normal form we can split this table into two tables, Course and Instructor (Figures 2.19 and 2.20). Now we have eliminated the transitive dependencies that are apparent in the Course table in Figure 2.18.

course_id	course	classroom	faculty_id	faculty_name	phone
CSC-131A	Computers in Society	MTC-109	A52990	Black Anderson	750-378-9987
CSC-131B	Computers in Society	MTC-114	B66750	Alice Brown	750-330-6650
CSC-131C	Computers in Society	MTC-109	A52990	Black Anderson	750-378-9987
CSC-131D	Computers in Society	MTC-109	B86590	Davis Bhalla	750-378-1061
CSC-131E	Computers in Society	MTC-301	B66750	Alice Brown	750-330-6650
CSC-131I	Computers in Society	MTC-109	A52990	Black Anderson	750-378-9987
CSC-132A	Introduction to Programming	MTC-303	J33486	Steve Johnson	750-330-1116
CSC-132B	Introduction to Programming	MTC-302	B78880	Ying Bai	750-378-1148

FIGURE 2.18 The old course table.

course_id	course	classroom
CSC-131A	Computers in Society	MTC-109
CSC-131B	Computers in Society	MTC-114
CSC-131C	Computers in Society	MTC-109
CSC-131D	Computers in Society	MTC-109
CSC-131E	Computers in Society	MTC-301
CSC-131I	Computers in Society	MTC-109
CSC-132A	Introduction to Programming	MTC-303
CSC-132B	Introduction to Programming	MTC-302

FIGURE 2.19 The new course table.

faculty_id	faculty_name	phone
A52990	Black Anderson	750-378-9987
B66750	Alice Brown	750-330-6650
A52990	Black Anderson	750-378-9987
B86590	Davis Bhalla	750-378-1061
B66750	Alice Brown	750-330-6650
A52990	Black Anderson	750-378-9987
J33486	Steve Johnson	750-330-1116
B78880	Ying Bai	750-378-1148
A77587	Debby Angles	750-330-2276

FIGURE 2.20 The new instructor table.

2.8 DATABASE COMPONENTS IN SOME POPULAR DATABASES

All databases allow for the storage, retrieval, and management of the data. Simple databases provide basic services to accomplish these tasks. Many database providers, such as Microsoft SQL Server and Oracle, provide additional services which necessitates storing many components in the database other than data. These components, such as views, stored procedures etc., are collectively called database objects. In this section we will discuss various objects that make up MS Access, SQL Server, and Oracle databases.

There are two major types of databases: *File Server* and *Client Server*:

In a File Server database, data is stored in a file and each user of the database retrieves the data, displays the data, or modifies the data directly from or to the file. In a Client Server database, the data is also stored in a file; however, all these operations are mediated through a master program called a server. MS Access is a File Server database, whereas Microsoft SQL Server and Oracle are

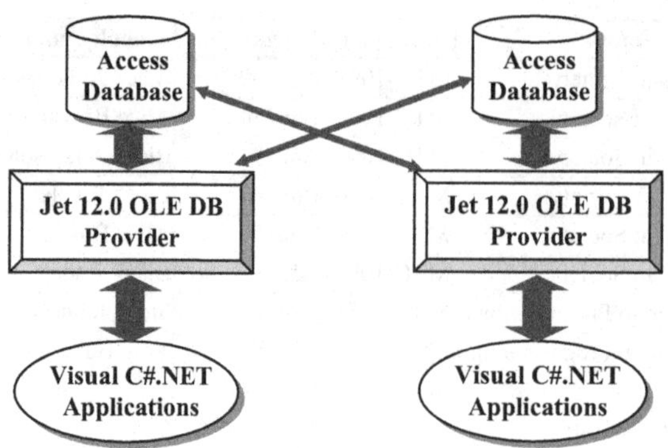

FIGURE 2.21 Microsoft Access database illustration.

Client Server databases. The Client Server databases have several advantages over the File Server databases. These include minimizing chances of crashes, the provision of features for recovery, the enforcement of security, better performance, and more efficient use of the network compared to the file server databases.

2.8.1 Microsoft Access Databases

Microsoft Access Database Engine is a collection of information stored in a systematic way that forms the underlying component of a database. Also called a Jet (Joint Engine Technology), it allows the manipulation of relational database. It offers a single interface that other software may use to access Microsoft databases. The supporting software is developed to provide security, integrity, indexing, record locking etc. By executing the MS Access program, MSACCESS.EXE, you can see the database engine at work and the user interface it provides. Figure 2.21 shows how a Java application accesses the MS Access database via ACE OLE database provider.

2.8.1.1 Database File

The Access database is made up of a number of components called objects, which are stored in a single file referred to as *database file*. As new objects are created or more data is added to the database, this file gets bigger. This is a complex file that stores objects like tables, queries, forms, reports, macros, and modules. The Access files have an .mdb (Microsoft DataBase) extension. Some of these objects help users to work with the database; others are useful for displaying database information in a comprehensible and easy to read format.

2.8.1.2 Tables

Before you can create a table in Access, you must create a database container and give it a name with the extension .mdb. Database creation is a simple process and is explained in detail with an example, which is given later in this chapter. Suffice it to say that a table is made up of columns and rows. Columns are referred to as fields, which are attributes of an entity. Rows are referred to as records, also called tuples.

2.8.1.3 Queries

One of the main purposes of storing data in a database is that the data may be retrieved later as needed, without having to write complex programs. This purpose is accomplished in Access and other databases by writing SQL statements. A group of such statements is called a query. It enables you to retrieve, update, and display data in the tables. You may display data from more than one table by using a Join operation. In addition, you may insert or delete data in the tables.

Access also provides a visual graphic user interface (GUI) to create queries. This bypasses writing SQL statements and makes it appealing to beginning and not so savvy users, who can use wizards or a GUI interface to create queries. Queries can extract information in a variety of ways. You can make them as simple or as complex as you like. You may specify various criteria to get desired information, perform comparisons, or you may want to perform some calculations and obtain the results. In essence, operators, functions, and expressions are the building blocks for Access operation.

2.8.2 SQL Server Databases

The Microsoft SQL Server Database Engine is a service for storing and processing data in either a relational (tabular) format or as XML documents. Various tasks performed by the Database Engine include:

- Designing and creating a database to hold the relational tables or XML documents.
- Accessing and modifying the data stored in the database.
- Implementing Web sites and applications.
- Building procedures.
- Optimizing the performance of the database.

The SQL Server database is a complex entity, made up of multiple components. It is more complex than the MS Access database, which can be simply copied and distributed. Certain procedures have to be followed for copying and distributing an SQL server database.

SQL Server is used by a diverse group of professionals with diverse needs and requirements. To satisfy different needs, SQL Server comes in five different editions: Enterprise edition, Standard edition, Workgroup edition, Developer edition, and Express edition. The most common editions are Enterprise, Standard, and Workgroup. It is noteworthy that the database engine is virtually the same in all of these editions.

SQL Server database can be stored on the disk using three types of files: primary data files, secondary data files, and transaction log files. Primary data files are created first and contain user-defined objects like tables and views, and system objects. These files have an extensions of .mdf. If the database grows too big for a disk, it can be stored as secondary files with an extension .ndf. The SQL Server still treats these files as if they are together. The data file is made up of many objects. The transaction log files carry an .ldf extension. All transactions to the database are recorded in this file.

Figure 2.22 illustrates the structure of the SQL Server Database. Each Java application has to access the server, which in turn accesses the SQL database.

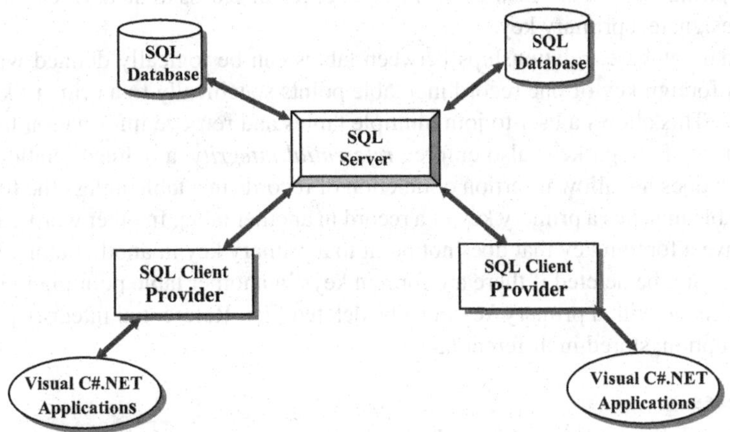

FIGURE 2.22 SQL Server database structure.

2.8.2.1 Data Files

A data file is a conglomeration of objects, which includes tables, keys, views, stored procedures and others. All these objects are necessary for the efficient operation of the database.

2.8.2.2 Tables

The data in a relational database resides in tables, which are the building blocks of the database. Each table consists of columns and rows. Columns represent various attributes or fields in a table. Each row represents one record. For example, one record in the Faculty table consists of name, office, phone, college, title, and email. Each field has a distinct data type, meaning that it can contain only one type of data such as numeric or character. Tables are the first objects created in a database.

2.8.2.3 Views

Views are virtual tables, meaning that they do not contain any data. They are stored as queries in the database, which are executed when needed. A view can contain data from one or more tables. The views can provide database security. Sensitive information in a database can be excluded by including non-sensitive information in a view and providing user access to the views instead of all tables in a database. The views can also hide the complexities of a database. A user can be using a view that is made up of multiple tables, whereas it appears as a single table to the user. The user can execute queries against a view just like a table.

2.8.2.4 Stored Procedures

Users write queries to retrieve, display or manipulate data in the database. These queries can be stored on the client machine or on the server. There are advantages associated with storing SQL queries on the server rather than on the client machine. It has to do with the network performance. Usually, users use same queries over and over again; frequently, different users are trying to access the same data. Instead of sending the same queries on the network repeatedly, it improves the network performance and executes queries faster if the queries are stored on the server where they are compiled and saved as stored procedures. The users can simply call the stored procedure with a simple command like *execute stored_procedure* A.

2.8.2.5 Keys and Relationships

A *primary key* is created for each table in the database to efficiently access records and to ensure *entity integrity*. This implies that each record in a table is unique in some way. Therefore no two records can have the same primary key. It is defined as a globally unique identifier. Moreover a primary key may not have null value, i.e. there may be missing data. SQL server creates a unique index for each primary key. This ensures the fast and efficient access to data. One or columns can be combined to designate a primary key.

In a relational database, relationships between tables can be logically defined with the help of *foreign keys*. A foreign key of one record in a table points specifically to a primary key of a record in another table. This allows a user to join multiple tables and retrieve information from more than one table at a time. Foreign keys also enforce *referential integrity*, a defined relationship between the tables which does not allow insertion or deletion of records in a table unless the foreign key of a record in one table matches a primary key of a record in another table. In other words, a record in one table cannot have a foreign key that does not point to a primary key in another table. Additionally a primary key may not be deleted if there are foreign keys in another table pointing to it. The foreign key values associated with a primary key must be deleted first. Referential integrity protects related data, from corruption, stored in different tables.

2.8.2.6 Indexes

The indexes are used to find records, quickly and efficiently, in a table just like one would use an index in a book. SQL server uses two types of indexes to retrieve and update data – clustered and non-clustered.

A *clustered index* sorts the data in a table so that the data can be accessed efficiently. It is akin to a dictionary or a phone book where records are arranged alphabetically. So one can go directly to a specific alphabet and from there search sequentially for the specific record. The clustered indexes are like an inverted tree. To index a structure is called a B-tree for binary-tree. You start with the root page at the top and find the location of other pages further down at secondary level, following to tertiary level and so on until you find the desired record. The very bottom pages are the leaf pages and contain the actual data. There can be only one clustered index per table because clustered indexes physically rearrange the data.

Non-clustered indexes do not physically rearrange the data in the same way as the clustered indexes. They do also consist of a binary tree with various levels of pages. The major difference, however, is that the leaves do not contain the actual data as in the clustered indexes; instead they contain pointers that point to the corresponding records in the table. These pointers are called row locators.

The indexes can be unique where the duplicate keys are not allowed, or not unique, which permits duplicate keys. Any column that can be used to access data can be used to generate an index. Usually, the primary and the foreign key columns are used to create indexes.

2.8.2.7 Transaction Log Files

A transaction is a logical group of SQL statements which carry out a unit of work. Client server database use log file to keep track of transactions that are applied to the database. For example, before an update is applied to a database, the database server creates an entry in the transaction log to generate a 'before' picture of the data in a table and then applies a transaction and creates another entry to generate an 'after' picture of the data in that table. This keeps track of all the operations performed on a database. Transaction logs can be used to recover data in the case of crashes or disasters. Transaction logs are automatically maintained by SQL Server.

2.8.3 Oracle Databases

Oracle was designed to be platform-independent, making it architecturally more complex than the SQL Server database. The Oracle database contains more files than SQL Server database.

The Oracle DBMS comes in three levels: Enterprise, Standard, and Personal. The Enterprise edition is the most powerful and is suitable for large installations using large number of transactions in multi-user environments. The Standard edition is also used by high-level multi-user installations. It lacks some of the utilities available in the Enterprise edition. The Personal edition is used in a single-user environment for the development of database applications. The database engine components are virtually the same for all three editions.

Oracle architecture is made up of several components, including an Oracle server, Oracle instance and an Oracle database. The Oracle server contains several files, processes, and memory structures. Some of these are used to improve the performance of the database and ensure database recovery in case of a crash. The Oracle server consists of an Oracle instance, and an Oracle database. An Oracle instance consists of background processes and memory structures. These background processes perform input/output and monitor other Oracle processes to ensure better performance and reliability. The Oracle database consists of data files that provide the actual physical storage for the data.

2.8.3.1 Data Files

The main purpose of a database is to store and retrieve data. It consists of a collection of data that is treated as a unit. An Oracle database has both a logical and physical structure. The logical layer consists of tablespaces, necessary for the smooth operation of an Oracle installation. Data files make up the physical layer of the database. These consist of three types of files: *data files*, which contain actual data in the database; *redo logfiles*, which contain records of modifications made to the database for future recovery in case of failure; and *control files*, which are used to maintain and verify database integrity. The Oracle server uses other files that are not part of the database. These include *parameter file*, which defines the characteristics of an Oracle instance; *password file*, which is used for authentication; and *archived redo logfiles*, which are copies of the redo log files necessary for recovery from failure. A partial list of some of the components follows.

2.8.3.2 Tables

Users can store data in a regular table, a partitioned table, an index-organized table, or a clustered table. A *regular table* is the default table, as in other databases. Rows can be stored in any order. A *partitioned table* has one or more partitions where rows are stored. Partitions are useful for large tables, which can be queried by several processes concurrently. *Index-organized tables* provide fast key-based access for queries involving exact matches. The table may have index on one or more of its columns. Instead of using two storage spaces for the table and a B-tree index, a single storage space is used to store both the B-tree and other columns. A *clustered table*(or group of tables) share(s) the same block, which is called a cluster. They are grouped together because they share common columns and are frequently used together. Clusters have a cluster key for identifying the rows that need to be stored together. Cluster keys are independent of the primary key and may be made up of one or more columns. Clusters are created to improve performance.

2.8.3.3 Views

Views are like virtual tables and are used in a similar fashion, as in the SQL Server databases discussed above.

2.8.3.4 Stored Procedures

In Oracle functions and procedures may be saved as stored program units. Multiple input arguments (parameters) may be passed as input to functions and procedures; however, functions return only one value as output, whereas procedures may return multiple values as output. The advantages to creating and using stored procedures are the same as mentioned above for the SQL Server. Because procedures are stored on the server, individual SQL statements do not have to be transmitted over the network, thus reducing the network traffic. In addition, commonly used SQL statements are saved as functions or procedures and may be used again and again by various users, thereby saving rewriting the same code repeatedly. The stored procedures should be made flexible so that different users are able to pass input information to the procedure in the form of arguments or parameters and get the desired output.

Figure 2.23 shows the syntax to create a stored procedure in Oracle. It has three sections – a header, a body, and an exception section. The procedure is defined in the header section. Input and output parameters, along with their data types, are declared here and transmit information to or from the procedure. The body section of the procedure starts with a key word BEGIN and consists of SQL statements. The exceptions section of the procedure begins with the keyword EXCEPTION

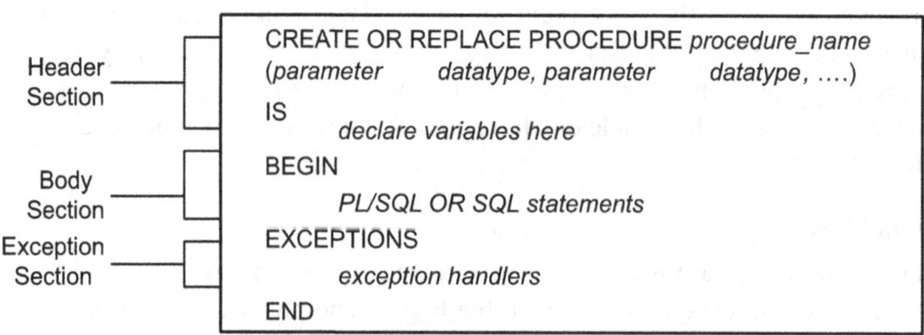

FIGURE 2.23 Syntax for creating a stored procedure in Oracle.

and contains exception handlers which are designed to handle the occurrence of some conditions that change the normal flow of execution.

Indexes are created to provide direct access to rows. An index is a tree structure. Indexes can be classified on their logic design or their physical implementation. Logical classification is based on an application perspective, whereas physical classification is based on how the indexes are stored. Indexes can be either partitioned or nonpartitioned. Large tables use partitioned indexes, which spreads an index to multiple table spaces, thereby decreasing contention for index look up and increasing manageability. An index may consist of a single column or multiple columns; it may be either unique or non-unique. Some of these indexes are outlined below:

Function based indexes precompute the value of a function or expression of one or more columns and stores it in an index. It can be created as a B-tree or as a bit map. It can improve the performance of queries performed on tables that rarely change.

Domain Indexes are application-specific and are created and managed by the user or applications. Single-column indexes can be built on text, spatial, scalar, object, or LOB data types.

B-tree indexes store a list of row IDs for each key. Structure of a *B-tree* index is similar to the ones in the SQL Server described above. The leaf nodes contain indexes that point to rows in a table. The leaf blocks allow scanning of the index in either ascending or descending order. Oracle server maintains all indexes when insert, update or delete operations are performed on a table.

Bitmap indexes are useful when columns have low cardinality and a large number of rows. For example, a column may contain few distinct values like Y/N for marital status, or M/F for gender. A bitmap is organized like a B-tree where the leaf nodes store a bitmap instead of row IDs. When changes are made to the key columns, bit maps must be modified.

2.8.3.4.1 Initialization Parameter Files

Oracle server must read the initialization parameter file before starting an oracle database instance. There are two types of initialization parameter files: a static parameter file and a persistent parameter file. An initialization parameter file contains a list of instance parameters, the name of the database the instance is associated with, the name and location of control files and information about the undo segments. Multiple initialization parameter files can exist to optimize performance.

2.8.3.4.2 Control Files

A control file is a small binary file that defines the current state of the database. Before a database can be opened, the control file is read to determine if the database is in a valid state or not. This maintains the integrity of the database. Oracle uses a single control file per database. It is maintained continuously by the server and can be maintained only by the Oracle server. It cannot be edited by a user or database administrator. A control file contains: database name and identifier; time stamp of database creation; tablespace name; names and location of data files and redo logfiles; current log files sequence number; and archive and backup information.

2.8.3.4.3 Redo Log Files

Oracle's redo log files provide a way to recover data in the event of a database failure. All transactions are written to a redo log buffer and passed on to the redo log files.

Redo log files record all changes to the data, provide a recovery mechanism, and can be organized into groups. A set of identical copies of online redo log files is called a redo log file group. The Oracle server needs a minimum of two online redo logfile groups for normal operations. The initial set of redo log file groups and members are created during the database creation. Redo log files are used in a cyclic fashion. Each redo log file group is identified by a log sequence number and is overwritten each time the log is reused. In other words, when a redo log file is full then the log writer moves to the second redo log file. After the second one is full first one is reused.

2.8.3.4.4 Password Files

Depending upon whether the database is administered locally or remotely, one can choose either operating system or password file authentication to authenticate database administrators. Oracle provides a password utility to create password file. Administrators use the GRANT command to provide access to the database using the password file.

2.9 CREATE MICROSOFT SQL SERVER 2019 EXPRESS SAMPLE DATABASE

After you finished the installation of SQL Server 2019 Express database and SQL Server Management Studio (refer to Appendix A on the CRC Press ftp site), you can begin to use it to connect to the server and build our database. Go to **Start | Microsoft SQL Server Tools 18 | Microsoft SQL Server Management Studio 18**. A connection dialog is opened as shown in Figure 2.24.

Your computer name followed by your server name should be displayed in the **Server name:** box. In this case, it is **DESKTOP-24JPUFB\SQL2019EXPRESS**. The Windows NT security engine is set by using the **Windows Authentication** method from the **Authentication** box. The User name box contains the name you entered when you register for your computer. Click on the **Connect** button to connect your client to the SQL database Server.

The server management studio is opened when this connection is completed, which is shown in Figure 2.25.

To create a new database, right-click on the **Databases** folder from the **Object Explorer** window, and select the **New Database** item from the popup menu. Enter **CSE_DEPT** into the **Database name** box in the New Database dialog as the name of our database, keep all other settings unchanged and then click the **OK** button. You can find that a new database named **CSE_DEPT** is created and located under the **Database** folder in the Object Explorer window, as shown in Figure 2.26.

Then you need to create data tables. For this sample database, you need to create five data tables: **LogIn, Faculty, Course, Student** and **StudentCourse**. Expand the **CSE_DEPT** database folder by clicking the

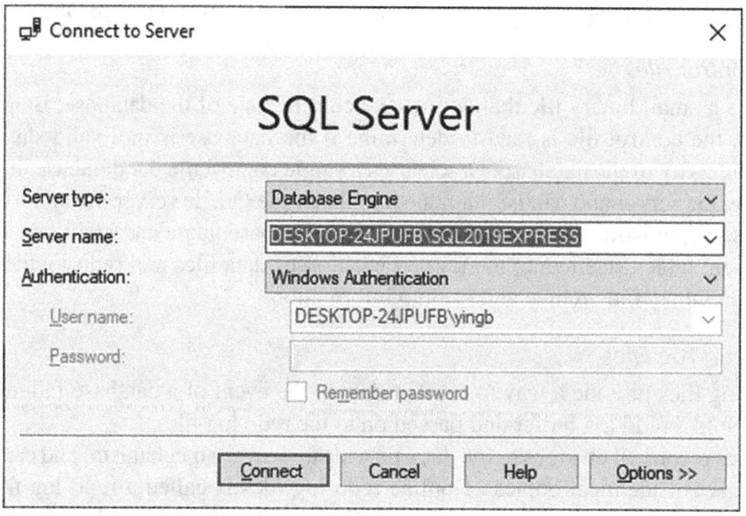

FIGURE 2.24 Connect to the SQL Server 2019 Express database.

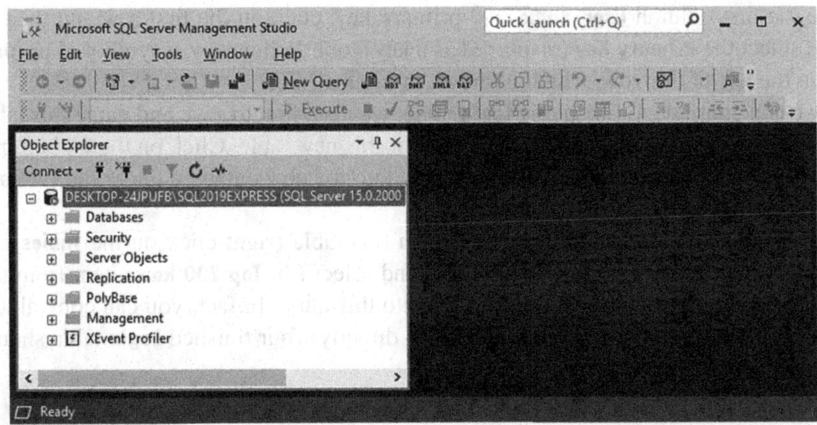

FIGURE 2.25 The opened server management studio.

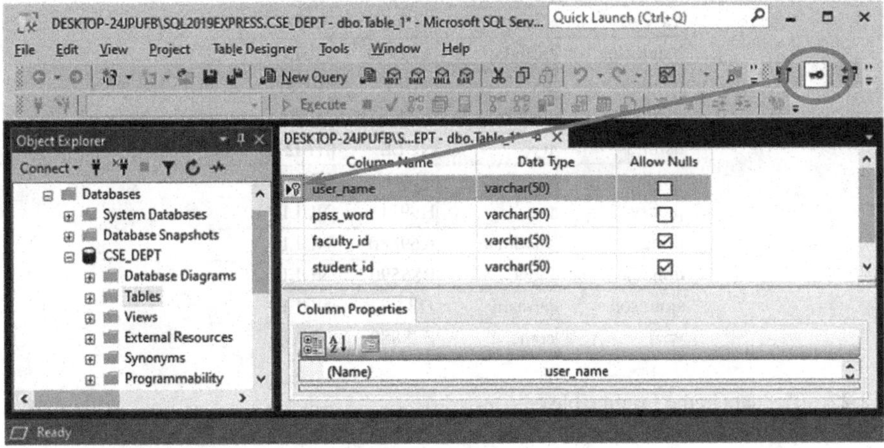

FIGURE 2.26 The new table window.

plus symbol next to it. Right-click on the **Tables** folder and select the **New→Table** item, a new table window is displayed, as shown in Figure 2.26.

2.9.1 Create the LogIn Table

A default data table **dbo.Table_1** is created as shown in Figure 2.26. Three columns are displayed in this new table: **Column Name, Data Type** and **Allow Nulls**, which allows you to enter the name, the data type and a null check mark for each column. You can check the checkbox if you allow that column to be empty; otherwise do not check it if you want that column to contain a valid data. Generally, for the column that works as the primary key, you should not make check for the checkbox associated with that column.

The first table is **LogIn** table, which has four columns with the following column names: **user_name, pass_word, faculty_id** and **student_id**. Enter those four names into four **Column Names** columns. The data types for these four columns are all **nvarchar(50)**, which means that this is a varied char type with a maximum letter count of 50. Enter those data types into each **Data Type** column. The top two columns, **user_name** and **pass_word**, cannot be empty, so leave those checkboxes blank and check other two checkboxes.

To make the first column **user_name** as a primary key, click on the first row and then go to the Toolbar and select the **Primary Key** (displayed as a key) tool. In this way, a symbol of primary key is displayed on the left of this row, which is shown in Figure 2.26.

Before we can continue to finish this **LogIn** table, we need first to save and name this table. Go to **File | Save Table_1** and enter the **LogIn** as the name for this new table. Click on the **OK** button to finish this saving. A new table, named **dbo.LogIn**, is added into the new database under the **Tables** folder in the Object Explorer window.

To add data into this **LogIn** table, right-click on this table (right-click on the **Tables** folder and select **Refresh** if you cannot find this **LogIn** table) and select **Edit Top 200 Rows** item from the popup menu. Enter all login data shown in Figure 2.27 into this table. In fact, you can copy all data rows from Figure 2.27 and paste them to the **LogIn** table directly. Your finished **LogIn** table should match one that is shown in Figure 2.28.

user_name	pass_word	faculty_id	student_id
abrown	america	B66750	NULL
ajade	tryagain	NULL	A97850
awoods	smart	NULL	A78835
banderson	birthday	A52990	NULL
bvalley	see	NULL	B92996
dangles	tomorrow	A77587	NULL
hsmith	try	NULL	H10210
terica	excellent	NULL	T77896
jhenry	test	H99118	NULL
jking	goodman	K69880	NULL
dbhalla	india	B86590	NULL
sjohnson	jermany	J33486	NULL
ybai	come	B78880	NULL

FIGURE 2.27 The data in the LogIn table.

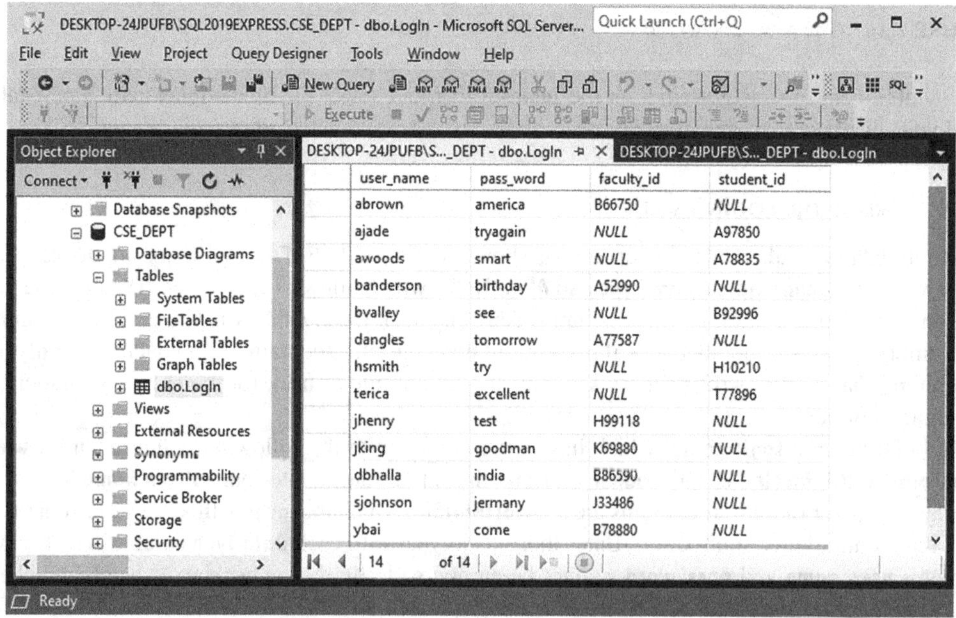

FIGURE 2.28 The finished LogIn table.

A point is that you must place an **NULL** for any field that has no value in this table since it is different with the blank field in the Microsoft Access file database. Go to the **File | Save All** item to save this table. Now let's continue to create the second table **Faculty**.

2.9.2 Create the Faculty Table

Right-click on the **Tables** folder under the **CSE_DEPT** database folder and select the **New→Table** item to open the design view of a new table, which is shown in Figure 2.29.

For this table, we have eight columns: **faculty_id, faculty_name, title, office, phone, college, email** and **fimage**. The data types for the columns **faculty_id** and **faculty_name** are **nvarchar(50)**, and all other data types, except for the **fimage** column, can be either **text** or **nvarchar(50)** since all of them are string variables. The data type for the **fimage** column is **image** since all faculty images are stored in this column. The reason we selected the **nvarchar(50)** as the data type for the **faculty_id** is that a primary key can work for this data type, but it does not work for the **text**. The finished design-view of the **Faculty** table should match one that is shown in Figure 2.29.

Since we selected the **faculty_id** column as the primary key, click on that row and then go to the Toolbar and select the **Primary Key** tool.

Now go to the **File** menu item and select the **Save Table_1**, and enter **Faculty** into the box for the **Choose Name** dialog as the name for this table, click **OK** to save this table.

Next you need to enter the data into this **Faculty** table. To do that, first open the table by right-clicking on the **dbo.Faculty** folder under the **CSE_DEPT** database folder in the Object Explorer window, and then select **Edit Top 200 Rows** item to open this table. Enter the data that is shown in Figure 2.30 into this **Faculty** table.

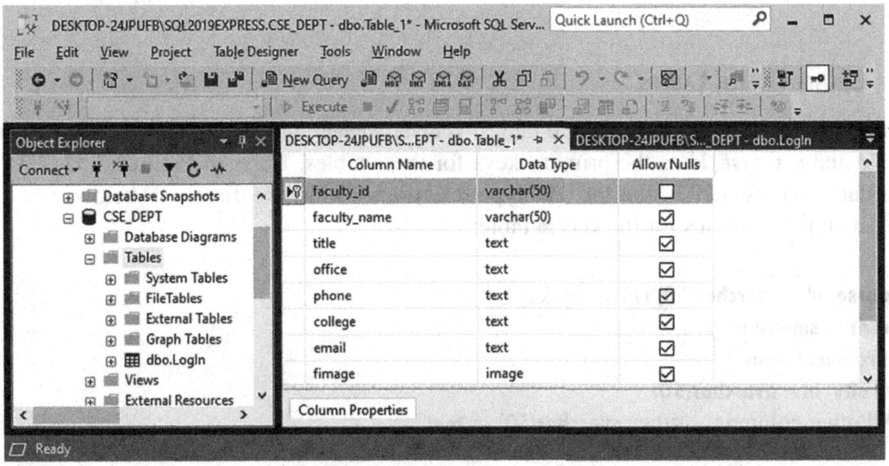

FIGURE 2.29 The design view of the Faculty table.

faculty_id	faculty_name	title	office	phone	college	email	fimage
A52990	Black Anderson	Professor	MTC-218	750-378-9987	Virginia Tech	banderson@college.edu	NULL
A77587	Debby Angles	Associate Professor	MTC-320	750-330-2276	University of Chicago	dangles@college.edu	NULL
B66750	Alice Brown	Assistant Professor	MTC-257	750-330-6650	University of Florida	abrown@college.edu	NULL
B78880	Ying Bai	Associate Professor	MTC-211	750-378-1148	Florida Atlantic University	ybai@college.edu	NULL
B86590	Davis Bhalla	Associate Professor	MTC-214	750-378-1061	University of Notre Dame	dbhalla@college.edu	NULL
H99118	Jeff Henry	Associate Professor	MTC-336	750-330-8650	Ohio State University	jhenry@college.edu	NULL
J33486	Steve Johnson	Distinguished Professor	MTC-118	750-330-1116	Harvard University	sjohnson@college.edu	NULL
K69880	Jenney King	Professor	MTC-324	750-378-1230	East Florida University	jking@college.edu	NULL

FIGURE 2.30 The data in the faculty table.

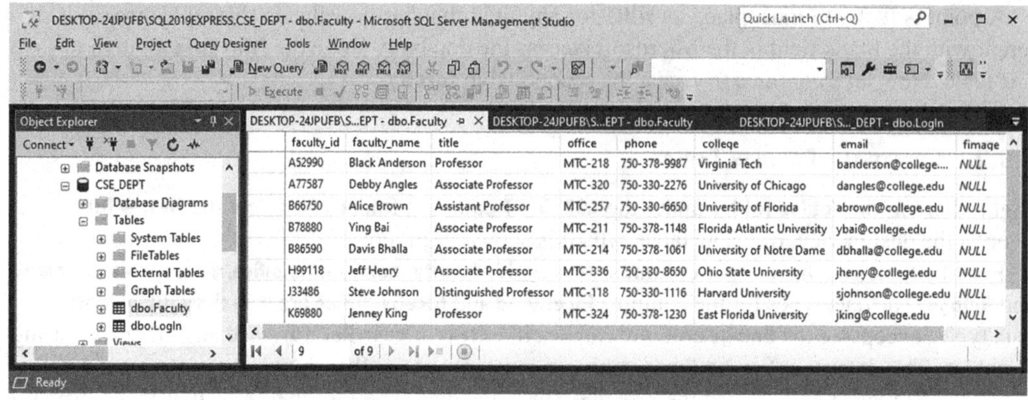

FIGURE 2.31 The completed faculty table.

Your finished **Faculty** table should match one that is shown in Figure 2.31.

Now go to the **File** menu item and select **Save All** to save this completed **Faculty** data table. Your finished **Faculty** data table will be displayed as a table named **dbo.Faculty** that has been added into the new database **CSE_DEPT** under the folder **Tables** in the Object Explorer window. At this moment just keep **NULL** for the **fimage** column and we will add actual faculty images later by using Visual Studio. NET and DevExpress controls.

2.9.3 Create Other Tables

In a similar way, create the rest of three tables: **Course, Student** and **StudentCourse**. Select **course_id, student_id** and **s_course_id** as the primary keys for these tables. Refer to Figures 2.32–2.34 to get detailed data for those tables. For the data type selections, follow the directions below:

The data type selections for the **Course** table:

- **course_id – nvarchar(50)** (Primary key)
- **credit – smallint**
- **enrollment – int**
- **faculty_id – nvarchar(50)**
- All other columns – either **nvarchar(50)** or **text**

The data type selections for the **Student** table:

- **student_id – nvarchar(50)** (Primary key)
- **student_name – nvarchar(50)**
- **gpa – float**
- **credits – int**
- **simage - image**
- All other columns – either **nvarchar(50)** or **text**

course_id	course	credit	classroom	schedule	enrollment	faculty_id
CSC-131A	Computers in Society	3	MTC-109	M-W-F: 9:00-9:55 AM	28	A52990
CSC-131B	Computers in Society	3	MTC-114	M-W-F: 9:00-9:55 AM	20	B66750
CSC-131C	Computers in Society	3	MTC-109	T-H: 11:00-12:25 PM	25	A52990
CSC-131D	Computers in Society	3	MTC-109	M-W-F: 9:00-9:55 AM	30	B86590
CSC-131E	Computers in Society	3	MTC-301	M-W-F: 1:00-1:55 PM	25	B66750
CSC-131I	Computers in Society	3	MTC-109	T-H: 1:00-2:25 PM	32	A52990
CSC-132A	Introduction to Programming	3	MTC-303	M-W-F: 9:00-9:55 AM	21	J33486
CSC-132B	Introduction to Programming	3	MTC-302	T-H: 1:00-2:25 PM	21	B78880
CSC-230	Algorithms & Structures	3	MTC-301	M-W-F: 1:00-1:55 PM	20	A77587
CSC-232A	Programming I	3	MTC-305	T-H: 11:00-12:25 PM	28	B66750
CSC-232B	Programming I	3	MTC-303	T-H: 11:00-12:25 PM	17	A77587
CSC-233A	Introduction to Algorithms	3	MTC-302	M-W-F: 9:00-9:55 AM	18	H99118
CSC-233B	Introduction to Algorithms	3	MTC-302	M-W-F: 11:00-11:55 AM	19	K69880
CSC-234A	Data Structure & Algorithms	3	MTC-302	M-W-F: 9:00-9:55 AM	25	B78880
CSC-234B	Data Structure & Algorithms	3	MTC-114	T-H: 11:00-12:25 PM	15	J33486
CSC-242	Programming II	3	MTC-303	T-H: 1:00-2:25 PM	18	A52990
CSC-320	Object Oriented Programming	3	MTC-301	T-H: 1:00-2:25 PM	22	B66750
CSC-331	Applications Programming	3	MTC-109	T-H: 11:00-12:25 PM	28	H99118
CSC-333A	Computer Arch & Algorithms	3	MTC-301	M-W-F: 10:00-10:55 AM	22	A77587
CSC-333B	Computer Arch & Algorithms	3	MTC-302	T-H: 11:00-12:25 PM	15	A77587
CSC-335	Internet Programming	3	MTC-303	M-W-F: 1:00-1:55 PM	25	B66750
CSC-432	Discrete Algorithms	3	MTC-206	T-H: 11:00-12:25 PM	20	B86590
CSC-439	Database Systems	3	MTC-206	M-W-F: 1:00-1:55 PM	18	B86590
CSE-138A	Introduction to CSE	3	MTC-301	T-H: 1:00-2:25 PM	15	A52990
CSE-138B	Introduction to CSE	3	MTC-109	T-H: 1:00-2:25 PM	35	J33486
CSE-330	Digital Logic Circuits	3	MTC-305	M-W-F: 9:00-9:55 AM	26	K69880
CSE-332	Foundations of Semiconductor	3	MTC-305	T-H: 1:00-2:25 PM	24	K69880
CSE-334	Elec. Measurement & Design	3	MTC-212	T-H: 11:00-12:25 PM	25	H99118
CSE-430	Bioinformatics in Computer	3	MTC-206	Thu: 9:30-11:00 AM	16	B86590
CSE-432	Analog Circuits Design	3	MTC-309	M-W-F: 2:00-2:55 PM	18	K69880
CSE-433	Digital Signal Processing	3	MTC-206	T-H: 2:00-3:25 PM	18	H99118
CSE-434	Advanced Electronics Systems	3	MTC-213	M-W-F: 1:00-1:55 PM	26	B78880
CSE-436	Automatic Control and Design	3	MTC-305	M-W-F: 10:00-10:55 AM	29	J33486
CSE-437	Operating Systems	3	MTC-303	T-H: 1:00-2:25 PM	17	A77587
CSE-438	Advd Logic & Microprocessor	3	MTC-213	M-W-F: 11:00-11:55 AM	35	B78880
CSE-439	Special Topics in CSE	3	MTC-206	M-W-F: 10:00-10:55 AM	22	J33486

FIGURE 2.32 The data in the course table.

student_id	student_name	gpa	credits	major	schoolYear	email	simage
A78835	Andrew Woods	3.26	108	Computer Science	Senior	awoods@college.edu	NULL
A97850	Ashly Jade	3.57	116	Info System Engineering	Junior	ajade@college.edu	NULL
B92996	Blue Valley	3.52	102	Computer Science	Senior	bvalley@college.edu	NULL
H10210	Holes Smith	3.87	78	Computer Engineering	Sophomore	hsmith@college.edu	NULL
T77896	Tom Erica	3.95	127	Computer Science	Senior	terica@college.edu	NULL

FIGURE 2.33 The data in the student table.

s_course_id	student_id	course_id	credit	major
1000	H10210	CSC-131D	3	CE
1001	B92996	CSC-132A	3	CS/IS
1002	T77896	CSC-335	3	CS/IS
1003	A78835	CSC-331	3	CE
1004	H10210	CSC-234B	3	CE
1005	T77896	CSC-234A	3	CS/IS
1006	B92996	CSC-233A	3	CS/IS
1007	A78835	CSC-132A	3	CE
1008	A78835	CSE-432	3	CE
1009	A78835	CSE-434	3	CE
1010	T77896	CSC-439	3	CS/IS
1011	H10210	CSC-132A	3	CE
1012	H10210	CSC-331	2	CE
1013	A78835	CSC-335	3	CE
1014	A78835	CSE-438	3	CE
1015	T77896	CSC-432	3	CS/IS
1016	A97850	CSC-132B	3	ISE
1017	A97850	CSC-234A	3	ISE
1018	A97850	CSC-331	3	ISE
1019	A97850	CSC-335	3	ISE
1020	T77896	CSE-439	3	CS/IS
1021	B92996	CSC-230	3	CS/IS
1022	A78835	CSE-332	3	CE
1023	B92996	CSE-430	3	CE
1024	T77896	CSC-333A	3	CS/IS
1025	H10210	CSE-433	3	CE
1026	H10210	CSE-334	3	CE
1027	B92996	CSC-131C	3	CS/IS
1028	B92996	CSC-439	3	CS/IS

FIGURE 2.34 The data in the StudentCourse table.

The data type selections for the **StudentCourse** table:

- **s_course_id** – **int**(Primary key)
- **student_id**– **nvarchar(50)**
- **course_id**– **nvarchar(50)**
- **credit** – **int**
- **major** – either **nvarchar(50)** or **text**

Enter the data that are shown in Figures 2.27, 2.29 and 2.31 into each associated table, and save each table as **Course, Student** and **StudentCourse**, respectively.

A possible problem you may encounter is that you cannot find the new created Table under the Tables folder in MSDM 2018 even when you complete a table creation. A simple solution is that you need to refresh that Tables folder by right-clicking on that folder and select Refresh item from the popup menu.

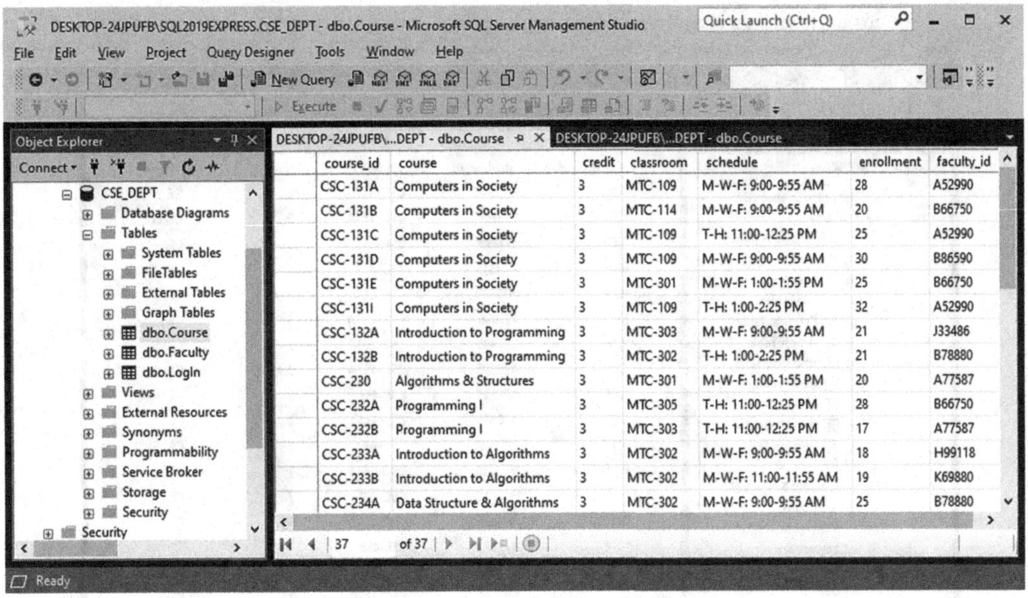
DESKTOP-24JPUFB\SQL2019EXPRESS.CSE_DEPT - dbo.Course - Microsoft SQL Server Management Studio
Quick Launch (Ctrl+Q)
File Edit View Project Query Designer Tools Window Help
New Query
Execute
Object Explorer
Connect
CSE_DEPT
Database Diagrams
Tables
System Tables
FileTables
External Tables
Graph Tables
dbo.Course
dbo.Faculty
dbo.LogIn
Views
External Resources
Synonyms
Programmability
Service Broker
Storage
Security
Security
DESKTOP-24JPUFB\...DEPT - dbo.Course
DESKTOP-24JPUFB\...DEPT - dbo.Course
course_id course credit classroom schedule enrollment faculty_id
CSC-131A Computers in Society 3 MTC-109 M-W-F: 9:00-9:55 AM 28 A52990
CSC-131B Computers in Society 3 MTC-114 M-W-F: 9:00-9:55 AM 20 B66750
CSC-131C Computers in Society 3 MTC-109 T-H: 11:00-12:25 PM 25 A52990
CSC-131D Computers in Society 3 MTC-109 M-W-F: 9:00-9:55 AM 30 B86590
CSC-131E Computers in Society 3 MTC-301 M-W-F: 1:00-1:55 PM 25 B66750
CSC-131I Computers in Society 3 MTC-109 T-H: 1:00-2:25 PM 32 A52990
CSC-132A Introduction to Programming 3 MTC-303 M-W-F: 9:00-9:55 AM 21 J33486
CSC-132B Introduction to Programming 3 MTC-302 T-H: 1:00-2:25 PM 21 B78880
CSC-230 Algorithms & Structures 3 MTC-301 M-W-F: 1:00-1:55 PM 20 A77587
CSC-232A Programming I 3 MTC-305 T-H: 11:00-12:25 PM 28 B66750
CSC-232B Programming I 3 MTC-303 T-H: 11:00-12:25 PM 17 A77587
CSC-233A Introduction to Algorithms 3 MTC-302 M-W-F: 9:00-9:55 AM 18 H99118
CSC-233B Introduction to Algorithms 3 MTC-302 M-W-F: 11:00-11:55 AM 19 K69880
CSC-234A Data Structure & Algorithms 3 MTC-302 M-W-F: 9:00-9:55 AM 25 B78880
37 of 37
Ready

FIGURE 2.35 The completed course table.

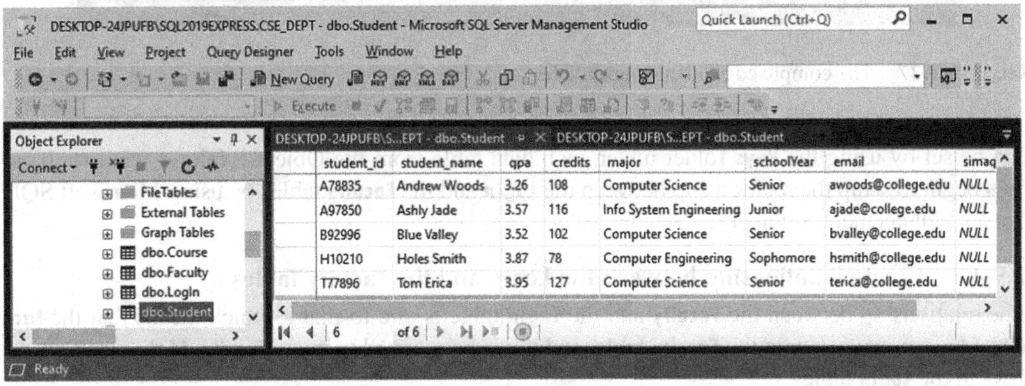
DESKTOP-24JPUFB\SQL2019EXPRESS.CSE_DEPT - dbo.Student - Microsoft SQL Server Management Studio
Quick Launch (Ctrl+Q)
File Edit View Project Query Designer Tools Window Help
New Query
Execute
Object Explorer
Connect
FileTables
External Tables
Graph Tables
dbo.Course
dbo.Faculty
dbo.LogIn
dbo.Student
DESKTOP-24JPUFB\S...EPT - dbo.Student
DESKTOP-24JPUFB\S...EPT - dbo.Student
student_id student_name gpa credits major schoolYear email simag
A78835 Andrew Woods 3.26 108 Computer Science Senior awoods@college.edu NULL
A97850 Ashly Jade 3.57 116 Info System Engineering Junior ajade@college.edu NULL
B92996 Blue Valley 3.52 102 Computer Science Senior bvalley@college.edu NULL
H10210 Holes Smith 3.87 78 Computer Engineering Sophomore hsmith@college.edu NULL
T77896 Tom Erica 3.95 127 Computer Science Senior terica@college.edu NULL
6 of 6
Ready

FIGURE 2.36 The completed student table.

Similar to the **Faculty** table, just keep **NULL** for the **simage** column in the **Student** table and we will add actual student images later by using Visual Studio.NET and DevExpress controls. The finished **Course**, **Student** and **StudentCourse** tables are shown in Figures 2.35–2.37, respectively.

One point you need to note is that you can copy the content of the whole table from the Microsoft Word tables (Figures 2.32–2.34) to the associated data table in the Microsoft SQL Server environment. To make these copies and pastes, first you must select all data rows from your Microsoft Word tables by highlighting them, and choose the **Copy** menu item. Next you must select a whole blank row from your destination table in the Microsoft SQL Server 2019 Express database, and paste those copied rows by clicking on that blank row and then click the **Paste** item from the **Edit** menu item.

2.9.4 Create Relationships Among Tables

Next we need to setup relationships among these five tables using the Primary and Foreign Keys. In the Microsoft SQL Server 2019 Express database environment, the relationship between tables

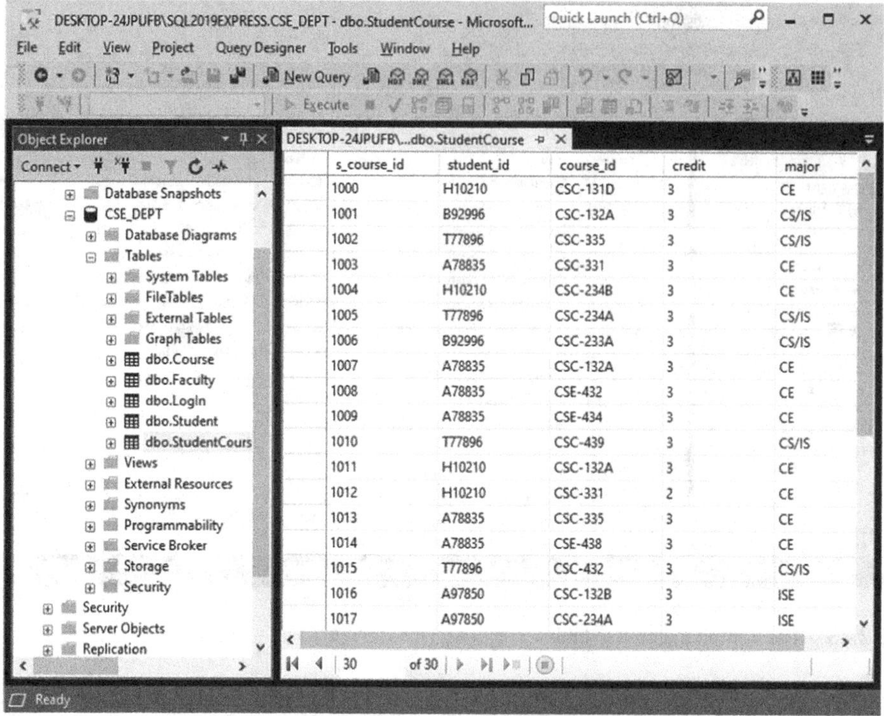

FIGURE 2.37 The completed StudentCourse table.

can be set by using the **Keys** folder under each data table from the Object Explorer window. Now let's begin to setup the relationship between the **LogIn** and the **Faculty** tables by using Microsoft SQL Server Management Studio 18.

2.9.4.1 Create Relationship between the LogIn and the Faculty Tables

The relationship between the **Faculty** and the **LogIn** table is one-to-many, which means that the **faculty_id** is a primary key in the **Faculty** table, and it can be mapped to many **faculty_id** that are foreign keys in the **LogIn** table.

To setup this relationship, expand the **LogIn** table and the **Keys** folder that is under the **LogIn** table in an opened Microsoft SQL Server Management Studio 18. Currently, only one primary key, **PK_LogIn**, is existed under the **Keys** folder.

To add a new foreign key, right-click on the **Keys** folder and select **New Foreign Key** item from the popup menu to open the **Foreign Key Relationships** dialog, which is shown in Figure 2.38.

The default foreign relationship is **FK_LogIn_LogIn***, which is displayed in the **Selected Relationship** box. Right now we want to create the foreign relationship between the **LogIn** and the **Faculty** tables, so change the name of this foreign relationship to **FK_LogIn_Faculty** by modifying its name in the **(Name)** box that is under the **Identity** pane.

Then select two tables by expanding the **Tables And Columns Specification** item that is under the **General** pane. Click the expansion button that is located on the right of the **Tables And Columns Specification** item to open the **Tables and Columns** dialog, which is shown in Figure 2.39.

Click the drop-down arrow from the **Primary key table** combobox and select the **Faculty** table since we need the primary key **faculty_id** from this table, then click on the blank row that is just below the **Primary key table** combobox and select the **faculty_id** column. You can see that the **LogIn** table has been automatically selected and displayed in the **Foreign key table** combobox. Click on the drop-down arrow from the box that is just under the **Foreign key table** combobox and select the **faculty_id**

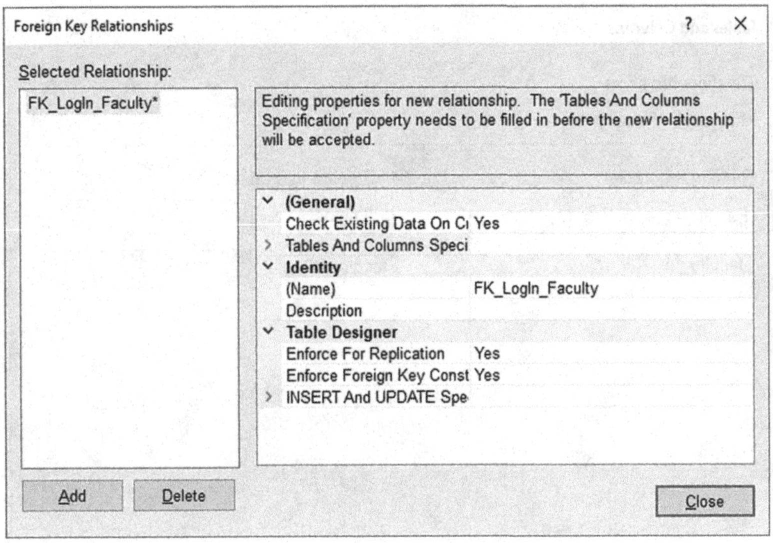

Foreign Key Relationships

Selected Relationship:

FK_LogIn_Faculty*

Editing properties for new relationship. The 'Tables And Columns Specification' property needs to be filled in before the new relationship will be accepted.

(General)
Check Existing Data On Cr Yes
Tables And Columns Speci
Identity
(Name) FK_LogIn_Faculty
Description
Table Designer
Enforce For Replication Yes
Enforce Foreign Key Const Yes
INSERT And UPDATE Spe

Add Delete Close

FIGURE 2.38 The opened foreign key relationships dialog box.

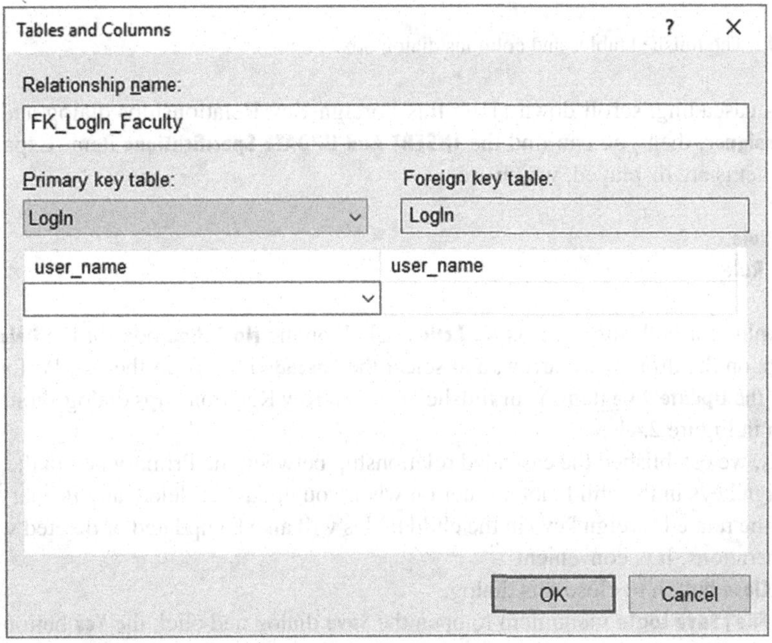

Tables and Columns

Relationship name:
FK_LogIn_Faculty

Primary key table: LogIn
Foreign key table: LogIn

user_name user_name

OK Cancel

FIGURE 2.39 The opened tables and columns dialog box.

as the foreign key for the **LogIn** table. Your finished **Tables and Columns** dialog should match one that is shown in Figure 2.40. Click on the **OK** button to close this dialog.

Before we can close this dialog, we need to do one more thing, which is to setup a cascaded relationship between the Primary key (**faculty_id**) in the parent table **Faculty** and the Foreign keys (**faculty_id**) in the child table **LogIn**. The reason we need to do this is because we want to simplify the data updating and deleting operations between these tables in a relational database such as **CSE_DEPT**. You will have a better understanding about this cascading later when you learn how to update and delete data against a relational database in Chapter 7.

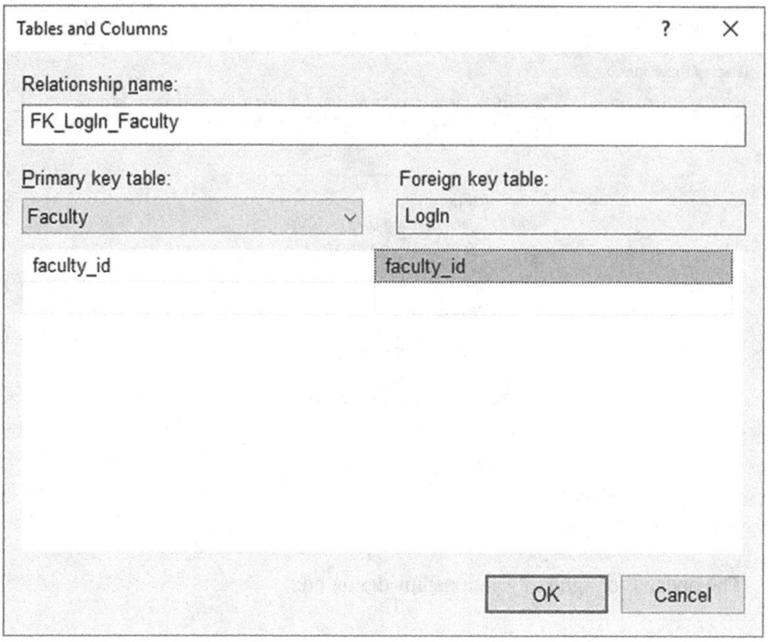

FIGURE 2.40 The finished tables and columns dialog box.

To do this cascading, scroll down along this Foreign Key Relationships dialog and expand the item **Table Designer**, then you can find the **INSERT And UPDATE Specifications** item. Expand this item and two sub items are displayed, which are:

- **Delete Rule**
- **Update Rule**

The default value for both sub items is **No Action**. Click on the **No Action** box for the **Delete Rule** item and then click on the drop-down arrow, and select the **Cascade** item from the list. Perform the same operation for the **Update Rule** item. Your finished Foreign Key Relationships dialog should match one that is shown in Figure 2.41.

In this way, we established the cascaded relationship between the Primary key in the parent table and the Foreign keys in the child table. Later on when you update or delete any Primary key from a parent table, the related foreign keys in the child tables will also be updated or deleted without other additional operations. It is convenient!

Click the **Close** button to close this dialog.

Go to the **File | Save LogIn** menu item to open the **Save** dialog and click the **Yes** button to save this relationship. You can select **Yes** or **No** to the **Save Change Script** dialog box if it appears.

Now right-click on the **Keys** folder under the **LogIn** table from the Object Explorer window, and select the **Refresh** item from the popup menu to refresh this **Keys** folder. Immediately you can find a new foreign key named **FK_LogIn_Faculty** appears under this **Keys** folder. This is our new created foreign key that sets the relationship between our **LogIn** and **Faculty** tables. You can also confirm and find this new created foreign key by right clicking on the **Keys** folder that is under the **Faculty** table.

2.9.4.2 Create Relationship between the LogIn and the Student Tables

In a similar way, you can create a foreign key for the **LogIn** table and setup a one-to-many relationship between the **Student** and the **LogIn** tables.

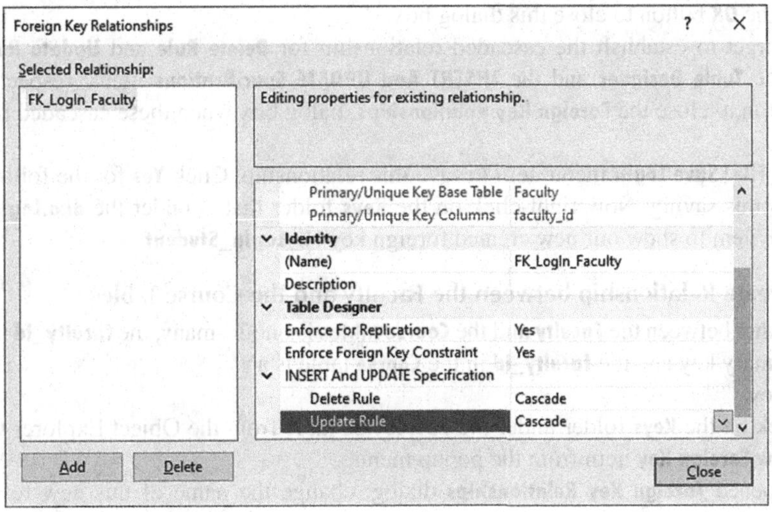

FIGURE 2.41 The finished foreign key relationships dialog.

Right-click on the **Keys** folder that is under the **dbo.LogIn** table and select **New Foreign Key** item from the popup menu to open the **Foreign Key Relationships** dialog. Change the name to **FK_LogIn_Student** by modifying it in the **(Name)** property under the **Identity** item on the right. Click on the three-dot button on right of the **Tables And Columns Specification** item to open the **Tables and Columns** dialog, then select the **Student** table from the **Primary key table** combobox and **student_id** from the box that is under the **Primary key table** combobox. Select the **student_id** from the box that is under the **Foreign key table** combobox. Your finished **Tables and Columns** dialog should match one that is shown in Figure 2.42.

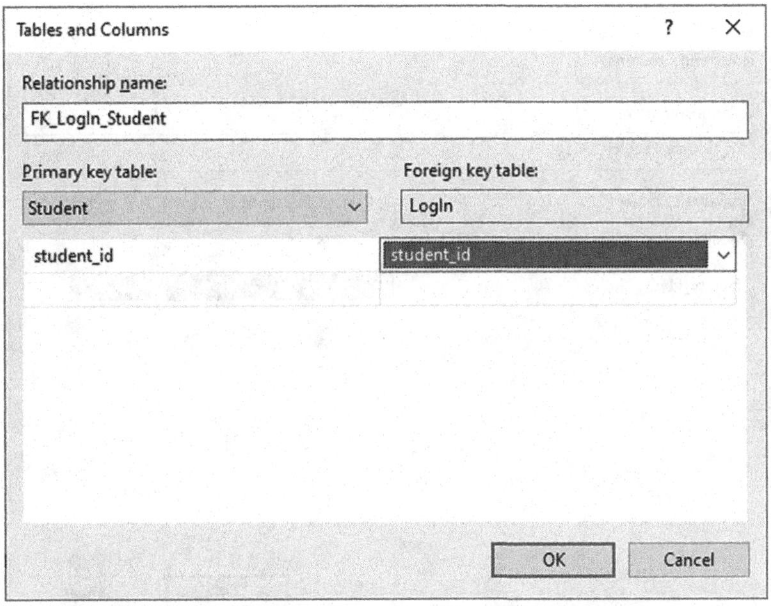

FIGURE 2.42 The completed tables and columns dialog.

Click on the **OK** button to close this dialog box.

Do not forget to establish the cascaded relationship for **Delete Rule** and **Update Rule** items by expanding the **Table Designer** and the **INSERT And UPDATE Specifications** items, respectively. Click the **Close** button to close the **Foreign Key Relationships** dialog box when these cascaded relationships are done.

Go to the **File | Save LogIn** menu item to save this relationship. Click **Yes** for the following dialog box to finish this saving. Now right-click on the **Keys** folder that is under the **dbo.LogIn** table, and select **Refresh** item to show our new created foreign key **FK_LogIn_Student**.

2.9.4.3 Create Relationship between the Faculty and the Course Tables

The relationship between the **Faculty** and the **Course** tables is one-to-many, the **faculty_id** in the **Faculty** table is a Primary key and the **faculty_id** in the **Course** table is a

Foreign key.

Right-click on the **Keys** folder under the **dbo.Course** table from the Object Explorer window and select the **New Foreign Key** item from the popup menu.

On the opened **Foreign Key Relationships** dialog, change the name of this new relationship to **FK_Course_Faculty** in the **(Name)** box under the **Identity** item on the right-hand side. Expand the **Tables and Columns Specifications** item and click on the three-dot button on the right to open the **Tables and Columns** dialog box.

In the opened **Tables and Columns** dialog box, select the **Faculty** table from the **Primary key table** combobox and select the **faculty_id** from the box that is just under the **Primary key table** combobox. Then select the **faculty_id** from the box that is just under the **Foreign key table** combobox. Your finished **Tables and Columns** dialog should match one that is shown in Figure 2.43.

Click on the **OK** button to close this dialog and setup the cascaded relationship for the **Delete Rule** and the **Update Rule** items. Then click the **Close** button to close the **Foreign Key Relationships** dialog box. Go to the **File | Save Course** menu item and click **Yes** for the Message Box to save this setting.

Now right-click on the **Keys** folder under the **dbo.Course** table, and select the **Refresh** item. Immediately you can find our new created relationship key **FK_Course_Faculty**.

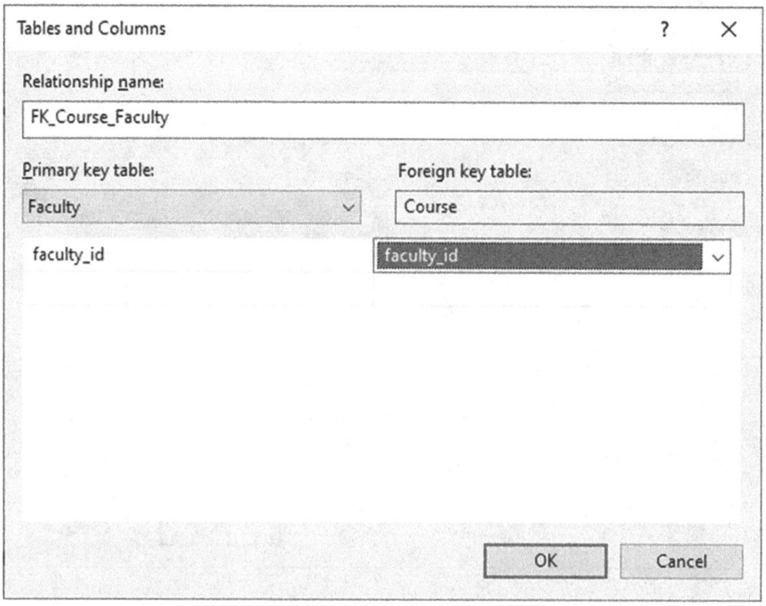

FIGURE 2.43 The finished tables and columns dialog.

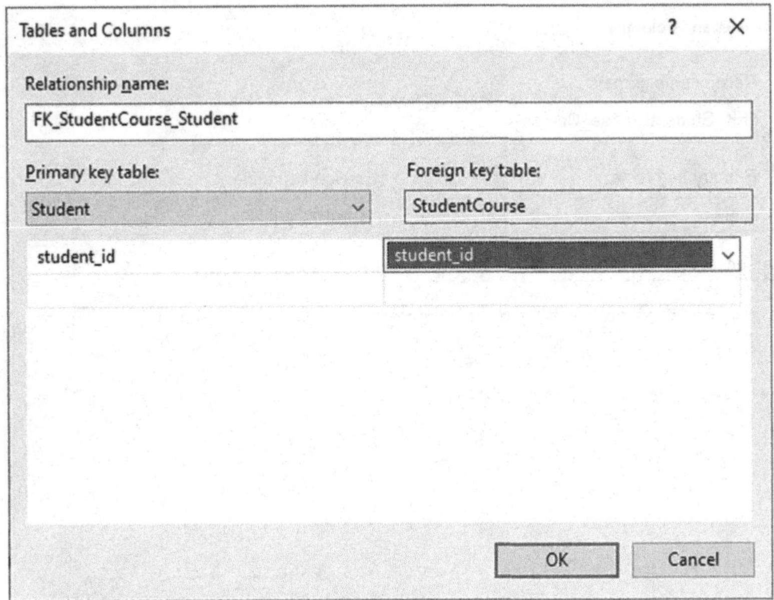

FIGURE 2.44 The finished tables and columns dialog.

2.9.4.4 Create Relationship between the Student and the StudentCourse Tables

The relationship between the **Student** and the **StudentCourse** tables is one-to-many, and the **student_id** in the **Student** table is a Primary key and the **student_id** in the **StudentCourse** table is a Foreign key.

Right-click on the **Keys** folder under the **dbo.StudentCourse** table from the Object Explorer window and select the **New Foreign Key** item from the popup menu.

On the opened **Foreign Key Relationships** dialog, change the name of this new relationship to **FK_StudentCourse_Student** in the **(Name)** box under the **Identity** item on the right hand side.

In the opened **Tables and Columns** dialog box, select the **Student** table from the **Primary key table** combobox and select the **student_id** from the box that is just under the **Primary key table** combobox. Then select the **student_id** from the box that is just under the **Foreign key table** combobox. The finished **Tables and Columns** dialog should match one that is shown in Figure 2.44.

Click on the **OK** button to close this dialog and setup the cascaded relationship for **Delete Rule** and the **Update Rule** items, and then click the **Close** button to close the **Foreign Key Relationships** dialog box. Go to the **File | Save StudentCourse** menu item and click **Yes** for the Message Box to save this relationship.

Now right-click on the **Keys** folder under the **dbo.StudentCourse** table, and select the **Refresh** item. Then you can find our created relationship key **FK_StudentCourse_Student**.

2.9.4.5 Create Relationship between the Course and the StudentCourse Tables

The relationship between the **Course** and the **StudentCourse** tables is one-to-many, the **course_id** in the **Course** table is a Primary key and the **course_id** in the **StudentCourse** table is a Foreign key.

Right-click on the **Keys** folder under the **dbo.StudentCourse** table from the Object Explorer window and select the **New Foreign Key** item from the popup menu.

On the opened **Foreign Key Relationships** dialog, change the name of this new relationship to **FK_StudentCourse_Course** in the **(Name)** box under the **Identity** item on the right hand side.

In the opened **Tables and Columns** dialog box, select the **Course** table from the **Primary key table** combobox and select the **course_id** from the box that is just under the **Primary key table** combobox. Then select the **course_id** from the box that is just under the **Foreign key table** combobox. Your finished **Tables and Columns** dialog should match one that is shown in Figure 2.45.

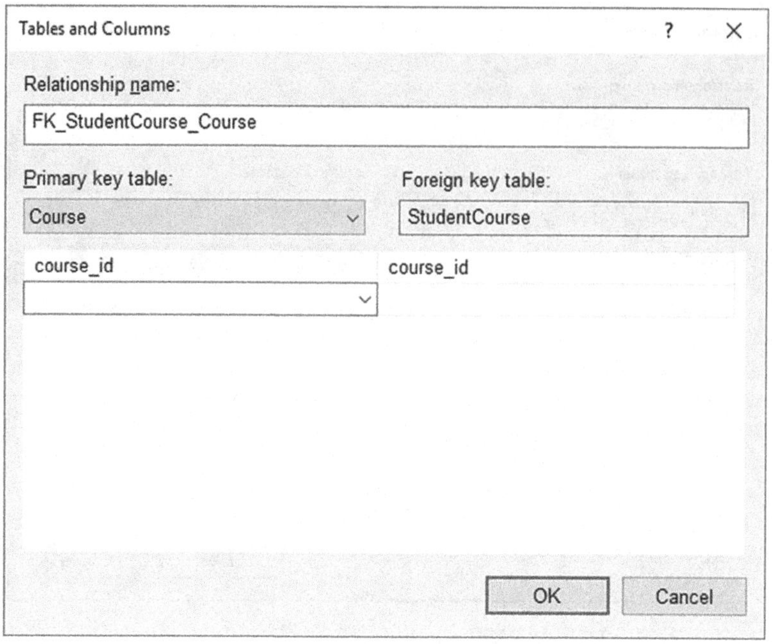

FIGURE 2.45 The finished tables and columns dialog.

Click the **OK** to close this dialog and do not forget to establish a cascaded relationship for the **Delete Rule** and the **Update Rule** items, and then click the **Close** button to close the **Foreign Key Relationships** dialog box. Then go to the **File | Save StudentCourse** menu item and click **Yes** for the Message Box to save this relationship.

Now right-click on the **Keys** folder under the **dbo.StudentCourse** table, and select the **Refresh** item. Then you can find our created relationship key **FK_StudentCourse_Course**.

At this point, we complete setting the relationships among our five data tables. You can close the SQL Server Management Studio 18 now.

A completed Microsoft SQL Server 2019 Express sample database **CSE_DEPT.mdf** can be found from the CRC Press ftp site, from a folder **Sample Database** that is located at the **Students** folder at that site (refer to Figure 1.2 in Chapter 1).The completed relationships among these tables are shown in Figure 2.46.

2.9.5 Store Images to the SQL Server 2019 Express Database

When building **Faculty** and **Student** tables in sections 2.9.2 and 2.9.3, we need to store faculty and student images into the SQL Server 2019 Express database directly. Due to the new property of SQL Server 2019 database, an image can be directly stored into the database column as an image object (in fact, it is a binary data array).

With the help of a product developed by Developer Express Incorporated, WindowsUI, we can directly insert an image into a SQL Server database's column via Microsoft Visual Studio.NET platform without any coding process. Follow Appendix F on the CRC Press ftp site to finish the downloading and installation of the WindowsUI component in your computer.

Now open Visual Studio.NET 2022 and click the link: **Continue without code** at the bottom to open the Visual Studio.NET. Go to **File | New Project** to open the platform selection page. Then go to the right-hand side and scroll down along the scroll bar to try to find our desired template, **Windows Forms App (.NET Framework)** with **C#** as the icon, as shown in Figure 2.47. Then click on it to select it and click on the **Next** button to continue.

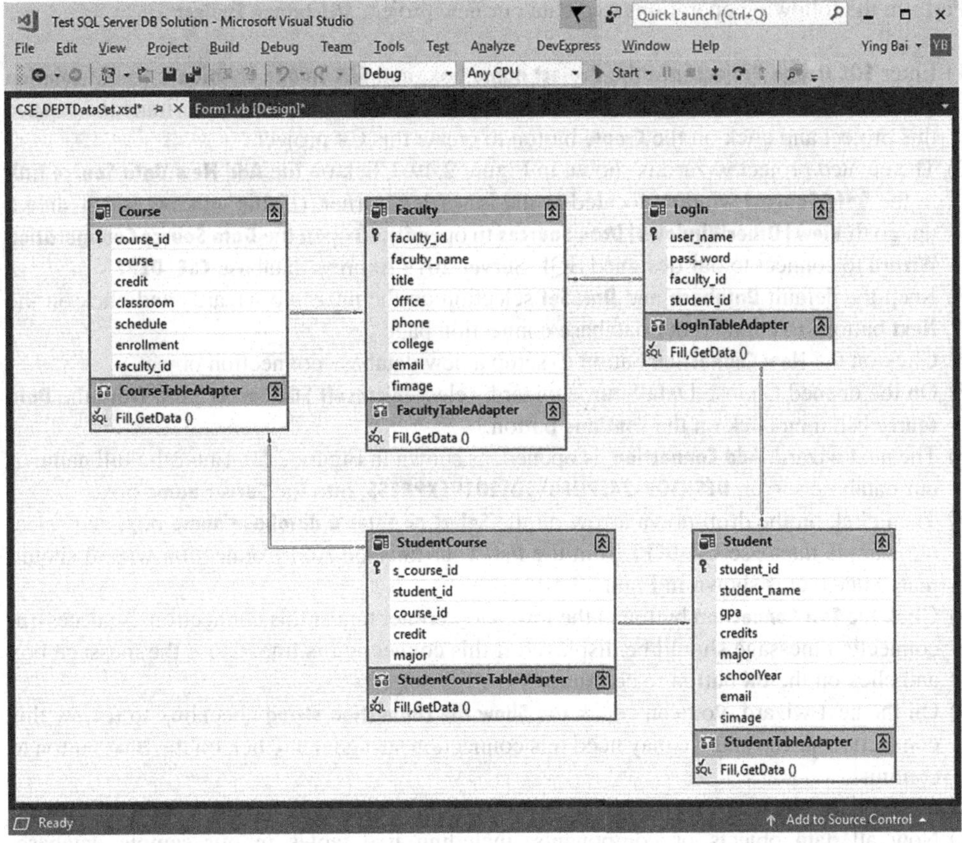

FIGURE 2.46 Relationships among tables.

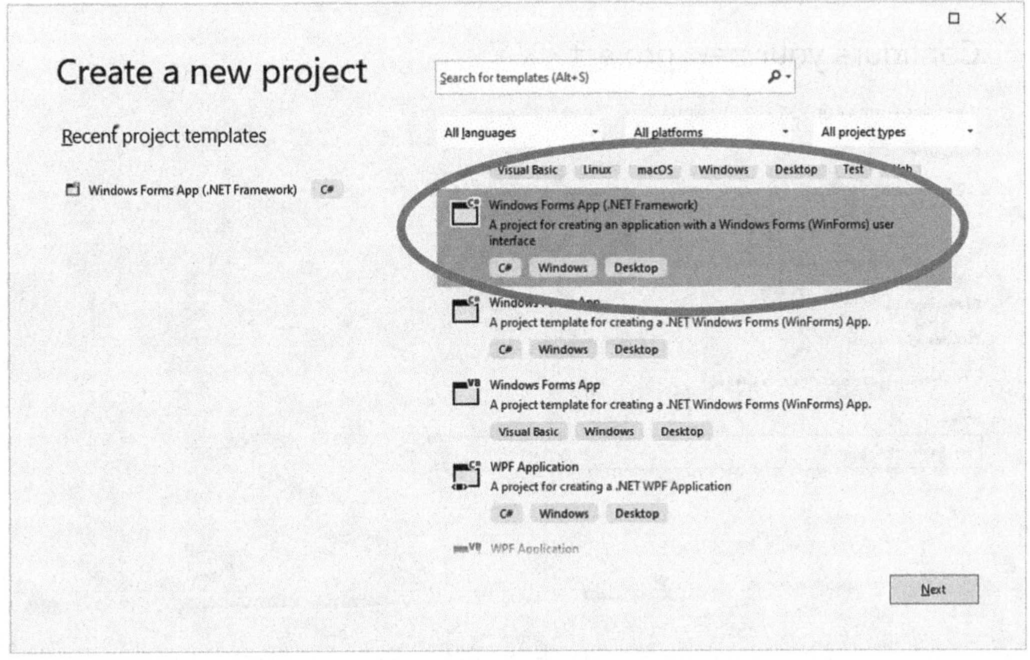

FIGURE 2.47 The create a new project wizard.

Perform the following operations to create our new project **SQL Image Project**:

1) Enter **SQL Image Project** into the **Project name** box, and **SQL Image Solution** into the **Solution name** box, as shown in Figure 2.48. Select a desired local folder on your machine to save this project and click on the **Create** button to create this C# project.
2) The created project wizard is shown in Figure 2.49. Click on the **Add New Data Source** link in the **Data Sources** window located at the lower-left corner, (if this window is not shown up, go to **View | OtherWindows | Data Sources** to open it), to open the **Data Source Configuration Wizard** to connect to our designed SQL Server 2019 Express database **CSE_DEPT**.
3) Keep the default **Database** and **DataSet** selection on the next two wizards and click on the **Next** buttons to come to our database connection page.
4) Click on the **New Connection** button to setup a new database connection object.
5) On the opened Choose Data Source wizard, select **Microsoft SQL Server** item from the **Data source** list, then click on the **Continue** button.
6) The next wizard, **Add Connection**, is opened, as shown in Figure 2.50. Enter the full name of our database server, **DESKTOP-24JPUFB\SQL2019EXPRESS**, into the **Server name** box.
7) Then click on the drop-down arrow on the **Select or enter a database name** box, and select our sample database **CSE-DEPT** from the list. Your finished Add Connection wizard should match one that is shown in Figure 2.50.
8) Click the **Test Connection** button at the lower-left corner to test this connection. A successful connection message should be displayed if this connection is fine. Close the message box and click on the **OK** button to continue.
9) On the next wizard, you can check the **Show the connection string** checkbox to review this connection string, and we may need this connection string later. Click on the **Next** button to continue.
10) Click on the **Next** button again on the next wizard to save our connection string.
11) Now all data objects or components, including five tables in our sample database, **CSE_DEPT**, are displayed, as shown in Figure 2.51.

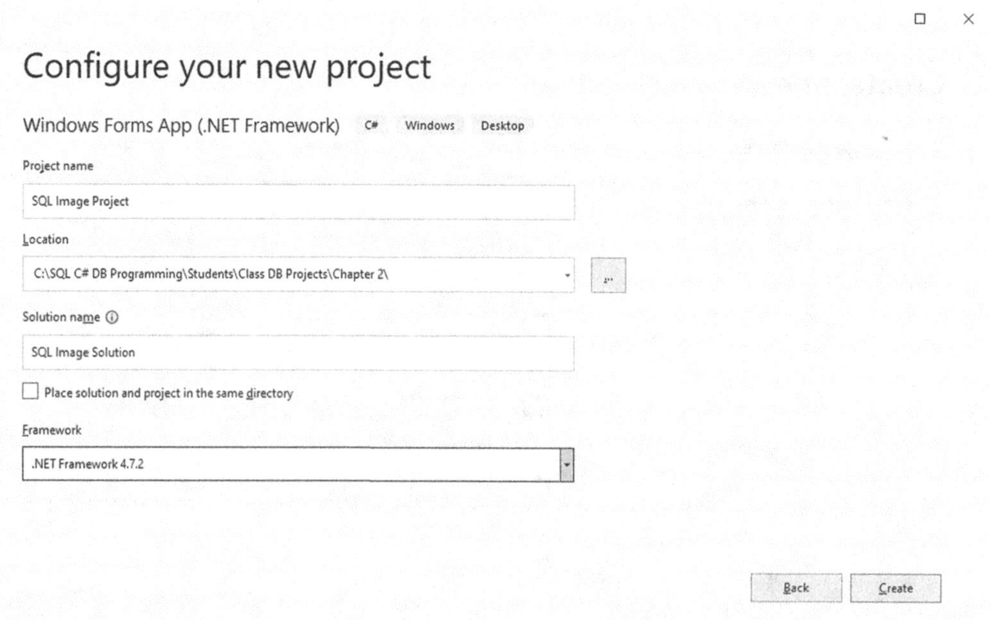

FIGURE 2.48 The name of new project and the solution wizard.

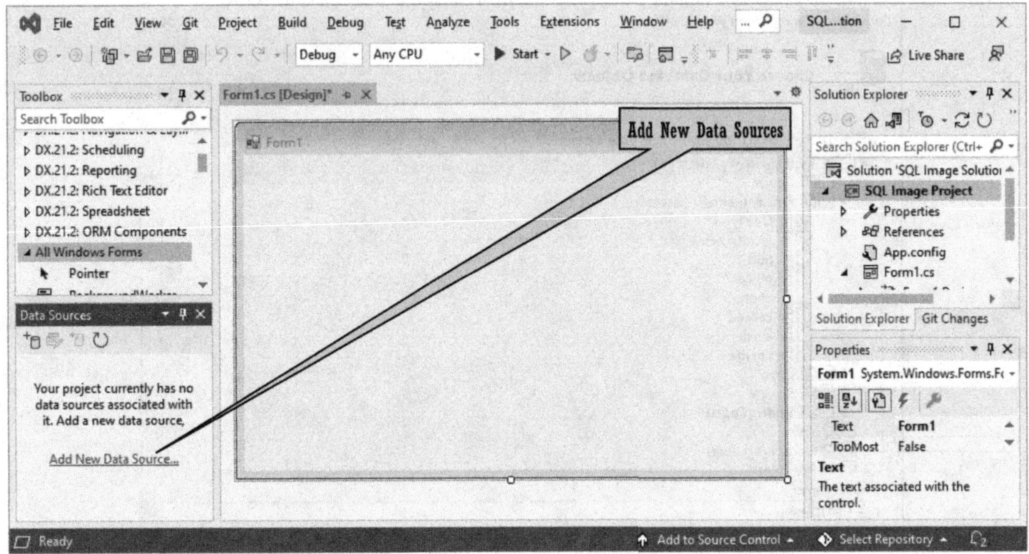

FIGURE 2.49 The new added project SQL image project.

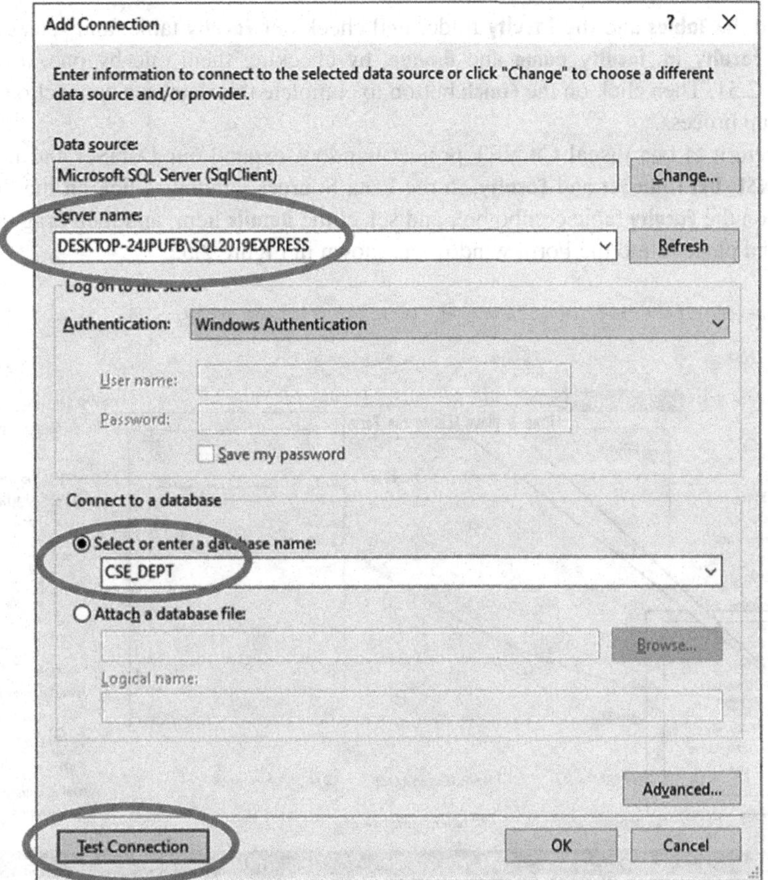

FIGURE 2.50 The opened add connection wizard.

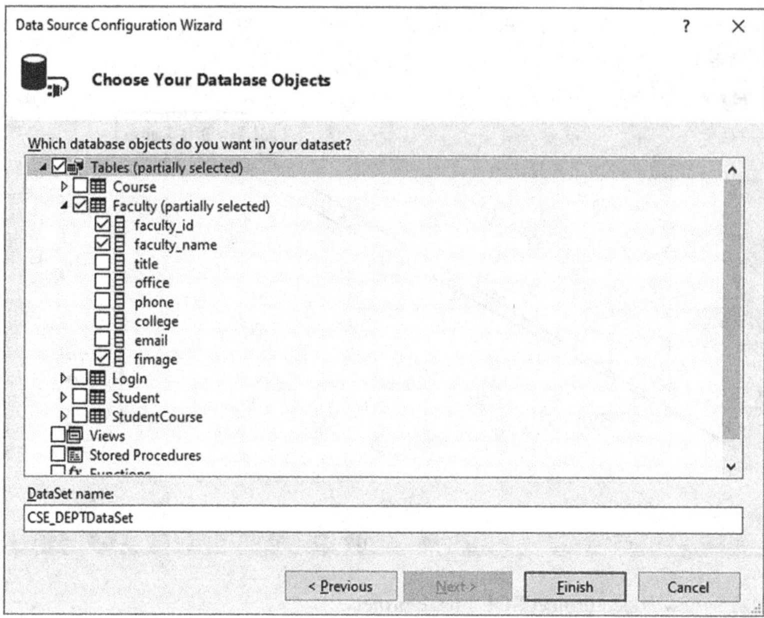

FIGURE 2.51 The connected database and our dataset CSE_DEPTDataSet.

12) Expand the **Tables** and the **Faculty** folder and check our **Faculty** table, and select three columns, **faculty_id, faculty_name** and **fimage**, by checking them one by one, as shown in Figure 2.51. Then click on the **Finish** button to complete this database connection and dataset setup process.
13) Now return to our Visual C#.NET project window, expand our DataSet and the Faculty table, **CSE_DEPTDataSet** and **Faculty**, in the Data Sources window. Click on the drop down arrow on the **Faculty** table combo box and select the **Details** item, and then drag this **Details** item and place it into the Form window, as shown in Figure 2.52.

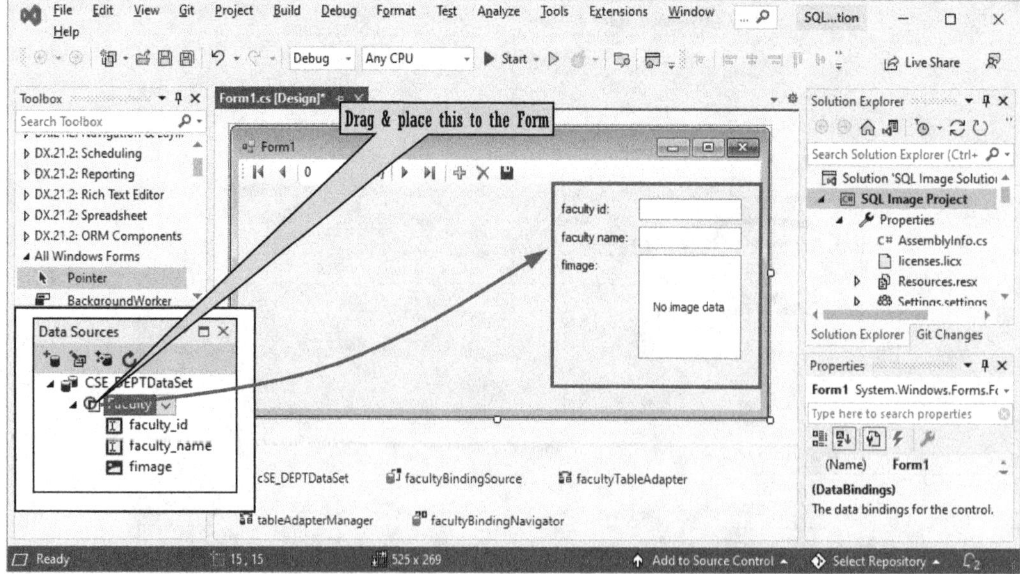

FIGURE 2.52 Drag and place three columns in details format on faculty table.

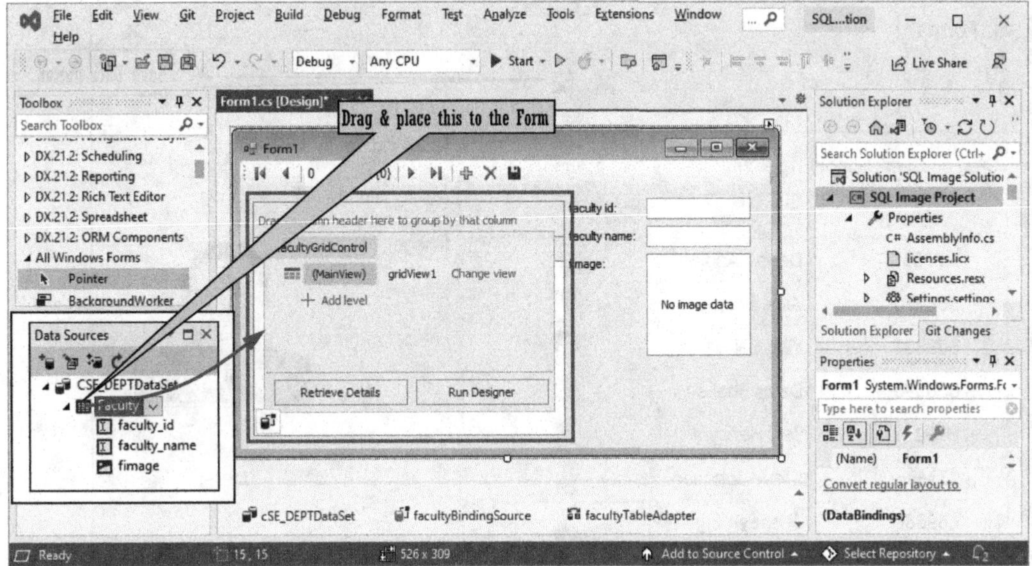

FIGURE 2.53 Drag and place three columns in GridView format on faculty table.

14) Now go to the **Image** object added on the Form window, **fimage**, and click on an arrow box ▶ located at the upper-right corner to open the **PictureEdit Tasks** dialog box, and select **Stretch** from the **Size Mode** combo box. Then click on any place on the Form window to close that PictureEdit Tasks dialog box.
15) Perform a similar operation as we did in step 12, click on the drop-down arrow on the **Faculty** table combo box and select the **GridView** item, and then drag this GridView item and place it into the Form window, as shown in Figure 2.53.
16) Now go to **File | Save All** item to save all of these additions and modifications to this Form window.
17) Then click on the **Start** button (green arrow on the tool bar) to run this Visual C# project. As the project runs, the contents of three columns for all faculty members in this **Faculty** table are displayed in both the Details and GridView except the faculty image **fimage**, as shown in Figure 2.54.
18) To add an image to the **fimage** box for the selected faculty, click on an arrow for that faculty and first click (left-click) on the **fimage** column in the GridView, and then right-click on the **fimage** column again. On the popup menu, select the **Load** item to try to load and add an image for the selected faculty member.
19) Browse to the related faculty image, in our case, all faculty images are stored in the folder: **Students\Images\Faculty** in the CRC Press ftp site. One can copy those images and save them in one of your local folder in your machine. Browse to that folder and select the associated faculty image, such as **Anderson.jpg** for the faculty member **Black Anderson**, by clicking on it, and click on the **Open** button to add it to the **CSE_DEPTDataSet**.
20) Then click on the **Save Data** button located at the upper-right corner on the tool bar to save this image into the database. Perform similar operations to add all faculty images into our sample database **CSE_DEPT.mdf**.

Your finished Form window is shown in Figure 2.54. Now you can stop the running of the Visual C#.NET project **SQL Image Project** by clicking on the **Close** button.

The relationships between each faculty member, student and related name of image file are shown in Figures 2.55 and 2.56.

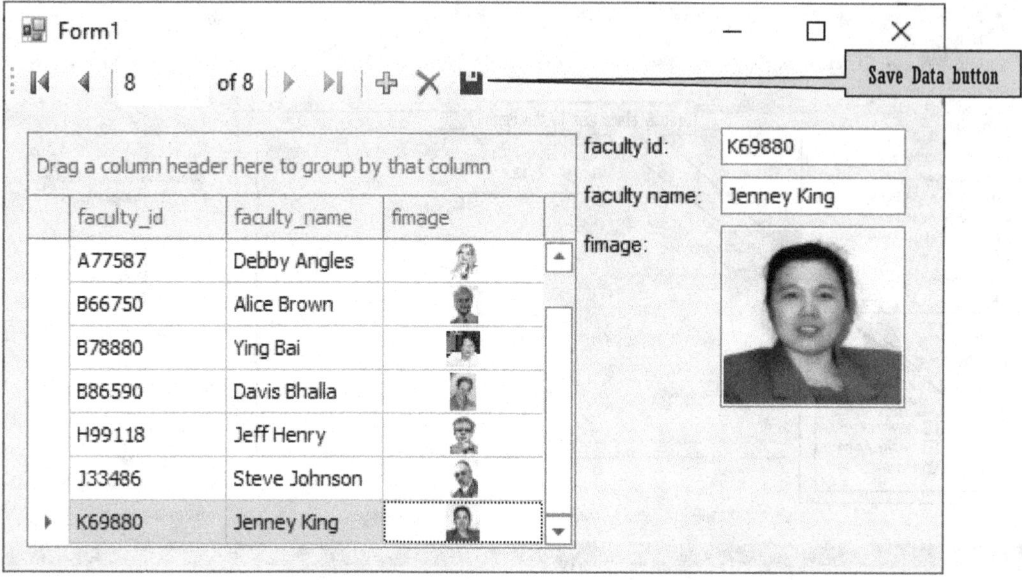

FIGURE 2.54 The completed form for adding faculty images.

faculty_id	faculty_name	fimage
A52990	Black Anderson	Anderson.jpg
A77587	Debby Angles	Angles.jpg
B66750	Alice Brown	Brown.jpg
B78880	Ying Bai	Bai.jpg
B86590	Davis Bhalla	Davis.jpg
H99118	Jeff Henry	Henry.jpg
J33486	Steve Johnson	Johnson.jpg
K69880	Jenney King	King.jpg

FIGURE 2.55 The image files in the faculty table.

student_id	student_name	simage
A78835	Andrew Woods	Woods.jpg
A97850	Ashly Jade	Jade.jpg
B92996	Blue Valley	Valley.jpg
H10210	Holes Smith	Smith.jpg
T77896	Tom Erica	Erica.jpg

FIGURE 2.56 The image files in the student table.

Now if you open the Microsoft SQL Server Management Studio 18 and the database **CSE_DEPT**, select and open the **Faculty** table with **Edit Top 200 Rows** item, you can find that all **NULL** in the **fimage** column become to **Binary data**, as shown in Figure 2.57.

In a similar way, you can add all students' images into the **Student** table in our database **CSE_DEPT.mdf**. All students' images can be found under a folder **Students\Images\Students** at the CRC Press ftp site (Figure 1.2 in Chapter 1). One can copy and store them in a local folder in your computer. The relationships between each student and related name of image file are shown in Figure 2.56.

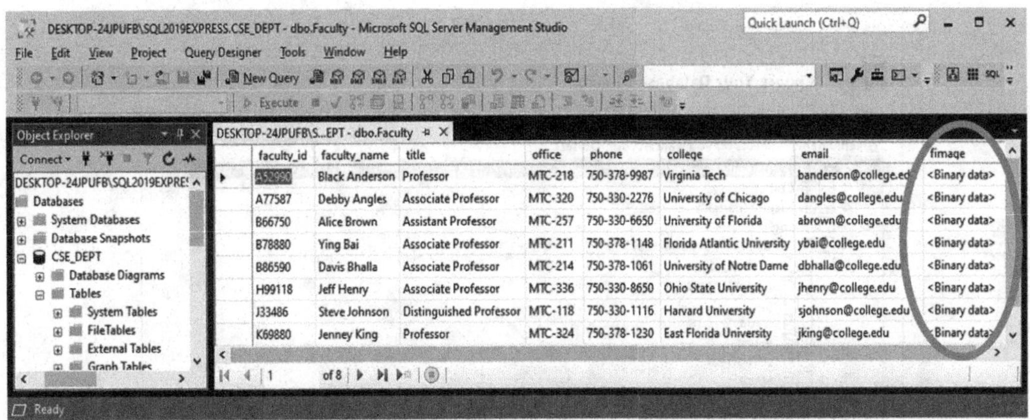

FIGURE 2.57 The modified fimage column.

Perform the following operations to add all students' images into the **Student** table in our sample database **CSE_DEPT**:

1) Open our project **SQL Image Project** if it is not opened, add another Windows Form object by right clicking on our project **SQL Image Project** in the Solution Explorer window, and select **Add | New Item** from the popup menu.
2) In the opened Add New Item wizard, select the item **Form (Windows Forms)** and enter **Form2.cs** into the **Name** box at the bottom. Then click on the **Add** button.
3) Now open the **Data Sources** window and right click on our added DataSet, **CSE_DEPTDataSet**, and select the **Configure Data Source with Wizard** item to configure or add our **Student** table into this DataSet.
4) In the opened Configuration Wizard, expand the **Tables** folder and the **Student** table, and check only three columns, **student_id, student_name** and **simage**.
5) Your finished **Student** table in the Configuration Wizard is shown in Figure 2.58. Click on the **Finish** button to complete this configuration process.
6) Now return to our Visual C#.NET project and focus on our added Form2 window. First expand our DataSet **CSE_DEPTDataSet** and the **Student** table in the Data Sources window. Click on the drop down arrow on the **Student** table combo box and select the **Details** item, and then drag this **Details** item and place it into the Form2 window.
7) Now go to the **Image** object added to the Form2 window, **simage**, and click on an arrow box ▶ located at the upper-right corner to open the **PictureEdit Tasks** dialog box, and select **Stretch** from the **Size Mode** combo box. Then click on any place on the Form2 window to close that PictureEdit Tasks dialog box.
8) Perform a similar operation as we did in step 6, click on the drop down arrow on the **Student** table combo box and select the **GridView** item, and then drag this GridView item and place it into the Form2 window.
9) Now go to **File | Save All** item to save all of these additions and modifications.
10) Now double click on the **C# Program.cs** file in the Solution Explorer window to open it, then go to coding line 19 and replace the code **Application.Run(new Form1())** with **Application.Run(new Form2())** since we need to run Form2 now.
11) Then click on the **Start** button (green arrow on the tool bar) to run this Visual C# project. As the project runs, the contents of three columns for all students in this **Student** table are displayed in both the Details and GridView except the student image **simage**, as shown in Figure 2.59.

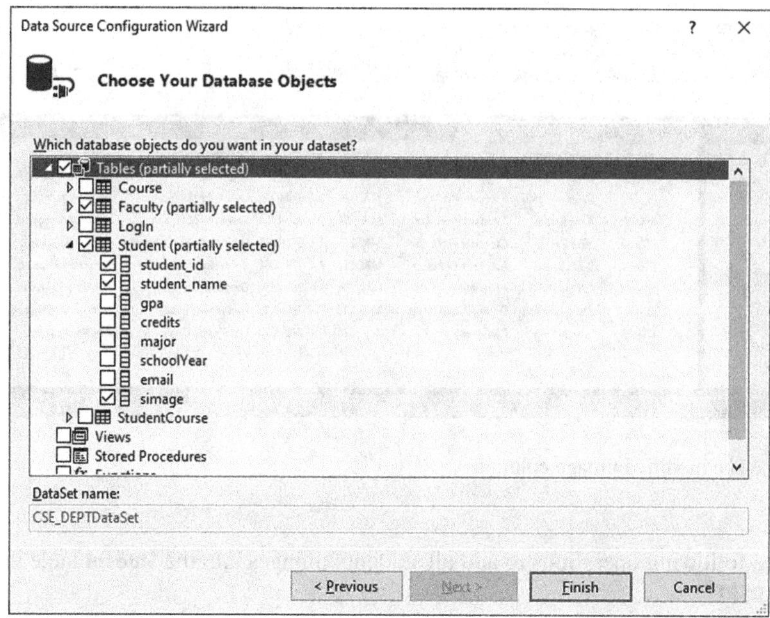

FIGURE 2.58 The finished student table in the data source configuration wizard.

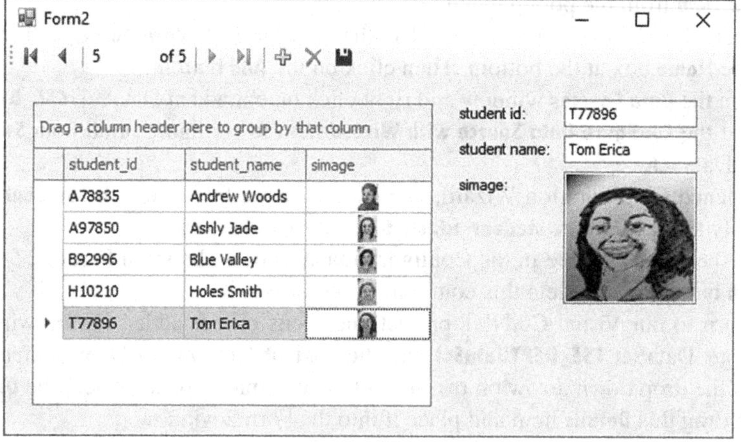

FIGURE 2.59 The completed form for adding student images.

12) To add an image to the **simage** box for the selected student, click on an arrow for that student and first click (left-click) on the **simage** column in the GridView, and then right-click on the **simage** column again. On the popup menu, select the **Load** item to try to load and add an image for the selected student.
13) Browse to the related student image, in our case, all student images are stored in the folder: **Students\Images\Students** in the CRC Press ftp site. One can copy those images and save them in one of your local folder in your machine. Browse to that local folder and select the associated student image, such as **Erica.jpg** for the student **Tom Erica**, by clicking on it, and click on the **Open** button to add it to the DataSet.
14) Then click on the **Save Data** button located at the upper-right corner on the tool bar to save this image into the database. Perform similar operations to add all student images into our sample database **CSE_DEPT.mdf**.

Your finished Form2 window is shown in Figure 2.59. Now you can stop the running of the Visual C#.NET project **SQL Image Project** by clicking on the **Close** button.

A completed complete projects, **SQL Image Project**, can be found from the folder **Class DB Projects\Chapter 2** under the **Students** folder in the CRC Press ftp site (refer to Figure 1.2 in Chapter 1).

2.10 A SHORT-CUT: HOW TO USE THE SAMPLE DATABASE WITHOUT BUILDING IT

If some users, for some reason or other, do not have time or do not like to create and build this sample database, **CSE_DEPT**, with these steps, they can take a short-cut to directly use this sample database without spending any time or efforts. The precondition is that the following components must be installed:

- Microsoft SQL Server 2019 Express Database
- Microsoft SQL Server Management Studio 18

Refer to Appendix A on the CRC Press ftp site to get more details in how to install Microsoft SQL Server 2019 Express Database and SQL Server Management Studio. Refer to Appendix E on the CRC Press ftp site to get more details in how to copy, paste this sample database file and attach it into the SQL Server 2019 Express Database via the SQL Server Management Studio.

2.11 CHAPTER SUMMARY

A detailed discussion and analysis of the structure and components about popular database systems are provided in this chapter. Some key technologies in developing and designing a database are also given and discussed in this part. The procedure and components used to develop a relational database are analyzed in detailed with some real-data tables in our sample database **CSE_DEPT**. The process in developing and building a sample database is discussed in detailed with the following points:

- Defining Relationships
- Normalizing the Data
- Implementing the Relational Database

In the second part of this chapter, a sample SQL Server 2019 Express database, **CSE_DEPT**, which is developed with an updated and popular database management system, Microsoft SQL Server Management Studio 18, is provided in detail. This sample database will be used in the following chapters throughout the entire book.

HOMEWORK

I. TRUE/FALSE SELECTIONS

____1. Database development process involves project planning, problem analysis, logical design, physical design, implementation and maintenance

____2. Duplication of data creates problems with data integrity.

____3. If the primary key consists of a single column, then the table in 1NF is automatically in 2NF.

____4. A table is in first normal form if there are no repeating groups of data in any column.

____5. When a user perceives the database as made up of tables, it is called a Network Model.

____6. The *entity integrity rule* states that no attribute that is a member of the primary (composite) key may accept a null value.

____7. When creating data tables for the Microsoft Access database, a blank field can be kept as a blank without any letter in it.

____8. To create data tables in SQL Server database, a blank field can be kept as a blank without any letter in it.

____9. The name of each data table in SQL Server database must be prefixed by the keyword dbo.

___10. In each relational database table, it can contain multiple primary keys, but only one unique foreign key.

II. Multiple Choice Questions

1. There are many advantages to using an integrated database approach over that of a file processing approach. These include
   a. Minimizing data redundancy
   b. Improving security
   c. Data independence
   d. All of the above
2. Entity integrity rule implies that no attribute that is a member of the primary key may accept ______
   a. Null value
   b. Integer data type
   c. Character data type
   d. Real data type
3. Reducing data redundancy will lead to _____
   a. Deletion anomalies
   b. Data consistency
   c. Loss of efficiency
   d. None of the above
4. ______ keys are used to create relationships among various tables in a database
   a. Primary keys
   b. Candidate keys
   c. Foreign keys
   d. Composite keys
5. In a small university the department of Computer Science has six faculty members. However, each faculty member belongs only to the Computer Science department. This type of relationship is called _________
   a. One-to-one
   b. One-to-many
   c. Many-to-many
   d. None of the above
6. The Client Server databases have several advantages over the File Server databases. These include ________
   a. Minimizing chances of crashes
   b. Provision of features for recovery
   c. Enforcement of security
   d. Efficient use of the network
   e. All of the above
7. One can create the foreign keys between tables ______
   a. Before any table can be created
   b. When some tables are created
   c. After all tables are created
   d. With no limitations

8. To create foreign keys between tables, first one must select the table that contains a _______ key and then select another table that has a _______ key.
   a. Primary, foreign
   b. Primary, primary
   c. Foreign, primary
   d. Foreign, foreign
9. The data type nvarchar(50) in SQL Server database is a string with _______
   a. Limited length up to 50 letters
   b. Fixed length of 50 letters
   c. Certain number of letters
   d. Varying length
10. For data tables in the SQL Server Database, a blank field must be ________
    a. Indicated by NULL Avoided
    b. Kept as a blank
    c. Either by NULL or a blank
    d. Indicated by NULL

III. Exercises

1. What are the advantages to using an integrated database approach over that of a file processing approach?
2. Define entity integrity and referential integrity. Describe the reasons for enforcing these rules.
3. Entities can have three types of relationships. It can be one-to-one, one-to-many, and many-to-many. Define each type of relationship. Draw ER diagrams to illustrate each type of relationship.
4. List all steps to create foreign keys between data tables for the SQL Server 2019 Express database in the SQL Server Management Studio. Illustrate those steps by using a real example. For instance, how to create foreign keys between the LogIn and the Faculty table.
5. List all steps to create Foreign keys between data tables for a SQL Server 2019 Express database in the SQL Server Management Studio. Illustrate those steps by using a real example. For instance, how to create foreign keys between the StudentCourse and the Course table.

3 Introduction to ADO.NET

It has been a long story for software developers to generate and implement sophisticated data processing techniques to improve and enhance data operations. The evolution of data access API has also been a long process, focusing predominantly on how to deal with relational data in a more flexible manner. The methodology development has been focused on Microsoft-based APIs, such as ODBC, OLEDB, Microsoft® Jet, Data Access Objects (DAO) and Remote Data Objects (RDO), in addition to many non-Microsoft-based APIs. These APIs did not bridge the gap between object-based and semi-structured (XML) data programming needs. Combine this problem with the task of dealing with many different data stores, non-relational data such as XML and applications applying across multiple languages are challenging topics and one should have a tremendous opportunity for complete re-architecture. The ADO.NET is a good solution for these challenges.

ADO.NET 2.0 was considered as a full solution between the relational database API and object-oriented data access API, which was released with the .NET Framework 2.0 and Visual Studio.NET 2005. Today the latest version of the ADO.NET is 4.3, which is released with the .NET Framework 4.0 and Visual Studio.NET 2017. In this chapter, first we will provide a detailed review of the history of ADO.NET, and then a full discussion and description about the components and architectures of ADO.NET 2.0 is given since most data components used for today's database actions are still covered by the ADO.NET 2.0. Finally we introduce some new features and components included in the ADO.NET 3.5.

3.1 THE ADO AND ADO.NET

ActiveX Data Object (ADO) is developed based on Object Linking and Embedding (OLE) and Component Object Model (COM) technologies. COM is used by developers to create re-usable software components, link components together to build applications, and take advantage of Windows services. In recent decades, ADO has been the preferred interface for Visual Basic programmers to access various data sources, with ADO 2.7 being the latest version of this technology. The development history of data accessing methods can be traced back to the mid-1990s, with Data Access Object (DAO);this was then followed by Remote Data Object (RDO), which was based on the Open Database Connectivity (ODBC). The late 1990s saw the development of ADO, which is based on OLEDB. This technology has been widely applied in most Object Oriented Programming and Database applications over the past decade.

ADO.NET 4.3 is the latest version of ADO.NET and is based principally on the Microsoft .NET Framework 4.0. The underlying technology applied in ADO.NET 4.3 is very different from the COM-based ADO. The ADO.NET Common Language Runtime provides bi-directional, transparent integration with COM. This means that COM and ADO.NET applications and components can use functionality from each system. However, the ADO.NET 4.3 Framework provides developers with a significant number of benefits, including a more robust, evidence-based security model, automatic memory management native Web services support and Language Integrated Query (LINQ). For new developments, the ADO.NET 4.3 is highly recommended as a preferred technology because of its powerful managed runtime environment and services.

This chapter will provide a detailed introduction to ADO.NET 2.0 and ADO.NET 4.3 and their components, and these components will be utilized for the rest of the book.

DOI: 10.1201/9781003319832-3

In this chapter, you will:

- Learn the basic classes in ADO.NET 2.0 and its architecture
- Learn the different ADO.NET 2.0 data providers
- Learn about the Connection and Command components
- Learn about the Parameters collection component
- Learn about the DataAdapter and DataReader components
- Learn about the DataSet and DataTable components
- Learn about the ADO.NET 4.3 Entity Framework (EF)
- Learn about the ADO.NET 4.3 Entity Framework Tools (EFT)
- Learn about the ADO.NET Entity Data Model (EDM)

First let's have a closer look at the ADO.NET 2.0 and have a global picture of its components.

3.2 OVERVIEW OF THE ADO.NET 2.0

ADO.NET is a set of classes that exposes data access services to the Microsoft .NET programmer. ADO.NET provides a rich set of components for creating distributed, data-sharing applications. It is an integral part of the Microsoft .NET Framework, providing access to relational, XML, and application data. ADO.NET supports a variety of development needs, including the creation of front-end database clients and middle-tier business objects used by applications, tools, languages, or Internet browsers.

All ADO.NET classes are located at the **System.Data** namespace with two files named **System.Data.dll** and **System.Xml.dll**. When compiling code that uses the **System.Data** namespace, reference both System.Data.dll and System.Xml.dll.

Basically speaking, ADO.NET provides a set of classes to support you to develop database applications and enable you to connect to a data source to retrieve, manipulate and update data with your database. The classes provided by ADO.NET are core to develop a professional data-driven application and they can be divided into the following three major components:

- Data Provider
- DataSet
- DataTable

These three components are located at the different namespaces. The DataSet and the DataTable classes are located at the System.Data namespace. The classes of the Data Provider are located at the different namespaces based on the types of the Data Providers.

Data Provider contains four classes: Connection, Command, DataAdapter and DataReader. These four classes can be used to perform the different functionalities to help you to:

1) Set a connection between your project and the data source using the Connection object
2) Execute data queries to retrieve, manipulate and update data using the Command object
3) Move the data between your DataSet and your database using the DataAdapter object
4) Perform data queries from the database (read-only) using the DataReader object

The DataSet class can be considered as a table container and it can contain multiple data tables. These data tables are only a mapping to those real data tables in your database. But these data tables can also be used separately without connecting to the DataSet. In this case, each data table can be considered as a DataTable object.

The DataSet and DataTable classes have no direct relationship with the Data Provider class; therefore they are often called Data Provider-independent components. Four classes, Connection,

Command, DataAdapter and DataReader, which belong to Data Provider, are often called Data Provider-dependent components.

To get a clearer picture of the ADO.NET, let's first take a look at the architecture of the ADO.NET.

3.3 THE ARCHITECTURE OF THE ADO.NET 2.0

The ADO.NET 2.0 architecture can be divided into two logical pieces: command execution and caching.

Command execution requires features such as connectivity, execution, and reading of results. These features are enabled with ADO.NET Data Providers. The caching of results is handled by the DataSet.

The Data Provider enables connectivity and command execution to underlying data sources. Note that these data sources do not have to be relational databases. Once a command has been executed, the results can be read using a DataReader. A DataReader provides efficient forward-only stream-level access to the results. In addition, results can be used to render a DataSet a DataAdapter. This is typically called "filling the DataSet."

Figure 3.1 shows a typical architecture of the ADO.NET 2.0.

In this architecture, the data tables are embedded into the DataSet as a DataTable-Collection and the data transactions between the DataSet and the Data Provider, such as SELECT, INSERT, UPDATE and DELETE, are made by using the DataAdapter via its own four different methods: SelectCommand, InsertCommand, UpdateCommand and DeleteCommand, respectively. The Connection object is only used to set a connection between your data source and your applications. The DataReader object is not used for this architecture. As you will see from the sample project in the following chapters, to execute the different methods under the DataAdapter to perform the data query is exactly to call the Command object with different parameters.

Another ADO.NET architecture is shown in Figure 3.2.

In this architecture, the data tables are not embedded into the DataSet but treated as independent data tables and each table can be considered as an individual DataTable object. The data transactions between the Data Provider and the DataTable are realized by executing the different methods of the Command object with the associated parameters. The ExecuteReader() method of the Command object is called when a data query is made from the data source, which is equivalent to execute an SQL SELECT statement, and the returned data should be stored to the DataReader object. When performing other data-accessing operations such as INSERT, UPDATE or DELETE, the ExecuteNonQuery() method of the Command object should be called with the suitable parameters attached to the Command object.

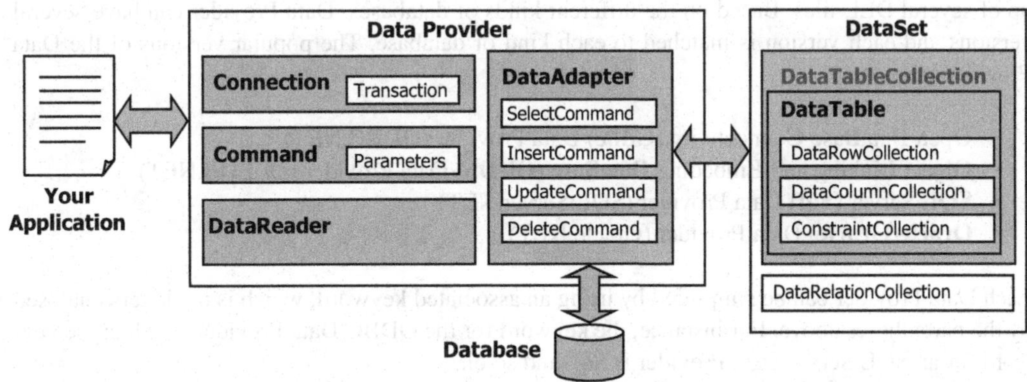

FIGURE 3.1 A typical architecture of the ADO.NET 2.0.

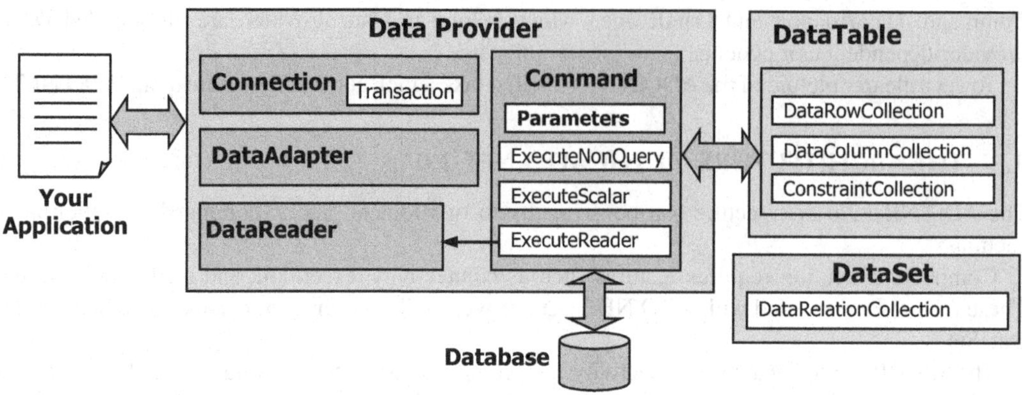

FIGURE 3.2 Another architecture of the ADO.NET 2.0.

Keep these two ADO.NET 2.0 architectures in mind; we will have a more detailed discussion for each component of the ADO.NET below. The sample projects developed in the following sections utilized these two architectures to perform the data query from and the data accessing to the data source.

3.4 THE COMPONENTS OF ADO.NET 2.0

As we discussed in Section 3.2, ADO.NET 2.0 is composed of three major components: Data Provider, DataSet and DataTable. First let's take a look at the Data Provider.

3.4.1 The Data Provider

The Data Provider can also be called a data driver and it can be used as a major component for your data-driven applications. The functionalities of the Data Provider, as its name means, are to:

- Connect your data source with your applications
- Execute different methods to perform the associated data query and data accessing operations between your data source and your applications
- Disconnect the data source when the data operations are done

The Data Provider is physically composed of a binary library file and this library is in the DLL file format. Sometimes this DLL file depends on other DLL files, so in fact a Data Provider can be made up of several DLL files. Based on the different kinds of databases, Data Provider can have several versions and each version is matched to each kind of database. The popular versions of the Data Provider are:

- **Open DataBase** Connectivity (**Odbc**) Data Provider (ODBC.NET)
- **Object Linking** and **Embeding DataBase** (**OleDb**) Data Provider (OLEDB.NET)
- **SQL** Server (**Sql**) Data Provider (SQL Server.NET)
- **Oracle**(**Oracle**) Data Provider (Oracle.NET)

Each Data Provider can be simplified by using an associated keyword, which is the letters enclosed by the parentheses above. For instance, the keyword for the ODBC Data Provider is Odbc; the keyword for an SQL Server Data Provider is Sql, and so on.

In order to distinguish this from the older Data Providers such as Microsoft ODBC, Microsoft OLE DB, Microsoft SQL Server and Oracle, in some books all different Data Providers included in

Namespaces	Descriptions
System.Data	Holds the DataSet and DataTable classes
System.Data.OleDb	Holds the class collection used to access an OLEDB data source
System.Data.SqlClient	Holds the classes used to access an SQL Server 7.0 data source or later
System.Data.Odbc	Holds the class collection used to access an ODBC data source
System.Data.OracleClient	Holds the classes used to access an Oracle data source

FIGURE 3.3 Namespaces for different data providers, DataSet and DataTable.

the ADO.NET are extended by a suffix '.NET', such as OLE DB.NET, ODBC.NET, SQL Server. NET and Oracle.NET. Since most Data Providers discussed in this book belong to ADO.NET, generally we do not need to add that .NET suffix but we will add this suffix if the old Data Providers are used.

The different data providers are located at the different namespaces, and these namespaces hold the various data classes that you must import into your code in order to use those classes in your project.

Figure 3.3 lists the most popular namespaces used by the different data providers and used by the DataSet and the DataTable.

Since the different Data Provider is located at the different namespace as shown in Figure 3.3, you must first add the appropriate namespace into your Visual C#.NET 2008 project, exactly into the each form's code window, whenever you want to use that Data Provider. Also all classes provided by that Data Provider must be prefixed by the associated keyword. For example, you must use 'using System.Data.OleDb' to add the namespace of the OLEDB.NET Data Provider if you want to use this Data Provider in your project, and also all classes belong to that Data Provider must be prefixed by the associated keyword OleDb, such as OleDbConnection, OleDbCommand, OleDbDataAdapter and OleDbDataReader. The same thing holds true for all other Data Providers.

Although different Data Providers are located at the different namespaces and have the different prefixes, the classes of these Data Providers have the similar methods or properties with the same name. For example, no matter what kind of Data Provider you are using such as an OleDb, an Sql or an Oracle, they have the methods or properties with the same name, such as Connection String property, Open() and Close() method as well as the ExecuteReader() method. This provides the flexibility for the programmers and allows them to use different Data Providers to access the different data source by only modifying the prefix applied before each class.

The following sections provide a more detailed discussion for each specific Data Provider. These discussions will give you a direction or guideline to help you to select the appropriate Data Provider when you want to use them to develop the different data-driven applications.

3.4.1.1 The ODBC Data Provider

The .NET Framework Data Provider for ODBC uses native ODBC Driver Manager (DM) through COM interop to enable data access. The ODBC data provider supports both local and distributed transactions. For distributed transactions, the ODBC data provider, by default, automatically enlists in a transaction and obtains transaction details from Windows 2000 Component Services.

The ODBC .NET data provider provides access to ODBC data sources with the help of native ODBC drivers in the same way that the OleDb .NET data provider accesses native OLE DB providers.

The ODBC.NET supports the following Data Providers:

- SQL Server
- Microsoft ODBC for Oracle
- Microsoft Access Driver (*.mdb)

Some older database systems only support ODBC as the data access technique, which include older versions of SQL Server and Oracle as well as some third-party database such as Sybase.

3.4.1.2 The OLEDB Data Provider

The System.Data.OleDb namespace holds all classes used by the .NET Framework 2.0 Data Provider for OLE DB. The .NET Framework Data Provider for OLE DB describes a collection of classes used to access an OLE DB data source in the managed space. Using the OleDbDataAdapter, you can fill a memory-resident DataSet that you can use to query and update the data source. The OLE DB.NET data access technique supports the following Data Providers:

- Microsoft Access
- SQL Server (7.0 or later)
- Oracle (9i or later)

One advantage of using the OLEDB.NET Data Provider is to allow users to develop a generic data-driven application. The so-called generic application means that you can use the OLEDB.NET Data Provider to access any data source such as Microsoft Access, SQL Server, Oracle and other data source that support the OLEDB.

Figure 3.4 shows the compatibility between the OLEDB Data Provider and the OLE DB.NET Data Provider.

3.4.1.3 The SQL Server Data Provider

This Data Provider provides access to a SQL Server version 7.0 or later database using its own internal protocol. The functionality of the data provider is designed to be similar to that of the .NET Framework data providers for OLE DB, ODBC, and Oracle. All classes related to this Data Provider are defined in a DLL file and is located at the System.Data.SqlClient namespace. Although Microsoft provides different Data Providers to access the data in SQL Server database, such as the ODBC and OLE DB, for the sake of optimal data operations, it is highly recommended to use this Data Provider to access the data in an SQL Server data source.

As shown in Figure 3.4, this Data Provider is a new version and it can only work for the SQL Server version 7.0 and later. If an old version of SQL Server is used, you need to use either an OLE DB.NET or a SQLOLEDB Data Provider.

3.4.1.4 The Oracle Data Provider

This Data Provider is an add-on component to the .NET Framework that provides access to the Oracle database. All classes related to this Data Provider are located in the **System.Data.OracleClient** namespace. This provider relies upon Oracle Client Interfaces provided by the Oracle Client Software. You need to install the Oracle Client software on your computer to use this Data Provider.

Microsoft provides multiple ways to access the data stored in an Oracle database, such as Microsoft ODBC for Oracle and OLE DB, you should use this Oracle Data Provider to access the data in an Oracle data source since this one provides the most efficient way to access the Oracle database.

This Data Provider can only work for the recent versions of the Oracle database such as 8.1.7 and later. For old versions of the Oracle database, you need to use either MSDAORA or an OLE DB.NET.

Provider Name	Descriptions
SQLOLEDB	Used for Microsoft SQL Server 6.5 or earlier
Microsoft.Jet.OLEDB.4.0	Use for Microsoft JET database (Microsoft Access)
MSDAORA	Use for Oracle version 7 and later

FIGURE 3.4 The compatibility between the OLEDB and OLEDB.NET.

As we mentioned in the previous parts, all different Data Providers use the similar objects, properties and methods to perform the data operations for the different databases. In the following sections, we will make a detailed discussion for these similar objects, properties and methods used for the different Data Providers.

3.4.2 The Connection Class

As shown in Figures 3.1 and 3.2, the Data Provider contains four sub-classes and the Connection component is one of them. This class provides a connection between your applications and the database you selected to connect to your project. To use this class to setup a connection between your application and the desired database, you need first to create an instance or an object based on this class. Depends on your applications, you can create a global connection instance for your entire project or you can create some local connection objects for each of your form windows. Generally, a global instance is a good choice since you do not need to perform multiple open and close operations for connection objects. A global connection instance is used in all sample projects in this book.

The Connection object you want to use depends on the type of the data source you selected. Data Provider provides four different Connection classes and each one is matched to one different database. Figure 3.5 lists these popular Connection classes used for the different data sources:

The new keyword is used to create a new instance or object of the Connection class. Although different Connection classes provide different overloaded constructors, two popular constructors are utilized widely for Visual C#.NET 2008. One of them does not accept any argument, but the other one accepts a connection string as the argument and this constructor is the most commonly used for data connections.

The connection string is a property of the Connection class and it provides all necessary information to connect to your data source. Regularly this connection string contains a quite few parameters to define a connection, but only five of them are popularly utilized for most data-driven applications:

1) Provider
2) Data Source
3) Database
4) User ID
5) Password

For different databases, the parameters contained in the connection string may have a little difference. For example, both OLE DB and ODBC databases need all of these five parameters to be included in a connection string to connect to OleDb or Odbc data source. But for the SQL Server database connection, you may need to use the Server to replace the Provider parameter, and for the Oracle database connection, you do not need the Provider and Database parameters at all for your connection string. You can find these differences in Section 5.15 in Chapter 5.

The parameter names in a connection string are case-insensitive, but some of parameters, such as the Password or PWD, may be case-sensitive. Many of the connection string properties can be read out separately. For example, one of the properties, state, is one of the most useful properties for your data-driven applications. By checking this property, you can get to know what is the current

Connection Class	Associated Database
OdbcConnection	ODBC Data Source
OleDbConnection	OLE DB Database
SqlConnection	SQL Server Database
OracleConnection	Oracle Database

FIGURE 3.5 The connection classes and databases.

connection status between your database and your project, and this checking is necessary for you to make the decision over which way your program is supposed to go. You can also avoid the unnecessary errors related to the data source connection by checking this property. For example, you cannot perform any data operation if your database has not been connected to your application. By checking this property, you can get a clear picture whether your application is connected to your database or not.

A typical data connection instance with a general connection string can be expressed by the following codes:

```
xxxConnection Connection = new xxxConnection("Provider=MyProvider;" +
                                              "Data Source=MyServer;" +
                                              "Database=MyDatabase;" +
                                              "User ID=MyUserID;" +
                                              "Password=MyPassWord;")
```

where xxx should be replaced by the selected Data Provider in your real application, such as OleDb, Sql or Oracle. You need to use the real parameter values implemented in your applications to replace those nominal values such as MyServer, MyDatabase, MyUserID and MyPassWord in your application.

The Provider parameter indicates the database driver you selected. If you installed a local SQL server and client such as the SQL Server 2019 Express on your computer, the Provider should be localhost. If you are using a remote SQL Server instance, you need to use that remote server's network name. If you are using the default named instance of SQLX on your computer, you need to use *.\SQLEXPRESS* as the value for your Provider parameter. For the Oracle server database, you do not need to use this parameter.

The Data Source parameter indicates the name of the network computer on which your SQL server or Oracle server is installed and running.

The Database parameter indicates your database name.

The User ID and Password parameters are used for the security issue for your database. In most cases, the default Windows NT Security Authentication is utilized.

Some typical Connection instances used for the different databases are listed below:

OLE DB Data Provider for Microsoft Access Database

```
OleDbConnection Connection = new OleDbConnection("Provider=Microsoft.Jet.
OLEDB.4.0;"+
                                    "Data Source=C:\database\CSE_DEPT.mdb;" +
                                    "User ID=MyUserID;" +
                                    "Password=MyPassWord;")
```

SQL Server Data Provider for SQL Server Database

```
SqlConnection Connection = new SqlConnection("Server=localhost;" +
                                             "Data Source=YBAI\SQLEXPRESS;" +
                                             "Database=CSE_DEPT;" +
                                             "Integrated Security=SSPI")
```

Oracle Data Provider for Oracle Database

```
OracleConnection Connection = new OracleConnection("Data Source=XE;" +
                                                   "User ID=system;" +
                                                   "Password=come")
```

Besides these important properties such as the connection string and state, the Connection class contains some important methods, such as the Open() and Close() methods. To make a real connection between your data source and your application, the Open() method is needed, and the Close() method is also needed when you finished the data operations and you want to exit your application.

3.4.2.1 The Open() Method of the Connection Class

To create a real connection between your database and your applications, the **Open()** method of the Connection class is called and it is used to open a connection to a data source with the property settings specified by the connection string. An important issue for this connection is that you must make sure that this connection is a bug-free connection; in other words, the connection is successful and you can use this connection to access data from your application to your desired data source without any problem. One of the efficient ways to do this is to use the **try-catch** block to embed this Open() operation to try to find and catch the typical possible errors caused by this connection. An example coding of opening an OLEDB connection is shown in Figure 3.6.

The Microsoft.ACE.OLEDB.12.0 driver, which is a driver for the Microsoft Access 2007, is used as the data provider and the Microsoft Access 2007 database file CSE_DEPT.accdb is located at the database\Access folder at our local computer. The Open() method, which is embedded inside the **try-catch** block, is executed after a new OleDbConnection object is created to open this connection. Two possible typical errors, either an OleDbException or an InvalidOperationException, could happen after this Open() method is executed. A related message would be displayed if any one of those errors occurred and caught.

To make sure that the connection is bug-free, one of the properties of the Connection class, State, is used. This property has two possible values: Open or Closed. By checking this property, we can inspect whether or not this connection is successful. The project will be exited if this connection is failed since we can do nothing without this connection object being setup and our database connection being successful.

```
string strConnectionString = "Provider=Microsoft.ACE.OLEDB.12.0;" +
                              "Data Source=C:\\database\\Access\\CSE_DEPT.accdb;";
accConnection = new OleDbConnection(strConnectionString);
try
{
    accConnection.Open();
}
catch (OleDbException e)
{
    MessageBox.Show("Access Error");
    MessageBox.Show("Error Code = " + e.ErrorCode);
    MessageBox.Show("Error Message = " + e.Message);
}
catch (InvalidOperationException e)
{
    MessageBox.Show("Invalid Message = " + e.Message);
}
if (accConnection.State != ConnectionState.Open)
{
    MessageBox.Show("Database connection is Failed");
    Application.Exit();
}
```

FIGURE 3.6 An example coding of the opening a connection.

3.4.2.2 The Close() Method of the Connection Class

The **Close()** method is a partner of the Open() method and it is used to close a connection between your database and your applications when you finished your data operations to the data source. You should close any connection object you connected to your data source after you finished the data access to any data source, otherwise a possible error may be encountered when you try to re-open that connection the next time you run your project.

Unlike the Open() method, which is a key to your data access and operation to your data source, the Close() method does not throw any exceptions when you try to close a connection that has already been closed. So you do not need to use a try… catch block to catch any error for this method.

3.4.2.3 The Dispose() Method of the Connection Class

The **Dispose()** method of the Connection class is an overloaded method and it is used to release the resources used by the Connection object. You need to call this method after the Close() method is executed to perform a clean-up job to release all resources used by the Connection object during your data access and operations to your data source. Although it is unnecessary for you to have to call this Dispose() method to do the clean-up job since one of the system tools, Garbage Collection, can periodically check and clean all resources used by unused objects in your computer, it is highly recommended for you to make this kind of coding to make your program more professional and efficient. A piece of example code is shown in Figure 3.7.

Now we have finished the discussion for the first component defined in a Data Provider, the Connection object, let's take a look at the next object, the Command object. Since a close relationship exists between the Command and the Parameter object, we discuss these two objects in one section.

3.4.3 The Command and the Parameter Classes

Command objects are used to execute commands against your database such as a data query, an action query, and even a stored procedure. In fact, all data accesses and data operations between your data source and your applications are achieved by executing the Command object with a set of parameters.

The Command class can be divided into different categories and these categories are based on the different Data Providers. In the case of the popular Data Providers, such as OLE DB, ODBC, SQL Server and Oracle, each has its own Command class. These Command classes are identified by the different prefix, such as OleDbCommand, OdbcCommand, SqlCommand and OracleCommand. Although these different Command objects belong to the different Data Providers, they share similar properties and methods, and they are equivalent in functionalities.

Depending on the architecture of the ADO.NET, the Command object can have two different roles whether you are using it to perform a data query or a data action. (Refer to Figures 3.1 and 3.2.) In Figure 3.1, if a TableAdapter is utilized to perform a data query and all data tables are embedded into the DataSet as a data-catching unit, the Command object is embedded into the different data query method of the TableAdapter, such as SelectCommand, InsertCommand, UpdateCommand and DeleteCommand, and is executed based on the associated query type. In this case, the Command object can be executed indirectly, which means that you do not need to use any Executing method to run the Command object directly; instead you can run it by executing the associated method of the TableAdapter.

```
' clean up the objects used
accConnection.Close();
accConnection.Dispose();
```

FIGURE 3.7 An example coding for the cleanup of resources.

In Figure 3.2, each data table can be considered as an individual table. The Command object can be executed directly based on the attached parameter collection that is created and initialized by the user.

No matter which role you want to use for the Command object, you should first create, initialize and attach the Parameters collection to the Command object before you can use it. In addition, you must initialize the Command object by assigning the suitable properties to it in order to use the Command object to access the data source to perform any data action. Some popular properties of the Command class are discussed below.

3.4.3.1 The Properties of the Command Class

The Command class contains more than ten properties, but only four of them are used popularly in most applications:

- Connection property
- CommandType property
- CommandText property
- Parameters property

The Connection property is used to hold a valid Connection object, and the Command object can be executed to access the connected database based on this Connection object.

The CommandType property is used to indicate what kind of command that is stored in the CommandText property should be executed. In other words, the CommandType property specifies how the CommandText property can be interpreted. In total, three CommandType properties are available: Text, TableDirect and StoredProcedure. The default value of this property is Text.

The content of the CommandText property is determined by the value of the CommandType property. It contains a complete SQL statement if the value of the CommandType property is Text. This may contain a group of SQL statements if the value of the CommandType property is StoredProcedure.

The Parameters property is used to hold a collection of the Parameter objects. You need to note that the Parameters is a collection but the Parameter is an object, which means that the former contains a group of objects and you can add the latter to the former.

You must first create and initialize a Parameter object before you can add that object to the Parameters collection for a Command object.

3.4.3.2 The Constructors and Properties of the Parameter Class

The Parameter class has four popular constructors, which are shown in Figure 3.8 (an SQL Server Data Provider is used as an example).

The first constructor is a blank one, and you need to initialize each property of the Parameter object one by one if you want to use this constructor to instantiate a new Parameter object. Three popular properties of a Parameter object are:

- ParameterName
- Value
- DbType

```
SqlParameter sqlParameter = new SqlParameter();
SqlParameter sqlParameter = new SqlParameter(ParamName, objValue);
SqlParameter sqlParameter = new SqlParameter(ParamName, sqlDbType);
SqlParameter sqlParameter = new SqlParameter(ParamName, sqlDbType, intSize);
```

FIGURE 3.8 Four constructors of the Parameter class.

Data Type	Associated Data Provider
OdbcType	ODBC Data Provider
OleDbType	OLE DB Provider
SqlDbType	SQL Server Data Provider
OracleType	Oracle Data Provider

FIGURE 3.9 The data types and the associated data provider.

The first property, ParameterName, contains the name of the selected parameter. The second property, Value, is the value of the selected parameter and it is an object. The third property, DbType, is used to define the data type of the selected parameter.

All parameters in the Parameter object must have a data type and you can indicate a data type for a selected parameter by specifying the DbType property. ADO.NET and ADO.NET Data Provider have different definitions for the data types they provided. The DbType is the data type used by ADO.NET, but ADO.NET Data Provider has another four different popular data types and each one is associated with a Data Provider. Figure 3.9 lists these data types as well the associated Data Providers.

Even the data types provided by ADO.NET and ADO.NET Data Provider are different, but they have a direct connection between them. As a user, you can use any data type you like, and the other one will be automatically changed to the corresponding value if you set one of them. For example, if you set the DbType property of an SqlParameter object to String, the SqlDbType parameter will be automatically set to Char. In this book, we will always use the data types defined in the ADO.NET Data Provider since all parameters discussed in this section are related to the different Data Provider.

The default data type for the DbType property is String.

3.4.3.3 Parameter Mapping

When you add a Parameter object to the Parameters collection of a Command object by attaching that Parameter object to the Parameters property of the Command class, the Command object needs to know the relationship between that added parameter and the parameters you used in your SQL query string such as an SELECT statement. In other words, the Command object needs to identify which parameter used in your SQL statement should be mapped to this added parameter. Different parameter mappings are used for different Data Providers. Figure 3.10 lists these mappings.

Both OLE DB and ODBC Data Providers used a so-called Positional Parameter Mapping, which means that the relationship between the parameters defined in an SQL statement and the added parameters into a Parameters collection is one-to-one in the order. In other words, the order in which the parameters appear in an SQL statement and the order in which the parameters are added into the Parameters collection should be exactly identical. The Positional Parameter Mapping is indicated with a question mark '?'.

For example, the following SQL statement is used for an OLE DB Data Provider as a query string:

```
SELECT user_name, pass_word FROM LogIn WHERE (user_name=?) AND
 (pass_word=?)
```

The **user_name** and **pass_word** are mapped to two columns in the **LogIn** data table. Two dynamic parameters are represented by two question marks '?' in this SQL statement.

Parameter Mapping	Associated Data Provider
Positional Parameter Mapping	ODBC Data Provider
Positional Parameter Mapping	OLE DB Provider
Named Parameter Mapping	SQL Server Data Provider
Named Parameter Mapping	Oracle Data Provider

FIGURE 3.10 The different parameter mappings.

To add a Parameter object to the Parameters collection of a Command object accCommand, you need to use the **Add()** method as below:

```
accCommand.Parameters.Add("user_name", OleDbType.Char).Value =
  txtUserName.Text;
accCommand.Parameters.Add("pass_word", OleDbType.Char, 8).Value =
  txtPassWord.Text;
```

You must be careful with the order in which you add these two parameters, user_name and pass_word, and make sure that this order is identical with the order in which those two dynamic parameters (?) appear in the above SQL statement.

Both SQL Server and Oracle Data Provider used the Named Parameter Mapping, which means that each parameter, either defined in an SQL statement or added into a Parameters collection, is identified by the name. In other words, the name of the parameter appeared in an SQL statement or a stored procedure must be identical with the name of the parameter you added into a Parameters collection.

For example, the following SQL statement is used for an SQL Server Data Provider as a query string:

```
SELECT user_name, pass_word FROM LogIn WHERE (user_name LIKE @Param1)
                                        AND (pass_word LIKE @Param2)
```

The user_name and pass_word are mapped to two columns in the LogIn data table. Compared with the above SQL statement, two dynamic parameters are represented by two nominal parameters **@Param1** and **@Param2** in this SQL statement. The equal operator is replaced by the keyword **LIKE** for two parameters. This changing is required by the SQL Server Data Provider.

Then you need two Parameter objects associated with your Command object, an example of initializing these two Parameter objects is shown in Figure 3.11.

Where two **ParameterName** properties are assigned with two dynamic parameters, "@Param1" and "@Param2", respectively. Both Param1 and Param2 are nominal names of the dynamic parameters and a @ symbol is prefixed before each parameter since this is the requirement of the SQL Server database when a dynamic parameter is utilized in an SQL statement.

You can see from this piece of code that the name of each parameter you used for each Parameter object must be identical with the name you defined in your SQL statement. Since the SQL Server and Oracle Data Provider use Named Parameter Mapping, however, you do not need to worry about the order in which you added Parameter objects into the Parameters collection of the Command object.

To add Parameter objects into a Parameters collection of a Command object, you need to use some methods defined in the **ParameterCollection** class.

3.4.3.4 The Methods of the ParameterCollection Class

Each ParameterCollection class has more than ten methods, but only two of them are most often utilized in the data-driven applications, which are the **Add()** and **AddWithValue()** methods. Each Parameter object must be added into the Parameters collection of a Command object before you can execute that Command object to perform any data query or data action.

```
SqlParameter paramUserName = new SqlParameter();
SqlParameter paramPassWord = new SqlParameter();

paramUserName.ParameterName = "@Param1";
paramUserName.Value = txtUserName.Text;
paramPassWord.ParameterName = "@Param2";
paramPassWord.Value = txtPassWord.Text;
```

FIGURE 3.11 An example of initializing the property of a Parameter object.

As we mentioned in the last section, you do not need to worry about the order in which you added the parameter into the Parameter object if you are using a Named Parameter Mapping Data Provider such as an SQL Server or an Oracle. However, you must pay attention to the order in which you added the parameter into the Parameter object if you are using a Positional Parameter Mapping Data Providers such as an OLE DB or an ODBC.

To add Parameter objects to an Parameters collection of a Command object, two popular ways are generally adopted, Add() method and AddWithValue() method.

The Add() method is an overloaded method and it has five different protocols, but only two of them are widely used. The protocols of these two methods are shown below.

```
ParameterCollection.Add(SqlParameter value);
ParameterCollection.Add(string parameterName, Object Value);
```

The first method needs a Parameter object as the argument, and that Parameter object should have been created and initialized before you call this Add() method to add it into the collection if you want to use this method.

The second method contains two arguments. The first one is a String that contains the ParameterName and the second is an object that includes the value of that parameter.

The AddWithValue() method is similar to the second Add() method with the following protocol:

```
ParameterCollection.AddWithValue(string parameterName, Object Value);
```

One example of using these two methods to add Parameter objects into a Parameters collection is shown in Figure 3.12. The top section is used to create and initialize the Parameter objects, which we have discussed in the previous sections.

First the Add() method is executed to add two Parameter objects, paramUserName and paramPassWord, to the Parameters collection of the Command object sqlCommand. To use this method, two Parameter objects should have been initialized.

The second way to do this job is to use the AddWithValue() method to add these two Parameter objects, which is similar to the second protocol of the Add() method.

The Parameters property in the Command class is a collection of a set of Parameter objects. You need first to create and initialize a Parameter object, and then you can add that Parameter object to the Parameters collection. In this way, you can assign that Parameter object to a Command object.

```
SqlParameter paramUserName = new SqlParameter();
SqlParameter paramPassWord = new SqlParameter();

paramUserName.ParameterName = "@Param1";
paramUserName.Value = txtUserName.Text;
paramPassWord.ParameterName = "@Param2";
paramPassWord.Value = txtPassWord.Text;

sqlCommand.Parameters.Add(paramUserName);
sqlCommand.Parameters.Add(paramPassWord);

sqlCommand.Parameters.AddWithValue("@Param1", txtUserName.Text);
sqlCommand.Parameters.AddWithValue("@Param2", txtPassWord.Text);
```

FIGURE 3.12 Two methods to add Parameter objects.

3.4.3.5 The Constructor of the Command Class

The constructor of the Command class is an overloaded method and it has multiple protocols. Four popular protocols are listed in Figure 3.13 (an SQL Server Data Provider is used as an example).

The first constructor is a blank one without any argument. You have to create and assign each property to the associated property of the Command object separately if you want to use this constructor to instantiate a new Command object.

The second constructor contains two arguments; the first one is the parameter name that is a string variable, and the second is the value that is an object. The following two constructors are similar to the second one, and the difference is that a data type and a data size argument are included.

A sample example of creating an SqlCommand object is shown in Figure 3.14. This example contains the following functionalities:

1) Create a **SqlCommand** object.
2) Create two **SqlParameter** objects.
3) Initialize two **SqlParameter** objects.
4) Initialize the **SqlCommand** object.
5) Add two Parameter objects into the **Parameters** collection of the Command object **sqlCommand**.

The top two lines of the coding create an SQL statement with two dynamic parameters, **user_name** and **pass_word**. Then two strings are concatenated to form a complete string. Two **SqlParameter** and a **SqlCommand** objects are created in the following lines.

Then two SqlParameter objects are initialized with nominal parameters and the associated text box's contents. After this, the SqlCommand object is initialized with four properties of the Command class.

Now let's take care of the popular methods used in the Command class.

```
SqlCommand sqlCommand = new SqlCommand();
SqlCommand sqlCommand = new SqlCommand (connString);
SqlCommand sqlCommand = new SqlCommand (connString, SqlConnection);
SqlCommand sqlCommand = new SqlCommand (connString, SqlConnection, SqlTransaction);
```

FIGURE 3.13 Three popular protocols of the constructor of the Command class.

```
string cmdString = "SELECT user_name, pass_word FROM LogIn "
cmdString += "WHERE (user_name = @Param1 ) AND (pass_word = @Param2)";
SqlParameter paramUserName = new SqlParameter();
SqlParameter paramPassWord = new SqlParameter();
SqlCommand sqlCommand As New SqlCommand();

paramUserName.ParameterName = "@Param1";
paramUserName.Value = txtUserName.Text;
paramPassWord.ParameterName = "@Param2";
paramPassWord.Value = txtPassWord.Text;
sqlCommand.Connection = sqlConnection;
sqlCommand.CommandType = CommandType.Text;
sqlCommand.CommandText = cmdString;
sqlCommand.Parameters.Add(paramUserName);
sqlCommand.Parameters.Add(paramPassWord);
```

FIGURE 3.14 An example of creating a SqlCommand object.

Method Name	Functionality
ExecuteReader()	Executes commands that return rows, such as a SQL SELECT statement. The returned rows are located in an **OdbcDataReader**, an **OleDbDataReader**, a **SqlDataReader** or an **OracleDataReader**, depending on which **Data Provider** you are using.
ExecuteScalar()	Retrieves a single value from the database.
ExecuteNonQuery()	Executes a non-query command such as SQL INSERT, DELETE, UPDATE, and SET statements.
ExecuteXmlReader (SqlCommand only)	Similar to the ExecuteReader method, but the returned rows must be expressed using XML. This method is only available for the SQL Server Data Provider.

FIGURE 3.15 Methods of the command class.

3.4.3.6 The Methods of the Command Class

In the last section, we discussed how to create an instance of the Command class and how to initialize the Parameters collection of a Command object by attaching Parameter objects to that Command object. Those steps are prerequisite to execute a Command object. The actual execution of a Command object is to run one of the methods of the Command class to perform the associated data queries or data actions. Four popular methods are widely utilized for most data-driven applications and Figure 3.15 lists these methods.

As we mentioned in the last section, the Command object is a Data Provider-dependent object, so four different versions of the Command object are developed and each version is determined by the Data Provider the user selected and used in the application, such as the OleDbCommand, OdbcCommand, SqlCommand and an OracleCommand. Although each Command object is dependent on the Data Provider, all methods of the Command object are similar in functionality and have the same roles in a data-driven application.

3.4.3.6.1 The ExecuteReader Method

The **ExecuteReader()** method is a data query method and it can only be used to execute a read-out operation from a database. The most popular matched operation is to execute an SQL SELECT statement to return rows to a **DataReader** by using this method. Depending on which Data Provider you are using, the different DataReader object should be utilized as the data receiver to hold the returned rows. Remember, the DataReader class is a read-only class and it can only be used as a data holder. You cannot perform any data updating by using the DataReader.

The following example coding can be used to execute an SQL SELECT statement, which is shown in Figure 3.16.

As shown in Figure 3.16, as the ExecuteReader() method is called, an SQL SELECT statement is executed to retrieve the id, user_name and pass_word from the LogIn table. The returned rows are

```
string cmdString = "SELECT user_name, pass_word FROM LogIn ";
SqlCommand sqlCommand = new SqlCommand();

sqlCommand.Connection = sqlConnection;
sqlCommand.CommandType = CommandType.Text;
sqlCommand.CommandText = cmdString;
sqlDataReader = sqlCommand.ExecuteReader();
```

FIGURE 3.16 The example coding of running of ExecuteReader method.

```
string cmdString = "SELECT pass_word FROM LogIn WHERE (user_name = ybai)";
SqlCommand sqlCommand = new SqlCommand();
string passWord = string.Empty;
 sqlCommand.Connection = sqlConnection;
 sqlCommand.CommandType = CommandType.Text;
 sqlCommand.CommandText = cmdString;
 passWord = sqlCommand.ExecuteScalar();
```

FIGURE 3.17 A sample coding of using the ExecuteScalar method.

assigned to the sqlDataReader object. Please note that the SqlCommand object should already be created and initialized before the ExecuteReader() method can be called.

3.4.3.6.2 The ExecuteScalar Method

The **ExecuteScalar()** method is used to retrieve a single value from a database. This method is faster and has substantially less overhead than the **ExecuteReader()** method. You should use this method whenever a single value needs to be retrieved from a data source.

A sample coding of using this method is shown in Figure 3.17.

In this sample, the SQL SELECT statement is used to try to pick up a password based on the username ybai, from the LogIn data table. This password can be considered as a single value. The ExecuteScalar() method is called after an SqlCommand object is created and initialized. The returned single value is a String and it is assigned to a String variable passWord.

Section 5.8 in Chapter 5 provides an example of using this method to pick up a single value, which is a password, from the LogIn data table in the **CSE_DEPT** database.

3.4.3.6.3 The ExecuteNonQuery Method

As we mentioned, the **ExecuteReader()** method is a read-only method and it can only be used to perform a data query job. To execute the different SQL Statements such as **INSERT, UPDATE** or **DELETE** commands, the **ExecuteNonQuery()** method is needed.

Figure 3.18 shows an example coding block of using this method to insert to and delete a record from the LogIn data table.

As shown in Figure 3.18, the first SQL statement is try to insert a new password into the **LogIn** data table with a value **come**. After an SqlCommand object is created and initialized, the **ExecuteNonQuery()** method is called to execute this **INSERT** statement. Similar procedure is performed for the **DELETE** statement.

Now let's look at the next class in the Data Provider, the DataAdapter.

```
string cmdString1 = "INSERT INTO LogIn (pass_word) VALUES ('reback')";
string cmdString2 = "DELETE FROM LogIn WHERE (user_name = ybai)";
SqlCommand sqlCommand = new SqlCommand();
 sqlCommand.Connection = sqlConnection;
 sqlCommand.CommandType = CommandType.Text;
 sqlCommand.CommandText = cmdString1;
 sqlCommand.ExecuteNonQuery();
 sqlCommand.CommandText = cmdString2;
 sqlCommand.ExecuteNonQuery();
```

FIGURE 3.18 An example coding block of using the ExecuteNonQuery method.

3.4.4 The DataAdapter Class

The **DataAdapter** serves as a bridge between a DataSet and a data source for retrieving and saving data. The DataAdapter provides this bridge by mapping **Fill()**, which changes the data in the DataSet to match the data in the data source, and Update, which changes the data in the data source to match the data in the DataSet.

The DataAdapter connects to your database using a Connection object and it uses Command objects to retrieve data from the database and populate those data to the DataSet and related classes such as DataTables, also the DataAdapter uses Command objects to send data from your DataSet to your database.

To perform a data query from your database to the DataSet, the DataAdapter uses the suitable Command objects and assign them to the appropriate DataAdapter properties such as SelectCommand, and execute that Command. To perform other data manipulations, the DataAdapter uses the same Command objects but assign them with different properties such as **InsertCommand, UpdateCommand** and **DeleteCommand** to complete the associated data operations.

As we mentioned in the previous section, the DataAdapter is a sub-component of the Data Provider, so it is a Data Provider-dependent component. This means that the DataAdapter has different versions based on the used Data Provider. Four popular DataAdapters are: OleDbDataAdapter, OdbcDataAdapter, SqlDataAdapter and OracleDataAdapter. Different DataAdapters are located at the different namespaces.

If you are connecting to a SQL Server database, you can increase overall performance by using the SqlDataAdapter along with its associated SqlCommand and SqlConnection objects. For OLE DB-supported data sources, use the **OleDbDataAdapter** with its associated **OleDbCommand** and **OleDbConnection** objects. For ODBC-supported data sources, use the **OdbcDataAdapter** with its associated **OdbcCommand** and **OdbcConnection** objects. For Oracle databases, use the **OracleDataAdapter** with its associated **OracleCommand** and **OracleConnection** objects.

3.4.4.1 The Constructor of the DataAdapter Class

The constructor of the DataAdapter class is an overloaded method and it has multiple protocols. Two popular protocols are listed in Figure 3.19 (an SQL Server Data Provider is used as an example).

The first constructor is most often used in the most data-driven applications.

3.4.4.2 The Properties of the DataAdapter Class

Some popular properties of the DataAdapter class are listed in Figure 3.20.

Constructor	Descriptions
SqlDataAdapter()	Initializes a new instance of a DataAdapter class
SqlDataAdapter(from)	Initializes a new instance of a DataAdapter class from an existing object of the same type

FIGURE 3.19 The constructors of the DataAdapter class.

Properties	Descriptions
AcceptChangesDuringFill	Gets or sets a value indicating whether AcceptChanges is called on a DataRow after it is added to the DataTable during any of the Fill operations.
MissingMappingAction	Determines the action to take when incoming data does not have a matching table or column.
MissingSchemaAction	Determines the action to take when existing DataSet schema does not match incoming data.
TableMappings	Gets a collection that provides the master mapping between a source table and a DataTable.

FIGURE 3.20 The public properties of the DataAdapter class.

Methods	Descriptions
Dispose	Releases the resources used by the DataAdapter.
Fill	Add or refreshe rows in the DataSet to match those in the data source using the **DataSet** name, and creates a DataTable.
FillSchema	Adds a DataTable to the specified DataSet.
GetFillParameters	Gets the parameters set by the user when executing an SQL SELECT statement.
ToString	Returns a String containing the name of the Component, if any. This method should not be overridden.
Update	Calls the respective INSERT, UPDATE, or DELETE statements for each inserted, updated, or deleted row in the specified DataSet from a named DataTable.

FIGURE 3.21 The public methods of the DataAdapter class.

3.4.4.3 The Methods of the DataAdapter Class

The DataAdapter has more than 10 methods available to help users to develop professional data-driven applications. Figure 3.21 lists some of the most frequently used methods.

Among these methods, the **Dispose(), Fill(), FillSchema()** and **Update()** are among the most often used methods. The **Dispose()** method should be used to release the used DataAdapter after the DataAdapter completes its job. The **Fill()** method should be used to populate a DataSet after the Command object is initialized and ready to be used. The **FillSchema()** method should be called if you want to add a new DataTable into the DataSet, and the **Update()** method should be used if you want to perform some data manipulations such as Insert, Update and Delete with the database and the DataSet.

3.4.4.4 The Events of the DataAdapter Class

Two popular events are widely used in the DataAdapter class, and these events are listed in Figure 3.22.

Before we can complete this section, an example coding is provided to show readers how to use the DataAdapter to perform some data access and data actions between your DataSet and your database. Figure 3.23 shows an example of using a SQL Server DataAdapter (assuming that a Connection object **sqlConnection** has been created).

Starting from step **A**, an SQL SELECT statement string is created with some other new object declarations, such as a new instance of SqlCommand class, a new object of SqlDataAdapter class and a new instance of the DataSet class. The DataSet class will be discussed in the following section and it is used as a table container to hold a collection of data tables. The **Fill()** method of the DataAdapter class can be used to populate the data tables embedded in the DataSet later.

In step **B**, the SqlCommand object is initialized with the Connection object, CommandType and the command string.

The instance of the SqlDataAdapter, sqlDataAdapter, is initialized with the command string and the SqlConnection object in step **C**.

In step **D**, the initialized SqlCommand object, sqlCommand, is assigned to the SelectCommand property of the sqlDataAdapter. Also the DataSet is initialized and cleared to make it ready to be filled by executing the **Fill()** method of the sqlDataAdapter to populate the data table in the DataSet later.

The **Fill()** method is called to execute a population of data from the Faculty data table into the mapping of that table in the DataSet in step **E**.

Events	Descriptions
Disposed	Occurs when the component is disposed by a call to the Dispose method.
FillError	Returned when an error occurs during a fill operation.

FIGURE 3.22 The events of the DataAdapter class.

```
A  string cmdString = "SELECT name, office, title, college FROM Faculty";
   SqlCommand sqlCommand = new SqlCommand();
   SqlDataAdapter sqlDataAdapter;
   DataSet sqlDataSet;
B  sqlCommand.Connection = sqlConnection;
   sqlCommand.CommandType = CommandType.Text;
   sqlCommand.CommandText = cmdString;
C  sqlDataAdapter = new SqlDataAdapter(cmdString, sqlConnection);
D  sqlDataAdapter.SelectCommand = sqlCommand;
   sqlDataSet = new DataSet();
   sqlDataSet.Clear();
E  int intValue = sqlDataAdapter.Fill(sqlDataSet);
   if (intValue == 0)
      MessageBox.Show("No valid faculty found!");
F  sqlDataSet.Dispose();
   sqlDataAdapter.Dispose();
   sqlCommand.Dispose();
```

FIGURE 3.23 An example of using the SqlDataAdapter to fill the DataSet.

An integer variable **Index** is used to hold the returned value of calling this **Fill()** method. This value is equal to the number of rows filled into the **Faculty** table in the DataSet. If this value is 0, which means that no matched row has been found from the Faculty table in the database and 0 row has been filled into the Faculty table in the DataSet, an error message is displayed. Otherwise, this fill is successful.

In step **F**, all components used for this piece of codes are released by using the **Dispose()** method.

3.4.5 The DataReader Class

The DataReader class is a read-only class and it can only be used to retrieve and hold the data rows returned from a database executing an ExecuteReader() method. This class provides a way of reading a forward-only stream of rows from a database. Depending on the Data Provider you are using, four popular DataReaders are provided by four Data Providers. These are OdbcDataReader, OleDbDataReader, SqlDataReader and OracleDataReader.

To create a DataReader instance, you must call the **ExecuteReader()** method of the Command object, instead of directly using a constructor since the DataReader class does not have any public constructor. The following code that is used to create an instance of the SqlDataReader is incorrect:

```
SqlDataReader sqlDataReader = newSqlDataReader();
```

While the DataReader object is being used, the associated Connection is busy serving the DataReader, and no other operations can be performed on the Connection other than closing it. This is the case until the Close() method of the DataReader is called. For instance, you cannot retrieve output parameters until after you call the Close() method to close the connected DataReader.

The IsClosed property of the DataReader class can be used to check if the DataReader has been closed or not, and this property returns a Boolean value. A *true* means that the DataReader has been closed. It is a good habit to call the Close() method to close the DataReader each time when you finished data query using that DataReader to avoid the troubles caused by the multiple connections to the database.

Figure 3.24 lists most public properties of the SqlDataReader class. All other DataReader classes have the similar properties.

Property Name	Value Type	Functionality
FieldCount	Integer	Gets the number of columns in the current row.
HasRows	Boolean	Gets a value that indicates whether the **SqlDataReader** contains one or more rows.
IsClosed	Boolean	Retrieves a Boolean value that indicates whether the specified **SqlDataReader** instance has been closed.
Item(Int32)	Native	Gets the value of the specified column in its native format given the column ordinal.
Item(String)	Native	Gets the value of the specified column in its native format given the column name.
RecordsAffected	Integer	Gets the number of rows changed, inserted, or deleted by execution of the Transact-SQL statement.
VisibleFieldCount	Integer	Gets the number of fields in the **SqlDataReader** that are not hidden.

FIGURE 3.24 Popular properties of the SqlDataReader class.

Method Name	Functionality
Close	Closes the opened SqlDataReader object.
Dispose	Releases the resources used by the DbDataReader.
GetByte	Gets the value of the specified column as a byte.
GetName	Gets the name of the specified column.
GetString	Gets the value of the specified column as a string.
GetValue	Gets the value of the specified column in its native format.
IsDBNull	Gets a value that indicates whether the column contains non-existent or missing values.
NextResult	Advances the data reader to the next result, when reading the results of batch Transact-SQL statements.
Read	Advances the **SqlDataReader** to the next record.
ToString	Returns a String that represents the current **Object**.

FIGURE 3.25 Popular methods of the SqlDataReader class.

The DataReader class has more than 50 public methods. Figure 3.25 lists the most useful methods of the SqlDataReader class. All other DataReader classes have the similar methods.

When you run the **ExecuteReader()** method to retrieve data rows from a database and assign them to a DataReader object, each time the DataReader can only retrieve and hold one row. So if you want to read out all rows from a data table, a loop should be used to sequentially retrieve each row from the database.

The DataReader object provides the most efficient ways to read data from the database, and you should use this object whenever you just want to read the data from the database from the start to finish to populate a list on a form or to populate an array or collection. It can also be used to populate a DataSet or a DataTable.

Figure 3.26 shows an example coding of using the SqlDataReader object to continuously retrieve all records (rows) from the Faculty data table suppose a Connection object sqlConnection has been created.

The functionality of this piece of code is explained below.

Starting from section **A**, a new SqlCommand and an SqlDataReader object is created with a SQL SELECT statement string object.

The Command object is initialized in section **B**. In section **C**, the **ExecuteReader()** method is called to retrieve data row from the **Faculty** data table and assign the resulted row to the SqlDataReader object. By checking the **HasRows** property (refer to Figure 3.24), one can determine whether a valid row has been collected or not. If a valid row has been retrieved, a **while()** and a **for()** loop are utilized to sequentially read out all rows one by one using the **Read()** method (refer to Figure 3.25).

```
A  string cmdString = "SELECT name, office, title, college FROM Faculty";
   SqlCommand sqlCommand = new SqlCommand();
   SqlDataReader sqlDataReader;
B  sqlCommand.Connection = sqlConnection;
   sqlCommand.CommandType = CommandType.Text;
   sqlCommand.CommandText = cmdString;
C  sqlDataReader = sqlCommand.ExecuteReader();
   if (sqlDataReader.HasRows == true)
   {
      while (FacultyReader.Read())
      {
         for (int intIndex = 0; intIndex <= FacultyReader.FieldCount – 1; intIndex++)
            FacultyLabel(intIndex).Text = FacultyReader.GetString(intIndex);
      }
   }
   else
D     MessageBox.Show("No matched faculty found!");
E  sqlDataReader.Close();
   sqlCommand.Dispose();
```

FIGURE 3.26 An example coding of using the SqlDataReader object.

Exception Name	Functionality
IndexOutOfRangeException	If an index does not exist within the range, array or collection, this exception occurs.
InvalidCastException	If you try to convert a database value using one of Get methods to convert a column value to a specific data type, this exception occurs.
InvalidOperationException	If you perform an invalid operation, either a property or a method, this exception occurs.
NotSupportedException	If you try to use any property or method on a DataReader object that has not been opened or connected, this exception occurs.

FIGURE 3.27 Popular exceptions of the DataReader class.

The **GetString()** method (refer to Figure 3.25) is used to populate the retrieved row to a Label control collection object. The **FieldCount** property (refer to Figure 3.24) is used as the termination condition for the **for()** loop, and its termination value is **FieldCount – 1** since the loop starts from 0, not 1. If the **HasRows** property returns a **false**, which means that no row has been retrieved from the Faculty table, an error message will be displayed in section **D**. Finally, before we can finish this data query job, we need to clean up the sources we used. In section **E**, the **Close()** and **Dispose()** (refer to Figure 3.25) methods are utilized to finish this cleaning job.

Before we can finish this section and move to the next one, we need to discuss one more staff, which is the DataReader Exceptions. Figure 3.27 lists often used Exceptions.

You can use the **try-catch** block to handle those Exceptions in your applications to avoid unnecessary debug process as your project runs.

3.4.6 The DataSet Component

The DataSet, which is an in-memory cache of data retrieved from a database, is a major component of the ADO.NET architecture. The DataSet consists of a collection of DataTable objects that you can relate to each other with DataRelation objects. In other words, a DataSet object can be considered as a table-container that contains a set of data tables with the DataRelation as a bridge to relate all tables together. The relationship between a DataSet and a set of DataTable objects can be defined:

- A DataSet class holds a data table collection, which contains a set of data tables or DataTable objects, and the Relations collection, which contains a set of DataRelation objects. This Relations collection sets up all relationships among those DataTable objects.
- A DataTable class holds the Rows collection, which contains a set of data rows or DataRow objects, and the Columns collection, which contains a set of data columns or DataColumn objects. The Rows collection contains all data rows in the data table and the Columns collection contains the actual schema of the data table.

The definition of the DataSet class is a generic idea, which means that it is not tied to any specific type of database. Data can be loaded into a DataSet by using a TableAdapter from many different databases, such as Microsoft Access, Microsoft SQL Server, Oracle, Microsoft Exchange, Microsoft Active Directory, or any OLE DB- or ODBC-compliant database.

Although not tied to any specific database, the DataSet class is designed to contain relational tabular data as one would find in a relational database.

Each table included in the DataSet is represented in the DataSet as a DataTable. The DataTable can be considered as a direct mapping to the real table in the database. For example, the LogIn data table, LogInDataTable, is a data table component or DataTable that can be mapped to the real table LogIn in the **CSE_DEPT** database. The relationship between any tables is realized in the DataSet as a DataRelation object. The DataRelation object provides the information that relates a child table to a parent table via a foreign key. A DataSet can hold any number of tables with any number of relationships defined between tables. From this point of view, a DataSet can be considered as a mini database engine, so it can contain all information of tables it holds such as the column name and data type, all relationships between tables, and, more importantly, it contains most management functionalities of the tables, such as browse, select, insert, update and delete data from tables.

A DataSet is a container and it keeps its data or tables in memory as XML files. In Visual Studio. NET 2022, when one wants to edit the structure of a DataSet, one must do that by editing an XML Schema or XSD file. Although there is a visual designer, the terminology and user interface are not consistent with a DataSet and its constituent objects. With the Visual Studio.NET 2022, one can easily edit the structure of a DataSet and make any changes to the structure of that DataSet by using the DataSet Designer in the Data Source window. More importantly, one can graphically manipulate the tables and queries in a manner more directly tied to the DataSet rather than having to deal with an XML Schema (XSD).

Summarily, the DataSet object is a very powerful component that can contain multiple data tables with all information related to those tables. By using this object, one can easily browse, access and manipulate data stored in it. We will explore this component in more detail in the following sections when a real project is built.

As we mentioned before, when you build a data-driven project and set up a connection between your project and a database by using ADO.NET, the data tables in the DataSet can be populated with data coming from your database by using the data query methods or the Fill method. From this point of view, you can consider the DataSet as a *data source* and it contains all mapped data tables from the database you connected to your project. In some books, the terminology *data source* means the DataSet.

Figure 3.28 shows a global relationship between the DataSet object, other data objects and the Visual C# 2022 application.

A DataSet can be typed or untyped; the difference between them is that the typed DataSet object has a schema and the untyped DataSet does not. In your data-driven applications, it is highly recommended to use the typed DataSet if that is possible because the typed DataSet has more support in Visual Studio 2022.

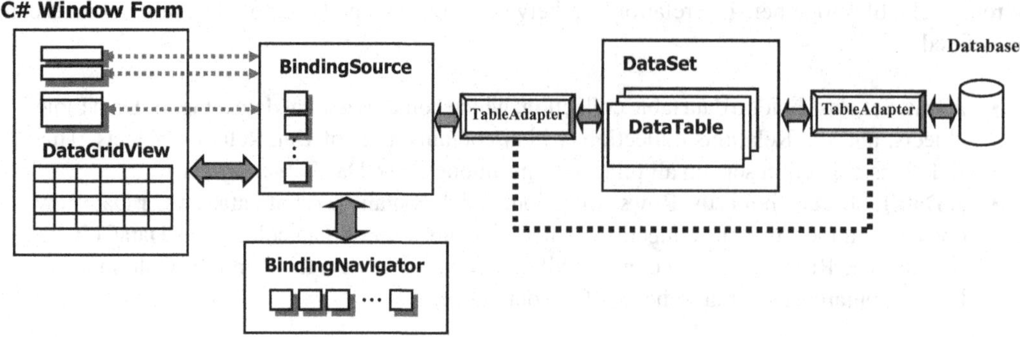

FIGURE 3.28 A global representation of the DataSet and other data objects.

Constructor	Functionality
DataSet()	Initializes a new instance of the **DataSet** class.
DataSet(String)	Initializes a new instance of a **DataSet** class with the given name.

FIGURE 3.29 Popular constructors of the DataSet class.

A typed DataSet object provides you with an easier way to access the content of the data table fields through strongly typed programming. The so-called strongly typed programming uses information from the underlying data scheme, which means that you can directly access and manipulate those data objects related to data tables. Another point is that a typed DataSet has a reference to an XML schema file and this file has an extension of the **.xsd**. A complete description of the structure of all data tables included in the DataSet is provided in this schema file.

3.4.6.1 The DataSet Constructor

The DataSet class has four public overloaded constructors, and Figure 3.29 lists two most often used constructors.

The first constructor is used to create a new instance of the DataSet class with a blank parameter. The second constructor is used to create a new instance of the DataSet with the specific name of the new instance.

3.4.6.2 The DataSet Properties

The DataSet class has more than 15 public properties. Figure 3.30 lists the most often used properties.

Property Name	Type	Functionality
DataSetName	String	Gets or sets the name of the current DataSet.
DefaultViewManager	DataViewManager	Gets a custom view of the data contained in the **DataSet** to allow filtering, searching, and navigating using a custom DataViewManager
HasErrors	Boolean	Gets a value indicating whether there are errors in any of the **DataTable** objects within this **DataSet**.
IsInitialized	Boolean	Gets a value that indicates whether the **DataSet** is initialized.
Namespace	String	Gets or sets the namespace of the **DataSet**.
Tables	DataTableCollection	Gets the collection of tables contained in the **DataSet**.

FIGURE 3.30 Public properties of the DataSet class.

Method Name	Functionality
BeginInit	Begins the initialization of a **DataSet** that is used on a form or used by another component. The initialization occurs at run time.
Clear	Clears the **DataSet** of any data by removing all rows in all tables.
Copy	Copies both the structure and data for this **DataSet**.
Dispose	Releases the resources used by the MarshalByValueComponent.
GetChanges	Gets a copy of the **DataSet** containing all changes made to it since it was last loaded, or since **AcceptChanges** was called.
HasChanges	Gets a value indicating whether the **DataSet** has changes, including new, deleted, or modified rows.
Load	Fills a **DataSet** with values from a data source using the supplied IDataReader.
Merge	Merges a specified **DataSet, DataTable**, or array of DataRow objects into the current **DataSet** or **DataTable**.
Reset	Resets the **DataSet** to its original state. Subclasses should override Reset to restore a **DataSet** to its original state.
ToString	Returns a String containing the name of the Component, if any. This method should not be overridden.
WriteXml	Writes XML data, and optionally the schema, from the **DataSet**.
WriteXmlSchema	Writes the **DataSet** structure as an XML schema.

FIGURE 3.31 Public methods of the DataSet class.

Event Name	Descriptions
Disposed	Adds an event handler to listen to the Disposed event on the component.
Initialized	Occurs after the DataSet is initialized.
Mergefailed	Occurs when a target and source DataRow have the same primary key value, and EnforceConstraints is set to true.

FIGURE 3.32 Public events of the DataSet class.

Among these properties, the DataSetName, IsInitialized and Tables are the most often used properties in your data-driven applications.

3.4.6.3 The DataSet Methods

The DataSet class has more than 30 public methods. Figure 3.31 lists the most frequently used methods.

Among those methods, the Clear(), Dispose() and Merge() methods are often used. Before you can fill a DataSet, it had better execute the Clear() method to clean up the DataSet to avoid any possible old data. Often in your applications, you need to merge other DataSets or data arrays into the current DataSet object by using the Merge() method. After you finished your data query or data action using the DataSet, you need to release it by executing the Dispose() method.

3.4.6.4 The DataSet Events

DataSet class has three public events and Figure 3.32 lists these events.

The Disposed event is used to trigger the Dispose() method as this event occurs. The Initialized event is used to make a mark to indicate that the DataSet has been initialized to your applications. The **Mergefailed** event is triggered when a conflict occurs and the **EnforceConstraints** property is set to **true** as you want to merge a DataSet with an array of DataRow objects, another DataSet, or a DataTable.

Before we can finish this section, we need to show your guys how to create, initialize and implement a real DataSet object in a data-driven application. A piece of codes shown in Figure 3.33 is used to illustrate these issues and a SQL Server Data Provider is utilized for this example. Assuming that an **SqlConnection** object, **sqlConnection**, has been created and initialized for this example.

```
A  string cmdString = "SELECT faculty_name, office, title, college FROM Faculty";
   SqlCommand sqlCommand = new SqlCommand();
   SqlDataAdapter sqlDataAdapter;
   DataSet sqlDataSet;
   int intValue = 0;
B  sqlCommand.Connection = sqlConnection;
   sqlCommand.CommandType = CommandType.Text;
   sqlCommand.CommandText = cmdString;
C  sqlDataAdapter.SelectCommand = sqlCommand;
   sqlDataSet = new DataSet();
   sqlDataSet.Clear();
D  intValue = sqlDataAdapter.Fill(sqlDataSet);
   if (intValue == 0)
      MessageBox.Show("No valid faculty found!");
E  sqlDataSet.Dispose();
   sqlDataAdapter.Dispose();
   sqlCommand.Dispose();
```

FIGURE 3.33 An example of using the DataSet.

Starting from step **A**, some initialization jobs are performed. An SQL SELECT statement is created, an SqlCommand object, an SqlDataAdapter object and a DataSet object are also created. The integer variable intValue is used to hold the returned value from calling the **Fill()** method.

In section **B**, the SqlCommand object is initialized by assigning the SqlConnection object to the Connection property, the **CommandType.Text** to the CommandType property and **cmdString** to the **CommandText** property of the SqlCommand object.

The initialized SqlCommand object is assigned to the SelectCommand property of the SqlDataAdapter object in step **C**. Then a new DataSet object **sqlDataSet** is initialized and the **Clear()** method is called to clean up the DataSet object before it can be filled.

In step **D**, the **Fill()** method of the **SqlDataAdapter** object is executed to fill the **sqlDataSet**. If this fill is successful, which means that the **sqlDataSet** (exactly the DataTable in the **sqlDataSet**) has been filled by some data rows, the returned value should be greater than 0. Otherwise it means that some errors occurred for this fill and an error message will be displayed to warn the user.

Before the project can be completed, all resources used in this piece of codes should be released and cleaned up. These cleaning jobs are performed in step **E** by executing some related method such as **Dispose()**.

You need to note that when the **Fill()** method is executed to fill a DataSet, The **Fill()** method retrieves rows from the data source using the SELECT statement specified by an associated the **CommandText** property. The Connection object associated with the SELECT statement must be valid, but it does not need to be open. If the connection is closed before the **Fill()** is called, the **Fill()** method will open the connection and retrieve the data, then close the connection. If the connection is open before the **Fill()** is called, it still remains open.

The fill operation then adds rows to the destination, DataTable objects in the DataSet, creates the DataTable objects if they are not existed. When creating DataTable objects, the fill operation normally creates only column name metadata. However, if the **MissingSchemaAction** property is set to **AddWithKey**, appropriate primary keys and constraints are also created.

If the **Fill()** returns the results of an **OUTER JOIN**, the DataAdapter does not set a **PrimaryKey** value for the resulting DataTable. You must explicitly define the primary key to ensure that duplicate rows are resolved correctly.

You can use the **Fill()** method multiple times on the same DataTable. If a primary key exists, incoming rows are merged with matching rows that already exist. If no primary key exists, incoming rows are appended to the DataTable.

3.4.7 The DataTable Component

DataTable class can be considered as a container that holds the Rows and Columns collections, and the **Rows** and **Columns** collections contain a set of rows (or **DataRow** objects) and a set of columns (or **DataColumn** objects) from a data table in a database. The **DataTable** is a directly mapping to a real data table in a database or a data source and it store its data in a mapping area, or a block of memory space that is associated to a data table in a database as your project runs. The **DataTable** object can be used in two ways as we mentioned in the previous sections. One way is that in a group of **DataTable** objects, each **DataTable** object is mapped to a data table in the real database, can be integrated into a **DataSet** object. All of these **DataTable** objects can be populated by executing the **Fill()** method of the DataAdapter object (refer to the example in Section 3.4.6.4). The argument of the **Fill()** method is not a **DataTable**, but a **DataSet** object since all **DataTable** objects are embedded into that **DataSet** object already. The second way to use the DataTable is that each DataTable can be considered as a single stand-alone data table object, and each table can be populated or manipulated by executing either the **ExecuteReader()** or **ExecuteNonQuery()** method of the **Command** object.

The DataTable class is located in the **System.Data** namespace and it is a Data Provider-independent component, which means that only one set of DataTable objects are existed no matter what kind of Data Provider you are using in your applications.

The DataTable is a central object in the ADO.NET library. Other objects that use the DataTable include the **DataSet** and the **DataView**.

When accessing DataTable objects, note that they are conditionally case-sensitive. For example, if one DataTable is named "**faculty**" and another is named "**Faculty**", a string used to search for one of the tables is regarded as case-sensitive. However, if "**faculty**" exists and "**Faculty**" does not, the search string is regarded as case-insensitive. A DataSet can contain two DataTable objects that have the same **TableName** property value but different **Namespace** property values.

If you are creating a DataTable programmatically, you must first define its schema by adding **DataColumn** objects to the **DataColumnCollection** (accessed through the **Columns** property). To add rows to a DataTable, you must first use the **NewRow()** method to return a new **DataRow** object. The **NewRow()** method returns a row with the schema of the DataTable, as it is defined by the table's DataColumnCollection. The maximum number of rows that a DataTable can store is 16,777,216.

The DataTable also contains a collection of Constraint objects that can be used to ensure the integrity of the data. The DataTable class is a member of the **System.Data** namespace within the .NET Framework class library. You can create and use a DataTable independently or as a member of a DataSet, and DataTable objects can also be used in conjunction with other .NET Framework objects, including the **DataView**. As we mentioned in the previous section, you access the collection of tables in a DataSet through the Tables property of the DataSet object.

In addition to a schema, a DataTable must also have rows to contain and order data. The **DataRow** class represents the actual data contained in a table. You use the **DataRow** and its properties and methods to retrieve, evaluate, and manipulate the data in a table. As you access and change the data within a row, the **DataRow** object maintains both its current and original state.

3.4.7.1 The DataTable Constructor

The DataTable has four overloaded constructors and Figure 3.34 lists the three most frequently used constructors.

You can create a DataTable object by using the appropriate DataTable constructor. You can add it to the DataSet by using the Add method to add it to the DataTable object's **Tables** collection.

You can also create DataTable objects within a DataSet by using the **Fill()** or **FillSchema()** methods of the DataAdapter object, or from a predefined or inferred XML schema using the **ReadXml()**, **ReadXmlSchema()**, or **InferXmlSchema()** methods of the DataSet. Note that after you have added a DataTable as a member of the **Tables** collection of one DataSet, you cannot add it to the collection of tables of any other DataSet.

Constructors	Descriptions
DataTable()	Initializes a new instance of the DataTable class with no arguments.
DataTable(String)	Initializes a new instance of the DataTable class with the specified table name.
DataTable(String, String)	Initializes a new instance of the DataTable class using the specified table name and namespace.

FIGURE 3.34 Three popular constructors of the DataTable class.

```
DataSet FacultyDataSet;
DataTable FacultyTable;

FacultyDataSet = new DataSet();
FacultyTable = new DataTable("Faculty");
FacultyDataSet.Tables.Add(FacultyTable);
```

FIGURE 3.35 An example of adding a DataTable into a DataSet.

When you first create a DataTable, it does not have a schema (that is, a structure). To define the schema of the table, you must create and add **DataColumn** objects to the **Columns** collection of the table. You can also define a primary key column for the table, and create and add **Constraint** objects to the **Constraints** collection of the table. After you have defined the schema for a DataTable, you can add rows of data to the table by adding **DataRow** objects to the **Rows** collection of the table.

You are not required to supply a value for the **TableName** property when you create a DataTable; you can specify the property at another time, or you can leave it empty.

However, when you add a table without a **TableName** value to a DataSet, the table will be given an incremental default name of **TableN**, starting with "**Table**" for **Table0**.

Figure 3.35 shows an example of creating a new DataTable and a DataSet, and then adding the DataTable into the DataSet object.

First, you need to create an instance for DataSet and DataTable classes. Then you can add this new DataTable instance into the new DataSet object by using the **Add()** method.

3.4.7.2 The DataTable Properties

The DataTable class has more than 20 properties. Figure 3.36 lists some most often used properties.

Among these properties, the **Columns** and **Rows** properties are very important to us, and both properties are collections of **DataColumn** and **DataRow** in the current DataTable object. The Columns property contains a collection of DataColumn objects in the current DataTable and each column in the table can be considered as a DataColumn object, and can be added into this Columns collection. A similar situation happened with the Rows property. The Rows property contains a collection of DataRow objects that are composed of all rows in the current DataTable object. You can get the total number of columns and rows from the current DataTable by calling these two properties.

3.4.7.3 The DataTable Methods

The DataTable class has about 50 different methods with 33 public methods, and Figure 3.37 lists some most often used methods.

Among these methods, three of them are important to us: **NewRow()**, **ImportRow()** and **LoadDataRow()**. Calling the NewRow() adds a row to the data table using the existing table schema, but with default values for the row, and sets the DataRowState to Added. Calling the ImportRow() preserves the existing DataRowState along with other values in the row. Calling the LoadDataRow() is to find and update a data row from the current data table. This method has two arguments, the **Value** (Object) and the **Accept Condition** (Boolean). The Value is used to update the data row if that row is found and

Properties	Descriptions
Columns	The data type of the Columns property is DataColumn-Collection, which means that it contains a collection of DataColumn objects. Each column in the DataTable can be considered as a DataColumn object. By calling this property, a collection of DataColumn objects existed in the DataTable can be retrieved.
DataSet	Gets the DataSet to which this table belongs.
IsInitialized	Gets a value that indicates whether the DataTable is initialized.
Namespace	Gets or sets the namespace for the XML representation of the data stored in the DataTable.
PrimaryKey	Gets or sets an array of columns that function as primary keys for the data table.
Rows	The data type of the Rows property is DataRowCollection, which means that it contains a collection of DataRow objects. Each row in the DataTable can be considered as a DataRow object. By calling this property, a collection of DataRow objects existed in the DataTable can be retrieved.
TableName	Gets or sets the name of the DataTable.

FIGURE 3.36 The popular properties of the DataTable class.

Methods	Descriptions
Clear	Clears the DataTable of all data.
Copy	Copies both the structure and data for this DataTable.
Dispose	Release the resources used by the MarshalByValue-Component.
GetChanges	Gets a copy of the DataTable containing all changes made to it since it was last loaded, or since AcceptChanges was called.
GetType	Gets the Type of the current instance.
ImportRow	Copies a DataRow into a DataTable, preserving any property settings, as well as original and current values.
Load	Fills a DataTable with values from a data source using the supplied IDataReader. If the DataTable already contains rows, the incoming data from the data source is merged with the existing rows.
LoadDataRow	Finds and updates a specific row. If no matching row is found, a new row is created using the given values.
Merge	Merge the specified DataTable with the current DataTable.
NewRow	Creates a new DataRow with the same schema as the table.
ReadXml	Reads XML schema and data into the DataTable.
RejectChanges	Rolls back all changes that have been made to the table since it was loaded, or the last time AcceptChanges was called.
Reset	Resets the DataTable to its original state.
Select	Gets an array of DataRow objects.
ToString	Gets the TableName and DisplayExpression, if there is one as a concatenated string.
WriteXml	Writes the current contents of the DataTable as XML.

FIGURE 3.37 The popular methods of the DataTable class.

the Condition is used to indicate whether the table allows this update to be made or not. If no matching row is found, a new row is created with the given Value.

3.4.7.4 The DataTable Events

The DataTable class contains 11 public events and Figure 3.38 lists these events.

The most often used events are **ColumnChanged**, **Initialized**, **RowChanged** and **RowDeleted**. By using these events, one can track and monitor the real situations occurred in the DataTable.

Events	Descriptions
ColumnChanged	Occurs after a value has been changed for the specified DataColumn in a DataRow.
ColumnChanging	Occurs when a value is being changed for the specified DataColumn in a DataRow.
Disposed	Adds an event handler to listen to the Disposed event on the component.
Initialized	Occurs after the DataTable is initialized.
RowChanged	Occurs after a DataRow has been changed successfully.
RowChanging	Occurs when a DataRow is changing.
RowDeleted	Occurs after a row in the table has been deleted.
RowDeleting	Occurs before a row in the table is about to be deleted.
TableCleared	Occurs after a DataTable is cleared.
TableClearing	Occurs when a DataTable is being cleared.
TableNewRow	Occurs when a new DataRow is inserted.

FIGURE 3.38 The public events of the DataTable class.

```
  //Create a new DataTable
A DataTable FacultyTable = new DataTable("FacultyTable");

  //Declare DataColumn and DataRow variables
B DataColumn column;
  DataRow row;

  //Create new DataColumn, set DataType, ColumnName and add to DataTable
C column = new DataColumn();
  column.DataType = System.Type.GetType("System.int32");
  column.ColumnName = "FacultyId";
  FacultyTable.Columns.Add(column);

  //Create another column.
D column = new DataColumn();
  column.DataType = Type.GetType("System.string");
  column.ColumnName = "FacultyOffice";
  FacultyTable.Columns.Add(column);

  //Create new DataRow objects and add to DataTable.
  int Index = 0;
E for (Index = 1; Index <= 10; Index++)
  {
    row = FacultyTable.NewRow();
    row("FacultyId") = Index;
    row("FacultyOffice") = "TC- " + Index;
F   FacultyTable.Rows.Add(row);
  }
```

FIGURE 3.39 An example of creating a new table and adding data into the table.

Before we can finish this section, we need to discuss how to create a data table and add data columns and rows into that new table. Figure 3.39 shows an example of creating a new data table object and adding columns and rows into this table named **FacultyTable**.

Refer to Figure 3.39, starting from step **A**, a new instance of the data table **FacultyTable** is created and initialized to a blank table.

In order to add data into this new table, you need to use the Columns and Rows collections, and these two collections contain the **DataColumn** and **DataRow** objects. So next you need to create **DataColumn** and **DataRow** objects, respectively. Step **B** finished these objects declarations.

In step **C**, a new instance of the DataColumn, **column**, is created by using the **new** keyword. Two DataColumn properties, **DataType** and **ColumnName**, are used to initialize the first DataColumn

FacultyId	FacultyOffice
1	TC-1
2	TC-2
3	TC-3
4	TC-4
5	TC-5
6	TC-6
7	TC-7
8	TC-8
9	TC-9
10	TC-10

FIGURE 3.40 The completed FacultyTable.

object with the data type as integer (**System.int32**) and with the column name as "**FacultyId**", respectively. Finally, the completed object of the DataColumn is added into the **FacultyTable** using the **Add()** method of the **Columns** collection class.

In step **D**, the second data column, with the column data type as string (**System.string**) and the column name as the "**FacultyOffice**", is added into the **FacultyTable** in a similar way as we did for the first data column **FacultyId**.

In step **E**, a **for()** loop is utilized to simplify the procedure of adding new data rows into this **FacultyTable**. First a loop counter **Index** is created, and a new instance of the DataRow is created with the method of the DataTable – **NewRow()**. In total, we create and add 10 rows into this FacultyTable object. For the first column **FacultyId**, the loop counter **Index** is assigned to this column for each row. But for the second column **FacultyOffice**, the building name, combined with the loop counter **Index**, is assigned to this column for each row. Finally, in step **F**, the DataRow object, **row**, is added into this **FacultyTable** using the **Add()** method which belongs to the **Rows** collection class.

When this piece of code runs, a complete **FacultyTable** can be obtained and it should match the one that is shown in Figure 3.40.

3.4.8 ADO.NET 4.3 Entity Framework

Most traditional databases,, such as Microsoft Access, SQL Server and Oracle, use the relational model of data. But today almost all programming languages are object-oriented languages and the object-oriented model of data structures are widely implemented in modern programs developed with those languages. Therefore a potential contradiction is existed between the relational model of data in databases and the object-oriented model of programming applied in our real world today. Although some new components were added into the ADO.NET 2.0 to try to solve this contradiction, this still does not give a full solution for this issue.

The latest version of ADO.NET is 4.3, but most of the key issues are closely related to those present in ADO.NET 3.5. A revolutionary solution of this problem came with the release of ADO.NET 3.5 based on the .NET Framework 3.5 and the addition of Language Integrated Query (LINQ) to Visual Studio.NET 2008. The main contributions of the ADO.NET 3.5 include the fact that some new components, ADO.NET 3.5 Entity Framework 6 (ADO.NET 3.5 EF6) and ADO.NET 3.5 Entity Data Model Tools, were added into ADO.NET 3.5. With these new components, the contradiction existed between the relational model of data used in databases and the object-oriented programming projects can be fully resolved.

A primary goal of the ADO.NET 3.5 EF is to raise the level of abstraction available for data programming, thus simplifying the development of data-aware applications and enabling developers to write less code. The Entity Framework is the evolution of ADO.NET that allows developers to program in terms of the standard ADO.NET 3.5 abstraction or in terms of persistent objects (ORM), and is built upon the standard ADO.NET 3.5 Provider model which allows access to third-party databases. The Entity Framework introduces a new set of services around the Entity Data Model (EDM).

ADO.NET 3.5 provides an abstract database structure that converts the traditional logic database structure to an abstract or object structure with three layers:

- Conceptual layer
- Mapping layer
- Logical layer

ADO.NET 3.5 EF6 defines these three layers using a group of XML files and these XML files provide a level of abstraction to enable users to program against the object-oriented Conceptual model instead of the traditional relational data model.

The Conceptual layer provides a way to allow developers to build object-oriented codes to access database and each component in databases can be considered as an object or entity in this layer. The Conceptual Schema Definition Language (CSDL) is used in those XML files to define entities and relationships that will be recognized and used by the Mapping layer to setup mapping between entities and relational data tables. The Mapping layer uses Mapping Schema Language (MSL) to establish mappings between entities in the Conceptual layer and the relational data structure in the Logical layer. The relational database schema is defined in an XML file using Store Schema Definition Language (SSDL) in the Logical layer. The Mapping layer works as a bridge or converter to connect the Conceptual layer to the Logical layer and interpret between the object-oriented data model in the Conceptual layer and the relational data model in the Logical layer. This mapping that is shown in Figure 3.41 allows users to code against the Conceptual layer and map those codes into the Logical layer.

A useful data component is provided by the Conceptual layer to enable users to develop object-oriented codes and it is called **EntityClient**. In essence, the EntityClient is a Data Provider with the associated components such as Connection (EntityConnection), Command (**EntityCommand**) and DataReader (**EntityDataReader**). The EntityClient is similar to other Data Providers we discussed in the previous sections in this chapter but it includes new components and functionalities.

The core of ADO.NET 3.5 EF is its **Entity Data Model** (EDM) and the user can access and use this model using the ADO.NET 3.5 Entity Data Model Tools, which include the Entity Data Model item template, the Entity Data Model wizard, the Entity Data Model Designer, entity mapping details, and the entity model browser.

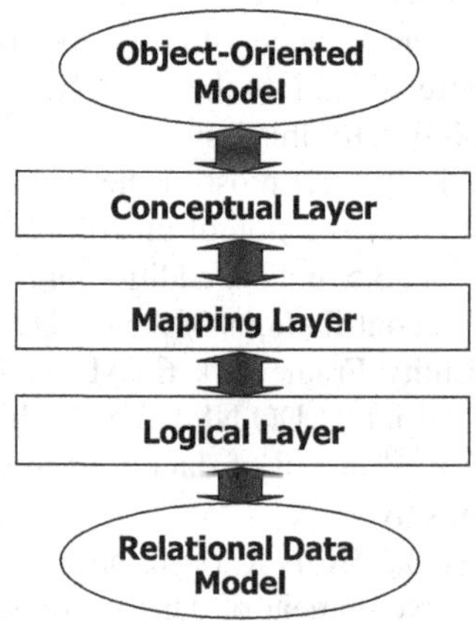

FIGURE 3.41 The mapping relationship between three layers.

In the following sections, we will discuss the Entity Data Model and how to use these Entity Data Model Tools to create, build and develop the Entity Data Model and implement it in your actual data-driven applications.

First let's take a closer look at the ADO.NET 3.5 Entity Data Model.

3.4.8.1 The ADO.NET 3.5 Entity Data Model

The ADO.NET 3.5 Entity Data Model (EDM) is a data model for defining application data as sets of entities and relationships on which common language runtime (CLR) types and storage structures can be mapped. This enables developers to create data access applications by programming against a conceptual application model instead of programming directly against a relational storage schema.

The following tools are designed to help you work with the EDM:

- The ADO.NET 3.5 Entity Data Model item template is available for Visual C# project type, and ASP.NET Web Site and Web Application projects, and launches the Entity Data Model Wizard.
- The Entity Data Model Wizard generates an EDM, which is encapsulated in an .edmx file. The wizard can generate the EDM from an existing database. The wizard also adds a connection string to the App.Config or Web.Config file and configures a single-file generator to run on the conceptual model contained in the .edmx file. This single-file generator will generate C# or VB code from the conceptual model defined in the .edmx file.
- The ADO.NET Entity Data Model Designer provides visual tools to view and edit the EDM graphically. You can open an .edmx file in the designer and create entities and map entities to database tables and columns.
- EdmGen.exe is a command-line tool that can be used to also generate models, validate existing models, and perform other functions on your EDM metadata files.

In the following sections we will provide a detailed discussion for each of these tools.

3.4.8.1.1 Entity Data Model Item Template

The ADO.NET 3.5 Entity Data Model item template is the starting point for the Entity Data Model tools. The ADO.NET 3.5 Entity Data Model item template is available for Visual C# and Visual Basic project types. It can be added to Console Application, Windows Application, Class Library, ASP.NET Web Service Application, ASP.NET Web Application, or ASP.NET Web Site projects. You can add multiple ADO.NET 3.5 Entity Data Model items to the same project, with each item containing files that were generated from a different database and/or tables within the same database.

When you add the ADO.NET 3.5 Entity Data Model item template to your project, Visual Studio:

- Adds references to the System.Data, System.Data.Entity, System.Core, System.Security, and System.Runtime.Serialization assemblies if the project does not already have them.
- Starts the Entity Data Model Wizard. The wizard is used to generate an Entity Data Model (EDM) from an existing database. The wizard creates an .edmx file, which contains the model information. You can use the .edmx file in the ADO.NET Entity Data Model Designer to view or modify the model.
- Creates a source code file that contains the classes generated from the conceptual model. The source code file is auto-generated, is updated when the .edmx file changes, and is compiled as part of the project.

Next let us consider the Entity Data Model Wizard.

3.4.8.1.2 Entity Data Model Wizard

The Entity Data Model Wizard starts after you add an ADO.NET 3.5 Entity Data Model to your project. The wizard is used to generate an Entity Data Model (EDM). It creates an .edmx file that contains the model information. The .edmx file is used by the ADO.NET 3.5 Entity Data Model Designer, which enables you to view and edit the mappings graphically.

You can select to create an empty model or to generate the model from an existing database. Generating the model from an existing database is the recommended practice for this release of the EDM tools.

The wizard also creates a source code file that contains the classes generated from the CSDL information encapsulated in the .edmx file. The source code file is auto-generated and is updated when the .edmx file changes.

Depending on your selections, the wizard will help you with the following steps.

- Choosing the Model Contents: It is recommended that you select to generate the model from an existing database. The Wizard takes you step by step through the selection of the data source, database, and database objects to include in the EDM.
- Choosing the Database Connection: You can choose an existing connection from the list of connections or click **New Database Connection** to open the **Connection Properties** dialog box and create a new connection to the database.
- Choosing your Database Objects: You can select the tables, views, and stored procedures to include in the EDM.

Now let's consider the real part – ADO.NET 3.5 Entity Data Model Designer.

3.4.8.1.3 Entity Data Model Designer

The ADO.NET 3.5 Entity Data Model Designer provides visual tools for the creation and editing of an Entity Data Model (EDM).

The ADO.NET Entity Data Model Designer includes the following components:

- A visual design surface for creating and editing the conceptual model. You can create, modify, or delete entities and associations.
- An Entity Mapping Details window to view and edit mappings. You can map entity types or associations to database tables and columns.
- An Entity Model Browser to give you a tree view of the EDM.
- Toolbox controls to create entities, associations and inheritance relationships.

The ADO.NET 3.5 Entity Data Model Designer is integrated with the Visual Studio.NET 2008 components. You can view and edit information using the Properties window and errors are reported in the Error List.

Figure 3.42 shows an example of the ADO.NET 3.5 Entity Data Model Designer. Two important functionalities of using the Entity Data Model Designer are.

3.4.8.1.3.1 Opening the ADO.NET Entity Data Model Designer The ADO.NET 3.5 Entity Data Model Designer is designed to work with an .edmx file. The .edmx file is an encapsulation of three EDM metadata artifact files, the Conceptual schema definition language (CSDL), the Store schema definition language (SSDL), and the Mapping specification language (MSL) files. When you run the EDM Wizard an .edmx file is created and added to your solution. You open the **ADO.NET Entity Data Model Designer** by double-clicking on the .edmx file in the Solution Explorer.

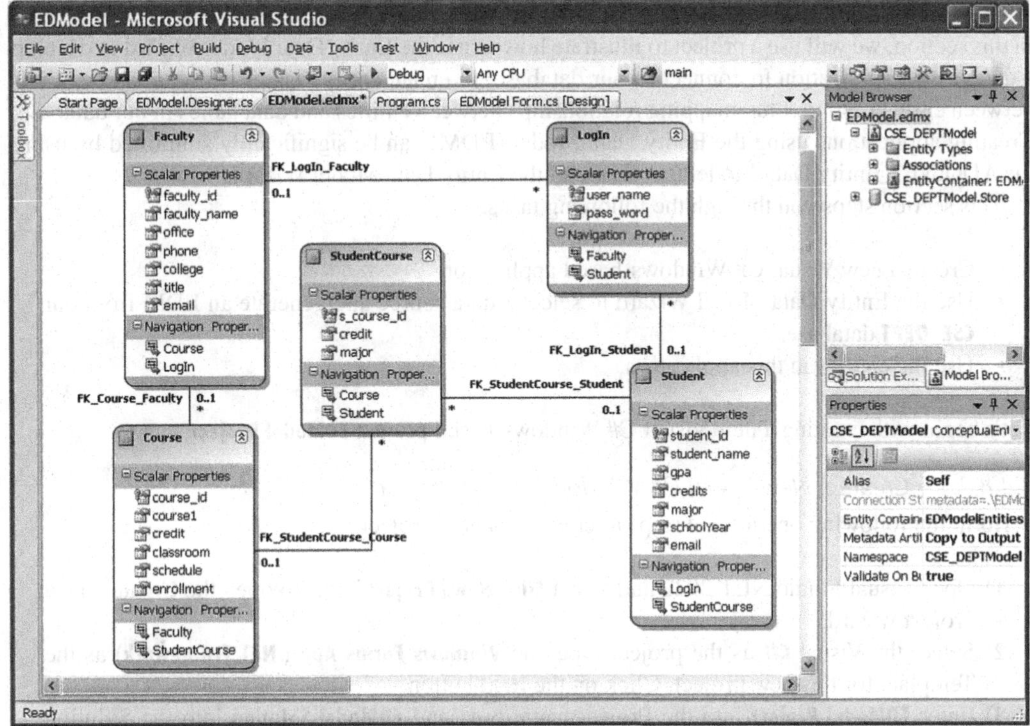

FIGURE 3.42 An example of the ADO.NET 3.5 entity data model designer.

3.4.8.1.3.2 Validating the EDM As you make changes to the EDM, the ADO.NET Entity Data Model Designer validates the modifications and reports errors in the Error List. You can also validate the EDM at any time by right-clicking on the design surface and selecting **Validate Model**.

3.4.8.1.4 Entity Model Browser

The Entity Model Browser is a Visual Studio tool window that is integrated with the ADO.NET 4.3 Entity Data Model Designer. It provides a tree view of the Entity Data Model (EDM). The Entity Model Browser groups the information into two nodes.

The first node shows you the conceptual model. By expanding the underlying nodes, you can view all entity types and associations in the model. The second node shows you the target database model. By expanding the underlying nodes you can see what parts of the database tables, views, and stored procedures have been imported into the model.

The Entity Data Model Browser enables you to do the following:

- Clicking on an item in the Entity Model Browser makes it active in the **Properties** window and the **Entity Mapping Details View** window. You can use these windows to modify the properties or entity mappings.
- Create a function import a stored procedure.
- Update the SSDL information from the database.

The Entity Model Browser opens when the ADO.NET 3.5 Entity Data Model Designer is opened. If the Entity Model Browser is not visible, right-click on the main design surface and select **Show Entity Model Browser**.

3.4.8.2 Using the ADO.NET 3.5 Entity Data Model Wizard

In this section, we will use a project to illustrate how to use the Entity Data Model Wizard to develop a data-driven application to connect to our database, to create entity classes, to setup associations between entities and to setup mapping relationships between entities and data tables in our database. Creating applications using the Entity Data Model (EDM) can be significantly simplified by using the ADO.NET Entity Data Model template and the Entity Data Model Wizard.

This section steps you through the following tasks:

- Create a new Visual C# Windows-based application.
- Use the Entity Data Model Wizard to select a data source and generate an EDM from our **CSE_DEPT** database.
- Use the entities in this application.

Let's begin with creating a new Visual C# Windows-based project **EDModel Project**.

3.4.8.2.1 Create a New Visual C# Windows-Based Project

Perform the following operational steps to create this new project:

1) Open Visual Studio.NET 2022 and select **File | New | Project** items to open the Create a new project wizard.
2) Select the Visual **C#** as the project type and **Windows Forms App (.NET Framework)** as the Template for this new project. Click on the **Next** button.
3) Enter **EDModel Project** into the Project name box, and **EDModel Solution** into the Solution name box. Select any folder in your machine as the **Location** to save this project (as shown in Figure 3.43). Then click on the **Create** button to create this new project with a new solution.
4) Change the **Text** property of the Form window to **Entity Data Model Form**.
5) Go to the Properties window and change the **StartPosition** property of the Form window to **CenterScreen**.
6) Add a Button control to the Form window and set its **Name** property to **cmdShow** and its **Text** property to **Show Faculty**. Set its **Font** style to Bold and Size to 10.

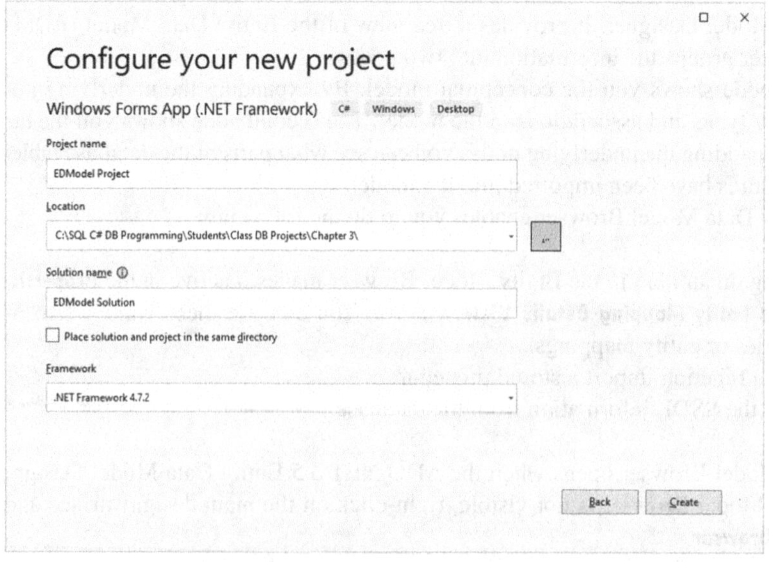

FIGURE 3.43 The finished wizard to create a new C# Windows Forms App project.

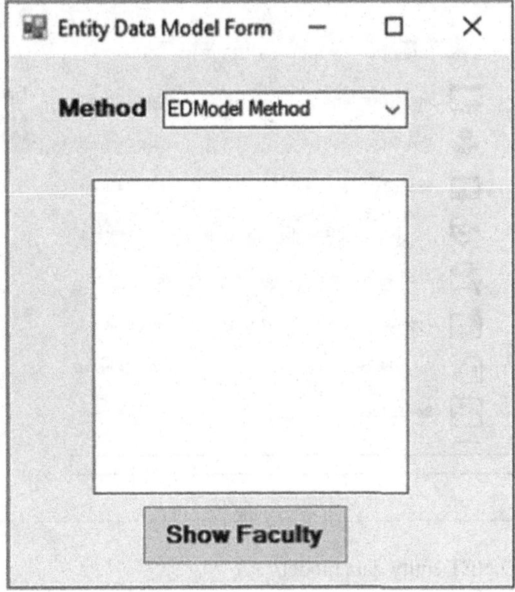

FIGURE 3.44 The EDModelForm window.

7) Add a Listbox control to the Form window and set its **Name** property to **FacultyList**. Set its **Font** style to Bold and Size to 10.
8) Add a Label control to the top of this Form1 and set its **Text** property to **Method**, font style to Bold and Size of 10.
9) Add a ComboBox control to the top of this From1 and set the **Name** property of this control to **ComboMethod**.

Your finished EDModelForm window should match one that is shown in Figure 3.44.

Now let's generate our Entity Data Model Wizard using the Entity Data Model Tools. The ADO.NET Entity Data Model item template is the starting point for the EDM tools.

3.4.8.2.2 Generate the Entity Data Model Files

Perform the following operations to generate our Entity Data Model Wizard:

1) Right click our project **EDModel Project** from the Solution Explorer window and select the **Add | New Item** from the popup menu.
2) In the opened Add New Item wizard, select the item **ADO.NET Entity Data Model** from the Templates box and enter **EDModel** into the **Name** box at the bottom. Your finished **Add New Item** wizard should match the one that is shown in Figure 3.45. Click on the **Add** button to add this component to our new project.
3) The Entity Data Model Wizard is opened with four options:
   a. EF Designer from database.
   b. Empty EF Designer model.
   c. Empty Code First model.
   d. Code First from database.

   Select the first item **EF Designer from database** since we want to create this EDM from our sample database **CSE_DEPT**. Click on the **Next** button to continue.

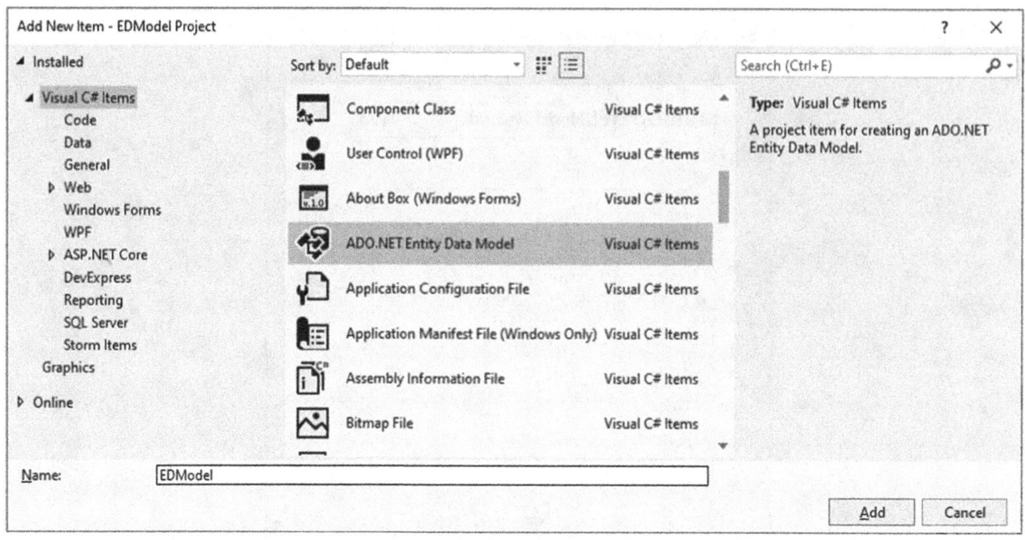

FIGURE 3.45 Add an ADO.NET entity data model.

4) The next wizard, **Choose Your Data Connection**, allows you to select our desired database to connect to. Click on the **New Connection** button to make a new connection. The Connection Properties wizard is displayed, then click on the **Change** button to select our desired data source.
5) On the opened Change Data Source wizard, select the **Microsoft SQL Server** and click on the **OK** button since we need to connect to a SQL Server database.
6) Enter our full server name, **DESKTOP-24JPUFB\SQL2019EXPRESS**, into the **Server name** box, and click on the drop-down arrow on the **Select or enter a database name** combo box, and select our sample database **CSE_DEPT** from that box.
7) Your finished **Add Connection** wizard is shown in Figure 3.46.
8) You can test this data source connection by clicking on the **Test Connection** button located at the lower-left corner, as shown in Figure 3.46. A **Test connection succeeded** message should be displayed if everything is fine.
9) Click on the **OK** button to close it and click on the **OK** button on that Add Connection wizard to return to the **Choose Your Data Connection wizard**.
10) Check on the **Show the connection string** checkbox if you like to keep and save this connection string in our project. Click on the **Next** button to continue.
11) The Choose Your Version wizard is shown up to enable us to select the EF version. Check the **Entity Framework 6.x** radio button since we need to use that version, and click on the **Next** button to continue.
12) The Choose Your Database Objects wizard appears and this wizard allows you to select our desired database objects such as tables, views and stored procedures. Make sure to expand and check the **Tables** checkbox since we may need all five tables including **LogIn, Faculty, Course, Student** and **StudentCourse**. Keep the default model name at the bottom, **CSE_DEPTModel**, with no change. An example of this wizard is shown in Figure 3.47. Click the **Finish** button to complete this process.
13) A message box may popup to confirm this generation, check the **Do not show this message again** checkbox and click on the **OK** button to confirm this process.

The Designer View of this generated Entity Data Model is displayed in the main window, as shown in Figure 3.48. Now open the Solution Explorer window and you can find that an Entity Data Model **EDModel.edmx** has been added into our project, which is also shown in Figure 3.48.

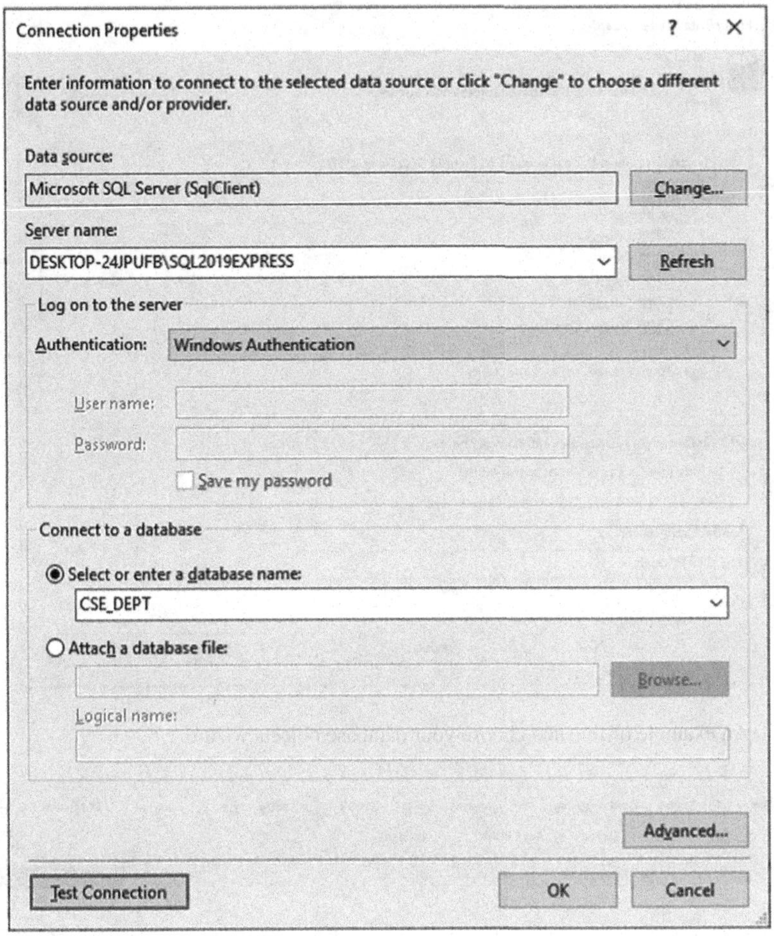

FIGURE 3.46 The finished connection properties wizard.

Five tables and connections between them are displayed in this view. On each table, two groups of entity properties are displayed, Scalar Properties and Navigation Properties. The first category contains all entity properties (mapped to columns in our physical table) and the second category contains all related entities (mapped to related tables by using the primary-foreign keys) in this database. The connections between each entity (mapped to data table) are called associations.

One can also open another tool, **Table Mapping**, to get detailed mapping information for each table. To open, for example, the detailed mapping for the **Faculty** table, just right-click on the **Faculty** table in this Designer View and select the item **Table Mapping** from the popup menu. An example of this Faculty table mapping is shown in Figure 3.49.

In addition to these tools, an XML mapping file associated with our Entity Data Model **EDModel** is also created. To open this file, right-click our new created **EDModel.edmx** from the Solution Explorer window and select the item **Open With** to open the Open With wizard, which is shown in Figure 3.50. Select the item **XML (Text) Editor** and then click the **OK** button to open this XML mapping file.

Now if you open the **App.Config** file by double-clicking it from the Solution Explorer window, you can find that our connection string, **CSE_DEPTEntities** we created using the Entity Data Model Wizard, is under the **<connectionStrings>** tag in this file.

At this point, we have finished creating our Entity Data Model, and now we can use this model to build our Visual C# data-driven application to show readers how to make it work.

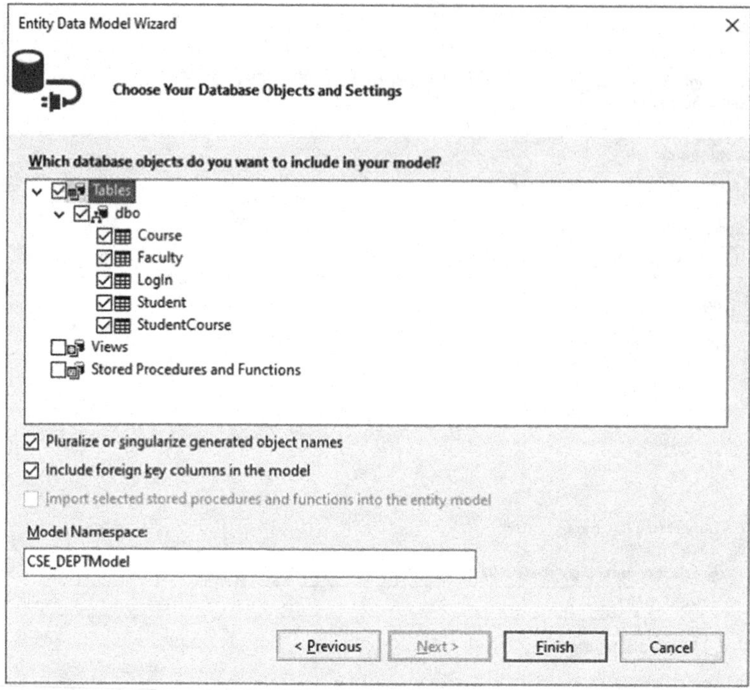

FIGURE 3.47 An example of finished choose your database objects wizard.

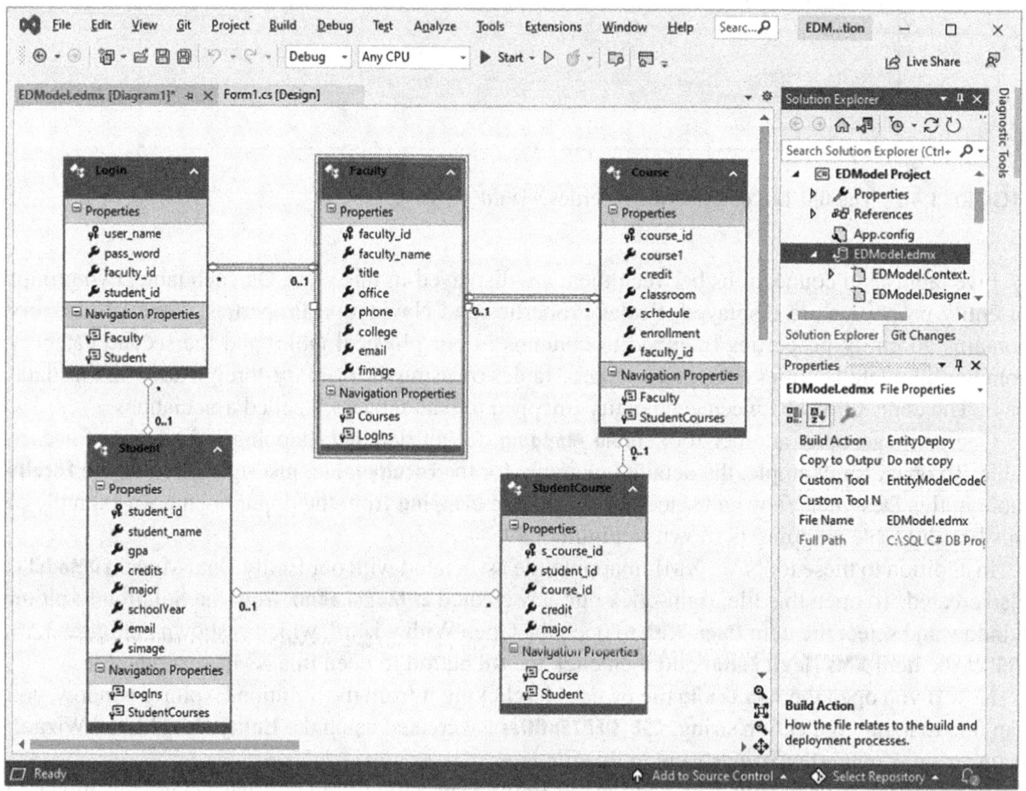

FIGURE 3.48 The added EDModel.

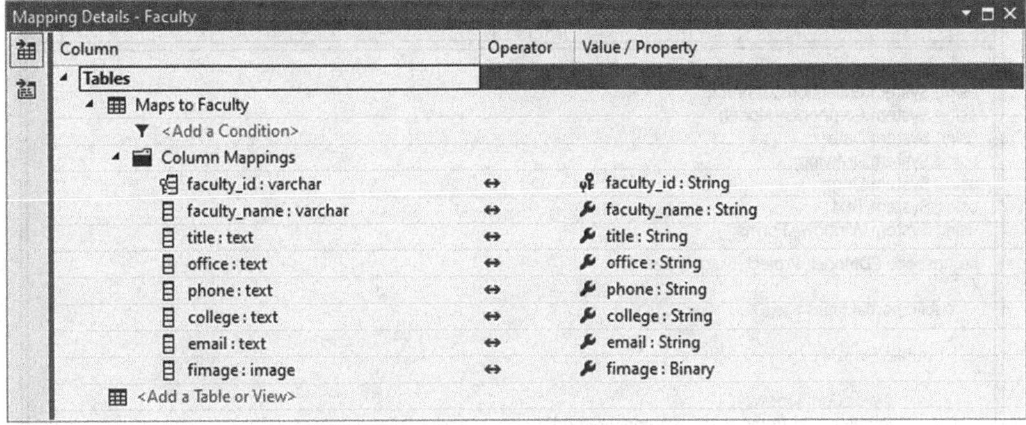

FIGURE 3.49 An example of table mapping – Faculty entity.

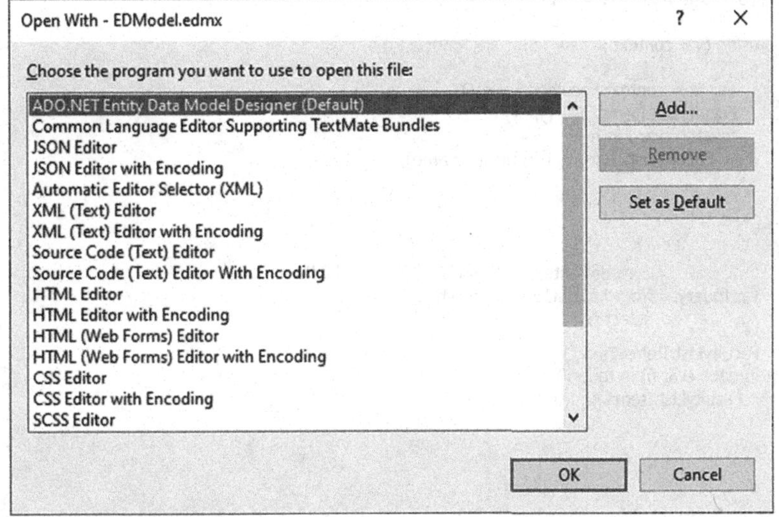

FIGURE 3.50 The Open With wizard.

3.4.8.2.3 Use the ADO.NET 3.5 Entity Data Model Wizard

The functionality of this project is that all faculty members in our **Faculty** table will be retrieved and displayed in a Listbox control **FacultyList** as the user clicks the **Show Faculty** button when the project runs. Now let's use the Entity Data Model to perform the coding development for the Form1 code window to realize this functionality.

Open the Code Window of this Form1 class and enter the codes shown in Figure 3.51 into this window. Let's have a closer look at this piece of code to see how it works.

A. The first coding job is to add two different query methods, **EDModel Method** and **LINQ Method**, since we allow users to perform this query with either **Entity Data Model** method or with **LINQ Method**.

B. Then we need to build the codes for the **Show Faculty** button's Click method. Right-click on the form object **Form1.cs** from the Solution Explorer window and click on the **View Designer**

```
EDModel Project                    cmdShow_Click(object sender, EventArgs e)

using System;
using System.Collections.Generic;
using System.ComponentModel;
using System.Data;
using System.Drawing;
using System.Linq;
using System.Text;
using System.Windows.Forms;

namespace EDModel_Project
{
  public partial class Form1 : Form
  {
    public Form1()
    {
      InitializeComponent();
A     ComboMethod.Items.Add("EDModel Method");
      ComboMethod.Items.Add("LINQ Method");
      ComboMethod.SelectedIndex = 0;
    }
    private void cmdShow_Click(object sender, EventArgs e)
    {
B     if (ComboMethod.Text == "EDModel Method")
      {
        using (var context = new CSE_DEPTEntities())
        {
C         var fn = context.Faculties.ToList();
D         FacultyList.Items.Clear();
E         foreach (var f in fn)
            FacultyList.Items.Add(f.faculty_name);
        }
      }
F     else
      {
        CSE_DEPTEntities dbContext = new CSE_DEPTEntities();
G       var fquery = from f in dbContext.Faculties
                     select f;

H       FacultyList.Items.Clear();
I       foreach (var fn in fquery)
          FacultyList.Items.Add(fn.faculty_name);
  }
    }
  }
}
```

FIGURE 3.51 The codes for the cmdShow_Click method.

button to open its Form Window. Double-click the **Show Faculty** button to open its Click method. First we need to check which query method is selected by the users. If the **EDModel Method** is selected, a new object of the Entity class **CSE_DEPTEntities**, **context**, is generated with the **using** command.

C. Then an Entities query is performed to retrieve all faculty names and convert them into a list with a system method **ToList()**. The query result is assigned to the query variable **fn**.
D. The **FacultyList** must be first cleaned up before it can be filled with all queried faculty names.
E. A **foreach()** loop is used to pick up each faculty name from the query variable **f** from the result **fn**, and add it into the **FacultyList**.
F. If the **LINQ Method** is chosen by the user, similarly a **CSE_DEPTEntities** object, **dbContext**, is generated.
G. Then a LINQ query is performed to get all faculty names. Refer to Chapter 4 to get more details about the structure and syntax of this LINQ query.

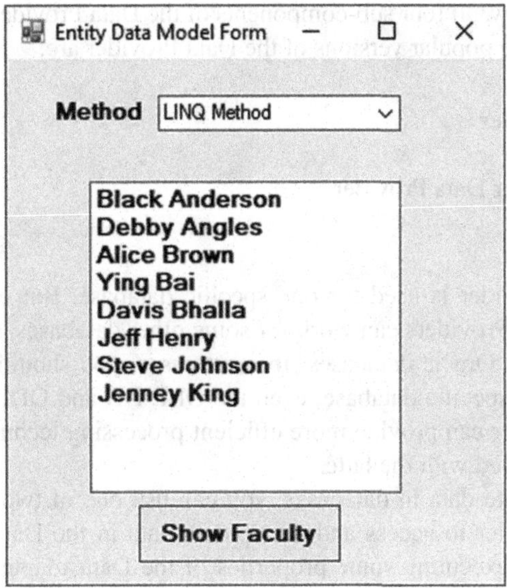

FIGURE 3.52 The running result of the project EDModel project.

H. The Listbox control **FacultyList** is cleaned up before it can be filled.
I. A **foreach()** loop is used to pick up each faculty name from the query variable **fn** from the result **fquery**, and add it into the **FacultyList**.

Now let's run the project to test our codes. Click the **Start** button to run the project. The Form1 window is displayed, as shown in Figure 3.52. Select any query method and click on the **Show Faculty** button to connect to our sample database and retrieve back all faculty names. The running result is shown in Figure 3.52.

Click the **Close** button that is located at the upper-right corner of this Form to close our project. It can be found from this piece of code that it is relatively simple and easy to use the Entity Data Model to access and manipulate data against the database.

3.5 CHAPTER SUMMARY

The main topic of this chapter is an introduction to the ADO.NET, which includes the architectures, organizations and components of the ADO.NET 2.0, 3.5 and 4.3.

Detailed discussions and descriptions are provided in this chapter to give readers both fundamental and practical ideas and pictures in how to use components in ADO.NET 2.0, ADO.NET 3.5 and ADO.NET 4.3 to develop professional data-driven applications. Two ADO.NET architectures are discussed to enable users to follow the directions to design and build their preferred projects based on the different organizations of the ADO.NET.

A history of the development of ADO.NET is first introduced in this chapter. Different data-related objects are discussed, such as Data Access Object (DAO), Remote Data Object (RDO), Open Database Connectivity (ODBC), OLE DB and the ADO. The difference between the ADO and the ADO.NET is also provided in detail.

Fundamentally, the ADO.NET is a class-container and it contains three basic components: Data Provider, DataSet and DataTable. Furthermore, the Data Provider contains four sub-components: Connection, Command, TableAdapter and DataReader. You should bear in mind that the Data Provider comes in multiple versions based on the type of the database you are using in your applications.

Thus, from this point of view, all four sub-components of the Data Provider are called Data Provider-dependent components. The popular versions of the Data Provider are:

- OLE DB Data Provider
- ODBC Data Provider
- Microsoft SQL Server Data Provider
- Oracle Data Provider

Each version of Data Provider is used for one specific database. But one exception is that both OLE DB and ODBC Data Providers can work for some other databases, such as Microsoft Access, Microsoft SQL Server and Oracle databases. In most cases, you should use the matched version of the Data Provider for a specific database; even the OLE DB and ODBC can work for that kind of database since the former can provide more efficient processing technique, faster accessing and manipulating speed compared with the latter.

To access and manipulate data in databases, you can use one of two ADO.NET architectures: you can use the DataAdapter to access and manipulate data in the DataSet that is considered as a DataTables collector by executing some properties of the DataAdapter, such as **SelectCommand, InsertCommand, UpdateCommand** and **DeleteCommand**. Alternatively, you can treat each DataTable as a single table object and access and manipulate data in each table by executing the different methods of the Command object, such as **ExecuteReader()** and **ExecuteNonQuery()**.

A key point in using the Connection object of the Data Provider to setup connection between your applications and your data source is the connection string, which has the different format and style depending on the database you are using. The popular components of the connection string include Provider, Data Source, Database, Use ID and Password. But some connection strings only use a limited number of components, such as the Data Provider for the Oracle database.

An important point in using the Command object to access and manipulate data in your data source is the **Parameter** component. The Parameter class contains all properties and methods that can be used to setup specific parameters for the Command object. Each Parameter object contains a set of parameters, and each Parameter object can be assigned to the Parameters collection that is one of property of the Command object.

The latest version of ADO.NET, ADO.NET 4.3, is discussed with some examples in the final section in this chapter. The properties and functionalities of the ADO.NET 4.3 Entity Framework (EF6) and ADO.NET 3.5 Entity Framework Tools (EFT) are discussed in detail. The core of ADO. NET 4.3 EF6, the Entity Data Model, and associated Item template, Wizard and Designer, is also discussed and analyzed with a real project example **EDModel Project**.

After finishing this chapter, you should be able to:

- Understand the architecture and organization of the ADO.NET.
- Understand three components of the ADO.NET, such as the Data Provider, the DataSet and the DataTable.
- Use the Connection object to connect to an Microsoft Access, Microsoft SQL Server and Oracle database.
- Use the Command and Parameter objects to select, insert and delete data using a string variable containing a SQL statement.
- Use the DataAdapter object to fill a DataSet using the **Fill()** method.
- Read data from the data source using the DataReader object.
- Read data from the DataTable using the SelectCommand property of the DataAdapter object.
- Create DataSet and DataTable objects and add data into the DataTable object
- Understand the ADO.NET 4.3 Entity Framework (EF6) and ADO.NET 3.5 Entity Framework Tools (EFT).

- Understand the ADO.NET 3.5 Entity Data Model (EDM) and the associated Item template, Wizard and Designer.
- Create and implement ADO.NET 4.3 Entity Data Model Tools to develop professional data-driven applications in Visual C# 2022 IDE.

In Chapter 4, we will discuss a popular technique, Language Integrated Query (LINQ), which was released with ADO.NET 3.5 and .NET Framework 3.5 in Visual Studio.NET 2008. With the help of this new technique, the operational process of the data queries and manipulations with different data sources can be significantly simplified and the efficiency of the data actions against the data sources can be greatly improved.

HOMEWORK

I. TRUE/FALSE SELECTIONS

____1. ADO.NET is composed of four major components: Data Provider, DataSet, DataReader and DataTable.
____2. ADO is developed based on Object Linking and Embedding (OLE) and Component Object Model (COM) technologies.
____3. ADO.NET 3.5 is based mainly on the Microsoft .NET Framework 2.0.
____4. The Connection object is used to setup a connection between your data-driven application and your data source.
____5. Both OLE DB and ODBC Data Providers can work for the SQL Server and Oracle databases.
____6. Different ADO.NET components are located at the different namespaces. The **DataSet** and **DataTable** are located at the **System.Data** namespace.
____7. The DataSet can be considered as a container that contains multiple data tables, but those tables are only a mapping of the real data tables in the database.
____8. The ExecuteReader() method is a data query method and it can only be used to execute a read-out operation from a database.
____9. Both SQL Server and Oracle Data Providers used a so-called Named Parameter Mapping technique.
___10. The DataTable object is a Data Provider-independent object.

II. MULTIPLE CHOICES

1. To populate data from a database to a DataSet object, one needs to use the _____
   a. Data Source
   b. DataAdapter (TableAdapter)
   c. Runtime object
   d. Wizards
2. The Parameters property of the Command class ________
   a. Is a Parameter object
   b. Contains a collection of Parameter objects
   c. Contains a Parameter object
   d. Contains the parameters of the Command object
3. To add a Parameter object to the Parameters property of the Command object, one needs to use the ______ method that belongs to the _______
   a. Insert, Command
   b. Add, Command
   c. Insert, Parameters collection
   d. Add, Parameters collection

4. DataTable class is a container that holds the _______ and _______ objects
   a. DataTable, DataRelation
   b. DataRow, DataColumn
   c. DataRowCollection, DataColumnCollection
   d. Row, Column
5. The _______ is a property of the DataTable class, and it is also a collection of DataRow objects. Each DataRow can be mapped to a _____ in the DataTable
   a. Rows, column
   b. Columns, column
   c. Row, row
   d. Rows, row
6. The ______ data provider can be used to execute the data query for ______ data providers
   a. SQL Server, OleDb and Oracle
   b. OleDb, SQL Server and Oracle
   c. Oracle, SQL Server and OleDb
   d. SQL Server, Odbc and Oracle
7. To perform a Fill() method to fill a data table, exactly it executes ______ object with suitable parameters
   a. DataAdapter
   b. Connection
   c. DataReader
   d. Command
8. The DataReader is a read-only class and it can only be used to retrieve and hold the data rows returned from a database when executing a(n) _______ method.
   a. Fill
   b. ExecuteNonQuery
   c. ExecuteReader
   d. ExecuteQuery
9. One needs to use ______ method to release all objects used for a data-driven application before one can exit the project
   a. Release
   b. Nothing
   c. Clear
   d. Dispose
10. To ____ data between the DataSet and the database, the ___ object should be used
    a. Bind, BindingSource
    b. Add, TableAdapter
    c. Move, TableAdapter
    d. Remove, DataReader

III. Exercises

1. Explain two architectures of the ADO.NET 2.0, and illustrate the functionality of these two architectures using block diagrams.
2. List three basic components of the ADO.NET 2.0 and the different versions of the Data Provider as well as their sub-components.
3. Explain the relationship between the Command and Parameter objects. Illustrate how to add Parameter objects to the Parameters collection that is a property of the Command object using an example. Assuming that an SQL Server Data Provider is used with two parameters: parameter_name: **username, password**, parameter_ value: **Name, Come**.

4. Explain the relationship between the DataSet and DataTable. Illustrate how to use the Fill method to populate a DataTable in the DataSet. Assuming that the data query string is an SQL SELECT statement: **SELECT faculty_id, faculty_name FROM Faculty**, and an SQL Server Data Provider is utilized.
5. Explain the components and functionalities of ADO.NET 3.5 Entity Framework (EF) and ADO.NET 3.5 Entity Framework Tools (EFT).
6. Illustrate the relationship between the ADO.NET 3.5 Entity Data Model and its associated components, such as Item template, Wizard and Designer.
7. Explain the relationship between three layers of the ADO.NET 3.5 Entity Data Model, Conceptual layer, Mapping layer and Logical layer.

4 Introduction to Language Integrated Query (LINQ)

Language-Integrated Query (LINQ) is a groundbreaking innovation in Visual Studio 2008 and the .NET Framework version 3.5, which bridges the gap between the world of objects and the world of data.

Traditionally, queries against data are expressed as simple strings without type checking at compile time or IntelliSense support. In addition, you have to learn a different query language for each type of data source: Microsoft Access, SQL databases, XML documents, various Web services, and Oracle databases. LINQ makes a query as a first-class language construct in C# and Visual Basic. You write queries against strongly typed collections of objects using language keywords and familiar operators.

In Visual Studio.NET you can write LINQ queries in C# with SQL Server databases, XML documents, ADO.NET DataSets, and any collection of objects that supports IEnumerable or the generic IEnumerable<T> interface. As we mentioned in Chapter 3, LINQ support for the ADO.NET 3.5 Entity Framework is also planned, and LINQ providers are being written by third parties for many Web services and other database implementations.

You can use LINQ queries in new projects, or alongside non-LINQ queries in existing projects. The only requirement is that the project should be developed under the .NET Framework 3.5 environment.

Before we can dig deeper into LINQ, we had better have a general and global picture about the LINQ. Let's start from the basic introduction about the LINQ.

4.1 OVERVIEW OF LANGUAGE INTEGRATED QUERY

The LINQ pattern is established on the basis of a group of methods called Standard Query Operators (SQO). Most of these methods operate on sequences, where a sequence is an object whose type implements the IEnumerable<T> interface or the IQueryable<T> interface. The standard query operators provide query capabilities, including filtering, projection, aggregation, sorting and more.

All SQO methods are located at the namespace System.Linq. To use these methods, one must declare this namespace with a directive such as: using System.Linq in the namespace declaration section of the code windows.

There are some potentially confusing signs and terminologies, such as IEnumerable, IEnumerable <T>, IQueryable and IQueryable<T> interfaces, so let's first have a closer look at these terminologies.

4.1.1 Some Special Interfaces Used in LINQ

Four interfaces, IEnumerable, IEnumerable<T>, IQueryable and IQueryable<T>, are widely used in LINQ queries via SQO. In fact, two interfaces, IEnumerable and IQueryable, are mainly used for the non-generic collections supported by the earlier versions of C#, such as C# 1.0 or earlier, and the other two interfaces, IEnumerable<T> and IQueryable<T>, are used to convert the data type of collections compatible with those in the System.Collection.Generic in C# 2.0 to either IEnumerable<T> (LINQ to Objects) or IQueryable<T> (LINQ to SQL) since LINQ uses a stronger typed collection or sequence as the data sources, and any data in those data sources must be converted to this stronger typed collection before the LINQ can be implemented. Most LINQ queries are performed on arrays or collections that implement the IEnumerable<T> or IEnumerable interfaces. But a LINQ to

DOI: 10.1201/9781003319832-4

SQL query is performed on classes that implement the IQueryable<T> interface. The relationship between the IEnumerable<T> and the IQueryable<T> interfaces is: IQueryable<T> implements IEnumerable<T>, therefore, in addition to the Standard Query Operator (SQO), the LINQ to SQL queries have additional query operators since it uses the IQueryable<T> interface.

4.1.1.1 The IEnumerable and IEnumerable<T> Interfaces

The IEnumerable<T> interface is a key part of LINQ to Objects and it allows all of the C# 2.0 generic collection classes to implement it. This interface permits the enumeration of a collection's elements. All of the collections in the System.Collections.Generic namespace support the IEnumerable<T> interface. Here T means the converted data type of the sequence or collection. For example, if you have an IEnumerable of *int*, expressed by IEnumerable<*int*>, it is exactly a sequence or a collection of *int*s.

In the case of the non-generic collections which existed in the old version of C#, such as C# 1.0 or older, they support the IEnumerable interface, but they do not support the IEnumerable<T> interface because of the stronger typed property of the latter. Therefore, you cannot directly call those SQO methods whose first argument is an IEnmerable<T> using non-generic collections. However, you can still perform LINQ queries using those collections by calling the Cast or OfType SQO to generate a sequence that implements IEnumerable<T>.

Here, a coding example of using LINQ to Object is shown in Figure 4.1.

The type IEnumerable<int> plays two important roles in this piece of code.

1) The query expression has a data source called **intArray** which implements IEnumerable<int>.
2) The query expression returns an instance of IEnumberable<int>.

Every LINQ to Objects query expression, including the one shown above, will begin with a line of this type:

```
From x in y
```

In each case, the data source represented by the variable **y** must support the IEnumerable<T> interface. As you have already seen, the array of integers shown in this example supports that interface.

The query shown in Figure 4.1 can also be re-written in such a way as is shown in Figure 4.2.

This piece of code makes explicit the type of the variable returned by this query, IEnumerable<int>. In practice, you will find that most LINQ to Objects queries return IEnumerable<T>, for different data type T.

```
// create an integer array
int[]  myArray = new int[] {1, 2, 3, 4, 5 };
IEnumerable<int> intArray = myArray.Select(i => i);
//LINQ query expression
var query = from num in intArray
            where num >= 3
            select num;
foreach (var intResult in query)
{
   Console.WriteLine(intResult);
}
```

FIGURE 4.1 A coding example of using LINQ to object query.

```
// create an integer array
int[]  myArray = new int[] {1, 2, 3, 4, 5 };
IEnumerable<int> query = from num in myArray
                         where num >= 3
                         select num;

foreach (var intResult in query)
{
    Console.WriteLine(intResult);
}
```

FIGURE 4.2 A modification of the coding example of using LINQ to object query.

By finishing these two examples, it should be clear to you that interfaces IEnumerable and IEnumerable<T> play a key role in LINQ to Objects queries. The former is used for the non-generic collections and the latter is used for the generic collections. The point is that a typical LINQ to Objects query expression not only takes a class that implements IEnumerable<T> as its data source, but also returns an instance with the same type.

4.1.1.2 The IQueryable and IQueryable<T> Interfaces

As we discussed in the previous section, IQueryable and IQueryable<T> are two of the interfaces used for LINQ to SQL queries. Similar to IEnumerable and IEnumerable<T> interfaces, in which the Standard Query Operator methods are defined as the static members in the Enumerable class, the Standard Query Operator methods applied for the IQueryable<T> interface are defined as static members of the Queryable class. The IQueryable interface is principally used for the non-generic collections and the IQueryable<T> is used for generic collections. Another point is that the IQueryable<T> interface is inherited from the IEnumerable<T> interface from the Queryable class and the definition of this interface is:

```
interface IQueryable<T> : IEnumerable<T>, Queryable
```

From this inheritance, one can treat an IQueryable<T> sequence as an IEnumerable<T> sequence. Figure 4.3 shows an example of using the IQueryable interface to perform query to a sample database CSE_DEPT. A database connection has been made using the DataContext object before this piece of code can be executed. The LogIn is the name of a table in this sample database and it has

```
//create a database connection using the DataContext object
public CSE_DEPTDataContext cse_dept = new CSE_DEPTDataContext();
//create local string variables
string username = string.Empty;
string password = string.Empty;

//LINQ query expression
IQueryable<LogIn> loginfo = from lg in cse_dept.LogIns
                            where lg.user_name == txtUserName.Text &&
                            lg.pass_word == txtPassWord.Text
                            select lg;
foreach (LogIn log in loginfo)
{
    username = log.user_name;
    password = log.pass_word;
}
```

FIGURE 4.3 A coding example of using LINQ to SQL query.

been converted to an entity before the LINQ query can be performed. An IQueryable<T> interface, exactly a Standard Query Operator, is utilized to perform this query. The LogIn works as a type in the IQueryable<T> interface to make sure that both the input sequence and returned sequence are strongly typed sequences with the type of LogIn. The Standard Query Operator fetches and returns the matched sequence and assigns them to the associated string variables using the foreach loop.

Now let's have a closer look at the Standard Query Operator (SQO).

4.1.2 Standard Query Operators

There are two sets of LINQ Standard Query Operators, one that operates on objects of type IEnumerable<T> and the other that operates on objects of type IQueryable<T>. The methods that make up each set are static members of the Enumerable and Queryable classes, respectively. They are defined as extension methods of the type that they operate on. This means that they can be called by using either static method syntax or instance method syntax.

In addition, several standard query operator methods operate on types other than those based on IEnumerable<T> or IQueryable<T>. The Enumerable type defines two such methods that both operate on objects of type IEnumerable. These methods, Cast<TResult>(IEnumerable) and OfType<TResult>(IEnumerable), allow you to enable a non-parameterized, or non-generic, collection to be queried in the LINQ pattern. They do this by creating a strongly typed collection of objects. The Queryable class defines two similar methods, Cast<TResult>(IQueryable) and OfType<TResult>(IQueryable), which operate on objects of type Queryable.

The standard query operators differ in the timing of their execution, depending on whether they return a singleton value or a sequence of values. Those methods that return a singleton value (for example, Average and Sum) execute immediately. Methods that return a sequence defer the query execution and return an enumerable object.

In the case of the methods that operate on in-memory collections, that is, those methods that extend IEnumerable<T>, the returned enumerable object captures the arguments that were passed to the method. When that object is enumerated, the logic of the query operator is employed and the query results are returned.

In contrast, methods that extend IQueryable<T> do not implement any querying behavior, but build an expression tree that represents the query to be performed. The query processing is handled by the source IQueryable<T> object.

Calls to query methods can be chained together in one query, which enables queries to become arbitrarily complex.

According to their functionality, the Standard Query Operator can be divided into two categories: Deferred Standard Query Operators and Non-deferred Standard Query Operators. Figure 4.4 lists some most often used Standard Query Operators.

Because of the limitations of space, we will select some most often used Standard Query Operator methods and give a detailed discussion for them one by one.

4.1.3 Deferred Standard Query Operators

Both deferred Standard Query Operators and non-deferred operators are organized based on their purpose and we start this discussion based on the alphabet order.

AsEnumerable (Conversion Purpose)

The AsEnumerable operator method has no effect other than to change the compile-time type of *source* from a type that implements IEnumerable<T> to IEnumerable<T> itself. This means that if an input sequence has a type of IEnumerable<T>, the output sequence will also be converted to one that has the same type, IEnumerable.

A piece of example codes of using this operator is shown in Figure 4.5.

Standard Query Operator	Purpose	Deferred
All	Quantifiers	No
Any	Quantifiers	No
AsEnumerable	Conversion	Yes
Average	Aggregate	No
Cast	Conversion	Yes
Distinct	Set	Yes
ElementAt	Element	No
First	Element	No
Join	Join	Yes
Last	Element	No
OfType	Conversion	Yes
OrderBy	Ordering	Yes
Select	Projection	Yes
Single	Element	No
Sum	Aggregate	No
ToArray	Conversion	No
ToList	Conversion	No
Where	Restriction	Yes

FIGURE 4.4 Most often used standard query operators.

```
FacultyDataAdapter.SelectCommand = accCommand;
FacultyDataAdapter.Fill(ds, "Faculty");
var facultyinfo = (from fi in ds.Tables["Faculty"].AsEnumerable()
                   where fi.Field<string>("faculty_name").Equals(ComboName.Text)
                   select fi);
foreach (var fRow in facultyinfo)
{
    //Display selected fRow elements...
}
```

FIGURE 4.5 An example coding for the operator AsEnumerable.

The key point for this query structure is the operator AsEnumerable(). Since different database systems use different collections and query operators, hose collections must be converted to the type of IEnumerable<T> in order to use the LINQ technique because all data operations in LINQ use a Standard Query Operator methods that can perform complex data queries on an IEnumerable<T> sequence. A compiling error would be encountered without this operator.

Cast (Conversion Purpose)

A Cast operator provides a method for explicit conversion of the type of an object in an input sequence to an output sequence with specific type. The compiler treats *cast-expression* as type *type-name* after a type cast has been made. A point to be noticed is that the Cast operator method works on the IEnumerable interface, but not the IEnumerable<T> interface, and it can convert any object with an IEnumerable type to IEnumerable<T> type.

An example coding of using this operator is shown in Figure 4.6.

Join(Join Purpose)

A join of two data sources is the association of objects in one data source with objects that share a common attribute in another data source.

Joining is an important operation in queries that target data sources whose relationships to each other cannot be followed directly. In object-oriented programming, this could mean a correlation between objects that is not modeled, such as the backwards direction of a

```
System.Collections.ArrayList fruits = new System.Collections.ArrayList();
fruits.Add("apple");
fruits.Add("mango");

IEnumerable<string> query = fruits.Cast<string>().Select(fruit => fruit);

foreach (string fruit in query)
   Console.WriteLine(fruit);

// the running result of this piece of codes is:
    apple
    mango
```

FIGURE 4.6 An example coding for the operator cast.

one-way relationship. An example of a one-way relationship is a Customer class that has a property of type City, but the City class does not have a property that is a collection of Customer objects. If you have a list of City objects and you want to find all the customers in each city, you could use a join operation to find them.

The join methods provided in the LINQ framework are Join and GroupJoin. These methods perform equi-joins or joins that match two data sources based on equality of their keys. In relational database terms, Join implements an inner join, that is, a type of join in which only those objects that have a match in the other data set are returned. The GroupJoin method has no direct equivalent in relational database terms, but it implements a superset of inner joins and left outer joins. A left outer join is a join that returns each element of the first (left) data source, even if it has no correlated elements in the other data source.

An example coding of using this operator is shown in Figure 4.7.

The issue is that we want to query all courses (course_id) taught by the selected faculty from the Course table based on the faculty_name. But the problem is that there is no faculty_name column in the Course table, and only faculty_id is associated with related course_id. Therefore we have to get the faculty_id from the Faculty table first based on the faculty_name, and then query the course_id from the Course table based on the queried faculty_id. This problem can be effectively solved by using a join operator method shown in Figure 4.7.

OfType (Conversion Purpose)

This operator method is implemented by using deferred execution. The immediate return value is an object that stores all the information that is required to perform the action. The query represented by this method is not executed until the object is enumerated either by calling its GetEnumerator method directly or by using **foreach** in Visual C#.

```
var courseinfo = Courses.
                    Join (Faculty, ci =>ci. faculty_id,  o => o.faculty_id).
                    Where (fi.faculty_name == ComboName.Text).
                    Select new
                    {
                         course_id = ci.course_id
                    };
foreach (var cid in courseinfo)
{
     CourseList.Items.Add(cid.course_id);
}
```

FIGURE 4.7 An example coding for the operator Join.

```
System.Collections.ArrayList fruits = new System.Collections.ArrayList(2);
fruits.Add("Mango");
fruits.Add("Orange");

// Apply OfType() to the ArrayList.
IEnumerable<string> query = fruits.OfType<string>();

Console.WriteLine("Elements of type 'string' are:");
foreach (string fruit in query)
   Console.WriteLine(fruit);

// the running result of this piece of codes is:

  Elements of type 'string' are:
  Mango
  Orange
```

FIGURE 4.8 An example coding for the operator OfType.

A piece of example codes of using this operator is shown in Figure 4.8.

The OfType<T>(IEnumerable) method returns only those elements in *source* that can be cast to type *TResult*. To instead receive an exception if an element cannot be cast to type *TResult*, use Cast<T>(IEnumerable).

This method is one of the few standard query operator methods that can be applied to a collection that has a non-parameterized type, such as an ArrayList. This is because OfType<TResult> extends the type IEnumerable. OfType<TResult> cannot only be applied to collections that are based on the parameterized IEnumerable<T> type, but may also be applied to collections that are based on the non-parameterized IEnumerable type.

By applying OfType<TResult> to a collection that implements IEnumerable, you gain the ability to query the collection by using the Standard Query Operators. For example, specifying a type argument of Object to OfType<TResult> would return an object of type IEnumerable<Object> in C#, to which the standard query operators can be applied.

OrderBy (Ordering Purpose)

This operator method is used to sort the elements of an input sequence in ascending order based on the keySelector method. The output sequence will be an ordered one in a type of IOrderedEnumerable<T>. Both IEnumerable and IQueryable classes contain this operator method. An example coding of using this operator is shown in Figure 4.9.

```
public static void OrderByEx()
{
   Pet[] pets = { new Pet { Name="Barley", Age=8 },
                  new Pet { Name="Boots", Age=4 },
                  new Pet { Name="Whiskers", Age=1 } };

   IEnumerable<Pet> query = pets.OrderBy(pet => pet.Age);

   foreach (Pet pet in query)
      Console.WriteLine("{0} - {1}", pet.Name, pet.Age);
}

// the running result of this piece of codes is:

   Whiskers - 1
   Boots - 4
   Barley - 8
```

FIGURE 4.9 An example coding for the operator OrderBy.

```
IEnumerable<int> squares = Enumerable.Range(1, 5).Select(x => x * x);
foreach (int num in squares)
   Console.WriteLine(num);

// the running result of this piece of codes is:
   1
   4
   9
   16
   25
```

FIGURE 4.10 A piece of example codes for the operator Select.

Select (Projection Purpose)

Both IEnumerable and IQueryable classes contain this operator method.

This operator method is implemented by using deferred execution. The immediate return value is an object that stores all the information that is required to perform the action. The query represented by this method is not executed until the object is enumerated either by calling its GetEnumerator method directly or by using **foreach** in Visual C#.

This projection method requires the transform function, *selector*, to produce one value for each value in the source sequence, *source*. If *selector* returns a value that is itself a collection, it is up to the consumer to traverse the subsequences manually. In such a situation, it might be better for your query to return a single coalesced sequence of values. To achieve this, use the SelectMany method instead of Select. Although SelectMany works similarly to Select, it differs in that the transform function returns a collection that is then expanded by SelectMany before it is returned. In query expression syntax, a **select** in Visual C# clause translates to an invocation of Select. A piece of example code of using this operator is shown in Figure 4.10.

Where (Restriction Purpose)

Both IEnumerable and IQueryable classes contain this operator method.

This method is implemented by using deferred execution. The immediate return value is an object that stores all the information that is required to perform the action. The query represented by this method is not executed until the object is enumerated either by calling its GetEnumerator method directly or by using **foreach** in Visual C#.

A piece of example codes of using this operator is shown in Figure 4.11.

In query expression syntax, a **where** in Visual C# clause translates to an invocation of Where <TSource>IEnumerable<TSource>, Func<TSource, Boolean>.

```
List<string> fruits = new List<string> { "apple", "banana", "mango", "orange",
                                         "blueberry", "grape", "strawberry" };
IEnumerable<string> query = fruits.Where(fruit => fruit.Length < 6);
foreach (string fruit in query)
   Console.WriteLine(fruit);
// the running result of this piece of codes is:
   apple
   mango
   grape
```

FIGURE 4.11 A piece of example code for the operator Where.

```
// Create a string array
string[] names = { "Hartono, Tommy", "Adams, Terry", "Andersen, Henriette","Hedlund, Magnus", "Ito, Shu" };
string name = names.ElementAt(2);
Console.WriteLine("The name chosen at random is '{0}'.", name);
// the running result of this piece of codes is:
   Andersen, Henriette
```

FIGURE 4.12 A piece of example code for the operator ElementAt.

4.1.4 Non-Deferred Standard Query Operators

Most often used non-deferred Standard Query Operator methods are discussed in this section.

ElementAt (Element Purpose)

This operator method returns the element at a specified index in a sequence. If the type of *source* implements IList<T>, that implementation is used to obtain the element at the specified index. Otherwise, this method obtains the specified element.

This method throws an exception if *index* is out of range. To instead return a default value when the specified index is out of range, use the ElementAtOrDefault<TSource> method.

A piece of example code using this operator is shown in Figure 4.12.

First (Element Purpose)

This operator method returns the first element of an input sequence. The method First<T Source>(IEnumerable<TSource> throws an exception if the source contains no elements. To instead return a default value when the source sequence is empty, use the FirstOrDefault method.

A piece of example code of using this operator is shown in Figure 4.13.

Last (Element Purpose)

This operator method returns the last element of a sequence. The method Last<TSource>(IE numerable<(TSource>)>) throws an exception if *source* contains no elements. To instead return a default value when the source sequence is empty, use the **LastOrDefault** method. A piece of example codes of using this operator is shown in Figure 4.14.

Single (Element Purpose)

This operator method returns a single, specific element of an input sequence of values. The Sin gle<TSource>(IEnumerable<TSource>) method throws an exception if the input sequence is empty. To instead return **nullNothingnullptra** null reference when the input sequence is empty, use **SingleOrDefault**. A piece of example codes of using this operator is shown in Figure 4.15.

```
// Create a string array
int[] numbers = { 9, 34, 65, 92, 87, 435, 3, 54, 83, 23, 87, 435, 67, 12, 19 };
int firstNum = numbers.First();
Console.WriteLine(firstNum);
// the running result of this piece of codes is:
  9
```

FIGURE 4.13 An example coding for the operator First.

```
int[] numbers = { 9, 34, 65, 92, 87, 435, 3, 54, 83, 23, 87, 67, 12, 19};
int last = numbers.Last();
Console.WriteLine(last);
// the running result of this piece of codes is 19
```

FIGURE 4.14 A piece of example code for the operator Last.

```
string[] fruits = { "orange" };
string fruit1 = fruits.Single();
Console.WriteLine(fruit1);
// the running result of this piece of codes is orange
```

FIGURE 4.15 A piece of example code for the operator Single.

ToArray (Conversion Purpose)

This operator method converts a collection to an array. This method forces query execution. The ToArray<TSource>(IEnumerable<TSource>) method forces immediate query evaluation and returns an array that contains the query results. You can append this method to your query in order to obtain a cached copy of the query results.

A piece of codes of using this operator is shown in Figure 4.16.

ToList (Conversion Purpose)

This operator method converts a collection to a List<T>. This method forces query execution. The ToList<TSource>(IEnumerable<TSource>) method forces immediate query evaluation and returns a List<T> that contains the query results. You can append this method to your query in order to obtain a cached copy of the query results.

A piece of code using this operator is shown in Figure 4.17.

Now we have a finished a detailed discussion about the Standard Query Operator methods and they are actual methods to be executed to perform a LINQ query. Next we will go ahead to discuss the LINQ query. We organize this part in the following sequence. First we will

```
public class ToArrayClass
{
    public static void Main()
    {
        string[] sArray = {"G", "H", "a", "H", "over", "Jack"};

        string[] names = sArray.OfType<string>().ToArray();
        foreach (string name in names)
            Console.WriteLine(name);
    }
}
// the running result of this piece of codes is:
    GHaHoverJack
```

FIGURE 4.16 A piece of example code for the operator ToArray.

```
string[] fruits = { "apple", "banana", "mango", "orange", "blueberry", "grape", "strawberry" };
List<int> lengths = fruits.Select(fruit => fruit.Length).ToList();
foreach (int length in lengths)
   Console.WriteLine(length);
// the running result of this piece of codes is:
 5
 6
 5
 6
 9
 5
 10
```

FIGURE 4.17 A piece of codes for the operator ToList.

provide an introduction about the LINQ query. Then we divide this discussion into seven sections:

1. Architecture and Components of LINQ
2. LINQ to Objects
3. LINQ to DataSet
4. LINQ to SQL
5. LINQ to Entities
6. LINQ to XML
7. C# 3.0 Language Enhancement for LINQ

Three components, LINQ to DataSet, LINQ to SQL, and LINQ to Entities, belong to LINQ to ADO.NET. Now let's start with the first part, introduction to LINQ query.

4.2 INTRODUCTION TO LINQ QUERY

A query is basically an expression that retrieves data from a data source. Queries are usually expressed in a specialized query language such as Microsoft Access, SQL Server, Oracle or XML document. Different languages have been developed over time for the various types of data sources, for example SQL for relational databases and XQuery for XML. Therefore, developers have had to learn a new query language for each type of data source or data format that they must support. LINQ simplifies this situation by offering a consistent model for working with data across various kinds of data sources and formats. In a LINQ query, you are always working with objects. You use the same basic coding patterns to query and transform data in XML documents, SQL databases, ADO.NET DataSets, .NET collections, and any other format for which a LINQ provider is available.

LINQ can be considered as a pattern or model that is supported by a collection of so-called Standard Query Operator methods we discussed in the previous section, and all those Standard Query Operator methods are static methods defined in either IEnumerable or IQueryable classes in the namespace *System.Linq*. The data operated in LINQ query are object sequences with the data type of either IEnumerable<T> or IQueryable<T>, where T is the actual data type of the objects stored in the sequence.

From another point of view, LINQ can also be considered as a converter or bridge that sets up a mapping relationship between the abstract objects implemented in Standard Query operators and the physical relational databases implemented in the real world. It is the LINQ that allows developers to directly access and manipulate data in different databases using objects with the same basic coding patterns. With the help of LINQ, the difficulty caused by learning and using different syntaxes, formats and query structures for different data sources in order to access and query them can be removed. The efficiency of database queries can be significantly improved and the query process can also be greatly simplified.

Structurally, all LINQ query operations consist of three distinct actions:

1) Obtain the data source.
2) Create the query.
3) Execute the query.

In order to help you to have a better understanding about the LINQ and its running process.

Let us use an example to illustrate how the three parts of a query operation are expressed in source code. The example uses an integer array as a data source for convenience; however, the same concepts apply to other data sources, too.

The example codes are shown in Figure 4.18.

The exact running process of this piece of codes is shown in Figure 4.19.

The key point is: in LINQ, the execution of the query is distinct from the query itself; in other words, when you create a query in step 2, you have not retrieved any data and the real data query occurs in step 3, Query Execution using the foreach loop.

Let's have a closer look at this piece of code and the mapped process to have a clear picture about the LINQ query and its process.

The **Data Source** used in this example is an integer array *numbers*, which implicitly supports the generic IEnumerable<T> interface. This fact means it can be queried with LINQ. A query is executed in a foreach statement, and foreach requires IEnumerable or IEnumerable<T>. Types that support IEnumerable<T> or a derived interface such as the generic IQueryable<T> are called queryable types.

The **Query** specifies what information to retrieve from the data source or sources. Optionally, a query also specifies how that information should be sorted, grouped, and shaped before it is returned. A query is stored in a query variable and initialized with a query expression. To make it easier to write queries, C# has introduced new query syntax.

A typical basic form of the query expression is shown in Figure 4.20.

Three clauses, **from**, **where** and **select**, are mostly used for most LINQ queries.

```
static void IntroLINQ()
{
    // The Three Parts of a LINQ Query:
    // 1. Data source.
    int[] numbers = new int[7] { 0, 1, 2, 3, 4, 5, 6 };

    // 2. Query creation. The numQuery is an IEnumerable<int>
    var numQuery = from num in numbers
                   where (num % 2) == 0
                   select num;

   // 3. Query execution.
   foreach (int num in numQuery)
   {
       Console.Write("{0,1} ", num);
   }
}
// the running result of this piece of codes is:
  0, 2, 4, 6
```

FIGURE 4.18 A piece of codes for the LINQ query.

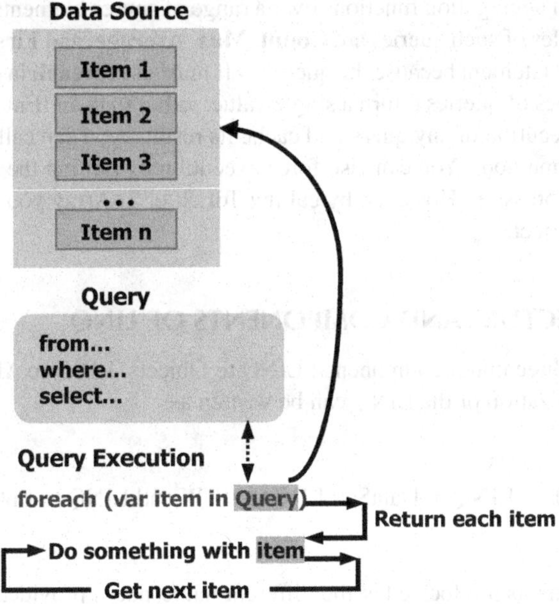

FIGURE 4.19 The running process of a LINQ query.

```
from [identifier] in [data source]
let [expression]
where [boolean expression]
order by [[expression](ascending/descending)], [optionally repeat]
select [expression]
group [expression] by [expression] into [expression]
```

FIGURE 4.20 A typical query expression of LINQ query.

The query used in this example returns all the even numbers from the integer array. The query expression contains three clauses: **from**, **where** and **select**. If you are familiar with SQL, you will have noticed that the ordering of the clauses is reversed from the order in SQL. The **from** clause specifies the data source, the **where** clause applies the filter, and the **select** clause specifies the type of the returned elements. For now, the important point is that in LINQ, the query variable itself takes no action and returns no data. It just stores the information that is required to produce the results when the query is executed at some later point.

The **Query Execution** in this example is a deferred execution since all operator methods used in this query are deferred operators (refer to Figure 4.4).

The **foreach** statement with an iteration variable *num* is used for this query execution to pick up each item from the data source and assign it to the variable *num*. A Console.WriteLine() method is executed to display each received data item, and this query process will continue until all data items have been retrieved from the data source.

Because the query variable itself never holds the query results, you can execute it as often as you like. For example, you may have a database that is being updated continually by a separate application. In your application, you could create one query that retrieves the latest data, and you could execute it repeatedly at some interval to retrieve different results every time.

Queries that perform aggregation functions over a range of source elements must first iterate over those elements. Examples of such queries are **Count**, **Max**, **Average**, and **First**. These execute without an explicit **foreach** statement because the query itself must use **foreach** in order to return a result. Note also that these types of queries return a single value, rather than an IEnumerable collection. To force the immediate execution of any query and cache its results, you can call the ToList<TSource> or ToArray<TSource> methods. You can also force execution by putting the **foreach** loop immediately after the query expression. However, by calling ToList or ToArray you also cache all the data in a single collection object.

4.3 THE ARCHITECTURE AND COMPONENTS OF LINQ

LINQ is composed of three major components: LINQ to Objects, LINQ to ADO.NET and LINQ to XML. A detailed organization or the LINQ can be written as:

1) LINQ to Objects
2) LINQ to ADO.NET (LINQ to DataSet, LINQ to SQL and LINQ to Entities)
3) LINQ to XML

All three of the components are located at the different namespaces provided by .NET Framework 3.5, which is shown in Figure 4.21.

A typical LINQ architecture is shown in Figure 4.22. Now let's give a brief introduction for each component in LINQ.

Namespace	Purpose
System.Linq	Classes and interfaces that support LINQ queries are located at this namespace
System.Collections.Generic	All components related to IEnumerable and IEnumerable<T> are located at this namespace (LINQ to Objects)
System.Data.Linq	All classes and interfaces related to LINQ to SQL are defined in this namespace
System.XML.Linq	All classes and interfaces related to LINQ to XML are defined in this namespace
System.Data.Linq.Mapping	Map a class as an entity class associated with a physical database

FIGURE 4.21 LINQ-related namespaces.

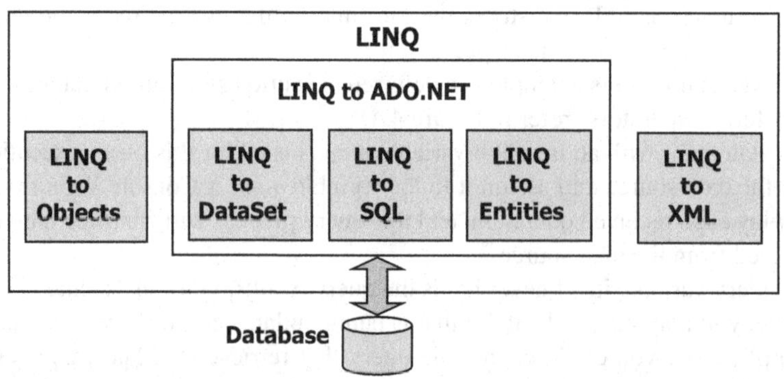

FIGURE 4.22 A typical LINQ architecture

4.3.1 Overview of LINQ to Objects

The LINQ to Objects refers to the use of LINQ queries with any IEnumerable or IEnumerable<T> collection directly, without the use of an intermediate LINQ provider or API such as LINQ to SQL or LINQ to XML. The actual LINQ queries are performed by using the Standard Query Operator methods that are static methods of the static System.Linq.Enumerable class that you use to create LINQ to Objects queries. You can use LINQ to query any enumerable collections such as List<T>, Array, or Dictionary<TKey, TValue>. The collection may be user-defined or may be returned by a .NET Framework API.

In a basic sense, LINQ to Objects represents a new approach to collections, which includes arrays and in-memory data collections. In the old process, you had to write complex foreach loops that specified how to retrieve data from a collection. In the LINQ approach, you write declarative code that describes what you want to retrieve.

In addition, LINQ queries offer three main advantages over traditional foreach loops:

1) They are more concise and readable, especially when filtering multiple conditions.
2) They provide powerful filtering, ordering, and grouping capabilities with a minimum of application code.
3) They can be ported to other data sources with little or no modification.

In general, the more complex the operation you want to perform on the data, the more beneficial it will be to use LINQ instead of traditional iteration techniques.

4.3.2 Overview of LINQ to DataSet

LINQ to DataSet belongs to LINQ to ADO.NET and it is a sub-component of LINQ to ADO.NET.

LINQ to DataSet makes it easier and faster to query over data cached in a DataSet object. Specifically, LINQ to DataSet simplifies querying by enabling developers to write queries from the programming language itself, instead of by using a separate query language. This is especially useful for Visual Studio developers, who can now take advantage of the compile-time syntax checking, static typing, and IntelliSense support provided by the Visual Studio in their queries.

LINQ to DataSet can also be used to query over data that has been consolidated from one or more data sources. This enables many scenarios that require flexibility in how data is represented and handled, such as querying locally aggregated data and middle-tier caching in Web applications. In particular, generic reporting, analysis, and business intelligence applications require this method of manipulation.

The LINQ to DataSet functionality is exposed primarily through the extension methods in the DataRowExtensions and DataTableExtensions classes. LINQ to DataSet builds on and uses the existing ADO.NET 2.0 architecture, and is not meant to replace ADO.NET 2.0 in application code. Existing ADO.NET 2.0 code will continue to function in a LINQ to DataSet application. The relationship of LINQ to DataSet to ADO.NET 2.0 and the data store can be illustrated in Figure 4.23.

It can be found from Figure 4.23 that LINQ to DataSet is built based on ADO.NET 2.0 and uses its all components, including Connection, Command, DataAdapter and DataReader. The advantage of this structure is that all developers using ADO.NET 2.0 can continue their database implementations and developments without problem.

4.3.3 Overview of LINQ to SQL

LINQ to SQL belongs to LINQ to ADO.NET and it is a sub-component of LINQ to ADO.NET.

LINQ to SQL is a component of .NET Framework version 3.5 that provides a run-time infrastructure for managing relational data as objects. As we discussed in Chapter 3, in LINQ to SQL, the data

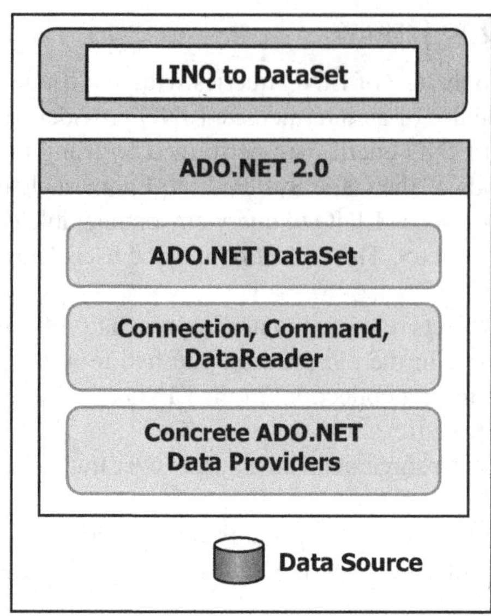

FIGURE 4.23 The relationship between LINQ to DataSet and ADO.NET 2.0

model of a relational database is mapped to an object model expressed in the programming language of the developer with three layers. When the application runs, LINQ to SQL translates into SQL the language-integrated queries in the object model and sends them to the database for execution. When the database returns the results, LINQ to SQL translates them back to objects that you can work with in your own programming language.

Two popular LINQ to SQL Tools, SQLMetal and Object Relational Designer, are widely used in developing applications of using LINQ to SQL. The SQLMetal provides a DOS-like template with a black-white window. Developers using Visual Studio typically use the Object Relational Designer, which provides a graphic user interface for implementing many of the features of LINQ to SQL.

4.3.4 Overview of LINQ to Entities

LINQ to Entities belongs to LINQ to ADO.NET and it is a sub-component of LINQ to ADO.NET.

Through the Entity Data Model we discussed in Section 3.4.8.1 in Chapter 3, ADO.NET 3.5 exposes entities as objects in the .NET environment. This makes the object layer an ideal target for Language-Integrated Query (LINQ) support. Therefore, LINQ to ADO.NET includes LINQ to Entities. LINQ to Entities enables developers to write queries against the database from the same language used to build the business logic. Figure 4.24 shows the relationship between LINQ to Entities and the Entity Framework, ADO.NET 2.0, and the data store.

It can be found that the Entities and Entity Data Model (EDM) released by ADO.NET 3.5 locates at the top of this LINQ to Entities, and they are converted to the logical model by the Mapping Provider and interfaced to the data components such as Data Providers defined in ADO.NET 2.0. The bottom components used for this model are still 'old' components that work for the ADO.NET 2.0.

Most applications are currently written on the relational databases and they are compatible with ADO.NET 2.0. At some point, these applications will have to interact with the data represented in a relational form. Database schemas are not always ideal for building applications, and the conceptual models of applications differ from the logical models of databases. The Entity Data Model (EDM)

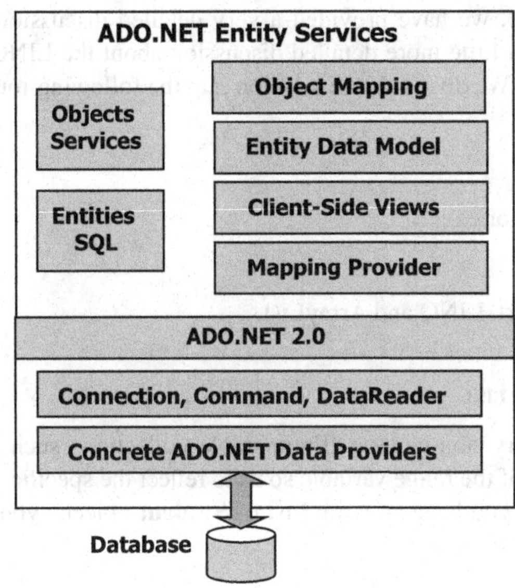

FIGURE 4.24 Relationship between LINQ to entities, entity framework and ADO.NET 2.0.

released with ADO.NET 3.5 is a conceptual data model that can be used to model the data of a particular domain so that applications can interact with data as entities or objects.

4.3.5 Overview of LINQ to XML

LINQ to XML is a LINQ-enabled, in-memory XML programming interface that enables you to work with XML from within the .NET Framework programming languages.

LINQ to XML provides an in-memory XML programming interface that leverages the .NET Language-Integrated Query (LINQ) Framework. LINQ to XML uses the latest .NET Framework language capabilities and is comparable to an updated, redesigned Document Object Model (DOM) XML programming interface. This interface had been known as XLing in older prereleases of LINQ.

The LINQ family of technologies provides a consistent query experience for objects (LINQ), relational databases (LINQ to SQL), and XML (LINQ to XML).

At this point, we have finished an overview of the LINQ family. Now let's go a little deeper into those topics to get a more detailed discussion for each of them.

4.4 LINQ TO OBJECTS

As we mentioned in the previous section, LINQ to Objects is used to query any sequences or collections that are either explicitly or implicitly compatible with IEnumerable sequences or IENumerable<T> collections. Since any IEnumerable collection contains a sequence of objects with a data type that is compatible with IEnumerable<T>, there is no need to use any LINQ API such as LINQ to SQL to convert or map this collection from an object model to a relational model, and the LINQ to Objects can be directly implemented to those collections or sequences to perform the queries.

Regularly, LINQ to Objects is mainly used to query arrays and in-memory data collections. In fact, it can be used to query for any enumerable collections such as List<T>, Array, or Dictionary<TKey, TValue>. All of these queries are performed by executing Standard Query Operator methods defined in the IEnumerable class. The difference between the IEnumerable and IEnumerable<T> interfaces is that the former is used for non-generic collections and the latter is used for generic collections.

In Sections 4.1.3 and 4.1.4, we have provided a very detailed discussion of the Standard Query Operators. Now let's give a little more detailed discussion about the LINQ to Objects using those Standard Query Operators. We divide this discussion into the following four parts:

1) LINQ and ArrayList
2) LINQ and Strings
3) LINQ and File Directories
4) LINQ and Reflection

Let's starts with the first part, LINQ and ArrayList.

4.4.1 LINQ and ArrayList

When using LINQ to query non-generic IEnumerable collections such as ArrayList, you must explicitly declare the type of the range variable so as to reflect the specific type of the objects in the collection. For example, if you have an ArrayList of **Student** objects, your *from* clause in a query should look like this:

```
var query = from Student s in arrList
```

By specifying the type of the range variable s with **Student**, you are casting each item in the ArrayList *arrList* to a Student.

The use of an explicitly typed range variable in a query expression is equivalent to calling the Cast<TResult> method. Cast<TResult> throws an exception if the specified cast cannot be performed. Cast<TResult> and OfType<TResult> are the two Standard Query Operator methods we discussed in Section 4.1.3 and these two methods operate on non-generic IEnumerable types.

Let's illustrate this query with a C# example project named **NonGenericLINQ.cs**. Open the Visual Studio 2022 and create a new C# Console project by going to **File | New | Project** menu item, then selecting the **C# Console App** template and name it as **NonGenericLINQ**, and entering the codes that are shown in Figure 4.25 into the opened code window of **C# Program.cs** file.

Let's have a closer look at this piece of code to see how it works.

A. The **System.Collections** namespace is first added into this project since all non-generic collections are defined in this namespace. In order to use any non-generic collection such as ArrayList, you must declare this namespace in this project before it can be used.
B. An new **Student** class with two members is created and this class is used as a protocol for those objects to be created and added into the ArrayList non-generic collection later.
C. A new instance of the ArrayList class **arrList** is created and initialized by adding four new Student objects.
D. A LINQ query is created with the **student** as the range variable whose type is defined as **Student** by a Cast operator method. The filtering condition is that all student objects should be selected as long as their first Scores's value is greater than 95.
E. A **foreach** loop is used to pick up all query results one by one and assign it to the iteration variable **s**. A **Console.WriteLine()** method is executed to display each received data item, including the student's name and scores.
F. Two code lines here allow users to run this project in the Debugging mode since the Console window cannot keep its opening status if you run the project in the Debugging mode.

Now you can Build and Run the project, the running result should be:

```
Svetlana Omelchenko: 98
Cesar Garcia: 97
```

```
NonGenericLINQ.Program                    Main()

  using System;
A using System.Collections;
  using System.Collections.Generic;
  using System.Linq;
  using System.Text;

  namespace NonGenericLINQ
  {
B    public class Student
     {
        public string StudentName { get; set; }
        public int[] Scores { get; set; }
     }
     class Program
     {
        static void Main(string[] args)
        {
C          ArrayList arrList = new ArrayList();
           arrList.Add(new Student { StudentName = "Svetlana Omelchenko", Scores = new int[] { 98, 92, 81, 60 }});
           arrList.Add(new Student { StudentName = "Claire O'Donnell", Scores = new int[] { 75, 84, 91, 39 }});
           arrList.Add(new Student { StudentName = "Sven Mortensen", Scores = new int[] { 88, 94, 65, 91 }});
           arrList.Add(new Student { StudentName = "Cesar Garcia", Scores = new int[] { 97, 89, 85, 82 }});

D          var query = from Student student in arrList
                       where student.Scores[0] > 95
                       select student;

E          foreach (Student s in query)
              Console.WriteLine(s.StudentName + ": " + s.Scores[0]);

F          // Keep the console window open in debug mode.
           Console.WriteLine("Press any key to exit... ");
           Console.ReadKey();
        }
     }
  }
```

FIGURE 4.25 The code for the example project NonGenericLINQ.

A complete C# Console project named **NonGenericLINQ** can be found from a folder **Class DB Projects\Chapter 4** that is located under the **Students** folder at the CRC Press ftp site (refer to Figure 1.2 in Chapter 1).

Next let's concentrate on the LINQ and Strings queries.

4.4.2 LINQ and Strings

LINQ can be used to query and transform strings and collections of strings. It can be especially useful with semi-structured data in text files. LINQ queries can be combined with traditional string functions and regular expressions. For example, you can use the Split or Split() method to create an array of strings that you can then query or modify by using LINQ. You can use the IsMatch() method in the **where** clause of a LINQ query. And you can use LINQ to query or modify the MatchCollection results returned by a regular expression.

You can query, analyze, and modify text blocks by splitting them into a queryable array of smaller strings by using the Split() method. You can split the source text into words, sentences, paragraphs, pages, or any other criteria, and then perform additional splits if they are required in your query. Many different types of text files consist of a series of lines, often with similar formatting, such as tab- or comma-delimited files or fixed-length lines. After you read such a text file into memory, you can use LINQ to query and/or modify the lines. LINQ queries also simplify the task of combining data from multiple sources.

Two example projects are provided in this part to illustrate 1) how to query a string to determine the number of numeric digits it contains, and 2) how to sort lines of structured text, such as comma-separated values, by any field in the line.

4.4.2.1 Query a String to Determine the Number of Numeric Digits

Because the String class implements the generic IEnumerable<T> interface, any string can be queried as a sequence of characters. However, this is not a common use of LINQ. For complex pattern matching operations, use the Regex class.

The following example queries a string to determine the number of numeric digits it contains. Note that the query is 'reused' after it is executed the first time. This is possible because the query itself does not store any actual results.

Create a new C# Console project and name it as **QueryStringLINQ**, and enter the codes that are shown in Figure 4.26 into the opened code window of the **C# Program.cs** file.

Let's have a closer look at this piece of codes to see how it works.

A. The namespace System.IO is added into the namespace declaration section of this project since we need to use some components defined in that namespace.

QueryStringLINQ.Program	Main()

```
    using System;
    using System.Collections.Generic;
    using System.Linq;
    using System.Text;
A   using System.IO;
    namespace QueryStringLINQ
    {
        class Program
        {
B           static void Main(string[] args)
            {
                string aString = "ABCDE99F-J74-12-89A";
                // Select only those characters that are numbers
C               IEnumerable<char> stringQuery = from ch in aString
                                                where Char.IsDigit(ch)
                                                select ch;
                // Execute the query
D               foreach (char c in stringQuery)
                   Console.Write(c + " ");
                // Call the Count method on the existing query.
E               int count = stringQuery.Count();
                Console.WriteLine("Count = {0}", count);
                // Select all characters before the first '-'
F               IEnumerable<char> stringQuery2 = aString.TakeWhile(c => c != '-');
                // Execute the second query
G               foreach (char c in stringQuery2)
                   Console.Write(c);
H               Console.WriteLine(System.Environment.NewLine + "Press any key to exit");
                Console.ReadKey();
            }
        }
    }
```

FIGURE 4.26 The codes for the example project QueryStringLINQ.

B. A string object or a generic collection **aString** is created and this will work as a data source to be queried by LINQ to Objects.
C. The LINQ to Objects query is created and initialized with three clauses. The method **IsDigit()** is used as the filtering condition for the where clause and **ch** is the range variable. All digital elements in this string collection will be filtered, selected and returned. A **Cast()** operator is used for the returned query collection with an IEnumerable<T> interface, and T is replaced by the real data type **char** here.
D. The query is executed by using a foreach loop and c is an iteration variable. The queried digits are displayed by using the **Console.WriteLine()** method.
E. The **Count()** method is executed to query the number of digits existing in the queried string. This query is 'reused' because the query itself does not store any actual results.
F. Another query or the second query is created and initialized. The purpose of this query is to retrieve all letters before the first dash line in the string collection.
G. The second query is executed and the result is displayed using the **Console.WriteLine()** method.
H. The purpose of these two coding lines is to allow users to run this project in a Debugging mode. Now you can run the project in Debugging mode by clicking **Debug | Start Debugging** menu item, and the running result of this project is:

9 9 7 4 1 2 8 9 Count = 8
ABCDE99F

A complete C# Console project named **QueryStringLINQ** can be found from a folder **Class DB Projects\Chapter 4** that is located under the **Students** folder at the CRC Press ftp site (refer to Figure 1.2 in Chapter 1).

Our first example project is successful. Now let's take a look at the second example.

4.4.2.2 Sort Lines of Structured Text by Any Field in the Line

This example shows readers how to sort lines of structured text, such as comma-separated values, by any field in the line. The field may be dynamically specified at runtime. Assume that the fields in a sample text file scores.csv represent a student's ID number, followed by a series of four test scores.

First let's create a new C# Console project named **SortLinesLINQ**. Then we need to create a sample text file **scores.csv**. Open the NotePad editor and enter the codes that are shown in Figure 4.27 into this opened Text Editor. This file represents a data spreadsheet. Column 1 is the student's ID, and columns 2 through 5 are test scores.

Click on the **File | Save As** menu item from the NotePad editor to open the Save As dialog box. Browse to the folder in which our new C# project is located, **C:\SortLinesLINQ\SortLinesLINQ**. Enter **"scores.csv"** into the **File name** box and click the **Save** button to save this sample file. The point to be

```
111, 97, 92, 81, 60
112, 75, 84, 91, 39
113, 88, 94, 65, 91
114, 97, 89, 85, 82
115, 35, 72, 91, 70
116, 99, 86, 90, 94
117, 93, 92, 80, 87
118, 92, 90, 83, 78
119, 68, 79, 88, 92
120, 99, 82, 81, 79
121, 96, 85, 91, 60
122, 94, 92, 91, 91
```

FIGURE 4.27 The content of the sample text file scores.csv.

noticed is that the file name **scores.csv** must be enclosed by a pair of double quotation marks when you save this file in the extension **.csv**. Otherwise the file will be saved with a text extension.

Close the NotePad editor and now let's develop the codes for our new project.

Open our new C# project **SortLinesLINQ** and open the **C# Program.cs** file, and enter the codes that are shown in Figure 4.28 into this code window to replace all original codes.

Let's have a closer look at this piece of codes to see how it works.

A. The namespace **System.IO** is added into the namespace declaration section of this project since we need to use some components defined in that namespace.

B. A string collection **scores** is created as the data source for this project and this collection is a generic collection that is compatible with the IEnumerable<T> data type. The method **ReadAllLines()** is executed to open and read the sample file scores.csv we created at the beginning of this section, and assign this file to the **scores** string collection.

```
SortLinesLINQ.Program                    Main()

  using System;
  using System.Collections.Generic;
  using System.Linq;
  using System.Text;
A using System.IO;
  namespace SortLinesLINQ
  {
      class Program
      {
          static void Main(string[] args)
          {
              // Create an IEnumerable data source
B             string[] scores = System.IO.File.ReadAllLines(@"../../../scores.csv");
              // Change this to any value from 0 to 4.
C             int sortField = 1;
              Console.WriteLine("Sorted highest to lowest by field [{0}]:", sortField);
              // Demonstrates how to return query from a method.
              // The query is executed here.
D             foreach (string str in RunQuery(scores, sortField))
              {
                  Console.WriteLine(str);
              }
              // Keep the console window open in debug mode.
E             Console.WriteLine("Press any key to exit");
              Console.ReadKey();
          }
          // Returns the query variable, not query results!
F          static IEnumerable<string> RunQuery(IEnumerable<string> source, int num)
          {
              // Split the string and sort on field[num]
G             var scoreQuery = from line in source
                               let fields = line.Split(',')
                               orderby fields[num] descending
                               select line;
H             return scoreQuery;
          }
      }
  }
```

FIGURE 4.28 The codes for the example project SortLinesLINQ.

```
Sorted highest to lowest by field [1]:
116, 99, 86, 90, 94
120, 99, 82, 81, 79
111, 97, 92, 81, 60
114, 97, 89, 85, 82
121, 96, 85, 91, 60
122, 94, 92, 91, 91
117, 93, 92, 80, 87
118, 92, 90, 83, 78
113, 88, 94, 65, 91
112, 75, 84, 91, 39
119, 68, 79, 88, 92
115, 35, 72, 91, 70
```

FIGURE 4.29 The running result of the project SortLinesLINQ.

C. A local integer variable **sortField** is initialized to 1, which means that we want to use the first column in this string collection, student ID, as the filtering criteria. You can change this criteria by selecting any other column if you like.

D. The query is built and executed by calling a method **RunQuery()** with two arguments: the data source **scores** and the filtering criteria **sortField**. The queried results are displayed by executing the method **Console.WriteLine()**.

E. The purpose of these two coding lines is to allow users to run this project in a Debugging mode.

F. The body of the method **RunQuery()** starts from here. One point to be noticed is that the keyword **static** must be prefixed in front of this method to indicate that this method is a static method. This is very important because this method will be called from inside the **main()** method that is a static method. Otherwise a compiling error would be encountered if you missed this keyword.

G. The query is built with four clauses. The **Split()** method is used in the **let** clause to allow the string to be split into different pieces at each comma. The queried result is distributed in a descending order by using the orderby operator.

H. The queried result is returned to the calling method.

Now run the project by clicking on the **Debug | Start Debugging** menu item, and the running result of this project is shown in Figure 4.29.

A complete C# Console project named **SortLinesLINQ** can be found from a folder **Class DB Projects\Chapter 4** that is located under the **Students** folder at the CRC Press ftp site (refer to Figure 1.2 in Chapter 1). Next let's take care of another LINQ to Objects query, LINQ and File Directories.

4.4.3 LINQ and File Directories

Many file system operations are essentially queries and are therefore well-suited to the LINQ approach. Note that the queries for those file system are read-only. They are not used to change the contents of the original files or folders. This follows the rule that queries should not cause any side-effects. In general, any code (including queries that perform create-update-delete operators) that modifies source data should be kept separate from the code that just queries the data.

Different file operations or queries are existed for the file systems. The most typical operations include

1) Query for Files with a Specified Attribute or Name
2) Group Files by Extension (LINQ)

3) Query for the Total Number of Bytes in a Set of Folders (LINQ)
4) Query for the Largest File or Files in a Directory Tree (LINQ)
5) Query for Duplicate Files in a Directory Tree (LINQ)
6) Query the Contents of Files in a Folder (LINQ)

There is some complexity involved in creating a data source that accurately represents the contents of the file system and handles exceptions gracefully. The examples in this section create a snapshot collection of FileInfo objects that represents all the files under a specified root folder and all its subfolders. The actual state of each FileInfo may change in the time between when you begin and end executing a query. For example, you can create a list of FileInfo objects to use as a data source. If you try to access the **Length** property in a query, the FileInfo object will try to access the file system to update the value of **Length**. If the file no longer exists, you will get a FileNotFoundException in your query, even though you are not querying the file system directly. Some queries in this section use a separate method that consumes these particular exceptions in certain cases. Another option is to keep your data source updated dynamically by using the FileSystemWatcher.

Because of the limitation of the space, here we only discuss one file operation or query, which is to open, inspect and query the contents of files in a selected folder (the 6th operation).

4.4.3.1 Query the Contents of Files in a Folder

This example shows how to query over all the files in a specified directory tree, open each file, and inspect its contents. This type of technique could be used to create indexes or reverse indexes of the contents of a directory tree. A simple string search is performed in this example. However, more complex types of pattern matching can be performed with a regular expression.

Create a new C# Console project named **QueryContentsLINQ**, and then open the code window of the **C# Program.cs** file in the Solution Explorer window and enter the codes that are shown in Figure 4.30 into the code window to replace all original codes.

Let's have a closer look at this piece of codes to see how it works.

A. A string object **startFolder** is created and the value of this object is the default path of the Visual Studio.NET 2022, in which all files of the Visual Studio.NET 2022 are installed. You can modify this path if you installed your Visual Studio.NET 2022 at a different folder in your computer.

B. An IEnumerable <T> interface is used to define the data type of the queried files fileList. The real data type applied here is **System.IO.FileInfo** that is used to replace the nominal type T. The method **GetFiles()** is executed to open and access the queried files with the file path as the argument of this method.

C. The query criteria '**Visual Studio**' that is a keyword to be searched by this query is assigned to a string object **searchTerm** that will be used in the following query process.

D. The LINQ query is created and initialized with four clauses, **from, let, where** and **select**. The range variable **file** is selected from the opened files **fileList**. The method **GetFileText()** will be executed to read back the contents of the matched files using the **let** clause. Two **where** clauses are used here to filter the matched files with both an extension **.htm** and a keyword '**Visual Studio**' in the file name.

E. The **Console.WriteLine()** method is executed to indicate that the following matched files contain the searched keyword '**Visual Studio**' in their file names.

F. The LINQ query is executed to pick up all files that have a file name that contains the keyword '**Visual Studio**', and all searched files are displayed by using the method **Console.WriteLine()**.

G. The purpose of these two coding lines is to allow users to run this project in a Debugging mode.

```
QueryContentsLINQ.Program                    Main()

  using System;
  using System.Collections.Generic;
  using System.Linq;
  using System.Text;
  namespace QueryContentsLINQ
  {
     class Program
     {
        static void Main(string[] args)
        {
           // Modify this path as necessary.
A          string startFolder = @"c:\program files\Microsoft Visual Studio\";
           // Take a snapshot of the file system.
B          IEnumerable<System.IO.FileInfo> fileList = GetFiles(startFolder);
C          string searchTerm = @"Visual Studio";
           // Search the contents of each file. The queryMatchingFiles is an IEnumerable<string>.
D          var queryMatchingFiles = from file in fileList
                                    where file.Extension == ".htm"
                                    let fileText = GetFileText(file.FullName)
                                    where fileText.Contains(searchTerm)
                                    select file.FullName;
           // Execute the query.
E          Console.WriteLine("The term \"{0}\" was found in:", searchTerm);
F          foreach (string filename in queryMatchingFiles)
           {
              Console.WriteLine(filename);
           }
           // Keep the console window open in debug mode.
G          Console.WriteLine("Press any key to exit ...");
           Console.ReadKey();
        }
        // Read the contents of the file.
H       static string GetFileText(string name)
        {
I          string fileContents = String.Empty;
           // If the file has been deleted since we took the snapshot, ignore it and return the empty string.
J          if (System.IO.File.Exists(name))
              fileContents = System.IO.File.ReadAllText(name);
K          return fileContents;
        }
        // This method assumes that the application has discovery permissions for all folders under the specified path.
L       static IEnumerable<System.IO.FileInfo> GetFiles(string path)
        {
M          if (!System.IO.Directory.Exists(path))
              throw new System.IO.DirectoryNotFoundException();
           string[] fileNames = null;
N          List<System.IO.FileInfo> files = new List<System.IO.FileInfo>();
O          fileNames = System.IO.Directory.GetFiles(path, "*.*", System.IO.SearchOption.AllDirectories);
P          foreach (string name in fileNames)
           {
              files.Add(new System.IO.FileInfo(name));
           }
Q          return files;
        }
     }
  }
```

FIGURE 4.30 The codes for the example project QueryContentsLINQ.

H. The body of the method **GetFileText()** starts from here. The point is that this method must be defined as a static method by prefixed with a keyword **static** in front of this method since it will be called from the **main()** method that is a static method, too.

I. The string object **fileContents** is initialized with an empty string object.

J. The system method **Exists()** is executed to find all files whose names contain the keyword '**Visual Studio**'. All of the matched files will be opened and the contents will be read back by the method **ReadAllText()**, and assigned to the string object **fileContents**.
K. The read out **fileContents** object is returned to the calling method.
L. The body of the method **GetFiles()** starts from here with the path as the argument of this method. The point is that this method must be defined as a static method and the returned data type is an IEnumerable<T> type.
M. An exception will be thrown out if the desired path did not exist in the current computer.
N. A new non-generic collection List<T> is created with a Cast to convert it to the IEnumerable<T> type.
O. The system method **GetFiles()** is executed to find the names of all files that are under the current path, and assign them to the string object array **fileNames**.
P. A **foreach** loop is executed to add all searched file names into the non-generic collection List<T> object files.
Q. All of those files are returned to the calling method.

Now you can build and run the project by clicking on the **Debug | Start Debugging** menu item. All files that have an extension **.htm**, and under the path **C:\Program Files\Microsoft Visual Studio** and whose name contains the keyword '**Visual Studio**' are found and displayed as this project runs. Press any key from the keyboard to exit this project.

A complete C# Console project **QueryContentsLINQ** can be found from a folder **Class DB Projects\Chapter 4** that is located under the **Students** folder at the CRC Press ftp site (refer to Figure 1.2 in Chapter 1). Next let's have a discussion about another query related to LINQ to Objects, the LINQ and Reflection.

4.4.4 LINQ and Reflection

The .NET Framework 3.5 class library reflection APIs can be used to examine the metadata in a .NET assembly and create collections of types, type members, parameters, and so on that are in that assembly. Because these collections support the generic IEnumerable interface, they can be queried by using LINQ to Objects query.

To make it simple and easy, in this section we use one example project to illustrate how LINQ can be used with reflection to retrieve specific metadata about methods that match a specified search criterion. In this case, the query will find the names of all the methods in the assembly that return enumerable types such as arrays.

Create a new C# Console project **QueryReflectionLINQ**. Open the code window of the **C# Program.cs** file in the Solution Explorer window and enter the codes shown in Figure 4.31 into this window to replace all original codes. Let's have a closer look at this piece of codes.

A. The namespace **System.Reflection** is added into the namespace declaration part of this project since we need to use some components defined in this namespace in this coding.
B. An **Assembly** object is created with the **Load()** method is executed to load and assign this new Assembly to the instance assembly.
C. The LINQ query is created and initialized with three clauses. The **GetTypes()** method is used to obtain the data type of all queried methods. The first **where** clause is used to filter methods in the **Public** type. The second **from** clause is used to get the desired methods based on the data type Public. The second **where** clause is used to filter all methods with three criteria: 1) the returning type of the method is array, 2) those methods should have a valid interface and 3) the returning type of those methods should not be **System.,string**. Also the queried methods' names are converted to string.

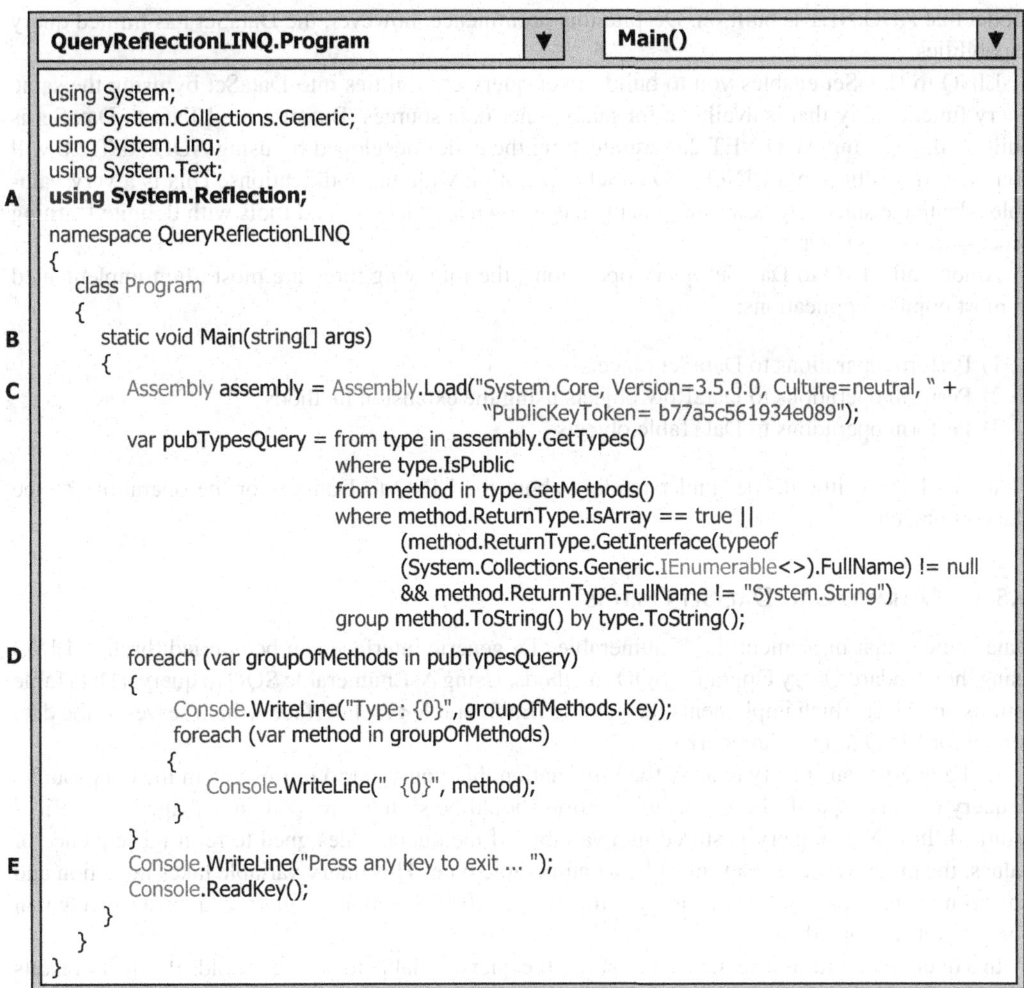

QueryReflectionLINQ.Program | Main()

```
  using System;
  using System.Collections.Generic;
  using System.Linq;
  using System.Text;
A using System.Reflection;
  namespace QueryReflectionLINQ
  {
     class Program
     {
B       static void Main(string[] args)
        {
C          Assembly assembly = Assembly.Load("System.Core, Version=3.5.0.0, Culture=neutral, " +
                                                  "PublicKeyToken= b77a5c561934e089");
           var pubTypesQuery = from type in assembly.GetTypes()
                               where type.IsPublic
                               from method in type.GetMethods()
                               where method.ReturnType.IsArray == true ||
                                    (method.ReturnType.GetInterface(typeof
                                    (System.Collections.Generic.IEnumerable<>).FullName) != null
                                    && method.ReturnType.FullName != "System.String")
                               group method.ToString() by type.ToString();
D          foreach (var groupOfMethods in pubTypesQuery)
           {
              Console.WriteLine("Type: {0}", groupOfMethods.Key);
              foreach (var method in groupOfMethods)
              {
                 Console.WriteLine("  {0}", method);
              }
           }
E          Console.WriteLine("Press any key to exit ... ");
           Console.ReadKey();
        }
     }
  }
```

FIGURE 4.31 The codes for the example project QueryReflectionLINQ.

D. Two **foreach** loops are utilized here. The first one is used to retrieve and display the datatype of the queried methods, and the second one is used to retrieve and display the names of the queried methods.

E. The purpose of these two coding lines is to allow users to run this project in a Debugging mode.

Now you can build and run the project by clicking the **Debug | Start Debugging** menu item. The running results are displayed in the console window.

A complete C# Console project named **QueryReflectionLINQ** can be found from a folder **Class DB Projects\Chapter 4** that is located under the **Students** folder at the CRC Press ftp site (refer to Figure 1.2 in Chapter 1).

4.5 LINQ TO DATASET

As we discussed in the previous section, LINQ to DataSet is a sub-component of LINQ to ADO.NET.

The DataSet, of which we provided a very detailed discussion in Chapter 3, is one of the most widely used components in ADO.NET, and it is a key element of the disconnected programming model that ADO.NET is built on. Despite this prominence, however, the DataSet has limited query capabilities.

LINQ to DataSet enables you to build richer query capabilities into DataSet by using the same query functionality that is available for many other data sources. Because the LINQ to DataSet is built on the existing ADO.NET 2.0 architecture, the codes developed by using ADO.NET 2.0 will continue to function in a LINQ to DataSet application without modifications. This is a very valuable advantage since any new components has its own architecture and tools with definite learning process to get it known.

Among all LINQ to DataSet query operations, the following three are most often implemented in most popular applications:

1) Perform operations to DataSet objects
2) Perform operations to DataRow objects using the extension methods
3) Perform operations to DataTable objects

First let's have a little deeper understanding about the LINQ to DataSet, or the operations to the DataSet objects.

4.5.1 Operations to DataSet Objects

Data sources that implement the IEnumerable<T> generic interface can be queried through LINQ using the Standard Query Operator (SQO) methods. Using AsEnumerable SQO to query a DataTable returns an object which implements the generic IEnumerable<T> interface, which serves as the data source for LINQ to DataSet queries.

In the query, you specify exactly the information that you want to retrieve from the data source. A query can also specify how that information should be sorted, grouped, and shaped before it is returned. In LINQ, a query is stored in a variable. If the query is designed to return a sequence of values, the query variable itself must be a enumerable type. This query variable takes no action and returns no data; it only stores the query information. After you create a query you must execute that query to retrieve any data.

In a query that returns a sequence of values, the query variable itself never holds the query results and only stores the query commands. Execution of the query is deferred until the query variable is iterated over in a **foreach** loop. This is called deferred execution; that is, query execution occurs sometime after the query is constructed. This means that you can execute a query as often as you want to. This is useful when, for example, you have a database that is being updated by other applications. In your application, you can create a query to retrieve the latest information and repeatedly execute the query, returning the updated information every time.

In contrast to deferred queries, which return a sequence of values, queries that return a singleton value are executed immediately. Examples of singleton queries include **Count**, **Max**, **Average**, and **First**. These execute immediately because the query results are required to calculate the singleton result. For example, in order to find the average of the query results the query must be executed so that the averaging function has input data to work with. You can also use the ToList<TSource> or ToArray<TSource> methods on a query to force immediate execution of a query that does not produce a singleton value. These techniques to force immediate execution can be useful when you want to cache the results of a query.

Basically, to perform a LINQ to DataSet query, three steps are needed:

1) Create a new DataSet instance
2) Populate the DataSet instance using the **Fill()** method
3) Query the DataSet instance using LINQ to DataSet

After a DataSet object has been populated with data, you can begin querying it. Formulating queries with LINQ to DataSet is similar to using Language-Integrated Query (LINQ) against other LINQ-enabled data sources. Remember, however, that when you use LINQ queries over a DataSet object you are querying an enumeration of DataRow objects, instead of an enumeration of a custom type. This means that you can use any of the members of the DataRow class in your LINQ queries. This lets you to create rich and complex queries.

As with other implementations of LINQ, you can create LINQ to DataSet queries in two different forms: query expression syntax and method-based query syntax. Basically, the query expression syntax will be finally converted to the method-based query syntax as the compiling time if the query is written as the query expression, and the query will be executed by calling the Standard Query Operator methods as the project runs.

4.5.1.1 Query Expression Syntax

A query expression is a query expressed in query syntax. A query expression is a first-class language construct. It is just like any other expression and can be used in any context in which a C# expression is valid. A query expression consists of a set of clauses written in a declarative syntax similar to SQL or XQuery. Each clause in turn contains one or more C# expressions, and these expressions may themselves be either a query expression or contain a query expression.

A query expression must begin with a **from** clause and must end with a **select** or **group** clause. Between the first **from** clause and the last **select** or **group** clause, it can contain one or more of these optional clauses: **where**, **orderby**, **join**, **let** and even additional **from** clauses. You can also use the **into** keyword to enable the result of a **join** or **group** clause to serve as the source for additional query clauses in the same query expression.

In all LINQ queries (including LINQ to DataSet), all of clauses will be converted to the associated Standard Query Operator methods, such as **From**, **Where**, **OrderBy**, **Join**, **Let** and **Select**, as the queries are compiled. Refer to Figure 4.4 in this Chapter to get the most often used Standard Query Operators and their definitions.

In LINQ, a query variable is always strongly typed and it can be any variable that stores a query instead of the results of a query. More specifically, a query variable is always an enumerable type that will produce a sequence of elements when it is iterated over in a **foreach** loop or a direct call to its method **IEnumerator.MoveNext**.

The coding example shown in Figure 4.32 illustrates a simple query expression with one data source, one filtering clause, one ordering clause, and no transformation of the source elements. The **select** clause ends the query.

An integer array is created here and this array works as a data source. The variable **scoreQuery** is a query variable and it contains only the query command and does not contain any query result. This query is composed of four clauses: **from**, **where**, **orderby** and **select**. Both the first and the last clause are required; the others are optional. The query is casted to a type of IEnumerable<int> by using an IEnumerable<T> interface. The **testScore** is an iteration variable that is scanned through the **foreach** loop to get and display each queried data when this query is executed. Exactly, when the **foreach** statement executes, the query results are not returned through the query variable **scoreQuery**. Rather, they are returned through the iteration variable **testScore**.

An alternative way to write this query expression is to use the so-called **implicit typing** of query variables. The difference between the explicit and implicit typing of query variables is that in the former situation, the relationship between the query variable **scoreQuery** and the **select** clause is clearly indicated by the IEnumerable<T> interface, and this makes sure that the type of returned collection is IEnumerable<T> that can be queried by LINQ. In the latter situation, we do not exactly know the data type of the query variable and therefore an implicit type **var** is used to instruct the compiler to infer the type of a query variable (or any other local variable) at the compiling time.

```
static void Main()
{
    // Data source.
    int[] scores = { 90, 71, 82, 93, 75, 82 };
    // Query Expression.
    IEnumerable<int> scoreQuery = from score in scores              //required
                                  where score > 80                  //optional
                                  orderby score descending          //optional
                                  select score;                     //must end with select or group
    // Execute the query to produce the results
    foreach (int testScore in scoreQuery)
    {
        Console.WriteLine(testScore);
    }
}

// Outputs: 90 82 93 82
```

FIGURE 4.32 The example codes for the query expression syntax.

```
static void Main()
{
    // Data source.
    int[] scores = { 90, 71, 82, 93, 75, 82 };
    // Query Expression.
    var scoreQuery = from score in scores              //required
                     where score > 80                  //optional
                     orderby score descending          //optional
                     select score;                     //must end with select or group
    // Execute the query to produce the results
    foreach (var testScore in scoreQuery)
    {
        Console.WriteLine(testScore);
    }
}

// Outputs: 90 82 93 82
```

FIGURE 4.33 The codes for the query expression in implicit typing of query variable.

The example codes written in Figure 4.32 can be expressed in another format that is shown in Figure 4.33 by using the implicit typing of query variable.

Here the implicit type **var** is used to replace the explicit type IEnumerable<T> for the query variable and it can be converted to the IEnumerable<int> automatically as the codes is compiled.

4.5.1.2 Method-Based Query Syntax

Most queries used in the general LINQ queries are written as query expressions by using the declarative query syntax introduced in C# 3.0. However, the .NET Common Language Runtime (CLR) has no notion of query syntax in itself. Therefore, at compile time, query expressions are converted to something that the CLR can understand - method calls. These methods are Standard Query Operators (SQO) methods, and they have names equivalent to query clauses such as **Where**, **Select**, **GroupBy**, **Join**, **Max**, **Average**, and so on. You can call them directly by using method syntax instead of query syntax. In Sections 4.1.3 and 4.1.4, we have provided a very detailed discussion about the Standard Query Operator methods. Refer to those sections to get more details for those methods and their implementations.

In general, we recommend query syntax because it is usually simpler and more readable; however, there is no semantic difference between method syntax and query syntax. In addition, some queries, such as those that retrieve the number of elements that match a specified condition, or that retrieve the element that has the maximum value in a source sequence, can only be expressed as method calls. The reference documentation for the Standard Query Operators in the **System.Linq** namespace generally uses method syntax. Therefore, even when getting started writing LINQ queries, it is useful to be familiar with how to use method syntax in queries and in query expressions themselves.

We have discussed the Standard Query Operator with a quite few examples of using the method syntax in Sections 4.1.3 and 4.1.4. Refer to those sections to get a clear picture in how to create and use method syntax to directly call SQO methods to perform LINQ queries. In this section, we give an example to illustrate the different format is using the query syntax and the method syntax for a given data source.

Create a new C# console project named **QueryMethodSyntax**. Open the code window of the **C# Program.cs** file and enter the codes that are shown in Figure 4.34 into this file to replace all original codes.

QueryMethodSyntax.Program ▼ **Main()** ▼

```
  using System;
  using System.Collections.Generic;
  using System.Linq;
  using System.Text;
  namespace QueryMethodSyntax
  {
     class Program
     {
        static void Main(string[] args)
        {
A          int[] numbers = {5, 10, 8, 3, 6, 12};
           //Query syntax:
B          IEnumerable<int> querySyntax = from num in numbers
                                          where num % 2 == 0
                                          orderby num
                                          select num;
           //Method syntax:
C          IEnumerable<int> methodSyntax = numbers.Where(num => num % 2 == 0).OrderBy(n => n);
           //Execute the query in query syntax
D          foreach (int i in querySyntax)
           {
              Console.Write(i + " ");
           }
           Console.WriteLine(System.Environment.NewLine);
           //Execute the query in method syntax
E          foreach (int i in methodSyntax)
           {
              Console.Write(i + " ");
           }
F          // Keep the console open in debug mode.
           Console.WriteLine(System.Environment.NewLine);
           Console.WriteLine("Press any key to exit ... ");
           Console.ReadKey();
        }
     }
  }
```

FIGURE 4.34 The codes for the example project QueryMethodSyntax.

Let's have a close look at this piece of codes to see how it works.

A. An integer array is created and it works as a data source for this project.
B. The first query that uses a query syntax is created and initialized with four clauses. The query variable is named **querySyntax** with a type of IEnumerable<int>.
C. The second query that uses a method syntax is created and initialized with the Standard Query Operator methods **Where()** and **OrderBy()**.
D. The first query is executed using a **foreach** loop and the query result is displayed by using the **Console.WriteLine()** method.
E. The second query is executed and the result is also displayed.
F. The purpose of these two coding lines is to allow users to run this project in a Debugging mode.

It can be found that the method syntax looks simpler in structure and easy to coding compared with the query syntax from this piece of code. In facts, the first query with the query syntax will be converted to the second query with the method syntax as the project is compiled.

Now you can build and run the project. You can find that the running result is identical for both syntaxes.

A complete C# Console project named **QueryMethodSyntax** can be found from a folder **Class DB Projects\Chapter 4** that is located under the **Students** folder at the CRC Press ftp site (refer to Figure 1.2 in Chapter 1).

In addition to the general and special properties of query expression discussed above, the following points are also important to understand query expressions:

1) Query expressions can be used to query and to transform data from any LINQ-enabled data source. For example, a single query can retrieve data from a DataSet, and produce an XML stream as output.
2) Query expressions are easy to master because they use many familiar C# language constructs.
3) The variables in a query expression are all strongly typed, although, in many cases, you do not have to provide the type explicitly because the compiler can infer it if an implicit type var is used.
4) A query is not executed until you iterate over the query variable in a **foreach** loop.
5) At compile time, query expressions are converted to Standard Query Operator method calls according to the rules set forth in the C# specification. Any query that can be expressed by using query syntax can also be expressed by using method syntax. However, in most cases query syntax is more readable and concise.
6) As a rule when you write LINQ queries, we recommend that you use query syntax whenever possible and method syntax whenever necessary. There is no semantic or performance difference between the two different forms. Query expressions are often more readable than equivalent expressions written in method syntax.
7) Some query operations, such as **Count** or **Max**, have no equivalent query expression clause and must therefore be expressed as a method call. Method syntax can be combined with query syntax in various ways.
8) Query expressions can be compiled to expression trees or to delegates, depending on the type that the query is applied to. IEnumerable<T> queries are compiled to delegates. IQueryable and IQueryable<T> queries are compiled to expression trees.

Now let's start the LINQ to DataSet with a single table query.

4.5.1.3 Query the Single Table

Language-Integrated Query (LINQ) queries work on data sources that implement the IEnumerable<T> interface or the IQueryable interface. The DataTable class does not implement either interface, so you must call the AsEnumerable method if you want to use the DataTable as a source in the **From** clause of a LINQ query.

As we discussed in Section 4.5.1, to perform LINQ to DataSet query, the first step is to create an instance of the DataSet and fill it with the data from the database. To fill a DataSet, a

DataAdapter can be used with the **Fill()** method that is attached to that DataAdapter. Each DataAdapter can only be used to fill a single DataTable in a DataSet.

In this section, we build an example to query a single DataTable using the LINQ to DataSet. Create a new C# Console project **DataSetSingleTableLINQ**. In this project, we need to use an OleDb Data Provider to access our SQL Server sample database **CSE_DEPT**. Microsoft provided this kind of provider to enable us to do this. Before we can build our codes, we need first to add this **System.Data.OleDb** package into our project to enable us to use it. Perform the following operations to add this package into our project:

1) Go to the menu item **Tools | NuGet Package Manager | Package Manager Console**.
2) In the opened Package Manager Console window at the bottom, type the command: **Install-Package System.Data.OleDb** and press the **Enter** key on your keyboard.
3) Some Successful Installation messages are displayed on that console window when it is done, which means that the package has been successfully installed and added into our project, and we can use it.

Now open the code window of the **C# Program.cs** file and enter the codes that are shown in Figure 4.35 into that window. Let's have a closer look at this piece of codes to see how it works.

A. Two namespaces, **System.Data** and **System.Data.OleDb**, must be added into this project since we need to use some OleDb data components.

B. A SQL query string is created to query all columns from the **Faculty** data table in the DataSet. Also all OleDb data components are created in this part including a non-OleDb data component, DataSet.

C. The connection string is declared since we need to use a SQL OleDb provider to connect to our sample database **CSE_DEPT** that is developed with Microsoft SQL Server 2019 Express. You may modify this string based on the server where you saved your database.

D. The Connection object **oleConnection** is initialized with the connection string and that connection is executed by calling the **Open()** method. Regularly a **try-catch** block should be used for this connection operation to catch up any possible exception. Here we skip it since we try to make this connection coding process simple.

E. The Command object is initialized with Connection, CommandType and CommandText properties.

F. The initialized Command object is assigned to the **SelectCommand** property of the DataAdapter and the DataSet is filled with the **Fill()** method. The point is that only a single table, **Faculty**, is filled in this operation.

G. A LINQ to DataSet query is created with three clauses, **from**, **where** and **select**. The data type of the query variable **facultyinfo** is implicit and it can be inferred by the compiler as the project is compiled. The **Faculty** data table works as a data source for this LINQ to DataSet query; therefore, the AsEnumerable() method must be used to convert it to an IEnumerable<T> type. The **where** clause filters the desired information for the selected faculty member (**faculty_name**). All of these clauses will be converted to the associated Standard Query Operator methods that will be executed to perform this query.

H. A **foreach** loop then enumerates the enumerable object returned by **select** and yields the query results. Since the query is an Enumerable type, it implements IEnumerable<T>, and the evaluation of the query is deferred until the query variable is iterated over using

```
DataSetSingleTableLINQ.Program                Main()

  using System;
A using System.Data;
  using System.Data.OleDb;
  using System.Linq;
  namespace DataSetSingleTableLINQ
  {
     class Program
     {
        static void Main(string[] args)
        {
B          string cmdString = "SELECT * FROM Faculty";
           OleDbDataAdapter dataAdapter = new OleDbDataAdapter();
           OleDbConnection oleConnection = new OleDbConnection();
           OleDbCommand oleCommand = new OleDbCommand();
           DataSet ds = new DataSet();
C          string oleString = "Provider=SQLOLEDB;" + "Data Source=DESKTOP-24JPUFB\\SQL2019EXPRESS;" +
                              "Database=CSE_DEPT;" + "User ID=SMART;" + "Password=Happy2022";
D          oleConnection = new OleDbConnection(oleString);
           oleConnection.Open();
E          oleCommand.Connection = oleConnection;
           oleCommand.CommandType = CommandType.Text;
           oleCommand.CommandText = cmdString;
F          dataAdapter.SelectCommand = oleCommand;
             dataAdapter.Fill(ds, "Faculty");
G          var facultyinfo = (from fi in ds.Tables["Faculty"].AsEnumerable()
                              where fi.Field<string>("faculty_name").Equals("Ying Bai")
                              select fi);
H          foreach (var fRow in facultyinfo)
           {
               Console.WriteLine("{0}\n{1}\n{2}\n{3}\n{4}", fRow.Field<string>("title"), fRow.Field<string>("office"),
                    fRow.Field<string>("phone"), fRow.Field<string>("college"), fRow.Field<string>("email"));
           }
I          oleConnection.Close();
        }
     }
  }
```

FIGURE 4.35 The codes for the example project DataSetSingleTableLINQ.

the **foreach** loop. Deferred query evaluation allows queries to be kept as values that can be evaluated multiple times, each time yielding potentially different results.

I. Finally, the connection to our sample database is closed by calling the **Close()** method.

Now you can build and run this project by clicking **Debug | Start Without Debugging**. Related information for the selected faculty will be retrieved and displayed in the console window.

A complete C# Console project named **DataSetSingleTableLINQ** can be found from a folder **Class DB Projects\Chapter 4** that is located under the **Students** folder at the CRC Press ftp site (refer to Figure 1.2 in Chapter 1).

4.5.1.4 Query the Cross Tables

A DataSet object must first be populated before you can query over it with LINQ to DataSet. There are several different ways to populate the DataSet. From the example we discussed in the last section, we used the DataAdapter class with the **Fill()** method to do this population operation.

In addition to querying a single table, you can also perform cross-table queries in LINQ to DataSet. This is done by using a **join** clause. A join is the association of objects in one data source with objects that share a common attribute in another data source, such as a **faculty_id** in the **LogIn** table and in the **Faculty** table. In object-oriented programming, relationships between objects are relatively easy to navigate because each object has a member that references another object. In external database tables, however, navigating relationships is not as straightforward. Database tables do not contain built-in relationships. In these cases, the **Join** operation can be used to match elements from each source. For example, given two tables that contain faculty information and course information, you could use a **join** operation to match course information and faculty for the same **faculty_id**.

The Language-Integrated Query (LINQ) framework provides two join operators, **Join** and **GroupJoin**. These operators perform equi-joins: that is, joins that match two data sources only when their keys are equal. (By contrast, Transact-SQL supports join operators other than **equals**, such as the **less than** operator.)

In relational database terms, **Join** implements an inner join. An inner join is a type of join in which only those objects that have a match in the opposite data set are returned.

In this section, we use an example project to illustrate how to use **Join** operator to perform a multi-table query using LINQ to DataSet. The functionality of this project is:

1) Populate a DataSet instance, exactly populate two data tables, **Faculty** and **Course**, with two DataAdapters.
2) Using LINQ to DataSet join query to perform the cross-table query.

Now create a new C# console project and name it **DataSetCrossTableLINQ**. Open the code window of the **C# Program.cs** and enter the codes shown in Figure 4.36 into this window.

Let's have a closer look at this piece of code to see how it works.

A. Two namespaces, **System.Data** and **System.Data.OleDb**, must be added into the namespace declaration section of this project since we need to use some OleDb data components such as DataAdapter, Command and Connection.

B. Two SQL query strings are created to query some columns from the **Faculty** and the **Course** data tables in the DataSet. In addition, all OleDb data components, include two sets of Command and DataAdapter objects, are created in this part, including a non-OleDb data component, DataSet. Each set of components is used to fill an associated data table in the DataSet.

C. The connection string is declared since we need to use a SQL OleDb provider to connect to our sample database **CSE_DEPT** that is developed with Microsoft SQL Server 2019 Express. You may modify this string based on the real server where you saved your database.

D. The Connection object **oleConnection** is initialized with the connection string and a connection is executed by calling the **Open()** method. Regularly a **try-catch** block should be used for this connection operation to catch up any possible exception. Here we skip it since we try to make this connection coding simple.

E. The **facultyCommand** object is initialized with Connection, CommandType and Command Text properties.

F. The initialized **facultyCommand** object is assigned to the SelectCommand property of the **facultyAdapter** and the DataSet is filled with the **Fill()** method. The point is that only a single table, **Faculty**, is filled in this operation.

G. The **courseCommand** object is initialized with Connection, CommandType and CommandText properties. The initialized **courseCommand** object is assigned to the SelectCommand property of the **courseAdapter** and the DataSet is filled with the **Fill()** method. The point is that only a single table, **Course**, is filled in this operation.

H. Two DataTable objects, **faculty** and **course**, are created and mapped to the DataSet.

I. A LINQ to DataSet query is created with a **join** clause. The data type of the query variable **courseinfo** is implicit and it can be inferred by the compiler as the project is compiled. Two data tables, **Faculty** and **Course**, work as a joined data source for this LINQ to DataSet query; therefore, the AsEnumerable() method must be used to convert them to an IEnumerable<T> type. Two identical fields, **faculty_id**, that is a primary key in the **Faculty** table and a foreign

DataSetCrossTableLINQ.Program | Main()

```
  using System;
A using System.Data;
  using System.Data.OleDb;
  using System.Collections.Generic;
  using System.Linq;
  using System.Text;

  namespace DataSetCrossTableLINQ
  {
     class Program
     {
        static void Main(string[] args)
        {
B          string strFaculty = "SELECT faculty_id, faculty_name FROM Faculty";
           string strCourse = "SELECT course_id, faculty_id FROM Course";
           OleDbDataAdapter facultyAdapter = new OleDbDataAdapter();
           OleDbDataAdapter courseAdapter = new OleDbDataAdapter();
           OleDbConnection oleConnection = new OleDbConnection();
           OleDbCommand facultyCommand = new OleDbCommand();
           OleDbCommand courseCommand = new OleDbCommand();
           DataSet ds = new DataSet();
C          string oleString = "Provider=SQLOLEDB;" + "Data Source=DESKTOP-24JPUFB\\SQL2019EXPRESS;" +
                              "Database=CSE_DEPT;" + "User ID=SMART;" + "Password=Happy2022";
D          oleConnection = new OleDbConnection(oleString);
           oleConnection.Open();
E          facultyCommand.Connection = oleConnection;
           facultyCommand.CommandType = CommandType.Text;
           facultyCommand.CommandText = strFaculty;
F          facultyAdapter.SelectCommand = facultyCommand;
           facultyAdapter.Fill(ds, "Faculty");
G          courseCommand.Connection = oleConnection;
           courseCommand.CommandType = CommandType.Text;
           courseCommand.CommandText = strCourse;
           courseAdapter.SelectCommand = courseCommand;
           courseAdapter.Fill(ds, "Course");
H          DataTable faculty = ds.Tables["Faculty"];
           DataTable course = ds.Tables["Course"];
I          var courseinfo = from ci in course.AsEnumerable()
                            join fi in faculty.AsEnumerable()
                            on ci.Field<string>("faculty_id") equals fi.Field<string>("faculty_id")
                            where fi.Field<string>("faculty_name") == "Ying Bai"
                            select new
                            {
                               course_id = ci.Field<string>("course_id")
                            };
J          foreach (var cid in courseinfo)
           {
              Console.WriteLine(cid.course_id);
           }
K          oleConnection.Close();
           facultyCommand.Dispose();
           courseCommand.Dispose();
           facultyAdapter.Dispose();
           courseAdapter.Dispose();
        }
     }
  }
```

FIGURE 4.36 The coding for the example project DataSetCrossTableLINQ.

key in the **Course** tables, works as a joined criterion to link two tables together. The **where** clause is used to filter the desired course information for the selected faculty member (**faculty_name**). All of these clauses will be converted to the associated Standard Query Operator methods that will be executed to perform and complete this query.

J. A **foreach** loop then enumerates the enumerable object returned by select and yields the query results. Because query is an Enumerable type, which implements IEnumerable<T>, the evaluation of the query is deferred until the query variable is iterated over using the **foreach** loop. Deferred query evaluation allows queries to be kept as values that can be evaluated multiple times, each time yielding potentially different results. All courses taught by the selected faculty are retrieved and displayed when this **foreach** loop is done.

K. Finally, the connection to our sample database is closed by calling the **Close()** method, and all data components used in this project are released.

In order to make this project work, you also need to install the **System.Data.OleDb** package by using the Package Manager Console as we did in the last section.

Now you can build and run this project. One point to be noticed is that the connection string implemented in this project. You need to modify this string in step **C** if you installed your database file **CSE_DEPT** in a different server.

Click on the **Debug | Start Without Debugging** menu item to run the project, and you can find that all courses (**course_id**) taught by the selected faculty are retrieved and displayed in this console window.

A complete C# Console project named **DataSetCrossTableLINQ** can be found from a folder **Class DB Projects\Chapter 4** that is located under the **Students** folder at the CRC Press ftp site (refer to Figure 1.2 in Chapter 1).

Next let's take a look at querying typed DataSet with LINQ to DataSet.

4.5.1.5 Query Typed DataSet

If the schema of the DataSet is known at application design time, it is highly recommended that you use a typed DataSet when using LINQ to DataSet. A typed DataSet is a class that derives from a DataSet. As such, it inherits all the methods, events, and properties of a DataSet.

Additionally, a typed DataSet provides strongly typed methods, events, and properties. This means that you can access tables and columns by name, instead of using collection-based methods. This makes queries simpler and more readable.

LINQ to DataSet also supports querying over a typed DataSet. With a typed DataSet, you do not have to use the generic **Field()** method or **SetField()** method to access column data. Property names are available at compile time because the type information is included in the DataSet. LINQ to DataSet provides access to column values as the correct type, so that the type mismatch errors are caught when the code is compiled instead of at run time.

Before we can begin querying a typed DataSet, we must generate a class by using the DataSet Designer in Visual Studio 2022.

In fact, it is easier to use LINQ to DataSet to query a typed DataSet as long as a typed DataSet has been created. There are two ways to create a typed DataSet: using the Data Source Configuration Wizard or using the DataSet Designer. Both belong to the Design Tools and Wizards provided by Visual Studio.NET.

We will use the second method, DataSet Designer, to create a typed DataSet. The database we will use is our sample database **CSE_DEPT** developed in Microsoft SQL Server 2019.

Create a new C# console project **TypedDataSetLINQ**. Now let's first create our typed DataSet. On the opened new project, right-click our new project from the Solution Explorer window. Select the **Add | New Item** from the popup menu to open the Add New item wizard, which is shown in Figure 4.37.

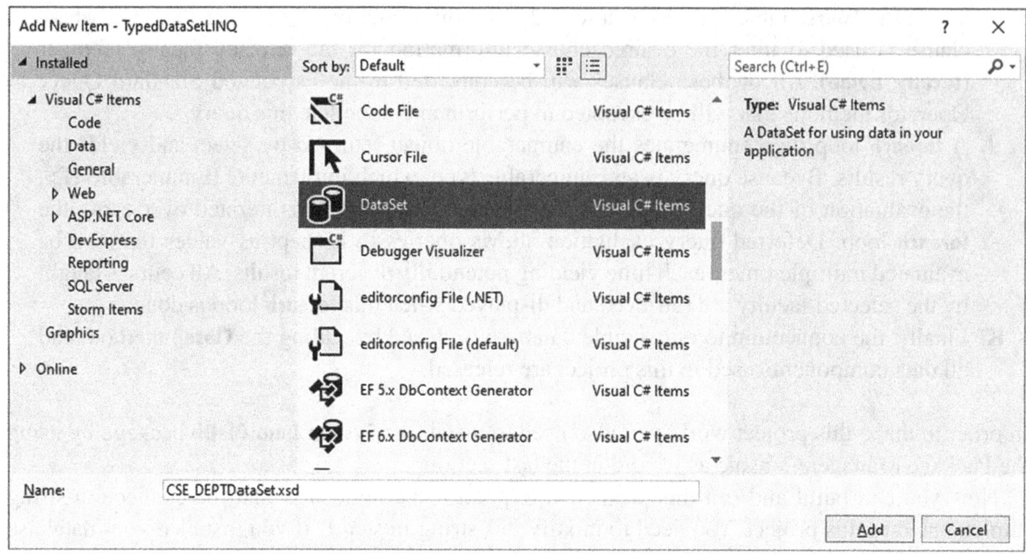

FIGURE 4.37 The opened add new item wizard.

Click the **DataSet** from the Template list and enter **CSE_DEPTDataSet.xsd** into the **Name** box as the name for this DataSet. Click on the **Add** button to add this DataSet into our project. Your finished Add New Item wizard should match one that is shown in Figure 4.37.

Next we need to select our data source for our new DataSet. Open the Server Explorer window and click on the arrow on the left of our Database Connection item if it has not been connected to connect it. Expand the **Tables** folder under that data source, you can find all five tables, which is shown in Figure 4.38.

Open the DataSet Designer by double-clicking the item **CSE_DEPTDataSet.xsd** from the Solution Explorer window if it is not opened. Drag the **Faculty** and the **Course** tables from the Server Explorer window and place them to the DataSet Designer. You can drag-place all five tables if you like, but here we only need to drag two of them. Exactly we only need to use the **Faculty** table in this project.

Now we have finished creating our typed DataSet and the connection to our data source. Next we need to perform the coding process to use LINQ to DataSet to perform the query to this typed DataSet.

Before we can develop and create our codes, we need first to add the **System.Data.SqlClient** package into our project to enable us to use it since we are using our sample database **CSE_DEPT**, which is built with the Microsoft SQL Server 2019 Express, as the data source in this project. Perform the following operations to add this package into our project:

1) Go to the menu item **Tools | NuGet Package Manager | Package Manager Console**.
2) In the opened Package Manager Console window at the bottom, type the command: **Install-Package System.Data.SqlClient** and press the **Enter** key on your keyboard.
3) Some Successful Installation messages are displayed on that console window when it is done, which means that the package has been successfully installed and added into our project, and we can use it.

Now double-click on the **C# Program.cs** file from the Solution Explorer window to open the code window of that file. Enter the codes that are shown in Figure 4.39 into this code window.

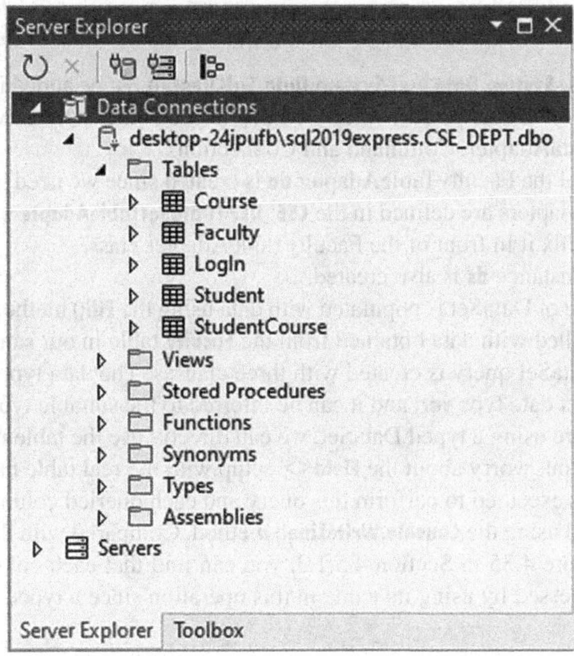

FIGURE 4.38 The add connection wizard and the server explorer window.

```
TypedDataSetLINQ.Program                    Main()

  using System;
A using System.Data;
  using System.Data.SqlClient;
  using System.Collections.Generic;
  using System.Linq;
  using System.Text;
  namespace TypedDataSetLINQ
  {
      class Program
      {
          static void Main(string[] args)
          {
B             CSE_DEPTDataSetTableAdapters.FacultyTableAdapter da = new
                                  CSE_DEPTDataSetTableAdapters.FacultyTableAdapter();
C             CSE_DEPTDataSet ds = new CSE_DEPTDataSet();
D             da.Fill(ds.Faculty);
E             var faculty = from fi in ds.Faculty
                            where fi.faculty_name == "Ying Bai"
                            select fi;
F             foreach (var f in faculty)
              {
                  Console.WriteLine("{0}\n{1}\n{2}\n{3}\n{4}", f.title, f.office, f.phone, f.college, f.email);
              }
          }
      }
  }
```

FIGURE 4.39 The codes for the example project TypedDataSetLINQ.

Let's have a closer look at this piece of codes to see how it works.

- **A.** Two namespaces, **System.Data** and **System.Data.SqlClient**, must be added into the namespace declaration section of this project since we need to use some SQL Server related components such as DataAdapter, Command and Connection.
- **B.** A new instance of the FacultyTableAdapter **da** is created since we need it to fill the DataSet later. All TableAdapters are defined in the **CSE_DEPTDataSetTableAdapters** namespace; therefore we must prefix it in front of the FacultyTableAdapter class.
- **C.** A new DataSet instance **ds** is also created.
- **D.** The new instance of DataSet is populated with data using the **Fill()** method. Exactly only the **Faculty** table is filled with data obtained from the **Faculty** table in our sample database.
- **E.** The LINQ to DataSet query is created with three clauses. The data type of the query variable is an implicit data type **var**, and it can be inferred to the suitable type as the compiling time. Since we are using a typed DataSet, we can directly use the table name, **Faculty**, after the DataSet without worry about the **Field<>** setup with the real table name.
- **F.** A **foreach** loop is executed to perform this query and each queried column from the **Faculty** table is displayed using the **Console.WriteLine()** method. Compared with the same displaying operation in Figure 4.35 in Section 4.5.1.3, you can find that each column in the queried result can be accessed by using its name in this operation since a typed DataSet is used in this project.

Now you can build and run the project. Click the **Debug | Start Without Debugging** item to run the project, and you can find all information related to the selected faculty is retrieved and displayed in this console window. Our project is successful!

A complete C# Console project named **TypedDataSetLINQ** can be found from a folder **Class DB Projects\Chapter 4** that is located under the **Students** folder at the CRC Press ftp site (refer to Figure 1.2 in Chapter 1).

4.5.2 Operations to DataRow Objects Using the Extension Methods

The LINQ to DataSet functionality is exposed primarily through the extension methods in the **DataRowExtensions** and **DataTableExtensions** classes. In C#, you can call either of these methods as an instance method on any object of type . When you use instance method syntax to call this method, omit the first parameter. The DataSet API has been extended with two new methods of the **DataRow** class, **Field()** and **SetField()**. You can use these to form Language-Integrated Query (LINQ) expressions and method queries against DataTable objects. They are the recommended methods to use for accessing column values within Language-Integrated Query (LINQ) expressions and method queries.

In this section, we discuss how to access and manipulate column values using the extension methods provided by the DataRow class, the **Field()** and the **SetField()** methods. These methods provide easier access to column values for developers, especially regarding **null** values. The DataSet uses **Value** to represent **null** values, whereas LINQ uses the nullable type support introduced in the .NET Framework 2.0. Using the pre-existing column accessor in DataRow requires us to cast the return object to the appropriate type. If a particular field in a DataRow can be **null**, you must explicitly check for a null value because the returning **Value** and implicitly casting it to another type throws an **InvalidCastException**.

The **Field()** method allows users to obtain the value of a column from the DataRow object and handles the casting of **DBNull**.Value. In total, the **Field()** method has six different prototypes. The **SetField()** method, which has three prototypes, allows users to set a new value for a column from the DataRow object, including handle a nullable data type whose value is **null**.

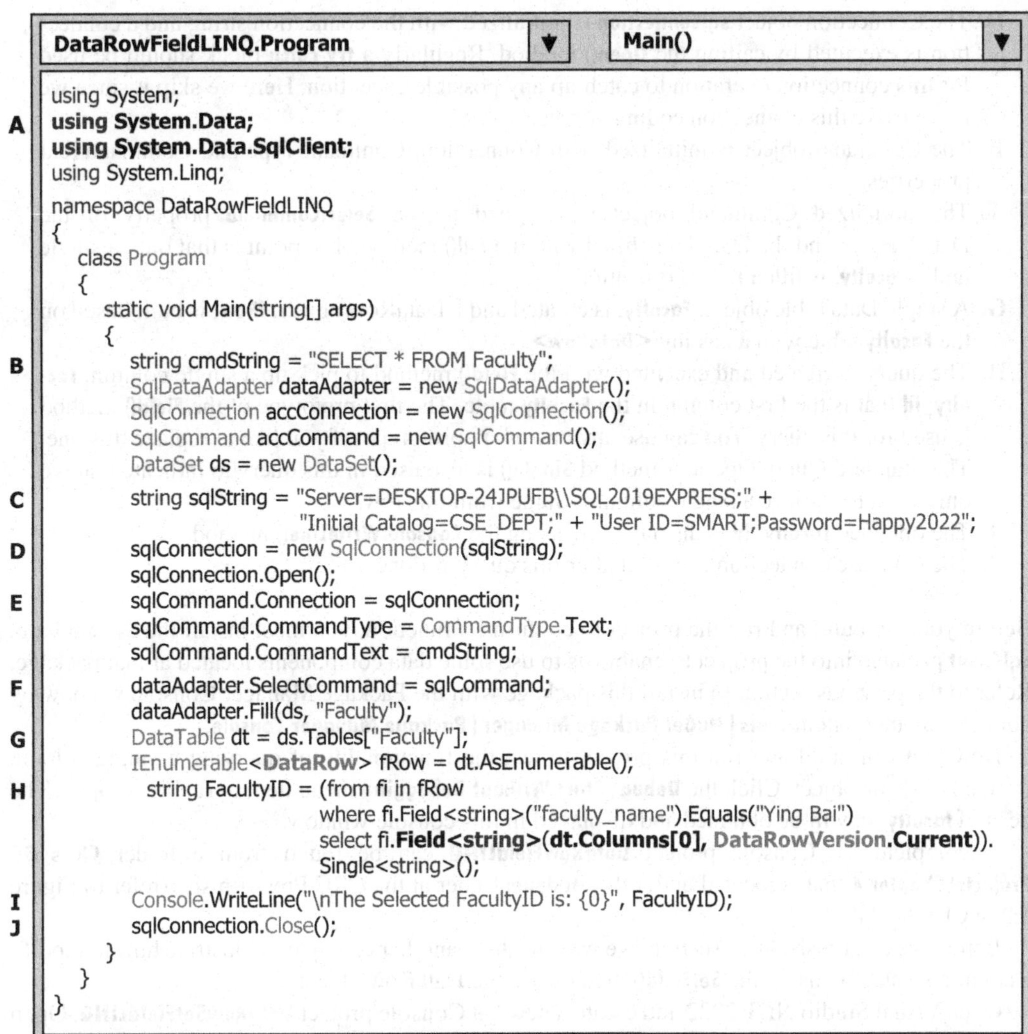

```
DataRowFieldLINQ.Program                    Main()

  using System;
A using System.Data;
  using System.Data.SqlClient;
  using System.Linq;
  namespace DataRowFieldLINQ
  {
     class Program
     {
        static void Main(string[] args)
        {
B          string cmdString = "SELECT * FROM Faculty";
           SqlDataAdapter dataAdapter = new SqlDataAdapter();
           SqlConnection accConnection = new SqlConnection();
           SqlCommand accCommand = new SqlCommand();
           DataSet ds = new DataSet();
C          string sqlString = "Server=DESKTOP-24JPUFB\\SQL2019EXPRESS;" +
                              "Initial Catalog=CSE_DEPT;" + "User ID=SMART;Password=Happy2022";
D          sqlConnection = new SqlConnection(sqlString);
           sqlConnection.Open();
E          sqlCommand.Connection = sqlConnection;
           sqlCommand.CommandType = CommandType.Text;
           sqlCommand.CommandText = cmdString;
F          dataAdapter.SelectCommand = sqlCommand;
           dataAdapter.Fill(ds, "Faculty");
G          DataTable dt = ds.Tables["Faculty"];
           IEnumerable<DataRow> fRow = dt.AsEnumerable();
H            string FacultyID = (from fi in fRow
                              where fi.Field<string>("faculty_name").Equals("Ying Bai")
                              select fi.Field<string>(dt.Columns[0], DataRowVersion.Current)).
                              Single<string>();
I          Console.WriteLine("\nThe Selected FacultyID is: {0}", FacultyID);
J          sqlConnection.Close();
        }
     }
  }
```

FIGURE 4.40 The codes for the example project DataRowFieldLINQ.

Now let's create a new C# console project to illustrate how to use the **Field()** method to retrieve some columns' values from the DataRow object. The database we will use is still our sample database **CSE_DEPT**. Open Visual Studio.NET 2022 and create a new C# console project and name it as **DataRowFieldLINQ**. Open the code window of the **C# Program.cs** file and enter the codes that are shown in Figure 4.40 into this code window.

Let's have a closer look at this piece of code to see how it works.

A. Two namespaces, System.Data and System.Data.SqlClient, must be added into the namespace declaration section of this project since we need to use some SQL data components such as DataAdapter, Command and Connection.

B. A SQL query string is created to query all columns from the **Faculty** data table in the DataSet. Also all SQL related data components are created in this part including a non-SQL data component, DataSet.

C. The connection string is declared since we need to use it to connect to our sample database **CSE_DEPT** that is developed in Microsoft SQL Server 2019 Express. You need to modify this string based on the real server in which you save your database.

D. The Connection object **sqlConnection** is initialized with the connection string and a connection is executed by calling the **Open()** method. Regularly a **try-catch** block should be used for this connection operation to catch up any possible exception. Here we skip it since we try to make this connection coding simple.
E. The Command object is initialized with Connection, CommandType and CommandText properties.
F. The initialized Command object is assigned to the **SelectCommand** property of the DataAdapter and the DataSet is filled with the **Fill()** method. The point is that only a single table, **Faculty**, is filled in this operation.
G. A single DataTable object, **Faculty**, is created and a DataRow object, **fRow**, is built based on the **Faculty** table with a casting **<DataRow>**.
H. The query is created and executed with the **Field()** method to pick up a single column, **faculty_id** that is the first column in the **Faculty** table. The first prototype of the **Field()** method is used for this query. You can use any one of six prototypes if you like to replace this one. The Standard Query Operator method **Single()** is also used in this query to indicate that we only need to retrieve a single column's value from this row.
I. The obtained **faculty_id** is displayed by using the **Console.WriteLine()** method.
J. The database connection is closed after this query is done.

Before you can build and run the project to confirm its function, you must install the **System.Data.SqlClient** package into the project to enable us to use some data components located at that package. Refer to the previous section to install this package with the Package Manager Console window by going to the menu item **Tools | NuGet Package Manager | Package Manager Console**.

Now you can build and run this project to test the functionality of querying a single column from a DataRow object. Click the **Debug | Start Without Debugging** menu item to run the project. The desired **faculty_id** will be obtained and displayed in this console window.

A complete C# Console project **DataRowFieldLINQ** can be found from a folder **Class DB Projects\Chapter 4** that is located under the **Students** folder at the CRC Press ftp site (refer to Figure 1.2 in Chapter 1).

Before we can finished this section, we want to show another example to illustrate how to modify a column's value by using the **SetField()** method via the DataRow object.

Open Visual Studio.NET 2022 and create a new C# Console project **DataRowSetFieldLINQ**. Open the code window of the **C# Program.cs** file and enter the codes shown in Figure 4.41 into this window.

The codes between steps **A** and **B** are identical with those we developed for our last project **DataRwoFieldLINQ**. Refer to that project to get more details for these codes and their functions.

Let's take a closer look at this piece of code to see how it works.

A. Two namespaces, **System.Data** and **System.Data.OleDb**, must be added into the namespace declaration section of this project since we need to use some OleDb data components such as DataAdapter, Command and Connection.
B. A LINQ to DataSet query is created with the **Field()** method via DataRow object. This query should return a complete data row from the **Faculty** table.
C. The **AcceptChanges()** method is executed to allow the DataRow object to accept the current value of each DataColumn object in the Faculty table as the original version of the value for that column. This method is very important and there would be no original version of the DataColumn object's values without this method.
D. Now we call **SetField()** method to set up a new value to the column **faculty_name** in the **Faculty** table. This new name will work as the current version of this DataColumn object's value. The second prototype of this method is used here and you can try to use any one of other two prototypes if you like.

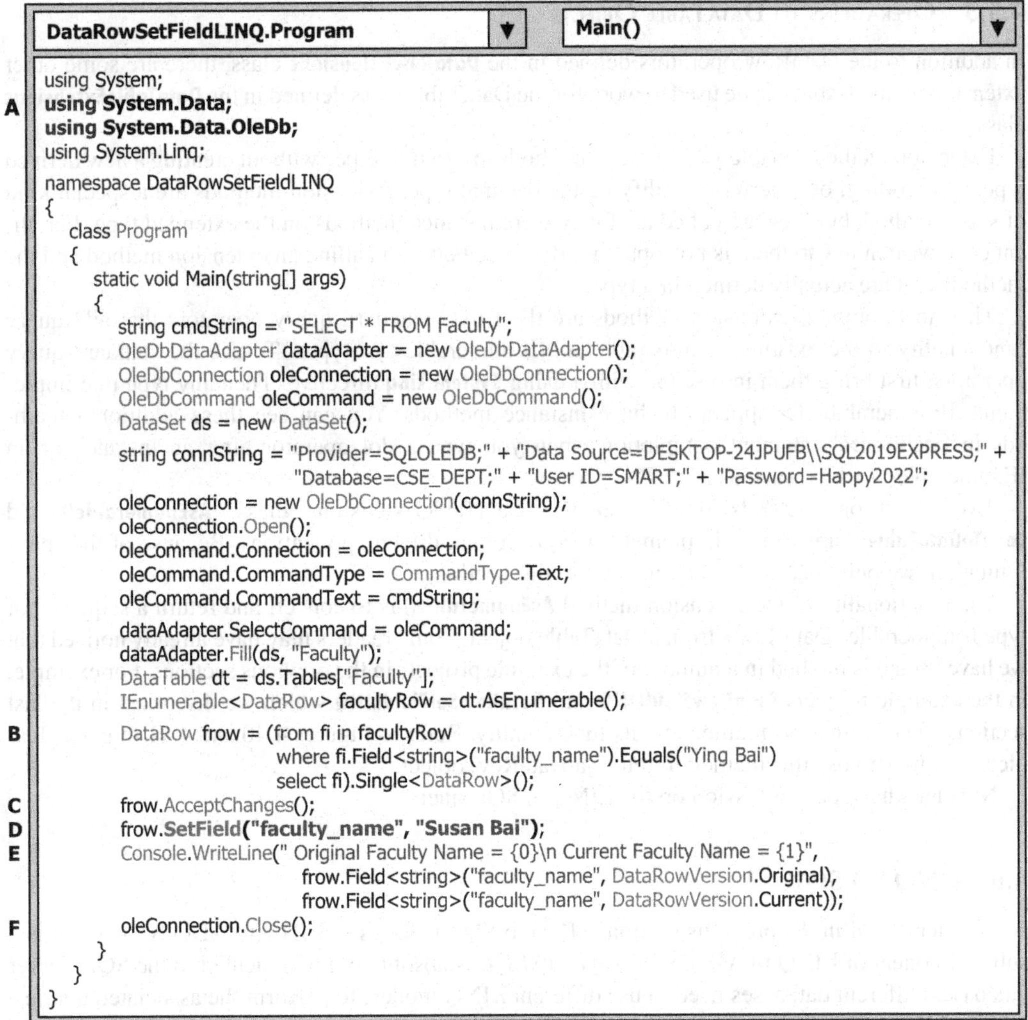

```
DataRowSetFieldLINQ.Program                Main()

  using System;
A using System.Data;
  using System.Data.OleDb;
  using System.Linq;
  namespace DataRowSetFieldLINQ
  {
     class Program
     {
        static void Main(string[] args)
        {
           string cmdString = "SELECT * FROM Faculty";
           OleDbDataAdapter dataAdapter = new OleDbDataAdapter();
           OleDbConnection oleConnection = new OleDbConnection();
           OleDbCommand oleCommand = new OleDbCommand();
           DataSet ds = new DataSet();
           string connString = "Provider=SQLOLEDB;" + "Data Source=DESKTOP-24JPUFB\\SQL2019EXPRESS;" +
                               "Database=CSE_DEPT;" + "User ID=SMART;" + "Password=Happy2022";
           oleConnection = new OleDbConnection(connString);
           oleConnection.Open();
           oleCommand.Connection = oleConnection;
           oleCommand.CommandType = CommandType.Text;
           oleCommand.CommandText = cmdString;
           dataAdapter.SelectCommand = oleCommand;
           dataAdapter.Fill(ds, "Faculty");
           DataTable dt = ds.Tables["Faculty"];
           IEnumerable<DataRow> facultyRow = dt.AsEnumerable();
B          DataRow frow = (from fi in facultyRow
                           where fi.Field<string>("faculty_name").Equals("Ying Bai")
                           select fi).Single<DataRow>();
C          frow.AcceptChanges();
D          frow.SetField("faculty_name", "Susan Bai");
E          Console.WriteLine(" Original Faculty Name = {0}\n Current Faculty Name = {1}",
                             frow.Field<string>("faculty_name", DataRowVersion.Original),
                             frow.Field<string>("faculty_name", DataRowVersion.Current));
F          oleConnection.Close();
        }
     }
  }
```

FIGURE 4.41 The codes for the example project DataRowSetFieldLINQ.

E. The **Console.WriteLine()** method is executed to display both original and the current values of the DataColumn object **faculty_name** in the **Faculty** table.
F. The database connection is closed after this query is done.

Before you can build and run the project to confirm its function, you must install the **System.Data.OleDb** package into the project to enable us to use some data components located at that package. Refer to Section 4.5.1.3 to install this package with the Package Manager Console window by going to the menu item **Tools | NuGet Package Manager | Package Manager Console**.

Now you can build and run the project to test the functionality of the method **SetField()**. Click on the **Debug | Start Without Debugging** menu item to run the project. You can find that both the original and the current version of the **DataColumn** object **faculty_name** is retrieved and displayed in the console window.

A complete C# Console project named **DataRowSetFieldLINQ** can be found from a folder **Class DB Projects\Chapter 4** that is located under the **Students** folder at the CRC Press ftp site (refer to Figure 1.2 in Chapter 1).

4.5.3 Operations to DataTable Objects

In addition to the DataRow operators defined in the **DataRowExtensions** class, there are some other extension methods that can be used to work for the DataTable class defined in the **DataTableExtensions** class.

Extension methods enable you to "add" methods to existing types without creating a new derived type, recompiling, or otherwise modifying the original type. Extension methods are a special kind of static method, but they are called as if they were instance methods on the extended type. For client code written in C#, there is no apparent difference between calling an extension method and the methods that are actually defined in a type.

The most common extension methods are the LINQ standard query operators that add query functionality to the existing IEnumerable and IEnumerable<T> types. To use the standard query operators, first bring them into scope with a using **System.Linq** directive. Then any type that implements IEnumerable<T> appears to have instance methods. You can see these additional methods in **IntelliSense** statement completion when you type a dot operator after an instance of an IEnumerable<T> type such as List<T> or Array.

Two extension methods defined in the DataTableExtensions class, **AsEnumerable()** and **CopyToDataTable()**, are widely implemented in most data-driven applications. Because of the space limitation, we only discuss the first method in this section.

The functionality of the extension method **AsEnumerable()** is to convert and return a sequence of type IEnumerable<DataRow> from a DataTable object. Some readers may have already noticed that we have used this method in a number of the example projects in the previous sections. For example, in the example projects **DataRowFieldLINQ** and **DataRowSetFieldLINQ** which we discussed in the last section, you can find this method and its functionality. Refer to Figures 4.40 and 4.41 to get a clear picture in how to use this method to return a DataRow object.

Next let's have our discussion on the LINQ to SQL query.

4.6 LINQ TO SQL

As we mentioned in the previous section, LINQ to SQL belongs to LINQ to ADO.NET and it is a sub-component of LINQ to ADO.NET. LINQ to SQL is absolutely implemented to the SQL Server database. Different databases need to use different LINQ models to perform the associated queries, such as LINQ to MySQL, LINQ to DB2 or LINQ to Oracle.

LINQ to SQL query is performed on classes that implement the IQueryable<T> interface. Since the IQueryable<T> interface is inherited from the IEnumerable<T> with additional components, therefore besides the Standard Query Operator (SQO), the LINQ to SQL queries have additional query operators since it uses the IQueryable<T> interface.

LINQ to SQL is an application programming interface (API) that allows users to easily and conveniently access the SQL Server database from the Standard Query Operators (SQO) related to the LINQ. To use this API, you must first convert your data tables in the relational database that is built based on a relational logic model to the related entity classes that are built based on the objects model. You then setup a mapping relationship between your relational database and a group of objects that are instantiated from entity classes. The LINQ to SQL or the Standard Query Operators will interface to these entity classes to perform the real database operations. In other words, each entity class can be mapped or is equivalent to a physical data table in the database, and each entity class's property can be mapped or is equivalent to a data column in that table. Only after this mapping relationship has been setup, one can use the LINQ to SQL to access and manipulate data against the databases.

After entity classes are created and the mapping relationships between each physical table and each entity class have been built, the conversion for data operations between the entity class and the real data table is needed. The class DataContext is the guy who will work in this role. Basically, the

DataContext is a connection class that is used to establish a connection between your project and your database. In addition to this connection role, the **DataContext** also provide the conversion function to convert or interpret operations of the Standard Query Operators for the entity classes to the SQL statements that can be run in real databases.

Two tools provided by LINQ to SQL are **SQLMetal** and the **Object Relational Designer** (**O/R Designer**). With the help of these tools, users can easily build all required entity classes, set the mapping relationships between the relational database and the objects model used in LINQ to SQL and create our **DataContext** object.

The difference between the **SQLMetal** and the **Object Relational Designer** is that the former is a console-based application, but the latter is a window-based application. This means that the **SQLMetal** provides a DOS-like template and the operations are performed by entering single command into a black-and-white window. The **Object Relational Designer** provides a graphic user interface (GUI) and allows user to drag-place tables represented by graphic icons into the GUI. Obviously, the second method, or tool, is more convenient and easier compared with the first one.

Due to the discontinuing in support for **SQLMetal** in Visual Studio 2022, we only concentrate on how to use the Object Relational Designer to build LINQ to SQL queries in Chapter 5.

4.6.1 LINQ to SQL Implementations

Some real projects that using LINQ to SQL queries with the **O/R Designer** will be developed in the following chapters, and those projects are categorized based on the following chapters:

- LINQ to SQL Select query projects: Chapters 5, 8 and 9
- LINQ to SQL Insert query projects: Chapters 8 and 9
- LINQ to SQL Update query projects: Chapters 7, 8 and 9
- LINQ to SQL Delete query projects: Chapters 7, 8 and 9

Refer to those chapters to get more detailed information and related codes developments for those projects.

4.7 LINQ TO ENTITIES

As we mentioned in the Introduction to LINQ section, LINQ to Entities belongs to LINQ to ADO.NET and it is a sub-component of LINQ to ADO.NET.

LINQ to Entities queries are performed under the control of the ADO.NET 3.5 Entity Framework (ADO.NET 3.5 EF) and ADO.NET 3.5 Entity Framework Tools (ADO.NET 3.5 EFT). ADO.NET 3.5 EF enables developers to work with data in the form of domain-specific objects and properties, such as customers and customer addresses, without having to think about the underlying database tables and columns where this data is stored.

To access and implement ADO.NET 3.5 EF and ADO.NET 3.5 EFT, developers need to understand the Entity Data Model, which is a core of ADO.NET 3.5 EF. LINQ allows developers to formulate set-based queries in their application code, without having to use a separate query language. Through the Object Services infrastructure of the Entity Framework, ADO.NET exposes a common conceptual view of data, including relational data, as objects in the .NET environment. This makes the object layer an ideal target for LINQ support.

This LINQ technology, LINQ to Entities, allows developers to create flexible, strongly typed queries against the Entity Framework object context by using LINQ expressions and the LINQ standard query operators directly from the development environment. The queries are expressed in the programming language itself and not as string literals embedded in the application code, as is usually the case in applications written on the Microsoft .NET Framework 2.0. Syntax errors, as well as errors in member names and data types, will be caught by the compiler and reported at compile time, reducing the potential for type problems between the Entity Data Model and the application.

LINQ to Entities queries use the Object Services infrastructure. The ObjectContext class is the primary class for interacting with an Entity Data Model as CLR objects. The developer constructs a generic ObjectQuery instance through the ObjectContext. The ObjectQuery generic class represents a query that returns an instance or collection of typed entities. The returned entity objects are updatable and are located in the object context. This is also true for entity objects that are returned as members of anonymous types.

4.7.1 The Object Services Component

Object Services is a component of the Entity Framework that enables you to query, insert, update, and delete data, expressed as strongly typed common language runtime (CLR) objects that are instances of entity types. Object Services supports both Language-Integrated Query (LINQ) and Entity SQL queries against types defined in an Entity Data Model (EDM). Object Services materializes returned data as objects, and propagates object changes back to the persisted data store.

It also provides facilities for tracking changes, binding objects to controls, and handling concurrency. Object Services is implemented by classes in the System.Data.Objects and System.Data.Objects.DataClasses namespaces.

4.7.2 The ObjectContext Component

The **ObjectContext** class encapsulates a connection between the .NET Framework and the database. This class serves as a gateway for Create, Read, Update, and Delete operations, and it is the primary class for interacting with data in the form of objects that are instances of entity types defined in an EDM. An instance of the ObjectContext class encapsulates the following:

- A connection to the database, in the form of an EntityConnection object.
- Metadata that describes the model, in the form of a MetadataWorkspace object.
- An ObjectStateManager object that manages objects persisted in the cache.

The Entity Framework tools consume a conceptual schema definition language (CSDL) file from a relational database and generate the object-layer code. This code is used to work with entity data as objects and to take advantage of Object Services functionality. This generated code includes the following data classes:

- A class that represents the EntityContainer for the model and is derived from ObjectContext.
- Classes that represent entities and inherit from EntityObject.

4.7.3 The ObjectQuery Component

The **ObjectQuery** generic class represents a query that returns a collection of zero or more typed entities. An object query always belongs to an existing object context. This context provides the connection and metadata information that is required to compose and execute the query.

4.7.4 LINQ to Entities Flow of Execution

Queries against the Entity Framework are represented by command tree queries, which execute against the object context. LINQ to Entities converts Language-Integrated Queries (LINQ) queries to command tree queries, executes the queries against the Entity Framework, and returns objects that can be used by both the Entity Framework and LINQ. The following is the process for creating and executing a LINQ to Entities query:

1) Construct an ObjectQuery instance from ObjectContext.
2) Compose a LINQ to Entities query in C# by using the ObjectQuery instance.
3) LINQ Standard Query Operators and expressions in query are converted to command trees.
4) The query, in command tree representation, is executed against the data store. Any exceptions thrown on the data store during execution are passed directly up to the client.
5) Query results are materialized back to the client.

Let's have a more detailed discussion for each of these steps.

4.7.4.1 Construct an ObjectQuery Instance

The ObjectQuery generic class represents a query that returns a collection of zero or more typed entities. An object query is typically constructed from an existing object context, instead of being manually constructed, and always belongs to that object context. This context provides the connection and metadata information that is required to compose and execute the query. The ObjectQuery generic class implements the IQueryable generic interface, whose builder methods enable LINQ queries to be incrementally built.

4.7.4.2 Compose a LINQ to Entities Query

Instances of the ObjectQuery generic class, which implements the generic IQueryable interface, serve as the data source for LINQ to Entities queries. In a query, you specify exactly the information that you want to retrieve from the data source. A query can also specify how that information should be sorted, grouped, and shaped before it is returned. In LINQ, a query is stored in a variable. This query variable takes no action and returns no data; it only stores the query information. After you create a query you must execute that query to retrieve any data.

LINQ to Entities queries can be composed in two different syntaxes: query expression syntax and method-based query syntax. We have provided a very detailed discussion about the query expression syntax and method-based query syntax with real example codes in Sections 4.5.1.1 and 4.5.1.2 in this chapter. Refer to those sections to get a clear picture for these two syntaxes.

4.7.4.3 Convert the Query to Command Trees

To execute a LINQ to Entities query against the Entity Framework, the LINQ query must be converted to a command tree representation that can be executed against the Entity Framework.

LINQ to Entities queries are comprised of LINQ Standard Query Operators (such as **Select**, **Where**, and **OrderBy**) and expressions. LINQ Standard Query Operators are not defined by a class, but rather are static methods on a class. In LINQ, expressions can contain anything allowed by types within the System.Expressions namespace and, by extension, anything that can be represented in a lambda function. This is a superset of the expressions that are allowed by the Entity Framework, which are by definition restricted to operations allowed on the database, and supported by ObjectQuery.

In the Entity Framework, both operators and expressions are represented by a single type hierarchy, which are then placed in a command tree. The command tree is used by the Entity Framework to execute the query. If the LINQ query cannot be expressed as a command tree, an exception will be thrown when the query is being converted. The conversion of LINQ to Entities queries involves two sub-conversions: the conversion of the Standard Query Operators and the conversion of the expressions. In general, expressions in LINQ to Entities are evaluated on the server, so the behavior of the expression should not be expected to follow CLR semantics.

An example of an expression used in LINQ to Entities is shown in Figure 4.42.

```
IQueryable<string> FacultyInfo = from fi in Faculties
                                 where fi.faculty_id == "B78880"
                                 select fi.faculty_name;
```

FIGURE 4.42 An example of expression used in LINQ to entities.

4.7.4.4 Execute the Query

After the LINQ query is created by the user, it is converted to a representation that is compatible with the Entity Framework (in the form of command trees), which is then executed against the store. At query execution time, all query expressions (or components of the query) are evaluated on the client or on the server. This includes expressions that are used in result materialization or entity projections.

A query expression can be executed in two ways. LINQ queries are executed each time the query variable is iterated over, not when the query variable is created; this is referred to as deferred execution. The query can also be forced to execute immediately, which is useful for caching query results. The following example shown in Figure 4.43 uses **Select** to return all the rows from *Faculty* and display the faculty names. Iterating over the query variable in the **foreach** loop causes the query to execute.

When a LINQ to Entities query is executed, some expressions in the query might be executed on the server and some parts might be executed locally on the client. Client-side evaluation of an expression takes place before the query is executed on the server. If an expression is evaluated on the client, the result of that evaluation is substituted for the expression in the query, and the query is then executed on the server. Because queries are executed on the data store, the data store configuration overrides the behavior specified in the client. Null value handling and numerical precision are examples of this. Any exceptions thrown during query execution on the server are passed directly up to the client.

4.7.4.5 Materialize the Query

Materialization is the process of returning query results back to the client as CLR types. In

LINQ to Entities, query results data records are never returned; there is always a backing CLR type, defined by the user or by the Entity Framework, or generated by the compiler (anonymous types). All object materialization is performed by the Entity Framework. Any errors that result from an inability to map between the Entity Framework and the CLR will cause exceptions to be thrown during object materialization.

Query results are usually returned as one of the following:

- A collection of zero or more typed entity objects or a projection of complex types in the Entity Data Model.
- CLR types supported by the Entity Data Model.

```
ObjectQuery<Faculty> faculties = cse_dept.Faculty;
IQueryable<string> FacultyNames = from f in faculties
                                  select f.faculty_name;
Console.WriteLine("Faculty Names:");
foreach (var fName in FacultyNames)
{
    Console.WriteLine(fName);
}
```

FIGURE 4.43 An example of executing the query.

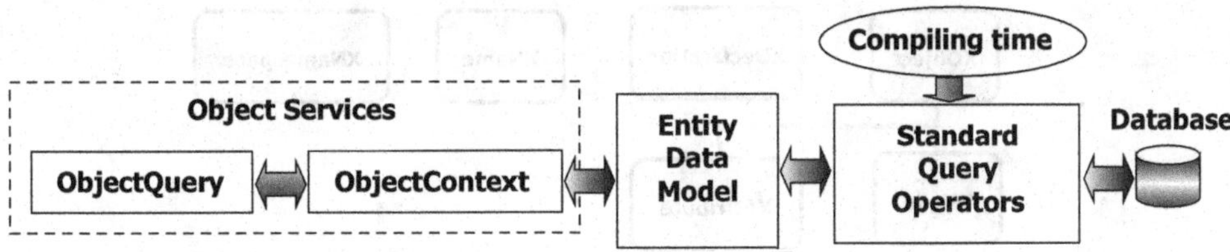

FIGURE 4.44 A simplified structure of LINQ to entities.

- Inline collections.
- Anonymous types.
- IGrouping instances.
- IQueryable instances.

A simplified structure of LINQ to Entities is shown in Figure 4.44.

We have provided a very detailed discussion about the structure and components used in LINQ to Entities query, next we need to illustrate these by using some examples.

4.7.5 Implementation of LINQ to Entities

In order to use LINQ to Entities query to perform data actions against databases, one needs to have a clear picture about the infrastructure and fully understanding about components used in LINQ to Entities. In Section 3.4.8 in Chapter 3, we have provided a very detailed discussion about the ADO.NET 3.5 Entity Framework and ADO.NET 3.5 Entity Data Model, including the Entity Data Model Wizard, Entity Data Model Designer and Entity Model Browser with a real example project **EDModel Project**. Review that section to get more details for the implementation of LINQ to Entities. A complete example project **EDModelProject** that uses LINQ to Entities query can be found from a folder **Class DB Projects\Chapter 3** that is under the **Students** folder at the CRC Press ftp site (refer to Figure 1.2 in Chapter 1).

4.8 LINQ TO XML

LINQ to XML was developed with Language-Integrated Query over XML in mind and takes advantage of standard query operators and adds query extensions specific to XML. LINQ to XML is a modernized in-memory XML programming API designed to take advantage of the latest .NET Framework language innovations. It provides both DOM- and XQuery/XPath-like functionality in a consistent programming experience across the different LINQ-enabled data access technologies.

There are two major perspectives for thinking about and understanding LINQ to XML. From one perspective you can think of LINQ to XML as a member of the LINQ Project family of technologies with LINQ to XML providing an XML Language-Integrated Query capability along with a consistent query experience for objects, relational database (LINQ to SQL, LINQ to DataSet, LINQ to Entities), and other data access technologies as they become LINQ-enabled. From another perspective you can think of LINQ to XML as a full feature in-memory XML programming API comparable to a modernized, redesigned Document Object Model (DOM) XML Programming API plus a few key features from XPath and XSLT.

LINQ to XML is designed to be a lightweight XML programming API. This is true both from a conceptual perspective, emphasizing a straightforward, easy to use programming model, and from a memory and performance perspective. Its public data model is aligned as much as possible with the W3C XML Information Set.

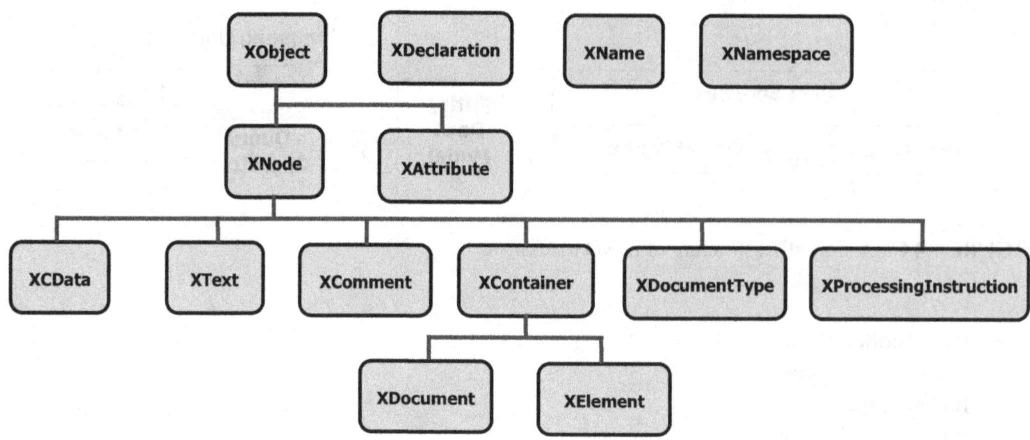

FIGURE 4.45 The LINQ to XML class hierarchy.

4.8.1 LINQ to XML Class Hierarchy

First let's have a global picture about the LINQ to XML Class Hierarchy that is shown in Figure 4.45.

The following important points should be noticed when study this class hierarchy:

1. Although XElement is low in the class hierarchy, it is the fundamental class in LINQ to XML. XML trees are generally made up of a tree of XElements. XAttributes are name/value pairs associated with an XElement. XDocuments are created only if necessary, such as to hold a DTD or top-level XML processing instruction (XProcessingInstruction). All other XNodes can only be leaf nodes under an XElement, or possibly an XDocument (if they exist at the root level).
2. XAttribute and XNode are peers derived from a common base class XObject. XAttributes are not XNodes because XML attributes are really name value pairs associated with an XML element not nodes in the XML tree. Contrast this with W3C DOM.
3. XText and XCData are exposed in this version of LINQ to XML, but, as discussed above, it is best to think of them as a semi-hidden implementation detail except when exposing text nodes is necessary. As a user, you can get back the value of the text within an element or attribute as a string or other simple value.
4. The only XNode that can have children is an XContainer, meaning either an XDocument or XElement. An XDocument can contain an XElement (the root element), an XDeclaration, an XDocumentType, or an XProcessingInstruction. An XElement can contain another XElement, an XComment, an XProcessingInstruction, and text (which can be passed in a variety of formats, but will be represented in the XML tree as text).

In addition to this class hierarchy, some other important components applied in XML also play key roles in LINQ to XML. One of them is the XML names.

XML names, often a complex subject in XML programming APIs, are represented simply in LINQ to XML. An XML name is represented by an XNamespace object (which encapsulates the XML namespace URI) and a local name. An XML namespace serves the same purpose that a namespace does in your .NET Framework-based programs, allowing you to uniquely qualify the names of your classes. This helps ensure that you don't run into a name conflict with other users or built-in names. When you have identified an XML namespace, you can choose a local name that needs to be unique only within your identified namespace.

```
XElement faculties = new XElement("faculties",
                     new XElement("faculty",
                     new XElement("faculty_name", "Patrick Tones"),
                     new XElement("phone", "750-378-0144"),
                     new XElement("title", "Associate Professor"),
                     new XElement("office", "MTC-387"),
                     new XElement("college", "Main University"),
                     new XElement("email", "ptones@college.edu"),
                     new XElement("faculty_id", "P68042")));
```

FIGURE 4.46 A sample XML file created using LINQ to XML.

4.8.2 Manipulate XML Elements

LINQ to XML provides a full set of methods for manipulating XML. You can insert, delete, copy, and update XML content. Before we can continue to discuss these data actions, first we need to show your guys how to create a sample XML element file using LINQ to XML.

4.8.2.1 Creating XML from Scratch

LINQ to XML provides a powerful approach to creating XML elements. This is referred to as *functional construction*. Functional construction lets you create all or part of your XML tree in a single statement. For example, to create a **facultiesXElement**, you could use the following code that is shown in Figure 4.46.

By indenting, the XElement constructor resembles the structure of the underlying XML. Functional construction is enabled by a XElement constructor that takes a **params** object. An example of the Functional construction is shown below.

```
public XElement(XName faculty_name, params object[] contents)
```

The *contents* parameter is extremely flexible, supporting any type of object that is a legitimate child of an XElement. Parameters can be any of the following:

- A *string*, which is added as text content. This is the recommended pattern to add a string as the value of an element; the LINQ to XML implementation will create the internal XText node.
- An **XText**, which can have either a string or **CData** value, added as child content. This is mainly useful for **CData** values; using a *string* is simpler for ordinary string values.
- An **XElement**, which is added as a child element.
- An **XAttribute**, which is added as an attribute.
- An **XProcessingInstruction** or **XComment**, which is added as child content.
- An IEnumerable, which is enumerated, and these rules are applied recursively.
- Anything else, **ToString()** is called and the result is added as text content.

The term CDATA, meaning *character data*, is used for distinct, but related purposes in the markup languages SGML and XML. The term indicates that a certain portion of the document is general *character data*, rather than non-character data or character data with a more specific, limited structure.

In the above example showing functional construction, a string ("Patrick Tones") is passed into the **faculty_name** XElement constructor. This could have been a variable (for example, **newXElement("faculty_name", facultyName)**), it could have been a different type besides string (for example, **new XElement("quantity", 55)**), and it could have been the result of a function call like the one that is shown in Figure 4.47.

```
{
    ...
    XElement qty = new XElement("quantity", GetQuantity());
    ...
}
public int GetQuantity() { return 55; }
```

FIGURE 4.47 A sample functional construction.

```
class Person
{
        public string faculty_name;
        public string[] PhoneNumbers;
}
var persons = new[] {new Person {
                                    faculty_name = "Patrick Tones",
                                    PhoneNumbers = new[] { "750-555-0144", "750-555-0145" }},
new Person { faculty_name = "Gretchen Rivas",
                    PhoneNumbers = new[] { "750-555-0163" }}};
XElement faculties = new XElement("faculties", from f in persons
                                                    select new XElement("faculty",
                                                    new XElement("fname", f.faculty_name),
                                                    from p in f.PhoneNumbers
                                                    select new XElement("phone", p)));
Console.WriteLine(faculties);
```

FIGURE 4.48 A sample query using LINQ to XML.

The code shown in Figure 4.48 reads faculties from an array of **Person** objects into a new XML element **faculties**.

Notice how the inner body of the XML, the repeating **faculty** element, and, for each **faculty**, the repeating **phone** were generated by queries that return an **IEnumerable**.

When an objective of your program is to create an XML output, functional construction lets you begin with the end in mind. You can use functional construction to shape your goal output document and either create the sub-tree of XML items inline, or call out to functions to do the work. Functional construction is instrumental in *transforms*, which belongs to XML Transformation. Transformation is a key usage scenario in XML, and functional construction is well-suited for this task.

Now let's use this sample XML file to discuss the data manipulations using LINQ to XML.

4.8.2.2 Insert XML

You can easily add content to an existing XML tree. To add another *phone* XElement, one can use the **Add()** method which is shown in section **A** in Figure 4.49.

This code fragment will add the **mobilePhone** XElement as the *last* child of faculty. If you want to add to the beginning of the children, you can use **AddFirst()**. If you want to add the child in a specific location, you can navigate to a child before or after your target location by using **AddBeforeSelf()** or **AddAfterSelf()**. For example, if you wanted **mobilePhone** to be the second **phone** you could do the coding that is shown in section **B** in Figure 4.49.

Let's look a little deeper at what is happening behind the scenes when adding an element child to a parent element. When you first create an XElement it is *unparented*. If you check its **Parent** property you will get back **null**, which is shown in section **C** in Figure 4.49.

When you use the **Add()**method to add this child element to the parent, LINQ to XML checks to see if the child element is unparented, if so, LINQ to XML *parents* the child element by setting the

```
A   XElement mobilePhone = new XElement("phone", "750-555-0168");
    faculty.Add(mobilePhone);

B   XElement mobilePhone = new XElement("phone", "750-555-0168");
    XElement firstPhone = faculty.Element("phone");
    firstPhone.AddAfterSelf(mobilePhone);

C   XElement mobilePhone = new XElement("phone", "750-555-0168");
    Console.WriteLine(mobilePhone.Parent);     // will print out null

D   faculty.Add(mobilePhone);
    Console.WriteLine(mobilePhone.Parent);     // will print out faculty

E   faculty2.Add(mobilePhone);

F   faculty2.Add(new XElement(mobilePhone));
```

FIGURE 4.49 Some sample codes of using LINQ to XML to insert XML.

child's **Parent** property to the XElement that **Add()** was called on. Section **D** in Figure 4.49 shows this situation.

This is a very efficient technique which is extremely important since this is the most common scenario for constructing XML trees.

To add **mobilePhone** to another faculty, such as faculty2, refer to the codes shown in section **E** in Figure 4.49.

Again, LINQ to XML checks to see if the child element is parented. In this case, the child is already parented. If the child *is* already parented, LINQ to XML *clones* the child element under subsequent parents. This situation can be illustrated by the codes that are shown in section **F** in Figure 4.49.

4.8.2.3 Update XML

To update XML, you can navigate to the XElement whose contents you want to replace, and then use the ReplaceNodes() method. For example, if you wanted to change the phone number of the first phone XElement of a **faculty**, you could do the codes that are shown in section **A** in Figure 4.50.

The method **SetElement()** is designed to work on simple content. With the **SetElement()**, you can operate on the parent. For example, we could have performed the same update we demonstrated above on the first phone number by using the code that is shown in section **B** in Figure 4.50.

The results would be identical. If there had been no phone numbers, an XElement named **"phone"** would have been added under **faculty**. For example, you might want to add an **office** to the **faculty**. If an **office** is already there, you can update it. If it does not exist, you can insert it. This situation is shown in section **C** in Figure 4.50.

If you use **SetElement()** with a value of **null**, the selected XElement will be deleted. You can remove the **office** element completely by using the code that is shown in section **D** in Figure 4.50.

```
A   faculty.Element("phone").ReplaceNodes("750-555-0155");
B   faculty.SetElement("phone", "750-555-0155");
C   faculty.SetElement("office", "MTC-119");
D   faculty.SetElement("office", null);
```

FIGURE 4.50 Some sample codes of using LINQ to XML to update XML.

```
A  faculty.Element("phone").Remove();
B  faculty.Elements("phone").Remove();
C  faculties.Element("faculty").Element("office").RemoveNodes();
D  faculty.SetElement("phone", null);
```

FIGURE 4.51 Some sample codes of using LINQ to XML to delete XML.

Attributes have a symmetric method called **SetAttribute()**, which has the similar functionality as **SetElement()**.

4.8.2.4 Delete XML

To delete XML elements, navigate to the content you want to delete and call the **Remove()**method. For example, if you want to delete the first phone number for a **faculty**, enter the following code that is shown in section **A** in Figure 4.51.

The **Remove()** method also works over an IEnumerable, so you could delete all of the phone numbers for a **faculty** in one call that is shown in section **B** in Figure 4.51.

You can also remove all of the content from an XElement by using the RemoveNodes() method. For example, you could remove the content of the first **faculty**'s first **office** with the statement that is shown in section **C** in Figure 4.51.

Another way to remove an element is to *set* it to **null** using the SetElement() method, which we talked about in the last section, Update XML. An example code is shown in section **D** in Figure 4.51.

4.8.3 Manipulate XML Attributes

There is substantial symmetry between working with XElement and XAttribute classes. However, in the LINQ to XML class hierarchy, XElement and XAttribute are quite distinct and do not derive from a common base class. This is because XML attributes are not nodes in the XML tree; they are unordered name/value pairs associated with an XML element. LINQ to XML makes this distinction; in practice, however, working with XAttribute is quite similar to working with XElement due to the nature of an XML attribute, where they diverge is understandable.

4.8.3.1 Add XML Attributes

Adding an XAttribute is very similar to adding a simple XElement. In the sample XML that is shown in Figure 4.52, notice that each phone number has a *type* attribute that states whether this is a home, work, or mobile phone number.

You create an XAttribute by using functional construction the same way you would create an XElement with a simple type. To create a **faculty** using functional construction, enter the following codes that are shown in Figure 4.53.

Just as you use the **SetElement()** method to update, add, or delete elements with simple types, you can do the same using the **SetAttribute(XName, object)**method on XElement. If the attribute exists, it

```
<faculties>
    <faculty>
      <faculty_name>Patrick Tones</faculty_name>
      <phone type="home">750-555-0144</phone>
      <phone type="work">750-555-0145</phone>
    </faculty>
```

FIGURE 4.52 A sample XML attributes.

```
XElement faculty = new XElement("faculty",
                        new XElement("faculty_name", "Patrick Tones"),
                        new XElement("phone",
                        new XAttribute("type", "home"),
                        "750-555-0144" ),
                        new XElement("phone",
                        new XAttribute("type", "work"),
                        "750-555-0145"));
```

FIGURE 4.53 A sample code to create an XAttribute.

will be updated. If the attribute does not exist, it will be added. If the value of the **object** is **null**, the attribute will be deleted.

4.8.3.2 Get XML Attributes

The primary method for accessing an XAttribute is by using the Attribute(XName) method on XElement. For example, to use the *type* attribute to obtain the contact's home phone number, one can use the following piece of codes that are shown in section **A** in Figure 4.54.

Notice that how the Attribute(XName) works similarly to the Element(XName) method. Also, notice that there are identical explicit cast operators, which lets you cast an XAttribute to a variety of simple types.

4.8.3.3 Delete XML Attributes

If you want to delete an attribute you can use **Remove()** or **SetAttribute(XName, object)** method, passing null as the value of object. For example, to delete the type attribute from the first phone using the **Remove()** method, use the code that is shown in section **B** in Figure 4.54.

Alternatively you can use the **SetAttribute()** method with a **null** argument to perform this deleting operation. An example code is shown in section **C** in Figure 4.54.

We have provided a very detailed discussion about the basic components on manipulating XML elements and attributes, now let's go a little deep on the query XML with LINQ to XML.

4.8.4 Query XML with LINQ to XML

The major differentiator for LINQ to XML and other in-memory XML programming APIs is Language-Integrated Query (LINQ). LINQ provides a consistent query experience across different data models as well as the ability to mix and match data models within a single query. This section describes how to use Language-Integrated Query with XML. The following section contains a few examples of using Language-Integrated Query across data models.

Standard query operators form a complete query language for IEnumerable<T>. Standard query operators show up as extension methods on any object that implements IEnumerable<T> and can be invoked like any other method. This approach, calling query methods directly, can be referred to as

```
A   foreach (p in faculty.Elements("phone"))
    {
        if ((string)p.Attribute("type") == "home")
          Console.Write("Home phone is: " + (string)p);
    }

B   faculty.Elements("phone").First().Attribute("type").Remove();

C   faculty.Elements("phone").First().SetAttribute("type", null);
```

FIGURE 4.54 A sample code to get and delete a XAttribute.

explicit dot notation. In addition to standard query operators are query expressions for five common query operators:

- Where
- Select
- SelectMany
- OrderBy
- GroupBy

Query expressions provide an ease-of-use layer on top of the underlying explicit dot notation similar to the way that foreach is an ease-of-use mechanism that consists of a call to GetEnumerator() and a while loop. When working with XML, you will probably find both approaches useful. An orientation of the explicit dot notation will give you the underlying principles behind XML Language-Integrated Query, and help you to understand how query expressions simplify things.

The LINQ to XML integration with Language-Integrated Query is apparent in three ways:

1) Leveraging standard query operators
2) Using XML query extensions
3) Using XML transformation

The first is common with any other Language-Integrated Query enabled data access technology and contributes to a consistent query experience. The last two provide XML-specific query and transform features.

4.8.4.1 Standard Query Operators and XML

LINQ to XML fully leverages standard query operators in a consistent manner exposing collections that implement the IEnumerable interface. We have provided a very detailed discussion about the Standard Query Operators in Sections 4.1.2–4.1.4 in this chapter. Review those sections for details on how to use standard query operators. In this section, we will cover two scenarios that occasionally arise when using standard query operators.

First let's create a XElement with multiple elements that can be queried by using a single Select Standard Query Operator. Enter the following codes that are shown in Figure 4.55 to create this sample XElement.

In this XElement, the faculty information is directly created under the root <faculties> element rather than under each separate <faculty> elements. In this way, we flatten out our faculty list and make it simple to be queried.

To use the Standard Query Operator Select to perform the LINQ to XML query, you can use a piece of sample codes that are shown in Figure 4.56. Notice that we used an array initializer to create the sequence of children that will be placed directly under the **faculties** element.

4.8.4.2 XML Query Extensions

XML-specific query extensions provide you with the query operations you would expect when working in an XML tree data structure. These XML-specific query extensions are analogous to the **XPath** axes. For example, the Elements() method is equivalent to the **XPath*** (star) operator. The following sections describe each of the XML-specific query extensions in turn.

The Elements query operator returns the child elements for each XElement in a sequence of XElements (IEnumerable<XElement>). For example, to get the child elements for every faculty in the faculty list, you could do the following:

```
foreach (XElement fi in faculties.Elements("faculty").Elements())
{
    Console.WriteLine(fi);
}
```

```
<faculties>
  <!-- contact -->
  <faculty_name>Patrick Tones</faculty_name>
  <phone type="home">750-555-0144</phone>
  <phone type="work">750-555-0145</phone>
  <office>MTC-319</office>
  <title>Associate Professor</title>
  <email>ptones@college.edu</email>
  <!-- contact -->
  <faculty_name>Greg River</faculty_name>
  <office>MTC-330</office>
  <title>Assistant Professor</title>
  <email>griver@college.edu</email>
  <!-- contact -->
  <faculty_name>Scott Money</faculty_name>
  <phone type="home">750-555-0134</phone>
   <phone type="mobile">750-555-0177</phone>
  <office>MTC-335</office>
  <title>Professor</title>
  <email>smoney@college.edu</email>
</faculties>
```

FIGURE 4.55 A sample code to create a XElement.

```
new XElement("faculties",
              from c in faculties.Elements("faculty")
              select new object[]
              {
                  new XComment("faculty"),
                  new XElement("faculty_name", (string)c.Element("faculty_name")),
                  c.Elements("phone"),
                  new XElement("office", c.Element("office"))
              });
```

FIGURE 4.56 A sample code to perform the query to a XElement.

Note that the two Elements() methods used in this example are different, although they do identical things. The first Elements is calling the XElement method Elements(), which returns an IEnumerable<XObject> containing the child elements in the single XElement faculties. The second Elements() method is defined as an extension method on IEnumerable<XObject>. It returns a sequence containing the child elements of every XElement in the list.

If you want all of the children with a particular name, you can use the Elements(XName) overload. A piece of sample codes is shown below:

```
foreach (XElement pi in faculties.Elements("faculty").Elements("phone"))
{
   Console.WriteLine(pi);
}
```

This would return all phone numbers related to all children.

4.8.4.3 Using Query Expressions with XML

There is nothing unique in the way that LINQ to XML works with query expressions so we will not repeat the information here. The following shows a few simple examples of using query expressions with LINQ to XML.

```
A  from f  in faculties.Elements("faculty")
   where (string) f.Element("office") == "MTC-3.*"
   orderby (string) f.Element("faculty_name")
   select (string) f.Element("faculty_name");

B  from f in faculties.Elements("faculty"), p in f.Elements("phone")
   where (string) f.Element("faculty_id") == "B.*" && p.Value.StartsWith("750")
   orderby (string) f.Element("faculty_name")
   select f;

C  from s in students.Elements("student"), average = students.Elements("student").
   Average(x => (int) x.Element("gpa"))
   where (int) s.Element("gpa") > average
   select s;
```

FIGURE 4.57 A sample code to perform the query using query expressions with XML.

The query shown in section **A** in Figure 4.57 retrieves all of the offices from the faculties, orders them by faculty_name, and then returns them as **string** (the result of this query is IEnumerable<string>).

The query shown in section **B** in Figure 4.57 retrieves all faculty members from faculty that have the **faculty_id** that starts from B and have an area code of 750 ordered by the **faculty_name**. The result of this query is IEnumerable<XElement>.

Another example shown in section **C** in Figure 4.57 retrieving the students that have a GPA that is greater than the average GPA.

4.8.4.4 Using XPath and XSLT with LINQ to XML

LINQ to XML supports a set of "bridge classes" that allow it to work with existing capabilities in the System.Xml namespace, including XPath and XSLT. A point to be noticed is that System.Xml supports only the 1.0 version of these specifications in "Orcas."

Extension methods supporting XPath are enabled by referencing the System.Xml.XPath namespace by adding this namespace typing: using System.Xml.XPath; in the namespace declaration section on the code window of each project.

This brings into scope CreateNavigator overloads to create XpathNavigator objects, XPathEvaluate overloads to evaluate an XPath expression, and XPathSelectElement[s] overloads that work much like SelectSingleNode and XPatheXelectNodes methods in the System.Xml DOM API. To use namespace-qualified XPath expressions, it is necessary to pass in a NamespaceResolver object, just as with DOM.

For example, to display all elements with the name "phone", the following codes can be developed:

```
foreach (var phone in faculties.XPathSelectElements("//phone"))
{
    Console.WriteLine(phone);
}
```

Likewise, XSLT is enabled by referencing the System.Xml.Xsl namespace by typing: using System.Xml.Xsl in the namespace declaration section on the code window of each project. That allows you to create an XPathNavigator using the XDocumentCreateNavigator() method and pass it to the Transform() method.

4.8.4.5 Mixing XML and Other Data Models

LINQ provides a consistent query experience across different data models via standard query operators and the use of Lambda Expressions that will be discussed in the next section. It also provides the ability to mix and match LINQ-enabled data models/APIs within a single query. This section provides a simple example of two common scenarios that mix relational data with XML, using our CSE_DEPT sample database.

4.8.4.5.1 Reading from a Database to XML

Figure 4.58 shows a simple example of reading from the CSE_DEPT database (using LINQ to SQL) to retrieve the faculties from the Faculty table, and then transforming them into XML.

4.8.4.5.2 Reading XML and Updating a Database

You can also read XML and put that information into a database. For this example, assume that you are getting a set of faculty members updates in XML format. For simplicity, the update records contain only the phone number changes.

First let's create a sample XML, which is shown in Figure 4.59.

To accomplish this update, you query for each facultyUpdate element and call the database to get the corresponding Faculty record. Then, you update the Faculty column with the new phone number. A piece of sample codes to fulfill this functionality is shown in Figure 4.60.

```
XElement Faculty Faculties = new XElement("Faculties",
                                from f in db.Faculties
                                where f.faculty_id == "B*"
                                select new XElement("Faculty",
                                new XAttribute("facultyName", f.faculty_name),
                                new XElement("Office", f.office),
                                new XElement("Title", f.title),
                                new XElement("Phone", f.phone),
                                new XElement("Email", f.email)));
Console.WriteLine(Faculty Faculties);
```

FIGURE 4.58 A sample code to perform the query using mixing XML.

```
facultyUpdates>
  <facultyUpdate>
    <faculty_id>D55990</faculty_id>
    <phone>750-555-0103</phone>
  </facultyUpdate>
  <facultyUpdate>
    <faculty_id>E23456</faculty_id>
    <phone>750-555-0143</phone>
  </facultyUpdate>
</facultyUpdates>
```

FIGURE 4.59 A sample XML.

```
foreach (var fi  in facultyUpdates.Elements("facultyUpdate"))
{
     Faculty faculty = db.Faculties.
     First(f => f.faculty_id == (string)fi.Element("faculty_id"));
     faculty.Phone = (string)fi.Element("phone");
}
db.SubmitChanges();
```

FIGURE 4.60 A piece of sample codes to read and update database.

At this point, we have finished the discussion about the LINQ to XML. Next we will have a closer look at the C# 3.0 language enhancement for LINQ.

4.9 C# 3.0 LANGUAGE ENHANCEMENT FOR LINQ

C# 3.0 introduces several language extensions that build on C# 2.0 to support the creation and use of higher-order, functional-style class libraries. The extensions enable construction of compositional APIs that have equal expressive power of query languages in domains such as relational databases and XML.

Compared with C# 2.0, significant enhancements have been added into C# 3.0, and these enhancements are mainly developed to support the Language-Integrated Query (LINQ). LINQ is a series of language extensions that supports data querying in a type-safe way; it is released with an elder version of Visual Studio, Visual Studio.NET 2008. The data to be queried, which we have discussed in the previous sections in this chapter, can take the form of objects (LINQ to Objects), databases (LINQ-enabled ADO.NET, which includes LINQ to SQL, LINQ to DataSet and LINQ to Entities), XML (LINQ to XML) and so on.

In addition to those general LINQ topics, special improvements on LINQ are made for C# and involved in C# 3.0. The main components of these improvements include:

- Lambda Expressions
- Extension Methods
- Implicitly Typed Local Variables
- Query Expressions

Let's have a detailed discussion for these topics one by one.

4.9.1 Lambda Expressions

Lambda expressions are a language feature that is similar in many ways to anonymous methods. In fact, if lambda expressions had been developed and implemented into the language first, there would have been no need for anonymous methods. The basic idea of using lambda expressions is that you can treat code as data. In the early versions of C#, such as C# 1.0, it is very common to pass strings, integers, reference types, and so on to methods so that the methods can work on those values. Anonymous methods and lambda expressions extend the range of the values to include code blocks. This concept is common in functional programming.

The syntax of lambda expressions can be expressed as a comma-delimited list of parameters with the lambda operator (=>) followed by an expression. For more complicated lambda expressions, a statement block can be followed after the lambda operator. A simple example of lambda expression used in C# looks like:

```
x => y
```

where x on the left side of the lambda operator is the input parameter and the *y* on the right side of the lambda operator is the output parameter. The data type of both input and the output parameters should be explicitly indicated by the delegate. Therefore, the lambda expressions are closely related to the delegate. This lambda expression can be read as *input x and output y*. The syntax of this kind of simple lambda expressions can be written as:

```
(param1, param2, ….   paramN) => output
```

A parenthesis should be used to cover all input parameters.

For more complicated lambda expressions, a statement block should be adopted. An example of this kind of syntax is shown below:

```
(x, y) => { if (x > y) return x; else return y; }
```

One point to be noticed is that the data type of both the input and the output parameters must be identical with those types defined in the delegate. For example, in the previous sample expression x => y, if the input x is defined as a string and the output is defined as an integer by the delegate, the output must be converted to an integer type by using the following lambda expression:

```
x => y.Length
```

where Length is a method to convert the input from a string to an integer.

Another example of using lambda expressions to perform LINQ query is:

```
IEnumerable<Faculty> faculty = EnumerableExtensions.Where(faculties, f =>
f.faculty_name == "Ying Bai");
```

Here the Standard Query Operator method Where() is used as a filter in this query. The input is an object with a type of faculties, and the output is a string variable. The compiler is able to infer that "f" refers to a faculty because the first parameter of the Where() method is IEnumerable<Faculty>, such that T must, in fact, be Faculty. Using this knowledge, the compiler also verifies that Faculty has a faculty_name member. Finally, there is no return keyword specified. In the syntactic form, the return member is omitted but this is merely syntactic convenience. The result of the expression is still considered to be the return value.

Lambda expressions also support a more verbose syntax that allows you to specify the types explicitly, as well as execute multiple statements. An example of this kind of syntax is:

```
return EnumerableExtensions.Where(faculties, (Faculty f) => {string id =
faculty_id; return f.faculty_id = id;});
```

Here the EnumerableExtensions class is used to allow us to access and use the static method Where() since all Standard Query Operator methods are static methods defined in either Enumerable or Queryable classes. As you know, a static method is defined as a class method and can be accessed and used by each class in which that method is defined. Is that possible for us to access a static method from an instance of that class? Generally, this will be considered as a stupid question since that is impossible. Is there any way to make it possible? The answer is maybe. To get that question answered correctly, let's go to the next topic.

4.9.2 Extension Methods

Regularly, static methods can only be accessed and used by classes in which those static methods are defined. For example, all Standard Query Operator methods, as we discussed in Sections 4.1.3 and 4.1.4, are static methods defined in either Enumerable or Queryable classes and can be accessed by those classes directly. But those static methods cannot be accessed by any instance of those classes. Let's use an example to make this story clear.

Figure 4.61 shows a piece of codes that defines both class and instance methods.

In this example, the method **ConvertToUpper()** is an instance method and **ConvertToLower()** is a class method. To call these methods, a different calling strategy must be utilized. To call and execute the instance method **ConvertToUpper()**, one must first create a new instance of the class Conversion, and then call that method. To call and execute the class method **ConvertToLower()**, one can directly call it

```
public static class Convertion
{
    public string ConvertToUpper(string input)
    {
        return input.ToUpper();
    }
    public static string ConvertToLower(string input)
    {
        return input.ToLower();
    }
}
```

FIGURE 4.61 An example of defining class and instance method.

```
// call instance method ConvertToUpper.
// first create a new instance of the class Conversion
Conversion conv = new Conversion();
string instResult = conv.ConvertToUpper("conversion");
// call class method ConvertToLower.
string classResult = Conversion.ConvertToLower("CONVERSION");
```

FIGURE 4.62 An example of calling class and instance method.

with the class name prefixed in front of that method. Figure 4.62 shows a piece of code to call these two methods.

In some situations, the query would become very complicated if one wants to call those static methods from any instance of those classes. To solve this complex issue, extension methods are developed to simplify the query structures and syntax.

To declare an extension method from existing static method, just add the keyword *this* to the first argument of that static method. For example, to make the class method **ConvertToLower()** an extension method, add the keyword *this* to the first argument of that method, as shown in Figure 4.63.

Now the class method **ConvertToLower()** has been converted to an extension method and can be accessed by any instance of the class Conversion.

The extension methods have the following important properties:

1) The extension method will work as an instance method of any object with the same type as the extension method's first argument's data type.
2) The extension methods can only be declared in static classes.
3) Both the class and the extension method are prefixed by the keyword *static*.

```
public static class Convertion
{
    // declare the class method ConvertToLower to extension method.
    public static string ConvertToLower(this string input)
    {
        return input.ToLower();
    }
}
```

FIGURE 4.63 Declare the class method ConvertToLower() to extension method.

Refer to Figure 4.63, the extension method **ConvertToLower()** has a data type of string since the first argument's type is string. This method is declared in a static class Conversion, and both class and this method are prefixed by the keyword *static*.

4.9.3 Implicitly Typed Local Variables

In LINQ query, there's another language feature known as implicitly typed local variables (or *var* for short) that instructs the compiler to infer the type of a local variable. As you know, with the addition of anonymous types to C#, a new problem becomes a main concern, which is that if a variable is being instantiated that is an unnamed type, as in an anonymous type, of what type variable would you assign it to? LINQ queries belong to strongly typed queries with two popular types: IEnumerable<T> and IQueryable<T>, as we discussed at the beginning of this chapter. Figure 4.64 shows an example of this kind of variable with an anonymous type.

A compiling error will be encountered when this piece of codes to be compiled since the data type of the variable faculty is not indicated. In C# 3.0 language enhancement for LINQ, a new terminology, implicitly typed local variable *var*, is developed to solve this kind of anonymous type problem. Refer to Figure 4.65. The codes written in Figure 4.64 can be re-written as those codes shown in Figure 4.65.

This time there would be no error if you compile this piece of codes since the keyword *var* informs the compiler to implicitly infer the variable type from the variable's initializer. In this example, the initializer for this implicitly typed variable faculty is a string collection. This means that all implicitly typed local variables are statically type checked at the compile time, therefore an initializer is required to allow compiler to implicitly infer the type from it.

The implicitly typed local variables mean that those variables are just local within a method, for example, the faculty is valid only inside the main() method in the previous example. It is impossible for them to escape the boundaries of a method, property, indexer, or other block because the type cannot be explicitly stated, and *var* is not legal for fields or parameter types.

Another important terminology applied in C# 3.0 language enhancement for LINQ is the object initializers. Object initializers basically allow the assignment of multiple properties or fields in a single expression. For example, a common pattern for object creation is shown in Figure 4.66.

In this example, there is no constructor of Faculty that takes a faculty id, name, office and title; however, there are four properties, faculty_id, faculty_name, office and title, which can be set once

```
public static class Main()
{
    // declare an anonymous type variable.
    faculty = new { faculty_id = "B78880", faculty_name = "Ying Bai" };
    Console.WriteLine("faculty information {0}, {1}", faculty.faculty_id + ". " + faculty.faculty_name);
}
```

FIGURE 4.64 Declare an anonymous type variable.

```
public static class Main()
{
    // declare an anonymous type variable.
    var faculty = new { faculty_id = "B78880", faculty_name = "Ying Bai" };
    Console.WriteLine("faculty information {0}, {1}", faculty.faculty_id + ". " + faculty.faculty_name);
}
```

FIGURE 4.65 Declare an anonymous type variable using implicitly typed local variable.

```
Faculty  faculty = new Faculty();
faculty.faculty_id = "B78880";
faculty.faculty_name = "Ying Bai";
faculty.office = "MTC-211";
faculty.title = "Associate Professor";
```

FIGURE 4.66 An example of using the object initializer.

an instance faculty is created. Object initializers allow creating a new instance with all necessary initializations being performed at the same time as the instantiation process.

4.9.4 Query Expressions

To perform any kind of LINQ query, such as LINQ to Objects, LINQ to ADO.NET, LINQ to XML, a valid query expression is needed. The query expressions implemented in C# 3.0 have a syntax that is closer to SQL statements and are composed of some clauses. One of the most popular query expressions is the foreach statement. As this foreach is executed, the compiler converts it into a loop with calls to methods such as **GetEnumerator()** and **MoveNext()**. The main advantage of using the foreach loop to perform the query is that it provides a significant simplicity in enumerating through arrays, sequences and collections and returns the terminal results in an easy way. A typical syntax of query expression is shown in Figure 4.67.

Generally, a query expression is composed of two blocks. The top block in Figure 4.67 is the from-clause block and the bottom block is the query-body block. The from-clause block only takes charge of the data query information (no query results), but the query-body block performs the real query and contains the real query results.

Referring to the syntax represented in Figure 4.67, the following components should be included in a query expression:

- A query variable must be defined first in either explicitly (IEnumerable<T>) or implicitly (var) type.
- A query expression can be represented in either query syntax or method syntax.
- A query expression must start with a **from** clause, and must end with a **select** or **group** clause. Between the first **from** clause and the last **select** or **group** clause, it can contain one or more of these optional clauses: **where**, **orderby, join, let** and even additional **from** clauses.

In all LINQ queries (including LINQ to DataSet), all of clauses will be converted to the associated Standard Query Operator methods, such as **From(), Where(), OrderBy(), Join(), Let()** and **Select()**, as the

```
var query_variable = from [identifier] in [data source]
                     let [expression]
                     where [boolean expression]
                     order by [[expression](ascending/descending)], [optionally repeat]
                     select [expression]
                     group [expression] by [expression] into [expression]

foreach (var range_variable  in query_variable)
{
    //pick up or retrieve back each element from the range_variable....
}
```

FIGURE 4.67 A typical syntax of query expression.

```
static void Main()
{
    IEnumerable<Faculty> faculty =  db.Faculties.Where(f => f.faculty_id == "D.*",
                                                  f => f.college == "U.*",
                                                  f => f.title == "Associate Professor");
    // Execute the query to produce the results
    foreach (Faculty  fi in faculty)
    {
      Console.WriteLine("{0}\n{1}\n{2}\n{3}\n{4}", f.faculty_name, f.title, f.office, f.phone, f.email);
    }
}
```

FIGURE 4.68 A real example of query expression.

queries are compiled. Refer to Figure 4.4 in this chapter to get the most often used Standard Query Operators and their definitions.

In LINQ, a query variable is always strongly typed and it can be any variable that stores a query instead of the results of a query. More specifically, a query variable is always an enumerable type that will produce a sequence of elements when it is iterated over in a **foreach** loop or a direct call to its method IEnumerator.MoveNext.

A very detailed discussion about the query expression has been provided in Sections 4.5.1.1 and 4.5.1.2 in this chapter. Refer to those sections to get more details for this topic.

Before we can finish this chapter, a real query example implemented in our project is shown in Figure 4.68.

4.10 CHAPTER SUMMARY

Language-Integrated Query (LINQ), which is built on .NET Frameworks 3.5, is a popular technology released with Visual Studio.NET 2008 by Microsoft. LINQ is designed to query general data sources represented in different formats, such as Objects, DataSet, SQL Server database, Entities and XML. The innovation of LINQ bridges the gap between the world of objects and the world of data.

An introduction to LINQ general programming guide is provided in the first part in this chapter. Some popular interfaces widely used in LINQ, such as IEnumerable, IEnumerable<T>, IQueryable and IQueryable<T>, and Standard Query Operators (SQO) including the deferred and non-deferred SQO, are discussed in that part.

An introduction to LINQ Query is given in the second part in this chapter. Following this introduction, a detailed discussion and analysis about the LINQ that is implemented for different data sources is provided based on a sequence listed below.

1) Architecture and Components of LINQ
2) LINQ to Objects
3) LINQ to DataSet
4) LINQ to SQL
5) LINQ to Entities
6) LINQ to XML
7) C# 3.0 Language Enhancement for LINQ

Both literal introductions and actual examples are provided for each part listed above to give readers not only a general and global picture about LINQ technique applied for different data, but also practical and real feeling about the program codes developed to realize the desired functionalities.

Twelve real projects are provided in this chapter to help readers to understand and follow up all techniques discussed in this chapter.

After finishing this chapter, readers should be able to:

- Understand the basic architecture and components implemented in LINQ
- Understand the functionalities of Standard Query Operators
- Understand general interfaces implemented in LINQ, such as LINQ to Objects, LINQ to DataSet, LINQ to SQL, LINQ to Entities and LINQ to XML.
- Understand the C# 3.0 language enhancement for LINQ
- Design and build real applications to apply LINQ queries to perform data actions to all different data sources
- Develop and build applications to apply C# 3.0 language enhancement for LINQ to perform all different queries to data sources

Starting from the next chapter, we will concentrate on the database programming with Visual C#.NET using the real projects.

HOMEWORK

I. True/False Selections

____1. LINQ queries are built based on .NET Frameworks 3.5.
____2. The most popular interfaces used for LINQ queries are: IEnumerable, IEnumerable<T>, IQueryable and IQueryable<T>.
____3. IEnumerable interface is used to convert data type of data source to IEnumerable<T> that can be implemented by LINQ queries.
____4. IEnumerable interface is inherited from the class IQueryable.
____5. All Standard Query Operator methods are static methods defined in the IEnumerable class.
____6. IEnumerable and IQueryable interfaces are mainly used for the non-generic collections supported by the earlier versions of C#, such as C# 1.0 or earlier.
____7. All LINQ query expressions can only be represented as query syntax.
____8. All LINQ query expressions will be converted to the Standard Query Operator methods during the compile time by CLR.
____9. The query variable used in LINQ queries contains both the query information and the returned query results.
___10. LINQ to SQL, LINQ to DataSet and LINQ to Entities belong to LINQ to ADO.NET.

II. Multiple Choice Questions

1. The difference between the interfaces IEnumerable and IEnumerable<T> is that the former is mainly used for ______, but the latter is used for _______
   a. Non-generic collections, generic collections
   b. Generic collections, non-generic collections
   c. All collections, partial collections
   d. .NET Frameworks 2.0, .NET Frameworks 3.5
2. The query variable used in LINQ queries contains ________
   a. Query information and query results
   b. Query information
   c. Query results
   d. Standard Query Operator

3. All Standard Query Operator (SQO) methods are defined as _______.This means that these methods can be called either as class methods or as instance methods
   a. Class methods
   b. Instance method
   c. Variable methods
   d. Extension methods
4. One of the SQO methods, the AsEnumerable() operator method, is used to convert the data type of the input object from _______ to _______
   a. IQuerable<T>, Ienumrable<T>
   b. IEnumerable<T>, IEnumerable<T>
   c. Any, IEnumerable<T>
   d. All of them
5. LINQ to Objects is used to query any sequences or collections that are either explicitly or implicitly compatible with ________ sequences or ________ collections
   a. Iquerable, Iquerable<T>
   b. IEnumerable, IENumerable<T>
   c. Deferred SQO, non-deferred SQO
   d. Generic, non-generic
6. LINQ to DataSet is built on the ________ architecture, the codes developed by using that version of ADO.NET will continue to function in a LINQ to DataSet application without modifications
   a. ADO.NET 2.0
   b. ADO.NET 3.0
   c. ADO.NET 3.5
   d. ADO.NET 4.0
7. Two popular LINQ to SQL Tools, _______ and _______, are widely used in developing applications of using LINQ to SQL
   a. Entity Data Model, Entity Data Model Designer
   b. IEnumerable, IEnumerable<T>
   c. SQLMetal, Object Relational Designer
   d. IQueryable, IQueryable<T>
8. LINQ to SQL query is performed on classes that implement the ________ interface. Since the ________ interface is inherited from the ________ with additional components, therefore the LINQ to SQL queries have additional query operators
   a. IEnumerable<T>, IEnumerable<T>, IQueryable<T>
   b. IEnumerable<T>, IQueryable<T>, IEnumerable<T>
   c. IQueryable<T>, IEnumerable<T>, IQueryable<T>
   d. IQueryable<T>, IQueryable<T>, IEnumerable<T>
9. LINQ to Entities queries are performed under the control of the ___________ and the ___________
   a. .NET Frameworks 3.5, ADO.NET 3.5
   b. ADO.NET 3.5 Entity Framework, ADO.NET 3.5 Entity Framework Tools
   c. IEnumerable<T>, IQueryable<T>
   d. Entity Data Model, Entity Data Model Designer
10. To access and implement ADO.NET 3.5 EF and ADO.NET 3.5 EFT, developers need to understand the ____________ that is a core of ADO.NET 3.5 EF
    a. SQLMetal
    b. Object Relational Designer
    c. Generic collections
    d. Entity Data Model

11. Lambda expressions, which is represented by ________, are a language feature that is similar in many ways to ________ methods
    a. =>, Standard Query Operator
    b. =>, anonymous
    c. =>, Generic collection
    d. =>, Iquerable
12. Extension methods are defined as those methods that can be called as either ________ methods or __________ methods
    a. Class, instance
    b. IEnumerable<T>, IQueryable<T>
    c. Generic, non-generic
    d. Static, dynamic
13. In LINQ queries, the data type ***var*** is used to define a(n) ____________, and the real data type of that variable can be inferred by the __________ during the compiling time.
    a. Generic variable, debugger
    b. implicitly typed local variable, compiler
    c. Non-generic variable, builder
    d. IEnumerable<T> variable, loader
14. In LINQ queries, the query expression must start with a ________ clause, and must end with a __________ or _________ clause
    a. begin, select, end
    b. select, where, orderby
    c. from, select, group
    d. query variable, range variable, foreach loop
15. The DataContext is a class that is used to establish a ________ between your project and your database. In addition to this role, the DataContext also provide the function to _______ operations of the Standard Query Operators to the SQL statements that can be run in real databases
    a. Relationship, perform
    b. Reference, translate
    c. Generic collections, transform
    d. Connection, convert

III. Exercises

1. Explain the architecture and components of the LINQ, and illustrate the functionality of these using a block diagram.
2. Explain the execution process of a LINQ query using the foreach statement.
3. Explain the definitions and functionalities of the Standard Query Operator methods.
4. Explain the relationship between the LINQ query expressions and Standard Query Operator methods
5. Explain the definitions and functionalities of IEnumerable, IEnumerable<T>, IQueryable and IQueryable<T> interfaces.
6. Explain the components and procedure used to perform LINQ to SQL queries.

```
List<string> fruits = new List<string> { "apple", "banana", "mango", "orange",
                                         "blueberry", "grape", "strawberry" };

var query = from fruit in fruits
            where fruit.Length < 6
            select fruit;

foreach (string f in query)
   Console.WriteLine(f);
```

FIGURE 4.69 A sample LINQ to object query.

7. A query used for LINQ to Objects, which is represented by a query syntax, is shown in Figure 4.69. Try to convert this query expression to a method's syntax.
8. Illustrate the procedure of creating each entity class for each data table in our sample database **CSE_DEPT** by using the Object Relational Designer, and adding a connection to the selected database using the DataContext class or the derived class from the DataContext class.
9. Explain the difference between the class method and the instance method, and try to illustrate the functionality of an extension method and how to build an extension method by using an example.
10. List three steps of performing the LINQ to DataSet queries.

5 Data Selection Query with Visual C#.NET

The newest Visual Studio release, Visual Studio 2022, adds more new components to simplify the data accessing, inserting and updating functionalities for database development and applications. First of all, Visual Studio 2022 is based on the latest .NET Framework 6.0 with powerful cross-platform 64-bit IDE for desktop and mobile App developments. There are a large number of new features, such as building responsive Web UIs in C# with Blazor, building, debugging, and testing .NET and C++ Apps in Linux environments, using hot reload capabilities across .NET and C++ Apps, and editing and running ASP.NET pages in the Web designer view.

In addition to those features, *Visual Studio 2022* also provides better cross-platform App development tools and the latest version of C++ build tools, including C++ 20 support. Coding with a new Razor editor that can refactor across files in a more quick and efficient way is another new feature. In addition, the diagnosis of issues with visualizations for async operations and automatic analyzers process is also greatly improved.

In summary, Visual Studio 2022 makes it quick and easy to build modern, cloud-based applications with Azure. Furthermore, the new version also has full support for .NET 6 and its unified framework for Web, client, and mobile Apps for both Windows and Mac developers. Visual Studio 2022 also includes robust support for the C++ workload with new productivity features, C++20 tooling, and IntelliSense.

On top of all these features, Visual Studio 2022 also supports some powerful design tools and wizards provided by Microsoft to help users to build and develop database programming easily and efficiently. The most popular design tools and wizards in the new software are

- Data Components in the Toolbox Window
- Wizards in the Data Source Window

Those design tools and wizards are still implemented in Visual Studio 2022, and they can be accessed and used by any .NET-compatible programming language, such as Visual C++, Visual Basic, Visual J# and Visual C#. The Toolbox window in Visual Studio 2022 contains data components that enable you to quickly and easily build simple database applications without needing to deal with complicated coding issues. Combining these data components with wizards, which are located in the Data Source wizard and related to ADO.NET, one can easily develop binding relationships between the data source and controls on the Visual C# windows form object., You can also build simple Visual C# projects to navigate, scan, retrieve and manipulate data stored in the data source with a few lines of code.

This chapter is divided into two parts; Part I provides a detailed description and discussion of how to use Visual Studio design tools and wizards to build simple but efficient database applications without any complicated coding process in the Visual C# environment. In Part II, a deeper digging into how to develop advanced database applications using runtime objects is presented. More complicated coding technology is provided in this part. Data query using the LINQ technology is also discussed in both parts with project examples. Five real examples are provided in detail with these two parts to enable readers to have a clear picture about the development of professional database applications in simple and efficient ways. This chapter concentrates only on the data query applications.

DOI: 10.1201/9781003319832-5

In this chapter, you will:

- Learn and understand the most useful tools and wizards used in developing data query applications
- Learn and understand how to connect a database with different components provided in data providers, and configure this connection with wizards
- Learn and understand how to use **BindingSource** object to display database tables' contents using **DataGridView**
- Learn and understand how to bind a **DataSet** (data source) to various controls in the windows form object
- Learn and understand how to configure, edit **DataAdapter** to build special queries
- Learn and understand how to retrieve data using the LINQ technology from the data source to simplify and improve the efficiency of the data querying
- Build and execute simple dynamic data query commands to retrieve desired data

To successfully complete this chapter, you need to understand topics such as Fundamentals of Databases, which is introduced in Chapter 2, and ADO.NET, which is discussed in Chapter 3. A sample database, **CSE_DEPT**, which was developed in Chapter 2, will be used throughout this chapter.

PART I DATA QUERY WITH VISUAL STUDIO DESIGN TOOLS AND WIZARDS

Before we can start this part a preview of a completed set of Visual Studio design tools and wizards is necessary. This preview can give readers some idea about how to access a database and query data via those design tools and wizards in an efficient and easy way. The database used for this project is SQL Server 2019.

5.1 VISUAL STUDIO DESIGN TOOLS AND WIZARDS

When developing and building a Windows application that needs to interface with a database, one powerful and simple way is to use design tools and wizards provided by Visual Studio. The size of the coding process can be significantly reduced, and the developing procedures can also be greatly simplified. Let us now first take a look at those components which are present in the Toolbox window.

5.1.1 Data Design Tools in the Toolbox Window

Each database-related Windows application contains three components that can be used to develop a database application using the data controls in the Toolbox: **DataSet**, **BindingSource** and **TableAdapter**. Two other useful components are the **DataGridView** and the **BindingNavigator**. All of these components, except for the TableAdapter, are located in the Toolbox window, as shown in Figure 5.1.

Compared with some earlier versions, such as Visual Studio 2003, in which only three components, **DataConnection**, **DataAdapter** and **DataSet**, are used to perform data operations for a data-driven Visual C# application. More components have been added into this Toolbox since Visual Studio 2010.

5.1.1.1 DataSet

A DataSet object can be considered as a container. It is used to hold data from one or more data tables. It maintains the data as a group of data tables with optional relationships defined between

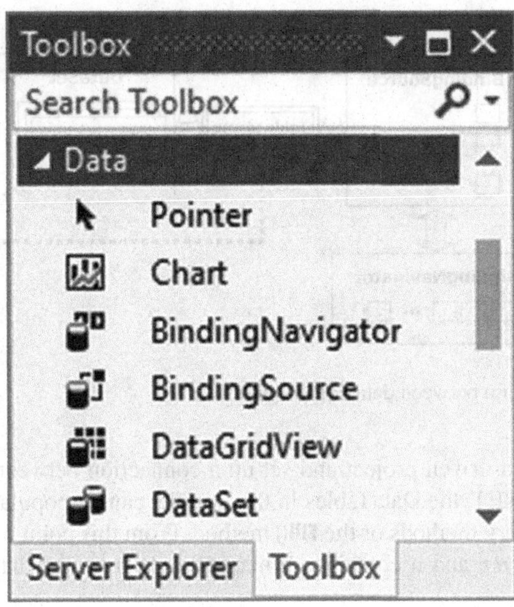

FIGURE 5.1 The data components in toolbox window.

those tables. The definition of the DataSet class is a generic idea, which means that it is not tied to any specific type of database. Data can be loaded into a DataSet by using a TableAdapter from many different databases such as Microsoft Access, Microsoft SQL Server, Oracle, Microsoft Exchange, Microsoft Active Directory, or any OLE DB- or ODBC-compliant database when your application begins to run or the **Form_Load()** event procedure is called if one used a **DataGridView** object.

Although not tied to any specific database, the DataSet class is designed to contain relational tabular data as one would find in a relational database. Each table included in the DataSet is represented in the DataSet as a DataTable. The DataTable can be considered as a direct mapping to the real table in the database. For example, the LogIn data table, LogInDataTable, is a data table component or DataTable that can be mapped to the real table LogIn in the CSE_DEPT database. The relationship between any tables is realized in the DataSet as a DataRelation object. The DataRelation object provides the information that relates a child table to a parent table via a foreign key. A DataSet can hold any number of tables with any number of relationships defined between tables. From this point of view, a DataSet can be considered as a mini database engine, meaning that it can contain all information of tables it holds, such as the column name and data type, all relationships between tables. More importantly, it contains most management functionalities of the tables such as browse, select, insert, update and delete data from tables.

A DataSet is a container and it keeps its data or tables in memory as XML files. In Visual Studio. NET 2003, when one wants to edit the structure of a DataSet, one must do that by editing an XML Schema or XSD file. Although there is a visual designer, the terminology and user interface are not consistent with a DataSet and its constituent objects.

With the Visual Studio 2022, one can easily edit the structure of a DataSet and make any changes to the structure of that DataSet by using the Dataset Designer in the Data Source window. More importantly, one can graphically manipulate the tables and queries in a manner more directly tied to the DataSet rather than having to deal with an XML Schema (XSD).

Summarily, the DataSet object is a very powerful component that can contain multiple data tables with all information related to those tables. By using this object, one can easily browse, access and manipulate data stored in it. We will explore this component in more detail in the following sections when a real project is built.

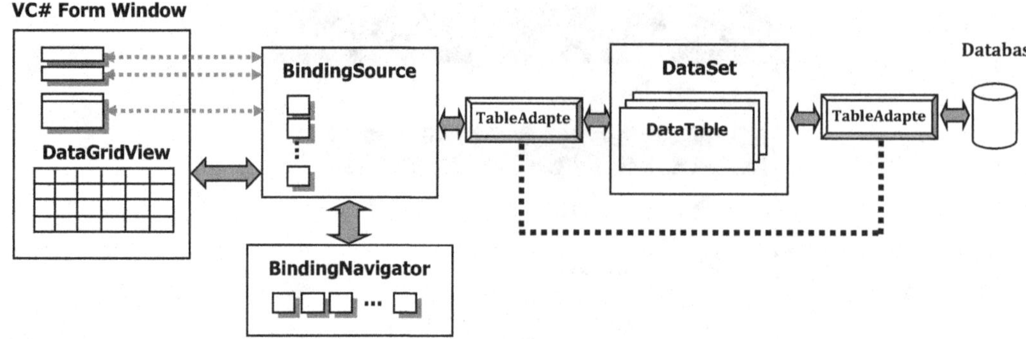

FIGURE 5.2 The relationship between data components.

When your build a data-driven project and set up a connection between your C# project and a database using the ADO.NET, the DataTables in the DataSet can be populated with data from your database by using data query methods or the **Fill()** method. From this point of view, you can consider the DataSet as a *data source* and it contains all mapped data from the database you connected to your project.

Refer to Figure 5.2 for a global picture of the DataSet and other components in the Toolbox window to obtain more detailed ideas for this issue.

5.1.1.2 DataGridView

The next useful data component defined in the Toolbox window is the DataGridView.

Like its name, you can consider the DataGridView as a view container, and it can be used to bind data from your database and display the data in a tabular or a grid format. You can use the DataGridView control to show read-only views of a small amount of data, or you can scale it to show editable views of very large sets of data. The DataGridView control provides many properties that enable you to customize the appearance of the view and properties that allow you to modify the column headers and the data displayed in the grid format. You can also easily customize the appearance of the DataGridView control by choosing among different properties. Many types of data stores can be used as a database, or the DataGridView control can operate with no data source bound to it.

By default, a DataGridView control has the following properties:

- It automatically displays column headers and row headers that remain visible as users scroll the table vertically.
- It has a row header that contains a selection indicator for the current row.
- It has a selection rectangle in the first cell.
- It has columns that can be automatically resized when the user double-clicks the column dividers.
- It automatically supports visual styles on Windows XP and the Windows Server 2003 family when the **EnableVisualStyles** method is called from the application's Main method.

Refer to Figure 5.2 to get a relationship between the DataGridView and other data components. A more detailed description on how to use the DataGridView control to bind and display data in Visual C# will be provided in Section 5.5 of this chapter.

5.1.1.3 BindingSource

The **BindingSource** component has two functionalities. First, it provides a layer of indirection when binding the controls on a form to data in the data source. This is accomplished by binding the BindingSource component to your data source, and then binding the controls on your form to the

BindingSource component. All further interactions with the data, including navigating, sorting, filtering, and updating, are accomplished with calls to the BindingSource component.

Second, the BindingSource component can act as a strongly typed data source. Adding a type to the BindingSource component with the Add method creates a list of that type.

Exactly, the BindingSource control works as a bridge to connect the data bound controls on your Visual C# forms with your data source (DataSet). The BindingSource control can also be considered as a container object and it holds all mapped data from the data source. As a data-driven project runs, the DataSet will be filled with data from the database by using a TableAdapter. In addition, the BindingSource control will create a set of data that are mapped to those filled data in the DataSet. The BindingSource control can hold this set of mapped data and create a one-to-one connection between the DataSet and the BindingSource. This connection is very useful when you perform data binding between controls on the Visual C# form and data in the DataSet. In fact, you set up a connection between your controls on the Visual C# form and those mapped data in the BindingSource object. As your project runs and the data are needed to be reflected on the associated controls, a request to BindingSource is issued and the BindingSource control will control the data accessing to the data source (DataSet) and data updating in those controls. For instance, the DataGridView control will send a request to the BindingSource control when a column sorting action is performed, and the latter will communicate with the data source to complete this sorting.

When perform a data binding in Visual Studio, you need to bind the data referenced by the BindingSource control to the **DataSource** property of your controls on the forms.

5.1.1.4 BindingNavigator

The **BindingNavigator** control allows users to scan and browse all records stored in the data source (DataSet) one by one in a sequence. The BindingNavigator component provides a standard UI with buttons and arrows to enable users to navigate to the first and the previous records as well as the next and the last records in the data source. It also provides textbox controls to display how many records existed in the current data table and the current displayed record's index.

As shown in Figure 5.2, the BindingNavigator is also bound to the BindingSource component as other components did. When the user clicks either the Previous or the Next button on the BindingNavigator UI, a request is sent to the BindingSource for the previous or the next record, and in turn, this request is sent to the data source for picking up the data.

5.1.1.5 TableAdapter

From Figure 5.2, one can find that a **TableAdapter** is equivalent to an adapter and it just works as a connection media between the database and DataSet, and between the BindingSource and the DataSet. This means that the TableAdapter has double functionalities when it works as different roles for the different purposes. For example, as you develop your data-driven applications using the design tools, the data in the database will be populated to the mapped tables in the DataSet using the TableAdapter's **Fill()** method. The TableAdapter also works as an adapter to coordinate the data operations between the BindingSource and the DataSet when the data bound controls in Visual C# form need to be filled or updated.

Prior to Visual Studio 2005, the Data Adapter was the only link between the DataSet and the database. If a change is needed to the data in the DataSet, you need to use a different Data Adapter for each table in the DataSet and have to call the Update method of each Data Adapter.

The TableAdapter is introduced in Visual Studio 2005 and you cannot find this component from the Toolbox window. The TableAdapter belongs to designer-generated component that connect your DataSet objects with their underlying databases, and it will be created automatically when you add and configure new data sources via design tools such as **Data Source Configuration Wizard**.

The TableAdapter is similar to DataAdapter in that both components can handle the data operations between DataSet and the database, but the TableAdapter can contain multiple queries to support multiple tables from the database, allowing one TableAdapter to perform multiple queries to your DataSet. Another important difference between the TableAdapter and the Data Adapter is that each TableAdapter is a unique class that is automatically generated by Visual Studio to work with only the fields you have selected for a specific database object.

The TableAdapter class contains queries used to select data from your database. In addition, it contains different methods to allow users to fill the DataSet with some dynamic parameters in your project with data from the database. You can also use the TableAdapter to build different SQL statements such as Insert, Update and Delete based on the different data operations. A more detailed exploration and implementation of TableAdapter with a real example will be provided in the following sections.

5.1.2 Data Design Wizards in the Data Source Window

Starting with Visual Studio 2005, two new Integrated Development Environment (IDE) features, the **Data Sources** Window and the **Data Source Configuration Wizard**, are added to assist you to set up data access by using the new classes, such as **DataConnector** and **TableAdapter**.

The Data Sources window is used to display the data sources or available databases in your project. You can use the Data Sources window to directly create a user interface (consisting of data-bound controls) by dragging items from the Data Sources window onto Visual C# forms in your project. Each item inside the Data Sources window has a drop-down control list where you can select the type of control to create prior to dragging it onto a form. You can also customize the control list with additional controls, such as controls that you have created.

A more detailed description on how to use the Data Sources window to develop a data-driven project is provided in Section 5.4.

5.1.2.1 Add New Data Source

The first time you create a new data-driven application project in Visual C# 2022 environment there is no any data source that has been added to your project and, therefore, the Data Source window is a blank one with no data source in there. For example, you can create a new Visual C# 2022 Windows application by selecting **File | New | Project** menu items and select the DataSource as the project name. After this new project is created and opened, you can find and open the **Data Sources** window by clicking the **View | OtherWindows | Data Sources** menu item from the menu bar, which is shown in Figure 5.3.

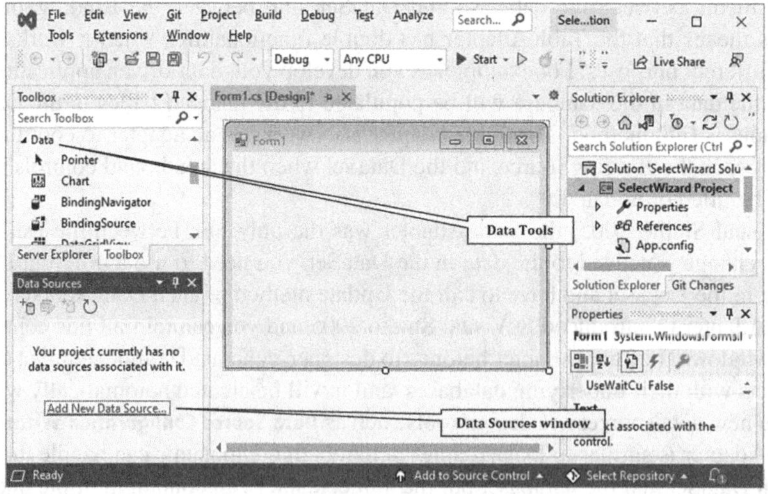

FIGURE 5.3 The data sources window.

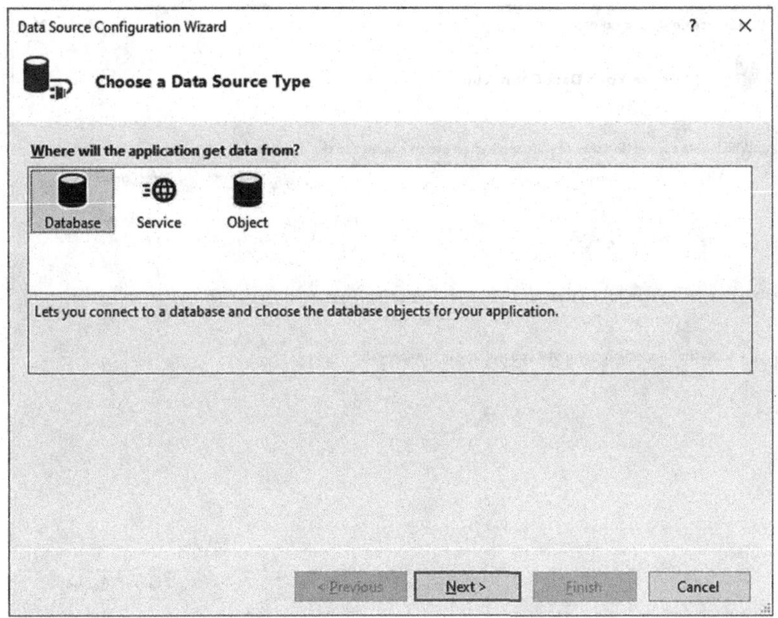

FIGURE 5.4 The data source configuration wizard.

When you create a new Visual C# database application project in the first time, the opened Data Sources window is a blank one sine you have no any previous database connected to this new project. To add a new data source or DataSet to this new project, you can click **Add New Data Source** link from the Data Sources window.

Once you click **Add New Data Source** link from the Data Sources window to add a new data source, The Data Source Configuration Wizard will be displayed. You need to use this wizard to select your desired database to be connected with your new project.

5.1.2.2 Data Source Configuration Wizard

The opened **Data Source Configuration Wizard** is shown in Figure 5.4.

By using the Data Source Configuration Wizard, you can select your desired data source or database that will be connected to your new project. The Data Source Configuration Wizard supports three types of data sources. The first option, **Database**, allows you to select a data source from a database server on your local computer or on a network server. The examples for this kind of data sources are Microsoft Access 2017, SQL Server 2019 Express, SQL Server 2019 or Oracle Database 18c XE. This option also allows you to choose either an .MDF SQL Server database file, a Microsoft Access .MDB or .ACCDB file. The difference between a SQL Server database and a SQL Server database file is that the former is a complete database that integrates the database management system with data tables to form a body or a package, but the latter is only a database file. The second option, **Service**, enables you to select a data source that is located at a Web service. The third option, **Object**, allows you to bind your user interface to one of your own database classes.

Click the **Next** button after you selected your desired source, and the next step in the Data Source Configuration Wizard allows you select your database model. Currently, only one model is available, which is **DataSet**. This means that you can set or build a DataSet to connect to your actual database and fill that DataSet with a data table, a data row, or a data column from the real database. That DataSet is only a mapping to your real database and it can be updated with any updating in your database. Select that DataSet model and click on the **Next** button to continue.

The next wizard, **Choose Your Data Connection**, allows you to either select an existing data connection or create a new connection to your data source, which is shown in Figure 5.5.

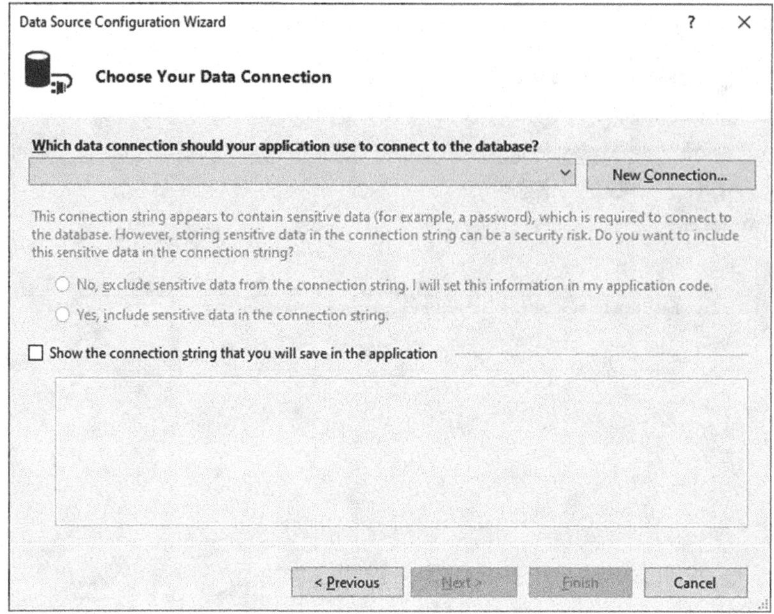

FIGURE 5.5 The next step in the data source configuration wizard.

The first time you run this wizard, there is no pre-existing database connection available. On subsequent uses of this wizard, however, you can reuse previously created connections. To make a new connection, click the **New Connection** button, then the **Choose Data Source** wizard is displayed, which is shown in Figure 5.6.

Six (6) popular data sources can be chosen based on your application, which are:

1) Microsoft Access Database File
2) Microsoft ODBC Data Source
3) Microsoft SQL Server
4) Microsoft SQL Server Database File
5) Oracle Database
6) Other

The second option is to allow users to select any kind of data source that is compatible with a Microsoft ODBC data source. The fourth option is for users who select a SQL Server 2005 Express as the data source.

Now let's use and connect to our SQL Server 2019 Express sample database, **CSE_DEPT**, which was built in Chapter 2, as an example to illustrate this Add Data Source procedure.

Perform the following operations to complete this adding procedure:

1) On the opened Choose Data Source wizard, as shown in Figure 5.6, select **Microsoft SQL Server** item from the **Data source** list (Figure 5.6), then click on the **Next** button.
2) The next wizard, **Add Connection**, is opened, as shown in Figure 5.7. Enter the full name of our database server, **DESKTOP-24JPUFB\SQL2019EXPRESS**, into the **Server name** box.
3) Then click on the drop-down arrow on the **Select or enter a database name** box, and select our sample database **CSE-DEPT** from the list. Your finished Add Connection wizard should match one that is shown in Figure 5.7.
4) You can test this database connection by clicking on the **Test Connection** button located in the lower-left corner. A successful connection dialog should be displayed if this connection is successful. Click on the **OK** button to close that dialog box.

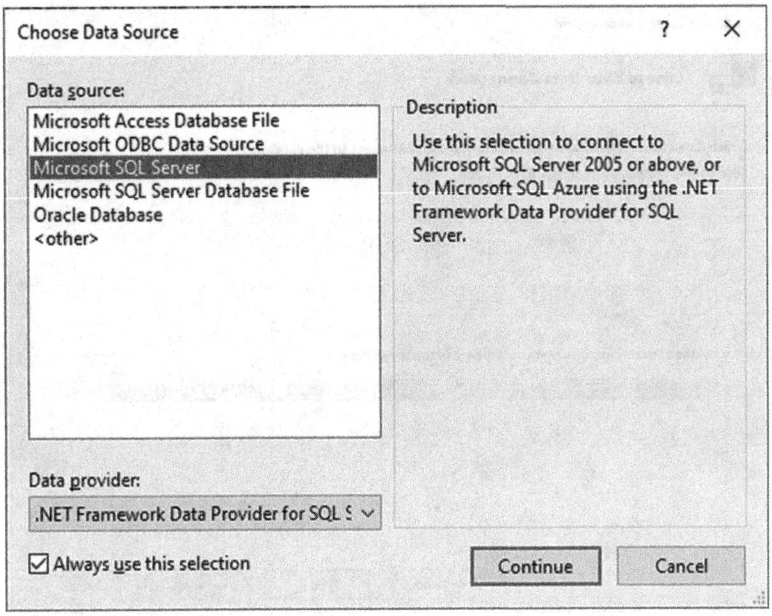

FIGURE 5.6 The opened choose data source wizard.

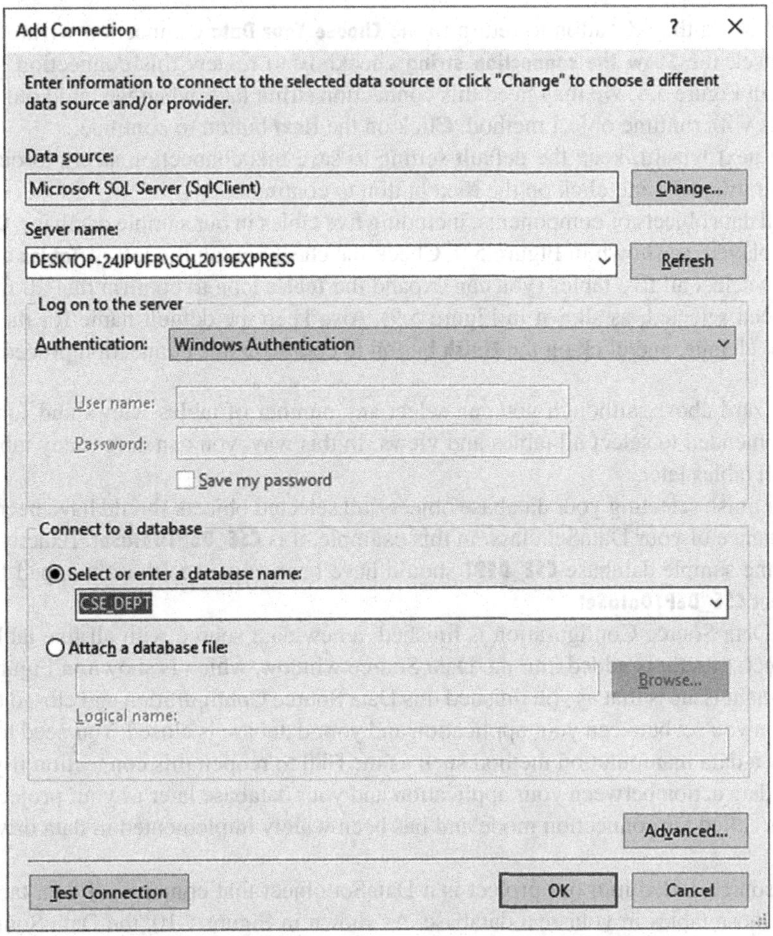

FIGURE 5.7 The opened add connection wizard.

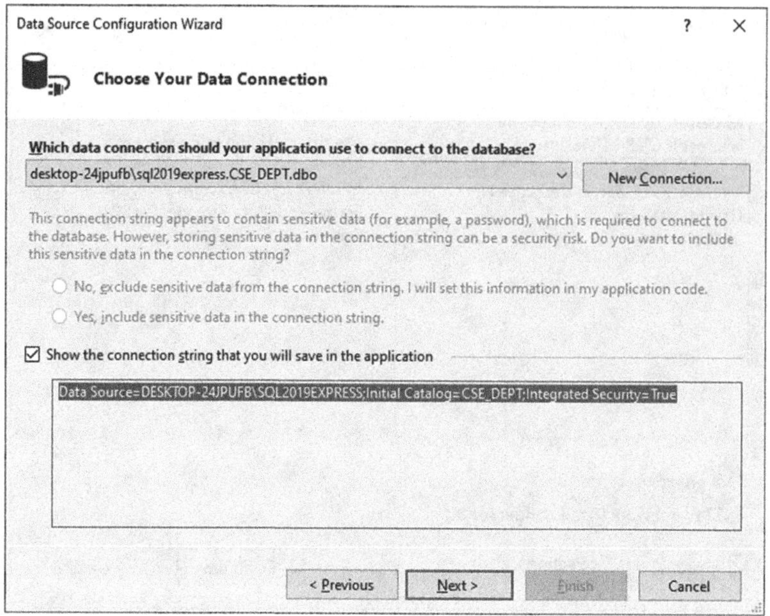

FIGURE 5.8 The database connection string.

5) Now click on the **OK** button to return to the **Choose Your Data** Connection wizard. You can also check the **Show the connection string** checkbox to review this connection string, as shown in Figure 5.8. We may need this connection string later when we build our database projects with runtime object method. Click on the **Next** button to continue.
6) On the next wizard, keep the default setting to save this connection string to our project configuration file, and click on the **Next** button to continue.
7) Now all data objects or components, including five tables in our sample database, **CSE_DEPT**, are displayed, as shown in Figure 5.9. Check the checkbox on the left of **Tables** and **Views** icons to select all five tables (you can expand the **Tables** icon to confirm that all five tables have been selected, as shown in Figure 5.9). Also keep the default name for the DataSet with no change, and click on the **Finish** button to complete this connection procedure.

In the last wizard above, although you can select any number of tables, views and functions, it is highly recommended to select all tables and views. In this way, you can access any table and view any data in all tables later.

When you finish selecting your database objects, all selected objects should have been added into your new instance of your DataSet class, in this example, it is **CSE_DEPTDataSet**. Exactly, the data in all tables in the sample database **CSE_DEPT** should have been copied to those mapped tables in the DataSet object **CSE_DEPTDataSet**.

After the Data Source Configuration is finished, a new data source with all five tables is added into our project, exactly is added into the Data Source window, which is shown in Figure 5.10.

One important issue is that as you finished this Data Source Configuration and closed this Wizard, the connection you set between your application and your database is closed. You need to use a valid data query or a data manipulation method such as the **Fill()** to reopen this connection if you want to perform any data action between your application and your database later as your project runs. This technology is called Disconnection mode and has been widely implemented in data driven applications today.

The data source added into our project is a DataSet object that contains all data tables that are mappings to those tables in your real database. As shown in Figure 5.10, the Data Source window

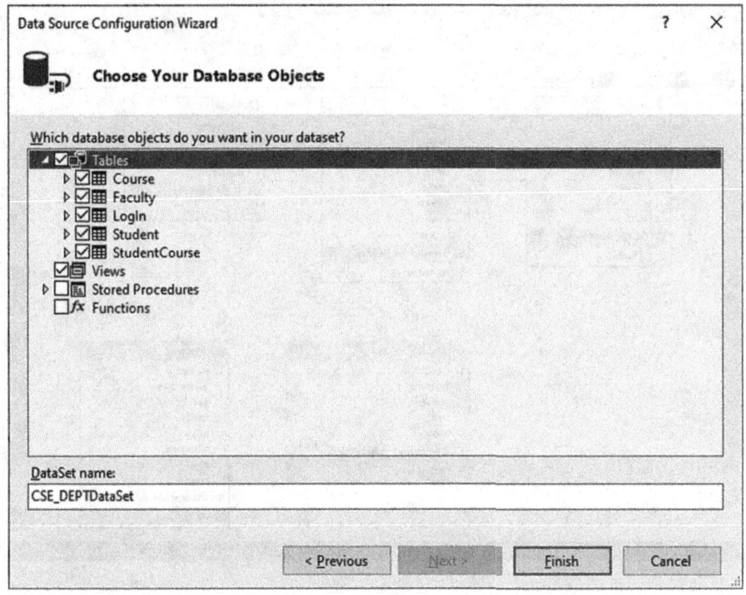

FIGURE 5.9 Select database objects in the configuration wizard.

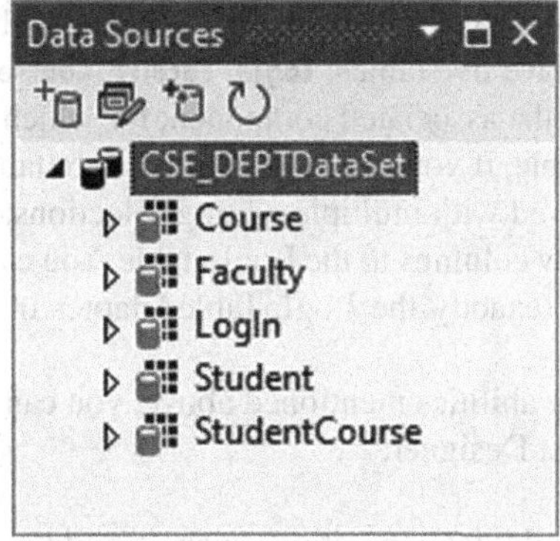

FIGURE 5.10 The added data source.

displays the data source and tables as a tree view, and each table is connected to this tree via a node. If you click a node (represented by a small '+' symbol surrounded with a box), all columns in the selected table will be displayed.

Even after the data source is added into your project, the story has not been finished and you still have some controllability over this data source. This means that you can still make some modifications to the data source, in fact, you can make modifications to the tables and data source-related methods. To do this job, you need to know something about another component, DataSet Designer, which is also located in the Data Source window.

5.1.2.3 DataSet Designer

The DataSet Designer is a group of visual tools used to create and edit a typed DataSet and the individual items that make up that DataSet.

The DataSet Designer provides visual representations of the objects contained in the DataSet. By using the **DataSet Designer**, you can create and modify TableAdapters, TableAdapter Queries, DataTables, DataColumns, and DataRelations.

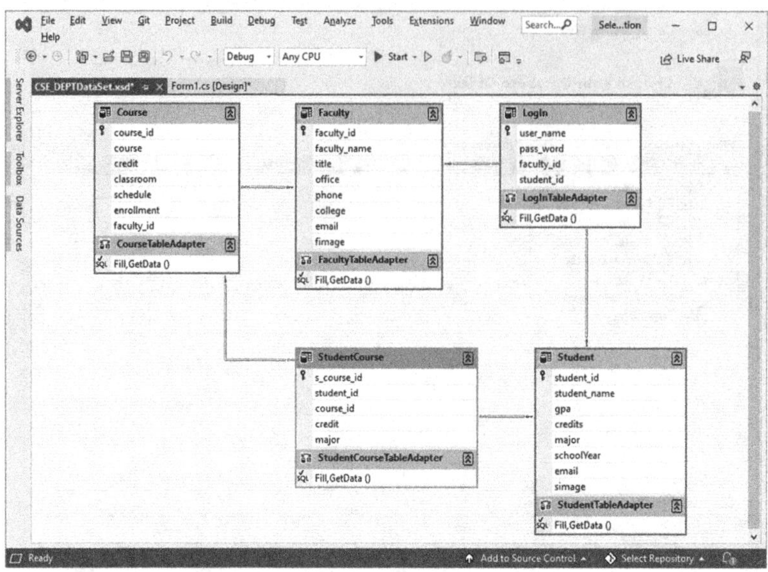

FIGURE 5.11 A sample DataSet designer.

To open the DataSet Designer, right-click on any place inside the Data Source window, then select the **Edit DataSet with Designer**. A sample DataSet Designer is shown in Figure 5.11.

In this sample database, we have five tables: **LogIn**, **Faculty**, **Course**, **Student** and **StudentCourse**. To edit any item, just right-click on the associated component for which you want to modify from each table to open a dialog. For example, if you want to edit the LogIn table, right-click on that table and a pop-up window will be displayed with multiple editing selections. You can add new queries, new relationships, new keys, even new columns to the LogIn table. You can also modify or edit any built-in method of the TableAdapter (exactly the LogInTableAdapter in this example), such as Select, Update, Insert or Delete.

In addition to multiple editing abilities mentioned above, you can perform the following popular data operations using the DataSet Designer:

- **Configure**: configure and build data operations such as building a data query by modifying the default methods of the TableAdapter such as **Fill()** and **GetData()**
- **Delete**: delete the whole table
- **Rename**: rename the table
- **Preview Data**: view the contents of the table in a grid format

The Preview Data is a very powerful tool and it allows users to preview the contents of a data table. Figure 5.12 shows an example of data table – **Faculty** table. To open the preview for this Faculty table, right-click on the Faculty table, and select the **Preview Data** item from the popup menu, and then click the **Preview** button.

Based on the above discussions, it can be seen that the DataSet Designer is a powerful tool to help users to design and manipulate a data source or DataSet, even the data source has been added into your project. But that is not enough! The reason I say that is because the DataSet Designer has one more important functionality, which is to allow users to add any missing table to your project.

Of course, you should not have this kind of problem in a normal situation as you develop a data-driven application using the DataSet Designer. In some cases, however, if you have forgotten to add a data table, or you add a wrong table (in my experience, this has happened a lot to students who

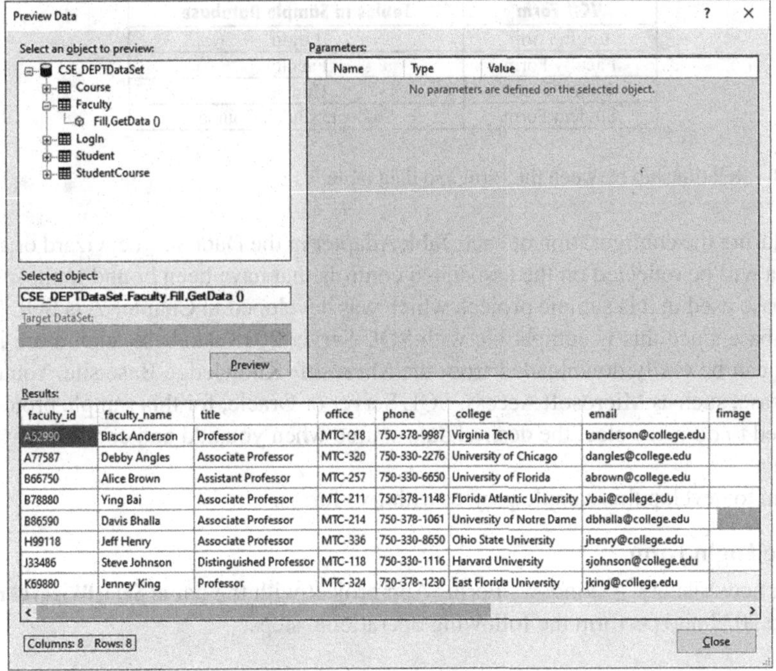

FIGURE 5.12 An example of preview data for faculty table.

selected the wrong data source). You need to use this functionality to add that missed table by first deleting the wrong table and then adding the correct one.

To add a missed table, just right-click a blank area of the designer surface and choose **Add | DataTable**. You can also use this functionality to add a TableAdapter, Query or a Relation to this DataSet.

A more detailed exploration of DataSet Designer will be provided in Section 5.4.3.

5.2 BUILD A SAMPLE DATABASE PROJECT – SELECTWIZARD WITH SQL SERVER DATABASE

So far, we have introduced most design tools and wizards located in both the Visual Studio Toolbox and the Data Source window. In the following sections, we will illustrate how to utilize those tools and wizards to build a data-driven application by using a real example. First, let's build a Visual C# project named **SelectWizardProject**, which means that we want to build this project with design tools and wizards provided by Visual Studio 2022.

5.2.1 Application User Interfaces

This project is composed of five forms, named LogIn Form, Selection Form, Faculty Form, Student Form and Course Form. The project is designed to map a Computer Science and Engineering Department in a university, and allow users to scan and browse all information about the department, including faculty, courses taught by selected faculty, student and courses taken by the associated student.

Each form, with the exception of the Selection form, is associated with one or two data tables in a sample database **CSE_DEPT**, which was developed in Chapter 2. The relationship between each form and tables is shown in Figure 5.13.

Controls on each form are bound to the associated fields in certain data tables located in the **CSE_DEPT** database. As the project runs, a data query will be executed via a dynamic SQL statement

VC# Form	Tables in Sample Database
LogIn Form	LogIn
Faculty Form	Faculty
Course Form	Course
Student Form	Student, StudentCourse

FIGURE 5.13 Relationship between the form and data table.

that is built during the configuration of each TableAdapter in the Data Source wizard or a LINQ. The retrieved data will be reflected on the associated controls that have been bound to those data fields.

The database used in this sample project, which was developed in Chapter 2, is SQL Server 2019 Express database since this is compatible with SQL Server 2018 database, and, more importantly, it is free and can be easily downloaded from the Microsoft Knowledge Base site. You can use any kind of database, such as Microsoft Access, SQL Server or Oracle, for this sample project. The only thing you need to do is to select the desired data source when you add and connect that data source to your project.

Let's begin to develop this sample project with five forms.

5.2.1.1 The LogIn Form

First create a new Visual C# Windows Forms App project with the name **SelectWizardProject**. Open Visual Studio 2022 and perform the following operational steps:

1) Launch Visual Studio 2022 by clicking its icon on either the desktop or the task bar.
2) Click on the **Continue without code** link located at the lower-right corner to open the standard Visual Studio window.
3) Go to the **File | New | Project** item to open the **Create a new project** wizard (Figure 5.14).
4) On the opened wizard, scroll down along the scroll bar on the right until you find our desired template, **Windows Forms App (.NET Framework)** as **C#** as the icon on the left, as shown in Figure 5.14, click it to select this template. Then click on the **Next** button to continue.
5) On the next wizard, **Configure your new project**, enter **SelectWizard Project** into the **Project name** box, and **SelectWizard Solution** into the **Solution name** box, respectively, as shown in Figure 5.15. Select your desired folder as the location from the **Location** box to save this new project. In our case, we used that location to save the project.
6) Click on the **Create** button to create this new project.

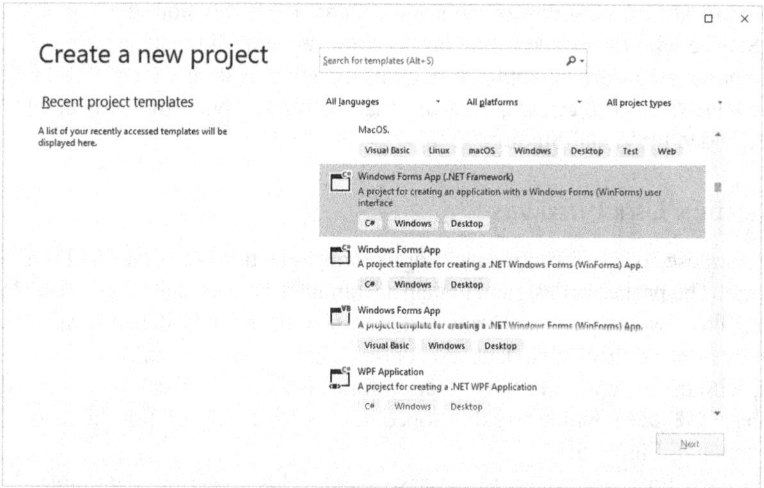

FIGURE 5.14 The finished new project wizard.

Configure your new project

Windows Forms App (.NET Framework) C# Windows Desktop

Project name

SelectWizard Project

Location

C:\SQL C# DB Programming\Students\Class DB Projects\Chapter 5

Solution name

SelectWizard Solution

Place solution and project in the same directory

Framework

.NET Framework 4.7.2

Back Create

FIGURE 5.15 The completed configure your new project wizard.

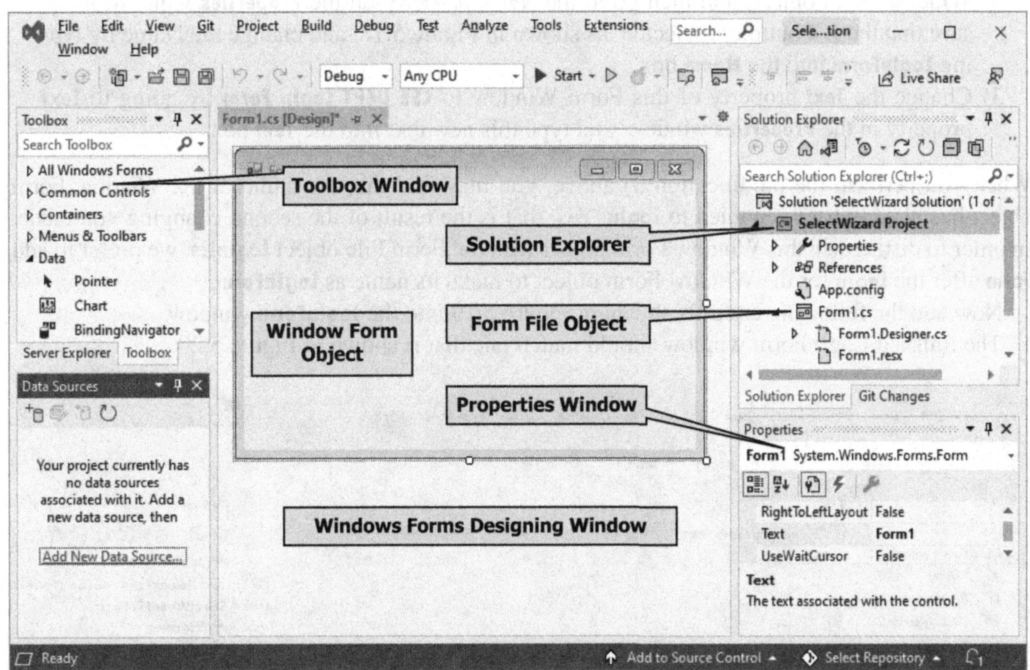

FIGURE 5.16 The new created project with its four windows.

When a new project is created with the default windows form being opened, which is shown in Figure 5.16, four windows are created and displayed and they are:

- Windows Form Designing window: Contains Window Form object and Form File object.
- Toolbox window: Contains all tools and components to be used to develop Visual C# application projects.
- Solution Explorer window: Contains all files and projects created and added into the current solution.
- Properties window: Contains all properties of the selected controls or objects.

Four folders are created and added into the Solution Explorer window for this new project, they are (Figure 5.16):

- **Properties**: Contains all properties of the selected objects.
- **References**: Contains all namespaces of the system classes, methods and events.
- **Form1.cs**: Contains all files of the graphic user interface and resources. It is also called Form File object.
- **C# Program.cs**: Contains the entry point of the project.

Perform the following modifications to this form to make it our project:

1) Change the name of the current Form File object from **Form1.cs** to **LogIn.cs** by right-clicking on the **Form1.cs** folder from the Solution Explorer window and select the **Rename** item from the popup menu, and change it by typing **LogIn** (do not touch **.cs**) into that folder. Then click on the Window Form object to exit this name changing.
   A Message will be displayed when you do this name changing. Just click on the **Yes** button to keep all related references to this object are also changed. The finished name changing of this object is shown in Figure 5.17.
2) Change the Window Form's object name from **LogIn** to **LogInForm** by first clicking on the Window Form object, and then go to the **Name** property on the **Properties** window, make sure that the **A-Z** button is selected, as shown in Figure 5.18, and change the Name by typing **LogInForm** into the **Name** box.
3) Change the **Text** property of this Form Window to **CSE DEPT LogIn Form** by going to **Text** property in the **Properties** window, and type this new text into the **Text** box.

When you perform the modification 3) above, you may find that the name of the Window Form object has already been renamed to **LogIn**. Yes, that is the result of the second changing you made. In order to distinguish this Window Form object with the Form File object **LogIn.cs**, we prefer to add **Form** after the **LogIn** for the Window Form object to make its name as **LogInForm**.

Now add the following controls shown in Figure 5.19 into the **LogInForm** window.

The finished LogInForm window should match one that is shown in Figure 5.20.

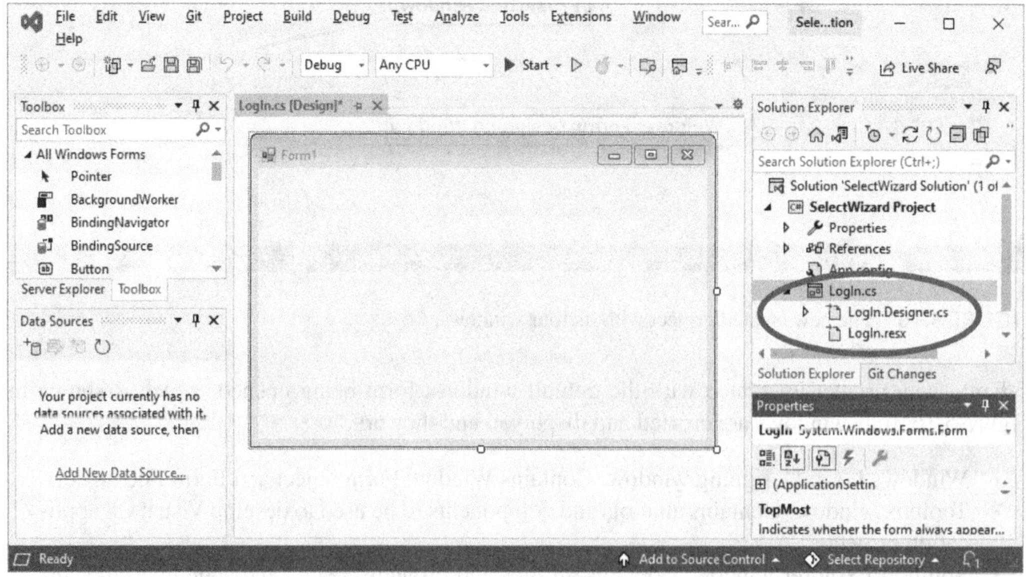

FIGURE 5.17 The changed names for the Form1.cs and related references.

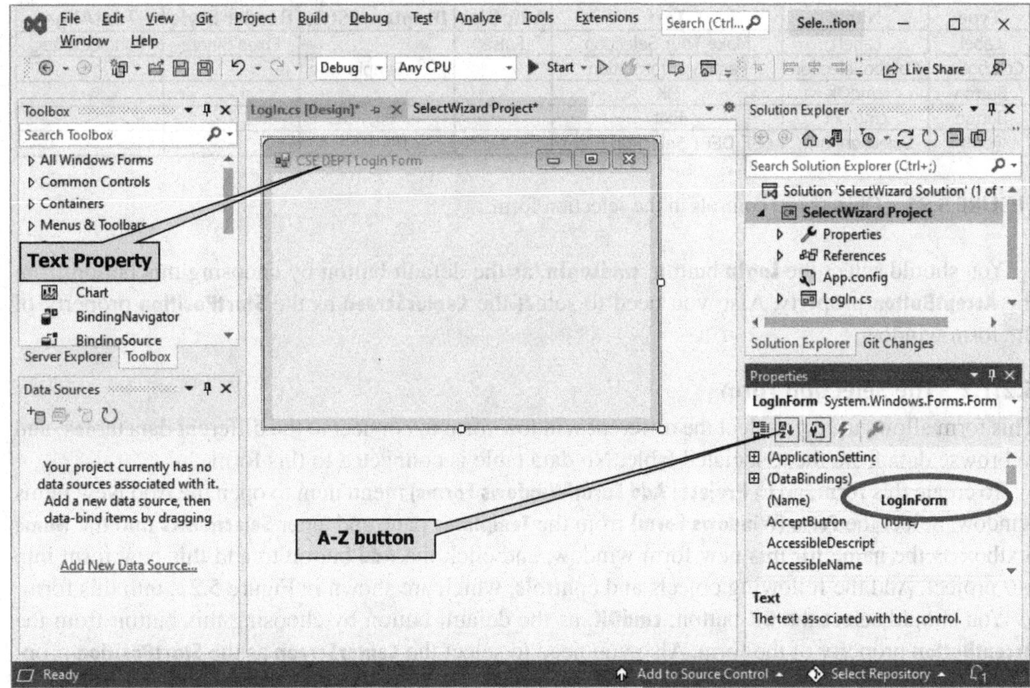

FIGURE 5.18 The finished modifications to our new project.

Type	Name	Text	TabIndex	AutoSize	BorderStyle	TextAlign
Label	Label1	Welcome to CSE Department	0	False	Fixed Single	MiddleCenter
Label	Label2	User Name	1	-	-	-
Textbox	txtUserName		2	-	-	-
Label	Label3	Pass Word	3	-	-	-
Textbox	txtPassWord		4	-	-	-
Button	cmdLogIn	LogIn	5	-	-	-
Button	cmdCancel	Cancel	6	-	-	-

FIGURE 5.19 Objects and controls in the LogIn Form.

FIGURE 5.20 The LogInForm window.

Type	Name	Text	AutoSize	DropDownStyle	Border Style	TextAlign
Label	Label1	Make Your Selection	False		Fixed Single	MiddleCenter
ComboBox	ComboSelection	Faculty Information	-	Simple	-	-
Button	cmdOK	OK	-		-	-
Button	cmdExit	Exit	-		-	-
Form	SelectionForm	CSE DEPT Selection Form	-		-	-

FIGURE 5.21 Objects and controls in the selection form.

You should select the **LogIn** button, **cmdLogIn**, as the default button by choosing this button from the **AcceptButton** property. Also you need to select the **CenterScreen** as the **StartPosition** property of the form window.

5.2.1.2 The Selection Form

This form allows users to select the different window form to connect to the different data tables, and to browse data from the associated table. No data table is connected to this form.

To create this form, go to **Project | Add Form(Windows Forms)** menu item to open the Add New Items window. Select the **Form (Windows Form)** from the **Templates** pane and enter **Selection.cs** into the **Name** textbox as the name for this new form window, and click the **Add** button to add this new form into our project. Add the following objects and controls, which are shown in Figure 5.21, into this form.

You should select the **OK** button, **cmdOK**, as the default button by choosing this button from the **AcceptButton** property of the form. Also you need to select the **CenterScreen** as the **StartPosition** property of the form.

The completed Selection form should match one that is shown in Figure 5.22.

5.2.1.3 The Faculty Form

The Faculty form contains controls that are related to faculty data or record stored in the database **CSE_DEPT**, which is a sample database we built in Chapter 2.

To create this new Faculty form, just right click on the project **SelectWizardProject** from the Solution Explorer window and select **Add | Form (Windows Forms)** item from the popup menu to open the **Add New Item** wizard. Select the **Form (Windows Forms)** item from the mid-list, and enter **Faculty.cs** into the **Name** box at the bottom as the name for this Form, and click on the **Add** button to add this form into our project.

Add the following objects and controls, as shown in Figure 5.23, into this Faculty form.

You should set up the **Select** button, **cmdSelect**, as the default button by choosing this button from the **AcceptButton** property of this form window. In addition, you need to select the **CenterScreen** as the **StartPosition** property of this form window.

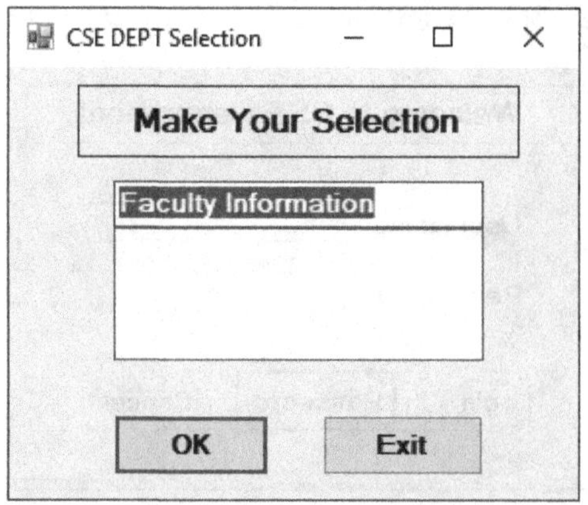

FIGURE 5.22 The selection form.

Type	Name	Text	TabIndex	DropDownStyle	SizeMode
GroupBox	GroupBox1	Faculty Image	0		
Label	Label1	Faculty Image	0.0		
TextBox	txtFacultyImage		0.1		
PictureBox	PhotoBox				StretchImage
GroupBox	GroupBox2	Faculty Name and Query Method	1		
Label	Label2	Faculty Name	1.0		
ComboBox	ComboName		1.1	DropDownList	
Label	Label3	Query Method	1.2		
ComboBox	ComboMethod		1.3	DropDownList	
GroupBox	GroupBox3	Faculty Information	2		
Label	Label4	Faculty ID	2.0		
TextBox	txtFacultyID		2.1		
Label	Label5	Faculty Name	2.2		
TextBox	txtFacultyName		2.3		
Label	Label6	Title	2.4		
TextBox	txtTitle		2.5		
Label	Label7	Office	2.6		
TextBox	txtOffice		2.7		
Label	Label8	Phone	2.8		
TextBox	txtPhone		2.9		
Label	Label9	College	2.10		
TextBox	txtCollege		2.11		
Label	Label10	Email	2.12		
TextBox	txtEmail		2.13		
Button	cmdSelect	Select	3		
Button	cmdInsert	Insert	4		
Button	cmdUpdate	Update	5		
Button	cmdDelete	Delete	6		
Button	cmdBack	Back	7		
Form	FacultyForm	CSE DEPT Faculty Form			

FIGURE 5.23 Objects and controls in the faculty form.

The finished Faculty form is shown in Figure 5.24.

In this chapter, we only use the **Select** and **Back** button to make data query from the Faculty table in our data source. Other buttons will be used in the following chapters.

5.2.1.4 The Course Form

This form is used to access the **Course** table in our data source to retrieve course information associated with a specific faculty member selected by the user. Recall how, in Chapter 2, we developed a sample database **CSE_DEPT** and the Course table is one of five tables built in that database. A one-to-many relationship exists between the Faculty and the Course table, which is connected by using a primary key **faculty_id** in the Faculty table and a foreign key **faculty_id** in the Course table. We will use this relationship to retrieve data from the Course table based on the selected **faculty_id** in both tables.

To create this Course Form, go to **Project | Add Form (Windows Forms)** menu item to open the **Add New Item** wizard. Select the **Form (Windows Forms)** from the mid-list and enter **Course.cs** into the **Name** box at the bottom. Click on the **Add** button to add this form into our current project. Then add the following objects and controls, which are shown in Figure 5.25, into this form window.

You should set up the **Select** button, **cmdSelect**, as the default button by choosing this button from the **AcceptButton** property of the Course form. Also you need to select the **CenterScreen** as the **StartPosition** property of the form.

The finished Course form should match one that is shown in Figure 5.26.

In this chapter, we only use the **Select** and the **Back** button to make data query from the Course table in our data source. The other buttons will be used in the following chapters.

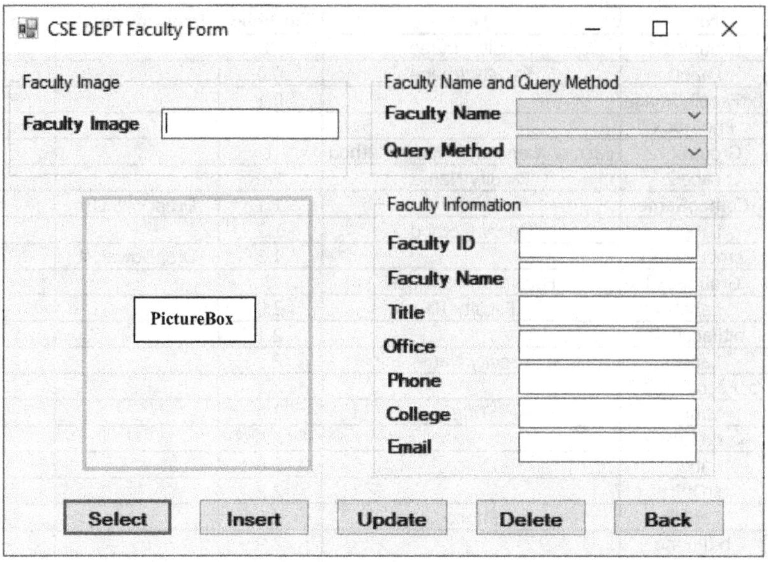

FIGURE 5.24 The finished faculty form.

Type	Name	Text	TabIndex	DropDownStyle
GroupBox	GroupBox1	Faculty Name and Query Method	0	
Label	Label1	Faculty Name	0.0	
ComboBox	ComboName		0.1	DropDownList
Label	Label2	Query Method	0.2	
ComboBox	ComboMethod		0.3	DropDownList
GroupBox	GroupBox2	Course ID List	1	
ListBox	CourseList		1.0	
GroupBox	GroupBox3	Course Information	2	
Label	Label3	Course ID	2.0	
TextBox	txtCourseID		2.1	
Label	Label4	Course	2.2	
TextBox	txtCourseName		2.3	
Label	Label5	Schedule	2.4	
TextBox	txtSchedule		2.5	
Label	Label6	Classroom	2.6	
TextBox	txtClassRoom		2.7	
Label	Label7	Credits	2.8	
TextBox	txtCredits		2.9	
Label	Label8	Enrollment	2.10	
TextBox	txtEnroll		2.11	
Button	cmdSelect	Select	3	
Button	cmdInsert	Insert	4	
Button	cmdUpdate	Update	5	
Button	cmdDelete	Delete	6	
Button	cmdBack	Back	7	
Form	CourseForm	CSE DEPT Course Form		

FIGURE 5.25 Objects and controls in the course form.

5.2.1.5 The Student Form

The Student form is used to collect and display student information, including the courses taken by the student. As we mentioned in Section 5.1, the Student form needs two data tables in the database; one is the **Student** table and the other one is the **StudentCourse** table. This is a typical example of using two data tables for one graphical user interface (form).

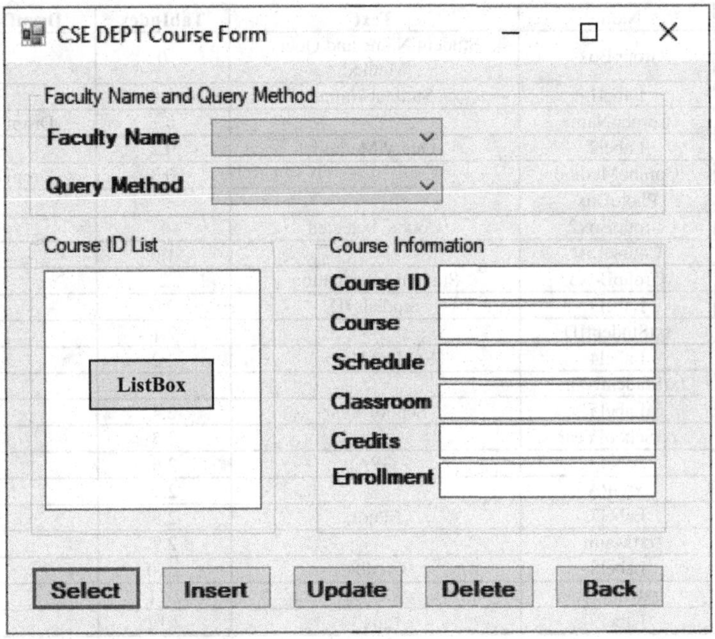

FIGURE 5.26 The finished course form.

To create this Student Form, go to the **Project | Add Form (Windows Forms)** menu item to add a new window form with a file name **Student.cs**. Add the following objects and controls, which are shown in Figure 5.27, into this form.

Make sure that you set up the following properties for controls and objects in this form:

- Make the **Select** button the default button by selecting this button from the **AcceptButton** property of the Student form.
- Select the **CenterScreen** from the **StartPosition** property of the form.
- Set the **BorderStyle** property of the ListBox control, **CourseList**, to **FixedSingle**.

Also the courses taken by the student is reflected and displayed in a ListBox control, **CourseList**.

Your finished Student form should match one that is shown in Figure 5.28. Go to the **File | Save All** menu item to save all forms we developed and built in these sections. All of these five windows forms are stored in the CRC Press ftp site, exactly under the folder **Students\Windows Forms**, and available to readers. If some readers want to use those forms without building them, they can add them into their project directly by going to that ftp site and inserting them one by one by following the operational steps in next section.

5.2.1.6 Using Five Windows Forms without Building Them

An easy way to use those five windows forms is to add those forms into your project directly. Perform the following operations to finish this adding process:

1) Create your new Windows Forms App (.NET Framework) C# project.
2) Right-click on your new C# project in the Solution Explorer window, and select the **Add | Existing Item** to open the **Add Existing Item** window.

Type	Name	Text	TabIndex	DropDownStyle
GroupBox	GroupBox1	Student Name and Query Method	0	
Label	Label1	Student Name	0.0	
ComboBox	ComboName		0.1	DropDownList
Label	Label2	Query Method	0.2	
ComboBox	ComboMethod		0.3	DropDownList
PictureBox	PhotoBox			
GroupBox	GroupBox2	Course Selected	1	
ListBox	CourseList		1.0	
GroupBox	GroupBox3	Student Information	2	
Label	Label3	Student ID	2.0	
TextBox	txtStudentID		2.1	
Label	Label4	Student Name	2.2	
TextBox	txtStudentName		2.3	
Label	Label5	School Year	2.4	
TextBox	txtSchoolYear		2.5	
Label	Label6	GPA	2.6	
TextBox	txtGPA		2.7	
Label	Label7	Major	2.8	
TextBox	txtMajor		2.9	
Label	Label8	Credits	2.10	
TextBox	txtCredits		2.11	
Label	Label9	Email	2.12	
TextBox	txtEmail		2.13	
Button	cmdSelect	Select	3	
Button	cmdInsert	Insert	4	
Button	cmdUpdate	Update	5	
Button	cmdDelete	Delete	6	
Button	cmdBack	Back	7	
Form	StudentForm	CSE DEPT Student Form		

FIGURE 5.27 Objects and controls in the student form.

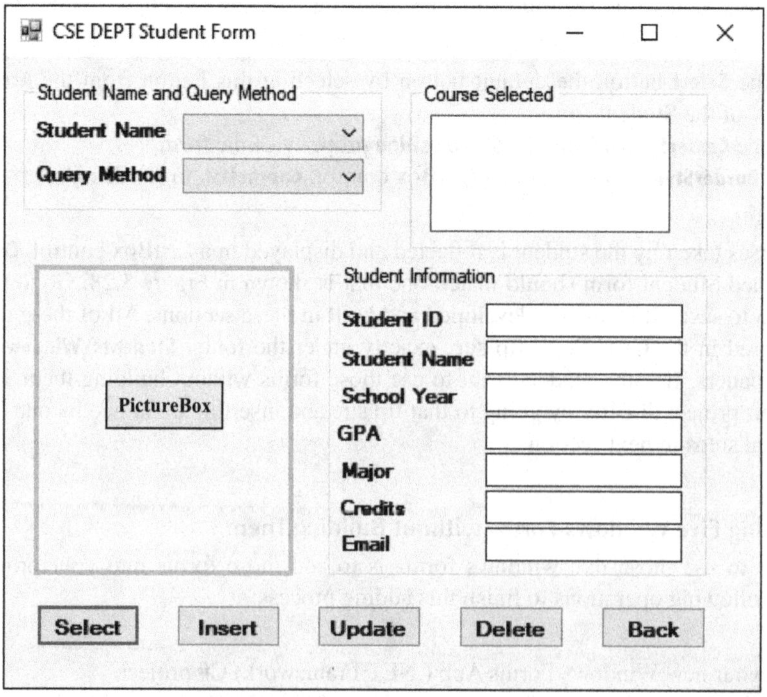

FIGURE 5.28 The finished student form.

3) Browse to the CRC Press ftp site to find the folder **Students\Windows Forms**, or you can copy all files under that folder and save them to one of your local folders.
4) Select the following files by checking the box in front of each of them **once a time**:
    a. **Course.cs**
    b. **Faculty.cs**
    c. **LogIn.cs**
    d. **Selection.cs**
    e. **Student.cs**
5) Then click on the **Add** button to add one of them into your project.

A trick is that each time you can only select and add **ONE** file to do this addition by selecting **Add | Existing Item**. Otherwise, the files you added would be failed.

Another trick is that when those files are first added into your project, they are prefixed with a C#, and you must wait for a moment to make them changed to the normal objects.

Next we need to select and add our desired data source to this project and connect our project with our database to perform the data query operations.

5.3 ADD AND UTILIZE VISUAL STUDIO.NET WIZARDS AND DESIGN TOOLS

After the graphical user interfaces are created, next we need to add a data source to this new project and set up a connection between our project and the database. In Section 5.1.2.2, we have discussed in detail how to add a new data source and how to configure it. In this section, we will illustrate these with a real Visual C# 2022 project, SelectWizard Project, we created in the last section.

5.3.1 Add and Configure a New Data Source

Open the SelectWizard Project if it is not opened and select the LogIn form window.

Go to **View | OtherWindows | Data Sources** menu item to open the Data Source window. Currently, this window is blank since we have not added and connected any data source to this project. Click on the link **Add New Data Source** as we did in Section 5.1.2.2 to add a new data source to our project. Perform the following operations to add our database into this project:

1) On the opened Data Source Configuration Wizard, keep the default selection **Database** and click the **Next** button to the next step. Still keep the default item **Dataset** and click on the **Next** button in the opened **Choose a Database Model** wizard.
2) In the opened **Choose Your Data Connection** wizard, click on the **New Connection** button to open the Add Connection wizard, as shown in Figure 5.29.
3) Keep the **Microsoft SQL Server (SqlClient)** in the top **Data source** box unchanged if this component is selected. Otherwise you need to click the **Change** button that is located on the right of the **Data source** box to select this component.
4) Enter the full server name, **DESKTOP-24JPUFB\SQL2019EXPRESS**, into the **Server name** box, and click on the drop-down arrow on the **Select or enter a database name** combobox, and select our sample database **CSE_DEPT** from that box.
5) Your finished **Add Connection** wizard should match one that is shown in Figure 5.29.
6) You can test this data source connection by clicking on the **Test Connection** button located at the lower-left corner, as shown in Figure 5.29. A **Test connection succeeded** message should be displayed if everything is fine.
7) Click on the **OK** button to that message box to close it and click on the **OK** button on that Add Connection wizard to return to the **Choose Your Data Connection** wizard.

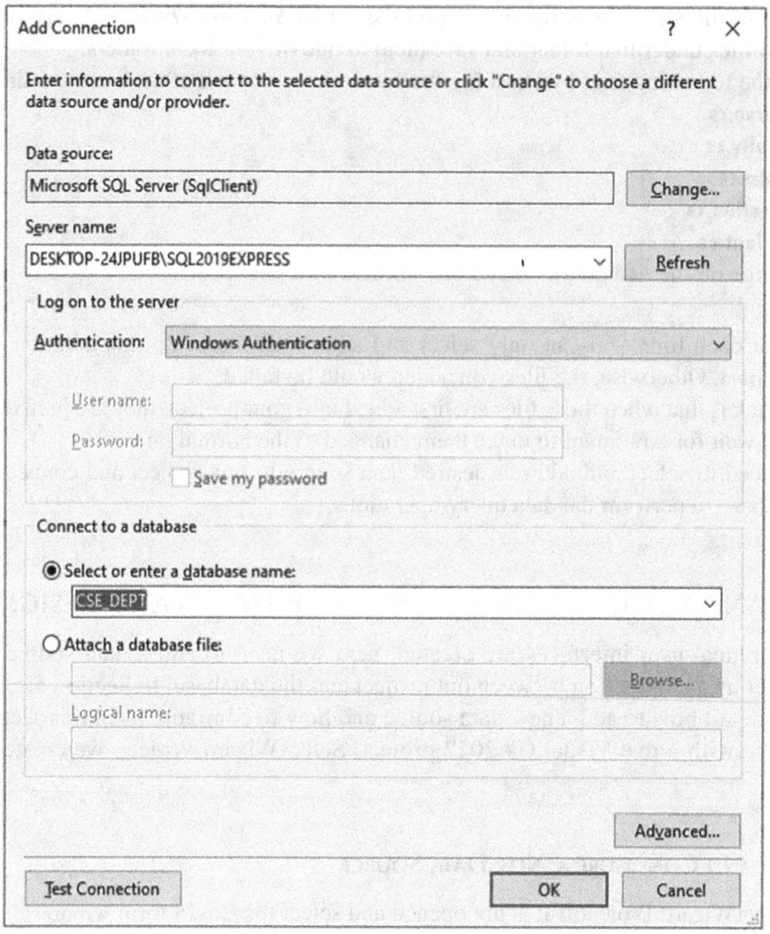

FIGURE 5.29 The finished add connection wizard.

8) Now you can check on the **Show the connection string** checkbox if you like to keep and save this connection string in your project, as shown in Figure 5.30. We may need to use this connection string when we build our database application project with runtime object method later. Click on the **Next** button to go to the next step.
9) In the next wizard, **Save the Connection String to the Application Configuration File**, keep the default settings and click on the **Next** button to continue.
10) In the next wizard, **Choose Your Database Objects**, as shown in Figure 5.31, expand the **Tables** folder and select all our five data tables, **Course, Faculty, LogIn, Student** and **StudentCourse**, by checking all of them one by one. Also check the **Views** folder to enable us to check all of five tables in a View format later.

Your finished **Choose Your Database Objects** wizard should match one that is shown in Figure 5.31. Click on the **Finish** button to complete this adding data source process.

Immediately, you can find that a new instance of the DataSet, **CSE_DEPTDataSet**, is added into our project, which is shown in Figure 5.32. Five data tables included in this DataSet are only mappings or copies of those real tables in our database. The connection you setup between the project and this database is closed as this Wizard is finished. You need to call some data query to reopen this connection as you perform data actions later in your project.

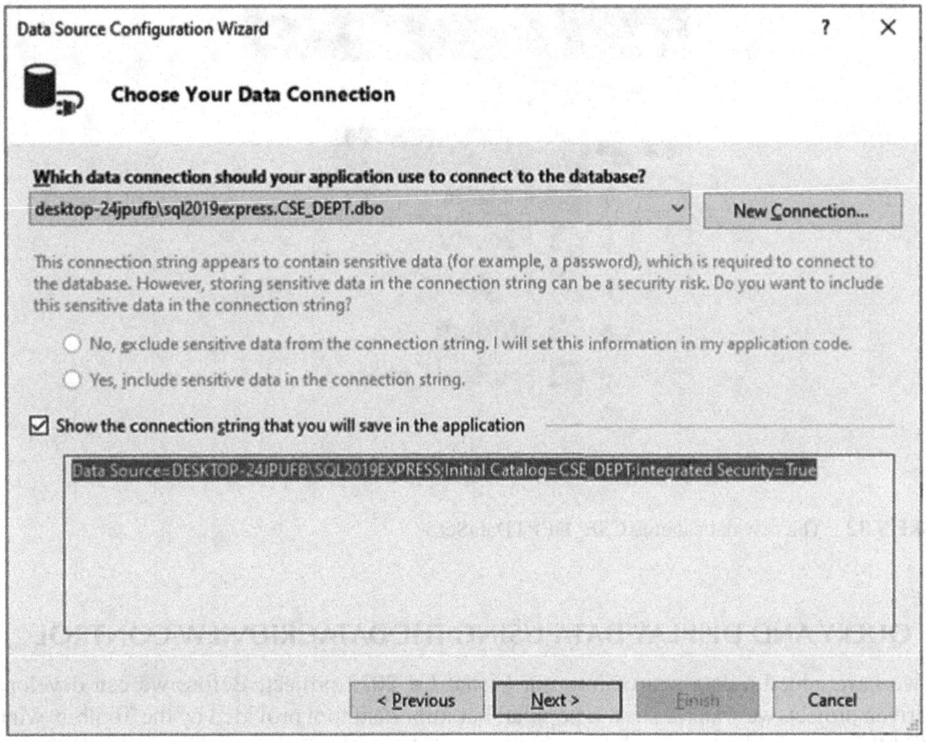

FIGURE 5.30 The database connection string.

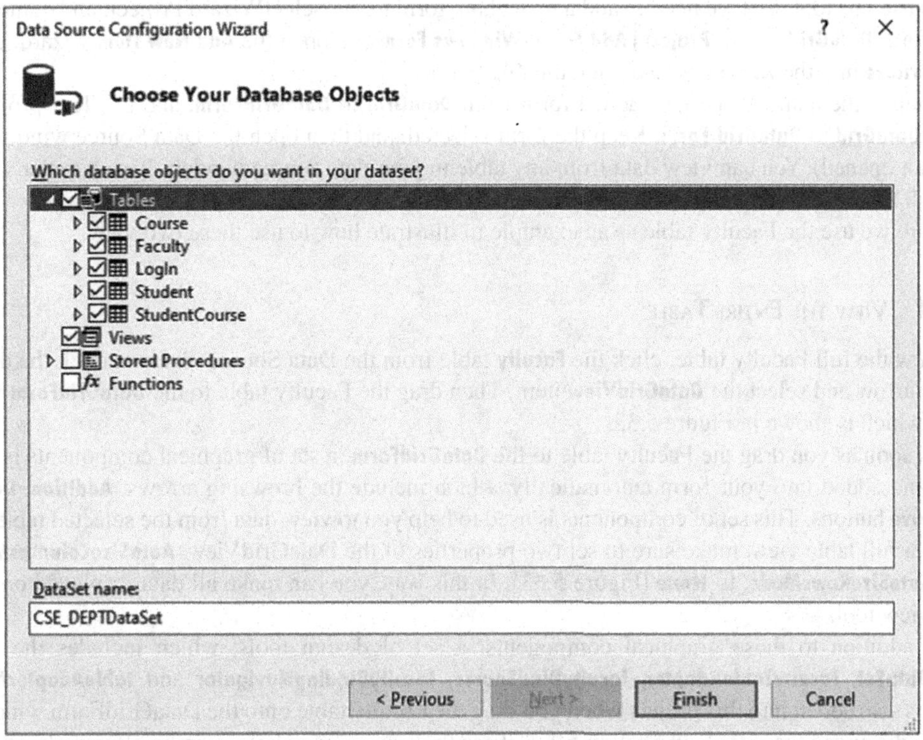

Data Source Configuration Wizard

Choose Your Database Objects

Which database objects do you want in your dataset?

- Tables
  - Course
  - Faculty
  - LogIn
  - Student
  - StudentCourse
- Views
- Stored Procedures
- Functions

DataSet name:

CSE_DEPTDataSet

< Previous | Next > | Finish | Cancel

FIGURE 5.31 The finished choose your database objects wizard.

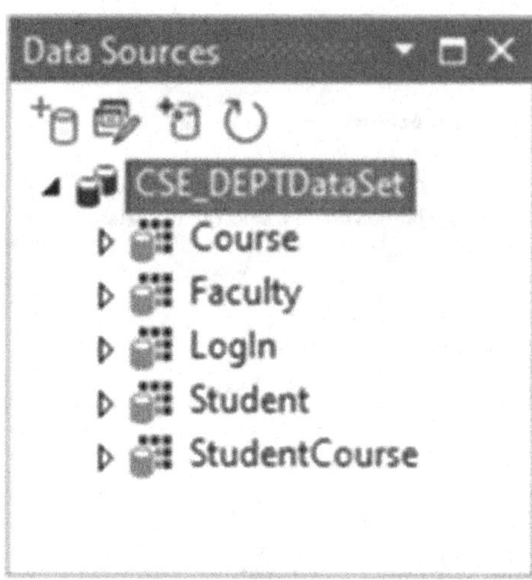

FIGURE 5.32 The new data source CSE_DEPTDataSet.

5.4 QUERY AND DISPLAY DATA USING THE DATAGRIDVIEW CONTROL

Now we have added a data source into our Visual C# 2022 project. Before we can develop this data-driven project, we want to show a popular, but important tool provided by the Toolbox window, **DataGridView**. As we discussed this tool in Section 5.1.1.2, the DataGridView is a view container and it can be used to bind data from your database and display the data in a tabular or a grid format in your Visual C# form windows.

To use this tool, first we need to add a new blank form to the SelectWizard Project, and name this new form **DataGrid**. Go to **Project | Add Form (Windows Forms)** to open the **Add New Item** wizard, enter **DataGrid.cs** into the **Name** box and click the **Add** button.

Change the name of the new added form from **DataGrid** to **DataGridForm**, and the Text property from **DataGrid** to **DataGrid Form**. Keep the form selected, and then open the Data Source window (if it is not opened). You can view data from any table in your data source window. Two popular views are **Full Table** view and **Detail** view for specified columns.

Here we use the Faculty table as an example to illustrate how to use these two views.

5.4.1 View the Entire Table

To view the full Faculty table, click the **Faculty** table from the Data Source window, click the drop-down arrow and select the **DataGridView** item. Then drag the Faculty table to the **DataGridForm** window, which is shown in Figure 5.33.

As soon as you drag the Faculty table to the **DataGridForm**, a set of graphical components is created and added into your form automatically, which include the browsing arrows, **Addition**, **Delete** and **Save** buttons. This set of components is used to help you to view data from the selected table. To make a full table view, make sure to set two properties of the DataGridView, **AutoSizeColumnsMode** and **AutoSizeRowsMode**, to **None** (Figure 5.33). In this way, you can make all data displayed on this grid view tool.

In addition to those graphical components, a set of design tools, which includes the **cSE_DEPTDataSet, facultyTableAdapter, facultyBindSource, facultyBindingNavigator** and **tableAdapterManager**, is also added into this project when you drag the Faculty table onto the DataGridForm window. As we discussed these tools in Section 5.1.1, these tools are used to help users to effectively access, translate and manipulate data between the Visual C# project and the DataSet.

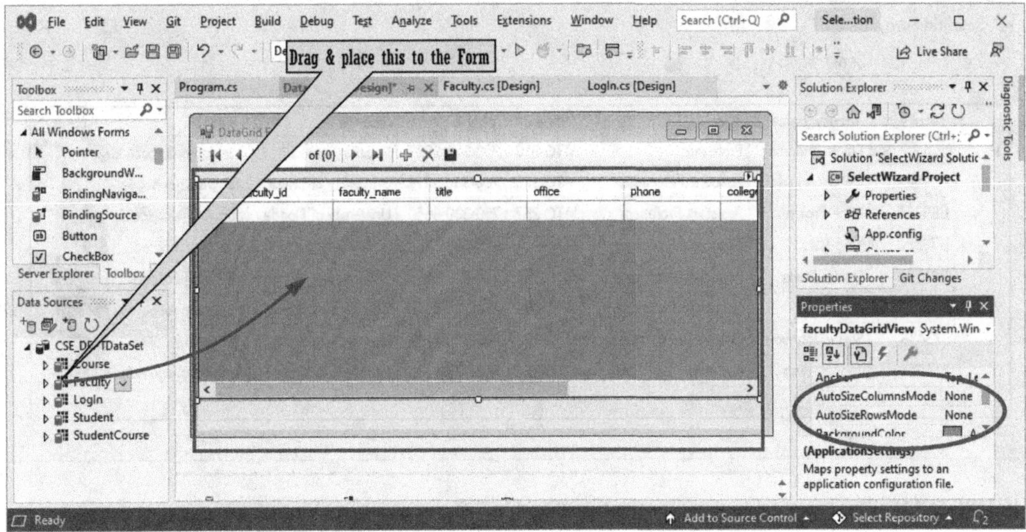

FIGURE 5.33 The DataGridView tool.

One important point to be noted is that those new added design tools (cSE_DEPTDataSet, facultyTableAdapter, ...) are exactly instances, not the classes, of those design tools. In Visual C#, they are called fields since these instances are class level and they are very similar to the Form level variables in Visual Basic.NET and the class variables in Java. This is the reason why the first letter of each those instances is lower case. This is a significant difference between Visual Basic.NET and Visual C#.NET. In Visual Basic.NET, all of those new added tools are classes, not instances. You must keep this in your mind when you develop data-driven applications in Visual C#.

Now you can run your project by clicking the **Start** button. But wait a moment! One more thing before you can run your project is to check whether you have selected your **DataGridForm** as the startup object. It is different to select a startup object for a project built in Visual C#.NET and Visual Basic.NET. In Visual Basic.NET, one can do that by going to the Project Properties window and selecting the startup form from the Startup object box. But in Visual C#.NET, you cannot do this job in that way. As you know, the **Program.cs** in the Solution Explorer window contains the entry point of each Visual C# project. this **Program.cs** contains the **Main()** method, from which the startup object can be defined.

To check the startup object for our current project, SelectWizard Project, open the **Program.cs** from the Solution Explorer window by double-clicking on it. You can find that one instruction,

```
Application.Run(new LogInForm());
```

is located inside this **Main()** method. The startup object is defined by calling a system method **Run()** with the constructor of the **LogInForm** as the argument. To change the startup object for our current project, modify this argument from **LogInForm()** to **DataGridForm()**, which means that we want to call the constructor of the **DataGridForm** class to create a new instance of the **DataGridForm** class, and start our project from this form. Now run our project by clicking on the Start button. The running result is shown in Figure 5.34.

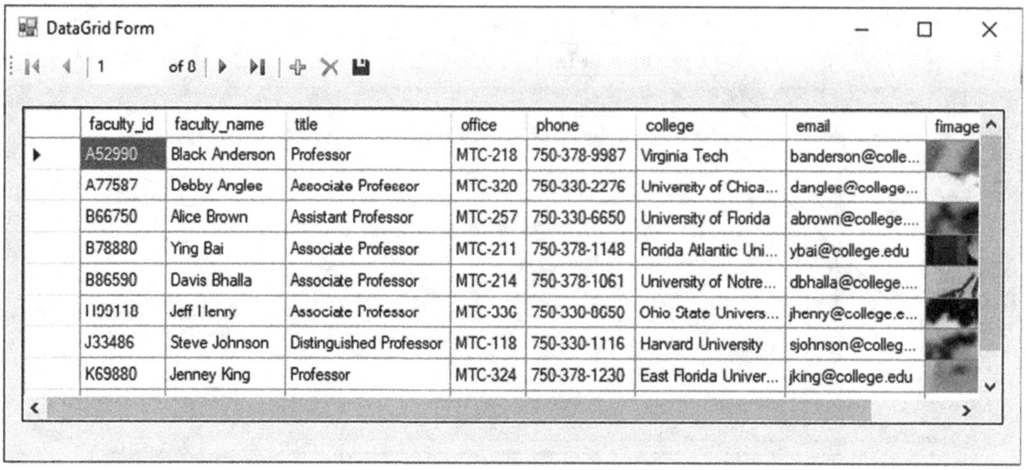

DataGrid Form

1 of 8

	faculty_id	faculty_name	title	office	phone	college	email	fimage
▶	A52990	Black Anderson	Professor	MTC-218	750-378-9987	Virginia Tech	banderson@colle...	
	A77587	Debby Anglee	Associate Professor	MTC-320	750-330-2276	University of Chica...	danglee@college...	
	B66750	Alice Brown	Assistant Professor	MTC-257	750-330-6650	University of Florida	abrown@college....	
	B78880	Ying Bai	Associate Professor	MTC-211	750-378-1148	Florida Atlantic Uni...	ybai@college.edu	
	B86590	Davis Bhalla	Associate Professor	MTC-214	750-378-1061	University of Notre...	dbhalla@college....	
	H99118	Jeff Henry	Associate Professor	MTC-336	750-330-8650	Ohio State Univers...	jhenry@college.e...	
	J33486	Steve Johnson	Distinguished Professor	MTC-118	750-330-1116	Harvard University	sjohnson@colleg...	
	K69880	Jenney King	Professor	MTC-324	750-378-1230	East Florida Univer...	jking@college.edu	

FIGURE 5.34 The entire table view for the faculty table.

Using this grid view tool, you can not only view data from the Faculty table, but also add new data into and delete data from the table by clicking the **Add** (+) or **Delete** (x) button to do that. Just type the new data in a new line after you click the **Add** button if you want to add new data, or move to the data you want to delete by clicking the browsing arrow on the top of the form window and then clicking the **Delete** button. One thing you need to know is that these modifications can only take effect to data in your data tables in the DataSet, it has nothing to do with data in your real database.

When you drag the Faculty table from the data source window to the DataGridForm, what was happened behind this dragging? Let's take a little more look at this issue. To do that, click the **Close** button to stop our project's running.

First, from the point of view of the graphical user interface, as we mentioned, five instances of design tools are created and added into this project. Second, from the point of view of the program codes, some instructions have been automatically added into this project, too. Open the code window of the DataGridForm by right-clicking on it from the Solution Explorer window and then clicking the **View Code** item from the popup menu. Browse to the method DataGridForm_Load() and you can find that a line of instruction is in there:

```
this.facultyTableAdapter.Fill(this.cSE_DEPTDataSet.Faculty);
```

The functionality of this instruction is that the Fill() method, which belongs to the FacultyTableAdapter class, is called to load data from the Faculty table in the database into the Faculty table in the DataSet, and furthermore into your DataGridView window. The **Fill()** is a very powerful method and it performs an equivalent operation to that of an SQL SELECT statement. To make this clearer, open the Data Source window, and right-click on any place inside that window. Select the **Edit the DataSet with Designer** item to open the **DataSet Designer Wizard**. Right-click on the bottom line, in which the **Fill()** and the **GetData()** methods are shown, on the Faculty table, and then select the **Configure** item to open the TableAdapter Configuration Wizard. You will find that a complete SQL SELECT statement is already in there:

```
SELECT faculty_id, faculty_name, title, office, college, phone,
Email, fimage FROM dbo.Faculty
```

This statement will be executed when the **Fill()** method is called by the facultyTable-Adapter as the **DataGridForm_Load()** event method runs when you start this project. The data returned from executing this statement will fill the grid view tool in the Faculty form.

5.4.2 View Each Record or Specified Columns

To view each record from the Faculty table, first delete the grid view tool from the Faculty form by right-clicking on that grid view tool and select **Delete** item from the popup menu. Then go to the Data Source window and click the Faculty table. Click the drop-down arrow and select the **Detail** item. Drag the Faculty table from the Data Source window to the Faculty form window. All column headers in the Faculty table are displayed, which is shown in Figure 5.35.

Now click the **Start** button to run your project, and the first record in the Faculty table is displayed in this grid tool, which is shown in Figure 5.36.

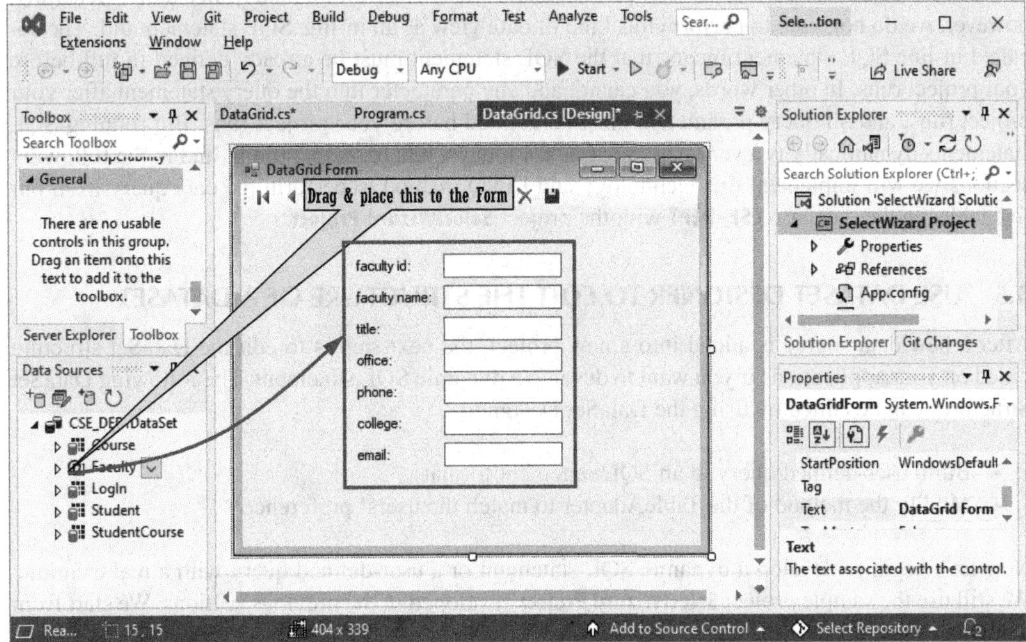

FIGURE 5.35 The grid view for specified columns.

DataGrid Form

1 of 8

faculty id: A52990

faculty name: Black Anderson

title: Professor

office: MTC-218

phone: 750-378-9987

college: Virginia Tech

email: banderson@college

faculty name: Black Anderson

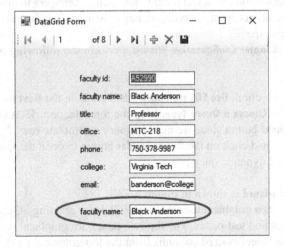

FIGURE 5.36 The running status of the grid view for each record.

To view each record, you can click the forward arrow on the top of the form to scan all records from the top to the bottom of the Faculty table.

If you only want to display some specified columns from the Faculty table, go to the Data Source window and select the Faculty table. Expand the table to display the individual columns, and drag the desired column from the Data Source window onto the DataGridForm window. For each column you drag, an individual data-bound control is created on the DataGridForm, accompanied by an appropriately titled label control. When you run this project, the first record with the specified columns will be retrieved and displayed on the form, and you can scan all records by clicking the forward arrow. One example of query a special column, **faculty name**, is shown at the bottom of Figure 5.36.

Well, the **DataGridView** is a powerful tool and allow users to view all data from a table. Generally, however, we do not want to perform this kind of data view as an in-line SQL statement did. The so-called in-line SQL statement means that the SQL statement must be already defined in full before your project runs. In other words, you cannot add any parameter into the query statement after your project runs, and all query parameters must be defined before your project runs. But running SQL statements dynamically is a very popular style for today's database operations, and in the following sections we will implement this technology and LINQ method to perform the data query from our five tables in the database **CSE_DEPT** with the project **SelectWizard Project**.

5.5 USE DATASET DESIGNER TO EDIT THE STRUCTURE OF A DATASET

After a new data source is added into a new project, the next step is to edit the DataSet structure based on your applications if you want to develop a dynamic SQL statement. The following DataSet Structures can be edited by using the DataSet Designer:

- Build user-defined query in an SQL statement format
- Modify the method of the TableAdapter to match the users' preference

Now let's begin to develop a dynamic SQL statement or a user-defined query with a real example. We still use the sample project **SelectWizard Project** developed in the previous sections. We start from the **LogIn** table.

Open the Data Source window and right-click any place inside the window, select **Edit DataSet with Designer** to open the DataSet Design Wizard. Locate the LogIn table and right-click on the last line, in which two methods – **Fill()** and **GetData()**–are displayed, and select the **Add Query** item from the popup menu. Of course, you can select other items such as **Configure** to modify an existing query. Right now, however, we do not want to configure any existing query; instead we just want to add a new query to perform our specified data query.

On the opened **TableAdapter Configuration Wizard**, perform the following operations to build our dynamic query:

1) Keep the default selection, **Use SQL statements**, and click on the **Next** button.
2) In the next wizard, **Choose a Query Type**, keep the top selection, **SELECT which returns rows**, and click on the **Next** button since we need to query a complete row.
3) In the next wizard, just click on the **Query Builder** button to open the Query Builder wizard to build our desired dynamic query.

The opened **Query Build wizard** is shown in Figure 5.37.

Query Builder provides a graphical user interface (GUI) for creating SQL queries, and it is composed of graphical panes and test panes. The top two panes are graphical panes and the third pane is the text pane. You can select desired columns from the top graphical pane, and each column you selected will be added into the second graphical pane. By using the second graphical pane, you can

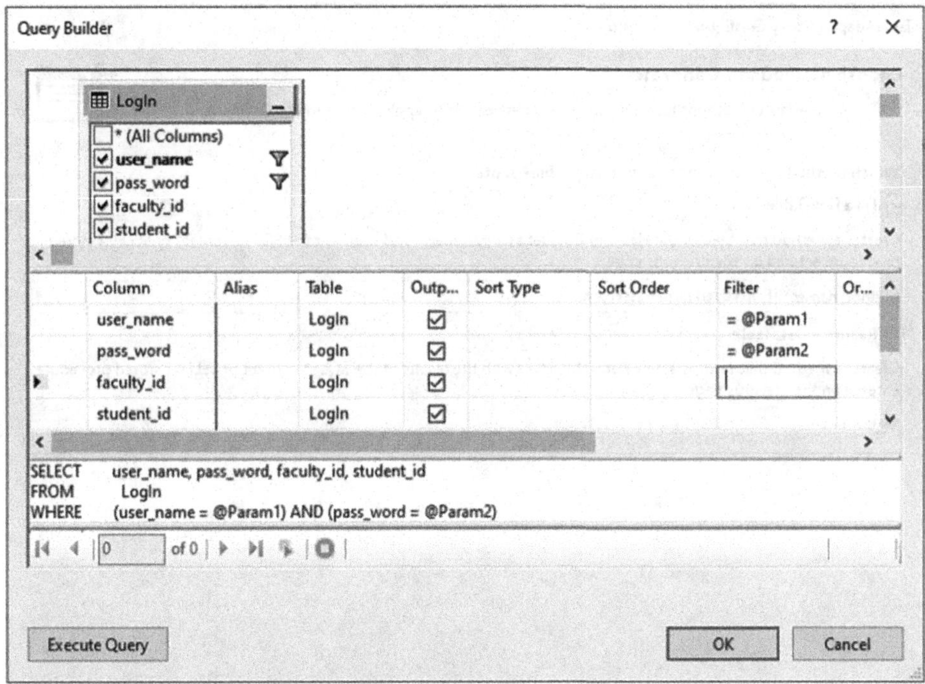

FIGURE 5.37 The opened query build wizard.

set up desired criteria to build user-defined queries. The query you built will be translated and presented by a real SQL statement in the text pane.

By default, all columns in the LogIn table are selected in the top graphical pane. You can decide which column you want to query by checking the associated checkbox in front of each column. In this application, we prefer to select all columns from the top graphical pane. The selected columns will be displayed in the second graphical pane, which is also shown in Figure 5.37.

Since we try to build a dynamic SQL query for the LogIn table, the login process is as follows. When the project runs, the **username** and **password** are entered by the user, and those two items will be embedded into an **SQL SELECT** statement that is sent to the data source, exactly to the LogIn table, to check if the username and password entered by the user can be found from the LogIn table. If a match is found, that matched record will be read back from the DataSet to the BindingSource via the TableAdapter, and furthermore reflected on the bound textboxes control on the Visual C# 2022 **LogIn** form window.

The problem is that when we build this query, we do not know the values of username and password, which will be entered by the user as the project runs. In other words, these two parameters are dynamic parameters. In order to build a dynamic query with two dynamic parameters, we need to use two question marks "?" to temporarily replace those two parameters in the SQL**SELECT** statement.

We do this by typing a question mark in the **Filter** column for **user_name** and **pass_word** rows in the second graphical pane, which is shown in Figure 5.37. The two question marks will become two dynamic parameters represented by **=@Param1** and **=@Param2**, respectively after you press the **Enter** key from the keyboard when you finish typing two question marks. This is a typical representation method for the dynamic parameters used in the SQL Server database query.

Now let's go to the text pane and you can find that a **WHERE** clause is attached at the end of the **SELECT** statement, which is shown in Figure 5.37. The clause

```
WHERE (user_name = @Param1) AND (pass_word = @Param2)
```

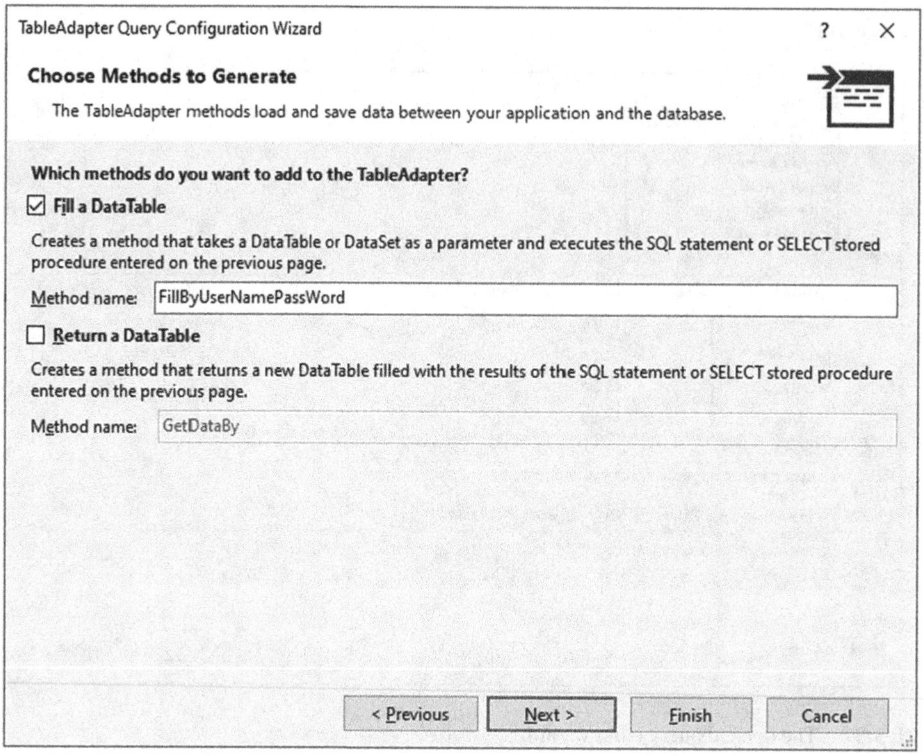

FIGURE 5.38 The finished choose methods to generate wizard.

is used to set up dynamic criteria for this **SELECT** statement. Two dynamic parameters, **Param1** and **Param2**, will be replaced by the actual username and password entered by the user as the project runs. You can consider the @ symbol as a * in C++, which works as an address. So we leave two addresses that will be filled later by two dynamic parameters, username and password, as the project runs.

Click the **OK** button to continue to the next step. The next wizard shows the complete query we build from the last step in the text format to ask your confirmation, and you can make any modification if you want; if not, just click the Next button to go to the next step.

The next wizard provides you with two options; the first one is to allow you to modify the **Fill()** method to meet your specified query for your application to fill a data table in the DataSet with your specified query criterion. The second option allows you to modify the **GetData()** method that returns a new data table filled with the executing results of the SQL statement above.

For this application, we only need to use and modify the **Fill()** method to return a single record from our LogIn table. To do that, keep the top checkbox, **Fill a DataTable**, checked and attach the word **ByUserNamePassWord** to the end of the **Fill** method in the **Method name** textbox, which is shown in Figure 5.38. Also uncheck the checkbox, **Return a DataTable**. We will use this modified **FillByUserNamePassWord**() method in our project to run the dynamic SQL statement we build in the last step to query one matched record. Click the **Next** button to go to the next wizard.

The next wizard shows the result of your TableAdapter configuration. If everything is going smoothly, all statements and methods should be created and modified successfully, as shown in Figure 5.39. Click on the **Finish** button to close this configuration.

Now you can find that a new query method, **FillByUserNamePassWord**(), has been added to the bottom of the LogIn table in the **TableAdapter Configuration Wizard**.

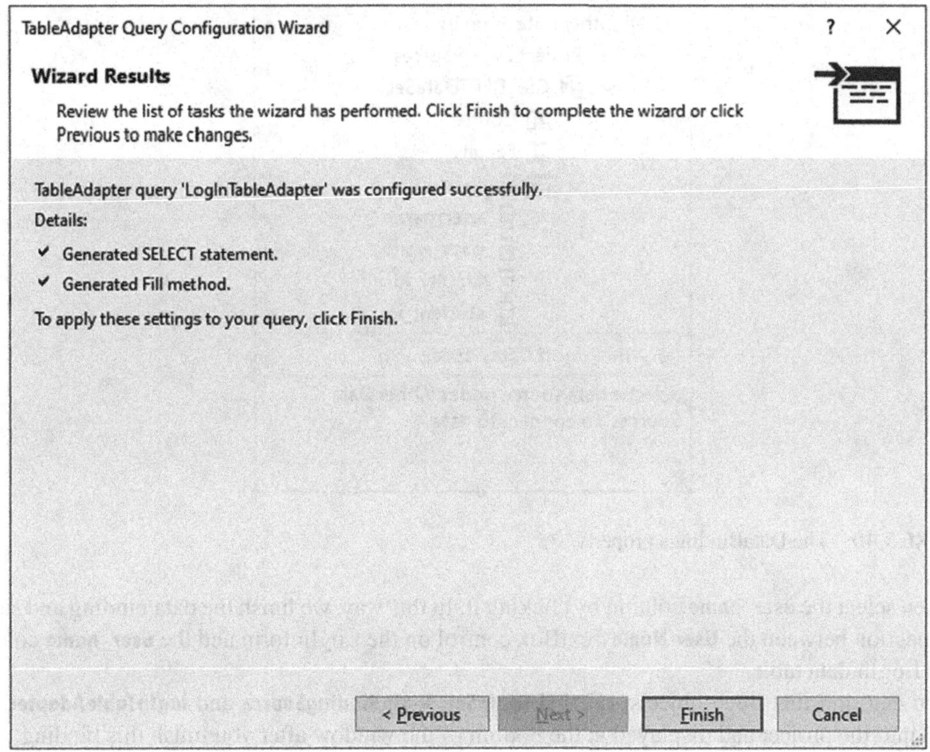

FIGURE 5.39 The result of the TableAdapter configuration wizard.

Before we can begin to do our coding job, we need to bind data to controls on the LogIn form to setup the connection between each control on the form and each data column on the data source.

5.6 BIND DATA TO THE ASSOCIATED CONTROLS IN LOGIN FORM

Open the Solution Explorer window and select the LogIn Form from that window, then click the View Designer button to open its GUI. Now we want to use the **BindingSource** to bind controls in the LogIn form, exactly the **User Name** and **Pass Word** TextBoxes, to the associated data fields in the LogIn table in the data source.

Click on the **User Name** TextBox, then go to the **DataBindings** property that is located in the top section of the Property window. Expand that property to display the individual items, and then select the **Text** item. Click the drop-down arrow to expand the following items:

- **Other Data Sources**
    - **Project Data Sources**
        - **CSE_DEPTDataSet**
            - **LogIn**
                - **user_name**

The expansion result is shown in Figure 5.40.

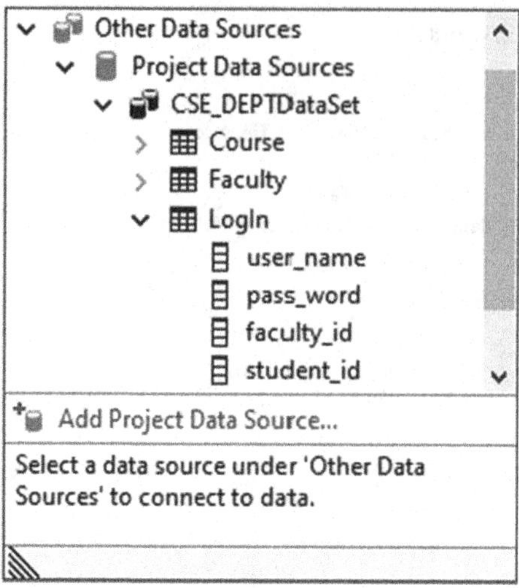

FIGURE 5.40 The DataBindings property.

Then select the **user_name** column by clicking it. In this way, we finish the data binding and set up a connection between the **User Name** TextBox control on the LogIn form and the **user_name** column in the LogIn data table.

You can find that three objects, **cSE_DEPTDataSet**, **logInBindingSource** and **logInTableAdapter**, are added into the project and displayed at the bottom of the window after you finish this binding.

Well, is that easy? Yes. Perform the similar operations for the **Pass Word** TextBox to bind it with the **pass_word** column in the LogIn table in the data source. But one point you need to note is: When we perform the data binding for the **User Name** TextBox, there is no pre-built or default BindingSource object available because we have not performed any data binding before, and the **User Name** is the first control you want to bind. After you finish the first binding, however, a new BindingSource object, **logInBindingSource**, is created. You need to use this created BindingSource object to handle all other data binding jobs for all other controls on the LogIn form.

When you perform the first data binding, there is no default BindingSource object available since you have not performed any binding before. You can browse to the desired data column and select it to finish this binding. Once you finish the first binding, a new BindingSource object is created, and all the following data bindings should use that new created BindingSource to perform all data bindings.

Let's perform the data binding for the **Pass Word** TextBox now.

Click that **Pass Word** TextBox to select it, and then go to the Properties window to expand the **DataBindings** property, select the **Text** item and click the drop-down arrow. This time you will find that a new BindingSource object, **logInBindingSource**, is shown up (Figure 5.41). Expand this new object and select the **pass_word** column in the LogIn table by clicking on it. The data binding for the **Pass Word** Textbox is done.

Some readers may have noted that when we built the **FillByUserNamePassWord()** method, we fill the LogIn form with four columns–**user_name**, **pass_word**, **faculty_id** and **student_id**–from the LogIn table. In fact, we only fill two textbox controls on the form, **txtUserName** and **txtPassWord**, with two associated columns in the LogIn table; **user_name** and **pass_word**. Because we only need to know if we can find the matched user name and password entered by the user from the LogIn table. If both

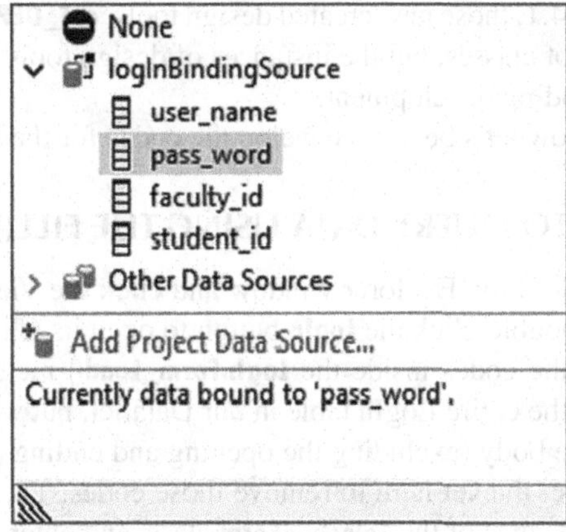

FIGURE 5.41 The new created BindingSource object.

matched items can be found from the LogIn table, this means that the login is successful and we can continue for the next step. Two bound-control on the form, **txtUserName** and **txtPassWord**, will be filled with the identical values stored in the LogIn table. It looks as if this does not make sense. In fact, we do not want to retrieve any column from the LogIn table; instead, we only want to find the matched items of user name and password from the LogIn table. If we can find matched user name and pas word, we do not care about the **faculty_id** and **student_id**. If no matched items can be found, this means that the login has failed and a warning message should be displayed.

To check the matched username and password entered by the user from the data source, one can use *Return a Single Value to Query Data* for LogIn table. But here in order to simplify this check, we use the Fill() method to fill four columns in a mapped data table in the DataSet. Then we can check whether this Fill() is successful. If it is, the matched data items have been found. Otherwise no matched data items are found.

Before we can go ahead with our coding, one thing we need to point out is the displaying style of the password in the textbox control **txtPassWord**. Generally, the password letters will be represented by a sequence of star * when users enter it as project runs. To make this happened to our project, you need to set the **PasswordChar** property of the textbox control **txtPassWord** to a star *.

Now it is time for us to develop codes that are related to those objects we created in the previous steps, such as the BindingSource and TableAdapter, to complete the dynamic query. The operational sequence of the login process is shown below:

1) When the project runs, the user needs to enter the username and password to two textbox controls, **txtUserName** and **txtPassWord**.
2) To start this login process, the user will click the LogIn button on the form to execute the LogIn button click method.
3) The LogIn button click method will first create some local variables or objects that will be used for the data query and a new object for the next form.
4) Then the method will call the **FillByUserNamePassWord()** method to fill the LogIn form.
5) If this Fill is successful, which means that the matched data items for username and password have been found from the LogIn table, the next window form, **SelectionForm**, will be displayed for the next operational step.
6) Otherwise, a warning message is displayed.

As we discussed in Section 5.4.1, those new created design tools, **cSE_DEPTDataSet**, **logInTableAdapter** and **logInBindingSource**, are not classes, but the instances of design tools. Therefore, we can directly use those instances for our coding development.

Keep this point in mind, now let's begin to develop the codes for the LogIn form.

5.7 DEVELOP CODES TO QUERY DATA USING THE FILL() METHOD

Select the **LogIn.cs** from the Solution Explorer window and click the View Designer button to open its graphical user interface. Double-click the **LogIn** button to open its Click method.

First we need to remove the codes inside the **LogInForm_Load()** method since this method performed a **Fill()** function to fill the entire LogIn table in our DataSet, but we do not need this function. Thus highlight the entire code body (excluding the opening and ending parentheses), right-click on this highlighted part and select the **Cut** item to remove those codes. Then we need to create a local object **selForm**, which is an instance of the **SelectionForm** class, and enter the codes that are shown in Figure 5.42 into this method.

Let's take a closer look at this piece of codes to see how it works.

A. A new namespace is created by the Visual C# and the name of this namespace is equal to the name of our project, **SelectWizard_Project**. By using the namespace technology, it is much easier to distinguish the different variables, methods, delegates and events that have the same name but located at different spaces.

```
SelectWizard Project                    cmdLogIn_Click(object sender, EventArgs e)

A  namespace SelectWizard_Project
   {
B     public partial class LogInForm : Form
      {
C        public LogInForm()
         {
            InitializeComponent();
         }
D        private void LogInForm_Load(object sender, EventArgs e) { }
E        private void cmdLogIn_Click(object sender, EventArgs e)
         {
F           SelectionForm selForm = new SelectionForm();
G           logInTableAdapter.ClearBeforeFill = true;
H           logInTableAdapter.FillByUserNamePassWord(cSE_DEPTDataSet.LogIn, txtUserName.Text, txtPassWord.Text);
I           if (cSE_DEPTDataSet.LogIn.Count == 0)
            {
               MessageBox.Show("No matched username/password found!");
               txtUserName.Clear();
               txtUserName.Focus();
               txtPassWord.Clear();
            }
J           else
            {
               this.Hide();
               selForm.ShowDialog();
               this.Close();
            }
         }
K        private void cmdCancel_Click(object sender, EventArgs e)
         {
            Application.Exit();
         }
      }
   }
```

FIGURE 5.42 The codes for the LogIn button click method.

B. This line indicates that our LogIn form class is derived from the system class Form.

C. The constructor of our LogInForm class contains a built-in method, **InitializeComponent()**. This method is used to initialize all new created instances and variables in this form. Starting Visual C# 2008, this method is moved to the **LogIn.Designer.cs** file.

D. The **LogInForm_Load()** is the first method to be executed when this LogInForm runs. All original codes inside this method have been removed since we do not need them.

E. Our LogIn button's Click method contains two arguments: the **sender** indicates the current object that triggers this method, and the second argument e contains the additional information for this event.

F. As this method is triggered and executed, first we need to create an instance of our next form window, **SelectionForm**.

G. Before we fill the LogIn data table, we need to clean up that table in the DataSet. As we mentioned in Section 5.1.1.1, the DataSet is a table holder and it contains multiple data tables. But these data tables are only mappings to those real data tables in the database. All data can be loaded into these tables in the DataSet by using the TableAdapter when the project runs. Here a property **ClearBeforeFill**, which belongs to the TableAdapter, is set to **True** to perform this cleaning job for that mapped LogIn data table in the DataSet.

H. Now we need to call the **FillByUserNamePassWord()** method we created in Section 5.5, to fill the LogIn data table in the DataSet. Because we have already bound two textbox controls on the LogIn form, **txtUserName** and **txtPassWord**, with two columns in the LogIn data table in the DataSet, **user_name** and **pass_word**, by using the **logInBindingSource**, so these two filled columns in the LogIn data table will also be reflected in those two bound textbox controls, **txtUserName** and **txtPassWord**, when this **FillByUserNamePassWord()** method is executed. This **Fill()** method has three arguments; the first one is the data table, in this case it is the LogIn table that is held by the DataSet, **CSE_DEPTDataSet**. The following two parameters are dynamic parameters that were temporarily replaced by two question marks "?" when we built this **Fill()** method in Section 5.5. Now we can use two real parameters, **txtUserName.Text** and **txtPassWord.Text**, entered by the user, to replace those two question marks in order to complete this dynamic query.

I. If no matched username and password can be found from the LogIn table in the database, the **FillByUserNamePassWord()** method cannot be executed to fill the LogIn table in the DataSet. This situation can be detected by checking the Count property of the LogIn table in the DataSet. This Count property represents the number of rows that have been successfully filled into the LogIn table in the DataSet. A zero value means that no matched username and password has been found and this fill is failed. A warning message is displayed if this happened and some cleaning jobs are performed for two textboxes in the LogIn form. By checking this property, we will know if this Fill is successful or not, or if a matched username and password has been found from the database.

J. Otherwise, if a matched username and password is found from the LogIn table in the database and the login process is successful, the current window or the LogInForm should be hidden by calling the **Hide()** method, and the next window form, **SelectionForm**, will be displayed to allow users to continue to the next step. After displaying the next form, the current LogIn form should be closed. The keyword **this** represents the current form.

K. The code for the **Cancel** button Click method is very simple. The **Application.Exit()** method should be called to terminate our project if this button is clicked by the user. Double-click on the Cancel button from the LogInForm Designer View to open this method, and enter this coding line.

Before we can test this piece of code by running the project, make sure that the LogIn form has been selected as the Startup form. To confirm this, double-click the **Program.cs** folder from the Solution Explorer window to open the **Main()** method. Make sure that the argument of the **Application.Run()**

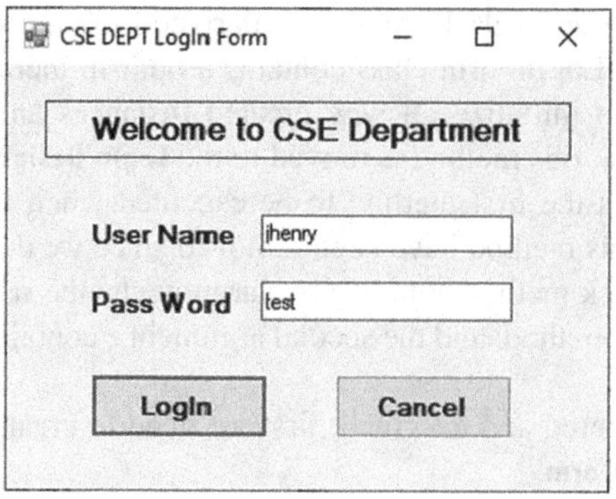

FIGURE 5.43 The running status of the project.

FIGURE 5.44 The warning message.

method is **new LogInForm()**. This means that a new instance of LogInForm class is created and displayed as this **Run()** method is executed.

Click the **Start** button to run the project and the LogIn form is shown up in Figure 5.43.

Enter a valid user name **jhenry** to the User Name textbox, and a valid password **test** to the Pass Word textbox, then click the LogIn button. The Fill method **FillByUserNamePassWord()** will be called to fill the LogIn table in the data source. Because we entered a correct username and password, this fill will be successful and the next form, **SelectionForm**, will be displayed to enable users to perform the next action. Now go to the **Debug | Stop Debugging** menu item to stop and terminate our project.

Now run the project again and try to enter a wrong username or password. To do this login process, a MessageBox will be displayed, as shown in Figure 5.44, to indicate this situation.

In this section, we used the LogIn form and LogIn table to show readers how to perform a dynamic data query and fill a mapped data table in the DataSet by using the Visual Studio design tools and wizards. The coding process is simple and easy to follow up. In the next section, we try to show the readers how to use another method provided by the TableAdapter to pick up a single value from the database.

5.8 USE RETURN A SINGLE VALUE TO QUERY DATA FOR LOGIN FORM

Many people may have experienced forgetting either the username or the password when they try to logon to a specified website to get some information, to order some merchandises or pay bills for their monthly utilities or cell phones. In this section, we show users how to use a method to retrieve a single data value from the database. This method belongs to the TableAdapter class.

We still use the LogIn form and LogIn table as an example. Suppose you forget your password, but you want to login to this project by using the LogIn form with your username. By using this example, you can retrieve your password by using your username.

The DataSet Designer allows us to edit the structure of the DataSet. As we discussed in Section 5.1.2.3, by using this Designer, you can configure an existing query, add a new query, and add a new column and even a new key to a database. The **Add Query** method allows us to add a new data query with a SQL SELECT statement which returns a single value.

Open the LogIn form window from the Solution Explorer window and open the Data Source window. Right-click on any place inside that window and select the **Edit DataSet with Designer**. Next locate the LogIn table and right-click on the last line of that table, which contains our modified method **FillByUserNamePassWord()** which we built in the last section. Then select **Add Query** to open the **TableAdapter Query Configuration Wizard**.

On the opened wizard, keep the default selection **Use SQL statements**, then click the **Next** and choose the **SELECT which returns a single value** radio button. Click the **Next** button to go to the next wizard and click the **Query Builder** button to build our query.

On the opened **Query Builder** wizard, perform the following operations to create this single data query:

1) Click the first row from the second pane to select it.
2) Then right-click on this row and select **Delete** from the popup menu to delete this row.
3) Go to the top pane and select the **pass_word** and **user_name** columns from the LogIn table by checking two checkboxes related to those two columns.
4) Go to the second pane and uncheck the checkbox for the **user_name** column from the **Output** column since we do not want to use it as the output, but instead we need to use it as a criterion to filter this query.
5) Still in the second pane, right-click on the **Group By** column and select **Delete** from the popup menu to remove this **Group By** choice.
6) Type a question mark '?' on the **Filter** field in the **user_name** column, and press the **Enter** key from your keyboard. Your finished Query Builder should match one that is shown in Figure 5.45.

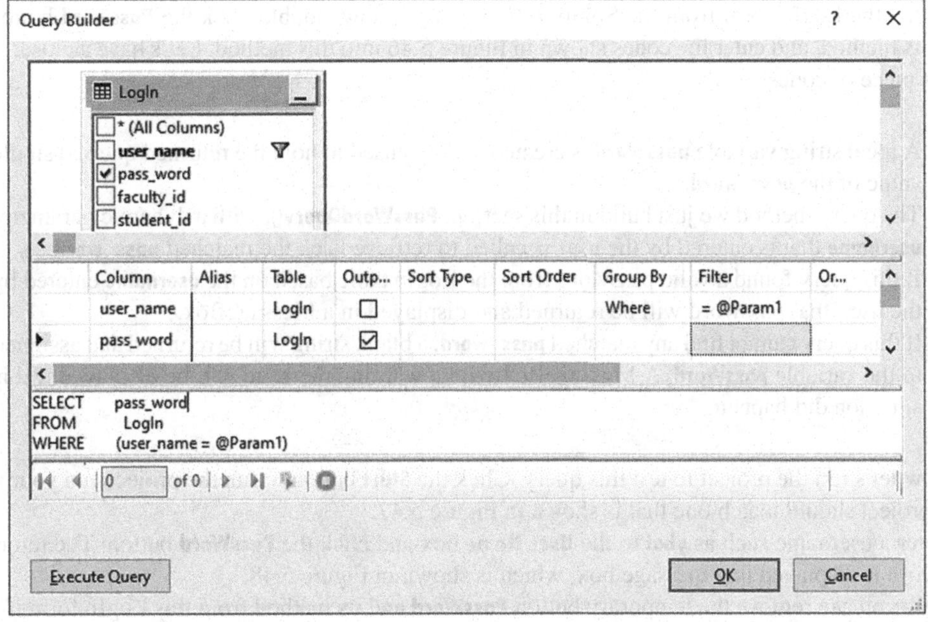

FIGURE 5.45 The finished query builder.

```
SelectWizard Project                         CmdPW_Click(object sender, EventArgs e)

    private void cmdPW_Click(object sender, EventArgs e)
    {
A           string passWord;
            logInTableAdapter.ClearBeforeFill = true;
B           passWord = logInTableAdapter.PassWordQuery(txtUserName.Text);
C           if (passWord != String.Empty)
               MessageBox.Show("The Password is: " + passWord);
D           else
               MessageBox.Show("No matched password found!");
    }
```

FIGURE 5.46 The codes for the cmdPW click button method.

The SQL statement

```
SELECTpass_wordFROMLogInWHERE (user_name = @Param1)
```

indicates that we want to select a password from the LogIn table based on the username that is a dynamic parameter, and this parameter will be entered by the user when the project runs. Click the **OK** button to go to the next wizard.

The next window is used to confirm your terminal SQL statement. Click the **Next** button to go to continue.

The next wizard allows you to choose a function name for this query. Change the default name to a meaningful name such as **PassWordQuery**, then click the **Next** button. A successful Wizard Result will be displayed if everything is fine. Click on the **Finish** button to complete this configuration.

Now let's do our coding process for the LogIn form. For the testing purpose, we need to add a temporary button with the name as **cmdPW** and the Text as **Password** to the LogIn form. Then select and open the LogIn form from the Solution Explorer window, double-click the **Password** button to open its method, and enter the codes shown in Figure 5.46 into this method. Let's have a closer look at this piece of codes.

A. A local string variable **passWord** is created and it is used to hold the returned queried single value of the **pass_word**.
B. The query method we just build in this section, **PassWordQuery()**, with a dynamic parameter **username** that is entered by the user is called to retrieve back the matched **pass_word**.
C. If this query found a valid password from the LogIn table based on the **username** entered by the user, that password will be returned and displayed in a MessageBox.
D. If this query cannot find any matched **pass_word**, a blank string will be returned and assigned to the variable **passWord**. A MessageBox with a warning message will be displayed if this situation did happen.

Now let's run the project to test this query. Click the **Start** button to run the project and your running project should match one that is shown in Figure 5.47.

Enter a username such as **ybai** to the **User Name** box and click the **PassWord** button. The returned password is displayed in a message box, which is shown in Figure 5.48.

Now you can remove the temporary button **PassWord** and its method from this LogIn form if you like since we do not need it any more for this project.

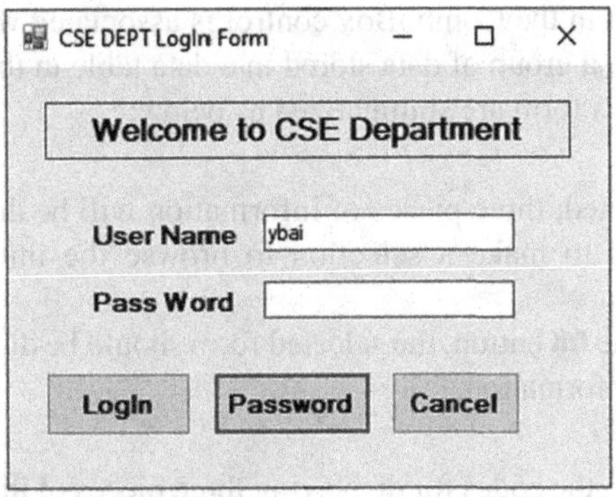

FIGURE 5.47 The running status of the LogIn form.

FIGURE 5.48 The returned password.

In the following sections, we will show the readers how to develop a more professional data-driven project by using more controls and methods. We still use the **SelectWizard Project** example project and continue with the SelectionForm.

5.9 CODING FOR THE SELECTION FORM

As we discussed in Section 5.6, if the login process is successful, the SelectionForm window should be displayed to allow users to continue for the next step. Figure 5.49 shows an opened SelectionForm window.

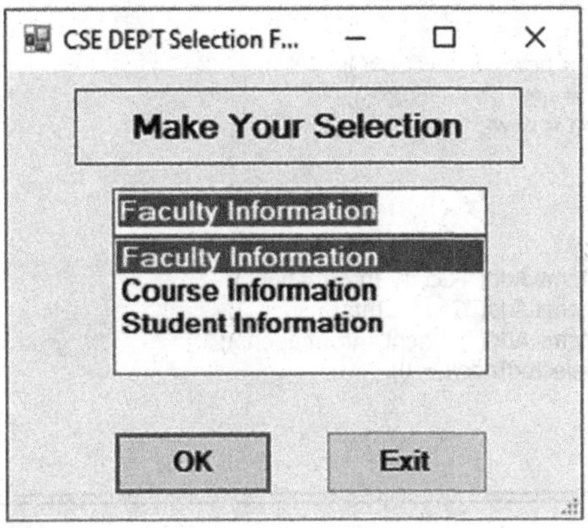

FIGURE 5.49 The opened selection form.

Each piece of information in the ComboBox control is associated with a form window and furthermore it is associated with a group of data stored in a data table in the database.

The operation steps for this form are summarized as below:

1) When this form is opened, three pieces of information will be displayed in a ComboBox control to allow users to make a selection to browse the information related to that selection.
2) When the user clicks the **OK** button, the selected form should be displayed to enable the user to browse the related information.

Based on the operation step 1, the codes for displaying three pieces of information should be located in the constructor of the **SelectionForm** since this constructor should be called first as an instance of the **SelectionForm** is created.

Open the SelectionForm window and click the **View Code** button to open its code window. Enter the codes, which are shown in Figure 5.50, into the constructor of the SelectionForm.

Let's have a closer look at this piece of codes to see how it works.

A. Three instances are created first, and each one is associated with a form class.

B. The **Add()** method of the ComboBox class is used to attach all three pieces of information to this ComboBox. The reference **this** represents the current form object, an instance of the SelectionForm class, and the property SelectedIndex is set to zero to select the first information as the default one.

According to operation step 2 described above, when users click the **OK** button, the related form selected by the user should be displayed to allow users to browse information from that form. Click the **View Designer** button to open the graphical user interface of the SelectionForm object. Then double click the **OK** button to open its **cmdOK_Click** method and enter the codes, which are shown in Figure 5.51, into this method.

Let's take a closer look at this piece of codes to see how it works.

```
SelectWizard Project                    SelectionForm

namespace SelectWizard_Project
{
    public partial class SelectionForm : Form
    {
A       FacultyForm facultyForm = new FacultyForm();
        CourseForm courseForm = new CourseForm();
        StudentForm studentForm = new StudentForm();

        public SelectionForm()
        {
            InitializeComponent();
B           this.ComboSelection.Items.Add("Faculty Information");
            this.ComboSelection.Items.Add("Course Information");
            this.ComboSelection.Items.Add("Student Information");
            this.ComboSelection.SelectedIndex = 0;
        }
    }
}
```

FIGURE 5.50 The detailed codes for the selection form.

```
SelectWizard Project                    CmdOK_Click(object sender, EventArgs e)

  private void cmdOK_Click(object sender, EventArgs e)
  {
A         if (this.ComboSelection.Text == "Faculty Information")
            facultyForm.Show();
B         else if (this.ComboSelection.Text == "Course Information")
            courseForm.Show();
C         else if (this.ComboSelection.Text == "Student Information")
            studentForm.Show();
D         else
            MessageBox.Show("Invalid Selection!");
  }
```

FIGURE 5.51 The coding for the OK button click method.

```
SelectWizard Project                    cmdExit.Click(object sender, EventArgs e)

  private void cmdExit_Click(object sender, EventArgs e)
  {
A         courseForm.Close();
          facultyForm.Close();
          studentForm.Close();
B         Application.Exit();
  }
```

FIGURE 5.52 The completed codes for the exit button click method.

The function for this piece of coding is straightforward and easily understood, and is outlined as below:

A. Open the FacultyForm window if the user selected the Faculty Information.
B. Open the StudentForm window if the user selected the Student Information.
C. Open the CourseForm window if the user selected the Course Information.
D. An error message is displayed if no information is selected.

The last coding process for this form is the **Exit** button. Open the GUI of the SelectionForm, double-click the **Exit** button to open its **cmdExit_Click()** method. Enter the following codes into this method, which is shown in Figure 5.52.

This piece of codes looks a little complicated. Let's see how this piece of codes works.

A. Three **Close()** methods attached to three instances, **facultyForm**, **courseForm** and **studentForm**, are executed to close the associated form object. The point is that you do not need to create any new instance for each of those classes since those instances are created in this SelectionForm as the class variables or called fields in Visual C# IDE.
B. Finally, the system method **Application.Exit()** is called to terminate the whole project.

Suppose the user selected the first information – **Faculty Information**. A Faculty form window will be displayed and this is supposed to be connected to a Faculty data table in the DataSet. If the user selected a faculty name from the ComboBox control and clicked the **Select** button on that form, all information related to that faculty should be displayed on that form, exactly on seven TextBoxes and a picturebox.

Now let's build the codes for the FacultyForm window. First let's see how to perform the data-binding to bind controls on the Faculty form to the associated columns in the database.

5.10 BIND DATA COLUMN TO THE ASSOCIATED CONTROLS IN FACULTY FORM

Open the Faculty Form window from the Solution Explorer window and perform the following data bindings.

1. Click the Faculty ID TextBox, **txtFacultyID**, to select it, then go to the Properties window to expand the **DataBindings** property, select the **Text** item and click its drop-down arrow. Expand the following items:

```
• Other Data Sources
      Project Data Sources
          CSE_DEPTDataSet
             Faculty
```

2. Then select the **faculty_id** column from the Faculty table by clicking on it. In this way, we finish the binding between the control **txtFacultyID** on the Faculty Form and the **faculty_id** column in the Faculty table. As soon as this data binding is finished, you can find that three instances are created and displayed under the form; **cSE_DEPTDataSet**, **facultyBindingSource** and **facultyTableAdapter**.
3. In a similar way, select and bind all other six TextBoxes, **txtFacultyName, txtTitle, txtOffice, txtPhone, txtCollege** and **txtEmail**, in the Faculty Information GroupBox. One important point to be noted is that when you bind the second TextBox control, **txtFacultyName**, you will find that a new object **facultyBindingSource** has been created under the **DataBindings** property. As we discussed in Section 5.6, as soon as you finished the first data binding, a new data-binding source is created and you need to use this data-binding source to bind our **txtFacultyName** control and all other controls. Expand this binding source and click on the **faculty_name** column to finish this binding. One example of this binding process is shown in Figure 5.53.

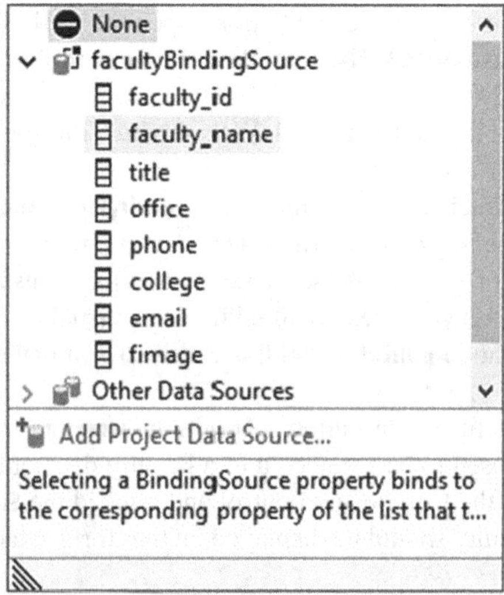

FIGURE 5.53 The expansion for the data binding.

4. Click on the **PhotoBox**, in which a selected faculty image will be displayed, to select it. Then go to the Properties window and expand the **DataBindings** property, select the **Image** item and click its drop-down arrow and expand the following items:

   - `facultyBindingSource`
     `fimage`

   Select the **fimage** item by clicking on it. Now we have completed the data binding process.

Next we need to use the DataSet Designer to build our data query with SQL SELECT statement and modify the name of the **FillBy()** method for the **facultyTableAdapter**.

Open the Data Source window and right-click on any place inside that window and select **Edit DataSet with** Designer item to open the DataSet Designer Wizard. Locate the **Faculty** table, then right-click on the last line of the Faculty table and select the **Add Query** item from the pop-up menu to open the **TableAdapter Configuration Wizard**.

On the opened Wizard, click on the **Next** button to keep the default command type – **Use SQL statements** and click the another **Next** button in the next wizard to keep the default query type – **SELECT which returns rows**. Then click the **Query Builder** button to open the Query Builder wizard.

In the middle graphical pane, move your cursor to the **Filter** column along the **faculty_name** line, then type a question mark "?" and press the **Enter** key from your keyboard. In this way, we add a **WHERE** clause with a dynamic parameter that is represented by = @Param1 in the SQL Server database.

Your finished Query Builder should match the one shown in Figure 5.54.

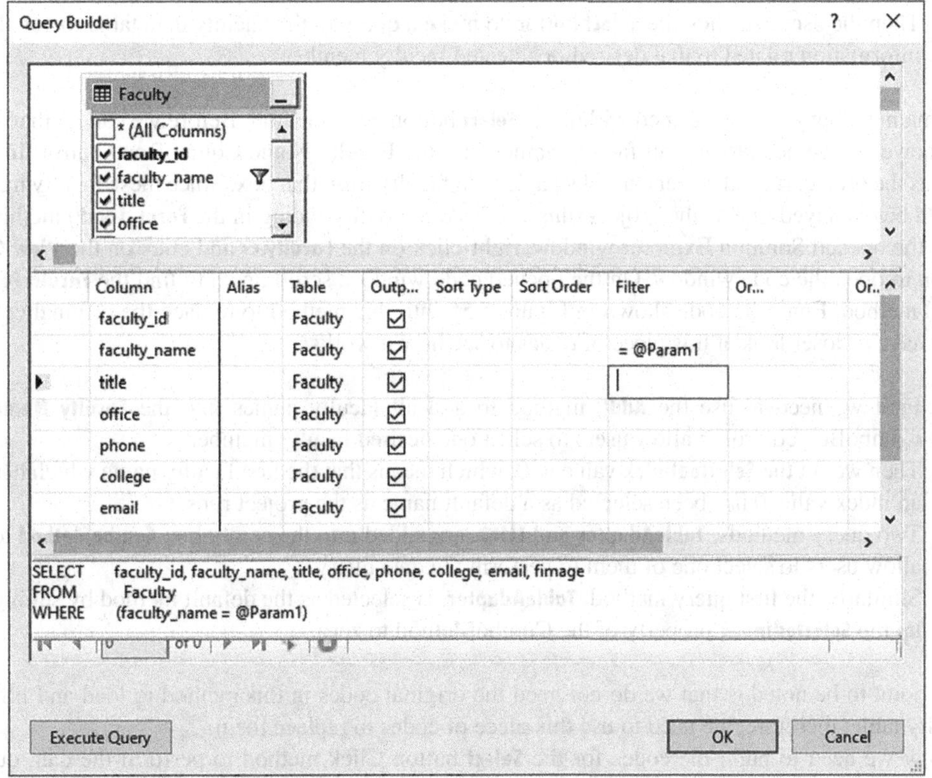

FIGURE 5.54 An example of the finished query builder.

Click on the **OK** and the **Next** buttons in the next two wizards to modify the name of the **FillBy()** method to **FillByFacultyName()**. Uncheck the **Return a DataTable** checkbox since we do not want to return any table. Click on the **Next** and then the **Finish** buttons for next two wizards to complete this configuration. You can find that this new method has been added to the bottom line for the Faculty table in the **TableAdapter Configuration Wizard**.

Now let's develop the codes for querying the faculty information using this Faculty form with the Faculty data table in the database, exactly in our DataSet.

5.11 DEVELOP CODES TO QUERY DATA FROM THE FACULTY TABLE

In this section, we divide the coding job into two parts with two methods. Querying data from the Faculty table using the SQL Select method is discussed in Section 5.11.1, and retrieving data using the LINQ method is explained in Section 5.11.2. Furthermore, we only take care of the coding developments for the **Select** and the **Back** buttons' click methods and the coding for all other buttons will be discussed and coded in the following sections.

5.11.1 Develop Codes to Query Data Using the SQL SELECT Method

As we mentioned above, the pseudo-code or the operation sequence of this data query can be described as below:

- After the project runs, the user has completed the login process. Now select the Faculty Information item from the Selection Form.
- The Faculty Form will be displayed to allow users to select the desired faculty name from the Faculty Name ComboBox control.
- Then the user can click the **Select** button to make a query to the Faculty data table to get all information related to that desired or selected faculty member.

The main coding job is performed within the **Select** button click method. Before we can do that coding, however, we need to add all faculty names into the Faculty Name ComboBox control. In this way, as the project runs, the user can select a desired faculty from that box. Since these faculty names should be displayed first as the project runs, we need to do this coding in the **Form_Load()** method.

In the opened Solution Explorer window, right-click on the **Faculty.cs** and click on the **View Code** button to open the code window. On the opened code window, scroll down to find the **FacultyForm_Load()** method. Enter the code shown in Figure 5.55 into this method to replace the original codes. Let's have a closer look at this piece of codes to see how it works.

A. First we need to use the **Add()** method to add all faculty names into the **Faculty Name** ComboBox control to allow users to select one desired faculty member.

B. Then we set the **SelectedIndex** value to 0, which means that the first faculty name which has an index value 0 has been selected as a default name as the project runs.

C. Two query methods, **TableAdapter** and **LINQ**, are added into the combobox **ComboMethod** to allow users to select one of them to perform the data query.

D. Similarly, the first query method, **TableAdapter**, is selected as the default method by setting up the **SelectedIndex** property of the ComboMethod to zero.

A point to be noted is that we do not need the original codes in this method to load and fill the Faculty table; therefore, we need to use this piece of codes to replace them.

Now we need to build the codes for the **Select** button Click method to perform the data query using the SQL SELECT query statement.

```
SelectWizard Project                     FacultyForm()

  private void FacultyForm_Load(object sender, EventArgs e)
  {
A         ComboName.Items.Add("Ying Bai");
          ComboName.Items.Add("Davis Bhalla");
          ComboName.Items.Add("Black Anderson");
          ComboName.Items.Add("Steve Johnson");
          ComboName.Items.Add("Jenney King");
          ComboName.Items.Add("Alice Brown");
          ComboName.Items.Add("Debby Angles");
          ComboName.Items.Add("Jeff Henry");
B         ComboName.SelectedIndex = 0;
C         ComboMethod.Items.Add("TableAdapter Method");
          ComboMethod.Items.Add("LINQ & DataSet Method");
D         this.ComboMethod.SelectedIndex = 0;
  }
```

FIGURE 5.55 The detailed codes for the FacultyForm_Load() event method.

```
SelectWizard Project                     cmdSelect_Click(object sender, EventArgs e)

  private void cmdSelect_Click(object sender, EventArgs e)
  {
A         this.facultyTableAdapter.ClearBeforeFill = true;
B         if (this.ComboMethod.Text == "TableAdapter Method")
          {
C           this.facultyTableAdapter.FillByFacultyName(cSE_DEPTDataSet.Faculty, ComboName.Text);
            if (cSE_DEPTDataSet.Faculty.Count == 0)
               MessageBox.Show("No Matched Faculty Found!");
          }
D         else
          {
          //   LINQtoDataSet();
          }
  }
```

FIGURE 5.56 The codes for the select button event procedure.

Click on the **View Designer** button to open the Faculty's GUI. On the opened Faculty form, double-click on the **Select** button to open this method, then enter the codes, which are shown in Figure 5.56, into this method.

Let's have a closer look at this piece of code to see how it works.

A. First we need to clean up the Faculty table in the DataSet before it can be filled by setting the **ClearBeforeFill** property to **True**.

B. Before we can perform this data query, we need to check which method has been selected. If the **TableAdapter Method** is selected, the method **FillByFacultyName()** we built in this section is called to fill the Faculty table with a dynamic parameter, which is selected by the user from the **Faculty Name** ComboBox control as the project runs.

C. By checking the **Count** property of the Faculty table in our DataSet, we should be able to know whether this fill is successful or not. If this property is 0, which means that no matched record has been found from the Faculty table in the database, and no any record or data has been filled into the Faculty table in our DataSet, a warning message is given

```
SelectWizard Project                    cmdBack_Click(object sender, EventArgs e)

private void cmdBack_Click(object sender, EventArgs e)
{
    this.Hide();
}
```

FIGURE 5.57 The codes for the back button.

for this situation to require users to handle this problem. The user can either continue to select correct faculty name or exit the project. If this property is non-zero, which indicates that this fill is successful and a matched faculty name is found and the Faculty table in our DataSet has been filled. A record related to the matched faculty will be displayed in seven TextBoxes and a PictureBox.

D. Otherwise, the **LINQ & DataSet Method** is selected and a user-defined method **LINQtoDataSet()** that will be developed below is called to retrieve back the faculty information with a LINQ query method.

The codes for the **Back** button Click method are very simple. The Faculty Form will be hidden when this button is clicked. A **Hide()** method is used for this purpose, which is shown in Figure 5.57.

5.11.2 Develop Codes to Query Data Using the LINQ Method

The LINQ query technique is one of the most popular query methods and widely implemented in the modern database programming applications. The query process can be significantly integrated and improved by using this technology. We have already provided a very detailed discussion about this technology in Chapter 4. Refer to that chapter to get a clear picture for this issue. In this part, we will concentrate on the implementations of this method.

Open the **Code Window** of the Faculty Form if it is not opened, create a user-defined method and enter the codes, which are shown in Figure 5.58, into this method.

```
SelectWizard Project                    LINQtoDataSet()

A  using System.IO;
   private void LINQtoDataSet()
   {
B      this.facultyTableAdapter.Fill(cSE_DEPTDataSet.Faculty);
C      var facultyinfo = (from fi in cSE_DEPTDataSet.Faculty
                          where fi.Field<string>("faculty_name").Equals(ComboName.Text)
                          select fi);
D      foreach (var fRow in facultyinfo)
       {
E          this.txtFacultyID.Text = fRow.faculty_id;
           this.txtFacultyName.Text = fRow.faculty_name;
           this.txtTitle.Text = fRow.title;
           this.txtOffice.Text = fRow.office;
           this.txtPhone.Text = fRow.phone;
           this.txtCollege.Text = fRow.college;
           this.txtEmail.Text = fRow.email;
F          this.PhotoBox.Image = Image.FromStream(new MemoryStream(fRow.fimage));
       }
   }
```

FIGURE 5.58 The detailed codes for the LINQ method.

Let's see how this piece of code works.

A. The **System.IO** namespace is added to enable us to use a method, **MemoryStream()**, to convert the column **fimage** whose data type is **byte[]** in the Faculty table to the **System.Drawing.Image** that can be accepted and displayed in the **PhotoBox** in our Faculty Form for a selected faculty image.
B. Then the default **Fill()** method of the **facultyTableAdapter** is executed to load data from the Faculty table in the database into the Faculty table in our DataSet. This step is necessary since the LINQ technique is applied with a DataSet and the DataSet must contain the valid data in all tables before this technique can be implemented.
C. A typical LINQ query structure is created and executed to retrieve back all related information for the selected faculty member. The facultyinfo is a C# implicitly typed local variable with a data type **var**. The C# will be able to automatically convert this **var** to any suitable data type. In this case, it is a DataSet, when it sees it. An iteration variable **fi** is used to iterate over the result of this query from the Faculty table. Then a similar SQL **SELECT** statement is executed with the **WHERE** clause.
D. A **foreach** loop is utilized to pick up each column from the selected data row **fRow**, which is obtained from the **facultyinfo** we get from the above LINQ query.
E. Assign each column to the associated TextBox to display them in the Faculty Form window.
F. Finally, we need to call a system method **FromStream()** with an argument, which is a new object of the class **MemoryStream()**, embedded with our **fimage** column in the Faculty table in our DataSet with an argument, to convert the latter from a **byte[]** type to a **System.Drawing.Image** type. The latter can be accepted and displayed in the **PhotoBox** in our Faculty Form for a selected faculty image.

At this point, we complete the coding process for this Form. Do not forget to remove the comment sign for the **LINQtoDataSet()** method in the **else** clause in the codes shown in Figure 5.56 since we have finished building of that method. Now we can run and test our project.

Click the **Build | Build Solution** menu item to build and link our project, and click the **Start** button to run the project. Enter **ybai** as the username and **come** as the password on the LogIn

Form. Click on the **LogIn** button to open the Selection Form window, select the **Faculty Information** item, and then click the **OK** button to open the Faculty Form. Select **Ying Bai** from the **Faculty Name** ComboBox, and click the **Select** button. All information related to this faculty with a selected faculty image will be displayed, as shown in Figure 5.59.

You can try to select either **TableAdapter Method** or **LINQ & DataSet** method from the **Query Method** ComboBox to perform different queries based on different faculty members to confirm the correctness of our project.

At this point, we complete the data query process for our Faculty table via the Faculty Form. Next we will take care of data query for our Course table via the Course Form.

5.12 BINDING DATA TO ASSOCIATED CONTROLS IN THE COURSE FORM

The functions of this form are illustrated by the following operational steps:

1) This Form allows users to find the course taught by the selected faculty from the Faculty Name ComboBox control when users click the **Select** button. All queried courses (exactly all **course_id**) are displayed in the Course ListBox.
2) The detailed information for each course, such as the course ID, course title, course schedule, classroom, credits and enrollment, can be obtained by clicking the desired **course_id** from the Course ListBox, and displayed in six TextBox controls.
3) The Back button allows users to return to the Selection Form to make other selection to obtain desired information related to that selection.

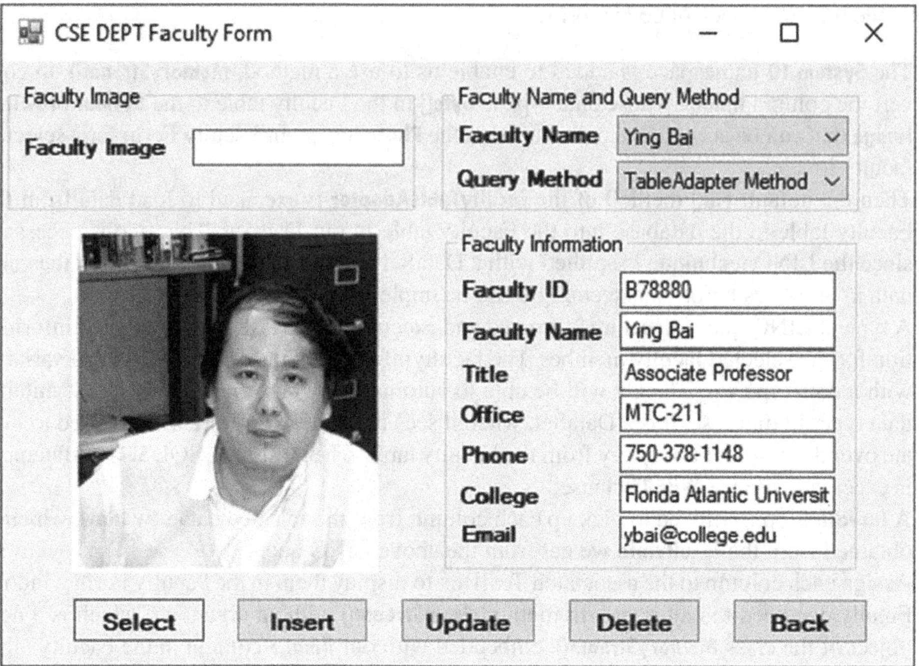

FIGURE 5.59 The running status of the faculty form window.

In this section, we only take care of two buttons; the **Select** and the **Back** buttons. The coding for the **Insert**, **Update** and **Delete** buttons will be discussed in the following chapters.

In above step 1, two queries need to be performed; In order to find the courses taught by the selected faculty, we need first to obtain the faculty ID that is associated with the selected faculty from the Faculty Name ComboBox when users clicked the **Select** button because no faculty name is available in the Course table. The only available information in the Course table is the **faculty_id**. So we need first to create a query that returns a single value (**faculty_id**) from the Faculty table; then we will create another query in the Course table to find the courses taught by the selected faculty based on the **faculty_id** we obtained from the Faculty table.

Now let's handle the first step, which is to create a query to obtain an associated **faculty_id** from the Faculty table based on the selected faculty name from the Faculty Name combobox in the Course form.

Open the DataSet Designer Wizard and right-click on the last line of the Faculty table and select Add Query to open the TableAdapter Query Configuration Wizard, keep the default selection **Use SQL statements** and click the **Next** button to go to the next wizard. Check the radio button in front of **SELECT which returns a single value** to choose this query type, and click the **Next** button to go the next wizard. Then click on the **Query Builder** to build our query.

Perform the following operations to complete this query building:

1) Click the first row (only one row) from the second pane to select it.
2) Then right-click on this row and select **Delete** from the popup menu to delete this row.
3) Go to the top pane and select the **faculty_id** and **faculty_name** columns from the **Faculty** table by checking two checkboxes related to those two columns.
4) Go to the second pane and uncheck the checkbox for the **faculty_name** column from the **Output** column since we do not want to use it as the output. Instead, we need to use it as a query criterion to filter this query.

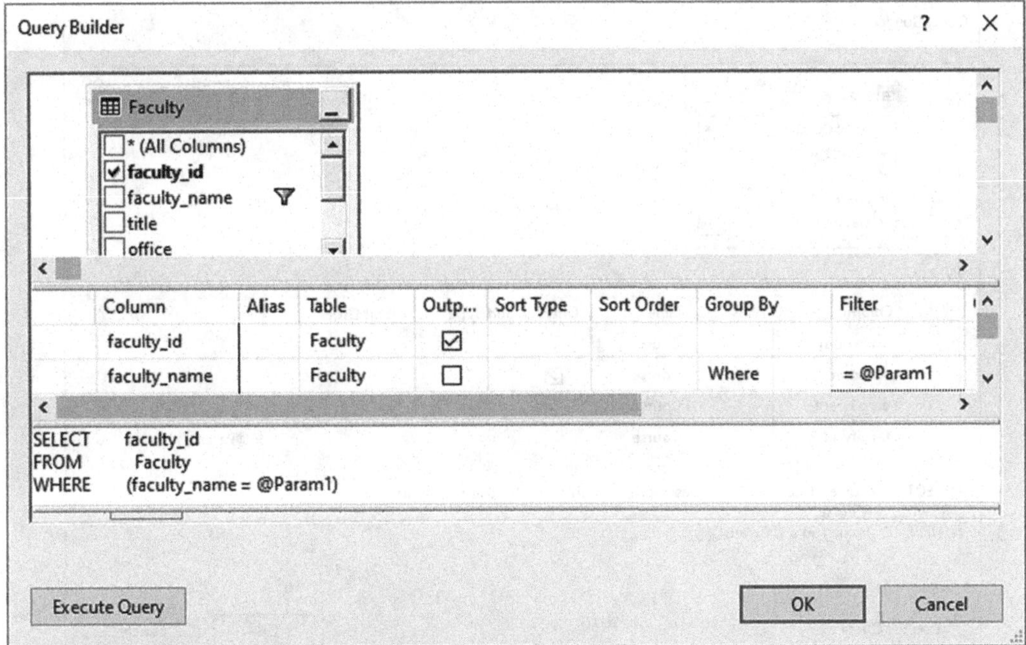

FIGURE 5.60 The finished query for the faculty_id.

5) Still in the second pane, right-click on the **Group By** column and select the **Delete** item from the popup menu to remove this **Group By** choice.
6) Type a question mark '?' on the **Filter** column along the **faculty_name** row, and press the **Enter** key from the keyboard. Your finished Query Builder should match one that is shown in Figure 5.60.

The SQL statement shown in the text pane or the third pane is:

```
SELECT faculty_id FROM Faculty WHERE (faculty_name = @Param1)
```

Click on the **OK** button and the **Next** button for the next wizard to continue to the next wizard. Enter the **FindFacultyIDByName** into the box as our function name and then click the **Next** and the **Finish** buttons to complete this query building.

Now let's continue to build our second query to find the courses taught by the selected faculty from the Course table. Open the DataSet Designer to create our desired query and modify the **Fill()** method for the CourseTableAdapter.

Open the Data Source window by clicking the **View | OtherWindows | Data Sources** menu item from the menu bar. Then right-click on any place inside that window and select the **Edit DataSet with Designer** item to open the DataSet Designer Wizard. Right-click on the last line of the **Course** table and choose the **Add Query** item to open the **TableAdapter Query Configuration Wizard**. Keep the default selection **Use SQL statements** and click on the **Next** button. Also keep the top selection **SELECT which returns rows** in the next wizard and click on the **Next** button. Then click the **Query Builder** button to open the Query Builder wizard, which is shown in Figure 5.61.

Keep the default selections for the top graphical pane. We only need the **course_id** column and we will explain why we need to keep this default items later. Go to the **Filter** column along the **faculty_id** row, type a question mark and press the **Enter** key from the keyboard. This is equivalent to us setting

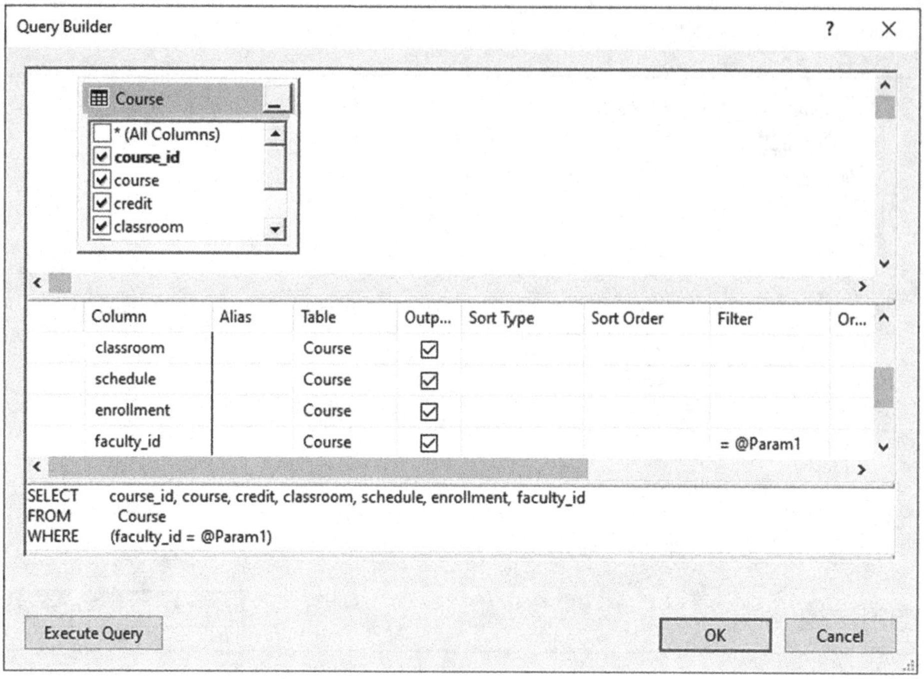

FIGURE 5.61 The finished query builder.

a dynamic parameter for this SQL SELECT statement. The completed SQL statement is displayed in the text pane, as shown in Figure 5.61, and the content of this statement is:

```
SELECT course_id, course, credit, classroom, schedule, enrollment,
 faculty_id
FROMCourse
WHERE (faculty_id = @Param1)
```

The dynamic parameter**@Param1** is a temporary parameter and it will be replaced by the real parameter, **faculty_id**, as the project runs.

Click on the **OK** and then the **Next** button to return to the TableAdapter Query Configuration Wizard to modify the **Fill()** method. Attach **ByFacultyID** to the end of the **Fill()** method to get a modified method: **FillByFacultyID()**. Uncheck the **Return a DataTable** checkbox since we do not need this method for this query. Then click on the **Next** and the **Finish** button for the following wizards to complete this configuration.

The next step is to binding six textbox controls in the CourseForm to the associated data column in the Course table in the DataSet. Select the **Course.cs** from the Solution Explorer window and click the **View** Designer button to open the CourseForm's graphical user interface.

First we need to bind the CourseList to the **course_id** column in the Course table in the DataSet. Recall that there are multiple **course_id**s with the same **faculty_id** in this Course table when we build our sample database in Chapter 2. Those multiple records with the same **faculty_id** are distinguished by the different course taught by that faculty. To bind a ListBox to those multiple records with the same **faculty_id**, we cannot continue to use the binding method we used for the TextBox controls as we did in the previous sections. This is the specialty of binding a ListBox control.

The special point is that the relationship between the ListBox and the data columns in a table is one-to-many, which means that a ListBox can contain multiple items. In that case, the CourseList

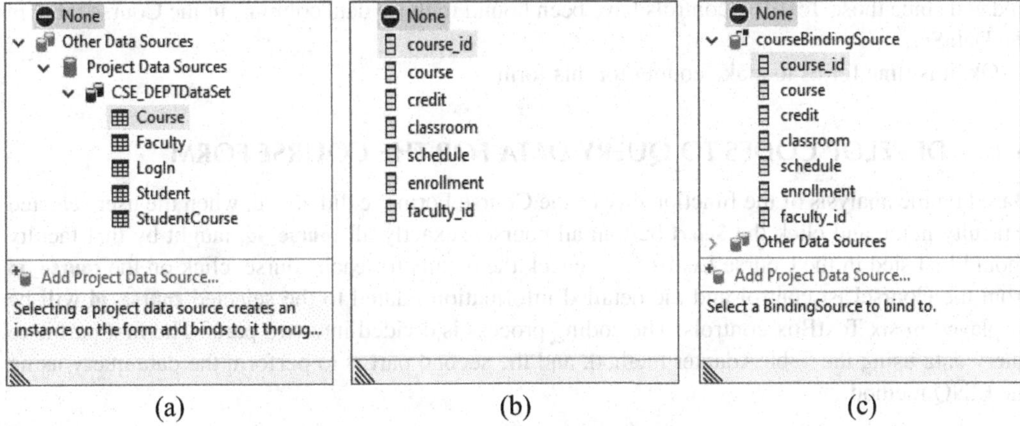

FIGURE 5.62 The expanded data binding source. (a–c) described in text.

can contain many **course_id**s. So the binding of a ListBox control is exactly to bind a ListBox to a table in the DataSet, exactly to the Course table in this application.

To do this binding, click the **CourseList** control from the Course Form, then go to the Properties window to find the **DataSource** property, and click the drop-down arrow to expand the items **Other Data Sources | Project Data Sources | CSE_DEPTDataSet** until the **Course** table is found. Select this table by clicking on it. Figure 5.62a shows this expansion situation.

Continue this binding by going to and expanding the **DisplayMember** property to find the **course_id** column, and select it by clicking on this item, as shown in Figure 5.62b.

In this way, we set up a binding relationship between the Course ListBox in the Course Form and the **Course** data table in the DataSet.

Now we need to bind six textbox controls in the Course Form to six columns in the Course data table in the DataSet. Perform the following operational step to complete these bindings:

1) Keep the Course Form opened and then select the **Course ID** TextBox from the Course Information GroupBox control.
2) Go to the **DataBindings** property and expand to the Text item, click the drop-down arrow and you will find that a **courseBindingSource** object is already in there for this project. This is due to the above data binding operation, CourseList binding.
3) Expand this **courseBindingSource** until you find the **course_id** column, which is shown in Figure 5.62c, and then choose it by clicking the **course_id** column. In this way, a binding is set up between the Course ID TextBox in the Course form and the **course_id** column in the Course table in the DataSet.
4) In a similar way, finish the binding for all other five TextBox controls: **Course**, **Schedule**, **Classroom**, **Credits** and **Enrollment**.

One point to be noted is the order in which to perform these two bindings. You must first perform the binding for the CourseList control, and then perform the binding for six TextBoxes.

Now we can answer the question why we need to keep the default selections at the top graphical pane when we built our query in the Query Builder (refer to Figure 5.60). The reason for this is that we need those columns to perform data binding for our six TextBox controls here. In this way, each TextBox control in the Course Form is bound with the associated data column in the Course table in the DataSet. After this kind of binding is setup, all data columns in the Course table in the DataSet will be updated by the data columns in the Course table in the real database each time a **FillByFacultyID()** method is executed. At the same time, all six TextBoxes' contents will also be updated since those TextBox controls have been bound to those data columns in the Course table in the DataSet.

Ok, it is time for us to make coding for this form.

5.13 DEVELOP CODES TO QUERY DATA FOR THE COURSE FORM

Based on the analysis of the functionality of the Course Form we did above, when the user selected a faculty name and click the **Select** button, all courses, exactly all **course_id**, taught by that faculty should be listed in the Course ListBox. To check the details for each course, click on the **course_id** from the CourseList control and the detailed information related to the selected **course_id** will be displayed in six TextBox controls. The coding process is divided into two parts. The first part is to query data using the TableAdapter method, and the second part is to perform the data query using the LINQ method.

5.13.1 QUERY DATA FROM THE COURSE TABLE USING THE TABLEADAPTER METHOD

Open the Course Form Code window by right-clicking on the **Course.cs** from the Solution Explorer window and click on the **View Code** item from the popup menu. Remove all default codes and enter the codes shown in Figure 5.63 into the **CourseForm_Load()** method.

This piece of cods is straightforward. A sequence of **Add()** method is used to add all faculty names into the Faculty Name ComboBox, and two methods into the Query Method ComboBox. Resetting the **SelectedIndex** property to 0 is to select the first faculty member and the first method as the default one from the ComboBox as the project runs.

Now open the Course Form window by right-clicking on the **Course.cs** from the Solution Explorer window, and select the **View Designer** item. Then double-click on the Select button to open its Click method. Enter the codes shown in Figure 5.64 into this method.

Let's have a closer look at this piece of codes to see how it works.

A. A new faculty table adapter object is created based on the FacultyTableAdapter class that is located at the namespace **CSE_DEPTDataSetTableAdapters**. Because we need this object to access the Faculty table to retrieve back the **faculty_id** based on the selected faculty name.

B. A local string variable **strFacultyID** is declared and it is used to hold the returned **faculty_id** when our built query **FindFacultyIDByName()** is executed.

```
SelectWizard Project ▼    CourseForm_Load(object sender, EventArgs e) ▼

private void CourseForm_Load(object sender, EventArgs e)
{
        this.ComboName.Items.Add("Ying Bai");
        ComboName.Items.Add("Davis Bhalla");
        ComboName.Items.Add("Black Anderson");
        ComboName.Items.Add("Steve Johnson");
        ComboName.Items.Add("Jenney King");
        ComboName.Items.Add("Alice Brown");
        ComboName.Items.Add("Debby Angles");
        ComboName.Items.Add("Jeff Henry");
        ComboName.SelectedIndex = 0;
        ComboMethod.Items.Add("TableAdapter Method");
        ComboMethod.Items.Add("LINQ & DataSet Method");
        this.ComboMethod.SelectedIndex = 0;
}
```

FIGURE 5.63 The detailed codes for the CourseForm_Load method.

```
SelectWizard Project                    cmdSelect_Click(object sender, EventArgs e)

    private void cmdSelect_Click(object sender, EventArgs e)
    {
A       CSE_DEPTDataSetTableAdapters.FacultyTableAdapter FacultyTableApt =
                                new CSE_DEPTDataSetTableAdapters.FacultyTableAdapter();
B       string strFacultyID = FacultyTableApt.FindFacultyIDByName(ComboName.Text);
C       if (strFacultyID != string.Empty)
        {
D           if (this.ComboMethod.Text == "TableAdapter Method")
            {
                this.courseTableAdapter.FillByFacultyID(cSE_DEPTDataSet.Course, strFacultyID);
E               if (cSE_DEPTDataSet.Course.Count == 0)
                    MessageBox.Show("No Matched Courses Found!");
            }
F           else
            {
             // LINQtoDataSet(strFacultyID);
            }
        }
G       else
            MessageBox.Show("No matched faculty_id found!");
    }
```

FIGURE 5.64 The detailed codes for the select button click method.

C. If the returned **faculty_id** is not an empty string, which means that a valid **faculty_id** has been obtained, then we can continue to perform the following faculty courses query based on this **faculty_id**.

D. If the user selected the **TableAdapter Method** to perform this query, the query we built in the DataSet Designer, **FillByFacultyID()**, is called to fill the Course table in our DataSet using the dynamic parameter **@Param1** that is replaced by our real parameter **strFacultyID** now.

E. By checking the **Count** property of the queried Course table, we can confirm whether or not the above query is successful. If that property is 0, which means that no any matched column has been found and no any record is returned, a MessageBox is used with a warning message being displayed to indicate this situation.

F. Otherwise the **TableAdapter Method** is chosen by the user and a user-defined method **LINQtoDataSet()**, which will be built later, is called to perform this data action. The argument is the **faculty_id** obtained from the first query we did above. This method is comment out now since we have not built this method so far.

G. If the returned **faculty_id** is an empty string, it means that no any valid **faculty_id** can be found from the Faculty table, a warning message is displayed to indicate this situation.

Return to the Course Form window by right-clicking on the **Course.cs** from the Solution Explorer window and select the **View Designer** item, then double-click the **Back** button to open its Click method and enter the code **this.Hide()** into this method.

That is it! The coding process for the data query using the TableAdapter is done. Next let's take care of the coding process for the data query using the LINQ to DataSet method.

5.13.2 Query Data from the Course Table Using the LINQ Method

In the coding we did for the last section (refer to Figure 5.64), the program will be directed to the **LINQtoDataSet()** method if the user selected the **LINQ & DataSet Method** from the **Query Method** ComboBox. Refer to Chapter 4 to get a detailed discussion about the data query between LINQ and DataSet. In this part, we will develop the codes to use this method to perform the data query from the Course table in our DataSet.

```
SelectWizard Project                    LINQtoDataSet()

  private void LINQtoDataSet(string facultyID)
  {
A     this.courseTableAdapter.FillByFacultyID(cSE_DEPTDataSet.Course, facultyID);
B     var courseinfo = (from ci in cSE_DEPTDataSet.Course.AsEnumerable()
                        where ci.Field<string>("faculty_id") == facultyID
                        select ci);
C     foreach (var cRow in courseinfo)
      {
          //this.txtCourseID.Text = cRow.course_id;
          //this.txtCourseName.Text = cRow.course;
          this.txtSchedule.Text = cRow.schedule;
          this.txtClassRoom.Text = cRow.classroom;
          this.txtCredits.Text = cRow.credit.ToString();
          this.txtEnroll.Text = cRow.enrollment.ToString();
      }
  }
```

FIGURE 5.65 The codes for the LINQ to DataSet method.

Open the Code Window of the Course Form if it is not opened, then create a new method **LINQtoDataSet()** and enter the codes, which are shown in Figure 5.65, into this method.

Let's see how this piece of code works.

A. First we need to call the query method **FillByFacultyID()** we built in Section 5.12 to load course data from the Course table in the database to the Course table in our DataSet. This operation is important and necessary for our next action, retrieving data from the Course table in the DataSet and displaying them in the CourseList box.

B. A typical LINQ query structure is created and executed to retrieve back all related course information for the selected faculty member. The **courseinfo** is a C# implicitly typed local variable with a data type **var**. The C# 2022 will be able to automatically convert this var to any suitable data type, in this case, it is a DataSet, when it sees it. An iteration variable **ci** is used to iterate over the result of this query from the Course table. Then a similar SQL SELECT statement is executed with the **WHERE** clause.

C. The **foreach** loop is utilized to pick up each column from the selected data row **cRow**, which is obtained from the **courseinfo** we get from the LINQ query.

Assign each column to the associated TextBox to display them in the Course Form window.

There is a complication in this assignment, which is the last running status of the **foreach** loop. When the **foreach** loop is done, the Course ID and the Course Name columns stored in the iteration variable **cRow** (**cRow.course_id** and **cRow.course**) will contain the last two columns, even if we want to assign the first **course_id** and **course** to those variables. To avoid this error occurring, the first two assignments must not be contained in this loop. Therefore, we should comment out the first two assignments (green coding lines in Figure 5.65). But how can we assign those columns to the **Course ID** and the **Course** TextBoxes in the Course Form window? This job can be handled by the BindingSource as you click and select the desired **course_id** from the **CourseList** box automatically.

At this point, we have completed all coding job for the Course Form. Before we can test our project, do not forget to remove the comment sign in front of the **LINQtoDataSet()** method in Figure 5.64 to make that method active.

Now click on the **Start** button to run our project. Enter **ybai** and **come** as the username and password for the LogIn form, and then select the **Course Information** from the Selection Form, and click on the **OK** button to open our Course Form, which is shown in Figure 5.66.

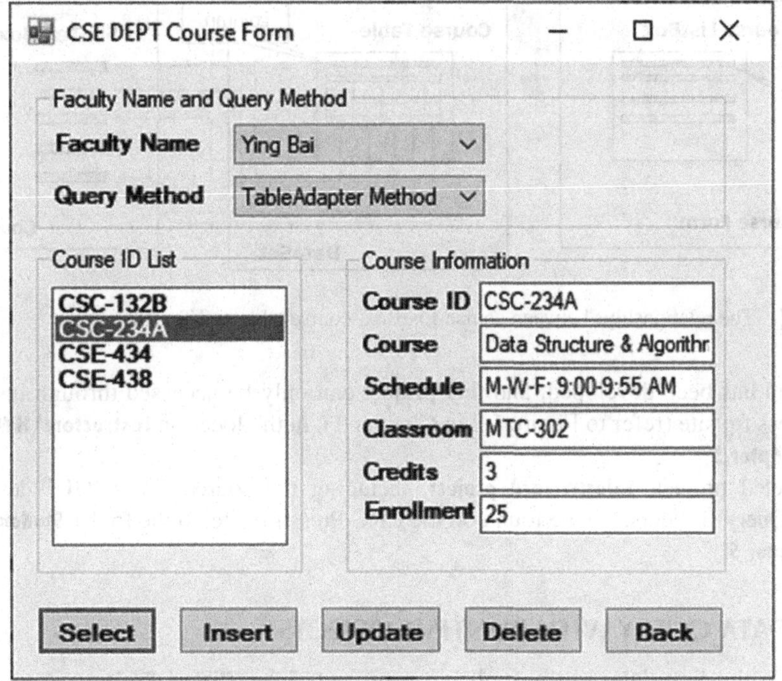

FIGURE 5.66 The running status of the course form.

On the opened Course Form window, select the default faculty name **Ying Bai** and click on the **Select** button to load and fill all courses (**course_id**) taught by this faculty into the Course table in our DataSet as well as the Course ListBox in this form.

The filled **course_id** are displayed in the Course ListBox, as shown in Figure 5.66.

Now let's go one more step forward by just clicking a **course_id** from the Course ListBox. Immediately, the detailed information about that selected course, including the course id, course name, schedule, classroom, credits and enrollment, will be displayed in the six TextBox controls. This makes sense since those TextBox controls have been bound to those six associated columns in the Course table in our DataSet. As you click one **course_id** from the Course ListBox, you have effectively selected and picked up one course record from the Course table. Recall that the Course ListBox is bound to the Course table in our DataSet by using the **CourseBindingSource** when we perform this data binding in Section 5.12. For the selected course record, six columns of that record have been bound to the six TextBox controls in the Form, so the data related to those six columns will also be reflected on these six TextBox controls. These relationships can be represented and illustrated by connections in Figure 5.67.

You can try to select the **LINQ to DataSet Method** to perform this data query, and a same querying result will be obtained without problem.

It is very interesting, is it not?

Yes! This is the power provided by Visual Studio 2022. By using those Design Tools and Wizards, it is very easy to develop professional database programming in the Visual C# 2022 environment, and it becomes fun to develop database programming in the template of Windows applications.

We have the last Window Form, which is the Student Form, but we want to leave this as homework for students to allow them to finish the developing of data connection and queries between the Student Form and the Student table as well as the StudentCourse table. For your reference, a completed project named **SelectWizard Student Project**, which contains the coding for

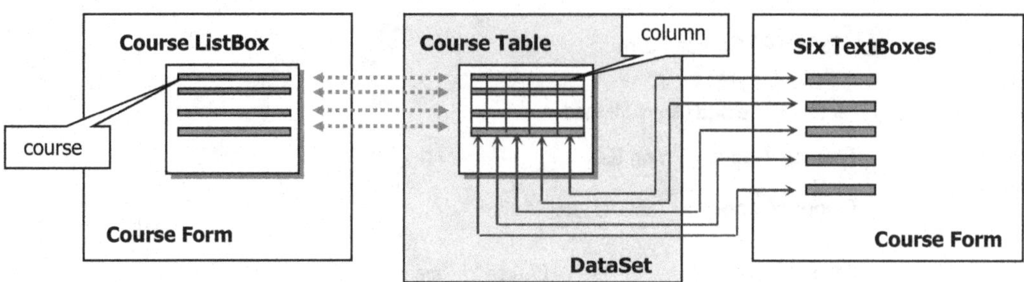

FIGURE 5.67 The relationships between course ListBox, course table and TextBox.

Student Form has been developed, and this project can only be accessed through instructors at the CRC Press ftp site (refer to Figure 1.2 in Chapter 1), in the location **Instructors\HW DB Project Solutions\Chapter 5**.

A completed project, **SelectWizard project**, including the source codes, GUI designs, Data Source and Query Builders, can be found on the CRC Press ftp site, in the folder **Students\Class DB Projects\Chapter 5**.

PART II DATA QUERY WITH RUNTIME OBJECTS

In contrast to the first data-driven application project, **SelectWizard Project**, we developed in Part I, in which a number of the design tools and wizards provided by Visual Studio, such as the DataSet, BindingSource, BindingNavigator and TableAdapter, are utilized to help readers to develop professional data-driven applications easily and conveniently, the sample projects developed in this part have nothing to do with those tools and wizards. This means that we create those ADO.NET objects by directly writing Visual C# codes without the aid of Visual Studio design-time tools and wizards as well as the auto-generated codes. All data-driven objects are created and implemented during the period of the project runs. In other words, all those objects are created dynamically.

The shortcoming of using those Visual Studio design tools and wizards to create data connections is that the auto-generated connection codes related to tools and wizards are embedded into the programs, and those connection codes are machine-dependent. Once that connection information in the programs is compiled, it cannot be modified. In other words, your programs cannot be distributed to and run in other platforms.

Compared with design tools and wizards, the advantages of using the runtime objects to make the data operations are: 1) it provides programmers with more flexibility in creating and implementing connection objects and data operation objects related to ADO.NET; and 2) it allows readers to use different methods to access and manipulate data from the data source and the database. But anything has both good and bad sides, and this is also the case here. The flexibility also brings some complex staff. For example, you have to create and use different data providers and different commands to access the different databases by using the different codes. Unlike the sample project we developed in the last part, in which you can use tools and wizards to select any data source you want and produce the same coding for the different data sources, in this part you must specify the data provider and command type based on your real data source to access the data in your project. The good news is that the LINQ technique released by Microsoft in Visual Studio provides an easier way to access different data sources from Visual C# projects. Before we can start to develop our projects, a detailed understanding of the connection and data operational classes is very important, and those classes are directly related to the ADO.NET. Although some discussions have been provided in Chapter 3, we will make a more detailed discussion for this topic in this section in order to provide readers with a clear picture of this issue.

5.14 INTRODUCTION TO RUNTIME OBJECTS

Runtime objects can be defined as: objects or instances used for data connections and operations in a data-driven application are created and implemented during the period of a project runs; in other words, those objects are created and utilized dynamically. To understand what kind of objects are most popularly used in a data-driven application, let's first have a detailed discussion about the most useful classes provided by ADO.NET.

According to Chapter 3, the ADO.NET architecture can be divided into three components: Data Provider, DataSet and a DataTable. These three components are directly related to different associated classes, which are shown in Figure 5.68.

The Data Provider contains four components

1) **Data Connection**
2) **Data Command**
3) **DataReader**
4) **TableAdapter (DataAdapter)**

All components inside the Data Provider are Data Provider-dependent components, which means that all components, including the Connection, Command, TableAdapter (DataAdapter) and DataReader, are identified and named based on the real data provider, or the database used. For example, the Data Provider used for SQL Server database must be identified and named by a prefix Sql, such as

- Data Connection component: SqlConnection
- Data Command component: SqlCommand
- DataAdapter (TableAdapter): SqlDataAdapter (SqlTableAdapter)
- DataReader components: SqlDataReader

and the same definition works for all other three Data Providers. All classes, methods, properties and constants of these four types of Data Provider are located at four different namespaces: **System.Data.OleDb, System.Data.SqlClient, System.Data.Odbc** and **System.Data.OracleClient**.

As shown in Figure 5.68, four kinds of data providers are popularly used in database programming in Visual C#. One must create the correct connection object based on the real database by using the specific prefix.

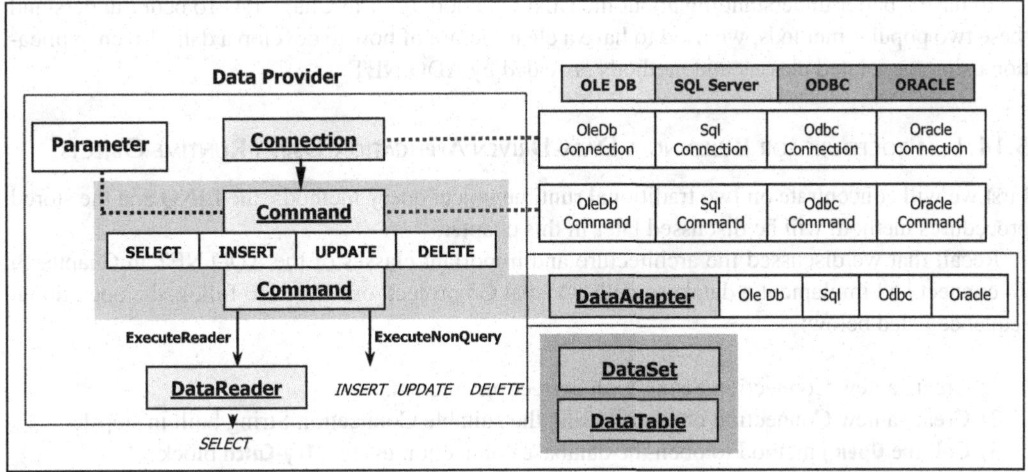

FIGURE 5.68 Classes provided by ADO.NET.

However, two components in the ADO.NET are Data Provider-independent: DataSet and DataTable. These two components are located at **System.Data** namespace. You do not need to use any prefix when you use these two components in your applications. Both DataSet and DataTable can be filled by using the DataAdapter or the TableAdapter components.

ADO.NET provides different classes to allow users to develop a professional data-driven application by using the different methods. Among those methods, two popular methods will be discussed in this part in detail.

The first method is to use the so-called DataSet-DataAdapter method to build a data-driven application. DataSet and DataTable classes can have different roles when they are implemented in a real application. Multiple DataTables can be embedded into a DataSet and each table can be filled, inserted, updated and deleted by using the different query method provided by the DataAdapter such as the SelectCommand, InsertCommand, UpdateCommand or DeleteCommand when one develops a data-driven application using this method. As shown in Figure 5.68, when you use this method, the Command and Parameter objects are embedded or attached to the DataAdapter object (represented by a shaded block) and the DataTable object is embedded into the DataSet object (represented by another shaded block). This method is relatively simple since you do not need to call some specific objects, such as the DataReader with specific method such as the ExecuteReader or ExecuteNonQuery to complete this data query. You just need to call the associated command of the TableAdapter to finish this data operation. But this simplicity brings some limitations for your applications. For instance, you cannot access different data tables separately to perform multiple specific data operations by using this single specified DataAdapter.

The second method allows you to use each object individually, which means that you do not have to use the DataAdapter to access the Command object, or embed the DataTable into the DataSet. This provides more flexibility. In this method, no DataAdapter or DataSet is needed, and you can only create a new Command object with a new Connection object, and then build a query statement and attach some useful parameter into that query for the newly created Command object. You can fill any DataTable by calling the ExecuteReader() method to a DataReader object, also you can perform any data manipulation by calling the ExecuteNonQuery() method to the desired DataTable.

In addition to these two traditional data query methods, the LINQ method that is a new method and released by Microsoft in Visual Studio 2008 is also discussed later in this Chapter.

In this section, we will provide four sample projects to cover these two popular methods and the LINQ method; **RTOSelect Project**, **SPSelect Project**, **LINQSelect Project**, and **LINQSPSelect Project**, which are associated with four kinds of query methods, Runtime Object method, Stored Procedures method, LINQ method and LINQ to SQL Stored Procedure method.

To have a better understanding about the LINQ method, refer to Chapter 4. To better understand these two popular methods, we need to have a clear picture of how to develop a data-driven application using the related classes and methods provided by ADO.NET.

5.14.1 Procedure for Building a Data-Driven Application Using Runtime Objects

First we will concentrate on two traditional runtime object query methods, the LINQ and the stored procedures method, will be discussed later in this chapter.

Recall that we discussed the architecture and important classes of the ADO.NET in Chapter 3. To connect and implement a database with a Visual C# project, one needs to follow the operational sequence listed below:

1) Create a new Connection String with correct parameters.
2) Create a new Connection object by using the suitable Connection String built in step 1.
3) Call the **Open()** method to open the database connection using a **Try-Catch** block.
4) Create a new **TableAdapter (DataAdapter)** object.
5) Create a new **DataTable** object that can be filled with data.

6) Call the suitable command/object such as a **SelectCommand** (or the **Fill()**) or a **DataReader** to make data query.
7) Fill the data to the bound-controls on the Visual C# Form window.
8) Release the used **TableAdapter**, **Command**, **DataTable** and the **DataReader** objects.
9) Close the database **Connection** object if no more database operation is needed.

Now let's first develop a sample project to access the data using the runtime object for SQL Server 2019 Express database via the Faculty Form.

5.15 QUERY DATA USING RUNTIME OBJECT TO SQL SERVER DATABASE

As we discussed in Chapter 3, one needs to use the different data providers to access the different databases, and the ADO.NET provides different namespaces for three different data providers: **System.Data.OleDb** for OLEDB, **System.Data.SqlClient** for SQL Server and **System.Data.OracleClient** for Oracle database.

We divide this discussion into two parts: 1) query data using the runtime object with general data query methods; and 2) data query using runtime objects with the LINQ to SQL method. LINQ to SQL is a good technique that is supplied with Visual Studio 2008 and it is exactly an API interface for working with SQL Server databases. We will first provide a detailed discussion about the general query methods for the SQL Server databases, and then we will concentrate on the LINQ to SQL with another project. The reason for us to divide this part into two separate projects is that the contradiction of the sharing of the same SQL Server 2019 Express database between the project using general runtime objects and the LINQ to SQL. As you know, SQL Server 2019 Express database allows only a single database instance to be created and applied for a data-driven application, meaning that it does not allow two or more users to access and use the same SQL Server 2019 Express database simultaneously. The first project we will develop is **RTOSelectFaculty Project**, which uses the general runtime objects and SQL command object to connect to our sample SQL Server database file **CSE_DEPT** in order to perform the data query. The second project we will develop is **LINQSelectFaculty Project**, which uses the LINQ to SQL technique and DataContext to connect to the same sample database to perform the similar data operations. As we discussed in Chapter 4, the DataContext is a special class that provides a connection to the database and translates Standard Query operators to the standard SQL statements to access our database. In order to avoid to access and use the same database simultaneously, we have to separate this discussion into two parts with two different projects.

First let's have a closer look at the Connection object with connection string.

5.15.1 Connect to SQL Server 2019 Express Databases

Basically, the similar runtime objects and structures are utilized to develop a data-driven project that can access the different databases. For example, all three kinds of data provide a need to use the Connection, Command, DataAdapter and DataReader objects to perform data queries to either a DataSet or a DataTable. The DataSet and the DataTable components are data provider-independent, but the first four objects are data provider-dependent. This means that one must use the different prefixes to specify what kind of data provider is utilized for certain databases. A prefix 'Sql' would be used if a SQL Server data provider is utilized, such as SqlConnection, SqlCommand, SqlDataAdapter and SqlDataReader. The same rule will be applied to the other data provider, such as the Oracle data provider.

Thus, the differences between the data-driven applications that can access the different database are the data provider-dependent components. Among them, the Connection String is a big issue. Different data providers need to use different connection strings to make the correct connection to the associated database.

Regularly a Connection String is composed of five parts:

- Provider
- Data Source
- Database
- User ID
- Password

A typical data connection instance with a general connection string can be expressed by the following codes:

```
Connection = new xxxConnection("Provider=MyProvider;" +
                              "Data Source=MyServer;" +
                              "Database=MyDatabase;" +
                              "User ID=MyUserID;" +
                              "Password=MyPassWord;");
```

where ***xxx*** should be replaced by the selected data provider in a real application, such as OleDb, Sql or Oracle. You need to use the real parameter values implemented in your applications to replace those nominal values such as MyServer, MyDatabase, MyUserID and MyPassWord in a real application.

The Provider parameter indicates the database driver you selected. If you installed a local SQL server and client such as the SQL Server 2019 Express on your computer, the provider should be *localhost*. If you are using a remote SQL Server instance, you need to use that *remote server's network name*. If you are using the default named instance of SQLX on your computer, you need to use *.\SQLEXPRESS* as the value for your provider parameter. Similar values can be used for the Oracle server database.

The Data Source parameter indicates the name of the network computer on which your SQL server or Oracle server is installed and running. The Database parameter indicates your database name. The User ID and Password parameters are used for the security issue for your database. In most cases, the default Windows NT Security Authentication is utilized.

You can also use the OLEDB as the SQL Server database provider. A sample connection string to be connected to a SQL Server database using the OLEDB data provider can be expressed:

```
Connection = new OleDbConnection("Provider=SQLOLEDB;" +
                                "Data Source=MyServer;" +
                                "Database=CSE_DEPT;" +
                                "User ID=MyUserID;" +
                                "Password=MyPassWord;");
```

You need to use the real parameter values implemented in your applications to replace those nominal values such as MyServer, MyUserID and MyPassWord for this connection object.

When you want to connect the SQL Server database using SqlClient with the **Windows Authentication Mode**, the connection string is a little different from those strings shown above. The Provider parameter should be replaced by the Server parameter and the User ID and the Password parameters should be replaced by the **Integrated Security** parameter. A sample connection string to be used to connect to a SQL Server database using the SqlClient is:

```
Connection = new SqlConnection("Server=SMART\\SQL2019EXPRESS;" +
                              "Database=CSE_DEPT;" +
                              "Integrated Security=SSPI");
```

where the value for the Server parameter is: *Computer Name\\SQL Server 2019 Express name* since we installed the Express version of the SQL 2019 Server in our local computer. We also installed the SQL 2019 Client on the same computer to make it work as both a server and a client.

However, if a **SQL Server Authentication Mode** is used for this connection, a completed connection string, including the Server, Database, User Name and Password, is needed, and it looks as:

```
Connection = new SqlConnection("Server=SMART\\SQL2019EXPRESS;" +
                              "Initial Catalog=CSE_DEPT;" +
                              "User ID=MyUserID;" +
                              "Password=MyPassWord;");
```

where the database name is replaced by the **Initial Catalog** and the **Integrated Security** is replaced by Username and Password.

By default, *SQL Server 2019 Express* used **Windows Authentication Mode** to authenticate connections when it is installed in your machine. However, in most popular database applications, a mixed or a **SQL Server Authentication Mode** is adopted for most database drivers. To match those applications, the default **Windows Authentication Mode** needs to be changed to the **SQL Server Authentication Mode**. Two ways can be utilized to change that connection mode:

1) Select the **SQL Server Authentication Mode** when installing SQL Server 2019 Express database in your machine.
2) Change the **Windows Authentication Mode** to the **SQL Server Authentication Mode** after the SQL Server 2019 Express database has been installed in your machine with the **Windows Authentication Mode**.

Refer to Appendix C on the CRC Press ftp site to perform this changing operation if one wants to use the **SQL Server Authentication Mode** to connect to our sample database.

In the above sections when we built the **SelectWizard Project**, to make thing simple, we created and added our DataSet into that project by using the default **Windows Authentication Mode** to connect to our sample database. If one wants to build a DataSet to connect to the sample database with **SQL Server Authentication Mode** via design tools and wizards, refer to Appendix D on the CRC Press ftp site, which provides details to carry out this connection. In the following projects, we will use both authentication modes to illustrate how to connect to our sample database to perform data queries.

In this section, we use an SQL Server 2019 Express database and connect it with our example project using the SQL Server data provider. The SQL Server database used in this sample project is **CSE_DEPT**, which was developed in Chapter 2. The advantages of using the Express version of SQL Server 2019 include, but are not limited to, the following:

- The SQL Server 2019 Express is fully compatible with SQL Server 2019 database and has the full functionalities of the latter.
- The SQL Server 2019 Express can be easily downloaded from the Microsoft site free of charge.
- The Microsoft SQL Server Management Studio 18 can also be downloaded and installed on your local computer free of charge. You can use this tool to build your database easily and conveniently.
- The SQL Client can be downloaded and installed on your local computer free of charge. You can install both SQL Server and Client on your local computer to develop professional data-driven applications to connect to your SQL Server database easily.

5.15.2 Create a New Visual C# Project RTOSelect Project

Now we need to create a new Visual C# 2022 project named **RTOSelect Project** to query data from some tables in our sample database. To make things simple, we only need to use some Windows Forms, such as **LogIn Form**, **Selection Form**, **Faculty Form** and **Course Form**, to perform related data queries. Therefore we only need to build those Forms in this new project. One easy way to build these Forms is to use some existing Forms, **LogIn.cs**, **Selection.cs**, **Faculty.cs**, and **Course.cs**, which can be found on the CRC Press ftp site, in the folder **Students\Windows Forms**. One can copy those files and save them to one of your local folders, and add them into the new project later.

Perform the following operational steps to create a new Visual C# Windows Forms App project **RTOSelect Project**:

1) Launch Visual Studio 2022 by clicking its icon on either the desktop or the task bar.
2) Click on the **Continue without code** link located at the lower-right corner to open the standard Visual Studio window.
3) Go to the **File | New | Project** item to open the **Create a new project** wizard.
4) On the opened wizard, select the template, **Windows Forms App (.NET Framework)** with **C#**, which is an icon on the left, and click it to select this template. Then click on the **Next** button to continue.
5) On the next wizard, **Configure your new project**, enter **RTOSelect Project** into the **Project name** box, and **RTOSelect Solution** into the **Solution name** box, respectively. Select your desired folder as the location from the **Location** box to save this new project.
6) Click on the **Create** button to create this new project.

To save the time, we can use and add five existing Window Forms, **LogIn.cs**, **Selection.cs**, **Faculty.cs**, **Student.cs** and **Course.cs**, into this new project. Perform the following operations to complete these Forms additions:

1) On the new opened project, go to the Solution Explorer window and right-click on the icon**Form1.cs**, and select the **Delete** item to remove this file.
2) Right-click on the project **RTOSelect Project** in the Solution Explorer window and select the **Add | Existing Item** to open the Add Existing Item wizard.
3) Browse to the CRC Press ftp site, in the folder **Students\Windows Forms** under that site, select the **LogIn.cs** by clicking its checkbox on the left.
4) Click on the **Add** button to add this Form into our project.
5) Immediately, a new item, **C# LogIn.cs**, is added into the Solution Explorer window. Wait a moment, this file will become a **LogIn.cs** folder with two subsidiary files, **LogIn.designer.cs** and **LogIn.resx**.
6) Repeat steps 2–5 above to add the other four Forms one by one. The point is that on each occasion you can only add one file. Otherwise, some exceptions or errors may be encountered.

Now we need to set and use the **LogIn.cs** as our starting object, and modify the namespaces in four added files to enable our new project to recognize them. Perform the following operations to complete this setup and namespaces modification processes:

1) Right-click on the **LogIn.cs** folder from the Solution Explorer window and select the **View Code** item to open the code window for this **LogIn.cs** class file.
2) Change its namespace from the original **SelectWizard_Project** to our current namespace, **RTOSelect_Project**.
3) Open the **LogIn.designer.cs** file by double-clicking on it from the Solution Explorer window (you need to expand the **LogIn.cs** folder to find this file).
4) Change the top line from the original namespace **SelectWizard_Project** to our current namespace, **RTOSelect_Project**.
5) Now open the main file, **C# Program.cs**, from the Solution Explorer window by double-clicking on that file.
6) On the opened **Program.cs** file, browse to the **Main()** method that is the entry or starting point for our project. Replace the third coding line **Application.Run(new Form1());** with **Application.Run(new LogInForm());**.

One point to be noted when performing the above operational steps is the order. One must follow up the operational order listed above to complete these modifications. Otherwise some exceptions may be encountered.

Perform a similar modification (steps 1–4 above) to namespaces on all other four Forms, **Faculty.cs**, **Course.cs**, **Student.cs** and **Selection.cs**, to make them compatible to our new project.

5.15.3 Query Data Using the General Runtime Objects For the LogIn Form

Open the LogInForm code window from the Solution Explorer window by clicking the **View Code** button to begin our coding process.

The first thing we need to do is to add the namespace SqlClient that contains all data components related to the SQL Server Data Provider since we need it to access the SQL Server databases in this project. Type the following code line in the namespace declaration section, which is in the top part, of this code window:

```
using System.Data.SqlClient;
```

Since the connection job is the first thing we need to do before we can make any data query, therefore we need to do the connection job in the constructor of this form object, to allow the connection to be made first as the project runs.

Open the Code window and find the constructor of this form, enter the following codes that are shown in Figure 5.69 into this part.

Let's have a closer look at this piece of codes to see how it works.

A. The namespace for the SQL Server Data Provider **System.Data.SqlClient** is added into this form to allow us to use all data components contained in that namespace.
B. A global SQL Connection object **SqlConnection** is declared here. The accessing mode for this object is **Public**, which means that any object or method defined in this project can use this connection object to access the sample SQL Server database **CSE_DEPT**.
C. A **SqlConnection** String is created here and it is used to connect our project with the SQL Server database selected. Please note that a **Windows Authentication Mode** is used for this database connection, thus the connection string contained the **Integrated Security=True** parameter that is used to indicate that connection mode. Currently this connection string is commented-out here since we prefer to use the next connection string in which a **SQL Server Authentication Mode** is used.
D. In this connection string, a **SQL Server Authentication Mode** is adopted and therefore both User ID and Password are added into this string at the end. The advantage of using this connection mode is that more parameters are included in this connection and make this connection more secured and safer. Refer to Appendix D on the CRC Press ftp site, exactly on Figure D.2, to get more details about this connection string.
E. A new instance of the **SqlConnection** class is created and initialized with the connection string as the argument.
F. A **try-catch** block is utilized to try to catch up any mistake or exception caused by opening this connection. The advantage of using this kind of strategy is to avoid unnecessary system debug process and simplify this debug procedure. Here multiple catch blocks are utilized to try to track and find any possible exception or error, including both **SqlException** and **InvalidOperationException**.
G. This step is used to confirm whether our database connection is successful or not. If not, an error message is displayed and the project is exited.

After a database connection is successful, we need next to use this connection to access the SQL Server database to perform our data query job.

```
RTOSelect Projct                                LogInForm()

  .......
  using System.Data;
A using System.Data.SqlClient;
  using System.Data.Linq;
  using System.Drawing;
  using System.Linq;
  using System.Text;
  using System.Windows.Forms;

  namespace RTOSelect_Project
  {
     public partial class LogInForm : Form
     {
B        public SqlConnection sqlConnection = null;
         public LogInForm()
         {
            InitializeComponent();
C           // string sqlString = "Server=DESKTOP-24JPUFB\\SQL2019EXPRESS;" +
            //                    "Initial Catalog=CSE_DEPT;" + "Integrated Security=True";
D           string sqlString = "Server=DESKTOP-24JPUFB\\SQL2019EXPRESS;" +
                               "Initial Catalog=CSE_DEPT;" + "User ID=SMART;Password=Happy2022";
E           sqlConnection = new SqlConnection(sqlString);
F           try
            {
               sqlConnection.Open();
            }
            catch (SqlException e)
            {
               MessageBox.Show("SQL Server Error");
               MessageBox.Show("Error Code = " + e.ErrorCode);
               MessageBox.Show("Error Message = " + e.Message);
            }
            catch (InvalidOperationException e)
            {
               MessageBox.Show("Invalid Message = " + e.Message);
            }
G           if (sqlConnection.State != ConnectionState.Open)
            {
               MessageBox.Show("Database connection is Failed");
               Application.Exit();
            }
         }
     }
```

FIGURE 5.69 The coding for the database connection.

5.15.3.1 Coding Method 1: Using the DataAdapter to Query Data

In this section, we discuss how to create and use the runtime objects to query the data from the SQL Server database by using the DataAdapter method.

Since we need to use two methods, TableAdapter (DataAdapter) and DataReader, to perform this login process, we need to add one more button to this Form. Perform the following operations to complete this addition:

1) Add one new button with **Name** as **cmdTabLogIn** and **Text** as **TabLogIn** into this Form.
2) Change the original login button with a new **Name** as **cmdReadLogIn** and **Text** as **ReadLogIn**, respectively.
3) Adjust the size of all three buttons to make them equal in the horizontal spaces.

The modified **LogInForm** window should match one that is shown in Figure 5.70.

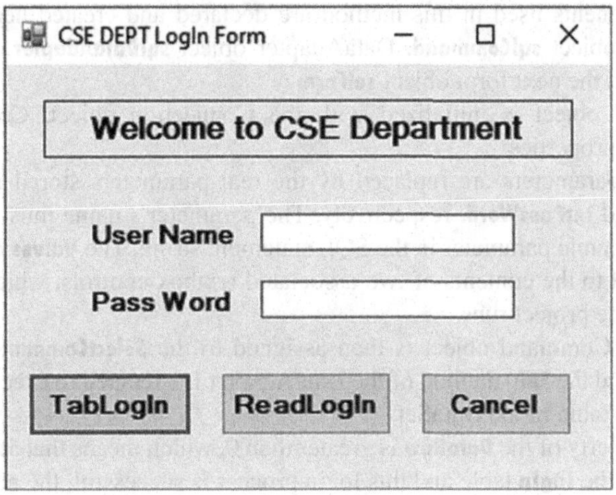

CSE DEPT LogIn Form

Welcome to CSE Department

User Name

Pass Word

TabLogIn ReadLogIn Cancel

FIGURE 5.70 The modified LogIn Form window.

Now open the LogInForm window by right-clicking on the **LogIn.cs** from the Explorer window and select the **View Designer** button, and then double-click the **TabLogIn** button to open its Click method. Enter the codes, which are shown in Figure 5.71, into this method.

Let's have a closer look at this piece of codes to see how it works.

A. The query string for the SQL Server database is declared first. This query string contained two dynamic parameters, **Username** and **Password**.

```
RTOSelect Projct                              cmdTabLogIn_Click(object sender, EventArgs e)

  private void cmdTabLogIn_Click(object sender, EventArgs e)
  {
A         string cmdString = "SELECT user_name, pass_word, faculty_id, student_id FROM LogIn ";
          cmdString += "WHERE (user_name=@Param1 ) AND (pass_word=@Param2)";
B         SqlDataAdapter LogInDataAdapter = new SqlDataAdapter();
          DataTable sqlDataTable = new DataTable();
          SqlCommand sqlCommand = new SqlCommand();
          SelectionForm selForm = new SelectionForm();
C         sqlCommand.Connection = sqlConnection;
          sqlCommand.CommandType = CommandType.Text;
          sqlCommand.CommandText = cmdString;
D         sqlCommand.Parameters.Add("@Param1", SqlDbType.Char).Value = txtUserName.Text;
          sqlCommand.Parameters.Add("@Param2", SqlDbType.Char, 8).Value = txtPassWord.Text;
E         LogInDataAdapter.SelectCommand = sqlCommand;
          LogInDataAdapter.Fill(sqlDataTable);
F         if (sqlDataTable.Rows.Count > 0)
          {
             this.Hide();
             selForm.ShowDialog();
             sqlConnection.Close();
             this.Close();
          }
G         else
             MessageBox.Show("No matched username/password found!");
H         sqlDataTable.Dispose();
          sqlCommand.Dispose();
          LogInDataAdapter.Dispose();
  }
```

FIGURE 5.71 The codes for the TabLogIn button click method.

B. All data components used in this method are declared and created here, which include the Command object **sqlCommand**, DataAdapter object **sqlDataAdapter**, DataTable object **sqlDataTable** and the next form object **selForm**.

C. The Command object is initialized with the Connection object, CommandType and CommandText properties.

D. Two dynamic parameters are replaced by the real parameters stored in two textboxes, **txtUserName** and **txtPassWord**, respectively. The parameter's name must be identical with the name of dynamic parameter in the SQL statement string. The **Values** of two parameters should be equal to the contents of two associated textbox controls, which will be entered by the user as the project runs.

E. The initialized Command object is then assigned to the **SelectCommand** property of the DataAdapter, and the **Fill()** method of the DataAdapter is executed to execute the Command to fill that **LogIn** table in the DataSet.

F. If the **Count** property of the **DataRow** is greater than 0, which means that at least one row has been filled into the **LogIn** table and this login process is successful, the next Form window, **SelectionForm**, is displayed to allow users to continue to query the desired information. The database connection is closed and the **LogInForm** should be removed from the project by executing the **Close()** method.

G. If the **Count** property is 0, which means that no row has been filled into the **LogIn** table and this fill is failed, an error message is displayed.

H. A cleaning job is performed to release all data components used in this method.

Now let's take a look at the codes for the second method.

5.15.3.2 Coding for Method 2: Using the DataReader to Query Data

Open the LogIn Form window and then double-click the ReadLogIn button to open its Click method. Enter the codes shown in Figure 5.72 into this method.

Most codes in the top section are identical with those codes in the **TabLogIn** button's Click method with two exceptions. First a **DataReader** object is created to replace the **DataAdapter** to perform the data query, and second a DataTable is removed from this method since we do not need it for our data query in this method.

Let's have a closer look at this piece of codes to see how it works.

A. The only modification for this query string is that we changed two of the nominal dynamic parameters' names to **@name** and **@word**, respectively. This is fine for the query string as long as the same parameters' names are used for both query string and the **Add()** method for the **Parameters** collection.

B. Two data components, **Command** and **DataTable**, are created here and they will be used in this method.

C. The **Command** object is initialized with **Connection** object, **CommandType** and **CommandText** properties.

D. Two nominal dynamic parameters are replaced by two real parameters whose values are stored in two TextBoxes, **txtUserName** and **txtPassWord**.

When using the Parameters collection to add dynamic parameters, the order of the dynamic parameters is very important. The order you add the dynamic parameters into the Parameters collection must be identical to the order in which the nominal parameters are placed in the SQL statement string.

```
RTOSelect Projct                 ▼   cmdReadLogIn_Click(object sender, EventArgs e)  ▼

  private void cmdReadLogIn_Click(object sender, EventArgs e)
  {
A         string cmdString = "SELECT user_name, pass_word, faculty_id, student_id FROM LogIn ";
          cmdString += "WHERE (user_name=@name ) AND (pass_word=@word)";
B         SqlCommand sqlCommand = new SqlCommand();
          SelectionForm selForm = new SelectionForm();
          SqlDataReader sqlDataReader;
C         sqlCommand.Connection = sqlConnection;
          sqlCommand.CommandType = CommandType.Text;
          sqlCommand.CommandText = cmdString;
D         sqlCommand.Parameters.Add("@name", SqlDbType.Char).Value = txtUserName.Text;
          sqlCommand.Parameters.Add("@word", SqlDbType.Char, 8).Value = txtPassWord.Text;
E         sqlDataReader = sqlCommand.ExecuteReader();
F         if (sqlDataReader.HasRows == true)
          {
            this.Hide();
            selForm.ShowDialog();
            sqlConnection.Close();
            this.Close();
          }
G         else
            MessageBox.Show("No matched username/password found!");
H         sqlCommand.Dispose();
          sqlDataReader.Close();
  }
```

FIGURE 5.72 The coding for the ReadLogIn button click method.

E. The **ExecuteReader()** method is called to perform the data query and the returned data should be filled in the **DataReader**.

F. If the returned **DataReader** contains some queried data, its **HasRows** property should be **true**, and then the project should go to the next step and the Selection Form should be displayed. The database connection is closed and the current Form, **LogIn Form**, should be removed from the project by executing of the **Close()** method.

G. Otherwise, an error message is displayed to indicate this situation.

H. A cleaning job is performed to release all data components used in this method.

The coding process for the **Cancel** command button's Click method is simple. The function of this method is to cancel the login process due to some reasons and exit the project. Open this method and enter the codes shown in Figure 5.73 into this method.

```
RTOSelect Project                ▼   cmdCancel_Click(object sender, EventArgs e)  ▼

private void cmdCancel_Click(object sender, EventArgs e)
{
      if (sqlConnection.State == ConnectionState.Open)
      {
          sqlConnection.Close();
          sqlConnection.Dispose();
      }
      Application.Exit();
}
```

FIGURE 5.73 The codes for the cancel button click method.

RTOSelect Projct | cmdExit_Click(object sender, EventArgs e)

```
   namespace RTOSelect_Project
   {
      public partial class SelectionForm : Form
      {
A        FacultyForm facultyForm = new FacultyForm();
         CourseForm courseForm = new CourseForm();
         StudentForm studentForm = new StudentForm();
         public SelectionForm()
         {
            InitializeComponent();
B           this.ComboSelection.Items.Add("Faculty Information");
            this.ComboSelection.Items.Add("Course Information");
            this.ComboSelection.Items.Add("Student Information");
C           this.ComboSelection.SelectedIndex = 0;
         }
         private void cmdOK_Click(object sender, EventArgs e)
         {
D           if (this.ComboSelection.Text == "Faculty Information")
               facultyForm.Show();
E           else if (this.ComboSelection.Text == "Course Information")
               courseForm.Show();
F           else
               studentForm.Show();
         }
         private void cmdExit_Click(object sender, EventArgs e)
         {
G          courseForm.Close();
           facultyForm.Close();
           studentForm.Close();
           Application.Exit();
         }
      }
   }
```

FIGURE 5.74 The complete codes for the Selection Form window.

5.15.4 The Coding Process for the Selection Form

The function of this Form is to enable users to select different items to perform related data query via different window Forms. When an item is selected and the **OK** button is clicked by the user, the selected window Form is opened to allow users to perform a related data query to the desired data table in our sample database. Double-click on the **OK** button from the Selection Form window to open its Click method, and enter the codes shown in Figure 5.74 into that method. Let's have a closer look at this piece of codes to see how it works.

A. Three new Form objects, **facultyForm**, **StudentForm** and **courseForm**, are created based on three classes, FacultyForm, StudentForm and CourseForm, since we need to show one of them if one is selected by the users to enable them to perform related data query to the related data table in our sample database.
B. Three selection items are added into the Selection ComboBox to enable users to select one of them as the project runs.
C. The **SelectedIndex = 0** indicates that the first item is selected as a default item.
D. If the **OK** button is clicked by the user, a sequence of **if-else** statements is used to identify which item has been selected. If the **Faculty Information** item is chosen, the **facultyForm** is displayed.
E. If the **Course Information** item is chosen, the **courseForm** is displayed.
F. Otherwise, the **Student Information** is selected and displayed.

G. If the **Exit** button is clicked by the users, all Form objects are closed and we exit the project by executing a system method **Application.Exit()**.

Next let's start to build the codes for the Faculty Form to perform data query from the Faculty table in our sample database.

5.15.5 Query Data Using the General Runtime Objects for the Faculty Form

First let's add two new namespaces, **System.IO** and **System.Data.SqlClient**, to the namespace declaration part in the code window of this Form. The former contained the general I/O related methods such as **MemoryStream()** that is used to convert a memory stream to an image and the latter contains components related to SQL Data Provider. These two new added namespaces have been highlighted in Figure 5.75.

Now open the Faculty Form **Code Window** and enter the codes shown in Figure 5.75 into the constructor of this class. The codes for the **Back** button Click method are also built following this constructor. The purpose of that method is to close a active database connection to our sample database and close the LogIn Form window as this button is clicked.

Let's have a closer look at this piece of codes to see how it works.

A. Two new namespaces, **System.IO** and **System.Data.SqlClient**, are first added into this code window since we need to use some components and methods defined in them.
B. A new object, **loginForm**, which is based on the **LogInForm** class is generated. The main reason we need this object is to set up and use an active connection to our sample database to perform the following data query to our Faculty table. Recall that in Figure 5.69, a database connection object **sqlConnection** was created in the constructor of that **LogInForm** class.
C. Inside the Faculty Form constructor, first all eight faculty names are added into the **Faculty Name** combobox. This operation will enable users to select one of them to perform data query for the selected faculty member as the project runs.
D. The first faculty member is selected as a default one by setting the **SelectedIndex = 0**.
E. Two different query methods, **DataAdapter Method** and the **DataReader Method**, are also added into the **Query Method** combobox to enable users to select one of them to perform related data query as the project runs.
F. Similarly, the first method is selected as a default query method by setting the **SelectedIndex** property to 0.
G. After a new object **loginForm** is generated in step **B**, we need to check whether a valid database connection object **sqlConnection**, which should be created when that new object is generated, is available. If that **sqlConnection** object returns a **null**, which means that the database connection is failed, a warning message is displayed to indicate that situation and the project should be exited if that situation is really happened.
H. The detailed codes for the **Back** button Click method start from here.
I. Before we can close this Faculty Form and return to the Selection Form, we need to check whether a valid database connection is still active. If it is, we need to close that connection and dispose it.
J. Close the created **loginForm** window by executing the **Close()** method since we no longer need it.
K. The current Faculty Form window is temporarily closed by executing the **Hide()** method since we can permanently close this Form as the **Exit** button on the Selection Form is clicked later.

Our next coding job is for the **Select** button Click method. When this button is clicked, the faculty name selected by the user from the ComboName box will be used as the query criterion to retrieve back all related information for that selected faculty and displayed in seven TextBoxes and a PictureBox control **PhotoBox** in the Faculty Form window.

```
RTOSelect Project                          FaculyForm()

     ........
     using System.Data;
A    using System.IO;
     using System.Data.SqlClient;
     using System.Data.OleDb;
     using System.Drawing;
     using System.Linq;
     using System.Text;
     using System.Windows.Forms;
     namespace RTOSelect_Project
     {
        public partial class FacultyForm : Form
        {
B          LogInForm loginForm = new LogInForm();
           public FacultyForm()
           {
              InitializeComponent();
C             ComboName.Items.Add("Ying Bai");
              ComboName.Items.Add("Davis Bhalla");
              ComboName.Items.Add("Black Anderson");
              ComboName.Items.Add("Steve Johnson");
              ComboName.Items.Add("Jenney King");
              ComboName.Items.Add("Alice Brown");
              ComboName.Items.Add("Debby Angles");
              ComboName.Items.Add("Jeff Henry");
D             ComboName.SelectedIndex = 0;
E             ComboMethod.Items.Add("DataAdapter Method");
              ComboMethod.Items.Add("DataReader Method");
F             ComboMethod.SelectedIndex = 0;
G             if (loginForm.sqlConnection == null)
              {
                 MessageBox.Show("The Database Connection Is Failed!");
                 Application.Exit();
              }
           }
H          private void cmdBack_Click(object sender, EventArgs e)
           {
I             if (loginForm.sqlConnection.State == ConnectionState.Open)
              {
                 loginForm.sqlConnection.Close();
                 loginForm.sqlConnection.Dispose();
J                loginForm.Close();
              }
K             this.Hide();
           }
        }
     }
```

FIGURE 5.75 The codes for the constructor of the FacultyForm and the back button method.

Open the Faculty Form window by right-clicking on the **Faculty.cs** from the Explorer window, and select the **View Designer** button. Then double-click on the **Select** button to open its Click method. Enter the codes shown in Figure 5.76 into this method.

Let's have a closer look at this piece of codes to see how it works.

A. The query string is first generated and this query is used to retrieve all eight columns from the Faculty table in our sample database **CSE_DEPT**. The dynamic parameter that located at the **WHERE** clause is a selected faculty name represented as **@name**.

B. A sequence of Data Provider-dependent objects are created here and they are used to perform the related data query operations shown below. A Data Provider-independent object, **sqlDataTable**, is also generated.

```
RTOSelect Project                    cmdSelect_Click(object sender, EventArgs e)

  private void cmdSelect_Click(object sender, EventArgs e)
  {
A     string cmdString = "SELECT faculty_id, faculty_name, title, office, phone, college, email, fimage FROM Faculty ";
      cmdString += "WHERE faculty_name = @name";
B     SqlDataAdapter FacultyDataAdapter = new SqlDataAdapter();
      SqlCommand sqlCommand = new SqlCommand();
      SqlDataReader sqlDataReader;
      DataTable sqlDataTable = new DataTable();
C     sqlCommand.Connection = loginForm.sqlConnection;
      sqlCommand.CommandType = CommandType.Text;
      sqlCommand.CommandText = cmdString;
D     sqlCommand.Parameters.Add("@name", SqlDbType.Char).Value = ComboName.Text;
E     if (ComboMethod.Text == "DataAdapter Method")
      {
         FacultyDataAdapter.SelectCommand = sqlCommand;
         FacultyDataAdapter.Fill(sqlDataTable);
F        if (sqlDataTable.Rows.Count > 0)
            FillFacultyTable(ref sqlDataTable);
G        else
            MessageBox.Show("No matched faculty found!");
H        sqlDataTable.Dispose();
         FacultyDataAdapter.Dispose();
      }
I     else if (ComboMethod.Text == "DataReader Method")
      {
         sqlDataReader = sqlCommand.ExecuteReader();
J        if (sqlDataReader.HasRows == true)
            FillFacultyReader(sqlDataReader);
K        else
            MessageBox.Show("No matched faculty found!");
L        sqlDataReader.Close();
      }
M     else                                          //Invalid method selected
         MessageBox.Show("Invalid Method Selected!");
  }
```

FIGURE 5.76 The completed codes for the select button click method.

C. Then the **sqlCommand** object is initialized with a group of related properties. One point to be noted is the **Connection** property, which should be assigned as a connection object that is generated in the LogIn Form constructor.

D. The data type of the dynamic parameter, **@name**, should be **SqlDbType.Char** since this type is equivalent to a string in C#.

E. If the **DataAdapter Method** is selected by the users, the **SelectCommand** property of a DataAdapter is initialized by the **sqlCommand** that has been initialized in the above step **C**, and the **Fill()** method is called to fill a DataTable, **sqlDataTable**, to perform a query to the Faculty table and fill a matched record into that DataTable.

F. By checking the **Count** property of the data row in the filled DataTable, we can confirm whether or not this fill operation is successful. When that **Count** property is greater than 0, which means that at least one data row has been matched and filled, and that query is successful, a user-defined method **FillFacultyTable()** is called with the filled DataTable as the argument to display all queried columns in the seven TextBoxes and a faculty image in the Faculty Form window.

G. Otherwise, if the **Count** property is less than or equal to 0, which means that no any row has been matched and retrieved, a warning message is displayed to indicate this case.

H. Some cleaning jobs are performed to close some used DataTable and the DataAdapter to keep our project neat.

I. If users selected the **DataReader Method** to perform this query, the **ExecuteReader()** method, which belongs to the initialized **sqlCommand** object in step **C**, is executed to perform this data query and return the queried result to the DataReader object.
J. By checking the **HasRows** property of the DataReader, we can confirm whether or not that **ExecuteReader()** method is running successfully. If that property returns a **true**, which means that at least one row has been matched and returned, then a user-defined method **FillFacultyReader()** is called to get that row and display each column on seven TextBoxes and a PictureBox in the Faculty Form window.
K. Otherwise, if the **HasRows** returns false, which means that the **ExecuteReader**() method is failed, a warning message is displayed to indicate that case.
L. A cleaning job is performed to close the DataReader object since we no longer need it.
M. If any other query method is selected by the users, a warning message is displayed.

Now let's take care of the coding process for two user-defined methods, **FillFacultyTable()** and **FillFacultyReader()**.

The first method is used to collect all eight queried data columns from a filled DataTable, **sqlDataTable**, and display each of them on the seven related TextBox on the Faculty Form window. Also the retrieved faculty image should be displayed in a PictureBox object, **PhotoBox**, in the Faculty Form window.

Open the **Code Window** of the Faculty Form and enter the codes shown in Figure 5.77 into this window. Let's have a closer look at this piece of codes to see how it works.

A. The type of the argument passed into this method is a reference, which is indicated by a keyword **ref**. This reference is similar to a fixed pointer in C++. When passing an argument in this way, it is equivalent to pass the address of that object into this method. Any modification to this object is permanent and can be returned to the calling program.
B. Some local variables and objects are declared first, including a local integer variable **index** that works as a loop counter later, and a TextBox array **fBox[]** that works as a data holder to store all seven pieces of queried faculty information to be displayed in seven TextBoxes later.

```
RTOSelect Project                    FillFacultyTable(ref DataTable FacultyTable)

A  private void FillFacultyTable(ref DataTable FacultyTable)
   {
B     int index = 0;
      TextBox[] fBox = { txtFacultyID, txtFacultyName, txtTitle, txtOffice, txtPhone, txtCollege, txtEmail };
C     foreach (DataRow row in FacultyTable.Rows)
      {
D        foreach (DataColumn column in FacultyTable.Columns)
         {
E           if (index <= 6)
            {
               fBox[index].Text = row[column].ToString();
               index++;
            }
F           else
            {
               byte[] bimage = (byte[])row["fimage"];
               PhotoBox.Image = Image.FromStream(new MemoryStream(bimage));
            }
         }
      }
   }
```

FIGURE 5.77 The codes for the user defined method FillFacultyTable().

C. To check and get all matched columns, two **foreach** loops are used. The outer loop is for the selected row and the inner loop is for each column. In fact, the outer loop can only be run once since only one row data is retrieved.
D. For the inner loop, a total of 8 columns should be checked and collected.
E. However, we only need the first 7 columns since they are 7 pieces of faculty information represented by String, and the last column is a faculty image represented by a **byte[]** array. Thus an **if** selection structure is used to enable us to only collect the first 7 columns (column order is arranged from 0 to 6). For each collected column, it is assigned to the related TextBox in the array **fBox[]** with the loop counter **index** as a position index. The loop counter is also updated for each loop.
F. Otherwise, if the last column or column 7 (the eighth column) is collected, it is converted to the **byte[]** and assigned to a new **byte[]** array **bimage**.

Two system methods, **FromStream()** and **MemoryStream()**, are used to convert the **byte[]** array to an image stream and assigned to the **Image** property of the PictureBox to display the queried faculty image in that PictureBox.

For the user-defined method **FillFacultyReader()**, open the Code Window of the Faculty Form window and enter the codes shown in Figure 5.78 into this window. Let's have a closer look at this piece of codes to see how it works.

A. Some local variables and objects are declared first, including a local integer variable **index** that works as a loop counter later, and a TextBox array **fBox[]** that works as a data holder to store all seven pieces of queried faculty information to be displayed in seven TextBoxes later.
B. A **while()** loop is used with the loop condition as the **Read()** method of the DataReader. This means that the **while()** loop will be continued as long as the **Read()** method returns a **true**, which means that a valid data column has been retrieved from the DataReader.
C. Inside the **while()** loop, a **for()** loop is utilized to pick up each queried column and assign it to the related TextBox in the Faculty Form window to display it. A point to be noted is the upper bound of this loop, which is **FieldCount – 2 = 6**, since we only need to pick up the first 7 columns and the column order starts from 0. Therefore the upper bound is 6 and that means column 7. The **FieldCount** is the total number of the collected columns, it should be 8, since each data row contains eight columns in our Faculty table.
D. For the last column, which is a faculty image stored as a **byte[]** array, a forced conversion is used to convert the **fimage** whose data type is object to a **byte[]** array.
E. The converted image **byte[]** array is further to be converted to an image stream by using two system methods, **FromStream()** and **MemoryStream()**, and assigned to the **Image** property of the PictureBox to be displayed in that PictureBox.

```
RTOSelect Project          FillFacultyReader(SqlDataReader FacultyReader)

  private void FillFacultyReader(SqlDataReader FacultyReader)
  {
A     int index;
      TextBox[] fBox = {txtFacultyID, txtFacultyName, txtTitle, txtOffice, txtPhone, txtCollege, txtEmail};
B     while (FacultyReader.Read())
      {
C        for (index = 0; index <= FacultyReader.FieldCount - 2; index++)
             fBox[index].Text = FacultyReader.GetString(index);
D        byte[] bimage = (byte[])FacultyReader["fimage"];
E        PhotoBox.Image = Image.FromStream(new MemoryStream(bimage));
      }
  }
```

FIGURE 5.78 The codes for the FillFacultyReader() method.

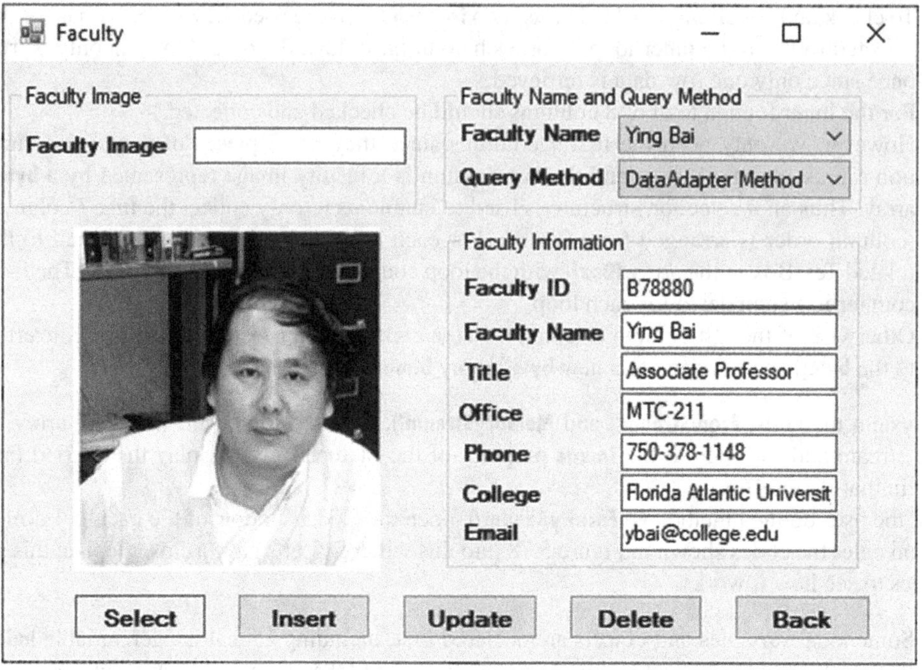

FIGURE 5.79 The running status of the faculty form.

Now we have completed all coding jobs for this Faculty Form and we can run the project to test the functionalities of the Faculty Form object.

Click on the **Start** button to build and run our project. Finish the login process by entering **jhenry** and **test** as a valid username and password, select the **Faculty Information** from the Selection Form to open the Faculty Form window, which is shown in Figure 5.79.

Keep the default faculty name **Ying Bai** and the **DataAdapter Method** with no change, click on the **Select** button to query this record. Immediately, the queried faculty record is displayed in seven TextBoxes and a PictureBox, as shown in Figure 5.79.

One can test a different query with the **DataReader Method** by selecting it from the **Query Method** combobox with other faculty member. Click on the Back and the Exit button to terminate our project.

Next let's handle how to query data from our Course table in our sample database with the Course Form window.

5.15.6 Query Data Using the General Runtime Objects for the Course Form

The function of this Course Form is to allow users to select all courses (**course_id**) taught by the selected faculty member. Furthermore, it enables users to get all detailed course information when users click on one **course_id** from the CourseList Box. Now let's begin our coding process.

As we did for the Faculty Form, first we need to add a namespace **System.Data.SqlClient** that contains the SQL Data Provider to the namespace declaration part in the code window of this form.

Then open the **Code Window** of this Course Form and enter the codes shown in Figure 5.80 into this window. Let's have a closer look at this piece of codes to see how it works.

- **A.** The **System.Data.SqlClient** namespace is added since we need to use a group of data components that are SQL Server Data Provider-dependent in this section.
- **B.** A new LogInForm object, **loginForm**, is declared and the purpose of generating this new object is to set up a valid connection to our sample database to get a connection object since we need to use it to query data from the Course table later.

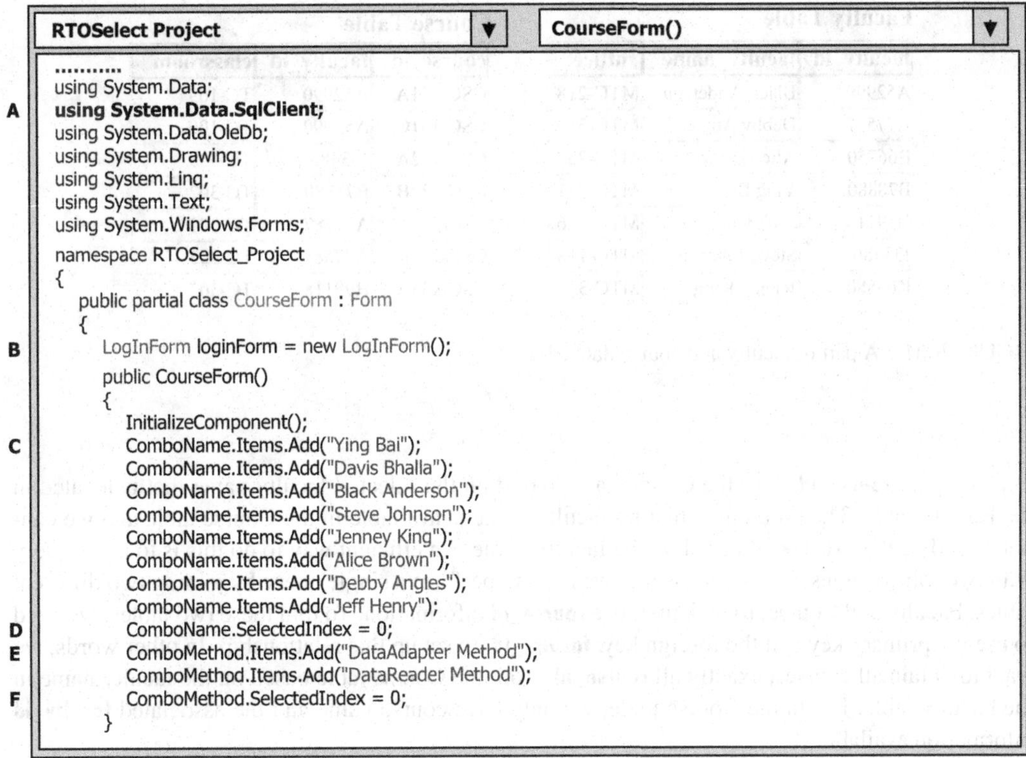

```
RTOSelect Project                    CourseForm()
  ..........
  using System.Data;
A using System.Data.SqlClient;
  using System.Data.OleDb;
  using System.Drawing;
  using System.Linq;
  using System.Text;
  using System.Windows.Forms;
  namespace RTOSelect_Project
  {
      public partial class CourseForm : Form
      {
B         LogInForm loginForm = new LogInForm();
          public CourseForm()
          {
              InitializeComponent();
C             ComboName.Items.Add("Ying Bai");
              ComboName.Items.Add("Davis Bhalla");
              ComboName.Items.Add("Black Anderson");
              ComboName.Items.Add("Steve Johnson");
              ComboName.Items.Add("Jenney King");
              ComboName.Items.Add("Alice Brown");
              ComboName.Items.Add("Debby Angles");
              ComboName.Items.Add("Jeff Henry");
D             ComboName.SelectedIndex = 0;
E             ComboMethod.Items.Add("DataAdapter Method");
              ComboMethod.Items.Add("DataReader Method");
F             ComboMethod.SelectedIndex = 0;
          }
```

FIGURE 5.80 The codes for the constructor of the CourseForm.

C. All eight faculty members are added into the **Faculty Name** combobox to enable users to select one of them to perform course query for that selected faculty member.
D. The **SelectedIndex = 0** makes the first faculty member in the **Faculty Name** combobox as a default faculty.
E. Two different query methods, **DataAdapter Method** and **DataReader Method**, are added into the **Query Method** combobox to enable users to select one of them to perform the related query.
F. Similarly, the first query method, **DataAdapter Method**, is selected as the default method by setting the **SelectedIndex** property as 0.

The next coding job is for the **Select** button Click method. Generally, we need to use two queries to retrieve back all courses (**course_id**) taught by the selected faculty in the Course form. The reason for that is because there is no faculty name column available in the Course table, and each course or **course_id** is related to a **faculty_id** in the Course table. In order to get a **faculty_id** that is associated with the selected faculty name, we must first perform a query to the Faculty table to obtain it. In order to simplify this data action, a join query is used in this method and it is a desired method to complete this functionality.

5.15.6.1 Retrieve Data From Multiple Tables Using the Joined Tables Method

To have a clear picture why we need to use the Join query method for this data action, let's first take a look at the data structure in our sample database. A part of Faculty and Course data table in the **CSE_DEPT** database is shown in Figure 5.81.

The **faculty_id** in the **Faculty** table is a primary key, but it is a foreign key in the Course table. The relationship between the Faculty and the Course table is one-to-many. What we want to do is

Faculty Table

faculty_id	faculty_name	office
A52990	Black Anderson	MTC-218
A77587	Debby Angles	MTC-320
B66750	Alice Brown	MTC-257
B78880	Ying Bai	MTC-211
H99118	Jeff Henry	MTC-336
J33486	Steve Johnson	MTC-118
K69880	Jenney King	MTC-324

Course Table

course_id	faculty_id	classroom
CSC-131A	A52990	TC-109
CSC-131C	A52990	TC-109
CSC-132A	J33486	TC-303
CSC-132B	B78880	TC-302
CSC-230	A77587	TC-301
CSC-232B	A77587	TC-303
CSC-233A	H99118	TC-302

FIGURE 5.81 A part of faculty and course data table.

to pick up all **course_id** from the Course table based on the selected faculty name that is located in the Faculty table. The problem is that no faculty name is available in the Course table and we cannot directly get all **course_id** based on the faculty name. An efficient way to do this is to use a query with two joined tables, which means that we need to perform a single query by joining two different tables, Faculty and Course, to pick up those **course_id** information. To join these two tables, we need to use the primary key and the foreign key, **faculty_id**, to set up this relationship. In other words, we want to obtain all courses, exactly all **course_id**, from the Course table based on the faculty name in the Faculty table. But in the Course table, we only have course name and the associated **faculty_id** information available.

Similarly, in the Faculty table, we only have faculty name and the associated **faculty_id** information available. The result is: We cannot set up a direct relationship between the faculty name in the Faculty table and the **course_id** in the Course table, but we can build an indirect relationship between them via **faculty_id** since it works as a bridge to connect two tables together using the primary and foreign key.

A SQL statement with two joined tables, **Faculty** and **Course**, can be represented as:

```
SELECT Course.course_id, Course.course FROM Course, Faculty
WHERE (Course.faculty_id = Faculty.faculty_id) AND (Faculty.faculty_name = @name)
```

The @name is a dynamic parameter and it will be replaced by the real faculty name selected by the user as the project runs.

One point to be noted is that the syntax of this SQL statement is defined in the ANSI 89 standard and is relatively out-of-date. Microsoft will not support this out-of-date syntax in the future. So it is highly recommended to use a new syntax for this SQL statement, which is defined in the ANSI 92 standard and looks as below:

```
SELECT Course.course_id, Course.course FROM Course JOIN Faculty
ON (Course.faculty_id = Faculty.faculty_id) AND (Faculty.faculty_name = @name)
```

Now let's use this inner join method to develop our query for this method. Double-click on the **Select** button from the Course Form window to open its Click method, and enter the codes shown in Figure 5.82 into this method.

Let's have a closer look at this piece of codes to see how it works.

A. The joined table query string is declared at the beginning of this method. Here only one column is queried, which is the **course_id**. An ANSI 92 standard is adopted and used for this query string.

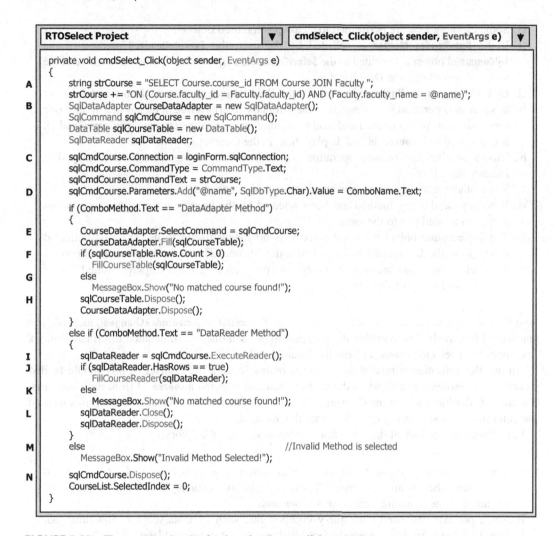

```
RTOSelect Project                cmdSelect_Click(object sender, EventArgs e)

   private void cmdSelect_Click(object sender, EventArgs e)
   {
A        string strCourse = "SELECT Course.course_id FROM Course JOIN Faculty ";
         strCourse += "ON (Course.faculty_id = Faculty.faculty_id) AND (Faculty.faculty_name = @name)";
B        SqlDataAdapter CourseDataAdapter = new SqlDataAdapter();
         SqlCommand sqlCmdCourse = new SqlCommand();
         DataTable sqlCourseTable = new DataTable();
         SqlDataReader sqlDataReader;

C        sqlCmdCourse.Connection = loginForm.sqlConnection;
         sqlCmdCourse.CommandType = CommandType.Text;
         sqlCmdCourse.CommandText = strCourse;
D        sqlCmdCourse.Parameters.Add("@name", SqlDbType.Char).Value = ComboName.Text;
         if (ComboMethod.Text == "DataAdapter Method")
         {
E            CourseDataAdapter.SelectCommand = sqlCmdCourse;
             CourseDataAdapter.Fill(sqlCourseTable);
F            if (sqlCourseTable.Rows.Count > 0)
                FillCourseTable(sqlCourseTable);
G            else
                MessageBox.Show("No matched course found!");
H            sqlCourseTable.Dispose();
             CourseDataAdapter.Dispose();
         }
         else if (ComboMethod.Text == "DataReader Method")
         {
I            sqlDataReader = sqlCmdCourse.ExecuteReader();
J            if (sqlDataReader.HasRows == true)
                FillCourseReader(sqlDataReader);
K            else
                MessageBox.Show("No matched course found!");
L            sqlDataReader.Close();
             sqlDataReader.Dispose();
         }
M        else                                              //Invalid Method is selected
            MessageBox.Show("Invalid Method Selected!");

N        sqlCmdCourse.Dispose();
         CourseList.SelectedIndex = 0;
   }
```

FIGURE 5.82 The completed codes for the select button click method.

B. All Data Provider-dependent objects, such as the CourseDataAdapter, Command, DataReader and DataTable, are generated here and those objects will be used later.

C. The SqlCommand object **sqlCmdCourse** is initialized with the connection object obtained from the constructor of the **LogInForm** class, connection string, command type, command text and command parameter.

D. The parameter's name must be identical to the dynamic nominal name **@name**, which is defined in the query string and it is exactly located in the **ON** clause. The parameter's value is the content of the Faculty Name combobox, which should be selected by the user as the project runs.

E. If the **DataAdapter Method** is selected by the user, the initialized **SqlCommand** object is assigned to the **SelectCommand** property of the DataAdapter and the **Fill()** method is executed to fill the Course table.

F. If the **Rows.Count** property of the filled Course table is greater than 0, which means that at least one row has been matched and filled into the data table. Then a user-defined method **FillCourseTable()** is called to fill all **course_id** into the CourseList box.

G. Otherwise, if the **Rows.Count** property is less than or equal to 0, this means that the fill operation is failed. A warning message is displayed for that case.

H. Some cleaning jobs are performed to cleanup some used objects.
I. If the **DataReader Method** is selected by the user, the **ExecuteReader()** method of the **SqlCommand** object is executed to the **SelectCommand** to query the Course table and read the matched record into the Data Reader.
J. By checking on the **HasRows** property of the Data Reader, we can confirm whether or not this reading operation is successful. If that property returns a **true**, it means that at least one row of data has been matched and read back, another user defined method **FillCourseReader()** is called to get all **course_id** and display them in the CourseList box.
K. Otherwise, that data reading operation is failed, and a warning message is displayed to indicate that situation.
L. Some other cleaning jobs are performed to remove some used objects.
M. If no any valid query method has been selected by the users, a warning message is displayed to remind this to the users.
N. The **SqlCommand** object is closed since it is no longer useful to us. The first collected **course_id** in the CourseList box is set as a default one. This setup is necessary since we must select one valid **course_id** to enable the program to get and display detailed course information for one of them later.

Next we need to take care of the coding jobs for the **CourseList_SelectedIndexChanged()** method. The function of that method is to enable the program to get and display all detailed information in six TextBoxes for a selected **course_id** from the CourseList box.

All detailed information related to a selected **course_id** from the CourseList box should be displayed in six textbox controls when the user clicked and selected a **course_id** from the CourseList box control. Double-click on the CourseList box in the Course Form window to open this method and enter the codes shown in Figure 5.83 into that method.

Let's have a closer look at these modified codes to see how they work.

A. The query string is created with six queried columns such as course_id, course, credit, classroom, schedule and enrollment. The query criterion is **course_id**. In addition, the nominal name of the dynamic parameter is **@courseid**.
B. Some popular and used data query components, such as DataAdapter, SqlCommand, DataTable and DataReader, are declared first and they will be used later.
C. The **SqlCommand** object is initialized by assigning related values to the property of that command object. The Connection object is obtained from generating a LogInForm instance and setting up a valid connection to our sample database via that constructor.
D. The nominal dynamic parameter, **@courseid**, is initialized by assigning a valid **course_id** selected by the users from the CourseList box.
E. If the **DataAdapter Method** is selected by the users, the initialized **SqlCommand** object is assigned to the **SelectCommand** property of that DataAdapter, and the **Fill()** method belongs to the DataAdapter is executed to query the Course table and fill the queried result into the DataTable.
F. By checking the **Rows.Count** property of the DataTable, we can confirm whether or not this query is successful. If that property is greater than 0, which means that at least one row has been matched, collected and filled into the DataTable, one user-defined method **FillCourseTextBox()** is executed to fill six TextBoxes to display the detailed course information for the selected **course_id** in the CourseList box.
G. Otherwise, if that property is less than or equal to 0, which means that the **Fill()** operation is failed, a warning message is displayed to indicate that case.
H. Some cleaning jobs are performed to remove some used objects.

```
RTOSelect Project                          CourseList_SelectedIndexChanged()

   private void CourseList_SelectedIndexChanged(object sender, EventArgs e)
   {
A      string cmdString = "SELECT course_id, course, credit, classroom, schedule, enrollment FROM Course ";
       cmdString += "WHERE course_id = @courseid";
B      SqlDataAdapter CourseDataAdapter = new SqlDataAdapter();
       SqlCommand sqlCommand = new SqlCommand();
       DataTable sqlDataTable = new DataTable();
       SqlDataReader sqlDataReader;

C      sqlCommand.Connection = loginForm.sqlConnection;
       sqlCommand.CommandType = CommandType.Text;
       sqlCommand.CommandText = cmdString;
D      sqlCommand.Parameters.Add("@courseid", SqlDbType.Char).Value = CourseList.SelectedItem;
E      if (ComboMethod.Text == "DataAdapter Method")
       {
          CourseDataAdapter.SelectCommand = sqlCommand;
          CourseDataAdapter.Fill(sqlDataTable);
F         if (sqlDataTable.Rows.Count > 0)
             FillCourseTextBox(sqlDataTable);
G         else
             MessageBox.Show("No matched course information found!");
H         sqlDataTable.Dispose();
          CourseDataAdapter.Dispose();
       }
I      else if (ComboMethod.Text == "DataReader Method")
       {
          sqlDataReader = sqlCommand.ExecuteReader();
J         if (sqlDataReader.HasRows == true)
             FillCourseReaderTextBox(sqlDataReader);
K         else
             MessageBox.Show("No matched course information found!");
L         sqlDataReader.Close();
          sqlDataReader.Dispose();
       }
M      else     //Invalid Method is selected
          MessageBox.Show("Invalid Method Selected!");

N      sqlCommand.Dispose();
   }
```

FIGURE 5.83 The codes for the CourseList_SelectedIndexChanged() method.

I. If the **DataReader Method** is selected, the **ExecuteReader()** method is executed to query the Course table and read back the detailed information for the selected **course_id**, and assign it to the DataReader.

J. If the **HasRows** property of the DataReader returns a **true**, which means that the operation of the **ExecuteReader()** is successful and a valid data row has been read back, another user-defined method **FillCourseReaderTextBox()** is called to fill the collected detailed course information to the six related TextBoxes in the Course Form.

K. Otherwise, if the **ExecuteReader()** method is failed, a warning message is displayed to remind and ask the users to handle it.

L. Some cleaning jobs are performed to close the used DataReader object since we no longer need it.

M. If no any valid query method has been selected, a warning message is shown up.

N. Finally, the used **SqlCommand** object is closed and disposed.

Next let's handle the coding process for two user defined methods, **FillCourseTextBox()** and **FillCourseReaderTextBox()**.

5.15.6.2 Build the Codes for Two User-Defined Methods

In the opened **Code Window** of the Course Form, enter the codes shown in Figure 5.84 into this code window. Let's have a closer look at this piece of codes to see how it works.

A. For the first method, **FillCourseTextBox()**, some local variables and objects are declared first, including a local integer variable **pos** that works as a loop counter later, and a TextBox array **cTextBox[]** that works as a data holder to store all six pieces of queried course information to be displayed in six TextBoxes later.
B. To check and get all matched columns, two **foreach** loops are used. The outer loop is for the selected row and the inner loop is for each column. In fact, the outer loop can only be run once since only one row data is retrieved.
C. For the inner loop, a total of 6 columns represented six pieces of course information should be checked and collected.
D. Each selected column is assigned to the related TextBox in the Course Form via a TextBox array **cTextBox[]** and display each of them via the **Text** property. One point to be noted is that the selected column, **row[column]**, is an object and it must be converted to a String via a **ToString()** method, and then assigned to the **Text** property.
E. The loop counter **pos** is updated for each loop to set up a correct position for the TextBox array to hold the related and collected column.
F. Similarly, for the second method, **FillCourseReaderTextBox()**, some local variables and objects are declared first, including a local integer variable **intIndex** that works as a loop counter later, and a TextBox array **cTextBox[]** that works as a data holder to store all six pieces of queried course information to be displayed in six TextBoxes later.
G. A **while()** loop is used with the loop condition as the **Read()** method of the DataReader. This means that the **while()** loop will be continued as long as the **Read()** method returns a true, which means that a valid data column has been retrieved from the DataReader.

```
RTOSelect Project                      FillCourseTextBox(DataTable CourseTable)

  private void FillCourseTextBox(DataTable CourseTable)
  {
A     int pos = 0;
      TextBox[] cTextBox = {txtCourseID, txtCourseName, txtCredits, txtClassRoom, txtSchedule, txtEnroll};
B     foreach (DataRow row in CourseTable.Rows)
      {
C        foreach (DataColumn column in CourseTable.Columns)
         {
D           cTextBox[pos].Text = row[column].ToString();
E           pos++;
         }
      }
  }
  private void FillCourseReaderTextBox(SqlDataReader CourseReader)
  {
F     int intIndex = 0;
      TextBox[] cTextBox = {txtCourseID, txtCourseName, txtCredits, txtClassRoom, txtSchedule, txtEnroll};
G     while (CourseReader.Read())
      {
H        for (intIndex = 0; intIndex <= CourseReader.FieldCount - 1; intIndex++)
            cTextBox[intIndex].Text = CourseReader.GetValue(intIndex).ToString();
      }
  }
```

FIGURE 5.84 The detailed codes for two user defined methods.

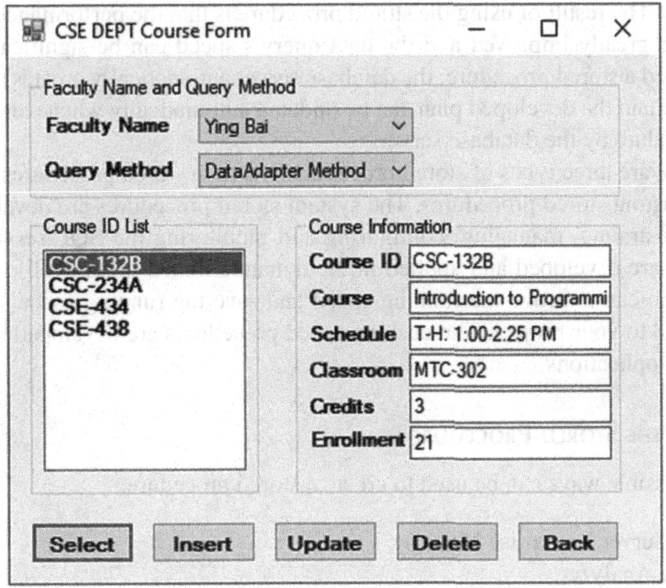

FIGURE 5.85 The running status of the course form.

H. Inside the **while()** loop, a **for()** loop is utilized to pick up each queried column and assign it to the related TextBox in the Course Form window to display it. A point to be noted is the upper bound of this loop is **FieldCount – 1 = 5**, since the column order starts from 0.

Now we have finished all coding jobs for this Course Form and we can start to run and test the codes we just developed for the CourseForm class. Click on the Start button on the top to run our project. Finish the login process by entering a valid username and password, such as **jhenry** and **test**. Then select the **Course Information** item and click on the **OK** button from the Selection Form to open the Course Form. Keep the default faculty name and query method, and click on the Select button to query the desired courses (**course_id**) for the selected faculty member. The running result is shown in Figure 5.85.

Now you can select other **course_id** by clicking one of them from the CourseList Box. Immediately, you can find that the related detailed information for that course (**course_id**) is displayed in six TextBoxes on the right.

One can also try to select the **DataReader Method** from the **Query Method** combobox to test the project to perform a different query on the Course table in our sample database.

A completed project **RTOSelect Project** can be found from the CRC Press ftp site, in the folder, **Class DB Projects\Chapter 5\RTOSelect Solution**, which is located under the **Students** folder on that site (refer to Figure 1.2 in Chapter 1).

Next let's discuss how to query data via the stored procedures method.

5.16 QUERY DATA USING STORED PROCEDURES

Stored Procedures are nothing more than functions or procedures applied in any project developed in any programming language. This means that stored procedures can be considered as functions or subroutines, and they can be called easily with any arguments and they can also return any data with certain types. One can integrate multiple SQL statements into a single stored procedure to perform multiple queries at a time, and those statements will be pre-compiled by the SQL Server to form an integrated target body. In this way, the pre-compiled body is insulated with your coding developed in Visual C# environment. You can easily call the stored procedure from your Visual C# 2022 project as the project runs. The result of using the stored procedure is that the performance of a data-driven application can be greatly improved and the data query's speed can be significantly faster. Also, when one developed a stored procedure, the database server automatically creates an execution plan for that procedure, and the developed plan can be updated automatically whenever a modification is made to that procedure by the database server.

Regularly, there are three types of stored procedures: System stored procedures, extended stored procedures and custom stored procedures. The system stored procedures are developed and implemented for administrating, managing, configuring and monitoring the SQL server. The extended stored procedures are developed and applied in the dynamic linked library (dll) format. This kind of stored procedure can improve the running speed and save the running space since they can be dynamically linked to your project. The custom stored procedures are developed and implemented by users for their applications.

5.16.1 Create the Stored Procedure

In general, five possible ways can be used to create a stored procedure.

1) Using SQL Server Enterprise Manager
2) Using Query Analyzer
3) Using ASP Code
4) Using Visual Studio.NET – Real Time Coding Method
5) Using Visual Studio.NET – Server Explorer

For Visual C# developers, one prefers to use the Server Explorer in Visual Studio.NET. A more complicated but flexible way to create a stored procedure is to use the real time coding method from Visual Studio.NET. In this section, we will concentrate on the fifth method listed above. A prototype or syntax of creating a stored procedure is shown in Figure 5.86.

For a SQL Server database, the name of the stored procedure is always prefixed by the keyword **dbo**. A sample stored procedure **StudentInfo** is shown in Figure 5.87.

```
CREATE PROCEDURE Stored Procedure's name
{
        @Param1's name    Param1's data type  Input/Output,
        @Param2's name    Param2's data type  Input/Output
        .......
}
AS
    (DECLARE Your local variables.... If you have)
    (Your SQL Statements)
    RETURN
```

FIGURE 5.86 The prototype of a SQL server stored procedure.

```
CREATE PROCEDURE dbo.StudentInfo
{
    @StudentName VARCHAR(50)
}
AS
    SELECT student_id FROM Student
    WHERE name = @StudentName
    RETURN
```

FIGURE 5.87 A sample SQL server stored procedure.

The parameters declared inside the braces are either input or output parameters used for this stored procedure. A @ symbol must be prefixed before the parameter in the SQL Server database. Any argument sent from the calling procedure to this stored procedure should be declared here. The other variables, which are created by using the keyword **DECLARE** located after the keyword **AS**, are local variables and they can only be used in this stored procedure. The keyword **RETURN** is used to return the queried data columns.

5.16.2 Call the Stored Procedure

When a stored procedure is created, it is ready to be called by your project developed in Visual C# 2022. You can use any possible ways to finish this calling. For example, you can use the **Fill()** method defined in the DataAdapter to fill a data table or you can use the **ExecuteReader()** method to return the reading result to a DataReader object. The above methods are good for the single-table query, which means that a group of SQL statements defined in that stored procedure is executed for only one data table. If you want to develop a stored procedure that makes multiple queries with multiple data tables, you need to use a system method **ExecuteNonQuery()**.

To call a developed stored procedure from Visual C# project via the **Fill()** method in the DataAdapter, one needs to follow the syntax described as below:

1) Create a Connection object and open it.
2) Create a Command object and initialize it.
3) Create any Parameter object and add it into the Command object if you have.
4) Execute the stored procedure by using the **Fill()** method in the TableAdapter class.

Figure 5.88 shows a piece of example codes that illustrates how to call a stored procedure named **dbo.StudentInfo** (assuming a Connection object has been created):

A. Some useful data components are declared here such as the DataAdapter, Command and DataTable.
B. The Command object is initialized by assigning the associated components to it. The first component is the Connection object.
C. In order to execute a stored procedure, the keyword StoredProcedure must be used here and assigned to the CommandType property of the Command object to indicate that a stored procedure will be called when this Command object is executed.
D. The name of the stored procedure must be assigned to the CommandText property of the Command object. This name must be identical with the name you used when you create the stored procedure.

```
A   SqlDataAdapter StudentDataAdapter = new SqlDataAdapter();
    SqlCommand sqlCmdStudent = New SqlCommand();
    DataTable sqlStudentTable = new DataTable();
B   sqlCmdStudent.Connection = LogInForm.sqlConnection;
C   sqlCmdStudent.CommandType = CommandType.StoredProcedure;
D   sqlCmdStudent.CommandText = "dbo.StudentInfo";
E   sqlCmdStudent.Parameters.Add("@StudentName", SqlDbType.Char).Value = ComboName.Text;
    StudentDataAdapter.SelectCommand = sqlCmdStudent;
F   StudentDataAdapter.Fill(sqlStudentTable);
    if (sqlStudentTable.Rows.Count > 0)
      Collect the retrieved data columns.....
    else
      MessageBox.Show("No matched student found!");
```

FIGURE 5.88 An example of calling the stored procedure.

E. The stored procedure **dbo.StudentInfo** needs one input parameter StudentName, so a real parameter that will be obtained from the Student Name combobox as the project runs is added into the Parameters collection, which is a property of the Command object. The initialized Command object is assigned to the Select-Command property of the DataAdapter and it will be used later.
F. The **Fill()** method is executed to call the stored procedure and fill the Student table. If this calling is successful, the returned data columns will be available, otherwise, an error message is displayed.

In the next part, we need to create a new Visual C# project **SPSelect Project** and use the Student Form to call two created stored procedures to perform data queries to the **Student** table in our sample database. First let's create our two new stored procedures with Server Explorer in the Visual Studio. NET 2022.

5.16.3 Query Data Using Stored Procedures for Student Form

First let's create two stored procedures for this Student Form. The first stored procedure is used to get the **student_id** from the **Student** table based on the selected student name, and the second is used to obtain the courses taken by the selected student based on the **student_id**. The reason why we need to use two queries is: we want to query all courses taken by the selected student based on the student's name, not the **student_id**, from the **StudentCourse** table. But there is only **student_id** column available in the **StudentCourse** table and no student name in that table. The student name can only be obtained from the **Student** table. So we need first to make a query to the **Student** table to get the **student_id** based on the student's name, and then make the second query to the **StudentCourse** table to get all courses (exactly all **course_id**) based on the **student_id** obtained from the first query.

The first stored procedure is named **dbo.StudentInfo** and we will create this stored procedure using the Server Explorer in the Visual Studio.NET IDE.

Open the Visual Studio.NET 2022 and open the Server Explorer window by clicking the **View | Server Explorer** menu item. To find our sample database **CSE_DEPT**, just expand the **Data Connections** folder, and one can find that our sample database **CSE_DEPT** has been inactively connected and added into this explorer, which is shown in Figure 5.89a.

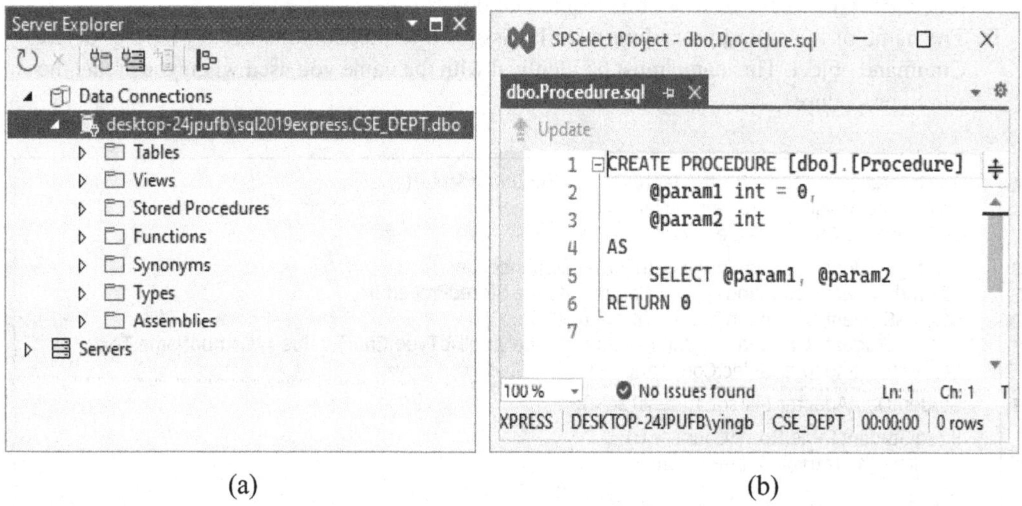

FIGURE 5.89 The finished server explorer window and the opened stored procedure wizard. (a and b) described in text.

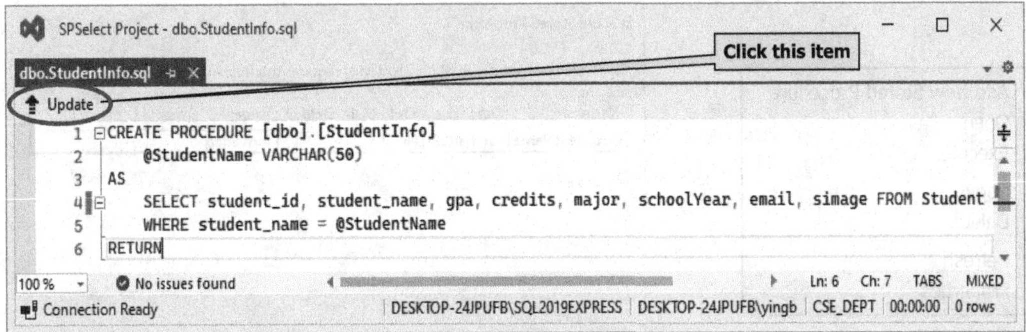

FIGURE 5.90 The first stored procedure – dbo.StudentInfo.

To make this connection active, right-click on our sample database and select **Refresh** item. Then expand our sample database and right-click on the **Stored Procedures** folder, and select the **Add New Stored Procedure** item to open a new stored procedure wizard, which is shown in Figure 5.89b.

The default name for a new stored procedure is **dbo.Procedure**, which is located immediately after the keyword **CREATE PROCEDURE**. The top default coding lines are used to create the parameters or parameter list. The bottom code line under the keyword **AS** is used to create the SQL statements. To create our first stored procedure, enter the codes shown in Figure 5.90 into this procedure.

The **@StudentName** is our only input parameter to this stored procedure, and this stored procedure will return eight pieces of information related to the selected student based on the input student name parameter. Don't forget to modify the stored procedure's name to **[dbo].[StudentInfo]**. Now click on the **Update** item on the upper-left corner, as shown in Figure 5.90, to save this stored procedure. Click on the **Update Database** button on the opened **Preview Database Updates** wizard to finish this saving process.

If everything is fine, an **Update completed successfully** message should be displayed.

Now if you go to or reopen the Server Explorer window, expand our database connection folder and the **Stored Procedures** folder, our new stored procedure may not be displayed. To see this procedure, just right-click on the **Stored Procedures** folder and select the **Refresh** item, and you can find our new stored procedure **StudentInfo** is in there.

In a similar way, we can create our second stored procedure **dbo.StudentCourseInfo**, which is shown in Figure 5.91.

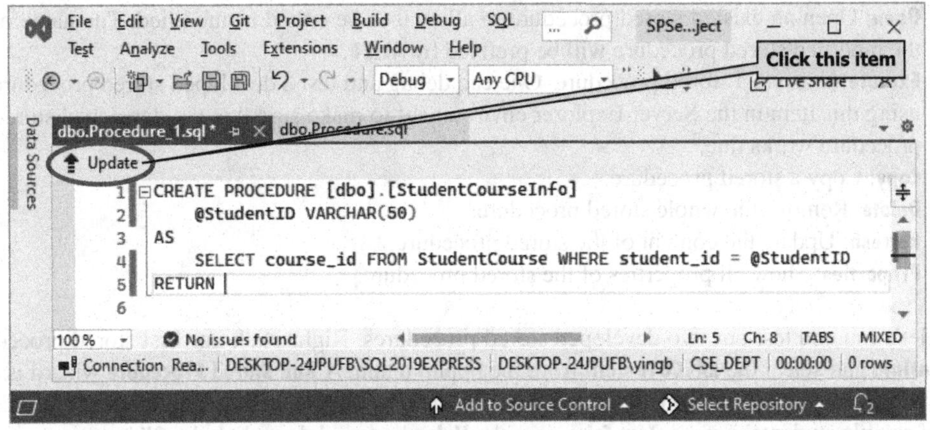

FIGURE 5.91 The second stored procedure – dbo.StudentCourseInfo.

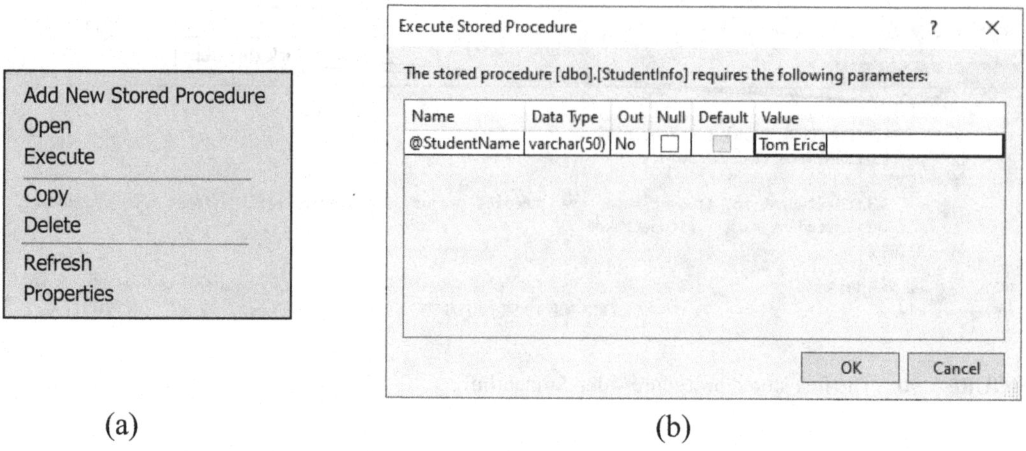

Add New Stored Procedure
Open
Execute
Copy
Delete
Refresh
Properties

(a)

Execute Stored Procedure

The stored procedure [dbo].[StudentInfo] requires the following parameters:

Name	Data Type	Out	Null	Default	Value
@StudentName	varchar(50)	No	☐	☐	Tom Erica

OK Cancel

(b)

FIGURE 5.92 The popup menu and the **EXECUTE** wizard. (a and b) described in text.

The only input parameter to this stored procedure is **@StudentID**, and this stored procedure will return all courses (exactly **course_id**) taken by the selected student based on the input parameter **student_id**. Click on the **Update** item on the upper-left corner, as shown in Figure 5.91, to save this stored procedure. Click on the **Update Database** button on the opened **Preview Database Updates** wizard to finish this saving process.

If everything is fine, an **Update completed successfully** message should be displayed.

OK, now we have finished creating our two stored procedures. Next we need to develop a new Visual C# project **SPSelect Project** and use the Student Form to query the **Student** and the **StudentCourse** tables in our sample database via these two stored procedures.

But wait for a moment. Before we can continue to develop our Visual C# project to call these two stored procedures, is there any way to check whether these two stored procedures work fine or not? The answer is yes! The Server Explorer in Visual Studio.NET allows us to debug and test custom stored procedures by using some popup menu items, as shown in Figure 5.92a.

Now go to the Server Explorer window, expand our database connection folder and our Stored Procedures folder. Then select one of our stored procedures, and then right-click that selected stored procedure. A popup menu will be displayed, which is shown in Figure 5.92a. The functionality for each item is explained below:

1) **Add New Stored Procedure**: Create a new stored procedure.
2) **Open**: Open an existed stored procedure to allow it to be edited or modified. The name of the modified stored procedure will be prefixed by **ALTER**.
3) **Execute**: Execute a stored procedure. One can debug and test a developed stored procedure using this item in the Server Explorer environment to make sure that the developed stored procedure works fine.
4) **Copy**: Copy a stored procedure.
5) **Delete**: Remove the whole stored procedure.
6) **Refresh**: Update the content of the stored procedure.
7) **Properties**: Show all properties of the stored procedure.

Now let's run and test our two developed stored procedures. Right-click our first stored procedure **StudentInfo** and select the **EXECUTE** item from the popup menu. A **Run Stored Procedure** wizard is displayed to allow you to enter any input parameter if you have, which is shown in Figure 5.92b. Enter one of sample students' names, **Tom Erica**, into the **Value** box, and then click the **OK** button to run our stored procedure. The testing result is displayed in the **Output** wizard, which is shown in Figure 5.93.

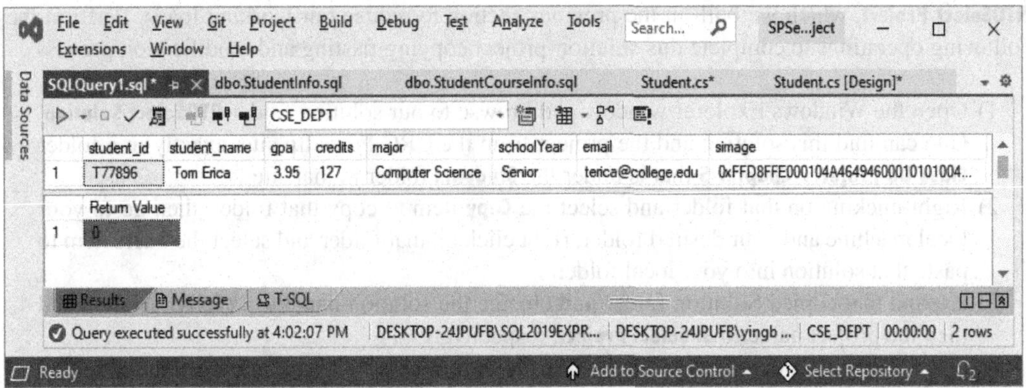

FIGURE 5.93 The testing result of our first stored procedure.

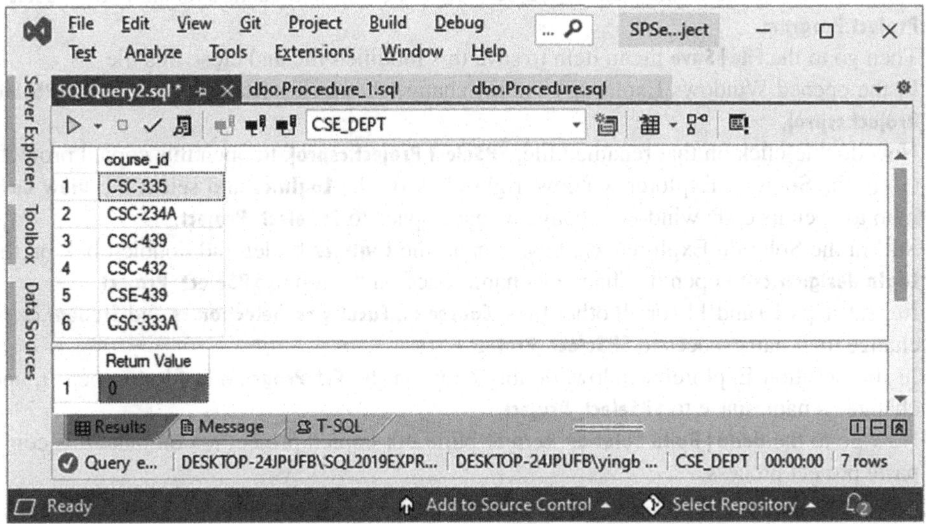

FIGURE 5.94 The testing result for our second stored procedure.

In total, there is one row with eight columns returned: **student_id, student_name, gpa, credits, major**, **schoolYear, email** and **simage**.

In a similar way, you can try to run our second stored procedure. You need to enter a valid **student_id** as the input parameter to run it. Of course, you can use the **student_id** obtained from our first stored procedure, which is **T77896**. The testing result for our second stored procedure **StudentCourseInfo** is shown in Figure 5.94.

Now that our two stored procedures have been tested successfully, it is time for us to develop a new Visual C# 2022 project SPSelect Project to call these two stored procedures to perform data query from the Student table in our sample database.

5.16.4 Create a New Visual C# Project SPSelect Project to Query Student Table

We can create a brand new Visual C# project to perform these data queries via our two stored procedures. However, in order to save time and space, we prefer to modify one of our projects,

RTOSelect Project, which we built in the previous section to reduce our working loads. Perform the following operations to complete this solution-project copying-pasting and modification process:

1) Open the Windows Explorer window and browse to our solution folder **RTOSelect Solution**. One can find this solution and the project from the CRC Press ftp site, exactly in a folder **Class DB Projects\Chapter 5** that is under the **Students** folder in that site.
2) Right-clicking on that folder and select the **Copy** item to copy that folder, then go to your local machine and your desired folder, right click on that folder and select the **Paste** item to paste that solution into your local folder.
3) Expand that copied Solution folder and change the solution name to **SPSelect Solution** and then the project name to **SPSelect Project**, respectively.
4) Open the project executed file **RTOSelect Project.csproj** via a NotePad under the renamed project **SPSelect Project** folder.
5) On the opened file, go to the **<RootNamespace>** (line 9) and **<AssemblyName>** (line 10) tags, change the RootNamespace to **SPSelect_Project** and the AssemblyName to **SPSelect Project**, respectively.
6) On the same file, go to the **<StartupObject>** tag (line 36), and change its name to **SPSelect_Project.Program**.
7) Then go to the **File | Save** menu item to save this modified file and close this file.
8) In the opened Windows Explorer window, change the name of that saved file to **SPSelect Project.csproj**.
9) Now double-click on that renamed file, **SPSelect Project.csproj**, to open this copied project.
10) Go to the Solution Explorer window, right-click on the **LogIn.cs** and select the **View Code** item to open its code window. Change its namespace to **SPSelect_Project**.
11) Still in the Solution Explorer window, expand the **LogIn.cs** folder and double-click on the **LogIn.designer.cs** to open it. Change its namespace on the top to **SPSelect_Project**.
12) Repeat steps 10 and 11 for all other files, **Course.cs**, **Faculty.cs**, **Selection.cs** and **Student.cs**, to change their namespaces to **SPSelect_Project**.
13) In the Solution Explorer window, double-click on the **C# Program.cs** file to open it, and change its namespace to **SPSelect_Project**.
14) Now go to the **Build | Build Solution** item to build our copied project to complete this copy-paste project process.

Next let's start our coding process for the Student Form window. First let's build the codes for the constructor of this Student class.

Go to the Solution Explorer window, right-click on the **Student.cs** folder and select the **View Code** item to open its code window. Enter the codes shown in Figure 5.95 into its constructor. Let's have a closer look at this piece of codes to see how it works.

A. The **System.Data.SqlClient** namespace is added first since we need to use a group of data components that are SQL Server Data Provider-dependent under that namespace in this section.
B. A new LogInForm object, **loginForm**, is declared and the purpose of generating this new object is to set up a valid connection to our sample database to get a connection object since we need to use it to query data from the Student table later.
C. All five student members are added into the **Student Name** combobox to enable users to select one of them to perform data query for that selected student. The **SelectedIndex = 0** makes the first student in the **Student Name** combobox as a default student.
D. Two query methods, **DataAdapter Method** and **DataReader Method**, are added into the **Query Method** combobox to enable users to select one to perform the related data query. Similarly, the first query method is selected as the default method by setting the **SelectedIndex** property

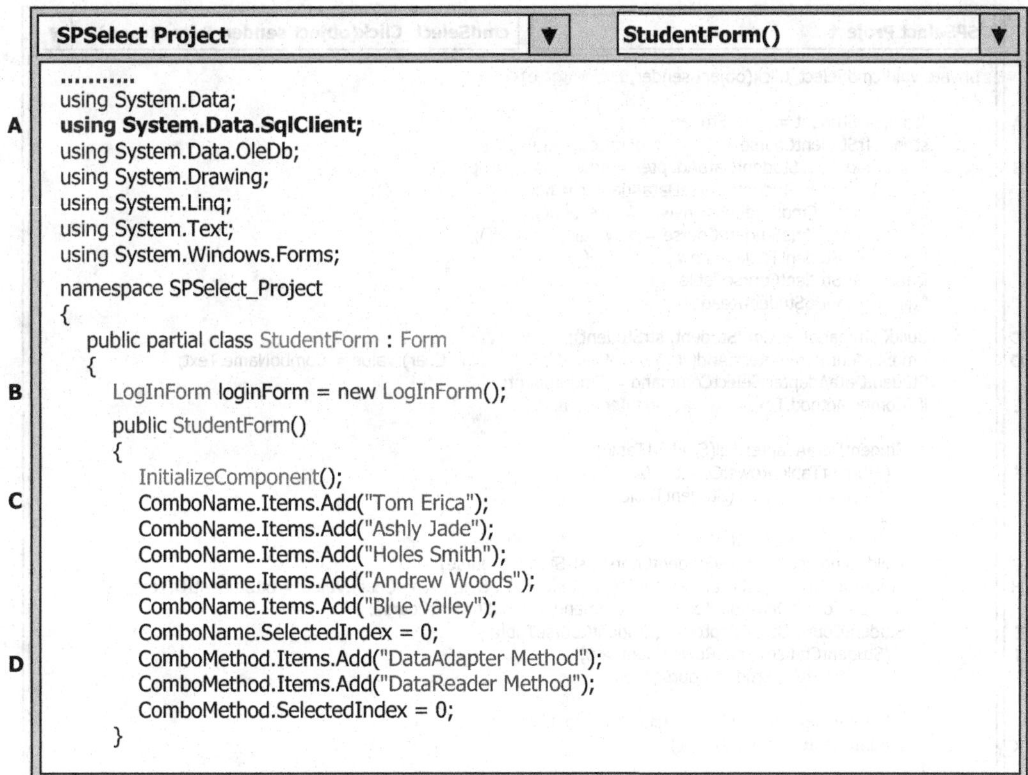

SPSelect Project | StudentForm()

```
    ..........
    using System.Data;
A   using System.Data.SqlClient;
    using System.Data.OleDb;
    using System.Drawing;
    using System.Linq;
    using System.Text;
    using System.Windows.Forms;
    namespace SPSelect_Project
    {
        public partial class StudentForm : Form
        {
B           LogInForm loginForm = new LogInForm();
            public StudentForm()
            {
                InitializeComponent();
C               ComboName.Items.Add("Tom Erica");
                ComboName.Items.Add("Ashly Jade");
                ComboName.Items.Add("Holes Smith");
                ComboName.Items.Add("Andrew Woods");
                ComboName.Items.Add("Blue Valley");
                ComboName.SelectedIndex = 0;
D               ComboMethod.Items.Add("DataAdapter Method");
                ComboMethod.Items.Add("DataReader Method");
                ComboMethod.SelectedIndex = 0;
            }
```

FIGURE 5.95 The codes for the constructor of the student form window.

to 0. A point to be noted is that although two query methods are available to the users, both methods need to call our stored procedures to perform related data queries to the **Student** table in our sample database.

Now open the Student Form by going to the Solution Explorer window, and right-clicking on the **Student.cs** and select the **View Designer** item.

Then open the **Select** button Click method by double-clicking on the **Select** button from the Student Form window, and enter the codes that are shown in Figure 5.96 into this method.

Let's take a closer look at this piece of codes to see how it works.

A. Two stored procedures' names are assigned to two string variables, **strStudent** and **strStudentCourse**, respectively. The names must be identical to those names we created in two stored procedures: **dbo.StudentInfo** and **dbo.StudentCourseInfo**.

B. All used data components are declared and created in the following section, which include two TableAdapters, two DataTables, two Command objects and one DataReader.

C. The user-defined method **BuildCommand()** is called to initialize the first Command object with the correct Connection, CommandType and CommandText properties. In order to execute our stored procedure, the properties should be set as follows:

- Connection = loginForm.**sqlConnection**
- CommandType = CommandType.**StoredProcedure**
- CommandText = "**dbo.StudentInfo**"

The content of the CommandText must be equal to the name of the stored procedure we developed above.

SPSelect Project | **cmdSelect_Click(object sender, EventArgs e)**

```
  private void cmdSelect_Click(object sender, EventArgs e)
  {
A     string strStudent = "dbo.StudentInfo";
      string strStudentCourse = "dbo.StudentCourseInfo";
B     SqlDataAdapter StudentDataAdapter = new SqlDataAdapter();
      SqlDataAdapter StudentCourseDataAdapter = new SqlDataAdapter();
      SqlCommand CmdStudent = new SqlCommand();
      SqlCommand CmdStudentCourse = new SqlCommand();
      DataTable StudentTable = new DataTable();
      DataTable StudentCourseTable = new DataTable();
      SqlDataReader StudentReader;
C     BuildCommand(ref CmdStudent, strStudent);
D     CmdStudent.Parameters.Add("@StudentName", SqlDbType.Char).Value = ComboName.Text;
      StudentDataAdapter.SelectCommand = CmdStudent;
E     if (ComboMethod.Text == "DataAdapter Method")
      {
         StudentDataAdapter.Fill(StudentTable);
F        if (StudentTable.Rows.Count > 0)
            FillStudentTextBox(StudentTable);
         else
            MessageBox.Show("No matched student found!");
G        BuildCommand(ref CmdStudentCourse, strStudentCourse);
H        CmdStudentCourse.Parameters.Add("@StudentID", SqlDbType.Char).Value = txtStudentID.Text;
         StudentCourseDataAdapter.SelectCommand = CmdStudentCourse;
I        StudentCourseDataAdapter.Fill(StudentCourseTable);
J        if (StudentCourseTable.Rows.Count > 0)
            FillCourseList(StudentCourseTable);
         else
            MessageBox.Show("No matched course_id found!");
K        CmdStudentCourse.Dispose();
      }
L     else    //DataReader Method is selected
      {
         SqlCommand CmdStudentCourse_dr = new SqlCommand();
         SqlDataReader StudentCourseReader;
M        StudentReader = CmdStudent.ExecuteReader();
N        if (StudentReader.HasRows == true)
            FillStudentReader(StudentReader);
O        else
            MessageBox.Show("No matched student found!");
         StudentReader.Close();
P        BuildCommand(ref CmdStudentCourse_dr, strStudentCourse);
Q        CmdStudentCourse_dr.Parameters.Add("@StudentID", SqlDbType.Char).Value = txtStudentID.Text;
R        StudentCourseReader = CmdStudentCourse_dr.ExecuteReader();
S        if (StudentCourseReader.HasRows == true)
            FillCourseReader(StudentCourseReader);
         else
            MessageBox.Show("No matched course_id found!");
T        StudentReader.Close();
         CmdStudentCourse_dr.Dispose();
         StudentCourseReader.Close();
      }
U     StudentTable.Dispose();
      StudentCourseTable.Dispose();
      StudentDataAdapter.Dispose();
      StudentCourseDataAdapter.Dispose();
      CmdStudent.Dispose();
      CmdStudentCourse.Dispose();
  }
```

FIGURE 5.96 The codes for the select button click method.

D. The unique input parameter to the stored procedure **dbo.StudentInfo** is a **StudentName**, which will be selected by the user from the student name combobox (**ComboName.Text**) as the project runs. This dynamic parameter must be added into the Parameters collection that is the property of the Command class by using the **Add()** method before the stored procedure can be executed. The initialized Command object **CmdStudent** is then assigned to the **SelectCommand** property of the DataAdapter to make it ready to be used in the next step.

E. If the user selected the **DataAdapter Method**, the **Fill()** method of the DataAdapter is called to fill the Student table via our first stored procedure.

F. If this calling is successful, the **Count** property should be greater than 0, which means that at least one row is filled into the Student table, and the user defined method **FillStudentTextBox()** is called to fill seven textboxes in the Student Form with seven retrieved columns from the stored procedure. Otherwise, an error message is displayed if this fill is failed.

G. The user-defined method **BuildCommand()** is called again to initialize our second Command object **CmdStudentCourse**. The values to be assigned to the properties of the Command object are:

- Connection = loginForm.**sqlConnection**
- CommandType = CommandType.**StoredProcedure**
- CommandText = "**dbo.StudentCourseInfo**"

The content of the CommandText must be equal to the name of the stored procedure we developed in the last section.

H. The unique input parameter to the stored procedure **dbo.StudentCourseInfo** is the **StudentID**, which is obtained from the calling of the first stored procedure and stored in the student ID textbox **txtStudentID**. This dynamic parameter must be added into the Parameters collection that is the property of the Command class by using the **Add()** method before the stored procedure can be executed. The initialized Command object **CmdStudentCourse** is then assigned to the **SelectCommand** property of the another DataAdapter to make it ready to be used in the next step.

I. The **Fill()** method of the DataAdapter is called to fill the **StudentCourse** table, which is exactly to call our second stored procedure to fill the **StudentCourse** table.

J. If this calling is successful, the **Count** property should be greater than 0, which means that at least one row is filled into the **StudentCourse** table, and the user-defined method **FillCourseList()** is called to fill the CourseList box in the Student Form with all courses (**course_id**) retrieved from the stored procedure. Otherwise, an error message is displayed if that fill operation is failed.

K. The used Command object **CmdStudentCourse** is removed by using the **Dispose()** method since we do not need it anymore in this method.

L. If the user selected the **DataReader Method**, first we need to create two local objects, a Command object **CmdStudentCourse_dr** and a DataReader object **StudentCourseReader**. The former works as an independent Command object to perform a query to the **StudentCourse** table via our second stored procedure to get all **course_id** taken by the selected student, and the later works as a Data Reader to get back all retrieved **course_id**.

M. Then the **ExecuteReader()** method is called to retrieve back all information related to the selected student and assign it to the **StudentReader** object.

N. If this method is executed successfully, which means that at least one row data is read back and assigned to the DataReader, the **HasRows** property of the DataReader should be **true**, and the user-defined method **FillStudentReader()** is executed to fill the related information to seven textboxes in the Student Form.

O. Otherwise, an error message is displayed to indicate this situation.

P. The **BuildCommand()** method is called to build the **StudentCourse** Command object with our second stored procedure. One point to be noted is the type of this first input parameter, which is a reference (**ref**). This means that an address of this Command object is passed into that method. The purpose of using this kind of type is that we need to get an initialized Command object to be returned to this method. Without using this **ref**, only a copy of that Command object is passed into that method and the returned object cannot be initialized.

Q. The unique input parameter to this stored procedure is the StudentID that is added to the Parameters collection that is a property of the Command object.

R. The **ExecuteReader()** method is called to run our second stored procedure to read out all courses taken by the selected student, and assign them to the **StudentCourse** DataReader object.

S. If the method **ExecuteReader()** runs successfully, the **HasRows** property of the DataReader object should be **true**, the user-defined method **FillCourseReader()** is executed to fill all courses (**course_id**) into the **CourseList** listbox. Otherwise, if this method fails, an error message is displayed.

T. Two student DataReader objects and one Command object are released before we can exit this method.

U. Some cleaning jobs are performed to release all other data objects used in this method.

The codes for the **BuildCommand()** method are shown in Figure 5.97.

This piece of codes is straightforward and easy to be understood. First a valid database connection object, which coming from a class-level connection object, **sqlConnection**, of the LogInForm class is assigned to the Connection property of the Command object. Then the Command object is initialized by assigning the related properties such as the CommandType and CommandText to it. The point is that the value assigned to the CommandType must be **StoredProcedure**, and the value assigned to the CommandText must be equal to the name of the stored procedure we developed in the last section.

The codes for two user-defined methods, **FillStudentTextBox()** and **FillCourseList()**, are shown in Figure 5.98. Let's have a closer look at these codes to see how they work.

A. For the first method, **FillStudentTextBox()**, two local variables are declared. The integer variable **pos** works as a loop counter for the inner foreach loop later to pick up each queried column from the retrieved row. A TextBox array, **sTextBox[]**, in which all seven TextBoxes in the Student Form are involved, is used to hold and display related data column retrieved from the **Student** table.

B. A nested foreach loop is used to retrieve each queried column from the returned row. In this case the outer loop is only executed one time since we have only retrieved back one data row from the **Student** table. Each retrieved column is assigned to the associated TextBox to be displayed in the Student Form.

C. In total, there are eight (8) columns are retrieved, of which seven columns are for matched student information to be displayed in seven TextBoxes in the Student Form and the final one is the student image. Thus, an **if** clause is used to only pick up the first seven columns and display them in seven TextBoxes via the array **sTextBox[]**.

D. The loop counter **pos** is updated for the next loop operation.

SPSelect Project	**BuildCommand()**

```
private void BuildCommand(ref SqlCommand cmdObj, string cmdString)
{
        cmdObj.Connection = loginForm.sqlConnection;
        cmdObj.CommandType = CommandType.StoredProcedure;
        cmdObj.CommandText = cmdString;
}
```

FIGURE 5.97 The codes for the BuildCommand() method.

```
SPSelect Project                    FillStudentTextBox(DataTable StudentTable)

  private void FillStudentTextBox(DataTable StudentTable)
  {
A     int pos = 0;
      TextBox[] sTextBox = {txtStudentID, txtStudentName, txtGPA, txtCredits, txtMajor, txtSchoolYear, txtEmail};
B     foreach (DataRow row in StudentTable.Rows)
      {
         foreach (DataColumn column in StudentTable.Columns)
         {
C           if (pos <= 6)
            {
               sTextBox[pos].Text = row[column].ToString();
D              pos++;
            }
E           else
            {
               byte[] bimage = (byte[])row["simage"];
               PhotoBox.Image = Image.FromStream(new System.IO.MemoryStream(bimage));
            }
         }
      }
  }
  private void FillCourseList(DataTable StudentCourseTable)
  {
F       CourseList.Items.Clear();
G       foreach (DataRow row in StudentCourseTable.Rows)
        {
           CourseList.Items.Add(row[0]);          //the 1st column is course_id - strStudentCourse
        }
  }
```

FIGURE 5.98 The codes for two user defined methods.

- **E.** For the last column, which contained a matched student image with an object data type, a forced conversion (**byte[]**) is used to convert that object to a **byte[]** type. Furthermore, it is converted to an image stream and assigned to the **Image** property of the Student Image box, **PhotoBox**, in the Student Form to be displayed.
- **F.** The functionality of the method **FillCourseList()** is to pick up each matched row (**course_id**) from the filled **StudentCourse** table and add them into the CourseList listbox. Prior to doing this fill action, the CourseList box is cleaned up.
- **G.** Another foreach loop is utilized to pick up each matched row (**course_id**) in the **StudentCourse** table and add each of them into the CourseList box. One point to be noted is the selected column number, it is 0, which means that this is the first column in the retrieved row. This makes sense since only one matched column could be retrieved, which is **course_id** and it is located at the first column in the returned row.

The codes for two other user-defined methods, **FillStudentReader()** and **FillCourseReader()**, are shown in Figure 5.99. Let's have a closer look at these codes to see how they work.

- **A.** For the first method, **FillStudentReader()**, two local variables are declared. The integer variable **index** works as a loop counter for a **for** loop later to pick up each queried column from the retrieved row. A TextBox array, **sTextBox**[], in which all seven TextBoxes in the Student Form are involved, is used to hold and display related data column retrieved from the **Student** table.

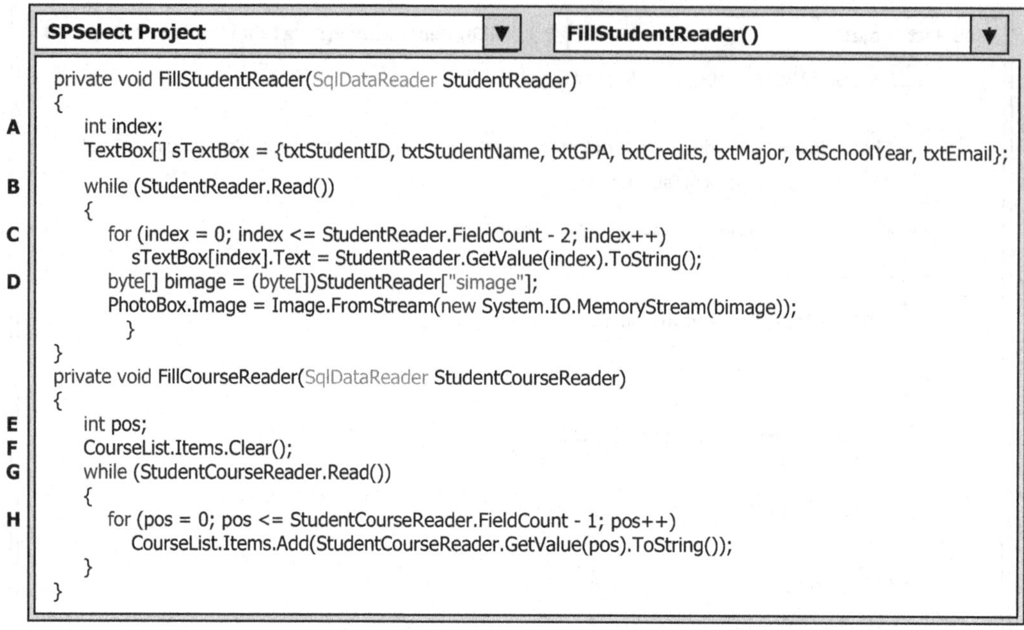

FIGURE 5.99 The codes for another two user defined methods.

B. A **while()** loop is then utilized to repeatedly pick up each column queried from the **Student** table as long as the **Read()** method of the DataReader is true, which means that a valid data column has been retrieved.

C. Inside that **while()** loop, a **for()** loop is used to conditionally pick up the first seven columns (0–6), in which seven pieces of a matched student information is involved, and assign them to seven TextBoxes in the Student Form via **sTextBox[]** array. Two points to be noted are: 1) The upper bound of this **for()** loop is **FieldCount – 2**, which is **8 – 2 = 6**, since the total column is 8 and the column number starts from 0, not 1. 2) To pick up each column, the system method **GetValue()** of the DataReader is used instead of using **GetString()** since two columns, **gpa** and **credits**, in the **Student** table are typed with **Double** and **Int32**. Also a forced conversion, **ToString()**, is used to convert both columns to String.

D. For the last column, which is a matched student image, a forced conversion (**byte[]**) is used to convert that object to a **byte[]** type. Furthermore, it is converted to an image stream and assigned to the **Image** property of the Student Image box, **PhotoBox**, in the Student Form to be displayed.

E. The function of the method **FillCourseReader()** is to pick up each matched row (**course_id**) from the filled **StudentCourse** table and add them into the CourseList listbox. First, a local integer variable **pos** is generated and it is used as a loop counter later for a **for()** loop to pick up each matched row (**course_id**).

F. Prior to doing this fill action, the CourseList box is cleaned up.

G. A **while()** loop is then utilized to repeatedly pick up each row queried from the **StudentCourse** table as long as the **Read()** method of the DataReader is **true**, which means that a valid data row has been retrieved.

H. Inside that **while()** loop, a **for()** loop is used to conditionally pick up all matched rows (**course_id**) and add them into the CourseList box in the Student Form to display them.

We have almost completed all coding development for this project. Finally, don't forget to build the codes for the **Back** command button. Open the Student Form or Designer View and double-click on this button to open its click method. Enter the codes shown in Figure 5.100 into this method.

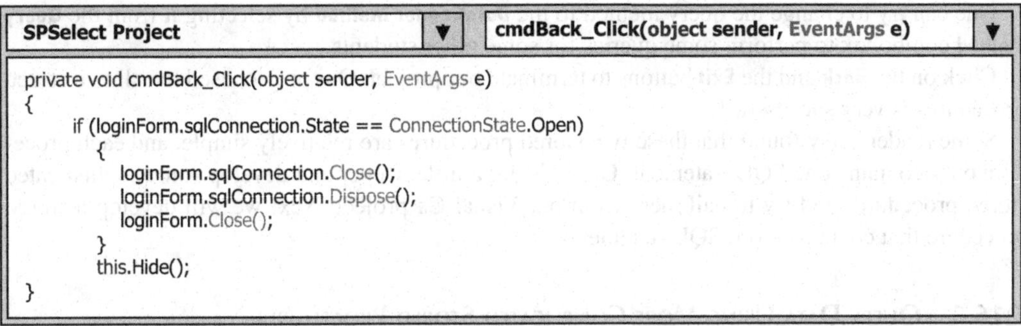

```
SPSelect Project                              cmdBack_Click(object sender, EventArgs e)

private void cmdBack_Click(object sender, EventArgs e)
{
    if (loginForm.sqlConnection.State == ConnectionState.Open)
    {
        loginForm.sqlConnection.Close();
        loginForm.sqlConnection.Dispose();
        loginForm.Close();
    }
    this.Hide();
}
```

FIGURE 5.100 The codes for the back button click method.

This piece of codes is straightforward. First, we need to check whether a valid database connection object is still active. If it is, we need to close this connection and the LogIn Form object. Then a system method **Hide()** is used to temporarily close this Student Form and return the control to the Selection Form.

Now we can begin to test to call those two stored procedures from our Visual C# project. Build the project and click the **Start** button to run our project, enter user name and password and select the **Student Information** item to open the Student Form window, which is shown in Figure 5.101.

Keep the default query method, DataAdapter Method and select the student **Ashly Jade** from the Student Name combobox. Then click on the **Select** button to perform a query to our **Student** and **StudentCourse** tables via our two stored procedures to get related student information. All information related to this student and the courses are displayed in seven TextBoxes, Student Image box and the CourseList box, which is shown in Figure 5.101.

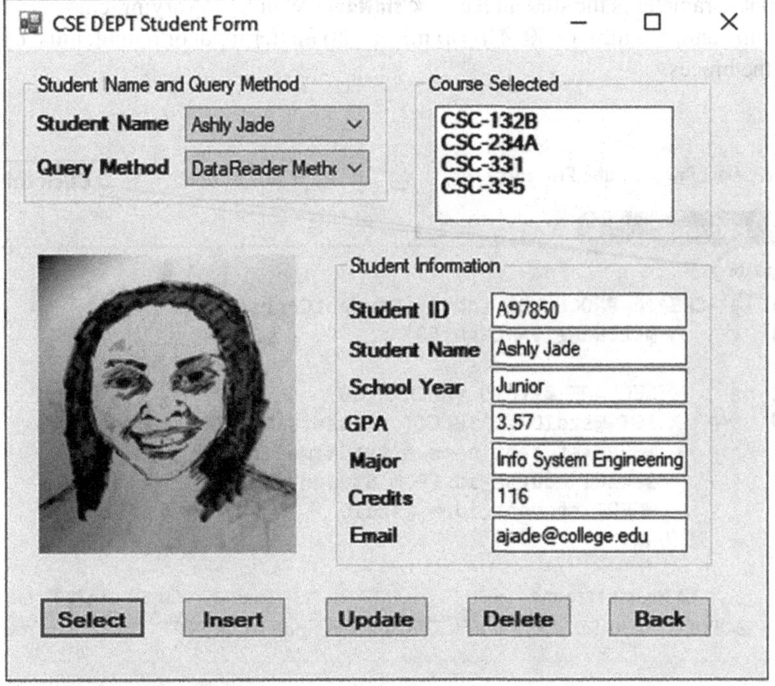

FIGURE 5.101 The running status of the student form.

One can try to change the query method to the **DataReader Method** by selecting it from the **Query Method** combobox to perform some queries for some other students.

Click on the **Back** and the **Exit** buttons to terminate our project. Our project used to call two stored procedures is very successful!

Some readers may found that these two stored procedures are relatively simple, and each procedure only contains one SQL statement. Ok, let's dig a little deeper and develop some sophisticated stored procedures and try to call them from our Visual C# project. Next we will develop a stored procedure that contains more SQL statements.

5.16.5 Query Data Using More Complicated Stored Procedures

Now what we want to do is to get all courses (exactly all **course_id**) taken by the selected student based only on the student name from the **StudentCourse** table. To do that, we must first go to the **Student** table to obtain the associated **student_id** based on the student name since there is no student name column available in the **StudentCourse** table. Then we can go to the **StudentCourse** table to pick up all **course_id** based on the selected **student_id**. Regularly we need to perform two queries to complete this data-retrieving operation. Now we try to combine these two queries into a single stored procedure to simplify our data-querying operation. First let's create our stored procedure.

Open Visual Studio.NET and the Server Explorer window, and click on the arrow-symbol icon on the left of our database folder to connect to our database if this database was added into the Server Explorer before. Otherwise you need to right click on the Data Connections folder to add and connect to our database.

Right-click on the **Stored Procedures** folder and select the **Add New Stored Procedure** item to open the Add Procedure wizard, and then enter the codes that are shown in Figure 5.102 into this new procedure.

Let's give a detailed discussion for this piece of codes.

A. The stored procedure is named **dbo.StudentCourseINTO**.

B. The input parameter is the student name, **@stdName**, which is a varying-char variable with a maximum character limit of 50. All parameters, no matter input or output, must be declared inside the braces.

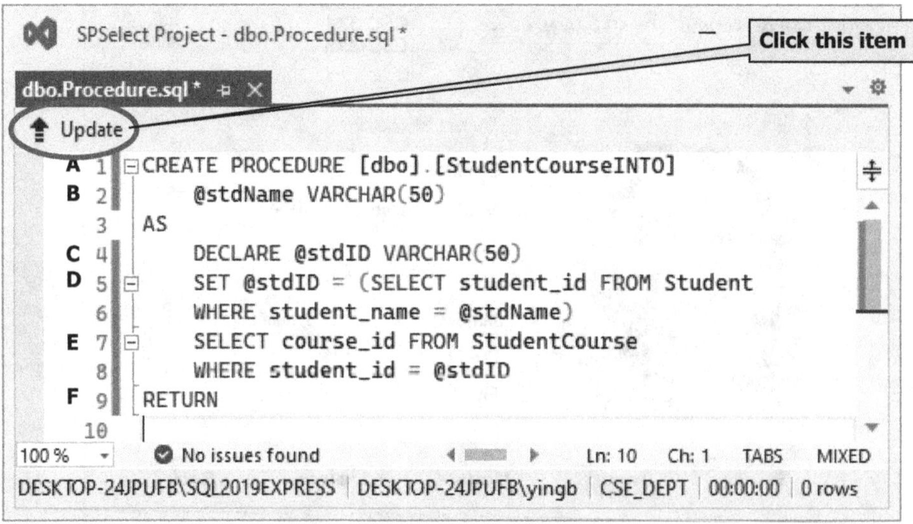

FIGURE 5.102 A new stored procedure – StudentCourseINTO.

C. The local variable **@stdID** is used to hold the returned query result from the first SQL statement that retrieves the **student_id**.
D. The first SQL statement is executed to get the **student_id** from the **Student** table based on the input parameter **@stdName**. A **SET** command must be used to assign the returned result from the first SQL query to the local variable (or intermediate variable) **@stdID**. The first SQL statement must be covered by the parenthesis to indicate that this whole query will be returned as a single data item.
E. The second SQL statement is executed and this query is used to retrieve all courses (**course_id**) taken by the selected student from the **StudentCourse** table based on the **student_id** that is obtained from the first query.
F. Finally the queried result, all courses or **course_id**, are returned.

Now click on the **Update** item on the upper-left corner, as shown in Figure 5.102, to save this stored procedure. Click on the **Update Database** button on the opened **Preview Database Updates** wizard to finish this saving process.

Now let's test our stored procedure in the Server Explorer window. Right-click on our new created stored procedure **StudentCourseINTO** and select the **Execute** item from the popup menu (right click on the **Stored Procedures** folder on the left and select the **Refresh** item to find this new stored procedure if you cannot find it). On the opened wizard, enter the student's name, **TomErica**, then click on the **OK** button to run our procedure. The running result is shown in Figure 5.103.

Next we need to develop a Visual C# project to call this stored procedure to test the functionality of the stored procedure. To save time and space, we added a new form window into this project and named it **SP_Student**.

Open our project **SPSelect Project** and select the **Project | Add Windows Form** item, enter **SP_Student Form.cs** into the **Name**: box and click the **Add** button to add this new Form into our project. Enter **SPForm** into the **name** property as the name for this Form.

Enlarge the size of this SP_Student Form by dragging the border of the form window, and then open the Student Form window. We need to copy all controls on the Student Form to our new SP_Student Form. On the opened Student Form, select **Edit | Select All** and **Edit | Copy** items, and then open the SP_Student Form and select **Edit | Paste** to paste all controls we copied from the Student Form.

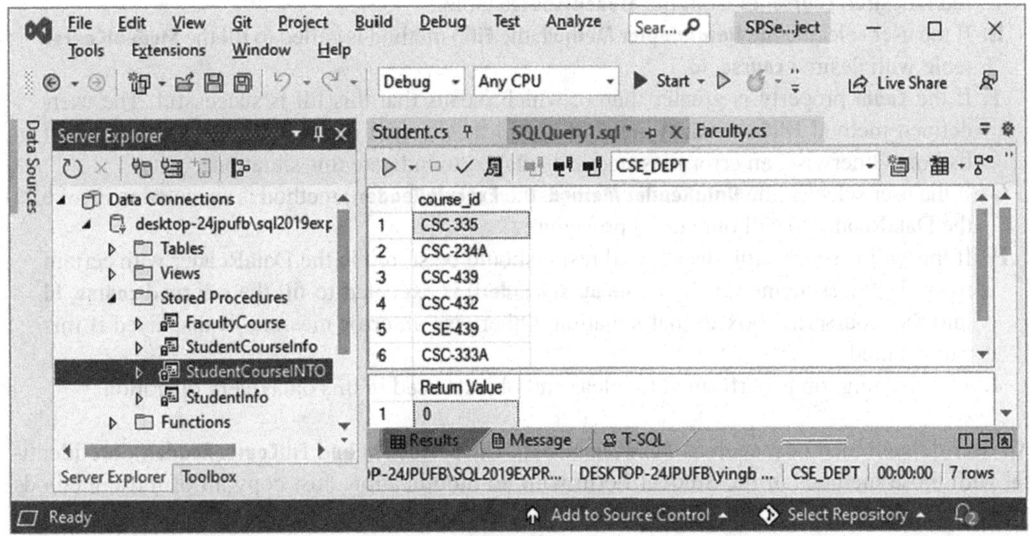

FIGURE 5.103 The running result of the stored procedure.

Now let's build codes for the SP_Student Form, and four coding parts are needed:

1) Coding for the constructor of this class.
2) Adding a new object of the LogInForm class, **LogInForm loginForm = new LogInForm()**; into the SP_Student Form class.
3) Coding for the **Select** and the **Back** button click methods.
4) Coding for the Selection Form class to add this SP_Student Form.

Open the constructor of the Student Form class, and copy all codes inside that constructor and paste them into the constructor of the SP_Student Form class. Next let's build the codes for the **Select** button Click method on the SP_Student Form. First we need to add the SQL Server related namespace **usingSystem.Data.SqlClient**; to the namespace declaration section on this SP_Student Form code window. Open the **Select** button Click method and enter the codes that are shown in Figure 5.104 into this method.

Let's discuss this piece of codes step by step to see how it works.

A. The name of our stored procedure, **dbo.StudentCourseINTO**, must be declared first and this name must be identical to the name we used when we created our stored procedure in the Server Explorer window.

B. All data components, including the Command, DataAdapter, DataTable and DataReader objects, are declared here since we need to use them for this data query.

C. The Command object is initialized with suitable properties by execution of the user-defined method **BuildCommand()**. The CommandType property must be **StoredProcedure** to indicate that this query is to execute a stored procedure. The CommandText property must be equal to the name of our stored procedure, **dbo.StudentCourseINTO**, which is stored in a string variable strStudentCourse.

D. The input parameter to the stored procedure is the student name, which is obtained from the **Student Name** combobox. It should be added into the Parameters collection property of the Command object. You need to note that the nominal name @stdName must be identical with the input parameter name we defined in our stored procedure **dbo.StudentCourseINTO**. The real parameter is entered by the user as the project runs. The finished Command object is assigned to the **SelectCommand** property of the DataAdapter, which will be used later to fetch desired **course_id** from the **StudentCourse** table.

E. If the user selected the **DataAdapter Method**, the **Fill()** method is called to fill the **StudentCourse** table with desired **course_id**.

F. If the **Count** property is greater than 0, which means that this fill is successful. The user-defined method **FillCourseList()** is called to fill the fetched **course_** id into the CourseList listbox. Otherwise, an error message is displayed to indicate this situation.

G. If the user selected the **DataReader Method**, the **ExecuteReader()** method is executed to invoke the DataReader to call our stored procedure.

H. If this call is successful, the queried result should be stored in the DataReader with certain rows. The user-defined method **FillCourseReader()** is executed to fill the returned **course_id** into the CourseList box in that situation. Otherwise an error message is displayed if this call is failed.

I. The cleaning job is performed to release all objects used in this data query operation.

All user-defined methods, such as **BuildCommand()**, **FillCourseList()** and **FillCourseReader()**, are identical with those methods in the Student Form with no modification. Just copy all of those methods

```
SPSelect Project                                   cmdSelect_Click()

using System.Data;
using System.Data.SqlClient;

namespace SPSelect_Project
{
    public partial class SPForm : Form
    {
        LogInForm loginForm = new LogInForm();
        public SPForm()
        {
            InitializeComponent();
            ComboName.Items.Add("Tom Erica");
            ComboName.Items.Add("Ashly Jade");
            ComboName.Items.Add("Holes Smith");
            ComboName.Items.Add("Andrew Woods");
            ComboName.Items.Add("Blue Valley");
            ComboName.SelectedIndex = 0;
            ComboMethod.Items.Add("DataAdapter Method");
            ComboMethod.Items.Add("DataReader Method");
            ComboMethod.SelectedIndex = 0;
        }
        private void cmdSelect_Click(object sender, EventArgs e)
        {
A           string strStudentCourse = "dbo.StudentCourseINTO";
B           SqlDataAdapter StudentCourseDataAdapter = new SqlDataAdapter();
            SqlCommand sqlCmdStudentCourse = new SqlCommand();
            DataTable sqlStudentCourseTable = new DataTable();
            SqlDataReader sqlStudentCourseReader;
C           BuildCommand(ref sqlCmdStudentCourse, strStudentCourse);
D           sqlCmdStudentCourse.Parameters.Add("@stdName", SqlDbType.Char).Value = ComboName.Text;
            StudentCourseDataAdapter.SelectCommand = sqlCmdStudentCourse;
E           if (ComboMethod.Text == "DataAdapter Method")
            {
                StudentCourseDataAdapter.Fill(sqlStudentCourseTable);
F               if (sqlStudentCourseTable.Rows.Count > 0)
                    FillCourseList(sqlStudentCourseTable);
                else
                    MessageBox.Show("No matched course_id found!");
            }
G           else    //DataReader Method is selected
            {
                sqlStudentCourseReader = sqlCmdStudentCourse.ExecuteReader();
                if (sqlStudentCourseReader.HasRows == true)
H                   FillCourseReader(sqlStudentCourseReader);
                else
                    MessageBox.Show("No matched course_id found!");
                sqlStudentCourseReader.Close();
            }
I           sqlStudentCourseTable.Dispose();
            StudentCourseDataAdapter.Dispose();
            sqlCmdStudentCourse.Dispose();
        }
    }
}
```

FIGURE 5.104 The codes for the select button click method.

```
SPSelect Project                    FillCourseList(DataTable StudentCourseTable)

private void FillCourseList(DataTable StudentCourseTable)
{
      CourseList.Items.Clear();
      foreach (DataRow row in StudentCourseTable.Rows)
      {
            CourseList.Items.Add(row[0]);               //the 1st column is course_id - strStudentCourse
      }
}
private void FillCourseReader(SqlDataReader StudentCourseReader)
{
    int pos;
    CourseList.Items.Clear();
    while (StudentCourseReader.Read())
    {
        for (pos = 0; pos <= StudentCourseReader.FieldCount - 1; pos++)
            CourseList.Items.Add(StudentCourseReader.GetValue(pos).ToString());
    }
}
```

FIGURE 5.105 The codes for two user-defined methods.

from the Student Form and paste them into the code window of the SP_Student Form class. Refer to Figures 5.97–5.99 to get detailed codes for those methods. For your convenience, we show two user defined methods **FillCourseList()** and **FillCourseReader()** again in Figure 5.105.

The codes for the **Back** button click method are identical with those codes in the **Back** button click method in the Student Form. Refer to Figure 5.100 to get more details about those codes. Just copy the codes in that method and paste them into the **Back** button click method.

Now let's add some codes to the Selection Form class to allow users to select this new SP_Student Form. Open the code window of the Selection Form and add the following codes:

1) Create a new field-level instance of the SP Form by entering the coding line: **SPFormspForm = new SPForm()**; inside the SPForm class.
2) Add a new item **SP Information** into the ComboSelection combobox by entering: **this.ComboSelection.Items.Add("SP Information")**; into the constructor of this form.
3) Add a selection branch for the **SP Information** by entering this code line into the **OK** button Click method: **else spForm.Show()**;
4) Add the code line: **spForm.Close()**; into the **Exit** button Click method.

The new added codes for the Selection Form class are shown in Figure 5.106. The modified parts have been highlighted in bold.

Now we can run the project to test this project to calling our stored procedure to query all courses (**course_id**) taken by the selected student.

As the project runs, enter the suitable username and password, and then select the **SP Information** from the Selection Form to open the SP Form window. Select a student name from the student combobox and click the **Select** button. All courses taken by selected student will be displayed in the CourseList box, which is shown in Figure 5.107.

Click on the **Back** and the **Exit** button to terminate our project.

The testing result for our stored procedure is very good, but we can do a little more to develop a more sophisticated stored procedure to meet our special requirement. What is our special requirement? We want to develop some nested stored procedures and call the nested stored procedure from our main or parent stored procedure. Sounds complicated, but is it? Yes, but we try to make this complicated issue simple by working through the following example.

```
SPSelect Project                          SelectionForm()

public partial class SelectionForm : Form
{
    FacultyForm facultyForm = new FacultyForm();
    CourseForm courseForm = new CourseForm();
    StudentForm studentForm = new StudentForm();
    SPForm spForm = new SPForm();
    public SelectionForm()
    {
        InitializeComponent();
        this.ComboSelection.Items.Add("Faculty Information");
        this.ComboSelection.Items.Add("Course Information");
        this.ComboSelection.Items.Add("Student Information");
        this.ComboSelection.Items.Add("SP Information");
        this.ComboSelection.SelectedIndex = 0;
    }
    private void cmdOK_Click(object sender, EventArgs e)
    {
        if (this.ComboSelection.Text == "Faculty Information")
            facultyForm.Show();
        else if (this.ComboSelection.Text == "Course Information")
            courseForm.Show();
        else if (this.ComboSelection.Text == "Student Information")
            studentForm.Show();
        else spForm.Show();
    }
    private void cmdExit_Click(object sender, EventArgs e)
    {
        courseForm.Close();
        facultyForm.Close();
        studentForm.Close();
        spForm.Close();
        Application.Exit();
    }
}
```

FIGURE 5.106 The modified codes for the SelectionForm class.

5.16.6 Query Data Using Nested Stored Procedures

The so-called nested stored procedure is very similar to subroutines or sub-query, which means that a main stored procedure can be considered as a parent stored procedure, and a sub stored procedure can be considered as a child stored procedure. The parent stored procedure can call the child stored procedure as it likes. In this section, we try to create two stored procedures, one is a main and the other is a child stored procedure. The main stored procedure, which is named **StudentAndCourse**, is used to get all courses taken by the selected student from the **StudentCourse** table based on a selected **student_id**, and the child stored procedure, which is named **StudentInfoID**, is used to get the **student_id** from the **Student** table based on the input student name.

Now open the Server Explorer window and connect to our database CSE_DEPT. After the database is connected, right-click on the Stored Procedures folder and select the **Add New Stored Procedure** item to open the Add Procedure wizard.

First let's create our main stored procedure – **dbo.StudentAndCourse**. Enter the codes that are shown in Figure 5.108 into our main stored procedure.

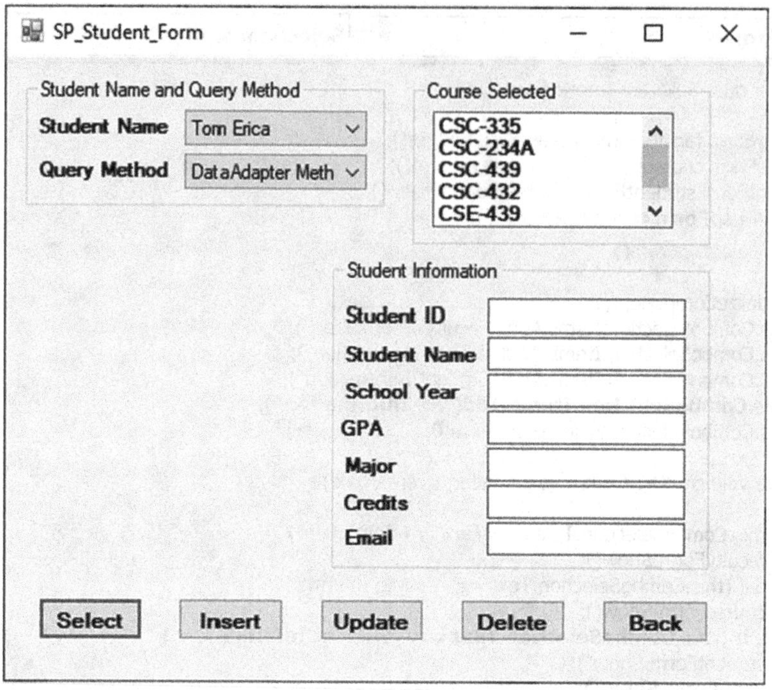

FIGURE 5.107 The running status of calling our stored procedure.

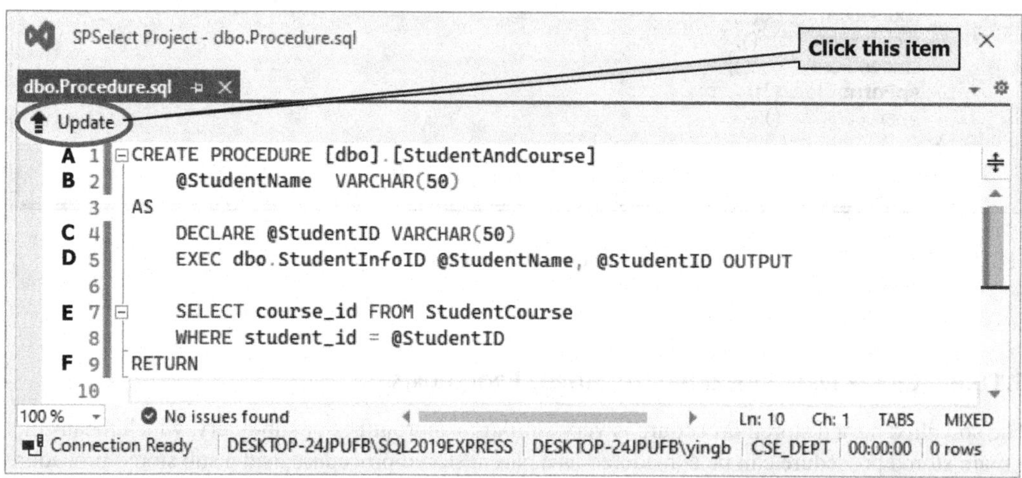

FIGURE 5.108 The main stored procedure.

The functionality of each coding line is:

A. The name of our main stored procedure is declared first, **dbo.StudentAndCourse**. This name must be identical with the name of the stored procedure used in our Visual C# project later.
B. The input parameter **@StudentName** is declared here.
C. The local variable **@StudentID** is used as an output parameter for the child stored procedure that will return this parameter, **student_id**, to our main procedure.
D. Call the child stored procedure to execute it using the command **EXEC**. This calling passes two parameters to the child stored procedure: the input parameter to the child procedure @

StudentName, and the output parameter **@StudentID**. The latter must be indicated with the keyword **OUTPUT**. Later in the child stored procedure, you must also declare this parameter as an output parameter using the keyword **OUTPUT** to match its definition defined in this main stored procedure.

E. After the child stored procedure is executed, it returns the **student_id**. Now we can perform our main query to obtain all courses taken by the selected student from the **StudentCourse** table based on the **student_id** returned by the child stored procedure.

F. The retrieved courses are returned to the calling procedure developed in Visual C# project.

Now click on the **Update** item on the upper-left corner, as shown in Figure 5.108, to save this stored procedure. Click on the **Update Database** button on the opened **Preview Database Updates** wizard to finish this saving process.

Second let's create our child stored procedure. Right click on the **Stored Procedures** folder in the Server Explorer window if our sample database **CSE_DEPT** has been connected and select the **Add New Stored Procedure** item from the popup menu. On the opened wizard, enter the codes that are shown in Figure 5.109 into this new child stored procedure.

The functionality for each coding line is explained below:

A. The name of our child stored procedure is declared first, which is: **dbo.StudentInfoID**. This name must be identical with the name used by our main stored procedure when this child procedure is called.

B. Two parameters are declared here; the first one, **@sName**, is the input and the second, **@sID**, is the output parameter. The default type of the parameter is **INPUT**, so the keyword **OUTPUT** must be attached for the second parameter since it is an output and will be returned to the main stored procedure.

C. The SQL statement is executed to get the desired **student_id** from the **Student** table based on the input student name. The returned **student_id** will be assigned to the output parameter @ **sID** by using the **SET** command.

D. The output parameter **@sID** is returned to the main stored procedure.

Now click on the **Update** item on the upper-left corner, as shown in Figure 5.109, to save this stored procedure. Click on the **Update Database** button on the opened **Preview Database Updates** wizard to finish this saving process.

To test both main and child stored procedure in the Server Explorer window, right-click on the main stored procedure **StudentAndCourse** item, and then select **Execute** item to open the Run Stored Procedure wizard.

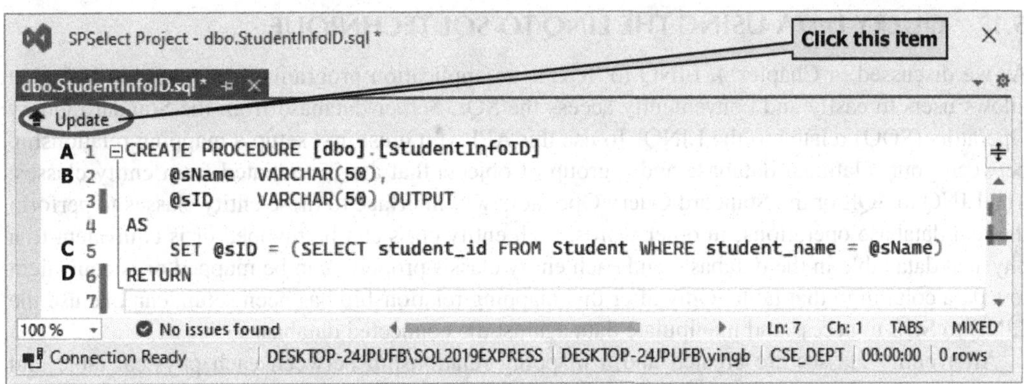

FIGURE 5.109 The child stored procedure.

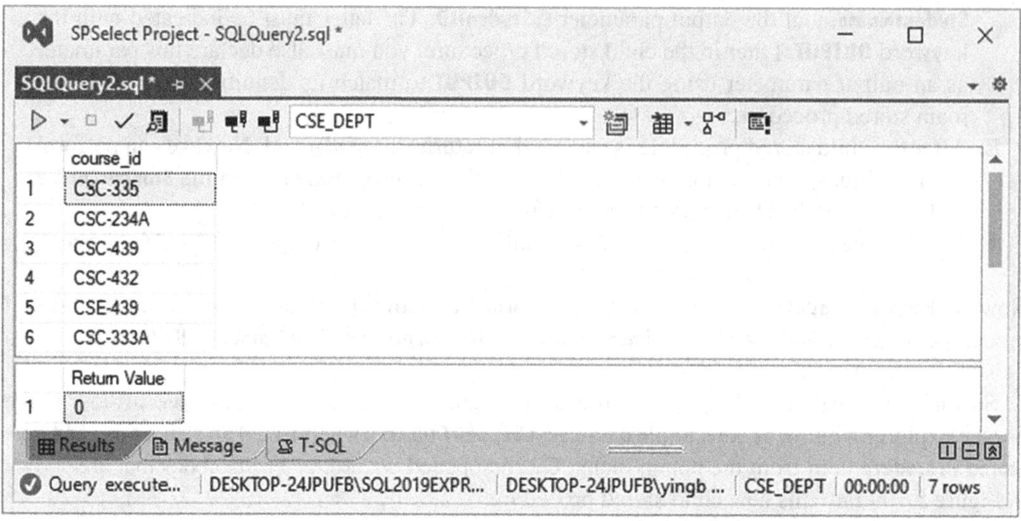

FIGURE 5.110 The running result of the nested stored procedure.

Enter a student name, such as **Tom Erica**, and click the **OK** button to run both stored procedures. The running result is shown in Figure 5.110.

Our nested stored procedures work fine!

To call this nested stored procedure, we need to develop a Visual C# project. In order to save time and space, we can use the codes we developed for the SP Form window in the last sub-section. All codes are same and the only modification is the stored procedure's name declared in the **cmdSelect_Click()** method, and the nominal input parameter name to the stored procedure. Change the name of the stored procedure from the **dbo.StudentCourseINTO** to the **dbo.StudentAndCourse** (refer to line **A** in Figure 5.104), and change the nominal parameter's name from **@stdName** to **@StudentName** (refer to line **D** in Figure 5.104).Then you can run that project to get the same result, which is shown in Figure 5.107, as we got from that project.

At this point, we finished developing a data-driven project using the stored procedure for the SQL Server database. A complete project **SPSelect Project** can be found from the CRC Press ftp site, in the folder **ClassDB Projects\Chapter 5\SPSelect Solution** that is located on the **Students** folder in that site

Now let's go to the next part in this chapter – develop a data-driven application using the LINQ to SQL with the SQL Server database.

5.17 QUERY DATA USING THE LINQ TO SQL TECHNIQUE

As we discussed in Chapter 4, LINQ to SQL is an application programming interface (API) that allows users to easily and conveniently access the SQL Server database from the Standard Query Operators (SQO) related to the LINQ. To use this API, you must first setup a mapping relationship between your relational database and a group of objects that are instantiated from entity classes. The LINQ to SQL or the Standard Query Operators will interface to these entity classes to perform the real database operations. In other words, each entity class can be mapped or is equivalent to a physical data table in the database, and each entity class's property can be mapped or is equivalent to a data column in that table. Only after this mapping relationship has been setup, can one use the LINQ to SQL to access and manipulate data against the connected databases.

After entity classes are created and a mapping relationship between each physical table and each entity class has been built, the conversion for data operations between the entity class and the real data table is needed. The class **DataContext** is the guy who will work in this role. Basically the

DataContext is a connection class that is used to establish a connection between your project and your database. In addition to this connection role, the DataContext also provides the conversion function to convert or interpret operations of the Standard Query Operators for the entity classes to the SQL statements that can be run in real databases.

The procedure to use LINQ to SQL to perform data actions against SQL Server database can be described in terms of the sequence listed below:

1) Add the **System.Data.Linq.dll** assembly into the project that will use LINQ to SQL by adding the reference **System.Data.Linq**.
2) Create an entity class for each data table by using one of two popular tools: **SQLMetal** or **Object Relational Designer**.
3) Add a connection to the selected database using the **DataContext** class or the derived class from the **DataContext** class.
4) Use LINQ to SQL to access the database to perform desired data actions.

As we mentioned in Chapter 4, the difference between the **SQLMetal** and the **Object Relational Designer** is that the former is a console-based application, whereas the latter is a window-based application. This means that the SQLMetal provides a DOS-like template and the operations are performed by entering single command into a black-white window. The Object Relational Designer, by contrast, provides a GUI and allows users to drag-place tables represented by graphic icons into it. Obviously, the second method or tool is more convenient and easier than the first one.

5.17.1 Create a New Visual C# Project and Setup LINQ to SQL Environment

In this section, we will develop a new Visual C# 2022 project LINQSelect Project and use it to illustrate how to perform the data query using the LINQ to SQL method step by step. Perform the following operational steps to create a new Visual C# Windows Forms App project **LINQSelect Project**:

1) Launch Visual Studio 2022 by clicking its icon on either the desktop or the task bar.
2) Click on the **Continue without code** link located at the lower-right corner to open the standard Visual Studio window.
3) Go to the **File | New | Project** item to open the **Create a new project** wizard.
4) On the opened wizard, select the template, **Windows Forms App (.NET Framework)** with **C#**, which is an icon on the left, and click it to select this template. Then click on the **Next** button to continue.
5) On the next wizard, **Configure your new project**, enter **LINQSelect Project** into the **Project name** box, and **LINQSelect Solution** into the **Solution name** box, respectively. Select your desired folder as the location from the **Location** box to save this new project.
6) Click on the **Create** button to create this new project.

To save time, we can use and add five existing Window Forms, **LogIn.cs**, **Selection.cs**, **Faculty.cs**, **Student.cs** and **Course.cs**, into this new project. Perform the following operations to complete these Forms additions:

1) On the new opened project, go to the Solution Explorer window and right click on the iconForm1.cs, and select the **Delete** item to remove this file.
2) Right click on the project **LINQSelect Project** in the Solution Explorer window and select the **Add | Existing Item** to open the Add Existing Item wizard.
3) Browse to the CRC Press ftp site, exactly to the folder **Students\Windows Forms** under that site, select the **LogIn.cs** by clicking its checkbox on the left.
4) Click on the **Add** button to add this Form into our project.

5) Immediately, a new item, **C# LogIn.cs**, is added into the Solution Explorer window. Wait a moment, this file will become a **LogIn.cs** folder with two subsidiary files, **LogIn.designer.cs** and **LogIn.resx**.
6) Repeat steps 2–5 above to add the other four Forms one by one. The point is that each time you can only add one file. Otherwise some exceptions or errors may be encountered.

Now we need to set and use the **LogIn.cs** as our starting object, and modify the namespaces in four added files to enable our new project to recognize them. Perform the following operations to complete this setup and namespaces modification processes:

1) Right-click on the **LogIn.cs** folder from the Solution Explorer window and select the **View Code** item to open the code window for this **LogIn.cs** class file.
2) Change its namespace from the original **SelectWizard_Project** to our current namespace, **LINQSelect_Project**.
3) Open the **LogIn.designer.cs** file by double-clicking on it from the Solution Explorer window (you need to expand the **LogIn.cs** folder to find this file).
4) Change the top line from the original namespace **SelectWizard_Project** to our current namespace, **LINQSelect_Project**.
5) Now open the main file, **C# Program.cs**, from the Solution Explorer window by double-clicking on that file.
6) On the opened **Program.cs** file, browse to the **Main()** method, which is the entry or starting point for our project. Replace the third coding line **Application.Run(new Form1());** with **Application.Run(new LogInForm());**.

One point to be noted when performing the above operational steps is the order. One must follow up the operational order listed above to complete these modifications. Otherwise, some exceptions may be encountered.

Perform a similar modification (steps 1–4 above) to namespaces on all other four Forms, **Faculty.cs**, **Course.cs**, **Student.cs** and **Selection.cs**, to make them compatible with our new project.

The procedure to use LINQ to SQL to perform data actions against SQL Server database can be described as a sequence listed below:

1) Add the **System.Data.Linq.dll** assembly into the project that will use LINQ to SQL by adding the reference **System.Linq**.
2) Create an entity class for each data table by using one of two popular tools: **SQLMetal** or **Object Relational Designer**.
3) Add a connection to the selected database using the DataContext class or the derived class from the DataContext class.
4) Use LINQ to SQL to access the database to perform desired data actions.

Open our new project and the LogIn Form window by clicking it from the Solution Explorer window. We need to develop this Form based on the steps listed above.

First we need to add the **System.Data.Linq.dll** assembly into the project by adding the reference System.Linq. We need to do this in two steps:

1) First, we need to add a reference to our project
2) Second, we need to add a namespace to the code window of the related form.

Let's start from the first step. Right-click our project **LINQSelect Project** from the Solution Explorer window, and select **Add | Reference** item from the popup menu to open the Add Reference wizard. Keep the default tab selected and scroll down the Reference List until you find the item **System.Data.**

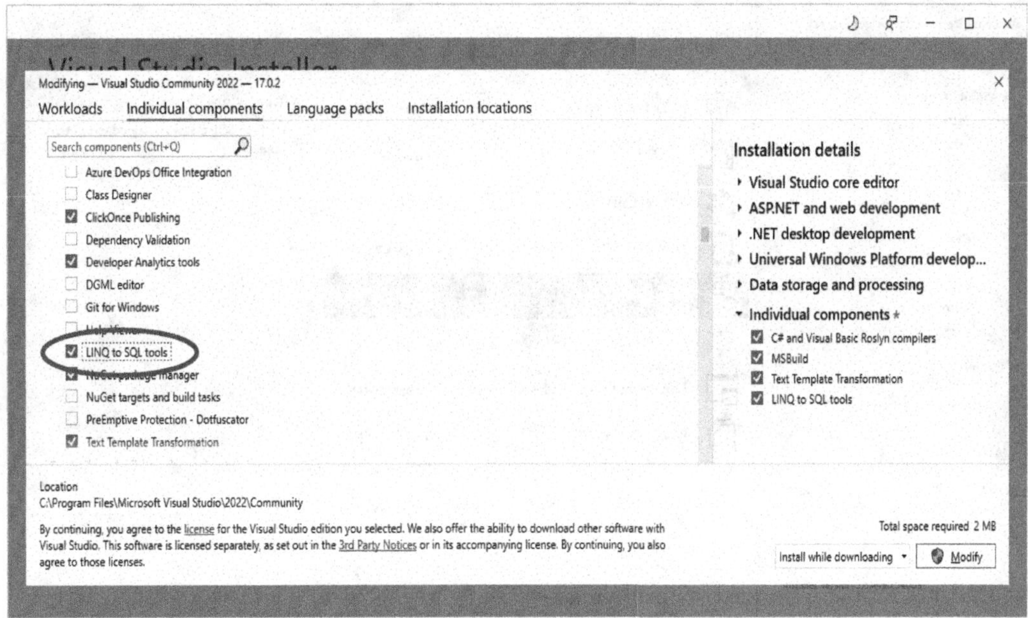

FIGURE 5.111 The opened Visual Studio.NET installer.

Linq. Select it by clicking the checkbox in front of it and click the **OK** button to add this reference to our project.

Next we need to create entity classes via **LINQ to SQL tools** provided by Visual Studio.NET to set up mapping relationships between each physical data table and the related entity class. We prefer to use the Object Relational Designer since it provides a GUI.

Starting Visual Studio.NET 2017, the **LINQ to SQL tools** is no longer available by default installation of that IDE. Perform the following operations to get and add it into our project:

1) On the opened project, go to **Tools | Get Tools and Features** item to open the Visual Studio Installer.
2) On the opened Installer, select the **Individual components** tab on the top, scroll down along the component list until you find the item, **LINQ to SQL tools** (Figure 5.111).
3) Check the checkbox in front of that item to select it, and click on the **Modify** button on the lower-right corner to download and add it into our project.

You can close the Visual Studio.NET Installer when that downloading process is complete.

One point to note is that you may need to close any currently opened Visual C# project to complete this downloading and installation process.

5.17.2 Create Entity Classes and Connect the DataContext to the Database

To open the Object Relational Designer, right-click our project **LINQSelect Project** from the Solution Explorer window, and select the item **Add | New Item** from the popup menu to open the Add New Item wizard. Then select the item **LINQ to SQL Classes** by clicking on it, and enter **CSE_DEPT.dbml** into the **Name** box as the name for this intermediate DBML file, as shown in Figure 5.112. Then click the **Add** button to open this Object Relational Designer.

The intermediate DBML file is an optional file when you created the entity classes and this file allows you to control and modify the names of those created entity classes and properties; it gives

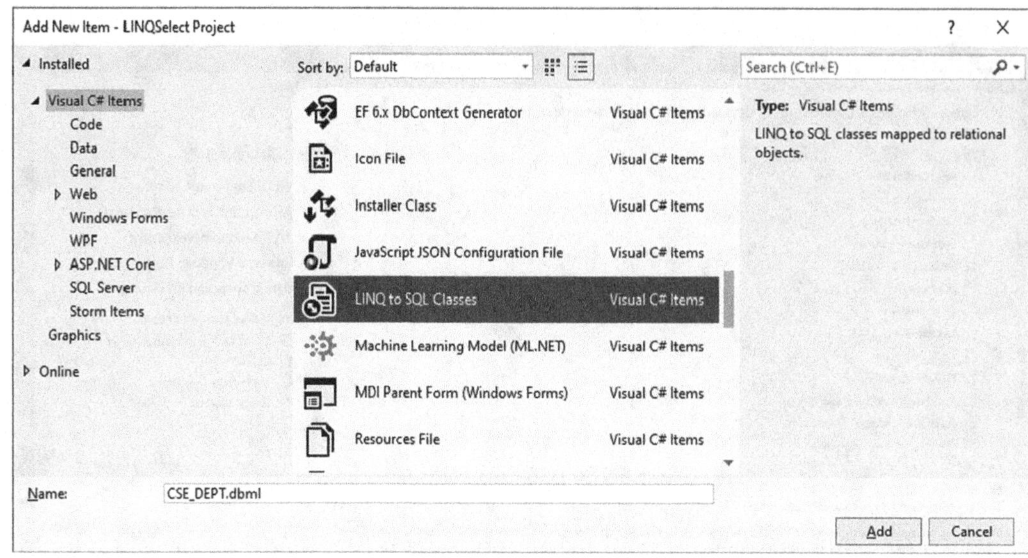

FIGURE 5.112 The opened add new item wizard.

you flexibility or controllability on entity classes. You can use any meaningful name for this DBML file, but generally the name should be identical to that of the database. Thus, we used **CSE_DEPT**, which is our database's name, as the name for this file.

The opened Object Relational Designer is shown in Figure 5.113.

You can find that a **CSE_DEPT.dbml** folder has been added into our project in the Solution Explorer window, which is shown in Figure 5.113. Two related files, **CSE_DEPT.dbml.layout** and **CSE_DEPT.designer.cs**, are attached under that folder. The first file is exactly the designer that is shown as a blank window in Figure 5.113, and the second file is auto-generated by the Object Relational Designer and it contains codes to create a child class **CSE_DEPTDataContext** that is derived from the

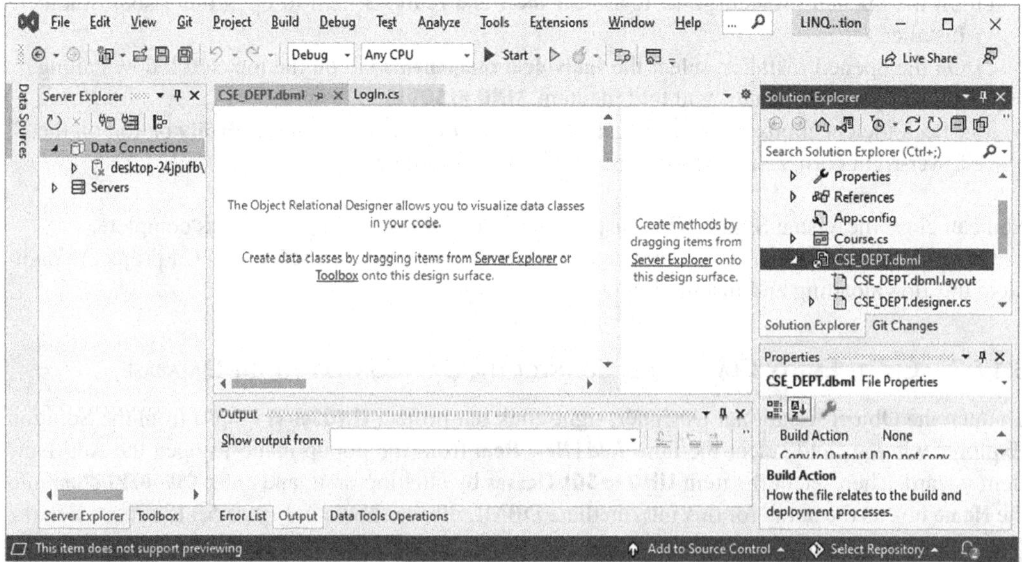

FIGURE 5.113 The opened object relational designer.

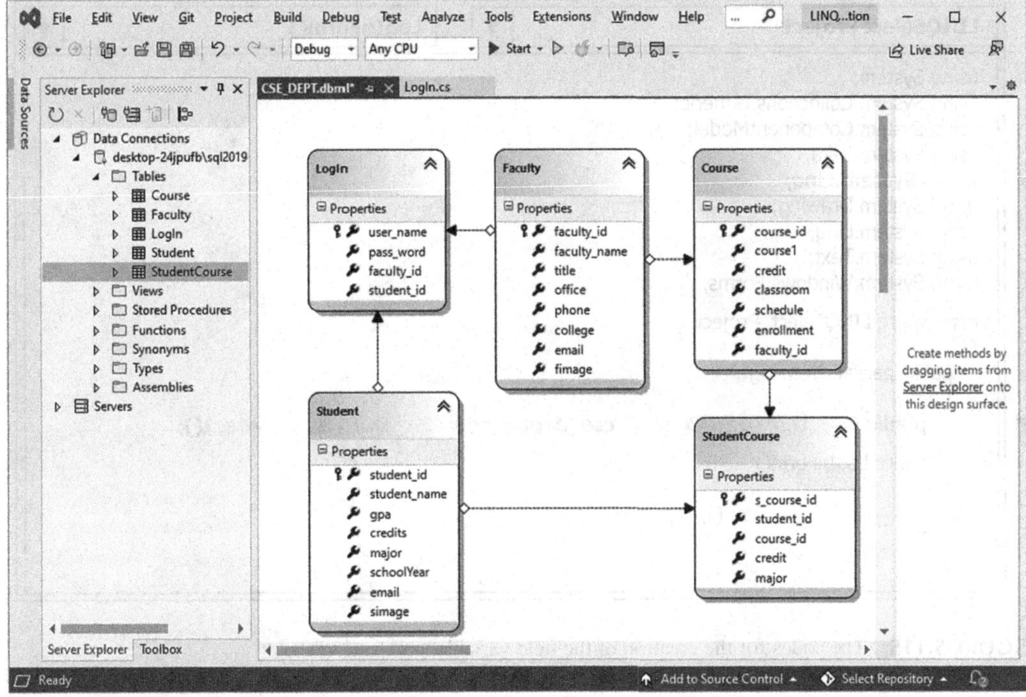

FIGURE 5.114 The finished designer.

DataContext class. Four overloaded constructors of the child class **CSE_DEPTDataContext** are declared in that file.

Now we need to connect our sample SQL Server database **CSE_DEPT** to this project using the DataContext object. One can directly open and connect our sample database **CSE_DEPT** from the Server Explorer window if it is already connected. Otherwise one must add a new connection to our sample database. To open and connect to our sample database **CSE_DEPT**, expand the **Data Connections** folder in the Server Explorer window, right-click on our database icon, and select the **Refresh** item on the popup menu. Expand this database to the Tables node and one can find all of our five data tables.

To create an entity class for each table, just perform a drag-place operation for each table between the Server Explorer window and the blank Design window. Starting from the **LogIn** table, drag it from the Server Explorer window and place it to the Design window. By dragging the LogIn table to the designer canvas, the source code for the LogIn entity class is created and added into the **CSE_DEPT.designer.cs** file. Then you can use this entity class to access and manipulate data from this project to the LogIn table in our sample database **CSE_DEPT**.

Perform similar drag-place operations to all other tables, and the finished design is shown in Figure 5.114. The arrow between the tables is called an association that is a new terminology used in the LINQ to SQL, which represents the relationship between tables.

Now we can start to use these entity classes and the DataContext object to perform desired data actions against our sample database using the LINQ to SQL technique.

5.17.3 Perform LINQ to SQL Query to LogIn Table via LogIn Form

We have provided a very detailed discussion about the entity classes and DataContext object as well as how to use the Object Relational Designer to create and add these components to a data-driven project to perform LINQ to SQL queries in Section 4.6.1 in Chapter 4. Prior to going to the next step, refer to that section to get a clear picture in how to create and use these components. When we

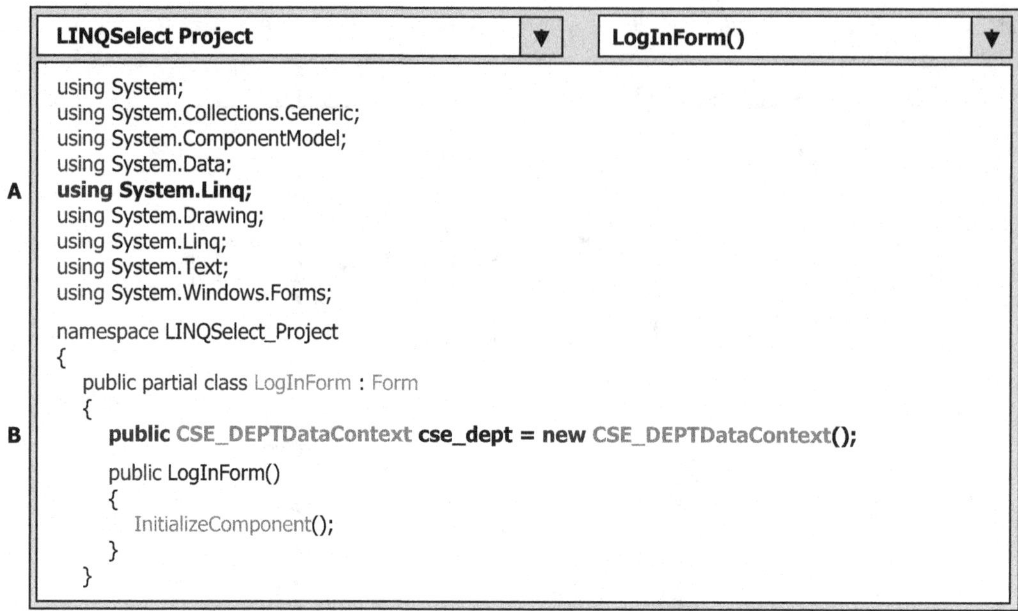

```
LINQSelect Project                                LogInForm()

  using System;
  using System.Collections.Generic;
  using System.ComponentModel;
  using System.Data;
A using System.Linq;
  using System.Drawing;
  using System.Linq;
  using System.Text;
  using System.Windows.Forms;

  namespace LINQSelect_Project
  {
      public partial class LogInForm : Form
      {
B         public CSE_DEPTDataContext cse_dept = new CSE_DEPTDataContext();
          public LogInForm()
          {
              InitializeComponent();
          }
      }
```

FIGURE 5.115 The codes for the creation of the field variable.

have finished reviewing Section 4.6.1 in Chapter 4, we can begin to build codes for our project. Let's start from our LogIn Form to access the LogIn table in our sample database.

First we need to create a field variable **cse_dept** based on our derived DataContext class **CSE_DEPTDataContext**. As we discussed, this object is used to connect to our sample database. Four overloaded constructors are available for this DataContext class, but in this application we only use the simplest one to simplify our coding process.

Now let's start the coding process for the LogIn Form class.

Open our new project **LINQSelect Project** and the code window of the **LogInForm**, and enter the codes shown in Figure 5.115 into this class.

Let's have a look at this piece of codes to see how it works.

A. The namespace **System.Linq** is added into this code section since we need to use all data components related to LINQ to SQL and this namespace contains all of them.

B. A new instance of our derived class **CSE_DEPTDataContext** is created with the first constructor. A trick in here is that no connection string is included in this connection object. Yes, where is the connection string? How can we connect to our database without connection string? While, the connection string is in there. Where? Ok, let's have a closer look at this issue now.

Open our application configuration file named **app.config** that is located at the Solution Explorer window by double-clicking on it. A sample file is shown in Figure 5.116.

It can be found from this XML file that our connection string is already in there under the **ConnectionString** tag, which includes the Data Source and the database Provider Name. In this application, it is a full name for our Data Source, including the database server, database name and authentication mode. Here a Windows Authentication Mode is used.

When you create a new instance of our derived DataContext class to connect to our sample database, the system can automatically locate this connection string from this configuration file and use it to do this connection even we did not clearly indicate this connection string. The instance **cse_dept** has finished the database connection when you create it and this connection has been saved when

LINQSelect Solution - App.config

App.config

```
<?xml version="1.0" encoding="utf-8" ?>
<configuration>
    <configSections>
    </configSections>
    <connectionStrings>
        <add name="LINQSelect_Project.Properties.Settings.CSE_DEPTConnectionString"
            connectionString="Data Source=DESKTOP-24JPUFB\SQL2019EXPRESS;Initial Catalog=CSE_DEPT;Integrated
            providerName="System.Data.SqlClient" />
    </connectionStrings>
    <startup>
        <supportedRuntime version="v4.0" sku=".NETFramework,Version=v4.7.2" />
    </startup>
</configuration>
```

100 % No issues found Ln: 1 Ch: 1 SPC CRLF

FIGURE 5.116 A piece of sample codes for the app.config file.

LINQSelect Project | cmdLogIn_Click(object sender, EventArgs e)

```
  private void cmdLogIn_Click(object sender, EventArgs e)
  {
A      string username = string.Empty;
       string password = string.Empty;
B      SelectionForm selForm = new SelectionForm();
C      IQueryable<LogIn> loginfo = from lg in cse_dept.LogIns
                                   where lg.user_name == txtUserName.Text &&
                                   lg.pass_word == txtPassWord.Text
                                   select lg;
D      foreach (LogIn log in loginfo)
       {
           username = (string)log.user_name;
           password = (string)log.pass_word;
       }
E      if (txtUserName.Text == string.Empty || txtPassWord.Text == string.Empty)
          MessageBox.Show("Enter a valid username/password");
F      else if (username == txtUserName.Text && password == txtPassWord.Text)
       {
           this.Hide();
           selForm.ShowDialog();
           cse_dept.Connection.Close();
           this.Close();
       }
G      else
          MessageBox.Show("The LogIn is failed!");
  }
```

FIGURE 5.117 The codes for the LogIn button click method.

it is created. Now we can use this connection object to perform our data actions against our sample database.

Now let's develop the codes for our login process. Double-click on the **LogIn** button from the LogIn Form window to open its Click method, and enter the codes shown in Figure 5.117 into this method. Let's have a closer look at this piece of codes to see how it works.

A. Two local-level string variables, **username** and **password**, are created and these two variables are used to hold the returned queried data from the **LogIn** table.

B. An instance of the next form class SelectionForm, **selForm**, is created and this form will be displayed if the login process is completed successfully.

C. As we discussed in the last section when we built the entity classes for this project, all five entity classes are related or bounded by using the associations (primary-foreign keys). Also recall that in Chapter 4, we discussed that most normal LINQ queries are performed on arrays or collections that apply the IEnumerable<T> or Ienumerable interfaces, but in LINQ to SQL queries, they are performed on entity classes that apply the Iqueryable<T> interface. This means that besides the Standard Query operators, LINQ to SQL queries have additional query operators available since Iqueryable<T> applies Ienumerable<T>. Here querying an associated entity class in LINQ to SQL is used with the Iqueryable<T> interface, and the <T> is the type of member variable of the related entity class. In this case, it is our **LogIn** table. An iteration variable **lg** is used to iterate over the result of this query from the **LogIn** table. Then a similar SQL **SELECT** statement is executed with the **WHERE** clause. Two criterions are used for this query, **user_name** and **pass_word**, and these two criterions are connected with a logic **AND** operator. One point to be noted is the member variable of our entity class LogIn, which is named LogIns in this query. The relationships or the associations between the **LogIn**, **Faculty** and **Student** tables are many-to-one, which means that Many **faculty_id** and **students_id** can exist in the **LogIn** table but only a single or unique **faculty_id** can be in the **Faculty** table and a unique **student_id** in the **Student** table. In other words, the LogIn class is in the *many* (child) side of a one-to-many relationship. Therefore, in general the member variable of this kind of entity class is named **LogIns**, and a'**s**' is attached to the name of the related entity class.

D. A **foreach** loop is utilized to pick up each column from the selected data row log, which is obtained from the **loginfo** we get from the LINQ query. Then, assign two columns, **log.user_name** and **log.pass_word**, to our two local string variables, **username** and **password**. The purpose of this assignment operation is to avoid the possible overhead cycles when identifying the validity of the username and password entered by the user. In other words, we prefer to do this validation outside of this **foreach** loop. You can try to do it inside this loop but you would definitely encounter some bugs. Since we are using a typed data table and database, we can directly access each column by using its name without using the **field<string>** and the column's name as the position for each of them.

E. An error message will be displayed if any input box is empty to remind users to enter a valid username and password.

F. If both **username** and **password** are correct and matched to both columns queried from the **LogIn** table, which means that this login process is successful, the **SelectionForm** is displayed and the current form is removed from the screen. The database connection should be closed to disconnect to our sample database.

G. If no matched **username** and **password** can be found, an error message is displayed to indicate this situation.

It appears that this query is quite simple and that all columns in the **LogIn** table have been collected, even if we did not explicitly perform any query to that table. The reason behind this simple query is that no login information is actually retrieved until all columns in the LogIn class are referenced, and this is called deferred loading. This terminology is used to describe the type of loading in which columns are not actually loaded from the database until they are required or referenced.

The codes for the **Cancel** button Click method is easy and they are shown in Figure 5.118. First the database connection is disconnected if it is still open, and the current LogIn Form is also closed. Our project is terminated by executing an **Exit()** command.

That completes all of the coding developments for the LogIn Form. Before we can test this Form, we prefer to finish the codes for the next form, Selection Form.

```
LINQSelect Project                      cmdCancel_Click(object sender, EventArgs e)

  private void cmdCancel_Click(object sender, EventArgs e)
  {
A      cse_dept.Connection.Close();
B      this.Close();
       Application.Exit();
  }
```

FIGURE 5.118 The codes for the cancel button click method.

5.17.4 Coding for the Selection Form

The coding for this form is basically identical with the same form we did for the previous project **RTOSelect Project** and the only difference is that the database connection object we used in this project is an instance of the derived class **CSE_DEPTDataContext**. Another point is that we do not need to add the namespace **System.Linq** to the namespace declaration section in this Form since the LINQ to SQL will not be used for this Form.

Open the SelectionForm and enter the codes that are shown in Figure 5.119 into the code window of this form. Most of the codes are identical with the same form we did for the project **RTOSelect Project**, with the exception of the following codes:

A. When the **Exit** button is clicked, first all three Forms are closed by executing the **Close()** method.
B. Then the project is exited by executing the **Application.Exit()** method.

Now let's run the project to test the codes we did for two forms, LogInFormand SelectionForm. Click on the **Start** button to run the project and the LogIn Form is displayed first. Enter a valid username and a password, such as **jhenry** and **test** into the **UserName** and **PassWord** boxes, and hit the **LogIn** button. The login process is successful and our next Form, Selection Form, is displayed. Click the Exit button on the SelectionForm to exit the project. Of course, you can test the login process by entering some incorrect username or password, and you will see what happened.

Next let's take care of the coding process for the Faculty Form.

5.17.5 Query Data Using the LINQ to SQL for the Faculty Form

In this section, we want to use two methods to perform the data query using the LINQ to SQL for this Form. The first method is a general LINQ to SQL method as we did for the LogInForm, but the second method is to query a single record from the **Faculty** table.

Open the code window of the FacultyForm and add the System.Linq to the namespace declaration section on this Form. Then enter the codes that are shown in Figure 5.120 into the constructor of this Form to perform the initialization jobs for this form.

Let's have a look at this piece of codes to see how it works.

A. The namespace **System.Linq** is added into the namespace declaration section on this Form to allow us to use all LINQ related components defined in that namespace.
B. Eight faculty members are added into the **Faculty Name** combobox and the first on is selected as a default one.
C. Two query methods are added into the **ComboMethod** combobox and the first method is selected at the default method.

```
LINQSelect Project                    SelectionForm()

using System;
using System.Collections.Generic;
using System.ComponentModel;
using System.Data;
using System.Drawing;
using System.Linq;
using System.Text;
using System.Windows.Forms;
namespace LINQSelect_Project
{
    public partial class SelectionForm : Form
    {
        FacultyForm facultyForm = new FacultyForm();
        CourseForm courseForm = new CourseForm();
        StudentForm studentForm = new StudentForm();
        public SelectionForm()
        {
            InitializeComponent();
            this.ComboSelection.Items.Add("Faculty Information");
            this.ComboSelection.Items.Add("Course Information");
            this.ComboSelection.Items.Add("Student Information");
            this.ComboSelection.SelectedIndex = 0;
        }
        private void cmdOK_Click(object sender, EventArgs e)
        {
            if (this.ComboSelection.Text == "Faculty Information")
                facultyForm.Show();
            else if (this.ComboSelection.Text == "Course Information")
                courseForm.Show();
            else if (this.ComboSelection.Text == "Student Information")
                studentForm.Show();
            else
                MessageBox.Show("Invalid Selection!");
        }
        private void cmdExit_Click(object sender, EventArgs e)
        {
A           courseForm.Close();
            facultyForm.Close();
            studentForm.Close();
B           Application.Exit();
        }
    }
}
```

FIGURE 5.119 The codes for the SelectionForm class.

The next coding job is for the **Select** button's Click method. When this button is clicked by the user as the project runs, all faculty information, including the faculty ID, name, title, office, phone, graduated college and email, will be queried and displayed in seven related TextBoxes with the faculty photo in the Faculty Form window. We can use the similar codes as we did for the LogInForm to perform the query in this form.

Now open the **Select** button's Click method by double-clicking this button from the design view of the FacultyForm, and enter the codes that are shown in Figure 5.121 into this method.

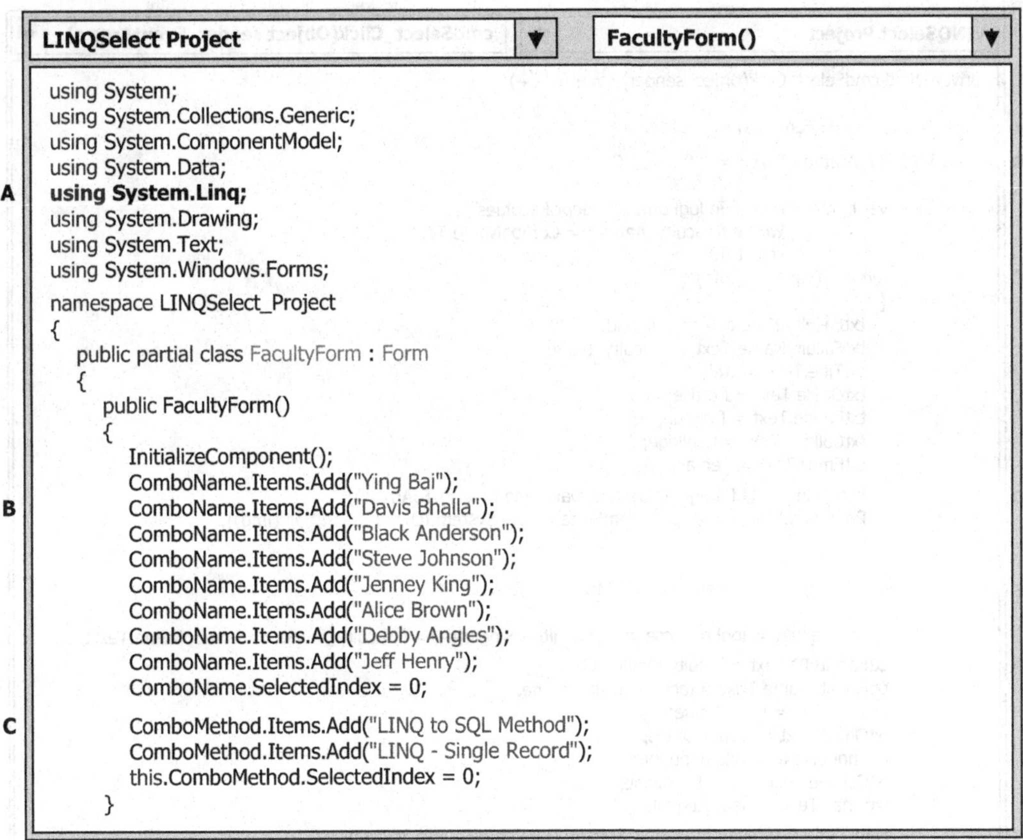

```
LINQSelect Project                FacultyForm()

using System;
using System.Collections.Generic;
using System.ComponentModel;
using System.Data;
A   using System.Linq;
using System.Drawing;
using System.Text;
using System.Windows.Forms;
namespace LINQSelect_Project
{
    public partial class FacultyForm : Form
    {
        public FacultyForm()
        {
            InitializeComponent();
            ComboName.Items.Add("Ying Bai");
B           ComboName.Items.Add("Davis Bhalla");
            ComboName.Items.Add("Black Anderson");
            ComboName.Items.Add("Steve Johnson");
            ComboName.Items.Add("Jenney King");
            ComboName.Items.Add("Alice Brown");
            ComboName.Items.Add("Debby Angles");
            ComboName.Items.Add("Jeff Henry");
            ComboName.SelectedIndex = 0;
C           ComboMethod.Items.Add("LINQ to SQL Method");
            ComboMethod.Items.Add("LINQ - Single Record");
            this.ComboMethod.SelectedIndex = 0;
        }
```

FIGURE 5.120 The codes for the constructor of the FacultyForm.

Let's have a closer look at this piece of codes to see how it works.

A. An instance of the LogInForm class, **logForm**, is created and the purpose of generating this instance is that we can use the global connection object **CSE_DEPTDataContext** we created in that class.

B. If the user selected the first method, **LINQ to SQL Method**, a standard LINQ query structure is adopted with an implicit typed local variable **f_info** with a data type **var**. The Visual C# 2022 can automatically convert this **var** to any suitable data type, in this case, it is a collection. An iteration variable **fi** is used to iterate over the result of this query from the **Faculty** table. Then a similar SQL **SELECT** statement is executed with the **WHERE** clause.

C. A **foreach** loop is utilized to pick up each column from the selected data row f, which is obtained from the **f_info** we get from the LINQ query. Then, assign each column to the associated TextBox control in the FacultyForm window to display them. Since we are using a typed database, we do not have to indicate each column clearly with the **field<string>** and the column's name as the position for each of them, instead we can directly use each column's name to access each of them.

D. The type of the queried faculty image via this LINQ to SQL is **System.Data.Linq.Binary**. To assign this image to the faculty image control, **PhotoBox**, in this Faculty Form to display it, we need to convert this type to the **System.Drawing.Image** in two steps: 1) convert that type to a **byte**[] array, and 2) convert that binary array to the desired type, **System.Drawing.Image**. Here an intermediate variable **img** and an **as** operator are used. The latter works as an indicator to indicate the data type of **f.fimage**.

```
LINQSelect Project                    cmdSelect_Click(Object sender, EventArgs e)

  private void cmdSelect_Click(object sender, EventArgs e)
  {
A       LogInForm logForm = new LogInForm();
B       if (ComboMethod.Text == "LINQ to SQL Method")
        {
            var f_info = from fi in logForm.cse_dept.Faculties
                         where fi.faculty_name == ComboName.Text
                         select fi;
C           foreach (var f in f_info)
            {
                txtFacultyID.Text = f.faculty_id;
                txtFacultyName.Text = f.faculty_name;
                txtTitle.Text = f.title;
                txtOffice.Text = f.office;
                txtPhone.Text = f.phone;
                txtCollege.Text = f.college;
                txtEmail.Text = f.email;
D               byte[] img = (f.fimage as System.Data.Linq.Binary).ToArray();
                PhotoBox.Image = Image.FromStream(new System.IO.MemoryStream(img));
            }
        }
E       else         // LINQ – Single Record Method selected
        {
            Faculty faculty = logForm.cse_dept.Faculties.Single(fi => fi.faculty_name == ComboName.Text);
F           txtFacultyID.Text = faculty.faculty_id;
            txtFacultyName.Text = faculty.faculty_name;
            txtTitle.Text = faculty.title;
            txtOffice.Text = faculty.office;
            txtPhone.Text = faculty.phone;
            txtCollege.Text = faculty.college;
            txtEmail.Text = faculty.email;
G           byte[] img = (faculty.fimage as System.Data.Linq.Binary).ToArray();
            PhotoBox.Image = Image.FromStream(new System.IO.MemoryStream(img));
        }
H       logForm.Close();
  }
```

FIGURE 5.121 The coding for the constructor of the FacultyForm.

E. If the user selected the **LINQ – Single Record Method**, a single LINQ query method is adopted and executed by calling the **Single()** method. The implicit variable **fi** is an **IQueryable<Faculty>** variable and the queried result is assigned to the faculty that is a typed Faculty variable.

F. Each column of the returned data is then assigned to the associated TextBox in the FacultyForm to display each of them one by one.

G. Similar to step **D** above, the type of the queried faculty image in the column **faculty.fimage** is converted to the **System.Drawing.Image**, and assigned to the faculty image control **PhotoBox** in the Faculty Form window.

H. Finally the new created instance **logForm** is closed since we no longer need to use it.

This appears quite simple in this piece of codes. Yes, it is indeed much simpler and shorter than those codes we did for the same method using the regular SQL Server database queries. No any Connection string, Command object, Connection object, or even DataAdapter and DataReader used for this query.

The codes for the **Back** button's Click method are very easy and simple, just put the coding line, this.Hide();, into this method.

Now let's run the project to test the function of this Faculty Form class. Click on the **Start** button (or **F5** key) to run the project. Enter a suitable username and password, such as **jhenry** and **test**, and

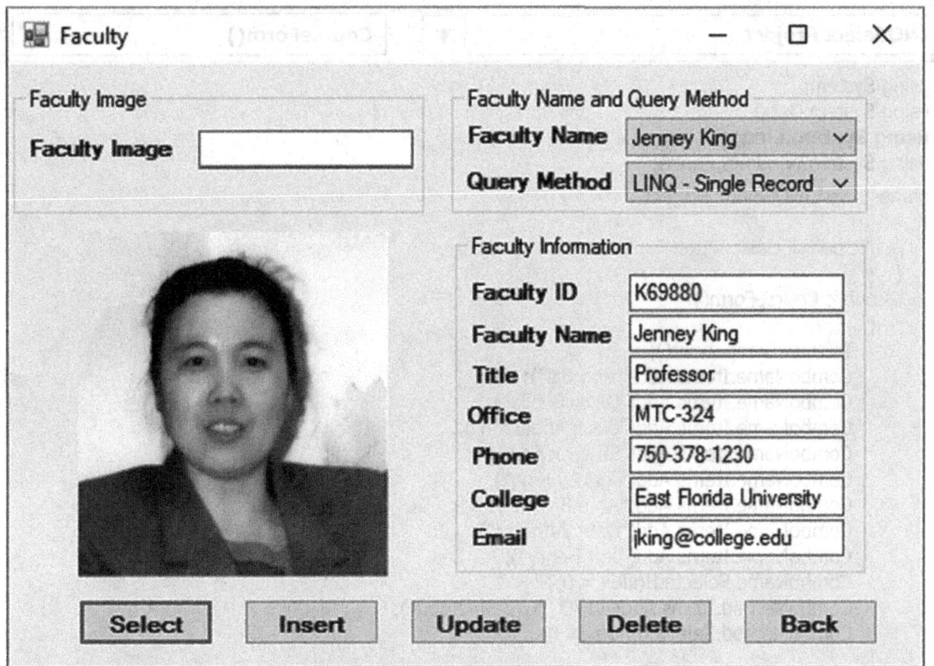

FIGURE 5.122 A running sample of the FacultyForm.

select the **Faculty Information** from the Selection Form to open the FacultyForm window, which is shown in Figure 5.122. Then keep the default faculty member in the Faculty Name combobox and click on the **Select** button to query that record. The information about the default faculty has been queried and displayed in seven TextBoxes and the PhotoBox. You can try to perform this query using the other faculty name via the second method, **LINQ – Single Record**. A sample of queried faculty information for the faculty member **Jenney King** is shown in Figure 5.122.

Our coding process for the Faculty Form with the LINQ to SQL is successful. Click the **Back** button to close this Form, and the **Exit** button to exit the project.

In the next section, we want to discuss how to use the joined LINQ to SQL technique to perform data queries to our **Course** table in our sample database via the Course Form window.

Now let's take care of the coding process for the CourseForm window.

5.17.6 Query Data Using the Joined LINQ to SQL For the Course Form

In this section, only one query method, joined LINQ to SQL, is used for this data query in the CourseForm. As we did before, first we need to add a **System.Linq** namespace to the namespace declaration section in the CourseForm code window. Then open the code window of the CourseForm and enter the codes into the constructor of the CourseForm, which are shown in Figure 5.123. Let's have a look at this piece of codes to see how it works.

A. The namespace System.Linq is added into the namespace declaration section on this form to allow us to use all LINQ related components defined in that namespace.

B. Eight faculty members are added into the **ComboName** combobox control in this Form to allow users to select one of them to perform the related course information query. The first faculty member is selected the default one by setting the **SelectedIndex** as 0.

C. The **LINQ to SQL Method** is added into the **ComboMethod** combobox control and this is the only method we want to use to perform the data query in this form.

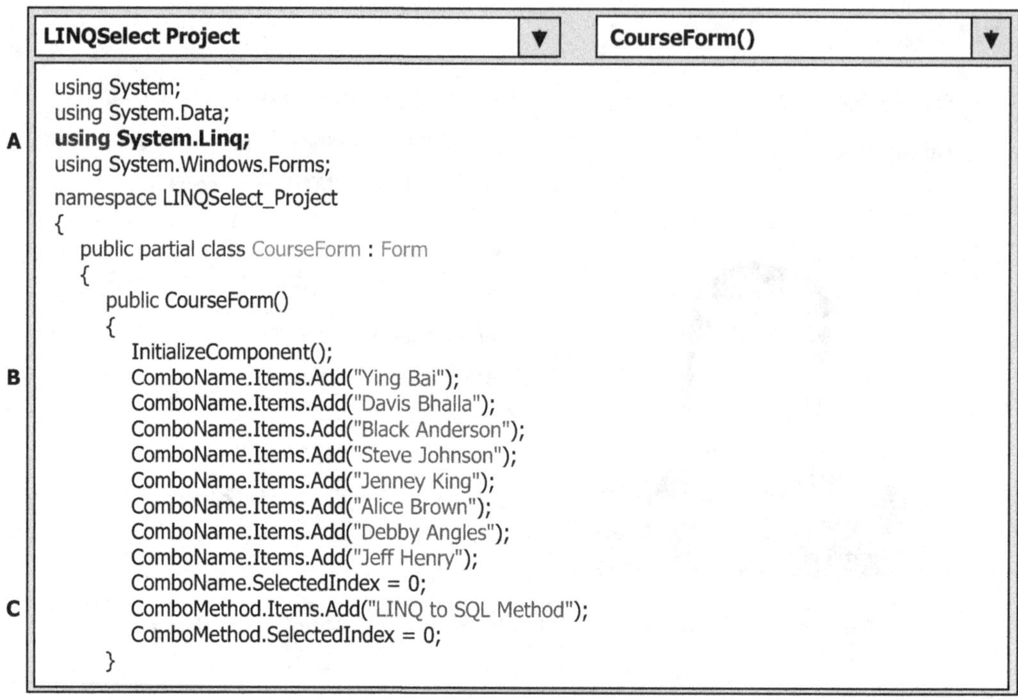

LINQSelect Project
CourseForm()
using System;
using System.Data;
A using System.Linq;
using System.Windows.Forms;
namespace LINQSelect_Project
{
public partial class CourseForm : Form
{
public CourseForm()
{
InitializeComponent();
B ComboName.Items.Add("Ying Bai");
ComboName.Items.Add("Davis Bhalla");
ComboName.Items.Add("Black Anderson");
ComboName.Items.Add("Steve Johnson");
ComboName.Items.Add("Jenney King");
ComboName.Items.Add("Alice Brown");
ComboName.Items.Add("Debby Angles");
ComboName.Items.Add("Jeff Henry");
ComboName.SelectedIndex = 0;
C ComboMethod.Items.Add("LINQ to SQL Method");
ComboMethod.SelectedIndex = 0;
}

FIGURE 5.123 The codes for the constructor of the CourseForm.

The next coding job is for the **Select** button's Click method. As this button is clicked, all courses (**course_id**) taught by the selected faculty will be displayed in the **CourseList** box. As you know, there is no **faculty_name** column available in the **Course** table and each course in the **Course** table is identified by the associated **faculty_id** column.

To query the course taught by the selected faculty based on the faculty name, we first need to perform a query to the **Faculty** table to get the desired **faculty_id**. Then we can query all **course_id** from the **Course** table based on the **faculty_id** we obtained from the first query. This means that we need to perform at least two queries from two tables to finish this **course_id** query. In this part, we try to use a joined LINQ to SQL method to simplify this process by developing a single query strategy.

Now open the **Select** button's Click method by double-clicking the **Select** button from the design view of the CourseForm window, and entering the codes that are shown in Figure 5.124 into this method. Let's have a closer look at this piece of codes to see how it works.

- **A.** An instance of the LogInForm class is created and the purpose of creating this instance is that we can access and use the global connection object **CSE_DEPTDataContext** we created in that class.
- **B.** The **CourseList** box control is cleaned up before it can be used to add queried **course_id** and display them in that control. This operation is very important and necessary, otherwise many duplicated **course_id**s will be added and displayed in this control without this cleaning action.
- **C.** A standard LINQ to SQL structure is generated with the implicit local variable **courseinfo**. The variables **ci** and **fi** are used to represent two iteration variables for two entity classes, **Courses** and **Faculties**, to iterate over the result of this query from both tables. The keyword **join** is used to connect these two classes together with the joined condition **on** both equaled **faculty_id** in two classes, respectively. The **where** clause is used to indicate the query criterion that is the **faculty_name** located in the **Faculty** entity class. Then a **select new**

```
LINQSelect Project                    cmdSelect_Click(object sender, EventArgs e)

  private void cmdSelect_Click(object sender, EventArgs e)
  {
A       LogInForm logForm = new LogInForm();
B       CourseList.Items.Clear();
C       var courseinfo = from ci in logForm.cse_dept.Courses
                         join fi in logForm.cse_dept.Faculties on ci.faculty_id equals fi.faculty_id
                         where fi.faculty_name == ComboName.Text
                         select new
                         {
                             course_id = ci.course_id
                         };
D       foreach (var cid in courseinfo)
        {
            CourseList.Items.Add(cid.course_id);
        }
E       CourseList.SelectedIndex = 0;
        logForm.Close();
  }
```

FIGURE 5.124 The codes for the select button click method.

statement is executed and the selected collection from the Course class is assigned to the column **course_id**. The point to be noted is that the relationship between the **Faculty** and the **Course** table is one-to-many, therefore a collection of **Courses** properties are stored in the Faculty entity class, but a single reference property **Faculties** is stored in the Course entity class.

D. A **foreach** loop is utilized to pick up each **course_id** from the selected data collection **courseinfo**, which is obtained using the joined LINQ to SQL query. Then, add each **course_id** to the **CourseList** box control in the CourseForm window to display them. Since we are using a typed database, therefore we do not have to indicate each column clearly with the **field<string>** and the column's name as the position for each of them, instead we can directly use each column's name to access each of them.

E. This line is very important since there will be no default **course_id** selected when all **course_id** are added into the **CourseList** box without this code line. Another purpose of this line is to trigger the **SelectedIndexChanged()** method to retrieve and display the detailed course information on six TextBoxes in the Course Form window based on the default or the selected **course_id** from the **CourseList** box when the Select button is clicked by the user. Also the created instance **logForm** is closed since its job is done.

Compared with those codes we did for the same method in the previous project, it can be found that this coding process is much simpler and shorter. Yes, it is very easy and convenient to develop this piece of codes to perform this data query. You can find the advantages of using the LINQ to SQL technique from this data query from our Course table.

The codes for the **Back** button's Click method are very easy; as we did before, just enter the code line: **this.Hide()**; to this method.

Now let's take care of the coding process for the **SelectedIndexChanged()** method. The function of this piece of codes is: after clicking the **Select** button to execute its Click method, all **course_id** taught by the selected faculty will be added and displayed in the **CourseList** box control. To get the detailed information for each course, the user can click each **course_id** from the **CourseList** box control, and all six pieces of detailed information related to the selected **course_id** are displayed in six TextBoxes in the Course Form.

Open this method by double clicking the **CourseList** box from the CourseForm window, and enter the codes that are shown in Figure 5.125 into this method.

```
LINQSelect Project                    CourseList_SelectedIndexChanged()

  private void CourseList_SelectedIndexChanged(object sender, EventArgs e)
  {
A     LogInForm logForm = new LogInForm();
B     IQueryable<Course> cinfo = from ci in logForm.cse_dept.Courses
                                 where ci.course_id == (string)CourseList.SelectedItem
                                 select ci;
C     foreach (Course c in cinfo)
      {
          txtCourseID.Text = c.course_id;
          txtCourseName.Text = c.course1;
          txtSchedule.Text = c.schedule;
          txtClassRoom.Text = c.classroom;
          txtCredits.Text = c.credit.ToString();
          txtEnroll.Text = c.enrollment.ToString();
      }
D     logForm.Close();
  }
```

FIGURE 5.125 The codes for the SelectedIndexChanged() method.

Let's have a closer look at this piece of codes to see how it works.

A. An instance of the LogInForm class, **logForm**, is created and the purpose of creating this instance is that we can use the global connection object **CSE_DEPTDataContext** we created in that class.

B. A standard LINQ to SQL query structure is adopted and the implicit variable **ci** is an **IQueryable<Course>** variable and the queried result is assigned to the **cinfo** that is a typed Course variable. The iteration variable ci is used to iterate over the result of this query from the **Course** table. Then a similar SQL **SELECT** statement is executed with the **WHERE** clause. The query criterion is the **course_id** selected from the **CourseList** box.

C. A **foreach** loop is utilized to pick up each column from the selected data row c, which is obtained from the **cinfo** we get from the LINQ query above. Then, assign each column to the associated TextBox control in the CourseForm window to display them. Since we are using a typed database, therefore we do not have to indicate each column clearly with the **field<string>** and the column's name as the position for each of them, instead we can directly use each column's name to access each of them. A trick is that the name of the second column on the Course entity class has been changed from **course** to **course1**. Recall that in Chapter 2, the name of this column is **course** in the **Course** table in our sample database. The reason for this change is that when we built the object-relational model for our sample database in Section 5.17.2 to create the Course entity class, there is a duplication between our **Course** table's name (**Course**) and the second column's name (**course**). Note that since SQL Server table and column names are not case sensitive, therefore in order to avoid this name duplication, the name of the second column in the **Course** table has been modified from **course** to **course1** in the entity class automatically by the Object Relational Designer.

D. Finally the created instance **logForm** is closed since we do not need it anymore.

Compared the codes in Figures 5.124 and 5.125 with those codes we developed in Figures 5.82 and 5.83, it can be found that the codes we developed in this section have been significantly simplified and shorten even they have the same functionalities, and this is the evidence of the advantage of using the LINQ to SQL over the traditional database query methods.

The last coding job we need to do for this form is the **Back** button's Click method. As we did before, open this method and enter: **this.Hide()**; into this method.

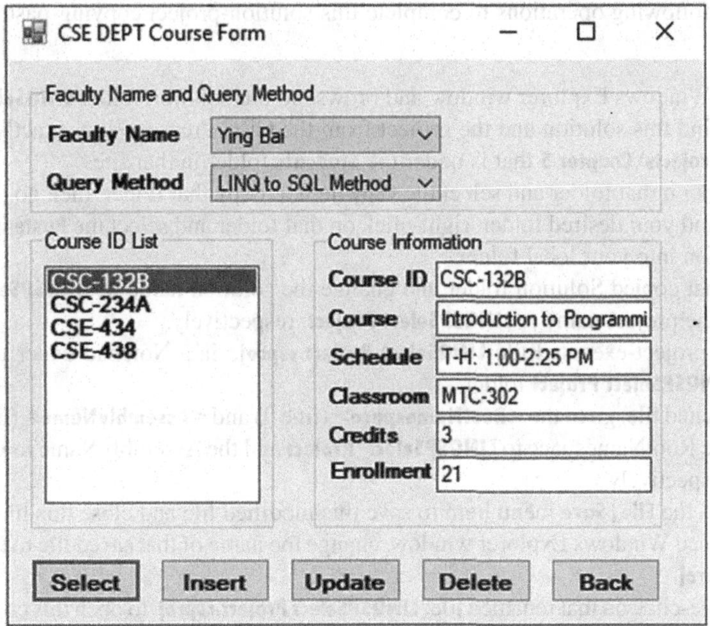

FIGURE 5.126 The running status of the CourseForm.

Now we have finished all coding jobs for this Course Form. Let's run the project to test the codes we developed for this Form. Click on the **Start** button to run the project. Complete the login process and select the **Course Information** from the SelectionForm to open the CourseForm, which is shown in Figure 5.126.

Keep the default faculty selected and click the **Select** button. All courses (**course_id**) taught by the selected faculty are displayed in the **CourseList** box. In addition, the detailed information about the first or the default **course_id** is displayed in six TextBoxes in this Form, which is shown in Figure 5.126. You can try to retrieve and display other faculty's courses by selecting different faculty name from the **Faculty Name** combobox with the **Select** button.

Our joined LINQ to SQL query is very successful! Click on the **Back** and the **Exit** button to terminate our project. A completed Visual C# project, **LINQSelect Project**, in which the LINQ to SQL techniques are used to perform data queries to our sample database, can be found from the CRC Press ftp site, exactly under a folder, **Class DB Projects\Chapter 5\LINQSelect Solution** that is located at the **Students** folder in that site.

Next let's handle the coding jobs for our last form, the StudentForm, with the LINQ to SQL Stored Procedure method.

5.18 QUERY DATA USING THE LINQ TO SQL STORED PROCEDURES FOR THE STUDENT FORM

In this section, we want to show readers how to call stored procedures with LINQ to SQL to perform the data query. The stored procedures discussed here are two procedures we developed in Section 5.16.3, **dbo.StudentInfo** and **dbo.StudentCourseInfo**. In order to call these two stored procedures in the LINQ to SQL environment, first we need to add these two procedures into the Object Relational Designer, exactly to the Methods pane.

First let's create a new **Visual C# Windows Forms App (.NET Framework)** project named **LINQSPSelect Project**. To save time and space, we can modify one of our projects, **LINQSelect Project**, we built in the last section to make it as our new project.

Perform the following operations to complete this solution-project copying-pasting and modification process:

1) Open the Windows Explorer window and browse to our solution folder **LINQSelect Solution**. One can find this solution and the project from the CRC Press ftp site, exactly in a folder **Class DB Projects\Chapter 5** that is under the **Students** folder in that site.
2) Right-click on that folder and select the **Copy** item to copy that folder, then go to your local machine and your desired folder, right-click on that folder and select the **Paste** item to paste that solution into your local folder.
3) Expand that copied Solution folder and change the solution name to **LINQSPSelect Solution** and then the project name to **LINQSPSelect Project**, respectively.
4) Open the project-executed file **LINQSelect Project.csproj** via a Notepad under the renamed project **LINQSPSelect Project** folder.
5) On the opened file, go to the **<RootNamespace>** (line 9) and **<AssemblyName>** (line 10) tags, change the RootNamespace to **LINQSPSelect_Project** and the AssemblyName to **LINQSPSelect Project**, respectively.
6) Then go to the **File | Save** menu item to save this modified file and close this file.
7) In the opened Windows Explorer window, change the name of that saved file to **LINQSPSelect Project.csproj**.
8) Now double-click on that renamed file, **LINQSPSelect Project.csproj**, to open this copied project.
9) Expand the folder **CSE_DEPT.dbml** from the Solution Explorer window, and double-click on the file **CSE_DEPT.designer.cs** to open it. Browse to line 51 and change the project name back to **base(global::LINQSelect_Project.Properties...)** since we have to use the original assembly reference for this new project.
10) Go to the Solution Explorer window, and right-click on the **LogIn.cs** and select the **View Code** item to open its code window. Change its namespace to **LINQSPSelect_Project**.
11) Still in the Solution Explorer window, expand the **LogIn.cs** folder and double-click on the **LogIn.designer.cs** to open this Designer file. Change its namespace on the top to **LINQSPSelect_Project**.
12) Repeat steps 10 and 11 for all other files, **Course.cs**, **Faculty.cs**, **Selection.cs** and **Student.cs**, to change their namespaces to **LINQSPSelect_Project**.
13) In the Solution Explorer window, double-click on the **C# Program.cs** file to open it, and Change its namespace to **LINQSPSelect_Project**.
14) Now go to the **Build | Build Solution** item to build our copied project to complete this copy-paste project process.

Now let's add two stored procedures we built in Section 5.16.3 into the Object Relational Designer, exactly to the Methods pane. Open the Object Relational Designer by double-clicking on the folder **CSE_DEPT.dbml** from the Solution Explorer window. The opened Object Relational Designer is shown in Figure 5.127.

Right-click the designer canvas and select the item **Show Methods Pane** from the popup menu to open the Methods pane if it has not been opened. We need to create our desired stored procedure by dragging each of them from the Server Explorer window to this Methods pane in this Object Relational Designer since the stored procedure is considered as a method in LINQ to SQL.

Now open the Server Explorer window if it has not been opened, and connect to our sample database **CSE_DEPT** if it has not been connected. Then expand the folders **CSE_DEPT** and **Stored Procedures** to display all stored procedures we developed for the previous projects. We need to use two stored procedures, **StudentInfo** and **StudentCourseInfo**. Just drag each of them from the Server Explorer window and place them to the Methods pane one by one. The finished Object Relational Designer should match one that is shown in Figure 5.127.

Now let's develop the codes for this Student Form. First we need to add namespace **System.Linq** to the namespace declaration section in this form. Then open the code window of the StudentForm and enter the codes shown in Figure 5.128 into the constructor of this Form.

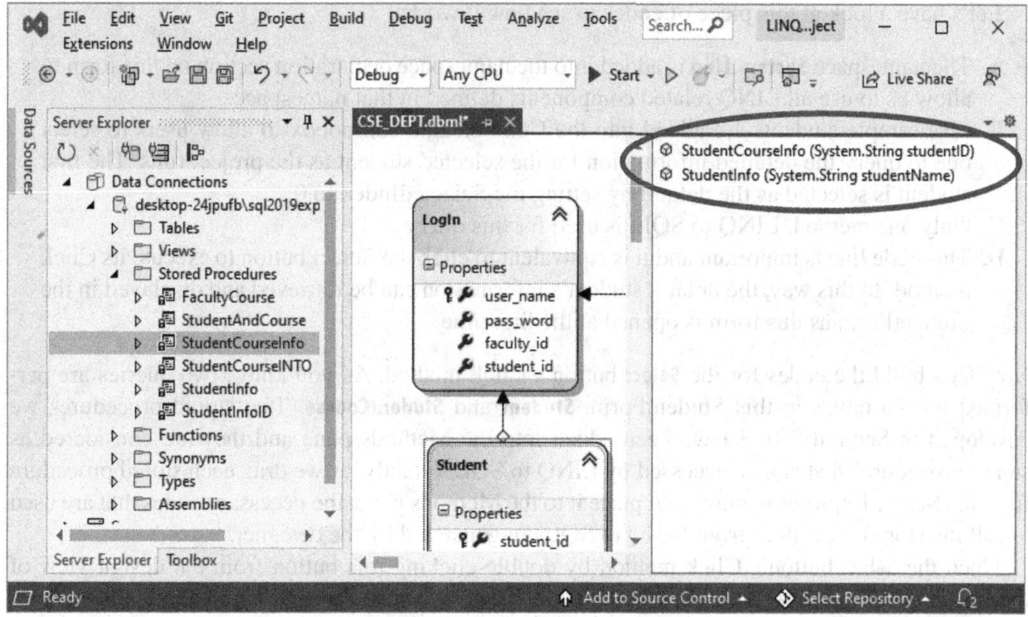

FIGURE 5.127 The opened and the finished object relational designer.

```
LINQSPSelect Project                    StudentForm()

  using System;
  using System.Collections.Generic;
  using System.ComponentModel;
  using System.Data;
A using System.Linq;
  using System.Drawing;
  using System.Linq;
  using System.Text;
  using System.Windows.Forms;
  namespace SQLSelectRTObjectLINQ
  {
     public partial class StudentForm : Form
     {
        public StudentForm()
        {
           InitializeComponent();
B          ComboName.Items.Add("Tom Erica");
           ComboName.Items.Add("Ashly Jade");
           ComboName.Items.Add("Holes Smith");
           ComboName.Items.Add("Andrew Woods");
           ComboName.Items.Add("Blue Valley");
           ComboName.SelectedIndex = 0;
C          ComboMethod.Items.Add("LINQ to SQL Method");
D          ComboMethod.SelectedIndex = 0;
        }
```

FIGURE 5.128 The codes for the constructor of the StudentForm.

Let's have a look at this piece of codes to see how it works.

A. The namespace **System.Linq** is added into the namespace declaration section on this form to allow us to use all LINQ related components defined in that namespace.
B. Five sample students are added into the ComboName combobox to allow users to select one to query the detailed information for the selected student as the project runs. The first student is selected as the default by setting the SelectedIndex to 0.
C. Only one method, LINQ to SQL, is used for this query.
D. This code line is important and it is equivalent to click the Select button to execute its Click method. In this way, the default student's information can be retrieved and displayed in the StudentForm as this form is opened at the first time.

Now let's build the codes for the **Select** button's Click method. As you know, two queries are performed to two tables in this StudentForm, **Student** and **StudentCourse**. Two stored procedures we developed in Section 5.16.3 have been added into the Methods pane and they are considered as stored procedures that can be accessed by LINQ to SQL. Exactly, as we drag each stored procedure from the Server Explorer window and place it to the Methods pane, the necessary codes that are used to call the stored procedure from LINQ to SQL are generated by the designer.

Open the **Select** button's Click method by double-clicking this button from the design view of the StudentForm window, and then enter the codes that are shown in Figure 5.129 into this method. Let's have a close look at this piece of codes to see how it works.

A. An instance of the LogInForm class, **logForm**, is created and the purpose of generating this object is that we can access and use the connection object **CSE_DEPTDataContext** we created in that class.
B. The stored procedure **StudentInfo()** is called to query the detailed information for the selected student. The returned queried collection is assigned to an implicit local variable **sinfo**. The argument of this stored procedure is the student's name stored in the **ComboName** combobox.

```
LINQSPSelect Project          cmdSelect_Click(object sender, EventArgs e)

  private void cmdSelect_Click(object sender, EventArgs e)
  {
A     LogInForm logForm = new LogInForm();
B     var sinfo = logForm.cse_dept.StudentInfo(ComboName.Text);
C     foreach (var si in sinfo)
      {
          txtStudentID.Text = si.student_id;
          txtStudentName.Text = si.student_name;
          txtSchoolYear.Text = si.schoolYear;
          txtGPA.Text = si.gpa.ToString();
          txtMajor.Text = si.major;
          txtCredits.Text = si.credits.ToString();
          txtEmail.Text = si.email;
D         byte[] img = (si.simage as System.Data.Linq.Binary).ToArray();
          PhotoBox.Image = Image.FromStream(new System.IO.MemoryStream(img));
      }
E     CourseList.Items.Clear();
F     var scinfo = logForm.cse_dept.StudentCourseInfo(txtStudentID.Text);
G     foreach (var sc in scinfo)
      {
          CourseList.Items.Add(sc.course_id);
      }
H     logForm.Close();
  }
```

FIGURE 5.129 The coding for the select button's click method.

C. A **foreach** loop is utilized to pick up each column from the selected data row **si**, which is obtained from the **sinfo** we get from the LINQ query above. Then, assign each column to the associated TextBox control in the StudentForm window to display them. Since we are using a typed database, we do not have to indicate each column clearly with the **field<string>** and the column's name as the position for each of them, instead we can directly use each column's name to access each of them.

D. The type of the queried student image via this LINQ to SQL stored procedure method is **System.Data.Linq.Binary**. To assign this image to the student image control, **PhotoBox**, exactly to the **Image** property, in this Student Form to display it, we need to convert this type to the **System.Drawing.Image** in two steps, 1) convert that type to a **byte[]** array, and 2) convert that binary array to the desired type, **System.Drawing.Image**. Here an intermediate variable **img** and an **as** operator are used. The latter works as an indicator to indicate the data type of **f.fimage**.

E. The **CourseList** box control is cleaned up before we can add any queried **course_id** into this control.

F. The second stored procedure **StudentCourseInfo()** is called to query the detailed course information for the selected student. The returned queried collection is assigned to an implicit local variable **scinfo**. The argument of this stored procedure is the **student_id** obtained from the calling of the first stored procedure and it is stored in the **txtStudentID** TextBox.

G. A **foreach** loop is utilized to pick up each **course_id** from the selected data rows **sc**, which is obtained from the **scinfo** we get from the LINQ query above. Then, each **course_id** is added into the **CourseList** box control in the StudentForm window to display them.

H. Finally, the generated instance **logForm** is closed since it finished its mission.

The codes for the **Back** button's Click method are easy. Just open that method and enter the code: **this.Hide()**; into that method.

At this point, we have finished all coding development for this project. Let's run the project to test it. Click on the **Start** button to run the project, complete the login process and select the item **Student Information** from the SelectionForm to open the StudentForm, which is shown in Figure 5.130.

Select the detailed student information by first choosing the desired student name, such as **Ashly Jade**, from the Student Name combobox, and then clicking the **Select** button. All information related to the selected student is displayed in seven TextBoxes and all courses taken by that student are displayed in the **CourseList** box, which is shown in Figure 5.130.

Click on the **Back** and then the **Exit** button to close our project. Our project is successful!

A complete project, **LINQSPSelect Project**, which used LINQ to SQL stored procedures method, can be found from the CRC Press ftp site, exactly at a folder **Class DB Projects\Chapter 5** under the **Students** folder at that site. You can copy and paste it in your computer to run it.

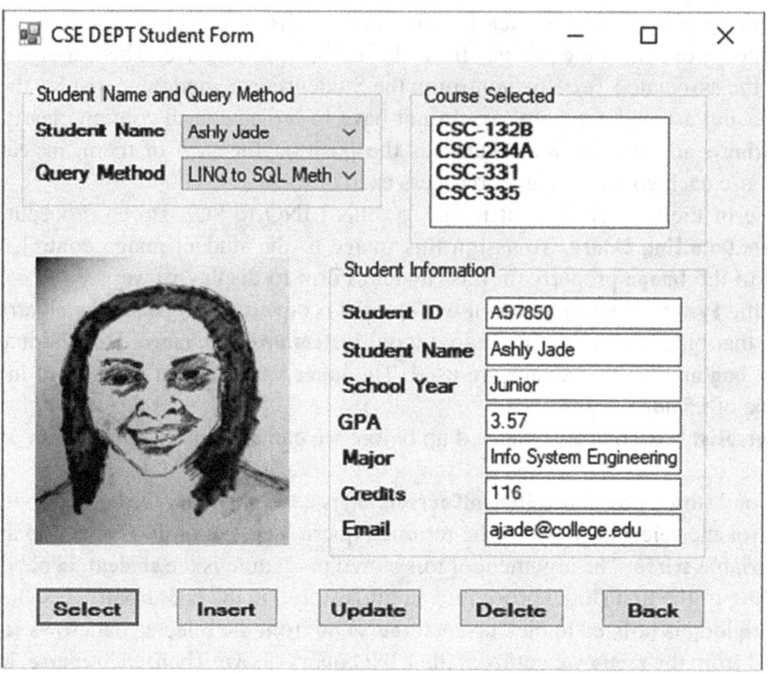

FIGURE 5.130 The running status of the StudentForm.

5.19 CHAPTER SUMMARY

The main discussion on this chapter is to develop professional data-driven applications in the Visual C#.NET 2022 environment by using different methods. The data query is the main topic of this chapter.

The first method is to utilize Design Tools and Wizards provided by Visual Studio.NET 2022 and ADO.NET to build simple, but powerful data query projects, and the second method is to use the runtime object method to build the portable data query projects. The third method is to use stored procedures to integrate multiple queries into a single function or procedure to simplify the query operations and to speed up the query processes. The fourth method is to use LINQ to SQL method to simplify the data query and improve the query efficiency.

Comparably, the first method is simple, and it is easy to be understood and learned by those students who are beginner to Visual C# and databases. That method utilizes a lot of powerful tools and wizards provided by Visual Studio.NET and ADO.NET to simplify the coding process, and most of the codes are auto-generated by the .NET Framework 4.7 and Visual C#.NET 2022 as the user uses those tools and wizards to perform data operations such as adding new data source, making data binding and connecting to the selected data source. The shortcoming of that method is that a lot of coding jobs are performed by the system behind the screen, so it is a little hard to allow users to have a clear picture about what is really happened behind those tools and wizards. The most codes are generated by the system automatically in the specific locations, so it is not easy to translate and execute those codes in other platforms.

The second method, the runtime objects, allows users to dynamically create all data-related objects and perform the associated data operations after the project runs. Because all objects are generated by the coding process, it is very easy to translate and execute this kind of projects in other platforms. This method provides a clear view for the users and enables users to have a global and detail picture in how to control the direction of the project with the codes based on the users' idea and feeling. The shortcoming of this method is that a lot of coding jobs may make the project complicated and it is hard to be accepted by the beginners.

The third method is to use stored procedures to integrate multiple queries into a single function or procedure to simplify the query operations and to speed up the query processes. This method is especially useful for some complicated query, in which multiple queries are needed to be performed to get the desired output results.

The fourth method, LINQ to SQL, is a good method and this technique was released with the Microsoft Visual Studio.NET 2008. The coding process can be significantly simplified and the query efficiency can be greatly improved by using this technique. These advantages can be found by comparing the codes we developed in some projects in this chapter.

A popular and powerful database is discussed in this chapter: Microsoft SQL Server Database, and it is explained in detail with some real sample projects. Different project uses different data query methods: DataAdapter method, runtime object method, stored procedures method, and LINQ to SQL method. Line-by-line illustrations are provided for each sample project. The readers can obtain the solid knowledge and practical experience in how to develop a professional data query application after they finish this chapter.

After finishing Part I in this chapter, you should be able to:

- Use the tools and wizards provided by Visual Studio.NET and ADO.NET to develop simple but powerful data-driven applications to perform data query to Microsoft SQL Server 2019 database.
- Use the SqlConnection class to connect to Microsoft SQL Server 2019 Express database.
- Perform data binding to a DataGridView using two methods.
- Use the SqlCommand class to execute the data query with dynamic parameters to Microsoft SQL Server 2019 Express database.
- Use the SqlDataAdapter to fill a DataSet and a DataTable object with Microsoft SQL Server 2019 Express database.
- Use the SqlDataReader class to query and process data with Microsoft SQL Server 2019 Express database.
- Use LINQ to SQL to simplify the data query process and improve the data query efficiency.
- Set properties for the SqlCommand object to construct a desired query string for Microsoft SQL Server 2019 Express database.

After reading Part II in this chapter, you should be able to:

- Use the runtime objects to develop the professional data-driven applications to perform data query to Microsoft SQL Server 2019 database.
- Use the SqlConnection class to dynamically connect to Microsoft SQL Server 2019 Express database.
- Use the SqlCommand class to dynamically execute the data query with dynamic parameters to Microsoft SQL Server 2019 Express database.
- Use the SqlDataAdapter to dynamically fill a DataSet and a DataTable object with Microsoft SQL Server 2019 Express database.
- Use the SqlDataReader class to dynamically read and process data with Microsoft SQL Server 2019 Express database.
- Use LINQ to SQL to significantly simplify the query process and improve the query efficiency.
- Set properties for the SqlCommand object dynamically to construct a desired query string for Microsoft SQL Server 2019 Express database.
- Use the Server Explorer to create, debug and test stored procedures in Visual Studio.NET environment.
- Use SQL stored procedure to perform the data query from Visual C#.NET.
- Use the SQL nested stored procedure to perform the data query from Visual C#.NET.

In Chapter 6, we will discuss the data insertion technique with Microsoft SQL Server 2019 Express database. Three methods are introduced in two parts: Part I: Using the Design Tools and Wizards provided by Visual Studio.NET to develop data inserting query, and Part II: Using the Runtime objects and LINQ to SQL to perform the data inserting job for Microsoft SQL Server 2019 Express database.

HOMEWORK

I. True/False Selections

____1. Data Provider-dependent objects are Connection, Command, TableAdapter and DataReader.
____2. LINQ to DataSet can be used to access any kind of databases.
____3. To move data between the bound controls on a form window and the associated columns in the data source, a BindingSource is needed.
____4. To set up the connection between the bound controls on a form window and the associated columns in the data source, a TableAdapter is needed.
____5. All TableAdapter classes are located in the namespace DataSetTableAdapters.
____6. Running the **Fill()** method is equivalent to executing the Command object.
____7. The DataSet can be considered as a container that contains multiple data tables, but those tables are only a mapping of the real data tables in the database.
____8. To run the **Fill()** method to fill a table is exactly to fill a data table that is located in the DataSet, not a real data table in the database.
____9. By checking the Count property of a data table, one can determine whether a fill-table-operation is successful or not.
____10. The DataTable object is a Data Provider-independent object.
____11. If one needs to include the SELECT statements in a SQL stored procedure, one can directly create a stored procedure and call it from Visual C#.NET.
____12. In order to use LINQ to SQL query method, one must create an entity class for each data table located in the target database.
____13. You can directly create, edit, manipulate and test stored procedures for the SQL Server database inside the Visual Studio.NET environment.
____14. To call a SQL Server stored procedure, one must set the CommandType property of the Command object to Procedure.
____15. To set up a dynamic parameter in an SELECT statement in the SQL Server database, a @ symbol must be prefixed before the nominal variable.
____16. To access different databases by using LINQ technique, different LINQ API must be used. For example, to access the SQL Server database, LINQ to SQL is used, to access the Oracle database, LINQ to Oracle must be used.
____17. To assign a dynamic parameter in an SELECT statement in the SQL Server database, the keyword LIKE must be used as the assignment operator.
____18. Two popular tools used to create an entity class are: SQLMetal and Object Relational Designer.
____19. Two popular ways to query data from any database are: using Fill() method that belongs to the TableAdapter class, or calling ExecuteReader method that belongs to the Command class.
____20. A DataTable can be considered as a collection of DataRowCollection and DataColumn Collection, and the latter contain DataRow and DataColumn objects.

II. Multiple Choices

1. To connect a database dynamically, one needs to use the _____
   a. Data Source
   b. TableAdapter
   c. Runtime object
   d. Tools and Wizards
2. Four popular data providers are ________
   a. ODBC, DB2, JDBC and SQL
   b. SQL, ODBC, DB2 and Oracle
   c. ODBC, OLEDB, SQL and Oracle
   d. Oracle, OLEDB, SQL and DB2
3. To modify the DataSet, one needs to use the ______ Wizard.
   a. DataSet configuration
   b. DataSet edit
   c. TableAdapter configuration
   d. Query Builder
4. To bind a control with the associated column in a data table, one needs to use ______
   a. BindingNavigator
   b. TableAdapter
   c. DataSet
   d. BindingSource
5. The ________ keyword should be used as an assignment operator for the WHERE clause with a dynamic parameter for a data query in SQL Server database.
   a. =
   b. LIKE
   c. :=
   d. @=
6. The ______ data provider can be used to execute the data query for ______ data providers.
   a. SQL Server, OleDb and Oracle
   b. OleDb, SQL Server and Oracle
   c. Oracle, SQL Server and OleDb
   d. SQL Server, Odbc and Oracle
7. To perform a Fill() method to fill a data table, exactly it executes ______ object with suitable parameters.
   a. DataAdapter
   b. Connection
   c. DataReader
   d. Command
8. To fill a list box or combobox control, one must ____ by using the ____ method.
   a. Remove all old items, Remove()
   b. Remove all old items, ClearBeforeFill()
   c. Clean up all old items, CleanAll()
   d. Clear all old items, ClearAll()
9. A _____ accessing mode should be used to define a connection object if one wants to use that connection object _______ for the whole project.
   a. Private, locally
   b. Protected, globally
   c. Public, locally
   d. Public, globally

10. To ____ data between the DataSet and the database, the ___ object should be used
    a. Bind, BindingSource
    b. Add, TableAdapter
    c. Move, TableAdapter
    d. Remove, DataReader
11. The keyword _______ will be displayed before the procedure's name if one modified an SQL Server stored procedure.
    a. CREATE
    b. CREATE OR REPLACE
    c. REPLACE
    d. ALTER
12. To perform a run-time data query to a SQL Server database, one needs to use ________
    a. OleDb Data Provider
    b. Oracle Data Provider
    c. Both (a) and (b)
    d. SQL Data Provider
13. To query data from any database using the run time object method, two popular methods are _______ and ________
    a. DataSet, TableAdapter
    b. TableAdapter, Fill
    c. DataReader, ExecuteReader
    d. TableAdapter, DataReader
14. To use a stored procedure to retrieve data columns from a SQL Server database, one needs to create a(n) _________
    a. Package
    b. Stored procedure
    c. SQL Trigger
    d. SQL Index
15. Two popular tools used to create an entity class are: ______ and ______.
    a. DataAdapter, DataReader
    b. Data Binder, Navigator
    c. DataTable, DataReader
    d. SQLMetal, Object Relational Designer

III. Exercises

1. Using design tools and wizards provided by Visual Studio.NET and ADO.NET to complete the data query for the Student Form in the **SelectWizard Project** (the project file can be found from the folder **Class DB Projects\Chapter 5** that is located under the **Students** folder at the CRC Press ftp site (refer to Figure 1.2 in Chapter 1).

   Hint 1: Need two TableAdapters and BindingSources, the former is used to **Student** table and the latter is for **StudentCourse** table.

   Hint 2: Use the first BindingSource to bind seven pieces of Student information to seven TextBoxes in Student Form, and use the second BindingSource to bind **CourseList** box to the **course_id** column in the **StudentCourse** table by setting up the **DataSource** and **DisplayMember** properties in the Properties window.

   Hint 3: Using DataSet Designer to build two queries, **FillByStudentName()** for the **Student** table and **FillByStudentID()** for the **StudentCourse** table. The input for the first query is a student name, and the input for the second query is a student_id.

2. Using the Runtime object method to complete the data query for the Student Form by using the DataReader query method in the **RTOSelect Project** (the project file can be found from the folder **Class DB Projects\Chapter 5** that is located under the **Students** folder at the CRC Press ftp site (refer to Figure 1.2 in Chapter 1).

   Hint1: Two queries are needed, one for **Student** table and the other for **StudentCourse** table. The first query is to get seven pieces of student information to be filled in seven TextBoxes in the Student Form, and the second query is to get **course_id** based on the selected **student_id**.

   Hint2: Two queries need to use two sets of **Command** and **DataReader** objects. Refer to codes for the Faculty and the Course Forms in the **RTOSelect Project**.

3. Adding some codes into the **cmdLogIn_Click()** method in the **RTOSelect Project** to allow users to try to login by 3 times. A warning message should be displayed and the project should be exited after 3 times of trying to login if all of them are failed.
4. Try to use the OleDb data provider to replace the SQL Server data provider for the **RTOSelect Project** to perform a similar data query job for the Faculty Form.

   Hint 1: The OleDb connection string should be: **Provider=SQLOLEDB;Data Source= DESKTOP-24JPUFB\\SQL2019EXPRESS;Database=CSE_DEPT;User ID=SMART; Password=Happy2020**;

   Hint 2: The dynamic position holder should be a question mark**?**. However in those parameters assignment method, such as **Add()**, any name can be used for those position parameter holder, such as **@uname** and **@pword**, since only the position is a key for those dynamic parameters.

   Hint 3: Add OleDb namespace to the project, which is **System.Data.OleDb**.

5. Using LINQ to SQL to build a project, **LINQStudent Project**, to perform the data query to **Student** and **StudentCourse** tables for the Student Form in **LINQSelect Project**. For your convenience, refer to a sample project, **LINQSelect Project**, which can be found from the folder **Class DB Projects\Chapter 5** that is located under the **Students** folder at the CRC Press ftp site (refer to Figure 1.2 in Chapter 1).

   Hint 1: When copying the project **LINQSelect Project** and making it a new project **LINQStudent Project**, in addition to changing the namespace from **LINQSelect_Project** to **LINQStudent_Project** for all class and class designer files, including the **C# Program.cs** file, one also needs to change the namespace for the **CSE_DEPT.designer.cs** file.

   Hint 2: When building the LINQ to SQL query statement, two queries should be built. The first one is for the **Student** table, and the second one is for the **StudentCourse** table.

6 Data Inserting with Visual C#.NET

In the previous chapter we spent a lot of time in the discussion and explanation of data query using two different methods. In this chapter, we will concentrate on inserting data into the DataSet and the database. Inserting data into the DataSet or exactly inserting data into the data tables embedded in the DataSet is totally different to inserting data into the database or inserting data into the data tables in the database. The former is only to insert data into the mapping of the data table in the DataSet, and this insertion has nothing to do with the real data tables in the database. In other words, the data inserted into the mapping data tables in the DataSet are not inserted into the data tables in the real database. The latter approach is to insert the data into the data tables in the real database.

As you know, ADO.NET provided a disconnected working mode for the database access applications. The so-called disconnected mode means that your data-driven applications will not always maintain their connection with your database, and this connection may be ended after you setup your DataSet and load all data from the data tables in your database into those data table mappings in your DataSet, and most of the time you are just working on the data between your applications and your data table mappings in your DataSet. The main reason for using this mode is to reduce the overhead of maintaining a large number of connections to the database and to improve the efficiency of data transferring and implementations between the users' applications and the data sources.

In this chapter, we will provide two parts to show readers how to insert data into the database; inserting data into the database using the Visual Studio.NET design tools and wizards is discussed in the first part, and inserting data to the database using the run-time object method is shown in the second part.

When you have finished this chapter, you will

- Understand the working principle and structure on inserting data to the database using the Visual Studio.NET design tools and wizards.
- Understand the procedures involved in configuring the TableAdapter object by using the TableAdapter Query Configuration Wizard and building the query to insert data into the database.
- Design and develop special procedures to validate data before and after accessing the database.
- Understand the working principle and structure with regard to inserting data in the database using the run-time object method.
- Insert data into the DataSet using LINQ to DataSet and insert data into the database using LINQ to SQL queries.
- Design and build stored procedures to perform the action of data insertion.

To successfully complete this chapter, you need to understand topics such as the Fundamentals of Databases, which was introduced in Chapter 2, ADO.NET, which was discussed in Chapter 3. Furthermore, a sample database **CSE_DEPT**, which was developed in Chapter 2, will be used through this chapter.

DOI: 10.1201/9781003319832-6

In order to save time and avoid repetition, we will use the project **SelectWizard Project** we developed in the previous chapter. You will recall that some command buttons on the different form windows in that project have not been coded, such as **Insert**, **Update** and **Delete**, and those buttons or exactly the event procedures related to those buttons will be developed and built on in this chapter. We only concentrate on the coding for the **Insert** button in this chapter.

PART I INSERT DATA WITH VISUAL STUDIO.NET DESIGN TOOLS AND WIZARDS

In this part, we discuss the insertion of data into the database using the Visual Studio.NET design tools and wizards. We develop two methods to perform this data inserting: First we use the TableAdapter DBDirect method, **TableAdapter.Insert()**, to directly insert data into the database. Second we discuss how to insert data into the database by first adding new records into the DataSet, and then updating those new records from the DataSet to the database using the **TableAdapter.Update()** method. Both of these methods utilize the TableAdapter's direct and indirect methods to complete the data insertion. The database we try to use is the SQL Server 2019 Express database, **CSE_DEPT**, which was developed in Chapter 2 and located at the folder **Students\Sample Database** at the CRC Press ftp site (refer to Figure 1.2 in Chapter 1).

6.1 INSERT DATA INTO A DATABASE

In general, there are many different ways to insert data into the database in Visual Studio.NET. Three methods are widely utilized:

1) Using the TableAdapter's DBDirect methods, specifically such as the **TableAdapter.Insert()** method.
2) Using the TableAdapter's **Update()** method to insert new records that have already been added into the DataTable in the DataSet
3) Using the Command object combined with the **ExecuteNonQuery()** method

When using method 1, one can directly access the database and execute commands such as the **TableAdapter.Insert()**, **TableAdapter.Update()** and **TableAdapter.Delete()** to manipulate data in the database without requiring DataSet or DataTable objects to reconcile changes in order to send updates to a database. As mentioned at the beginning of this chapter, inserting data into a table in the DataSet is different with inserting data into a table in the database. If you are using a DataSet to store data in your applications, you need to use the **TableAdapter.Update()** method since the **Update()** method can trigger and send all changes (updates, inserts, and deletes) to the database.

A good choice is to try to use the **TableAdapter.Insert()** method when your application uses objects to store data (for example, you are using TextBoxes to store your data), or when you want finer control over creating new records in the database.

In addition to inserting data into the database, method 2 can be used for other data operations such as update and delete data from the database. You can build associated command objects and assign them to the appropriate TableAdapter's properties such as the **UpdateCommand** and **DeleteCommand**. The point is that when these properties are executed, the data manipulations only occur to the data table in the DataSet, not in the database. In order to make those data modifications occur in the real database, the **TableAdapter'sUpdate()** method is needed.

Exactly, the terminal execution of inserting, updating and deleting data of both methods 1 and 2 is performed by method 3. In other words, both methods 1 and 2 need method 3 to complete those data manipulations, which means that both methods need to execute the Command object, more precisely, the **ExecuteNonQuery()** method of the Command object to finish those data operations again the database.

Because methods 1 and 2 are relatively simple, in this part we will concentrate on inserting data into the database using the TableAdapter methods. First we discuss how to insert new records directly into the database using the **TableAdapter.Insert()** method, and then we discuss how to insert new records into the DataSet and then into a database using the **TableAdapter.Update()** method. Method 3 will be discussed in Part II since it contains more completed coding process related to the runtime objects.

6.1.1 Insert New Records into a Database Using the TableAdapter.Insert Method

When you use this TableAdapter DBDirect method to perform data manipulations to a database, the main query must provide enough information in order for the DBDirect methods to be created correctly. The so-called main query is the default or original query methods such as **Fill()** and **GetData()** when you initially open any TableAdapter by using the TableAdapter Configuration Wizard. Enough information means that the data table must contain completed definitions. For example, if a TableAdapter is configured to query data from a table that does not have a primary key column defined, it does not generate DBDirect methods.

Figure 6.1 lists three TableAdapter DBDirect methods.

It can be seen from Figure 6.1 that the **TableAdapter.Update()** method has two functions: one is to directly make all changes in the database based on the parameters contained in the **Update()** method; the other is to update all changes made in the DataSet to the database based on the associated properties of the TableAdapter such as the InsertCommand, UpdateCommand and DeleteCommand.

In this chapter, we only take care of the inserting data, so only top two methods are discussed in this chapter. The third method will be discussed in Chapter 7.

6.1.2 Insert New Records into a Database Using the TableAdapter.Update Method

To use this method to insert data into the database, one needs to perform the following two steps:

1) Add new records to the desired DataTable by creating a new DataRow and adding it to the Rows collection.
2) After the new rows are added to the DataTable, call the **TableAdapter.Update()** method. You can control the amount of data to be updated by passing an entire DataSet, a DataTable, an array of DataRows, or a single DataRow.

TableAdapter DBDirect Method	Description
TableAdapter.Insert	Adds new records into a database allowing you to pass in individual column values as method parameters.
TableAdapter.Update	Updates existing records in a database. The Update method takes original and new column values as method parameters. The original values are used to locate the original record, and the new values are used to update that record. The TableAdapter.Update method is also used to reconcile changes in a dataset back to the database by taking a DataSet, DataTable, DataRow, or array of DataRows as method parameters.
TableAdapter.Delete	Deletes existing records from the database based on the original column values passed in as method parameters.

FIGURE 6.1 TableAdapter DBDirect methods.

In order to provide a detailed discussion and explanation how to use these two methods to insert new records into the database, a real example will be very helpful. Let's first create a new Visual Basic. NET project to handle these issues.

6.2 INSERT DATA INTO THE SQL SERVER DATABASE USING THE PROJECT INSERTWIZARD PROJECT

We have provided a very detailed introduction about the design tools and wizards in Visual Studio. NET in Section 5.1 in the previous chapter, such as DataSet, BindingSource, TableAdapter, Data Source window, Data Source Configuration window and DataSet Designer. We need to use those components to develop our data-inserting sample project based on the **SelectWizardProject** developed in the previous chapter. First let's copy that project and carry out some modifications to get our new project. The advantage of creating our new project in this way is that you don't need to redo the data source connection and configuration since those jobs have been performed in the previous chapter.

6.2.1 Create a New Project Based on the SelectWizard Project

Open the Windows Explorer and create a new folder **DB Projects\Chapter 6** on your local driver. Then browse for the solution **SelectWizard Solution**, which was developed and built in the previous chapter and located at the folder **ClassDB Projects\Chapter 5**,which is under the **Students** folder at the CRC Press ftp site (refer to Figure 1.2 in Chapter 1). Copy this solution folder with the project to our new folder **DB Projects\Chapter 6**.

We can use this as our new project to perform data insertion function to the some tables in our sample database.

6.2.2 Application User Interfaces

As you know from the last chapter, five Form Windows work as the user interfaces for the **SelectWizardProject**: **LogIn, Selection, Faculty, Course** and **Student**. All of these five Form Windows contain five buttons: **Select**, **Insert**, **Update**, **Delete** and **Back**. We used two buttons, **Select** and **Back** buttons in the last chapter, to discuss how to query data from our sample database using that button. In fact, we do not need to build any other new Form to perform the data insertion; instead we can use the **Insert** button defined in those Forms to carry out that function. Initially, let's concentrate on the Faculty Form to perform the data insertion into our **Faculty** table in our sample database.

First, let's concentrate on the data validation before the data can be inserted into the database.

6.2.3 Validate Data Before the Data Insertion

The most popular validation is to make sure that each datum is not empty and that it contains a certain value. In other words, we want to make sure that each piece of data has a value, either a real value or a NULL value, before they can be inserted into the database.

In this application, we try to validate each piece of faculty information, which is stored in the associated TextBox, is not an empty string unless the user intends to leave it as an empty datum. In that case, an NULL must be entered. To make this validation simple, we develop a control collection and add all of those TextBoxes into that collection. In this way, we don't need to check each TextBox; instead we can use the **For Each ...Next** loop to scan the whole collection to find the empty TextBox.

6.2.3.1 The .NET Framework Collection Classes

The .NET Framework provides a control collection class and this class can be used to store objects of either the same type or different types in an order. One important issue is that the index value in the .NET Framework collection class is 0-based, which means that the index starts from 0, not 1. The namespace for the .NET Framework control collection class is **System.Collections.Generic**. A generic collection is useful when every item in the collection has the same data type.

To create a .NET Framework collection object **newCSCollection**, one can use one of the following declarations:

```
privateDictionary<string, string>newCSCollection =
                         new System.Collections.Generic. Dictionary
                          <string, string>();
or
private Dictionary<string, string>newCSCollection = newDictionary
  <string, string>();
```

The **Dictionary(Key, Value)** generic class provides a mapping from a set of keys to a set of values. The first declaration uses the full name of the collection class, which means that both the class name and the namespace are included. The second declaration uses only the collection class name with the default namespace. The new created collection object contains two arguments, the **item key** and the **item content**, and both are in the string format. Besides **Dictionary()** class, there are some other classes available to store object collections, such as **Queue()**, **List()** and **Stack()**. The **Dictionary()** class is more powerful and easier to implement compared with other classes.

Now let's begin to develop the codes for this data validation using this collection component for our application.

6.2.3.2 Validate Data Using the Generic Collection

First we need to create the generic collection object for our Faculty Form. Since this collection will be used by the different methods in this form, so a class-level object or a field object should be created. Open the Code Window of the Faculty Form by clicking the **View Code** button from the Solution Explorer window, and enter the codes that are shown in Figure 6.2 into the fields-declaration section.

The so-called fields-declaration section, which is located just under the class header, is used to create all class-level variables or objects. The generic collection object, **FacultyCollection**, is created with two arguments: the item key and the item content. The green color code in which the default namespace is utilized also works fine. Here we comment it out to illustrate that we prefer to use the full class name to create this collection object.

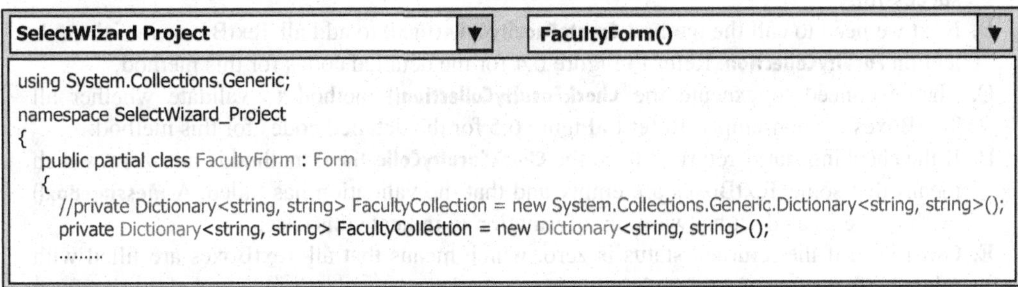

SelectWizard Project
FacultyForm()
using System.Collections.Generic;
namespace SelectWizard_Project
{
public partial class FacultyForm : Form
{
//private Dictionary<string, string> FacultyCollection = new System.Collections.Generic.Dictionary<string, string>();
private Dictionary<string, string> FacultyCollection = new Dictionary<string, string>();
....

FIGURE 6.2 Declare the class level collection object.

SelectWizard Project | cmdInsert_Click(object sender, EventArgs e)

```
  private void cmdInsert_Click(object sender, EventArgs e)
  {
A         int check = 0;
B         CreateFacultyCollection();
C         check = CheckFacultyCollection();
D         if (check != 0)
             MessageBox.Show("Please fill all textboxes...");
E         else
          {
             // continue to perform the data insertion......
          }
F         RemoveFacultyCollection();
  }
```

FIGURE 6.3 The codes for the insert button event procedure.

In order to use the collection object to check all TextBoxes, one needs to add all TextBoxes into the collection object after the collection object **FacultyCollection** is created by using the **Add()** method. One point we need to emphasize is the order to perform this validation check. When the project starts, all TextBoxes are blank. The user needs to enter all faculty information into the appropriate TextBox, and then clicks the **Insert** button to perform this data insertion. The time to add all TextBoxes into the collection object should be after the user has finished entering all pieces of information into all TextBoxes, not before. In addition, each time that the user finished data validation by checking all TextBoxes, all TextBoxes should be removed from that collection since the collection only allows those TextBoxes to be added by one time.

Another point to be noted is that in order to simplify this data validation, in this application we need all TextBoxes to be filled with certain information or a NULL value needs to be entered if no information available. In other words, we don't allow any TextBox to be empty. The data insertion will not be performed until all TextBoxes are non-empty in this application.

Based on these descriptions, we need to create three user-defined methods to perform these adding, checking and removing TextBoxes from the collection object, respectively.

Open the graphical user interface (GUI) window of the Faculty Form, and then double-click on the **Insert** button to open its Click method. Enter the codes that are shown in Figure 6.3 into this method.

Let's take a look at this piece of code to see how it works.

A. First we need to create an integer variable **check** and initialize it to zero. The purpose of using this variable is to hold the returned checking status of the execution of the method **CheckFacultyCollection()** built later to indicate whether the validation for all TextBoxes is successful.

B. Next we need to call the method **CreateFacultyCollection()** to add all TextBoxes into the collection **FacultyCollection**. Refer to Figure 6.4 for the detailed codes for this method.

C. Then we need to execute the **CheckFacultyCollection()** method to validate whether all TextBoxes are non-empty. Refer to Figure 6.5 for the detailed codes for this method.

D. If the checking status returned from the **CheckFacultyCollection()** method is non-zero, which means that some TextBoxes are empty and that the validation has failed. A **MessageBox()** method is executed with a warning information to indicate this case.

E. Otherwise, if the returned status is zero, which means that all TextBoxes are filled with related information and this validation is successful, we need to build our codes to perform the data insertion process.

```
SelectWizard Project                    CreateFacultyCollection()

private void CreateFacultyCollection()
{
        FacultyCollection.Add("Faculty ID", txtFaculyID.Text);
        FacultyCollection.Add("Faculty Name", txtFacultyName.Text);
        FacultyCollection.Add("Faculty Title", txtTitle.Text);
        FacultyCollection.Add("Faculty Office", txtOffice.Text);
        FacultyCollection.Add("Faculty Phone", txtPhone.Text);
        FacultyCollection.Add("Faculty College", txtCollege.Text);
        FacultyCollection.Add("Faculty Email", txtEmail.Text);
}
```

FIGURE 6.4 The codes for the method CreateFacultyCollection().

```
SelectWizard Project                    CheckFacultyCollection()

  private int CheckFacultyCollection()
  {
A       int check = 0;
B       foreach (KeyValuePair<string, string> strCheck in FacultyCollection)
        {
C           if (strCheck.Value == string.Empty)
            {
                MessageBox.Show(strCheck.Key + " is empty!");
                check++;
            }
        }
D       return check;
  }
```

FIGURE 6.5 The codes for the method CheckFacultyCollection().

```
SelectWizard Project                    RemoveFacultyCollection()

private void RemoveFacultyCollection()
{
        FacultyCollection.Remove("Faculty ID");
        FacultyCollection.Remove("Faculty Name");
        FacultyCollection.Remove("Faculty Title");
        FacultyCollection.Remove("Faculty Office");
        FacultyCollection.Remove("Faculty Phone");
        FacultyCollection.Remove("Faculty College");
        FacultyCollection.Remove("Faculty Email");
}
```

FIGURE 6.6 The codes for the method RemoveFacultyCollection().

F. Finally the **RemoveFacultyCollection()** method is called to remove all TextBoxes that have been added into the collection in the **CreateFacultyCollection()** method since the collection only allows those TextBoxes to be added one at a time. The detailed codes for the **RemoveFacultyCollection()** method are shown in Figure 6.6.

Now let's take care of the codes for the **CreateFacultyCollection()** method, which are shown in Figure 6.5.

This piece of code is very simple and straightforward. Each TextBox is added into the collection by using the **Add()** method with two parameters: **Key** and **Value**. The **Key** parameter works as an identifier for the object, and the **Value** parameter contains the content of the object – TextBox in this case. Both parameters are represented in a string format. In this way, each object, or TextBox can be identified by its **Key**. Of course, each TextBox can also be identified by its index, but remember that the index starts from 0, not 1 since it is a .NET Framework collection.

To check and validate all TextBoxes from the collection, the **CheckFacultyCollection()** method is executed. The codes for this method are shown in Figure 6.5.

Let's take a look at this piece of code to see how it works.

A. First we need to create an integer variable **check** and initialize it to zero. The purpose of this variable is to hold the returned checking status of execution of this method and return this status to the calling method.
B. A **foreach** loop is executed to scan each TextBox stored in the **FacultyCollection** collection. A point to be noted is that the data type of the loop variable or the iteration variable **strCheck** must be an IEnumerable or IEnumerable<T> (refer to Sections 4.2 and 4.4.2 in Chapter 4). Also the **foreach** statement of the C# requires the **type** of the elements in the collection. Since each element of a collection based on **Dictionary(Key, Value)** is a **Key/Value** pair, the element **type** is not the type of the **Key** or the type of the **Value**. Instead, the element type is **KeyValuePair(Key, Value)**. Since both **Key** and **Value** are in String format, therefore the **string** type is used for both of them for the element **strCheck**.
C. An **if** block is used to check whether any TextBox is empty or not by using the **Value** of each TextBox. A message will be displayed if any TextBox is empty with the **Key** as the identifier. The **check** variable is increased by 1 if an empty TextBox is detected.
D. Finally, the checking status variable **check** is returned to the calling method.

To remove all TextBoxes from the collection, the **RemoveFacultyCollection()** method should be called, and the codes for this subroutine are shown in Figure 6.6.

The **Key** parameter of each TextBox is used as the identifier for each TextBox and the **Remove()** method is called to remove all TextBoxes from the collection object.

At this point, we completed the coding process for the data validation. Next we need to handle some initialization and termination coding jobs for the data insertion.

6.2.4 Validate Data After the Data Insertion

After a new record has been inserted into the **Faculty** table in our sample database, we need to check and confirm whether that data insertion is successful or not. Fortunately, we do not need to create any new method to do that confirmation; instead we can use the **Select** button with its method to do that checking. But we need to update all faculty names stored in the Faculty Name combobox, **ComboName**, to enable users to select the desired or the new-inserted faculty member to do that checking. Thus, we need to build a new method **CurrentFaculty()** in our project and use a default query method **Fill()** built with design tools and wizards to do that job. Let's start from the new method **CurrentFaculty()**.

On the opened Code Window of the Faculty Form, enter the codes that are shown in Figure 6.7 into that window. Let's have a closer look at this piece of code to see how it works.

A. Two local integer variables, **result** and **index**, are created first. The former is used as a returned variable to indicate whether this method is executed successfully or not, and the

```
SelectWizard Project                    CurrentFaculty()

  private int CurrentFaculty()
  {
A     int result = 0, index;
B     facultyTableAdapter.ClearBeforeFill = true;
C     facultyTableAdapter.Fill(cSE_DEPTDataSet.Faculty);
D     if (cSE_DEPTDataSet.Faculty.Count != 0)
      {
          ComboName.Items.Clear();
E         for (index = 0; index < cSE_DEPTDataSet.Faculty.Count; index++)
              ComboName.Items.Add(cSE_DEPTDataSet.Faculty.Rows[index].ItemArray[1].ToString());
F         ComboName.SelectedIndex = 0;
G         return result;
      }
H     else
          return result++;
  }
```

FIGURE 6.7 The codes for the method CurrentFaculty().

latter works as a loop counter in a **for()** loop to pick up all selected faculty names acquired from the **Faculty** table in our sample database.

B. Prior to performing the **Fill()** method, the TableAdapter is first cleared.

C. Then the **Fill()** method is executed to fill the **Faculty** table in our DataSet by retrieving all faculty records from the **Faculty** table in our sample database.

D. By checking the **Count** property in the filled **Faculty** table, we can confirm whether or not that filling operation is successful. If that **Count** property is non-zero, which means that at least one row data has been retrieved and the fill operation is good, we need to pick up all queried data columns and display them in the Faculty Name combobox, **ComboName**. Prior to doing that, we need first to make sure that combobox is empty by using the **Clear()** method.

E. A **for()** loop is used to pick up all queried faculty names with the **Count** property as the upper bound. All retrieved faculty names will be added into the combobox **ComboName** by using the **Add()** method. A key issue is how to find and locate the required faculty name column from all queried faculty records by using the **Fill()** method. Here we used **Rows[index].ItemArray[1]** to find this column location. The **Rows[index]** is used to define the row location and the **ItemArray[1]** is used to find the column location. The **ItemArray[1]** can be considered as **Column[1]**, that is the second column or **faculty_name** column in the **Faculty** table, and the **Column[0]** is the first column, **faculty_id**, in the **Faculty** table. The **index** works as a loop counter to scan and pick up all data rows in the **Faculty** table.

F. After all faculty names have been added into the combobox, the first faculty name is selected as a default one.

G. The running result, which is 0, is returned to the calling method to indicate that this method is executed successfully.

H. Otherwise, a value of 1 is returned to indicate that this method is failed.

The reason we used the default query method **Fill()** is because that method queries all columns based on the main schema without missing any column in the **Faculty** table and we do not need to create any new query method. Another reason is that we cannot query or select only some desired columns, for our case, in fact we only need to query the **faculty_name** column. But we cannot do that and we have to select all columns from this **Faculty** table since it is required by the main schema in the DataSet and the TableAdapter. Otherwise some mismatching query error may be encountered.

6.2.5 Initialization Coding for the Data Insertion

In this section, we need to build the codes for the following method:

- Coding for the **Form_Load** method to initialize the combobox **ComboMethod** by adding and displaying two data insertion methods, **TableAdapter.Insert()** and **TableAdapter.Update()**,since we want to use two different methods to perform this data insertion action.

As the project runs and the Faculty Form window is shown up, two different methods should be displayed in this box to allow users to select one to perform the data insertion, either the **TableAdapter.Insert()** or the **TableAdapter.Update()** method. The displaying of this selection should be made first as the Form Window is loaded and displayed; therefore, we need to put these codes into the **Form_Load()** method.

Open the **Form_Load()** method in the Faculty Form and add the codes that are shown in Figure 6.8 into this method. The new added codes have been highlighted in bold.

Now we need to take care of the detailed codes for the data insertion. Because we are using the design tools to perform this job, we need first to configure the TableAdapter and build the insert query using the TableAdapter Query Configuration Wizard.

6.2.6 Build the Insert Query

As we mentioned, two methods will be discussed in this part; one is to insert new records using the TableAdapter DBDirect method **TableAdapter.Insert()** to insert data into the database, and the other is to use the **TableAdapter.Update()** method to insert new records into the database. First let's concentrate on the first method.

SelectWizard Project | **FacultyForm_Load()**

```
private void FacultyForm_Load(object sender, EventArgs e)
{
        ComboName.Items.Add("Ying Bai");
        ComboName.Items.Add("Davis Bhalla");
        ComboName.Items.Add("Black Anderson");
        ComboName.Items.Add("Steve Johnson");
        ComboName.Items.Add("Jenney King");
        ComboName.Items.Add("Alice Brown");
        ComboName.Items.Add("Debby Angles");
        ComboName.Items.Add("Jeff Henry");
        ComboName.SelectedIndex = 0;
        ComboMethod.Items.Add("TableAdapter Method");
        ComboMethod.Items.Add("LINQ & DataSet Method");
        ComboMethod.Items.Add("TableAdapter Insert");
        ComboMethod.Items.Add("TableAdapter Update");
        this.ComboMethod.SelectedIndex = 0;
}
```

FIGURE 6.8 The added codes for the Form_Load() method.

6.2.6.1 Configure the TableAdapter and Build the Data Insertion Query

In order to use the **TableAdapter.Insert()** DBDirect method to access the database, we need first to configure the TableAdapter and build the Insert query. Perform the following operations to build this Insert query:

1) Open the Data Source window by going to **View | OtherWindows | Data Sources** menu item.
2) On the opened window, click the **Edit the DataSet with Designer** button that is located at the second left on the toolbar in the Data Source window to open this Designer. Then right-click on the bottom item from the **Faculty** table and select the **Add Query** item from the popup menu to open the TableAdapter Query Configuration Wizard.
3) Keep the default selection, **Use SQL statements**, unchanged and click the **Next** button to go to the next wizard.
4) Select and check the **INSERT** item from this wizard since we need to perform inserting new records query, and then click the **Next** button again to continue.
5) Click the **Query Builder** button to build our insert query. The opened Query Builder wizard is shown in Figure 6.9.
6) The default Insert query statement is identical with our requirement since we want to insert a new faculty record that contains new information about that inserted faculty, which includes the **faculty_id, faculty_name, office, phone, college, title, email** and **fimage**. Click on the **OK** button to go to the next wizard.
7) Click on the **Next** button to confirm this query and continue to the next step.
8) Modify the query function name from the default one to the **InsertFaculty** and click on the **Next** button to go to the last wizard.
9) Click on the **Finish** button to complete this query building and close the wizard.

Immediately, you can find that a new query function has been added into the **FacultyTableAdapter** as the last item.

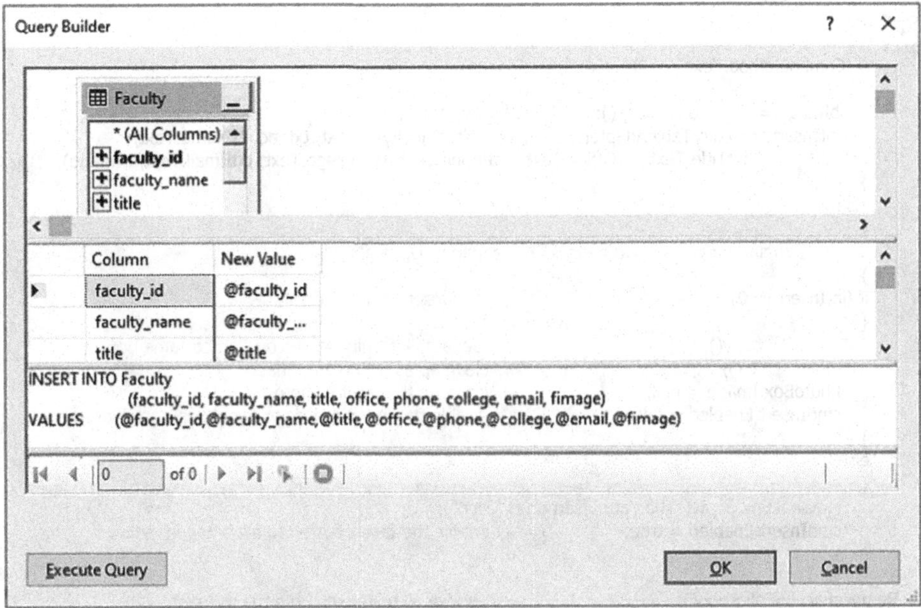

FIGURE 6.9 The opened query builder wizard.

Now that we finished the configuration of the TableAdapter and building of the insert query, it is time for us to develop the codes to run the TableAdapter to complete this data-inserting query.

Now let's start our coding job. First we need to develop the codes for the first method, using the TableAdapter DBDirect method, **TableAdapter.Insert()**.

6.2.7 Develop Codes to Insert Data Using the TableAdapter.Insert Method

Open the GUI of the Faculty Form, and then double-click on the **Insert** button to open its Click method and add the codes that are shown in Figure 6.10 into this method.

Recall that we have created some codes for this method in Section 6.2.3.2 to perform the data validation, so those codes are indicated with the gray color in the background.

Let's have a look at this piece of new added code to see how it works.

A. A local byte[] array **bImage** and an integer variable **intInsert** are declared here and the former is used to hold the selected faculty image to be inserted into our **Faculty** table and the latter is used to hold the returned value from execution of the **TableAdapter.Insert()** method. The value of this returned integer, which indicates how many records have been successfully inserted or affected in the database, can be used to determine whether or not this data insertion is successful. A returned value of zero means that no record has been added or affected to the database; in other words, that insertion is failed.

SelectWizard Project | **cmdInsert_Click(object sender, EventArgs e)**

```
    private void cmdInsert_Click(object sender, EventArgs e)
    {
A       byte[] bImage = null;
        int check = 0; IntInsert = 0;

        CreateFacultyCollection();
        check = CheckFacultyCollection();
        if (check != 0)
           MessageBox.Show("Please fill all textboxes...");
        else
        {
B          if (ComboMethod.Text == "TableAdapter Insert")
           {
              bImage = getFacultyImage();
              intInsert = facultyTableAdapter.InsertFaculty(txtFacultyID.Text, txtFacultyName.Text,
                          txtTitle.Text, txtOffice.Text, txtPhone.Text, txtCollege.Text, txtEmail.Text, bImage);
           }
C          else
           {
                // coding for the second method TableAdapter Update()......
           }
D          if (intInsert != 0)                        // data insertion is successful
           {
              CurrentFaculty();                        // update all faculty names on ComboName box
              ClearFaculty();                          // clean up all faculty information
              PhotoBox.Image = null;                   // clean up the faculty photo
              cmdInsert.Enabled = false;               // disable the Insert button to avoid duplicated insertion
           }
E          else
           {
              MessageBox.Show("The data insertion is failed");
              cmdInsert.Enabled = true;                // enable the Insert button to allow the insertion
           }
        }
        RemoveFacultyCollection();                     // remove all textboxes from the collection
    }
```

FIGURE 6.10 The modified codes for the insert button click method.

B. If the user selected the **TableAdapter Insert** method to perform this data insertion, first a user-defined method, **getFacultyImage()**,which will be built later, is called to get the selected faculty image to be inserted, and the query function **InsertFaculty()**, which we built in the last section by using the TableAdapter Query Configuration Wizard, is executed to complete this data insertion. Eight pieces of new information, which is about the new inserted faculty and entered by the user into seven TextBoxes with a selected faculty image, will be inserted into the **Faculty** table in our sample database.
C. If the user selected the **TableAdapter.Update()** method to perform this data insertion, the data insertion should be performed by calling that method. The coding development for this method will be discussed in the next section.
D. If this data insertion is successful, the returned integer value will reflect the number of records that have been inserted into the database correctly. As we mentioned in step **A**, a returned value of non-zero indicates that this insertion is successful. Some updating and cleaning jobs are performed. First, all faculty names in the combobox **ComboName** are updated by calling the user-defined method **CurrentFaculty()** built in the last section, and another user-defined method, **ClearFaculty()**,which will be built later, is executed to cleanup all inserted faculty information, including cleaning up the faculty photo and disabling the **Insert** button to avoid any possible duplicated insertion action.
E. If the **intInsert** returns a zero, which means that this data insertion is failed, a MessageBox will be displayed with a warning message to indicate this situation to the user. The **Insert** button is also enabled to allow all future insertions.

One point we need to emphasize is that when performing a data insertion, the same data can only be inserted into the database by one time, and the database does not allow multiple insertions of the same data item. To avoid multiple insertions, in this application (exactly in most popular applications) we need to disable the **Insert** button once a record is inserted successfully (refer to step **D**). If the insertion is failed, we need to recover or re-enable the **Insert** button to allow the user to try another insertion later (step **E**).

From the above explanations, we know that it is a good way to avoid the multiple insertions of the same data item into the database by disabling the **Insert** button after that insertion is successfully completed. A question arises: When and how can this button be enabled again to allow us to insert some other different new records if we want to do that later? The solution to this question is to develop another method to handle this issue. Try to think about it; the time when we want to insert new different data item into the database, first we must enter each piece of new faculty information into each associated TextBox, such as **txtFacultyID, txtFacultyName, txtOffice, txtPhone, txtTitle, txtCollege** and **txtEmail**. In other words, anytime that the content of a TextBox is changed, which means that a new different record will be inserted, we should enable the **Insert** button at that moment to allow users to perform this new insertion.

Most databases, including the Microsoft Access, SQL Server and Oracle, do not allow multiple data insertions of the same data item into the databases. Each data item or record can only be added or inserted into the database by one time. In other words, no duplicating record can be added or existed in the database. Each record in the database must be unique. The popular way to avoid this situation to be happened is to disable the Insert button after one insertion is done.

Visual C#.NET did provide an event called **TextChanged** and an associated method for the TextBox control. Therefore, we can use this event and method to enable the **Insert** button as long as a **TextChanged** event occurs. Well, another question arises: when a TextBox's **TextChanged** event

```
SelectWizard Project                    txtFacultyID_TextChanged()

private void txtFacultyID_TextChanged(object sender, EventArgs e)
{
        cmdInsert.Enabled = true;
}
```

FIGURE 6.11 The codes for the TextChanged() method.

is occurring, we should trigger the associated method to enable the **Insert** button to allow users to insert a new record. Which TextBox's **TextChanged** event should be used? To answer this question, we need to review the data issue in the database. As you know, in our sampling database **CSE_DEPT** (exactly in our **Faculty** data table), it identifies a record based on its primary key. In other words, only those records with different primary keys can be considered as different records. So the solution to our question is: if only the content of the TextBox that stores the primary key, in our case it is the **txtFacultyID** who stores the **faculty_id**, is changed, this means that a new record will be inserted, and as this happened, that TextBox's **TextChanged** method should be triggered to enable the **Insert** button.

To open the **TextChanged** method for the Faculty ID TextBox, open the GUI of the Faculty Form window, and double-click on the TextBox, **txtFacultyID**, and then enter the codes shown in Figure 6.11 into this method. The codes for this method are simple: enable the **Insert** button by setting the **Enabled** property of that button to **true** as the **txtFacultyID** TextChanged event occurs.

Now we continue to build codes for some user defined methods. Two methods, **getFacultyImage()** and **ClearFaculty()**, should be taken care of next.

6.2.7.1 Develop the Codes for Two User Defined Methods

First let's take care of the codes for the method **getFacultyImage()**. Open the Code Window of the Faculty Form window and enter the codes shown in Figure 6.12 into that window. Let's have a closer look at this piece of code to see how it works.

A. Some local objects are first declared, including a MemoryStream class and an OpenFileDialog class object, **ms** and **dlg**. The former is used as an intermediate translation image variable array and the latter provides a File Dialog to enable users to select a desired faculty image to be inserted into our database. A byte[] array variable **bimage** is also

```
SelectWizard Project                    getFacultyImage()

  private byte[] getFacultyImage()
  {
A         MemoryStream ms = new MemoryStream();
          OpenFileDialog dlg = new OpenFileDialog();
          byte[] bimage = null;
B         dlg.Filter = "JPG Files (*.jpg)|*.jpg|All Files (*.*)|*.*";
          dlg.Title = "Select the Faculty Image";
C         if (dlg.ShowDialog() == DialogResult.OK)
          {
             PhotoBox.Image = Image.FromFile(dlg.FileName);
             PhotoBox.Image.Save(ms, PhotoBox.Image.RawFormat);
D            bimage = ms.ToArray();
          }
E         return bimage;
  }
```

FIGURE 6.12 The codes for the method getFacultyImage().

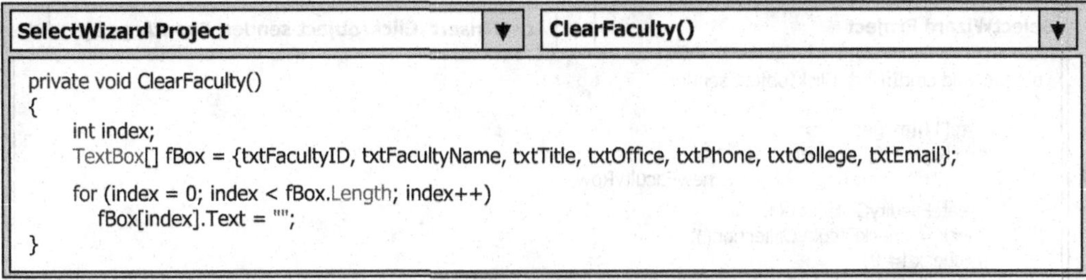
SelectWizard Project | ClearFaculty()

```
private void ClearFaculty()
{
    int index;
    TextBox[] fBox = {txtFacultyID, txtFacultyName, txtTitle, txtOffice, txtPhone, txtCollege, txtEmail};

    for (index = 0; index < fBox.Length; index++)
       fBox[index].Text = "";
}
```

FIGURE 6.13 The codes for the method ClearFaculty().

generated and it works as a returned image array since the only data type used to store an image in a SQL Server database is byte[].

B. The OpenFileDialog class object **dlg** is initialized with the Filter and Title properties. The former is used to define the image type to be selected and the latter provides a title for that dialog.
C. If the system method **ShowDialog()** is executed successfully, returning a system constant, **DialogResult.OK**, this means that the OpenFileDialog is opened successfully and the user has selected a valid faculty image. First, that selected image is read out by using the **FromFile()** method. It is then assigned to the **Image** property of the Faculty Image control, **PhotoBox**, in the Faculty Form window, and then that image is converted to the MemoryStream format and saved to the MemoryStream class object **ms** via the system method **Save()**.
D. Finally, that converted image is further to be converted to a byte array via the **ToArray()** method.
E. The converted image array is returned to the calling method.

Next let's handle the codes for the **ClearFaculty()** method. The purpose of this method is to clean up all inserted faculty information from seven TextBoxes after a faculty record has been successfully inserted into our sample database, and then to enable users to test that data insertion action.

On the opened Code Window of the Faculty Form window, enter the codes shown in Figure 6.13 into that window to generate this method.

The function of this piece of code is straightforward. First, a local integer variable **index** and a TextBox array **fBox** are generated, then a **for()** loop is used to set the **Text** property of each TextBox to an empty string "" to clean each of them.

Next let's finish the coding development for the **TableAdapter.Update()** method.

6.2.8 Develop Codes to Insert Data Using the TableAdapter.Update Method

When a data-driven application uses DataSet to store data, as we did for this application by using the CSE_DEPTDataSet, one can use the **TableAdapter.Update()** method to insert (or add) a new record into the database.

To insert a new record into the database using this method, two steps are needed:

1) Add new records to the desired data table in the DataSet. For example, in this application, the **Faculty** table in the DataSet CSE_DEPTDataSet.
2) Call the **TableAdapter.Update()** method to update new added records from the data table in the DataSet to the data table in the database. The amount of data to be updated can be controlled by passing the different argument in the **Update()** method, either an entire DataSet, a DataTable, an array of DataRow, or a single DataRow.

Now let's develop our codes based on the above two steps to insert data using this method.

```
SelectWizard Project                      cmdInsert_Click(object sender, EventArgs e)

private void cmdInsert_Click(object sender, EventArgs e)
{
        byte[] bImage;
        int check = 0, intInsert = 0;
A       CSE_DEPTDataSet.FacultyRow newFacultyRow;
        CreateFacultyCollection();
        check = CheckFacultyCollection();
        if (check != 0)
            MessageBox.Show("Please fill all textboxes...");
        else
        {
            if (ComboMethod.Text == "TableAdapter Insert")
            {
                bImage = getFacultyImage();
                intInsert = facultyTableAdapter.InsertFaculty(txtFacultyID.Text, txtFacultyName.Text,
                        txtTitle.Text, txtOffice.Text, txtPhone.Text, txtCollege.Text, txtEmail.Text, bImage);
            }
            else
            {
B               newFacultyRow = this.cSE_DEPTDataSet.Faculty.NewFacultyRow();
C               InsertFacultyRow(ref newFacultyRow);
D               cSE_DEPTDataSet.Faculty.Rows.Add(newFacultyRow);
E               intInsert = facultyTableAdapter.Update(cSE_DEPTDataSet.Faculty);
            }
            if (intInsert != 0)                  // data insertion is successful
            {
                CurrentFaculty();                // update all faculty names on ComboName box
                ClearFaculty();                  // clean up all faculty information
                PhotoBox.Image = null;           // clean up the faculty photo
                cmdInsert.Enabled = false;       // disable the Insert button to avoid duplicated insertion
            }
            else
            {
                MessageBox.Show("The data insertion is failed");
                cmdInsert.Enabled = true;        // enable the Insert button to allow the insertion
            }
        }
        RemoveFacultyCollection();
}
```

FIGURE 6.14 The codes for the second data insertion method.

Re-open the graphical user interface of the Faculty Form window and double-click on the **Insert** button to open its Click method. We have already developed most codes for this method in the last section, and now we need to add the codes to perform the second data insertion method. Browse to the **else** block (step E in Figure 6.10), and enter the codes that are shown in Figure 6.14 into this block.

In order to distinguish between the new codes and the old codes that have been added before, all old codes are indicated with the gray background color.

Let's take a close look at this piece of new inserted codes to see how it works.

A. First we need to declare a new object of the **DataRow** class, **newFacultyRow**. Each DataRow object can be mapped to a real row in a data table. Since we are using the DataSet to manage all data tables in this project, the DataSet must be prefixed before the **DataRow** object. In addition, we need to create a row in the **Faculty** data table, the **FacultyRow** is selected as the DataRow class.

B. Next we need to create a new object of the **newFacultyRow** class.

C. A user-defined method **InsertFacultyRow()** is called to add all pieces of faculty information about the new inserting faculty, which is stored in seven TextBoxes and a PhotoBox, into this new created DataRow object. The codes and the function of this user-defined method are explained later. The method returns a completed **DataRow** that contains all the pieces of faculty information about the new record. One point to be noted is that a reference parameter, **ref newFacultyRow**, is passed into the method, which means that the address (not the value) of the object **newFacultyRow** is passed into the method, and any modification to this object is permanent. We need this permanent property to keep our returned **newFacultyRow** object updated.

D. The completed DataRow is added into the **Faculty** table in our DataSet object. One point to be noted is that adding a new record into a data table in the DataSet is nothing to do with adding a new record into a data table in the database. The data tables in the DataSet are only mappings of those real data tables in the database. To add this new record into the database, one needs to perform the next step.

E. The TableAdapter's method **Update()** is executed to make this new record be added into the real database. As we mentioned before, you can control the amount of data to be added into the database by passing the different arguments. Here we only want to add one new record into the **Faculty** table, so a data table is passed as the argument. This **Update()** method supposes to return an integer value to indicate whether this update is successful or not. The value of this returned integer is equal to the number of rows that have been successfully added into the database. A returned value of zero means that this update is failed since no new row has been added into the database.

Now let's develop the codes for the user-defined method **InsertFacultyRow()**. Open the Code Window of the Faculty Form and enter the codes that are shown in Figure 6.15 into that window for this method.

The function of this piece of codes is straightforward and easily understood. First a local byte[] array, **bImage**, is generated and the user-defined method, **getFacultyImage()**, is called to get the selected faculty image to be inserted. Then seven pieces of new faculty information stored in the associated TextBoxes with the selected faculty image are added into the new DataRow object, exactly added into a new row of the faculty table in the DataSet. Since the argument **facultyRow** is passed into this method using a reference value, any modification to this object **facultyRow** is permanent, which means that this modification can be returned to the calling method and keep valid until the project is terminated or exited.

At this point, we have completed the coding development for our data insertion through the use of two methods. Now let's test our coding by running our project.

Click on the Start button to run the project. Enter the correct username and password to the LogIn Form, and select the Faculty Information from the Selection Form window to open the Faculty Form window, which is shown in Figure 6.16.

SelectWizard Project ▼	InsertFacultyRow() ▼

```
private void InsertFacultyRow(ref CSE_DEPTDataSet.FacultyRow facultyRow)
{
    byte[] bImage;

    bImage = getFacultyImage();
    facultyRow.faculty_id = txtFacultyID.Text;
    facultyRow.faculty_name = txtFacultyName.Text;
    facultyRow.title = txtTitle.Text;
    facultyRow.office = txtOffice.Text;
    facultyRow.phone = txtPhone.Text;
    facultyRow.college = txtCollege.Text;
    facultyRow.email = txtEmail.Text;
    facultyRow.fimage = bImage;
}
```

FIGURE 6.15 The codes for the user-defined method InsertFacultyRow().

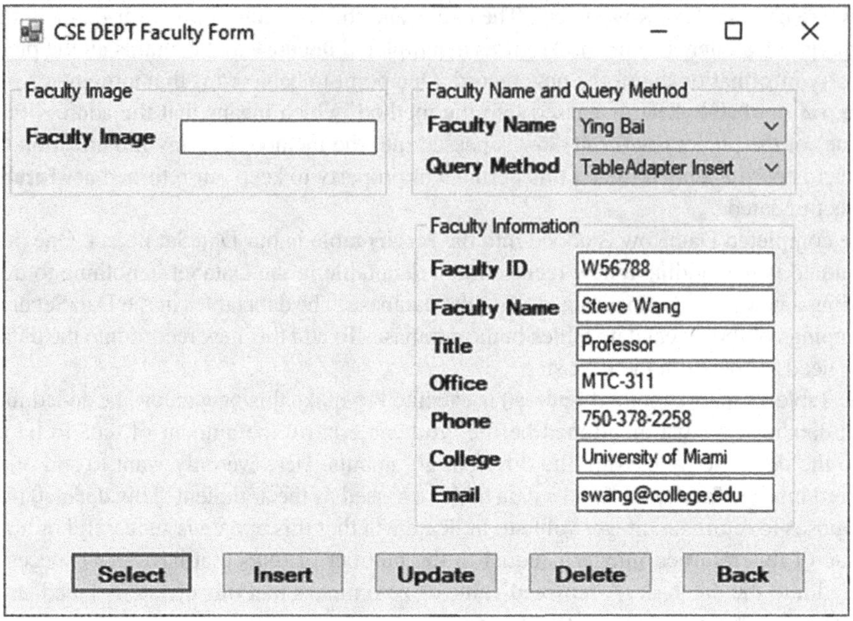

FIGURE 6.16 The running status of the faculty form window.

Now let's test the first method, **TableAdapter.Insert()**, by selecting it from the Query Method combobox, and then entering seven pieces of information into the related TextBox as a new faculty record as below:

Faculty ID:	**W56788**
Faculty Name:	**Steve Wang**
Title:	**Professor**
Office:	**MTC-311**
Phone:	**750-378-2258**
College:	**University of Miami**
Email:	**swang@college.edu**

Then click on the **Insert** button to open a FileDialog to select a desired faculty image. Browse the desired folder in your local machine to select a faculty image, **Wang.jpg**, and click on the **Open** button to select it and close that FileDialog. All faculty images are available and stored in the CRC Press ftp site, in a folder **Images\Faculty** that is located under the **Students** folder on that site (refer to Figure 1.2 in Chapter 1). One can copy those images and save them into a local folder on your local machine.

If this insertion is successful, the contents on all TextBoxes are cleaned up and the **Insert** button is disabled to avoid the same data to be inserted into the database more than one time.

To check or confirm this data insertion, two ways can be used; 1) using the **Select** button click method to retrieve back that inserted faculty record, 2) open the **Faculty** table via Server Explorer or Microsoft SQL Server Management Studio 18.

Now let's first use the **Select** button click method to do that checking. Just open and browse the Faculty Name combobox, **ComboName**, and you can find that the new inserted faculty name, **Steve Wang**, has been added into this combobox. Choose it and click on the **Select** button to try to retrieve this new record. The new inserted faculty with all related information is displayed in this Form, as shown in Figure 6.17.

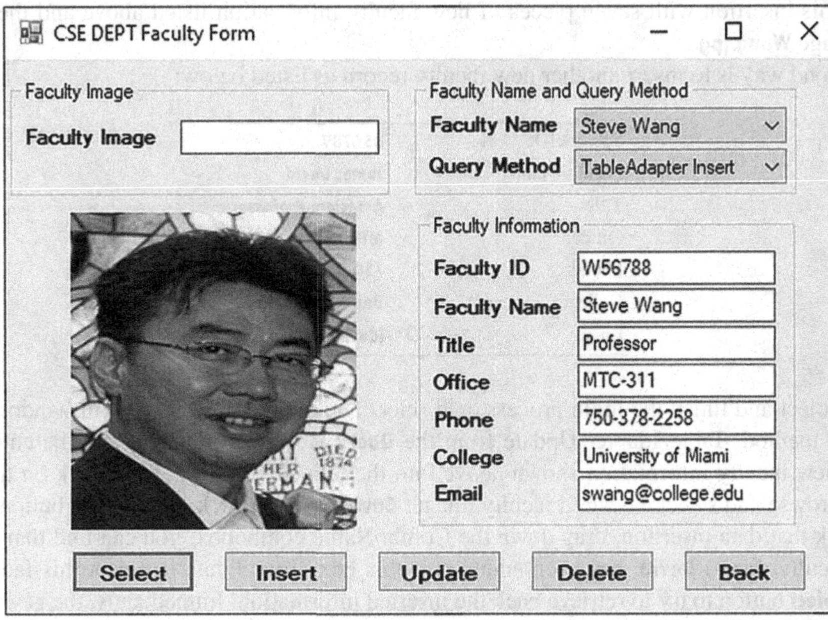

FIGURE 6.17 The retrieved new inserted faculty record.

Click on the **Back** and the **Exit** button to terminate our project.

To use the second way to do this checking, just open the Server Explorer window and click on the arrow on the left of our sample database to connect to it. Then expand the **Tables** folder and right click on the **Faculty** table, select the item **Show Table Data** from the popup menu to open the **Faculty** table. You can find that the new faculty member, **Steve Wang**, has been inserted into this table at the bottom line, as shown in Figure 6.18.

To test to insert a new faculty record into the **Faculty** table with another method, the **TableAdapter. Update()** method, two ways could be adopted; the first one can insert the same new faculty record but had better first remove that inserted new faculty record from the **Faculty** table. To do that removing in the Server Explorer window, on the opened **Faculty** table, right-click on the new inserted faculty record, and select the **Delete** item. Then go to the **File | Save All** menu item to save this change. Now one can run the project and select the method **TableAdapter Update** from the **Query Method** combobox,

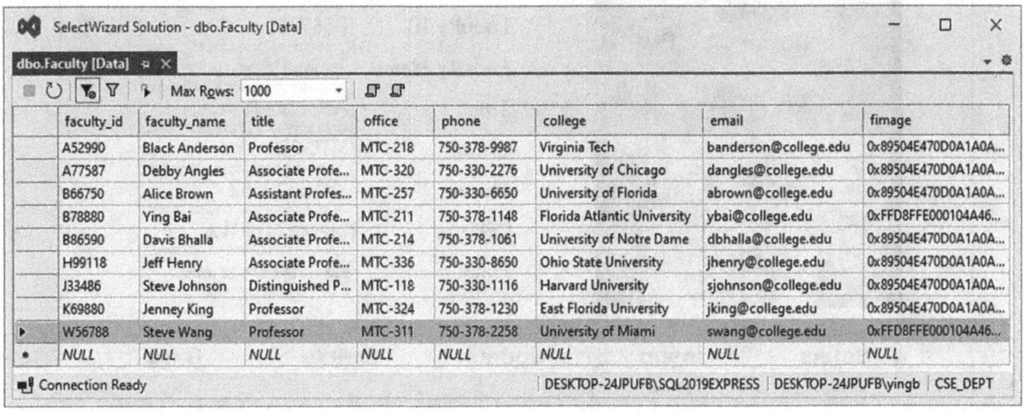

faculty_id	faculty_name	title	office	phone	college	email	fimage
A52990	Black Anderson	Professor	MTC-218	750-378-9987	Virginia Tech	banderson@college.edu	0x89504E470D0A1A0A...
A77587	Debby Angles	Associate Profe...	MTC-320	750-330-2276	University of Chicago	dangles@college.edu	0x89504E470D0A1A0A...
B66750	Alice Brown	Assistant Profes...	MTC-257	750-330-6650	University of Florida	abrown@college.edu	0x89504E470D0A1A0A...
B78880	Ying Bai	Associate Profe...	MTC-211	750-378-1148	Florida Atlantic University	ybai@college.edu	0xFFD8FFE000104A46...
B86590	Davis Bhalla	Associate Profe...	MTC-214	750-378-1061	University of Notre Dame	dbhalla@college.edu	0x89504E470D0A1A0A...
H99118	Jeff Henry	Associate Profe...	MTC-336	750-330-8650	Ohio State University	jhenry@college.edu	0x89504E470D0A1A0A...
J33486	Steve Johnson	Distinguished P...	MTC-118	750-330-1116	Harvard University	sjohnson@college.edu	0x89504E470D0A1A0A...
K69880	Jenney King	Professor	MTC-324	750-378-1230	East Florida University	jking@college.edu	0x89504E470D0A1A0A...
W56788	Steve Wang	Professor	MTC-311	750-378-2258	University of Miami	swang@college.edu	0xFFD8FFE000104A46...
NULL	NULL	NULL	NULL	NULL	NULL	NULL	NULL

FIGURE 6.18 The opened faculty table.

and redo this insertion with seven pieces of new faculty information listed above and the desired faculty image **Wang.jpg**.

The second way is to insert another new faculty record as listed below:

Faculty ID:	**D56789**
Faculty Name:	**James David**
Title:	**Associate Professor**
Office:	**MTC-222**
Phone:	**750-330-1662**
College:	**University of Main**
Email:	**jdavid@college.edu**

Run the project and finish the login process, and select and open the Faculty Form window. Select the second method, TableAdapter Update from the **Query Method** combobox, and the enter seven pieces of new faculty information shown above into the related TextBox. Then click on the Insert button to browse and select a desired faculty image, **David.jpg**, and click on the **Open** button.

To check that data insertion, drag down the ComboName combobox, you can find that our new inserted faculty, **James David**, has been added into this box. To validate it, select this faculty and click the **Select** button to try to retrieve back the inserted information. Immediately, the new inserted faculty information is retrieved back from the database and displayed in the associated TextBoxes, as shown in Figure 6.19.

Click the **Back** and then the **Exit** buttons from the Faculty Form and the Selection Form windows to terminate the project.

A completed project, **SelectWizard Project**, with the data insertion function, can be found from a folder **Class DB Project\Chapter 6\SelectWizard Solution** that is located under the **Students** folder on the CRC Press ftp site (refer to Figure 1.2 in Chapter 1).

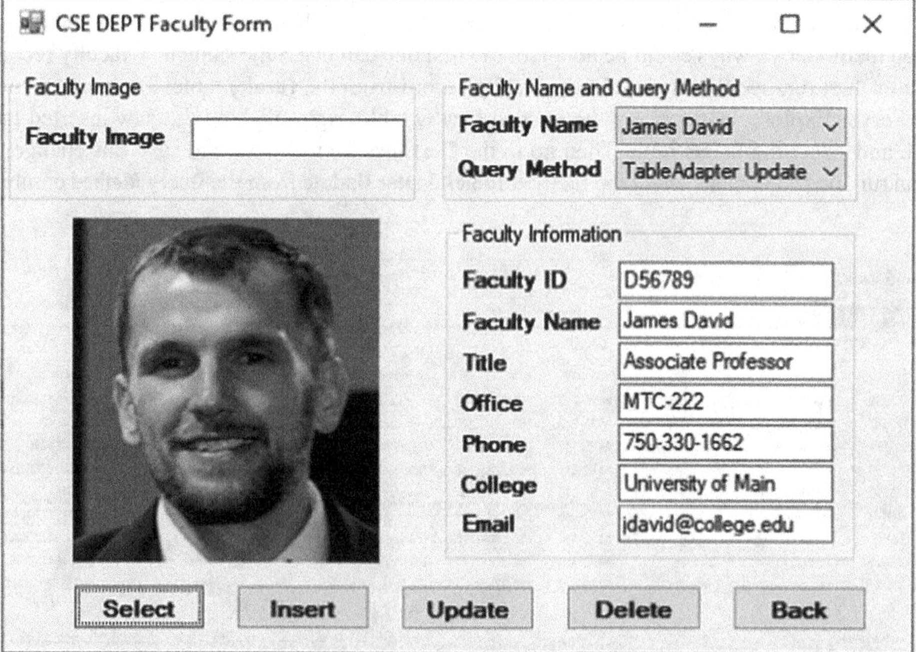

FIGURE 6.19 The testing status of the data insertion with the TableAdapter.Update().

6.3 INSERT DATA INTO THE COURSE TABLE WITH THREE METHODS

In this section, we want to discuss how to insert new records into the database using three different methods; **TableAdapter Insert**, **TableAdapter Update** and **Stored Procedure** methods. To make it simple, we will use the Course Form windows in our project **SelectWizard Project** built in the previous section to insert a new course record into the **Course** table in our sample database via these methods.

To use those different methods to insert new records into the database, we need to perform the following tasks to build our project:

1) First we need to add some class-level variables and modify the codes in the **Form_Load()** method of the Course Form window by adding three query methods to allow users to select one of them to perform the related data insertion action.
2) To use the **TableAdapter.Insert()** method, we need to build a query **InsertCourse()** via the TableAdapter Query Configuration Wizard.
3) To use the stored procedure method, we need to create a stored procedure named **InsertCourseSP()** under the **Course** table using the TableAdapter Query Configuration Wizard.
4) Build the codes for the **Insert** button's Click method to call one of the methods to insert a new course record into the **Course** table in our sample database.

Let's do our jobs, starting from step 1 listed above.

6.3.1 Add Class Variables and Modify the Codes in the Form_Load() Method

Open the Code Window and the **Form_Load()** method of the Course Form window, and enter the code, which is shown in Figure 6.20, into that code window to replace all original codes to allow users to select one of them to perform the related data insertion.

```
SelectWizard Project                    CourseForm_Load(object sender, EventArgs e)

public partial class CourseForm : Form
  {
     string strFacultyID;
     string[] CourseInfo = new string[6];
     public CourseForm()
     {
        InitializeComponent();
     }
     private void CourseForm_Load(object sender, EventArgs e)
     {
        ComboName.Items.Add("Ying Bai");
        ComboName.Items.Add("Davis Bhalla");
        ComboName.Items.Add("Black Anderson");
        ComboName.Items.Add("Steve Johnson");
        ComboName.Items.Add("Jenney King");
        ComboName.Items.Add("Alice Brown");
        ComboName.Items.Add("Debby Angles");
        ComboName.Items.Add("Jeff Henry");
        ComboName.SelectedIndex = 0;
        ComboMethod.Items.Add("TableAdapter Method");
        ComboMethod.Items.Add("LINQ & DataSet Method");
        ComboMethod.Items.Add("TableAdapter Insert");
        ComboMethod.Items.Add("TableAdapter Update");
        ComboMethod.Items.Add("Stored Procedure");
        ComboMethod.SelectedIndex = 0;
     }
```

FIGURE 6.20 The new added codes in the Form_Load() method.

Refer to Figure 6.20, two class string variables, **strFacultyID**, and an array, **CourseInfo[]**, are generated, and these variables will be used later. In total, five query methods are listed in the Query Method combobox **ComboMethod**. The top two methods are used for the **Select** query and the bottom three are used for the data **Insertion** action.

Next let's build a new query **InsertCourse()** via the TableAdapter Query Configuration Wizard, which will be called by the **TableAdapter.Insert()** method.

6.3.2 Build the Query Method InsertCourse()

Perform the following operations to build this new query method:

1) On the opened Data Sources window, right-click on any location inside the **Data Sources** window and select the **Edit the DataSet with Designer** item from the popup menu to open this wizard.
2) Right-click the last item from the **Course** table and select the **Add Query** item from the popup menu to open the TableAdapter Query Configuration Wizard.
3) Keep the default selection, **Use SQL statements**, and click on the **Next** button.
4) Check the **INSERT** radio button and click **Next** to continue.
5) Click the **Query Builder** button on the opened wizard since we need to build a new query. The opened **Query Builder** wizard is shown in Figure 6.21.
6) Click the **OK** button to the next wizard to confirm our built query function, which is shown in Figure 6.22.
7) The default query includes a **SELECT ... FROM** statement and it is used to select the desired columns from this **Course** table and insert those columns to another target table. Here we only need to insert a record into the **Course** table without any other target table, so just highlight the second **SELECT** statement and delete it by pressing the **Delete** key from your keyboard.

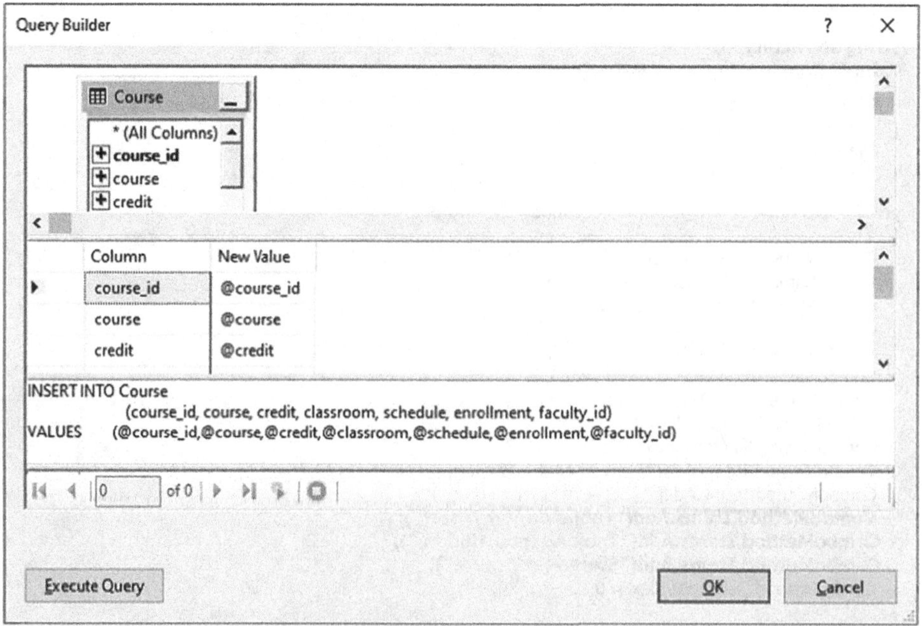

FIGURE 6.21 The opened query builder wizard.

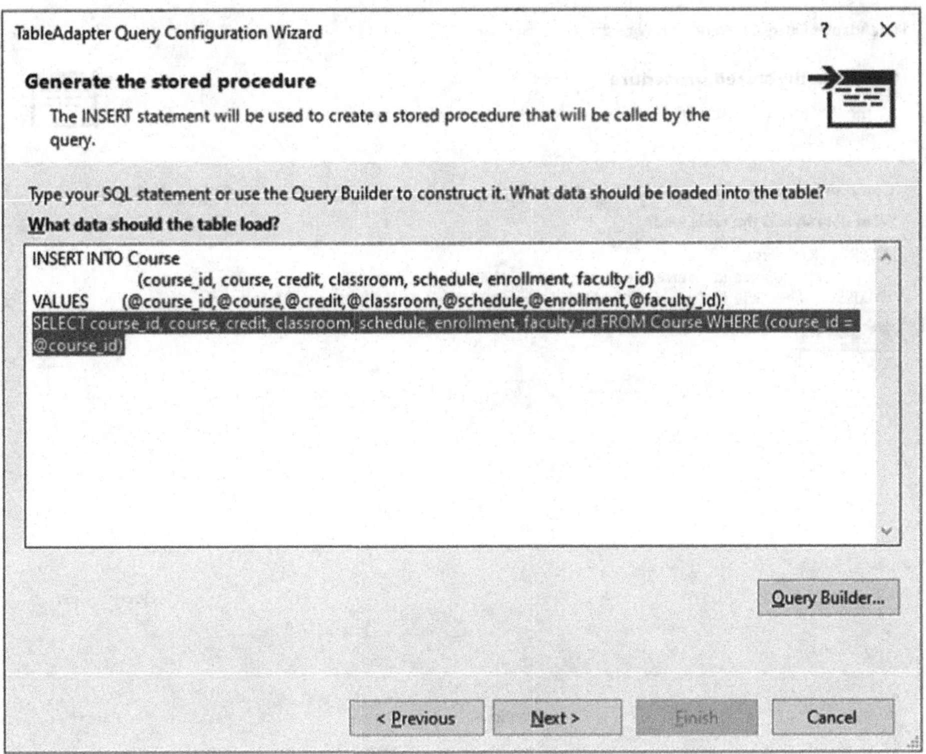

FIGURE 6.22 The data insertion confirmation wizard.

8) Click on the **Next** button to go to the next wizard.
9) On the next wizard, enter **InsertCourse** into the name box as the name of this query method. Click on the **Next** and then the **Finish** buttons for the following wizards to finish and close this process.

Next let's create a stored procedure named **InsertCourseSP()** under the **Course** table using the TableAdapter Query Configuration Wizard.

6.3.3 Create the Stored Procedure Using the TableAdapter Query Configuration Wizard

Open the **Data Source** window by clicking the **View | OtherWindows | Data Sources** menu item, and then right-click on any location inside the **Data Source** window and select the **Edit the DataSet with Designer** item from the popup menu to open this wizard. Right-click the last item from the **Course** table and select the **Add Query** item from the popup menu to open the TableAdapter Query Configuration Wizard. Perform the following operations to build this query:

1) Check the **Create new stored procedure** radio button since we want to create a new stored procedure to do the data insertion, and click the **Next** button to go to the next wizard.
2) Check the **INSERT** radio button and click **Next** to continue.
3) Click the **Query Builder** button on the opened wizard since we need to build a new query.
4) Click the **OK** button to the next wizard to confirm our built query function, which is shown in Figure 6.23.

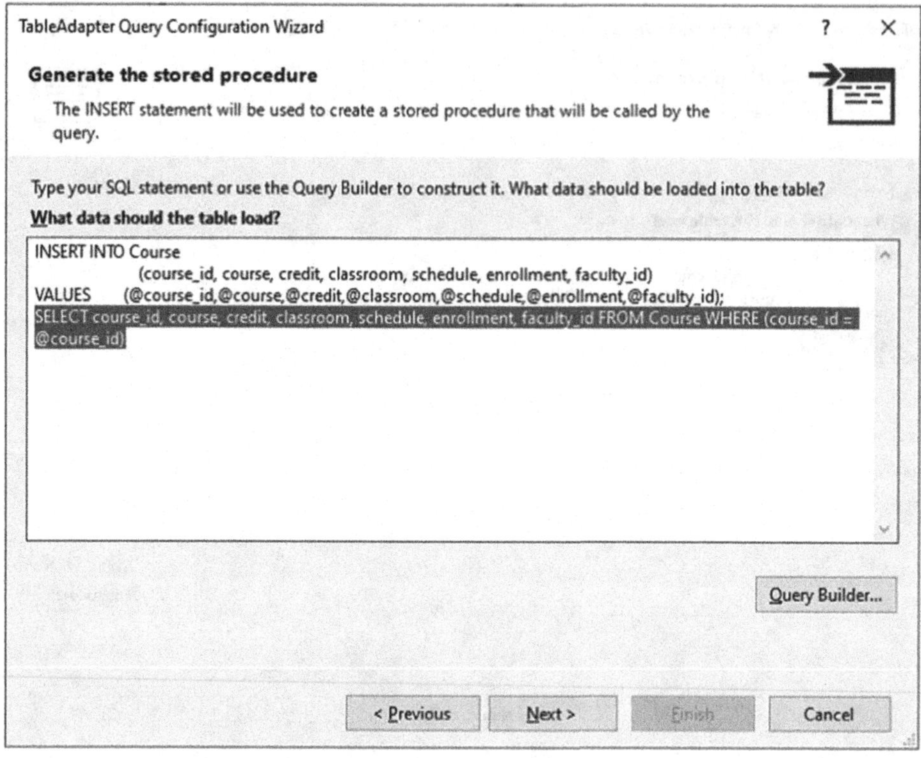

FIGURE 6.23 The data insertion confirmation wizard.

5) The default query includes a **SELECT … FROM** statement and it is used to select the desired columns from this **Course** table and insert those columns to another target table. Here we only need to insert a record into the **Course** table without any other target table, so just highlight the second **SELECT** statement and delete it by pressing the **Delete** key from your keyboard.
6) Click on the **Next** button to go to the next wizard.
7) On the next wizard, enter **InsertCourseSP** into the name box as the name of this query stored procedure. Click on **Next** and then **Finish** for the following wizards to finish and close this process.

Next let's build the codes for the **Insert** button's Click method of the Course Form to perform this data insertion action.

6.3.4 Build the Codes for the Insert Button's Click Method

Open the **Insert** button's Click method from the Course Form window and add the codes that are shown in Figure 6.24 into this method.

Let's have a closer look at these codes to see how they work.

A. Some local objects and variables are generated first, which include two integer variables, **check** and **intInsert**. The former is used as a holder to hold the running result of one of user-defined methods, **CheckCourseInfo()** that will be built later, and the latter also works as a holder to hold the running result of the query stored procedure **InsertCourseSP()** that was built in the last section. A new **CourseRow** object, **newCourseRow**, and a **FacultyTableAdapter** object **FacultyTableApt**, are declared here since we need to use them later to perform related queries.

```
SelectWizard Project                    cmdInsert_Click(object sender, EventArgs e)

  private void cmdInsert_Click(object sender, EventArgs e)
  {
A     int check = 0, intInsert = 0;
      CSE_DEPTDataSet.CourseRow newCourseRow;
      CSE_DEPTDataSetTableAdapters.FacultyTableAdapter FacultyTableApt =
                  new CSE_DEPTDataSetTableAdapters.FacultyTableAdapter();
B     InitCourseInfo();
C     check = CheckCourseInfo();
D     if (check == 0)
      {
        FacultyTableApt.ClearBeforeFill = true;
E       strFacultyID = FacultyTableApt.FindFacultyIDByName(ComboName.Text);
F       if (ComboMethod.Text == "TableAdapter Insert")
        {
          intInsert = courseTableAdapter.InsertCourse(txtCourseID.Text, txtCourseName.Text,
          Convert.ToInt16(txtCredits.Text), txtClassRoom.Text, txtSchedule.Text, int.Parse(txtEnroll.Text), strFacultyID);
        }
G       else if (ComboMethod.Text == "TableAdapter Update")
        {
          newCourseRow = cSE_DEPTDataSet.Course.NewCourseRow();
H         newCourseRow = InsertCourseRow(ref newCourseRow);
I         cSE_DEPTDataSet.Course.Rows.Add(newCourseRow);
          intInsert = courseTableAdapter.Update(cSE_DEPTDataSet.Course);
        }
J       else           // stored procedure method is selected
          intInsert = courseTableAdapter.InsertCourseSP(txtCourseID.Text, txtCourseName.Text,
                                   Convert.ToInt16(txtCredits.Text), txtClassRoom.Text, txtSchedule.Text,
                                   Convert.ToInt16(txtEnroll.Text), strFacultyID);
K       if (intInsert != 0)                   // data insertion is successful
        {
          ClearCourse();                      // clean up all faculty information
          cmdInsert.Enabled = false;          // disable the Insert button
        }
L       else
        {
          MessageBox.Show("The course insertion is failed");
          cmdInsert.Enabled = true;
        }
      }
M     else
        MessageBox.Show("Fill all Course Information box, enter a NULL for any blank column");
  }
```

FIGURE 6.24 The codes for the insert button's click method.

B. A user-defined method, **InitCourseInfo()** that will be built later, is executed to initialize and build a **CourseInfo[]** array, which is a class-level array variable declared in Figure 6.20, to facilitate the pre-checking and post-checking of this data insertion action later.

C. Another user-defined method, **CheckCourseInfo()** that will be built later, is called to check and make sure that all TextBoxes in the Course Form have been filled with a valid value to be inserted into the **Course** table. The running result is assigned to the local integer variable **check**.

D. If the running result is 0, which means that all TextBoxes have been filled with valid values, the data insertion will be performed. First the FacultyTableAdapter object, **FacultyTableApt**, is cleaned up to avoid any duplicated insertion. The reason why we used this FacultyTableAdapter is that we need to use one of query methods, **FindFacultyIDByName()** we built in Section 5.12 in Chapter 5 since there is no **faculty_name** column available in the **Course** table, and the only available column is **faculty_id**. Thus we need to get a matched **faculty_id** based on the selected **faculty_name** by the users in this Course Form.

E. Then the query method **FindFacultyIDByName()** that belongs to the FacultyTableAdapter is executed to get a matched **faculty_id** based on the selected faculty name. The retrieved **faculty_id** is reserved to a class-level String variable **strFacultyID** for future usage.
F. If the **TableAdapter Insert** method is selected, the query method **InsertCourse()** we built in Section 6.3.2 is executed to insert a new course record by picking up six pieces of new course information from six TextBoxes in this Course Form with the queried **faculty_id**.
G. Alternatively, if the **TableAdapter Update** method is selected, a new CourseRow object, **newCourseRow**, is generated.
H. Then the generated **newCourseRow** is inserted into the **Course** table via a user-defined method, **InsertCourseRow()** that will be built later. A point to be noted is that both the input argument and the returned object look identical, but they are different. The key is that the input argument is a reference object and it should be executed first. Therefore the returned object is a running result of this method.
I. The finished **newCourseRow** cannot be exactly inserted into the **Course** table until the following two methods, **Add()** and **Update()**, are executed.
J. If the **Stored Procedure** method is selected, the query made by a stored procedure **InsertCourseSP()** we built in Section 6.3.3 is executed to insert a new course record into the **Course** table. One point to be noted is the data types for columns **Credits** and **Enrollment**. The former is a short integer (two bytes) but the latter is a normal integer (four bytes). Therefore, an appropriate conversion method should be used.
K. For any insertion method, if it returns a non-zero value, which means that the data insertion is successful and at least one row has been inserted into the database, another user-defined method, **ClearCourse()** that will be built later, is called to cleanup all six TextBoxes in this Course Form to enable users to perform some checking and confirming jobs for that insertion. In addition, the **Insert** button is disabled to avoid any possible duplicated insertion for the same record.
L. Otherwise, if any insertion method returns a zero, which means that the data insertion is failed, a MessageBox with a warning message is displayed to indicate that case, and the **Insert** button is enabled to allow users to perform next insertion.
M. If the **CheckCourseInfo()** method returns a non-zero value, which means that some TextBoxes may be not filled with valid values, a MessageBox with a warning message is displayed to indicate that case.

Next let's continue to finish the building of the codes for all user-defined methods used in that **Insert** button's Click method. In total, we have four user-defined methods that need to be coded:

- InitCourseInfo()
- CheckCourseInfo()
- InsertCourseRow()
- ClearCourse()

Let's start from the first one, **InitCourseInfo()**.

6.3.5 Build the Codes for Four User-Defined Methods

The function of the method **InitCourseInfo()** is to combine all six TextBoxes in the Course Form window into a single text or a String array **CourseInfo[]**. With the help of this text array, one can access and edit each piece of information stored in a related TextBox easily.

Open the code window of the Course Form window and enter the codes shown in Figure 6.25 into this window. All six TextBoxes are assigned to a class-level string array **CourseInfo[]**, which makes it easier to be accessed and modified later.

```
SelectWizard Project                    InitCourseInfo()

private void InitCourseInfo()
{
    CourseInfo[0] = txtCourseID.Text;
    CourseInfo[1] = txtCourseName.Text;
    CourseInfo[2] = txtSchedule.Text;
    CourseInfo[3] = txtClassRoom.Text;
    CourseInfo[4] = txtCredits.Text;
    CourseInfo[5] = txtEnroll.Text;
}
```

FIGURE 6.25 The detailed codes for the method InitCourseInfo().

```
SelectWizard Project                    CheckCourseInfo()

private int CheckCourseInfo()
{
    int pos = 0, check = 0;
    for (pos = 0; pos < 6; pos++)
    {
        if (CourseInfo[pos] == string.Empty)
            check++;
    }
    return check;
}
```

FIGURE 6.26 The codes for the method CheckCourseInfo().

In the same opened code window of the Course Form, enter the codes that are shown in Figure 6.26 into that window as the body of the method **CheckCourseInfo()**.

The function of this method is straightforward. Two local integer variables, **pos** and **check**, are generated first. The former works as a loop counter and the latter is used as a returned indicator to indicate the running status of execution of this method. A **for()** loop is used to check each TextBox to see whether any of them is empty. If anyone is empty, which means that the user may have forgotten to fill it, the returned variable **check** is increased by 1 to indicate this error. Otherwise a zero is returned to indicate that this method is executed successfully.

Next let's take care of the third method, **InsertCourseRow()**. Open the code window of the Course Form and enter the codes shown in Figure 6.27 into this window. Let's have a closer look at the codes inside this method to see how they work.

A. The returned variable of this method and the argument passed into this method are **CourseRow** objects. In fact, the argument has a reference as its data type, which means that any modification or change to this object will be returned to the calling method. Thus, we may not need to use returned variable from this method; instead we can directly use the argument. To make things clear, here we still used the returned variable.

B. All seven pieces of new inserted course information are initialized by assigning the contents of six TextBoxes and queried **faculty_id**.

C. The data type for the **credit** column is a short integer, and thus a conversion is needed to convert the Text to a short integer value.

D. Similarly, a conversion from a Text to an integer for the **enrollment** column is performed to match the data type used for that column in our sample database.

E. Lastly, the initialized **CourseRow** object is returned.

```
SelectWizard Project                                  InsertCourseRow()

A  private CSE_DEPTDataSet.CourseRow InsertCourseRow(ref CSE_DEPTDataSet.CourseRow courseRow)
   {
B      courseRow.faculty_id = strFacultyID;
       courseRow.course_id = txtCourseID.Text;
       courseRow.course = txtCourseName.Text;
       courseRow.schedule = txtSchedule.Text;
       courseRow.classroom = txtClassRoom.Text;
C      courseRow.credit = short.Parse(txtCredits.Text);
D      courseRow.enrollment = int.Parse(txtEnroll.Text);

E      return courseRow;
   }
```

FIGURE 6.27 The codes for the method InsertCourseRow().

```
SelectWizard Project                                  ClearCourse()

   private void ClearCourse()
   {
A          int index;
           TextBox[] cBox = {txtCourseID, txtCourseName, txtCredits, txtClassRoom, txtSchedule, txtEnroll};

B          for (index = 0; index < cBox.Length; index++)
              cBox[index].Text = "";
   }
```

FIGURE 6.28 The detailed codes for the method ClearCourse().

Finally, let's handle the codes for the method **ClearCourse()**. On the opened code window of the Course Form, enter the codes that are shown in Figure 6.28 into this window as the body for this method.

The function of this method is to clean up the contents of all six TextBoxes after a data insertion action is finished to enable users to check and confirm that data insertion.

Let's have a closer look at this piece of codes to see how it works.

A. First some local variables, including an integer and a TextBox array, **index** and **cBox[]**, are declared. The former works as a loop counter and the latter is used as a container to hold all six TextBoxes objects.

B. A **for()** loop is used to setup an zero-length or an empty string to the **Text** property of each TextBox to make it empty.

Before we can run and test our project, the last coding job is for the **TextChanged** event method for the **Insert** button. As we discussed above, if a new course record has been successfully inserted into the **Course** table, the **Insert** button will be disabled to avoid any possible duplicated insertion for the same record. However, when another new course needs to be inserted, a new **course_id** must be first inserted into this Course ID TextBox. This will trigger the occurrence of a **TextChanged** event of the Course ID TextBox. In that case, the **Insert** button should be enabled to allow users to do that new insertion action. To do this coding job, just double-click on the Course ID TextBox on the Designer View of the Course Form window to open that method, and enter **cmdInsert.Enabled = True**; into that method.

At this point, we have completed all coding jobs to perform a new course record insertion function for this Course Form window.

Now let's run the project to test to insert data using three different methods, **TableAdapter Insert**, **TableAdapter Update**, and the stored procedures. We need to use three sample course records as new course records to test our project.

Click on the **Run** button to run our project, complete the login process by entering a matched username and password, such as **jhenry** and **test**, and select the **Course Information** from the Selection Form to open the Course Form window. Keep the default faculty member **Ying Bai** and select the **TableAdapter Insert** method from the **Query Method** combobox, and enter the following data as a new course record into six TextBoxes:

Course ID:	**CSE-548**
Course Name:	**Fuzzy Logic Designs**
Schedule:	**M-W-F: 9:00-9:50 AM**
Classroom:	**MTC-309**
Credits:	**3**
Enrollment:	**18**

Click on the **Insert** button to perform this data insertion action. Immediately, all six TextBoxes become blank to indicate that our data insertion is successful.

To check and confirm this insertion action, just click on the **Select** button to try to retrieve back that new inserted course. All courses taught by the faculty member **Ying Bai** are retrieved back and displayed in the CourseList box, as shown in Figure 6.29. Click on the new course **CSE-548** from the CourseList box; all detailed information for that course is shown up in six TextBoxes, as shown in Figure 6.29.

One can use the following two sets of data as two new course records to test the **TableAdapter Update** and stored procedure methods, respectively.

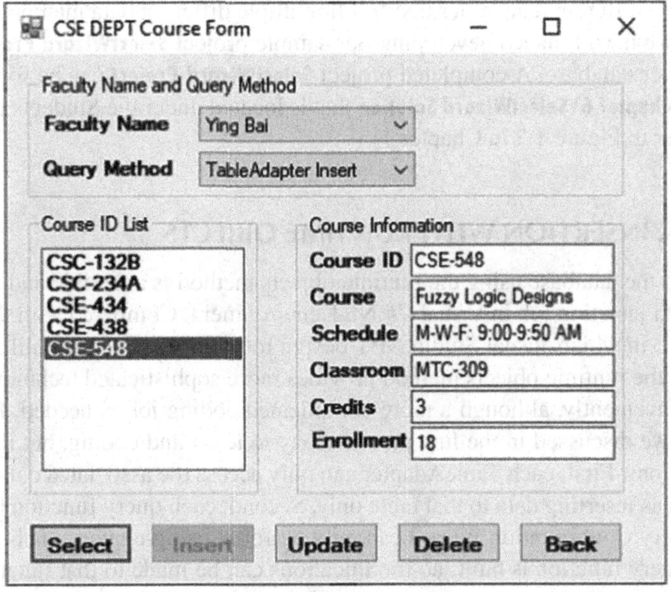

FIGURE 6.29 The new inserted course CSE-548.

To test the **TableAdapter Update** method, select this method from the **Query Method** combobox and enter the following data as a new course record:

Course ID:	**CSE-520**
Course Name:	**AdvancedFuzzy Designs**
Schedule:	**T-H:1:30-2:45 PM**
Classroom:	**MTC-109**
Credits:	**4**
Enrollment:	**25**

To test the **Stored Procedure** method, select this method from the **Query Method** combobox and enter the following data as a new course record:

Course ID:	**CSE-534**
Course Name:	**Neural Networks**
Schedule:	**T-H: 9:30-10:45 AM**
Classroom:	**MTC-114**
Credits:	**3**
Enrollment:	**28**

It can be found that there is no difference between calling a query function and calling a stored procedure to perform this data insertion. That is indeed true for this data action because the stored procedure is exactly a function or a collection of functions used to perform some special functionality or functionalities. However, we cannot create a stored procedure that can be used to perform multiple data actions to the multiple different data tables by using the TableAdapter Query Configuration Wizard since each TableAdapter can only access the associated data table. To insert data into the database using the run time object method, which we will discuss in Part II, one stored procedure can access multiple different data tables and fulfill multiple different data manipulation operations.

At this point, we have finished developing our sample project **SelectWizard Project** to insert data into the SQL Server database. A completed project **SelectWizard Project** can be found from a folder **Class DB Projects\Chapter 6\SelectWizard Solution** that is located under the Students folder at the CRC Press ftp site (refer to Figure 1.2 in Chapter 1).

PART II DATA INSERTION WITH RUNTIME OBJECTS

Inserting data into the database using the runtime objects method is a flexible and professional way to perform the data insertion job in Visual C#.NET environment. Compared with those methods we discussed in Part I, in which Visual Studio.NET design tools and wizards are utilized to insert data into the database, the runtime objects method provides more sophisticated techniques to do this job efficiently and conveniently, although a more complicated coding job is needed. Relatively speaking, the methods we discussed in the first part are easy to learn and coding, but these methods did have some limitations. First, each TableAdapter can only access the associated data table to perform data actions, such as inserting data to that table only. Second, each query function built by using the TableAdapter Query Configuration Wizard can only perform a single query, such as data selection. Third, after the query function is built, no modifications can be made to that function dynamically, which means that the only times that the query function can be modified are either before the project runs or after the project terminates. In other words, you cannot modify that query function during the project run.

To overcome those shortcomings, we will discuss how to insert data using the runtime object method in this part. Three sections are covered in this part: inserting data using the general runtime object method is discussed first. Inserting data into the database using the LINQ to DataSet and LINQ to SQL queries is introduced in the second section. Inserting data using the stored procedures is presented in the third part.

Generally, you need to use the TableAdapter to perform data actions again the database if you developed your applications using the Visual Studio.NET design tools and wizards in the design time. However, you should use the DataAdapter to make those data manipulations if you developed your projects using the run time objects method.

6.4 THE GENERAL RUNTIME OBJECTS METHOD

We have provided a very detailed introduction and discussion about the runtime objects method in Section 5.14 in Chapter 5. Refer to that section to get more detailed information about this method. For your convenience, we highlight some important points and general methodology of this method as well as some keynotes in using this method to perform the data actions again the databases.

As you know, ADO.NET provides different classes to help users to develop professional data-driven applications by using the different methods to perform specific data actions such as inserting data, updating data and deleting data. For the data insertion, two popular methods are widely applied:

1) Add new records into the desired data table in the DataSet, and then call the **DataAdapter.Update()** method to update the new added records from the table in the DataSet to the table in the database.
2) Build the **INSERT** command using the Command object, and then call the command's method **ExecuteNonQuery()** to insert new records into the database. Or you can assign the built command object to the **InsertCommand** property of the DataAdapter and call the **ExecuteNonQuery()** method from the **InsertCommand** property.

The first method is to use the so-called DataSet-DataAdapter method to build a data-driven application. DataSet and DataTable classes can have different roles when they are implemented in a real application. Multiple DataTables can be embedded into a DataSet and each table can be filled, inserted, updated and deleted by using the different properties of a DataAdapter such as the **SelectCommand, InsertCommand, UpdateCommand** or **DeleteCommand** when the DataAdapter's **Update()** method is executed.

The DataAdapter will perform the associated operations based on the modifications you made for each table in the DataSet. For example, if you add new rows into a table in the DataSet, and then you call this DataAdapter's **Update()** method. This will perform an **InsertCommand** based on your modifications. The **DeleteCommand** will be executed if you delete rows from the table in the DataSet and call this **Update()** method. This method is relatively simple since you do not need to call some specific methods such as the **ExecuteNonQuery**() to complete these data queries. But this simplicity brings some limitations for your applications. For instance, you cannot access different data tables individually to perform multiple specific data operations. This method is very similar to the second method we discussed in Part I, so we will not continue to provide any discussion for this method in this part.

The second method is to allow you to use each object individually, which means that you do not have to use the DataAdapter to access the Command object, or use the DataTable with DataSet together. This provides more flexibility. In this method, no DataAdapter or DataSet is needed, and you only need to create a new Command object with a new Connection object, and then build a query statement and attach some useful parameter into that query for the new created Command object. You can insert data into any data table by calling the **ExecuteNonQuery()** method that belongs to the Command class. We will concentrate on this method in this part.

In this section, we provide a sample project named **RTOInsert Project** to illustrate how to insert new records into a SQL Server database using the runtime object method.

Now let's start to build the sample project **RTOInsert Project** to insert data into the SQL Server database using the runtime object method. Recall in Sections 5.15.5, 5.15.6 and 5.16.3 in Chapter 5, we discussed how to select data for the Faculty, Course and Student Form windows using the runtime object method. For the Faculty Form, a regular runtime selecting query is performed, and for the Course Form, a runtime joined-table selecting query is developed. For the Student table, the stored procedures are used to perform the runtime data query.

We will concentrate on inserting data to the **Faculty** table from the Faculty Form window using the runtime object method in this part.

In order to avoid the duplication on the coding process, we will modify an existing project named **RTOSelect Project** we developed in Chapter 5 to create our new project RTOInsert Project used in this section.

6.5 INSERT DATA INTO THE SQL SERVER DATABASE USING THE RUN TIME OBJECT METHOD

Open the Windows Explorer and create a new folder **C:\Chapter 6** if you have not yet done so. Then browse the folder **Class DB Projects\Chapter 5\RTOSelect Solution** that is located under the **Students** folder at the CRC Press ftp site, and copy the entire solution **RTOSelect Solution** to our new folder **C:\Chapter 6**. Perform the following operational steps to make that copied solution as our new solution and project:

1) Change the names of the solution and the project from **RTOSelect Solution** to **RTOInsert Solution**, and **RTOSelect Project** to **RTOInsert Project**.
2) Change the project file name from **RTOSelect Project.csproj** to **RTOInsert Project.csproj**. Double-click on the **RTOInsert Project.csproj** to open this project.

On the opened project, perform the following modifications to get our desired project:

1) Go to **Project | RTOInsert Project Properties** menu item to open the project's property window. Change the **Assembly name** from **RTOSelect Project** to **RTOInsert Project** and the **Default namespace** from **RTOSelect_Project** to **RTOInsert_Project**, respectively.
2) Click on the **Assembly Information** button to open the Assembly Information wizard, change the **Title** and the **Product** to **RTOInsert Project**. Click on the **OK** button to close this wizard.
3) Change the **Startup object** from **RTOSelect_Project.Program** to **(Not set)**.
4) Go to the **File | Save All** menu item to save those modifications. Click on the **Save** button on the opened File Explorer window and **Overwrite** and **Save** button to save this project.
5) Now right-click on the **LogIn.cs** folder in the Solution Explorer window and select the **View Code** item to open the code window for this **LogIn.cs** class file.
6) Change its namespace from the original **RTOSelect_Project** to our new namespace, **RTOInsert_Project**.
7) Open the **LogIn.designer.cs** file by double-clicking on it from the Solution Explorer window (you need to expand the **LogIn.cs** folder to find this file).
8) Change the top line from the original namespace **RTOSelect_Project** to our current namespace, **RTOInsert_Project**.
9) Repeat steps 5–7 above for all other files, such as **Faculty.cs**, **Course.cs**, **Selection.cs** and **Student.cs**, to change the namespaces for all of those files.

10) Now open the main file, **C# Program.cs**, from the Solution Explorer window by double-clicking on that file, and change its namespace to **RTOInsert_Project**.

Go to the **File | Save All** menu item again to save those modifications. Now you can build the project to confirm those modifications by going to the menu item **Build | Build Solution**. A 'building successful' message should be displayed in the **Output** window.

Now we are ready to develop the codes our new project to perform data insertions. The coding process for this data insertion is divided into three steps;

1) The data validation before the data insertion.
2) The data validation after the data insertion.
3) The data insertion using the run time object method.

The purpose of the first step is to confirm that all inserted data that stored in each associated TextBox should be complete and valid. In other words, all TextBoxes should be non-empty. The second step is used to confirm that the data insertion is successful, in other words, the new inserted data should be in the desired table in the database and can be read back and displayed in the related Form window.

Unlike the returned-data query such as SELECT, in which a system query method Fill() is executed to try to open a new database connection if no any valid connection is existed between the database and the application, all non-returned data queries such as INSERT, UPDATE and DELETE do not have this functionality to open a new connection between the database and the application if no any valid connection is existed. Therefore the user must develop codes to provide this kind of functionality to those non-returned data queries.

In this section, we want to use the Faculty Form to perform data insertion to the **Faculty** table in our sample database. Let's start from the first step.

6.5.1 The Coding Process for the Data Validation before the Data Insertion

This data validation can be considered as a pre-validation and can be performed by calling two user-defined methods. The first method is **InitFacultyInfo()** and it is used to set up a mapping relationship between each item in the string array **FacultyInfo[]** and each TextBox stored the faculty information. The second method is **CheckFacultyInfo()** and it is used to scan and check all TextBoxes to make sure that no one of them is empty.

Open the code window of the Faculty Form, and enter the codes that are shown in Figure 6.30 to create two user-defined methods, **InitFacultyInfo()** and **CheckFacultyInfo()**.

Let's have a closer look at this piece of codes to see how it works.

A. A class-level string array, **FacultyInfo[]**, is added into this class and this array can be used to store all seven TextBoxes stored a new inserted faculty record.

B. Inside the user-defined method, **InitFacultyInfo()**, All seven TextBoxes stored a new faculty record are assigned to the **FacultyInfo[]** array, which is a zero-based string array that starts its index from 0. In this way, it is easier for us to scan and check each of the TextBoxes to make sure that no one of them is empty later.

C. Inside the user-defined method, **CheckFacultyInfo()**, a **for** loop is used to scan each TextBox in the **FacultyInfo[]** string array to check whether any of them is empty. A message will be displayed if this situation happened and the checking status is returned to allow user to fill up all TextBoxes.

```
RTOInsert Project                    FacultyInfo()

  public partial class FacultyForm : Form
  {
     LogInForm loginForm = new LogInForm();
A    string[] FacultyInfo = new string[7];
     .........
B private void InitFacultyInfo()
  {
       FacultyInfo[0] = txtFacultyID.Text;
       FacultyInfo[1] = txtFacultyName.Text;
       FacultyInfo[2] = txtTitle.Text;
       FacultyInfo[3] = txtOffice.Text;
       FacultyInfo[4] = txtPhone.Text;
       FacultyInfo[5] = txtCollege.Text;
       FacultyInfo[6] = txtEmail.Text;
  }
C private int CheckFacultyInfo()
  {
       int pos = 0, check = 0;
       for (pos = 0; pos <= 6; pos++)
       {
           if (FacultyInfo[pos] == string.Empty)
              check++;
       }
       return check;
  }
```

FIGURE 6.30 The codes for the InitFacultyInfo() and CheckFacultyInfo().

Now let's develop the codes for the data validation process after a new record has been inserted into the **Faculty** table in our sample database.

6.5.2 The Coding Process for the Data Validation after the Data Insertion

After a new record has been inserted into the **Faculty** table in our sample database, we need to check and confirm whether that data insertion is successful or not. Fortunately, we do not need to create any new method to do that confirmation; instead we can use the **Select** button with its Click method to do that checking. But we need to update all faculty names stored in the Faculty Name combobox, **ComboName**, to enable users to select the desired or the newly inserted faculty member to do that checking. Thus, we need to build a new method **CurrentFaculty()** in our project to do that job.

On the opened Code Window of the Faculty Form, enter the codes that are shown in Figure 6.31 into that window. Let's have a closer look at this piece of code to see how it works.

A. First a **SQLDataReader** object, **sqlReader**, is declared since we like to use the Data Reader method to get all current faculty names.

B. A database connection object, **conn**, is initialized by assigning the Connection object, **sqlConnection**, which is created in the LogIn Form class.

C. Then a SQLCommand object, **sqlCommand**, is generated and initialized with a query string and the connection object. To make things simple, here we directly use this kind of initialization method to make this query shorter.

D. The **sqlCommand** is executed by calling its **ExecuteReader()** method, and the query result is stored to the **sqlReader** object.

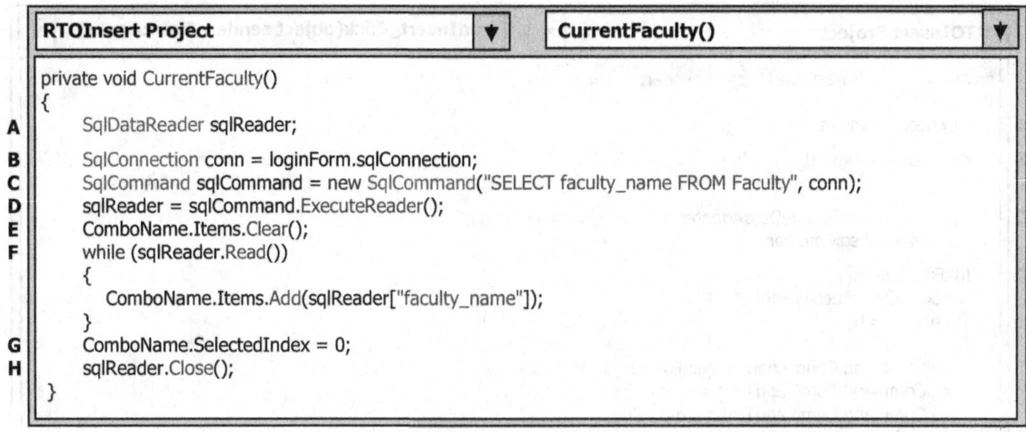

RTOInsert Project | CurrentFaculty()

```
  private void CurrentFaculty()
  {
A       SqlDataReader sqlReader;
B       SqlConnection conn = loginForm.sqlConnection;
C       SqlCommand sqlCommand = new SqlCommand("SELECT faculty_name FROM Faculty", conn);
D       sqlReader = sqlCommand.ExecuteReader();
E       ComboName.Items.Clear();
F       while (sqlReader.Read())
        {
          ComboName.Items.Add(sqlReader["faculty_name"]);
        }
G       ComboName.SelectedIndex = 0;
H       sqlReader.Close();
  }
```

FIGURE 6.31 The codes for the method CurrentFaculty().

E. Before we can retrieve all queried faculty names and add them into the combobox, **ComboName**, we need to clean up that combobox to make it ready.

F. A **while()** loop is used with the **sqlReader.Read()** method as its condition to scan and read out all queried faculty names one by one, and add each of them into the combobox, **ComboName**. An issue is that one can use either the column name or the column index for the **sqlReader** object to get each faculty name.

G. By resetting the **SelectedIndex** property to zero, the first added faculty name can be selected as the default one and displayed in the top of the combobox.

H. Finally the **sqlReader** is closed by using the **Close()** method.

Now let's develop the codes for the **Insert** button's Click method to call those two methods to perform the data validation, and then perform the data insertion action.

6.5.3 The Coding Process for the Data Insertion Action

Now open the **Insert** button's Click method by double-clicking on it from the Faculty Form window, and enter the codes that are shown in Figure 6.32 into this method.

The function of this piece of code is straightforward and easy to be understood. First, the user-defined method **InitFacultyInfo()** is called to set up the mapping relationship between each item in the string array **FacultyInfo[]** and each TextBox. Then another user-defined method, **CheckFacultyInfo()**,is executed to check and make sure that no one TextBox is empty. If any of the TextBoxes is empty, this method returns a non-zero value to allow users to re-fill any missed information to the associated TextBoxes until all of them are non-empty. Let's have a look at this piece of code to see how it works.

A. Two local integer variables, **check** and **intInsert**, are created first. The former is used as a status holder for the running result of our user-defined method **CheckFacultyInfo()** to be executed later and the latter works as a status holder for the running a system method **ExecuteNonQuery()** later.

B. The insert query string is declared with eight pieces of new faculty information to be inserted into the **Faculty** table in our sample database.

C. Some data components used to perform the data insertion are declared here, including the **SqlDataAdapter** and **SqlCommand** objects.

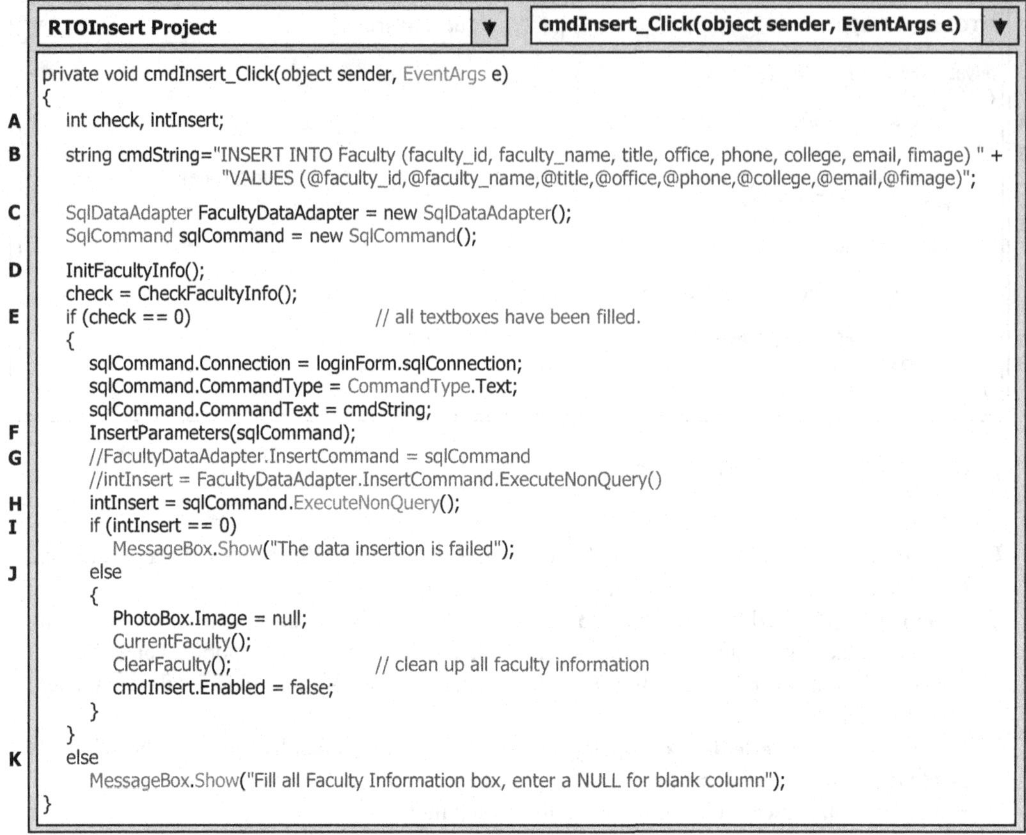

```
RTOInsert Project        cmdInsert_Click(object sender, EventArgs e)

  private void cmdInsert_Click(object sender, EventArgs e)
  {
A    int check, intInsert;
B    string cmdString="INSERT INTO Faculty (faculty_id, faculty_name, title, office, phone, college, email, fimage) " +
                      "VALUES (@faculty_id,@faculty_name,@title,@office,@phone,@college,@email,@fimage)";
C    SqlDataAdapter FacultyDataAdapter = new SqlDataAdapter();
     SqlCommand sqlCommand = new SqlCommand();
D    InitFacultyInfo();
     check = CheckFacultyInfo();
E    if (check == 0)                    // all textboxes have been filled.
     {
        sqlCommand.Connection = loginForm.sqlConnection;
        sqlCommand.CommandType = CommandType.Text;
        sqlCommand.CommandText = cmdString;
F       InsertParameters(sqlCommand);
G       //FacultyDataAdapter.InsertCommand = sqlCommand
        //intInsert = FacultyDataAdapter.InsertCommand.ExecuteNonQuery()
H       intInsert = sqlCommand.ExecuteNonQuery();
I       if (intInsert == 0)
           MessageBox.Show("The data insertion is failed");
J       else
        {
           PhotoBox.Image = null;
           CurrentFaculty();
           ClearFaculty();              // clean up all faculty information
           cmdInsert.Enabled = false;
        }
     }
K    else
        MessageBox.Show("Fill all Faculty Information box, enter a NULL for blank column");
  }
```

FIGURE 6.32 The completed codes for the insert button click method.

D. Two user-defined methods, **InitFacultyInfo()** and **CheckFacultyInfo()**, are executed to setup a mapping between each element in the class-level string array **FacultyInfo[]** and each TextBox stored a new faculty record in this Faculty Form, and check whether all TextBoxes have been filled with valid values.

E. If the returned **check** is zero, which means that all TextBoxes have been filled with valid values, the Command object is initialized with the related properties, such as Connection, CommandType and CommandText properties of the Command class. A point to be noted is that we do not need to create any new connection, instead we can use a class-level Connection object generated in the LogIn Form class.

F. Another user-defined method, **InsertParameters()**, which will be built later, is called to add eight pieces of new faculty information into the Properties of the Command object.

G. These two instructions are used to perform this data insertion with another method, the **DataAdapter Method**. Both of them have been commented out to concentrate our data insertion with the **ExecuteNonQuery()** method shown below. This method provides the same function as the **ExecuteNonQuery()** method.

H. The data insertion function is executed by calling the **ExecuteNonQuery()** method to physically insert this new record into the Faculty table in our sample database. The running result of execution of that method is returned and assigned to our local integer variable **intInsert**.

I. If the returned value of **intInsert** is zero, which means that the data insertion is failed with no any data row being inserted. A MessageBox is displayed with a warning message to indicate that case.

J. Otherwise our data insertion is successful, and some cleaning jobs are performed to clear all TextBoxes and a **PhotoBox** in the Faculty Form. The user-defined method **CurrentFaculty()** is executed to get back all current faculty names, including the newly inserted one, and add them into the Faculty Name combobox, **ComboName**, to enable users to perform a checking or confirmation job later. The **Insert** button is disabled to avoid any possible duplicated inserting action.

K. If the integer variable check returns a non-zero value, which means that some TextBoxes have not been filled with valid values, a MessageBox is displayed with a warning message to indicate that case.

Now let's take care of some user-defined methods used in that **Insert** button's Click method, which include the method **InsertParameters()**, **ClearFaculty()** and **getFacultyImage()**. The first one is used to add all pieces of new inserting faculty information into the **Parameters** properties of the Command object to complete the configuration of the Command object, and the second one works as a cleaning method to clean the contents of all TextBoxes stored a new faculty record to be inserted into the **Faculty** table in our sample database. The third method is used to get a selected faculty image by the user.

The detailed codes for the user-defined method **InsertParameters()** are shown in Figure 6.33. On the opened code window of the Faculty Form, enter this piece of codes to make this method available.

The function of this piece of codes is easy, first a byte[] array, **bImage**, is generated and this array is used to hold a faculty image selected by the user and to be inserted into the database. Then the user-defined method **getFacultyImage()** is called to get a selected faculty image and assign it to the byte[] array **bImage**. The reason to use this kind of byte[] format for that image is because this is the requirement to store an image in the SQL Server database.

Next, each piece of faculty-related information stored on the associated TextBox is assigned to each matched parameter by using the **Add()** method. One point to be noted is that the @ symbol must be prefixed before each parameter since this is the requirement of the SQL Server database operations.

Now, remaining in the opened code window, enter the codes shown in Figure 6.34 into that window to get the second method, **ClearFaculty()**. To clean up all TextBoxes in this Faculty Form, first a local variable **index** is generated and it works as a loop counter for a **for()** loop shown below. A TextBox array **fBox[]** is created by adding all TextBoxes into that array. Then each TextBox stored in that array is cleaned up by assigning a zero-length or an empty string to the **Text** property of each of them with the help of the **for()** loop. The **fBox.Length** property value works as the upper bound for that loop.

Finally, let's take care of the getFacultyImage() method. On the opened code window of the Faculty Form window, enter the codes that are shown in Figure 6.35 into that window as the coding body of that method.

RTOInsert Project	InsertParameters(SqlCommand cmd)

```
private void InsertParameters(SqlCommand cmd)
{
    byte[] bImage = null;

    bImage = getFacultyImage();
    cmd.Parameters.Add("@faculty_id", SqlDbType.Char).Value = txtFacultyID.Text;
    cmd.Parameters.Add("@faculty_name", SqlDbType.Char).Value = txtFacultyName.Text;
    cmd.Parameters.Add("@office", SqlDbType.Char).Value = txtOffice.Text;
    cmd.Parameters.Add("@phone", SqlDbType.Char).Value = txtPhone.Text;
    cmd.Parameters.Add("@college", SqlDbType.Char).Value = txtCollege.Text;
    cmd.Parameters.Add("@title", SqlDbType.Char).Value = txtTitle.Text;
    cmd.Parameters.Add("@email", SqlDbType.Char).Value = txtEmail.Text;
    cmd.Parameters.Add("@fimage", SqlDbType.Binary).Value = bImage;
}
```

FIGURE 6.33 The codes for the user-defined method InsertParameters().

RTOInsert Project	ClearFaculty()

```
private void ClearFaculty()
{
    int index;
    TextBox[] fBox = {txtFacultyID, txtFacultyName, txtTitle, txtOffice, txtPhone, txtCollege, txtEmail};
    for (index = 0; index < fBox.Length; index++)
       fBox[index].Text = "";
}
```

FIGURE 6.34 The detailed codes for the method ClearFaculty().

RTOInsert Project	getFacultyImage()

```
  private byte[] getFacultyImage()
  {
A     MemoryStream ms = new MemoryStream();
      OpenFileDialog dlg = new OpenFileDialog();
      byte[] bimage = null;
B     dlg.Filter = "JPG Files (*.jpg)|*.jpg|All Files (*.*)|*.*";
      dlg.Title = "Select the Faculty Image";
C     if (dlg.ShowDialog() == DialogResult.OK)
      {
         PhotoBox.Image = Image.FromFile(dlg.FileName);
         PhotoBox.Image.Save(ms, PhotoBox.Image.RawFormat);
D        bimage = ms.ToArray();
      }
E     return bimage;
  }
```

FIGURE 6.35 The codes for the method getFacultyImage().

Let's have a closer look at this piece of codes to see how it works.

A. Some local objects are first declared, including a MemoryStream class and an OpenFileDialog class objects, **ms** and **dlg**. The former is used as an intermediate translation image variable array and the latter provides a File Dialog to enable users to select a desired faculty image to be inserted into our database. A byte[] array variable **bimage** is also generated and it works as a returned image array since the only data type used to store an image in a SQL Server database is byte[].

B. The OpenFileDialog class object **dlg** is initialized with the Filter and Title properties. The former is used to define the image type to be selected and the latter provides a title for that dialog.

C. If the system method **ShowDialog()** is executed successfully, which returns a system constant, **DialogResult.OK**, it means that the OpenFileDialog is opened successfully and the user has selected a valid faculty image. First, that selected image is read out by using the **FromFile()** method and assigned to the **Image** property of the Faculty Image control, **PhotoBox**, in the Faculty Form window, and then that image is converted to the MemoryStream format and saved to the MemoryStream class object **ms** via the system method **Save()**.

D. Finally, that converted image is further to be converted to a byte array via the **ToArray()** method.

E. The converted image array is returned to the calling method.

RTOInsert Project	txtFacultyID_TextChanged()

```
private void txtFacultyID_TextChanged(object sender, EventArgs e)
{
        cmdInsert.Enabled = true;
}
```

FIGURE 6.36 The codes for the faculty ID TextBox TextChanged method.

The last coding job is for the Faculty ID TextBox, exactly for the **TextChanged** event and its method of the Faculty ID TextBox. As we mentioned, in order to avoid multiple insertions of the same data, the **Insert** button will be disabled after one data insertion is completed. This **Insert** button should be enabled again when the content of the Faculty ID TextBox is changed, which means that a different new record is ready to be inserted into the database.

Double-click the Faculty ID TextBox from the Faculty Form window to open this method and enter the codes that are shown in Figure 6.36 into this method.

Now we are ready to run the project to test the codes we have developed to try to insert a new record into the **Faculty** data table in our sample database. Click on the **Start** button to run the project, complete the login process and open the Faculty Form window. Then enter the following data into the related TextBox as a new faculty record:

Faculty ID:	**W56788**
Faculty Name:	**Steve Wang**
Title:	**Professor**
Office:	**MTC-311**
Phone:	**750-378-2258**
College:	**University of Miami**
Email:	**swang@college.edu**

Click on the **Insert** button to try to insert this new record into the **Faculty** table in the database.

On the opened File Dialog wizard, browse to the folder where all faculty images are stored. In fact, all faculty images are stored in a folder **Images\Faculty** under the **Students** folder located on the CRC Press ftp site (refer to Figure 1.2 in Chapter 1). One can copy all faculty images from that folder and save them in a local folder at the user's machine. Now browse to that local folder and select a faculty image **Wang.jpg**, and click on the **Open** button.

Immediately, all TextBoxes and the faculty image box, **PhotoBox**, become empty and the **Insert** button is disabled. This means that our data insertion is successful!

To check and validate this new inserted faculty record, two methods can be used: 1) use the **Select** button's Click method to try to retrieve back this new inserted faculty record from our database, 2) open our sample database and the **Faculty** table to confirm this data insertion action.

First let's use method 1 to do this checking.

Go to the **Faculty Name** combobox and click on its drop-down arrow, one can find that the new inserted faculty member, **Steve Wang**, has been added into this box. Select it and click on the **Select** button to try to get that record back. Immediately, all pieces of that new inserted faculty information, including a selected faculty image, are displayed in this Faculty Form window, as shown in Figure 6.37.

FIGURE 6.37 The retrieved new inserted faculty record.

Click on the **Back** and the **Exit** button from the Faculty Form and the Selection Form windows to close our project.

To use the second method to confirm this data insertion, just open the Server Explorer window and perform the following operations to open our **Faculty** table to do this confirmation:

1) Connect to our sample database by clicking on the arrow on the left of our database server in the Server Explorer window.
2) Expand our database folder and the **Tables** folder to find the **Faculty** table.
3) Right click on our **Faculty** table and select the **Show Table Data** item to open the **Faculty** table.
4) Browse to the bottom of this table, one can find the new inserted faculty record, as shown in Figure 6.38.

RTOInsert Project - dbo.Faculty [Data]

dbo.Faculty [Data]

Max Rows: 1000

	faculty_id	faculty_name	title	office	phone	college	email	fimage
	A52990	Black Anderson	Professor	MTC-218	750-378-9987	Virginia Tech	banderson@col...	0x89504E470D0...
	A77587	Debby Angles	Associate Profe...	MTC-320	750-330-2276	University of C...	dangles@colle...	0x89504E470D0...
	B66750	Alice Brown	Assistant Profes...	MTC-257	750-330-6650	University of Fl...	abrown@colleg...	0x89504E470D0...
	B78880	Ying Bai	Associate Profe...	MTC-211	750-378-1148	Florida Atlantic ...	ybai@college.e...	0xFFD8FFE0001...
	B86590	Davis Bhalla	Associate Profe...	MTC-214	750-378-1061	University of N...	dbhalla@colleg...	0x89504E470D0...
	H99118	Jeff Henry	Associate Profe...	MTC-336	750-330-8650	Ohio State Univ...	jhenry@college...	0x89504E470D0...
	J33486	Steve Johnson	Distinguished P...	MTC-118	750-330-1116	Harvard Univer...	sjohnson@coll...	0x89504E470D0...
	K69880	Jenney King	Professor	MTC-324	750-378-1230	East Florida Uni...	jking@college....	0x89504E470D0...
▸	W56788	Steve Wang	Professor	MTC-311	750-378-2258	University of Mi...	swang@college...	0xFFD8FFE0001...
•	NULL	NULL	NULL	NULL	NULL	NULL	NULL	NULL

Connection Ready | DESKTOP-24JPUFB\SQL2019EXPRESS | DESKTOP-24JPUFB\yingb | CSE_DEPT

FIGURE 6.38 The opened faculty data table in our sample database.

A completed Visual C#.NET project **RTOInsert Project** can be found at a folder **Class DB Projects\Chapter 6\RTOInsert Solution** under the **Students** folder at the CRC Press ftp site (refer to Figure 1.2 in Chapter 1).

6.6 INSERT DATA INTO THE SQL SERVER DATABASE USING STORED PROCEDURES

In this section, we discuss how to use stored procedures to perform data insertion actions. To save time and space, we can modify the project **RTOInsert Project** we built in the last section to create a new project **RTOInsertSP Project** to perform the data insertion using the stored procedures. We try to use the stored procedure method to insert a new course record into the Course table in our sample database to illustrate the operations of using this method. Perform the following operations to modify the project **RTOInsert Project** and make it as our new project **RTOInsertSP Project**:

1) Open the Windows Explorer and create a new folder **C:\Chapter 6** if you have not yet done so. Then browse to the folder **Class DB Projects\Chapter 6\RTOInsert Solution** that is located under the **Students** folder at the CRC Press ftp site. Then copy the entire solution **RTOInsert Solution** to our new folder **C:\Chapter 6**.
2) Change the names of the solution and the project from **RTOInsert Solution** to **RTOInsertSP Solution**, and **RTOInsert Project** to **RTOInsertSP Project**.
3) Change the project file name from **RTOInsert Project.csproj** to **RTOInsertSP Project.csproj**. Double-click on the **RTOInsertSP Project.csproj** to open this project.

On the opened project, perform the following modifications to get our desired project:

1) Go to **Project | RTOInsertSP Project Properties** menu item to open the project's property window. Change the **Assembly name** from **RTOInsert Project** to **RTOInsertSP Project** and the **Default namespace** from **RTOInsert_Project** to **RTOInsertSP_Project**.
2) Click on the **Assembly Information** button to open the Assembly Information wizard, change the **Title** and the **Product** to **RTOInsertSP Project**. Click on the **OK** button to close this wizard.
3) Change the **Startup object** from **RTOInsert_Project.Program** to **(Not set)**.
4) Go to the **File | Save All** menu item to save those modifications. Click on the **Save** button on the opened File Explorer window, and the **Overwrite** and **Save** button again to save this project.
5) Now right-click on the **LogIn.cs** folder in the Solution Explorer window and select the **View Code** item to open the code window for this **LogIn.cs** class file.
6) Change its namespace from the original **RTOInsert_Project** to our new namespace, **RTOInsertSP_Project**.
7) Open the **LogIn.designer.cs** file by double-clicking on it from the Solution Explorer window (you need to expand the **LogIn.cs** folder to find this file).
8) Change the top line from the original namespace **RTOInsert_Project** to our current namespace, **RTOInsertSP_Project**.
9) Repeat steps 5–7 above for all other files, such as **Faculty.cs**, **Course.cs**, **Selection.cs** and **Student.cs**, to change the namespaces for all of those files.
10) Now open the main file, **C# Program.cs**, from the Solution Explorer window by double-clicking on that file, and change its namespace to **RTOInsertSP_Project**.

Go to the **File | Save All** menu item again to save those modifications. Now you can build the project to confirm those modifications by going to the menu item **Build | Build Solution**. A 'building successful' message should be displayed in the **Output** window.

Next let's begin to develop the codes for the Course Form. However, we need first to take care of our stored procedures issue.

6.6.1 Develop Stored Procedures of SQL Server Database

Recall that when we built our sample database **CSE_DEPT** in Chapter 2, there is no faculty name column in the **Course** table, and the only relationship existed between the **Faculty** and the **Course** tables is the **faculty_id**, which is a primary key in the **Faculty** table but a foreign key in the **Course** table.

As the project runs and the Course Form window is shown up, the user needs to insert new course data based on the faculty name, not the faculty ID. Therefore, for this new course data insertion, we need to perform two queries with two tables: first, we need to make a query to the **Faculty** table to get the **faculty_id** based on the faculty name selected by the user; second, we can insert a new course record based on the **faculty_id** we obtained from our first query. These two queries can be combined into a single stored procedure.

Compared with the stored procedure, another solution to avoid performing two queries is to use a joined-table query to combine these two queries together to complete a course query, as we did for the Course Form in Section 5.15.6.1 in Chapter 5. However, it is more flexible and convenient to use stored procedures to perform this kind of multiple queries, especially when the queries are performed for multiple different data tables.

Now let's develop our stored procedures to combine these two queries to complete this data insertion. The stored procedure is named **dbo.InsertFacultyCourse.**

On the opened Visual Studio.NET, open the Server Explorer window and click on the arrow-symbol icon that is next to the **CSE_DEPT** database folder to connect to our database if this database was added into the Server Explorer before. Otherwise you need to right-click on the **Data Connections** folder to add and connect to our sample database. Refer to Section 5.3.1 in Chapter 5 for the detailed information of adding and connecting to our sample database.

Then expand our connected database and right-click on the **Stored Procedures** folder, and select the **Add New Stored Procedure** item to open the Add Procedure wizard. Enter the codes that are shown in Figure 6.39 into this new procedure. Do not forget to change the procedure's name to **dbo.InsertFacultyCourse** which is located at the top of this procedure.

The functionality of this stored procedure is:

A. All input parameters are listed in this part. The **@FacultyName** is selected by the user from the **ComboName** combobox as the project runs, and all other input parameters should be entered by the user to the associated TextBox in the Course Form window.

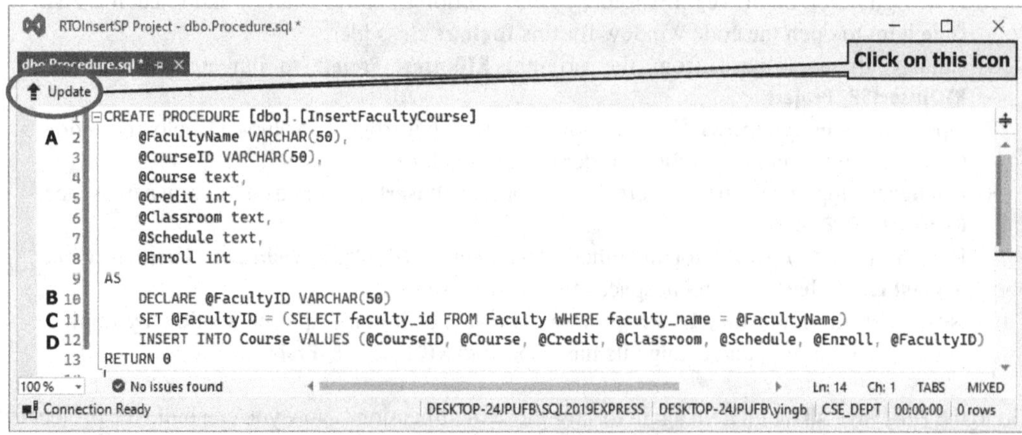

FIGURE 6.39 The finished stored procedure dbo.InsertFacultyCourse().

B. A local variable **@FacultyID** is declared and it is used to hold the returned value from the execution of the first query to the **Faculty** table in step **C**.
C. The first query is executed to pick up a matched **faculty_id** from the **Faculty** table based on the first input parameter, **@FacultyName**.
D. The second query is used to insert a new course record into the **Course** table. The last parameter in the **VALUES** parameter list is the **@FacultyID**, which is obtained from the first query.

The coding process for this stored procedure is simple and easy to be understood. One point you should know is the order of parameters in the **VALUES** parameter list. This order must be identical with the column order in the **Course** table. Otherwise, an error may be encountered when this stored procedure is saved.

Click on the **Update** icon located at the upper-left corner, as shown in Figure 6.39, to save this stored procedure into our database. On the opened **Preview Database Updates** wizard, click on the **Update Database** button, a successful updating message should be displayed in the **Data Tools Operations** wizard located at the bottom.

We can run and test this new stored procedure in this Visual Studio IDE. To do this, go to the Server Explorer window and right click on the Stored Procedures folder, and Select the **Refresh** item to refresh that folder. Immediately, our new stored procedure **dbo.InsertFacultyCourse** should be displayed in this Server Explorer window. Now right-click on our new stored procedure and select the **Execute** item from the popup menu to open the **Run Stored Procedure** wizard. Enter the input parameters into the associated box for a new course record, and the finished parameters wizard is shown in Figure 6.40.

Now click on the **OK** button to run this stored procedure. The running result is displayed in the **Query T-SQL** and the **Message** window at the bottom, which is shown in Figure 6.41.

To check and confirm this course insertion action, go to the Server Explorer window and open the **Course** table in our sample database by right-clicking on the **Course** table and select the **Show Table Data** item. Browse to the bottom of that **Course** table, our new inserted course, **CSE-538**, can be found at the last row, as shown in Figure 6.42.

Next we need to develop the codes in Visual C#.NET environment to call this stored procedure to insert a new course record into the database from our Course Form window.

Name	Data Type	Out	Null	Default	Value
@FacultyName	varchar(50)	No	☐	☐	Ying Bai
@CourseID	varchar(50)	No	☐	☐	CSE-538
@Course	text	No	☐	☐	Advanced Robotics
@Credit	int	No	☐	☐	3
@Classroom	text	No	☐	☐	MTC-336
@Schedule	text	No	☐	☐	T-H: 1:30-2:45 PM
@Enroll	int	No	☐	☐	32

FIGURE 6.40 The opened run stored procedure wizard.

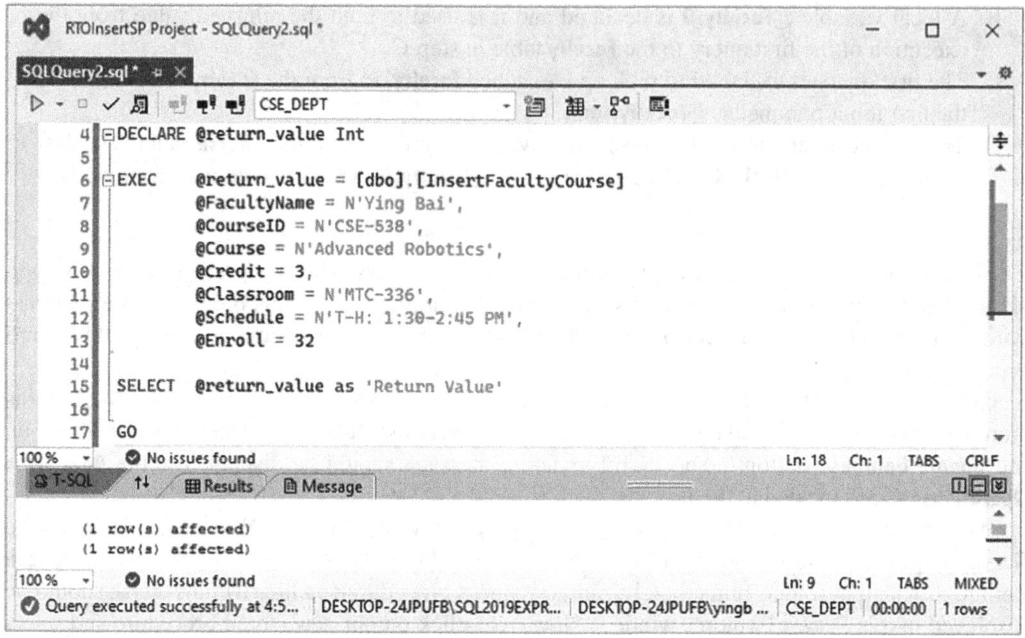

FIGURE 6.41 The running result of the stored procedure dbo.InsertFacultyCourse().

RTOInsertSP Project - dbo.Course [Data]

course_id	course	credit	classroom	schedule	enrollment	facult...
CSE-334	Elec. Measurement & Design	3	MTC-212	T-H: 11:00-12:25 PM	25	H99118
CSE-430	Bioinformatics in Computer	3	MTC-206	Thu: 9:30-11:00 AM	16	B86590
CSE-432	Analog Circuits Design	3	MTC-309	M-W-F: 2:00-2:55 PM	18	K69880
CSE-433	Digital Signal Processing	3	MTC-206	T-H: 2:00-3:25 PM	18	H99118
CSE-434	Advanced Electronics Systems	3	MTC-213	M-W-F: 1:00-1:55 PM	26	B78880
CSE-436	Automatic Control and Design	3	MTC-305	M-W-F: 10:00-10:55 AM	29	J33486
CSE-437	Operating Systems	3	MTC-303	T-H: 1:00-2:25 PM	17	A77587
CSE-438	Advd Logic & Microprocessor	3	MTC-213	M-W-F: 11:00-11:55 AM	35	B78880
CSE-439	Special Topics in CSE	3	MTC-206	M-W-F: 10:00-10:55 AM	22	J33486
CSE-520	Advanced Fuzzy Designs	4	MTC-109	T-H: 1:30-2:45 PM	25	B78880
CSE-534	Neural Networks	3	MTC-114	T-H: 9:30-10:45 AM	28	B78880
CSE-538	Advanced Robotics	3	MTC-336	T-H: 1:30-2:45 PM	32	B78880
NULL	NULL	NULL	NULL	NULL	NULL	NULL

Connection Ready | DESKTOP-24JPUFB\SQL2019EXPRESS | DESKTOP-24JPUFB\yingb | CSE_DEPT

FIGURE 6.42 The new inserted course record CE-538 in the course table.

6.6.2 Develop Codes to Call Stored Procedures to Insert Data into the Course Table

The coding development for this data insertion is divided into three steps; the data validation before the data insertion; data insertion using the stored procedure; and the data validation after the data insertion. The purpose of the first step is to confirm that all inserted data that stored in each associated

TextBox should be complete and valid. In other words, all TextBoxes should be non-empty. The third step is used to confirm that the data insertion is successful; in other words, the new inserted data should be in the desired table in the database and can be read back and displayed in the Course Form window. Let's begin with the coding process for the first step.

6.6.2.1 Validate Data before the Data Insertion

Prior to building the codes to do the pre-data insertion inspection, we need first to add a new query method, **Stored Procedure**, into the Query Method combobox, **ComboMethod**, in the constructor of the Course Form to enable users to select and use this method to do a new course insertion. Also we need to create a class-level array **CourseInfo[]** to hold six TextBoxes stored six pieces of new inserted course information. Open the code window of the Course Form window and the constructor of the **CourseForm**, then add one coding line into that constructor, which is shown in step **A** in Figure 6.43. Then create a class-level String array **CourseInfo[]**, which is shown in step **B** in Figure 6.43.

Then three user-defined methods, **InitCourseInfo()**, **CheckCourseInfo()** and **ClearCourse()**, are built to facilitate the pre-checking for the data insertion action. The first method is used to set up a structure or a mapping between the class-level array **CourseInfo[]** and six TextBoxes in the Course Form window. The purpose of the second method is to check and confirm no any TextBox is empty; in other words, all TextBoxes are filled with valid values, which is a new course record to be inserted into the **Course** table in our sample database. The **ClearCourse()** method works as a cleaner to clean up the contents for all six TextBoxes after a new course record has been inserted to enable users to perform a validation check to confirm the data insertion action.

The detailed codes for these three methods are shown in steps **C**, **D** and **E** in Figure 6.43. The functions of those pieces of code are straightforward, with no further explanation required. Now let's build the codes for the **Insert** button's Click method to perform the data pre-checking and data insertion operations.

6.6.2.2 Build the Codes for the Insert Click Method to Perform Data Insertion

Open the **Insert** button's Click method by double-clicking on the **Insert** button from the Course Form window, and enter the codes that are shown in Figure 6.44 into this method. Let's take a look at those new added codes to see how they work.

- **A.** Some local variables and objects are declared first, including two integer variables, **check** and **intInsert**, a query string **cmdString** and a SqlCommand object. Two integer variables are used for running status holder to keep the running results for two methods, the user-defined methods, **CheckCourseInfo()**, and a system method **ExecuteNonQuery()**, to be called later. The query string is used for the query to our stored procedure to perform this data insertion action later. The SqlCommand object is a main object to perform this data insertion action.
- **B.** Two user-defined methods, **InitCourseInfo()** and **CheckCourseInfo()**, are executed to perform the data pre-checking functions to do the pre-insertion validation jobs.
- **C.** If the checking result is fine, which means that all TextBoxes have been filled with valid data values, the SqlCommand object is initialized by assigning it with appropriate values to the related properties. One point to ne noted is the **CommandType** property, here a **StoredProcedure** value must be assigned since we need to call a stored procedure to perform this data insertion function.
- **D.** Another user-defined method, **InsertParameters()** that will be built later, is executed to fill the Parameters property of the SqlCommand object with a new course record to be inserted into our database. A passing-by-reference mode is used for that method since we want to make sure that all modifications to the passed parameters are permanent.
- **E.** The **ExecuteNonQuery()** method of the Command class is executed to call the stored procedure to perform the new data insertion. The running result of this method is returned and assigned to one local variable **intInsert**.

```
RTOInsertSP Project                    CourseForm()

  .........
  namespace RTOInsertSP_Project
  {
    public partial class CourseForm : Form
    {
A     string[] CourseInfo = new string[6];
      LogInForm loginForm = new LogInForm();

      public CourseForm()
      {
        InitializeComponent();
        ComboName.Items.Add("Ying Bai");
        ComboName.Items.Add("Davis Bhalla");
        ComboName.Items.Add("Black Anderson");
        ComboName.Items.Add("Steve Johnson");
        ComboName.Items.Add("Jenney King");
        ComboName.Items.Add("Alice Brown");
        ComboName.Items.Add("Debby Angles");
        ComboName.Items.Add("Jeff Henry");
        ComboName.SelectedIndex = 0;
        ComboMethod.Items.Add("DataAdapter Method");
        ComboMethod.Items.Add("DataReader Method");
B       ComboMethod.Items.Add("Stored Procedure");
        ComboMethod.SelectedIndex = 0;
      }

C     private void InitCourseInfo()
      {
        CourseInfo[0] = txtCourseID.Text;
        CourseInfo[1] = txtCourseName.Text;
        CourseInfo[2] = txtSchedule.Text;
        CourseInfo[3] = txtClassRoom.Text;
        CourseInfo[4] = txtCredits.Text;
        CourseInfo[5] = txtEnroll.Text;
      }
D     private int CheckCourseInfo()
      {
        int pos = 0, check = 0;

        for (pos = 1; pos <= 6; pos++)
        {
          if (CourseInfo[pos] == String.Empty)
            check++;
        }
        return check;
      }
E     private void ClearCourse()
      {
        int index;
        TextBox[] cBox = {txtCourseID, txtCourseName, txtSchedule, txtClassRoom, txtCredits, txtEnroll};

        for (index = 0; index < cBox.Length; index++)
          cBox[index].Text = "";
      }
    }
  }
```

FIGURE 6.43 The codes used for pre-data insertion inspection.

F. The Command object is cleaned up after the data insertion.
G. The returned value of calling the **ExecuteNonQuery()** method equals to the number of rows or records that have been successfully inserted into the database. A zero means that no row or record has been inserted into the database and this data insertion is failed. In that case, a warning message is displayed.

```
RTOInsert Project | cmdInsert_Click(object sender, EventArgs e)

  private void cmdInsert_Click(object sender, EventArgs e)
  {
A       int check, intInsert;
        string cmdString = "dbo.InsertFacultyCourse";
        SqlCommand sqlCommand = new SqlCommand();
B       InitCourseInfo();
        check = CheckCourseInfo();
C       if (check == 0)
        {
            sqlCommand.Connection = loginForm.sqlConnection;
            sqlCommand.CommandType = CommandType.StoredProcedure;
            sqlCommand.CommandText = cmdString;
D           InsertParameters(ref sqlCommand);
E           intInsert = sqlCommand.ExecuteNonQuery();
F           sqlCommand.Dispose();
G           if (intInsert == 0)
                MessageBox.Show("The data insertion is failed");
H           else
            {
                ClearCourse();                          // clean up all course information
                cmdInsert.Enabled = false;
            }
        }
I       else
            MessageBox.Show("Fill all Course Information box, enter a NULL for blank column");
  }
```

FIGURE 6.44 The codes for the insert button's click method.

H. Otherwise, this data insertion is successful. The information stored in all six TextBoxes is cleaned up to make it ready for the users to perform a checking or a validation for that data insertion. In addition, the **Insert** button is disabled to avoid multiple insertions of the same data into the database.

I. If the returned **check** value is not zero, which means that some TextBoxes are empty, a warning message is displayed to remind users to fill them immediately.

The detailed codes for the user-defined method **InsertParameters()** are shown in Figure 6.45. The function of this piece of code is straightforward and needs no further explanations.

Now we have finished all coding jobs for this data insertion operation.

Let's run the project to test the new data insertion using the stored procedure method. Click on the **Start** button to run the project, enter the suitable username and password such as **jhenry** and **test**

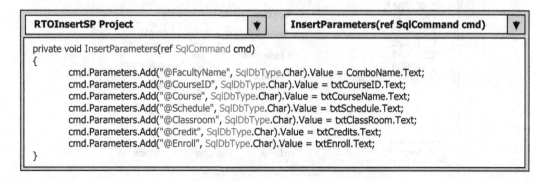

```
RTOInsertSP Project | InsertParameters(ref SqlCommand cmd)

private void InsertParameters(ref SqlCommand cmd)
{
     cmd.Parameters.Add("@FacultyName", SqlDbType.Char).Value = ComboName.Text;
     cmd.Parameters.Add("@CourseID", SqlDbType.Char).Value = txtCourseID.Text;
     cmd.Parameters.Add("@Course", SqlDbType.Char).Value = txtCourseName.Text;
     cmd.Parameters.Add("@Schedule", SqlDbType.Char).Value = txtSchedule.Text;
     cmd.Parameters.Add("@Classroom", SqlDbType.Char).Value = txtClassRoom.Text;
     cmd.Parameters.Add("@Credit", SqlDbType.Char).Value = txtCredits.Text;
     cmd.Parameters.Add("@Enroll", SqlDbType.Char).Value = txtEnroll.Text;
}
```

FIGURE 6.45 The codes for the method InsertParameters().

to finish the login process. Select the **Course Information** item from the Selection Form to open the Course Form window.

Enter the following data into the associated TextBox as a new course record:

Faculty Name:	**Ying Bai**
Course ID:	**CSE-668**
Course Name:	**Modern Controls**
Schedule:	**M-W-F: 9:00 – 9:50 AM**
Classroom:	**MTC-309**
Credits:	**3**
Enrollment:	**30**

Keep the default faculty name **Ying Bai** in the Faculty Name combobox with no change and click on the **Insert** button to call our stored procedure to insert this new course record into the database. Immediately, the **Insert** button is disabled after this data insertion. Is our data insertion successful? To answer this question, we need to perform the data validation in the next section.

6.6.2.3 Validate Data Insertion after the Course Data Insertion

To confirm or validate this course insertion, we can use the **Select** button, exactly the **Select** button's Click method to try to retrieve back all courses, including that new inserted course, taught by the selected faculty member **Ying Bai**.

To do that checking, just click on the **Select** button to try to retrieve back all courses taught by that faculty and display them in the CourseList Box in this Course Form window. All courses taught by the selected faculty are displayed in the CourseList box. The last item, **CSE-668**, is just the course we added into the **Course** table for this insertion. Click that item and all information related to that new course is displayed in six TextBoxes in this Course Form, which is shown in Figure 6.46. This is the evidence that our data insertion using the stored procedure is successful!

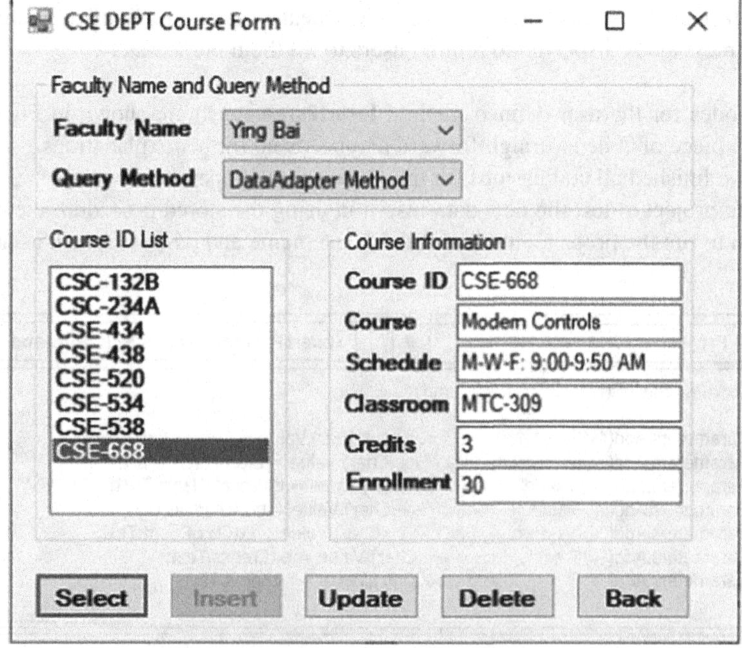

FIGURE 6.46 The data validation process.

RTOInsertSP Project - dbo.Course [Data]

dbo.Course [Data]

Max Rows: 1000

course_id	course	credit	classroom	schedule	enrollment	faculty_id
CSE-334	Elec. Measurement & Design	3	MTC-212	T-H: 11:00-12:25 PM	25	H99118
CSE-430	Bioinformatics in Computer	3	MTC-206	Thu: 9:30-11:00 AM	16	B86590
CSE-432	Analog Circuits Design	3	MTC-309	M-W-F: 2:00-2:55 PM	18	K69880
CSE-433	Digital Signal Processing	3	MTC-206	T-H: 2:00-3:25 PM	18	H99118
CSE-434	Advanced Electronics Systems	3	MTC-213	M-W-F: 1:00-1:55 PM	26	B78880
CSE-436	Automatic Control and Design	3	MTC-305	M-W-F: 10:00-10:55 AM	29	J33486
CSE-437	Operating Systems	3	MTC-303	T-H: 1:00-2:25 PM	17	A77587
CSE-438	Advd Logic & Microprocessor	3	MTC-213	M-W-F: 11:00-11:55 AM	35	B78880
CSE-439	Special Topics in CSE	3	MTC-206	M-W-F: 10:00-10:55 AM	22	J33486
CSE-520	Advanced Fuzzy Designs	4	MTC-109	T-H: 1:30-2:45 PM	25	B78880
CSE-534	Neural Networks	3	MTC-114	T-H: 9:30-10:45 AM	28	B78880
CSE-538	Advanced Robotics	3	MTC-336	T-H: 1:30-2:45 PM	32	B78880
CSE-668	Modern Controls	3	MTC-309	M-W-F: 9:00-9:50 AM	30	B78880
NULL	NULL	NULL	NULL	NULL	NULL	NULL

Connection Ready | DESKTOP-24JPUFB\SQL2019EXPRESS | DESKTOP-24JPUFB\yingb | CSE_DEPT

FIGURE 6.47 The inserted new course CSE-668.

Another way to confirm this data insertion is to open the Course table from the Server Explorer window. On the opened Course table, one can find that our new inserted course, CSE-668, can be found at the bottom of that table, as shown in Figure 6.47.

A completed project **RTOInsertSP Project** that includes the data insertion using the stored procedure method can be found from a folder **Class DB Projects\Chapter 6 \RTOInsertSP Solution**, which is located under the **Students** folder on the CRC Press ftp site (refer to Figure 1.2 in Chapter 1).

6.7 CHAPTER SUMMARY

Four popular data insertion methods are discussed and analyzed with three project examples for our SQL Server 2019 Express database in this chapter:

1) Using TableAdapter's DBDirect methods **TableAdapter.Insert()** method.
2) Using the **TableAdapter's Update()** method to insert new records that have already been added into the DataTable in the DataSet.
3) Using the Command object's **ExecuteNonQuery()** method.
4) Using the stored procedures method.

Method 1 is developed using the Visual Studio.NET design tools and wizards and it allows users to directly access the database and execute the TableAdapter's methods, such as **TableAdapter.Insert()** and **TableAdapter.Update()**,to manipulate data in the database without requiring DataSet or DataTable objects to reconcile changes in order to send updates to a database. As we mentioned at the beginning of this chapter, inserting data into a table in a DataSet is different to inserting data into a table in the database. If you are using the DataSet to store data in your applications, you need to use the **TableAdapter.Update()** method since the **Update()** method can trigger and send all changes (updates, inserts, and deletes) to the database.

One good habit is to try to use the **TableAdapter.Insert()** method when your application uses objects to store data (for example, you are using TextBoxes to store your data), or when you want finer control over creating new records in the database.

Method 2 allows users to insert new data into a database with two steps. First, the new record should be added into the data table that is located in a DataSet; second, the **TableAdapter.Update()**

method can be executed to update the whole table in the DataSet to the associated table in the database.

Method 3 is a run time object method and this method is more flexible and convenient since it allows users to insert data into multiple data tables with the different functionalities.

Method 4 uses stored procedures to replace the general query functions. This method promises users with more powerful controllability and flexibility on data insertions, especially for data insertions with multiple queries to multiple tables.

This chapter is divided into two parts. Part I provides a detailed discussion and analysis of inserting data into a SQL Server database using the Visual Studio.NET design tools and wizards. It is simple and easy to develop a data insertion project with these tools and wizards. The disadvantage of using these tools and wizards is that the data can only be inserted into limited destinations, for example, a certain data table. Part II presents the run time object method and stored procedure method to improve the efficiency of the data insertion and provides more flexibility in data insertion.

Three real projects are provided in this chapter to give readers a clear and direct picture in developing professional data insertion applications in the Visual C#.NET environment.

HOMEWORK

I. True/False Selections

____1. Three popular data insertion methods are the **TableAdapter.Insert()**, **TableAdapter.Update()** and **ExecuteNonQuery()** methods of the Command class.

____2. Unlike the **Fill()** method, a valid database connection must be set before a new data can be inserted into a database.

____3. One can directly insert new data or new records into a database with a single step using the **TableAdapter.Update()** method.

____4. When executing an **INSERT** query, the order of the input parameters in the **VALUES** list can be different with the order of the data columns in the database.

____5. To insert an image into a SQL Server database, the data type for that image should be **Image**.

____6. In addition to using the **ExecuteNonQuery()** method of a Command class to insert a new record, one can use the **InsertCommand.ExecuteNonQuery()** method, which belongs to a DataAdapter class, to perform a data insertion.

____7. When performing the data insertion, the same data can be inserted into the database on multiple occasions.

____8. To insert data into the database using the **TableAdapter.Update()** method, the new data should be first inserted into the table in the DataSet. Then the **Update()** method is executed to update that new data into the table in the database.

____9. To insert data into the SQL Server database using the stored procedures, one can create and test a new stored procedure in the Server Explorer window.

___10. To call stored procedures to insert data into a database, the parameters' names must be identical with those names of the input parameters defined in the stored procedures.

II. Multiple Choice Questions

1. To insert data into the database using the **TableAdapter.Insert()** method, one needs to use the ________ to build the ________.
   a. Data Source, Query Builder
   b. TableAdapter Query Configuration Wizard, Insert query
   c. Runtime object, Insert query
   d. Server Explorer, Data Source

2. To insert data into the database using the **TableAdapter.Update()** method, one needs first to add new data into the _______, and then update that data into the database.
   a. Data table
   b. Data table in the database
   c. DataSet
   d. Data table in the DataSet
3. To insert data into the database using the **TableAdapter.Update()** method, one can update ___________
   a. One data row only
   b. Multiple data rows
   c. The whole data table
   d. Either of above
4. Because the ADO.NET provides a disconnected mode to the database, to insert a new record into the database, a valid ________ must be established.
   a. DataSet
   b. TableAdapter
   c. Connection
   d. Command
5. The _______ operator should be used as an assignment operator in the **WHERE** clause for a dynamic parameter of a data query in SQL Server database.
   a. =:
   b. LIKE
   c. =
   d. @
6. To confirm a stored procedure built in the Server Explorer window in SQL Server database, one can _______ that stored procedure to make sure it works.
   a. Build
   b. Execute
   c. Debug
   d. Compile
7. To create a new stored procedure in the Server Explorer window for a SQL Server database, one can _______ that stored procedure and test it.
   a. Build
   b. Execute
   c. Debug
   d. Compile
8. To insert a data record into a SQL Server database using the **INSERT** query, the parameters' data type must be ________.
   a. OleDbType
   b. SqlDbType
   c. OracleDbType
   d. OracleType
9. To call a stored procedure to insert a record into a database, the CommandType property of the Command object must be equal to ___________.
   a. CommandType.InsertCommand
   b. CommandType.StoredProcedure
   c. CommandType.Text
   d. CommandType.Insert

10. To insert data using stored procedures, the CommandText property of the Command object must be equal to __________.
    a. The content of the CommandType.InsetCommand
    b. The content of the CommandType.Text
    c. The name of the Insert command
    d. The name of the stored procedure

III. Exercises

1. Following is a stored procedure developed in SQL Server database. Please develop a piece of codes in Visual C#.NET to call this stored procedure to insert a new data into the database.

```
CREATE OR REPLACE PROCEUDRE dbo.InsertStudent
  @Name VARCHAR(20),
  @Major text,
  @SchoolYear int,
  @Credits float,
  @Email text
AS
INSERT INTO Student VALUES (@Name, @Major, @SchoolYear, @Credits, @Email)
RETURN
```

2. Following is a piece of codes developed in Visual C#.NET and this piece of codes is used to call a stored procedure in a SQL Server database to insert a new record into the database. Please create the associated stored procedure via the Server Explorer window (assume a valid database connection has been set).

```
string cmdString = "dbo.Insert_Course";
int intInsert = 0;
SqlCommand sqlCommand = new SqlCommand();
sqlCommand.Connection = sqlConnection;
sqlCommand.CommandType = CommandType.StoredProcedure;
sqlCommand.CommandText = cmdString;
sqlCommand.Parameters.Add("FacultyName", SqlDbType.Char).Value = ComboName.Text;
sqlCommand.Parameters.Add("CourseID", SqlDbType.Char).Value = txtCourseID.Text;
sqlCommand.Parameters.Add("Course", SqlDbType.Char).Value = txtCourseName.Text;
sqlCommand.Parameters.Add("Schedule", SqlDbType.Char).Value = txtSchedule.Text;
sqlCommand.Parameters.Add("Classroom", SqlDbType.Char).Value = txtClassRoom.Text;
sqlCommand.Parameters.Add("Credit", SqlDbType.Char).Value = txtCredits.Text;
intInsert = sqlCommand.ExecuteNonQuery();
```

3. Using the tools and wizards provided by Visual Studio.NET and ADO.NET to perform the data insertion for the **Student** table via the Student Form in the **SelectWizard Project** (the project is located at a folder **Class DB Projects\Chapter 6\SelectWizard Solution** under the **Students** folder at CRC Press ftp site (refer to Figure 1.2 in Chapter 1)).
4. Using the Runtime objects method to complete the inserting data query for the **Student** table via the Student Form by using the **RTOInsert Project** (the project is located at a folder **Class DB Projects\Chapter 6\RTOInsert Solution** under the **Students** folder at CRC Press ftp site (refer to Figure 1.2 in Chapter 1)).

5. Using a stored procedure to complete the inserting data query for the **Student** table via the Student Form by using the **RTOInsertSP Project** (the project is located at a folder **Class DB Projects\Chapter 6\RTOInsertSP Solution** under the **Students** folder at CRC Press ftp site (refer to Figure 1.2 in Chapter 1)).

   Hint: When building the stored procedure, **dbo.InsertStudent()**, the data type of the last input parameter **@simage** is **image**.

7 Data Updating and Deleting with Visual C#.NET

In this chapter, we will discuss how to update and delete data against the databases. In general, many different methods are provided and supported by Visual C#.NET and .NET Framework to help users to perform the data updating and deleting against the database. Among them, three popular methods are widely implemented:

1) Using TableAdapter DBDirect methods such as **TableAdapter.Update()** and **TableAdapter.Delete()** to update and delete data directly against the databases.
2) Using **TableAdapter.Update()** method to update and execute the associated TableAdapter's properties such as **UpdateCommand** or **DeleteCommand** to save changes made for the table in the DataSet to the table in the database.
3) Using the run time object method to develop and execute the Command's method **ExecuteNonQuery()** to update or delete data against the database directly.

Methods 1 and 2 each need to use Visual Studio.NET Design Tools and Wizards to create and configure suitable TableAdapters, build the associated queries using the Query Builder, and call those queries from Visual C#.NET applications. The difference between methods 1 and 2 is that method 1 can be used to directly access the database to perform the data updating and deleting in a single step, whereas method 2 needs two steps to finish the data updating or deleting. In method 2, first, the data updating or deleting are performed to the associated tables in the DataSet, and then those updated or deleted data are updated to the tables in the database by executing the **TableAdapter.Update()** method.

This chapter is divided into two parts; Part I provides discussions on data updating and deleting using methods 1 and 2, or, in other words, using the **TableAdapter.Update()** and **TableAdapter.Delete()** methods developed in Visual Studio.NET Design Tools and Wizards. Part II presents the data updating and deleting using the run time object method by developing command objects to execute the **ExecuteNonQuery()** method dynamically. Updating and deleting data using stored procedures and the LINQ to SQL query are also discussed in that part.

When you have finished this chapter, you will be able to:

- Understand the working principle and structure on updating and deleting data against the database using the Visual Studio.NET Design Tools and Wizards.
- Understand the procedures in how to configure the TableAdapter object by using the TableAdapter Query Configuration Wizard and build the query to update and delete data against the database.
- Design and develop special procedures to validate data before and after data updating and deleting.
- Understand the working principle and structure on updating and deleting data against the database using the run-time object method.
- Design and build stored procedures to perform the data updating and deleting.
- Design and build LINQ to SQL query to update and delete data.

To successfully complete this chapter, you need to understand topics such as Fundamentals of Databases, which was introduced in Chapter 2, and ADO.NET, which was discussed in Chapter 3.

DOI: 10.1201/9781003319832-7

In addition, a sample database **CSE_DEPT**, which was developed in Chapter 2, will be used throughout this chapter.

In order to save time and avoid the repeatability, we will use the sample projects such as SelectWizard Project, RTOInsert Project, and RTOInsertSP Project we developed in the previous chapter and modify them to create new associated projects, and use them in this chapter. Recall that some command buttons on the different form windows in those projects have not been coded, such as Update and Delete, and that those buttons, or, more accurately, the methods related to those buttons will be developed and built upon in this chapter. We only concentrate on the coding for the **Update** and **Delete** buttons in this chapter.

PART I DATA UPDATING AND DELETING WITH VISUAL STUDIO.NET DESIGN TOOLS AND WIZARDS

In this part, we discuss updating and deleting data against the database using the Visual Studio Design Tools and Wizards. We will develop two methods to perform these data actions: First we use the TableAdapter DBDirect methods, **TableAdapter.Update()** and **TableAdapter.Delete()**, to directly update or delete data in the database. Secondly, we will discuss how to update or delete data in the database by first updating or deleting records in the DataSet, and then updating those records' changes from the DataSet to the database using the **TableAdapter.Update()** method.

Both methods utilize the so-called TableAdapter's direct and indirect methods to complete the data updating or deleting. The database we try to use is the Microsoft SQL Server 2019 Express database, **CSE_DEPT**, which was developed in Chapter 2 and it can be found from a folder **Sample Database** located under the Students folder at the CRC Press ftp site (refer to Figure 1.2 in Chapter 1).

7.1 UPDATE OR DELETE DATA AGAINST SQL SERVER DATABASES

We have already provided a very detailed discussion about the TableAdapter DBDirect methods in Section 6.1.1 in Chapter 6. To use these methods to directly access the database to make the desired manipulations to the data stored in that database, one needs to use Visual Studio.NET Design Tools and Wizards to create and configure the associated TableAdapter. There are some limitations existed when using these DBDirect methods to update or delete data against databases. For example, each TableAdapter is associated with a unique data table in the DataSet; therefore, the data updating or deleting can only be executed for that unique data table by using the associated TableAdapter. In other words, the specified TableAdapter cannot update or delete data from any other data tables other than the data table that is related to the created TableAdapter.

7.1.1 Updating and Deleting Data against Related Tables in a DataSet

When updating or deleting data against related tables in a DataSet, it is important to update or delete data in the proper sequence in order to reduce the chance of violating referential integrity constraints. The order of command execution will also follow the indices of the **DataRowCollection** in the DataSet. To prevent data integrity errors from being raised, the best practice is to update or delete data against the database in the following sequence:

1) Child table: delete records.
2) Parent table: insert, update, and delete records.
3) Child table: insert and update records.

For our sample database **CSE_DEPT**, all five tables are related with different primary keys and foreign keys. For example, among the **LogIn**, **Faculty** and **Course** tables, the **faculty_id** works as a key to relate these three tables together. The **faculty_id** is a primary key in the **Faculty** table, but a foreign key in both **LogIn** and the **Course** tables. In order to update or delete data from any of those tables, one needs to follow the sequence above. As a case of updating or deleting a record against the database, the following data operation sequence needs to be performed:

1) First, remove or delete that record from the child tables, **LogIn** and **Course** tables, respectively.
2) Then update or delete that record in the parent table, **Faculty** table.
3) Finally, that updated record can be inserted into the child tables such as **Login** and **Course** tables for the data updating operation. There is no any data action for the data deleting operations for the child tables.

It would be terribly complicated if we update a full record (including update the primary key) for an existing record in our sample database. In practice, it is unnecessary to update a primary key for any record since the primary key has the same lifetime as a database. A better and popular way to do this updating is to remove those undesired records and then insert new records with new primary keys. Therefore, in this chapter, we will concentrate on updating existing data in our sample database without touching the primary key. For data deleting, we can delete a full record with the primary key involved and all related records in the child tables will also be deleted since all tables have been set in a **Cascade Delete** mode when we built these data tables for our sample database **CSE_DEPT** in Section 2.9.4 in Chapter 2.

7.1.2 Update or Delete Data against Database Using TableAdapter DBDirect Methods

Three typical TableAdapter's DBDirect methods are listed in Figure 6.1 in Chapter 6. For your convenience, we redraw that table in here, which is shown as in Figure 7.1.

Both DBDirect methods, **TableAdapter.Update()** and **TableAdapter.Delete()**, need the original column values as the parameters when these methods are executed. The **TableAdapter.Update()** method needs both the original and the new column values to perform the data updating. Another point to be noted is that when the application uses the object to store the data, for instance, in our sample project we use TextBox objects to store our data; one should use this DBDirect method to perform the data manipulations against the database.

7.1.3 Update or Delete Data against Database Using TableAdapter.Update Method

You can use the **TableAdapter.Update()** method to update or edit records in a database. The **TableAdapter.Update()** method provides several overloads that perform different operations depending on

TableAdapter DBDirect Method	Description
TableAdapter.Insert	Adds new records into a database allowing you to pass in individual column values as method parameters.
TableAdapter.Update	Updates existing records in a database. The Update method takes original and new column values as method parameters. The original values are used to locate the original record, and the new values are used to update that record. The TableAdapter.Update method is also used to reconcile changes in a dataset back to the database by taking a DataSet, DataTable, DataRow, or array of DataRows as method parameters.
TableAdapter.Delete	Deletes existing records from the database based on the original column values passed in as method parameters.

FIGURE 7.1 TableAdapter DBDirect methods.

Update Method	Description
TableAdapter.Update(DataTable)	Attempt to save all changes in the DataTable to the database. (This includes removing any rows deleted from the table, adding rows inserted to the table, and updating any rows in the table that have changed)
TableAdapter.Update(DataSet)	Although the parameter takes a dataset, the TableAdapter attempts to save all changes in the TableAdapter's associated DataTable to the database. (This includes removing any rows deleted from the table, adding rows inserted in the table, and updating any rows in the table that have changed)
TableAdapter.Update(DataRow)	Attempt to save changes in the indicated DataRow.
TableAdapter.Update(DataRows())	Attempt to save changes in any row in the array of DataRows to the database.
TableAdapter.Update("new column values", "original column values")	Attempts to save changes in a single row that is identified by the original column values.

FIGURE 7.2 Variations of TableAdapter.Update() method.

the parameters passed in. It is important to understand the results of calling these different method signatures.

To use this method to update or delete data against the database, one needs to perform the following two steps:

1) Change or delete records from the desired DataTable based on the selected data rows from the table in the DataSet.
2) After the rows have been modified or deleted from the DataTable, call the **TableAdapter.Update()**method to reflect those modifications to the database. You can control the amount of data to be updated by passing an entire DataSet, a DataTable, an array of DataRows, or a single DataRow.

Figure 7.2 describes the behavior of the various **TableAdapter.Update()** methods.

Different parameters or arguments can be passed into these five variations of this method. The parameter DataTable, which is located in a DataSet, is a data table mapping to a real data table in the database. When a whole DataTable is passed, any modification to that table will be updated and reflected in the associated table in the database. Similarly, if a DataSet is passed, all DataTables in that DataSet will be updated and reflected to those tables in the database.

The last variation of this method is to pass the original columns and the new columns of a data table to perform this updating. In fact, this method can be used as a DBDirect method to access the database to manipulate data.

In order to provide a detailed discussion and explanation of how to use these two methods to update or delete records against the database, a real example will be very helpful. Let's first create a new Visual C#.NET project to handle those issues.

7.2 UPDATE AND DELETE DATA FOR THE FACULTY TABLE IN OUR SQL SERVER DATABASE

In order to save the time and the space, we can still modify an existing project **SelectWizardProject** we built in Chapter 5 but modified in Chapter 6 to create our new project and use it in this chapter. In this section, we try to perform data updating and deleting actions for the **Faculty** table in our sample database.

Open the Windows Explorer and create a new folder such as **C:\Chapter 7** in your local machine (if you have not yet created it), and browse to our project **SelectWizardProject**, which can be found from a folder **Class DB Projects\Chapter 6\SelectWizard Solution** that is under the **Students** folder on the CRC Press ftp site. Copy the entire solution folder **SelectWizard Solution** and paste it to our new folder **C:\Chapter 7**.

Prior to developing the codes for our new project, we need first to build two queries, **UpdateFaculty()** and **DeleteFaculty()**, via the Data Source window.

7.2.1 Configure the TableAdapter and Build the Data Updating and Deleting Queries

Perform the following operational steps to build the data updating query:

1) Open the Data Source window and the **TableAdapter Query Configuration Wizard** by right-clicking on any place inside the Data Source window. Then select the item **Edit DataSet with Designer** from the popup menu.
2) On the opened wizard, go to the **Faculty** table, right-click on the last item in the **Faculty** table, and select **Add Query** item from the popup menu.
3) Keep the default selection, **Use SQL statements**, unchanged and click on the **Next** button to go to the next wizard.
4) Select and check the **UPDATE** item from this wizard since we need to perform updating data query, and then click on the **Next** button again to continue.
5) Click the **Query Builder** button to open the Query Builder wizard to build our updating query. The opened Query Builder wizard is shown in Figure 7.3.
6) Remove all contents from the **faculty_id** and **faculty_name** rows under the **Filter** and **Or** columns.
7) Uncheck the **Set** checkbox from the **faculty_id** row under the column **Set**, and enter a question mark (**?**) to the **faculty_id** row under the column **Filter**, press the **Enter** key from the keyboard.
8) Change the name of the parameter **@Param1** to **@fid** for the **Filer** column in the **faculty_id** row.

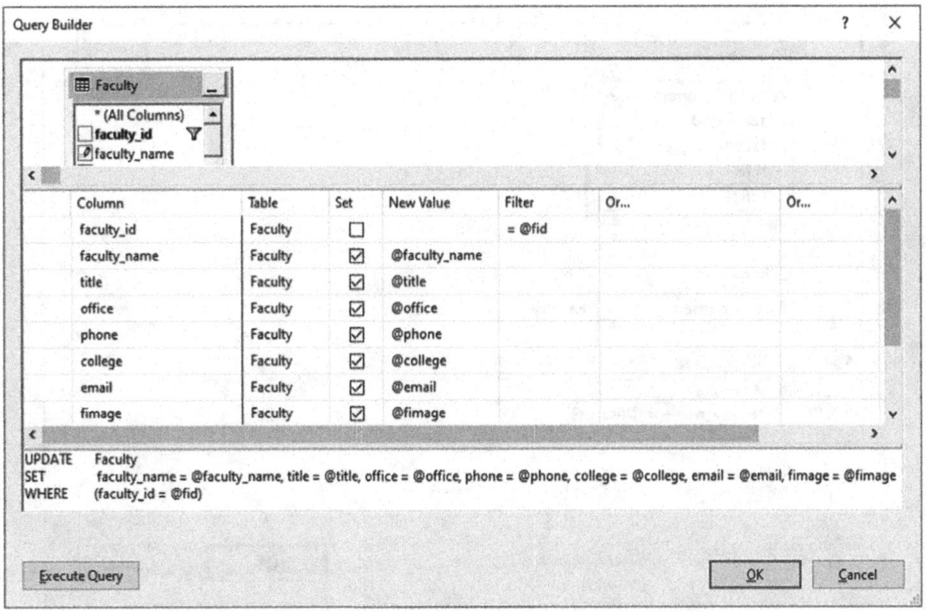

FIGURE 7.3 The update query builder.

9) Remove the contents for all rows under the last row, **fimage**, and your finished query builder wizard should match one that is shown in Figure 7.3.
10) Click on the **OK** button to go to the next wizard. Remove the **SELECT** statement under the **WHERE** clause since we do not need this function. Click on the **Next** button to confirm this query and continue to the next step.
11) Modify the query function name from the default one to the **UpdateFaculty** and click on the **Next** button to go to the last wizard.
12) Click on the **Finish** button to complete this Query Builder and close the wizard.

Perform the following operations to build the data-deleting query:

1) Open the Data Source window and the **TableAdapter Query Configuration Wizard** by right-clicking on any place inside the Data Source window, and select the item **Edit DataSet with Designer** from the popup menu.
2) On the opened wizard, go to the **Faculty** table, right-click on the last item in the **Faculty** table, and select **Add Query** item from the popup menu.
3) Keep the default selection, **Use SQL statements**, unchanged and click on the **Next** button to go to the next wizard.
4) Select and check the **DELETE** item from this wizard since we need to perform deleting data query. Then click on the **Next** button again to continue to the next wizard.
5) Click on the **Query Builder** button since we want to build our deleting query. The opened Query Builder wizard is shown in Figure 7.4.
6) Delete the whole line of the row **faculty_id** and the row **@IsNull_faculty_name**. Remove the contents of the columns **Filter** and **Or** for the **faculty_name** row.
7) Enter a question mark (**?**) into the **Filter** column alongside the **faculty_name** row and press the **Enter** key on the keyboard.

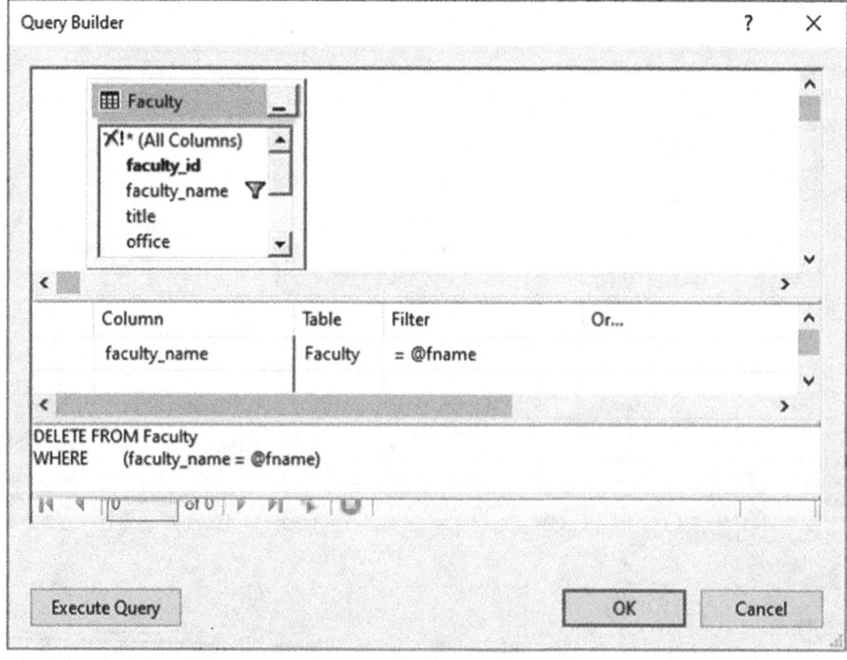

FIGURE 7.4 The delete query builder.

8) Change the name of the dynamic parameter **@Param1** to **@fname**, and press the **Enter** key from the keyboard.
9) Your finished query builder should match one that is shown in Figure 7.4. Click on the **OK** button to go to the next wizard.
10) Click on the **Next** button to confirm this query and continue to the next step.
11) Modify the query function name to the **DeleteFaculty** and click on the **Next** button to go to the last wizard.
12) Click on the **Finish** button to complete this query building and close the wizard. Immediately, you can find that a new query function **DeleteFaculty** has been added into the Faculty TableAdapter as the last item.

Next let's develop the codes to call these built query methods to perform the related data updating and deleting actions. First let's build codes for the data-updating action.

7.2.2 Develop Codes to Update Data Using the TableAdapter DBDirect Method

To perform the data updating using the built query method, some modifications to the original codes in the Faculty Form are necessary. We divided these modifications into two subsections: codes modifications and codes creations.

First let's make some modifications to the codes in the Faculty Form class.

7.2.2.1 The Codes Modifications

The first modification is to modify the codes inside the **Form_Load()** method in the Faculty Form class. Two modifications are involved:

1) Add the user-defined method, **CurrentFaculty()**, built in Section 6.5.2 in Chapter 6, into this method to update all faculty names in the **Faculty Name** combobox to enable users to validate the data updating action.
2) Add two new updating methods into the **Query Method** combobox:
   a) TableAdapter DBDirect Method
   b) TableAdapter Update Method

Open the Code Window of the Faculty Form and add those items into the **Form_Load()** method using the **Add()** method. The modified codes for this method are shown in steps **A** and **B** in Figure 7.5. The new added codes have been highlighted in bold.

```
SelectWizard Project                FacultyForm_Load(object sender, EventArgs e)

  private void FacultyForm_Load(object sender, EventArgs e)
  {
A         CurrentFaculty();
          ComboMethod.Items.Add("TableAdapter Method");
          ComboMethod.Items.Add("LINQ & DataSet Method");
          ComboMethod.Items.Add("TableAdapter Insert");
          ComboMethod.Items.Add("TableAdapter Update");
B         ComboMethod.Items.Add("TableApt DBDirect Method");
          ComboMethod.Items.Add("TableApt Update Method");
          this.ComboMethod.SelectedIndex = 0;
  }
```

FIGURE 7.5 The modified codes for the Form_Load method.

7.2.2.2 The Codes Creations

The main coding process to perform this data updating is developed inside the **Update** button's Click method in the Faculty Form window. Open this method and enter the codes that are shown in Figure 7.6 into that method.

Let's have a closer look at this piece of new added codes to see how it works.

A. Some local variables and objects are declared first, including a FacultyRow class object **FacultyRow** and it is used to store a new faculty row to be updated in the **Faculty** table, a String variable **strFacultyID** that works as a holder to save the retrieved **faculty_id** based on the selected faculty name. Both variables are used for the TableAdapter Update data updating method later. The integer variable **intUpdate** also works as a status holder to save the returned running status of execution of the **UpdateFaculty()** query method to perform a faculty record updating action. The byte[] array **bImage** is used to store a selected faculty image to be updated for a faculty record.

B. If the **TableApt DBDirect Method** is selected, a user-defined method **getFacultyImage()**we built in Section 6.5.3 in Chapter 6 is executed to get an updated faculty image and then assigned to the byte[] array **bImage**.

C. Then the query **UpdateFaculty()**we built in Section 7.2.1 is called to perform this faculty record updating action based on eight pieces of faculty information stored in seven TextBoxes in the Faculty Form window and a selected faculty image. The running status of execution of that query is returned and assigned to the local integer variable **intUpdate** that will be used later.

D. If the **TableAdapter Update Method** is selected, we need to build the codes in the next section to perform that kind of data updating operation.

E. By checking the returned running status stored in the variable **intUpdate**, we can determine whether or not that data updating action is successful. If a zero value is returned, which means that some error had been encountered and the data updating is failed, a MessageBox with a warning message is displayed to indicate that case.

SelectWizard Project | **cmdUpdate_Click(object sender, EventArgs e)**

```
  private void cmdUpdate_Click(object sender, EventArgs e)
  {
A     CSE_DEPTDataSet.FacultyRow FacultyRow;
      string strFacultyID = null;
      int intUpdate = 0;
      byte[] bImage;
B     if (ComboMethod.Text == "TableApt DBDirect Method")
      {
        bImage = getFacultyImage();
C       intUpdate = facultyTableAdapter.UpdateFaculty(txtFacultyName.Text, txtTitle.Text, txtOffice.Text, txtPhone.Text,
                                                       txtCollege.Text, txtEmail.Text, bImage, txtFacultyID.Text);
      }
D     else          //TableAdapter Update method selected
      {

      }
E     if (intUpdate == 0)
        MessageBox.Show("Faculty Table Updating is failed!");
F     else
        CurrentFaculty();
  }
```

FIGURE 7.6 The codes for the update command button's click method.

F. Otherwise the data updating action is successful and at least one row has been updated (**intUpdate** = 1). Another user-defined method, **CurrentFaculty()**, we built in Section 6.5.2 in Chapter 6 is executed to get all updated faculty names and display them in the Faculty Name combobox.

Now let's continue to develop the codes for the second data updating method.

7.2.3 Develop Codes to Update Data Using the TableAdapter.Update Method

Open the **Update** button's Click method if it is not opened and add the codes that are shown in Figure 7.7 into this method, precisely into the **else** block. The codes we developed in the previous section have been highlighted by the gray background color.

Let's take a look at this piece of new added codes to see how it works.

A. In order to update a selected row from the **Faculty** table in the DataSet, we need first to identify that row. Visual Studio.NET provides a default method, **FindBy()**, to do that. But that method needs a primary key as a criterion to perform a query to locate the desired row from the table. In our case, the primary key for our **Faculty** table is the **faculty_id**. To find that **faculty_id**, we can use a query function **FindFacultyIDByName()** we built in Section 5.12 in Chapter 5 with the Faculty Name as a criterion. One key point to run this function is that the parameter Faculty Name must be an old faculty name because in order to update a faculty, we must first find the old faculty row based on the old **faculty_name**. Therefore the combobox **ComboName.Text** is used as the old faculty name.

B. After the **faculty_id** is found, the default system method **FindByfaculty_id()** is executed to locate the desired row from the **Faculty** table, and the desired data row is returned and assigned to the local variable **FacultyRow**.

SelectWizard Project	**cmdUpdate_Click(object sender, EventArgs e)**

```
private void cmdUpdate_Click(object sender, EventArgs e)
{
    CSE_DEPTDataSet.FacultyRow FacultyRow;
    string strFacultyID = null;
    int intUpdate = 0;
    byte[] bImage;
    if (ComboMethod.Text == "TableApt DBDirect Method")
    {
        bImage = getFacultyImage();
        intUpdate = facultyTableAdapter.UpdateFaculty(txtFacultyName.Text, txtTitle.Text, txtOffice.Text, txtPhone.Text,
                                                      txtCollege.Text, txtEmail.Text, bImage, txtFacultyID.Text);
    }
    else          //TableAdapter Update method selected
    {
A       strFacultyID = facultyTableAdapter.FindFacultyIDByName(ComboName.Text);
B       FacultyRow = cSE_DEPTDataSet.Faculty.FindByfaculty_id(strFacultyID);
C       FacultyRow = UPFacultyRow(ref FacultyRow);
D       this.Validate();
E       facultyBindingSource.EndEdit();
F       intUpdate = facultyTableAdapter.Update(cSE_DEPTDataSet.Faculty);
    }
    if (intUpdate == 0)
        MessageBox.Show("Faculty Table Updating is failed!");
    else
        CurrentFaculty();
}
```

FIGURE 7.7 The codes for the second data updating method.

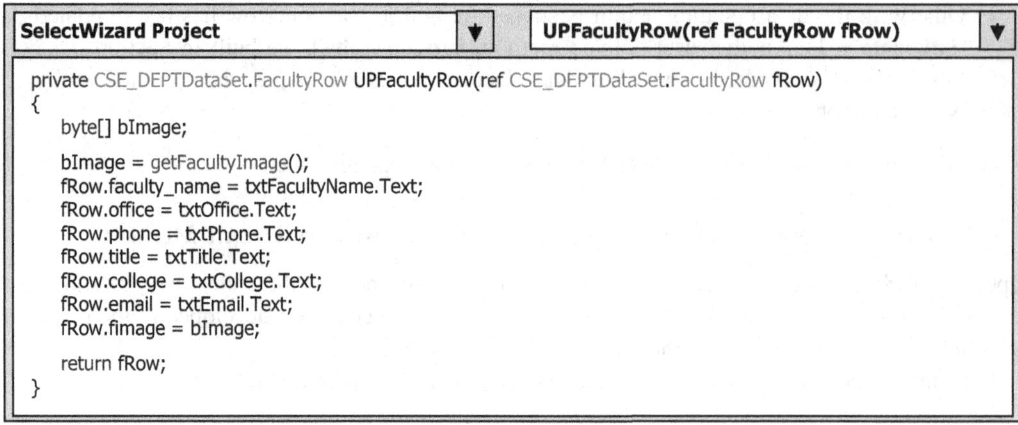


```
private CSE_DEPTDataSet.FacultyRow UPFacultyRow(ref CSE_DEPTDataSet.FacultyRow fRow)
{
    byte[] bImage;

    bImage = getFacultyImage();
    fRow.faculty_name = txtFacultyName.Text;
    fRow.office = txtOffice.Text;
    fRow.phone = txtPhone.Text;
    fRow.title = txtTitle.Text;
    fRow.college = txtCollege.Text;
    fRow.email = txtEmail.Text;
    fRow.fimage = bImage;

    return fRow;
}
```

FIGURE 7.8 The codes for the user-defined method UPFacultyRow().

C. A user-defined method **UPFacultyRow()** that will be built later is called to assign all updated faculty information to the selected row. In this way, the faculty information, exactly a row in the **Faculty** table in the DataSet, is updated.
D. The **Validate()** command closes out the editing of a control. In our case, it closes any editing for TextBox control in the Faculty Form window.
E. The **EndEdit()** method of the binding source writes any edited data in the controls back to the record in the DataSet. In our case, any updated data entered into the TextBox control will be reflected to the associated column in the DataSet.
F. Finally, the **Update()** method of the TableAdapter sends updated data back to the database. The argument of this method can be either a whole DataSet, a DataTable in the DataSet or a DataRow in a DataTable. In our case, we used the Faculty DataTable as the argument for this method.

The codes for the user-defined method **UPFacultyRow()** are shown in Figure 7.8. The functionality of this method is straightforward and easy to be understood.

The argument of this method is a DataRow object and it is passed by a Reference to the method. The advantage of passing an argument in this way is that any modifications performed to DataRow object inside the method can be returned to the calling procedure without requiring the creation of another returned variable. The updated faculty information stored in the associated TextBox is assigned to the associated column of the DataRow in the **Faculty** table in the DataSet. In this way, the selected DataRow in the **Faculty** table is updated.

At this point, we finished the coding development for two methods to update the data in a database. Next we discuss how to delete data from the database.

7.2.4 Develop Codes to Delete Data Using the TableAdapter DBDirect Method

To delete data from a database, you can use either the TableAdapter DBDirect method **TableAdapter.Delete()** or the **TableAdapter.Update()**method. Or, if your application does not use TableAdapters, you can use the run time object method to create a command object to delete data from a database (for example, **ExecuteNonQuery()** method).

The **TableAdapter.Update()** method is typically used when your application uses a DataSet to store data, whereas the **TableAdapter.Delete()** method is typically used when your application uses objects, for example in our case we used TextBoxes, to store data.

As we mentioned in the previous section, to delete a record from our sample database, no new user interface is needed and we can use the Faculty Form window to perform this data deleting

```
SelectWizard Project                    cmdDelete_Click(object sender, EventArgs e)

    private void cmdDelete_Click(object sender, EventArgs e)
    {
A           MessageBoxButtons vbButton = MessageBoxButtons.YesNo;
            CSE_DEPTDataSet.FacultyRow FacultyRow;
            DialogResult Answer;
            string strFacultyID = null;
            int intDelete = 0;
B           Answer = MessageBox.Show("Sure to delete this record?", "Delete", vbButton);
C           if (Answer == System.Windows.Forms.DialogResult.Yes)
            {
D               if (ComboMethod.Text == " TableApt DBDirect Method ")
E                   intDelete = facultyTableAdapter.DeleteFaculty(ComboName.Text);
F               else
                {
                    // TableAdapter Update() method is selected.....
                }
                CurrentFaculty();
            }
G           if (intDelete == 0)
                MessageBox.Show("Faculty Table Deleting is failed!");
    }
```

FIGURE 7.9 The codes for the delete button's click method.

action. Open the Faculty Form window with the Designer View and double-click on the **Delete** button to open its Click method. Then enter the codes that are shown in Figure 7.9 into this method.

Let's have a look at this piece of code to see how it works.

A. All data components and objects as well as variables used in this method are declared and created here. A button object of the **MessageboxButtons** class is created and we need to use these two buttons to confirm the data deleting later. The **FacultyRow** is used to locate the DataRow in the Faculty DataTable and it is used for the second deleting method. The local variable **Answer** is an instance of **DialogResult** and it is used to hold the returned value from the calling of the system method **MessageBox.Show()**.This variable can be replaced by an integer variable if you like.

B. First, the system method **MessageBox.Show()**is called to confirm that a data deletion will be performed from the **Faculty** data table.

C. If the returned value of calling this **MessageBox.Show()** is **Yes**, meaning that the user has confirmed that this data deleting is fine, the data deletion will be performed in the next step.

D. If the user selected the first method, the **TableApt DBDirect Method**, the query function we built in Section 7.2.1 will be called to perform the data deleting from the **Faculty** table in the database.

E. The execution result of the first method is stored in the local variable **intDelete**.

F. If the user selected the second method, **TableApt Update Method**, the associated codes that will be developed in the next section will be executed to delete data, first from the DataTable in the DataSet, and then from the data table in the database by executing the **Update**() method.

G. The returned value of calling either the **TableAdapter.Delete**() method or the **TableAdapter.Update**()method is an integer value and stored in the local variable **intDelete**. The value of this returned data is equal to the number of deleted data rows in the database or deleted DataRows in the DataSet. A returned zero value means that no data row has been deleted and that data deleting is failed. In that case, a warning message is displayed.

Now let's continue to develop the codes for the second data deleting method.

```
SelectWizard Project    cmdDelete_Click(object sender, EventArgs e)

private void cmdDelete_Click(object sender, EventArgs e)
{
        MessageBoxButtons vbButton = MessageBoxButtons.YesNo;
        CSE_DEPTDataSet.FacultyRow FacultyRow;
        DialogResult Answer;
        string strFacultyID = null;
        int intDelete = 0;

        Answer = MessageBox.Show("Sure to delete this record?", "Delete", vbButton);
        if (Answer == System.Windows.Forms.DialogResult.Yes)
        {
            if (ComboMethod.Text == " TableApt DBDirect Method ")
               intDelete = facultyTableAdapter.DeleteFaculty(ComboName.Text);
            else   // TableAdapter Update() method is selected.....
            {
A              strFacultyID = facultyTableAdapter.FindFacultyIDByName(ComboName.Text);
B              FacultyRow = cSE_DEPTDataSet.Faculty.FindByfaculty_id(strFacultyID);
C              FacultyRow.Delete();          // delete data from the DataTable in DataSet
D              intDelete = facultyTableAdapter.Update(cSE_DEPTDataSet.Faculty);
            }
            CurrentFaculty();
        }
        if (intDelete == 0)
            MessageBox.Show("Faculty Table Deleting is failed!");
}
```

FIGURE 7.10 The codes for the second method of the data deleting.

7.2.5 Develop Codes to Delete Data Using the TableAdapter.Update Method

On the opened Code Window, exactly on the opened Delete button's Click method, of the Faculty Form window, add the codes that are shown in Figure 7.10 into the **else** block of that method. The codes we developed in the previous section have been highlighted with the gray color as the background.

Let's have a close look at this piece of new added codes to see how it works.

- **A.** To identify the DataRow to be deleted from the DataTable, a default system method **FindByfaculty_id()** will be utilized. However, that method needs to use the **faculty_id** as a criterion. Therefore, we need first to retrieve the **faculty_id** from the **Faculty** table based on the Faculty Name selected by the user by using a user-built method **FindFacultyIDByName()**.
- **B.** After a desired **faculty_id** is found, the default system method **FindByfaculty_id()** is executed to locate the desired DataRow from the **Faculty** table, and the desired DataRow is returned and assigned to the local variable **FacultyRow**.
- **C.** The **Delete()** method of the **FacultyRow** is executed to delete the selected DataRow from the **Faculty** DataTable in the DataSet.
- **D.** The **TableAdapter.Update()** method is executed to update that deleted DataRow from the DataSet to the data row in the database.

At this point we have completed all coding developments for this project. Now let's run our project to test and confirm data updating and deleting actions.

7.2.6 Run Project to Validate the Data after the Data Updating and Deleting

Click on the Run button to run our project. Complete the login process and select the **Faculty Information** from the Selection Form to open the Faculty Form window. Select a desired faculty member, such as **Ying Bai** from the **Faculty Name** combobox, then click on the **Select** button to retrieve this faculty record.

Enter the following information to update this faculty record:

Faculty Name:	**Susan Bai**
Title:	**Professor**
Office:	**MTC-218**
Phone:	**750-378-2800**
College:	**Duke University**
Email:	**sbai@college.edu**

Select the **TableApt DBDirect Method** from the **Query Method** combobox and click on the **Update** button to update this record. Browse to your local image folder and select the desired faculty image **White.jpg** from the opened File Dialog, and click on the **Open** button to load and update this faculty image. All faculty images can be found from a folder **Images\Faculty** under the **Students** folder on the CRC Press ftp site (refer to Figure 1.2 in Chapter 1). You can copy all of those faculty images and store them at one of your local folders to make it easy to get one of them to test this project.

To confirm or validate this data updating, just go to the updated **Faculty Name** combobox and select the updated faculty member, **Susan Bai**, and click on the Select button to try to retrieve back that updated record. Immediately, all updated information for that selected faculty are displayed in this Faculty Form window, as shown in Figure 7.11.

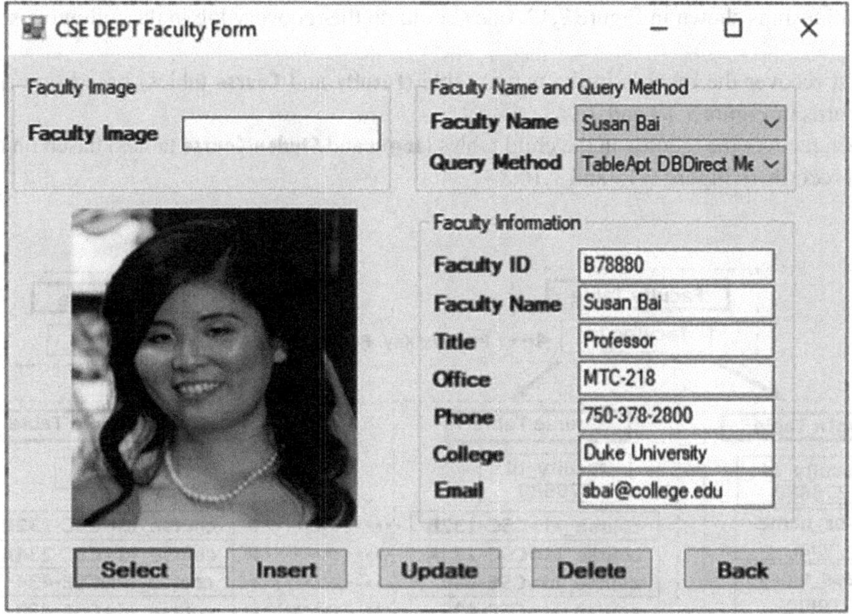

FIGURE 7.11 The updated faculty record by using the TableAdapter DBDirect method.

One can try to use the second method, **TableAdapter.Update() Method**, to do another updating action to recover it to the original faculty record for the faculty member **Ying Bai** with the following data items:

Faculty Name:	**Ying Bai**
Title:	**AssociateProfessor**
Office:	**MTC-211**
Phone:	**750-378-1148**
College:	**Florida Atlantic University**
Email:	**ybai@college.edu**
Faculty Image:	**Bai.jpg**

To test to delete a faculty record, the best way is to delete a new inserted faculty member, **Steve Wang**, which was inserted into our database in Section 6.2.8 in Chapter 6 and it is not an original faculty member when we built our database. To test this deletion, select that faculty name from the **Faculty Name** combobox and click on the **Delete** button.

To confirm that data deleting action, just open the **Faculty Name** combobox again, and the faculty member **Steve Wang** has disappeared from this box. Another way to do this validation job is to open the Faculty table to confirm it.

One needs to do a lot of recovering jobs to recover that deleted faculty record if an original faculty member were deleted due to the relationships among the parent and child tables. For example, if an original faculty member **Ying Bai** were deleted from the Faculty table, not only would this faculty member have been deleted from the Faculty table, but also more than 10 records would be deleted from all related child tables. Figure 7.12 shows the relationships between the **Faculty** table and other tables in our sample database **CSE_DEPT**.

In order to recover that deleted faculty member, one needs to recover all of those records shown in Figure 7.12, which is a terribly complicated recovery job to be done!

An import issue for this data recovery is the order of recovering these deleted records. Based on those relationships shown in Figure 7.12, one should do the recovery job in the following sequence:

- First recover the records in the parent table (**Faculty** and **Course** tables) based on original records in Figure 7.13 and 7.14.
- Then recover the records in the child tables (**LogIn** and **StudentCourse** tables) based on original records in Figure 7.15 and 7.16.

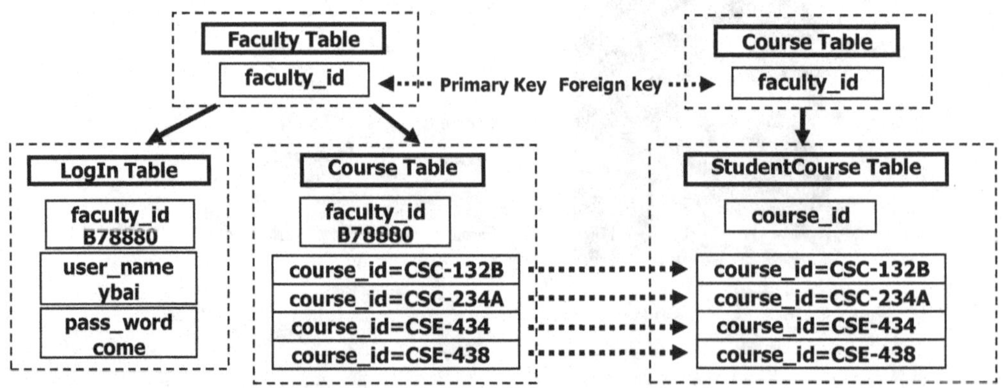

FIGURE 7.12 The relationships among parent and child tables.

faculty_id	faculty_name	title	office	phone	college	email	fimage
B78880	Ying Bai	Associate Professor	MTC-211	750-378-1148	Florida Atlantic University	ybai@college.edu	NULL

FIGURE 7.13 The data to be recovered in the faculty table.

course_id	course	credit	classroom	schedule	enrollment	faculty_id
CSC-132B	Introduction to Programming	3	MTC-302	T-H: 1:00-2:25 PM	21	B78880
CSC-234A	Data Structure & Algorithms	3	MTC-302	M-W-F: 9:00-9:55 AM	25	B78880
CSE-434	Advanced Electronics Systems	3	MTC-213	M-W-F: 1:00-1:55 PM	26	B78880
CSE-438	Advd Logic & Microprocessor	3	MTC-213	M-W-F: 11:00-11:55 AM	35	B78880

FIGURE 7.14 The data to be recovered in the course table.

user_name	pass_word	faculty_id	student_id
ybai	come	B78880	NULL

FIGURE 7.15 The data to be recovered in the login table.

s_course_id	student_id	course_id	credit	major
1005	T77896	CSC-234A	3	CS/IS
1009	A78835	CSE-434	3	CE
1014	A78835	CSE-438	3	CE
1016	A97850	CSC-132B	3	ISE
1017	A97850	CSC-234A	3	ISE

FIGURE 7.16 The data to be recovered in the StudentCourse table.

Follow the table order in Figure 7.12 and refer to Figures 7.13–7.16 to complete these records recovery.

A complete project **SelectWizard Project** can be found from a folder **Class DB Projects\ Chapter 7\ SelectWizard Solution** under the **Students** folder at the CRC Press ftp site (refer to Figure 1.2 in Chapter 1).

PART II DATA UPDATING AND DELETING WITH RUNTIME OBJECTS

To update or delete data against the database using the run time objects method is a flexible and professional way to perform the data modification jobs in the Visual C#.NET environment. Compared with the method we discussed in Part I, in which Visual Studio.NET Design Tools and Wizards are utilized to update or delete data against the database, the run time object method provides more sophisticated techniques to do this job efficiently and conveniently even a more complicated coding job is needed. Relatively speaking, the method we discussed in the first part is easy to learn and code, but the method does have some limitations. First, each TableAdapter can only access the associated data table to perform data actions such as updating or deleting data against that table only. Second, each query function built by using the TableAdapter Query Configuration Wizard can only perform a single query such as data updating or deletion. Third, after the query function is built, no modifications can be made to that function dynamically, which means that the only times that you can modify that query function are either before the project runs or after the project terminates. In other words, you cannot modify that query function during the project runs.

To overcome those shortcomings, we will discuss how to update or delete data using the run time object method in this part.

Basically, you need to use the TableAdapter to perform data actions against the database if you develop your applications using the Visual Studio.NET Design Tools and Wizards in the design time. However, you should use the DataAdapter to make those data manipulations if you develop your project using the run time objects method.

7.3 THE RUN TIME OBJECT METHOD

We have provided a very detailed introduction and discussion about the run time objects method in Section 5.14 in Chapter 5. Refer to that section to get more detailed information about this method. For your convenience, we highlight some important points and general methodologies of this method as well as some keynotes in using this method to perform the data updating and deleting again the databases in this part.

As you know, ADO.NET provides different classes to help users to develop professional data-driven applications by using the different methods to perform specific data actions such as updating and deleting data items. Among them, two popular methods are widely implemented for most applications:

1) Update or delete records from the desired data table in the DataSet, and then call the **DataAdapter.Update()** method to update the updated or deleted records from the table in the DataSet to the table in the database.
2) Build the update or delete command using the Command object, and then call the Command's method **ExecuteNonQuery()** to update or delete records against the database. Or you can assign the built command object to the **UpdateCommand** or **DeleteCommand** properties of the DataAdapter and call the **ExecuteNonQuery()** method from the **UpdateCommand** or the **DeleteCommand** property.

The first method is to use the so-called DataSet-DataAdapter method to build a data-driven application. DataSet and DataTable classes can have different roles when they are implemented in a real application. Multiple DataTables can be embedded into a DataSet and each table can be filled, inserted, updated and deleted by using the different properties of a DataAdapter such as the **SelectCommand**, **InsertCommand**, **UpdateCommand** or **DeleteCommand** when the DataAdapter's **Update()** method is executed. The DataAdapter will perform the associated operations based on the modifications you made for each table in the DataSet. For example, if you deleted rows from a table in the DataSet, and then you label this DataAdapter's **Update()** method. This method will perform a **DeleteCommand** based on your modifications. This method is relatively simple since you do not need to call some specific methods, such as the **ExecuteNonQuery()** to complete these data queries. But this simplicity brings some limitations for your applications. For instance, you cannot access different data tables individually to perform multiple specific data operations. This method is very similar to the second method we discussed in Part I; therefore we will not continue to provide any discussion for this method in this part.

The second method allows us to use each object individually, which means that you do not have to use the DataAdapter to access the Command object, or use the DataTable with DataSet together. This provides more flexibility. In this method, no DataAdapter or DataSet is needed, and you only need to create a new Command object with a new Connection object, and then build a query statement and attach some useful parameters into that query for that new created Command object. Then you can update or delete data against any data table by calling the **ExecuteNonQuery()** method which belongs to the Command class. We will concentrate our discussions on this method in this part.

In this section, we provide two sample projects, **RTOUpdateDelete Project** and **SPUpdateDelete Project**, to illustrate how to update or delete records against our sample SQL Server database using the run time object and stored procedure method.

In addition to that sample project, we will also discuss the data updating and deleting against our sample databases using the LINQ to SQL query method. A sample project, **LINQUpdateDelete Project**, will be developed in this chapter to show readers how to build an actual data-driven project to update and delete data against our sample databases using the LINQ to SQL query method.

7.4 UPDATE AND DELETE DATA USING THE RUN TIME OBJECT METHOD

Now let's first create and develop the sample project **RTOUpdateDelete Project** to update and delete data against the SQL Server database using the run time object method. In this part, we divide this discussion into two sections:

1) Update and delete data against the **Faculty** table via the Faculty Form window using the run time object method.
2) Update and delete data against the **Faculty** table via the Faculty Form using the run time stored procedure method.

In order to avoid duplication in the coding process, we can modify two existing projects we developed in Chapter 6, **RTOInsert Project** and **RTOInsertSP Project**, to create our new projects **RTOUpdateDelete Project** and **SPUpdateDelete Project** used in this section. First let's concentrate on our first project, **RTOUpdateDelete Project**.

Open the Windows Explorer and create a new folder such as **C:\Chapter 7** if you have not already done so. Then browse to the folder **Class DB Projects\Chapter 6**, which is located under the **Students** folder on the CRC Press ftp site. Copy the entire folder **RTOInsert Solution** and save it to the new folder **C:\Chapter 7** we have just created. Perform the following operations to make it our new project:

1) Change the name of the Solution and the project from **RTOInsert Solution** to **RTOUpdateDelete Solution**, and from **RTOInsert Project** to **RTOUpdateDelete Project**.
2) Also change the **RTOInsert Project.csproj** to **RTOUpdateDelete Project.csproj**. Then double-click on the project **RTOUpdateDelete Project.csproj** to open this project.
3) Go to the menu item **Project | RTOUpdataDelete Project Properties** to open the project's property window. Change the **Assembly name** and the **Default namespace** to **RTOUpdataDelete Project** and **RTOUpdateDelete_Project**, respectively.
4) Click on the **Assembly Information** button to open the **Assembly Information** wizard, change the **Title** and the **Product** to **RTOUpdataDelete Project**. Click on the **OK** button to close this wizard.
5) Change the project namespace for all Form windows classes, including **LogIn.cs, Faculty.cs, Course.cs, Selection.cs** and **Student.cs**, as well as related class **Designer.cs** files, from **RTOInsert_Project** to **RTOUpdateDelete_Project** using the **Find and Replace** dialog box.
6) Double-click on the **C# Program.cs** file from the Solution Explorer window to open it, and change the namespace to **RTOUpdateDelete_Project**.

Go to the File | **Save All** to save those modifications. Click on the **Save**, the **Overwrite** and then the **Save** button again to save this project. Now we are ready to develop our codes on our new project to perform data updating and deleting actions.

7.4.1 Update Data for the Faculty Table in the SQL Server Database

Let's first discuss updating data against the **Faculty** table for the SQL Server database. To update data against the **Faculty** data table, we do not need to add any new Windows Form and we can use the Faculty Form as the user interface. We need to perform the following two steps to complete this data updating action:

1) Develop codes to update the faculty data.
2) Validate the data updating.

First let's develop the codes for our data updating action.

7.4.1.1 Develop Codes to Update Data

As we mentioned in the previous sections, to update or delete an existing record from our related tables, one must follow the three steps listed in Section 7.1.1.

Open the **Update** button's Click method by double-clicking the **Update** button from the Faculty Form Designer View and enter the codes that are shown in Figure 7.17 into this method.

Let's take a look at this piece of codes to see how it works.

A. The Update query string is defined first at the beginning of this method. All eight data columns in the **Faculty** table, with the exception of the **faculty_id**, are input parameters. The dynamic parameter **@fid** represents the original **faculty_id**, which is a primary key in the **Faculty** table and will not be updated.

B. All data components and local variables are declared here, such as the Command object and integer variable **intUpdate**. The latter is used to hold the returned running status of the calling of the **ExecuteNonQuery()** method.

C. The Command object is initialized and built using the Connection object and the Parameter object.

```
RTOUpdateDelete Project        cmdUpdate_Click(object sender, EventArgs e)

  private void cmdUpdate_Click(object sender, EventArgs e)
  {
A     string cmdString = "UPDATE Faculty SET faculty_name = @name, title = @title, office = @office, " +
            "phone = @phone, college = @college, email = @email, fimage = @fimage WHERE (faculty_id = @fid)";
B        SqlCommand sqlCommand = new SqlCommand();
         int intUpdate = 0;
C        sqlCommand.Connection = loginForm.sqlConnection;
         sqlCommand.CommandType = CommandType.Text;
         sqlCommand.CommandText = cmdString;
D        UpdateParameters(ref sqlCommand);
E        intUpdate = sqlCommand.ExecuteNonQuery();
F        sqlCommand.Dispose();
         CurrentFaculty();
G        if (intUpdate == 0)
            MessageBox.Show("The data updating is failed");
  }
H private void UpdateParameters(ref SqlCommand cmd)
  {
      byte[] bImage;
      bImage = getFacultyImage();
      cmd.Parameters.Add("@name", SqlDbType.Char).Value = txtFacultyName.Text;
      cmd.Parameters.Add("@title", SqlDbType.Char).Value = txtTitle.Text;
      cmd.Parameters.Add("@office", SqlDbType.Char).Value = txtOffice.Text;
      cmd.Parameters.Add("@phone", SqlDbType.Char).Value = txtPhone.Text;
      cmd.Parameters.Add("@college", SqlDbType.Char).Value = txtCollege.Text;
      cmd.Parameters.Add("@email", SqlDbType.Char).Value = txtEmail.Text;
      cmd.Parameters.Add("@fimage", SqlDbType.Binary).Value = bImage;
      cmd.Parameters.Add("@fid", SqlDbType.Char).Value = txtFacultyID.Text;
  }
```

FIGURE 7.17 The codes for the data updating operation.

D. A user-defined method, **UpdateParameters()**, whose codes will be built later, is called to add all updating parameters into the Command's Parameters property. The passing mode used for the passed argument is passing-by-reference, which means that a valid starting address of that Command object is passed into the method, and any modification to this Command object is permanent and it can be returned to the calling method.
E. Then the **ExecuteNonQuery()** method of the Command class is executed to update a faculty row in the **Faculty** table. The running result of this method is returned and stored in the local variable **intUpdate**.
F. The Command object is released after this data updating and the updated faculty member (name) is refreshed in the Faculty Name combobox by executing a user-defined method **CurrentFaculty**().
G. The returned value from calling of the **ExecuteNonQuery()** method is equal to the number of rows that have been updated in the **Faculty** table. A zero means that no row has been updated; an error message is displayed to indicate it if this situation is really occurred.
H. The detailed codes for the user-defined method **UpdateParameters()** are shown in this step. Seven pieces of updated faculty information are assigned to the associated columns in the **Faculty** table.

At this point, we finished the coding development for the data updating operation for the **Faculty** table by using the runtime object method. Next let's take care of the data validation after this data updating to confirm that our data updating is successful.

7.4.1.2 Validate the Data Updating

We do not need to add any new Form window or button to perform this data validation; instead we can use the Faculty Form window and the **Select** button, precisely the **Select** button's Click method, to perform this validation job. By clicking the **Select** button on the Faculty Form window with the selected updated faculty name from the **Faculty Name** combobox, we can perform the selection query to retrieve the updated faculty record from the database and display it on the Faculty Form.

Before we can run the project to test the data updating function, we prefer to first complete the coding process for the data deleting operation.

7.4.2 Delete Data From the Faculty Table for the SQL Server Database

As we mentioned in the previous section, to delete a faculty record from our database, we have to follow up two steps listed below:

1) First, delete records from the child tables (**LogIn**, **Course** and **StudentCourse** tables).
2) Second, delete record from the parent table (**Faculty** table).

The data deleting function can be performed by using the **Delete** button's Click method in the Faculty Form window. Therefore, the main coding job for this function is developed inside that method.

7.4.2.1 Develop Codes to Delete Data

Open the **Delete** button's Click method by double-clicking on the **Delete** button from the Designer View of the Faculty Form window, and enter the codes that are shown in Figure 7.18 into that method.

Let's have a close look at this piece of codes to see how it works.

A. The deleting query string is declared first at the beginning of this method. The only input parameter is the **faculty_name**. Although the primary key of the **Faculty** table is **faculty_id**, in order to make it convenient to the user, the **faculty_name** is used as the criterion for this data-deleting query. A potential problem of using the **faculty_name** column as the deleting

```
RTOUpdateDelete Project                    cmdDelete_Click(object sender, EventArgs e)

  private void cmdDelete_Click(object sender, EventArgs e)
  {
A       string cmdString = "DELETE FROM Faculty WHERE (faculty_name = @fname)";
B       MessageBoxButtons vbButton = MessageBoxButtons.YesNo;
C       SqlCommand sqlCommand = new SqlCommand();
        DialogResult Answer;
        int intDelete;
D       Answer = MessageBox.Show("Do you want to delete this record?", "Delete", vbButton);
E       if (Answer == System.Windows.Forms.DialogResult.Yes)
        {
           sqlCommand.Connection = loginForm.sqlConnection;
           sqlCommand.CommandType = CommandType.Text;
           sqlCommand.CommandText = cmdString;
F          sqlCommand.Parameters.Add("@fname", SqlDbType.Char).Value = ComboName.Text;
G          intDelete = sqlCommand.ExecuteNonQuery();
H          sqlCommand.Dispose();
I          CurrentFaculty();
J          if (intDelete == 0)
              MessageBox.Show("The data Deleting is failed");
K          else
           {
              ClearFaculty();
              PhotoBox.Image = null;
           }
        }
  }
```

FIGURE 7.18 The codes for the data-deleting query.

criterion is that no duplicated **faculty_name** should be existed in the **Faculty** table for this application. In other words, each faculty name must be unique in the **Faculty** table. A solution to this potential problem is that we can use the **faculty_id** as the criterion for the data-deleting query as an option.

B. A MessageBox's button's object is created and this object is used to display both buttons in the MessageBox, **Yes** and **No**, when the project runs.

C. All data components and local variables used in this method are declared here. The data type of the variable **Answer** is **DialogResult**. However, one can use an integer variable to replace it. The integer variable **intDelete** is used to hold the returned data from calling the **ExecuteNonQuery()** method to delete a record from the **Faculty** table.

D. As the **Delete** button is clicked when the project runs, first a MessageBox is displayed to confirm that the user wants to delete the selected member from the **Faculty** table.

E. If the user's answer is **Yes**, then the deleting operation begins to be processed. The Command object is initialized and built by using the Connection object and the Command string we defined at the beginning of this method.

F. The dynamic parameter **@fname** is replaced by the real parameter, the faculty name stored in the Faculty Name combobox **ComboName**. A key point to be noted is that you must use the faculty name stored in the combobox control, which is an existing faculty name, but you cannot use the faculty name stored in the Faculty Name TextBox since that may be an updating faculty name.

G. The **ExecuteNonQuery()** method of the Command class is called to execute the data-deleting query to the **Faculty** table. The running result of calling that method is stored in the local variable **intDelete**.

H. The Command object is released after the data deleting.

I. The user-defined method **CurrentFaculty()** is executed to update all faculty names in the Faculty Name combobox after this data deleting action to allow users to check and confirm that data deleting action.
J. The returned value from calling of the **ExecuteNonQuery()** method is equal to the number of rows that have been successfully deleted from the **Faculty** table. If a zero returns, which means that no row has been deleted from the **Faculty** table and this data deleting is failed, an error message is displayed if that situation occurred.
K. After the data deleting is completed, all faculty information stored in seven TextBoxes and the faculty image stored in the PhotoBox should be cleaned up to enable users to check and confirm this data deleting action.

Finally let's take care of the coding process to validate the data-deleting query.

7.4.2.2 Validate the Data Updating and Deleting

As we did for the validation for the data updating in the last section, we do not need to create any new Form window to do this validation, and we can use the Faculty Form, exactly use the **Select** button's Click method, to perform this data validation.

Before we can run this project to test the data updating and deleting actions against our **Faculty** table, make sure to create a local folder in your machine to store all faculty image files that can be found from the folder **Students\Images\Faculty** at the CRC Press ftp site (refer to Figure 1.2 in Chapter 1).

Now let's run the project to test both data updating and deleting operations. Click on the **Start** button to run the project, enter the suitable username and password to the LogIn Form, and select the **Faculty Information** item from the Selection Form to open the Faculty Form window. First let's select a faculty member and retrieve back all information related to the selected faculty from our database, and display those pieces of information in this form. Then we can update this faculty by modifying some pieces of information stored in related TextBoxes. In this test, we select **Ying Bai** as a faculty member and enter the following updated information to the related textboxes:

Faculty Name:	**Susan Bai**
Title:	**Professor**
Office:	**MTC-218**
Phone:	**750-378-2800**
College:	**Duke University**
Email:	**sbai@college.edu**

Click on the **Update** button in the Faculty Form window to try to update this record. On the opened File Image Selection wizard, browse to your local folder where all faculty image files are located, and select a desired faculty image file, **White.jpg**, and click on the **Open** button to perform this data updating action.

To validate this data updating, first select another faculty from the combobox control ComboName and click the **Select** button to retrieve back all information for that faculty. Then go to the Faculty Name combobox again, and one can find that the updated faculty member, **Susan Bai**, has been in there. Select that updated faculty name **Susan Bai** from the box and click the **Select** button to retrieve back the updated information for that selected faculty member. Immediately, you can find that all pieces of updated information related to the selected faculty are displayed in this Form. This means that our data updating is successful. Your updated faculty information window should match one that is shown in Figure 7.19.

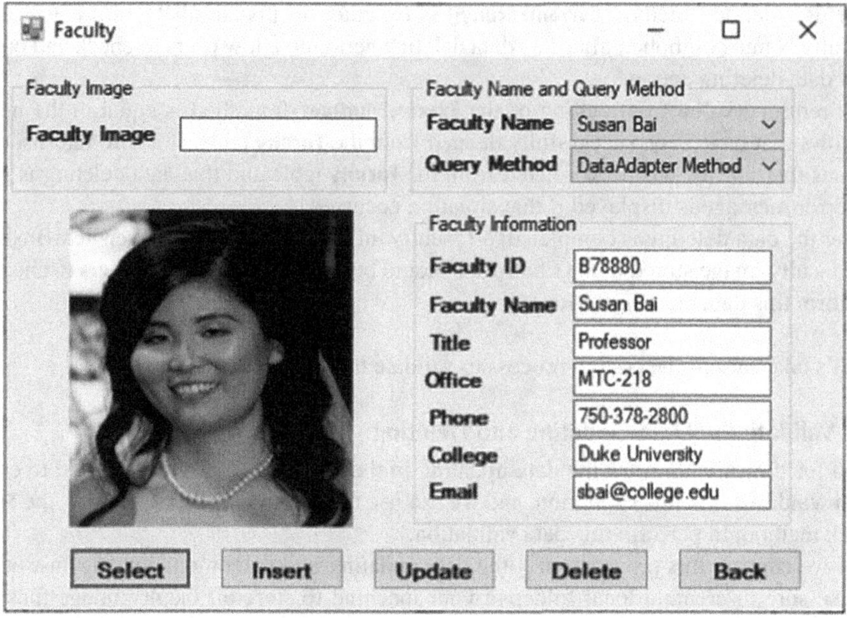

FIGURE 7.19 The updated faculty information.

To keep our sample database identical, it is highly recommended to recover the updated faculty record to the original faculty record. To do that, one can perform another updating action to get the original faculty record **Ying Bai**, which is shown below, to replace that updated one:

Faculty Name:	**Ying Bai**
Title:	**AssociateProfessor**
Office:	**MTC-211**
Phone:	**750-378-1148**
College:	**Florida Atlantic University**
Email:	**ybai@college.edu**
Faculty Image:	**Bai.jpg**

Next let's test the data deleting function. In order to avoid a complicated data recovering job, we prefer not to delete any original faculty record. The so-called original faculty record is a faculty record that was created when we built our sample database in Chapter 2 since those faculty members contained some complicated relationships with other tables, such as **Course**, **LogIn** and **StudentCourse** tables, by using primary and foreign keys. Refer to Section 7.2.6 to get more details for these relationships.

Now go to the **Faculty Name** combobox to select a faculty member **James David**, which is not an original faculty record, but it was inserted in Section 6.2.8 in Chapter 6. Click on the **Delete** button to try to delete this faculty record from the **Faculty** table. Then click **Yes** to the MessageBox and all faculty information displayed in seven TextBoxes is gone. Is our data deleting successful? To answer this question, open the **Faculty Name** combobox and the deleted faculty member, **James David**, cannot be found from that box. This means that the selected faculty with all information have been successfully deleted from the **Faculty** table. Yes, our data deleting is successful.

However, if an original faculty record, such as **Ying Bai**, were deleted, due to the complicated relationships in existence, not only would that faculty record be deleted from the **Faculty** table, but so also would some other data records in the related tables be deleted. Refer to Figure 7.20 to get a clear picture for those relationships.

In order to recover that deleted faculty member, the following points must be kept in mind and the following procedures must be followed:

1) Recall that when we built our sample database **CSE_DEPT**, exactly when we setup the relationships among tables, we selected the **Cascade** mode for both **Update** and **Delete Rules** for **INSERT** and **UPDATE Specification** field between the **Faculty** and **LogIn**, **Faculty** and **Course**, and **Course** and **StudentCourse** tables. This means that among these tables, the **Faculty** is a parent table for the **LogIn** and the **Course** tables and the **LogIn** and the **Course** are child tables to the **Faculty** table. Similarly, the **Course** is a parent table for the **StudentCourse** table and the **StudentCourse** is a child table to the **Course** table. The cascade updating and deleting means that when a record in the parent table is updated or deleted, all related records in the child tables are also updated or deleted. An example of cascade updating and deleting is shown in Figure 7.20. The faculty member **Ying Bai** with a **faculty_id=B78880** is selected for this cascade updating and deleting example.
2) As shown in Figure 7.20, if the faculty member with a **faculty_id=B78880**, which is a primary key in the **Faculty** table, but a foreign key in the **LogIn** and the **Course** tables, is updated or deleted from the **Faculty** table, the related records in the child tables, **LogIn** and **Course**, with the same **faculty_id** will also be updated or deleted with the associated columns. Two associated columns, **user_name** and **pass_word**, located in the **LogIn** table and four associated columns, **course_id**, located in the **Course** table will also be updated or deleted. Similarly, if a **course_id** that is a primary key in the **Course** table but a foreign key in the **StudentCourse** table is updated or deleted from the **Course** table, all related records in the child table, **StudentCourse**, will also be updated or deleted. Figure 7.20 shows the associated columns that will be affected when this cascade updating or deleting actions are performed for the selected faculty member **Ying Bai**.
3) An import issue is the order to recover these deleted records. You have to first recover the records in the parent table (**Faculty** and **Course** tables), and then recover the records in the child tables. Following the table order in Figure 7.20 and refer to Sections 2.9.4.1–2.9.4.5 in Chapter 2, as well as Figures 7.21–7.24 to complete these records recovering jobs.

A complete project **RTOUpdateDelete Project** can be found from a folder **Class DB Projects\Chapter 7\RTOUpdateDelete Solution** under the **Students** folder on the CRC Press ftp site (refer to Figure 1.2 in Chapter 1).

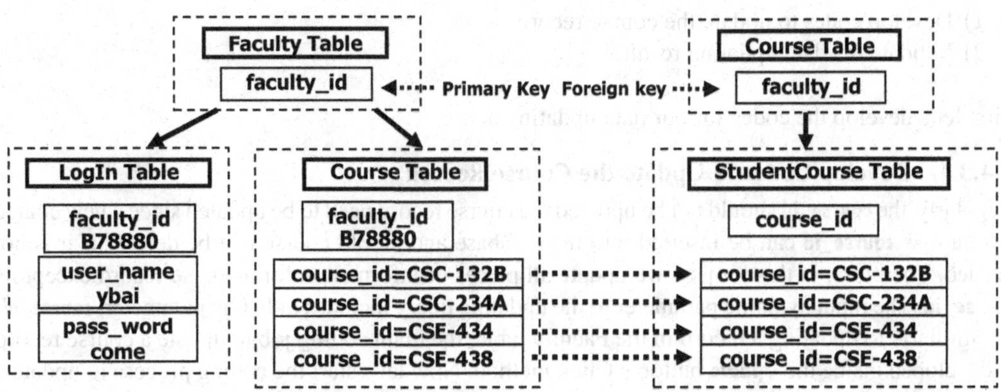

FIGURE 7.20 The relationships among tables.

faculty_id	faculty_name	title	office	phone	college	email	fimage
B78880	Ying Bai	Associate Professor	MTC-211	750-378-1148	Florida Atlantic University	ybai@college.edu	NULL

FIGURE 7.21 The data to be recovered in the faculty table.

user_name	pass_word	faculty_id	student_id
ybai	come	B78880	NULL

FIGURE 7.22 The data to be recovered in the LogIn table.

course_id	course	credit	classroom	schedule	enrollment	faculty_id
CSC-132B	Introduction to Programming	3	MTC-302	T-H: 1:00-2:25 PM	21	B78880
CSC-234A	Data Structure & Algorithms	3	MTC-302	M-W-F: 9:00-9:55 AM	25	B78880
CSE-434	Advanced Electronics Systems	3	MTC-213	M-W-F: 1:00-1:55 PM	26	B78880
CSE-438	Advd Logic & Microprocessor	3	MTC-213	M-W-F: 11:00-11:55 AM	35	B78880

FIGURE 7.23 The data to be recovered in the course table.

s_course_id	student_id	course_id	credit	major
1005	T77896	CSC-234A	3	CS/IS
1009	A78835	CSE-434	3	CE
1014	A78835	CSE-438	3	CE
1016	A97850	CSC-132B	3	ISE
1017	A97850	CSC-234A	3	ISE

FIGURE 7.24 The data to be recovered in the StudentCourse table.

7.4.3 Update Data for the Course Table in the SQL Server Database

In this section, we discuss how to perform data updating for the **Course** table in our sample database via the Course Form window in our project **RTOUpdateDelete Project** built in the last section.

Let's first discuss updating data against the **Course** table for the SQL Server database. To update data against the **Course** data table, we do not need to add any new Windows Form and we can use the Course Form window as the user interface. We need to perform the following two steps to complete this data updating action:

1) Develop codes to update the course record.
2) Validate the data updating result.

First let's develop the codes for our data updating action.

7.4.3.1 Develop Codes to Update the Course Record

Regularly, the **course_id** should not be updated if a course record need to be updated since a new course with a new **course_id** can be inserted into the database and an old course can be deleted if it is not needed. Therefore, in this project, we update all pieces of information for a course record except its **course_id**. The input dynamic parameter to the updating query includes only one parameter, **course_id**.

Similarly to updating a record in the Faculty table, the main coding job to update a course record is developed inside the **Update** button's Click method. Now let's start the coding process to update a course record in our sample database.

RTOUpdateDelete Project	cmdUpdate_Click(object sender, EventArgs e)

```
  private void cmdUpdate_Click(object sender, EventArgs e)
  {
A     string cmdString = "UPDATE Course SET course = @Cname, credit = @Credit, classroom = @Classroom, " +
          "schedule = @Schedule, enrollment = @Enroll WHERE (course_id = @cid)";
B     SqlCommand sqlCommand = new SqlCommand();
      int intUpdate;
C     sqlCommand.Connection = loginForm.sqlConnection;
      sqlCommand.CommandType = CommandType.Text;
      sqlCommand.CommandText = cmdString;
D     UpdateParameters(ref sqlCommand);
E     intUpdate = sqlCommand.ExecuteNonQuery();
F     sqlCommand.Dispose();
G     if (intUpdate == 0)
          MessageBox.Show("The data updating is failed");
  }
H private void UpdateParameters(ref SqlCommand cmd)
  {
      cmd.Parameters.Add("@Cname", SqlDbType.Char).Value = txtCourseName.Text;
      cmd.Parameters.Add("@Credit", SqlDbType.Char).Value = txtCredits.Text;
      cmd.Parameters.Add("@Classroom", SqlDbType.Char).Value = txtClassRoom.Text;
      cmd.Parameters.Add("@Schedule", SqlDbType.Char).Value = txtSchedule.Text;
      cmd.Parameters.Add("@Enroll", SqlDbType.Char).Value = txtEnroll.Text;
      cmd.Parameters.Add("@cid", SqlDbType.Char).Value = txtCourseID.Text;
  }
```

FIGURE 7.25 The codes for the course data updating operation.

Open the project **RTOUpdateDelete Project** and the Course Form window, then double-click on the **Update** button to open its Click method. Enter the codes shown in Figure 7.25 into this method. Let's have a close look at this piece of codes to see how it works.

A. The Update query string is defined first at the beginning of this method. All five data columns in the **Course** table, except the **course_id**, are input parameters. The dynamic parameter **@cid** represents the original **course_id**, which is a primary key in the **Course** table and will not be updated.

B. All data components and local variables are declared here such as the Command object and integer variable **intUpdate**. The latter is used to hold the returned running status of the calling of the **ExecuteNonQuery()** method.

C. The Command object is initialized and built using the Connection object and the Parameter object.

D. A user-defined method **UpdateParameters()** whose codes are shown in step **H** is called to add all updating parameters into the Command's Parameters property. The passing mode used for the passed argument is passing-by-reference, which means that a valid starting address of that Command object is passed into the method, and any modification to this Command object is permanent and it can be returned to the calling method.

E. Then the **ExecuteNonQuery()** method of the Command class is executed to update a course row in the **Course** table. The running result of this method is returned and stored in the local variable **intUpdate**.

F. The Command object is released after this data updating action.

G. The returned value from calling of the **ExecuteNonQuery()** method is equal to the number of rows that have been updated in the **Course** table. A zero means that no row has been updated, an error message is displayed to indicate it if this situation is really occurred.

H. The detailed codes for the user-defined method **UpdateParameters()** are shown in this step. Five pieces of updated course information with the original **course_id** are assigned to the associated columns in the **Course** table.

At this point, we finished the coding development for the data updating operation for the **Course** table by using the runtime object method. Next let's take care of the data validation after this data updating to confirm that our data updating is successful.

7.4.3.2 Validate the Course Data Updating

We do not need to add any new Form window or button to perform this data updating validation; instead we can use the Course Form window and the **Select** button, exactly the **Select** button's Click method, to perform this validation job. By clicking the **Select** button on the Course Form window with the selected faculty name from the **Faculty Name** ComboBox, we can perform the selection query to retrieve back the updated course record from the database and display it on the Course Form window to confirm it.

Now let's run the project to test the data updating function. Click on the **Start** button to run the project, enter the suitable username and password to the LogIn Form, and select the **Course Information** item from the Selection Form to open the Course Form window.

First let's select a faculty member and click on the **Select** button to retrieve all course information related to the selected faculty, such as **Ying Bai**, from our database, and display those pieces of information in this Form. Then we can update a selected course, such as **CSE-438**, by selecting it from the CourseList box, and updating it by modifying some pieces of information stored in related TextBoxes. Enter the following updated information to the related textboxes:

Course Name:	**Artificial Controls**
Schedule:	**T-H: 1:30 – 2:45 PM**
Classroom:	**MTC-212**
Credit:	**4**
Enrollment:	**26**

Now click on the **Update** button to start this course updating action.

To validate this updating action, first select another faculty, such as **Davis Bhalla**, from the **Faculty Name** combobox and click on the **Select** button to display all courses taught by that faculty. Then re-select the **Ying Bai** from the **Faculty Name** combobox, and click on the **Select** button to show all courses. Now click on the course_id, **CSE-438**, from the **CourseList** box, you can find that the course has been updated, as shown in Figure 7.26.

To keep our database neat and identical, it is highly recommended to recover this updated course record back to the original one. Enter the following data into the related TextBoxes in this Course Form and perform another data updating action to complete this course data recovery job:

Course Name:	**Adv Logic & Microprocessor**
Schedule:	**M-W-F: 11:00-11:55 AM**
Classroom:	**MTC-213**
Credit:	**3**
Enrollment:	**35**

Click on the **Back** and the **Exit** button to terminate this project. Our course data updating is successful. Next let's discuss how to delete a course record from the **Course** table in our sample database.

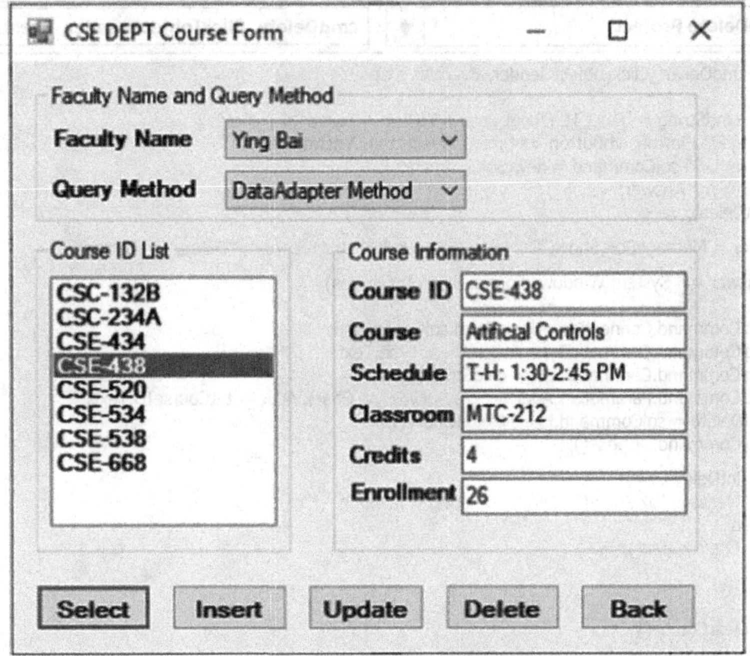

FIGURE 7.26 The confirmation result of a course data updating action.

7.4.4 Delete Data for the Course Table in the SQL Server Database

In this section, we discuss how to perform data deleting for the **Course** table in our sample database via the Course Form window in our project **RTOUpdateDelete Project** built in the last section.

Let's concentrate our discussions on deleting data from the **Course** table in the SQL Server database. To delete data against the **Course** data table, we do not need to add any new Windows Form and we can use the Course Form window as the user interface with the help of the **Delete** button, exactly the **Delete** button's Click method, to perform this deleting action. We need to perform the following two steps to complete this data updating action:

1) Develop codes to delete the course record.
2) Validate the data deleting result.

Now let's develop the codes to perform our data deleting action.

7.4.4.1 Develop Codes to Delete the Course Record

In a similar manner to deleting a record from the Faculty table, the main coding job to delete a course record is developed inside the **Delete** button's Click method. Now let's start the coding process to delete a course record from our sample database.

Open the project **RTOUpdateDelete Project** and the Course Form window, then double-click on the **Delete** button to open its Click method. Enter the codes shown in Figure 7.27 into this method.

Let's have a close look at this piece of code to see how it works.

A. The deleting query string is declared first at the beginning of this method. The only input parameter is a **course_id**, which is a primary key in the **Course** table in our sample database.
B. A MessageBox button's object is created and this object is used to display both buttons in the MessageBox, **Yes** and **No**, when the project runs.

```
RTOUpdateDelete Project                     cmdDelete_Click(object sender, EventArgs e)

  private void cmdDelete_Click(object sender, EventArgs e)
  {
A       string cmdString = "DELETE FROM Course WHERE (course_id = @cid)";
B       MessageBoxButtons vbButton = MessageBoxButtons.YesNo;
C       SqlCommand sqlCommand = new SqlCommand();
        DialogResult Answer;
        int intDelete;
D       Answer = MessageBox.Show("Do you want to delete this record?", "Delete", vbButton);
E       if (Answer == System.Windows.Forms.DialogResult.Yes)
        {
           sqlCommand.Connection = loginForm.sqlConnection;
           sqlCommand.CommandType = CommandType.Text;
           sqlCommand.CommandText = cmdString;
F          sqlCommand.Parameters.Add("@cid", SqlDbType.Char).Value = txtCourseID.Text;
G          intDelete = sqlCommand.ExecuteNonQuery();
H          sqlCommand.Dispose();
I          if (intDelete == 0)
              MessageBox.Show("The data Deleting is failed");
J          else
              ClearCourse();
        }
  }
K private void ClearCourse()
  {
     int index;
     TextBox[] cBox = {txtCourseID, txtCourseName, txtSchedule, txtClassRoom, txtCredits, txtEnroll};
     for (index = 0; index < cBox.Length; index++)
        cBox[index].Text = "";
  }
```

FIGURE 7.27 The codes for the course data-deleting query.

C. All data components and local variables used in this method are declared here. The data type of the variable **Answer** is **DialogResult**. However, one can use an integer variable to replace it. The integer variable **intDelete** is used to hold the returned data from calling the **ExecuteNonQuery()** method to delete a record from the **Course** table.

D. As the **Delete** button is clicked when the project runs, first a MessageBox is displayed to confirm that the user wants to delete the selected course from the **Course** table.

E. If the user's answer is **Yes**, then the deleting operation begins to be processed. The Command object is initialized and built by using the Connection object and the Command string we defined at the beginning of this method.

F. The dynamic parameter **@cid** is replaced by the real parameter, a **course_id** stored in the Course Listbox, **CourseList**.

G. The **ExecuteNonQuery()** method of the Command class is called to execute the data-deleting query to the **Course** table. The running result of calling that method is stored in the local variable **intDelete**.

H. The Command object is released after the data deleting.

I. The returned value from calling of the **ExecuteNonQuery()** method is equal to the number of rows that have been successfully deleted from the **Course** table. If a zero returns, which means that no row has been deleted from that table and this data deleting is failed, an error message is displayed if that situation occurred.

J. Otherwise, the course data deleting action is executed successfully. After a data deleting action is completed, all course information stored in six TextBoxes should be cleaned up to enable users to check and confirm that data deleting action. This cleaning job can be done by executing a user defined method, **ClearCourse()**, whose detailed codes are shown in next step, step **K.**

K. The function of this method is to clean up all six TextBoxes. A TextBox[] array is generated first, and then a **for()** loop is used to clean each of them one by one by assigning a blank or a zero-length string to the **Text** property of each TextBox.

Finally let's take care of the coding process to validate the data-deleting query.

7.4.4.2 Validate the Course Data Deleting

As we did for the validation for the data updating in the last section, we do not need to create any new Form window to do this validation, and we can use the Course Form, exactly use the **Select** button's Click method, to perform this data deleting validation.

Now let's test this course data deleting function by clicking on the **Start** button to run our project. As the project runs, complete the login process and open the Course Form window by selecting the **Course Information** from the Selection Form, then click on the **Select** button to retrieve and display all courses taught by the faculty member **Ying Bai**. Now we try to delete one course, **CSE-438**, from the Course table in our sample database. Select that **course_id** from the CourseList box and click on the **Delete** button.

Immediately one can find that all course information related to that course is removed from all related textboxes. Now click the **Select** button again to try to retrieve all courses taught by the faculty member **Ying Bai**, one can find that the course (course_id) **CSE-438** has been removed from the CourseList box.

Another way to check this deletion action is to go to the Server Explorer window. Then right-click on the **Course** table and select **Show Table Data** item from the popup menu to open the **Course** table. You can find that the course **CSE-438** has been deleted from this table.

In order to keep our database neat, we prefer to recover this deleted course record with the original data. Recall in Section 2.9.4.5 in Chapter 2, when a course record is deleted from the **Course** table (parent table), all records related to that course in the **Course** and the **StudentCourse** table (child table) will also be deleted. Therefore a total of 2 records in our sample database is deleted from two tables:

- One course record **CSE-438** from the **Course** table (parent table)
- One student course record **CSE-438** from the **StudentCourse** table (child table)

Open those tables in the Server Explorer window and add those deleted records back to each associated table one by one. Figures 7.28–7.29 shown those deleted course records in both tables. You can use the copy/paste functions to first copy all rows from each table, and then paste them at the end of each table in our sample database.

Another important point in recovering these deleted records is the order in which you performed those copy/paste actions. You must first recover the course deleted from the parent table, Course

course_id	course	credit	classroom	schedule	enrollment	faculty_id
CSE-438	Advd Logic & Microprocessor	3	MTC-213	M-W-F: 11:00-11:55 AM	35	B78880

FIGURE 7.28 The data to be recovered in the course table.

s_course_id	student_id	course_id	credit	major
1014	A78835	CSE-438	3	CE

FIGURE 7.29 The data to be recovered in the StudentCourse table.

table, and then you can recover all other related records in all other child tables. The reason for this is that the **Course** is a parent table with the **course_id** as a primary key, and you cannot recover any other record without first recovering the deleted record from the parent table.

Click on the **File | Save All** menu item when you finished these recoveries to save those recovered records.

A complete project **RTOUpdateDelete Project** that contained the updating and deleting function for the **Course** table can be found from a folder **Class DB Projects\Chapter 7\ RTOUpdateDelete Solution** under the **Students** folder at the CRC Press ftp site (refer to Figure 1.2 in Chapter 1).

7.5 UPDATE AND DELETE DATA FROM THE DATABASE USING STORED PROCEDURES

As we mentioned in the previous sections, performing the data updating among related tables is a very challenging topic. But the good news is that most of the time it is unnecessary to update the primary key, or the **faculty_id**, in our **Faculty** table if we want to update any other faculty information from the **Faculty** table in the database. Basically, it is much better to insert a new faculty record with a new **faculty_id** into the **Faculty** table than to update that record, including the primary key **faculty_id**, because the primary key **faculty_id** is good for the lifetime of the database in actual applications. Therefore, based on the analysis above, we will perform the data updating for all columns in the **Faculty** table except the **faculty_id** in this section.

To delete records from related tables, we need to perform two steps: First we need to delete records from the child tables, and then we can delete those records from the parent table. For example, if we want to delete a record from the **Faculty** table, first we need to delete those records that are related to the record to be deleted from the **Faculty** table from the **LogIn** and the **Course** tables (child tables), and then we can delete the record from the **Faculty** table (parent table).

To save time and space, we can modify an existing project to make it our new project.

7.5.1 Update and Delete Data against SQL Server Database Using Stored Procedures

To update and delete data using the stored procedures developed in the SQL Server database is very similar to the data updating and deleting we performed in the last section. With a small modification to the existing project **RTOUpdateDelete Project**, we can easily create our new project **SPUpdateDelete Project** to perform the data updating and deleting by calling stored procedures developed in the SQL Server database.

To develop our new project in this section, we divide it into three sections:

1) Modify the existing project **RTOUpdateDelete Project** to create our new project **SPUpdateDelete Project**.
2) Develop the data updating and deleting stored procedures in the SQL Server database.
3) Call stored procedures to perform the data updating and deleting functions for the faculty information using the Faculty Form window.

Now let's start with the first step.

7.5.1.1 Modify an Existing Project to Create Our New Project

Open the Windows Explorer and create a new folder such as **C:\Chapter 7** in your local machine if you have not, and then browse to the folder **Students\Class DB Projects\ Chapter 7** that is located on the CRC Press ftp site (refer to Figure 1.2 in Chapter 1). Copy the entire solution folder **RTOUpdateDelete**

Solution and paste it to our new folder **C:\Chapter 7**. Perform the following operations to make it as our new project:

1) Change the name of the Solution and the project from **RTOUpdateDelete Solution** to **SPUpdate Delete Solution**, from **RTOUpdateDelete Project** to **SPUpdateDelete Project**.
2) Also change the **RTOUpdateDelete Project.csproj** to **SPUpdateDelete Project.csproj**. Then double click on the project **SPUpdateDelete Project.csproj** to open this project.
3) Go to the menu item **Project | SPUpdataDelete Project Properties** to open the project's property window. Change the **Assembly name** and the **Default namespace** to **SPUpdataDelete Project** and **SPUpdateDelete_Project**, respectively.
4) Click on the **Assembly Information** button to open the **Assembly Information** wizard, change the **Title** and the **Product** to **SPUpdataDelete Project**. Click on the **OK** button to close this wizard.
5) Change the project namespace for all Form windows classes, including **LogIn.cs**, **Faculty.cs**, **Course.cs**, **Selection.cs** and **Student.cs**, as well as related class **Designer.cs** files, from **RTO UpdateDelete_Project** to **SPUpdateDelete_Project** using the **Find and Replace** dialog box.
6) Double click on the **C# Program.cs** file from the Solution Explorer window to open it, and change the namespace to **SPUpdateDelete_Project**.

Go to the **File | Save All** to save those modifications. Click on the **Save**, the **Overwrite** and then the **Save** button again to save this project. Now we are ready to modify the codes in our new project to perform data updating and deleting actions by calling the stored procedures. The code modifications include the following parts:

1) Replace the query string in the **Update** button's Click method in the Faculty Form with the name of the data updating stored procedure that will be developed in the next section to allow the method to call the related stored procedure to perform the data updating action.
2) Replace the query string in the **Delete** button's Click method in the Faculty Form with the name of the data deleting stored procedure that will be developed in the next section to allow the method to call the related stored procedure to perform the data deleting action.

Regularly, these two modifications should be performed after the stored procedures have been created in the SQL Server database since we need some information from those created stored procedures, such as the name of the stored procedure and the names of the input parameters, to execute these modifications to call the stored procedures. Because of the similarity between this project and the last one, we assumed that we have known those pieces of information and we can put those pieces of information into these two methods in advance. The assumed information includes:

1) The name of the data updating stored procedure is **dbo.UpdateFacultySP**.
2) The names of the input updated parameters are identical with those names used for the user defined method **UpdateParameters**().
3) The name of the input dynamic parameter is **@FacultyID**.
4) The name of the data deleting stored procedure is **dbo.DeleteFacultySP**.
5) The name of the input dynamic parameter is **@fname**.

Based on those assumptions, we can first modify our coding in the **Update** button's Click method. The key point is that we need to remember the names of those input parameters and the name of the stored procedure, and put them into our stored procedure later when we developed it in the next section.

```
SPUpdateDelete Project                          cmdUpdate_Click(object sender, EventArgs e)

  private void cmdUpdate_Click(object sender, EventArgs e)
  {
A       string cmdString = "dbo.UpdateFacultySP";
        SqlCommand sqlCommand = new SqlCommand();
        int intUpdate = 0;
        sqlCommand.Connection = loginForm.sqlConnection;
B       sqlCommand.CommandType = CommandType.StoredProcedure;
        sqlCommand.CommandText = cmdString;
        UpdateParameters(ref sqlCommand);
        intUpdate = sqlCommand.ExecuteNonQuery();
        sqlCommand.Dispose();
        CurrentFaculty();
        if (intUpdate == 0)
           MessageBox.Show("The data updating is failed");
  }
```

FIGURE 7.30 The modified codes for the update button's click method.

Open the **Update** button's Click method and modify its coding. Your finished modifications to this method are shown in Figure 7.30. The modified parts have been highlighted with the bold words. Let's see how this piece of modified codes works.

A. The content of the query string now should be equal to the name of the stored procedure, **dbo.UpdateFacultySP**, to be built in the next section.
B. The **CommandType** property of the Command object should be **StoredProcedure** to tell the project that a stored procedure should be called to perform the data updating job as the project runs.

There is no modification to the user-defined method **UpdateParameters()**. But in order to clarify the correctness of those input updated parameters for the stored procedure to be built in the next section, the codes for that method are shown here again in Figure 7.31.

Try to remember those parameters' names since we need to use them later when build our stored procedure **dbo.UpdateFaculty()** in the next section.

Next let's modify the codes in the **Delete** button's Click method. Open this method and perform two modifications to this method. Your finished method should match one that is shown in Figure 7.32.

```
SPUpdateDelete Project                          UpdateParameters(ref SqlCommand cmd)

private void UpdateParameters(ref SqlCommand cmd)
{
    byte[] bImage;
    bImage = getFacultyImage();
    cmd.Parameters.Add("@name", SqlDbType.Char).Value = txtFacultyName.Text;
    cmd.Parameters.Add("@title", SqlDbType.Char).Value = txtTitle.Text;
    cmd.Parameters.Add("@office", SqlDbType.Char).Value = txtOffice.Text;
    cmd.Parameters.Add("@phone", SqlDbType.Char).Value = txtPhone.Text;
    cmd.Parameters.Add("@college", SqlDbType.Char).Value = txtCollege.Text;
    cmd.Parameters.Add("@email", SqlDbType.Char).Value = txtEmail.Text;
    cmd.Parameters.Add("@fimage", SqlDbType.Binary).Value = bImage;
    cmd.Parameters.Add("@fid", SqlDbType.Char).Value = txtFacultyID.Text;
}
```

FIGURE 7.31 The codes for the user defined method UpdateParameters().

```
SPUpdateDelete Project                    cmdDelete_Click(object sender, EventArgs e)

private void cmdDelete_Click(object sender, EventArgs e)
{
A       string cmdString = "dbo.DeleteFacultySP";
        MessageBoxButtons vbButton = MessageBoxButtons.YesNo;
        SqlCommand sqlCommand = new SqlCommand();
        DialogResult Answer;
        int intDelete = 0;
        Answer = MessageBox.Show("Do you want to delete this record?", "Delete", vbButton);
        if (Answer == System.Windows.Forms.DialogResult.Yes)
        {
           sqlCommand.Connection = loginForm.sqlConnection;
B          sqlCommand.CommandType = CommandType.StoredProcedure;
           sqlCommand.CommandText = cmdString;
           sqlCommand.Parameters.Add("@fname", SqlDbType.Char).Value = ComboName.Text;
           intDelete = sqlCommand.ExecuteNonQuery();
           sqlCommand.Dispose();
           CurrentFaculty();
           if (intDelete == 0)
              MessageBox.Show("The data Deleting is failed");
           else
           {
              ClearFaculty();
              PhotoBox.Image = null;
           }
        }
}
```

FIGURE 7.32 The modified codes for the delete button's click method.

The modified parts have been highlighted with the bold words. Let's see how this piece of modified codes works.

A. The content of the query string now should be equal to the name of the stored procedure, **dbo.DeleteFacultySP**, to be built in the next section.
B. The **CommandType** property of the Command object should be **StoredProcedure** to tell the project that a stored procedure should be called to perform a data updating job as the project runs.

Now we have finished all coding modifications in Visual C#.NET environment. Next let's create our two stored procedures. There are two ways to create a stored procedure:

1) Create it in the Microsoft SQL Server Management Studio 18.
2) Create it in the Server Explorer in the Visual Studio.NET environment.

Since we are working on Visual C#.NET project, thus we prefer to use the second way to create our stored procedures.

7.5.1.2 Develop Stored Procedures with the Server Explorer Window

On the Server Explorer window and click on the arrow-symbol icon that is next to **CSE_DEPT** database folder to connect to our database if this database was added into the Server Explorer before. Otherwise you need to right click on the **Data Connections** folder to add and connect to our sample database. Refer to Section 5.3.1 in Chapter 5 for the detailed information of adding and connecting to our sample database.

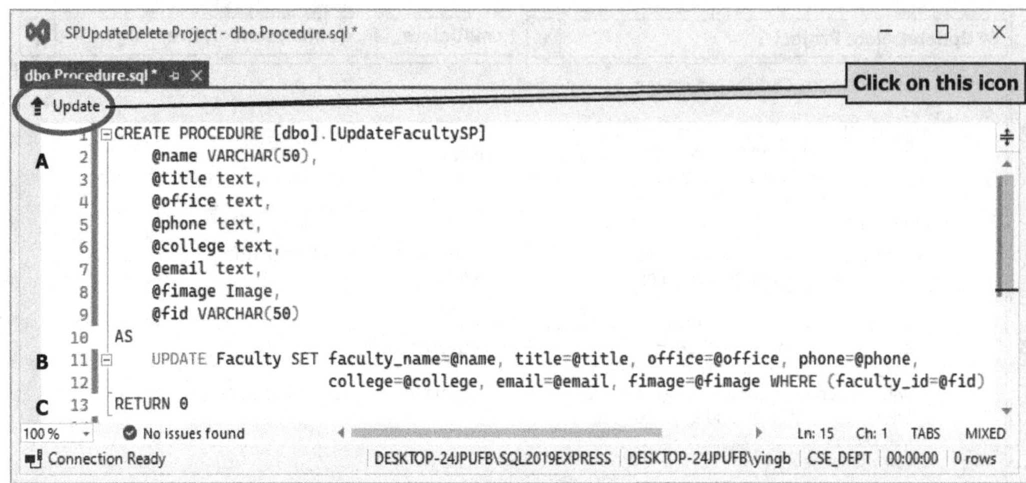

FIGURE 7.33 The created data updating stored procedure.

Perform the following operations to create our stored procedure **dbo.UpdateFacultySP**:

1) Expand our connected database and right click on the **Stored Procedures** folder.
2) Select the **Add New Stored Procedure** item to open the Add Procedure wizard.
3) Enter the codes that are shown in Figure 7.33 into this new procedure.
4) Do not forget to change the procedure's name to **dbo.UpdateFacultySP** that is located at the top of this procedure.

Refer to Section 2.9.2 in Chapter 2 for the data types of those input parameters, and the data types of those input parameters should be identical with those data types of the associated columns defined in the **Faculty** table.

The functionality of this stored procedure is:

A. All input updated parameters are listed in this part. All those parameters' names must be identical with those used in the user-defined method **UpdateParameters()**shown in Figure 7.31 in the last section.

B. The **Update** query is generated by assigning all those updated parameters to the associated columns in the **Faculty** table. The dynamic parameter **@fid** is assigned to the **WHERE** clause as the updating condition or criterion.

C. If the updating query is executed successfully, a zero is returned to indicate that case.

Click on the **Update** icon located at the upper-left corner, as shown in Figure 7.33, to save this stored procedure into our database. On the opened **Preview Database Updates** wizard, click on the **Update Database** button, a successful updating message should be displayed in the **Data Tools Operations** wizard located at the bottom.

Now let's build our second stored procedure. Perform the following operations to create our stored procedure **dbo.DeleteFacultySP**:

1) Expand our connected database and right-click on the **Stored Procedures** folder.
2) Select the **Add New Stored Procedure** item to open the Add Procedure wizard.
3) Enter the codes that are shown in Figure 7.34 into this new procedure.
4) Do not forget to change the procedure's name to **dbo.DeleteFacultySP** that is located at the top of this procedure.

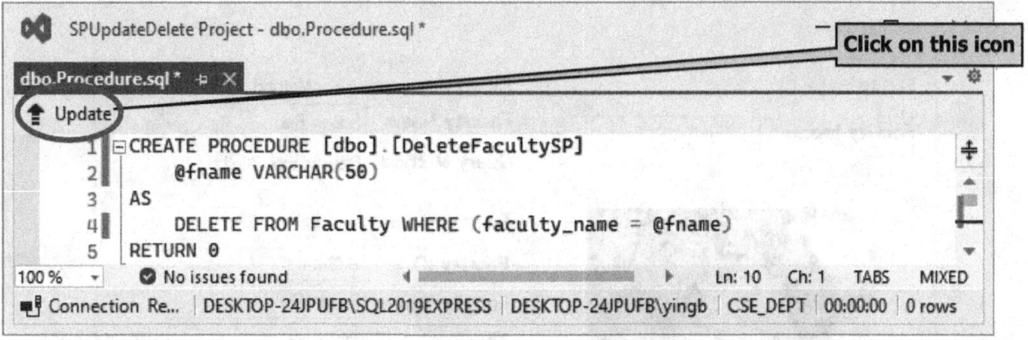

FIGURE 7.34 The created data deleting stored procedure.

The only input dynamic parameter to this stored procedure is a desired **faculty_name**, which can be obtained from the Faculty Name combobox in the Faculty Form window. The only one point to be noted is that this input dynamic parameter or faculty name must be identical with one we used for the coding line of adding this parameter in the **Delete** button's Click method, which is **@fname**, as shown in Figure 7.32.

The function of this stored procedure is straightforward. A SQL **Delete** query is executed to remove a selected faculty record from the **Faculty** table in our sample database with a selected faculty name, indicated by the input parameter **@fname**.

Click on the **Update** icon located at the upper-left corner, as shown in Figure 7.34, to save this stored procedure into our database. On the opened **Preview Database Updates** wizard, click on the **Update Database** button, a successful updating message should be displayed in the **Data Tools Operations** wizard located at the bottom.

Next let's run our Visual C# project to call those stored procedures to perform data updating and deleting actions for the **Faculty** table in our sample database.

7.5.1.3 Call the Stored Procedures to Perform Data Updating and Deleting Actions

Run our project by clicking the Start button, enter a suitable username and password to complete the login process, and then select the **Faculty Information** item from the Selection Form to open the Faculty Form window. Select the faculty name **Ying Bai** from the Faculty Name combobox control, and click the **Select** button to get and display the information for the selected faculty.

To update this faculty record, enter the following data into the associated textboxes to perform this data updating:

Faculty Name:	**Susan Bai**
Title:	**Professor**
Office:	**MTC-218**
Phone:	**750-378-2800**
College:	**Duke University**
Email:	**sbai@college.edu**

Click on the **Update** button in the Faculty Form window to try to update this record. On the opened File Image Selection wizard, browse to your local folder where all faculty image files are located, select a desired faculty image file, **White.jpg**, and click on the **Open** button to perform this data updating action.

To validate this data updating, first select another faculty from the combobox control **ComboName** and click the **Select** button to retrieve back all information for that faculty. Then go to the Faculty Name combobox again, and one can find that the updated faculty member, **Susan Bai**, is in there.

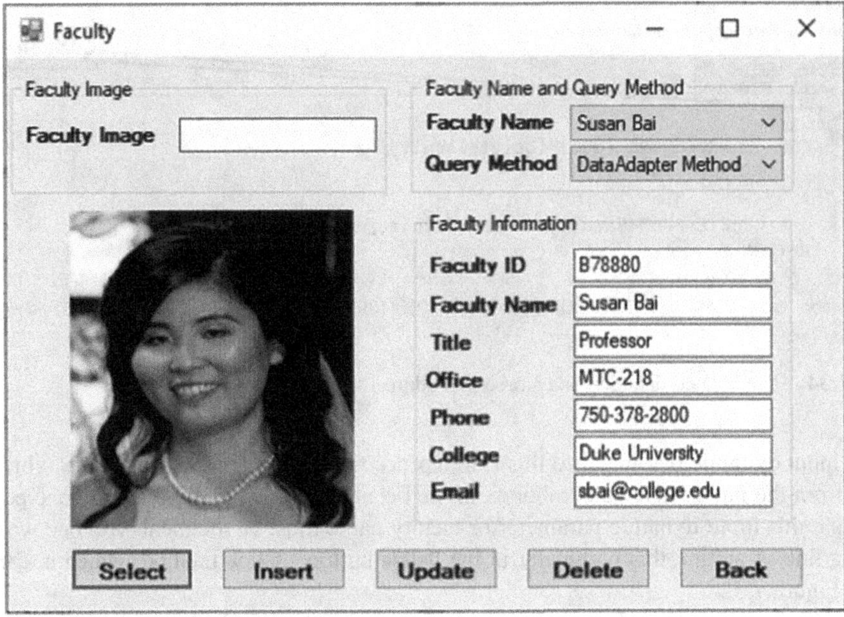

FIGURE 7.35 The updated faculty information.

Select that updated faculty name **Susan Bai** from the box and click the **Select** button to retrieve back the updated information for that selected faculty member. Immediately, you can find that all pieces of updated information related to the selected faculty are displayed in this Form. This means that our data updating is successful. Your updated faculty information window should match one that is shown in Figure 7.35.

To keep our sample database identical, it is highly recommended to recover the updated faculty record to the original faculty record. To do that, one can perform another updating action to get the original faculty record **Ying Bai**, which is shown below, to replace that updated one:

Faculty Name:	**Ying Bai**
Title:	**Associate Professor**
Office:	**MTC-211**
Phone:	**750-378-1148**
College:	**Florida Atlantic University**
Email:	**ybai@college.edu**
Faculty Image:	**Bai.jpg**

Next let's test the data deleting function. In order to avoid a complicated data recovering job, we prefer not to delete any original faculty record. The so-called original faculty record is a faculty record that was created when we built our sample database in Chapter 2 since those faculty members contained some complicated relationships with other tables, such as **Course**, **LogIn** and **StudentCourse** tables, because of the use of primary and foreign keys. Refer to Section 7.2.6 to get more details of these relationships. If an original faculty record were deleted, not only would the selected faculty member be deleted from the **Faculty** table, but so also would about 10 records related to that deleted faculty member in other tables, such as **Course**, **LogIn** and **StudentCourse** tables, due to the Cascaded Updating and Deleting property set in our sample database. The recovering jobs to recover those deleted records would be time-consuming and very complicated.

Another important point in recovering those deleted records is the order in which you performed those recovering jobs. You must first recover the faculty member deleted from the parent table, **Faculty** table, and then you can recover all other related records in all other child tables. The reason for this is that the **Faculty** is a parent table with the **faculty_id** as a primary key, you cannot recover any other record without first recovering the deleted record from the parent table.

To avoid those recovering troubles, we prefer to delete some new inserted faculty record. Recall that in Section 6.2.8 in Chapter 6, we inserted a new faculty member **Steve Wang** with the following data items:

Faculty ID:	**W56788**
Faculty Name:	**Steve Wang**
Title:	**Professor**
Office:	**MTC-311**
Phone:	**750-378-2258**
College:	**University of Miami**
Email:	**swang@college.edu**
Faculty Image:	**Wang.jpg**

The main reason we try to delete this record is that no other record in any other tables is related to this new inserted faculty member, and this makes the recovering job much easier and simpler. Therefore, prior to performing this deleting action, run our current project to first insert that record into the **Faculty** table in our sample database.

Now go to the **Faculty Name** combobox, one can find that new inserted faculty member **Steve Wang**. Select that faculty member and click on the **Delete** button to try to delete this faculty record from the **Faculty** table. Then click **Yes** to the MessageBox and all faculty information displayed in seven TextBoxes is gone. Is our data deleting successful? To answer this question, open the **Faculty Name** combobox and the deleted faculty member, **Steve Wang**, cannot be found from that box, and this means that the selected faculty with all information have been successfully deleted from the **Faculty** table. Yes, our data deleting is successful.

Another way to confirm this deleting action is to open the **Faculty** table from the Server Explorer window to do that checking.

A complete project **SPUpdateDelete Project** can be found from a folder **Class DB Projects\Chapter 7\SPUpdateDelete Solution** that is under the **Students** folder located at the CRC Press ftp site (Refer to Figure 1.2 in Chapter 1).

7.6 UPDATE AND DELETE DATA AGAINST DATABASES USING THE LINQ TO SQL QUERY

As we discussed in Chapter 4, LINQ to SQL queries can perform all kinds of data query operations, including the data selections, data insertion, data updating and deleting actions. Standard LINQ to SQL queries include the following all four queries:

- Select
- Insert
- Update
- Delete

To perform any of these operations or queries, we need to use entity classes and DataContext we discussed in Section 4.6 in Chapter 4 to do LINQ to SQL actions against our sample database. To make thing simple, in this section we want to use an existing project **LINQSelect Project** built in Chapter 5 to make it our new project to perform the data updating and deleting actions to the **Faculty** table in our sample database **CSE_DEPT** by using the LINQ to SQL query. We leave the data insertion coding as a homework to readers.

Now let's perform the following steps to create our new project **LINQSelect Project**:

1) Create a new folder **C:\Chapter 7** on your local machine if you did not do it.
2) Browse to the solution **LINQSelect Solution**, which is developed in Chapter 5 and located at the folder **ClassDB Projects\Chapter 5** that is under the **Students** folder at the CRC Press ftp site (refer to Figure 1.2 in Chapter 1).
3) Copy this solution folder with the project and paste it to your new local folder **C:\Chapter 7**.

We can use this project as our new project to perform data updating and deleting functions to the Faculty table in our sample database.

The reason we adopted this project as our new project is that we do not need to create any new data entity class **CSE_DEPTDataContext** and Database Model **CSE_DEPT.dbml** components, instead we can use those objects generated in the project **LINQSelect Project** to save our time and efforts.

Now let's concentrate on the coding for our data updating and deleting actions. Open the Visual Studio, our new project **LINQSelect Project** and Faculty Form window.

The first coding job is to modify the codes inside the Faculty Form Constructor to use a user defined method **CurrentFaculty()** to be built in Section 7.6.2 to enable all faculty members to be updated and added into the **Faculty Name** combobox.

7.6.1 Modify the Codes for the Faculty Form Constructor

The function of the original codes inside the Constructor is to add all default faculty members manually into the **Faculty Name** combobox to enable users to select one of them to perform a related data query. However, those faculty members may not be the updated members. To solve this issue, we prefer to build a user defined method **CurrentFaculty()** to get the updated faculty members from the **Faculty** table in our sample database and display them in the Faculty Name combobox.

Open the code window of the Faculty Form window and browse to the Constructor of this **Faculty.cs** class. Enter the codes shown in Figure 7.36 into this Constructor. The only modification is to use the user defined method **CurrentFaculty()** to replace original eight coding lines, **ComboName.Items.Add()**;, and the new added method has been highlighted with bold words. Next let's build our user defined method **CurrentFaculty()**.

```
LINQSelect Project                    FacultyForm()

public partial class FacultyForm : Form
{
    public FacultyForm()
    {
        InitializeComponent();
        CurrentFaculty();

        ComboMethod.Items.Add("LINQ to SQL Method");
        ComboMethod.Items.Add("LINQ - Single Record");
        this.ComboMethod.SelectedIndex = 0;
    }
    .........
}
```

FIGURE 7.36 The modified codes for the constructor of the faculty form window.

```
LINQSelect Project                          CurrentFaculty()

  private void CurrentFaculty()
  {
A     LogInForm logForm = new LogInForm();
B     ComboName.Items.Clear();
C     var f_info = from fi in logForm.cse_dept.Faculties
                   select fi;
D     foreach (var f in f_info)
        ComboName.Items.Add(f.faculty_name);
E     ComboName.SelectedIndex = 0;
F     logForm.Close();
  }
```

FIGURE 7.37 The codes for the method CurrentFaculty().

7.6.2 Build the User-Defined Method CurrentFaculty() with SQO Method

We did build this method in Sections 6.2.4 and 6.5.2 in Chapter 6 with two different methods, TableAdapter and SqlDataReader, but now we are using LINQ method to perform the data updating action, thus we need to use SQO method to build that method.

On the opened code window of the Faculty Form window, add the codes that are shown in Figure 7.37 into this window as our method, **CurrentFaculty()**.

Let's have a closer look at this piece of codes to see how it works.

- **A.** A LogInForm object **logForm** is declared first since we need to use a valid database Connection object built in its constructor later to perform our data updating actions.
- **B.** The **Faculty Name** combobox is cleaned up first before we can add any current faculty member into it.
- **C.** A SQO query statement is executed via a valid database connection to query all faculty records from the **Faculty** table.
- **D.** A **foreach()** loop is used to collect all current faculty names from the queried result obtained from the last query, and assign them to the **Faculty Name** combobox **ComboName** by adding them one by one.
- **E.** The **SelectedIndex** property of the **ComboName** combobox is set to zero to select the top faculty member as a default one.
- **F.** Finally, the LogInForm object **logForm** is closed. The side-effect of this closing is to close the valid database connection, too.

Now let's build the codes for the **Update** button's Click method.

7.6.3 Develop the Codes for the Update Button Click Method

Double-click on the **Update** button from our Faculty Form window to open its Click method and enter the codes that are shown in Figure 7.38 into this method.

Let's have a close look at this piece of codes to see how it works.

- **A.** Some local variables and objects are generated first, including a byte[] array **img** that is used to hold the updated faculty image by executing a user-defined method **getFacultyImage()** later, and a LogInForm object **logForm** since we need to use a valid database Connection object built in its constructor later.
- **B.** The user-defined method **getFacultyImage()**, built in Section 6.2.7.1 in Chapter 6, is called to collect a desired faculty image used to update the selected faculty image.

```
LINQSelect Project | cmdUpdate_Click(object sender, EventArgs e)

  private void cmdUpdate_Click(object sender, EventArgs e)
  {
A       byte[] img = null;
        LogInForm logForm = new LogInForm();
B       img = getFacultyImage();
C       Faculty fi = logForm.cse_dept.Faculties.Where(f => f.faculty_id == txtFacultyID.Text).First();
D       fi.faculty_name = txtFacultyName.Text;
        fi.title = txtTitle.Text;
        fi.office = txtOffice.Text;
        fi.phone = txtPhone.Text;
        fi.college = txtCollege.Text;
        fi.email = txtEmail.Text;
        fi.fimage = img;
E       logForm.cse_dept.SubmitChanges();
F       CurrentFaculty();
        logForm.Close();
  }
```

FIGURE 7.38 The codes for the update button click method.

C. A LINQ selection query is executed using the Standard Query Operator (SQO) method with the **faculty_id** as the query criterion. The **First()** method is used to return only the first matched record. It does not matter for our application since we have only one record that is associated with this specified **faculty_id**.
D. All seven columns, with the exceptio of the **faculty_id**, for the selected faculty member are updated by assigning the updated value stored in the associated TextBox to each column in the **Faculty** table in our sample database. The collected faculty image is assigned to the **fimage** column in the **Faculty** table.
E. This data updating cannot be really occurred until the **SubmitChanges()** method is executed.
F. The Faculty Name ComboBox control is cleaned up and the user-defined method **CurrentFaculty()** to be built in the next section is executed to refresh the updated faculty members stored in that control. In addition, the LogInForm object **logForm** is closed since we no longer need it.

For the detailed codes of the user-defined method **getFacultyImage()**, which was built in Section 6.2.7.1 in Chapter 6, refer to that section, exactly Figure 6.12 in that section, to get more details about it. The function of that method is to get a desired faculty image as an updated one to complete a faculty record updating. For your convenience, we redisplay the codes with that method in Figure 7.39.

Now we can run the project to perform the faculty record updating action for any selected faculty member, such as **Ying Bai**. As the project runs, open the Faculty Form and select the faculty member **Ying Bai** from the **Faculty Name** combobox, then click on the **Select** button to get and display that record on this Form.

Now enter the following information as an updated faculty record into the related TextBox to begin this data updating action:

Faculty Name:	**Susan Bai**
Title:	**Professor**
Office:	**MTC-218**
Phone:	**750-378-2800**
College:	**Duke University**
Email:	**sbai@college.edu**

```
LINQSelect Project                    getFacultyImage()

    private byte[] getFacultyImage()
    {
A       MemoryStream ms = new MemoryStream();
        OpenFileDialog dlg = new OpenFileDialog();
        byte[] bimage = null;
B       dlg.Filter = "JPG Files (*.jpg)|*.jpg|All Files (*.*)|*.*";
        dlg.Title = "Select the Faculty Image";
C       if (dlg.ShowDialog() == DialogResult.OK)
        {
            PhotoBox.Image = Image.FromFile(dlg.FileName);
            PhotoBox.Image.Save(ms, PhotoBox.Image.RawFormat);
D           bimage = ms.ToArray();
        }
E       return bimage;
    }
```

FIGURE 7.39 The codes for the method getFacultyImage().

Click on the **Update** button in the Faculty Form window to try to update this record. On the opened File Image Selection wizard, browse to your local folder where all faculty image files are located, select a desired faculty image file, **White.jpg**, and click on the **Open** button to perform this data updating action. All faculty images can be found from a folder **Students\Images\Faculty** on the CRC Press ftp site. One can go to that folder, copy all faculty image files and save them to one of your local folders in your machine.

To validate this data updating, first select another faculty from the combobox control **ComboName** and click the **Select** button to retrieve back all information for that faculty. Then go to the **Faculty Name** combobox again, and one can find that the updated faculty member, **Susan Bai**, has been in there. Select it from that box and click on the **Select** button to retrieve back the updated information for that faculty member. Immediately, you can find that all pieces of updated information related to the selected faculty are displayed in this Form. This means that our data updating is successful. Your updated faculty information window should match one that is shown in Figure 7.40.

To keep our sample database identical, it is recommended to recover the updated faculty record to the original one. To do that, one can perform another updating to get the original faculty record **Ying Bai**, which is shown below, to replace the updated one:

Faculty Name:	**Ying Bai**
Title:	**Associate Professor**
Office:	**MTC-211**
Phone:	**750-378-1148**
College:	**Florida Atlantic University**
Email:	**ybai@college.edu**
Faculty Image:	**Bai.jpg**

Next let's perform the coding for the data deleting action.

7.6.4 Develop the Codes for the Delete Button Click Method

Double-click on the **Delete** button from the Faculty Form window to open its Click method and enter the codes that are shown in Figure 7.41 into this method.

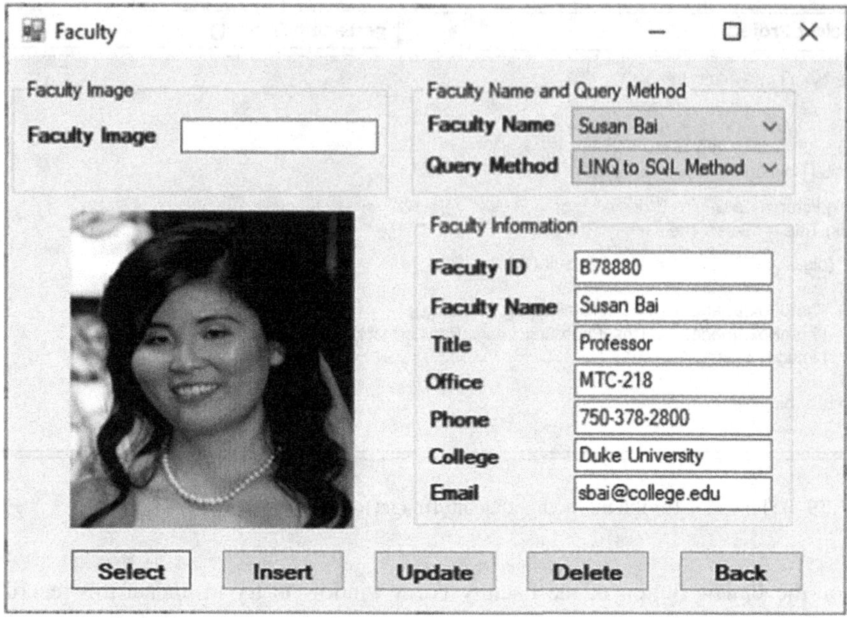

FIGURE 7.40 The faculty record updating result.

```
LINQSelect Project                      cmdDelete_Click(object sender, EventArgs e)

  private void cmdDelete_Click(object sender, EventArgs e)
  {
A      LogInForm logForm = new LogInForm();
B      var faculty = (from fi in logForm.cse_dept.Faculties
                      where fi.faculty_name == ComboName.Text
                      select fi).Single<Faculty>();
C      logForm.cse_dept.Faculties.DeleteOnSubmit(faculty);
D      logForm.cse_dept.SubmitChanges();
E      CurrentFaculty();
F      ClearFaculty();
G      logForm.Close();
  }
```

FIGURE 7.41 The codes for the delete button click method.

Let's have a close look at this piece of codes to see how it works.

A. A LogInForm object **logForm** is declared first since we need to use a valid database Connection object built in its constructor later to perform our data deleting actions.
B. A LINQ query is created and initialized with three clauses, **from**, **where** and **select**. The range variable **fi** is selected from the **Faculty**, which is exactly an instance of our entity class Faculty and the **faculty_name** works as the query criterion for this query. All information related to the selected faculty members (**faculty_name**) will be retrieved back and stored in the query variable **faculty**. The keyword **Single** means that only a single record is queried.
C. The system method **DeleteOnSubmit()** is executed to issue a deleting action to the faculty instance, **Faculties**.
D. Another system method **SubmitChanges()** is executed to exactly perform this deleting action against the **Faculty** tables in our sample database. Only after this method is executed, the deleting action is actually performed and the desired faculty record is deleted from our sample database.

```
LINQSelect Project                    ClearFaculty()

  private void ClearFaculty()
  {
A     int index;
      TextBox[] fBox = { txtFacultyID, txtFacultyName, txtTitle, txtOffice, txtPhone, txtCollege, txtEmail };
B     for (index = 0; index < fBox.Length; index++)
          fBox[index].Text = "";
C     PhotoBox.Image = null;
  }
```

FIGURE 7.42 The codes for the method ClearFaculty().

E. The user-defined method, **CurrentFaculty()**, is called to update the **Faculty Name** combobox to get and display all updated faculty members in there.
F. Another user-defined method, **ClearFaculty()**, is executed to clean up all seven TextBoxes in the Faculty Form window to allow users to confirm that data deleting action.
G. Finally, the LogInForm object **logForm** is closed. The side-effect of this closing is to close the valid database connection, too.

The codes for the user-defined method, **ClearFaculty()**, are shown in Figure 7.42. Let's have a close look at this piece of codes to see how it works.

A. A local integer variable **index** is created first and it is used as a loop counter for **for()** loop later to collect all seven TextBoxes. A TextBox[] array **fBox** is also generated and initialized with seven TextBoxes in the Faculty Form window.
B. A **for()** loop is used to get all seven TextBoxes and reset each of them to blank.
C. Finally, the Faculty Image box, **PhotoBox**, is cleaned up by assigning a **null** to the **Image** property of that box.

Now let's test the data deleting function. In order to avoid a complicated data recovering job, we prefer not to delete any original faculty record. The so-called original faculty record is a faculty record that was created when we built our sample database in Chapter 2 since those faculty members contained some complicated relationships with other tables, such as **Course**, **LogIn** and **StudentCourse** tables, by using primary and foreign keys. Refer to Section 7.2.6 to get more details for these relationships. If an original faculty record were deleted, not only would the selected faculty member be deleted from the **Faculty** table, but also about 10 records related to that deleted faculty member in other tables, such as **Course**, **LogIn** and **StudentCourse** tables, would also be deleted due to Cascaded Updating and Deleting property set in our sample database. The recovering jobs to recover those deleted records would be time-consuming and very complicated.

To avoid those recovering troubles, we prefer to delete some new inserted faculty record. Recall that in Section 6.2.8 in Chapter 6, we inserted a new faculty member **Steve Wang** with the following data items:

Faculty ID:	**W56788**
Faculty Name:	**Steve Wang**
Title:	**Professor**
Office:	**MTC-311**
Phone:	**750-378-2258**
College:	**University of Miami**
Email:	**swang@college.edu**
Faculty Image:	**Wang.jpg**

The main reason we try to delete this record is that no other record in any other tables is related to this new inserted faculty member, and this makes the recovering job much easier and simpler.

Prior to performing this data deleting action, first run one of our previous projects, **SPUpdateDelete Project**, to insert that record into the **Faculty** table in our sample database since we may have deleted that inserted record in some of our previous projects when we tested it. To confirm that data insertion action, one may need to open the **Faculty** table in our sample database to check it via the Server Explorer.

Now run our current project **LINQSelect Project**, then go to the **Faculty Name** combobox, one can find that new inserted faculty member **Steve Wang**. Select that faculty member and click on the **Delete** button to try to delete this faculty record from the **Faculty** table. Immediately all faculty information displayed in seven TextBoxes and the faculty image are gone.

To check and confirm our data deleting action, open the **Faculty Name** combobox and the deleted faculty member, **Steve Wang**, cannot be found from that box, and this means that the selected faculty with all information have been successfully deleted from the **Faculty** table. Yes, our data deleting is successful.

Another way to confirm this deleting action is to open the **Faculty** table from the Server Explorer window to do that checking.

A complete project **LINQSelect Project** can be found from a folder **Class DB Projects\ Chapter 7\ LINQSelect Solution** that is under the **Students** folder located at the CRC Press ftp site (Refer to Figure 1.2 in Chapter 1).

7.7 CHAPTER SUMMARY

Data updating and deleting queries are discussed in this chapter with a sample SQL Server database **CSE_DEPT**.

Four popular data updating and deleting methods are discussed and analyzed with four real project examples:

1) Using TableAdapter DBDirect methods such as **TableAdapter.Update()** and **TableAdapter.Delete()** to update and delete data directly again the databases.
2) Using **TableAdapter.Update()** method to update and execute the associated TableAdapter's properties such as **UpdateCommand** or **DeleteCommand** to save changes made for the table in the DataSet to the table in the database.
3) Using the run time object method to develop and execute the Command's method **ExecuteNonQuery()** to update or delete data again the database directly.
4) Using LINQ to SQL query method to update and delete data against our sample SQL Server database **CSE_DEPT**.

Both methods 1 and 2 need to use Visual Studio.NET Design Tools and Wizards to create and configure suitable TableAdapters, build the associated queries using the Query Builder and call those queries from Visual C#.NET applications.

The difference between methods 1 and 2 is that method 1 can be used to directly access the database to perform the data updating and deleting in a single step, whereas method 2 needs two steps to finish the data updating or deleting. First, the data updating or deleting are performed to the associated tables in the DataSet, and then those updated or deleted data are updated to the tables in the database by executing the **TableAdapter.Update()** method.

This chapter is divided into two parts; Part I provides discussions on data updating and deleting using methods 1 and 2, or in other words, using the **TableAdapter.Update()** and **TableAdapter.Delete()** methods developed in the Visual Studio.NET Design Tools and Wizards. Part II presents the data updating and deleting using the run time object method to develop command objects to execute the **ExecuteNonQuery()** method dynamically. Updating and deleting data against our sample database using the stored procedure method and LINQ to SQL query method are also discussed in the second part.

Four real sample projects are provided in this chapter to help readers to understand and design the professional data driven applications to update or delete data against a sample SQL Server 2019 Express database.

HOMEWORK

I. True/False Selections

____1. Three popular data updating methods are: the TableAdapter DBDirect method, **TableAdapter.Update()** and **ExecuteNonQuery()** method of the Command class.

____2. Unlike the **Fill()** method, a valid database connection must be set before a data can be updated in the database.

____3. One can directly update data or delete records against the database using the **TableAdapter.Update()** method.

____4. When executing an **UPDATE** query, the order of the input parameters in the **SET** list can differ according to the order of the data columns in the database.

____5. To update data against a SQL Server database using LINQ to SQL, the target record cannot be updated until a system method **SubmitChanges()** is executed.

____6. One can directly delete records from the database using the TableAdapter DBDirect method such as **TableAdapter.Delete()** method.

____7. When performing data updating actions, one record can be updated in the database multiple times with the same input parameters.

____8. To delete data from the database using the **TableAdapter.Update()** method, the data should be first deleted from the table in the DataSet, and then the **Update()** method is executed to update that deletion to the table in the database.

____9. To update data in the SQL Server database using the stored procedures, one can create and test the created stored procedure in the Server Explorer window.

____10. To call stored procedures to update data against a database, the input parameters' names must be identical with those names of the input parameters defined in the stored procedures.

II. Multiple Choice Questions

1. To update data in the database using the **TableAdapter.Update()** method, one needs to use the ________ to build the _________.
   a. Data Source, Query Builder
   b. TableAdapter Query Configuration Wizard, Update query
   c. Runtime object, Insert query
   d. Server Explorer, Data Source
2. To delete data from the database using the **TableAdapter.Update()** method, one needs first to delete data from the _______, and then update that data into the database.
   a. Data table
   b. Data table in the database
   c. DataSet
   d. Data table in the DataSet
3. To delete data from the database using the **TableAdapter.Update()** method, one can delete ____________
   a. One data row only
   b. Multiple data rows
   c. The whole data table
   d. Either of above

4. Because the ADO.NET provides a disconnected mode to the database, to update or delete a record against the database, a valid ________ must be established.
   a. DataSet
   b. TableAdapter
   c. Connection
   d. Command
5. The _______ operator should be used as an assignment operator for the **WHERE** clause with a dynamic parameter for a data query in a SQL Server database.
   a. =:
   b. LIKE
   c. =
   d. @
6. To test a data deleting stored procedure built in the Server Explorer, one can _______ the stored procedure to make sure that it is correctly stored into the database.
   a. Build
   b. Execute
   c. Debug
   d. Compile
7. To test a data updating stored procedure built in the Server Explorer window for the SQL Server database, one can _______ the stored procedure to make sure it works.
   a. Build
   b. Execute
   c. Debug
   d. Compile
8. To update data in a SQL Server database using the UPDATE command, the data types of the input parameters should be ________ those data types in the database.
   a. Different from
   b. Basically identical to
   c. A little different from
   d. Exactly identical to
9. To update data using stored procedures, the **CommandType** property of the Command object used in the C# codes must be equal to ___________.
   a. CommandType.InsertCommand
   b. CommandType.StoredProcedure
   c. CommandType.Text
   d. CommandType.Insert
10. To update data using stored procedures, the **CommandText** property of the Command object must be equal to ___________.
    a. The content of the CommandType.InsetCommand
    b. The content of the CommandType.Text
    c. The name of the Insert command
    d. The name of the stored procedure

III. Exercises

1. Build a stored procedure with the codes shown below. Also develop a piece of codes in Visual C#.NET to call this stored procedure to update a record in the **Student** table in our sample database via the **Update** button in the project **SPUpdateDelete Project**.

   Hint: Using the **Update** button on the Student Form in the **SPUpdateDelete Project** located at the folder **Class DB Projects\Chapter 7**which is under the **Students** folder at the CRC Press ftp site.

```
CREATE OR REPLACE PROCEUDRE dbo.UpdateStudent
   @Name VARCHAR(20),
   @GPA float,
   @Credits smallint,
   @Major text,
   @SchoolYear text,
   @Email text,
   @simage Image,
   @StudentID VARCHAR(20)
AS
UPDATE Student SET student_name=@Name, major=@Major, schoolYear=@SchoolYear,
                   credits=@Credits, gpa=@GPA, email=@Email, simage=@simage
WHERE (student_id=@StudentID)
RETURN 0
```

2. Below is a piece of codes developed in Visual C#.NET and this coding is used to call a stored procedure in a SQL Server database to update a record in the **Course** table via the Course Form. Please create the associated stored procedure in SQL Server database via the Server Explorer window under the Visual C# environment.

```
string cmdString = "dbo.UpdateCourse";
int  intUpdate;
SqlCommand  sqlCommand =  new SqlCommand();
sqlCommand.Connection = loginForm.sqlConnection;
sqlCommand.CommandType = CommandType.StoredProcedure;
sqlCommand.CommandText = cmdString;
sqlCommand.Parameters.Add("@CourseID", SqlDbType.Char).Value = txtCourseID.Text;
sqlCommand.Parameters.Add("@CourseName", SqlDbType.Char).Value = txtCourseName.Text;
sqlCommand.Parameters.Add("@Schedule", SqlDbType.Char).Value = txtSchedule.Text;
sqlCommand.Parameters.Add("@Classroom", SqlDbType.Char).Value = txtClassRoom.Text;
sqlCommand.Parameters.Add("@Credit", SqlDbType.Char).Value = txtCredits.Text;
sqlCommand.Parameters.Add("@Enroll", SqlDbType.Char).Value = txtEnroll.Text;
intUpdate = sqlCommand.ExecuteNonQuery();
```

3. Using the tools and wizards provided by Visual Studio.NET and ADO.NET to perform the data updating for the **Student** table via the Student Form in the **SelectWizard Project** (the project file is located at a folder **Class DB Projects\Chapter 7\SelectWizard Solution** under the **Students** folder at the CRC Press ftp site (refer to Figure 1.2 in Chapter 1).

   Hint1: The binding to all TextBoxes in the Student Form to all columns in the **Student** table in our sample database had been done and all related components had been generated.

   Hint2: Build the query function **UpdateStudent()**, with DataSet Designer.

   Hint3: Develop codes in the **Student.cs** code window, exactly inside the **Update** button's Click method, to call the query function to perform this data updating.

4. Using the Runtime objects to complete the update data query for the Student Form to the **Student** table by using the project **RTOUpdateDelete Project** (the project file is located at the folder, **Class DB Projects\Chapter 7\RTOUpdateDelete Solution** located under the **Students** folder at the CRC Press ftp site (refer to Figure 1.2 in Chapter 1).
5. Using the stored procedure to complete the data-updating query for the Course Form to the **Course** table by using the project **SPUpdateDelete Project** (the project file is located at the folder: **Class DB Projects\Chapter 7\SPUpdateDelete Solution** located under the **Students** folder at the CRC Press ftp site (refer to Figure 1.2 in Chapter 1).

   Hint: One can use the codes built in Exercise 2 with the built stored procedure **dbo.UpdateCourse** in that exercise.

6. Using the LINQ to SQL method to complete the data-deleting query for the Student Form to the **Student** table by using the project **LINQSelect Project** (the project file is located at the folder: **Class DB Projects\Chapter 7\LINQSelect Solution** located under the **Students** folder at the CRC Press ftp site (refer to Figure 1.2 in Chapter 1).

   Hint1: It is highly recommended to delete a new inserted student member to avoid the complicated data recovery process. A good way is to run any exercise projects, such as exercise 3, 4 or 5, in the Homework part of Chapter 6, to first insert a new student member with the following information (then delete this new inserted student record):

Student ID:	**B36588**
Student Name:	**Susan Bai**
GPA:	**3.88**
Credits:	**96**
Major:	**Computer Science**
SchoolYear:	**Junior**
Email:	**sbai@college.edu**
simage:	**White.jpg**

   Hint2: Four tables are involved in this data deleting action: **Student**, **LogIn**, **Course** and **StudentCourse** tables if an original student record were deleted. The recovery order is: first, recover the record from the parent table (**Student** table), and then recover all other records for all other child tables.

8 Accessing Data in ASP.NET

We have provided a very detailed discussion on database programming with Visual C#.NET using the Windows-based applications in the previous chapters. From this chapter on, we will concentrate on the database programming with Visual C#.NET using the Web-based applications. To develop the Web-based application and allow users to access the database through the Internet, you need to understand an important component: Active Server Page.NET or ASP.NET.

Essentially, ASP.NET allows users to write software to access databases through a Web browser rather than a separate program installed on computers. With the help of ASP.NET, the users can easily create and develop an ASP.NET Web application and run it on the server as a server-side project. The user then can send requests to the server to download any Web page, to access the database to retrieve, display and manipulate data via the Web browser. The actual language used in the communications between the client and the server is Hypertext Markup Language (HTML).

When finished this chapter, you will be able to:

- Understand the structure and components of ASP.NET Web applications.
- Understand the structure and components of .NET Framework.
- Select data from the database and display data in a Web page.
- Understand the Application state structure and implement it to store global variables.
- Understand the AutoPostBack property and implement it to communicate with the server effectively.
- Insert, Update and Delete data from the database through a Web page.
- Use the stored procedure to perform the data actions against the database via a Web application.
- Use LINQ to SQL query to perform the data actions against the database via a Web application.
- Perform client-side data validation in Web pages.

In order to help readers to successfully complete this chapter, first we need to provide a detailed discussion about the ASP.NET. A historical review for the ASP.NET is an essential issue to all readers who are not familiar with this new component.

8.1 HISTORICAL REVIEW FOR ASP.NET FRAMEWORK

The first version, ASP.NET 1.0, was released in 2002 with Visual Studio.NET 2002 together. Since then it was always released with Visual Studio.NET, exactly, with the .NET Frameworks (4.8) together until ASP.NET 4.8 in 2019. After that, a branch of ASP.NET called ASP.NET Core was developed; the first version was 1.0built in 2016. Today the latest version of ASP.NET Core is 6.0 released in November, 2021.

The ASP.NET Core is called a cross-platform framework and it enables any Web application to run on different platforms, such as Windows, MacOS, and Linux. Compared with traditional ASP.NET 4.x, the ASP.NET Core provides some advantages to enable users to build Web applications with higher performances. However, for most Web applications, the similar functions can be developed by using ASP.NET 4.x frameworks, and the difference is that a .NET Framework runtime is used by ASP.NET 4.x but a .NET Core runtime is used by ASP.NET Core.

DOI: 10.1201/9781003319832-8

Another difference between the ASP.NET 4.x and ASP.NET Core is the third-party language used to build Web applications. The ASP.NET Core only allows users to use Visual Studio with C# or F# languages, but the ASP.NET 4.x allows users to use Visual Studio with C#, Visual Basic and F#.

In fact, both .NET Framework and .NET Core support building Web applications with ASP MVC, and they also share a lot of same APIs which are called .NET Standard. However, the .NET Core does not support any desktop applications with the user interfaces.

Although ASP.NET Core provides some advantages, such as cross-platform and cloud-based Web application developments, the third-party languages are limited to only C# and F#, and it does not support to build desktop applications with user interfaces. Therefore, in this book we still concentrate our study on the ASP.NET 4.x framework and use it to build our Web applications.

The prerequisite to understand the ASP.NET is the .NET Framework since the ASP.NET is a part of .NET Framework; in other words, the .NET Framework is a foundation of the ASP.NET. Thus we need first to give a detailed discussion about the .NET Framework.

8.2 WHAT IS .NET FRAMEWORK?

The .NET Framework is a model that provides a foundation to develop and execute different applications at an integrated environment such as Visual Studio.NET. In other words, the .NET Framework can be considered as a system to integrate and develop multiple applications such as Windows applications, Web applications or XML Web Services by using a common set of tools and codes such as Visual C#.NET or Visual Basic.NET.

The current version of the .NET Framework is 4.8. Basically, the .NET Framework consists of the following components:

- The Common Language Runtime – CLR (called runtime). The runtime handles runtime services such as language integration, security and memory management. During the development stage, the runtime provides features that are needed to simplify the development.
- Class Libraries. Class libraries provide reusable codes for most common tasks such as data access, XML Web service development, Web and Windows forms.

The main goal to develop the .NET Framework is to overcome several limitations on Web applications since different clients may provide different client browsers. To solve these limitations, .NET Framework provides a common language called Microsoft Intermediate Language (MSIL) that is language-independent and platform-independent, and allows all programs developed in any .NET-based language to be converted into this MSIL. The MSIL can be recognized by the Common Language Runtime (CLR) and the

CLR can compile and execute the MSIL codes by using the Just-In-Time compiler located at the local machines or clients.

You need to access the .NET Framework by using the class libraries provided by the .NET Framework and implement the .NET Framework by using the tools such as Visual Studio.NET provided by the .NET Framework, too. All class libraries provided by the

.NET Framework are located at the different namespaces. All .NET-based languages access the same libraries.

A typical .NET Framework model is shown in Figure 8.1. The .NET Framework supports three types of user interfaces:

- Windows Forms that run on Windows 32 client computers. All projects we developed in the previous chapters used this kind of user interface.
- Web Forms that run on Server computers through ASP.NET and the Hypertext Transfer Protocol (HTTP).
- The Command Console.

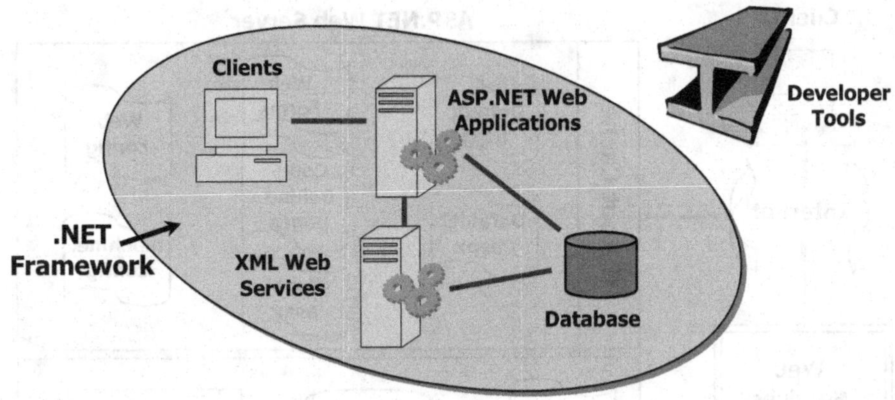

FIGURE 8.1 A .NET framework model.

Summarily, the advantages of using the .NET Framework to develop Windows-based and Web-based applications include, but are not limited to:

- The .NET Framework is based on Web standards and practices, and it fully supports Internet technologies, including the Hypertext Markup Language (HTML), HTTP, XML, Simple Object Access Protocol (SOAP), XML Path Language (XPath) and other Web standards.
- The .NET Framework is designed using unified application models, so the functionality of any class provided by the .NET Framework is available to any .NET-compatible language or programming model. The same piece of code can be implemented in Windows applications, Web applications and XML Web services.
- The .NET Framework is easy for developers to use since the code in the .NET Framework is organized into hierarchical namespaces and classes. The .NET Framework provides a common type system, which is called the unified type system; it can be used by any .NET-compatible language. In the unified type system, all language elements are objects that can be used by any .NET application written in any .NET-based language.

Now let's have a closer look at the ASP.NET.

8.3 WHAT IS ASP.NET AND ASP.NET 4.8?

ASP.NET is a programming framework built on the .NET Framework and is used to build Web applications. Developing ASP.NET Web applications in the .NET Framework is very similar to developing Windows-based applications. An ASP.NET Web application is composed of many different parts and components, but the fundamental component of ASP.NET is the Web Form. A Web Form is the Web page that users view in a browser and an ASP.NET Web application can contain one or more Web Forms. A Web Form is a dynamic page that can access server resources.

The current version of the ASP.NET is 4.8, which is combined with .NET Framework 4.8 to provide a professional and convenient way to help users to build and develop a variety of data-driven applications in .NET programming languages. Compared with the progression from ASP.NET 2.0, the features in ASP.NET 4.8 are *additive*, which means that the core assemblies installed from the .NET Framework 2.0 are still used by the 4.8 versions. In short, ASP.NET 4.8 does not change, take away or break any functionality, concepts, or code present in 2.0, but it simply adds new types and features and capabilities to the framework. Therefore, ASP.NET 4.8 is a rather minor upgrade from ASP.NET 2.0; that is, there are comparatively few new ASP.NET-specific features in the .NET Framework 4.8.

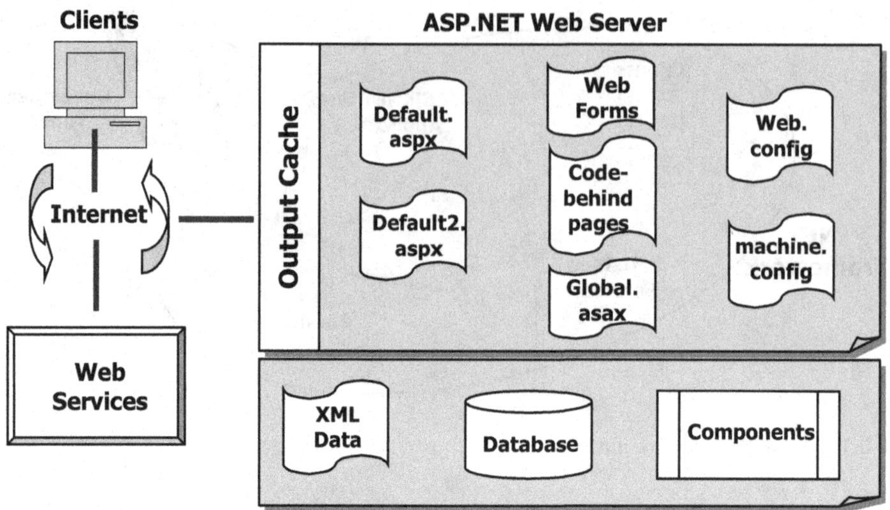

FIGURE 8.2 The structure of an ASP.NET web application.

There are some new features worth noting in ASP.NET 4.8:

- Core Services
- Integrated ASP.NET AJAX support
- Web Forms
- ASP.NET Model View Controller (MVC)
- Dynamic Data
- The ListView control
- The DataPager control

In addition to these new features, one of the most significant differences between ASP.NET 4.8 and ASP.NET 2.0 is that the LINQ support is added into ASP.NET 4.8. LINQ provides a revolutionary solution between the different query syntaxes used in the different databases, and bridges the gap between the world of objects and the world of data.

A completed structure of an ASP.NET Web application is shown in Figure 8.2.

Unlike a traditional Web page that can run scripts on the client, an ASP.NET Web Form can also run server-side codes to access databases, to create additional Web Forms or to take advantage of the built-in security of the server. In addition, since an ASP.NET Web Form does not rely on client-side scripts, it is independent of the client's browser type or operating system. This independence allows users to develop a single Web Form that can be viewed on any device that has Internet access and a Web browser.

Because ASP.NET is part of the .NET Framework, the ASP.NET Web application can be developed in any .NET-based language.

The ASP.NET technology also supports XML Web services. These are distributed applications that use XML for transferring information between clients, applications and other XML Web services.

The main parts of an ASP.NET Web application include:

- Web Forms or **Default.aspx** pages. The Web Forms or **Deafult.aspx** pages provide the user interface for the Web application, and they are very similar to the Windows Forms in the Windows-based application. The Web Forms files are indicated with an extension of **.aspx**.
- Code-behind pages. The so-called code-behind pages are related to the Web Forms and contain the server-side codes for the Web Form. This code-behind page is very similar to

the code window for the Windows Forms in a Windows-based application we discussed in the previous chapters. Most event methods or handlers associated with controls on the Web Forms are located in this code-behind page. The code-behind pages are indicated with an extension of **.aspx.cs**.

- Web Services or **.asmx** pages. Web services are used when you create dynamic sites that will be accessed by other programs or computers. ASP.NET Web services may be supported by a code-behind page that is designed by the extension of **.asmx.cs**.
- Configuration files. The Configuration files are XML files that define the default settings for the Web application and the Web server. Each Web application has one **Web.config** configuration file, and each Web server has one **machine.config** file.
- **Global.asax** file. The **Global.asax** file, also known as the ASP.NET application file, is an optional file that contains code for responding to application-level events that are raised by ASP.NET or by HttpModules. At runtime, **Global.asax** is parsed and compiled into a dynamically generated .NET Framework class that is derived from the HttpApplication base class. This dynamic class is very similar to the **Application class** or main thread in Visual C++, and this class can be accessed by any other objects in the Web application.
- XML Web service links. These links are used to allow the Web application to send and receive data from an XML Web service.
- Database connectivity. The Database connectivity allows the Web application to transfer data to and from database sources. Generally, it is not recommended to allow users to access the database from the server directly because of the security issues, instead, in most industrial and commercial applications, the database can be accessed through the application-layer to strengthen the security of the databases.
- Caching. Caching allows the Web application to return Web Forms and data more quickly after the first request.

8.3.1 ASP.NET Web Application File Structure

When you create an ASP.NET Web application, Visual Studio.NET creates two folders to hold the files that related to the application. When the project is compiled, a third folder is created to store the terminal dll file. In other words, the final or terminal file of an ASP.NET Web application is a dynamic linked library file (.dll).

Figure 8.3 shows a typical file structure of an ASP.NET Web application.

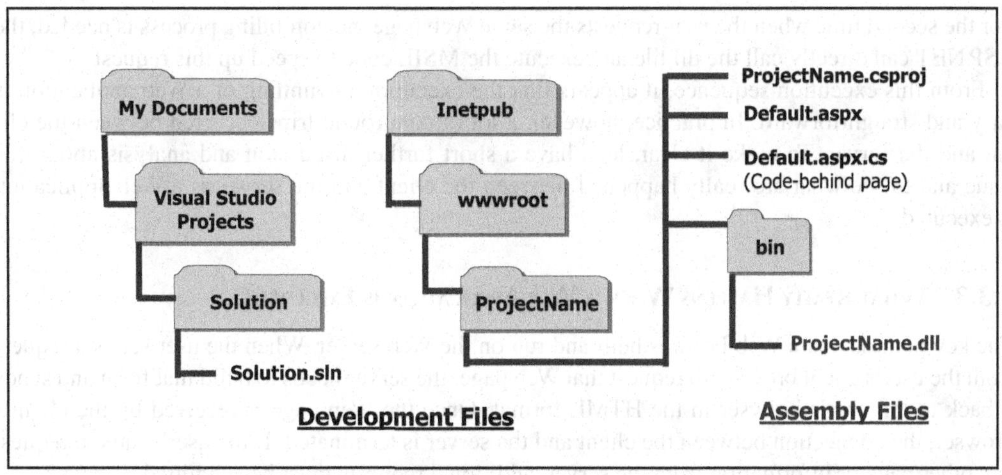

FIGURE 8.3 ASP.NET web application file structure.

Those folders listed on the left side in Figure 8.3 are very familiar to us since they are created by the Windows-based applications. But the folders created on the right side are new to us, and the functionalities of those folders are:

- The **Inetpub** folder contains another folder named **wwwroot** and it is used to hold the root address of the Web project whose name is defined as **ProjectName**. The project file **ProjectName.csproj** is an XML file that contains references to all project items, such as forms and classes.
- The bin folder contains the assembly file or the terminal file of the project with the name of **ProjectName.dll**. All ASP.NET Web applications will be finally converted to a dll file and stored in the server's memory.

8.3.2 ASP.NET Execution Model

When you finished an ASP.NET Web application, the Web project is compiled and two terminal files are created:

1) Project Assembly files (.dll). All code-behind pages (.aspx.cs) in the project are compiled into a single assembly file that is stored as **ProjectName.dll**. This project assembly file is placed in the **bin** directory of the Web site and will be executed by the Web server as a request is received from the client at the running time.
2) **AssemblyInfo.cs** file. This file is used to write the general information, specially assembly version and assembly attributes, about the assembly.

As a Web project runs and the client requests a Web page for the first time, the following events occur:

1) The client browser issues a GET HTTP request to the server.
2) The ASP.NET parser interprets the course code.
3) Based on the interpreting result, ASP.NET will direct the request to the associated assembly file (.dll) if the code has been compiled into the dll files. Otherwise, the ASP.NET invokes the compiler to convert the code into the dll format.
4) Runtime loads and executes the Microsoft Intermediate Language (MSIL) codes and sends back the required Web page to the client in the HTML file format.

For the second time when the user requests the same Web page, no compiling process is needed, the ASP.NET can directly call the dll file and execute the MSIL code to speed up this request.

From this execution sequence, it appears that the execution or running of a Web application is easy and straightforward. In practice, however, a lot of data round trips occurred between the client and the server. To make it clear, let's have a short further discussion and analysis about this issue and to see what are really happened between the client and the server as a Web application is executed.

8.3.3 What Really Happens When a Web Application is Executed?

The key point is that a Web Form is built and run on the Web server. When the user sends a request from the user's client browser to request that Web page, the server needs to build that form and sends it back to the user's browser in the HTML format. Once the Web page is received by the client's browser, the connection between the client and the server is terminated. If the user wants to request any other page or information from the server, additional requests must be submitted.

To make this issue more clear, we can use our LogIn Form as an example. The first time the user sends a request to the server to ask to start a logon process, the server builds the LogIn Form and sends it back to the client in the HTML format. After that, the connection between the client and the server is gone. After the user received the LogIn Web page and enter the necessary logon information, such as the username and password to the LogIn Form, the user needs to send another request to the server to ask the server to process those pieces of logon information. After the server received and processed the logon information, if the server found that the logon information is invalid, the server needs to re-build the LogIn Form and send it back to the client with some warning message. Therefore, you can see how many round trips occurred between the client and the server as a Web application is executed.

A good solution to try to reduce those round trips is to make sure that all information entered from the client side should be as correct as possible. In other words, try to make as much validation as possible in the client side to reduce the burden of the server.

Now we have finished the discussion about the .NET Framework and ASP.NET as well as the ASP.NET Web applications. Next we will create and develop some actual Web projects using the ASP.NET Web Forms to illustrate how to access the database through the Web browser to select, display and manipulate data on Web pages.

8.3.4 The Requirements to Test and Run a Web Project

Before we can start to create our real Web project using the ASP.NET, we need the following requirements to test and run our Web project:

1) Web server: To test and run our Web project, you need a Web server either on your local computer or on your network. By default, if you installed Visual Studio 2022 Community on your local computer, the **IIS 10.0 Express** should have been installed on your local computer. This software allows your Web development tools such as Visual Studio.NET to connect to the server to upload or download pages from the server.
2) In this chapter, in order to make our Web project simple and easy, we always use our local computer as a pseudo server. In other words, we always use the localhost, which is the IP name of our local computer, as our Web server to communicate with our browser to perform the data accessing and manipulating.

If you have not enabled the IIS on your computer, following the steps below to enable this component on your computer:

- Click **Start**, then click Control Panel, and click on the **Programs**.
- Under the **Programs and Features** item, click on the link **Turn Windows features on or off** to open the Windows Features wizard, as shown in Figure 8.4.
- Check the checkbox for the **Internet Information Services** item from the list to enable the IIS on your computer.
- To confirm that this enabling function, expand this **Internet Information Services** item, and make sure that both items, **Web Management Tools** and **World Wide Web Services**, are enabled, too. This can be indicated with a selection mark for both checkboxes, as shown in Figure 8.4.
- Click the **OK** button to activate this IIS and close the Windows Features wizard.
- The activation function starts to enable this IIS on the next wizard, and a completion message is displayed when this is done. Just click on the **Close** button to finish this enabling process. Finally close the Control Panel.

You may need to re-boot your computer to make this enabling function effect.

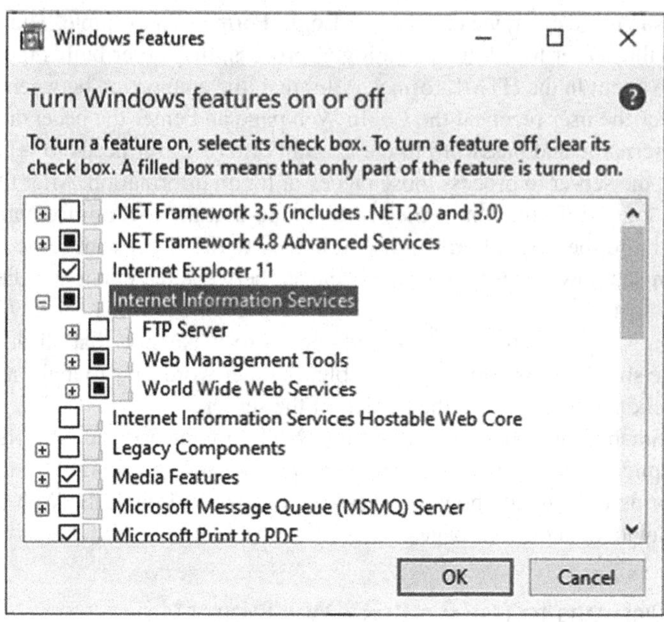

FIGURE 8.4 The opened Windows features wizard.

As you know, the .NET Framework includes two Data Providers for accessing enterprise databases: the .NET Framework Data Provider for OLE DB and the .NET Framework Data Provider for SQL Server. Because there is no significant difference between the Microsoft Access database and the SQL Server database, in this chapter, we only use the SQL Server database as our target database to illustrate how to select, display and manipulate data against our sample database through the Web pages.

This chapter is organized in the following ways:

1) Develop ASP.NET Web application to select and display data from the Microsoft SQL Server database.
2) Develop ASP.NET Web application to insert data into the Microsoft SQL Server database.
3) Develop ASP.NET Web application to update and delete data against the Microsoft SQL Server database.
4) Develop ASP.NET Web application to select and manipulate data against the Microsoft SQL Server database using LINQ to SQL query.

Let's start from the first one in this list to create and build our ASP.NET Web application. However, before we can continue, we need to set up and configure the Visual Studio 2022 Community IDE to add one missed but important component, **ASP.NET Template for .NET Framework**, which is not installed by default.

8.3.5 Install Missed Component to Get ASP.NET Template for .NET Framework

Perform the following operations to add the missed ASP.NET Template for .NET Framework:

1) Open Visual Studio 2022 Community IDE and click on the **Continue without code** link to open the traditional studio wizard.
2) Go to **Tools | Get Tools and Features** menu item to open the Visual Studio Installer.
3) On the opened Installer, click on the **Individual Components** tab on the top to open this wizard.

4) Scroll down along the scrolling bar on the right until you find three components:
    a. .NET Framework project and item templates
    b. .NET WebAssembly build tools
    c. Advanced ASP.NET features
5) Select all of these three components by checking them one by one.
6) Click on the **Modify** button on the lower-right corner to install these components.
7) Finally, click on the **Close** button when these installations are done.

8.4 DEVELOP ASP.NET WEB APPLICATION TO SELECT DATA FROM SQL SERVER DATABASES

Let's start a new ASP.NET Web application project **SQLWebSelect** to illustrate how to access and select data from the database via the Internet. Open the Visual Studio.NET 2022 and click the **Continue without code** link.

Then go to the menu **File | New | Project** to create a new ASP.NET Web application project. On the opened New Template wizard, which is shown in Figure 8.5, select the template **ASP.NET Web Application (.NET Framework)** and click on the **Next** button. Enter **SQLWebSelectProject** into the **Project name** box and **SQLWebSelect Solution** into the **Solution name** box, and select a desired location to save this project. Then click on the **Create** button to create this new Web application project.

On the next wizard, as shown in Figure 8.6, select the **Web Forms** template by clicking on it, and then click on the **Create** button again to continue.

You can place your new project in any folder you like in your computer. In our case, we place it in our folder **C:\Chapter 8**. Click the **OK** button to create this new Web application project.

On the opened new project, the default Web Form is named **Default.aspx** and it is located at the Solution Explorer window. This is the Web Form that works as a user interface in the server-side. Now let's perform some modifications to this form to make it our LogIn Form page.

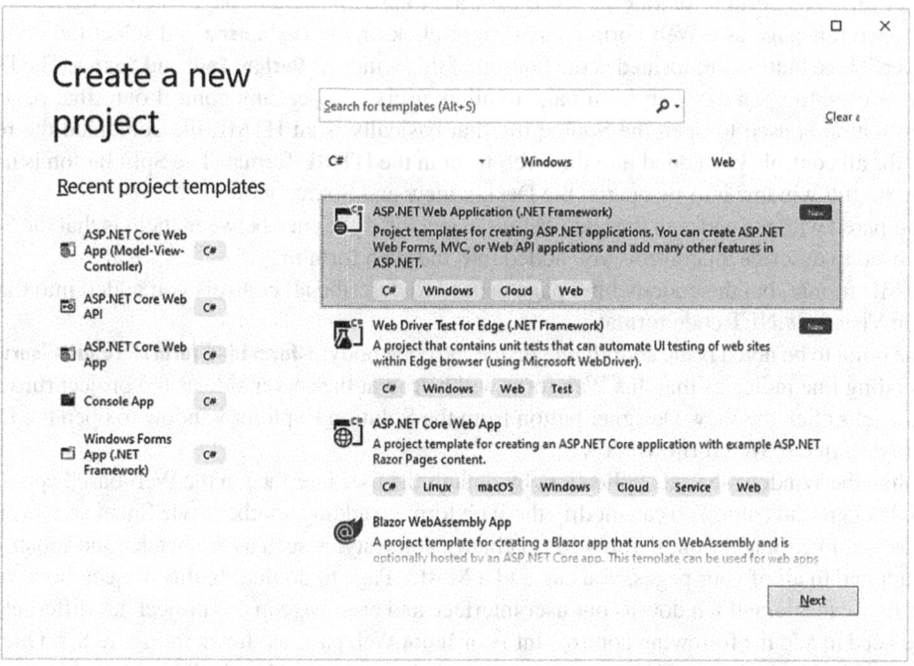

FIGURE 8.5 The opened template wizard.

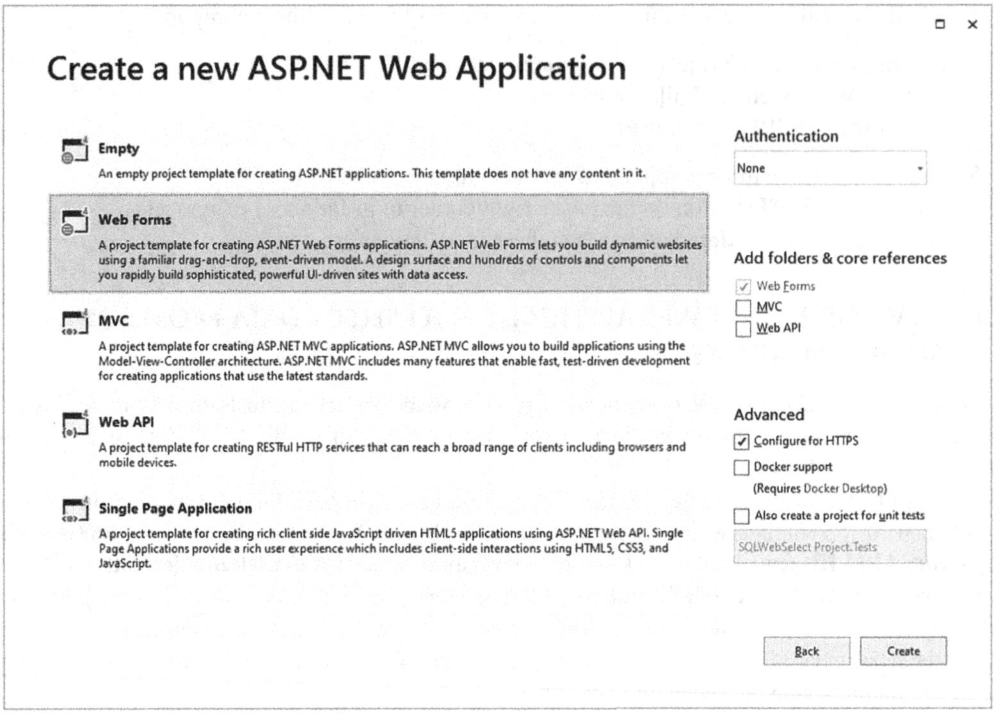

Create a new ASP.NET Web Application

Empty
An empty project template for creating ASP.NET applications. This template does not have any content in it.

Web Forms
A project template for creating ASP.NET Web Forms applications. ASP.NET Web Forms lets you build dynamic websites using a familiar drag-and-drop, event-driven model. A design surface and hundreds of controls and components let you rapidly build sophisticated, powerful UI-driven sites with data access.

MVC
A project template for creating ASP.NET MVC applications. ASP.NET MVC allows you to build applications using the Model-View-Controller architecture. ASP.NET MVC includes many features that enable fast, test-driven development for creating applications that use the latest standards.

Web API
A project template for creating RESTful HTTP services that can reach a broad range of clients including browsers and mobile devices.

Single Page Application
A project template for creating rich client side JavaScript driven HTML5 applications using ASP.NET Web API. Single Page Applications provide a rich user experience which includes client-side interactions using HTML5, CSS3, and JavaScript.

Authentication
None

Add folders & core references
Web Forms
MVC
Web API

Advanced
Configure for HTTPS
Docker support
(Requires Docker Desktop)
Also create a project for unit tests
SQLWebSelect Project.Tests

Back
Create

FIGURE 8.6 The selected web form wizard.

8.4.1 Create the User Interface – LogIn Form

Right click this **Default.aspx** item and select the **Rename** item from the popup menu and change the name of this Web Form to **LogIn.aspx** since we want to use this default page as our LogIn page.

To open this page as a Web Form format, right-click on the **LogIn.aspx** and select the item **View Designer**. Three buttons are located at the bottom of this window: **Design**, **Split** and **Source**. The Design button is used to open the Web form page to allow users to insert any control onto that page. The Source button is used to open the Source file that basically is an HTML file contained the related codes for all controls you added into this Web form in the HTML format. The Split button is used to divide the full window into two parts: the Design view and Source view.

Compared with the codes in the code-behind page, the difference between them is that the Source file is used to describe all controls you added into the Web form in

HTML format, but the code-behind page is used to describe all controls you added into the Web form in Visual C#.NET code format.

One point to be noted is the coding line inside the code body: **<form id="form1" runat="server">**. This coding line indicates that this Web form will be run at the server side as the project runs.

Now let's click the View Designer button from the Solution Explorer window to open the Design view to design our Web form window.

Unlike the Windows-based application, by default the user interface in the Web-based application has no background color. You can modify the Web form by adding another Style Sheet and format the form as you like. In addition, if you want to change some styles such as the header and footer of the form applied to all of your pages, you can add a Master Page to do that. In this project, however, we prefer to use the default window as our user interface and each page in our project has different style.

We need to add the following controls into our **LogIn** Web page as shown in Figure 8.7. One point to be noted is that there is no **Name** property available for any control in the Web form object, instead a property **ID** is used to replace the **Name** property and it works as a unique identifier for each control you added into the Web form.

Type	ID	Text	TabIndex	BackColor	TextMode	Font
Label	Label1	Welcome to CSE DEPT	0	#E0E0E0		Bold/Large
Label	Label2	User Name	1			Bold/Small
Textbox	txtUserName		2			
Label	Label3	Pass Word	3			Bold/Small
Textbox	txtPassWord		4		Password	
Button	cmdLogIn	LogIn	5			Bold/Medium
Button	cmdCancel	Cancel	6			Bold/Medium

FIGURE 8.7 Controls for the LogIn form.

Another difference with the Windows-based form is that when you add these controls into our Web form, first you must locate a position for the control to be added using the **Space** key and the **Enter** key on your keyboard in the Web form, and then pick up a control from the Toolbox window and drag it to that location. You cannot pick and drag a control to a random location as you want in this Web form and this is a significant difference between the Windows-based form and the Web-based form windows.

However, an exception or good news is that for Visual Studio 2022, you can still add and place any control to this Web form in any random location as you did on a Windows Form as long as you set the **Position** property of each control to **Absolute** value. To do that, one needs to:

1) Add a control to the Web Form at a location.
2) Select that control by clicking on it.
3) Go to **Format | Set Position** menu item and select and check the **Absolute** property.

After this setup, you can move any control to any random location as you like, and this greatly increased the flexibility and efficiency of building our Web Form.

Your finished user interface should match the shown in Figure 8.8.

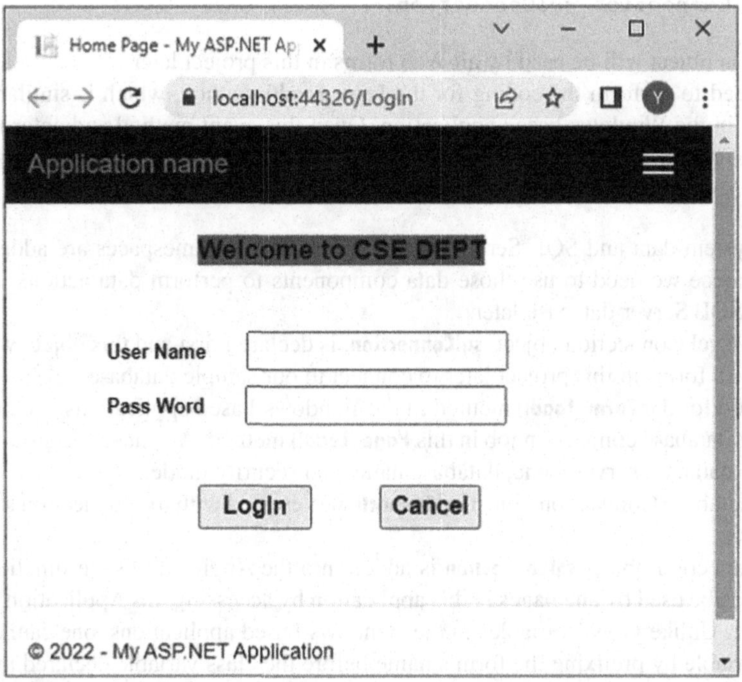

FIGURE 8.8 The finished LogIn web form.

Before we can add the codes into the code-behind page to response to the controls to perform the logon process, first we must run the project to allow the **Web.config** file to recognize those controls we have added into the Web form. Click the **IIS Express** button on the toolbar to run our project. You may need to click the **Yes** to two prompted dialogs to enable our Web page to be certificated and recognized by the local server. The running Web page should match one that is shown in Figure 8.8. Click on the **Close** button that is located at the upper-right corner of the form to close this page.

One important and interesting point to add a control to a Web Form to a random location is to set the **Position** property of each control to the **Absolute** value. After this setting, one can add any control and move it to any location as one did for the Windows Form

Now let's develop the codes to access the database to perform the logon process.

8.4.2 Develop the Codes to Access and Select Data from the Database

Open the code-behind page **LogIn.aspx** by right-clicking on it and select the **View Code** button from the Solution Explorer window. First we need to add a SQL Server data provider-related namespace as we did for those projects in the previous chapters. Add the following namespace to the top of this code window to involve the namespaces for the Data and the SQL Server Data Provider:

```
using System.Data;
using System.Data.SqlClient;
```

Next we need to create a class or field-level variable, **sqlConnection**, for our connection object. Enter the following code under the class header:

```
publicSqlConnection sqlConnection;
```

This connection object will be used by all Web forms in this project later.

Now we need to perform the coding for the **Page_Load()** method, which is similar to the **Form_Load()** method in the Windows-based application. Open this event method and enter the codes that are shown in Figure 8.9 into this method.

Let's have a closer look at this piece of codes to see how it works.

- **A.** Some system data and SQL Server data provider-related namespaces are added into this project since we need to use those data components to perform data actions against our sample SQL Server database later.
- **B.** A class-level Connection object, **sqlConnection**, is declared first and this object will be used by all Web forms in this project later to connect to our sample database.
- **C.** As we did for the **Form_Load()** method in the Windows-based applications, we need to perform the database connection job in this **Page_Load()** method. A connection string is created with the database server name, database name and security mode.
- **D.** A new database Connection object **sqlConnection** is created with the connection string as the argument.
- **E.** The Connection object **sqlConnection** is added into the Application state function and this object can be used by any pages in this application by accessing this Application state function later. Unlike global variables in the Windows-based applications, one cannot access a class variable by prefixing the form's name before the class variable declared in that form

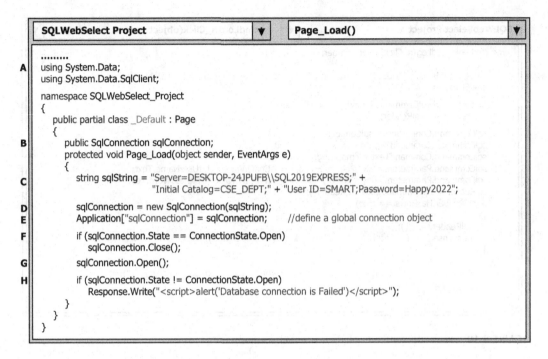

```
SQLWebSelect Project                    Page_Load()

  ........
A using System.Data;
  using System.Data.SqlClient;

  namespace SQLWebSelect_Project
  {
     public partial class _Default : Page
     {
B       public SqlConnection sqlConnection;
        protected void Page_Load(object sender, EventArgs e)
        {
C          string sqlString = "Server=DESKTOP-24JPUFB\\SQL2019EXPRESS;" +
                              "Initial Catalog=CSE_DEPT;" + "User ID=SMART;Password=Happy2022";

D          sqlConnection = new SqlConnection(sqlString);
E          Application["sqlConnection"] = sqlConnection;      //define a global connection object

F          if (sqlConnection.State == ConnectionState.Open)
              sqlConnection.Close();
G          sqlConnection.Open();
H          if (sqlConnection.State != ConnectionState.Open)
              Response.Write("<script>alert('Database connection is Failed')</script>");
        }
     }
  }
```

FIGURE 8.9 The codes for the Page_Load method.

from other pages. In the Web-based application, the Application state function is a good place to store any global variable. In ASP.NET Web application, Application state is stored in an instance of the **HttpApplicationState** class that can be accessed through the Application property of the **HttpContext** class in the server side and is faster than storing and retrieving information in a database.

F. First we need to check whether this database connection has been made. If it is, we need first to disconnect this connection by using the **Close()** method.
G. Then we can call the **Open()** method to set up the database connection.
H. By checking the database connection state property, we can confirm the connection we made. If the connection state is not equal to **Open**, which means that the database connection is failed, a warning message is displayed and the procedure is exited.

One significant difference in using the Message box to display some debug information in the Web form is that you cannot use a Message box as you did in the Windows-based applications. In the Web form development, no Message box available and you can only use the Javascript **alert()** method to display a Message box in ASP.NET. Two popular objects are widely utilized in the ASP.NET Web applications: The **Request** and the **Response** objects. The ASP **Request** object is used to get information from the user, and the ASP **Response** object is used to send output to the user from the server. The **Write()** method of the **Response** object is used to display the message sent by the server. You must add the script tag **<script>……</script>** to indicate that the content is written in Javascript language.

Now let's perform the coding for the **LogIn** button's Click method.

The function of this piece of codes is to access the **LogIn** table located in our sample SQL Server database based on the username and password entered by the user to try to find the matched logon information. Currently, we have not created our next page, the– **Selection** page, so we just display a Message box to confirm the success of the logon process if it is.

```
SQLWebSelect Project    cmdLogIn_Click(object sender, EventArgs e)

  protected void cmdLogIn_Click(object sender, EventArgs e)
  {
A      string cmdString = "SELECT user_name, pass_word, faculty_id, student_id FROM LogIn ";
       cmdString += "WHERE (user_name=@name) AND (pass_word=@word)";
B      SqlCommand sqlCommand = new SqlCommand();
       SqlDataReader sqlReader;
C      sqlCommand.Connection = sqlConnection;
       sqlCommand.CommandType = CommandType.Text;
       sqlCommand.CommandText = cmdString;
       sqlCommand.Parameters.Add("@name", SqlDbType.Char).Value = txtUserName.Text;
       sqlCommand.Parameters.Add("@word", SqlDbType.Char, 8).Value = txtPassWord.Text;
D      sqlReader = sqlCommand.ExecuteReader();
E      if (sqlReader.HasRows == true)
       {
          sqlReader.Close();
          Response.Write("<script>alert('LogIn is successful!')</script>");
       }
F      else
          Response.Write("<script>alert('No matched username/password found!')</script>");
G      sqlCommand.Dispose();
  }
```

FIGURE 8.10 The codes for the LogIn button's click method.

Right click on the **LogIn.aspx** page from the Solution Explorer window and select the **View Designer** button, and then double-click on the **LogIn** button to open its Click method. Enter the codes that are shown in Figure 8.10 into this method.

Let's have a closer look at this piece of codes to see how it works.

- **A.** A SQL query statement is declared first since we need to use this query statement to retrieve the matched username and password from the **LogIn** table. Because this query statement is relatively long, we split it into two sub-strings.
- **B.** All data objects related to the SQL Server Data Provider are created here such as the Command object and DataReader object.
- **C.** The Command object is initialized and built by assigning it with the Connection object, commandType and Parameters collection properties of the Command class. The **Add()** method is utilized to add two actual dynamic parameters to the Parameters collection of the Command class.
- **D.** The **ExecuteReader()** method of the Command class is executed to access the database, retrieve the matched username and password and return them to the **DataReader** object.
- **E.** If the **HasRows** property of the **DataReader** is **true**, which means that at least one matched username and password has been found and retrieved from the database. First the used **SqlDataReader** must be closed, and a successful message is created and sent back from the server to the client to display it in the client browser.
- **F.** Otherwise, no matched username or password has been found from the database, and a warning message is created and sent back to the client and displayed in the client browser.
- **G.** The used object, such as the Command, is released since it is no longer to be used.

Next let's make the coding for the **Cancel** button's Click method.

The function of this method is to close the current Web page if this **Cancel** button is clicked, which means that the user wants to terminate the ASP.NET Web application. Double-click the **Cancel** button from the Design View of the LogIn Form to open this method and enter the codes that are shown in Figure 8.11 into this method.

SQLWebSelect Project | cmdCancel_Click(object sender, EventArgs e)

```
    protected void cmdCancel_Click(object sender, EventArgs e)
    {
A       if (sqlConnection.State == ConnectionState.Open)
            sqlConnection.Close();
B       Response.Write("<script>window.close()</script>");
    }
```

FIGURE 8.11 The codes for the cancel button's click method.

The function of this piece of codes is:

A. First we need to check whether the database is still connected to our Web form. If it is, we need to close this connection before we can terminate our Web application.
B. The server sends back a command with the **Response** object's method **Write()** to issue a Javascript statement **window.close()** to close the Web application.

One key point to be noted to use this **Cancel** button to terminate our Web application is that you must reset the **CausesValidation** property of this **Cancel** button to **false** to skip the validation process to be built in the next section for two textboxes, **txtUserName** and **txtPassWord**. Otherwise, you must go through this validation process by entering a username and a password to close our project even when this **Cancel** button is clicked.

To reset that property, on the opened Design View of the **LogIn** page, select the **Cancel** button and go to the Properties window, and select the **false** from the **CausesValidation** property. In this way, you can directly close or terminate our project without going through the validation process.

At this point, we have finished developing the codes for the **LogIn** Web form. Before we can run the project to test our Web page, we need to add some data validation functionalities in the client side to reduce the burden of the server.

8.4.3 Validate the Data in the Client Side

As we mentioned in Section 8.3.3, in order to reduce the burden of the server, we should make every efforts to perform the data validation in the client side. In other words, before we can send requests to the server, we need to make sure that our information to be sent to the server should be as correct as possible. ASP.NET provides some tools to help us to complete this data validation. These tools include five validation controls that are shown in Figure 8.12.

Validation Control	Functionality
RequiredFieldValidator	Validate whether the required field has valid data (not blank).
RangeValidator	Validate whether a value is within a given numeric range. The range is defined by the MaximumValue and MinimumValue properties provided by users.
CompareValidator	Validate whether a value fits a given expression by using the different Operator property such as 'equal', 'greater than', 'less than' and the type of the value, which is setting by the Type property.
CustomValidator	Validate a given expression using a script function. This method provides the maximum flexibility in data validation but one needs to add a function to the Web page and sends it to the server to get the feedback from it.
RegularExpressionValidator	Validate whether a value fits a given regular expression by using the ValidationExpression property, which should be provided by the user.

FIGURE 8.12 Validation controls.

All of these five controls are located at the **Validation** tab in the Toolbox window in Visual Studio. NET environment.

Here we want to use the first control, **RequiredFieldValidator**, to validate our two textboxes, **txtUserName** and **txtPassWord**, in the **LogIn** page to make sure that both of them are not empty when the **LogIn** button is clicked by the user as the project runs.

Open the Design View of the **LogIn** Web form, go to the Toolbox window and click the **Validation** tab to expand it. Drag the **RequiredFieldValidator** control from the Toolbox window and place it next to the username textbox. Set the following properties to this control in the property window:

ErrorMessage:	**UserName is Required**
ControlToValidate:	**txtUserName**

Perform the similar dragging and placing operations to place the second **RequiredFieldValidator** just next to the password textbox. Set the following properties for this control in the property window:

ErrorMessage:	**PassWord is Required**
ControlToValidate:	**txtPassWord**

Your finished **LogIn** Web form should match one that is shown in Figure 8.13.

Now run our project to test this data validation by clicking the **IIS Express** button, without entering any data into two textboxes, and then click the **LogIn** button. Immediately, two error messages, which are created by the **RequiredFieldValidators**, are displayed to ask users to enter these two pieces of information. After entering the username and password, click the **LogIn** button again, a successful

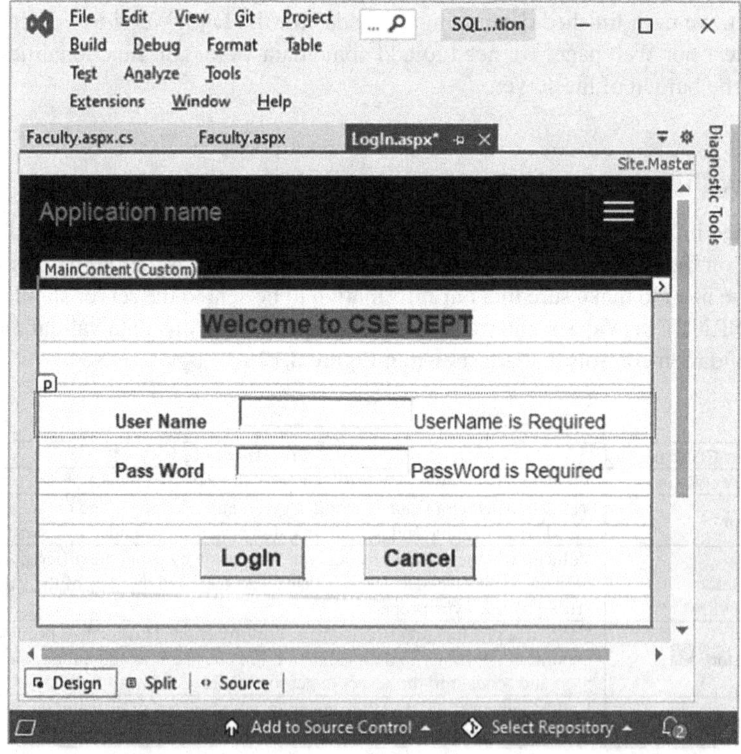

FIGURE 8.13 Adding the data validation – RequiredFieldValidator.

login message is displayed. So you can see how the **RequiredFieldValidator** works to reduce the processing load for the server.

When we run our Web application project above, we did not specify or select a Web browser, instead we just used the default browser, **Google Chrome**. However, to effectively run and execute our Web application projects built in this chapter, we should use our desired Web browser, **Internet Explorer**. The reason for that is because this kind of browser contained more powerful tools and classical components to meet the functions and requirements for our applications.

8.4.4 Select a Desired Web Browser to Effectively Run Our Web Application Project

To select the Internet Explorer as our Web browser, perform the following operational steps:

1) In the opened Visual Studio 2022 and our **SQLWebSelect Project**, click on the drop-down arrow located at the right of the **IIS Express** button on the top.
2) On the opened sub-menu, click on the **Web Browser (Google Chrome)** item.
3) Select the **Internet Explorer** item by checking it from the sub-menu.

Now the default Web browser is changed to **Internet Explorer** attached with the **IIS Express** button on the top.

One of the most important features when using this Internet Explorer as our Web browser is to execute some classical Web API functions to effectively run our Web applications to perform our desired functions. For example, to effectively terminate our Web application project, we used a Javascript method, **window.close()**. This method can be used to effectively stop our Web applications. However, this method can only be worked under the Internet Explorer browser but not any other browser.

8.4.5 Create the Second User Interface – Selection Page

Now let's continue to develop our Web application by adding another Web page, the Selection page. As we did in the previous chapters, after the logon process is finished, the next step is to allow users to select different functionalities from the Selection form to perform the associated database actions.

The function of this Selection page is to allow users to visit different pages to perform different database actions such as selecting, inserting, updating or deleting data against the database via the different tables by selecting the different items. Therefore, this Selection page needs to perform the following jobs:

1) Provide and display all available selections to allow users to select them.
2) Open the associated page based on the users' selection.

Now let's build this page. To do that, we need to add a new Web page. Right-click our project **SQLWebSelect Project** from the Solution Explorer window and select the **Add | New Item** from the popup menu. On the opened wizard, select the **Web Form** as our Template, and enter **Selection.aspx** into the **Name** box as the name for this new page, and then click the **Add** button to add this page into our project.

On the opened Web form, add the controls shown in Figure 8.14 into this page. Your finished Selection page should match the one that is shown in Figure 8.15.

As we mentioned in the last section, before you pick up those controls from the Toolbox window and drag them into the page, you must first use the Space or the Enter keys from the keyboard to locate the positions on the page for those controls. An exception is that when you set the Position property for all controls to **Absolute**, then you

Next let's create the codes for this Selection page to allow users to select the different page to perform the associated data actions.

Type	ID	Text	TabIndex	BackColor	Font
Label	Label1	Make Your Selection:	0	#E0E0E0	Bold/Large
DropDownList	ComboSelection		1		
Button	cmdSelect	Select	2		Bold/Medium
Button	cmdExit	Exit	3		Bold/Medium

FIGURE 8.14 Controls for the selection form can move any of those controls to any desired location on the Web page.

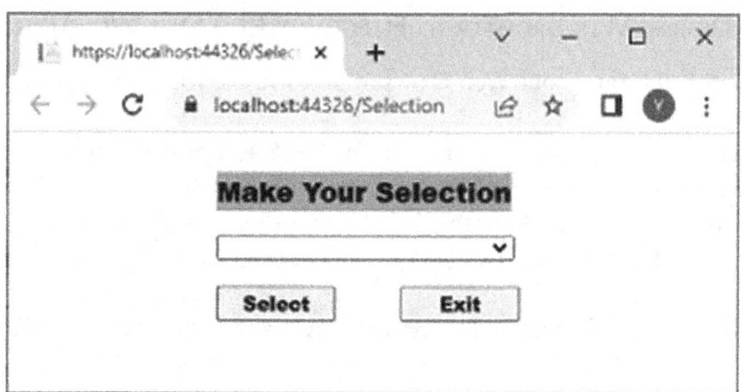

FIGURE 8.15 The finished Selection page.

8.4.6 Develop the Codes for the Selection Page to Open the Other Page

First let's run the Selection page to build the Web configuration file. Click on the **IIS Express** button to run this page, and then click the **Close** button that is located on the upper-right corner of the page to close it.

Right-click on the **Selection.aspx** from the Solution Explorer window and click on the **View Code** item to open the code page for the Selection Web form. First let's add a SQL Data Provider-related namespaces on the top of this page to provide a reference to all data components of the SQL Data Provider:

```
using System.Data;
using System.Data.SqlClient;
```

Then enter the codes that are shown in Figure 8.16 into the **Page_Load()** method to add all selection items into the combobox control **ComboSelection** to allow users to make their selection as the project runs.

The function of this piece of coding is straightforward. Three pieces of CSE Dept related information are added into the combobox **ComboSelection** by using the **Add()** method, and these pieces of information will be selected by the user as the project runs.

Next we need to create the codes for two buttons' Click methods. First let's do the coding for the **Select** button. Right-click on the **Selection.aspx** from the Solution Explorer window and click on the **View Designer** item to open the Selection Web form, and then

Double-click the **Select** button to open its method. Enter the codes that are shown in Figure 8.17 into this method.

The function of this piece of coding is easy. Based on the information selected by the user, the related Web page is opened by using the server's **Response** object, precisely by using the **Redirect()** method of the server's **Response** object. All of these three pages will be created and discussed in the following sections.

```
SQLWebSelect Project                 Page_Load(object sender, EventArgs e)

using System.Data;
using System.Data.SqlClient;

namespace SQLWebSelect_Project
{
   public partial class Selection : System.Web.UI.Page
   {
      protected void Page_Load(object sender, EventArgs e)
      {
         ComboSelection.Items.Add("Faculty Information");
         ComboSelection.Items.Add("Course Information");
         ComboSelection.Items.Add("Student Information");
      }
   ........
```

FIGURE 8.16 The coding for the Page_Load() method of the selection page.

```
SQLWebSelect Project                 cmdSelect_Click(object sender, EventArgs e)

protected void cmdSelect_Click(object sender, EventArgs e)
{
     if (ComboSelection.Text == "Faculty Information")
         Response.Redirect("Faculty.aspx");
     else if (ComboSelection.Text == "Student Information")
         Response.Redirect("Student.aspx");
     else if (ComboSelection.Text == "Course Information")
         Response.Redirect("Course.aspx");
}
```

FIGURE 8.17 The coding for the select button's click method.

Finally let's take care of the coding for the **Exit** button's Click method. The function of this piece of code is to close the database connection and the Web application. Double click the **Exit** button from the Design View of the Selection page to open this method. Enter the codes that are shown in Figure 8.18 into this method.

Let's have a closer look at this piece of codes to see how it works.

First we need to check if the database is still connected to our application. If it is, the global connection object stored in the Application state is activated with the **Close()** method to close the database connection. Then the **Write()** method of the server **Response** object is called to close the Web application. A key point is that the Application state function stores an object, Connection object in this case. In order to access and use that Connection object stored in the Application global function, a casting **(SqlConnection)** must be clearly prefixed before that object; therefore, a two-layer

```
SQLWebSelect Project                 cmdExit_Click(object sender, EventArgs e)

protected void cmdExit_Click(object sender, EventArgs e)
{
     if (((SqlConnection)Application["sqlConnection"]).State == ConnectionState.Open)
         ((SqlConnection)Application["sqlConnection"]).Close();
     Response.Write("<script>window.close()</script>");
}
```

FIGURE 8.18 The coding for the exit button's click method.

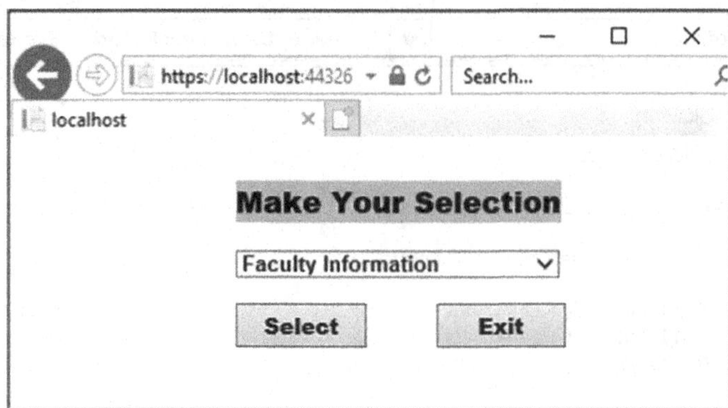

FIGURE 8.19 The running status of the second page – selection page.

parenthesis is used to complete this casting. Otherwise a compiling error will be encountered since the compiler cannot recognize and convert the general object stored in the Application state function to a specific Connection object.

Now we have finished the coding for the Selection page. Before we can run the project to test this page, we need to do some modifications to the codes in the **LogIn** button's Click method in the **LogIn** page to allow the application to switch from the **LogIn** page to the **Selection** page as the **LogIn** process is successful.

Open the **LogIn** page and the **LogIn** button's Click method, replace the code body that is located inside **if(sqlReader.HasRows == true)** block (under the line **sqlReader.Close();**):

```
Response.Write("<script>alert('LogIn is successful!')</script>");
```

with the following code:

```
Response.Redirect("Selection.aspx");
```

In this way, as long as the login process is successful, the next page, the **Selection** page, will be opened by executing the **Redirect()** method of the server **Response** object. The argument of this method is the URL address of the **Selection** page. Since the **Selection** page is located at the same application as the **LogIn** page does, a direct page name is used.

Now let's run the application to test two pages. Make sure that the **LogIn** page is the starting page for our application. To do that, right click the **LogIn.aspx** from the Solution Explorer window and select the item **Set As Start Page** from the popup menu. Click the IIS Express button to run our project. Enter the suitable username and password such as **ybai** and **come**, then click the **LogIn** button. The **Selection** page is displayed if the login process is successful, as shown in Figure 8.19.

Click on the **Exit** button to close our application. Now let's begin to develop our next page, **Faculty** page.

8.4.7 Create the Third User Interface – Faculty Page

Right-click our project folder **SQLWebSelect Project** from the Solution Explorer window and select the **Add | New Item** from the popup menu. On the opened wizard, select the Template **Web Form** and then enter **Faculty.aspx** into the **Name** box as the name for this new page, and click the **Add** button to add this new page into our project.

On the opened Web form, add the controls that are shown in Figure 8.20 into this page.

As we mentioned in the last section, before you can drag those controls from the Toolbox window and place them into the page, you must first use the Space or the Enter keys from the keyboard

Type	ID	Text	HorizontalAlign	BackColor	Font
Label	Label1	CSE_DEPT Faculty Page		#E0E0E0	Bold/Large
FileUpload	FileUploadImage				
Label	Label3	Faculty Name			Bold/Small
DropDownList	ComboName				
Image	PhotoBox				
Panel	Panel1		Right	#FFFFCC	
Label	Label4	Faculty ID			Bold/Small
TextBox	txtFacultyID				
Label	Label5	Name			Bold/Small
TextBox	txtName				
Label	Label6	Title			Bold/Small
TextBox	txtTitle				
Label	Label7	Office			Bold/Small
TextBox	txtOffice				
Label	Label8	Phone			Bold/Small
TextBox	txtPhone				
Label	Label9	College			Bold/Small
TextBox	txtCollege				
Label	Label10	Email			Bold/Small
TextBox	txtEmail				
Button	cmdSelect	Select			Bold/Small
Button	cmdInsert	Insert			Bold/Small
Button	cmdUpdate	Update			Bold/Small
Button	cmdDelete	Delete			Bold/Small
Button	cmdBack	Back			Bold/Small

FIGURE 8.20 Controls for the faculty form.

to locate the positions on the page for those controls. However, if you want to add and place those controls onto the Web form at any random location as you did for the Windows Form object, you need to set the **Position** property of each control to the **Absolute** value (refer to Section 8.4.1 to get more details for this issue).

When building this **Faculty** Web Page, the following points should be kept in mind:

1) The first important point to be noted is the position of the **Image** control on the page form. After drag and place the **Image** control into this page, go to the **Properties** window and set the **ImageAlign** property to **Left**.
2) The second important point is the position style of this Web Form. Click on any place in this page and go to the **Properties** window. Select the **Style** property and click on the expansion button to open the **Modify Style** wizard. Click on the **Position** item from the left pane and select the **absolute** item from the **position**: combobox in the right pane.
3) The third important point is the horizontal alignment property for the **Panel1**. This panel works as a container and all six textboxes to be added into this panel should be aligned to the right to make them in correct format. To set this up, select the **Panel1** and go to its **Properties** window, and set the **HorizontalAlign** property to **Right** in its Properties window.
4) The fourth important point is the font style and size for all labels' captions. For example, for the **Label1** control, its caption is **CSE DEPT Faculty Page**. To setup its style and size, select this label by clicking on it and go to the **Format** menu item and select the lower **Font** item from the sub-menu to set its style as **Arial Black** and size as **medium (14 pt)**, and click on the **OK** button.
5) For all other labels, set its caption's style as **Arial Black** and size as **small (12 pt)**.

Now you can enlarge this Image and place it in the left side of this Web page. Your finished **Faculty** page should match one that is shown in Figure 8.21.

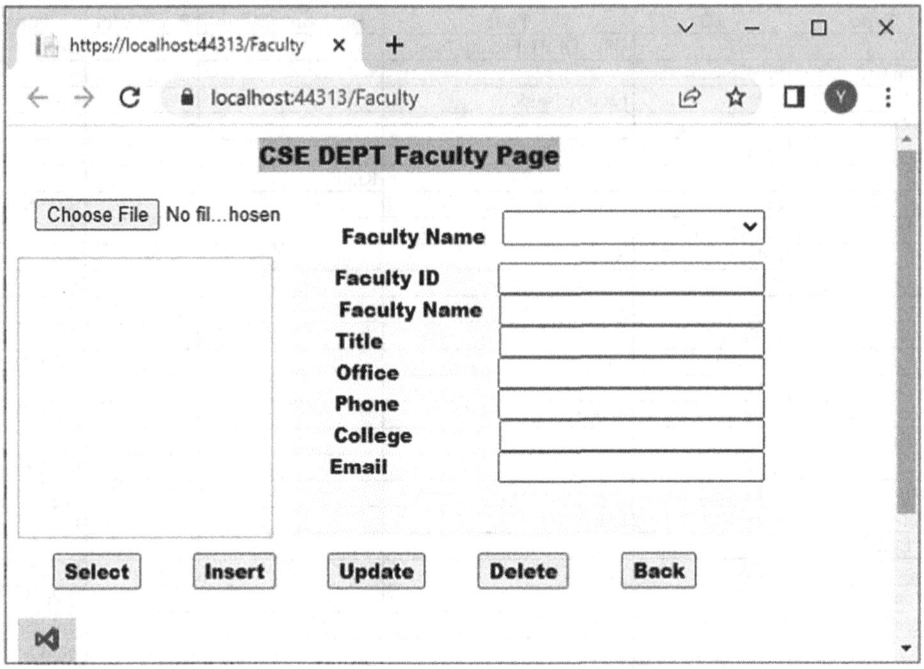

FIGURE 8.21 The finished faculty page.

Another easier way to build this Faculty page is to add an existing **Faculty** page **Faculty.aspx** that can be found from the folder **Web Forms** under the **Students** folder in the CRC Press ftp site (refer to Figure 1.2 in Chapter 1). Perform the following operations to add this existing **Faculty** page into our project:

1) Right-click on our project **SQLWebSelect Project** from the Solution Explorer window, and select the **Add | Existing Item**.
2) Browse to the folder **Students\Web Forms** on the CRC Press ftp site and select three items, **Faculty.aspx** , **Faculty.aspx.designer.cs** and **Faculty.aspx.cs**. Then click the **Add** button to add them into our project. You can also download and save these pages into a temporary folder in your computer and then perform this adding action.

Although we have added five buttons into this **Faculty** page; however, in this section we only take care of the **Select** and the **Back** buttons, exactly two buttons' Click methods, since we want to discuss how to retrieve the queried data from our database and display them in this **Faculty** page. Other buttons will be used in the following sections later.

Now let's begin to develop the codes for the **Faculty** page.

8.4.8 Develop the Codes to Select the Desired Faculty Information

First let's run the project to build the configuration file **Web.config** to configure all controls we just added into the Faculty page. Click on the **IIS Express** button to run the project, enter the suitable username and password to open the **Selection** page. Select the **Faculty Information** item from this page to open the **Faculty** page. Click on the **Close** button that is located at the upper-right corner of this page to close the project.

Open the code page of the **Faculty** form and, as we did before, let's first add a SQL Data Provider related namespaces to the top of this page to provide a reference to all data components of the SQL Data Provider:

```
using System.Data;
using System.Data.SqlClient;
```

The coding for this page can be divided into three parts: Coding for the **Page_Load()** method, coding for the **Select** button's Click method and coding for other methods. First let's take care of the coding for the **Page_Load()** method.

8.4.8.1 Develop the Codes for the Page_Load Method

In the opened code page, open the **Page_Load()** method and enter the codes that are shown in Figure 8.22 into this method.

Let's have a closer look at this piece of codes to see how it works.

A. Some SQL Server Data Provider-related namespaces are first added into this namespace area since we need to use some SQL Server data components located in those namespaces.

B. A field-level textbox array, **FacultyTextBox[]**, is created since we need this array to hold seven pieces of faculty information and display them in those textboxes later.

C. Before we can perform the data actions against the database, we need to make sure that a valid database connection is set to allow us to transfer data between our project and the database. An Application state, which is used to hold our global connection object variable, is utilized to perform this checking and connecting to our database if it has not been connected.

SQLWebSelect Project | **Page_Load(object sender, EventArgs e)**

```
  using System;
  using System.Web.UI.WebControls;
A using System.Data;
  using System.Data.SqlClient;

  namespace SQLWebSelect_Project
  {
     public partial class Faculty : System.Web.UI.Page
     {
B       private TextBox[] FacultyTextBox = new TextBox[7];
        protected void Page_Load(object sender, EventArgs e)
        {
C          if (((SqlConnection)Application["sqlConnection"]).State != ConnectionState.Open)
               ((SqlConnection)Application["sqlConnection"]).Open();
D          if (!IsPostBack)
           {
              ComboName.Items.Add("Ying Bai");
              ComboName.Items.Add("Davis Bhalla");
              ComboName.Items.Add("Black Anderson");
              ComboName.Items.Add("Steve Johnson");
              ComboName.Items.Add("Jenney King");
              ComboName.Items.Add("Alice Brown");
              ComboName.Items.Add("Debby Angles");
              ComboName.Items.Add("Jeff Henry");
           }
        }
     }
  }
```

FIGURE 8.22 The codes for the Page_Load() method.

D. As the project runs, each time as the user clicks the **Select** button to perform a data query, a request is sent to the database server and the Web server (it can be the same server as the database server). Then the Web server will post back a refreshed **Faculty** page to the client when it received this request (**IsPostBack = true**). Each time this happened, the **Page_Load()** method will be activated and the eight faculty members will be duplicated and attached to the end of the combobox control **ComboName** again. To avoid this duplication, we need to check the **IsPostBack** property of the page and add eight faculty members into the combobox control only one time when the project starts (**IsPostBack = false**). Refer to Section 8.4.9.1 for more detailed discussion about the **AutoPostBack** property.

Next we need to develop the codes for the **Select** button's Click method to perform the data query actions against the database.

8.4.8.2 Develop the Codes for the Select Button Method

The function of this piece of codes is to make a query to the database to retrieve the faculty information based on the selected faculty member by the user from the **Faculty Name** combobox control, and display those pieces of retrieved information in seven textbox controls and faculty image on the **Faculty** page.

Open this **Select** button's Click method by double-clicking on this button from the Design View of the **Faculty** form, and enter the codes that are shown in Figure 8.23 into this method.

Let's take a closer look at this piece of codes to see how it works.

A. The query string that contains a SELECT statement is declared here since we need to use this string as our command text. The dynamic parameter of this query is the **@name**, which is the selected faculty name by the user as the project runs.

B. All data components such as the Command and DataReader objects are declared here since we need to use them to perform the data query later.

C. The Command object is initialized by assigning the associated components to it. These components include the global Connection object that is stored in the Application state function, the CommandType and the CommandText properties.

```
SQLWebSelect Project                cmdSelect_Click(object sender, EventArgs e)

    protected void cmdSelect_Click(object sender, EventArgs e)
    {
A       string cmd = "SELECT faculty_id, faculty_name, title, office, phone, college, email, fimage FROM Faculty ";
        string cmdString = cmd + "WHERE faculty_name = @name";
B       SqlCommand sqlCommand = new SqlCommand();
        SqlDataReader sqlDataReader;

C       sqlCommand.Connection = (SqlConnection)Application["sqlConnection"];
        sqlCommand.CommandType = CommandType.Text;
        sqlCommand.CommandText = cmdString;
D       sqlCommand.Parameters.Add("@name", SqlDbType.Char).Value = ComboName.Text;

E       sqlDataReader = sqlCommand.ExecuteReader();
F       if (sqlDataReader.HasRows == true)
            FillFacultyReader(sqlDataReader);
G       else
            Response.Write("<script>alert('No matched faculty found!')</script>");

H       sqlDataReader.Close();
        sqlCommand.Dispose();
    }
```

FIGURE 8.23 The codes for the select button's click method.

D. The Parameter object is initialized by assigning the dynamic parameter's name and value to it.

E. The **ExecuteReader()** method of the Command object is called to execute the query command to retrieve back the selected faculty information, and assign it to the DataReader object.

F. By checking the **HasRows** property of the DataReader, we can determine whether this query is successful or not. If this property is greater than zero, which means that at least one row is retrieved from the **Faculty** table in the database and therefore the query is successful, a user-defined method **FillFacultyReader()**, which we will be built in the next part, is called to fill seven textboxes on the **Faculty** page with the retrieved faculty image.

G. Otherwise if the **HasRows** property is equal to zero, which means that no row has been retrieved from the database and the query is failed. A warning message is displayed in the client by calling the **Write()** method of the server **Response** object.

H. All data components used for this data query are released after this query.

At this point we finished the first part-coding for the **Select** button's Click method. Now let's handle the second part coding process for this method.

8.4.8.3 Develop the Codes for Other Methods

Next let's take care of the coding for other methods in this **Faculty** page. This includes the coding for the following methods:

1) User-defined method **FillFacultyReader**().
2) **Back** button's Click method.

First let's take care of the user-defined method **FillFacultyReader()**. The function of this method is to fill seven textboxes with seven pieces of queried faculty information and display the queried faculty image in this page.

One significant difference in displaying an image between the Windows-based and the Web-based application is that the **Image.Url** property, which belongs to the control **System.Web.UI.WebControls.Image**, is utilized to access the matched faculty photo file and only the name of an image file is needed to display the associated image in the Web-based application. In the Windows-based application, a **System.Drawing()** method must be used to display an image based on the image file's name.

Open the code page of the **Faculty** Web form, and type the codes that are shown in Figure 8.24 to create this user-defined method inside the Faculty class.

```
SQLWebSelect Project          FillFacultyReader(SqlDataReader FacultyReader)

  private void FillFacultyReader(SqlDataReader FacultyReader)
  {
A      int intIndex;
B      TextBox[] fBox = { txtFacultyID, txtName, txtTitle, txtOffice, txtPhone, txtCollege, txtEmail };
C      while (FacultyReader.Read())
       {
D         for (intIndex = 0; intIndex <= FacultyReader.FieldCount - 2; intIndex++)
             fBox[intIndex].Text = FacultyReader.GetString(intIndex);
E         byte[] bimage = (byte[])FacultyReader["fimage"];
F         string img = Convert.ToBase64String(bimage);
          PhotoBox.ImageUrl = String.Format("data:image/jpg;base64,{0}", img);
       }
  }
```

FIGURE 8.24 The coding for the user defined method FillFacultyReader().

Let's have a closer look at this piece of codes to see how it works.

A. First a loop counter **intIndex** is declared and it is used for the **for()** loop later to pick up each column retrieved from the **Faculty** table in our sample database.
B. A textbox array **fBox[]** is generated to hold seven textboxes to be filled later via the **for()** loop with seven data columns stored in the **FacultyReader**.
C. A **while()** loop is executed as long as the loop condition **Read()** method is **true**, which means that a valid record is read out from the DataReader. This method will return a **false** if no valid record can be read out from the DataReader, which means that all data has been read out. In this application, in fact, this **while()** loop is only executed one time since we have only one row (one record) read out from the DataReader.
D. A **for()** loop is utilized to pick up each data column read out from the DataReader object, and assign each of them to the associated textbox control on the Faculty page window via the textbox array **fBox[]**. The **intIndex** is used here to identify each column from the DataReader. The terminal column number is equal to **FieldCount – 2** since the last column (7) in the **Faculty** table is a faculty image, **fimage**, which is an image object and it cannot be counted as a text. Thus the 7 columns contained the text information for a faculty record are arranged from column 0 to column 6 (**FieldCount = 8**).
E. Since the faculty image is stored at the last column with a format of binary data, therefore we need to get and convert it to a byte[] array.
F. Because there is no **PictureBox** object available in a Web page, we need to convert that image from a byte[] array to a 64-bit String, and assign it to the **ImageUrl** property of the **Image** object in the Faculty page, **PhotoBox**.

Finally, let's take care of the coding for the **Back** button's click method. The function of this piece of codes is to return the control to the **Selection** page as this button is clicked. Double-click the **Back** button from the Design View of the **Faculty** page window to open this method and enter the coding line into this method, which is shown in Figure 8.25.

This coding is straightforward and easily understood. The **Redirect()** method of the server **Response** object is executed to direct the client from the current **Faculty** page back to the **Selection** page when this button is clicked by the user. Exactly, the server resends the **Selection** page to the client when this button is clicked and a request is sent to the server.

Now we have finished all coding development for the **Faculty** page. It is the time for us to run the project to test our pages. Click the **IIS Express** button to run our project. Enter the suitable username and password, such as **jhenry** and **test**, to the LogIn page, then select the **Faculty Information** from the Selection page to open the Faculty page. Select one faculty member, such as **Ying Bai**, and then click the **Select** button to retrieve the selected faculty information from the database. All information related to that selected faculty is retrieved and displayed in this **Faculty** page, as shown in Figure 8.26.

Click on the **Back** button to return to the Selection page, and then click the **Exit** button to terminate our project. So far our Web application is successful.

SQLWebSelect Project ▼	cmdBack_Click(object sender, EventArgs e) ▼

```
protected void cmdBack_Click(object sender, EventArgs e)
{
    Response.Redirect("Selection.aspx");
}
```

FIGURE 8.25 The codes for the back button's click method.

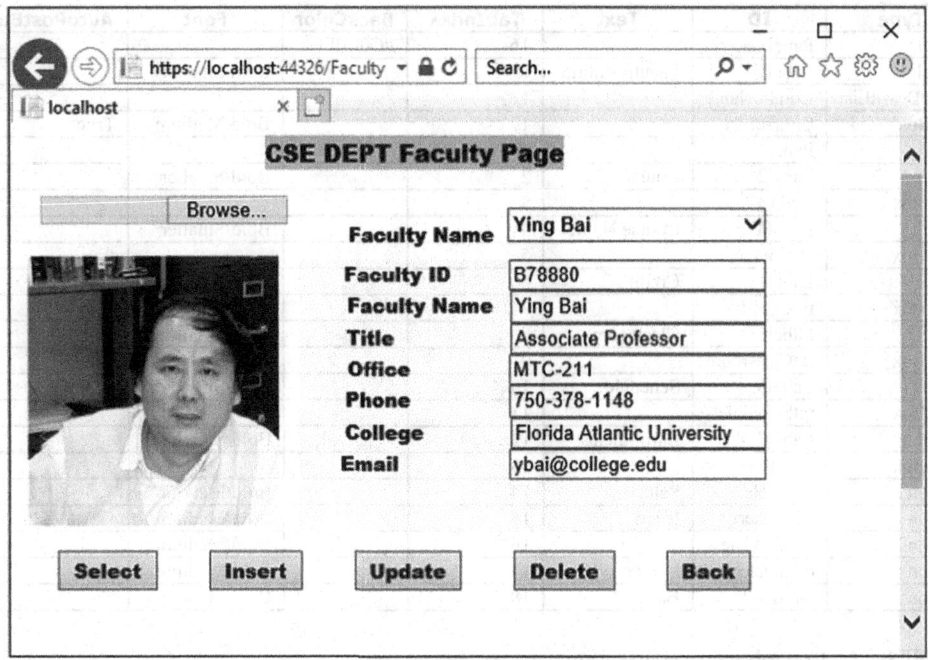

FIGURE 8.26 The running status of the faculty page.

Next we need to create our next Web page, **Course** page, and add it into our project to select and display all courses taught by the selected faculty member.

8.4.9 Create the Fourth User Interface – Course Page

To create a new Web page and add it into our project, go to the Solution Explorer window and right-click our project **SQLWebSelect Project**, then select **Add | New Item** from the popup menu to open the **Add New Item** wizard. On the opened wizard, select the template **Web Form**, and enter **Course.aspx** into the **Name** box as the name for our new page and click the **Add** button to add it into our project.

On the opened Web form, add the controls that are shown in Figure 8.27 into this page.

As we mentioned before, you cannot place a control in any position on the form as you like. Now we try to show a technology to place a control to your desired position on the page window just as you did for your Windows-based application. The key element is the **Position** property for each control you added into the page window. For example, in this **Course** page, we added two panel controls, one list box control, six textbox controls and five button controls. In order to locate those controls to the desired position on the page, you must set up the **Format | Set Position** property to **Absolute** for all controls added into this page, with the exception of the label controls. This position setup is especially important to the ListBox control, otherwise the second panel cannot be added into the correct location.

Another issue is the panel size and background color. As you add a new panel into the page, the background color of that new panel is transparency, which means that you cannot see that new added panel. To see that panel, you need to define the size of the panel by performing the following steps:

1) Click the new added panel to select it and go to the **Property** window.
2) Set the **Height** and the **Width** properties to the desired dimensions in pixels.

Type	ID	Text	TabIndex	BackColor	Font	AutoPostBack
Panel	Panel1		16	#C0C0FF		
Label	Label1	Faculty Name	0		Bold/Smaller	
DropDownList	ComboName		1			
ListBox	CourseList		17		Bold/Medium	True
Panel	Panel2		18	#C0C0FF		
Label	Label2	Course ID	2		Bold/Smaller	
TextBox	txtID		3			
Label	Label3	Course Name	4		Bold/Smaller	
TextBox	txtCourse		5			
Label	Label4	Credit	6		Bold/Smaller	
TextBox	txtCredit		7			
Label	Label5	Classroom	8		Bold/Smaller	
TextBox	txtClassroom		9			
Label	Label6	Schedule	10		Bold/Smaller	
TextBox	txtSchedule		11			
Label	Label7	Enrollment	12		Bold/Smaller	
TextBox	txtEnroll		13			
Button	cmdSelect	Select	14		Bold/Medium	
Button	cmdInsert	Insert	15		Bold/Medium	
Button	cmdUpdate	Update	16		Bold/Medium	
Button	cmdDelete	Delete	17		Bold/Medium	
Button	cmdBack	Back	18		Bold/Medium	

FIGURE 8.27 Controls on the course form.

In this application, set the **Height** and **Width** properties for panel1 and panel2 to:

- Panel1: **Height** – 40px, **Width** – 458px
- Panel2: **Height** – 161px, **Width** – 327px

Your finished Course page should match the one shown in Figure 8.28. Before we can continue to develop the codes for this page, we must emphasize one key point for the list box control used in the Web-based applications. There is a significant different process issue existed for the list box control between the Windows-based and Web-based applications.

8.4.9.1 The AutoPostBack Property of the List Box Control

One important property applied to a list box control is the **AutoPostBack** property. In contrast to the list box control used in the Windows-based application, a **SelectedIndexChanged** event will not be created in the server side if the user clicked and selected an item from the list box. The reason for that is because the default value for the **AutoPostBack** property of a list box control is set to **false** when you add a new list box to your Web form. This means that even if the user clicked an item from the list box, a **SelectedIndexChanged** event can only be created in the client side and it cannot be sent to the server. As you know, the list box is running at the server side when your project runs. Therefore, no matter how many times you clicked and changed the items in the list box at the client side, no event can be created in the server side. Therefore, it looks like that your clicking on the list box control cannot be responded by your project as the project runs.

However, in this project we need to use this **SelectedIndexChanged** event to trigger its event method to perform the course information query. In order to solve this problem, the **AutoPostBack** property should be set to **true**. In this way, each time you click an item to select it from the list box, this **AutoPostBack** property will be set to post back to the server to indicate that the user has interacted with that control.

In this section, we only discuss the coding for the **Select** and the **Back** buttons' click methods to perform the course data query. The operations for the other buttons such as **Insert**, **Update** and **Delete**

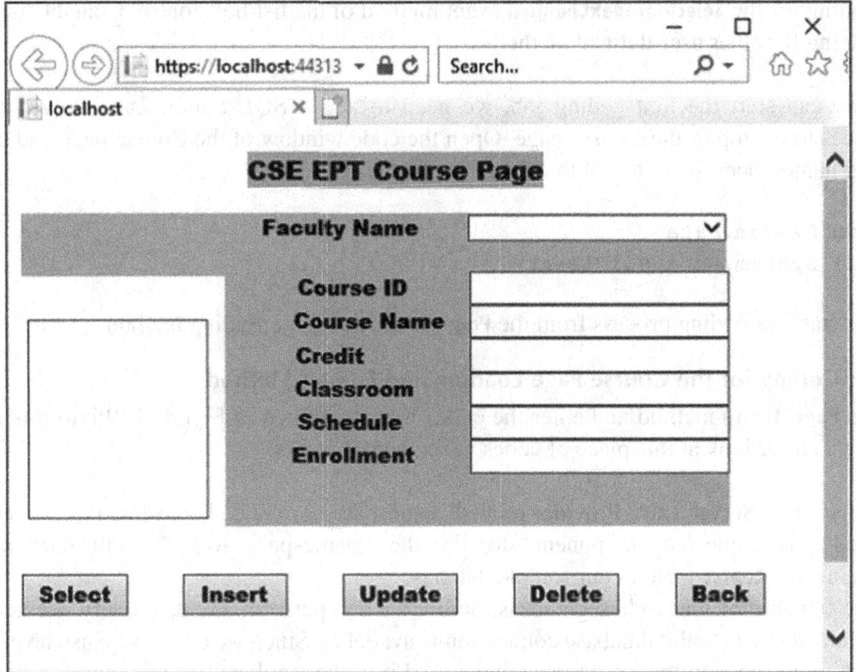

FIGURE 8.28 The finished course web page.

will be discussed later in the following sections when we perform the data inserting or updating against the database using the Web pages.

Now let's develop the codes for the **Select** and the **Back** buttons' click methods to pick up the course data from the database using the Course Web page.

8.4.9.2 Develop the Codes to Select the Desired Course Information

The general functions of the Course page are:

1) When the user selected the desired faculty member from the Faculty Name combobox control and clicks the **Select** button, the IDs of all courses (**course_id**) taught by the selected faculty should be retrieved from the database and displayed in the list box control **CourseList** on the Course page.
2) When the user clicks any **course_id** from the list box control **CourseList**, the detailed course information related to the selected **course_id** in the list box will be retrieved from the database and displayed in six textboxes on the Course page.

Based on the function analysis above, we need to concentrate our coding on two methods; one is the **Select** button's click method and the other is the **SelectedIndexChanged** event method of the list box control **CourseList**. The first coding is used to retrieve and display all **course_id** related to courses taught by the selected faculty in the list box control, and the second coding is to retrieve and display the detailed course information such as course title, schedule, classroom, credit and enrollment related to the selected **course_id** from the CourseList.

The above coding jobs can be divided into four parts:

1) Coding for the Course page loading and ending event methods. These methods include the **Page_Load()** and the **Back** button's click method.
2) Coding for the **Select** button's click method.

3) Coding for the **SelectedIndexChanged** event method of the list box control CourseList.
4) Coding for other user-defined methods.

Before we can start the first coding job, we need to add a SQL Server Data Provider related namespaces to the top of the Course page. Open the code window of the Course page and enter the following namespaces to the top of that page:

```
using System.Data;
using System.Data.SqlClient;
```

Now let's start our coding process from the **Page_Load()** and Page Ending methods.

8.4.9.3 Coding for the Course Page Loading and Ending Methods

Open the **Page_Load()** method and enter the codes that are shown in Figure 8.29 into this method. Let's take a closer look at this piece of codes to see how it works.

A. Some SQL Server Data Provider-related namespaces are added into this page since we need to use some data components stored in those namespaces to perform the data actions against the **Course** table in our sample database.

B. The function of this code segment is: before we can perform any data query, we need to check whether a valid database connection is available. Since we created a class-level connection instance in the LogIn page and stored it in the Application state, now we need to check this connection object and re-connect it to the database if our application has not been connected to the database.

C. The following codes are used to initialize the **Faculty Name** combobox control, and the **Add()** method is utilized to add all faculty members into this combobox control to allow users to

```
SQLWebSelect Project                    Page_Load(object sender, EventArgs e)

   using System;
   using System.Web.UI.WebControls;
A  using System.Data;
   using System.Data.SqlClient;
   namespace SQLWebSelect_Project
   {
      public partial class Course : System.Web.UI.Page
      {
         protected void Page_Load(object sender, EventArgs e)
         {
B           if (((SqlConnection)Application["sqlConnection"]).State != ConnectionState.Open)
               ((SqlConnection)Application["sqlConnection"]).Open();
C           if (!IsPostBack)          //these items can only be added into the combo box in one time
            {
               ComboName.Items.Add("Ying Bai");
               ComboName.Items.Add("Davis Bhalla");
               ComboName.Items.Add("Black Anderson");
               ComboName.Items.Add("Steve Johnson");
               ComboName.Items.Add("Jenney King");
               ComboName.Items.Add("Alice Brown");
               ComboName.Items.Add("Debby Angles");
               ComboName.Items.Add("Jeff Henry");
            }
         }
      }
   }
```

FIGURE 8.29 The coding for the Page_Load() method.

select one to get the course information as the project runs. Here a potential bug is existed for this piece of codes. As we mentioned in Section 8.4.9.1, an **AutoPostBack** property will be set to **true** whenever the user clicked and selected an item from the list box control, and this property will be sent back to the server to indicate that an action has been taken by the user to this list box. After the server received this property, it will send back a refreshed **Course** page to the client; therefore, the **Page_Load()** method of the Course page will be triggered and run again as a refreshed **Course** page is sent back. The result of execution of this **Page_Load()** method is to attach another copy of all faculty members to the end of those faculty members that have been already added into the combobox control **ComboName** when the **Course** page is displayed for the first time. As the number you clicked an item from the CourseList box increases, the number of copies of all faculty members will also be increased and displayed in the **ComboName** box. To avoid this duplication, we only need to add all faculty members in the first time as the Course page is displayed, but do nothing if any another **AutoPostBack** property occurred.

The coding for the **Back** button's click method is similar to that for the **Back** button in the **Faculty** page. When this button is clicked by the user, the **Course** page should be switched back to the **Selection** page. The **Redirect()** method of the server **Response** object is used to fulfill this switching back function. Double click on the **Back** button from the Design View of the **Course** page and enter the following codes into this method:

```
Response.Redirect("Selection.aspx");
```

Next let's continue to do the coding for the **Select** button's click method.

8.4.9.4 Coding for the Select Button Click Method

As we mentioned at the beginning of this section, the function of this method is: when the user selected a desired faculty member from the **Faculty Name** combobox control and clicks the **Select** button, all **course_id** related to courses taught by the selected faculty should be retrieved from the database and displayed in the list box control **CourseList** on the **Course** page.

Double-click on the **Select** button from the Design View of the **Course** page window to open its Click method, and enter the codes that are shown in Figure 8.30 into this method.

```
SQLWebSelect Project        cmdSelect_Click(object sender, EventArgs e)

  protected void cmdSelect_Click(object sender, EventArgs e)
  {
A     string strCourse = "SELECT Course.course_id FROM Course JOIN Faculty ";
      strCourse += "ON (Course.faculty_id = Faculty.faculty_id) AND (Faculty.faculty_name = @name)";
B     SqlCommand sqlCommand = new SqlCommand();
      SqlDataReader sqlDataReader;
C     sqlCommand.Connection = (SqlConnection)Application["sqlConnection"];
      sqlCommand.CommandType = CommandType.Text;
      sqlCommand.CommandText = strCourse;
      sqlCommand.Parameters.Add("@name", SqlDbType.Char).Value = ComboName.Text;
D     sqlDataReader = sqlCommand.ExecuteReader();
E     if (sqlDataReader.HasRows == true)
         FillCourseReader(sqlDataReader);
F     else
         Response.Write("<script>alert('No matched course found!')</script>");
G     sqlDataReader.Close();
      sqlCommand.Dispose();
  }
```

FIGURE 8.30 The codes for the select button's click method.

Let's have a look at this piece of codes to see how it works.

A. The joined table query string is declared at the beginning of this method. Here only one column or the first column, **course_id**, is queried. The reason for this is that we need to use this **course_id**, not course name, as the identifier to pick up each course's detailed information from the **Course** table when the user clicked and selected that **course_id** from the **CourseList** box. The assignment operator = is used for the criteria in the **ON** clause in the definition of the query string, and this is required by SQL Server database operation. For a more detailed discussion about the joined table query, refer to Section 5.15.6.1 in Chapter 5.
B. Some SQL data objects, such as Command and DataReader, are created here. All of these objects should be prefixed by the keyword **sql** to indicate that all those components are related to the SQL Server database.
C. The **sqlCommand** object is initialized with the connection string, command type, command text and command parameter. The parameter's name must be identical with the dynamic nominal parameter's name **@name**, which is defined in the query string and it is exactly located after the assignment operator in the **ON** clause. The parameter's value is the content of the **Faculty Name** combobox, which should be selected by the user as the project runs later.
D. The **ExecuteReader()** method of the Command class is executed to read back all courses (**course_id**) taught by the selected faculty and assign them to the DataReader object.
E. If the **HasRows** property of the DataReader is **true**, which means that at least one row data has been retrieved from the database, the **FillCourseReader()** method to be built later is called to fill the **CourseList** box with all queried **course_id**.
F. Otherwise, this joined query is failed and a warning message is displayed.
G. Finally some cleaning jobs are performed to release objects used for this query.

Now let's take care of the coding for the user-defined method **FillCourseReader**(), which is shown in Figure 8.31. Open the code page of the Course Web form and enter the codes that are shown in Figure 8.31 to create this method inside the **Course** class.

Let's have a closer look at this piece of codes to see how it works.

A. A local string variable **strCourse** is created and this variable can be considered as an intermediate variable holder that is used to temporarily hold the queried data row from the **Course** table.
B. The **CourseList** box is cleaned up before it can be filled by the **course_id**.
C. A **while()** loop is utilized to retrieve the first column for each row (**GetString(0)**), whose column index is 0 and the data value is the **course_id**. The queried data is first assigned to the intermediate variable **strCourse**, and then it is added into the **CourseList** box by using the **Add()** method.

SQLWebSelect Project | **FillCourseReader()**

```
  private void FillCourseReader(SqlDataReader CourseReader)
  {
A        string strCourse = string.Empty;

B        CourseList.Items.Clear();
C        while (CourseReader.Read())
         {
            strCourse = CourseReader.GetString(0);        //the 1st column is course_id
            CourseList.Items.Add(strCourse);
         }
  }
```

FIGURE 8.31 The coding for the method FillCourseReader.

Now let's start to develop the codes for the **SelectedIndexChanged()** event method of the list box control **CourseList**. The function of this method is: when the user clicks any **course_id** from the list box control **CourseList**, the detailed course information related to the selected **course_id** in the list box such as course title, schedule, credit, classroom and enrollment will be retrieved from the database and displayed in six textboxes on the **Course** page form.

8.4.9.5 Coding for the SelectedIndexChanged Method of the List Box Control

Double-click the list box control **CourseList** from the Design View of the **Course** Web form to open this event method, and then enter the codes that are shown in Figure 8.32 into this method.

Let's take a closer look at this piece of codes to see how it works.

- **A.** The query string is created with six queried columns, such as course_id, course, credit, classroom, schedule and enrollment. The query criterion is **course_id**, which is selected by the user by clicking a valid **course_id** from the **CourseList** box control as the project runs.
- **B.** Two SQL data objects are created and these objects are used to perform the data operations between the database and our project.
- **C.** The **sqlCommand** object is initialized with the connection object, command type, command text and command parameter. The parameter's name must be identical with the dynamic nominal name **@courseid**, which is defined in the query string, exactly after the assignment operator in the **WHERE** clause. The parameter's value is the **course_id** selected by the user from the **CourseList** box control.
- **D.** The **ExecuteReader()** method is executed to read back the detailed information for the selected course, and assign it to the DataReader object.
- **E.** If the **HasRows** property of the DataReader is **true**, which means that at least one row data has been retrieved from the database, the user-defined method **FillCourseReaderTextBox()** is called to fill those pieces of information into six textboxes in the Course page.
- **F.** Otherwise, this query is failed and a warning message is displayed.
- **G.** Finally, some cleaning jobs are performed to release objects used for this query.

Next let's build the codes for our user-defined method **FillCourseReaderTextBox()** to fill six textboxes in the Course page with six queried columns from the Course table in our sample database.

```
SQLWebSelect Project                    CourseList_SelectedIndexChanged()

  protected void CourseList_SelectedIndexChanged(object sender, EventArgs e)
  {
A     string cmdString = "SELECT course_id, course, credit, classroom, schedule, enrollment FROM Course ";
      cmdString += "WHERE course_id = @courseid";
B     SqlCommand sqlCommand = new SqlCommand();
      SqlDataReader sqlDataReader;

C     sqlCommand.Connection = (SqlConnection)Application["sqlConnection"];
      sqlCommand.CommandType = CommandType.Text;
      sqlCommand.CommandText = cmdString;
      sqlCommand.Parameters.Add("@courseid", SqlDbType.Char).Value = CourseList.SelectedItem.ToString();
D     sqlDataReader = sqlCommand.ExecuteReader();
E     if (sqlDataReader.HasRows == true)
          FillCourseReaderTextBox(sqlDataReader);
F     else
          Response.Write("<script>alert('No matched course information found!')</script>");
G     sqlDataReader.Close();
      sqlCommand.Dispose();
  }
```

FIGURE 8.32 The codes for the SelectedIndexChanged() event method.

```
SQLWebSelect Project                          FillCourseReaderTextBox()

private void FillCourseReaderTextBox(SqlDataReader CourseReader)
{
A       int intIndex;
        TextBox[] cBox = { txtCourseID, txtCourse, txtCredit, txtClassroom, txtSchedule, txtEnroll };
B       while (CourseReader.Read())
        {
          for (intIndex = 0; intIndex <= CourseReader.FieldCount - 1; intIndex++)
             cBox[intIndex].Text = CourseReader.GetValue(intIndex).ToString();
        }
}
```

FIGURE 8.33 The codes for the method FillCourseReaderTextBox().

8.4.9.6 Coding for the User-Defined Method FillCourseReaderTextBox()

On the opened code page of the Course Web form, enter the codes that are shown in Figure 8.33 into the Course class to create this user-defined method.

Let's take a look at this piece of codes to see how it works.

A. A loop counter **intIndex** and a textbox array **cBox[]**, are created first. The former is used for a loop counter for the **for()** loop to pick up each queried column from the **CourseReader**, and the latter works as a data holder to receive each column and display it on the related textbox in the course page.

B. A **while()** and a **for()** loop are used to pick up all six pieces of course-related information from the DataReader one by one. The **Read()** method is used as the Condition for the **While()** loop. A returned **true** means that a valid data is read out from the DataReader, and a returned **false** means that no any valid data can been read out from the DataReader, in other words, no more data is available and all data has been read out. The **for()** loop uses the **FieldCount – 1** as the termination condition since the index of the first data column is 0, not 1, in the DataReader object. Each read-out data is converted to a string and assigned to the associated textbox control in the textbox object array.

At this point, we have finished all coding developments for the Course Web form. Now let's run the project to test the function of this form. Click the **IIS Express** button to run the project. Enter the suitable username and password, such as **jhenry** and **test**, to the

LogIn page and select the **Course Information** item from the **Selection** page to open the **Course** page. On the opened page, select a faculty member from the combobox control and then click the **Select** button to retrieve all courses taught by that faculty and display them in the CourseList box. Your running result is shown in Figure 8.34.

Click any **course_id** from the CourseList box to select it; immediately the detailed information related to that selected **course_id** is displayed in six textboxes, which is shown in Figure 8.35.

Click on the **Back** button to return to the **Selection** page, and you can click any other item from the **Selection** page to perform the associated information query or you can click the **Exit** button to terminate the application. Our Web application is successful.

A complete Web application project **SQLWebSelect Project** used to query data from the SQL Server database can be found from the folder **Class DB Projects\Chapter 8** that is under the **Students** folder on the CRC Press ftp site (refer to Figure 1.2 in Chapter 1).

When running the project, a possible bug is that no response comes from the server when one selects a **couse_id** from the **CourseList** box by clicking on it. This is because the **AutoPostBack** property of the Course List box is not set up correctly. This issue can be solved by setting that property to **true** to enable the server to post it back to the client.

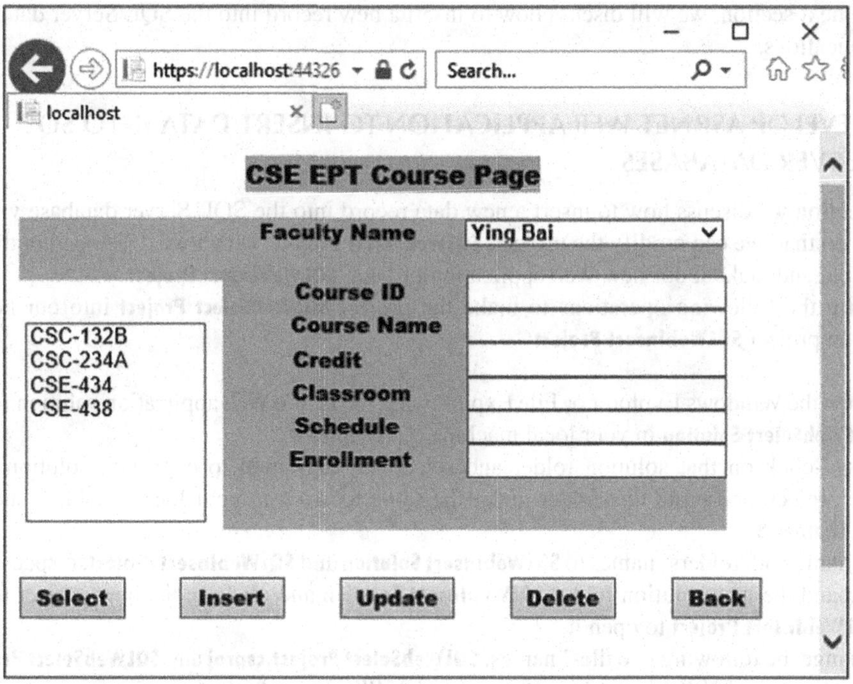

FIGURE 8.34 The running status of the course page.

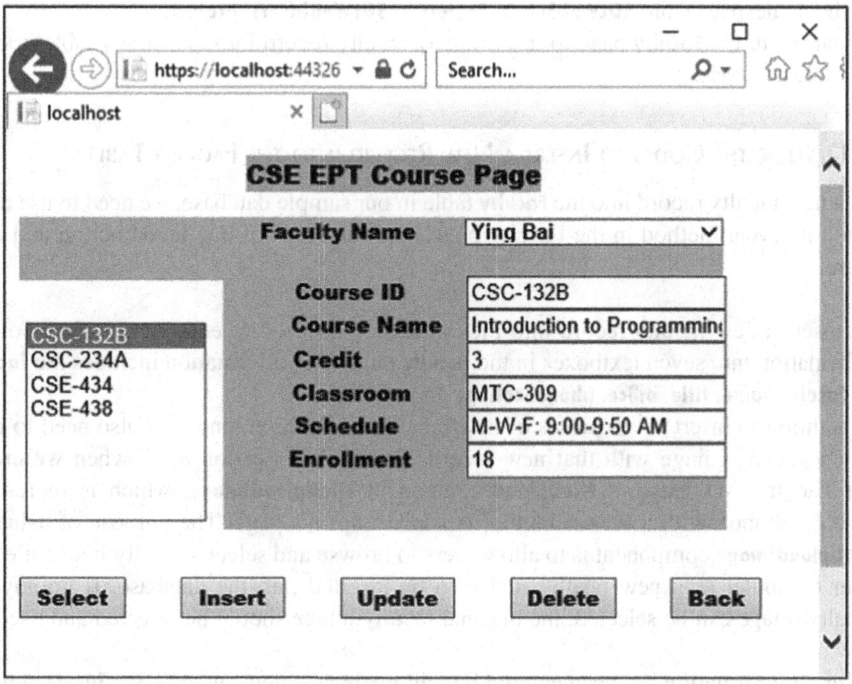

FIGURE 8.35 The detailed course information.

In the next section, we will discuss how to insert a new record into the SQL Server database via Web applications.

8.5 DEVELOP ASP.NET WEB APPLICATION TO INSERT DATA INTO SQL SERVER DATABASES

In this section we discuss how to insert a new data record into the SQL Server database via a Web page. To do that, we can modify the project, **SQLWebSelect Project**, which we developed in the previous section, and make it our new Web application project, **SQLWebInsert Project**.

Perform the following operations to make the project **SQLWebSelect Project** into our new Web application project **SQLWebInsert Project**:

1) Open the Windows Explorer or File Explorer and locate the Web application solution folder **SQLWebSelect Solution** in your local machine (**C:\Chapter 8**).
2) Right-click on that solution folder and select the **Copy** item to copy that solution with the project, and paste that folder under the same location in your local machine, such as **C:\Chapter 8**.
3) Rename both folders' names to **SQLWebInsert Solution** and **SQLWebInsert Project**, respectively.
4) Expand the new solution folder **SQLWebInsert Solution** and click on the new project folder **SQLWebInsert Project** to open it.
5) Change the following two files' names, **SQLWebSelect Project.csproj** and **SQLWebSelect Project.csproj.user**, to **SQLWebInsert Project.csproj** and **SQLWebInsert Project.csproj.user**.
6) Now double click on the new project **SQLWebInsert Project.csproj** to open it in the Visual Studio 2022.

A key point to be noted is that even we changed the solution and the project's names, but the project's namespace is kept with no change because it would be a very complicated process if we changed the namespace from **SQLWebSelect_Project** to **SQLWebInsert_Project**.

Let's start from the **Faculty** page to insert a new faculty record into the **Faculty** table in our SQL Server sample database.

8.5.1 Develop the Codes to Insert a New Record into the Faculty Table

To insert a new faculty record into the **Faculty** table in our sample database, we need to use the **Insert** button with its event method in the Faculty page. The functions of this **Insert** button and its event method are:

1) To insert a new faculty record into the database, you need to enter seven pieces of new information into seven textboxes in the **Faculty** page. The information includes the **faculty_id**, **faculty name**, **title**, **office**, **phone**, **college** and **email**.
2) In addition to insert seven pieces of new faculty information, one may also need to insert a new faculty image with that new record. Recalled in Section 8.4.7 when we created our Faculty Web page, a **FileUpload** component **FileUploadImage**, which is represented by a combobox with a **Browse** button, is added into this page. The purpose of using this **FileUploadImage** component is to allow users to browse and select a faculty image file from your computer as a new faculty image to be inserted into the database. If no any new faculty image can be selected, the original faculty image should be selected and used as a new one.
3) After all information has been entered into all textboxes, you can click the **Insert** button to insert this new record into the **Faculty** table in our sample database via the Web page.

Now let's start creating the codes for this Faculty page. The coding process can be divided into three parts: The coding for the **Page_Load()**, the coding for the **Insert** button's click method and coding for other user-defined methods.

8.5.2 Develop the Codes for the Page_Load Method

We need to modify the codes inside this **Page_Load()** method to enable it to retrieve the current or updated faculty members from our sample database. The reason for that is because the faculty members will be updated after this data inserting action and we need to get and display the updated faculty members in the **ComboName** combobox to enable users to query detailed information for any of them.

Open the **Page_Load()** method and enter the codes that are shown in Figure 8.36 into the bottom of this method.

The only modification is that a new user-defined method, **CurrentFaculty()**, is added into this method. The purpose of using this method is to get the current or updated faculty members from the **Faculty** table in our sample database and display them in the **Faculty Name** combobox to enable users to select them to perform related query.

On the opened Code Window of the **Faculty** page, enter codes shown in Figure 8.37 to generate this method. Let's have a closer look at this piece of codes to see how it works.

A. The query string is declared first to query all current faculty names from the **Faculty** table.
B. Two data objects, **sCommand** and **sReader**, are generated and they are to be used to perform this data query. A point to be noted is that a special initialization method is used for the

```
SQLWebSelect Project ▼        Page_Load(object sender, EventArgs e) ▼
  ………
    protected void Page_Load(object sender, EventArgs e)
    {
        if (((SqlConnection)Application["sqlConnection"]).State != ConnectionState.Open)
            ((SqlConnection)Application["sqlConnection"]).Open();
        if (!IsPostBack)
A           CurrentFaculty();
    }
```

FIGURE 8.36 The modified codes for the Page_Load() method.

```
SQLWebSelect Project ▼        CurrentFaculty() ▼
  private void CurrentFaculty()
  {
A     string cmd = "SELECT faculty_name FROM Faculty";
B     SqlCommand sCommand = new SqlCommand(cmd, (SqlConnection)Application["sqlConnection"]);
      SqlDataReader sReader = sCommand.ExecuteReader();
C     ComboName.Items.Clear();
D     while (sReader.Read())
         ComboName.Items.Add(sReader.GetString(0));
E     sReader.Close();
      sCommand.Dispose();
  }
```

FIGURE 8.37 Detailed codes for the user defined method CurrentFaculty().

SqlCommand object, in which the query string and the connection object work together as two arguments to simplify this assignment process. Then the **ExecuteReader()** method of the SqlCommand object is called to run this query. The query result is returned and assigned to the SqlDataReader object **sReader**.

C. Before the **Faculty Name** combobox can be filled with all updated faculty names, it must be cleaned up first and this step is necessary, otherwise all previous faculty names will be added together with this new addition.

D. A **while()** loop with the **Read()** method as the loop condition is used to check and pick up each retrieved data rows from the first column (column 0) in the **Faculty** table since only one data column (**faculty_name**) is retrieved. Then each row is assigned or added into the **Faculty Name** combobox. A system method **GetString(0)** is used to convert the retrieved row from an object type to a string value.

E. Finally two used objects, **sReader** and **sCommand**, are released.

Next let's build the codes for the **Insert** button event method.

8.5.3 Develop the Codes for the Insert Button Click Method

Open the **Insert** button's Click method by double-clicking the **Insert** button from the Design View of the **Faculty** page, and enter the codes that are shown in Figure 8.38 into this method.

Let's have a closer look at this piece of codes to see how it works.

A. The insert query string is declared first and it contains eight pieces of information that is related to eight columns in the **Faculty** table in the database.

B. The data components and local variables used in the method are declared here. The SqlCommand object, **sqlCommand**, and a local integer variable, **intInsert**, are used to execute the data insertion action and hold the returned data from the execution of the data insertion command.

```
SQLWebInsert Project                    cmdInsert_Click(object sender, EventArgs e)

  protected void cmdInsert_Click(object sender, EventArgs e)
  {
A    string cmdString = "INSERT INTO Faculty (faculty_id, faculty_name, title, office, phone, college, email, fimage) " +
                        "VALUES (@faculty_id,@faculty_name,@title, @office,@phone,@college,@email, @fimage)";
B    SqlCommand sqlCommand = new SqlCommand();
     int intInsert;
C    if (!FileUploadImage.HasFile)
       Response.Write("<script>alert('Select an image first using FileUpload!')</script>");
     else
     {
D      sqlCommand.Connection = (SqlConnection)Application["sqlConnection"];
       sqlCommand.CommandType = CommandType.Text;
       sqlCommand.CommandText = cmdString;
E      InsertParameters(sqlCommand);
F      intInsert = sqlCommand.ExecuteNonQuery();
G      sqlCommand.Dispose();
H      if (intInsert == 0)
         Response.Write("<script>alert('The data insertion is failed')</script>");
I      CurrentFaculty();
J      cmdInsert.Enabled = false;                       //disable the Insert button
     }
  }
```

FIGURE 8.38 The codes for the insert button's click method.

C. A FileUpload object, **FileUploadImage**, is used to allow users to select and get a faculty image to be inserted in our database. If the user entered all seven pieces of information into seven textboxes as a new faculty record to be inserted, but forgot to select a faculty image, by checking the **HasFile** property of that **FileUploadImage**, we can determine whether or not a valid faculty image has been selected. If that property is **false**, which means that no faculty image has been selected, a warning message is displayed to ask users to do that image selection first.

D. Otherwise, if the property **HasFile** returns a **true**, which means that a valid faculty image has been selected, then the **sqlCommand** object can be initialized to be ready to perform this data insertion action.

E. A user-defined method, **InsertParameters()**, which will be built later, is executed to assign all eight input parameters to the **Parameters** collection of the command object.

F. The **ExecuteNonQuery()** method of the command object is called to run the insert query to perform this data insertion action.

G. A cleaning job is performed to release all objects used in the method.

H. The **ExecuteNonQuery()** method will return a data value to indicate whether or not this data insertion is successful. The value of this returned data equals to the number of rows that have been successfully inserted into the **Faculty** table in the database. If a zero returned, which means that no row has been inserted into the database, a warning message is displayed to indicate this situation. Otherwise, the data insertion is successful.

I. Another user-defined method, **CurrentFaculty()**, is executed to get the current or updated faculty members from our database after this data insertion action is done, and display those updated faculty names on the **Faculty Name** combobox.

J. The **Insert** button is disabled after the current record is inserted into the database. This is to avoid the multiple insertions of the same record into the database. The **Insert** button will be enabled again when the content of the **Faculty ID** textbox is changed, which means that a new different faculty record will be inserted.

Next let's take care of the coding development for all other methods, including all related user-defined methods that will be used for this data insertion action.

8.5.4 Develop the Codes for Other Methods

The coding for other methods includes the following methods:

1) The system **TextChanged** event method for the **faculty_id** textbox.
2) The user-defined method **InsertParameters()**.
3) The user-defined method **getFacultyImage()**.

As we mentioned, after a new faculty record is successfully inserted into the **Faculty** table in our sample database, the **Insert** button should be disabled to avoid duplicated insertion to be occurred. However, this button should be enabled again when another new faculty record is ready to be inserted. By checking the content of the **faculty_id** textbox, we can identify whether or not a new faculty record is ready to be inserted. If that content is changed, which means that a new **faculty_id** is entered, the **TextChanged** event of that textbox is triggered, and, based on this event, we should enable the **Insert** button.

To do that coding, just double-click on the **faculty_id** textbox from the Design View of the **Faculty** page to open its **TextChanged** event method, and enter the coding line:

```
cmdInsert.Enabled = true;
```

The detailed codes for the user-defined method **InsertParameters()** are shown in Figure 8.39.

```
SQLWebInsert Project                InsertParameters(SqlCommand cmd)

private void InsertParameters(SqlCommand cmd)
{
    byte[] bImage;
    bImage = getFacultyImage();
    cmd.Parameters.Add("@faculty_id", SqlDbType.Char).Value = txtFacultyID.Text;
    cmd.Parameters.Add("@faculty_name", SqlDbType.Char).Value = txtName.Text;
    cmd.Parameters.Add("@title", SqlDbType.Char).Value = txtTitle.Text;
    cmd.Parameters.Add("@office", SqlDbType.Char).Value = txtOffice.Text;
    cmd.Parameters.Add("@phone", SqlDbType.Char).Value = txtPhone.Text;
    cmd.Parameters.Add("@college", SqlDbType.Char).Value = txtCollege.Text;
    cmd.Parameters.Add("@email", SqlDbType.Char).Value = txtEmail.Text;
    cmd.Parameters.Add("@fimage", SqlDbType.Binary).Value = bImage;
}
```

FIGURE 8.39 The codes for the method InsertParameters().

```
SQLWebSelect Project                getFacultyImage()

A   using System.IO;
    private byte[] getFacultyImage()
    {
B       int length;
C       string imgPath = Server.MapPath("~/FacultyImage/");
D       if (!Directory.Exists(imgPath))
           Directory.CreateDirectory(imgPath);
E       FileUploadImage.SaveAs(imgPath + Path.GetFileName(FileUploadImage.FileName));
F       PhotoBox.ImageUrl = "~/FacultyImage/" + FileUploadImage.FileName;
G       length = FileUploadImage.PostedFile.ContentLength;
H       byte[] img = new byte[length];
        FileUploadImage.PostedFile.InputStream.Read(img, 0, length);
I       return img;
    }
```

FIGURE 8.40 Detailed codes for the user defined method getFacultyImage().

This coding is straightforward and easy to be understood. First a local byte[] array, **bImage**, is generated and another user-defined method, **getFacultyImage()**, is called to get the selected faculty image. Then each piece of new faculty information is assigned to the associated input parameter by using the **Add()** method of the **Parameters** collection of the Command object.

The detailed codes for the user-defined method **getFacultyImage()** are shown in Figure 8.40. Let's have a closer look at this piece of codes to see how it works.

A. A new namespace **System.IO** should be added first since we need to use some components under that namespace, such as **Directory** and **Path**, in this method.
B. A local integer variable **length** is declared and this variable works as a holder to hold the length of the byte[] array of the selected faculty image.
C. A default folder, **FacultyImage**, which will be used to store our selected faculty image, is declared and it should be located under the current project folder. The ~ indicated that this is the current folder **SQLWebInsert Project**. The system method **MapPath()** is used to set up this path or folder and assign it to the local string variable **imgPath**.
D. First we need to check if this default folder is already existed in the machine by using the system method **Exists()**. If not, another system method, **CreateDirectory()**, is used to create it in our machine.

E. Then the selected faculty image file is saved to that default or new created folder via a system method **SaveAs()**.
F. The selected faculty image is displayed in the Faculty Image box, **PhotoBox**, by assigning the faculty image file's name to the **ImageUrl** property.
G. Now we need to convert that faculty image file to the byte[] format. First we need to get the length in bytes for that image file with the method **ContentLength()**.
H. A new byte[] array, **img**, is generated with the **length** as the argument. Another system method, **Read()**, is utilized to read that file and convert it to a byte[] array.
I. Finally, the converted faculty image array is returned to the calling method.

At this point, we have completed all coding developments for this data insertion function. Now we can run the project to test the data insertion functionality via the Web site. Click the **IIS Express** button to run the project. Enter the suitable username and password, such as **jhenry** and **test**, to finish the login process, and select the **Faculty Information** item from the Selection page to open the **Faculty** page. First keep the default faculty name in the **Faculty Name** combobox and click on the **Select** button to perform a faculty query action to get all information for that selected faculty member.

To insert a new faculty record, enter the following seven pieces of information into seven textboxes:

Faculty ID:	**D99866**
Faculty Name:	**David Smith**
Title:	**Professor**
Office:	**MTC-215**
Phone:	**750-378-1258**
College:	**University of Michigan**
Email:	**dsmith@college.edu**

Now try to click on the **Insert** button to insert this new record into the database. A warning message is displayed to indicate that a valid faculty image has not been selected. Click **OK** for that message, go to the FileUpload box and click on the **Browse** button to select a desired faculty image for this new inserted faculty member. All faculty images can be found from a folder **Images\Faculty** under the **Students** folder on the CRC Press ftp site. One can copy all of those image files and save them into one of your local folder.

In the opened FileUpload window, browse to your local folder and select the faculty image **David.jpg**, and click on the **Open** button to close that window.

Now click on the **Insert** button again to try to insert this new record into our database. The **Insert** button is immediately disabled and the selected faculty image is displayed in the **PhotoBox**, which is shown in Figure 8.41.

Next we need to perform the data validation to confirm that our data insertion is successful.

8.5.5 Validate the Data Insertion

To check and confirm this data insertion action, first perform another query for any other faculty member. Then go to the **Faculty Name** combobox, one can find that the new inserted faculty name has been there. Click that name to select it and click on the **Select** button to get that record back. The queried result is identical with that shown Figure 8.41. This means that our data insertion action is successful!

Click on the **Back** and then **Exit** button to close our project.

A complete Web application project **SQLWebInsert Project** can be found from a folder **Class DB Projects\Chapter 8\SQLWebInsert Solution** that is under the **Students** folder on the CRC Press ftp site (refer to Figure 1.2 in Chapter 1).

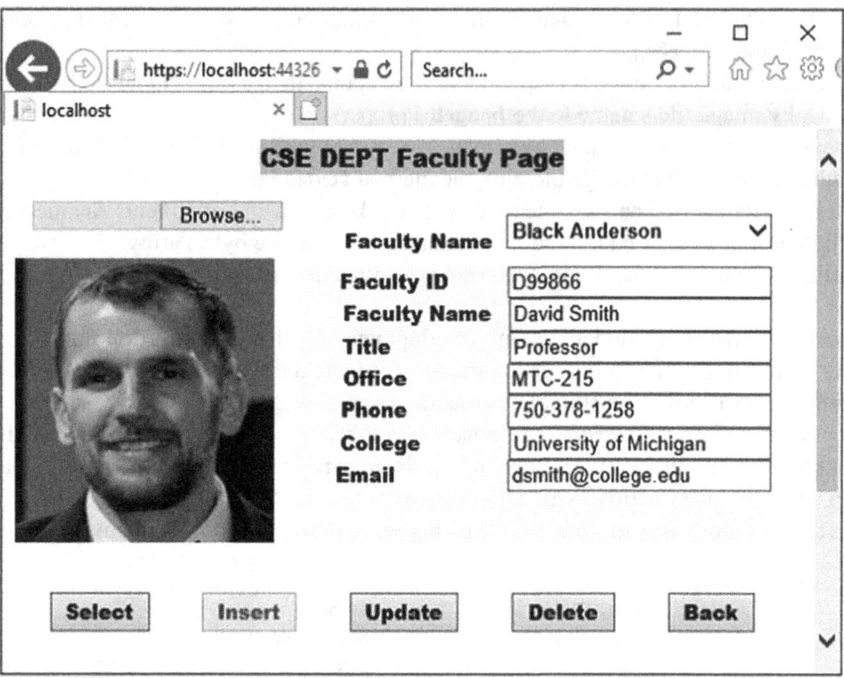

FIGURE 8.41 The running status of the faculty page.

In the next section, we will discuss how to perform the data updating and deleting actions against our SQL Server database via the Web applications.

8.6 DEVELOP WEB APPLICATIONS TO UPDATE AND DELETE DATA IN SQL SERVER DATABASES

To update or delete data against the relational databases is a challenging topic. We have provided a very detailed discussion and analysis for this topic in Section 7.1.1. Refer to that section to get more detailed information for these data actions. Here we want to emphasize some important points related to the data updating and deleting.

1) When updating or deleting data against related tables in a database, it is important to update or delete data in the proper sequence in order to reduce the chance of violating referential integrity constraints. The order of command execution will also follow the indices of the **DataRowCollection** in the database. To prevent data integrity errors from being raised, the best practice is to update or delete data against the database in the following sequence:

   A. Child table: delete records.
   B. Parent table: insert, update, and delete records.
   C. Child table: insert and update records.

2) To update an existing data against the database, generally it is unnecessary to update the primary key for that record. It is much better to insert a new record with a new primary key into the database than updating the primary key for an existing record because of the complicated operations listed above. In practice, it is very rare to update a primary key for an existing record against the database in most real applications. Therefore, in this section, we concentrate our discussion on updating the existing records by modifying all data columns except the primary key column.

3) To delete a record from a relational database, the normal operation sequence listed above must be followed. For example, to delete a record from the **Faculty** table in our application, one must first delete those records that are related to the data to be deleted in the **Faculty** table from the child table such as the **LogIn** and **Course** tables, and then one can delete the record from the **Faculty** table. The reason for this deleting sequence is because the **faculty_id** is a foreign key in the **LogIn** and the **Course** tables, but it is a primary key in the **Faculty** table. One must first delete data with the foreign keys and then delete the data with the primary key from the database.

Keep these three points in mind, and now let's begin to build our project.

We can modify one of our existing projects, **SQLWebInsert Project**, and make it our new project **SQLWebUpdateDelete Project**. Perform the following operations to create our new Web application project **SQLWebUpdateDelete Project**:

1) Open the Windows Explorer and create a new folder **C:\Chapter 8** if you have not done that. Then copy the solution **SQLWebInsert Solution** from the folder **ClassDB Projects\Chapter 8** that is under the **Students** folder on the CRC Press ftp site and paste it to our new folder **C:\Chapter 8**.
2) Rename both solution and the project folders' names to **SQLWebUpdateDelete Solution** and **SQLWebUpdateDelete Project**, respectively.
3) Expand the new solution folder **SQLWebUpdateDelete Solution** and click on the new project folder **SQLWebUpdateDelete Project** to open it.
4) Change two files' names, **SQLWebInsert Project.csproj** and **SQLWebInsert Project.csproj.user**, to **SQLWebUpdateDelete Project.csproj** and **SQLWebUpdateDelete Project.csproj.user**.
5) Now double-click on the new project **SQLWebUpdateDelete Project.csproj** to open it in the Visual Studio 2022.

A key point to be noted is that even we changed the solution and project's names, but the project's namespace is kept with no change because it would be a very complicated process if we changed the namespace from **SQLWebSelect_Project** to **SQLWebUpdateDelete_ Project**.

Let's start from the **Faculty** page to update an existing faculty record in the **Faculty** table for our SQL Server sample database.

8.6.1 Develop the Codes for the Update Button Click Method

The function of using this button is to update an existing faculty record as the user updated six pieces of information (excluding the **faculty_id**) on the **Faculty** page and clicked the **Update** button.

Open this method by double-clicking on the **Update** button from the Design View of the **Faculty** Web form and enter the codes that are shown in Figure 8.42 into this method.

Let's take a closer look at this piece of codes to see how it works.

A. An updating query string is declared first with the **faculty_id** as the query dynamic parameter. This is because when you want to update an existing faculty record, you can update all other six pieces of information without touching the **faculty_id** since it is a primary key in the **Faculty** table.

B. The data component, Command object, used in this method is created here. A local integer variable **intUpdate** is also created and it is used as a value holder to keep the returned updating result from the executing the **ExecuteNonQuery()** method later.

C. A FileUpload object, **FileUploadImage**, is used to allow users to select and get a faculty image to be updated in our database. If the user entered all six pieces of information into

```
SQLWebUpdateDelete Project                    cmdUpdate_Click(object sender, EventArgs e)

   protected void cmdUpdate_Click(object sender, EventArgs e)
   {
A      string cmdString = "UPDATE Faculty SET faculty_name = @name, title = @title, office = @office, " +
                          "phone = @phone, college = @college, email = @email, fimage = @fimage " +
                          "WHERE (faculty_id = @fid)";
B      SqlCommand sqlCommand = new SqlCommand();
       int intUpdate;
C      if (!FileUploadImage.HasFile)
          Response.Write("<script>alert('Select an updating image using FileUpload!')</script>");
D      else
       {
          sqlCommand.Connection = (SqlConnection)Application["sqlConnection"];
          sqlCommand.CommandType = CommandType.Text;
          sqlCommand.CommandText = cmdString;
E         UpdateParameters(ref sqlCommand);
F         intUpdate = sqlCommand.ExecuteNonQuery();
G         sqlCommand.Dispose();
H         if (intUpdate == 0)
             Response.Write("<script>alert('The data updating is failed')</script>");
I         CurrentFaculty();
       }
   }
```

FIGURE 8.42 The codes for the update button's click method.

six textboxes as an updated faculty record, but forgot to select an updated faculty image, by checking the **HasFile** property of that **FileUploadImage**, we can determine whether or not an updated faculty image has been selected. If that property is **false**, which means that no faculty image has been selected, a warning message is displayed to ask users to do that image selection first.

D. Otherwise, if the property **HasFile** returns a **true**, which means that an updated faculty image has been selected, then the **sqlCommand** object can be initialized to be ready to perform this data updating action.

E. A user-defined method **UpdateParameters()**, whose detailed codes will be shown below, is called to assign all input parameters to the command object.

F. The **ExecuteNonQuery()** method of the Command class is called to execute the data updating operation. This method returns a feedback value to indicate whether this data updating is successful or not, and this returned value is stored into the local integer variable **intUpdate**.

G. A cleaning job is performed to release all data objects used in this method.

H. The data value returned from calling the **ExecuteNonQuery()** is exactly equal to the number of rows that have been successfully updated in the database. If this value is zero, which means that no any row has been updated and this data updating is failed, a warning message is displayed. Otherwise, if this value is non-zero, which means that this data updating is successful.

I. Finally the user-defined method **CurrentFaculty()** is called to update all faculty members, exactly all faculty names, and display them in the **Faculty Name** combobox to allow users to select any one to perform other query.

The detailed coding for the method **UpdateParameters()** is shown in Figure 8.43.

This coding is straightforward and easily understood. First a local byte[] array, **bImage**, is generated and another user-defined method, **getFacultyImage()**, is called to get the updated faculty image.

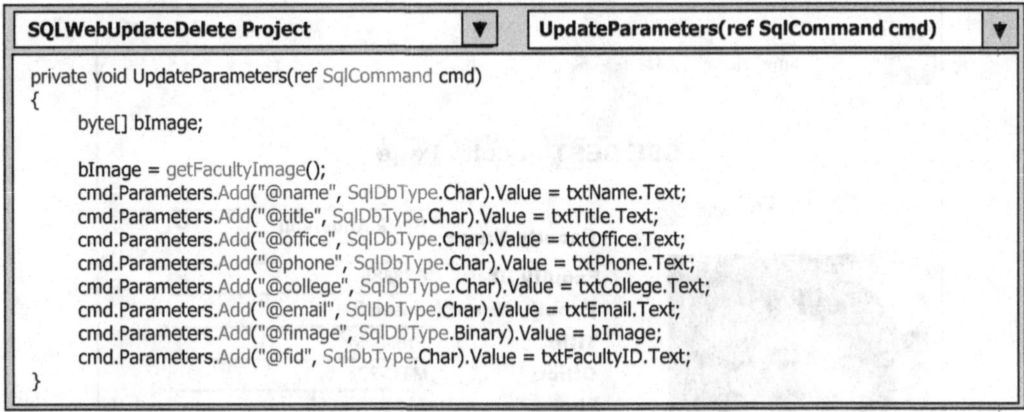
SQLWebUpdateDelete Project | UpdateParameters(ref SqlCommand cmd)

```
private void UpdateParameters(ref SqlCommand cmd)
{
    byte[] bImage;

    bImage = getFacultyImage();
    cmd.Parameters.Add("@name", SqlDbType.Char).Value = txtName.Text;
    cmd.Parameters.Add("@title", SqlDbType.Char).Value = txtTitle.Text;
    cmd.Parameters.Add("@office", SqlDbType.Char).Value = txtOffice.Text;
    cmd.Parameters.Add("@phone", SqlDbType.Char).Value = txtPhone.Text;
    cmd.Parameters.Add("@college", SqlDbType.Char).Value = txtCollege.Text;
    cmd.Parameters.Add("@email", SqlDbType.Char).Value = txtEmail.Text;
    cmd.Parameters.Add("@fimage", SqlDbType.Binary).Value = bImage;
    cmd.Parameters.Add("@fid", SqlDbType.Char).Value = txtFacultyID.Text;
}
```

FIGURE 8.43 The coding for the method UpdateParameters().

Then each piece of new faculty information is assigned to the associated input parameter by using the **Add()** method of the **Parameters** collection of the Command object.

A point to be noted is for the argument **cmd** passed into this method. The type is **ref**, which means that a reference or an address of that object is passed. When argument is passed in this way, any modification will be reflected and returned to the calling method. This passing mode is very similar to a pointer in C++.

Another key point is the last or dynamic parameter **faculty_id**, which is a primary key in the **Faculty** table but a foreign key in the **LogIn** and the **Course** tables. As we mentioned above, to update an existing faculty record, this key cannot be modified but all other six parameters can be changed without any issue. For the detailed codes built for the user-defined method **getFacultyImage()**, refer to Figure 8.40 in Section 8.5.4 in this chapter.

At this point we have finished all coding jobs for the data updating actions against the SQL Server database in the **Faculty** page. Before we can run the project to test this data updating function, make sure that the starting page is the **LogIn** page. To check and set the starting page, right-click on the **LogIn.aspx** page from the Solution Explorer window, select the **Set As Start Page** item by clicking on it.

Now let's run the project to test the data updating actions. Click on the **IIS Express** button to run the project, enter the suitable username and password to the **LogIn** page, and select the **Faculty Information** item from the **Selection** page to open the **Faculty** page. Let's try to update the faculty member **Ying Bai** to test this updating function.

Select the faculty name **Ying Bai** from the combobox control **ComboName** and click on the **Select** button to retrieve back the information for this faculty.

Now let's do updating action for this faculty member by entering the following six pieces of information into six textboxes:

Faculty Name:	**Susan Bai**
Title:	**Professor**
Office:	**MTC-228**
Phone:	**750-378-8655**
College:	**DukeUniversity**
Email:	**sbai@college.edu**

Then click on the **Browse** button for the FileUpload object to browse to your local folder where all faculty images are stored, select the faculty image **White.jpg**, and click on the **Open** button. Then click

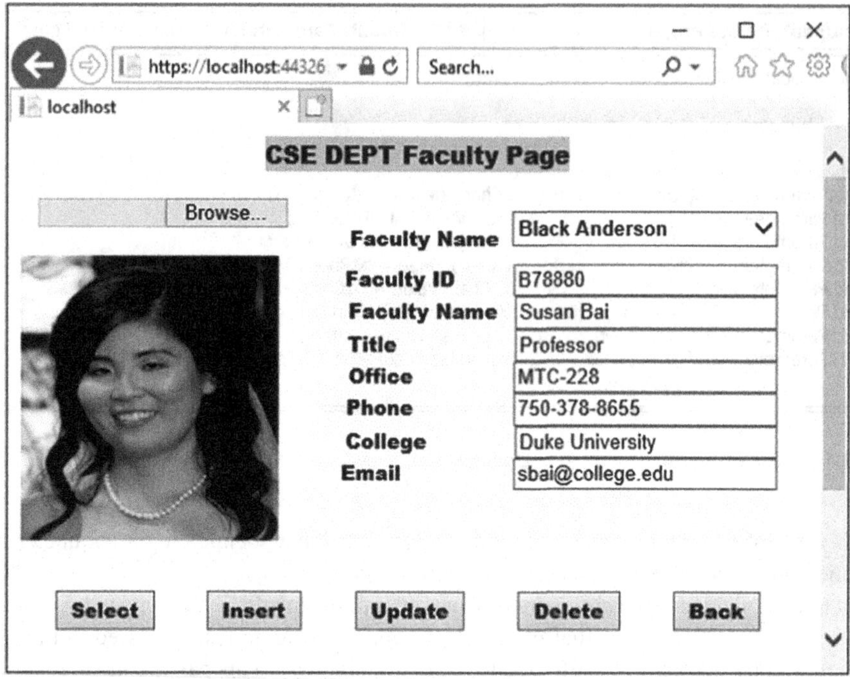

FIGURE 8.44 The data updating process for the faculty page.

the **Update** button to update this faculty record in the **Faculty** table in our sample database. Your finished **Faculty** page is shown in Figure 8.44.

To confirm this data updating, in a similar way, let's first select another faculty from the **Faculty Name** combobox and click the **Select** button to retrieve and display that faculty information. Then go to the **Faculty Name** combobox; one can find that the updated faculty name, **Susan Bai**, has been placed there. Click that name to select it and click on the **Select** button to retrieve and display that updated faculty record. You can see that the selected faculty information has been updated, which is shown in Figure 8.45.

It is highly recommended to recover the updated faculty record to the original one if possible. One can complete that recovery job by performing another data updating action.

Next let's take care of the data deleting action against the SQL Server database. Similarly to the data updating, for the data deleting we don't need any new Web page and we can still use the **Faculty** page to perform the data deleting actions.

8.6.2 Develop Codes for the Delete Button Click Method

Since deleting a record from a relational database is a complex issue, we divide this discussion into five sections:

1) Relationships between five tables in our sample database.
2) Data deleting sequence.
3) Use the Cascade deleting option to simplify the data deleting action.
4) Create the stored procedure to perform the data deleting action.
5) Call the stored procedure to perform the data deleting action.

Let's start with the first section.

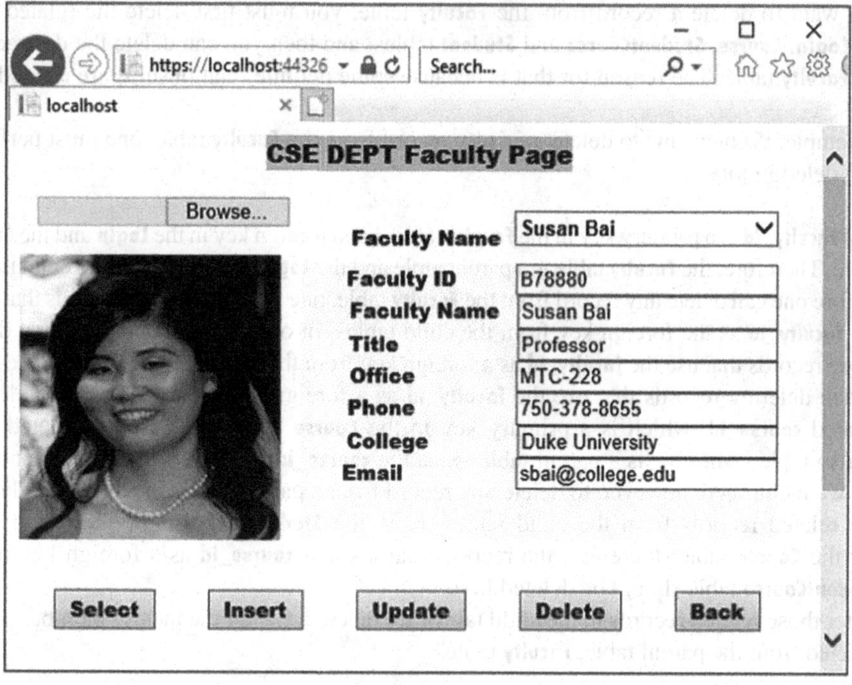

FIGURE 8.45 The updated faculty record in the faculty page.

8.6.2.1 Relationships between Five Tables in Our Sample Database

As we discussed at the beginning of this section, to delete a record from a relational database, one must follow a correct sequence. In other words, one must first delete the records that are related to the record to be deleted in the parent table from the child tables. In our sample database, five tables are related together by using the primary and foreign keys. In order to make these relationships clear, we re-draw Figure 2.12 in Chapter 2, which is Figure 8.46 in this section, to illustrate this issue.

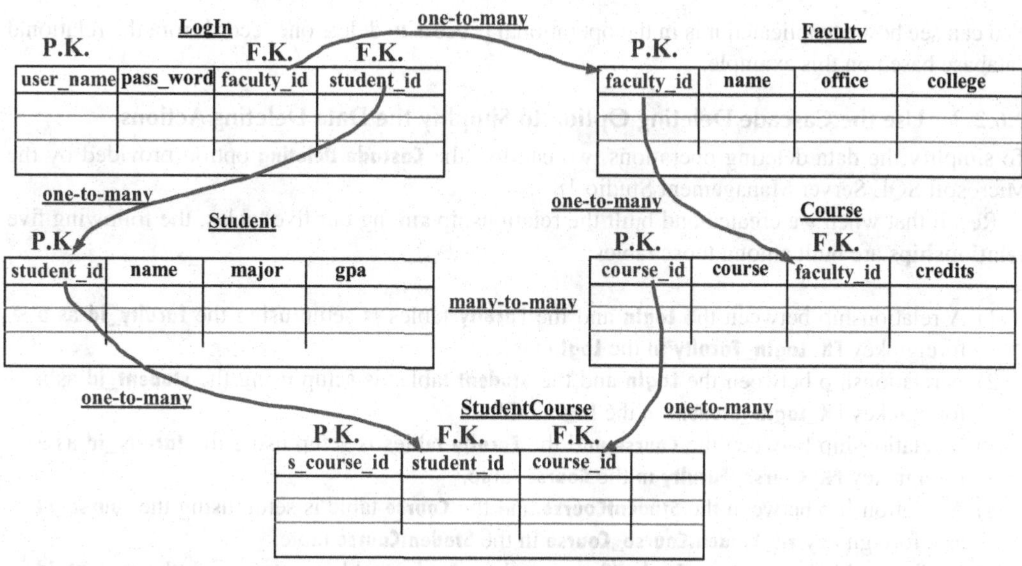

FIGURE 8.46 The relationships among five tables.

If you want to delete a record from the **Faculty** table, you must first delete the related records from the **LogIn**, **Course**, **StudentCourse** and **Student** tables, and then you can delete the desired record from the **Faculty** table. The reason for that is because some definite relationships are existed among five tables.

For example, if one wants to delete a faculty record from the **Faculty** table, one must perform the following deleting jobs:

- The **faculty_id** is a primary key in the **Faculty** table, but a foreign key in the **LogIn** and the **Course** table. Therefore, the **Faculty** table is a parent table and the **LogIn** and the **Course** are child tables. Before one can delete any record from the **Faculty** table, one must first delete records that have the **faculty_id** as the foreign key from the child tables. In other words, one must first delete those records that use the **faculty_id** as a foreign key from the **LogIn** and the **Course** tables.
- When deleting records that use the **faculty_id** as a foreign key from the **Course** table, the related **course_id**, which is a primary key in the **Course** table, will also be deleted. The **Course** table right now is a parent table since the **course_id** is a primary key for that table. As we mentioned, however, to delete any record from a parent table, one must first deleted the related records from the child tables. Now the **StudentCourse** table is a child table for the **Course** table; therefore, the records that use the **course_id** as a foreign key in the **StudentCourse** table should be deleted first.
- After those related records in the child tables are deleted, finally the faculty member can be deleted from the parent table, **Faculty** table.

8.6.2.2 Data Deleting Order Sequence

In summary, to delete a record from the **Faculty** table, one needs to perform the following deleting jobs in the order or sequence shown below:

1) Delete all records that use the **course_id** as the foreign key from the **StudentCourse** table.
2) Delete all records that use the **faculty_id** as the foreign key from the **LogIn** table.
3) Delete all records that use the **faculty_id** as the foreign key from the **Course** table.
4) Delete the desired faculty member from the **Faculty** table.

You can see how complicated it is in the operational process to delete one record from the relational database based on this example.

8.6.2.3 Use the Cascade Deleting Option to Simplify the Data Deleting Actions

To simplify the data deleting operations, we can use the **Cascade Deleting** option provided by the Microsoft SQL Server Management Studio 18.

Recall that when we created and built the relationship among our five tables, the following five **relationships** are built among those tables:

1) A relationship between the **LogIn** and the **Faculty** tables is setup using the **faculty_id** as a foreign key **FK_LogIn_Faculty** in the **LogIn** table.
2) A relationship between the **LogIn** and the **Student** tables is setup using the **student_id** as a foreign key **FK_LogIn_Student** in the **LogIn** table.
3) A relationship between the **Course** and the **Faculty** tables is setup using the **faculty_id** as a foreign key **FK_Course_Faculty** in the **Course** table.
4) A relationship between the **StudentCourse** and the **Course** table is setup using the **course_id** as a foreign key **FK_StudentCourse_Course** in the **StudentCourse** table.
5) A relationship between the **StudentCourse** and the **Student** table is setup using the **student_id** as a foreign key **FK_StudentCourse_Student** in the **StudentCourse** table.

Based on the data deleting order sequence (1–4) listed in the last section, in order to delete a record from the **Faculty** table, one needs to perform four deleting operations in that sequence. Compared with those four deleting operations, the first one is the most difficult and the reason for that is:

To perform the first data deleting, one must first find all **course_id** that use the **faculty_id** as the foreign key from the **Course** table, and then, based on those **course_id**, one needs to delete all records that use those **course_ids** as the foreign keys from the **StudentCourse** table. To delete operations in sequences 3 and 4, they are very easy and each deleting operation only needs one deleting query. The conclusion for this discussion is: how can we find an easy way to complete the deleting operation in sequence 1?

A good solution to that question is to use the **Cascade** option, as we did in Chapter 2, to perform the data deleting and updating in a cascaded mode. This **Cascade** option allows the SQL Server database engine to perform that deleting operation in sequence 1 as long as a **Cascade** option is selected for relationships 4 and 5 listed above.

Now let's use a real example to illustrate how to use this **Cascade** option to simplify the data deleting operations, especially for the first data deleting in that sequence.

Perform the following operations to open Microsoft SQL Server Management Studio 18:

1) Go to **Start | All Programs | Microsoft SQL Server Tools 18 | SQL Server Management Studio 18**.
2) On the opened Studio window, select the **SQL Server Authentication** mode to finish the login process by entering **SMART** and **Happy2022** as username and password, and click on the **Connect** button to connect to our database server.
3) Then expand the **Databases** folder, our sample database folder **CSE_DEPT**, and the **Tables** folder to display all five tables. Since we only have interesting on relationships 4 and 5, so just expand the **dbo.StudentCourse** table and the **Keys** folder to display all Keys we established in Section 2.9.4 in Chapter 2. Double click the key **FK_StudentCourse_Course** to open it, which is shown in Figure 8.47.

On the opened Foreign Key Relationships wizard, keep our desired foreign key **FK_StudentCourse_Course** selected on the left pane, and then click the small plus icon before the item **INSERT And UPDATE Specification** and you can find that a **Cascade** mode has been set for both **Delete Rule** and **Update Rule** items, which is shown in Figure 8.47.

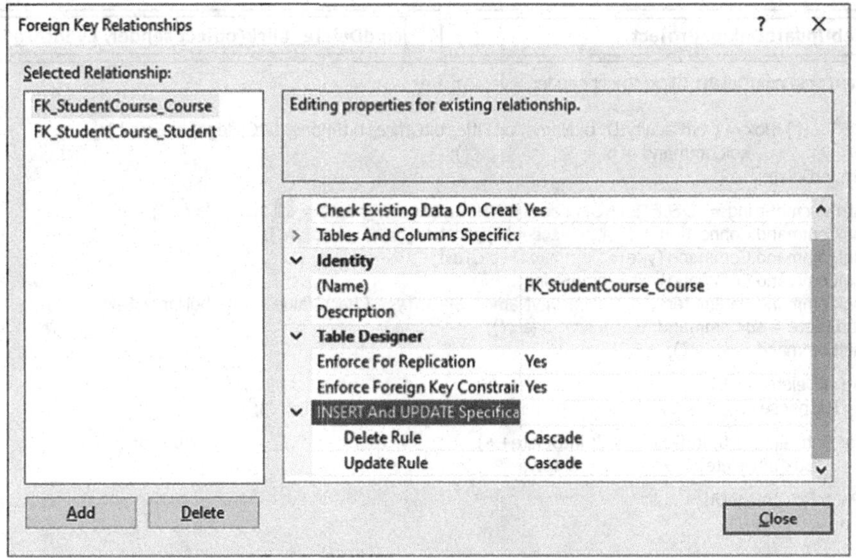

FIGURE 8.47 The foreign key relationship wizard.

After this **Cascade** option is setup, each time when you want to delete all records that use the **course_id** or the **student_id** as the foreign keys in the **StudentCourse** table, the SQL Server engine will perform those data deleting operations automatically for you in that cascaded sequence. Therefore, you can see how easy it is to perform the data deletion in sequence 1. Click on the **Close** button to close that wizard.

Now let's create our codes for the Delete button's Click method to perform this data deleting operation.

8.6.2.4 Develop the Codes to Perform the Data Deleting Action

Open Visual Studio.NET and our Web application project **SQLWebUpdateDelete Project**. Then open the **Delete** button's click method from the Design View of the **Faculty** Web form by double-clicking on the **Delete** button. Then enter the codes that are shown in Figure 8.48 into this method.

Let's take a closer look at this piece of codes to see how it works.

- **A.** First a textbox array **fBox[]** is generated to hold seven textboxes to be emptied later via the **for()** loop to clean up this deleted faculty record from this page.
- **B.** A Command object and a local variable used in this method are declared here. The integer variable **intDelete** is used to hold the returned value from calling of the **ExecuteNonQuery()** method of the Command class later.
- **C.** The data deleting query string is declared first with the **faculty_name** as the query criterion.
- **D.** The Command object is initialized by using the Connection object, Command Type, Command Text and Parameters properties.
- **E.** After the Command object is initialized, the **ExecuteNonQuery()** method of the Command class is called to perform the data deleting action. This method will return an integer value and it is assigned to the local variable **intDelete.**
- **F.** A cleaning job is performed to release all objects used in this deleting action.
- **G.** The returned value from calling the **ExecuteNonQuery()** method is exactly equal to the number of rows that have been successfully deleted from our sample database. If this value is zero, which means that no row has been deleted or affected from our database and this data deletion has failed, a warning message is displayed. Otherwise, a non-zero value is returned, which means that at least one row in our database has been deleted from our database and this data deleting is successful.

```
SQLWebUpdateDelete Project          cmdDelete_Click(object sender, EventArgs e)

  protected void cmdDelete_Click(object sender, EventArgs e)
  {
A     TextBox[] fBox = { txtFacultyID, txtName, txtTitle, txtOffice, txtPhone, txtCollege, txtEmail };
B     SqlCommand sqlCommand = new SqlCommand();
      int intDelete;

C     string cmdString = "DELETE FROM Faculty WHERE (faculty_name = @FacultyName)";
D     sqlCommand.Connection = (SqlConnection)Application["sqlConnection"];
      sqlCommand.CommandType = CommandType.Text;
      sqlCommand.CommandText = cmdString;
      sqlCommand.Parameters.Add("@FacultyName", SqlDbType.Char).Value = ComboName.Text;
E     intDelete = sqlCommand.ExecuteNonQuery();
F     sqlCommand.Dispose();

G     if (intDelete == 0)
         Response.Write("<script>alert('The data deleting is failed')</script>");

H     for (intDelete = 0; intDelete < 7; intDelete++)          // clean up the Faculty textbox array
          fBox[intDelete].Text = string.Empty;

I     PhotoBox.ImageUrl = null;
J     CurrentFaculty();
  }
```

FIGURE 8.48 The coding for the delete button's click method.

H. A cleaning job is performed to clean up the contents of all textboxes that stored the deleted faculty information.
I. The deleted faculty image is also removed from the **PhotoBox** object in this page.
J. The user-defined method **CurrentFaculty()** is called to query the **Faculty** table to get updated faculty names, and display them in the **Faculty Name** combobox.

At this point, we have finished all coding jobs to delete data against the SQL Server database via Web pages. Before we can run the project to test this deleting function, make sure that the starting page is the LogIn page.

After the project runs, enter the suitable username and password to complete the login process, then open the **Faculty** page by clicking the **Faculty Information** item from the **Selection** page, select the default faculty member **Ying Bai** from the combobox control and then click the **Select** button to retrieve and display this faculty's information.

Now click on the **Delete** button to delete this faculty record from our database. Immediately, all seven pieces of faculty information stored in the related seven textboxes are removed. The selected faculty image is also removed.

To confirm this data deleting, open the **Faculty Name** combobox, and the deleted faculty member, **Ying Bai**, cannot be found from this box, which means that this faculty member has been deleted from our sample database.

Another way to confirm this data deleting is to open our sample database via the Microsoft SQL Server Management Studio 18, and you can find that all records related to that deleted faculty member, **Ying Bai**, as shown in Figures 8.49–8.52, have been deleted from our database. Yes, our data deleting action is successful.

Before we can close the SQL Server Management Studio, it is highly recommended that you recover all records that have been deleted from our sample database. To do that recovering job, you need to take the following actions in the following orders:

1) Recover the **Faculty** table by inserting the deleted faculty record, which is shown in Figure 8.49, into the **Faculty** table via the **Insert** button on this **Faculty** page.
2) Recover the **LogIn** table by adding the deleted login record, as shown in Figure 8.50, into the **LogIn table** via the Microsoft SQL Management Studio 18.

faculty_id	faculty_name	office	phone	college	title	email	fimage
B78880	Ying Bai	MTC-211	750-378-1148	Florida Atlantic University	Associate Professor	ybai@college.edu	Bai.jpg

FIGURE 8.49 The data deleted from the faculty table.

user_name	pass_word	faculty_id	student_id
ybai	come	B78880	NULL

FIGURE 8.50 The data deleted from the LogIn table.

course_id	course	credit	classroom	schedule	enrollment	faculty_id
CSC-132B	Introduction to Programming	3	MTC-302	T-H: 1:00-2:25 PM	21	B78880
CSC-234A	Data Structure & Algorithms	3	MTC-302	M-W-F: 9:00-9:55 AM	25	B78880
CSE-434	Advanced Electronics Systems	3	MTC-213	M-W-F: 1:00-1:55 PM	26	B78880
CSE-438	Advd Logic & Microprocessor	3	MTC-213	M-W-F: 11:00-11:55 AM	35	B78880

FIGURE 8.51 The data deleted from the course table.

s_course_id	student_id	course_id	credit	major
1005	T77896	CSC-234A	3	CS/IS
1009	A78835	CSE-434	3	CE
1014	A78835	CSE-438	3	CE
1016	A97850	CSC-132B	3	ISE
1017	A97850	CSC-234A	3	ISE

FIGURE 8.52 The data deleted from the StudentCourse table.

3) Recover the **Course** table by adding the deleted courses records, which are shown in Figure 8.51, into the **Course** table via the Microsoft SQL Management Studio 18.
4) Recover the **StudentCourse** table by adding the deleted courses taken by the associated students, as shown in Figure 8.52, into the **StudentCourse** table via the Microsoft SQL Management Studio 18.

When performing the first recovery job above, one can run this project and use the **Insert** button and its Click method to perform another data insertion action to insert that deleted faculty record.

To perform the recovery jobs 2–4 above, one can use the Microsoft SQL Server Management Studio 18 to open our sample database and related tables, and add those records one by one manually. One can copy all rows from Figures 8.51 and 8.52, and paste them on the bottom of each related table.

A complete Web application project **SQLWebUpdateDelete Project** can be found from a folder **Class DB Projects\Chapter 8\SQLWebUpdateDelete Solution** that is located under the **Students** folder on the CRC Press ftp site (refer to Figure 1.2 in Chapter 1).

8.7 DEVELOP ASP.NET WEB APPLICATIONS WITH LINQ TO SQL QUERY

In this section, we provide a fundamental end-to-end LINQ to SQL scenario for selecting, adding, modifying, and deleting data against our sample database via Web pages. As you know, LINQ to SQL queries can perform not only the data selections, but also the data insertion, updating and deletion. The standard LINQ to SQL queries include

- Select
- Insert
- Update
- Delete

To perform any of these operations, we need to use entity classes and DataContext we discussed in Section 4.6.1 in Chapter 4 to do LINQ to SQL actions against our sample database. We have already created a Windows-based application project **LINQSelect Project** in Section 5.17.1 in Chapter 5 to illustrate how to use LINQ to SQL to perform data queries to our **LogIn**, **Faculty**, **Course** and **Student** tables in our sample database **CSE_DEPT**. However, in this section, we want to create a Web-based project to perform the data selection, data insertion, data updating and deleting actions against related tables in our sample database **CSE_DEPT** using the LINQ to SQL query via Web pages.

Now let's perform the following steps to create our new project **WebLINQSQL Project**:

1) Create a new ASP.NET Web Application (.NET Framework) C# project and set the Project name as **WebLINQSQL Project** and Solution name as **WebLINQSQL Solution**, respectively. Select the **C:\Chapter 8** as the location to save this project and click on the **Create** button.
2) On the next wizard, select the **Web Forms** as the template, and click on the **Create** button again to create this project.

3) On the new created Web project, go to the Solution Explorer window and select the **Default.aspx** by right clicking on it, and select the **Delete** item to remove it since we do not need this page in this project, and we can use the **LogIn** page as our default or start page.

Next we need to add all four Web pages we built in Sections 8.4.1, 8.4.5, 8.4.7 and 8.4.9 into this new project and add some reference related to LINQ to SQL. Perform the following operations to complete those additions:

1) Right-click on our new project **WebLINQSQL Project** from the Solution Explorer window, and select the **Add | Existing Item** menu item from the popup menu.
2) On the opened **Add Existing Item** wizard, browse to the folder **Students\Web Forms** that is located on the CRC Press ftp site, and select all of those pages with all extensions, such as **.aspx**, **aspx.cs** and **aspx.designer.cs**, by checking each of them. (An example is: **LogIn.aspx, LogIn.aspx.cs** and **LogIn.aspx.designer.cs**). Then click on the **Add** button to add them into our project. One can copy all of those pages and save them to one of your local folders, and get them from that folder.
3) Next we need to add **System.Data.Linq** reference to this new project. Right-click on our new project from the Solution Explorer window, and select **Add | Reference** item from the popup menu to open the Add Reference wizard. Keep the default tab selected and scroll down along the Reference List until you find the item **System.Data.Linq**, select it by checking the checkbox in front of it and click the **OK** button to add this reference to our project.

A point to be noted is that all of those added pages are generated under the namespace **SQLWebSelect_Project**; thus, that namespace cannot be changed even we add them into our current project.

Next we need to create entity classes via **LINQ to SQL tools** provided by Visual Studio.NET to set up mapping relationships between each physical data table and the related entity class. We prefer to use the Object Relational Designer since it provides a graphic user interface.

8.7.1 Create Entity Classes and Connect the DataContext to the Database

We need to create this new entity class and object of the DataContext class since we need to use this object to connect to our sample database to perform data queries. In fact, we need first to create entity classes via **LINQ to SQL tools** provided by Visual Studio.NET to set up mapping relationships between each physical data table and the related entity class. We prefer to use the Object Relational Designer since it provides a graphic user interface.

We have provided a detailed discussion about how to install this **LINQ to SQL tools** in Section 5.17.1 in Chapter 5. Refer to that section to get detailed descriptions for that tools and finish installation for it if you have not installed it.

We also provided detailed discussion about how to create entity class and its object in Section 5.17.2 in Chapter 5. For your convenience, we redo this discussion in this section to make it easy to be built and applied.

Perform the following operations to create this entity class and its object:

1) Right-click our project **WebLINQSQL Project** from the Solution Explorer window, and select the item **Add | New Item** from the popup menu to open the Add New Item wizard.
2) On the opened wizard, select the **Visual C#** item as the template from the left pane. Then select the item **LINQ to SQL Classes** from the list at the center by clicking on it, and enter **CSE_DEPT.dbml** into the **Name** box at the bottom as the name for this intermediate DBML file, as shown in Figure 8.53.
3) Then click the **Add** button to open this Object Relational Designer.

You can find that a **CSE_DEPT.dbml** folder has been added into our project in the Solution Explorer window, which is shown in Figure 8.54. Two related files, **CSE_DEPT.dbml.layout** and **CSE_DEPT.designer.cs**,

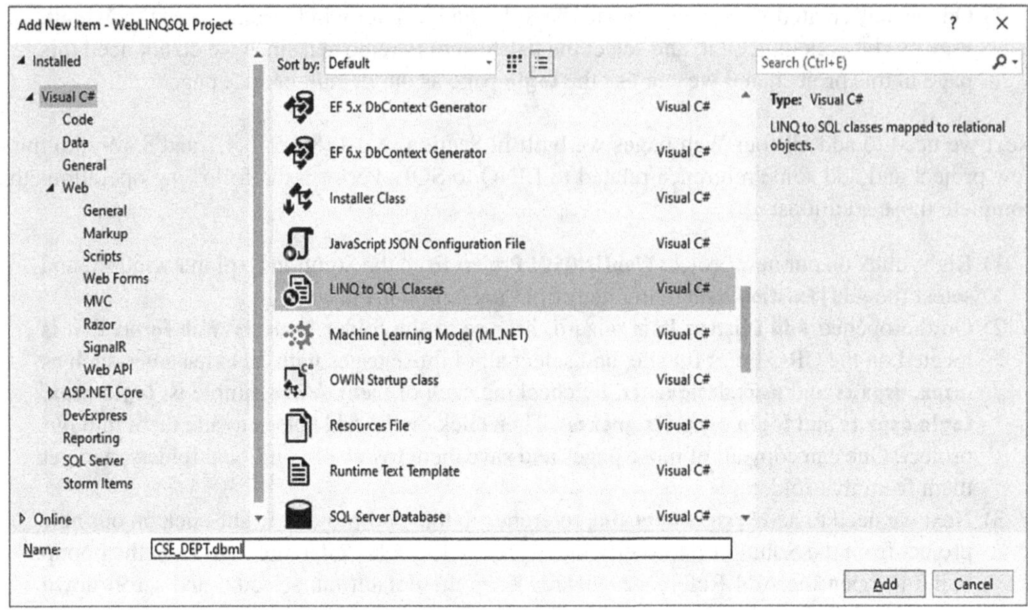

FIGURE 8.53 The finished add new item wizard.

are attached under that folder. The first file is exactly the designer that is shown as a blank window in Figure 8.54, and the second file is auto-generated by the Object Relational Designer and it contains codes to create a child class **CSE_DEPTDataContext** that is derived from the DataContext class. Four overloaded constructors of the child class **CSE_DEPTDataContext** are declared in that file.

To open the Object Relational Designer, double-click on the item **CSE_DEPT.dbml** from the Solution Explorer window. The opened Object Relational Designer is shown in Figure 8.54.

Prior to creating the entity class, we need to connect to our sample database. To do that, just click on the arrow in front of our ample database, **desktop-24jpufb\sql2019 express.CSE_DEPT.dbo**, and then expand the **Tables** folder to show all our five tables.

To create an entity class for each table, just perform a drag-place operation for each table between the Server Explorer window and the blank Design window. Starting from the **LogIn** table, drag it from the Server Explorer window and place it into the Design window. By dragging the **LogIn** table to the designer canvas, the source code for the **LogIn** entity class is created and added into the **CSE_DEPT.designer.cs** file. Then you can use this entity class to access and manipulate data from this project to the LogIn table in our sample database **CSE_DEPT**.

Perform similar drag-place operations to all other tables, and the finished designer is shown in Figure 8.55. The arrow between tables is called an association that is a new terminology used in the LINQ to SQL, which represents the relationship between tables.

Now we can start to use these entity classes and the DataContext object to perform desired data actions against our sample database using the LINQ to SQL technique.

Let's start from our **LogIn** page to access the **LogIn** table in our sample database.

8.7.2 Perform LINQ to SQL Query to LogIn Table via LogIn Page

First we need to create a field variable **cse_dept** based on our derived DataContext class **CSE_DEPTDataContext**. As we discussed, this object is used to connect to our sample database. Four overloaded constructors are available for this DataContext class, but in this application we only use the simplest one to simplify our coding process.

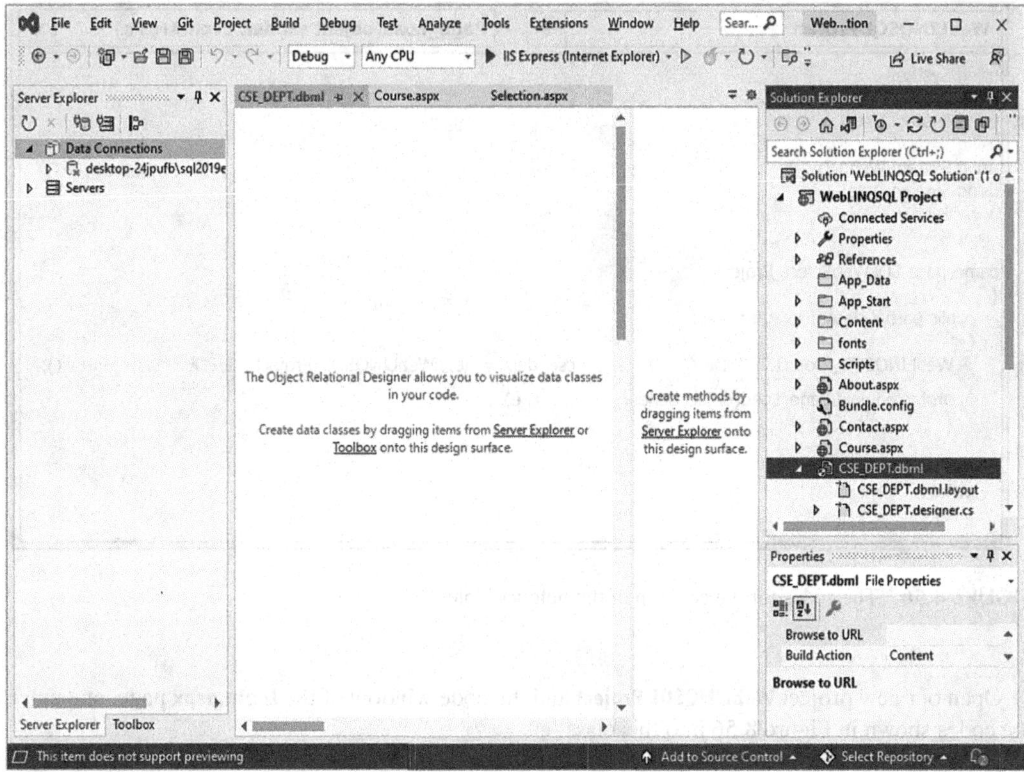

FIGURE 8.54 The opened object relational designer.

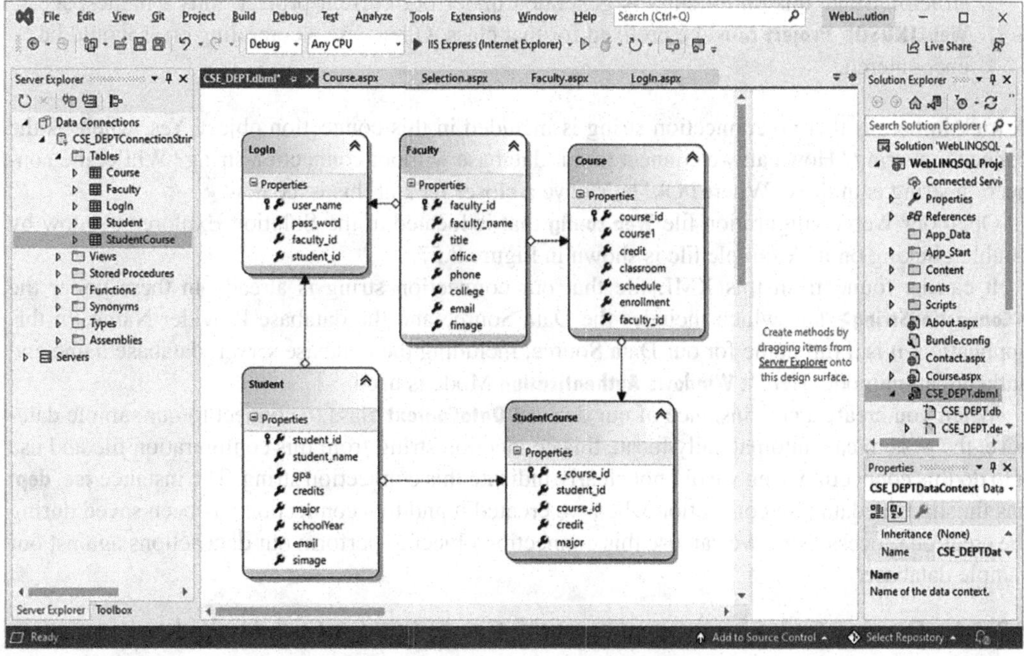

FIGURE 8.55 The finished designer.

```
WebLINQSQL Project                    Page_Load(object sender, EventArgs e)

  using System;
  using System.Collections.Generic;
A using System.Linq;
  using System.Web;
  using System.Web.UI;
  using System.Data;
  using System.Data.SqlClient;
  using System.Web.UI.WebControls;
  namespace SQLWebSelect_Project
  {
     public partial class _Default : Page
     {
B       WebLINQSQL_Project.CSE_DEPTDataContext cse_dept = new WebLINQSQL_Project.CSE_DEPTDataContext();
        protected void Page_Load(object sender, EventArgs e)
        {

        }
     .........
```

FIGURE 8.56 The codes for the creation of the field variable.

Open our new project **WebLINQSQL Project** and the code window of the **LogIn.aspx** page, and enter the codes shown in Figure 8.56 into this class.

Let's have a closer look at this piece of codes to see how it works.

A. The namespace **System.Linq** is automatically added into this code section and we need to use all data components related to LINQ to SQL and this namespace contains all of them.

B. A new instance of our derived class **CSE_DEPTDataContext** is created with the first constructor. Since this entity class is generated under our current project, thus a namespace **WebLINQSQL_Project** must be prefixed for that class. Otherwise a compiling error would be encountered.

A trick in here is that no connection string is included in this connection object. Yes, where is the connection string? How can we connect to our database without connection string? While, the connection string is in there. Where? Ok, let's have a closer look at this issue now.

Open our Web configuration file **Web.config** that is located at the Solution Explorer window by double-clicking on it. A sample file is shown in Figure 8.57.

It can be found from this XML file that our connection string is already in there under the **<ConnectionString>** tag, which includes the Data Source and the database Provider Name. In this application, it is a full name for our Data Source, including the database server, database name and authentication mode. Here a **Windows Authentication** Mode is used.

When you create a new instance of our derived **DataContext** class to connect to our sample database, the system can automatically locate this connection string from this configuration file and use it to do this connection even we did not clearly indicate this connection string. The instance **cse_dept** has finished the database connection when we created it and this connection has been saved during the creation process. Now we can use this connection object to perform our data actions against our sample database.

8.7.2.1 Develop Codes for the LogIn and the Cancel Buttons Click Methods

Double-click on the **LogIn** button from the Design View of the **LogIn** page to open its Click event method, and enter the codes shown in Figure 8.58 into this method.

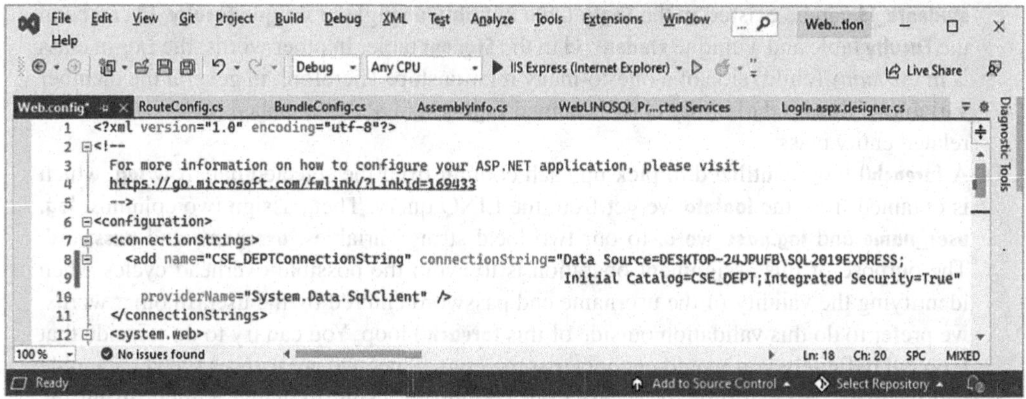

FIGURE 8.57 A piece of sample codes for the Web.config file.

```
WebLINQSQL Project                    cmdLogIn_Click(object sender, EventArgs e)

  private void cmdLogIn_Click(object sender, EventArgs e)
  {
A       string username = string.Empty;
        string password = string.Empty;
B       Selection selForm = new Selection();
C       var loginfo = (from lg in cse_dept.LogIns
                      where lg.user_name == txtUserName.Text && lg.pass_word == txtPassWord.Text
                      select lg);
D       foreach (var log in loginfo)
        {
           username = (string)log.user_name;
           password = (string)log.pass_word;
        }
E       if (txtUserName.Text == string.Empty || txtPassWord.Text == string.Empty)
           Response.Write("<script>alert('Enter a valid username/password!')</script>");
F       else if (username == txtUserName.Text && password == txtPassWord.Text)
        {
           Response.Redirect("Selection.aspx");
           cse_dept.Connection.Close();
           cse_dept.Dispose();
        }
G       else
           Response.Write("<script>alert('The LogIn is failed!')</script>");
  }
```

FIGURE 8.58 The codes for the login button click Method.

Let's have a closer look at this piece of codes to see how it works.

A. Two local-level string variables, **username** and **password**, are created and these two variables are used to hold the returned queried data from the **LogIn** table.

B. An instance of the next page class Selection, **selForm**, is created and this page will be displayed if the login process is completed successfully.

C. An iteration variable **lg** is used to iterate over the result of this query from the **LogIn** table. Then a similar SQL **SELECT** statement is executed with the **WHERE** clause. Two criterions are used for this query, **user_name** and **pass_word**, and these two criterions are connected with a logic **AND** operator. One point to be noted is the member variable of our entity class LogIn, which is named **LogIns** in this query. The relationships or the associations between the **LogIn**, **Faculty** and **Student** tables are many-to-one, which means that many **faculty_id** and

students_id can be existed in the **LogIn** table but only a single or unique **faculty_id** can be in the **Faculty** table and a unique **student_id** in the **Student** table. In other words, the LogIn class is in the *many* (child) side of a one-to-many relationship. Therefore, in general the member variable of this kind of entity class is named **LogIns**, and a'**s**' is attached to the name of the related entity class.

D. A **foreach()** loop is utilized to pick up each column from the selected data row **log**, which is obtained from the **loginfo** we get from the LINQ query. Then, assign two columns, **log.user_name** and **log.pass_word**, to our two local string variables, **username** and **password**. The purpose of this assignment operation is to avoid the possible overhead cycles when identifying the validity of the username and password entered by the user. In other words, we prefer to do this validation outside of this **foreach()** loop. You can try to do it inside that loop but definitely you would encounter some bugs. Since we are using a typed data table and database, we can directly access each column by using its name without using the **field<string>** and the column's name as the position for each of them.

E. An error message will be displayed if any input box is empty to remind the user to enter valid username and password.

F. If both **username** and **password** are correct and matched to both columns queried from the **LogIn** table, which means that this login process is successful, the **Selection** page is displayed. The database connection is closed to disconnect to our sample database, and all resources used by that object are released.

G. If no matched **username** and **password** can be found, an error message is displayed to indicate this situation.

Next let's do the coding for the **Cancel** button in this **LogIn** page.

Double-click on the **Cancel** button from the Design View of the **LogIn** page to open its click method. Enter the following coding line to that method:

```
Response.Write("<script>window.close()</script>");
```

Next let's build the codes for the Selection page.

8.7.3 Build the Codes for the Selection Page

Open the code window of the **Selection** page by right-clicking on the **Selection.aspx** from the Solution Explorer window, and click on the **View Code** item. Enter the codes shown in Figure 8.59 into this window.

Let's have a closer look at this piece of codes to see how it works.

A. First, three field-level or class-level objects are generated for three page classes.

B. Three pages are added into the **Selection** combobox to enable users to select and open one of them to perform related query actions on that page. The condition for adding these three pages is to make sure that that adding is not a **PostBack** page by the server.

C. The first page is selected and displayed as a default page as the project runs.

Next let's build the codes for the **Select** and **Exit** buttons, exactly for their event methods.

Double-click on the **Select** and the Exit buttons from the Design View of the **Selection.aspx** page to open their click methods, and enter codes shown in Figure 8.60 into these methods. Let's have a closer look at these pieces of codes to see how they work.

A. If users select any page from the Selection combobox, the related page is opened to direct users to go to that page to perform the related query job. The **Redirect()** method in the server side is a powerful method to perform this kind of job. A point to be noted is that a **Student**

```
WebLINQSQL Project                    Page_Load(object sender, EventArgs e)

  using System;
  namespace SQLWebSelect_Project
  {
     public partial class Selection : System.Web.UI.Page
     {
A        Faculty facultyPage = new Faculty();
         Course coursePage = new Course();
         Student studentPage = new Student();
         protected void Page_Load(object sender, EventArgs e)
         {
            if (!IsPostBack)
            {
B              ComboSelection.Items.Add("Faculty Information");
               ComboSelection.Items.Add("Course Information");
               ComboSelection.Items.Add("Student Information");
C              ComboSelection.SelectedIndex = 0;
            }
         }
  }
```

FIGURE 8.59 The codes for the selection page class.

```
WebLINQSQL Project                    cmdSelect_Click(object sender, EventArgs e)

  protected void cmdSelect_Click(object sender, EventArgs e)
  {
A     if (ComboSelection.Text == "Faculty Information")
         Response.Redirect("Faculty.aspx");
      else if (ComboSelection.Text == "Course Information")
         Response.Redirect("Course.aspx");
      else if (ComboSelection.Text == "Student Information")
         Response.Redirect("Student.aspx");
B     else
         Response.Write("<script>alert('Invalid Selection!')</script>");
  }
  protected void cmdExit_Click(object sender, EventArgs e)
  {
C     facultyPage.Dispose();
      coursePage.Dispose();
      studentPage.Dispose();
D     Response.Write("<script>window.close()</script>");
  }
```

FIGURE 8.60 The codes for the select-exit button click methods in the selection page.

page is also involved in this selection process, but we did not discuss the building process for that page. The reason for that is to save the readers' time and efforts. A completed **Student** page has been built and located at the **Students\Web Forms** folder on the CRC Press ftp site. One needs to add this page as we did in Section 8.7 with all other pages together.

B. If no any page is selected, an error message is displayed to indicate that situation.

C. When the Exit button is clicked, the first three pages are released to make them ready to be removed from the memory.

D. Finally, the Web application is closed by calling a system method **window.close()**.

Next let's continue to build codes for the **Faculty** page to perform the related data query from the **Faculty** table in our sample database.

8.7.4 Perform LINQ to SQL Query to Faculty Table via Faculty Page

In this section, we need to divide our coding process into the following six parts:

1) Create a new object of the DataContext class and do some initialization coding.
2) Develop the codes for the **Select** button's Click method to retrieve back the selected faculty information using the LINQ to SQL query.
3) Develop the codes for the **Insert** button's Click method to insert new faculty member using the LINQ to SQL query.
4) Develop the codes for the **Update** button's Click method to update the selected faculty member using the LINQ to SQL query.
5) Develop codes for the **Delete** button's Click method to delete the selected faculty member using the LINQ to SQL query.
6) Develop codes for the **Back** button click method to return to the Selection page.

Now let's start our coding process from the first one listed above.

8.7.4.1 Create a New Object of the DataContext Class

Open the code window and the **Page_Load()** method of the **Faculty** Web page, and enter the codes that are shown in Figure 8.61 into this method.

Let's have a close look at this piece of codes to see how it works.

A. A new field-level object of the DataContext class, **cse_dept**, is created first since we need to use this object to connect our sample database to this Web project to perform the data actions later.

B. A user-defined method **CurrentFaculty()** is executed to retrieve back all current faculty members from our sample database and display them in the **ComboName** combobox control to allow the user to select a desired faculty later. To avoid multiple displaying of retrieved

```
WebLINQSQL Project        Page_Load(object sender, EventArgs e)

  using System;
  using System.Linq;
  public partial class _Default : System.Web.UI.Page
  {
A    CSE_DEPTDataContext cse_dept = new CSE_DEPTDataContext();
     protected void Page_Load(object sender, EventArgs e)
     {
        if (!IsPostBack)
        {
B          CurrentFaculty();
           ComboName.SelectedIndex = 0;
        }
     }
     void CurrentFaculty()
     {
C       ComboName.Items.Clear();
D       var faculty = (from fi in cse_dept.Faculties
                       let fields = "faculty_name"
                       select fi);
E       foreach (var f in faculty)
           ComboName.Items.Add(f.faculty_name);
  }
```

FIGURE 8.61 Initialization codes for the faculty web page.

faculty members, an **if** selection structure is adopted to make sure that we only displaying those current faculty members in the combobox at the first time as this Web page is loaded, and will not display them each time as the server sends back a refreshed **Faculty** page to the client.

C. Before we can update the combobox control **ComboName** by adding all current faculty members into this control, a cleaning job is performed to avoid the multiple adding and displaying of those faculty members.

D. The LINQ query is created and initialized with three clauses, **from**, **let** and **select**. The range variable **fi** is selected from the **Faculty** entity in our sample database. All current faculty members (**faculty_name**) will be read back using the **let** clause and assigned to the query variable **faculty**.

E. The LINQ query is executed to pick up all queried faculty members and add them into the ComboName combobox control in our Faculty page.

Next let's take care of the coding for the **Select** button to query detailed information for a selected faculty member.

8.7.4.2 The Coding for the Data Selection Query

Double-click on the **Select** button in the Design View of the **Faculty** page to open its Click method and enter the codes that are shown in Figure 8.62 into this method.

The function of this piece of codes is to retrieve back detailed information for a selected faculty member from the **Faculty** table in our sample database and display them in seven textboxes in the **Faculty** page with the selected faculty image as this **Select** button is clicked by the user.

Let's have a close look at this piece of codes to see how it works.

A. The LINQ query is created and initialized with three clauses, **from**, **where** and **select**. The range variable **fi** is selected from the **Faculty** entity in our sample database based on a matched faculty members (**faculty_name**).

B. The LINQ query then is executed to pick up all columns for the selected faculty member and display them on the associated textbox in our **Faculty** page.

```
WebLINQSQL Project                    cmdSelect_Click(object sender, EventArgs e)

  protected void cmdSelect_Click(object sender, EventArgs e)
  {
A     var f_info = from fi in cse_dept.Faculties
                   where fi.faculty_name == ComboName.Text
                   select fi;
B     foreach (var f in f_info)
      {
        txtFacultyID.Text = f.faculty_id;
        txtName.Text = f.faculty_name;
        txtTitle.Text = f.title;
        txtOffice.Text = f.office;
        txtPhone.Text = f.phone;
        txtCollege.Text = f.college;
        txtEmail.Text = f.email;
C       byte[] img = (f.fimage as System.Data.Linq.Binary).ToArray();
        string bimg = Convert.ToBase64String(img);
D       PhotoBox.ImageUrl = String.Format("data:image/jpg;base64,{0}", bimg);
      }
  }
```

FIGURE 8.62 The codes for the select button click method.

C. The selected faculty image is converted to a byte array **img[]**, and furthermore converted to a String with a **Base64String** format.
D. Finally, that String is formatted and assigned to the **ImageUrl** property of the Faculty Image box, **PhotoBox**, to be displayed there.

Now let's concentrate on the coding for our data insertion actions.

However, before we can continue building our codes to insert a new record into our database with the LINQ to SQL method, let's have a discussion about a key component, the DataContext class, with its methods to provide us a clear picture about that class and its implementations.

8.7.4.3 The DataContext Class and Its Implementations

As we discussed in Chapter 4, the DataContext is the source of all entities mapped over a database connection. It tracks changes that you made to all retrieved entities and maintains an identity cache that guarantees that entities retrieved more than one time are represented by using the same object instance.

In general, a DataContext instance is designed to last for one unit of work; however, your application defines that term. A DataContext is lightweight and is not expensive to create. A typical LINQ to SQL application creates DataContext instances at method scope or as a member of short-lived classes that represent a logical set of related database operations.

Four constructors are involved with this class, which are shown in Figure 8.63.

The DataContext class contains 30 methods, some most popular methods are listed in Figure 8.64. Among these popular methods, the following methods are important in the real LINQ to SQL implementations:

- ExecuteCommand()
- ExecuteQuery()

Constructor	Functions
DataContext(Connection)	Initializes a new instance of the DataContext class by referencing the connection used by the .NET Framework.
DataContext(Connection, Source)	Initializes a new instance of the DataContext class by referencing a connection and a mapping source.
DataContext(String)	Initializes a new instance of the DataContext class by referencing a file source.
DataContext(String, Source)	Initializes a new instance of the DataContext class by referencing a file source and a mapping source.

FIGURE 8.63 Constructors of the DataContext class.

Methods	Functions
CreateDatabase()	Dynamically creates a new database on the server.
DatabaseExists()	Determines whether the associated database can be opened.
DeleteDatabase()	Deletes the associated database.
ExecuteCommand(String, Object[])	Executes SQL commands directly on the database.
ExecuteQuery(Type, String, Object[])	Executes SQL queries directly on the database.
ExecuteQuery<TResult>(String, Object[])	Determines whether the associated database can be opened.
SubmitChanges()	Computes the set of modified objects to be inserted, updated, or deleted, and executes the appropriate commands to implement the changes to the database.
ToString()	Returns a string that represents the current object (Inherited from Object).

FIGURE 8.64 Most popular methods in the DataContext class.

The **ExecuteCommand()** is a popular and powerful method, and, in fact, this method is a pass-through mechanism for cases where LINQ to SQL does not adequately provide for a particular scenario. This method returns an integer (**Int32**) to indicate the number of rows that have been modified by execution of this method

The syntax for the command is almost the same as the syntax used to create an ADO.NET **DataCommand**. The only difference is in how the parameters are specified. Specifically, you specify parameters by enclosing them in braces ({...}) and enumerate them starting from 0. The parameter is associated with the equally numbered object in the parameters array.

The first argument represents a non-query SQL command to be executed, and it should be in a **String** format. The second argument is an object array or a parameter array to be passed into the command. If the number of objects in the array is less than the highest number identified in the command string, an exception is thrown. If the array contains objects that are not referenced in the command string, no exception is thrown.

If any one of the parameters is null, it is converted to **DBNull.Value**.

The **ExecuteCommand()** method can execute any SQL related command, such as:

1) Create a new data table in a selected database dynamically.
2) Execute any non-query command, such as Insert, Update and Delete to the selected table from the target database.

Some example codes of using this method are shown in Figure 8.65.

Another useful method is the **ExecuteQuery()** and it can be used to perform any query SQL command. A coding example by using this method is shown in Figure 8.66.

Based on the discussion above, we should have a clear picture in how to use those methods to perform related queries to get our desired results.

The main reason to provide that discussion for those methods in the DataContext class is to enlarge or expand our views to select or adopt more other ways to perform data queries in different

```
// using ExecuteCommand() to create a new table newFaculty
CSE_DEPTDataContext cse_dept = new CSE_DEPTDataContext();
cse_dept.ExecuteCommand("create table newFaculty(faculty_id varchar(50), faculty_name varchar(50),
                        title text, office text, phone text, college text, email text, fimage image)");
cse_dept.SubmitChanges();

// using ExecuteCommand() to insert a new record into the Course table
cse_dept.ExecuteCommand("INSERT INTO Course Values ({0}, {1}, {2}, {3}, {4}, {5})",
                        course_id, course, credit, classroom, schedule);

// using ExecuteCommand() to update a record in the Product table
cse_dept.ExecuteCommand("UPDATE Product SET Quantity = {0} WHERE ProductID = {1}", "20 boxes", 50);

// using ExecuteCommand() to delete a record from the Order table
cse_dept.ExecuteCommand("DELETE FROM Order WHERE OrderID = {0}", 12);
```

FIGURE 8.65 Some real coding examples of using the ExecuteCommand() method.

```
// using ExecuteQuery() to query a record from the Student table
CSE_DEPTDataContext cse_dept = new CSE_DEPTDataContext();
var sr = cse_dept.ExecuteQuery<Student>(@"SELECT * FROM Student WHERE student_id = {0}", "J86577");
```

FIGURE 8.66 A coding example to query student table via ExecuteCommand() method.

or various methods. Because sometimes for some applications, the LINQ to SQL method does not adequately provide for a particular scenario, and this is true to our situation since we declared **Faculty** as the name for our ASP page name (**Faculty.aspx**), but that name is duplicated with our **Faculty** data table. To solve this issue, we can use the **ExecuteCommand()** method to perform our non-query commands, such as **Insert**, **Update** or **Delete**, in the following sections.

One point to be clarified is that the **ExecuteCommand()** method is a more powerful method and it can be used to perform many SQL commands.

Next let's use that method to perform our data insertion action to the **Faculty** table in our sample database.

8.7.4.4 The Coding for the Data Insertion Query

Double-click on the **Insert** button from the Design View of our **Faculty** page to open its Click method and enter the codes that are shown in Figure 8.67 into this method.

Let's have a closer look at this piece of codes to see how it works.

A. A byte[] array **bImage** object and an integer variable **intInsert** are declared first since we need to insert a new faculty image with this data insertion action. The integer variable is used to get the running result of the **ExecuteCommand()** method.

B. Prior to inserting any data into our database, we need to check whether a valid faculty image has been selected if this **Insert** button is clicked by the user. This can be done by checking the **HasFile** property of the **FileUpload** class. If no faculty image has been selected, a warning message is displayed to remind the users to do that first.

```
WebLINQSQL Project                    cmdInsert_Click(object sender, EventArgs e)

   protected void cmdInsert_Click(object sender, EventArgs e)
   {
A     byte[] bImage;
      int intInsert;
B     if (!FileUploadImage.HasFile)
         Response.Write("<script>alert('Select an image first using FileUpload!')</script>");
      else
      {
C        bImage = getFacultyImage();
D        intInsert = cse_dept.ExecuteCommand("INSERT INTO Faculty Values ({0}, {1}, {2}, {3}, {4}, {5}, {6}, {7}) ",
                        txtFacultyID.Text, txtName.Text, txtTitle.Text, txtOffice.Text, txtPhone.Text, txtCollege.Text,
                        txtEmail.Text, bImage);
E        CurrentFaculty();
F        if (intInsert == 0)
            Response.Write("<script>alert('The data insertion is failed')</script>");
G        else
         {
            ClearFaculty();
            cmdInsert.Enabled = false;
         }
      }
   }
H  private void ClearFaculty()
   {
      TextBox[] fBox = {txtFacultyID, txtName, txtTitle, txtOffice, txtPhone, txtCollege, txtEmail};
      for (int index = 0; index < fBox.Length; index++)
         fBox[index].Text = String.Empty;
   }
```

FIGURE 8.67 The codes for the insert button's click method.

C. Otherwise a user-defined method **getFacultyImage()** is called to get the selected faculty image to be inserted into our sample database.

D. Then the **ExecuteCommand()** method of the DataContext class is executed to insert a new record into the **Faculty** table in our database. One point is the format of calling this method. The value holders must be in the braces { } format and embedded by the parameters' order numbers starting from 0. Following these value holders, the real parameters' values will be attached with the same order.

E. After a new record has been inserted into our database, we need to update our **Faculty Name** combobox control **ComboName** to reflect that insertion by calling another user defined method **CurrentFaculty()**.

F. As we discussed above, the **ExecuteCommand()** method returns an integer value, which is equal to the number of rows that have been modified. If the value of that returned integer is zero, which means that our data insertion is failed and no any record has been inserted. A warning message is displayed to indicate that case.

G. Otherwise, the data insertion is successful. All textboxes in the **Faculty** page are cleaned up by calling another user-defined method **ClearFaculty()** whose codes are shown below. In addition, the **Insert** button is disabled to avoid multiple duplicated records to be inserted.

H. The codes for the user-defined method, **ClearFaculty()**, are straightforward with no any trick. First a Textbox array, **fBox[]**, is generated to include all seven textboxes in this **Faculty** page. Then all textboxes are cleaned up by using a for loop process.

Now let's concentrate on the coding for our data updating action.

8.7.4.5 The Coding for the Data Updating Query

Double-click on the **Update** button from the Design View of the Faculty page to open its Click method and enter the codes that are shown in Figure 8.68 into this method.

```
WebLINQSQL Project    cmdUpdate_Click(object sender, EventArgs e)

  protected void cmdUpdate_Click(object sender, EventArgs e)
  {
A     byte[] bImage;
B     if (!FileUploadImage.HasFile)
         Response.Write("<script>alert('Select an updating image using FileUpload!')</script>");
      else
      {
C        bImage = getFacultyImage();
D        var fi = cse_dept.Faculties.Where(f => f.faculty_id == txtFacultyID.Text).First();
         // updating the existing faculty information
E        fi.faculty_name = txtName.Text;
         fi.title = txtTitle.Text;
         fi.office = txtOffice.Text;
         fi.phone = txtPhone.Text;
         fi.college = txtCollege.Text;
         fi.email = txtEmail.Text;
         fi.fimage = bImage;

F        cse_dept.SubmitChanges();
G        ComboName.Items.Clear();
         CurrentFaculty();
H        ClearFaculty();
      }
  }
```

FIGURE 8.68 The codes for the update button click method.

Let's have a close look at this piece of codes to see how it works.

A. A byte[] array **bImage** object is declared first since we need to get an image to update the selected faculty's image with this data updating action.
B. Prior to updating a data record in our database, we need to check whether an updated faculty image has been selected if this **Update** button is clicked by the user. This can be done by checking the **HasFile** property of the **FileUpload** class. If no faculty image has been selected, a warning message is displayed to remind the users to make that selection first.
C. Otherwise, a user-defined method **getFacultyImage()** is called to get the selected faculty image to be updated in our sample database.
D. A selection query is executed using the Standard Query Operator method with the **faculty_id** as the query criterion. The **First()** method is used to return only the first matched record. It does not matter to our application since we have only one record that is associated with this specified **faculty_id**.
E. An updated faculty record, which is stored in six textboxes, except the **faculty_id** textbox, and a selected faculty image, are updated by assigning each of them to the related column in the **Faculty** instance in our DataContext class object **cse_dept**.
F. This data updating can be really performed only after a system method **SubmitChanges()** is executed.
G. The **Faculty Name** combobox control **ComboName** is cleaned up to make it ready to be updated. Another user-defined method, **CurrentFaculty()**, is called to update all faculty names on that combobox.
H. Finally, the user-defined method **ClearFaculty()** is executed to clean up all textboxes in the **Faculty** page to make it ready for a validation for that updating next.

Before we can run our Web project to test these data actions, let's complete the coding for our data deleting action.

8.7.4.6 The Coding for the Data Deleting Query

Double-click on the **Delete** button from the Design View of our **Faculty** page to open its Click method and enter the codes that are shown in Figure 8.69 into this method.

WebLINQSQL Project | **cmdDelete_Click(object sender, EventArgs e)**

```
  protected void cmdDelete_Click(object sender, EventArgs e)
  {
A     var faculty = (from fi in cse_dept.Faculties
                     where fi.faculty_id == txtFacultyID.Text
                     select fi).Single();
B     cse_dept.Faculties.DeleteOnSubmit(faculty);
C     cse_dept.SubmitChanges();
      // clean up all textboxes
D     txtFacultyID.Text = string.Empty;
      txtName.Text = string.Empty;
      txtTitle.Text = string.Empty;
      txtOffice.Text = string.Empty;
      txtPhone.Text = string.Empty;
      txtCollege.Text = string.Empty;
      txtEmail.Text = string.Empty;
E     PhotoBox.ImageUrl = null;
F     ComboName.Items.Clear();
      CurrentFaculty();
  }
```

FIGURE 8.69 The codes for the delete button click method.

Let's have a close look at this piece of codes to see how it works.

A. A LINQ selection query is first executed to pick up the faculty member to be deleted. This query is initialized with three clauses, **from**, **where** and **select**. The range variable **fi** is selected from the **Faculties**, which is an instance of our entity class **Faculty** and the **faculty_id** works as the query criterion for this query. All information related to the selected faculty members (**faculty_id**) will be retrieved back and stored in the query variable **faculty**. The **Single**() means that only a single or the first record is queried.
B. The system method **DeleteOnSubmit()** is executed to issue a deleting action to the faculty instance, **Faculties** in our DataContext class object **cse_dept**.
C. Another system method,**SubmitChanges()**, is executed to exactly perform this deleting action against data tables in our sample database. Only after this method is executed can the selected faculty record can be deleted from our database.
D. All textboxes stored information related to the deleted faculty are cleaned up by assigning an empty string to each of them.
E. The Faculty Image box, **PhotoBox**, is also cleaned up by assigning a **null** to its **ImageUrl** property.
F. The **Faculty Name** combobox is cleaned up to be ready to be updated, and then the user-defined method,**CurrentFaculty()**, is executed to get all current faculty names to reflect this faculty record deleting for all faculty members stored in that control.

Finally, let's do our coding for the **Back** button click method.

8.7.4.7 The Coding for the Back Button Click Method

The main function of this method is to close the database connection setup by the

DataContext object, release all resources used by the DataContext object during all data queries and actions, and transfer the program control back to the **Selection** page to enable users to perform the next preferred query.

Double-click on the **Back** button from the Design View of the **Faculty** page to open its click method and enter the codes shown in Figure 8.70 into that method. Let's have a closer look at this piece of codes to see how it works.

A. As this **Back** button is clicked, which means that all query actions have been completed, the connection to our sample database is no longer to be used. Thus, that connection should be closed by calling the system method **Close**().
B. In addition, all resources used by the DataContext instance, **cse_dept**, should be released by executing another system method **Dispose()**.
C. Finally, the program control is transferred back to the **Selection** page to enable users to perform any other preferred data query based on that page.

WebLINQSQL Project	cmdBack_Click(object sender, EventArgs e)

```
  protected void cmdBack_Click(object sender, EventArgs e)
  {
A     cse_dept.Connection.Close();
B     cse_dept.Dispose();
C     Response.Redirect("Selection.aspx");
  }
```

FIGURE 8.70 The codes for the Back button's click method.

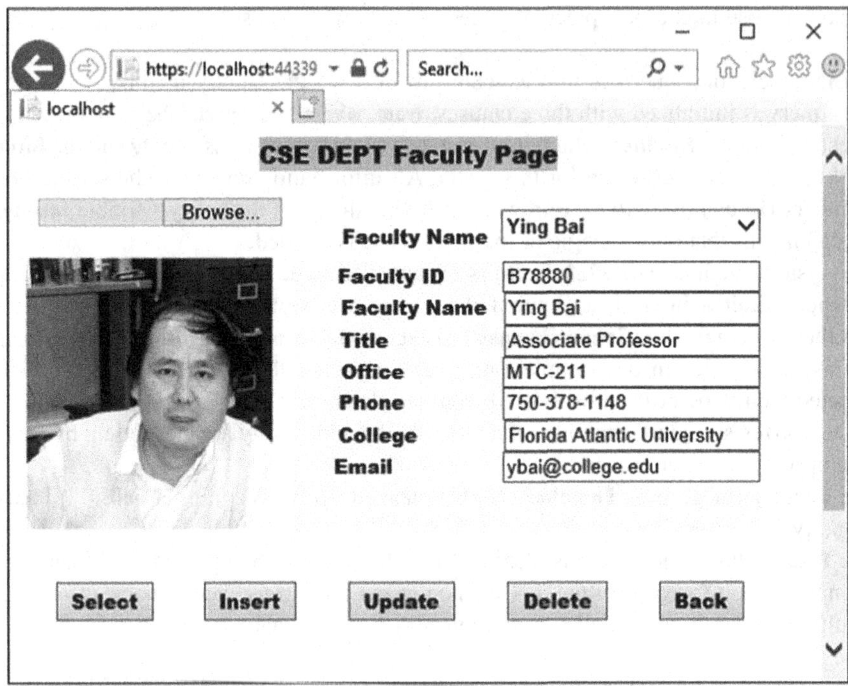

FIGURE 8.71 The queried result for a selected faculty record.

Now we can build and run our Web project **WebLINQSQL Project** to test the data query actions against our sample database.

First let's test the data selection query by opening the **Faculty** page after the login process is done. On the opened Faculty page, select the faculty member **Ying Bai** from the **Faculty Name** combobox, and click on the **Select** button to try to retrieve back all information related to that selected faculty. The query result is shown in Figure 8.71.

To insert a new faculty member into the **Faculty** table in our sample database, enter the following information into seven textboxes in the **Faculty** page:

Faculty ID textbox:	**S52877**
Faculty Name textbox:	**Smith Lane**
Title textbox:	**Assistant Professor**
Office textbox:	**MTC-200**
Phone textbox:	**750-330-2288**
College textbox:	**University of Kansas**
Email textbox:	**slane@college.edu**

Your finished faculty insertion page should match one that is shown in Figure 8.72.

Then click on the **Insert** button when you finish these data entering to all textboxes to try to perform this data insertion. A warning message is displayed to remind us to first select a valid faculty image via the **FileUpLoadImage** component. Go to that component by clicking on the **Browse** button to browse to the folder **Images\Faculty** under the **Students** folder on the CRC Press ftp site. One can copy those faculty images and save them into a folder on your local machine. Then select a desired faculty image, such as **Wang.jpg**, and click on the **Insert** button again to perform this data insertion action.

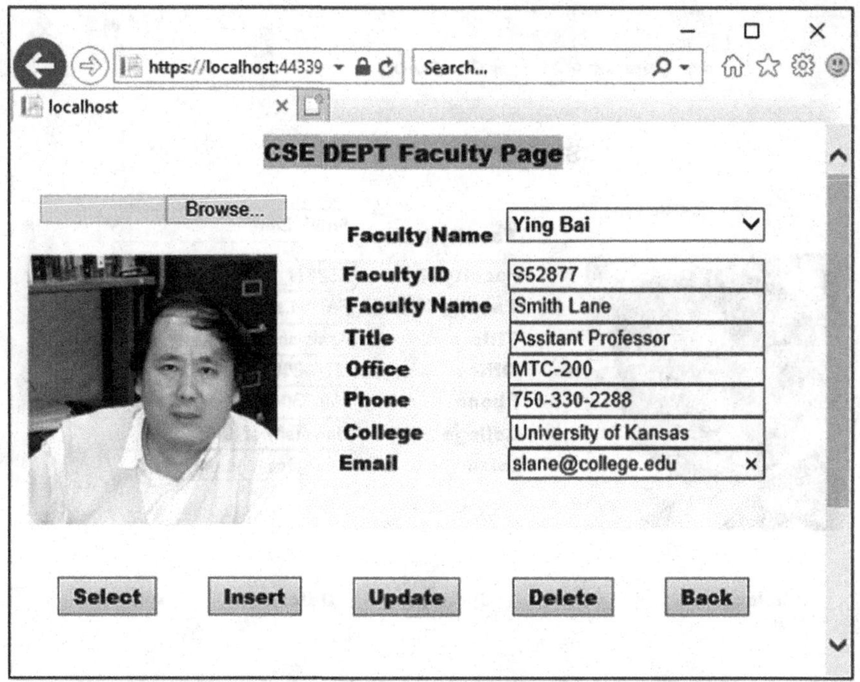

FIGURE 8.72 The finished new faculty record to be inserted.

Immediately, all seven textboxes contained a new inserted faculty record are cleaned up with the **Insert** button being disabled. To test and confirm this data insertion, go to the **Faculty Name** combobox, and the new inserted faculty member, **Smith Lane**, has been in there. Select that member and click on the **Select** button to try to retrieve that new record. Your confirmation page should match one that is shown in Figure 8.73.

Now let's test the data updating and deleting functions. First let's take care of the data updating action.

Select the faculty name, **Ying Bai**, from the **Faculty Name** combobox by clicking on it and then click on the **Select** button to get that record. Next, update that faculty record by entering the following data items into the associated textbox as an updated record:

Faculty Name:	**Susan Bai**
Title:	**Professor**
Office:	**MTC-228**
Phone:	**750-378-8655**
College:	**DukeUniversity**
Email:	**sbai@college.edu**

Now, click on the **Browse** button on the **FileUploadImage** object to browse to your local folder where all faculty images are stored, select the faculty image **White.jpg**, and click on the **Open** button. Then click the **Update** button to update this faculty record in the **Faculty** table in our sample database.

To confirm this data updating action, go to the **Faculty Name** combobox, and one can find that the updated faculty member, **Susan Bai**, has been there. Select that member and click on the **Select** button to try to get that updated record back. Immediately the updated faculty record is displayed in this page, as shown in Figure 8.74.

FIGURE 8.73 The testing and confirmation status of the data insertion action.

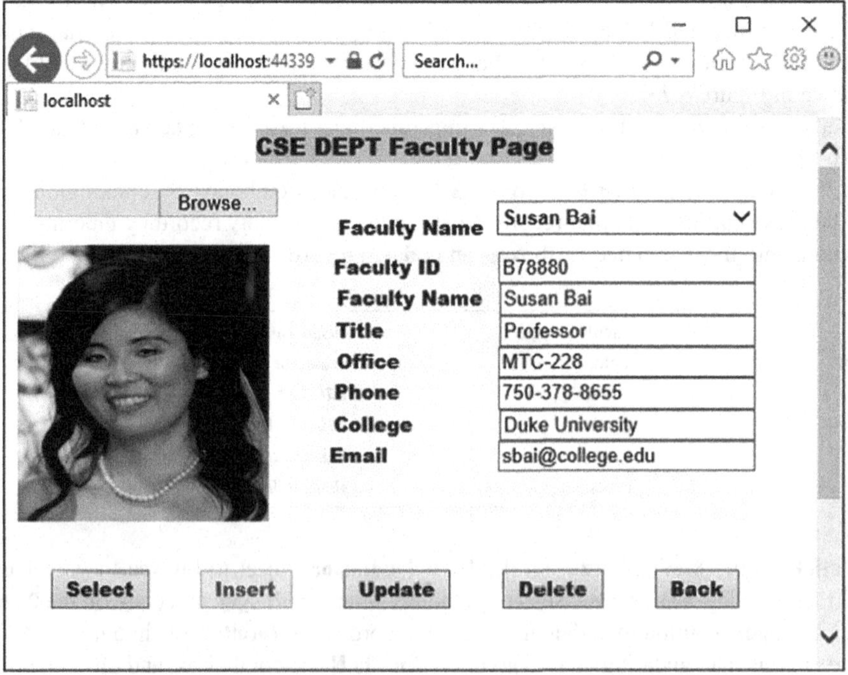

FIGURE 8.74 The confirmation page for the updated faculty record.

It is highly recommended that you recover this updated faculty record back to its original one. Just perform another data updating action with this **Update** button again to complete that recovery job.

Finally, let's test the data deleting function.

As we discussed in Section 8.6.2, to delete an original faculty record from the **Faculty** table in our sample database is a very complicated and time-consuming process due to the primary and foreign keys relationships among tables. To delete an original faculty member, not only is the faculty record in the **Faculty** table removed, but also all records related to that faculty member in all child tables are also deleted. Moreover, it would be a terrible process to recover that deleted faculty record since one must first recover that deleted record from the parent table, and then recover the related records in the child tables.

Therefore to make this data deleting easier, here we want to delete a faculty record that was inserted in this section but not an original faculty record (the so-called original faculty member is a member that is created when the database is generated).

To perform that deleting action, select the faculty member, **Smith Lane**, from the **Faculty Name** combobox, and click on the **Delete** button to try to delete it. Immediately, all seven textboxes and the faculty image box become blank, which means that our data deleting action is successful.

To test and confirm that data deleting action, go to the **Faculty Name** combobox, and one can find that the faculty member, **Smith Land**, has gone.

One point to be noted is that you had better recover that deleted faculty record if any original faculty record, such as **Ying Bai**, is deleted since we want to keep our database neat and complete. Refer to Figures 8.49–8.52 in Section 8.6.2.4 to recover that deleted faculty record **Ying Bai** in our sample database.

A complete Web page application project **WebLINQSQL Project** can be found from the folder **Class DB Projects\Chapter 8\WebLINQSQL Solution** that is under the **Students** folder on the CRC Press ftp site (refer to Figure 1.2 in Chapter 1).

In the following sections, we discuss how to query data from another data table in our sample database, **Course** table, with the LINQ to SQL method via the ASP.NET Web applications.

8.8 DEVELOP WEB APPLICATIONS TO QUERY COURSE TABLE WITH LINQ TO SQL METHOD

We do not need to create any new Web application project to perform any query from the **Course** table by using the LINQ to SQL technique; instead, we can modify one of our Web application projects, **WebLINQSQL Project**, to make it our new project **WebLINQSQL_Course Project**. Perform the following operations to complete this modification and creation for our new Web application project:

1) Open the Windows Explorer or File Explorer and locate the Web application solution folder **WebLINQSQL Solution** in your local machine (**C:\Chapter 8**).
2) Right-click on that solution folder and select the **Copy** item to copy that solution with the project, and paste that folder under the same location in your local machine, such as **C:\Chapter 8**.
3) Rename both folders' names to **WebLINQSQL_Course Solution** and **WebLINQSQL_ Course Project**, respectively.
4) Expand the new solution folder **WebLINQSQL_Course Solution** and click on the new project folder **WebLINQSQL_Course Project** to open it in the File Explorer.
5) Change the following two files' names, **WebLINQSQL Project.csproj** and **WebLINQSQL Project.csproj.user**, to **WebLINQSQL_Course Project.csproj** and **WebLINQSQL_Course Project.csproj.user**.
6) Now double-click on the new project **WebLINQSQL_Course Project.csproj** to open it in the Visual Studio 2022.

A key point to be noted is that even we changed the solution and project's names, but the project's namespace is kept with no change because it would be a very complicated process if we changed the namespace from **SQLWebSelect_Project** to **WebLINQSQL_Course _Project**.

Now let's start from the **Course** page to perform a data query from the **Course** table in our SQL Server sample database.

8.8.1 Develop the Codes to Query Course Record from the Course Table

In this section, we need to divide our coding process into the following seven parts:

1) Create a new object of the DataContext class and do some initialization coding.
2) Develop the codes for the **Select** button's Click method to retrieve back all courses, exactly **course_id**, taught by the selected faculty member using the LINQ to SQL query.
3) Develop the codes for the **SelectedIndexChanged** event method of the **CourseList** box to get back details for a selected **course_id** and display them in six textboxes in this **Course** page.
4) Develop the codes for the **Insert** button's Click method to insert new course record into the **Course** table using the LINQ to SQL query.
5) Develop the codes for the **Update** button's Click method to update an existing course using the LINQ to SQL query.
6) Develop codes for the **Delete** button's Click method to delete an existing course from the **Course** table in our sample database using the LINQ to SQL query.
7) Develop codes for the **Back** button click method to return to the **Selection** page.

First let's take care of the coding process for the **Page_Load()** method.

8.8.1.1 Create a New Object of the DataContext Class

Open the code window and the **Page_Load()** method of the **Course** Web page, and enter the codes that are shown in Figure 8.75 into this method.

Let's have a close look at this piece of codes to see how it works.

A. A new field-level object of the DataContext class, **cse_dept**, is created first since we need to use this object to connect our sample database to this Web project to perform the data actions later. A point is that a namespace **WebLINQSQL_Project** must be prefixed to that class since that class is generated in that project.

B. A user-defined method,**CurrentFaculty()**, is executed to retrieve back all current faculty members from our sample database and display them in the **ComboName** combobox control to allow users to select a desired faculty later. To avoid the multiple displaying of retrieved faculty members, an **if** selection structure is adopted to make sure that we only displaying those current faculty members in the combobox at the first time as this Web page is loaded, and will not display them each time as the server sends back a refreshed **Course** page to the client.

C. The first faculty member is selected as a default one to be selected in that control.

D. Inside the user-defined method, before we can update the combobox control **ComboName** by adding all current faculty members into this control, a cleaning job is performed to avoid the multiple adding and displaying of those faculty members later.

E. The LINQ query is created and initialized with three clauses, **from**, **let** and **select**. The range variable **fi** is selected from the **Faculty** entity in our sample database. All current faculty members (**faculty_name**) will be read back using the **let** clause and assigned to the query variable **faculty**.

F. The LINQ query is executed to pick up all queried faculty members and add them into the **ComboName** combobox control in our **Course** page.

Next let's concentrate on the coding for the **Select** button's click method.

```
WebLINQSQL_Course Project   ▼   Page_Load(object sender, EventArgs e)   ▼

using System;
using System.Linq;
namespace SQLWebSelect_Project
{
    public partial class Course : System.Web.UI.Page
    {
A       WebLINQSQL_Project.CSE_DEPTDataContext cse_dept = new WebLINQSQL_Project.CSE_DEPTDataContext();
        protected void Page_Load(object sender, EventArgs e)
        {
            if (!IsPostBack)
            {
B               CurrentFaculty();
C               ComboName.SelectedIndex = 0;
            }
        }
        void CurrentFaculty()
        {
D           ComboName.Items.Clear();
E           var faculty = (from fi in cse_dept.Faculties
                           let fields = "faculty_name"
                           select fi);
F           foreach (var f in faculty)
                ComboName.Items.Add(f.faculty_name);
        }
    }
}
```

FIGURE 8.75 Initialization codes for the faculty web page.

```
WebLINQSQL_Course Project   ▼   cmdSelect_Click(object sender, EventArgs e)   ▼

protected void cmdSelect_Click(object sender, EventArgs e)
{
A   var c_info = from ci in cse_dept.Courses
                 join fi in cse_dept.Faculties on ci.faculty_id equals fi.faculty_id
                 where (fi.faculty_name == ComboName.Text)
                 select ci;
B   CourseList.Items.Clear();
C   foreach (var cid in c_info)
        CourseList.Items.Add(cid.course_id);
}
```

FIGURE 8.76 The codes for the select button click method.

8.8.1.2 The Coding for the Data Selection Query

The function of this click method is: when the user selected a desired faculty member from the **Faculty Name** combobox and clicks the **Select** button, all **course_id** related to courses taught by the selected faculty member should be retrieved from the database and displayed in the list box control **CourseList** on the **Course** page.

Double-click on the **Select** button from the Design View of the **Course** page to open its Click method, and enter the codes that are shown in Figure 8.76 into this method.

Let's have a close look at this piece of codes to see how it works.

A. An inner joined LINQ query is generated first due to the relationships between the **Course** and the **Faculty** tables in our sample database. As we know, there is no **faculty_name** column available in the **Course** table, and the only column related to the **Faculty** table is the

faculty_id, which is a primary key in the **Faculty** table but a foreign key in the **Course** table. In order to get all matched **course_id** taught by the selected faculty member (**faculty_name**), an inner joined query is necessary. This kind of query joins two tables, **Faculty** and **Course**, together to meet two query criteria: **faculty_id** in both tables must be identical and the **faculty_name** must be equal to the selected **faculty_name** in the **Faculty Name** combobox in this page.

B. Prior to displaying all queried **course_id** in the **CourseList** box, that control must be cleaned up to avoid possible multiple query results to be displayed later.

C. The joined LINQ query is executed to pick up all matched **course_id** and add them into the **CourseList** box to display them in that box.

Now let's handle the coding for the **SelectedIndexChanged** event method of the course listbox control **CourseList** to get back details for a selected **course_id** and display them in six textboxes in this **Course** page.

8.8.1.3 The Coding for the SelectedIndexChanged Method of the CourseList Box

The function of this method is: when the user clicks any **course_id** from the list box control **CourseList**, the detailed course information related to the selected **course_id** in the list box, such as course id, course title, schedule, credit, classroom and enrollment, will be retrieved from the database and displayed in six textboxes on the **Course** page.

Double-click on the list box control **CourseList** from the Design View of the **Course** Web form to open this event method, and enter the codes that are shown in Figure 8.77 into this method.

Let's take a closer look at this piece of codes to see how it works.

A. A LINQ query is created and initialized with three clauses, **from**, **where** and **select**. The range variable **ci** is selected from the **Courses** entity in our sample database. All course details for the selected **course_id** will be read back using the **select** clause and assigned to the query variable **c_info**.

B. The LINQ query is executed to pick up each piece of course details and add each of them into the related textbox to display it in our **Course** page.

A point to be noted for this piece of codes is the data type for two columns, **credit** and **enrollment**, in the **Course** table. The former is a float and the latter is an integer. Thus, a system method **ToString()** must be used to convert both of them to text and then assign them to the related textbox.

```
WebLINQSQL_Course Project        CourseList_SelectedIndexChanged()

  protected void cmdSelect_Click(object sender, EventArgs e)
  {
A     var c_info = from ci in cse_dept.Courses
                   where ci.course_id == CourseList.SelectedItem.ToString()
                   select ci;
B     foreach (var c in c_info)
      {
        txtCourseID.Text = c.course_id;
        txtCourse.Text = c.course1;
        txtCredit.Text = c.credit.ToString();
        txtClassroom.Text = c.classroom;
        txtSchedule.Text = c.schedule;
        txtEnroll.Text = c.enrollment.ToString();
      }
  }
```

FIGURE 8.77 The codes for the SelectedIndexChanged() method.

As the project runs, another important point to be noted is the **AutoPostBack** property of the **CourseList** box control. Refer to Section 8.4.9.1 in this chapter to get more details about that property and its affection. Double check to make sure that it is set to **true**; otherwise, there is no any response when you click and select a **course_id** from the **CourseList** box to try to display details for each selected **course_id**.

Now let's test the codes we built to confirm the functions of this data query via LINQ to SQL method.

Click on the **IIS Express** button to run our project. Complete the login process and open the **Course** page. On the opened **Course** page, select a desired faculty member, such as **Ying Bai**, from the **Faculty Name** combobox, and click on the **Select** button to get all courses (**course_id**) taught by that faculty member. The results of this selection are shown in Figure 8.78. All **course_id** are retrieved and displayed in the **CourseList** box.

Then select one course by clicking a **course_id** from the **CourseList** box, the details for that selected course are shown in six textboxes, as shown in Figure 8.78.

Now just click on the **Close** button located at the upper-right corner of this page to close and terminate our project since we have not do our coding for the **Back** button.

Next let's discuss how to insert a new course record into the **Course** table in our sample database. However we need to emphasize one compiling issue prior to doing that.

One possible bug when compiling or building this project is that a missed file under the **packages** folder cannot be found. The possible reason for that is due to our creation of this project, which is modified from one of our projects, **SQLWebSelect Project**. The project Solution name may have not been changed correctly. To solve this issue, go to our current project solution folder, **WebLINQSQL_Course Solution** and remove the original solution, **WebLINQSQL Solution.sln**, from that folder. Then go to **File | Save All** menu item to save the current solution. Click the **Yes** and **Overwrite** button to make it our new project solution.

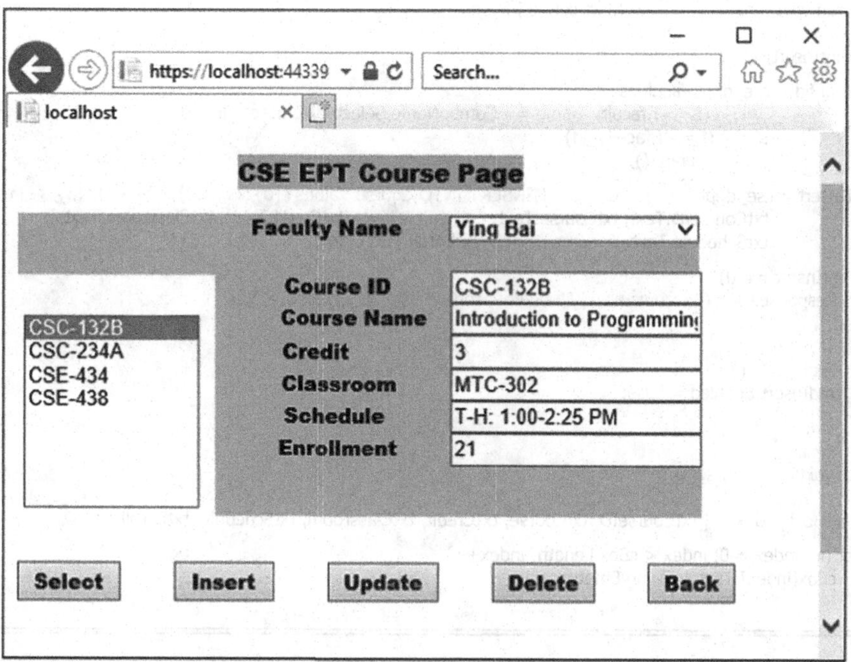

FIGURE 8.78 The running result for our course data query.

8.8.2 Develop the Codes to Insert a New Course Record into the Course Table

To insert a new course record into the **Course** table in our sample database via the LINQ to SQL method, we need to use the **Insert** button's click method. The function of this method is: when the user enters all six pieces of new course information, such as course id, course title, schedule, credit, classroom and enrollment, into the six related textboxes in this **Course** page with a selected faculty member, and click on the **Insert** button, a new course record will be inserted into our database.

Double-click on the **Insert** button from the Design View of the **Course** Web page to open this event method, and enter the codes that are shown in Figure 8.79 into this method. Let's take a closer look at this piece of codes to see how it works.

- **A.** A local integer variable **intInsert** is first generated and it will be used to hold the running result of the **ExecuteCommand()** method later.
- **B.** Since there is no faculty name column available and the only available column is **faculty_id** in the **Course** table, we need to perform two queries to perform this data insertion; first query a matched **faculty_id** from the **Faculty** table based on a selected faculty name by the user, and then perform a new course insertion action based on that **faculty_id** to the **Course** table. The first query starts in step **B**, where the Lambda expression (=>) is used for this LINQ query (refer to Section 4.9.1 in Chapter 4 to get more details about that expression). The query criterion in the **Where** clause is a selected faculty name from the **ComboName** combobox and it must be converted from an object type to a String type. The **FirstOrDefault()** method is used to select the first matched **faculty_id**, exactly only one or a single **faculty_id** available for that query.
- **C.** The **ExecuteCommand()** is called to perform this data insertion action with the selected **faculty_id** from the above query. One point to be noted is the parameter object part; the data

```
WebLINQSQL_Course Project        cmdInsert_Click(object sender, EventArgs e)

  protected void cmdInsert_Click(object sender, EventArgs e)
  {
A     int intInsert;
B     string fid = cse_dept.Faculties
                 .Where(f => f.faculty_name == ComboName.SelectedItem.ToString())
                 .Select(f => f.faculty_id)
                 .FirstOrDefault();
C     intInsert = cse_dept.ExecuteCommand("INSERT INTO Course Values ({0}, {1}, {2}, {3}, {4}, {5}, {6}) ",
                 txtCourseID.Text, txtCourse.Text, Convert.ToInt16(txtCredit.Text), txtClassroom.Text,
                 txtSchedule.Text, Convert.ToInt32(txtEnroll.Text), fid);
D     if (intInsert == 0)
         Response.Write("<script>alert('The data insertion is failed')</script>");
E     else
      {
         ClearCourse();
         cmdInsert.Enabled = false;
      }
  }
  private void ClearCourse()
  {
F     TextBox[] cBox = { txtCourseID, txtCourse, txtCredit, txtClassroom, txtSchedule, txtEnroll };
G     for (int index = 0; index < cBox.Length; index++)
         cBox[index].Text = String.Empty;
  }
```

FIGURE 8.79 The codes for the insert button click method.

types for the **Credit** and **Enrollment** columns are small integer and integer, thus the related parameters must be converted to the matched types.

D. The running result of **ExecuteCommand()** method is assigned to the local variable **intInsert**, that result is represented as an integer number and its value is equal to the number of records that have been inserted into the database successfully. If a value of zero is returned, which means that no any record has been inserted into our database and that insertion action is failed. A warning message is displayed for that case.

E. Otherwise, our data insertion is successful, a user-defined method **ClearCourse()** is called to clean up all six textboxes in the **Course** page to indicate that case, and the **Insert** button is disabled to avoid multiple duplicated insertions to be occurred.

F. Inside the user-defined method **ClearCourse()**, a textbox array **cBox[]** is declared first to hold all six textboxes as a collection object.

G. Then a **for()** loop is utilized to assign an empty string to each textbox in the textbox array **cBox[]** to clean all of them one by one.

Now let's test the codes we built to confirm the functions of this data insertion via LINQ to SQL method.

Click on the **IIS Express** button to run our project. Complete the login process and open the **Course** page. On the opened **Course** page, select a desired faculty member, such as **Ying Bai**, from the **Faculty Name** combobox, and click on the **Select** button to get all courses (**course_id**) taught by that faculty member.

Then select one course by clicking a **course_id** from the **CourseList** box, the details for that selected course are shown in six textboxes. Keep the selected faculty name with no changed and enter the following data items into six textboxes as a new course record:

Faculty Name:	**Ying Bai**
Course ID:	**CSE-668**
Course Name:	**Modern Controls**
Credits:	**3**
Classroom:	**MTC-309**
Schedule:	**M-W-F: 9:00 – 9:50 AM**
Enrollment:	**30**

Now click on the **Insert** button to insert this new record into the **Course** table in our sample database. Immediately, all textboxes become empty.

To check or confirm this data insertion action, just click the **Select** button again to get back all courses (**course_id**) taught by the faculty member **Ying Bai**. The new inserted course, **CSE-668**, can be found from the **CourseList** box. Select that new course by clicking on it from the listbox and the details for that course are shown in six textboxes, as shown in Figure 8.80. Just click on the **Close** button on the upper-right corner on this page to close our project. Later on we will build codes for the **Back** button to do this closing.

Next let's concentrate on the coding for the **Update** button's click method to handle our data updating function.

8.8.3 Develop the Codes to Update a Course Record in the Course Table

The purpose of using the **Update** button's click method is to update an existing course record as the user updated five pieces of information (exclude the **course_id**) on the **Course** page and clicked the **Update** button.

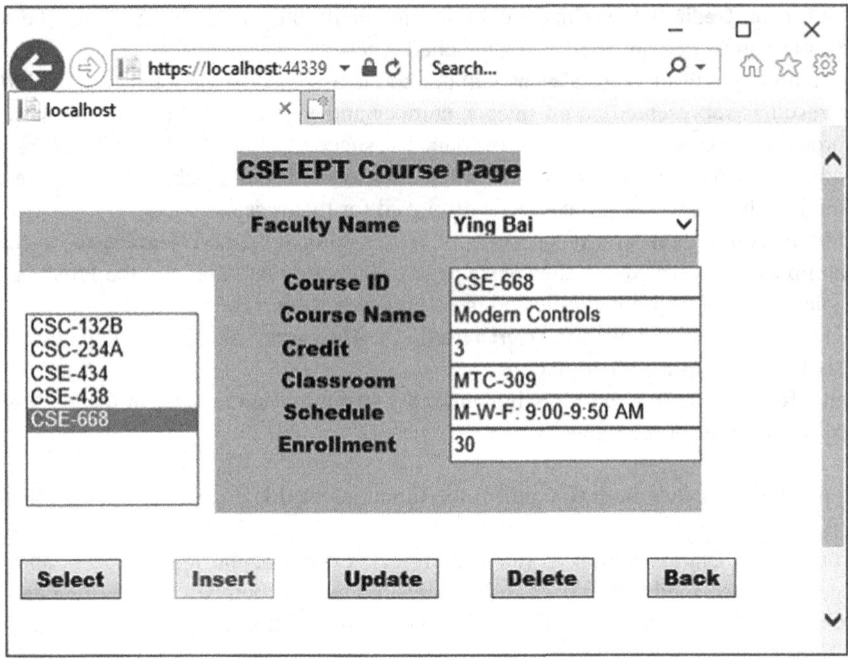

FIGURE 8.80 The running result of inserting a new record into the course table.

```
WebLINQSQL_Course Project          cmdUpdate_Click(object sender, EventArgs e)

  protected void cmdUpdate_Click(object sender, EventArgs e)
  {
A     int intUpdate;
B     intUpdate = cse_dept.ExecuteCommand("UPDATE Course SET course = {0}, credit = {1}, classroom = {2},
                              schedule = {3}, enrollment = {4} WHERE course_id = {5}", txtCourse.Text,
                              Convert.ToInt16(txtCredit.Text), txtClassroom.Text, txtSchedule.Text,
                              Convert.ToInt32(txtEnroll.Text), txtCourseID.Text);
C     if (intUpdate == 0)
         Response.Write("<script>alert('The data updating is failed')</script>");
D     else
         ClearCourse();
  }
```

FIGURE 8.81 The codes for the update button click method.

Open this method by double-clicking on the **Update** button from the Design View of the **Course** Web page and enter the codes that are shown in Figure 8.81 into this method.

Let's take a closer look at this piece of codes to see how it works.

A. A local integer variable **intUpdate** is created and it works as a holder to keep the returned updating result from the execution of the **ExecuteCommand()** method later.

B. The data updating query command string is generated with a format as we discussed in Section 8.7.4.3. Each specified dynamic parameter must be enclosed with a brace ({…}) and enumerated starting from 0.

C. The running result of **ExecuteCommand()** method, which is an integer number, is assigned to our local variable **intUpdate**. If this value is zero, which means that no any record has been updated and that data updating action is failed. A warning message is displayed to indicate that case.

D. Otherwise the data updating action is successful. The user-defined method **ClearCourse()** is called to clean up all six textboxes in the **Course** page to enable users to check and confirm that data updating action.

Now let's test the codes we built to confirm the functions of this data updating via LINQ to SQL method.

Click on the **IIS Express** button to run our project. Complete the login process and open the **Course** page. On the opened **Course** page, select a desired faculty member, such as **Ying Bai**, from the **Faculty Name** combobox, and click on the **Select** button to get all courses (**course_id**) taught by that faculty member.

Then select one course by clicking a **course_id** from the **CourseList** box, the details for that selected course are shown in six textboxes. Keep the selected faculty name with no changed and select a **course_id**, **CSE-668**, from the **CourseList** box. Then enter the following data items into five textboxes as an updated course record:

Course Name:	**Deep Learning**
Credits:	**3**
Classroom:	**MTC-228**
Schedule:	**M-W-F: 1:00 – 1:50 PM**
Enrollment:	**22**

Now click on the **Update** button to update this course record in the **Course** table in our sample database. Immediately, all textboxes become empty.

To check or confirm this data updating action, just click the **Select** button again to get back all courses (**course_id**) taught by the faculty member **Ying Bai**. The updated course, **CSE-668**, can be found from the **CourseList** box. Select that course by clicking on it from the listbox and the details for that course are shown in six textboxes, as shown in Figure 8.82.

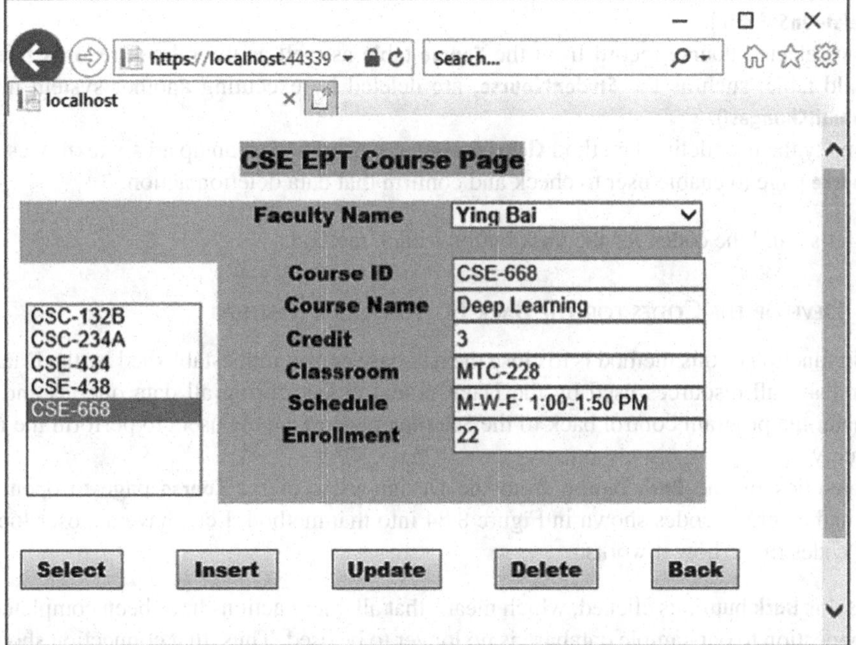

FIGURE 8.82 The running result of data updating for the course table.

```
WebLINQSQL_Course Project          cmdDelete_Click(object sender, EventArgs e)

  protected void cmdDelete_Click(object sender, EventArgs e)
  {
A     var course = (from ci in cse_dept.Courses
                    where ci.course_id == txtCourseID.Text
                    select ci).Single();

B     cse_dept.Courses.DeleteOnSubmit(course);
C     cse_dept.SubmitChanges();
D     ClearCourse();
  }
```

FIGURE 8.83 The codes for the delete button click method.

One can find that the course record is really updated after this data updating action.

Just click on the **Close** button on the upper-right corner on this page to close our project. Later on, we will build codes for the **Back** button to do this closing.

Next let's concentrate on the coding for the **Delete** button's click method to handle our data deleting function.

8.8.4 Develop the Codes to Delete a Course Record from the Course Table

The function of this method is to delete an existing course record from the **Course** table as this Delete button is clicked by the user. Double-click on the **Delete** button from the Design View of our **Course** page to open its Click method and enter the codes that are shown in Figure 8.83 into this method.

Let's have a closer look at this piece of codes to see how it works.

A. First a Select query is created and performed to retrieve a course record to be deleted from the **Course** table. The query criterion is a specific **course_id** located at the Course ID textbox. The Standard Query Operator method **Single()** is used to retrieve back only a single course record.

B. The queried course record is placed into the deleting pool with a system method **DeleteOnSubmit()**.

C. The selected course record from the **Course** table as well as the related records from the child table, such as the **StudentCourse**, are deleted by executing another system method **SubmitChanges()**.

D. Finally the user defined method **ClearCourse()** is executed to clean up all six textboxes in the **Course** page to enable user to check and confirm that data deletion action.

Finally, let's build the codes for the **Back** button's click method.

8.8.5 Develop the Codes for the Back Button Click Method

The main function of this method is to close the database connection established by the DataContext object, release all resources used by the DataContext object during all data queries and actions, and transfer the program control back to the **Selection** page to enable users to perform the next preferred query.

Double-click on the **Back** button from the Design View of the **Course** page to open its click method and enter the codes shown in Figure 8.84 into that method. Let's have a closer look at this piece of codes to see how it works.

A. As this **Back** button is clicked, which means that all query actions have been completed, the connection to our sample database is no longer to be used. Thus, that connection should be closed by calling the system method **Close**().

```
WebLINQSQL Project                    cmdBack_Click(object sender, EventArgs e)

    protected void cmdBack_Click(object sender, EventArgs e)
    {
A       cse_dept.Connection.Close();
B       cse_dept.Dispose();
C       Response.Redirect("Selection.aspx");
    }
```

FIGURE 8.84 The codes for the back button's click method.

B. Also all resources used by the DataContext instance, **cse_dept**, should be released by executing another system method **Dispose()**.
C. Finally, the program control is transferred back to the **Selection** page to enable users to perform any other preferred data query based on that page.

At this point, we have all coding development for the course record queries and implementations via the LINQ to SQL method.

Now let's test the codes we built to confirm the functions of this data deletion and **Back** button click method via the LINQ to SQL method.

Click on the **IIS Express** button to run our project. Complete the login process and open the **Course** page. On the opened **Course** page, select a desired faculty member, such as **Ying Bai**, from the **Faculty Name** combobox, and click on the **Select** button to get all courses (**course_id**) taught by that faculty member.

Then select one course by clicking a **course_id** from the **CourseList** box, the details for that selected course are shown in six textboxes. Keep the selected faculty name with no changed and select a **course_id**, **CSE-668**, from the **CourseList** box. Click on the **Delete** button to try to delete this record from the **Course** table in our sample database.

To check and confirm this data deleting action, keep the selected faculty member with no changed, and click on the **Select** button to try to retrieve all courses (**course_id**) taught by that faculty member. One can find that the course **CSE-668** has been disappeared or removed from the **CourseList** box. This means that our data deleting action is successful.

Since the course **CSE-668** is a new inserted or added course into the **Course** table in our database in Section 8.8.2; thus, no any related record in the child table **StudentCourse** to be deleted. However, if an original course record that is created as our sample database is generated is deleted, some related records in the child table, such as **StudentCourse**, will also be deleted.

Now click on the **Back** button, and then the **Exit** button from the **Selection** page to terminate our project.

A complete Web page application project **WebLINQSQL_Course Project** can be found from the folder **Class DB Projects\Chapter 8\WebLINQSQL_Course Solution** that is under the **Students** folder on the CRC Press ftp site (refer to Figure 1.2 in Chapter 1).

8.9 DEVELOP WEB APPLICATIONS TO QUERY STUDENT TABLE WITH STORED PROCEDURE METHOD

In Section 5.16 in Chapter 5, we discussed how to perform queries to the **Student** table in our sample database using the stored procedure method. Five stored procedures, **dbo.StudentInfo**, **dbo.StudentCourseInfo**, **dbo.StudentCourseINTO**, **dbo.StudentAndCourse**, and **dbo.StudentInfoID**, were generated to enable us to call them from C# Windows-based projects to perform related queries.

In this section, we try to use some of those stored procedures in our Web application projects to perform similar queries with LINQ to SQL technique.

We do not need to create any new Web application project to perform any query from the **Student** table; instead we can modify one of our previous Web application projects, **WebLINQSQL Project**, to make it our new project **WebSP_Student Project**. Perform the following operations to complete this modification and creation for our new Web application project:

1) Open the Windows Explorer or File Explorer and locate the Web application solution folder **WebLINQSQL Solution** in your local machine (**C:\Chapter 8**).
2) Right-click on that solution folder and select the **Copy** item to copy that solution with the project, and paste that folder under the same location in your local machine, such as **C:\Chapter 8**.
3) Rename both folders' names to **WebSP_Student Solution** and **WebSP_ Student Project**, respectively.
4) Expand the new solution folder **WebSP_Student Solution** and click on the new project folder **WebSP_Student Project** to open it in the File Explorer.
5) Change the following two files' names, **WebLINQSQL Project.csproj** and **WebLINQSQL Project.csproj.user**, to **WebSP_Student Project.csproj** and **WebSP_Student Project.csproj.user**.
6) Now double-click on the new project **WebSP_Student Project.csproj** to open it in the Visual Studio 2022.

A key point to be noted is that even we changed the solution and project's names, but the project's namespace is kept with no change because it would be a very complicated process if we changed the namespace from **SQLWebSelect_Project** to **WebSP_Student _Project**.

Now let's start to work for the **Student** page to perform data query from the **Student** and **StudentCourse** tables in our SQL Server sample database.

8.9.1 Develop the Codes to Query Student Record from the Student Table

In this section, we need to divide our coding process into the following four parts:

1) Create a new object of the DataContext class and do some initialization coding.
2) Develop the codes for the **Select** button's Click method to call the related stored procedure via LINQ to SQL to retrieve back selected student information.
3) Develop the codes for the **Select** button's method to call related stored procedures via LINQ to SQL to get all courses enrolled by the selected student.
4) Develop codes for the **Back** button Click method to return to the **Selection** page.

First let's take care of the coding process for the **Page_Load()** method.

8.9.1.1 Create a New Object of the DataContext Class

Open the code window and the **Page_Load()** method of the **Student** Web page, and enter the codes that are shown in Figure 8.85 into this method.

Let's have a closer look at this piece of codes to see how it works.

A. A new field-level object of the DataContext class, **cse_dept**, is created first since we need to use this object to connect our sample database to this Web project to perform the data actions later. A point is that the namespace **WebLINQSQL_Project** must be prefixed to that class since that class is generated in that project.
B. A user-defined method, **CurrentStudent()**, is executed to retrieve back all current students' names from our sample database and display them in the **ComboName** combobox control to allow users to select a desired student later. To avoid multiple displaying of retrieved student members, an **if** selection structure is adopted to make sure that we are only displaying

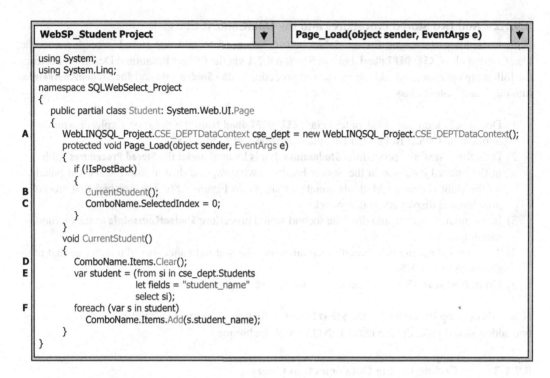

```
WebSP_Student Project    Page_Load(object sender, EventArgs e)

  using System;
  using System.Linq;
  namespace SQLWebSelect_Project
  {
     public partial class Student: System.Web.UI.Page
     {
A       WebLINQSQL_Project.CSE_DEPTDataContext cse_dept = new WebLINQSQL_Project.CSE_DEPTDataContext();
        protected void Page_Load(object sender, EventArgs e)
        {
           if (!IsPostBack)
           {
B             CurrentStudent();
C             ComboName.SelectedIndex = 0;
           }
        }
        void CurrentStudent()
        {
D          ComboName.Items.Clear();
E          var student = (from si in cse_dept.Students
                          let fields = "student_name"
                          select si);
F          foreach (var s in student)
              ComboName.Items.Add(s.student_name);
        }
  }
```

FIGURE 8.85 Initialization codes for the student web page.

those current students in the combobox at the first time as this Web page is loaded, and will not display them each time as the server sends back a refreshed **Student** page to the client.

C. The first student is selected as a default one to be selected in that control.

D. Inside the user-defined method, before we can update the combobox control **ComboName** by adding all current students' names into that control, a cleaning job is performed to avoid the multiple adding and displaying of those students.

E. A LINQ query is created and initialized with three clauses, **from**, **let** and **select**. The range variable **si** is selected from the **Student** entity in our sample database. All current students (**student_name**) will be read back using the **let** clause and assigned to the query variable **student**.

F. The LINQ query is executed to pick up all queried students' names and add them into the **ComboName** combobox control in our **Student** page.

The reason we still used the LINQ to SQL method to perform this student query is because of its simplicity in coding structure. One can use a different query method to do this query job. Perform the following operations to save our new project and our solution:

1) Go to **File | Save All** menu to save our new project with solution. On the opened File Explorer, click on the **Save** and **Overwrite** button, and the **Save** button again.
2) Then open the Windows Explorer or File Explorer and click on our new solution folder **WebSP_Student Solution**, and delete the original solution file, **WebLINQSQL Solution.sln** since we no longer need that file.
3) Go to **Build | Rebuild WebSP_Student Project** menu item to rebuild our project.

Next let's do the coding for the Select button's click method. However, before we can do that coding process, we need to add two stored procedures into our DataContext class.

8.9.1.2 Add Two Stored Procedures into the DataContext Class

Prior to building the codes for the **Select** button, we need to add our stored procedures to the DataContext class, **CSE_DEPT.dbml**, built in Section 8.7.1 via the Object Relational Designer. Perform the following operations to add our two stored procedures, **dbo.StudentInfo** and **dbo.StudentCourseInfo**, into our DataContext class:

1) Double-click on our DataContext class **CSE_DEPT.dbml** from the Solution Explorer window to open the Object Relational Designer, as shown in Figure 8.86.
2) Drag the first stored procedure, **StudentInfo** that is located under the **Stored Procedures** folder in the opened database in the Server Explorer window, and drop it into the second panel on the right (Creating Methods panel), as shown in Figure 8.86. The finished first stored procedure is displayed on that panel.
3) In a similar way, drag and drop the second stored procedure **StudentCourseInfo** to the method panel, too.
4) The finished adding two stored procedures into the method panel should match one that is shown in Figure 8.86.
5) Go to **File | Save All** menu item to save those added operations.

Now let's develop the codes for the **Select** button's click method to query student records by calling two added stored procedures via the LINQ to SQL technique.

8.9.1.3 The Coding for the Data Selection Query

The function of this click method is: when the user selected a desired student from the **Student Name** combobox and clicks the **Select** button, a stored procedure **dbo.StudentInfo** built in Section 5.16.3, should be called to get all detailed information related to that student and displayed in seven textboxes with a selected student image in the **Student** page. In addition to displaying detailed student

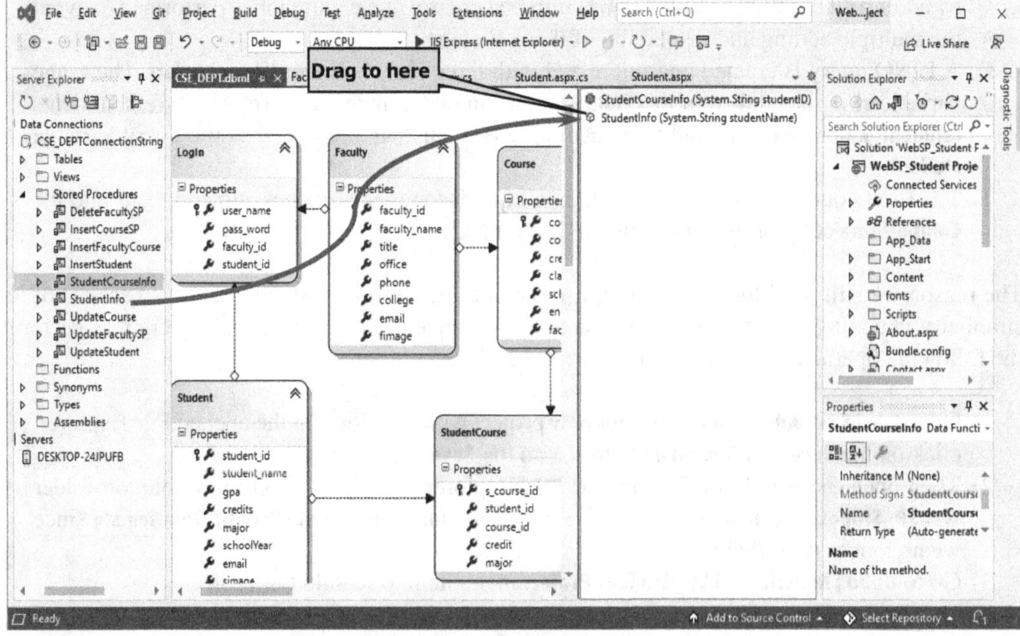

FIGURE 8.86 The added two stored procedures as methods or functions.

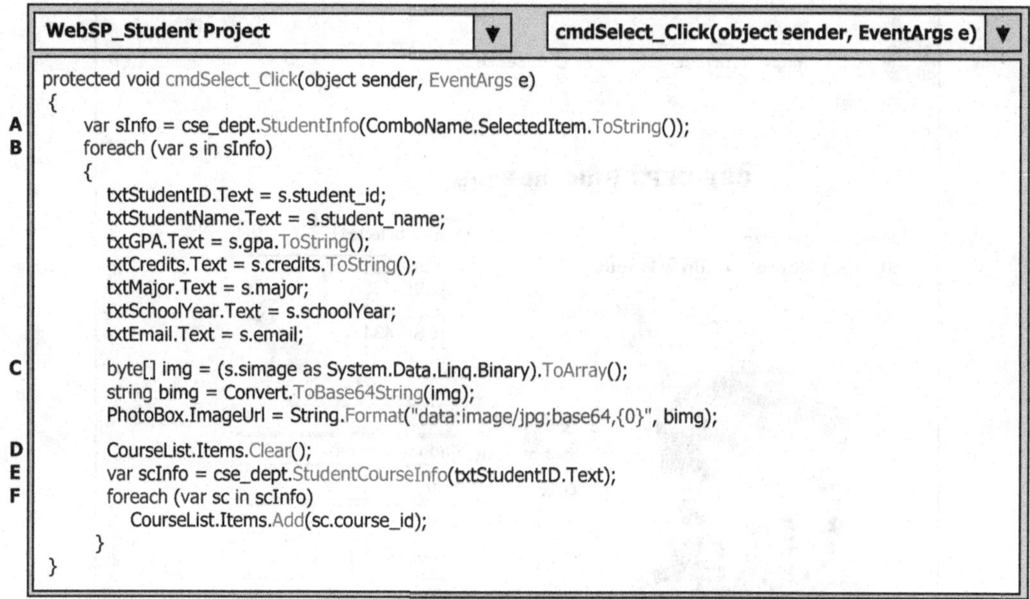


```
  protected void cmdSelect_Click(object sender, EventArgs e)
  {
A     var sInfo = cse_dept.StudentInfo(ComboName.SelectedItem.ToString());
B     foreach (var s in sInfo)
      {
          txtStudentID.Text = s.student_id;
          txtStudentName.Text = s.student_name;
          txtGPA.Text = s.gpa.ToString();
          txtCredits.Text = s.credits.ToString();
          txtMajor.Text = s.major;
          txtSchoolYear.Text = s.schoolYear;
          txtEmail.Text = s.email;
C         byte[] img = (s.simage as System.Data.Linq.Binary).ToArray();
          string bimg = Convert.ToBase64String(img);
          PhotoBox.ImageUrl = String.Format("data:image/jpg;base64,{0}", bimg);
D         CourseList.Items.Clear();
E         var scInfo = cse_dept.StudentCourseInfo(txtStudentID.Text);
F         foreach (var sc in scInfo)
              CourseList.Items.Add(sc.course_id);
      }
  }
```

FIGURE 8.87 The completed codes for the select button's click method.

information, all courses enrolled by the selected student should also be displayed in the **CourseList** box by calling another stored procedure **dbo.StudentCourseInfo**.

Double-click on the **Select** button from the Design View of the **Student** page to open its Click method, and enter the codes that are shown in Figure 8.87 into this method.

Let's have a closer look at this piece of codes to see how it works.

A. The first stored procedure **StudentInfo()** is called with the LINQ to SQL format to query a student record based on the selected student name from the **Student Name** combobox. That stored procedure can be recognized and called after we added it into the DataContext class.
B. Then a **foreach()** loop is utilized to execute the LINQ to SQL command to pick up each column of the queried student record and assign it to the associated textbox to display them in the **Student** page.
C. A selected student image is converted to an array, and then to an appropriate format **Base64String**, and displayed in the student image box, **PhotoBox**.
D. Prior to executing the second stored procedure, **StudentCourseInfo()**, the **CourseList** box is first cleaned up to make it ready to collect and display all courses (**course_id**) enrolled by the selected student.
E. The second stored procedure is called to query all courses for the selected student.
F. Finally each course is picked up from the queried result and added into the **CourseList** box.

Now let's test the codes in the **Select** button's click method to confirm its function.

Click on the **IIS Express** button to run our project. Complete the login process and open the **Student** page by selecting it from the **Selection** page. On the opened **Student** page, select a desired student name, such as **Andrew Woods**, and click on the **Select** button to retrieve the record for that student. Immediately all seven pieces of information related to that student is queried and displayed in seven textboxes in this **Student** page with the selected student image, as shown in Figure 8.88.

Now just click on the **Close** button located at the upper-right corner of this page to terminate our project. We will build the codes for the **Back** button click method to return our project to the Selection page to do the termination function later.

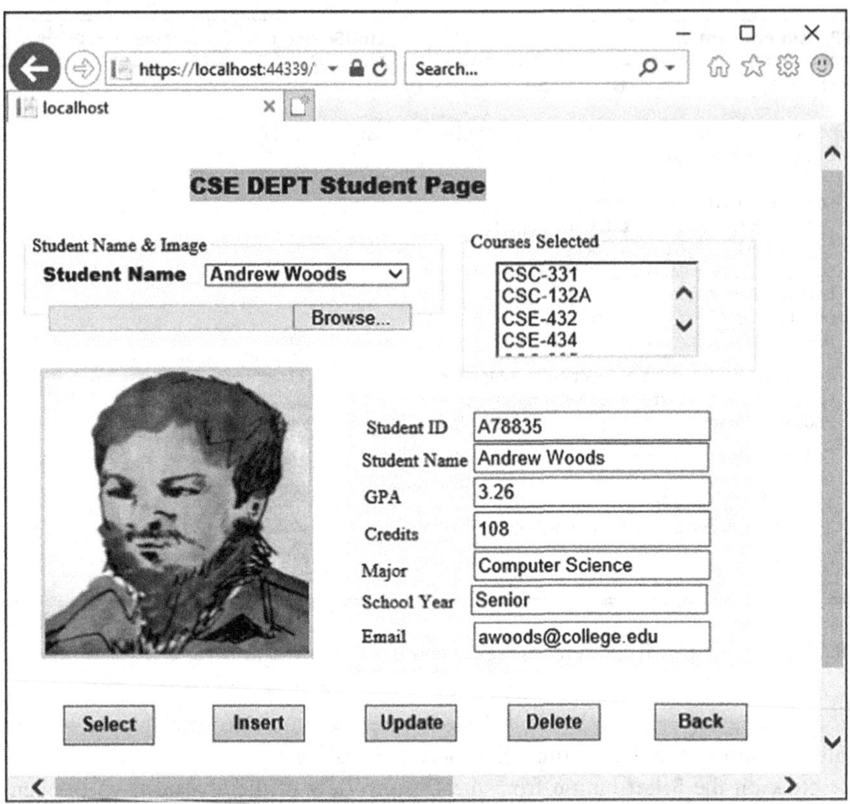

FIGURE 8.88 The running result of querying a student record.

8.9.2 Develop the Codes to Insert a Student Record into the Student Table

In this section, we discuss how to insert a new student record into the **Student** table in our sample database by calling stored procedure via the LINQ to SQL technique. We need to use the **Insert** button's click method to perform this data insertion action. As that button is clicked, a new student record stored in seven textboxes and a selected student image are inserted into the **Student** table.

Recall in Exercise 5 in homework on Chapter 6, a stored procedure **dbo.InsertStudent** should be generated for that exercise. Now let's first create that stored procedure if that exercise is not performed or completed.

8.9.2.1 Create a User-Defined Stored Procedure dbo.InsertStudent

Open Visual Studio 2022 and Server Explorer window, connect and open our sample database and expand the **Stored Procedures** folder. If that stored procedure, **dbo.InsertStudent**, cannot be found, we need to create it. Perform the following operations to generate this stored procedure:

1) Right-click on the **Stored Procedure** folder and select the **Add New Stored Procedure** item to open the default new procedure wizard.
2) Enter the codes shown in Figure 8.89 into this wizard as the body of that stored procedure.
3) Click on the **Update** icon, as shown in Figure 8.89, to save this stored procedure into our database.
4) Then click on the **Update Database** button to complete this saving action.

The codes for this stored procedure are straightforward and easily understood. The first eight pieces of input information are generated as a new student record to be inserted into the **Student** table.

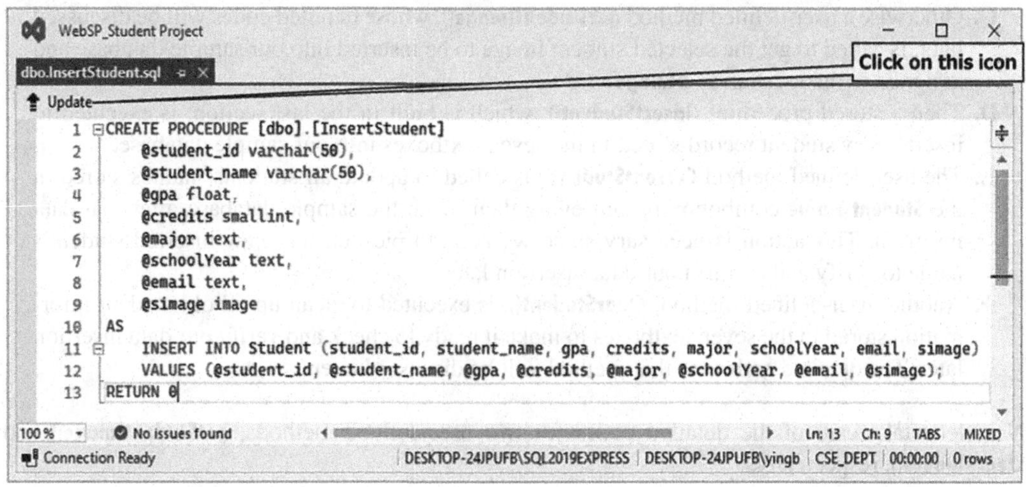

FIGURE 8.89 The detailed codes for the stored procedure dbo.InsertStudent().

Then the **Insert** command is executed to insert that record into the database. The only point to be noted is the data type for the student image, which should be **image**, not **Binary**.

Refer to Section 8.9.1.2 to add this stored procedure into our DataContext class to enable the latter to recognize and use it later. Next let's build the codes to call that stored procedure to perform data insertion action.

8.9.2.2 The Coding for the Data Insertion Query

Double-click on the **Insert** button from the Design View of the Student page to open its click method, and enter the codes shown in Figure 8.90 into that method.

Let's have a closer look at that piece of codes to see how it works.

A. A byte[] array **bImage** is declared first since we need to insert a new student image with this data insertion action later.

B. Prior to inserting any data into our database, we need to check whether a valid student image has been selected if this **Insert** button is clicked by the user. This can be done by checking the **HasFile** property of the **FileUpload** class. If no student image has been selected, a warning message is displayed to remind the users to do that first.

```
WebSP_Student Project                    cmdInsert_Click(object sender, EventArgs e)

protected void cmdInsert_Click(object sender, EventArgs e)
{
A    byte[] bImage;
B    if (!FileUploadImage.HasFile)
        Response.Write("<script>alert('Select an image first using FileUpload!')</script>");
C    else
     {
        bImage = getStudentImage();
D       cse_dept.InsertStudent(txtStudentID.Text, txtStudentName.Text, Convert.ToDouble(txtGPA.Text),
              Convert.ToInt16(txtCredits.Text), txtMajor.Text, txtSchoolYear.Text, txtEmail.Text, bImage);
E       CurrentStudent();
F       ClearStudent();
     }
}
```

FIGURE 8.90 The detailed codes for the insert button's click method.

C. Otherwise a user-defined method **getStudentImage()**, whose detailed codes will be discussed later, is called to get the selected student image to be inserted into our sample database and assigned to the local array **bImage**.
D. Then a stored procedure, **InsertStudent()**, which is built in the last section, is executed to insert a new student record stored in the seven textboxes into our sample database.
E. The user-defined method **CurrentStudent()** is called to update all students' names stored in the **Student Name** combobox by retrieving them from the sample database after that data insertion. This action is necessary since we need to pick up that new inserted student's name to verify and confirm our data insertion later.
F. Another user-defined method, **ClearStudent()**, is executed to clean up all old student information stored in the seven textboxes to make it ready to check and verify our data insertion later. The detailed codes for that method will be discussed later.

Next let's take care of the detailed codes for two user-defined methods, **getStudentImage()** and **ClearStudent()**, respectively.

8.9.2.3 The Coding for Two User Defined Methods

The coding for the first method is similar to that used for the **getFacultyImage()** method. The detailed codes for that method are shown in Figure 8.91. Let's have a quick look about those codes to see how they work.

A. A local integer variable **length** is declared and this variable works as a holder to hold the length of the byte[] array of the selected student image.
B. A default folder, **StudentImage**, which will be used to store our selected student image, is declared and it should be located under the current project folder. The ~ indicated that this is the current folder **WebSP_Student Project**. The system method **MapPath()** is used to set up this path or folder and assign it to the local string variable **imgPath**.
C. First we need to check if this default folder is already existed in the machine by using the system method **Exists()**. If not, another system method **CreateDirectory()** is used to create it in our machine.
D. Then the selected student image file is saved to that default or new created folder via a system method **SaveAs()**.
E. The selected student image is displayed in the Student Image box, **PhotoBox**, by assigning the student image file's name to the **ImageUrl** property.

```
WebSP_Student Project                    getStudentImage()

  private byte[] getStudentImage()
  {
A     int length;
B     string imgPath = Server.MapPath("~/StudentImage/");
C     if (!System.IO.Directory.Exists(imgPath))
         System.IO.Directory.CreateDirectory(imgPath);
D     FileUploadImage.SaveAs(imgPath + System.IO.Path.GetFileName(FileUploadImage.FileName));
E     PhotoBox.ImageUrl = "~/StudentImage/" + FileUploadImage.FileName;
F     length = FileUploadImage.PostedFile.ContentLength;
G     byte[] img = new byte[length];
      FileUploadImage.PostedFile.InputStream.Read(img, 0, length);
H     return img;
  }
```

FIGURE 8.91 Detailed codes for the user defined method getStudentImage().

```
WebSP_Student Project          ClearStudent()

  private void ClearStudent()
  {
A     TextBox[] sBox = { txtStudentID, txtStudentName, txtGPA, txtCredits, txtMajor, txtSchoolYear, txtEmail };
B     for (int index = 0; index < sBox.Length; index++)
         sBox[index].Text = String.Empty;
  }
```

FIGURE 8.92 The codes for the user-defined method ClearStudent().

F. Now we need to convert that student image file to the **byte[]** format. First we need to get the length in bytes for that image file with the method **ContentLength()**.
G. A new **byte[]** array **img** is generated with the **length** as the argument. Another system method **Read()** is utilized to read that file and convert it to a **byte[]** array.
H. Finally the converted student image array is returned to the calling method.

The codes for the user-defined method **ClearStudent()** are shown in Figure 8.92.

The function of this piece of codes is to clean up the content stored in all seven textboxes to make it ready for us to confirm and check the correctness of that student record insertion action. The line-by-line explanations are:

A. First a **TextBox** array, **sBox**, is generated and it is used to store all seven textboxes in the Student page. The advantage of using this kind of array is to simplify this cleaning process by using a loop body later.
B. Then a **for** loop is utilized with the length of the **TextBox** as a terminating index to clean up all seven textboxes.

Before we can build and run our Web application to test the data insertion function, the last job we need to do is to complete the coding for the **Back** button's Click method to enable our application to return to the Selection page from which we can terminate our application.

Double-click on the **Back** button from the Design View of the Student page to open its click method, and enter the codes shown in Figure 8.93 into that method.

Let's have a closer look at that piece of codes to see how it works.

A. First we need to close the connection between our Web application and our sample database by executing a system method **close()**. Also we need to dispose that database context object by using another system method **Dispose()**.
B. Finally, we need to transfer our application to the Selection page by using a system method **Redirect()**.

```
WebSP_Student Project          cmdBack_Click(Object sender, EventArgs e)

  protected void cmdBack_Click(object sender, EventArgs e)
  {
A     cse_dept.Connection.Close();
      cse_dept.Dispose();
B     Response.Redirect("Selection.aspx");
  }
```

FIGURE 8.93 The codes for the Back button's Click method.

At this point, we have completed all coding developments for this data insertion function. Now we can run the project to test the data insertion functionality via the Web site. Click the **IIS Express** button to run the project. Enter the suitable username and password, such as **jhenry** and **test**, to finish the login process, and select the **Student Information** item from the Selection page to open the **Student** page. First keep the default student name in the **Student Name** combobox and click on the **Select** button to perform a student query action to get all information for that selected student.

To insert a new student record, enter the following seven pieces of information into seven textboxes:

Student ID:	**B56822**
Student Name:	**Susan Bai**
GPA:	**3.95**
Credits:	**86**
Major:	**Computer Science**
SchoolYear:	**Sophomore**
Email:	**sbai@college.edu**

Now try to click on the **Insert** button to insert this new record into the database. A warning message is displayed to indicate that a valid student image has not been selected. Click **OK** for that message, go to the FileUpload box and click on the **Browse** button to select a desired student image for this new inserted student. All student images can be found from a folder **Images\Students** under the **Students** folder on the CRC Press ftp site. One can copy all of those image files and save them into one of your local folder.

In the opened FileUpload window, browse to your local folder and select the student image **White.jpg**, and click on the **Open** button to close that window.

Now click on the **Insert** button again to try to insert this new record into our database. The **Insert** button is immediately disabled and the selected student image is displayed in the **PhotoBox**, which is shown in Figure 8.94.

Next let's perform the data validation to confirm that our data insertion is successful.

8.9.2.4 Validate the Student Data Insertion

There are two ways to check and verify our data insertion action. The first way is easy and simple. It is to perform another query for the inserted student. First perform a query for any other student. Then go to the **Student Name** combobox; one can find that the new inserted student name has been there. Click that name to select it and click on the **Select** button to get that record back. The queried result is identical with that shown Figure 8.94. This means that our data insertion action is successful!

Click on the **Back** button to return our application to the Selection page, and then click on the **Exit** button to terminate our Web application.

Another way to test this student record insertion is to open the **Student** table via the Server Explorer window to verify whether that new student record has been inserted.

A complete Web application project **WebSP_Student Project** can be found from a folder **Class DB Projects\Chapter 8\WebSP_Student Solution** that is under the **Students** folder on the CRC Press ftp site (refer to Figure 1.2 in Chapter 1).

In the next section, we will discuss how to perform the data updating and deleting actions against our SQL Server database via the Web applications.

8.9.3 Update and Delete a Student Record in the Student Table via Stored Procedures

As we discussed in Section 8.6, to update or delete data against the relational databases is a challenging topic. We have provided a very detailed discussion and analysis for this topic in Section 7.1.1. Refer to that section to get more detailed information for these data actions. Here we want to emphasize

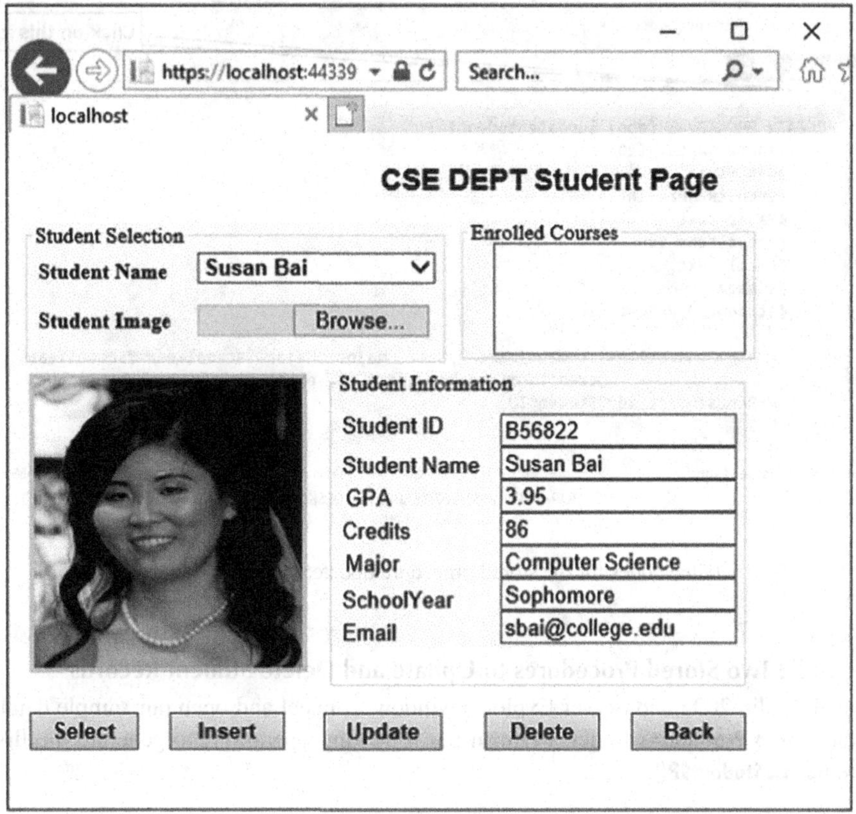

FIGURE 8.94 The running result of inserting a new student.

some important points related to updating and deleting a student record from the **Student** table in our sample database:

1) When updating or deleting data against related tables in a database, it is important to update or delete data in the proper sequence in order to reduce the chance of violating referential integrity constraints.
2) To update an existing record against the database, it is unnecessary to update the primary key for that record. It is much better to insert a new record with a new primary key into the database than updating the primary key for an existing record because of the complicated operations. Therefore, in this section, we concentrate our discussion on updating the existing student records by modifying all data columns except the primary key column.
3) To delete a record from a relational database, the normal operation sequence must be followed. For example, to delete a record from the **Student** table in our application, one must first delete those records related to the data to be deleted in the **Student** table from the child table such as the **LogIn** and **StudentCourse** tables, and then one can delete the record from the **Student** table. The reason for that deleting sequence is because the **student_id** is a foreign key in the **LogIn** and the **StudentCourse** tables, but it is a primary key in the **Student** table. One must first delete data with the foreign keys and then delete the data with the primary key from the database.

Keep these three points in mind, and now let's begin to build our project. First let's concentrate on building our two stored procedures, **updateStudentSP()** and **deleteStudentSP**. Also we need to add those two stored procedures into our DataContext class.

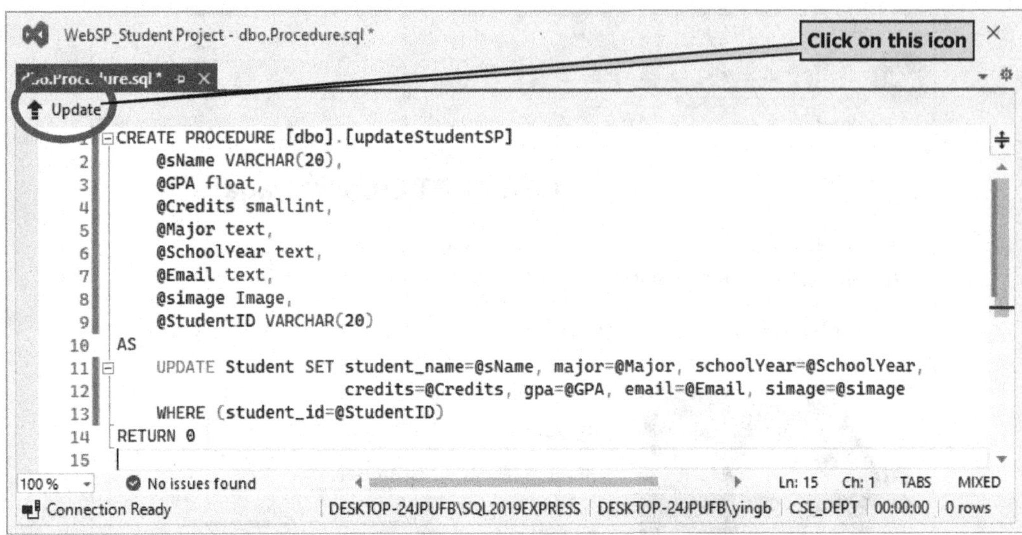

FIGURE 8.95 The detailed codes for the stored procedure updateStudentSP().

8.9.3.1 Build Two Stored Procedures to Update and Delete Student Records

Open Visual Studio 2022 and Server Explorer window, connect and open our sample database and expand the **Stored Procedures** folder. Perform the following operations to generate the first stored procedure **updateStudentSP()**:

1) Right click on the **Stored Procedure** folder and select the **Add New Stored Procedure** item to open the default new procedure wizard.
2) Enter the codes shown in Figure 8.95 into this wizard as the body of that stored procedure.
3) Click on the **Update** icon, as shown in Figure 8.95, to save this stored procedure into our database.
4) Then click on the **Update Database** button to complete this saving action.

The codes for this stored procedure are straightforward and easily understood. First seven pieces of input information are generated as an updated student record to be updated in the **Student** table. Then the **UPDATE** command is executed to update that record in the database with the **student_id** as the query criterion. The only point to be noted is the data type for the student image, which should be **Image**, not **Binary**.

Refer to Section 8.9.1.2 to add this stored procedure into our DataContext class to enable the latter to recognize and use it later. Next let's build the second stored procedure **deleteStudentSP()**.

Similarly, as we did above, open Visual Studio 2022 and Server Explorer window, connect and open our sample database and expand the **Stored Procedures** folder. Perform the following operations to generate the second stored procedure **deleteStudentSP()**:

1) Right click on the **Stored Procedure** folder and select the **Add New Stored Procedure** item to open the default new procedure wizard.
2) Enter the codes shown in Figure 8.96 into this wizard as the body of that stored procedure.
3) Click on the **Update** icon, as shown in Figure 8.96, to save this stored procedure into our database.
4) Then click on the **Update Database** button to complete this saving action.

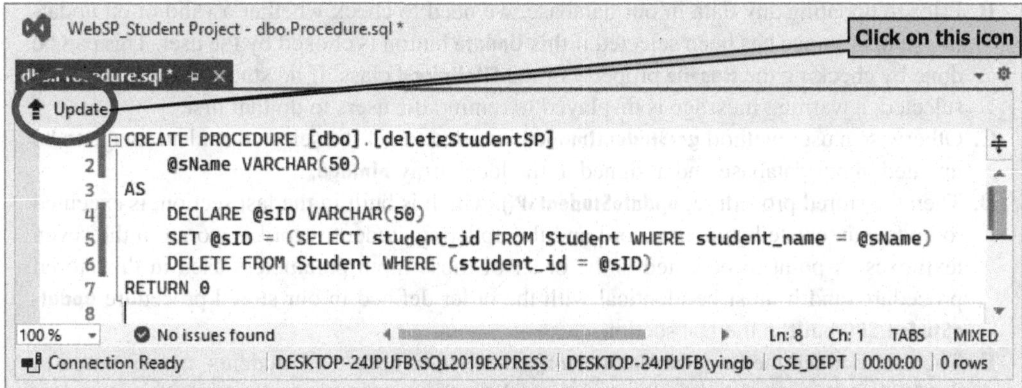

FIGURE 8.96 The detailed codes for the stored procedure deleteStudentSP().

The codes for this stored procedure are straightforward and easily understood. First an input parameter, **sName**, which is a student's name selected by the user, is declared. Then a local variable **sID** is generated since we prefer to delete a student's record based on the **student_id**, not **student_name**. An internal query is performed to get a matched **student_id** based on the selected student's name. Finally the student's record is deleted from the **Student** table.

Refer to Section 8.9.1.2 to add these two stored procedures into our DataContext class to enable the latter to recognize and use them later. Next let's build the codes to call that stored procedures to perform data updating and deleting actions.

8.9.3.2 The Coding for the Data Updating Query

Open our project **WebSP_Student Project** and double-click on the **Update** button from the Design View of the Student page to open its click method, and enter the codes shown in Figure 8.97 into that method.

Let's have a closer look at that piece of codes to see how it works.

A. A byte[] array **bImage** is declared first since we need to update a student image with this data updating action later.

```
WebSP_Student Project        cmdUpdate_Click(object sender, EventArgs e)

  protected void cmdUpdate_Click(object sender, EventArgs e)
  {
A     byte[] bImage;
B     if (!FileUploadImage.HasFile)
         Response.Write("<script>alert('Select an updating image using FileUpload!')</script>");
      else
      {
C        bImage = getStudentImage();
D        cse_dept.updateStudentSP(txtStudentName.Text, Convert.ToDouble(txtGPA.Text),
         Convert.ToInt16(txtCredits.Text), txtMajor.Text, txtSchoolYear.Text, txtEmail.Text, bImage,
         txtStudentID.Text);
E       CurrentStudent();
F       ClearStudent();
      }
  }
```

FIGURE 8.97 The codes for the update button's click method.

B. Prior to updating any data in our database, we need to check whether a valid or an updating student image has been selected if this **Update** button is clicked by the user. This can be done by checking the **HasFile** property of the **FileUpload** class. If no student image has been selected, a warning message is displayed to remind the users to do that first.

C. Otherwise a user method **getStudentImage()** is called to get the selected student image to be updated in our database and assigned to the local array **bImage**.

D. Then the stored procedure, **updateStudentSP()**, which is built in the last section, is executed to update an existed student record and the updating student record is stored in the seven textboxes. A point to be noted is the order of those input parameters used in this stored procedure, and it must be identical with the order defined in our stored procedure **updateStudentSP()** built in the last section.

E. The user-defined method, **CurrentStudent()**, is called to update all students' names stored in the **Student Name** combobox by retrieving them from the sample database after that data updating. This action is necessary since we need to pick up that updated student's name to verify and confirm our data updating later.

F. Another user-defined method, **ClearStudent()**, is executed to clean up all old student information stored in the seven textboxes to make it ready to check and verify our data updating later. The detailed codes for that method can be found from Section 8.9.2.3.

Now let's run the project to test the data updating functionality via the Web site. Click the **IIS Express** button to run the project. Enter the suitable username and password, such as **jhenry** and **test**, to finish the login process, and select the **Student Information** item from the Selection page to open the **Student** page. First select a student **Susan Bai** from the **Student Name** combobox and click on the **Select** button to perform a student query action to get all information for that selected student.

To update an existing student record, such as **Susan Bai**, enter the following six pieces of information (without **student_id**) into six textboxes as an updated student record:

Student Name:	**Jennifer Bai**
GPA:	**3.80**
Credits:	**121**
Major:	**Computer Engineering**
SchoolYear:	**Senior**
Email:	**jbai@college.edu**

Now click on the **Update** button to update this record in the database. A warning message is displayed to indicate that a valid student image has not been selected. Click **OK** for that message, go to the FileUpload box and click on the **Browse** button to select a desired student image for this updating record. All student images can be found from a folder **Images\Students** under the **Students** folder on the CRC Press ftp site. One can copy all of those image files and save them into one of your local folder.

In the opened FileUpload window, browse to your local folder and select the student image **David.jpg**, and click on the **Open** button to close that window.

Now click on the **Update** button again to try to update this student record in our sample database. The selected student image is displayed in the **PhotoBox**, which is shown in Figure 8.98.

To confirm that data updating action, just select the updated student's name, **Jennifer Bai**, from the **Student Name** combobox, and click on the **Select** button to try to retrieve back that updated student's record, as shown in Figure 8.98. One can find that that student's record has been really updated.

Click on the **Back** button to return our application to the Selection page, and then click on the **Exit** button to terminate our Web application.

FIGURE 8.98 The running result of updating an existing student record.

Another way to test this student record updating action is to open the **Student** table via the Server Explorer window to verify whether or not that new student record has been updated.

Next let's take care of data deleting action by building our codes in the **Delete** button's Click method in the current project.

8.9.3.3 The Coding for the Data Deleting Query

Open our project **WebSP_Student Project**, double-click on the **Delete** button from the Design View of the Student page to open its click method, and enter the codes shown in Figure 8.99 into that method.

```
WebSP_Student Project                cmdDelete_Click(object sender, EventArgs e)

  protected void cmdDelete_Click(object sender, EventArgs e)
  {
A      cse_dept.deleteStudentSP(txtStudentName.Text);
B      PhotoBox.ImageUrl = null;
C      CurrentStudent();
       ClearStudent();
    }
  }
```

FIGURE 8.99 The detailed codes for the delete button's click method.

The function of this piece of codes is straightforward and easily understood.

A. First the stored procedure **deleteStudentSP()** we built in Section 8.9.3.1 is executed to delete the selected student record based on the student's name.
B. The selected student's image is also deleted from the **PhotoBox** by assigning a **null** to the property **ImageUrl**.
C. Then all current students' names in our sample database are retrieved and added into the **Student Name** combobox. Also, all seven textboxes are cleaned up to indicate that the selected student's record has been deleted from our database.

Now run our project, finish the login process and open the Student page. To test our data deleting action, select a student's name, such as **Jennifer Bai**, from the **Student Name** combobox, and click on the **Delete** button to try to delete that record.

To confirm that data deletion action, just go to the **Student Name** combobox, and one can find that the selected student has been deleted and cannot be found from there. Another way to test this student record deleting action is to open the **Student** table via the Server Explorer window to verify whether that new student record has been deleted.

Click on the **Back** button to return our application to the Selection page, and then click on the **Exit** button to terminate our Web application project.

A complete Web application project **WebSP_Student Project** that contains the data updating and deleting actions can be found from a folder **Class DB Projects\Chapter 8\WebSP_Student Solution** that is under the **Students** folder on the CRC Press ftp site (refer to Figure 1.2 in Chapter 1).

8.10 CHAPTER SUMMARY

A detailed and completed introduction to the ASP.NET and the .NET Framework, including the ASP.NET 4.8, is provided at the beginning of this chapter. This part is especially useful and important to readers or students who do not have any knowledge or background in the Web application developments and implementations.

Following the introduction section, a detailed discussion on how to install and configure the environment to develop the ASP.NET Web applications is provided. Some essential tools, such as the Web server, IIS and FrontPage Server Extension 2000, as well as the installation process of these tools, are introduced and discussed in detail.

Starting from Section 8.3, detailed developments and building processes of ASP.NET Web applications to access SQL Server database are discussed with seven real Web application projects. The seven real ASP.NET Web application projects are as follows:

1) ASP.NET Web application to select and display data from the Faculty table in the Microsoft SQL Server database.
2) ASP.NET Web application to insert data into the Faculty table in the Microsoft SQL Server database.
3) ASP.NET Web application to update and delete data against the Faculty table in the Microsoft SQL Server database.
4) ASP.NET Web application to perform data actions with LINQ to SQL query.
5) ASP.NET Web application to select and display data for the Course table.
6) ASP.NET Web application to insert data into the Course table.
7) ASP.NET Web application to update and delete data from the Student table in the SQL Server database with the stored procedures.

The stored procedures with the entity class and object of the DataContext class are utilized in the last project to help readers or students to perform different data actions against our sample SQL

Server database more efficiently and conveniently. The detailed discussion on the data action order is provided to help readers to understand the integrity constraint built in the relational database. It is a tough topic to update or delete data from related tables in a relational database, and a clear and deep discussion on this topic will significantly benefit readers and improve their knowledge and hands-on experience of these issues.

HOMEWORK

I. True/False Selections

____1. The actual language used in the communications between the client and the server is HTML.

____2. ASP.NET and .NET Framework are two different models that provide the development environments to the Web programming.

____3. The .NET Framework is composed of the Common Language Runtime (called runtime) and a collection of class libraries.

____4. You access the .NET Framework by using the class libraries provided by the .NET Framework, and you implement the .NET Framework by using the tools such as Visual Studio.NET provided by the .NET Framework, too.

____5. ASP.NET 4.8 is a programming framework built on the .NET Framework 4.8 and it is used to build Web applications.

____6. The fundamental component of ASP.NET is the Web Form. A Web Form is the Web page that users view in a browser and an ASP.NET Web application can contain one or more Web Forms.

____7. A Web Form is a dynamic page that runs on the server side. It can access server resources when it is viewed by users via the client browser.

____8. Similar to traditional Web pages, an ASP.NET 4.x Web page can only run scripts on the client side.

____9. The controls you added to the Web form will run on the Web server when this Web page is requested by the user through a client browser.

___10. To allow a List Box control to response to a user click as the Web page runs, the **AutoPostBack** property of that List Box must be set to **False**.

II. Multiple Choices

1. When the user sends a request from the user's client browser to request a Web page, the server needs to build that form and sends it back to the user's browser in the ______ language format.
   a. ASP.NET
   b. .NET Framework
   c. XML
   d. HTML
2. Once a requested Web page is received by the client's browser, the connection between the client and the server is ________.
   a. Still active
   b. Terminated
   c. Not active
   d. Either active or inactive

3. As a Web application runs, the programs developed in any .NET-based language are converted into the ______ codes that can be recognized by the CLR, and the CLR can compile and execute the MSIL codes by using the Just-In-Time compiler.
   a. Visual Studio.NET
   b. Visual Basic.NET
   c. Microsoft Intermediate Language (MSIL)
   d. C#
4. The terminal file of an ASP.NET Web application is a ________ file.
   a. Dynamic Linked Library (dll)
   b. MSIL
   c. XML
   d. HTML
5. Because Web pages are frequently refreshed by the server, one must use the _______ to store the global variable.
   a. Global.asax file
   b. Defaulty.aspx file
   c. Config file
   d. Application state function
6. One needs to use the ______ method to display a message box in Web applications.
   a. MessageBox.Show()
   b. MessageBox.Display
   c. Javascript alert()
   d. Response.Write()
7. Unlike the Windows-based applications that use the Form_Load as the first event method, a Web-based application uses the _______ as the first event method.
   a. Start_Page
   b. Page_Load
   c. First_Page
   d. Web_Start
8. To delete data from a relational database, one must first delete the data from the _______ tables, and then one can delete the target data from the ______ table.
   a. Major, minor
   b. Parent, child
   c. Parent, parent
   d. Child, parent
9. To allow the SQL Server database engine to delete all related records from the child tables, the Delete Rule item in the INSERT And UPDATE Specifications box of the Foreign Key Relationship dialog box must be set to _______.
   a. No action
   b. Cascade
   c. Set default
   d. Set Null
10. To display any message on a running Web page, one must use the ______ method.
   a. MessageBox.Show()
   b. Response()
   c. Response.Redirect()
   d. Response.Write()

III. Exercises

1. Write a paragraph to answer and explain the following questions:
   a. What is ASP.NET?
   b. What is the main component of the ASP.NET Web application?
   c. How is an ASP.NET Web application executed?
2. Suppose we want to delete one record from the **Student** table in our sample database CSE_DEPT based on one student_id = 'H10210'. List all deleting steps and deleting queries including the data deleting from the child and the parent tables.
3. Figure 8.100 shows a piece of codes developed in the Page_Load() method. Explain the functionality of the statement **if (!IsPostBack)** block.

```
Course                                    Page_Load()

protected void Page_Load(object sender, EventArgs e)
{
    if (((OracleConnection)Application["oraConnection"]).State != ConnectionState.Open)
        ((OracleConnection)Application["oraConnection"]).Open();

    if (!IsPostBack)
    {
        ComboName.Items.Add("Ying Bai");
        ComboName.Items.Add("Davis Bhalla");
        ComboName.Items.Add("Black Anderson");
        ComboName.Items.Add("Steve Johnson");
        ComboName.Items.Add("Jenney King");
        ComboName.Items.Add("Alice Brown");
        ComboName.Items.Add("Debby Angles");
        ComboName.Items.Add("Jeff Henry");
    }
}
```

FIGURE 8.100 The codes for the Page_Load method.

4. Use Web page **Course.aspx** and develop codes to the **Delete** button's Click method to delete a course record in the **SQLWebUpdateDelete Project**, which can be found from the folder **Class DB Projects\Chapter 8** that is located on the CRC Press ftp site (refer to Figure 1.2 in Chapter 1)). Refer to Section 8.8.2 to first insert a new course **CSE-668** by running project **WebLINQSQL_Course Project**, and then test this deleting action since the course **CSE-668** is a new course without any relationship with any other tables.
5. Use the Web page **Course.aspx** and develop the codes to the **Update** button's Click method to update a course record in that page at the **SQLWebUpdateDelete Project**, which can be found from the folder **Class DB Projects\Chapter 8** that is located on the CRC Press ftp site (refer to Figure w in Chapter 1)). It is highly recommended that you restore the updated course record back to the original one.
6. Use the Web page **Student.aspx** and develop the codes to call two stored procedures, **dbo.StudentInfo** and **dbo.StudentCourseInfo**, built into the previous projects, to select one record from the Student table by using the project **SQLWebSelectProject** (the project can be found from the folder **Class DB Projects\Chapter 8** that is located on the CRC Press ftp site (refer to Figure 1.2 in Chapter 1)). Use the **Select** button's Click method to perform this query action.

9 ASP.NET Web Services

We provided a very detailed discussion about the ASP.NET Web applications in the last chapter. In this chapter, we will concentrate on another ASP.NET related topic – ASP.NET Web Services.

Unlike the ASP.NET Web applications, in which the user needs to access the Web server through the client browser by sending requests to the server to obtain the desired information, ASP.NET Web Services provide an automatic way to search, identify and return the desired information required by the user through a set of methods installed in the Web server Those methods can be accessed by a computer program, not the user, via the Internet. Another important difference between the ASP. NET Web applications and ASP.NET Web services is that the latter does not provide any graphic user interfaces (GUIs) and the users need to create those GUIs themselves to access the Web services via the Internet.

When finished this chapter, you will

- Understand the structure and components of ASP.NET Web Services, such as Simple Object Access Protocol (SOAP), Web Services Description Language (WSDL) and Universal Description, Discovery and Integration (UDDI).
- Create correct SOAP Namespaces for the Web Services to make used names and identifiers unique in the user's document.
- Create suitable security components to protect the Web methods.
- Build the professional ASP.NET Web Service projects to access our sample database to obtain required information.
- Build client applications to provide GUIs to consume a Web Service.
- Build the professional ASP.NET Web Service projects to insert new records into our sample database.
- Build the professional ASP.NET Web Service projects to update and delete data against our sample database.

In order to help readers to successfully complete this chapter, first we need to provide a detailed discussion about the ASP.NET Web Services and their components.

9.1 WHAT ARE WEB SERVICES AND THEIR COMPONENTS?

Essentially, the Web services can be considered a set of methods installed in a Web server and can be called by computer programs installed on the clients through the Internet. Those methods can be used to locate and return the target information required by the computer programs. Web services do not require the use of browsers or HTML, and therefore Web services are sometimes called *application services.*

To effectively find, identify and return the target information required by computer programs, a Web service needs the following components:

1) XML (Extensible Markup Language).
2) SOAP (Simple Object Access Protocol).
3) UDDI (Universal Description, Discovery and Integration).
4) WSDL (Web Services Description Language).

DOI: 10.1201/9781003319832-9

The function of each component is listed below:

XML is a text-based data storage language which uses a series of tags to define and store data. The so-called tags are used to **mark up** data to be exchanged between applications. The **marked up** data then can be recognized and used by different applications without any problem. As you know, the Web services platform is XML + HTTP (Hypertext Transfer Protocol) and the HTTP protocol is the most popular Internet protocol. But the XML provides a kind of language that can be used between different platforms and programming languages to express complex messages and functions. In order to make the codes used in the Web services to be recognized by applications developed in different platforms and programming languages, the XML is used for the coding in the Web services to make up them line by line.

SOAP is a communication protocol used for communications between applications. Essentially, SOAP is a simple XML-based protocol to help applications developed in different platforms and languages to exchange information over HTTP. Therefore, SOAP is a platform-independent and language-independent protocol, which means that it can run at any operating systems with any programming languages. In essence, a SOAP works as a carrier to transfer data or requests between applications. Whenever a request is made to the Web server to request a Web service, this request is first wrapped into a SOAP message and sent over the Internet to the Web server. Similarly, as the Web service returns the target information to the client, the returned information is also wrapped into a SOAP message and sent over the Internet to the client browser.

WSDL is an XML-based language for describing Web services and how to access them. In WSDL terminology, each Web service is defined as an abstract endpoint or a Port and each Web method is defined as an abstract operation. Each operation or method can contain some SOAP messages to be transferred between applications. Each message is constructed by using the SOAP protocol as a request is made from the client. WSDL defines two styles for how a Web service method can be formatted in a SOAP message: Remote Procedure Call (RPC) and Document. Both RPC- and Document-style messages can be used to communicate with a Web Service using a RPC.

A single endpoint can contain a group of Web methods and that group of methods can be defined as an abstract set of operations called a Port Type. Therefore, WSDL is an XML format for describing network services as a set of endpoints operating on SOAP messages containing either document-oriented or procedure-oriented information. The operations and messages are described abstractly, and then bound to a concrete network protocol and message format to define an endpoint.

UDDI is an XML-based directory for businesses to list themselves on the Internet and the goal of this directory is to enable companies to find one another on the Web and make their systems interoperable for e-commerce. UDDI is often considered as a telephone book's yellow and white pages. By using those pages, it allows businesses to list themselves by name, products, locations, or the Web services they offer.

Summarily, based on these components and their roles discussed above, we can conclude:

- XML is used to tag the data to be transferred between applications.
- SOAP is used to wrap and pack the data tagged in the XML format into the messages represented in the SOAP protocol.
- WSDL is used to map a concrete network protocol and message format to an abstract endpoint, and describe the Web services available in an WSDL document format.
- UDDI is used to list all Web services that are available to users and businesses.

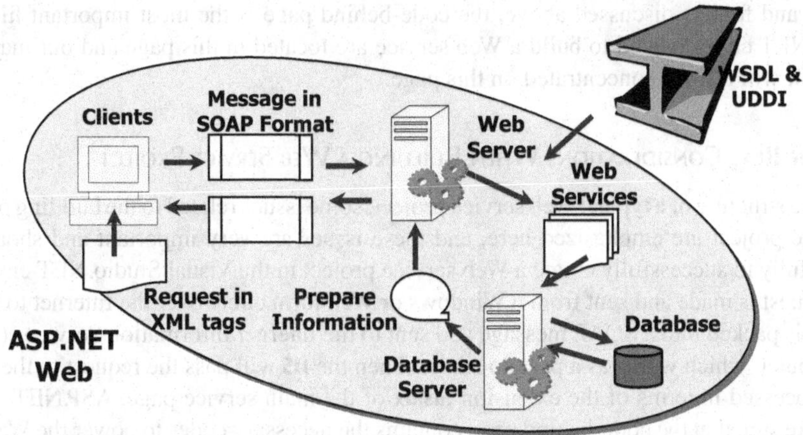

FIGURE 9.1 A typical process of a web service.

Figure 9.1 shows a diagram to illustrate these components and their roles in an ASP.NET Web service process.

By now, we have obtained the fundamental knowledge about the ASP.NET Web services and their components, next let's see how to build a Web service.

9.2 PROCEDURES TO BUILD A WEB SERVICE

Different methods and languages can be used to develop different Web services such as the C# Web services, Java Web services and Perl Web services. In this section we only concentrate on developing the ASP.NET Web services using the Visual C#.NET. Before we can start to build a real Web service project, let's first take a closer look at the structure of a Web service project.

9.2.1 The Structure of a Typical Web Service Project

A typical Web service project contains the following components:

1) As a new Web service project is created, two page files and one folder are created under this new project. The folder **App_Data** is used to store all project data.
2) The code-behind page **IService1.cs**. This page contains the real C#.NET codes for a simple Web service. Visual Web Developer includes two default declarations to help users to develop Web services on the top of this page, which are:
   - **using System.Runtime.Serialization;**
   - **using System.ServiceModel;**
3) Another file is named **Service1.svc**. As we know, WCF services hosted in IIS are represented as special content files or **.svc** files inside the IIS application. This model is similar to the way in which ASMX pages are represented inside of an IIS application as **.asmx** files. A **.svc** file contains a WCF-specific processing directive that allows the WCF hosting infrastructure to activate hosted services in response to incoming messages.
4) The configuration file **Web.config**, which is an XML-based file, is used to setup a configuration for the new created Web service project, such as the namespaces for all kinds of Web components, Connection string and default authentication mode. Each Web service project has its own configuration file.

Of all files and folders discussed above, the code-behind page is the most important file since all Visual C#.NET codes related to build a Web service are located in this page and our major coding development will also be concentrated on this page.

9.2.2 The Real Considerations When Building a Web Service Project

Based on the structure of a typical Web service project, some issues related to the building of an actual Web service project are emphasized here, and these issues are very important and should be followed carefully to successfully create a Web service project in the Visual Studio.NET environment.

As a request is made and sent from a Windows or Web form client over the Internet to the server, the request is packed into a SOAP message and sent to the Internet Information Services (**IIS**) on the client computer, which works as a pseudo server. Then the **IIS** will pass the request to the ASP.NET to get it processed in terms of the extension **.asmx** of the main service page. ASP.NET checks the page to make sure that the code-behind page contains the necessary codes to power the Web Service, exactly to trigger the associated Web methods to search, find, and retrieve the information required by the client, pack it to the SOAP message and return it to the client.

During this process, the following detailed procedures must be performed:

1) When ASP.NET checks the received request represented in a SOAP message, the ASP.NET will make sure that the names and identifiers used in the SOAP message must be unique, in other words, those names and identifiers cannot be conflicted with any name and identifier used by any other message. To make names and identifiers unique, we need to use our specific namespace to place and hold our SOAP message.
2) In general, a request contains a set of information, rather than a single piece of information. To request those pieces of information, we need to create a Web service proxy class to consume Web services. In other words, we do not want to develop a separate Web method to query each piece of information, and that will make our project's size terribly large if we need a lot of information. A good solution is to instantiate an object based on that class and integrate those pieces of information into that object. All information can be embedded into that object and can be returned if that object returns. Another choice is to design a Web method to make it return a DataSet. This is a convenient way to return all data.
3) As a professional application, we need to handle the exceptions to make our Web service as perfect as possible. In that case, we need to create a base class to hold some error-checking codes to protect our real class that will be instantiated to an object that contains all the information we need, so this real class should be a child class inherited from the base class.
4) Since the Web services did not provide any GUI, we need to develop some GUIs in either Windows-based or Web-based applications to interface to the Web services to display returned information on GUIs.

Starting from .NET Frameworks 4.0, a good platform, Windows Communication Foundation (WCF), is provided to support to build professional Web Services projects. First let's have a basic understanding about this new tool.

9.2.3 Introduction to the Windows Communication Foundation (WCF)

As the advanced development of the service-oriented communications, the software development has been significantly changed. Whether the message is done with SOAP or in some other way, applications that interact through services have become the norm. For Windows developers, this change is made possible by using the Windows Communication Foundation (WCF). First released as part of the .NET Framework 3.0 in 2006, then updated in the .NET Framework 3.5, and the most recent version of this technology is included in the .NET Framework 4.8. For a substantial share of new software built on .NET, WCF is the right foundation.

9.2.3.1 What is the WCF?

The Windows Communication Foundation (WCF) is a framework for building service-oriented applications. Using WCF, you can send data as asynchronous messages from one service endpoint to another. A service endpoint can be part of a continuously available service hosted by IIS, or it can be a service hosted in an application. An endpoint can be a client of a service that requests data from a service endpoint.

WCF is a unified framework for creating secure, reliable, transacted, and interoperable distributed applications. In earlier versions of Visual Studio, there were several technologies that could be used for communicating between applications.

If you wanted to share information in a way that enabled it to be accessed from any platform, you would use a Web service (also known as an ASMX Web service). If you wanted to just move data between a client and server that are running on the Windows operating system, you would use .NET Remoting. If you wanted transacted communications, you would use Enterprise Services (DCOM), and if you wanted a queued model you would use Message Queuing (also known as MSMQ).

WCF brings together the functionality of all those technologies under a unified programming model. This simplifies the experience of developing distributed applications.

In fact, WCF is implemented primarily as a set of classes on the top of the .NET Framework's Common Language Runtime (CLR). This allows .NET developers to build service-oriented applications easily. In addition, WCF allows the creation of clients that access services in a mutual way, which means that both the client and the service can run in pretty much the same way as any Windows process. WCF doesn't define a required host. Wherever they run, clients and services can interact via SOAP, via a WCF-specific binary protocol, and in other ways.

9.2.3.2 WCF Data Services

WCF Data Services, formerly known as ADO.NET Data Services, is a component of the .NET Framework that enables you to create services that use the Open Data Protocol (OData) to expose and consume data over the Web or intranet by using the semantics of representational state transfer (REST). OData exposes data as resources that are addressable by URIs. Data is accessed and changed by using standard HTTP verbs of GET, PUT, POST, and DELETE. OData uses the entity-relationship conventions of the Entity Data Model to expose resources as sets of entities that are related by associations.

WCF Data Services uses the OData protocol for addressing and updating resources. In this way, you can access these services from any client that supports OData. OData enables you to request and write data to resources by using well-known transfer formats: Atom, a set of standards for exchanging and updating data as XML, and JavaScript Object Notation (JSON), a text-based data exchange format used extensively in AJAX application.

WCF Data Services can expose data that originates from various sources as OData feeds. Visual Studio tools make it easier for you to create an OData-based service by using an ADO.NET Entity Framework data model. You can also create OData feeds based on common language runtime (CLR) classes and even late-bound or un-typed data.

WCF Data Services also includes a set of client libraries, one for general .NET Framework client applications and another specifically for Silverlight-based applications.

These client libraries provide an object-based programming model when you access an OData feed from environments such as the .NET Framework and Silverlight.

9.2.3.3 WCF Services

A WCF service is based on an interface that defines a contract between the service and the client. It is marked with a **OperationContract** attribute, as a piece of codes shown in Figure 9.2.

```
public interface IService1
{
    [OperationContract]
    string GetData(int value);

    [OperationContract]
    CompositeType GetDataUsingDataContract(CompositeType composite);

    // TODO: Add your service operations here
}
```

FIGURE 9.2 The service interface and contract.

You define functions or methods that are exposed by a WCF service by marking them with an **OperationContractAttribute** attribute. In addition, you can expose serialized data by marking a composite type with a **DataContractAttribute** attribute. This enables data binding in a client.

After an interface and its methods are defined, they are encapsulated in a class that implements the interface. A single WCF service class can implement multiple service contracts. A WCF service is exposed for consumption through what is known as an **endpoint**. The endpoint provides the only way to communicate with the service; you cannot access the service through a direct reference as you would with other classes.

An endpoint consists of an address, a binding, and a contract. The address defines where the service is located; this could be a URL, an FTP address, or a network or local path. A binding defines the way that you communicate with the service. WCF bindings provide a versatile model for specifying a protocol such as HTTP or FTP, a security mechanism such as Windows Authentication or user names and passwords, and much more. A contract includes the operations that are exposed by the WCF service class.

Multiple endpoints can be exposed for a single WCF service. This enables different clients to communicate with the same service in different ways. For example, a banking service might provide one endpoint for employees and another for external customers, each using a different address, binding, and/or contract.

9.2.3.4 WCF Clients

A WCF client consists of a **proxy** that enables an application to communicate with a WCF service, and an endpoint that matches an endpoint defined for the service. The proxy is generated on the client side in the **app.config** file and includes information about the types and methods that are exposed by the service. For services that expose multiple endpoints, the client can select the one that best fits its needs, for example, to communicate over HTTP and use Windows Authentication.

After a WCF client has been created, you reference the service in your code just as what you could do for any other object. For example, to call the **GetData**() method shown in Figure 9.2, you would write the codes shown in Figure 9.3.

In most cases, you need to create a proxy to setup a reference to the server in the client to access the operations defined in the server.

9.2.3.5 WCF Hosting

From a developer perspective, WCF provides two alternatives for hosting services, which are both mostly identical under the covers. The easier of the two alternatives is to host services inside an ASP.NET application; the more flexible and more explicit alternative is to host services yourself and in whichever application process you choose.

```
Protected void Button1_Click(object sender, EventArgs e)
{
    var client = New ServiceReference1.Service1Client;
    String returnString;
    returnString = client.GetData(5);
    Label1.Text = returnString;
}
```

FIGURE 9.3 The codes in the client side to call the operation GetData() in the server.

Hosting WCF services in ASP.NET is very simple and straightforward and very similar to the ASMX model. You can either place your entire service implementation in a ***.svc** file just as with ASP.NET Web services ***.asmx** files, or reference a service implementation residing in a code-behind file or some other assembly. With respect to how the service implementation class is located (and possibly compiled), none of these options differ much from how you would typically create an ASMX Web service. Even the attributes of the **@Service** directive are the same as those for the **@WebService** directive.

The important difference between WCF and ASMX is that the WCF service will not do anything until you specify precisely how it shall be exposed to the outside world. An ASMX service will happily start talking to the world once you place the ***.asmx** file into an IIS virtual directory. A WCF service will not talk to anybody until you tell it to do so, and how to do so.

9.2.3.6 WCF Visual Studio Templates

Visual Studio.NET provides a set of WCF templates to help developers to build different Web services and applications. In fact, WCF Visual Studio templates are predefined project and item templates you can use in Visual Studio to quickly build WCF services and surrounding applications.

WCF Visual Studio templates provide a basic class structure for service development. Specifically, these templates provide the basic definitions for service contract, data contract, service implementation, and configuration. You can use these templates to create a simple service with minimal code interaction, as well as a building block for more advanced services.

Two of the most popular templates are **WCF Service Application** template and **WCF Service Library** template.

9.2.3.6.1 WCF Web Service Application Template

When you create a new Visual C#.NET project using the **WCF Web ServiceApplication** template, the project includes the following three major files:

1) Service Contract file (**IService1.cs**): The service contract file is an interface that has WCF service attributes applied. This file provides a definition of a simple service to show you how to define your services, and includes parameter-based operations and a simple data contract sample. This is the default file displayed in the code editor after creating a WCF service project.
2) Service Implements file (**Service1.svc**): This file is an implement file for the class **IService1** interface file, and it implements the contract defined in the service contract file.
3) Web Configuration file (**Web.config**): The configuration file provides the basic elements of a WCF service model with a secure HTTP binding. It also includes an endpoint for the service and enables metadata exchange.

The template automatically creates a Web site that will be deployed to a virtual directory and hosts a service in it.

9.2.3.6.2 WCF Service Library Project Template

When you create a new Visual C#.NET project using the **WCF Service Library** template, the new project automatically includes the following three files:

1) Service contract file (**IService1.cs**).
2) Service implementation file (**Service1.svc**).
3) Application configuration file (**App.config**).

Now let's start to build our Web service project using the WCF template. We prefer to use the **WCF ServiceApplication** template and include our Web service in our ASP.NET application project.

Starting from Visual Studio.NET 2022, the WCF template is not bound with the Studio and no longer to be installed with the installation of Visual Studio.NET together. To use that tool, one must download and install it separately. Next let's discuss how to download and install that tool and add it into our project.

9.2.4 Download and Install WCF Component in the Visual Studio.NET Environment

Perform the following operations to complete this downloading and installation process:

1) Launch Visual Studio.NET 2022 Community version and click on the **Continue without code** link to open the traditional Visual Studio IDE.
2) Go to the **Tools | Get Tools and Features** menu to open the Visual Studio Installer.
3) Click on the **Individual components** tab on the top to open that wizard.
4) Scroll down the list until you find the tool, **Windows Communication Foundation**, which is located under the **Development activities** group. Check the checkbox in front of that tool to select it.
5) Click on the **Modify** button located at the lower-right corner to starting the download and installation process.
6) Click on the **Yes** button on the popup MessageBox to confirm this process.
7) Click on the **Close** button located at the upper-right corner to close this installer when the downloading and installation process is done.

Now we are ready to build our C# Web Service projects and applications with WCF Template. Let's have a clear picture about the procedures of building process.

9.2.5 Procedures to Build an ASP.NET Web Service

The advantages of using the WCF templates to build our Web services are obvious; for instance, the protocols of the interface and contract have been predefined. However, you must follow up those protocols to fill your codes such as operations and methods. An easy way to do these is to directly add our Web service with our operations in our ways. In the following sections, we will not use the protocols provided by WCF and directly create our Web services and place them into an ASP.NET Web services ***.asmx** file.

Web service is basically composed of a set of Web methods that can be called by the computer programs in the client side. To build those methods, generally one needs to perform the following steps:

1) Create a new WCF Web Service project.
2) Add a new ASP.NET Web Service project.
3) Create a base class to handle the error checking to protect our real class.
4) Create our real Web service class to hold all Web methods and codes to response to requests.
5) Add all Web methods into our Web service class.
6) Develop the detail codes for those Web methods to perform the Web services.

7) Build a Windows-based or Web-based project to consume the Web service to pick up and display the required information on the GUI.
8) Store our ASP.NET Web service project files in a safe location.

In this chapter, we try to develop the following projects to illustrate the building and implementation process of Web services project:

- Build a professional ASP.NET Web Service project to access the SQL Server database to obtain required information for the Faculty table.
- Build client applications to provide GUIs to consume a Web Service.
- Build a professional ASP.NET Web Service project to insert new information into the SQL Server database with the Faculty table.
- Build a professional ASP.NET Web Service project to update and delete information against the SQL Server database with the Faculty table.
- Build a professional ASP.NET Web Service project to access the SQL Server database to obtain required information for the Course table.
- Build a professional ASP.NET Web Service project to insert new information into the SQL Server database with the Course table.
- Build a professional ASP.NET Web Service project to update and delete information against the SQL Server database with the Course table.
- Build client applications to provide GUIs to consume a Web Service.

Based on procedures discussed above, we can start to build our first Web service project **WebServiceSelect Project**.

9.3 BUILD ASP.NET WEB SERVICE PROJECT TO ACCESS SQL SERVER DATABASE

To create a new ASP.NET Web Service project, perform the following operations:

1) Open the Windows Explorer or File Explorer to create a new folder **Chapter 9** under your root drive C.
2) Open the traditional Visual Studio.NET and go to **File | New | Project** item.
3) On the opened New Project wizard, type **WFC Service** into the **Search for templates** box at the top to try to find and locate our desired WFC Template. The search results are shown in Figure 9.4.
4) Make sure to select the item **WCF Service Application** with the C# icon in front of that item, as shown in Figure 9.4, from the Templates list since we need to create our Web service project to be hosted in IIS. Then click on the **Next** button.
5) Enter **WebServiceSelect Project** into the **ProjectName** box and **WebServiceSelect Solution** into the **Solution name** box. Enter or select **C:\Chapter 9** into the **Location** box, which is shown in Figure 9.5.
6) Click on the **Create** button to create this new Web service project.

9.3.1 Files and Items Created in the New Web Service Project

After this new WCF Web service project is created, four items are produced in the Solution Explorer window, which are shown in Figure 9.6. These components include:

1) Additional connected service files (**Connected Services**)
2) Service contract file (**IService1.cs**).
3) Service implements file (**Service1.svc**).
4) Web configuration file (**Web.config**).

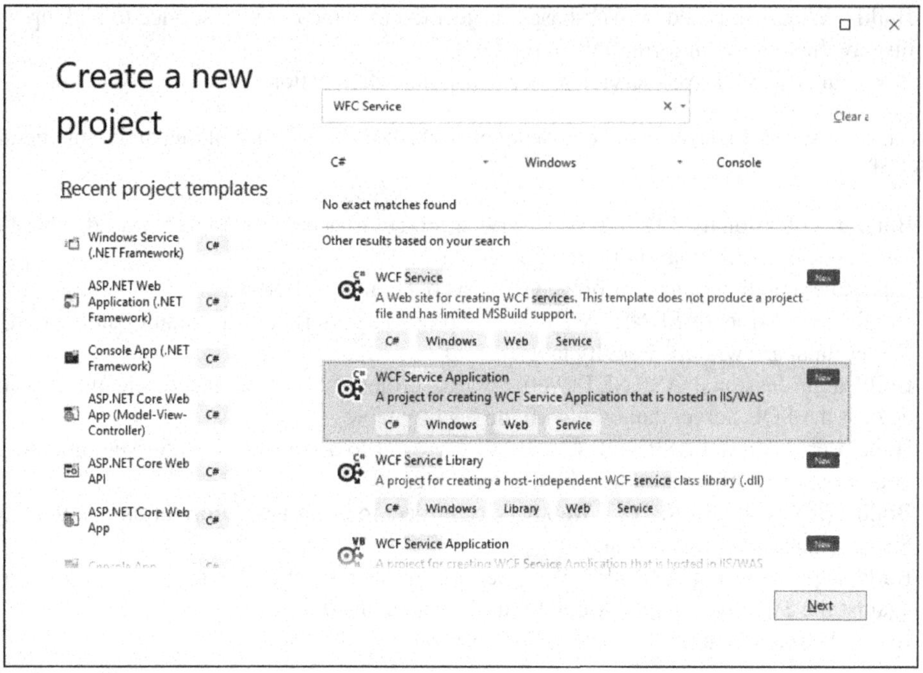

FIGURE 9.4 The searching results for WFC component.

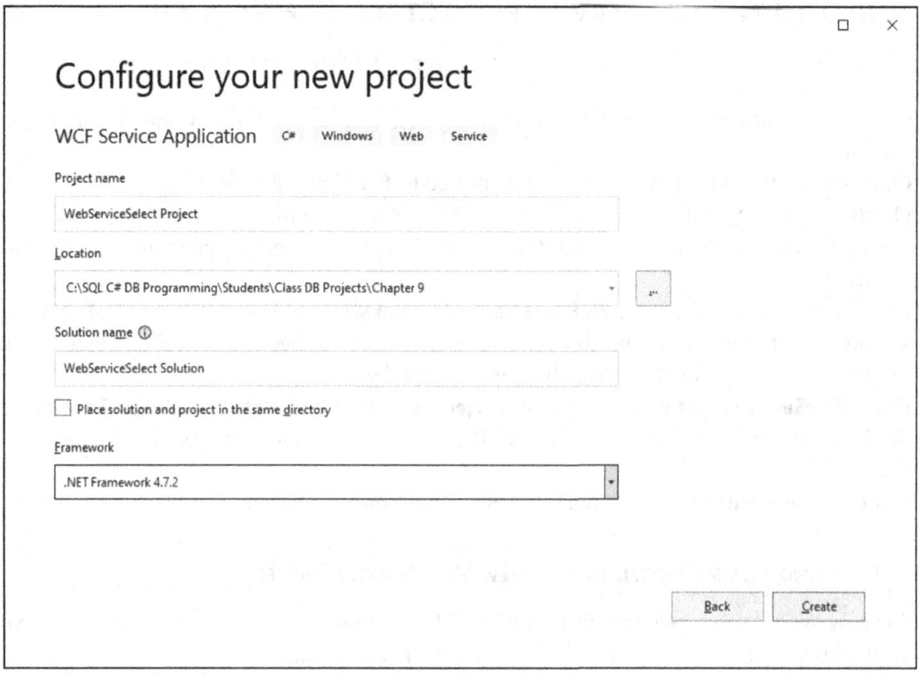

FIGURE 9.5 Create a new WCF web service project.

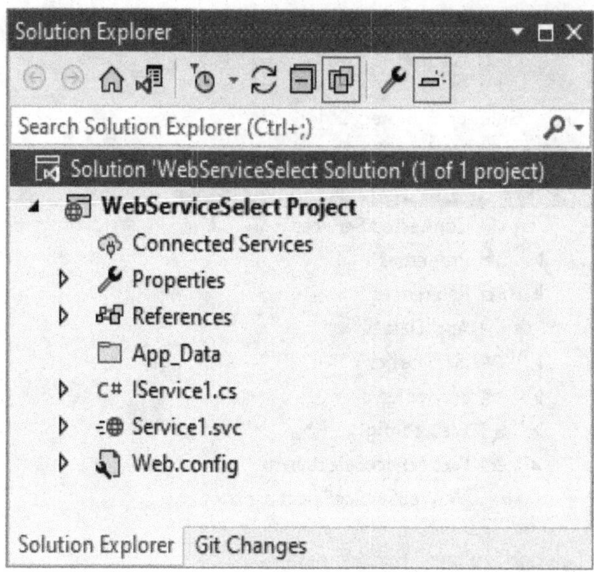

FIGURE 9.6 New created items for a WCF web service project.

As we discussed in the previous sections, files 2 and 3 are used to provide some default functions to get some system data and operations.

We can add our operations or methods to the default service file **IService1.cs** to build our project. But here we want to build our Web service with our own code-behind page in our customer way, thus perform the following operations to add a new Web main service into our project:

1) Right-click on our new project **WebServiceSelect Project** from the Solution Explorer window and select the **Add | New Item**.
2) On the **Add New Item** wizard, select **Web Service (ASMX)** from the Template list.
3) Enter **WebServiceSelect.asmx** into the **Name** box.
4) Click on the **Add** button to complete this item addition operation.

The modified Web service project is shown in Figure 9.7.

The main Web Service file, **WebServiceSelect.asmx**, is a code-behind page and it is the place we need to create and develop the codes for our Web services. This page contains a default class that is derived from the base class **WebService**. The class defined a default Web method **HelloWorld** that is a placeholder and we can replace it with our own method or methods later based on the requirement of our Web service project. This file is also used to display information about the Web service's methods and provide access to the Web service's WSDL information.

The configuration file **Web.config** is used to setup a configuration for our new Web service project, such as the namespaces for all kinds of Web components, connection strings for data components and Web services and Windows authentication mode. All of these components are automatically created and added into our new project. More important, the page file **WebServiceSelect.asmx** is designed to automatically create extensible WSDL, dispatch Web methods, serialize and de-serialize parameters, and provide hooks for message interception within our applications. But now it only contains a compile directive when a new Web service project is created and opened from the File System.

Now double-click on the code-behind page **WebServiceSelect.asmx** to open this file that is shown in Figure 9.8, and let's have a closer look at the codes in this page.

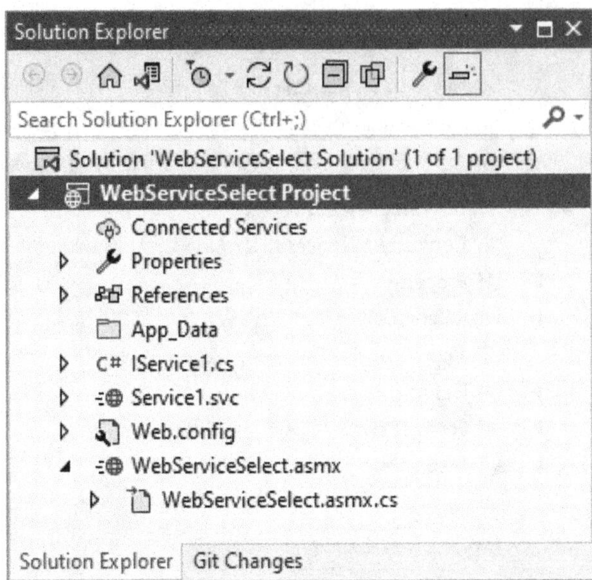

FIGURE 9.7 The modified web service project.

```
WebServiceSelect Project                    HelloWorld()

A   using System;
    using System.Collections.Generic;
    using System.Linq;
    using System.Web;
    using System.Web.Services;
B   namespace WebServiceSelect_Project
    {
        /// <summary>
        /// Summary description for WebServiceSelect
        /// </summary>
        [WebService(Namespace = "http://tempuri.org/")]
C       [WebServiceBinding(ConformsTo = WsiProfiles.BasicProfile1_1)]
D       [System.ComponentModel.ToolboxItem(false)]
        // To allow this Web Service to be called from script, using ASP.NET AJAX, uncomment the following line.
        // [System.Web.Script.Services.ScriptService]
E       public class WebServiceSelect : System.Web.Services.WebService
        {
F           [WebMethod]
            public string HelloWorld()
            {
                return "Hello World";
            }
        }
    }
```

FIGURE 9.8 The default codes for the code-behind page WebServiceSelect.asmx.

A. The Web services related namespaces that contains the Web service components are imported first to allow us to access and use those components to build our Web service project. A detailed description about those namespaces and their functionalities is shown in Figure 9.9.

B. Some WebService attributes are defined in this part. Generally WebService attributes are used to identify additional descriptive information about deployed Web Services. The namespace attribute is one of examples. As we discussed in the last section, we need to use

Namespace	Functionality
using System	Enable you to use the System library in your project. Which gives you some useful classes and functions like Console class or the WriteLine function/method.
using System.Collections.Generic	Contains interfaces and classes that define generic collections, which allow users to create strongly typed collections that provide better type safety and performance than non-generic strongly typed collections.
using System.Web	Contains classes and interfaces that enable browser-server communication. These classes include the HttpRequest class, which provides extensive information about the current HTTP request.
using System.Web.Services	Contains classes that enable you to create XML Web services using ASP.NET and XML Web service clients. XML Web services are applications that provide the ability to exchange messages in a loosely coupled environment using standard protocols such as HTTP, XML, XSD, SOAP, and WSDL.

FIGURE 9.9 The web service namespaces.

our own namespace to store and hold names and identifiers used in our SOAP messages to distinguish them with any other SOAP messages used by other Web services. Here in this new project, Microsoft used a default namespace **http://tempuri.org/**, which is a temporary system defined namespace to identify all Web Services code generated by the .NET framework, to store this default Web method. We need to use our own namespace to store our Web methods later when we deploy our Web services in a real application.

C. This Web Service Binding attribute indicates that the current Web service complies with the Web Services Profiles Basic, **BasicProfile1_1**. Here exactly a binding is equivalent to an interface in which it defines a set of concrete operations.
D. This attribute indicates a base implementation of a toolbox item class.
E. Our Web service class **WebServiceSelect** is a child class that is derived from the parent class **WebService** located in the namespace **System.Web.Services**.
F. The default Web method HelloWorld is defined as a global function and this function returns a string "**Hello World**" when it is returned to the client.

Now let's run the default **HelloWorld()** Web service project to get a feeling about what it looks like and how it works.

Click on the **IIS Express** button to run the default HelloWorld method.

9.3.2 A Feeling of the Hello World Web Service Project as It Runs

Our **WebServiceSelect.asmx** page should be the starting page and the following Internet Explorer (IE) page is displayed as shown in Figure 9.10.

This page displays the Web service class name **WebServiceSelect** and all Web methods or operations developed in this project. By default, only one method **HelloWorld**() is created and used in this project.

Below the method, the default namespace in which the current method or operation is located is shown up, and a recommendation that suggests us to create our own namespace to store our Web service project is displayed. Following this recommendation, some example namespaces used in C#, Visual Basic and C++ are listed.

Now let's access our Web service by clicking on the **HelloWorld** method or link. The test method page is shown up, which is shown in Figure 9.11.

The **Invoke** button is used to test our HelloWorld method using the HTTP Protocol. Below the **Invoke** button, some message examples that are created by using different protocols are displayed. These include the requesting message and responding message created in SOAP 1.1, SOAP 1.2 and HTTP Post. The placeholder that is the default namespace **http://tempuri.org/** should be replaced by the actual namespace when this project is modified to a real application.

Now click on the **Invoke** button to run and test the default method **HelloWorld()**.

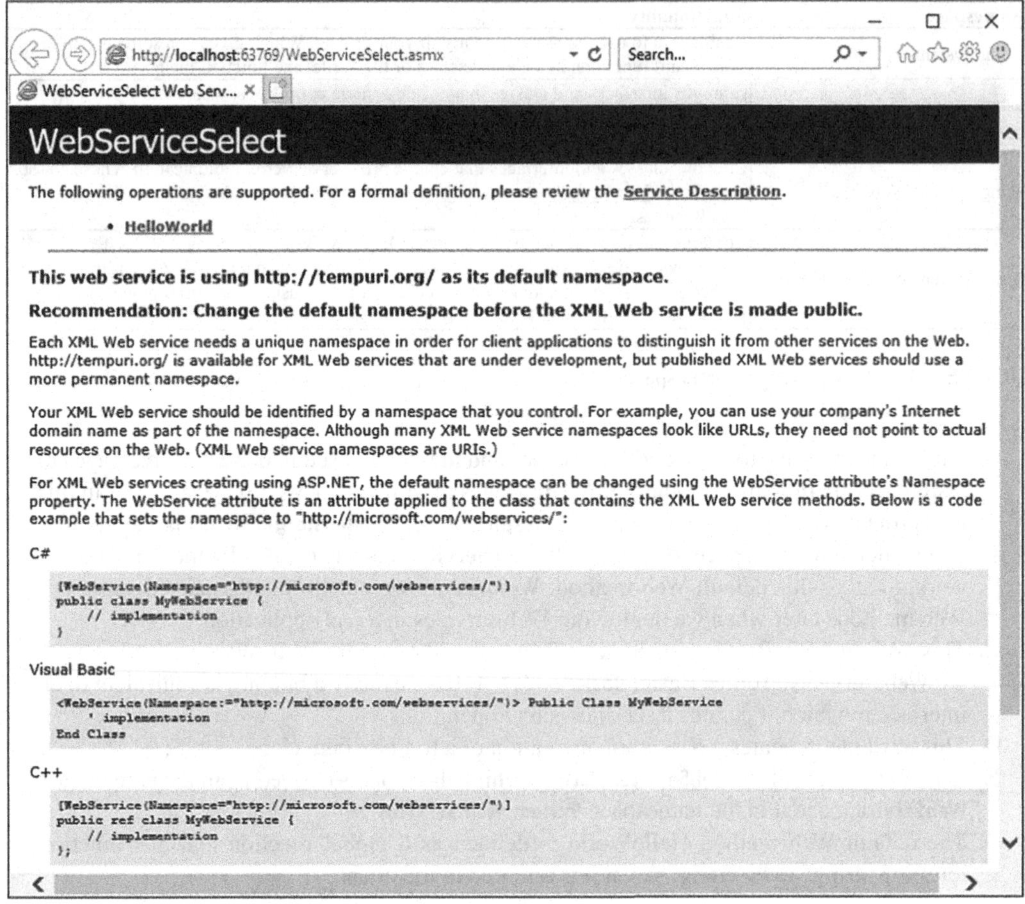

FIGURE 9.10 The running status of the default web service project.

As the **Invoke** button is clicked, an URL that contains the default namespace and the default HelloWorld method's name is activated, and a new browser window that is shown in Figure 9.12 is displayed. When the default method HelloWorld is executed, the main service page **WebServiceSelect.asmx** sends a request to the IIS, and furthermore, the IIS sends it to the ASP.NET runtime to process this request based on that URL.

The ASP.NET runtime will execute the HelloWorld method, pack the returned data as a SOAP message, and then send it back to the client. The returned message contains only a string object, exactly a string of **"Hello World"** for this default method.

In this returned result, the version and the encoding of the used XML code is indicated first. The **xmlns** attribute is used to indicate the namespace used by this String object that contains only a string of "Hello World".

As we discussed in the previous section, ASP.NET Web service did not provide any GUI, so the running result of this default project is represented by using the XML codes in some Web interfaces we have seen. This is because those Web interfaces are only provided and used for the testing purpose for the default Web service. In a real application, no such Web interface will be provided and displayed.

Click on the **Close** button that is located on the upper-right corner of the browser to close two browser pages. You may also click on the **Stop** button to stop this project.

At this point, we should have a basic understanding and feeling about a typical Web service project and its structure as well as its operation process. Next we will build our own Web service project

http://localhost:63769/WebServiceSelect.asmx?op=HelloWorld

WebServiceSelect Web Serv...

WebServiceSelect

Click here for a complete list of operations.

HelloWorld

Test

To test the operation using the HTTP POST protocol, click the 'Invoke' button.

Invoke

SOAP 1.1

The following is a sample SOAP 1.1 request and response. The placeholders shown need to be replaced with actual values.

```
POST /WebServiceSelect.asmx HTTP/1.1
Host: localhost
Content-Type: text/xml; charset=utf-8
Content-Length: length
SOAPAction: "http://tempuri.org/HelloWorld"

<?xml version="1.0" encoding="utf-8"?>
<soap:Envelope xmlns:xsi="http://www.w3.org/2001/XMLSchema-instance" xmlns:xsd="http://www.w3.org/2001/XMLSchema" xmlns:sc
  <soap:Body>
    <HelloWorld xmlns="http://tempuri.org/" />
  </soap:Body>
</soap:Envelope>
```

```
HTTP/1.1 200 OK
Content-Type: text/xml; charset=utf-8
Content-Length: length

<?xml version="1.0" encoding="utf-8"?>
<soap:Envelope xmlns:xsi="http://www.w3.org/2001/XMLSchema-instance" xmlns:xsd="http://www.w3.org/2001/XMLSchema" xmlns:sc
  <soap:Body>
    <HelloWorldResponse xmlns="http://tempuri.org/">
      <HelloWorldResult>string</HelloWorldResult>
    </HelloWorldResponse>
  </soap:Body>
</soap:Envelope>
```

SOAP 1.2

The following is a sample SOAP 1.2 request and response. The placeholders shown need to be replaced with actual values.

```
POST /WebServiceSelect.asmx HTTP/1.1
Host: localhost
Content-Type: application/soap+xml; charset=utf-8
Content-Length: length

<?xml version="1.0" encoding="utf-8"?>
<soap12:Envelope xmlns:xsi="http://www.w3.org/2001/XMLSchema-instance" xmlns:xsd="http://www.w3.org/2001/XMLSchema" xmlns:
  <soap12:Body>
    <HelloWorld xmlns="http://tempuri.org/" />
  </soap12:Body>
</soap12:Envelope>
```

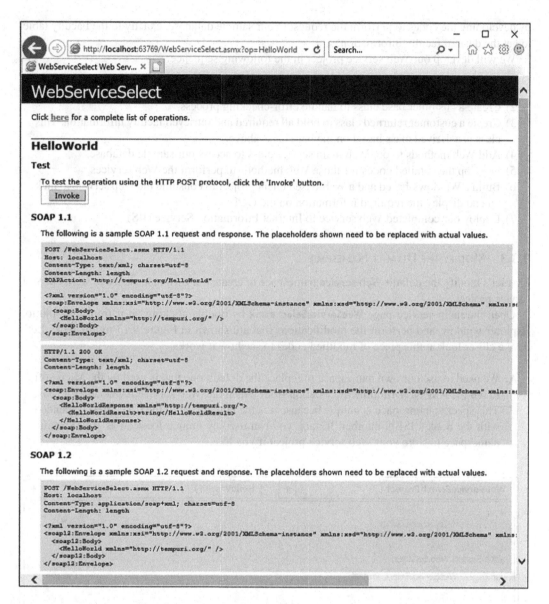

FIGURE 9.11 The test method page.

FIGURE 9.12 The running status of the default method.

by developing the codes to perform the request to our sample database, exactly to the Faculty table, to get the desired faculty information.

We will develop our Web service project in the following sequence:

1) Modify the default namespace to create our own Web service namespace.
2) Create a customer base class to handle error-checking process.
3) Create a customer returned class to hold all required and retrieved faculty information. This class is a derived class based on the base class above.
4) Add Web methods to our Web main service class to access our sample database.
5) Develop the detailed codes for those Web methods to perform the Web services.
6) Build a Windows-based and a Web-based client project to consume the Web service to pick up and display the required information on the GUI.
7) Deploy our completed Web service to Internet Information Service (IIS).

9.3.3 Modify the Default Namespace

First let's modify the default Web service namespace to create our own namespace to store our Web service project.

Open the main service page **WebServiceSelect.asmx** by double-clicking on it from the Solution Explorer window, and perform the modifications that are shown in Figure 9.13 to this page. Let's have a closer look at this piece of modified codes to see how it works.

A. We need to use our own namespace to replace the default one that is used by the Microsoft to tell the ASP.NET runtime the location from which our Web service is loaded as it runs. This specific namespace is unique because it is the home page of the CRC Press appended with the book's ISBN number. In fact, you can use any unique location as your specific namespace to store your Web service project if you like.

```
WebServiceSelect Project          HelloWorld()

using System;
using System.Collections.Generic;
using System.Linq;
using System.Web;
using System.Web.Services;

namespace WebServiceSelect_Project
{
    /// <summary>
    /// Summary description for WebServiceSelect
    /// </summary>
A   [WebService(Namespace = "https://www.routledge.com/978-1032312354/")]
    [WebServiceBinding(ConformsTo = WsiProfiles.BasicProfile1_1)]
    [System.ComponentModel.ToolboxItem(false)]
    // To allow this Web Service to be called from script, using ASP.NET AJAX, uncomment the following line.
    // [System.Web.Script.Services.ScriptService]
    public class WebServiceSelect : System.Web.Services.WebService
    {
        [WebMethod]
        public string HelloWorld()
        {
            return "Hello World";
        }
    }
}
```

FIGURE 9.13 The modified main service page.

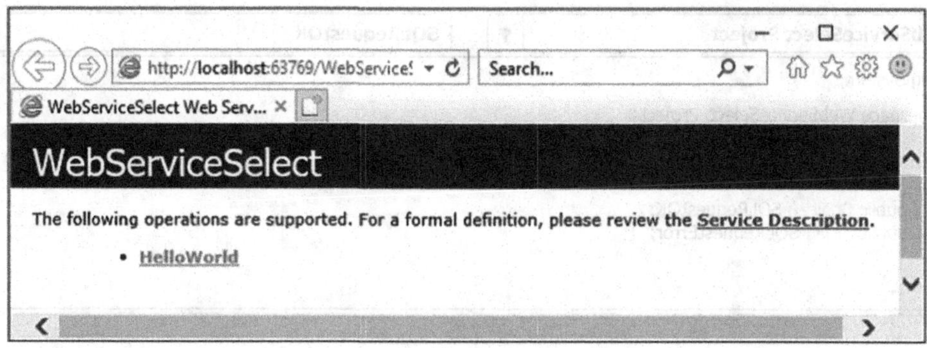

FIGURE 9.14 The running status of the modified web service project.

Now click on the **IIS Express** button to run our new Web service project, a default Web interface is displayed with our project name, as shown in Figure 9.14.

If you click on the default method **HelloWorld** and then **Invoke** button to test that method, you can find that the namespace has been updated to our new specific namespace, **https://www.routledge.com/978-1032312354/**.

A point to be noted is that you must set the service file **WebServiceSelect.asmx** as the start page before you can run our service project since this file is the entry point of our Web service project. To do that, right-click on our page **WebServiceSelect.asmx** from the Solution Explorer window and select the item **Set As Start Page**.

9.3.4 Create a Base Class to Handle Error Checking for Our Web Service

In this section we want to create a parent or base class and use it to handle some possible errors or exceptions as our project runs. It is possible for some reasons that our requests cannot be processed and returned improperly. One of the most possible reasons for that is the security issue. To report any errors or problems that occurred in the processing of requests, a parent or base class is a good candidate to perform those jobs. We name this base class as **SQLSelectBase** and it has two member data:

- **Boolean SQLRequestOK**: True if the request is fine; otherwise a False is set.
- **String SQLRequestError**: A string used to report the errors or problems.

To create a new base class in our new project, right-click on our new service project **WebServiceSelect Project** from the Solution Explorer window. Then select the **Add | New Item** from the popup menu. On the opened Add New Item wizard, select the **Class** item from the center under the **Visual C#** Template on the left, and enter **SQLSelectBase.cs** into the **Name** box as our new class name. Then click on the **Add** button to add this new class into our project.

Now double-click on this new added class and enter the codes that are shown in Figure 9.15 into this class as the class member data.

Two public class member data, **SQLRequestOK** and **SQLRequestError**, are added into this new base class. These two data will work together to report possible errors or problems during the request processing.

9.3.5 Create a Customer Returned Class to Hold All Retrieved Data

Now we need to create our returned Web service class which will be instantiated and returned to us with our required information as the project runs. This class should be a child class of our base class **SQLSelectBase** we just created. We name this class **SQLSelectResult**.

```
WebServiceSelect Project            SQLRequestOK

using System;
namespace WebServiceSelect_Project
{
   public class SQLSelectBase
   {
      public Boolean SQLRequestOK;
      public String SQLRequestError;
   }
}
```

FIGURE 9.15 The class member data.

```
WebServiceSelect Project            SQLSelectResult

using System;
namespace WebServiceSelect_Project
{
   public class SQLSelectResult:SQLSelectBase
   {
      public String FacultyID;
      public String FacultyTitle;
      public String FacultyOffice;
      public String FacultyPhone;
      public String FacultyCollege;
      public String FacultyEmail;
      public Byte[] FacultyImage;
   }
}
```

FIGURE 9.16 The member data for the class SQLSelectResult.

Right-click on our new Web service project **WebServiceSelect Project** from the Solution Explorer window, and select the **Add | New Item** from the popup menu. On the opened Add New Item wizard, select the **Class** item from the Template list. Then enter **SQLSelectResult.cs** into the **Name** box as the name for this new class, and then click on the **Add** button to add this new class into our project.

Double-click on this new added class and enter the codes that are shown in Figure 9.16 into this class as the member data to this class.

Since this class will be instantiated to an object that will be returned with our desired faculty information to us as the Web method is called, so all desired faculty information should be added into this class as the member data. When we make a request to this Web service project, and furthermore, to our sample database, the following desired faculty data should be included and returned (exclude the **faculty_name** since it will be input to a related Web Method later to be called to get all of these pieces of faculty information):

- Faculty_id
- Faculty title
- Faculty office
- Faculty phone
- Faculty college
- Faculty email
- Faculty image

All of these pieces of information, which can be exactly mapped onto all columns in the **Faculty** table in our sample database, are needed to be added into this class as the member data. It is true that this does not look like a professional schema. Another, better option is that we do not need to create any class that will be instantiated to an object to hold these pieces of information, instead we can use a DataSet to hold those pieces of information and allow the Web method to return that DataSet as a whole package for those pieces of faculty information. But that better option is relatively complicated compared with our current class. So right now we prefer to start our project with an easier way, and later on we will discuss how to use the DataSet to return our desired information in the following sections.

As we mentioned before, this class is a child class of our base class **SQLSelectBase;** in other words, this class is inherited from that base class. Seven pieces of faculty information without **faculty_name** are declared here as the member data for this class.

Next we need to take care of our Web method that will response to our request and return our desired faculty information to us as this method is called.

9.3.6 Add Web Methods into Our Web Service Class

Before we can add a Web method to our project and perform the coding process for it, we want to emphasize an important point that is easily confused by users, which is the Web service class and those classes we just created in the last section.

The Web service class **WebServiceSelect.asmx** is a system class and it is used to contain all codes we need to access the Web service and Web methods to execute our requests. The base class **SQLSelectBase** and the child class **SQLSelectResult** are created by us and they belong to application classes. These application classes will be instantiated to the associated objects that will be used by the Web methods developed in the system class **WebServiceSelect.asmx** to return the requested information as the project runs. Keep this difference in mind and this will help you to understand them better as you develop a new Web service project.

We can add a new Web method or modify the default method **HelloWorld** and make it as our new Web method in our system class **WebServiceSelect.asmx**. This method will use an object instantiated from the application class **SQLSelectResult** we created in the previous section to hold and return the faculty information we requested.

9.3.7 Develop the Codes for the Modified Web Methods to Perform the Web Services

The name of this Web method is **GetSQLSelect()**, and it contains an input parameter Faculty Name with the following functions as this method is called:

1) Setup a valid connection to our sample database.
2) Create all required data objects and local variables to perform the necessary data operations.
3) Instantiate a new object from the application class **SQLSelectResult** and use it as the returned object that contains all required faculty data.
4) Execute the associated data object's method to perform the data query to the Faculty table based on the input parameter, Faculty Name.
5) Assign each piece of acquired information obtained from the Faculty table to the associated class member data defined in the class **SQLSelectResult**.
6) Release and clean up all data objects used.
7) Return the object to the client.

9.3.7.1 Web Service Connection Strings

Among those functions listed above, function 1 is one of the most challenging tasks. There are two ways to perform this database connection in Web service applications. One way is to directly use the connection string and connection object in the Web service class as we did in the previous projects. Another way is to define the connection string in the **Web.config** file. The second way is better since the **Web.config** file provides an attribute **<connectionStrings/>** for this purpose and ASP.NET 4.7 recommends to store the data components' connection string in the **Web.config** file.

In this project, we will use the second way to store our connection string. To do that, open our Web service project the **Web.config** file by double-clicking on it, move to the end of that file, and enter either of the following code segments into this configuration file (just above the configuration ending tag **</configuration>**):

```
<connectionStrings>
<add name="sql_conn"connectionString="Server=localhost\SQL2019EXPRESS; _
 Integrated Security=SSPI;Database=CSE_DEPT;"/>
</connectionStrings>
```
or
```
<connectionStrings>
 <add name="sql_conn" connectionString="Server=localhost\
   SQL2019EXPRESS; _
  Initial Catalog=CSE_DEPT;User ID=SMART;Password=Happy2022;"/>
</connectionStrings>
```

The following important points should be noted when create this connection string:

1) You need only to enter either the upper or the lower segment as the connection string, not both since we setup our sample database with two accessing modes; **Windows Authentication mode** and **SQL Server Authentication mode**. The upper one is used for the former and the lower is used for the latter mode.
2) This **connectionStrings** attribute must be written in a **single line** in the **Web.config** file. However, due to the space limitation, here we used two lines to represent this attribute. But in your real codes, you must place this attribute in a single line in your **Web.config** file; otherwise, a grammar problem will be encountered.
3) Web services that require a database connection in this project use either a SQL Server Authentication mode with a login ID and password for a user account, or a Windows Authentication mode without those credentials. Because we used **Windows Authentication mode** during we created our sample database in Chapter 2, but we modified that accessing mode to the **Server Authentication mode** in Chapter 5. Thus in this project you can use either mode as you like.

To test and confirm this **connectionString**, we can develop some codes and modify the codes in the default **HelloWorld** Web method in the main service page to do that. Close the **Web.config** file and open the main service page **WebServiceSelect.asmx** by double clicking on it from the Solution Explorer window, and enter the codes shown in Figure 9.17 into this page. All modified codes have been highlighted with the bold words, and let's see how this piece of codes works to test our connection string.

A. The namespaces that contains the SQL Server Data Provider and Web service as well as the system configurations are added into this page with the **using** commands since we need to use those data components in this page.

B. The **ConnectionStrings** property of the **ConfigurationManager** class is used to pick up the connection string we defined in the **Web.config** file, which can be considered as a default connection configuration. The connection name **sql_conn** that works as an argument for this property must be identical with the name we used for the connection name in the **Web.config** file. When this property is used, it returns a **ConnectionStringSettingsCollection** object

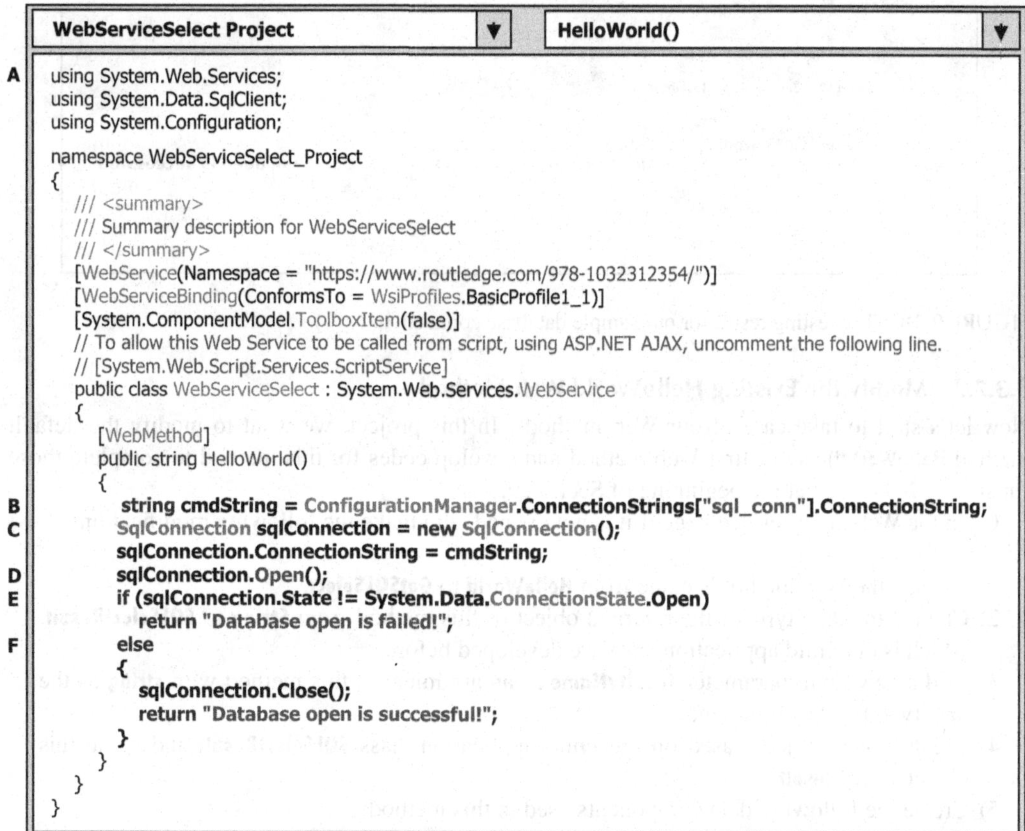

```
WebServiceSelect Project                 HelloWorld()

A   using System.Web.Services;
    using System.Data.SqlClient;
    using System.Configuration;

    namespace WebServiceSelect_Project
    {
      /// <summary>
      /// Summary description for WebServiceSelect
      /// </summary>
      [WebService(Namespace = "https://www.routledge.com/978-1032312354/")]
      [WebServiceBinding(ConformsTo = WsiProfiles.BasicProfile1_1)]
      [System.ComponentModel.ToolboxItem(false)]
      // To allow this Web Service to be called from script, using ASP.NET AJAX, uncomment the following line.
      // [System.Web.Script.Services.ScriptService]
      public class WebServiceSelect : System.Web.Services.WebService
      {
        [WebMethod]
        public string HelloWorld()
        {
B          string cmdString = ConfigurationManager.ConnectionStrings["sql_conn"].ConnectionString;
C          SqlConnection sqlConnection = new SqlConnection();
           sqlConnection.ConnectionString = cmdString;
D          sqlConnection.Open();
E          if (sqlConnection.State != System.Data.ConnectionState.Open)
              return "Database open is failed!";
F          else
           {
              sqlConnection.Close();
              return "Database open is successful!";
           }
        }
      }
    }
```

FIGURE 9.17 The modified codes to test the connection string.

containing the contents of the **ConnectionStringsSection** object for the current application's default configuration, and a **ConnectionStringsSection** object contains the contents of the configuration file's **connectionStrings** section.

C. A new SQL Connection object is created and initialized with the connection string we obtained above.

D. The **Open()** method of the SQL Connection object is executed to try to open our sample database and setup a valid connection.

E. By checking the **State** property of the Connection object, we can determine whether or not this connection is successful. If the **State** property is not equal to the **ConnectionState.Open**, which means that a valid database connection has not been installed, a warning message is returned and displayed.

F. Otherwise, the connection is successful, a successful message is displayed and the connection is closed.

Now you can run the project by clicking on the **IIS Express** button. Click on the **HelloWorld** method from the built-in Web interface, and then click on the **Invoke** button to execute that method to test our database connection.

A successful message should be displayed if this connection is fine, as shown in Figure 9.18. Click on the **Close** button located at the upper-right corner on that page to terminate our Web service project.

A point is that this piece of codes is only used for the testing purpose and we will modify this piece of codes and place it into a user-defined function **SQLConn()** later when we develop our real project.

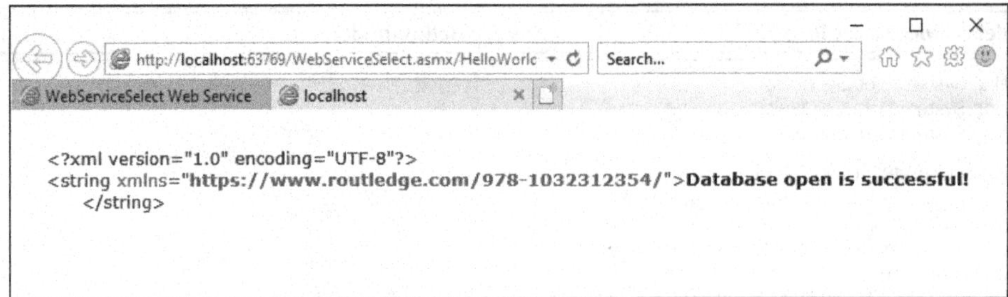

FIGURE 9.18 The testing result for our sample database connection.

9.3.7.2 Modify the Existing HelloWorld Web Method

Now let's start to take care of our Web methods. In this project, we want to modify the default method **HelloWorld()** as our first Web method and develop codes for this method to complete those functions (2–7) listed at the beginning of Section 9.3.7.

Open the Web main service page if it is not opened, and make the following modifications:

1) Change the Web method's name from **HelloWorld** to **GetSQLSelect**.
2) Change the data type of the returned object of this method from **String** to **SQLSelectResult**, which is our child application class we developed before.
3) Add a new input parameter **FacultyName** as an argument to this method with **string** as the data type for that argument.
4) Create a new object based on our child application class **SQLSelectResult** and name this object as **SQLResult**.
5) Create the following data components used in this method:
   a. SQL Command Object **sqlCommand**.
   b. SQL Data Reader Object **sqlReader**.
6) Replace the default returned object in the method from the "Hello World" string to the new created object **SQLResult**.
7) Move the connection testing codes we developed in the last section into a user defined function **SQLConn()**.

Your finished Web method **GetSQLSelect()** is shown in Figure 9.19. Let's take a closer look at this piece of modified codes to see how it works.

A. Modification steps 1, 2 and 3 listed above are performed at this line. The method's name and the returned data type are modified to **GetSQLSelect** and **SQLSelectResult**, respectively. Also an input parameter **FacultyName** is added into this method as an argument.

B. Modification step 4 is performed at this line, and an instance of the application class **SQLSelectResult** is created here.

C. Modification step 5 is performed at this line and two SQL data objects are created; **sqlCommand** and **sqlReader**, respectively.

D. Modification step 6 is performed at this line, and the original returned data is updated to the current object **SQLResult**.

E. Modification step 7 is performed here and a new user-defined function **SQLConn()** is created with the codes we developed to test the connection string above.

F. If this connection is failed, a **null** is returned. Otherwise, a successful connection object is assigned to the returned connection object **conn**.

G. The connection object is returned to the Web method.

```
WebServiceSelect Project                    GetSQLSelect(string FacultyName)

   [WebMethod]
A  public SQLSelectResult GetSQLSelect(string FacultyName)
   {
      SqlConnection sqlConnection = new SqlConnection();
B     SQLSelectResult SQLResult = new SQLSelectResult();
C     SqlCommand sqlCommand = new SqlCommand();
      SqlDataReader sqlReader;

      .........
D     return SQLResult;
   }
E  protected SqlConnection SQLConn()
   {
      string cmdString = ConfigurationManager.ConnectionStrings["sql_conn"].ConnectionString;
      SqlConnection conn = new SqlConnection();
      conn.ConnectionString = cmdString;
      conn.Open();
F     if (conn.State != System.Data.ConnectionState.Open)
         conn = null;
G     return conn;
   }
```

FIGURE 9.19 The modified web method – GetSQLSelect().

Next we need to develop the codes to execute the associated data object's method to perform the data query to the Faculty table based on the input parameter, **Faculty Name**.

9.3.7.3 Develop the Codes to Perform the Database Queries

To perform the database query via our Web service project, we need to perform the following coding developments:

- Add the major codes into our Web method to perform the data query.
- Create a user-defined subroutine **FillFacultyReader()** to handle the data assignments to our returned object.
- Create an error or exception-processing subroutine **ReportError()** to report any errors encountered during the project runs.

Now let's first concentrate on adding the codes to perform the data query to our sample database **CSE_DEPT**.

Open our main service page and add the codes that are shown in Figure 9.20 into our Web method. The codes we developed in the previous sections have been highlighted with the gray color as the background.

Let's take a closer look at these new added codes to see how they work.

A. The namespace **System.Data** is added into this page since some basic data components and data types are defined in this namespace and we need to use those components in this page.

B. The query string is declared at the beginning of this method. One point you may have already noted is that a **+** symbol is used here to connect two segments as a single query string. The Web service page allows us to use this one as the concatenating operator. Another point is that a space must be attached at the end of the first part of this query string, **"...FROM Faculty"** since this space works as a separator between the first and the second part of this query string. The query function could not be executed correctly without this space.

```
WebServiceSelect Projct                    GetSQLSelect(string FacultyName)

  using System.Web.Services;
  using System.Data.SqlClient;
  using System.Configuration;
A using System.Data;
  namespace WebServiceSelect_Project
  {
     /// <summary>
     /// Summary description for WebServiceSelect
     /// </summary>
     [WebService(Namespace = "https://www.routledge.com/978-1032312354/")]
     [WebServiceBinding(ConformsTo = WsiProfiles.BasicProfile1_1)]
     [System.ComponentModel.ToolboxItem(false)]
     // To allow this Web Service to be called from script, using ASP.NET AJAX, uncomment the following line.
     // [System.Web.Script.Services.ScriptService]
     public class WebServiceSelect : System.Web.Services.WebService
     {
       [WebMethod]
        public SQLSelectResult GetSQLSelect(string FacultyName)
        {
           SqlConnection sqlConnection = new SqlConnection();
           SQLSelectResult SQLResult = new SQLSelectResult();
           SqlCommand sqlCommand = new SqlCommand();
           SqlDataReader sqlReader;
B          string cmdString = "SELECT faculty_id, title, office, phone, college, email, fimage  FROM Faculty " +
                              "WHERE faculty_name = @facultyName";
C          SQLResult.SQLRequestOK = true;
D          sqlConnection = SQLConn();
E          if (sqlConnection == null)
           {
              SQLResult.SQLRequestError = "Database connection is failed";
              ReportError(SQLResult);
              return null;
           }
F          sqlCommand.Connection = sqlConnection;
           sqlCommand.CommandType = CommandType.Text;
           sqlCommand.CommandText = cmdString;
           sqlCommand.Parameters.Add("@facultyName", SqlDbType.NVarChar).Value = FacultyName;
G          sqlReader = sqlCommand.ExecuteReader();
H          if (sqlReader.HasRows == true)
              FillFacultyReader(ref SQLResult, sqlReader);
I          else
           {
              SQLResult.SQLRequestError = "No matched faculty found";
              ReportError(SQLResult);
           }
J          sqlReader.Close();
           sqlConnection.Close();
           sqlCommand.Dispose();
K          return SQLResult;
        }
```

FIGURE 9.20 The modified codes for the web method.

C. Initially, we assume that our Web method works fine by setting the Boolean variable **SQLRequestOK**, which we defined in our base class **SQLSelectBase**, to **True**. This variable will keep this value until an error or exception is encountered.

D. The user-defined function **SQLConn()**, whose detailed codes are shown in Figure 9.19, is called to perform the database connection. This function will return a connection object if the connection is successful. Otherwise, the function will return a **null** object.

E. If a **null** is returned from calling the function **SQLConn()**, which means that the database connection has something wrong, the user-defined subroutine **ReportError()**, whose codes are shown later in Figure 9.22, is executed to report the encountered error.

F. The Command object is initialized with the connection object that is obtained from the function **SQLConn()**, command type and command text. Also the input Parameter **@facultyName** is assigned with the real input parameter **FacultyName** that is an input parameter to the Web method. One issue is the data type for that parameter. For this application, the data type must be a **SqlDbType.NvarChar** since the data type of the **faculty_name** column was defined as the **nvarchar(50)** in the Faculty table when our sample database was built in Chapter 2.

G. The ExecuteReader() method of the command class is called to invoke the DataReader to perform the data query from our Faculty table.

H. By checking the **HasRows** property of the DataReader, we can determine whether or not this query is successful. If this property is **True**, which means that at least one row has been returned and the query is successful, the user defined subroutine **FillFacultyReader()** is called to assign all queried data columns to the associated member data we created in our child class **SQLSelectResult**. Two arguments, **SQLResult,** that is our returning object, and **sqlReader,** that is our DataReader object, are passed into that subroutine. The difference between these two arguments is the passing mode; the returning object **SQLResult** is passed by using a passing-by-reference mode, which means that an address of that object is passed into the subroutine and all assigned data columns to that object can be brought back to the calling procedure. This is very similar to a returned object from calling a function. But the DataReader **sqlReader** is passed by using a passing-by-value mode, which means that only a copy of that object is passed into the subroutine and any modification to that object is temporary.

I. If the **HasRows** property returns **False**, which means that the data query is failed, an error message is assigned to the member data **SQLRequestError** defined in our base class **SQLSelectBase**, and our **ReportError()** method is called to report this error.

J. A cleaning job is performed to release all data objects used in this method.

K. The object **SQLResult** is returned as the query result from our Web service.

Next let's take care of developing the codes for our two user-defined methods or procedures **FillFacultyReader()** and **ReportError()**.

9.3.7.4 Develop the Codes for Two Methods Used in the Web Method

The codes for the method **FillFacultyReader()** are shown in Figure 9.21. Let's have a closer look at this piece of codes in this subroutine to see how it works.

A. The **Read()** method of the DataReader is executed to read out the queried data row, In our case, only one row that is matched to the input faculty name is read out and feed into the DataReader object **sReader**.

B. Each data column in the Faculty table, except the faculty image, can be identified by using its name from the DataReader object **sReader** and converted to a string using the **Convert** class method **ToString()**. The data type of the faculty image column is a binary array byte[], thus a forced conversion is performed to convert its type to the byte[]. Finally all columns are assigned to the associated member data in our returning object.

Optionally, you can use the **GetString()** method to retrieve each column from the DataReader **sReader**. An index that is matched to the position of each column in the query string **cmdString** must be used to locate each piece of data if that method is used.

```
WebServiceSelect Project    FillFacultyReader()

  protected void FillFacultyReader(ref SQLSelectResult sResult, SqlDataReader sReader)
  {
A     if (sReader.Read() == true)
      {
B        sResult.FacultyID = Convert.ToString(sReader["faculty_id"]);
         sResult.FacultyTitle = Convert.ToString(sReader["title"]);
         sResult.FacultyOffice = Convert.ToString(sReader["office"]);
         sResult.FacultyPhone = Convert.ToString(sReader["phone"]);
         sResult.FacultyCollege = Convert.ToString(sReader["college"]);
         sResult.FacultyEmail = Convert.ToString(sReader["email"]);
         sResult.FacultyImage = (byte[])sReader["fimage"];
      }
  }
```

FIGURE 9.21 The codes for the method FillFacultyReader().

```
WebServiceSelect Project    ReportError(SQLSelectResult ErrSource)

protected void ReportError(SQLSelectResult ErrSource)
{
    ErrSource.SQLRequestOK = false;
}
```

FIGURE 9.22 The codes for the subroutine ReportError().

The key point for this method is the passing mode for the first argument. A passing-by-reference mode is used for our returning object and this is equivalent to return an address of the passed object from a function.

The codes for another user-defined method **ReportError()** are shown in Figure 9.22.

The input parameter to this subroutine is our returning object. A **False** is assigned to the **SQLRequestOK** member data and the error message is assigned to the **SQLRequestError** string variable defined in our base class **SQLSelectBase**. Since our returning object is instantiated from our child class **SQLSelectResult** that is inherited from our base class, so our returning object can access and use those member data defined in the base class.

At this point, we finished all coding jobs for our Web service project. Now let's run our project to test the data query functionality. Click on the **IIS Express** button to run the project and the built-in Web interface is displayed, which is shown in Figure 9.23.

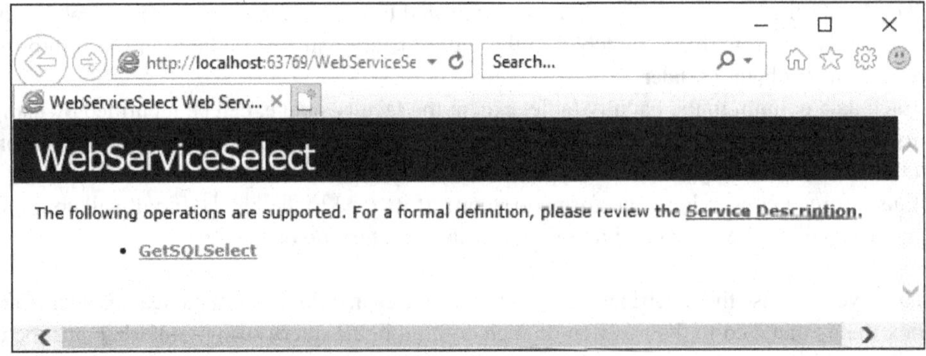

FIGURE 9.23 The running status of the web service.

WebServiceSelect

Click here for a complete list of operations.

GetSQLSelect

Test

To test the operation using the HTTP POST protocol, click the 'Invoke' button.

Parameter	Value
FacultyName:	Ying Bai

Invoke

SOAP 1.1

The following is a sample SOAP 1.1 request and response. The placeholders shown need to be replaced

FIGURE 9.24 The running status of our web method.

Click on our Web method **GetSQLSelect** to open the built-in Web interface for our Web method, which is shown in Figure 9.24. Enter the faculty name **Ying Bai** into the **FacultyName** box as an input Value, and then click on the **Invoke** button to execute the Web method to trigger the ASP.NET runtime to perform our data query.

The running result is returned and displayed in the XML format, which is shown in Figure 9.25. Each returned data is enclosed by a pair of XML tags to indicate or markup its facility. For example, the **B78880**, which is the queried **faculty_id**, is enclosed by the tag **<FacultyID>...</FacultyID>**, and the name of this tag is defined in our child class **SQLSelectResult**. Our first Web service method is very successful.

As we mentioned before, a Web service did not provide any user interface and one needs to develop some user interfaces to consume the Web service if one wants to display those pieces of information obtained from the Web services. Here, a built-in Web interface is provided by Microsoft

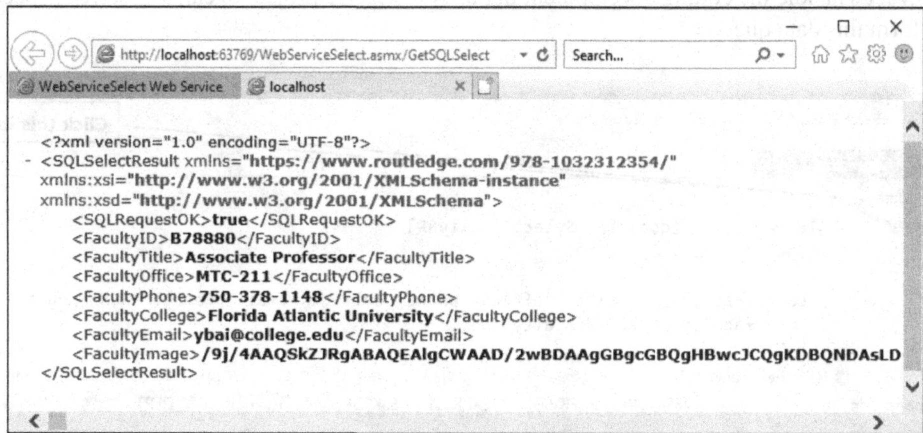

FIGURE 9.25 The running result of our web service project.

to help users to display queried information from the Web services. In most real applications, users need to develop user interfaces themselves to perform these data displaying or other data operations.

Click on the **Close** button that is located at the upper-right corner of the page to close our Web service project.

9.3.8 Develop a Stored Procedure to Perform the Data Query in Web Service

An optional and better way to perform the data query via Web service is to use the stored procedures. The advantage of using this method is that the coding process can be greatly simplified and most query jobs can be performed in the database side. Therefore, the query execution speed can be faster. The query efficiency can also be improved and the query operations can be integrated into a single group or block of code body to strengthen the integrity of the query.

9.3.8.1 Develop the Stored Procedure WebSelectFacultySP

Now let's first develop our stored procedure in the Server Explorer window in Visual Studio.NET environment.

Open the Visual Studio.NET and open the Server Explorer window, then click on the small arrow icon in front of our SQL Server database to expand our sample database. Then right click on the **Stored Procedures** folder and select the item **Add New Stored Procedure** from the popup menu to open a new stored procedure. Enter the codes that are shown in Figure 9.26 into this code body as our new stored procedure.

Click on the **Update** item shown in Figure 9.26 and the **Update Database** button to save this new stored procedure with a name of **dbo.WebSelectFacultySP**.

Now one can expand the **Stored Procedures** folder in the Server Explorer to check and confirm this new created stored procedure. Right click on that folder and select the **Refresh** item if you cannot find it.

We can run this stored procedure in the Visual Studio.NET environment to confirm its function. Right click on this new created stored procedure from the Server Explorer

Window and select the **Execute** item from the popup menu to open the Run Stored Procedure wizard. Enter the faculty name **Ying Bai** to the **Value** box as the input parameter and click on the **OK** button to run it. The running result is displayed in the **Output** window that is located at the bottom of this wizard, which is shown in Figure 9.27.

All queried seven (7) columns, that include the **faculty_id**, **title**, **office**, **phone**, **college**, **email** and **fimage** in the Faculty table, are displayed in this **Result** window. You need to move the horizontal bar at the bottom to see all of these columns.

Our stored procedure is successful.

Now let's handle the coding development in our Web service project to call this stored procedure to perform this data query.

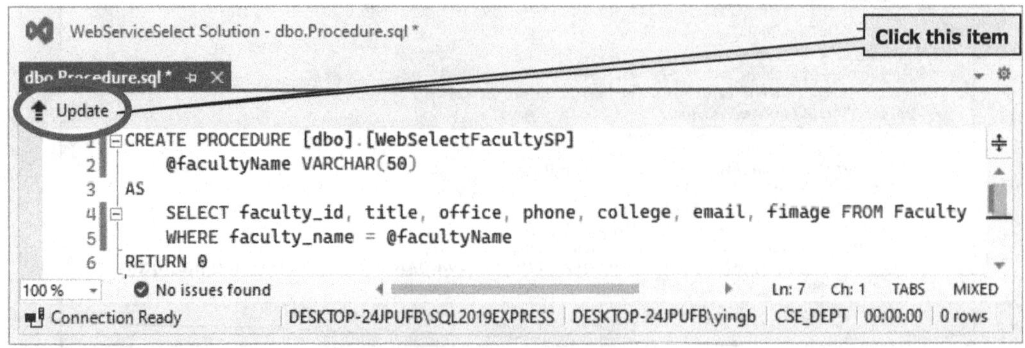

FIGURE 9.26 The stored procedure dbo.WebSelectFacultySP.

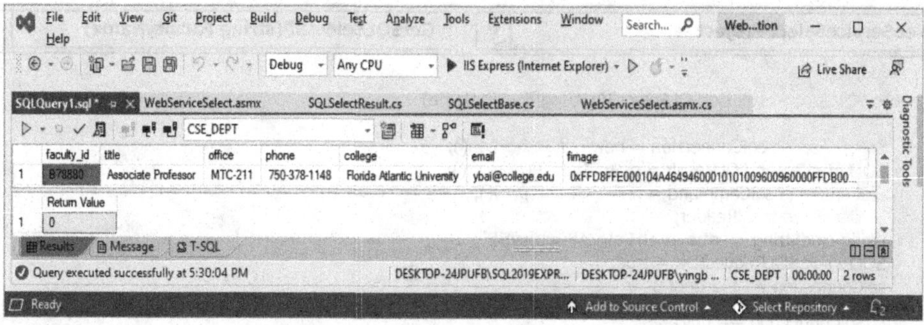

FIGURE 9.27 The running result of the stored procedure.

9.3.8.2 Add Another Web Method to Call the Stored Procedure

To distinguish from the first Web method we developed in the previous section, we had better add another Web method to perform this data query by calling the stored procedure. To do that, highlight and select the whole coding body of our first Web method **GetSQLSelect()**, including both the method header and the code body. Then copy this whole coding body and paste it to the bottom of our code-behind page (must be inside our Web service class).

Perform the modifications shown in Figure 9.28 to this copied Web method to make it as our second Web method **GetSQLSelectSP()**. The modified parts have been highlighted in bold. Let's have a closer look at this piece of codes to see how this method works.

A. Change the Web method's name by attaching two letters **SP** to the end of the original Web method's name, and the new method's name becomes **GetSQLSelectSP**.
B. Change the content of the query string **cmdString** to "**dbo.WebSelectFacultySP**". To call a stored procedure from a Web service project, the content of the query string must be exactly equal to the name of the stored procedure we developed in the last section. Otherwise a running error may be encountered during the project runs because the project cannot find the desired stored procedure.
C. Change the CommandType property of the Command object from the **CommandType.Text** to the **CommandType.StoredProcedure**. This changing is very important since we need to call a stored procedure to perform the data query. Therefore we must tell the ASP.NET runtime that a stored procedure should be called when the command object is executed.

Now run the project to test this new Web method. Click on the second Web method **GetSQLSelectSP** as the project runs, enter a desired faculty member such as **Ying Bai** into the **FacultyName** box and click on the **Invoke** button to run it. The same running result as we got from the last project can be obtained. You can see how easy it is to develop codes to perform the data query by calling the stored procedure in the Web service project.

Next we will discuss how to use a DataSet as a returning object to contain all pieces of queried information we need from running a Web service project.

9.3.9 Use DataSet as the Returning Object for the Web Method in Web Service

The advantage of using a DataSet as the returning object for a Web method is that we do not need to create any application class to instantiate a returning object. Another advantage is that a DataSet can contain multiple records coming from the different tables, and we do not need to create multiple member data in our application class to hold those data items. Finally, the size of our coding body could be greatly reduced when a DataSet is used, especially for a large block of data that are queried via the Web service project.

```
WebServiceSelect Project                    GetSQLSelectSP(string FacultyName)

    [WebMethod]
A   public SQLSelectResult GetSQLSelectSP(string FacultyName)
    {
        SqlConnection sqlConnection = new SqlConnection();
        SQLSelectResult SQLResult = new SQLSelectResult();
        SqlCommand sqlCommand = new SqlCommand();
        SqlDataReader sqlReader;
B       string cmdString = "dbo.WebSelectFacultySP";
        SQLResult.SQLRequestOK = true;
        sqlConnection = SQLConn();
        if (sqlConnection == null)
        {
            SQLResult.SQLRequestError = "Database connection is failed";
            ReportError(SQLResult);
            return null;
        }
        sqlCommand.Connection = sqlConnection;
C       sqlCommand.CommandType = CommandType.StoredProcedure;
        sqlCommand.CommandText = cmdString;
        sqlCommand.Parameters.Add("@facultyName", SqlDbType.NVarChar).Value = FacultyName;
        sqlReader = sqlCommand.ExecuteReader();
        if (sqlReader.HasRows == true)
            FillFacultyReader(ref SQLResult, sqlReader);
        else
        {
            SQLResult.SQLRequestError = "No matched faculty found";
            ReportError(SQLResult);
        }
        sqlReader.Close();
        sqlConnection.Close();
        sqlCommand.Dispose();
        return SQLResult;
    }
```

FIGURE 9.28 The modified codes for the web method – GetSQLSelectSP().

To distinguish from those Web methods we developed in the previous sections, we can create another new Web method **GetSQLSelectDataSet()** and add it into our Web service project. To do that, open our code-behind page if it is not opened, highlight and select the whole coding body of our first Web method **GetSQLSelect()**, including the method header and coding body. Copy and paste it to the bottom of our page (must be inside our Web service class).

Perform the modifications shown in Figure 9.29 to this copied Web method to make it as our third Web method. The modified codes have been highlighted in bold. Let's have a closer look at this modified Web method to see how it works.

A. The Web method's name is modified by attaching the **DataSet** to the end of the original method name. In addition, the data type of the returning object is the **DataSet**, which means that this Web method will return a DataSet.

B. Two new data objects, **FacultyAdapter** and **dsFaculty**, are created. The first object works as a DataAdapter and the second works as a DataSet, respectively. A local integer variable **intResult** is also created and it will be used to hold the returning value by calling the **Fill()** method of the DataAdapter to perform the data query later.

C. The initialized Command object is assigned to the SelectCommand property of the DataAdapter class. This Command object will be executed when the **Fill()** method is called to perform the data query, exactly to fill the faculty table in the DataSet **dsFaculty**.

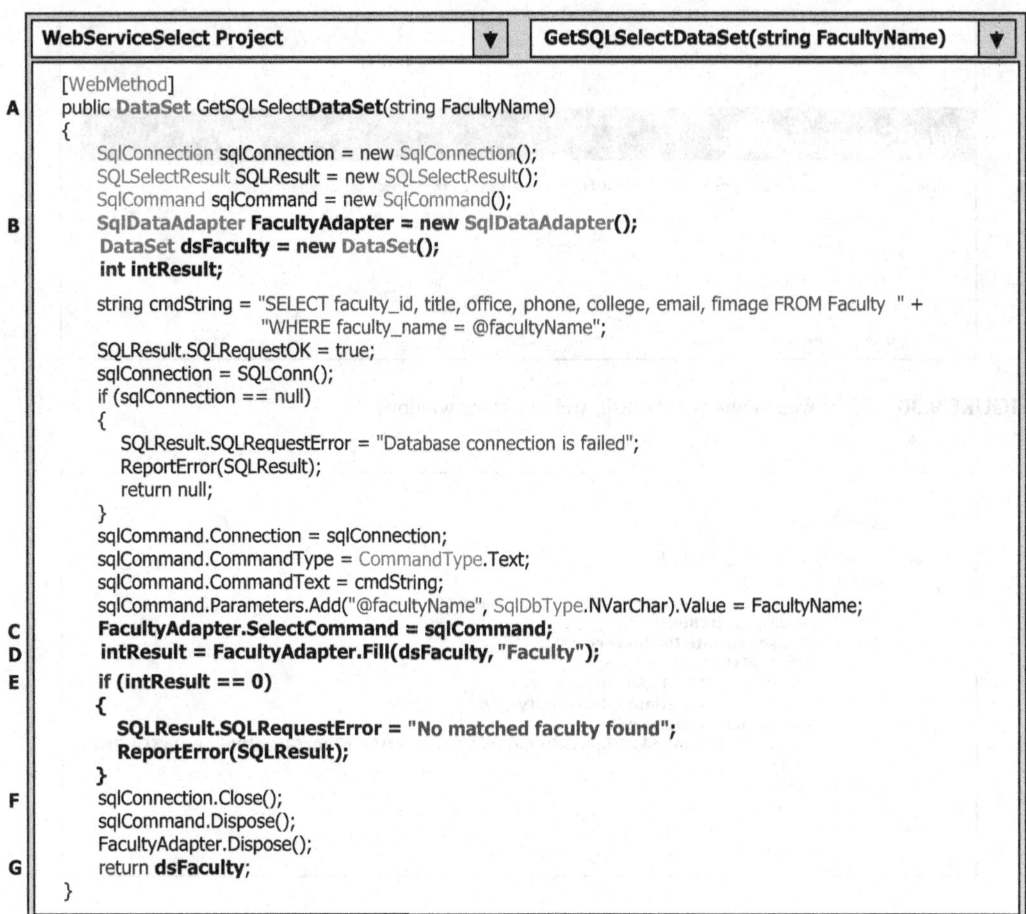

```
WebServiceSelect Project                GetSQLSelectDataSet(string FacultyName)

    [WebMethod]
A   public DataSet GetSQLSelectDataSet(string FacultyName)
    {
        SqlConnection sqlConnection = new SqlConnection();
        SQLSelectResult SQLResult = new SQLSelectResult();
        SqlCommand sqlCommand = new SqlCommand();
B       SqlDataAdapter FacultyAdapter = new SqlDataAdapter();
        DataSet dsFaculty = new DataSet();
        int intResult;
        string cmdString = "SELECT faculty_id, title, office, phone, college, email, fimage FROM Faculty " +
                           "WHERE faculty_name = @facultyName";
        SQLResult.SQLRequestOK = true;
        sqlConnection = SQLConn();
        if (sqlConnection == null)
        {
           SQLResult.SQLRequestError = "Database connection is failed";
           ReportError(SQLResult);
           return null;
        }
        sqlCommand.Connection = sqlConnection;
        sqlCommand.CommandType = CommandType.Text;
        sqlCommand.CommandText = cmdString;
        sqlCommand.Parameters.Add("@facultyName", SqlDbType.NVarChar).Value = FacultyName;
C       FacultyAdapter.SelectCommand = sqlCommand;
D       intResult = FacultyAdapter.Fill(dsFaculty, "Faculty");
E       if (intResult == 0)
        {
           SQLResult.SQLRequestError = "No matched faculty found";
           ReportError(SQLResult);
        }
F       sqlConnection.Close();
        sqlCommand.Dispose();
        FacultyAdapter.Dispose();
G       return dsFaculty;
    }
```

FIGURE 9.29 The modified web method – GetSQLSelectDataSet().

D. The **Fill()** method of the DataAdapter class is executed to fill the **Faculty** table in our DataSet. This method will return an integer value stored in the local integer variable **intResult** to indicate whether that filling is successful or not.
E. If the returned value is zero, which means that no any row has been retrieved from the **Faculty** table in our sample database and no any row has been filled into our **Faculty** table in our DataSet **dsFaculty**. Therefore that data query is failed. An error message will be sent to our member data in our base class and that error will be reported by using the **ReportError()** method later.
F. Otherwise, if the returned value is non-zero, which means that at least one row has been retrieved and filled into the **Faculty** table in our DataSet, a cleaning job is performed to release all objects used for this Web method. Typically this returned value is equal to the number of rows that have been successfully retrieved from the **Faculty** table in our database and filled into the **Faculty** table in our DataSet. In our application, this value should be equal to one since only one record is returned from our sample database and filled into the DataSet.
G. Finally, the filled DataSet **dsFaculty**, exactly the filled Faculty table in this DataSet, is returned from the Web service.

Now run the project to test this returned DataSet function by clicking on the **IIS Express** button. Now three Web methods available to this Web service, which are shown in Figure 9.30.

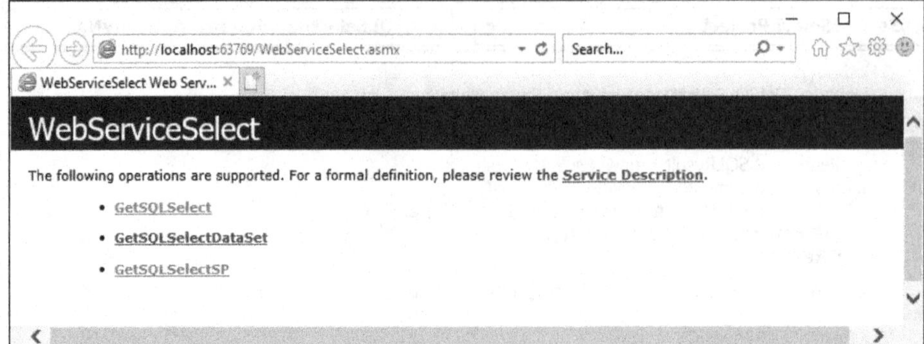

FIGURE 9.30 Three web methods in built-in web interface window.


```
http://localhost:63769/WebServiceSelect.asmx/GetSQLSelectDat
WebServiceSelect Web Service    localhost
    - <NewDataSet xmlns="">
      - <Faculty diffgr:id="Faculty1" msdata:rowOrder="0">
          <faculty_id>B78880</faculty_id>
          <title>Associate Professor</title>
          <office>MTC-211</office>
          <phone>750-378-1148</phone>
          <college>Florida Atlantic University</college>
          <email>ybai@college.edu</email>
          <fimage>/9j/4AAQSkZJRgABAQEAlgCWAAD/2wBDAAgGBgcGBQgHBwcJCQgKDBQND/
        </Faculty>
      </NewDataSet>
    </diffgr:diffgram>
</DataSet>
```


FIGURE 9.31 The running result of the web method GetSQLSelectDataSet().

Click on the second Web method **GetSQLSelectDataSet** from the built-in Web interface window and enter the faculty name **Ying Bai** into the **Value** box as our desired faculty Member. Then click on the **Invoke** button to call this Web method to perform the data query. The running result is returned and shown in Figure 9.31.

A new DataSet is created since we used a non-typed DataSet in this application and all seven pieces of faculty information related to the desired faculty member **Ying Bai** are retrieved and filled into the **Faculty** table in our DataSet. These pieces of information are also returned to our Web service project and displayed in the built-in Web interface window, as shown in Figure 9.31. You can add another Web method to get back the object **SQLSelectResult** to check the returning status of the DataSet if you like.

At this point, we have finished all codes developing jobs in our Web service project in the server side. A complete Web service project **WebServiceSelect Project** that contains three Web methods can be found from the folder **ClassDB Projects\Chapter 9\WebService-Select Solution** that is under the **Students** folder located at the CRC Press ftp site (refer to Figure 1.2 in Chapter 1).

Next we need to develop some professional Windows-based or Web-based applications with beautiful GUIs to use or consume our Web service project. Those Windows-based or Web-based applications can be considered as Web service clients.

9.3.10 Build Windows-Based Client Project to Consume the Web Services

To use or consume a Web service, first we need to create a Web service proxy class in our Windows-based or Web-based applications. Then we can create a new instance of that Web service proxy class and execute the desired Web methods located in that Web service class. The process of creating a Web service proxy class is equivalent to add a Web reference to our Windows-based or Web-based application projects.

9.3.10.1 Create a Web Service Proxy Class

Basically, adding a Web reference to our Windows-based or Web-based applications is to execute a searching process. During this process, Visual Studio.NET 2022 will try to find all Web services available to our applications. The following operations will be performed by Visual Studio.NET 2022 during this process:

1) When looking for Web services from the local computers, Visual Studio.NET will check all files that include a Web service main page with an **.asmx** extension, a WSDL file with a **.wsdl** extension or a Discovery file with a **.disco** extension.
2) When searching for Web services from the Internet, Visual Studio.NET 2022 will try to find a UDDI file that contains all registered Web services with their associated Discovery documents.
3) When all available Web services are found, either from your local computer or from the Internet, you can select your desired Web services from them by adding them into the Web client project as Web references. Also you can open each of them to take a look at the detail description for each Web service and its Web methods. Once you selected the desired Web services, you can modify the names of the selected Web services as you want. The point is that even if the name of the Web service is changed in the Web client side, the ASP.NET runtime can remember and still use the original name of that Web service as it is consumed.
4) As those Web services have been referenced to the client project, a group of necessary files or documents are also created by Visual Studio.NET 2022. These files include:

   A. A Discovery Map file that provides the necessary SOAP interfaces for communications between the client project and the Web services.
   B. A Discovery file that contains all available XML Web services on a Web server, and these Web services are obtained through a process called XML Web services Discovery.
   C. A WSDL file that provides a detailed description and definition about those Web services in an abstract manner.

To add a Web reference to our client project, we need first to create a client project.

Open Visual Studio.NET 2022 in the Administrator mode and create a new Visual C# Windows Forms App (.NET Framework) or Windows-based project and name it as **WinClientSelect Project** and save it in the folder **C:\Chapter 9**. Now let's add a Web reference to our new project.

There are two ways to select the desired Web services and add it as a reference to our client project; one way is to use the **Browser** provided by the Visual Studio.NET to find the desired Web service, and the other way is to copy and paste the desired Web service URL to the URL box located in this Add Web Reference wizard. In order to use the second way, you need first to run the Web service, and then copy its URL and paste it to the URL box in this wizard if you have not deployed that Web service to IIS. If you did deploy that Web service, you can directly type that URL into the **Address** box in this wizard.

Because we developed our Web service on our local computer and have not deployed our Web service to IIS, we should use the second way to find our Web service. Perform the following operations to add this Web reference:

1) Open Visual Studio.NET 2022 and our Web service project **WebServiceSelect Project**, and click on the **IIS Express** button to run it. Copy the URL from the **Address** bar in the running Web service project.

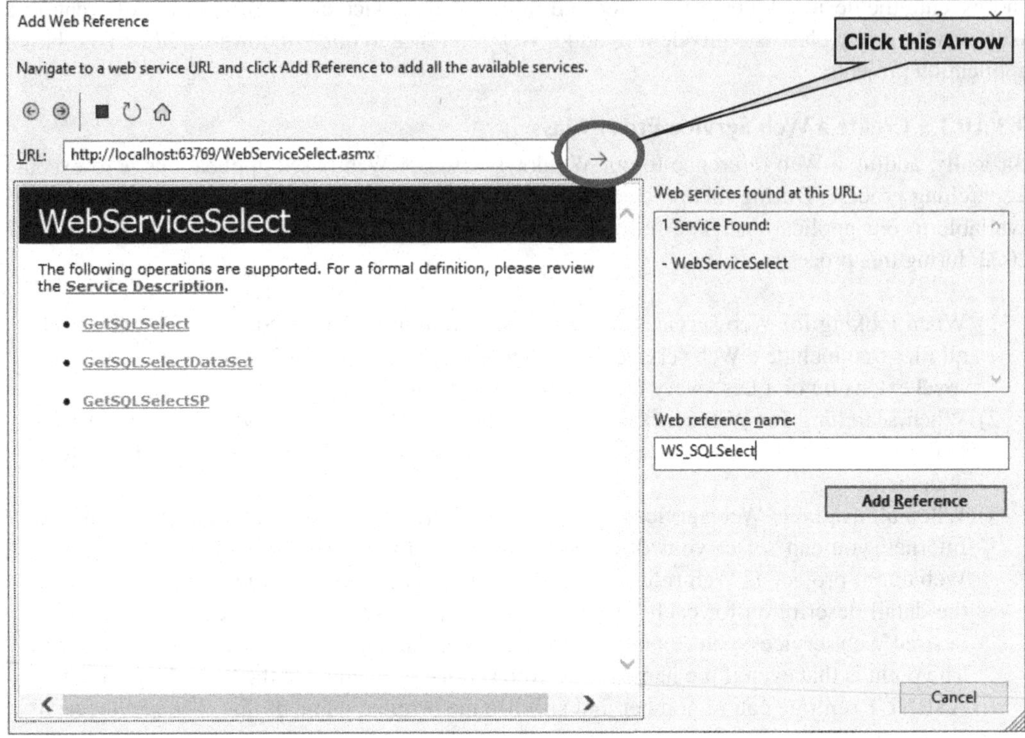

FIGURE 9.32 The add web reference wizard.

2) Then open another Visual Studio.NET 2022 in the Administrator mode and open our client project **WinClientSelect Project**.
3) Right click on our client project **WinClientSelect Project** from the Solution Explorer window, and select the item **Add | Service Reference** from the popup menu to open the Add Service Reference wizard.
4) Click on the **Advanced** button located at the lower-left corner on that wizard to open the Service Reference Settings wizard.
5) Click on the **Add Web Reference** button in the lower-left corner to open the Add Web Reference wizard, which is shown in Figure 9.32.
6) Paste that URL we copied from step 1 into the URL box in the Add Web Reference wizard and click on the **Arrow** button to enable the Visual Studio.NET to begin to search it.
7) When the Web service is found, the name of our Web service is displayed in the right pane, which is shown in Figure 9.32.
8) Alternately you can change the name for this Web reference from **localhost** to any meaningful name such as **WS_SQLSelect** in our case. Click on the **Add Reference** button to add this Web service as a reference to our new client project.
9) Click on the **Close** button from our Web service built-in Web interface window to terminate our Web service project.

Immediately you can find that the Web service **WS_SQLSelect**, which is under the folder **Web References**, has been added into the Solution Explorer window in our client project. This reference is the so-called Web service proxy class.

Next let's develop the graphic user interface by adding useful controls to interface to our Web service and display the queried information.

9.3.10.2 Develop the Graphic User Interface for the Windows-Based Client Project

Perform the following modifications to our new project:

1) Rename the Form File object from the default name **Form1.cs** to our desired name **WinClient Form.cs**.
2) Rename the Window Form object from the default name **Form1** to our desired name **FacultyForm** by modifying the **Name** property of the form window.
3) Rename the form title from the default title **Form1** to **CSE_DEPT Faculty Form** by modifying the **Text** property of the form.

To save time and space, we can use the GUI located in the project **RTOUpdateDelete Project** we developed in Chapter 7. Open that project from the folder **ClassDB Projects\Chapter 7** that is under the **Students** folder at the CRC Press ftp site (refer to Figure 1.2 in Chapter 1). Then open the Faculty form window and select all controls from that form by going to the menu item **Edit | Select All**, and then **Edit | Copy** menu item to copy all controls selected from this form window.

Return to our new Windows-based Web service client project **WinClientSelect Project**, open our form window and paste those controls we copied from the Faculty form in the project **RTOUpdateDelete Project**.

The purpose of the combobox control **Query Method** is to select one of three different query methods developed in our Web service project to get the desired faculty information:

1) Method 1: Uses an object to return our queried information.
2) Method 2: Uses a stored procedure to return our queried information.
3) Method 3: Uses a DataSet to return our queried information.

The **Faculty Name** combobox control is used to select the desired faculty member as the input parameter for the Web method to pick up our desired faculty information. In this application, only the **Select** and **Back** buttons are used.

The function of this project is: when the project runs, as the desired method and the faculty name have been selected from the associated controls, the **Select** button will be clicked by the user. Our client project will be connected to our Web service based on the Web reference we provided, and the selected method will be called based on the method chosen from the **Query Method** combobox control, to perform the data query to retrieve the desired faculty record from our sample database, and display it in this graphic user interface.

Now let's take care of the coding process for this project to connect to our Web service using the Web reference we developed in the last section.

9.3.10.3 Develop the Code to Consume the Web Service

The coding job can be divided into four parts:

1) The coding for the constructor of the FacultyForm class to initialize the **Query Method** combobox control and the **Faculty Name** combobox control. The first initialization will setup three Web methods that can be selected by the user to perform the data query from the Web Service. The second one is to setup a default list of faculty members that can be selected by the user to perform the associated faculty information query.
2) The coding for the **Back** button's Click method to terminate the project.
3) The coding for the **Select** button's Click method.
4) The coding for other user-defined methods, such as **ShowFaculty()**, **ProcessObject()**, **FillFaculty Object()** and **FillFacultyDataSet()**.

The main coding job is performed inside the **Select** button's Click method. As we discussed, when this button is clicked by the user, a connection to our Web Service needs to be established using the

Web reference we setup in the previous section. Therefore, we need first to create an object based on that Web reference or instantiate that Web Service to get an instance, then we can access the different Web methods to perform our data query via that instance. This process is called to instantiate the proxy class and invoke the Web methods. The protocol to instantiate a proxy class is:

```
WebReference.WebService newInstance = new WebReference.WebService();
```

After this new instance is created, then a connection between our client project and our Web service can be setup by using this instance. The pseudo-codes for this method are listed below:

A. A new Web Service instance **wsSQLSelect** is created using the protocol given above.
B. A new object **wsSQLResult** is also created and it can be used as a mapping of the real object **SQLSelectResult** developed in the Web Service. We can easily access the Web method to perform our data query and pick up the result from that returning object by assigning it to the mapping object.
C. A new DataSet object is created and it is used to call the Web method that returns a DataSet.
D. Based on the method selected by the user from the **Query Method** combobox control, different Web methods can be called to perform the data query.
E. The returned data that are stored in the real object are assigned to our mapping object, and each piece of information can be retrieved from this object and displayed in our graphic user interface.
F. If a DataSet method is used, the returned DataSet object is assigned to our mapping DataSet and the method **FillFacultyDataSet()** is called to fill the textboxes in the client form with the information picked up from the DataSet.

Now let's start our coding process for the constructor of the Faculty Form.

9.3.10.3.1 Develop the Codes for the Constructor of the FacultyForm Class

Now let's begin to develop codes for the constructor of the FacultyForm class to complete the initialization jobs listed in step 1 above.

Open the constructor of the FacultyForm class and enter the following codes that are shown in Figure 9.33 into this method.

```
WinClientSelect FacultyForm                FacultyForm()

    public FacultyForm()
    {
            InitializeComponent();
A           ComboName.Items.Add("Ying Bai");
            ComboName.Items.Add("Davis Bhalla");
            ComboName.Items.Add("Black Anderson");
            ComboName.Items.Add("Steve Johnson");
            ComboName.Items.Add("Jenney King");
            ComboName.Items.Add("Alice Brown");
            ComboName.Items.Add("Debby Angles");
            ComboName.Items.Add("Jeff Henry");
            ComboName.SelectedIndex = 0;
B           ComboMethod.Items.Add("Object Method");
            ComboMethod.Items.Add("Stored Procedure Method");
            ComboMethod.Items.Add("DataSet Method");
            ComboMethod.SelectedIndex = 0;
    }
```

FIGURE 9.33 The coding for the constructor of the FacultyForm class.

Let's take a closer look at this piece of codes to see how it works.

A. Eight default faculty members are added into the combobox control **ComboName** using the **Add()** method, and this will allow users to select one desired faculty from this combobox control to perform the data query as the project runs. The default-selected faculty is the first one by setting the SelectedIndex property to zero.

B. Three Web methods are also added into another combobox control **ComboMethod** to allow users to select one of them to perform the associated data query via our Web service. The default method is selected as the first one.

Next let's develop the codes for the **Back** button's Click method.

9.3.10.3.2 Develop Codes for the Back Button Click Method

This coding is very easy; just open the **Back** button's Click method by double-clicking it from the Faculty Form window and enter the following one line code into this method:

```
Application.Exit();
```

The purpose of this coding line is to terminate our project as this button is clicked by the user. Next let's build the codes for the **Select** button's Click method.

9.3.10.3.3 Develop the Codes for the Select Button Click Event Procedure

Open the **Select** button's click method and enter the codes that are shown in Figure 9.34 into this method. Let's have a closer look at this piece of codes to see how it works.

A. Some data objects are created at the beginning of this method, which include a new Web Service instance **wsSQLSelect** that is created using the protocol given above, a new object **wsSQLResult** that can be used as a mapping of the real object **SQLSelectResult** developed in

```
WinClientSelect Project          cmdSelect_Click(object sender, EventArgs e)

  private void cmdSelect_Click(object sender, EventArgs e)
  {
A         WS_SQLSelect.WebServiceSelect wsSQLSelect = new WS_SQLSelect.WebServiceSelect();
          WS_SQLSelect.SQLSelectResult wsSQLResult = new WS_SQLSelect.SQLSelectResult();
          DataSet wsDataSet = new DataSet();

B         if (ComboMethod.Text == "Object Method")
          {
             try{wsSQLResult = wsSQLSelect.GetSQLSelect(ComboName.Text);}
C            catch (Exception err) {MessageBox.Show("Web service is wrong: " + err.Message);}
D            ProcessObject(ref wsSQLResult);
          }
E         else if (ComboMethod.Text == "Stored Procedure Method")
          {
             try { wsSQLResult = wsSQLSelect.GetSQLSelectSP(ComboName.Text); }
F            catch (Exception err) { MessageBox.Show("Web service is wrong: " + err.Message); }
G            ProcessObject(ref wsSQLResult);
          }
H         else
          {
             try { wsDataSet = wsSQLSelect.GetSQLSelectDataSet(ComboName.Text); }
I            catch (Exception err) { MessageBox.Show("Web service is wrong: " + err.Message); }
J            FillFacultyDataSet(ref wsDataSet);
          }
  }
```

FIGURE 9.34 The codes for the select button click method.

our Web Service and we can easily access the Web method to perform our data query and pick up the result from that returning object by assigning it to this mapping object later, and a new DataSet object that is used to call the Web method that returns a DataSet.

B. If the user selected the **Object Method** from the **ComboMethod** control, a **try-catch** block is used to call the associated Web method **GetSQLSelect()**, which is developed in our Web Service, through the instantiated reference class to perform the data query. The selected faculty that is located in the **Text** property of the **ComboName** combobox control is passed as a parameter for this calling.
C. The **catch** statement is used to collect any possible exceptions if any error occurred for this calling, and the error message is displayed using a message box.
D. If no exception occurred, a user-defined method **ProcessObject()**, whose codes will be built later, is executed to pick up all pieces of retrieved information from the returned object and display them in this form window.
E. If the user selected the **Stored Procedure Method**, the associated Web method **GetSQLSelectSP()**, which is developed in our Web Service, is called via the instance of the Web reference class to perform the data query.
F. The **catch** statement is used to collect any possible exceptions if any error occurred for this calling, and the error message is displayed by using a message box.
G. Similarly, the user-defined method **ProcessObject()**, whose codes will be built later, is executed to pick up all pieces of retrieved information from the returned object and display them in this form window.
H. If users selected the **DataSet Method**, the Web method **GetSQLSelectDataSet()** is called through the instance of the Web reference class, and the method returns a DataSet that contains our desired faculty information.
I. The **catch** statement is used to collect any possible exceptions if any error occurred for this calling, and the error message is displayed by using a message box.
J. Another user-defined method **FillFacultyDataSet()**, whose codes will be developed later, is called to pick up all pieces of retrieved information from the returned DataSet and display them in this form.

Next let's take care of the coding development for all user-defined methods.

9.3.10.3.4 Develop the Codes for All User-Defined Methods

The codes for the user defined methods **ProcessObject()** and **FillFacultyObject()** are shown in Figure 9.35. Both methods use our child class **SQLSelectResult** as the data type of the passed argument since our returned object is an instance of this class.

The function of this piece of codes is:

A. If the member data **SQLRequestOK** that is stored in the instance of our child class or returned object is set to **True**, which means that our Web method is executed successfully, the user defined method **FillFacultyObject()** is called and executed. This method picks up each piece of information from the queried object **wsResult** and displays it in this form window.
B. Otherwise, some exceptions were occurred and a warning message is displayed with a message box.
C. As the method **FillFacultyObject()** is called, all seven pieces of faculty information stored in the returned object are picked up and assigned to the associated textbox in this form to be displayed. The faculty name can be obtained directly from the Faculty Name combobox control from this form window.

The codes for the subroutine **FillFacultyDataSet()** are shown in Figure 9.36. The argument passed into this subroutine is an instance of DataSet we created in the **Select** button click method. Let's take a look at this piece of codes to see how it works.

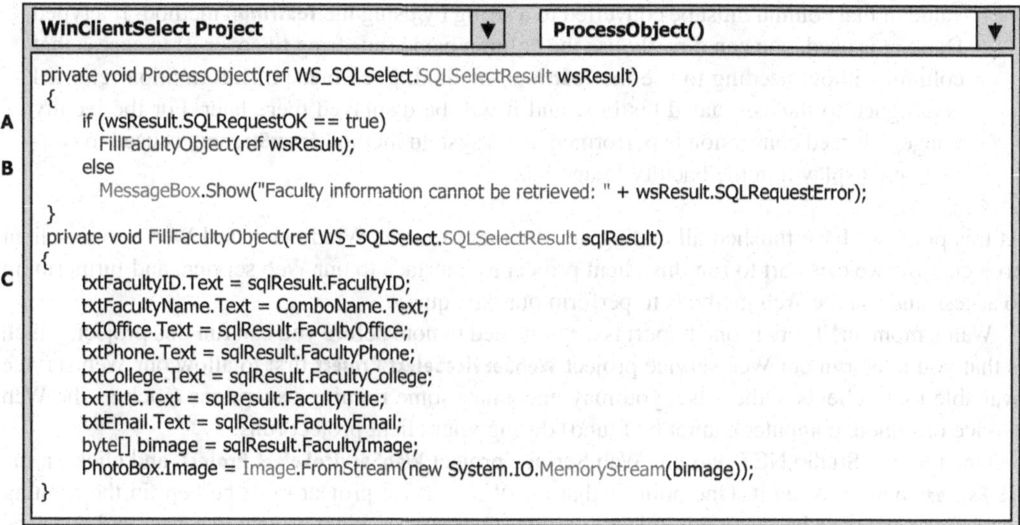

```
WinClientSelect Project                    ProcessObject()

  private void ProcessObject(ref WS_SQLSelect.SQLSelectResult wsResult)
  {
A      if (wsResult.SQLRequestOK == true)
         FillFacultyObject(ref wsResult);
B      else
         MessageBox.Show("Faculty information cannot be retrieved: " + wsResult.SQLRequestError);
  }
  private void FillFacultyObject(ref WS_SQLSelect.SQLSelectResult sqlResult)
  {
C      txtFacultyID.Text = sqlResult.FacultyID;
       txtFacultyName.Text = ComboName.Text;
       txtOffice.Text = sqlResult.FacultyOffice;
       txtPhone.Text = sqlResult.FacultyPhone;
       txtCollege.Text = sqlResult.FacultyCollege;
       txtTitle.Text = sqlResult.FacultyTitle;
       txtEmail.Text = sqlResult.FacultyEmail;
       byte[] bimage = sqlResult.FacultyImage;
       PhotoBox.Image = Image.FromStream(new System.IO.MemoryStream(bimage));
  }
```

FIGURE 9.35 The codes for two user defined methods.

```
WinClientSelect Project                    FillFacultyDataSet(ref DataSet ds)

  private void FillFacultyDataSet(ref DataSet ds)
  {
A        DataTable FacultyTable = new DataTable();
         DataRow FacultyRow;
B        FacultyTable = ds.Tables["Faculty"];
C        FacultyRow = FacultyTable.Rows[0];                    //only one row in the Faculty table
D        txtFacultyID.Text = FacultyRow["faculty_id"].ToString();
         txtFacultyName.Text = ComboName.Text;
         txtOffice.Text = FacultyRow["office"].ToString();
         txtPhone.Text = FacultyRow["phone"].ToString();
         txtCollege.Text = FacultyRow["college"].ToString();
         txtTitle.Text = FacultyRow["title"].ToString();
         txtEmail.Text = FacultyRow["email"].ToString();
         byte[] bimage = (byte[])FacultyRow["fimage"];
         PhotoBox.Image = Image.FromStream(new System.IO.MemoryStream(bimage));
  }
```

FIGURE 9.36 The codes for the user-defined method FillFacultyDataSet().

A. Two data objects, **FacultyTable,** which is a new object of the DataTable class, and **FacultyRow, which** is a new instance of the DataRow class, are created first since we need to use these two objects to access the DataSet to pick up all requested faculty information later.

B. The returned **Faculty** table that is embedded in our returned DataSet is assigned to our new created object **FacultyTable**. Because the DataSet we created in the **Select** button click method is an untyped DataSet, the table name must be clearly indicated with a string '**Faculty**'. For typed DataSet, you can directly use the table name to access the desired table without needing any string.

C. Since we only request one record or one row from the **Faculty** table, the returned **Faculty** table contains only one row information that is located at the top row with an index of zero. This one row information is assigned to our **FacultyRow** object we created above.

D. We can access each column from the returned data row using the column name represented by a string with a class method **ToString()**. As we mentioned, the DataSet we are using is an untyped DataSet; therefore, the column name must be indicated with a string and the value of that column must be converted to a string by using the **ToString()** method. If a typed DataSet is used, you can directly use the column name (no string to cover it) to access that column without needing to use the **ToString()** method. Each piece of information returned is assigned to the associated textbox, and it will be displayed there later. For the faculty image, a forced conversion is performed and a system method **FromStream()** is used to convert and display it in the Faculty Image box.

At this point we have finished all coding development for this Windows-based Web service client project. Now we can start to run this client project to interface to our Web service, and furthermore to access and use the Web methods to perform our data query.

Wait a moment! There is one import issue you need to note before you can run this project, which is that you must run our Web service project **WebServiceSelect Project** first to allow our Web service available to all clients. Otherwise, you may encounter some running exceptions (such as the Web service or remote computer cannot be found) during your client project runs.

Open Visual Studio.NET and our Web Service project **WebServiceSelect Project**, and click on the **IIS Express** button to run it. One point is that our Web service project must be kept in the running status (even the page has been minimized) in order to allow our client project to access and interface to it. An exception will be encountered if you stop our Web service when you try to access it from our client project.

Make sure that our Web service has been run once and it is in the running status, which can be identified by a small **IIS Express** icon in the task bar on the bottom of your screen. You may need to click on the **Show hidden icons** item (∧) on the bottom of the task bar to find this **IIS Express** icon. Then open it by right clicking on it and select **Show All Applications** item. The opened running status of this Web service project is shown in Figure 9.37.

Then start our client project by clicking on the **Start** button from the project **WinClientSelect Project**. The running status is shown in Figure 9.38.

Select any query method and a faculty name, such as **Jenney King**, from the Faculty Name combobox, and click on the **Select** button to call the associated Web service method to retrieve the desired faculty record. The returned faculty record is displayed in the associated textboxes with the faculty photo, which is shown in Figure 9.38.

You can try to select any other Web service method, either the **Stored Procedure** or the **DataSet** method, and other faculty members to perform this data query. The running result confirmed that

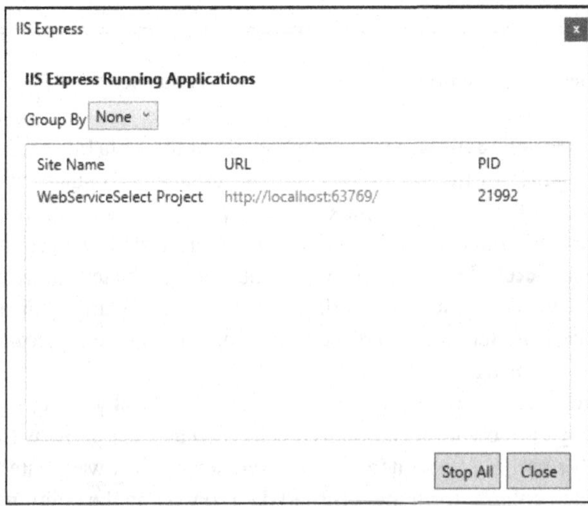

FIGURE 9.37 The running status of our web service WebServiceSelect project.

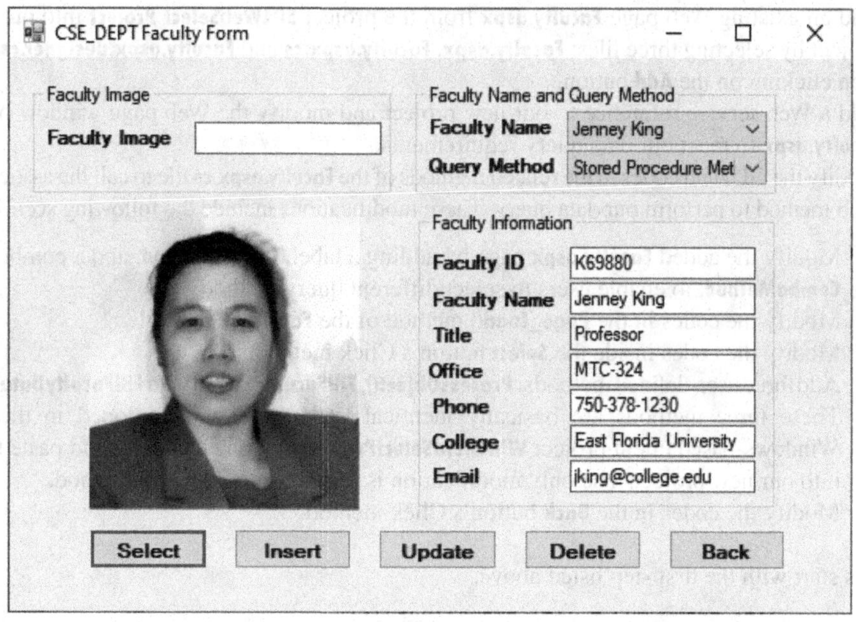

FIGURE 9.38 The running status of our client project.

both our Web service and our Windows-based client projects are very successful. Click on the **Back** button to terminate our project.

A complete Windows-based client project **WinClientSelect Project** can be found from a folder **ClassDB Projects\Chapter 9\WinClientSelect Solution** that is under the **Students** folder on the CRC Press ftp site (refer to Figure 1.2 in Chapter 1). You need to load both our client and our Web service projects from that site and install them in your computer if you want to run and test this client project. Also you must run our Web service project first to make sure that our Web service is ready to be consumed by that client project.

Next we want to develop a Web-based client project to consume our Web service by retrieving the desired faculty information.

9.3.11 Build Web-Based Client Project to Consume the Web Service

Developing a Web-based client application to consume a Web service is very similar to developing a Windows-based client project to reference and accessing a Web service as we did in the last section. As long as a Web service is referenced by the Web-based client project, one can access and call any Web method developed in that Web service to perform the desired data queries via the Web-based client project without any problem. Visual Studio.NET will create the same document files, such as the Discovery Map file, the WDSL file and the DISCO file, for the client project no matter whether this Web service is consumed by a Windows-based or a Web-based client application.

To save time and space, we can modify an existing ASP.NET Web application **SQLWebSelect Project** we developed in Chapter 8 to make it our new Web-based client project **WebClientSelect Project**. In fact, we can copy and rename that entire project as our new Web-based client project. However, we prefer to create a new ASP.NET Web site application project and only copy and modify the Faculty page.

The developing process in this section can be divided into the following parts:

1) Create a new ASP.NET Web Application (.NET Framework) project and name it as **WebClientSelect Project** with **Web Forms** as Template.

2) Add an existing Web page **Faculty.aspx** from the project **SQLWebSelect Project** into our new project by selecting three files; **Faculty.aspx**, **Faculty.aspx.cs** and **Faculty.aspx.designer.cs**, and then clicking on the **Add** button.
3) Add a Web service reference to our new project and modify the Web page window of the **Faculty.aspx** to meet our data query requirements.
4) Modify the GUI and codes in the related methods of the **Faculty.aspx.cs** file to call the associated Web method to perform our data query. These modifications include the following sections:

   a. Modify the added **Faculty.aspx** page by adding a label, **Query Method**, and a combobox, **ComboMethod**, to enable users to select different query method.
   b. Modify the codes in the **Page_Load()** method of the **Faculty.aspx.cs** file.
   c. Modify the codes inside the **Select** button's Click method.
   d. Add three user-defined methods: **ProcessObject()**, **FillFacultyObject()** and **FillFacultyDataSet()**. These three methods are basically identical with those we developed in the last Windows-based client project **WinClientSelectProject**, and one can copy and paste them into our new project. The only modification is for the **ProcessObject()** method.
   e. Modify the codes in the **Back** button's Click method.

Now let's start with the first step listed above.

9.3.11.1 Create a New Web Site Project and Add an Existing Web Page

Open Visual Studio.NET and go to the **File | New | Project** menu item to create a new ASP.NET Web Application project. Enter **WebClientSelect Project** and **WeClientSelect Solution** into the **Project name** and **Solution name** box, respectively, and **C:\Chapter 9** into the **Location** box. Click on the **Create** button, select the **Web Forms** item, and click on the **Create** button again to create this new Web application project.

Perform the following operations to add all existing Web page files related to **Faculty.aspx** into our new Web application project:

1) Right-click on our new project **WebClientSelect Project** from the Solution Explorer window, and select the item **Add | Existing Item** from the popup menu.
2) Browse to our Web project **SQLWebSelect Project** that can be found from the folder **ClassDB Projects\Chapter 8** that is under the **Students** folder located on the CRC Press ftp site (refer to Figure 1.2 in Chapter 1). Select the Web page files, **Faculty.aspx**, **Faculty.aspx.cs** and **Faculty.aspx.designer.cs**, from the list and click on the **Add** button to add those Web page files into our new Web project.

Now let's handle to add a Web reference to our project to access the Web service we built in the previous section.

9.3.11.2 Add a Web Service Reference and Modify the Web Form Window

Perform the following operations to add this Web reference:

1) Open Visual Studio.NET 2022 and our Web service project **WebServiceSelect Project**, and click on the **IIS Express** button to run it.
2) Copy the URL from the **Address** bar in our running Web service project.
3) Then open another Visual Studio.NET and our Web client application project **WebClientSelect Project**.
4) Right-click on our client project **WebClientSelect Project** from the Solution Explorer window, and select the item **Add | Service Reference** from the popup menu to open the Add Service Reference wizard.

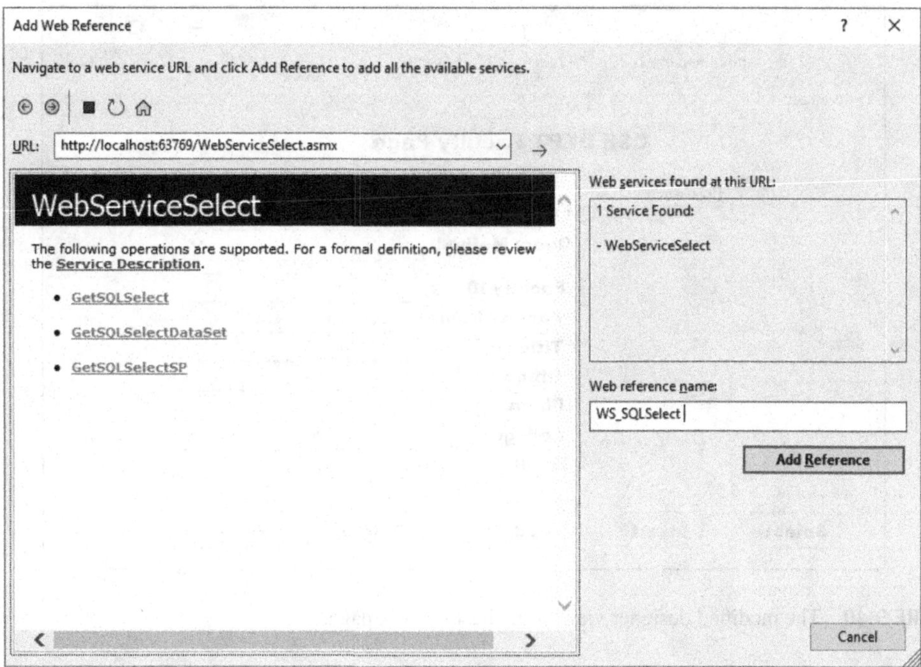

FIGURE 9.39 Add a web reference.

5) Click on the **Advanced** button located at the lower-left corner on that wizard to open the Service Reference Settings wizard.
6) Click on the **Add Web Reference** button in the lower-left corner to open the Add Web Reference wizard, which is shown in Figure 9.39.
7) Paste the URL we copied from step 2 into the URL box in this Add Web Reference wizard and click on the **Arrow** button to enable the Visual Studio.NET to begin to search it.
8) When the Web service is found, the name of our Web service is displayed in the right pane, which is shown in Figure 9.39.
9) Alternately, you can change the name for this Web reference from **localhost** to any meaningful name, such as **WS_SQLSelect** in our case. Click on the **Add Reference** button to add this Web service as a reference to our client project.
10) Click on the **Close** button from our Web service built-in Web interface window to close our Web service page.

Immediately, you can find that the Web service **WS_SQLSelect**, which is under the folder **Web References**, has been added into the Solution Explorer window in our client project. This reference is the so-called Web service proxy class.

Next let's modify the added **faculty.asmx** page, precisely the Faculty Web Form, by adding two controls to enable users to select different query methods.

Open the Designer view of the **Faculty.aspx** page and add one DropDownList control **ComboMethod** and an associated label **Query Method** just under the Faculty Name combobox control in that page. Your modified **Faculty.aspx** page should match one that is shown in Figure 9.40.

That modified page can be found from a folder **Web Forms\Chapter 9** that is under the **Students** folder on the CRC Press ftp site (refer to Figure 1.2 in Chapter 1) if one wants to use it but without time and efforts to build it.

Next let's concentrate our efforts on the modifications of codes on some methods. Fist let's start from the **Page_Load()** method.

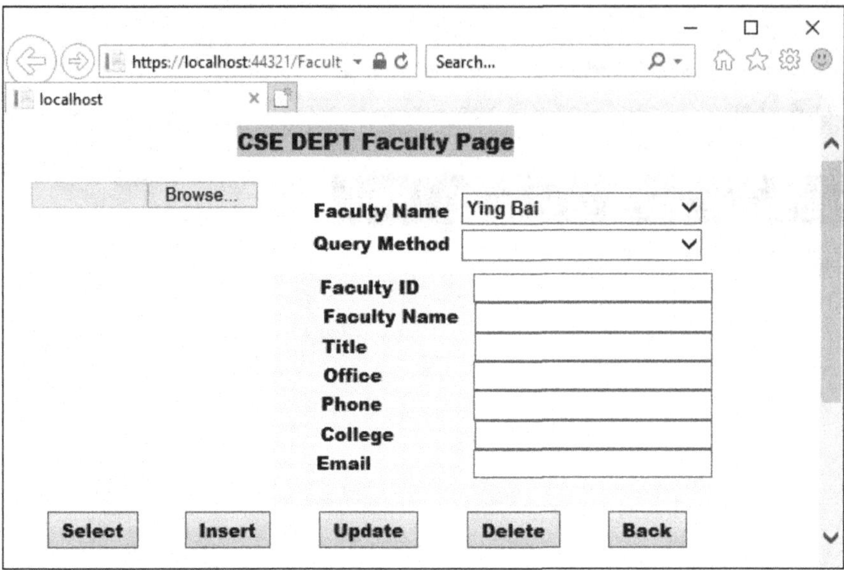

FIGURE 9.40 The modified designer view of the Faculty.aspx page.

9.3.11.3 Modify the Codes in the Page_Load Event Method

Perform the following changes to complete this modification:

1) Remove the namespace directory **using System.Data.SqlClient**; from the top of this page since we do not need it in this application.
2) Remove the entire **if** block and the associated global connection object that is stored in the Application state function **Application["sqlConnection"]**.
3) Add codes to display three Web methods in the combobox control **ComboMethod** by using the system method **Add()**.
4) Setup the first item as a default one for both combobox controls.

Your finished codes for the **Page_Load()** method should match one that is shown in Figure 9.41. The new added codes have been highlighted in bold.

The next modification is to change the codes inside the **Select** button's click method.

9.3.11.4 Modify the Codes in the Select Button Click Method

Replace all codes in this method with the following coding sequences:

A. First let's create three new instances:

1. **wsSQLSelect** for the proxy class of our Web Service
2. **wsSQLResult** for the child class of our Web Service
3. **wsDataSet** for our DataSet class

The coding for the first two objects, **wsSQLSelect** and **wsSQLResult**, can be represented by two lines, not four lines. But in order to make those lines shorter, we separate them with the declaration and assignment in two lines. In fact, they can be combined together by using one coding line for each of them. The reason for those long lines is because the proxy class is added into our current project; thus, our current project, which works as a namespace, must be prefixed for that proxy class to enable the compiler to know and use it.

B. Create a local DataSet object **wsDataSet** and a string variable **errMsg**. The former is used to work as a DataSet object and the latter is used to store any possible error message.

C. If the user selected the **Object Method**, a **try...catch** block is used to call the first Web method **GetSQLSelect()** that we developed in our Web Service project with the selected faculty name

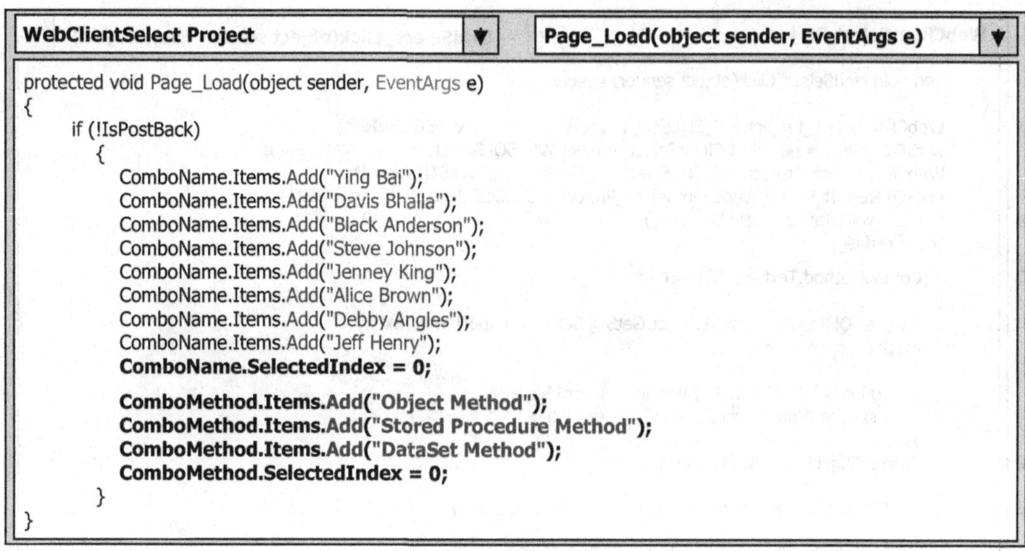

```
WebClientSelect Project                Page_Load(object sender, EventArgs e)

protected void Page_Load(object sender, EventArgs e)
{
    if (!IsPostBack)
    {
        ComboName.Items.Add("Ying Bai");
        ComboName.Items.Add("Davis Bhalla");
        ComboName.Items.Add("Black Anderson");
        ComboName.Items.Add("Steve Johnson");
        ComboName.Items.Add("Jenney King");
        ComboName.Items.Add("Alice Brown");
        ComboName.Items.Add("Debby Angles");
        ComboName.Items.Add("Jeff Henry");
        ComboName.SelectedIndex = 0;

        ComboMethod.Items.Add("Object Method");
        ComboMethod.Items.Add("Stored Procedure Method");
        ComboMethod.Items.Add("DataSet Method");
        ComboMethod.SelectedIndex = 0;
    }
}
```

FIGURE 9.41 The modified Page_Load() method.

as the input parameter. The returned object that contains our queried faculty information is assigned to our local mapping object **wsSQLResult** if that calling is successful. Otherwise, an error message is displayed using the **Write()** method of the Response object of the server.

D. The user-defined method **ProcessObject()** is executed to assign the retrieved faculty information to the associated textbox in our Web page to display them.

E. If the user selected the **Stored Procedure Method**, the associated Web method **GetSQLSelectSP()**, which is developed in our Web Service, is called via the instance of the Web reference class to perform the data query. The **catch** statement is used to collect any possible exceptions if any error occurred for this calling, and the error message is displayed using the **Write()** method of the **Response** object of the server. Similarly, the user-defined method **ProcessObject()** is executed to pick up all pieces of retrieved information from the returned object and displays them in this Web page.

F. If users selected the **DataSet Method**, the Web method **GetSQLSelectDataSet()** is called through the instance of the Web reference class, and the method returns a DataSet that contains our desired faculty information. The **catch** block is used to collect any possible exceptions if any error occurred for this calling, and the error message is displayed using the **Write()** method of the **Response** object of the server.

G. The method **FillFacultyDataSet()** is called to pick up all pieces of retrieved information from the returned DataSet and displays them in this Web page.

All of these modification steps are shown in Figure 9.42.

Next let's add three user-defined methods **ProcessObject()**, **FillFacultyObject()** and **FillFacultyDataSet()**, into this project.

9.3.11.5 Add Three User-Defined Methods

We need to add three user-defined methods, **ProcessObject()**, **FillFacultyObject()** and **FillFacultyDataSet()**, into this project. The codes for these three methods are basically identical with those we developed in the last Windows-based Web Service client project **WinClientSelect Project**, and one can copy and paste them into our new project with a little modifications.

Open our Windows-based client project **WinClientSelectProject**, copy these three methods from that project and paste them into the code page of our current Faculty page. The only modification for the first method **ProcessObject()** we need to make is to replace the **MessageBox()** with the **Write()**

```
WebClientSelect Project                    cmdSelect_Click(object sender, EventArgs e)

  protected void cmdSelect_Click(object sender, EventArgs e)
  {
A       WebClientSelect_Project.WS_SQLSelect.WebServiceSelect wsSQLSelect;
        wsSQLSelect = new WebClientSelect_Project.WS_SQLSelect.WebServiceSelect();
        WebClientSelect_Project.WS_SQLSelect.SQLSelectResult wsSQLResult;
        wsSQLResult = new WebClientSelect_Project.WS_SQLSelect.SQLSelectResult();
B       DataSet wsDataSet = new DataSet();
        string errMsg;
C       if (ComboMethod.Text == "Object Method")
        {
          try {wsSQLResult = wsSQLSelect.GetSQLSelect(ComboName.Text);}
          catch (Exception err)
          {
            errMsg = "Web service is wrong: " + err.Message;
            Response.Write("<script>alert('" + errMsg + "')</script>");
          }
D         ProcessObject(ref wsSQLResult);
        }
E       else if (ComboMethod.Text == "Stored Procedure Method")
        {
          try { wsSQLResult = wsSQLSelect.GetSQLSelectSP(ComboName.Text); }
          catch (Exception err)
          {
            errMsg = "Web service is wrong: " + err.Message;
            Response.Write("<script>alert('" + errMsg + "')</script>");
          }
          ProcessObject(ref wsSQLResult);
        }
F       else
        {
          try { wsDataSet = wsSQLSelect.GetSQLSelectDataSet(ComboName.Text); }
          catch (Exception err)
          {
            errMsg = "Web service is wrong: " + err.Message;
            Response.Write("<script>alert('" + errMsg + "')</script>");
          }
G         FillFacultyDataSet(ref wsDataSet);
        }
  }
```

FIGURE 9.42 The modified codes for the select button's click method.

```
WebClientSelect Project                    ProcessObject(ref SQLSelectResult wsReult)

private void ProcessObject(ref WebClientSelect_Project.WS_SQLSelect.SQLSelectResult wsResult)
{
    string errMsg;
    errMsg = "Faculty information cannot be retrieved: " + wsResult.SQLRequestError;
    if (wsResult.SQLRequestOK == true)
      FillFacultyObject(ref wsResult);
    else
      Response.Write("<script>alert('" + errMsg + "')</script>");
}
```

FIGURE 9.43 The modified codes for the ProcessObject() method.

method provided by the **Response** object of the server class to display an error message. Create a local string variable **errMsg** in this method to hold the possible error message. The modified codes for this method should match one that is shown in Figure 9.43. The modified parts have been highlighted with the bold style words.

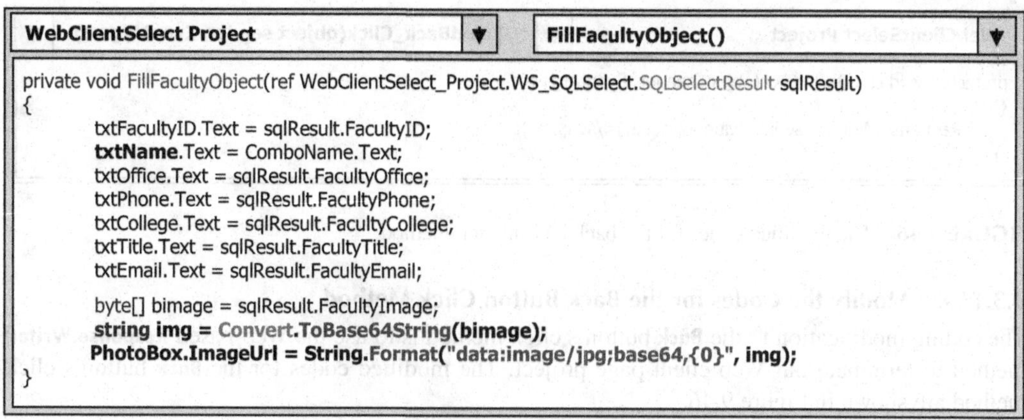

```
WebClientSelect Project                    FillFacultyObject()

private void FillFacultyObject(ref WebClientSelect_Project.WS_SQLSelect.SQLSelectResult sqlResult)
{
        txtFacultyID.Text = sqlResult.FacultyID;
        txtName.Text = ComboName.Text;
        txtOffice.Text = sqlResult.FacultyOffice;
        txtPhone.Text = sqlResult.FacultyPhone;
        txtCollege.Text = sqlResult.FacultyCollege;
        txtTitle.Text = sqlResult.FacultyTitle;
        txtEmail.Text = sqlResult.FacultyEmail;

        byte[] bimage = sqlResult.FacultyImage;
        string img = Convert.ToBase64String(bimage);
        PhotoBox.ImageUrl = String.Format("data:image/jpg;base64,{0}", img);
}
```

FIGURE 9.44 The modified codes for the FillFacultyObject() method.

The modifications for the second method **FillFacultyObject()** include changing the name of the faculty name textbox from **txtFacultyName** to **txtName** and add some conversions between the faculty image **byte[]** array and **Base64String** since the latter can be recognized and used by the **ImageUrl** property of the faculty image box, **PhotoBox,** which can be displayed in that box.

The modified codes for this method have been highlighted in Figure 9.44.

The modifications for the third method **FillFacultyDataSet()**are similar to the second method, in which the name of the faculty name textbox is changed from **txtFacultyName** to **txtName** and the faculty image is converted to a string and assigned to the **ImagUrl** property of the faculty image control **PhotoBox**.

The modified codes for this method have been highlighted in Figure 9.45.

Finally, let's modify the codes inside the Back button's click method to terminate our Web client project as that button is clicked.

```
WebClientSelect Project                    FillFacultyDataSet()

private void FillFacultyDataSet(ref DataSet ds)
{
        DataTable FacultyTable = new DataTable();
        DataRow FacultyRow;

        FacultyTable = ds.Tables["Faculty"];
        FacultyRow = FacultyTable.Rows[0];                    //only one row in the Faculty table
        txtFacultyID.Text = FacultyRow["faculty_id"].ToString();
        txtName.Text = ComboName.Text;
        txtOffice.Text = FacultyRow["office"].ToString();
        txtPhone.Text = FacultyRow["phone"].ToString();
        txtCollege.Text = FacultyRow["college"].ToString();
        txtTitle.Text = FacultyRow["title"].ToString();
        txtEmail.Text = FacultyRow["email"].ToString();

        byte[] bimage = (byte[])FacultyRow["fimage"];
        string img = Convert.ToBase64String(bimage);
        PhotoBox.ImageUrl = String.Format("data:image/jpg;base64,{0}", img);
}
```

FIGURE 9.45 The modified codes for the FillFacultyDataSet() method.

```
WebClientSelect Project        cmdBack_Click(object sender, EventArgs e)

protected void cmdBack_Click(object sender, EventArgs e)
{
    Response.Write("<script>window.close()</script>");
}
```

FIGURE 9.46 The modified codes for the back button click method.

9.3.11.6 Modify the Codes for the Back Button Click Method

The coding modification to the **Back** button's click method is to use the Web-based **Response.Write()** method to terminate our Web client page project. The modified codes for the **Back** button's click method are shown in Figure 9.46.

Now it is the time for us to run our Web-based client project to test the functions of our data query for our Web service. However, before we can run our project, we need to make sure that the following two things have been done:

1) Make sure that the **Faculty.aspx** page is the starting page as the project runs. To confirm that, right click our **Faculty.aspx** page from the Solution Explorer window and select the item **Set As Start Page** from the popup menu.
2) Make sure that our Web service **WebServiceSelect Project** has been run at least one time and that Web service status is running. This can be identified by a small white icon located in the task bar at the bottom of the screen.

Now click on the **IIS Express** button to run our Web client project. The Faculty page is displayed and it is shown in Figure 9.47.

Keep the default Web query method, **Object Method**, in the Query Method combobox control selected and the faculty name in the Faculty Name combobox control unchanged. Then click on the **Select** button to call the associated Web method developed in our Web service to retrieve the selected faculty information from our sample database via the Web server. The query result is shown in Figure 9.47.

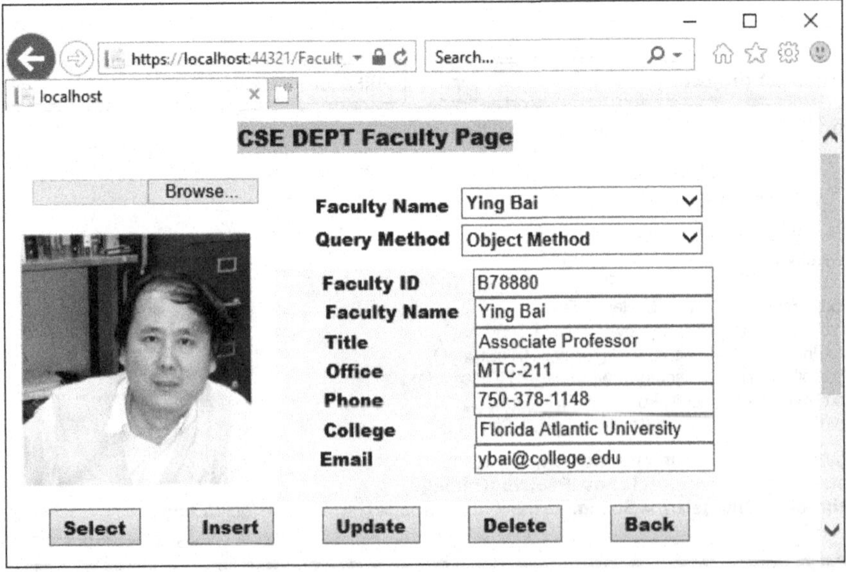

FIGURE 9.47 The running status of our web-based client project.

You can try to select different Web query methods with different faculty members to test this project. Our Web-based client project is very successful. Click on the **Back** button to terminate our client project.

A complete Web-based Web service client project **WebClientSelect Project** can be found from a folder **Class DB Projects\Chapter 9** that is under the Students folder at the CRC Press ftp site (refer to Figure 1.2 in Chapter 1).

9.3.12 Deploy the Completed Web Service to Production Servers

When we finished developing and testing our Web service in our local machine, we need to deploy it to the .NET SDK or an IIS 5 or higher virtual directory to allow users to access and use it via a production server. We may discuss this topic in the early section when we finished developing our Web service project. The reason we delay this discussion until this section is that we do not have to perform this Web service deployment if we running our Web service and accessing it using a client project in our local computer (development server). However, we must deploy our Web service to IIS if we want to run it in a formal Web server (production server).

Basically, we have two ways to do this deployment; one way is to simply copy our Web service files to a server running the IIS 5 or higher, or to the folder that is or contains our virtual directory. Another way is to use the Builder provided by Visual Studio.NET to pre-compile the Web pages and copy the compiled files to our virtual directory. The so-called virtual directory is a default directory that can be recognized and accessed by a Web server such as IIS to run our Web services. In both ways, we need a virtual directory to store our Web service files and allow Web server to pick up and run our Web service from that virtual directory. Now let's see how to create an IIS virtual directory.

The following steps describe how to add a target Web service and create an IIS virtual directory using the Internet Information Services (IIS) Manager:

1) First create a folder to save our virtual directory's files. Typically, we need to create this folder under the default Web service root folder **C:\Inetpub\wwwroot**. In our case, create a new folder named **WS_Select** and place it under the root folder **C:\Inetpub\wwwroot**.
2) Open the Control Panel and select the item **System and Security**, then click on the **Administrative Tools** icon. On the opened list, double click on the icon **Computer Management**, then expand the item **Services and Applications** from the left pane and click the item **Internet Information Services (IIS) Manager**. Then click the **Current View** tab on the bottom of this wizard. Two items are listed under this icon: **Application Pools** and **Sites**.
3) Right-click on the item **Sites** and select **Add Website** item, as shown in Figure 9.48.
4) Enter **WebServiceSelect Project** into the **Site name** box as the name for this site, and click on the expansion button on the right of the **Physical path** to browse to the location of our Web service project located, in this case, it is **C:\SQL C# DB Programming\Students\Class DB Projects\Chapter 9\WebServiceSelect Solution\ WebServiceSelect Project**. Click on the **OK** button. In your case, however, it should be **C:\Chapter 9\ WebServiceSelect Solution\ WebServiceSelect Project**.
5) In our case, enter the server name **DESKTOP-24JPUFB** into the **Host name** box. However, you need to enter your server name into this box. Then click on the **Test Settings** button to test the Pass-through authentication of this service.
6) Click on the **Close** and the **OK** button to complete this adding operation.

After our Web service is added into the IIS, next we can deploy our Web service by either copying files to this virtual directory or performing a pre-compile process. Starting from Visual Studio.NET 2017, Microsoft provides an easy way to help users to build, configure, perform settings and deploy the Web service on the IIS with a Publish tool.

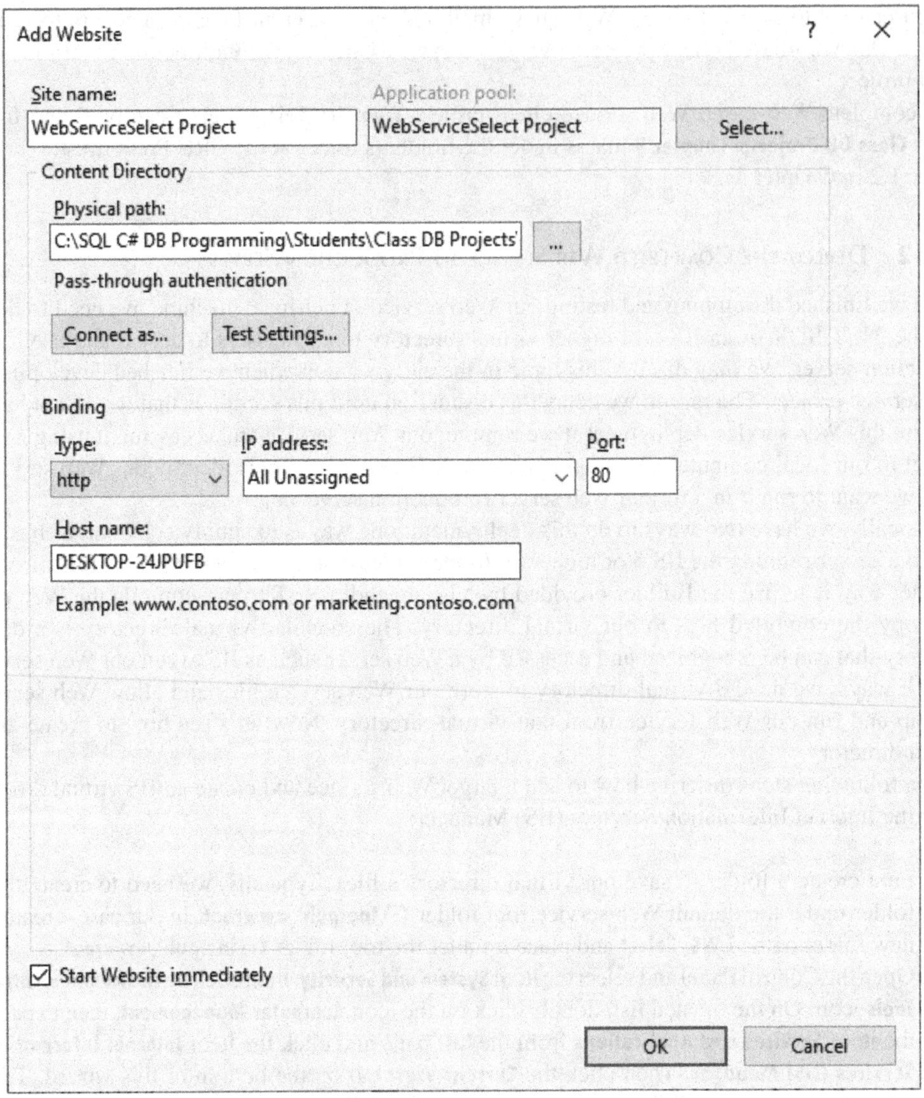

FIGURE 9.48 The completed add website wizard.

Next we will discuss how to publish a Web service to the production server using the Publish tool.

9.3.12.1 Publish the Desired Web Service

Perform the following steps to complete this publish process for our Web service:

1) Open Visual Studio.NET in the **Administrator Mode** and our Web service project **WebService Select Project**.
2) Right-click on our opened project and select **Publish** item from the popup menu.
3) Select the item **Web Server (IIS)** and click on the **Next** button to continue.
4) Keep the default **Web Deploy** and click on the **Next** button.
5) Enter the server name into the **Server** box; in our case, it is our computer name, **DESKTOP-24JPUFB**. You need to use your computer name in your case.

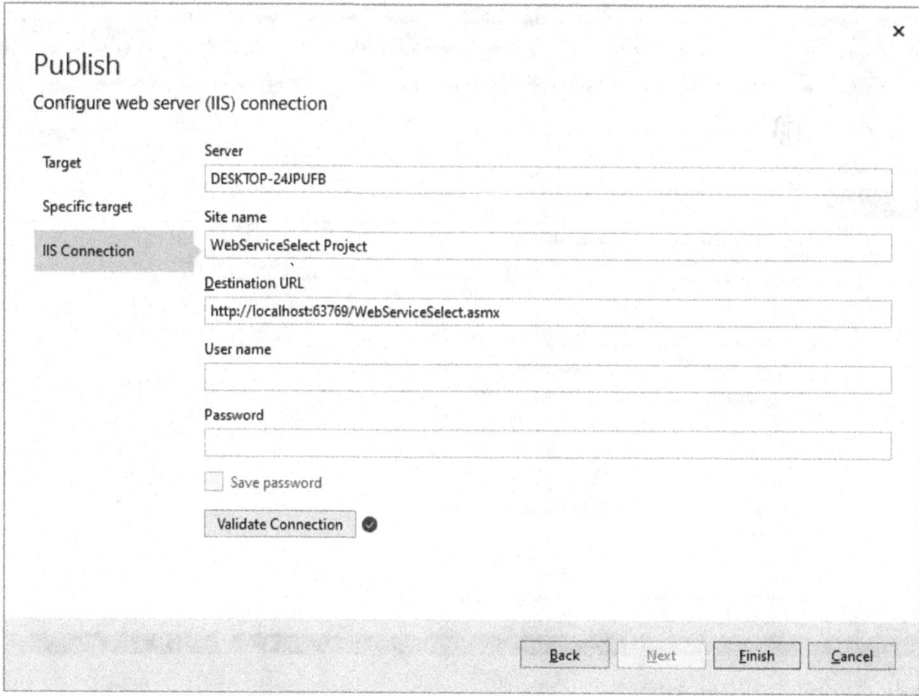

FIGURE 9.49 The customer profile setup wizard.

6) Enter the site name into the **Site name** box. In our case, it is **WebServiceSelect Project** (refer to step 5 in the last section when we add the Web site to the IIS).
7) Enter our target URL, **http://localhost:63769/WebServiceSelect.asmx**, into the **Destination URL** box (refer to Add Web Service Reference in Section 9.3.11.2 for this URL).
8) Now click the **Validate Connection** button to check and test the connection for this Web site if you like. A green check mark should be displayed in the right of this button if this test is successful, which is shown in Figure 9.49.

Now click on the **Finish** and then the **Publish** button to reserve this profile and start the publishing process.

The Visual Studio.NET begins the building and publishing process. If everything is fine, our Web site will be published successfully, which is shown in Figure 9.50.

One key point to make this publishing process success is that the Visual Studio.NET 2022 must be opened in the **Administrator Mode**, otherwise a running error may be encountered to ask you to do that since only the Administrator has the authentication and power to do this page publishing process. One can right-click on the Visual Studio icon and select the item **Run as administrator** to open it as the administrator mode.

If, for some reason, your Web service cannot be deployed or published successfully, you may need to go to site https://www.microsoft.com/web/downloads/platform.aspx to download and install Web Platform Installer 5.0 (WebPI 5.0) provided by Microsoft to make sure that a valid and updated IIS is installed in your computer.

At this point, we have finished discussion about how to create and consume a Web service using a Windows-based and a Web-based client project. In the following sections, we will expand these discussions to perform the data insertion, data updating and deleting actions against the database through the Web services.

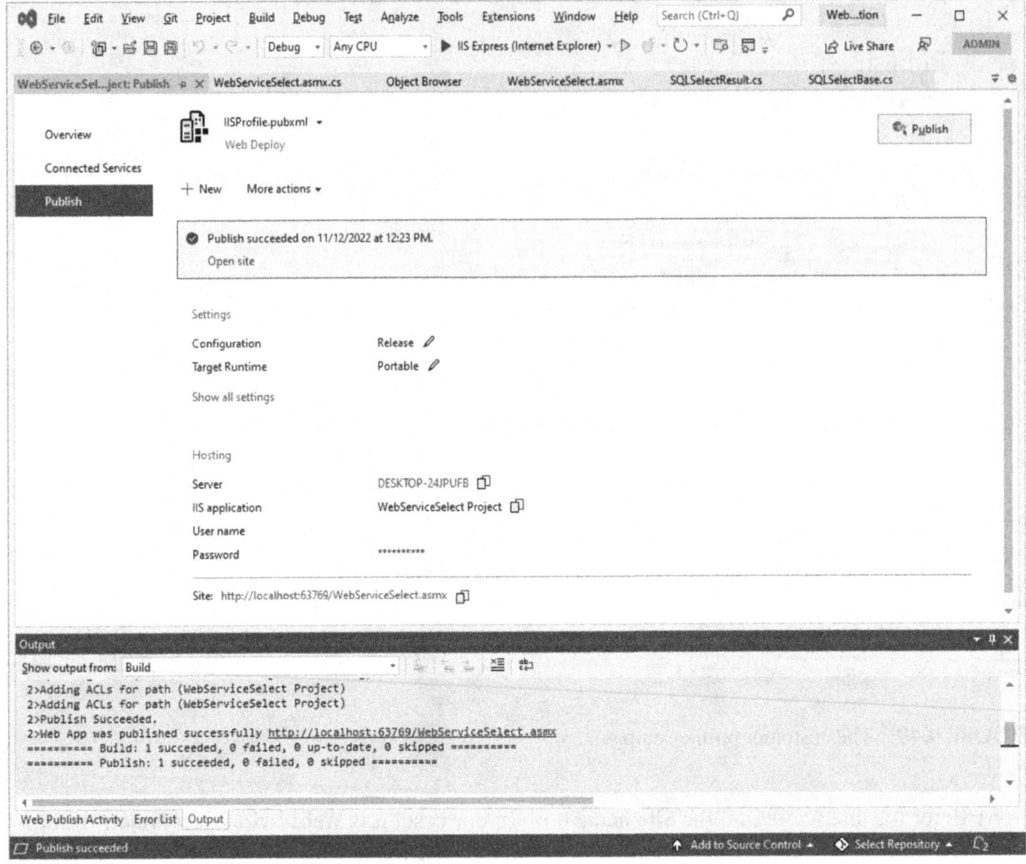

FIGURE 9.50 The web site publishing result.

9.4 BUILD ASP.NET WEB SERVICE PROJECT TO INSERT DATA INTO SQL SERVER DATABASE

In this section we will discuss how to insert data into our sample database through a Web service developed in Visual Studio.NET. The data table we try to use for this data action is the **Course** table. In other words, we want to insert a new course record for the selected faculty into the **Course** table via a Web service we will develop in the next section.

9.4.1 Create a New Web Service Project WebServiceInsert Project

First let's create a new folder such as **Chapter 9** in your root directory using the Windows Explorer. Then create a new **WCF Service Application** project **WebServiceInsert Project** (refer to Section 9.3) and place it into our new created folder **C:\Chapter 9**.

Perform the following operations to add a new Web main service into our project:

1) Right-click on our new project **WebServiceInsert Project** from the Solution Explorer window and select the **Add | New Item**.
2) On the **Add New Item** wizard, select **Web Service (ASMX)** from the Template list.
3) Enter **WebServiceInsert.asmx** into the **Name** box.
4) Click on the **Add** button to complete this item addition operation.

Based on Section 9.3.2 in this chapter, the complete procedure to build a Web service project can be summarized as:

1) Modify the default namespace to make it our own Web service namespace.
2) Add a new database connection string into the Web configuration file **Web.config**.
3) Create a customer base class to handle error-checking codes to protect our real Web service class.
4) Create a customer returned class to hold all required course information. This class is a derived class based on the base class above.
5) Add Web methods to our Web main service class to access our sample database.
6) Develop the detail codes for those Web methods to perform the Web services.

Let's perform those procedures one by one in the following sequence.

1) Refer to Section 9.3.3 to modify the default namespace to make it our Web service namespace, **https://www.routledge.com/978-1032312354/**.
2) Refer to Section 9.3.7.1 to add a new database connection string into the Web configuration file **Web.config** as below:

```
<connectionStrings>
  <add name="sql_conn" connectionString="Server=localhost\SQL2019EXPRESS; _
  Initial Catalog=CSE_DEPT;User ID=SMART;Password=Happy2022;"/>
</connectionStrings>
```

3) Create a customer base class **SQLInsertBase.cs** by going to **Add | New Item** menu with the following member data (refer to Section 9.3.4):
   - **public Boolean SQLInsertOK**: True if the inserting is fine, otherwise is False.
   - **public string SQLInsertError**: A string used to report the errors or problems.

4) Create a customer derived class **SQLInsertRecord.cs** based on the **SQLInsertBase** class with the following seven member data (refer to Section 9.3.4):
   - **publicstring[] CourseID = newstring[10];**
   - **publicstring Course;**
   - **public int Credit;**
   - **public string Classroom;**
   - **public string Schedule;**
   - **public int Enrollment;**
   - **public string FacultyID;**

   Go to the **File | Save All** menu item to save above modifications.

Next let's *take* care of creating the different Web methods with detailed codes to perform the course record insertion actions.

9.4.2 Develop Four Web Service Methods

We try to develop or add four Web methods in our Web service project, two of them are used to insert the desired course information into our sample database and two of them are used to retrieve the new inserted course record from the database to test the data insertion. One of two latter methods is used to retrieve the detailed course information based on the **course_id**. The functions of these methods are described below:

1) Develop a Web method **SetInsertSP()** to call a stored procedure to perform a new course insertion.
2) Develop a Web method **GetInsert()** to retrieve the new inserted course information from the database using a joined table query.
3) Develop a Web method **InsertDataSet()** to perform a data insertion by using multi-query and return a DataSet that contains the updated **Course** table.
4) Develop a Web method **GetInsertCourse()** to retrieve the detailed course information based on the input **course_id**.

The reason we use two different methods (1 and 3) to perform this data insertion is to try to compare them. As you know, there is no faculty name column in the **Course** table and each course is related to an associated **faculty_id**. In order to insert a new course into the **Course** table, one must first perform a query to the **Faculty** table to get the desired **faculty_id** based on the selected faculty name, and then one can perform an insertion query to insert a new course based on that **faculty_id** obtained from the first query. The first method combines those two queries into a stored procedure and the third method uses a DataSet to return the whole **Course** table to make this data insertion convenient.

First let's take care of building our Web methods.

9.4.2.1 Develop Codes for the First Web Method SetInsertSP()

Open our new project **WebServiceInsert Project** and the code window of our main service page **WebServiceInsert.asmx** and enter the codes shown in Figure 9.51 to replace the default Web method, **HelloWorld()**, with our first new Web method **SetInsertSP()**.

This Web method uses a stored procedure to perform the data insertion. Recall that in Section 6.5.1.1 in Chapter 6, we developed a stored procedure **dbo.InsertFacultyCourse** in the SQL Server database and used it to insert a new course into the Course table. We will use this stored procedure again in this Web method to reduce our coding load. Refer to that section to get more detailed information about how to develop this stored procedure. Seven input parameters are used for this stored procedure, **@FacultyName**, **@CourseID**, **@Course**, **@Schedule**, **@Classroom**, **@Credit** and **@Enroll**. All of these parameters will be input by the user as this Web service project runs.

Let's take a closer look at the codes for this Web method to see how they work.

- **A.** The **System.Data.SqlClient** namespace is imported first since we need to use some class and objects defined in that namespace.
- **B.** The Web method name is also changed to **SetInsertSP**, which means that this Web method will call a stored procedure to perform the data insertion action. Seven input parameters are passed into this method as a new course record to be inserted into the Course table. The returned object should be an instance of our modified base class **SQLInsertBase**.
- **C.** Recalled that we built a stored procedure named **dbo.InsertFacultyCourse()** in Section 6.6.1 in Chapter 6. Here we like to use that procedure in this project. The content of the query string must be equal to the name of that stored procedure. Otherwise a possible running error may be encountered as this Web service is executed since the stored procedure is identified by its name when it is called.
- **D.** A returned object **SQLInsertResult** is created based on our customer base class **SQLInsertBase**. To be exact, there is no any data supposed to be returned for the data insertion action. However, in order to enable our client project to get a clear feedback from execution of this Web service, we prefer to return an object that contains the information indicating whether this Web service is successful or not.
- **E.** A local integer variable **intInsert** is declared and this variable is used to hold the returned value from calling of the **ExecuteNonQuery()** method of the Command class, and that method will call the stored procedure to perform the data insertion action. This returned value is equal to the number of rows that have been successfully inserted into our database.

```
WebServiceInsert Project                SetInsertSP()

   using System.Web.Services;
   using System.Data;
A  using System.Data.SqlClient;

   namespace WebServiceInsert_Project
   {
      /// Summary description for WebServiceInsert
      [WebService(Namespace = "https://www.routledge.com/978-1032312354/")]
      [WebServiceBinding(ConformsTo = WsiProfiles.BasicProfile1_1)]
      [System.ComponentModel.ToolboxItem(false)]
      // To allow this Web Service to be called from script, using ASP.NET AJAX, uncomment the following line.
      // [System.Web.Script.Services.ScriptService]
      public class WebServiceInsert : System.Web.Services.WebService
      {
         [WebMethod]
B        public SQLInsertBase SetInsertSP(string FacultyName, string CourseID, string Course, int Credit,
                                          string Classroom, string Schedule, int Enroll)
         {
C           string cmdString = "dbo.InsertFacultyCourse";
            SqlConnection sqlConnection = new SqlConnection();
D           SQLInsertBase SQLInsertResult = new SQLInsertBase();
            SqlCommand sqlCommand = new SqlCommand();
E           int intInsert = 0;
F           SQLInsertResult.SQLInsertOK = true;
G           sqlConnection = SQLConn();
H           if (sqlConnection == null)
            {
               SQLInsertResult.SQLInsertError = "Database connection is failed";
               ReportError(SQLInsertResult);
               return null;
            }
            sqlCommand.Connection = sqlConnection;
I           sqlCommand.CommandType = CommandType.StoredProcedure;
            sqlCommand.CommandText = cmdString;
J           sqlCommand.Parameters.Add("@FacultyName", SqlDbType.Text).Value = FacultyName;
            sqlCommand.Parameters.Add("@CourseID", SqlDbType.Char).Value = CourseID;
            sqlCommand.Parameters.Add("@Course", SqlDbType.Text).Value = Course;
            sqlCommand.Parameters.Add("@Schedule", SqlDbType.Char).Value = Schedule;
            sqlCommand.Parameters.Add("@Classroom", SqlDbType.Text).Value = Classroom;
            sqlCommand.Parameters.Add("@Credit", SqlDbType.Int).Value = Credit;
            sqlCommand.Parameters.Add("@Enroll", SqlDbType.Int).Value = Enroll;
K           intInsert = sqlCommand.ExecuteNonQuery();
L           sqlConnection.Close();
            sqlCommand.Dispose();
M           if (intInsert == 0)
            {
               SQLInsertResult.SQLInsertError = "Data insertion is failed";
               ReportError(SQLInsertResult);
            }
N           return SQLInsertResult;
         }
      }
   }
```

FIGURE 9.51 Detailed codes for the first web method.

F. Initially we set the member data **SQLInsertOK** that is located in our customer base class **SQLInsertBase** to **True** to indicate our Web service running status is good.

G. The user-defined method, **SQLConn()**, whose detailed codes can be found in Figure 9.19 in Section 9.3.7.3, is called to perform a valid database connection.

H. If that connection to our sample database is failed, which is indicated by a returned Connection object containing a **Null**, an error message is assigned to another member data **SQLInsertError** that is also located in our customer base class **SQLInsertBase** to log on this error. Another user-defined method, **ReportError()**, whose codes will be shown later, is called to report this error.

I. The property value **CommandType.StoredProcedure** must be assigned to the **CommandType** property of the Command object to tell the project that a stored procedure should be called as this command object is executed.

J. Seven input parameters are assigned to the Parameters collection property of the Command object, and the last six parameters work as a new course record to be inserted into the **Course** table. One important point to be noted is that these input parameters' names must be identical with those names defined in the stored procedure **dbo.InsertFacultyCourse()** developed in Section 6.6.1 in Chapter 6. Refer to that section to get a detailed description of those parameters' names defined in that stored procedure.

K. The **ExecuteNonQuery()** method is executed to call the stored procedure to perform this data insertion. This method returns an integer value that is stored in our local variable **intInsert**.

L. A cleaning job is performed to release data objects used in this method.

M. The returned value from calling of the **ExecuteNonQuery()** method, which is stored in the variable **intInsert**, is equal to the number of rows that have been successfully inserted into the **Course** table. If this value is zero, which means that no any row has been inserted into our database and that data insertion is failed, a warning message is assigned to the member data **SQLInsertError** that will be reported by using our user defined method **ReportError()**.

N. Finally the instance of our base class, **SQLInsertResult**, is returned to the calling procedure to indicate the running result of this Web method.

Next let's take care of the coding for two user-defined methods used in this page.

9.4.2.2 Develop Codes for the User Defined Methods

Two user-defined methods, **SQLConn()** and **ReportError()**, are included in this project. Refer to Figure 9.19 in Section 9.3.7.3 and Figure 9.22 in Section 9.3.7.4 to get more details about those user-defined methods. For your convenience, the detailed codes for those two methods are shown again in Figure 9.52.

At this point we have finished the coding development and modification to this Web method. Now we can run this Web service project to insert a new course record to our sample database via this Web service. Click on the **IIS Express** button to run the project. The built-in Web interface is shown in Figure 9.53.

Click on the Web method **SetInsertSP** to open another built-in Web interface to display the input parameters window, which is shown in Figure 9.54.

Enter the following parameters as a new course record into this Web method:

FacultyName:	**Ying Bai**
CourseID:	**CSE-556**
Course:	**Advanced Fuzzy Systems**
Schedule:	**M-W-F: 1:00-1:55 PM**
Classroom:	**MTC-315**
Credit:	**3**
Enroll:	**28**

Click on the **Invoke** button to run this Web method to call the stored procedure to perform this data insertion. The running result is displayed in the built-in Web interface, which is shown in Figure 9.55.

Based on the returned member data **SQLInsertOK = True**, it indicates that our data insertion is successful. To confirm this, first click on the **Close** button that is located at the upper-right corner of

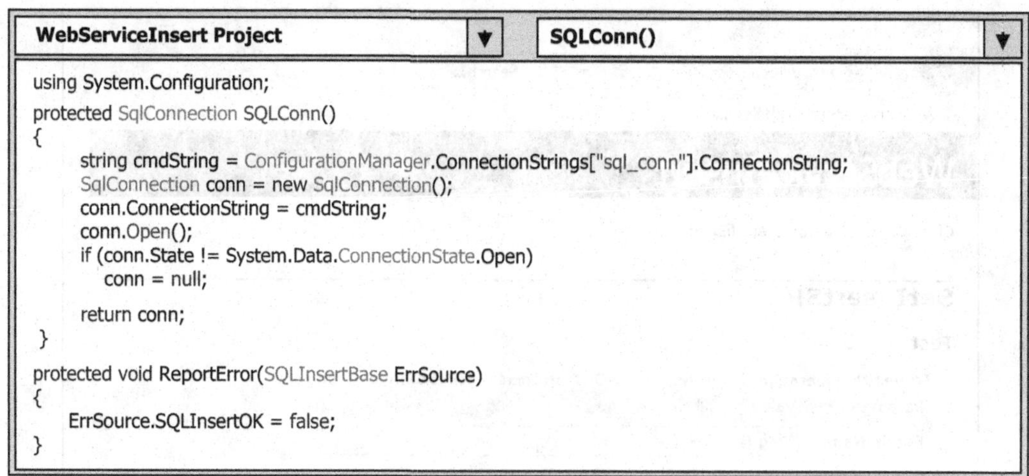
WebServiceInsert Project | SQLConn()

```
using System.Configuration;
protected SqlConnection SQLConn()
{
      string cmdString = ConfigurationManager.ConnectionStrings["sql_conn"].ConnectionString;
      SqlConnection conn = new SqlConnection();
      conn.ConnectionString = cmdString;
      conn.Open();
      if (conn.State != System.Data.ConnectionState.Open)
         conn = null;

      return conn;
}
protected void ReportError(SQLInsertBase ErrSource)
{
    ErrSource.SQLInsertOK = false;
}
```

FIGURE 9.52 Detailed codes for two user defined methods.

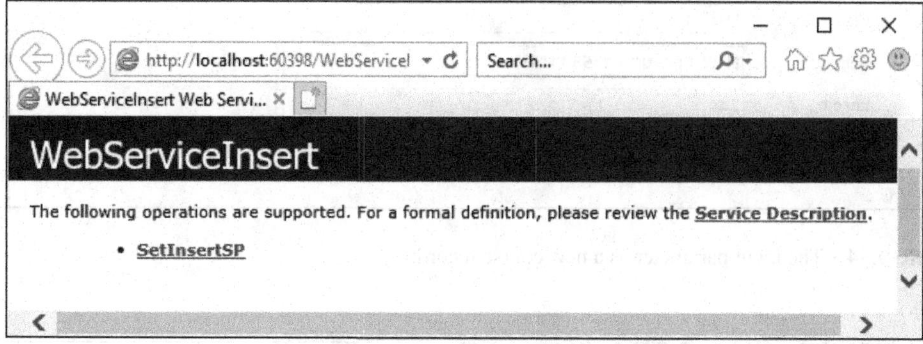

FIGURE 9.53 The running status of the built-in web interface.

this Web interface to terminate our Web service project. Then open the **Course** table in our sample database **CSE_DEPT.mdf** using either the Sever Explorer or the Microsoft SQL Server Management Studio to check this new inserted course.

One can find that the new inserted course record with **course_id = CSE-556** has been inserted into the last line in our **Course** table with a **faculty_id = B78880**. This confirmed that our data insertion is successful.

9.4.2.3 Develop the Second Web Method GetInsert()

The function of this Web method is to retrieve all **course_id**, which includes the original and the new inserted **course_id**, from the **Course** table based on the input faculty name. This Web method will be called or consumed by a client project later to get back and display all **course_id** in a ListBox control in the client project.

Recall that in Section 5.15.6.1 in Chapter 5, we developed a joined-table query to perform the data query from the **Course** table to get all **course_id**s based on the faculty name. The reason for that is because there is no faculty name column available in the **Course** table, and each course or **course_id** is related to a **faculty_id** in that table. In order to get the **faculty_id** that is associated with the selected faculty name, one must first perform a query from the **Faculty** table to obtain it. In this situation, a join query is a desired method to perform this function.

We will use the same strategy to perform this data query in this section.

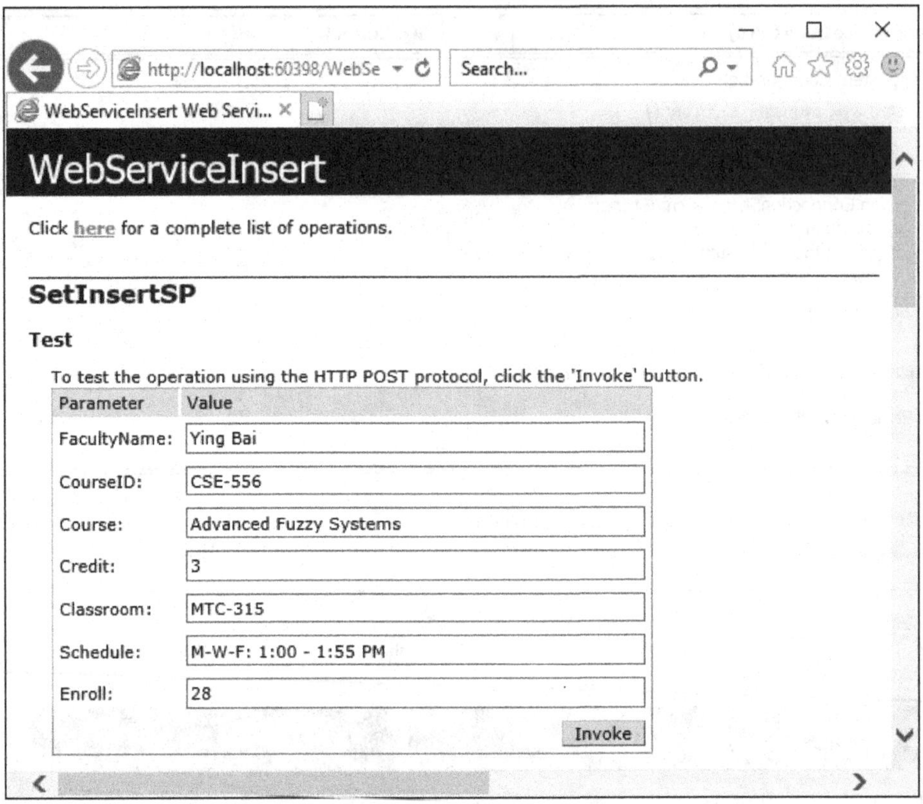

FIGURE 9.54 The input parameter as a new course record.

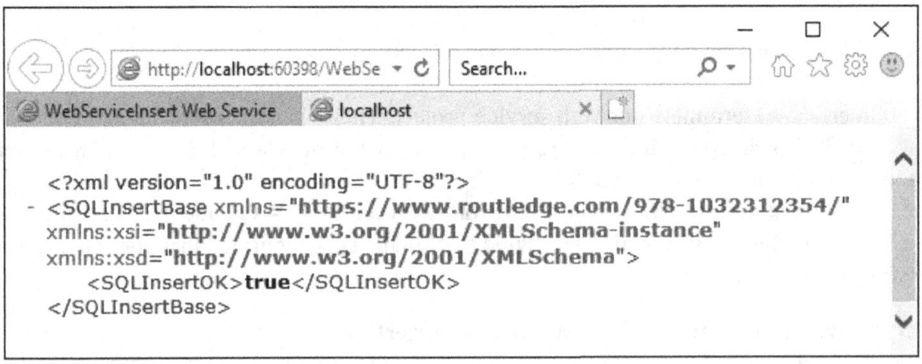

FIGURE 9.55 The running result of the first web method.

Open the code window of our main service page **WebServiceInsert.asmx** and enter the codes that are shown in Figure 9.56 into this page to create our new Web method **GetInsert()**.

Let's have a closer look at the codes in this Web method to see how they work.

A. The returning data type for this Web method is our modified derived class **SQLInsertRecord**, and an entire course record is stored in the different member data in that class. The input parameter to this Web method is a selected faculty name.

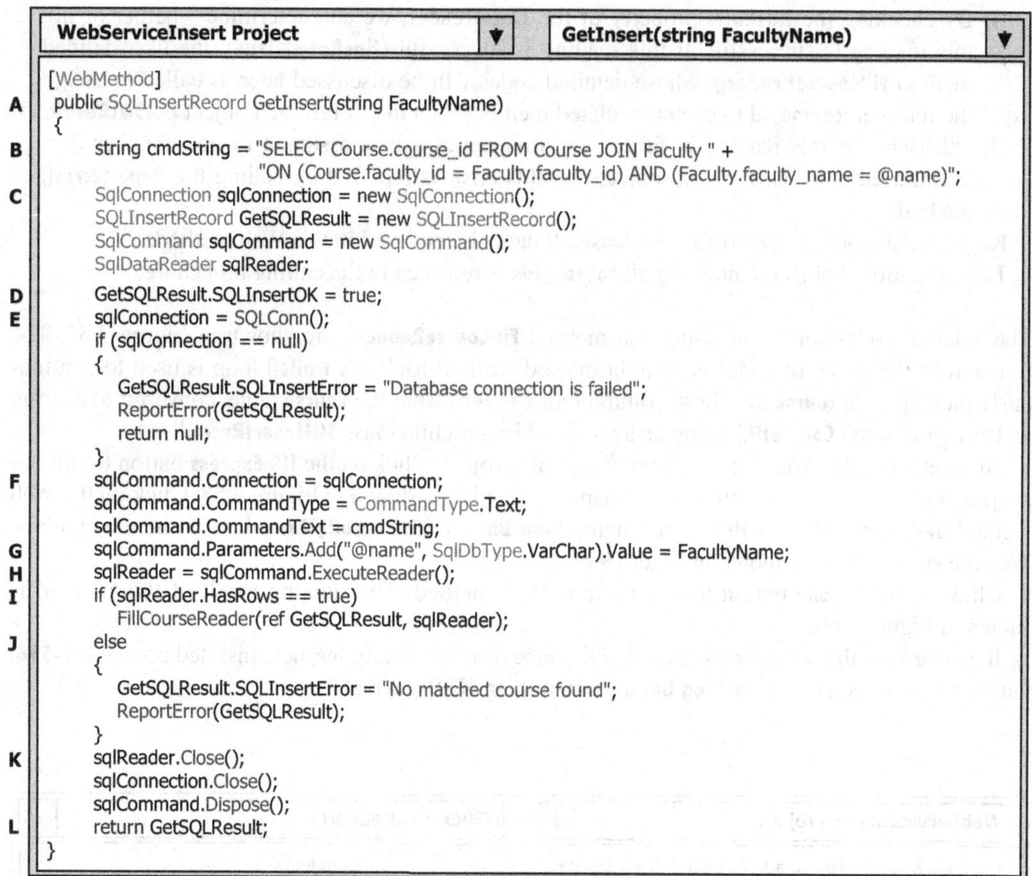

```
WebServiceInsert Project          GetInsert(string FacultyName)

  [WebMethod]
A public SQLInsertRecord GetInsert(string FacultyName)
  {
B     string cmdString = "SELECT Course.course_id FROM Course JOIN Faculty " +
              "ON (Course.faculty_id = Faculty.faculty_id) AND (Faculty.faculty_name = @name)";
C     SqlConnection sqlConnection = new SqlConnection();
      SQLInsertRecord GetSQLResult = new SQLInsertRecord();
      SqlCommand sqlCommand = new SqlCommand();
      SqlDataReader sqlReader;
D     GetSQLResult.SQLInsertOK = true;
E     sqlConnection = SQLConn();
      if (sqlConnection == null)
      {
         GetSQLResult.SQLInsertError = "Database connection is failed";
         ReportError(GetSQLResult);
         return null;
      }
F     sqlCommand.Connection = sqlConnection;
      sqlCommand.CommandType = CommandType.Text;
      sqlCommand.CommandText = cmdString;
G     sqlCommand.Parameters.Add("@name", SqlDbType.VarChar).Value = FacultyName;
H     sqlReader = sqlCommand.ExecuteReader();
I     if (sqlReader.HasRows == true)
         FillCourseReader(ref GetSQLResult, sqlReader);
J     else
      {
         GetSQLResult.SQLInsertError = "No matched course found";
         ReportError(GetSQLResult);
      }
K     sqlReader.Close();
      sqlConnection.Close();
      sqlCommand.Dispose();
L     return GetSQLResult;
  }
```

FIGURE 9.56 The codes for our second web method GetSQLInsert().

B. The joined-table query string is defined here and an ANSI92 standard that is an up-to-date standard is used for the syntax of this query string. The ANSI 89, which is an out-of-date syntax standard, can still be used for this query string definition. But the up-to-date standard is recommended. Refer to Section 5.15.6.1 in Chapter 5 to get more detailed descriptions for this topic. The nominal name of the input dynamic parameter to this query is **@fname**.

C. All used data objects are declared here, such as the Connection, Command and DataReader objects. A returned object, **GetSQLResult**, that is instantiated from our child class **SQLInsertRecord** is also created and it will be returned to the calling procedure with the queried course information.

D. Initially, we set the running status of our Web method to OK.

E. The user-defined function **SQLConn()** is called to connect to our sample database. A warning message is assigned to the member data in our returned object and the user-defined method **ReportError()** is executed to report any exception occurred during this connection.

F. The Command object is initialized with appropriate properties such as the Connection object, command type and command text.

G. The real input parameter **FacultyName** is assigned to the dynamic parameter **@fname** using the **Add()** method, and the data type for it must be **VarChar**.

H. The **ExecuteReader()** method is called to trigger the DataReader and perform the data query. This method is a read-only method and the returned reading result is assigned to the DataReader object **sqlReader**.

I. By checking the **HasRows** property of the DataReader, we can determine whether or not this reading is successful. If this reading is successful (**HasRows=True**), the user-defined method **FillCourseReader()**, whose detailed codes will be discussed later, is called to assign the returned **course_id** to each associated member data in our returned object **GetSQLResult**.

J. Otherwise, if this reading is failed, a warning message is assigned to our member data **SQLInsertError** in our returned object and this error is reported by calling the **ReportError()** method.

K. A cleaning job is performed to release all data objects used in this Web method.

L. The returned object containing all **course_id**s is returned to the calling procedure.

The detailed codes for our user-defined method **FillCourseReader()** are shown in Figure 9.57. The function of this piece of codes is straightforward without tricks. A **while()** loop is used to continuously pick up each **course_id** whose column index is zero from the **Course** table, convert it to a string and assign it to the **CourseID()** string array defined in our child class **SQLInsertRecord**.

Now let's test this Web method by running this project. Click on the **IIS Express** button to run our project and the built-in Web interface is displayed, which is shown in Figure 9.58. Click on the Web method **GetInsert** and enter the faculty name **Ying Bai** into the **FacultyName** box in the next built-in Web interface, which is shown in Figure 9.59.

Click on the **Invoke** button to execute this Web method. The running result of this method is shown in Figure 9.60.

It can be seen that all courses (exactly all **course_ids**), including our new inserted course **CSE-556**, taught by the selected faculty **Ying Bai** are listed in an XML format.

WebServiceInsert Project | **FillCourseReader()**

```
protected void FillCourseReader(ref SQLInsertRecord sResult, SqlDataReader sReader)
{
   int pos = 0;
   while (sReader.Read())
   {
      sResult.CourseID[pos] = System.Convert.ToString(sReader.GetSqlString(0));    //the 1st column is course_id
      pos++;
   }
}
```

FIGURE 9.57 The codes for the FillCourseReader() method.

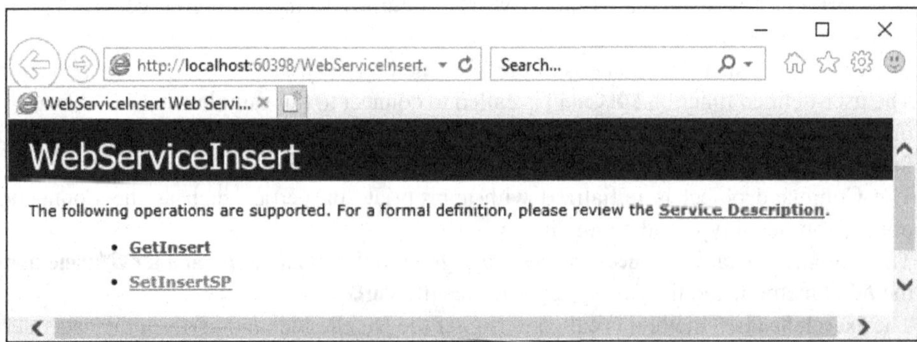

FIGURE 9.58 The running status of our web service project.

FIGURE 9.59 The input parameter wizard for the web method GetSQLInsert().

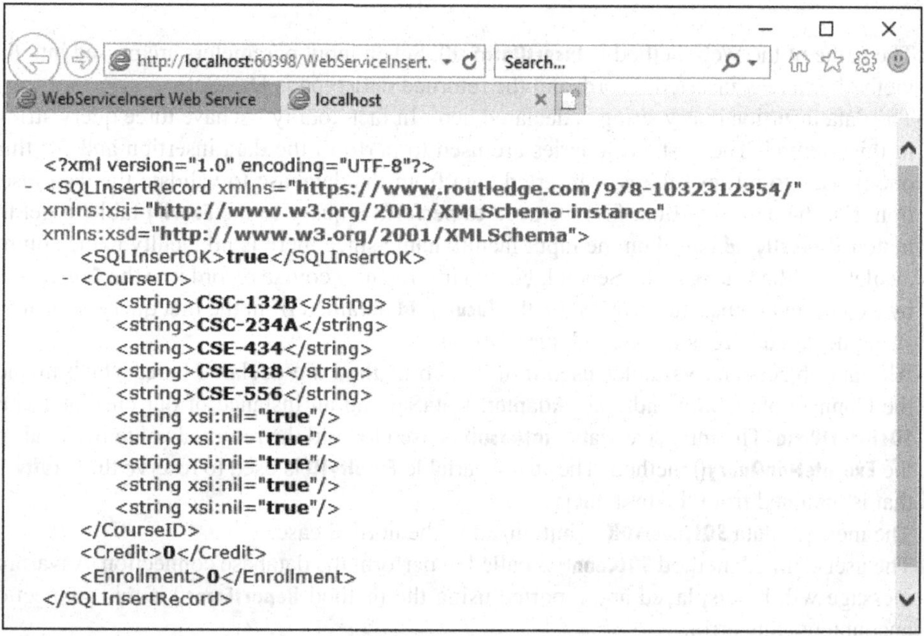

```
http://localhost:60398/WebServiceInsert.   Search...
WebServiceInsert Web Service   localhost

<?xml version="1.0" encoding="UTF-8"?>
- <SQLInsertRecord xmlns="https://www.routledge.com/978-1032312354/"
xmlns:xsi="http://www.w3.org/2001/XMLSchema-instance"
xmlns:xsd="http://www.w3.org/2001/XMLSchema">
    <SQLInsertOK>true</SQLInsertOK>
  - <CourseID>
        <string>CSC-132B</string>
        <string>CSC-234A</string>
        <string>CSE-434</string>
        <string>CSE-438</string>
        <string>CSE-556</string>
        <string xsi:nil="true"/>
        <string xsi:nil="true"/>
        <string xsi:nil="true"/>
        <string xsi:nil="true"/>
        <string xsi:nil="true"/>
    </CourseID>
    <Credit>0</Credit>
    <Enrollment>0</Enrollment>
</SQLInsertRecord>
```

FIGURE 9.60 The running result of our web method GetInsert().

Our second Web method is successful. Click on the **Close** button that is located at the upper-right corner of this page to terminate our Web service project. Then go to **File | Save All** to save all methods we have developed.

Next let's take care of building our third Web method **InsertDataSet()** to insert data into the **Course** table using the DataSet method.

9.4.2.4 Develop the Third Web Method InsertDataSet()

The function of this Web method is similar to that of the first Web method, which is to insert a new course record into the **Course** table based on the selected faculty member. The difference is that this

Web method uses a multi-query way to insert a new course record into the **Course** table and uses a DataSet as the returned object. Furthermore, the returned DataSet contains the updated **Course** table that includes the new inserted course record. The advantages of using a DataSet as the returned object include:

1) Unlike Web methods 1 and 2, which are a pair of methods, and in which the first one is used to insert data into the database and the second one is used to retrieve the new inserted data from the database to confirm the data insertion, Web method 3 contains both data insertion and retrieving functions. Later, when a client project is developed to consume this Web service, methods 1 and 2 must be called together from that client project to perform both data insertion and data validation jobs. However, method 3 has both data insertion and data validation functions, so it can be called independently.
2) Because a DataSet is returned, we do not need to create any new instance for our customer class as the returned object. However, in order to report or log on any exception encountered during the project runs, we still need to create and use an instance of our customer class to handle those error-processing issues.

Create and add a new Web method **InsertDataSet()**, and enter the codes that are shown in Figure 9.61 into that method. Let's have a closer look at the codes in this Web method to see how they work.

A. The name of the Web method is **InsertDataSet()**. Seven input parameters are passed into this method as a new inserted record, and the returned data type is DataSet.
B. The data insertion query string is declared here. In fact, totally we have three query strings in this method. The first two queries are used to perform the data insertion and the third one is used to retrieve the new inserted data from the database to validate the data insertion. For the data insertion, first we need to perform a query to the **Faculty** table to get the matched **faculty_id** based on the input faculty name since there is no faculty name column available in the **Course** table. Second, we can insert a new course record into the **Course** table by executing another query based on the **faculty_id** obtained from the first query. The query string declared here is the second query string.
C. All data objects and variables used in this Web method are declared here, which include the Connection, Command, DataAdapter, DataSet and an instance of our customer class **SQLInsertBase**. The integer variable **intResult** is used to hold the returned value from calling the **ExecuteNonQuery()** method. The string variable **FacultyID** is used to reserve the **faculty_id** that is obtained from the first query.
D. The member data **SQLInsertOK** is initialized to the normal case.
E. The user-defined method **SQLConn()** is called to perform the database connection. A warning message will be displayed and reported using the method **ReportError()** if this connection encountered any error.
F. The Command object is first initialized to perform the first query – get **faculty_id** from the **Faculty** table based on the input faculty name.
G. The first query string is assigned to the CommandText property.
H. The dynamic parameter **@fname** is assigned with the actual input parameter **FacultyName**. The key point is the data type for that parameter, which should be **VarChar** or **NVarChar**, otherwise a running error maybe encountered.
I. The **ExecuteScalar()** method of the Command object is called to perform the first query to pick up the **faculty_id** and assign it to the local string variable **FacultyID**. One point to be noted is the data type that the **ExecuteScalar()** method returned. An **Object** type is returned from calling of that method in the normal case, but it can be automatically converted to a **String** type by Visual C#.NET if it is assigned to a variable with the **String** type.

WebServiceInsert Project | InsertDataSet()

```
  [WebMethod]
A public DataSet InsertDataSet(string FacultyName, string CourseID, string Course, string Schedule,
                              string Classroom, int Credit, int Enroll)
  {
B    string cmdString = "INSERT INTO Course VALUES (@course_id, @course, @credit, @classroom, " +
                        "@schedule, @enrollment, @faculty_id)";
C    SqlConnection sqlConnection = new SqlConnection();
     SQLInsertBase SetSQLResult = new SQLInsertBase();
     SqlCommand sqlCommand = new SqlCommand();
     SqlDataAdapter CourseAdapter = new SqlDataAdapter();
     DataSet dsCourse = new DataSet();
     int intResult = 0;
     string FacultyID;
D    SetSQLResult.SQLInsertOK = true;
E    sqlConnection = SQLConn();
     if (sqlConnection == null)
     {
        SetSQLResult.SQLInsertError = "Database connection is failed";
        ReportError(SetSQLResult);
        return null;
     }
F    sqlCommand.Connection = sqlConnection;
     sqlCommand.CommandType = CommandType.Text;
G    sqlCommand.CommandText = "SELECT faculty_id FROM Faculty WHERE faculty_name = @Name";
H    sqlCommand.Parameters.Add("@Name", SqlDbType.VarChar).Value = FacultyName;
I    FacultyID = (string)sqlCommand.ExecuteScalar();
J    sqlCommand.CommandText = cmdString;
K    sqlCommand.Parameters.Add("@faculty_id", SqlDbType.VarChar).Value = FacultyID;
     sqlCommand.Parameters.Add("@course_id", SqlDbType.VarChar).Value = CourseID;
     sqlCommand.Parameters.Add("@course", SqlDbType.Text).Value = Course;
     sqlCommand.Parameters.Add("@schedule", SqlDbType.Char).Value = Schedule;
     sqlCommand.Parameters.Add("@classroom", SqlDbType.Text).Value = Classroom;
     sqlCommand.Parameters.Add("@credit", SqlDbType.Int).Value = Credit;
     sqlCommand.Parameters.Add("@enrollment", SqlDbType.Int).Value = Enroll;
L    CourseAdapter.InsertCommand = sqlCommand;
M    intResult = CourseAdapter.InsertCommand.ExecuteNonQuery();
N    if (intResult == 0)
     {
        SetSQLResult.SQLInsertError = "No matched course found";
        ReportError(SetSQLResult);
     }
O    sqlCommand.CommandText = "SELECT * FROM Course WHERE faculty_id = @FacultyID";
P    sqlCommand.Parameters.Add("@FacultyID", SqlDbType.VarChar).Value = FacultyID;
Q    CourseAdapter.SelectCommand = sqlCommand;
R    CourseAdapter.Fill(dsCourse, "Course");
S    CourseAdapter.Dispose();
     sqlConnection.Close();
     sqlCommand.Dispose();
T    return dsCourse;
  }
```

FIGURE 9.61 The codes for the web method InsertDataSet().

- **J.** The second query string is assigned to the CommandText property to make it ready to perform the second query – insert new course record into the **Course** table.
- **K.** All seven input parameters to the **INSERT** command are initialized by assigning them with the actual input values. The point to be noted is the data types of the last two parameters. Both **credit** and **enrollment** are integers, so the data type **SqlDbType.Int** is used for each of them.
- **L.** The initialized Command object is assigned to the InsertCommand property of the DataAdapter.

M. The **ExecuteNonQuery()** method is called to perform this data insertion query to insert a new course record into the Course table in our sample database. This method will return an integer to indicate the number of rows that have been successfully inserted into the database.
N. If this returned integer is zero, which means that no row has been inserted into the database and this insertion is failed, a warning message is assigned to the member data **SQLInsertError** and our method **ReportError()** is called to report this error.
O. The third query string, which is used to retrieve all courses, including the new inserted course, from the database based on the input **faculty_id**, is assigned to the CommandText property of the Command object.
P. The dynamic parameter **FacultyID** is initialized with the actual **faculty_id** obtained from the first query as we did above.
Q. The initialized Command object is assigned to the SelectCommand property of the DataAdapter.
R. The **Fill()** method of the DataAdapter is executed to retrieve all courses, including the new inserted courses, from the database and add them into the DataSet **dsCourse**.
S. A cleaning job is performed to release all objects used in this Web method.
T. Finally the DataSet that contains the updated course information is returned to the calling procedure.

Compared with the first Web method, it appears that more codes are involved in this method. Yes, it is true. However, this method has two functions: inserting data into the database and validating the inserted data from the database. In order to validate the data insertion for the first method, the second Web method must be executed. Therefore, from the point of view of data insertion and data validation process, the third Web method has less code compared with the first one.

Now let's run our Web service project to test this Web method using the built-in Web interface. Click on the **IIS Express** button to run the project and click on our third Web method **InsertDataSet** from the built-in Web interface to start it. The parameters wizard is displayed, which is shown later in Figure 9.62. Enter the following parameters into each associated **Value** box as the data of a new course:

FacultyName:	**Ying Bai**
CourseID:	**CSE-665**
Course:	**Advanced Robotics**
Schedule:	**T-H: 1:30-2:45 PM**
Classroom:	**MTC-309**
Credit:	**3**
Enroll:	**32**

Your finished parameter wizard should match one that is shown in Figure 9.62.

Click on the **Invoke** button to run this Web method to perform this new course insertion. The running result is shown in Figure 9.63.

All six courses, including the sixth course **CSE-665** that is the new inserted course, are displayed in the XML format or tags in this running result interface.

A point to be noted is that you can only insert this new course record into the database one time, which means that after this new course has been inserted into the database, you cannot continue to click on the **Invoke** button to perform another insertion with the same course information since the data to be inserted into the database must be unique.

Click on the **Close** button that is located at the upper-right corner of this Web interface to terminate our service. Next let's develop our fourth Web method.

http://localhost:60398/WebServiceInsert.

WebServiceInsert Web Servi...

WebServiceInsert

Click here for a complete list of operations.

InsertDataSet

Test

To test the operation using the HTTP POST protocol, click the 'Invoke' button.

Parameter	Value
FacultyName:	Ying Bai
CourseID:	CSE-665
Course:	Advanced Robotics
Schedule:	T-H: 1:30-2:45 PM
Classroom:	MTC-309
Credit:	3
Enroll:	32

Invoke

FIGURE 9.62 The finished input parameter wizard.

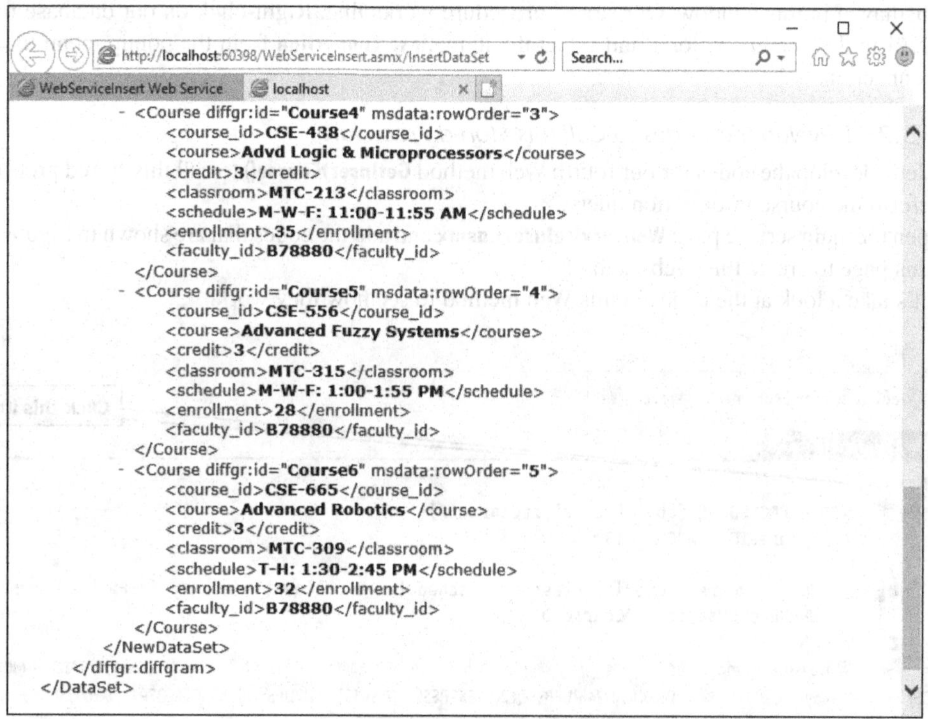

FIGURE 9.63 The running result of the third web method.

9.4.2.5 Develop the Fourth Web Method GetInsertCourse()

The function of this method is to retrieve the detailed course information from the database based on the input **course_id**. This method can be consumed by a client project when users want to get the detailed course information such as the course name, schedule, classroom, credit, enrollment and **faculty_id** when a **course_id** is selected from a ListBox control.

Because this query is a single query, you can use either a normal query or a stored procedure if you want to reduce the coding load for this method. Relatively speaking, a stored procedure is more efficient compared with a normal query, so we prefer to use a stored procedure to perform this query.

Now let's first create our stored procedure WebSelectCourseSP.

9.4.2.5.1 Create the Stored Procedure WebSelectCourseSP()

Open Visual Studio.NET 2022 and the Server Explorer window, click on the arrow in front of our sample database folder **CSE_DEPT** to connect it and then expand to the **Stored Procedures** folder. To create a new stored procedure, right click on this folder and select the item **Add New Stored Procedure** to open the Add New Stored Procedure wizard.

Enter the codes that are shown later in Figure 9.64 into this wizard to create our new stored procedure **WebSelectCourseSP()**. Click on the **Update** item as shown in Figure 9.64, and click on the **Update Database** button on the opened **Review Database Updates** wizard to save this new stored procedure. A successful updating message should be displayed in the **Data Tools Operations** box at the bottom if everything is fine.

To test this stored procedure, right-click on this new created stored procedure (you may need to refresh the **Stored Procedure** folder to see this new added one). Then select the item **Execute** from the popup menu to open the Run Stored Procedure wizard.

Enter **CSE-438** into the **Value** box in this wizard as the input **course_id** and click on the **OK** button to run this stored procedure. The running result is displayed in the **Results** window, which is shown in Figure 9.65. All queried 6 columns are retrieved from our sample database, from the **Course** table, and displayed in this window. Our stored procedure works fine. Right-click on our database folder **CSE_DEPT** in the Server Explorer and select the item **Close Connection** from the popup menu to close this connection.

9.4.2.5.2 Develop the Codes to Call this Stored Procedure

Now let's develop the codes for our fourth Web method **GetInsertCourse()** to call this stored procedure to perform the course information query.

Open the main service page **WebServiceInsert.asmx** and add the codes that are shown in Figure 9.66 into this page to create this Web method.

Let's take a look at the codes in this Web method to see how they work.

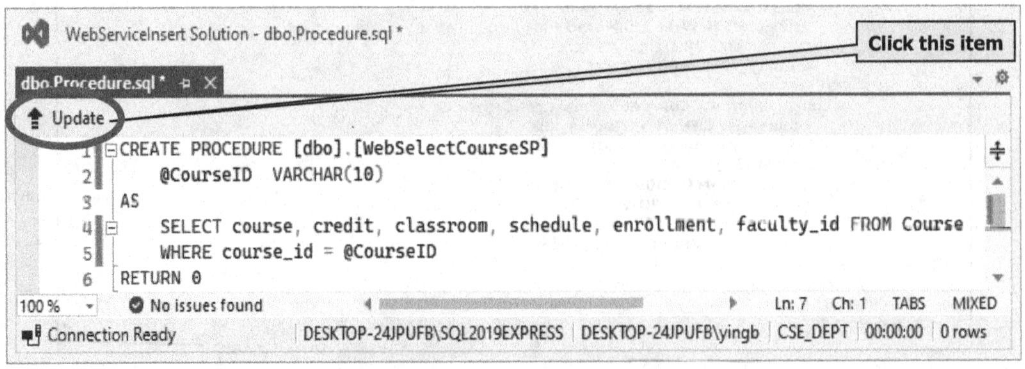

FIGURE 9.64 The codes for the stored procedure WebSelectCourseSP().

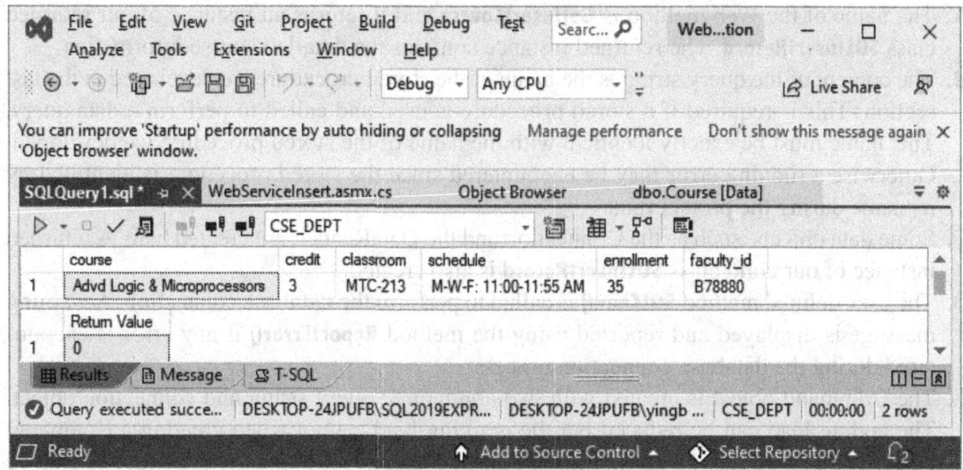

FIGURE 9.65 The running result of the stored procedure WebSelectCourseSP().

```
WebServiceInsert Project                    GetInsertCourse()

    [WebMethod]
A   public SQLInsertRecord GetInsertCourse(string CourseID)
    {
B       string cmdString = "dbo.WebSelectCourseSP";
C       SqlConnection sqlConnection = new SqlConnection();
        SQLInsertRecord GetSQLResult = new SQLInsertRecord();
        SqlDataReader sqlReader;
        GetSQLResult.SQLInsertOK = true;
D       sqlConnection = SQLConn();
        if (sqlConnection == null)
        {
            GetSQLResult.SQLInsertError = "Database connection is failed";
            ReportError(GetSQLResult);
            return null;
        }
E       SqlCommand sqlCommand = new SqlCommand(cmdString, sqlConnection);
F       sqlCommand.CommandType = CommandType.StoredProcedure;
G       sqlCommand.Parameters.Add("@CourseID", SqlDbType.VarChar).Value = CourseID;
H       sqlReader = sqlCommand.ExecuteReader();
I       if (sqlReader.HasRows == true)
            FillCourseDetail(ref GetSQLResult, sqlReader);
J       else
        {
            GetSQLResult.SQLInsertError = "No matched course found";
            ReportError(GetSQLResult);
        }
K       sqlReader.Close();
        sqlConnection.Close();
        sqlCommand.Dispose();
L       return GetSQLResult;
    }
```

FIGURE 9.66 The codes for the web method GetInsertCourse().

A. The name of the Web method is **GetInsertCourse** and it returns an instance of our returned class **SQLInsertRecord**. The returned instance contains the detailed course information.
B. The content of the query string is the name of the stored procedure we developed in the last section. This is required if a stored procedure is used and called to perform a data query. This name must be exactly identical with the name of the stored procedure we developed. Otherwise a running error may be encountered since the stored procedure is identified by its name during the project runs.
C. Some data objects, such as the Connection and the DataReader, are created here. A returned instance of our child class **SQLInsertRecord** is also created.
D. The user-defined method **SQLConn()** is called to perform the database connection. A warning message is displayed and reported using the method **ReportError()** if any error is encountered during the database connection process.
E. The Command object is created with two arguments: query string and connection object. The coding load can be reduced but the working load cannot when creating a Command object in this way. As you know, the Command class has four kinds of constructors and we used the third one here.
F. The CommandType property of the Command object must be set to the value of **Stored Procedure** since we need to call a stored procedure to perform this course information query in this method.
G. The dynamic parameter **@CourseID** is assigned with the actual parameter **CourseID** that will be entered as an input parameter by the user as the project runs. One point to be noted is that the nominal name of this dynamic parameter must be identical with the name of input parameter defined in the stored procedure we developed in the last section.
H. After the Command object is initialized, the **ExecuteReader()** method is called to trigger the DataReader and to run the stored procedure to perform the course information query. The returned course information is stored to the DataReader.
I. By checking the **HasRows** property of the DataReader, we can determine whether the course information query is successful or not. If this property is **True**, which means that at least one row has been found and returned from our database, the user-defined method **FillCourseDetail()**, whose detailed codes are shown in Figure 9.67, is executed to assign each piece of course information to the associated member data defined in our derived class, and an instance of this class will be returned as a reference when this method is done.
J. Otherwise, if this property returns **False**, which means that no row has been selected and returned from our database, a warning message is displayed and reported using the **ReportError()** method.
K. A cleaning job is performed to release all data objects used in this Web method.
L. Finally, an instance of our returned class SQLInsertRecord, **GetSQLResult** that contains the detailed information for a queried course, is returned to the calling procedure.

The detailed codes for the user-defined method **FillCourseDetail()** are shown in Figure 9.67. Let's have a closer look at this piece of codes to see how it works.

A. Two arguments are passed into this method: the first one is our returned object that contains all member data and the second one is the DataReader that contains queried course information. The point is that the passing mode for the first argument is passing-by-reference, which means that an address of our returned object is passed into this method. In this way, all modified member data that contain the course information in this returned object can be returned to the calling procedure or our Web method – **GetInsertCourse()**. From this point of view, this method works just as a function and our object can be returned as this method is completed.
B. The **Read()** method of the DataReader is executed to read course record from the DataReader.

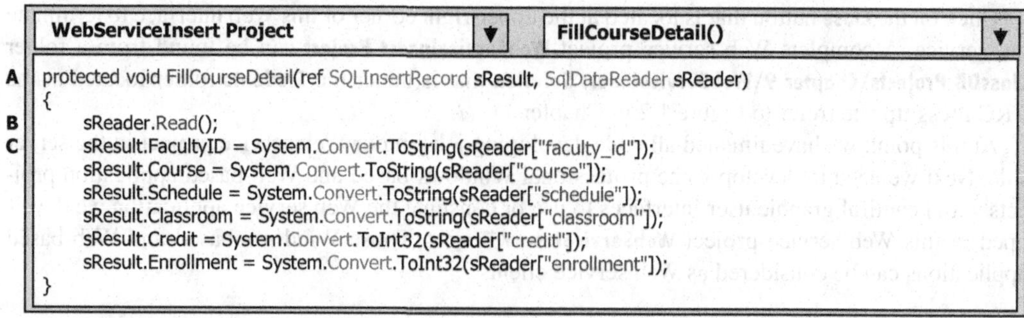

```
WebServiceInsert Project        FillCourseDetail()

A  protected void FillCourseDetail(ref SQLInsertRecord sResult, SqlDataReader sReader)
   {
B      sReader.Read();
C      sResult.FacultyID = System.Convert.ToString(sReader["faculty_id"]);
       sResult.Course = System.Convert.ToString(sReader["course"]);
       sResult.Schedule = System.Convert.ToString(sReader["schedule"]);
       sResult.Classroom = System.Convert.ToString(sReader["classroom"]);
       sResult.Credit = System.Convert.ToInt32(sReader["credit"]);
       sResult.Enrollment = System.Convert.ToInt32(sReader["enrollment"]);
   }
```

FIGURE 9.67 The codes for the FillCourseDetail() method.

C. Each column of queried course record is assigned to the associated member data in our child class. Two system methods, **Convert.ToString()** and **Convert.ToInt32()**, are used to convert all data to the associated data types for that assignment. A point is that one can use a **System** namespace on the top of this page by adding it as **using System;** to directly use the **Convert** class without prefixing the **System**.

Now let's build and run our project to test this Web method. Click on the **IIS Express** button to run the project. Select our Web method **GetInsertCourse** from the built-in Web interface, enter **CSE-665** as the **course_id** into the **Value** box, and then click on the **Invoke** button to run this Web method. The running result of this Web method is shown in Figure 9.68.

Six pieces of course information are displayed in XML tags except the **course_id**. Recall that we defined the **course_id** as a string array **CourseID[]** with a dimension of **10** in our child class. This member data is used for our second Web method – **GetInsert()** that returns an array contains all **course_id**. Since we did not use it in this method ten elements on this **CourseID[]** array are set to **true** and displayed in this resulting file.

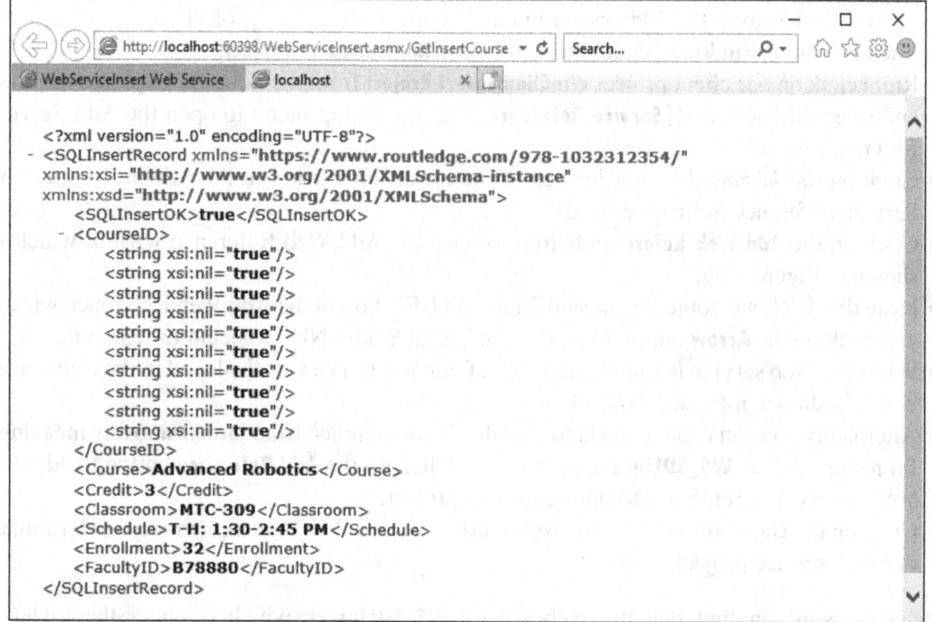


```
<?xml version="1.0" encoding="UTF-8"?>
- <SQLInsertRecord xmlns="https://www.routledge.com/978-1032312354/"
  xmlns:xsi="http://www.w3.org/2001/XMLSchema-instance"
  xmlns:xsd="http://www.w3.org/2001/XMLSchema">
    <SQLInsertOK>true</SQLInsertOK>
  - <CourseID>
        <string xsi:nil="true"/>
        <string xsi:nil="true"/>
        <string xsi:nil="true"/>
        <string xsi:nil="true"/>
        <string xsi:nil="true"/>
        <string xsi:nil="true"/>
        <string xsi:nil="true"/>
        <string xsi:nil="true"/>
        <string xsi:nil="true"/>
        <string xsi:nil="true"/>
    </CourseID>
    <Course>Advanced Robotics</Course>
    <Credit>3</Credit>
    <Classroom>MTC-309</Classroom>
    <Schedule>T-H: 1:30-2:45 PM</Schedule>
    <Enrollment>32</Enrollment>
    <FacultyID>B78880</FacultyID>
</SQLInsertRecord>
```

FIGURE 9.68 The running result of our web method GetInsertCourse().

Click on the **Close** button that is located at the upper-right corner of this Web interface to terminate our service. A complete Web service project **WebServiceInsert Project** can be found from a folder **ClassDB Projects\Chapter 9\WebServiceInsert Solution** that is under the **Students** folder located at the CRC Press ftp site (refer to Figure 1.2 in Chapter 1).

At this point, we have finished all code developing jobs in our Web service project in the server side. Next we need to develop some professional Windows-based and Web-based application projects with beautiful graphic user interfaces to use or consume the Web service application we developed in this Web service project **WebServiceInsert Project**. Those Windows-based and Web-based applications can be considered as Web service clients.

9.4.3 Build Windows-Based Clients to Consume the Web Services

To use or consume a Web service, first we need to create a Web service proxy class in our Windows-based or Web-based applications. Then we can create a new instance of the Web service proxy class and execute the desired Web methods located in that Web service class. The process of creating a Web service proxy class is equivalent to add a Web reference to our Windows-based or Web-based project applications.

9.4.3.1 Create a Windows-Based Consume Project and a Web Service Proxy Class

Basically, adding a Web reference to our Windows-based or Web-based applications is to execute a searching process. During this process, Visual Studio.NET 2022 will try to find all Web services available to our applications.

Open Visual Studio.NET 2022 in the Administrator mode and create a new Visual C# Windows Forms App (.NET Framework) project and name it as **WinClientInsert Project** and save it to the folder **C:\Chapter 9**. Now let's add a Web reference to our new project.

Refer to Section 9.3.11.2 to start this adding Web reference process. Perform the following operations to finish this procedure:

1) Open our Web service project **WebServiceInsert Project**, and click on the **IIS Express** button to run it.
2) Copy the URL from the **Address** bar in our running Web service project.
3) Then open our Windows-based client project **WinClientInsert Project**.
4) Right click on our client project **WinClientInsert Project** from the Solution Explorer window, and select the item **Add | Service Reference** from the popup menu to open the Add Service Reference wizard.
5) Click on the **Advanced** button located at the lower-left corner on this wizard to open the Service Reference Settings wizard.
6) Click on the **Add Web Reference** button to open the Add Web Reference wizard, which is shown in Figure 9.69.
7) Paste that URL we copied from step 2 into the URL box in the Add Web Reference wizard and click on the **Arrow** button to enable the Visual Studio.NET to begin to search it.
8) When the Web service is found, the name of our Web service is displayed in the right pane, which is shown in Figure 9.69.
9) Alternately you can change the name for this Web reference from **localhost** to any meaningful name, such as **WS_SQLInsert**, in our case. Click on the **Add Reference** button to add this Web service as a reference to our new client project.
10) Click on the **Close** button from our Web service built-in Web interface window to terminate our Web service project.

Immediately, you can find that the Web service **WS_SQLInsert**, which is under the folder **Web References**, has been added into the Solution Explorer window in our client project. This reference is the so-called Web service proxy class.

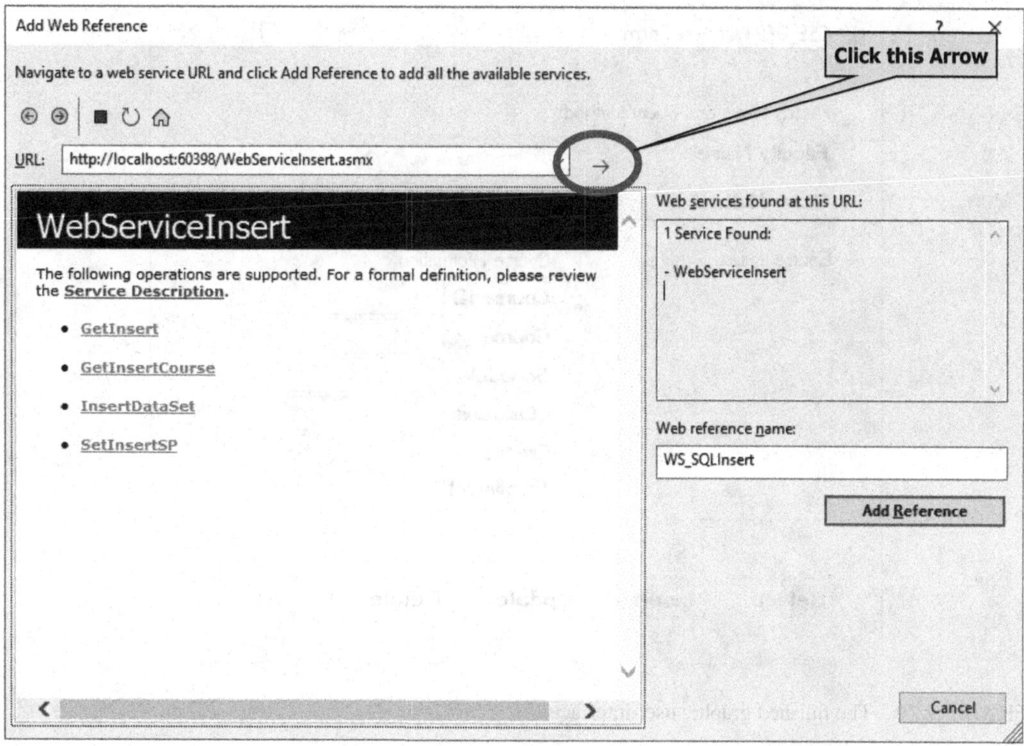

FIGURE 9.69 The finished add web reference wizard.

Next let's develop the graphic user interface by adding useful controls to interface to our Web service and to display the queried course information.

9.4.3.2 Develop the Graphic User Interface for the Client Project

Perform the following modifications to our new client project:

1) Rename the Form File object from the default name **Form1.cs** to our desired name **WinClient Form.cs**.
2) Rename the Window Form object from the default name **Form1** to our desired name **CourseForm** by modifying the **Name** property of the form window.
3) Rename the form title from the default title **Form1** to **CSE_DEPT Course Form** by modifying the **Text** property of the form.
4) Change the **StartPosition** property of the form window to **CenterScreen**.

To save time and space, we can use the Course Form located in the project **RTOUpdateDelete Project** we developed in Chapter 7 as our graphic user interface. You can find this project from the folder **ClassDB Projects\Chapter 7\RTOUpdateDelete Solution** that is under the **Students** folder on the CRC Press ftp site (refer to Figure 1.2 in Chapter 1). Perform the following operations to add this Course Form into our new client project:

1) Open the project **RTOUpdateDelete Project** and the **Course** form window from the CRC Press ftp site.
2) Select all controls from that form by going to the item **Edit | Select All**, and go to **Edit | Copy** menu item to copy all controls selected from this form window.
3) Return to our new Windows-based client project **WinClientInsert Project**, open our form window **CourseForm** and paste those controls we copied from step 2 into this form.

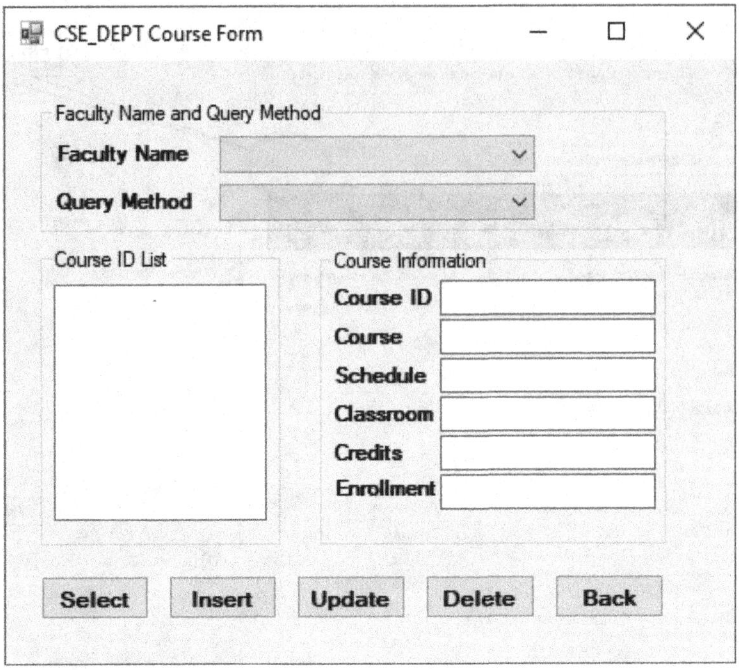

FIGURE 9.70 The finished graphic user interface.

Your finished graphic user interface is shown in Figure 9.70.

The purpose of the **Query Method** combobox control is used to select two different methods developed in our Web service project to get our desired course information:

1) **Stored Procedure Method** that uses a stored procedure to insert a new course record into the database.
2) **DataSet Method** that uses three queries to insert a new course record into the database and return a DataSet that contains the detailed course information.

The **Faculty** Name combobox control is used to select a desired faculty member as the input parameter to the Web methods to insert and pick up the desired course record.

In this application, only the **Insert**, **Select** and **Back** buttons are used. The **Insert** button is used to trigger a data insertion action, the **Select** button is to trigger a data validation action to confirm that data insertion and the **Back** button is used to terminate our project.

The detailed functions of this project include:

1) **Insert Data Using the Stored Procedure Method**: when the project runs, as this method and a faculty name as well as a new course record that is stored in six textboxes have been selected and entered. Then the **Insert** button is clicked by the user. Our client project will be connected to our Web service via the Web reference we provided, and call the selected Web method **SetInsertSP()** to run the stored procedure to insert that new course record into our sample database.
2) **Insert Data Using the DataSet Method**: if this method is selected, the Web method **InsertDataSet()** built in our Web service will be called to execute two queries to perform this new course insertion. In addition, all courses, which include the new inserted course, taught by the selected faculty that works as an input to this method, will be retrieved and stored into a DataSet, and that DataSet will be returned to our client project.

3) **Validate Data Insertion Using the Stored Procedure Method**: to confirm this data insertion, the **Select** button, exactly the **Select** button's click method that will be developed later, is used to validate that data insertion. If the **Stored Procedure Method** is selected, the Web method **GetInsert()** is called to perform a joined-table query to retrieve all **course_id**, which include the new inserted **course_id**, from the database and stored them into an instance of our returned class **SQLInsertRecord** in our Web service. This instance will be returned to our client project and all **course_id** stored in that instance will be taken out and displayed in the list box control **CourseList** in our client form window.
4) **Validate Data Insertion Using the DataSet Method**: if this method is selected and the **Select** button is clicked, the **Select** button's click method that will be built later is executed to pick up all **course_id** from a DataSet that is returned in step 2. Also all **course_id** will be displayed in the list box control **CourseList** in our client form window.
5) **Get Detailed Course Information for a Specific Course**: when this method is selected and a **course_id** in the list box control **CourseList** is clicked, the Web method **GetInsertCourse()** in our Web service will be called to run a stored procedure to retrieve all six pieces of information related to that selected **course_id** and store them into an instance of our returned class **SQLInsertRecord** in our Web service. This instance will be returned to our client project and all six pieces of course information stored in that instance will be taken out and displayed in six textbox controls in our client form window.

Now let's take care of the coding development for this project to connect to our Web service using the Web reference we developed in the last section to call the associated Web methods to perform the different data actions.

9.4.3.3 Develop the Code to Consume the Web Service

The coding development can be divided into the following four parts:

1) Initialize and terminate the client project.
2) Insert a new course record into the database using both methods.
3) Validate the data insertion using both methods.
4) Get the detailed information for a specific course using both methods.

Now **let's** start our coding process based on these four steps.

9.4.3.3.1 Develop the Codes to Initialize and Terminate the Client Project

This coding includes the developing codes for the constructor of the **CourseForm** class, the **Back** button's Click method and some other initialization codes such as the field-level variables declarations.

Open Visual Studio.NET 2022 and our client project **WinClientInsert Project** if it has not been opened, then open the Code Window of the **WinClient Form.cs**, and enter the codes that are shown in Figure 9.71 into this Code Window.

Let's have a closer look at this piece of codes to see how it works.

A. Three field-level variables are created here. The first one is a Boolean variable **dsFlag** and it is used to set a flag to indicate whether the **InsertDataSet()** Web method has been executed or not. Because this Web method performs both data insertion and data retrieving, it can only be called once from the **Insert** button's Click method before you can perform the data retrieving from the **Select** button's Click method. The second is a DataSet object since we need to use this DataSet in multiple methods and multiple processes in this project, such as the data insertion and the data validation processes later. The third one is an instance of the child class **SQLInsertRecord** developed in our Web Service project, and this instance is

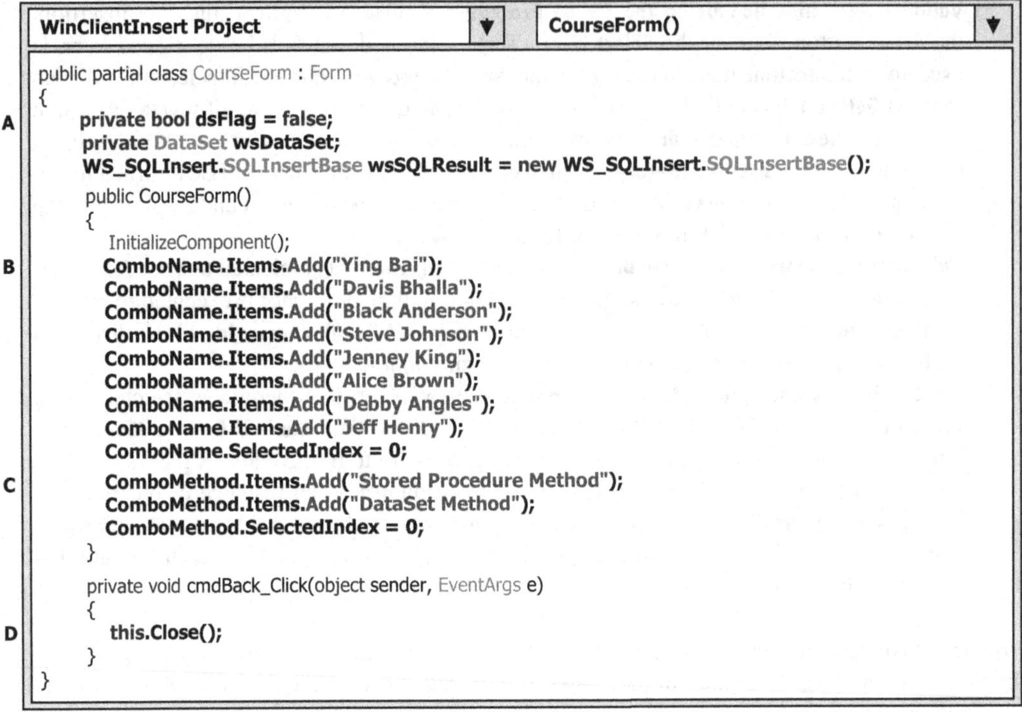

```
WinClientInsert Project                CourseForm()

public partial class CourseForm : Form
{
A       private bool dsFlag = false;
        private DataSet wsDataSet;
        WS_SQLInsert.SQLInsertBase wsSQLResult = new WS_SQLInsert.SQLInsertBase();
        public CourseForm()
        {
            InitializeComponent();
B           ComboName.Items.Add("Ying Bai");
            ComboName.Items.Add("Davis Bhalla");
            ComboName.Items.Add("Black Anderson");
            ComboName.Items.Add("Steve Johnson");
            ComboName.Items.Add("Jenney King");
            ComboName.Items.Add("Alice Brown");
            ComboName.Items.Add("Debby Angles");
            ComboName.Items.Add("Jeff Henry");
            ComboName.SelectedIndex = 0;
C           ComboMethod.Items.Add("Stored Procedure Method");
            ComboMethod.Items.Add("DataSet Method");
            ComboMethod.SelectedIndex = 0;
        }
        private void cmdBack_Click(object sender, EventArgs e)
        {
D           this.Close();
        }
}
```

FIGURE 9.71 The codes of the constructor and the back button click method.

used to receive the returned instance from calling the first Web method **SetInsertSP()** when perform a data insertion action.

B. Inside the constructor, eight default faculty members are added into the combobox control **ComboName** using the **Add()** method. These faculty members will be displayed and selected by the user as the input parameter to call different Web methods to perform either data insertion or data validation operation as the project runs. The first faculty member is selected as the default one by setting the **SelectedIndex** property to zero.

C. Two Web methods, the **Stored Procedure Method** and the **DataSet Method**, are added into the combobox control **ComboMethod**, and these methods can be selected by the user to call the associated Web method to perform the desired data operation as the project runs. Similarly, the first method, the **Stored Procedure Method**, is selected as the default one.

D. The coding for the **Back** button's Click method is very simple. The **Close()** method is called to terminate our client project as this button is clicked. A point to be noted is that when doing this piece of codes, one needs to first double click on the **Back** button from the Designer View of the Form window to open this method, and then enter this coding line into that method.

The first coding job is done and let's continues to perform the next coding process.

9.4.3.3.2 Develop the Codes to Insert a New Course Record into the Database

This coding development can be divided into two parts based on two methods: the **Stored Procedure Method** and the **DataSet Method**. Because of the similarity between the codes in these two methods, we combine them together.

To insert a new course record into the database via our Web service, the following three jobs should have been completed before the **Insert** button can be clicked:

1) The Web method has been selected from the **Query Method** combobox control.
2) The faculty name has been selected from the **Faculty Name** combobox control.
3) Six textboxes have been filled with six pieces of information related to a new course to be inserted.

Besides those conditions, one more important requirement for this data insertion is that any new course record can only be inserted into the database once. In other words, no duplicated record can be inserted into the database. This duplication can be identified by checking the content of the textbox **Course ID**, or the column **course_id** in the Course table in the database. As you know, the **course_id** is the primary key in the **Course** table and each record is identified by using this primary key. As long as the **course_id** is different, no duplication could be occurred. Based on this analysis, in order to avoid the duplicated insertion occurs, the **Insert** button should be disabled after a new course record is inserted into the database and this button should be kept in disabled until a different or a new **course_id** is entered into the **Course ID** textbox, which means that a new record is ready to be inserted into the database.

Keep this in mind and now let's start to develop the codes for the **Insert** button's click method. Double-click on the **Insert** button from the Design View of our client project to open the **Insert** button's click method. Then enter the codes that are shown in Figure 9.72 into this method. Let's have a closer look at this piece of codes to see how it works.

A. An integer variable **intInsert** is generated and it is used to hold the returned running status of a user defined method **CheckCourse()** whose codes will be built later. An instance of the Web reference to our Web service or our proxy class is also created here since we need it to access our Web methods to perform different data actions later. This instance works as a bridge between our client project and Web methods developed in our Web service project.
B. A user defined function **CheckCourse()** is called to check whether all course-related textboxes have been filled with all pieces of course information.
C. If the returned value from calling of the method **CheckCourse()** is non-zero, which means that all course information has been entered into the related textbox, it means that we can continue to perform our data insertion function.
D. If users selected the **Stored Procedure Method** to perform the data insertion, a **Try-Catch** block is used to call the Web method **SetInsertSP()** with seven pieces of new course information as arguments to insert a new course record into the database. The calling result is returned and assigned to our class-level variable **wsSQLResult** that will be checked later. A point is that the order of those passed arguments must be identical with that defined in the same method in our Web method.
E. If any error is encountered, the error message is displayed.
F. Besides the error-checking performed by the **Catch** statement, we also need to check the member data defined in our returned class to make sure that the running status of our Web method is fine. One of member data **SQLInsertOK** is used to store this running status. If this status is **False**, which means that something is wrong during the execution of this Web method, the error message is displayed using another member data **SQLInsertError** that stored the error source.
G. Otherwise, if users selected the **DataSet Method**, first the Boolean variable **dsFlag** is set to **True** to indicate that the Web method **InsertDataSet()** has been executed once. This flag should be reset to **False** if users want to retrieve the course information from the database by clicking on the **Select** button but they have not called this Web method to first insert

```
WinClientInsert Project                     cmdInsert_Click(object sender, EventArgs e)

  private void cmdInsert_Click(object sender, EventArgs e)
  {
A     int intInsert;
      intInsert = CheckCourse();
B     WS_SQLInsert.WebServiceInsert wsSQLInsert = new WS_SQLInsert.WebServiceInsert();
C     if (intInsert != 0)
      {
D        if (ComboMethod.Text == "Stored Procedure Method")
         {
            try
            {
               wsSQLResult = wsSQLInsert.SetInsertSP(ComboName.Text, txtCourseID.Text, txtCourseName.Text,
               Convert.ToInt32(txtCredits.Text), txtClassRoom.Text, txtSchedule.Text,
               Convert.ToInt32(txtEnroll.Text));
            }
E           catch (Exception err) { MessageBox.Show("Web service is wrong: " + err.Message); }
F           if (wsSQLResult.SQLInsertOK == false)
               MessageBox.Show(wsSQLResult.SQLInsertError);
         }
G        else
         {
            dsFlag = true;           //indicate the DataSet insert is performed
            try
            {
               wsDataSet = wsSQLInsert.InsertDataSet(ComboName.Text, txtCourseID.Text,
                           txtCourseName.Text, txtSchedule.Text, txtClassRoom.Text,
                           Convert.ToInt32(txtCredits.Text), Convert.ToInt32(txtEnroll.Text));
            }
H           catch (Exception err) { MessageBox.Show("Web service is wrong: " + err.Message); }
         }
I        cmdInsert.Enabled = false;
      }
J     else
         MessageBox.Show("Enter valid course information for all textboxes");
  }
```

FIGURE 9.72 The codes for the insert button click method.

a new course record. If this happened, a message is displayed to direct the users to first execute this Web method to insert a new record into the database. Another **Try-Catch** block is used to call the Web method **InsertDataSet()** with seven pieces of new course information as arguments to insert a new course record into the database. In addition to performing the new course insertion, this Web method also performed a data query to retrieve all courses, including the new inserted course, from the database and assign them to the DataSet that is returned to our client project.

H. If any running error is detected by the **Catch** statement, the error message is displayed.

I. Finally, the **Insert** button is disabled to avoid multiple insertions of the same record into the database.

J. If the returned value from calling of the method **CheckCourse()** is zero, which means that not all course information has been entered into the related textbox, a warning message is displayed to remind the user to fill all required course information to all textboxes.

The codes for the user-defined method **CheckCourse()** are shown in Figure 9.73.

Let's have a closer look at this piece of codes to see how it works.

A. Two integer variables, **index** and **ret**, are declared first. The former works as a loop counter and the latter works as a returned status for this method. The **ret** is initialized to a non-zero value as a default one. To make this checking easy, a textbox array, **tCourse[]**, is used to store all six textboxes in this form.

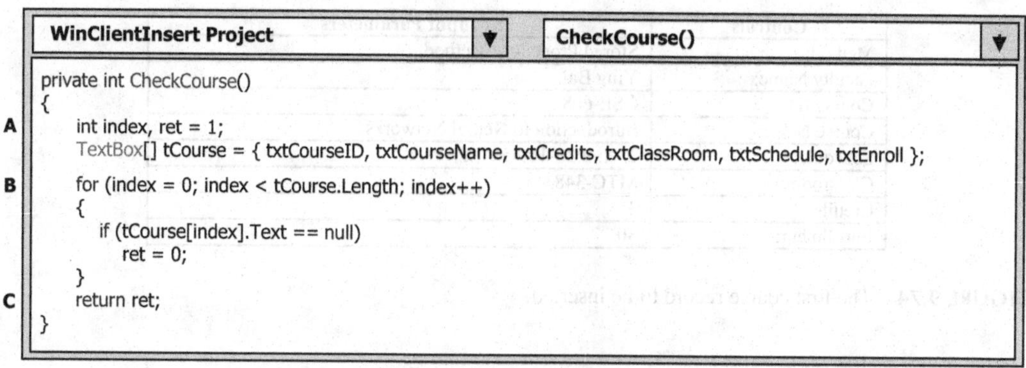

WinClientInsert Project
CheckCourse()
private int CheckCourse()
{
A int index, ret = 1;
TextBox[] tCourse = { txtCourseID, txtCourseName, txtCredits, txtClassRoom, txtSchedule, txtEnroll };
B for (index = 0; index < tCourse.Length; index++)
{
if (tCourse[index].Text == null)
ret = 0;
}
C return ret;
}

FIGURE 9.73 The codes for the user-defined method CheckCourse().

B. A loop is executed to check whether any textbox is empty. If it is, the returned variable **ret** is cleared to 0.

C. Otherwise, a successful value of 1 is returned to indicate that this data insertion checking is fine.

Another coding development is for the **Course ID** textbox, exactly to the **TextChanged** event of the **Course ID** textbox and the combobox, **ComboMethod**, exactly to the **SelectedIndexChanged** event. As we mentioned, the **Insert** button should be disabled after one new course record has been inserted into the database to avoid the multi-insertion of the same data. However, this button should be enabled when a new different course record is ready to be inserted into the database. As soon as the content of the **Course ID** textbox changed or the insert method is changed, which means that a new record is ready and the **Insert** button should be enabled. To do these codes, double click on the textbox **Course ID** and combobox **ComboMethod** from the Design View of our WinClient Form window to open both **TextChanged** and **SelectedIndexChanged** event triggering methods. Enter the following codes into these two event methods:

```
cmdInsert.Enabled = true;
```

At this point, we have finished all coding developments for the data insertion process. Before we can continue to develop the rest of our project, we prefer to first run the client project to test this data insertion function.

The prerequisite to run our client project is to make sure that our Web service is in the running status in this local computer. To check and confirm that, open our Web service project **WebServiceInsert Project** and click on the **IIS Express** button to run it. Then you may minimize our Web service page by clicking on the **Minimize** button (make sure that our Web service is still in the running status even when the page has disappeared).

Now you should find that a small white icon has been added into the status bar on the bottom of the screen. This small white icon means that our Web service is in the running status and any client can access and use it now.

Now run our Windows-based client project **WinClientInsert Project** by clicking on the **Start** button. As the **CourseForm** window is displayed, perform the following two insertions by using two Web methods with the following operations and parameters:

1) Insert the first new course record shown in Figure 9.74 using the **Stored Procedure Method**. Click on the **Insert** button to finish this data insertion.
2) Insert the second new course record shown in Figure 9.75 using the **DataSet Method**.

Click on the **Insert** button to finish this data insertion action.

Controls	Input Parameters
Method:	Stored Procedure Method
Faculty Name:	Ying Bai
Course ID:	CSE-668
Course Name:	Introduction to Neural Networks
Schedule:	T-H: 9:30-10:45 AM
Classroom:	MTC-348
Credits:	3
Enrollment:	30

FIGURE 9.74 The first course record to be inserted.

Controls	Input Parameters
Method:	DataSet Method
Faculty Name:	Ying Bai
Course ID:	CSE-526
Course Name:	Embedded Microcontrollers
Schedule:	M-W-F: 9:00-9:55 AM
Classroom:	MTC-308
Credits:	3
Enrollment:	32

FIGURE 9.75 The second course record to be inserted.

Now click on the **Back** button to terminate our client project. To confirm these two data insertions, open the Server Explorer or Microsoft SQL Server Management Studio. Then open our sample database **CSE_DEPT** and our **Course** table. You can find that these two records have been added into our **Course** table in the last two rows.

9.4.3.3.3 Develop the Codes to Perform the Inserted Data Validation

To confirm or validate a data insertion action, we can open our database and data table to check it. However, a professional way to do that confirmation is to use codes to perform this validation. In this section, we discuss how to perform this validation by developing the codes in the **Select** button's click method in our client project.

As we mentioned in the previous sections, as this **Select** button is clicked after a new course insertion, all **course_id**, including the new inserted **course_id**, will be retrieved from the database and displayed in a ListBox control in this **CourseForm** window. This data validation is also divided into two parts according to the method adopted by the user: either the **Stored Procedure Method** or the **DataSet Method**. Different processes will be performed based on these two methods. Because of the coding similarity between those two methods, we combine these codes together and put them into this **Select** button's click method.

Now double-click on the **Select** button from the Design View of our Course Form **WinClient Form.cs** to open it Click method and enter the codes that are shown in Figure 9.76 into this method. Let's take a closer look at this piece of codes to see how it works.

A. First an instance of our derived class SQLInsertRecord, **wsSQLResult**, is re-declared here since we declared this instance as a class variable before as our base class SQLInsertBase. Also another instance of our Web service reference or proxy class is created and this instance works as a bridge to connect our client project with the Web methods developed in our Web service together.

B. If the **Stored Procedure Method** has been selected by the user, a **Try-Catch** block is used to call our Web method **GetInsert()** with the selected faculty name as the input to retrieve all **course_id** from the database. This method returns an instance of our derived class defined in

```
WinClientInsert Project | cmdSelect_Click(object sender, EventArgs e)

  private void cmdSelect_Click(object sender, EventArgs e)
  {
A     WS_SQLInsert.SQLInsertRecord wsSQLResult = new WS_SQLInsert.SQLInsertRecord();
      WS_SQLInsert.WebServiceInsert wsSQLInsert = new WS_SQLInsert.WebServiceInsert();
B     if (ComboMethod.Text == "Stored Procedure Method")
      {
         try { wsSQLResult = wsSQLInsert.GetInsert(ComboName.Text); }
         catch (Exception err) { MessageBox.Show("Web service is wrong: " + err.Message); }
C        if (wsSQLResult.SQLInsertOK == false)
            MessageBox.Show(wsSQLResult.SQLInsertError);
D        ProcessObject(ref wsSQLResult);
      }
E     else
      {
         if (dsFlag == false)
            MessageBox.Show("No DataSet Insert performed, do data insertion first");
F        FillCourseDataSet(ref wsDataSet);
G        dsFlag = false;
      }
  }
```

FIGURE 9.76 The codes for the select button click method.

the Web service and it contains all **course_id** retrieved from the database, and it is assigned to our local instance **wsSQLResult** to be processed later. An error message is displayed if any error were encountered during the execution of that Web method.

C. In addition to the error checking performed by the system in the **Catch** statement, we also need to perform our error-checking process by inspecting the status of the member data **SQLInsertOK**. The error source will be displayed if any error is occurred.
D. If that Web method works fine, a user defined method **ProcessObject()**, whose detailed codes are shown in Figure 9.77, is called to extract all course columns from that returned instance **wsSQLResult**.
E. If the user selected the **DataSet Method**, first we need to check whether the Web method **InsertDataSet()** has been executed or not by checking the status of the class-level variable **dsFlag**. Because prior to using this method to retrieve the course information from the database, a new course record should have been inserted into the database by using the method **InsertDataSet()** in the **Insert** button's click method. In fact, that method performs both data insertion and data retrieving. An error may be encountered if you use this method to retrieve the course information from the **Select** button's click method without first performing the data insertion from the **Insert** button's click method since nothing has been inserted. Therefore nothing can be obtained from the returned DataSet. If this **dsFlag** is **False**, which means that nothing has been inserted, an information message is displayed to ask you to first perform the data insertion.
F. If the Web method **InsertDataSet()** has been executed, a user-defined method **FillCourse DataSet()**, whose detailed codes are shown in Figure 9.78, is called to fill the list box control with all retrieved **course_id**.
G. Finally, the **dsFlag** is reset to **False** to indicate that the method **InsertDataSet()** has not been executed.

The detailed codes for the methods **ProcessObject()** and **FillCourseListBox()** are shown in Figure 9.77. Let's have a look at the codes in these two subroutines to see how they work.

```
WinClientInsert Project                    ProcessObject()

  private void ProcessObject(ref WS_SQLInsert.SQLInsertRecord wsResult)
  {
A     if (wsResult.SQLInsertOK == true)
         FillCourseListBox(ref wsResult);
B     else
         MessageBox.Show("Course information cannot be retrieved: " + wsResult.SQLInsertError);
  }
  private void FillCourseListBox(ref WS_SQLInsert.SQLInsertRecord sqlResult)
  {
C     int index = 0;
D     CourseList.Items.Clear();            //clean up the course listbox
E     for (index = 0; index <= sqlResult.CourseID.Length - 1; index++)
      {
          if (sqlResult.CourseID[index] != null)
             CourseList.Items.Add(sqlResult.CourseID[index]);
      }
  }
```

FIGURE 9.77 The codes for the methods ProcessObject() and FillCourseListBox().

```
WinClientInsert Project                    FillCourseDataSet()

  private void FillCourseDataSet(ref DataSet ds)
  {
A     DataTable CourseTable = new DataTable();
B     CourseList.Items.Clear();                    //clean up the course listbox
C     CourseTable = ds.Tables["Course"];
D     foreach (DataRow CourseRow in CourseTable.Rows)
      {
          CourseList.Items.Add(CourseRow[0]);      //the 1st column is course_id
      }
  }
```

FIGURE 9.78 The codes for the FillCourseDataSet() method.

A. First we need to check the member data **SQLInsertOK** to make sure whether the Web method is executed successfully or not. If it is, the user defined method **FillCourseListBox()** is called to fill all **course_id** contained in the returned instance to the list box control in our client form.
B. A warning message is displayed if any error was encountered during the execution of that Web method.
C. In the user-defined method **FillCourseListBox()**, first a local integer variable **index** is created and it works as a loop count for a **for()** loop to continuously pick up all **course_id** from the returned instance and add them into the list box control.
D. The course list box control is cleaned up first before any **course_id** can be added into it. This process is very important in displaying all **course_id**, otherwise any new **course_id** will be attached at the end of the original **course_id** in this control and the displaying result is messy.
E. A **for()** loop is used to continuously pick up each **course_id** from the **CourseID()** array defined in our returned class **SQLInsertResult**. One point to be noted is the upper bound or the length of this array. The length or the size of this array is 11 but the upper bound of this array is 10 since the index of this array starts from 0, not 1. Therefore the upper bound of this array is equal to the length of this array minus by 1. As long as the content of the **CourseID(index)** is not Null, the remaining **course_id** is added into the list box control by using the **Add()** method.

The codes for the subroutine **FillCourseDataSet()** is shown in Figure 9.78. Let's have a look at the codes in this subroutine to see how they work.

A. A DataTable object is declared at the beginning of this method since we need to use it to perform the data extraction from the returned instance and data addition to the list box control.
B. The list box control is first cleaned up to avoid messy displaying of multiple **course_id**.
C. The **CourseTable** object is initialized by adding a new data table named **"Course"** and is assigned to the DataSet object **ds**.
D. A **foreach**() loop is used to continuously pick up each row from the first column that is the **course_id** column, and add each of them into the list box control. One point to be noticed is that the first column has an index value of 0, not 1, since the index starts from 0.

At this point we finished all coding process for the **Select** button's click method. In other words, all codes related to the data validation are completed.

Now let's run our client project to perform the data validation after the data insertion process. Before we can start to run the project, make sure that the following two conditions are met:

1) Our Web service is in the running status and this can be checked by locating a small white icon on the status bar on the bottom of the screen. If you cannot find this icon, open our Web service project **WebServiceInsert Project** and click on the **IIS Express** button to run it. After the Web service starts to run, you can minimize the Web page if you like but make sure that it is still in the running status.
2) Two new course records, **CSE-668** and **CSE-526**, which we inserted in Section 9.4.3.3.2 by testing the **Insert** button's click method, have been deleted from the **Course** table in our sample database since we want to insert the same course records in the following test.

Now click on the **Start** button to run our client project. Enter the same input parameters as shown in Figure 9.74 in Section 9.4.3.3.2, and click on the **Insert** button to finish this data insertion using the **Stored Procedure Method**. Next enter the same input parameters as shown in Figure 9.75 in Section 9.4.3.3.2, and click on the **Insert** button to finish this data insertion using the **DataSet Method**.

To check or validate these data insertions, make sure that the selected method in the **Query Method** combobox is still the **DataSet Method** and the Faculty Name is **Ying Bai**. Then click on the **Select** button to retrieve all **course_id** from the database. It can be found that all eight courses taught by the selected faculty are listed in the list box control with the **course_id** as the identifier for each course, as shown in Figure 9.79.

To test the **Stored Procedure Method**, make sure that the **Stored Procedure Method** is selected from the **Query Method** combobox. Now we can select another faculty from the **Faculty Name** combobox, and click on the **Select** button to pick up all **course_id** taught by the selected faculty. Next reselect the default Faculty Name **Ying Bai**, and then click on the **Select** button to try to retrieve all **course_id** taught by the selected faculty. You can find the same results obtained using the **DataSet Method** are displayed in the list box control.

The running result, or the data validation, is shown in Figure 9.79. It can be found that our new inserted two courses,**CSE-668** and **CSE-526,** have been added and displayed in the list box control and our data insertion is successful. Click on the **Back** button to terminate our project.

Next let's concentrate on the coding development to display the detailed course information for a selected **course_id** from the list box control.

9.4.3.3.4 Develop the Codes to Get the Detailed Information for a Specific Course

The function of this piece of codes is that the detailed course information, such as the course name, schedule, classroom, credit and enrollment, will be displayed in the associated textbox control as the

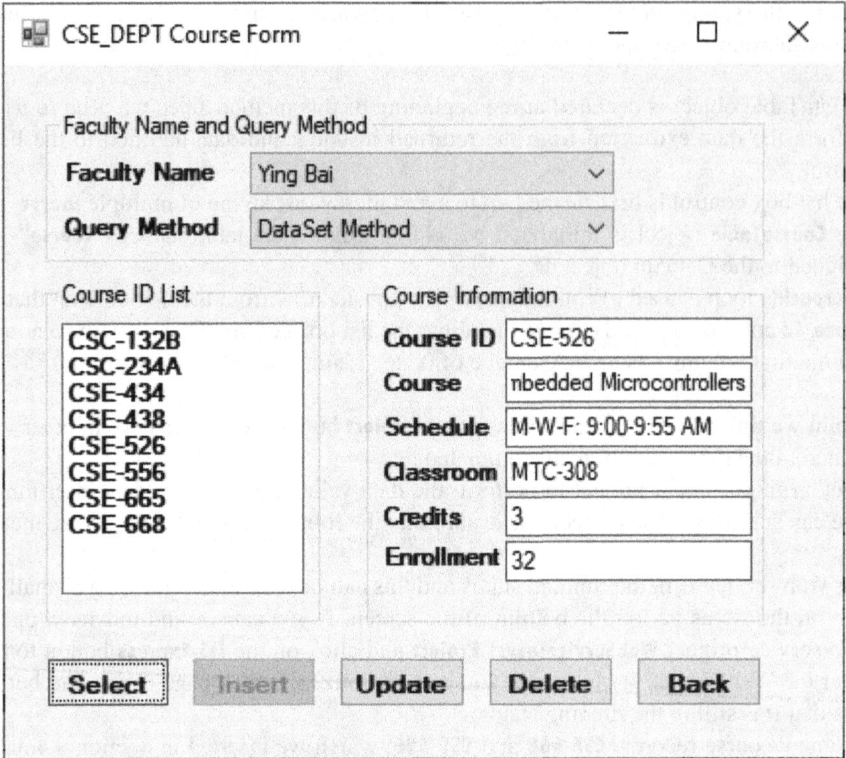

FIGURE 9.79 The running result of the data validation.

user clicked and selected one **course_id** from the list box control. The main coding job is performed inside the **SelectedIndexChanged** event method of the list box control **CourseList**. Because when user clicks or selects a **course_id** from the list box control, a **SelectedIndexChanged** event is issued and this event is passed to the associated **SelectedIndexChanged** event method to be processed.

To pick up the detailed course information for the selected **course_id**, the Web method **GetInsert Course()** in our Web service project **WebServiceInsert Project** is called. This method returns an instance of the returned class **SQLInsertRecord** to our client project. The detailed course information is stored in that returned instance.

Double-click on the list box control **CourseList** from the Design View of our Course Form **WinClient Form.cs** from the Solution Explorer window to open the **SelectedIndexChanged** event method, and enter the codes that are shown in Figure 9.80 into this method. Let's take a closer look at this piece of codes to see how it works.

- **A.** Two instances, one our Web service reference or the proxy class **wsSQLInsert**, and the other our returned **SQLInsertRecord** class, **wsSQLResult**, are created here. These instances work as a bridge between our client project and the Web methods developed in the Web service project.
- **B.** A **Try-Catch** block is used to call the Web method **GetInsertCourse()** with the selected **course_id** from the list box control as the argument to perform this course information retrieving. The selected **course_id** is stored in the **Text** property of the **CourseList** control.
- **C.** An exception message is displayed if any error was encountered during the execution of that Web method and caught by the system method **Catch**.
- **D.** In addition to the error checking performed by the system, we also need to perform our exception checking by inspecting the member data **SQLInsertOK** in the returned class

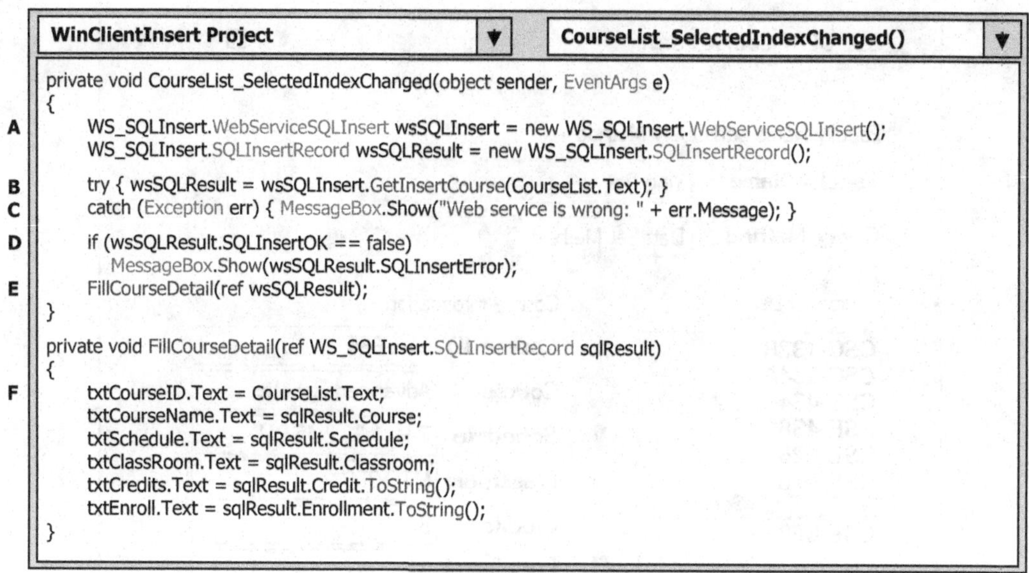

```
WinClientInsert Project                    CourseList_SelectedIndexChanged()

  private void CourseList_SelectedIndexChanged(object sender, EventArgs e)
  {
A     WS_SQLInsert.WebServiceSQLInsert wsSQLInsert = new WS_SQLInsert.WebServiceSQLInsert();
      WS_SQLInsert.SQLInsertRecord wsSQLResult = new WS_SQLInsert.SQLInsertRecord();
B     try { wsSQLResult = wsSQLInsert.GetInsertCourse(CourseList.Text); }
C     catch (Exception err) { MessageBox.Show("Web service is wrong: " + err.Message); }
D     if (wsSQLResult.SQLInsertOK == false)
         MessageBox.Show(wsSQLResult.SQLInsertError);
E     FillCourseDetail(ref wsSQLResult);
  }
  private void FillCourseDetail(ref WS_SQLInsert.SQLInsertRecord sqlResult)
  {
F     txtCourseID.Text = CourseList.Text;
      txtCourseName.Text = sqlResult.Course;
      txtSchedule.Text = sqlResult.Schedule;
      txtClassRoom.Text = sqlResult.Classroom;
      txtCredits.Text = sqlResult.Credit.ToString();
      txtEnroll.Text = sqlResult.Enrollment.ToString();
  }
```

FIGURE 9.80 The codes for the methods SelectedIndexChanged() and FillCourseDetail().

SQLInsertRecord. If that data value is **False**, which means that an application error was occurred during the running of that Web method, an error message is displayed.

E. If everything is fine, a user defined method **FillCourseDetail()** is executed to extract the detailed course information from the returned instance and assign it to each associated textbox control in our client window form.

F. The codes for the subroutine **FillCourseDetail()** are simple. The **course_id** can be directly obtained from the list box control and all other pieces of information can be extracted from the returned instance and assigned to the associated textbox.

When performing this function to get the detailed course information from the database, no difference is existed between the **Stored Procedure Method** and the **DataSet Method**. Both methods use the same process.

At this point, we have finished all coding jobs for our Windows-based client project. Now we can run the client project to test all functions of this project as well as the functions of our Web service project. Before we can do this, make sure that the following jobs have been performed:

1) Our Web service is in the running status and this can be checked by locating a small white icon on the status bar on the bottom of the screen. If you cannot find this icon, open our Web service project **WebServiceInsert Project** and click on the **IIS Express** button to run it.
2) Two new courses, **CSE-668** and **CSE-526**, which we inserted in Section 9.4.3.3.2 by testing the **Insert** button's click method, should have been deleted from the **Course** table in our sample database since we want to insert the same course records in this test.

Now click on the **Start** button to run our client project. Insert two new course records by entering parameters listed in Figure 9.74 in Section 9.4.3.3.2 with **Stored Procedure** method and Figure 9.75 in Section 9.4.3.3.2 with **Data Set** method. Then perform the data validation by clicking on the **Select** button. To get the detailed course information for the selected **course_id** from the list box control, click one **course_id**, and immediately the detailed information about the selected **course_id** is displayed in those associated textboxes, which is shown in Figure 9.81.

Click on the **Back** button to terminate our client project.

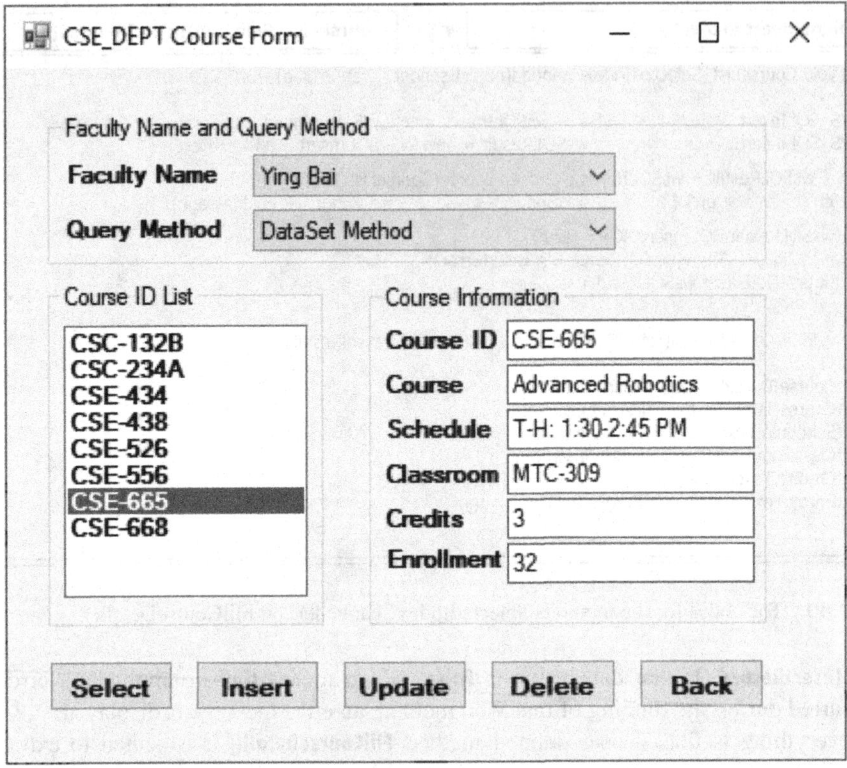

FIGURE 9.81 The running status of getting the detailed course information.

A complete Windows-based client project **WinClientInsert Project** can be found from the folder **ClassDB Projects\Chapter 9\WinClientInsert Solution** that is located on the CRC Press ftp site (refer to Figure 1.2 in Chapter 1).

9.4.4 Build Web-Based Client Project to Consume the Web Services

As we saw in Section 9.3.11, it can be found that there is no significant difference between developing a Web-based client application and a Windows-based client project to consume a Web service. As long as the Web service is referenced by the Web-based client project, one can access and call any Web method developed in that Web service to perform the desired data queries via the Web-based client project. Visual Studio.NET will create the same document files, such as the Discovery Map file and the WDSL file, for the client project no matter whether this Web service is consumed by a Windows-based or a Web-based client application.

To save time and space, we can refer one existing ASP.NET Web application project **SQLWebInsert Project** we developed in Chapter 8 to make it our new Web-based client project **WebClientInsert Project**. In fact, we can copy and rename that entire project as our new Web-based client project, but we prefer to create a new ASP.NET Web Application (.NET Framework) project and only create or add a new **Course** page.

This project can be developed if this sequence is followed:

A. Create a new **ASP.NET Web Application (.NET Framework)** project **WebClientInsert Project** and add a new Web page,**Course.aspx**, into our new project.

B. Add a Web service reference to our new project and build the codes for the Web form page **Course.aspx** to meet our data insertion requirements.

C. Develop the codes in the related methods of the **Course.aspx.cs** file to call the associated Web method to perform our data insertion. The code creations include the following sections:
   a. Build the codes in the **Page_Load()** method of the **CourseForm** class.
   b. Develop the codes for the **Insert** button's Click method.
   c. Develop the codes for the TextChanged event method of the Course ID textbox.
   d. Build the codes in the **Select** button's Click method. Also add four user-defined methods: **ProcessObject()**, **FillCourseListBox()**, **FillCourseDataSet()** and **FillCourseDetail()**. These four methods are basically identical with those we developed in the last Windows-based client project **WinClientInsert Project**, and one can copy and paste them into our new project with a few modifications.
   e. Build the codes in the **SelectedIndexChanged()** event method.
   f. Develop the codes in the **Back** button's Click method.

Now let's start our jobs with the first step listed above.

9.4.4.1 Create a New Web Application Project and Add a New Web Page

Open Visual Studio.NET and create a new ASP.NET Web Application (.NET Framework) C# project. Enter **WebClientInsert Project** and **WebClientInsert Solution** into the **Projectname** and **Solution name** boxes, and **C:\Chapter 9** into the **Location** box, and click on the **Create** button to continue. On the next wizard, select the **Web Forms** item from the list to create this new project.

To save time, we can use an existed but updated **Course** page that is located at a folder **Web Forms\Chapter 9** under the **Students** folder on the CRC Press ftp site (refer to Figure 1.2 in Chapter 1). To do that, on the opened new project window, right-click on our new project **WebClientInsert Project** from the Solution Explorer window, and select the item **Add | Existing Item** to open the Add Existing Item wizard. Browse to the folder **Web Forms\Chapter 9** that is under the **Students** folder on the CRC Press ftp site, select three items **Course.aspx**, **Course.aspx.cs** and **Course.aspx.designer.cs** by checking them from the list and click on the **Add** button to add these items into our new Web application project.

9.4.4.2 Add a Web Service Reference and Modify the Web Form Window

Perform the following operations to add our Web reference:

1) Open Visual Studio.NET and our Web service project **WebServiceInsert Project**, and click on the **IIS Express** button to run it.
2) Copy the URL from the **Address** bar in our running Web service project.
3) Then return to our Web client project **WebClientInsert Project**.
4) Right click on our client project **WebClientInsert Project** from the Solution Explorer window, and select the item **Add | Service Reference** to open the Add Web Reference wizard, which is shown in Figure 9.82.
5) Click on the **Advanced** button located at the lower-left corner on this wizard to open the Service Reference Settings wizard.
6) Click on the **Add Web Reference** button to open the Add Web Reference wizard, which is shown in Figure 9.82.
7) Paste the URL we copied from step 2 into the URL box in the Add Web Reference wizard and click on the **Arrow** button to enable the Visual Studio.NET to search and find it.
8) When the Web service is found, the name of our Web service is displayed in the right pane, which is shown in Figure 9.82.
9) Alternately you can change the name for this Web reference from **localhost** to any meaningful name such as **WS_SQLInsert** in our case. Click on the **Add Reference** button to add this Web service as a reference to our new client project.
10) Click on the **Close** button from our Web service built-in Web interface window to close our Web service page.

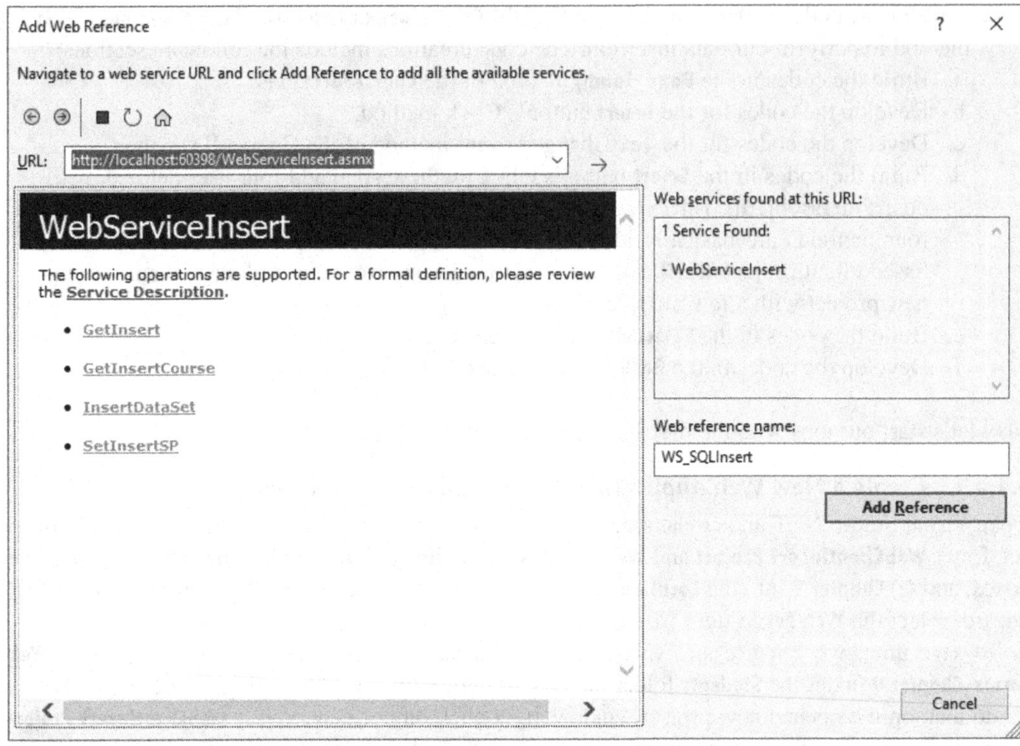

FIGURE 9.82 The finished add web reference wizard.

The coding process for the Designer View of the page **Course.aspx** include two steps:

1) Open the Designer view and set the **AutoPostBack** property of the **Course ID** textbox to **True**. **This is very important** since when the content of this textbox is changed during the project runs, a **TextChanged** event occurs. However, this event only occurs in the client side, not the server side. Thus this event cannot be transferred to and responded by the server. Therefore, the command inside this event method cannot be executed (the **Insert** button cannot be enabled) even the content of the Course ID textbox is changed when the project runs. To solve this problem, we must set the **AutoPostBack** property of this textbox to **True** to allow the server to send back a **TextChanged** event to the client automatically as the content of this textbox is changed. Similar things are happened to the **Method** combobox **ComboMethod** and listbox **CourseList**. Set their **AutoPostBack** property to **True**.
2) Change the **ID** property of the **Credit** textbox from **txtCredit** to **txtCredits**.

Now open the Designer View of the added Course page, **Course.aspx**, which is shown in Figure 9.83. Go to the **File | Save All** menu item to save these coding modifications.

9.4.4.3 Build the Codes for the Related Methods

The first coding process is for the **Page_Load()** method and some global variables.

9.4.4.3.1 Build the Codes for the Page_Load() Method

Enter the codes shown in Figure 9.84 into the **Page_Load()** method with some global variables. Let's have a closer look at this piece of codes to see how it works.

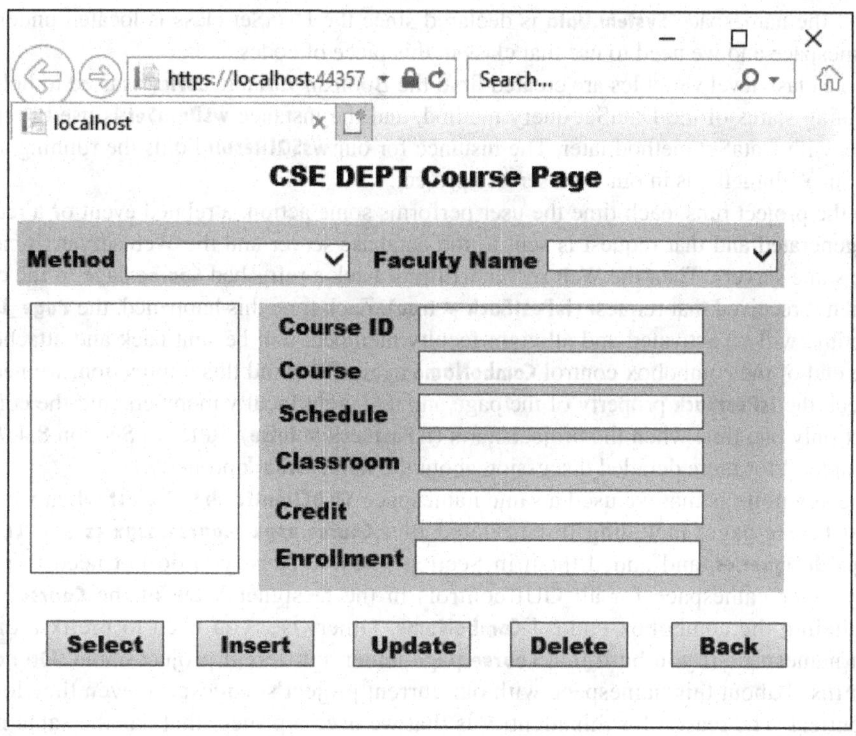

FIGURE 9.83 The updated course page window.

```
WebClientInsert Project                    Page_Load()

  using System;
A using System.Data;
  namespace WebClientInsert_Project
  {
     public partial class Course : System.Web.UI.Page
     {
B       private bool dsFlag = false;
        private DataSet wsDataSet = new DataSet();
        WS_SQLInsert.SQLInsertBase wsSQLResult = new WS_SQLInsert.SQLInsertBase();
        protected void Page_Load(object sender, EventArgs e)
        {
C          if (!IsPostBack)   //these items can only be added into the combo box in one time
           {
D             ComboName.Items.Add("Ying Bai");
              ComboName.Items.Add("Davis Bhalla");
              ComboName.Items.Add("Black Anderson");
              ComboName.Items.Add("Steve Johnson");
              ComboName.Items.Add("Jenney King");
              ComboName.Items.Add("Alice Brown");
              ComboName.Items.Add("Debby Angles");
              ComboName.Items.Add("Jeff Henry");
E             ComboName.SelectedIndex = 0;
F             ComboMethod.Items.Add("Stored Procedure Method");
              ComboMethod.Items.Add("DataSet Method");
              ComboMethod.SelectedIndex = 0;
           }
        }
     }
  }
```

FIGURE 9.84 The codes for the Page_Load() method.

A. First the namespace **System.Data** is declared since the DataSet class is located under that namespace and we need to use that class in this piece of codes.

B. Three class-level variables are created first; the Boolean variable **dsFlag** is used to hold the running status of the DataSet query method, and the instance **wsDataSet** is used to query data with DataSet method later. The instance for our **wsSQLResult** holds the running status of our Web methods in our Web service project.

C. As the project runs, each time the user performs some action, a related event or a request is generated and that request is sent to the database server and the Web server (it can be the same server). Then the Web server will post back a refreshed **Course** page to the client when it received that request (**IsPostBack = true**). Each time this happened, the **Page_Load()** method will be activated and all eight faculty members will be sent back and attached to the end of the combobox control **ComboName** again. To avoid this duplication, we need to check the **IsPostBack** property of the page and add eight faculty members into the combobox only one time when the project starts (**IsPostBack = false**). Refer to Section 8.4.9.1 in Chapter 8 for more detailed discussion about the **AutoPostBack** property.

D. One key point is that we used a same namespace **WebClientInsert_Project** when we built that **Course** page, including three related files,**Course.aspx**, **Course.aspx.cs** and **Course.aspx.designer.cs**, and added them in Section 9.4.4.1. Thus, you do not need to prefix any other namespace for all GUI controls in the Designer View of the **Course** page, including the combobox control **ComboName**. Otherwise, you need to prefix a different namespace if you built that **Course** page under a different project name. Do not be confused about this namespace with our current project's namespace even they looked identical. The reason for this identity is that we used a project that has the same name as our current project's name to build the **Course** page to reduce the coding jobs by using the same namespace.

E. The first faculty name is selected as a default one and displayed in the combobox control **ComboName** as the project runs.

F. Two inserting methods, **Stored Procedure Method** and the **DataSet Method**, are added into another combobox control, **ComboMethod**, to enable users to select one of them to perform related inserting action as the project runs. The first method is selected as a default one.

Your finished codes for the **Page_Load()** method should match one that is shown in Figure 9.84. The next step is to develop the codes for the **Insert** button's click method.

9.4.4.3.2 Develop Codes for the Insert Button Click Method

The function of this piece of codes is to insert a new course record that is stored in six textboxes in the Web page into the database as the **Insert** button is clicked. This piece of codes is basically identical with those in the same method on the Windows-based client project we developed in the last section. Therefore, we can copy those codes from that method and paste them into our current method with a few modifications.

Open the Windows-based client project **WinClientInsert Project** from the folder **ClassDB Projects\Chapter 9\WinClientInsert Solution** under the **Students** folder on the CRC Press ftp site (refer to Figure 1.2 in Chapter 1). Copy all codes from **Insert** button's click method and paste them into the **Insert** button's click method in our current Web-based client project **WebClientInsert Project**.

The only modification is to add one more String variable **errMsg** that is used to store the returned error information from calling different Web methods. In addition, all message box functions **MsgBox()** should be replaced by the **Write()** method of the Response object of the server class since the **MsgBox()** can only be used in the client side.

Your finished codes for the **Insert** button's click method should match one that is shown in Figure 9.85. The modification parts have been highlighted in bold.

```
WebClientInsert Project        cmdInsert_Click(object sender, EventArgs e)

  protected void cmdInsert_Click(object sender, EventArgs e)
  {
      int intInsert;
A     string errMsg;
      intInsert = CheckCourse();
      WS_SQLInsert.WebServiceInsert wsSQLInsert = new WS_SQLInsert.WebServiceInsert();
      if (intInsert != 0)
      {
B         if (ComboMethod.Text == "Stored Procedure Method")
          {
              try
              {
                  wsSQLResult = wsSQLInsert.SetInsertSP(ComboName.Text, txtCourseID.Text, txtCourseName.Text,
                  Convert.ToInt32(txtCredits.Text), txtClassRoom.Text, txtSchedule.Text,
                  Convert.ToInt32(txtEnroll.Text));
              }
              catch (Exception err) {
                  errMsg = "Web service is wrong: " + err.Message;
                  Response.Write("<script>alert('" + errMsg + "')</script>"); }
              if (wsSQLResult.SQLInsertOK == false)
                  Response.Write("<script>alert('" + wsSQLResult.SQLInsertError + "')</script>");
          }
C         else
          {
              dsFlag = true;                        //indicate the DataSet insert is performed
D             Application["dsFlag"] = dsFlag;       //reserve this flag as a global flag
              try
              {
E                 wsDataSet = wsSQLInsert.InsertDataSet(ComboName.Text, txtCourseID.Text,
                              txtCourseName.Text, txtSchedule.Text, txtClassRoom.Text,
                              Convert.ToInt32(txtCredits.Text), Convert.ToInt32(txtEnroll.Text));
              }
              catch (Exception err) {
                  errMsg = "Web service is wrong: " + err.Message;
                  Response.Write("<script>alert('" + errMsg + "')</script>"); }
          }
F         Application["wsDataSet"] = wsDataSet;     //reserve the global DataSet
G         cmdInsert.Enabled = false;
      }
H     else
      {
          errMsg = "Enter valid course information for all textboxes";
          Response.Write("<script>alert('" + errMsg + "')</script>");
      }
  }
```

FIGURE 9.85 The codes for the insert button click method.

Let's have a quick review for this piece of codes to see how it works.

A. A string variable **errMsg** is created and this variable is used to store the possible error message to be displayed via a Java **alert()** method if any error is occurred during the data insertion action processing.

B. If the user selected the **Stored Procedure Method** to perform this data insertion, the Web method **SetInsertSP()**, which is developed in the Web Service, is executed to call the associated stored procedure to insert a new course record into our sample database. Any error encountered during the execution of this Web method will be displayed and reported. The ID of the **Credit** textbox is changed to **txtCredits**.

C. If the user chooses the **DataSet Method** to perform this data insertion, we need to set a flag to tell the project that a DataSet data insertion has been performed.

D. This flag is stored into a global variable using the **Application** state function. The reason we need to use this step is that the Web method **InsertDataSet()** has two functionalities: insert data into the database and retrieve back data from the database. However, in order to perform the data retrieving using this method, first we must insert data using this method. Otherwise, no data can be retrieved if no data insertion is performed using this DataSet method. The reason we use an **Application** state to store this flag is that our Web client project will run on a Web server and the server will send back a refreshed page to the client each time a request is sent to the server, therefore all global variables' values will also be refreshed when a refreshed page is sent back. However, the Application state is never changed no matter how many times our client page is refreshed.
E. The associated Web method **InsertDataSet()** is called to insert this new course record into the database. Similarly, if any error is encountered during this calling process, it will be displayed and reported immediately.
F. The returned DataSet object **wsDataSet** that contains all **course_id** is a class-level variable. Because of the same reason as we discussed in step **D**, we need to use an **Application** state to store this DataSet since we need to pick up all **course_id** from it when we perform the validation process later by clicking the **Select** button. Otherwise the content of this DataSet will be refreshed each time a refreshed **Course** page is sent back.
G. Finally, the **Insert** button is disabled to avoid multi-insertion of the same data into the database.
H. If the user-defined method **CheckCourse()** returns a 0, which means that not all textboxes have been filled and some of them are blank. In that case, a warning message is displayed to remind the users to fill them up.

The codes for the user-defined method **CheckCourse()** are shown in Figure 9.86. The function of this method is straightforward and easy to be understood. A **for()** loop is used to check all textboxes to make sure that all of them are filled. Otherwise a zero is returned to indicate that some of them are still empty.

9.4.4.3.3 Develop Codes for the TextChanged Method of the CourseID Textbox

The **Insert** button should be enabled either when the content of the **course_id** textbox is changed or when the content of the **ComboMethod** DropDownList is changed, in either case, it indicates that a new course record should be ready to be inserted into the database. The events related to these two cases are **TextChanged** for **course_id** textbox and **SelectedIndexChanged** for **ComboMethod** control. Open these two event methods by double-clicking on them from the Designer View of the Web page window and enter the following code into these methods:

```
cmdInsert.Enabled = True
```

WebClientInsert Project ▼	**CheckCourse()** ▼

```
private int CheckCourse()
{
    int index, ret = 1;
    TextBox[] tCourse = { txtCourseID, txtCourseName, txtCredits, txtClassRoom, txtSchedule, txtEnroll };
    for (index = 0; index < tCourse.Length; index++)
    {
      if (tCourse[index].Text == null)
        ret = 0;
    }
    return ret;
}
```

FIGURE 9.86 The detailed codes for the user defined method CheckCourse().

As we mentioned, after a new course record has been inserted into the database, the **Insert** button must be disabled to avoid a possible multi-insertion of the same record into the database. But as a new course record is ready to be inserted into the database, this **Insert** button should be enabled. To distinguish between the existed and a new course record, the content of the Course ID textbox is a good candidate since it is a primary key in our **Course** data table. Each **course_id** is a unique identifier for each course record, and therefore as long as the content of this Course ID textbox changed, which means that a new course record is ready to be inserted, the **Insert** button should be enabled. A similar situation is true for the **ComboMethod** DropDownList control.

Another important point is that making sure that the **AutoPostBack** property of this Course ID textbox is set to **True** to allow the server to send back a **TextChanged** event to the client when its content is changed.

9.4.4.3.4 Build the Codes in the Select Button's Click Method

The codes for this method are similar to those codes we developed in the same method in our Windows-based client project **WinClientInsert Project**. So we can copy those codes and paste them into our current **Select** button's click method with a few modifications. Open the **Select** button's click method from our Windows-based client project **WinClientInsert Project**, copy those codes and paste them into our **Select** button's click method. The only modifications to this piece of copied codes are to change the Windows-based message box function **MsgBox()** to the Web-based message box function. Your finished codes for this method are shown in Figure 9.87. The modified parts have been highlighted in bold.

Let's take a quick review for this piece of codes to see how it works.

A. Two instances, one for our **SQLInsertRecord** class, and the other for our Web service reference **WebServiceSQLInsert**, are created first and these instances work as a bridge to connect this client project with the associated Web methods built in the Web service together.

```
WebClientInsert Project                cmdSelect_Click(object sender, EventArgs e)

  protected void cmdSelect_Click(object sender, EventArgs e)
  {
A       WS_SQLInsert.SQLInsertRecord wsSQLResult = new WS_SQLInsert.SQLInsertRecord();
        WS_SQLInsert.WebServiceSQLInsert wsSQLInsert = new WS_SQLInsert.WebServiceSQLInsert();
B       string errMsg;
C       if (ComboMethod.Text == "Stored Procedure Method")
        {
           try { wsSQLResult = wsSQLInsert.GetInsert(ComboName.Text); }
           catch (Exception err) { errMsg = "Web service is wrong: " + err.Message;
                                   Response.Write("<script>alert('" + errMsg + "')</script>"); }
D          if (wsSQLResult.SQLInsertOK == false)
              Response.Write("<script>alert('" + wsSQLResult.SQLInsertError + "')</script>");
E          ProcessObject(ref wsSQLResult);
        }
F       else
        {
           dsFlag = (bool)Application["dsFlag"];
G          if (dsFlag == false)
           {
              errMsg = "No DataSet Insertion performed, do that first";
              Response.Write("<script>alert('" + errMsg + "')</script>");
           }
H          wsDataSet = (DataSet)Application["wsDataSet"];
           FillCourseDataSet(ref wsDataSet);
I          Application["dsFlag"] = false;
        }
  }
```

FIGURE 9.87 The codes for the select button click method.

WebClientInsert Project	ProcessObject()

```
  private void ProcessObject(ref WS_SQLInsert.SQLInsertRecord wsResult)
  {
A     string errMsg;
B     if (wsResult.SQLInsertOK == true)
         FillCourseListBox(ref wsResult);
C     else
      {
         errMsg = "Course information cannot be retrieved: " + wsResult.SQLInsertError;
         Response.Write("<script>alert('" + errMsg + "')</script>");
      }
  }
  private void FillCourseListBox(ref WS_SQLInsert.SQLInsertRecord sqlResult)
  {
D     int index = 0;

E     CourseList.Items.Clear();                          //clean up the course listbox
F     for (index = 0; index <= sqlResult.CourseID.Length - 1; index++)
      {
         if (sqlResult.CourseID[index] != null)
            CourseList.Items.Add(sqlResult.CourseID[index]);
      }
  }
```

FIGURE 9.88 The codes for subroutines ProcessObject() and FillCourseListBox().

B. Also an **errMsg** string variable is created and it is used to store the error message to be displayed and reported later.

C. If the **Stored Procedure Method** is selected by the user, the associated Web method **GetInsert()** is executed to call the stored procedure to pick up all **course_id** taught by the selected faculty based on the input faculty name. If any error were occurred during the execution of this Web method, the error source is reported and displayed with an **alert()** script method.

D. Besides the system error checking, we also need to inspect any application error, and this can be performed by checking the status of the member data **SQLInsertOK** that is defined in the base class **SQLInsertBase** in our Web service project.

E. If no error is detected, the user-defined method **ProcessObject()**, whose detailed codes are shown later in Figure 9.88, is called to extract all retrieved **course_id** from the returned instance and add them into the list box control.

F. If the user selected the **DataSet Method**, first we need to check the **dsFlag** stored in an Application state to make sure that the Web method **InsertDataSet()** has been executed once since our current data query needs to extract all **course_id**s from the DataSet that is returned from the last execution of the Web method **InsertDataSet()**.

G. If this **dsFlag** is **False**, which means that this Web method has not been called and executed; therefore, we do not have any returned DataSet available. A warning message is displayed to indicate that situation.

H. If the **dsFlag** is **True**, which means that the Web method **InsertDataSet()** has been executed and a returned DataSet that contains all **course_ids** are available. Another user-defined method, **FillCourseDataSet()**, is executed to extract all **course_id** from that returned DataSet and add them into the list box control in our client page. The global DataSet object **wsDataSet**, which is stored in an Application state, is passed as an argument for this method calling.

I. Finally, the **dsFlag** stored in an Application state is reset to **False**.

The detailed codes for the methods **ProcessObject()** and **FillCourseListBox()** are shown in Figure 9.88. Let's have a closer look at this piece of codes to see how it works.

A. A local string variable **errMsg** is declared and it is used to hold any error message to be displayed and reported later.
B. First we need to check the member data **SQLInsertOK** to make sure that the Web method is executed successfully. If it is, a user defined method **FillCourseListBox()** is called to fill all **course_id** contained in the returned instance to the list box control **CourseList** in our client page.
C. A warning message is displayed if any error was encountered during the execution of that Web method.
D. In the method **FillCourseListBox()**, first a local integer variable **index** is created and it works as a loop number for a **for()** loop to continuously pick up all **course_id** from the returned instance and add them into the list box control.
E. The course list box control is cleaned up first before any **course_id** can be added into it. This process is very important in displaying all **course_id**, otherwise any new **course_id** will be attached at the end of the original **course_id** in this control and the displaying result is messy.
F. A **for()** loop is used to continuously pick up the **course_id** from the **CourseID[]** array defined in our returned class **SQLInsertRecord**. One point to be noted is the upper bound and the length of this array. The length or the size of this array is 11 but the upper bound of this array is 10 since the index of this array starts from 0, not 1. Therefore the upper bound of this array is equal to the length of this array minus by 1. As long as the content of the **CourseID[index]** is not Null, a valid **course_id** is added into the list box control by using the **Add()** method.

The codes for the user-defined method **FillCourseDataSet()** are shown in Figure 9.89.

The codes in this method are identical with those in the same method we built in our Windows-based client project **WinClientInsert Project**. You can copy and paste them from that project into our current project.

Let's have a look at the codes in this method to see how they work.

A. A **DataTable** object is declared at the beginning of this method since we need to use it to perform the data extraction from the returned instance and the data addition to the list box control later.
B. The list box control **CourseList** is first cleaned up to avoid messy displaying of multiple **course_id**.
C. The **CourseTable** object is initialized by adding a new data table named **Course** and is attached to the DataSet object **ds**.
D. A **foreach()** loop is used to continuously pick up the first column that is the **course_id** column from all returned rows, and add each of them into the list box control. One point to be noticed is that the first column has an index value of 0, not 1 since the index starts from 0.

```
WebClientInsert Project        FillCourseDataSet(ref DataSet ds)
   private void FillCourseDataSet(ref DataSet ds)
   {
A       DataTable CourseTable = new DataTable();
B       CourseList.Items.Clear();                              //clean up the course listbox
C       CourseTable = ds.Tables["Course"];
D       foreach (DataRow CourseRow in CourseTable.Rows)
        {
            CourseList.Items.Add(CourseRow[0].ToString());    //the 1st column is course_id
        }
   }
```

FIGURE 9.89 The codes for the method FillCourseDataSet().

Next we need to build the codes in the **SelectedIndexChanged()** event method for the **CourseList** box and add the fourth user-defined method **FillCourseDetail()**. First let's build the codes in the **SelectedIndexChanged** event method for the **CourseList** box.

9.4.4.3.5 Build the Codes in the SelectedIndexChanged Method

The function of this piece of codes is that the detailed course information, such as the course name, schedule, classroom, credit and enrollment, will be displayed in the associated textbox control as the user clicked and selected one **course_id** from the list box control. In fact, the main coding job is performed inside the **SelectedIndexChanged()** event method of the list box control **CourseList**. Because when user clicks or selects a **course_id** from the list box control, a **SelectedIndexChanged** event is issued and this event is passed to the associated **SelectedIndexChanged()** event method.

To pick up the detailed course information for a selected **course_id**, the Web method **GetInsertCourse()** in our Web service project **WebServiceInsert Project** is called, and this method returns an instance of the derived class **SQLInsertRecord** to our client project. The detailed course information is stored in that returned instance.

The codes in this event method are identical with those we did for the same event method in our Windows-based client project **WinClientInsert Project**. So we can copy those codes from there and paste them into our current project with a few modifications.

Double-click on the list box control **CourseList** from the Designer View of our client page to open the **SelectedIndexChanged()** event method of the list box control. Copy and paste those codes into our current Web-based project. The only modification is to change the Windows-based **MsgBox()** method to the Web-based script message method **alert()**. Your finished **SelectedIndexChanged()** event method is shown in Figure 9.90. The modified parts have been highlighted in bold.

Let's take a closer look at this piece of codes to see how it works.

A. Two instances, one is for our Web service reference class **WS_SQLInsert** and the other is for our derived class **SQLInsertRecord**, are created first. These instances work as a bridge between our client project and the Web methods developed in the Web service project.

B. A local string variable **errMsg** is declared and it is used to hold the error message to be displayed and reported later.

C. A **Try-Catch** block is used to call the Web method **GetInsertCourse()** with the selected **course_id** from the list box control as the argument to perform this course information retrieving. The selected **course_id** is stored in the **Text** property of the **CourseList** control. An exception

```
WebClientInsert Project                 CourseList_SelectedIndexChanged()

protected void CourseList_SelectedIndexChanged(object sender, EventArgs e)
{
A    WS_SQLInsert.WebServiceSQLInsert wsSQLInsert = new WS_SQLInsert.WebServiceSQLInsert();
     WS_SQLInsert.SQLInsertRecord wsSQLResult = new WS_SQLInsert.SQLInsertRecord();
B    string errMsg;
C    try { wsSQLResult = wsSQLInsert.GetInsertCourse(CourseList.Text); }
     catch (Exception err) { errMsg = "Web service is wrong: " + err.Message;
                             Response.Write("<script>alert('" + errMsg + "')</script>"); }
D    if (wsSQLResult.SQLInsertOK == false)
        Response.Write("<script>alert('" + wsSQLResult.SQLInsertError + "')</script>");
E    else
        FillCourseDetail(ref wsSQLResult);
}
```

FIGURE 9.90 The modified codes for the SelectedIndexChanged() event method.

message is displayed if any error was encountered during the execution of this Web method and caught by the system method **Catch**.

D. In addition to the system error checking, we also need to perform our exception checking by inspecting the member data **SQLInsertOK** in the base class **SQLInsertBase**. If this data value is **False**, which means that an application error was occurred during the running of that Web method. A related error message is displayed.

E. If everything is fine, a user-defined method **FillCourseDetail()** is executed to extract the detailed course information from the returned instance and assign it to each associated textbox control in our client page form.

The detailed codes for the method **FillCourseDetail()** is shown in Figure 9.91.

This piece of codes is identical with that we developed in the same method in our Windows-based client project **WinClientInsert Project**. You can copy and paste it from that project into this project.

The function of this piece of codes is straightforward. Each piece of course information is extracted from the returned instance and assigned to the associated textbox control in our client page window.

9.4.4.3.6 Build the Codes for the Back Button's Click Method

The final coding job is to build the codes for the **Back** button's click method. When this button is clicked by the user, our client project should be terminated. Open this event method and enter the following codes into this method to close our client project:

```
Response.Write("<script>window.close()</script>");
```

In this way, our client page will be terminated when the script command **close()** is executed.

At this point, we have finished all coding jobs for this Web-based client project. Before we can run this project to test the data insertion and validation functions, make sure that the following tasks have been performed:

- Our main Web page **Course.aspx** has been set as the starting page. This can be done by right-clicking on our main Web page and select the item **Set As Start Page** from the popup menu.
- Our Web service **WebServiceInsert Project** is in the running status and this can be checked by locating a small white icon on the status bar on the bottom of the screen. If you cannot find that icon, open our Web service project and click on the **IIS Express** button to run it.
- Two new course records, **CSE-668** and **CSE-526**, which we inserted before by testing the **Insert** button's click method in our Windows-based project, should have been deleted from the **Course** table in our sample database since we want to insert the same course records in this testing.

WebClientInsert Project | **FillCourseDetail()**

```
private void FillCourseDetail(ref WS_SQLInsert.SQLInsertRecord sqlResult)
{
    txtCourseID.Text = CourseList.Text;
    txtCourseName.Text = sqlResult.Course;
    txtSchedule.Text = sqlResult.Schedule;
    txtClassRoom.Text = sqlResult.Classroom;
    txtCredits.Text = sqlResult.Credit.ToString();
    txtEnroll.Text = sqlResult.Enrollment.ToString();
}
```

FIGURE 9.91 The codes for the method FillCourseDetail().

- The **AutoPostBack** property for three controls, **ComboMethod**, **txtCourseID** and **CourseList**, have been set to **True**. This is very important, otherwise no any event can be sent back from the server to our client if it is the default value, **False**.

Now click on the **IIS Express** button to run our Web client project. First let's test the data insertion function. Select the **Stored Procedure Method** from the **Method** combobox control. Then select the default faculty **Ying Bai** from the Faculty Name combobox control, enter the first new course record (shown in Figure 9.74 in Section 9.4.3.3.2) into the associated textboxes, and then click on the **Insert** button.

Perform a similar operation to insert the second new course record (shown in Figure 9.75 in Section 9.4.3.3.2) with the **DataSet Method** selected. Your running Web page is shown in Figure 9.92.

To validate these data insertions, click on the **Select** button for **DataSet Method** and then the **Stored Procedure Method**. The running result is shown in Figure 9.93.

You can find that our two new inserted courses,**CSE-668** and **CSE-526**, have been added into and retrieved from our database, and displayed in the list box control.

To get detailed course information for a specific course, click a desired **course_id** from the list box control. Immediately, the detailed course information for the selected **course_id** is displayed on each associated textbox, which is shown in Figure 9.94.

You can try to get the detailed information for different courses by selecting different **course_id**s from the list box control via either DataSet or Stored Procedure method. Click on the **Back** button to terminate our Web client project.

A completed Web-based Web service client project **WebClientInsert Project** can be found from the folder **Class DB Projects\Chapter 9\WebClientInsert Solution** that is under the **Students** folder on the CRC Press ftp site (refer to Figure 1.2 in Chapter 1).

Next we need to take care of updating and deleting data via Web services.

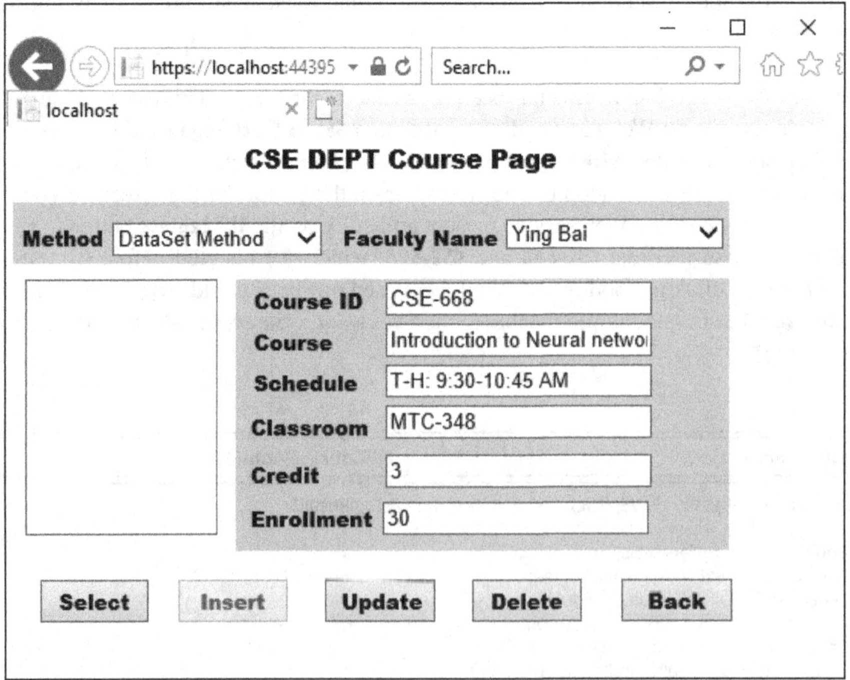

FIGURE 9.92 The running status of inserting new course records.

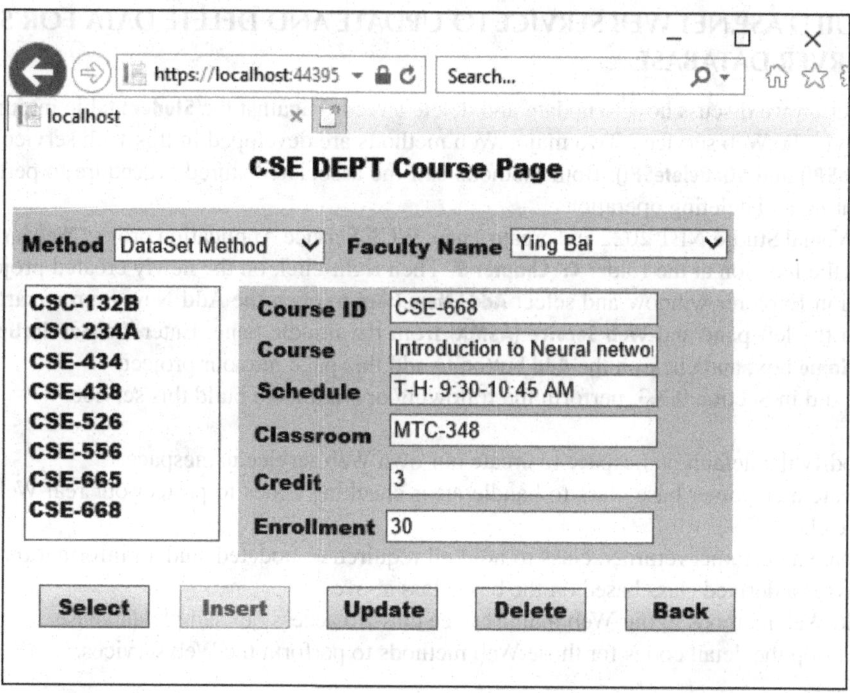

FIGURE 9.93 The running status of the data validation process.

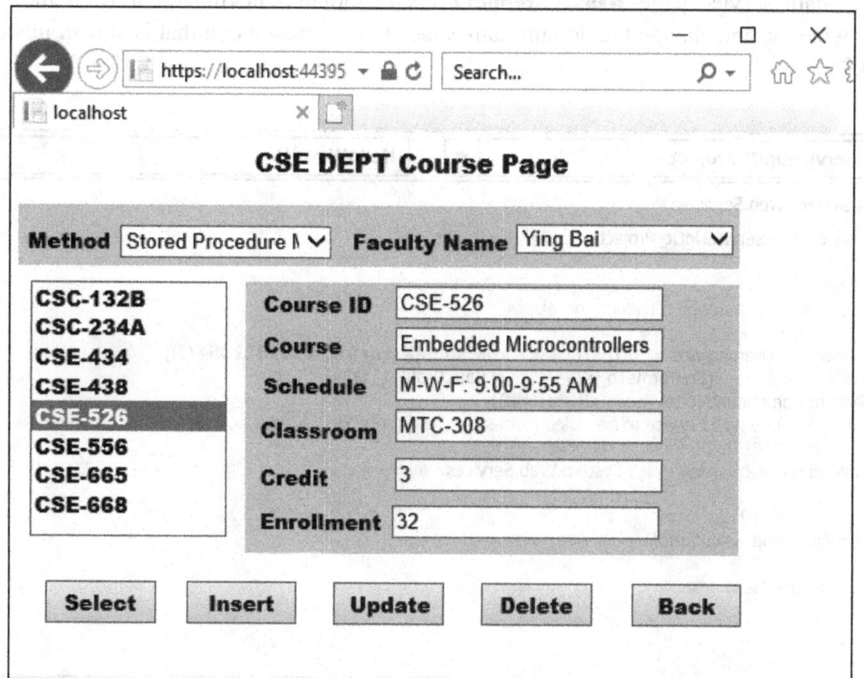

FIGURE 9.94 The running status of getting the detailed course information.

9.5 BUILD ASP.NET WEB SERVICE TO UPDATE AND DELETE DATA FOR SQL SERVER DATABASE

In this section we discuss how to update and delete a record against the **Student** table in our sample database via the Web services. Two major Web methods are developed in this Web service project: **SQLUpdateSP()** and **SQLDeleteSP()**. Both methods call the associated stored procedure to perform the data updating and deleting operations.

Open Visual Studio.NET 2022 and create a new WCF Service Application project **WebServiceUpDt Project** in the location at the folder **C:\Chapter 9**. Then right-click on the newly created project from the Solution Explorer window and select **Add | New Item** to open the Add New Item wizard. Select **Web** from the left pane and **Web Service (ASMX)** from the middle pane. Enter **WebServiceUpDt.asmx** into the **Name** box, and click on the **Add** button to add this page into our project.

As we did in Section 9.3.3, perform the following operations to build this service:

1) Modify the default namespace to create our own Web service namespace.
2) Create a customer base class to handle error-checking codes to protect our real Web service class.
3) Create a customer returned class to hold all required or updated student information. This class is a derived class based on the base class above.
4) Add Web methods to our Web main service class to access our sample database.
5) Develop the detail codes for those Web methods to perform the Web services.

Let's start our jobs based on this sequence now.

9.5.1 Modify the Default Namespace and Add Database Connection String

Open the main service page **WebServiceUpDt.asmx** by double-clicking on it from the Solution Explorer window, and change the default namespace to our special one that is shown in step **A** on Figure 9.95.

```
WebServiceUpDt Project                    HelloWorld()

using System.Web.Services;
namespace WebServiceUpDt_Project
{
   /// <summary>
   /// Summary description for WebServiceUpDt
   /// </summary>
A  [WebService(Namespace = "https://www.routledge.com/978-1032312354/")]
   [WebServiceBinding(ConformsTo = WsiProfiles.BasicProfile1_1)]
   [System.ComponentModel.ToolboxItem(false)]
   // To allow this Web Service to be called from script, using ASP.NET AJAX, uncomment the following line.
   // [System.Web.Script.Services.ScriptService]
   public class WebServiceUpDt : System.Web.Services.WebService
   {
      [WebMethod]
      public string HelloWorld()
      {
         return "Hello World";
      }
   }
}
```

FIGURE 9.95 The modified namespace.

We need to use our own namespace to replace the default namespace used by the Microsoft to tell the ASP.NET runtime the location from which our Web service is loaded as it runs. This specific namespace is unique because it is the home page of the CRC Press appended with the book's ISBN number. In fact, you can use any unique location as your specific namespace to store your Web service project if you like.

Now, as we did before, open the configuration file **Web.config** and add the database connection string by entering the following tabs into the end of this file:

```
<connectionStrings>
  <add name="sql_conn" connectionString="Server=localhost\SQL2019EXPRESS;
   Initial Catalog=CSE_DEPT;User ID=SMART;Password=Happy2022;"/>
</connectionStrings>
```

Make sure that this **<add name=...>** tag is a completed single-line code without any break-connection symbol in it. Here we used a break-connection symbol to make this line looks better on this limited length for this space.

One can add this connection string tab at any location inside this configuration file, such as by the end of this file or just before the end tag **</configuration>**.

9.5.2 Create Our Customer-Built Base and Returned Classes

Right-click on our new project in the Solution Explorer and select **Add | New Item** to add a new C# class **SQLBase.cs** with two member data:

1) **public Boolean SQLOK;**
2) **public string SQLError;**

In a similar way to create another class **SQLResult.cs**, which is a derived class based on the **SQLBase** class with eight members, as shown in Figure 9.96.

Go to the **File | Save All** menu item to save these operations. Next let's concentrate on adding and creating related Web methods to perform data updating and deleting actions.

```
WebServiceUpDt Project                    StudentID
namespace WebServiceUpDt_Project
{
  public class SQLResult:SQLBase
  {
     public string StudentID;
     public string StudentName;
     public float GPA;
     public int Credits;
     public string Major;
     public string SchoolYear;
     public string Email;
     public byte[] SImage;
  }
```

FIGURE 9.96 The member data for the class SQLResult.

9.5.3 Create a Web Method to Call Stored Procedure to Update Student Records

The function of this Web method **SQLUpdateSP()** is to call a SQL Server stored procedure **dbo.WebUpdateStudentSP()** that will be developed in Section 9.5.5 to perform the data updating for a student record based on a student's name.

Regularly, we do not need to update the primary key for a record to be updated because it is better to insert a new record with a new primary key than to update that record with a new primary key. Another reason for this issue is that it would be very complicated if one wanted to update a primary key in a parent table since that primary key may also be used as foreign keys in many other child tables. Therefore, one has to update those foreign keys first in many child tables before the primary key can be updated in the parent table. In this application, we concentrate on updating all columns for a student record without touching the primary key column **student_id**.

Now we just assume that our stored procedure is available and let's first to build our Web method **SQLUpdateSP()**. Open our new Web service project **WebServiceUpDt Project** and use a new Web method **SQLUpdateSP()**, whose codes are shown in Figure 9.97, to replace the default method **HelloWorld()**.

Let's have a closer look at these codes to see how they work.

A. First some useful namespaces are declared since we need to use some classes included and covered by those namespaces.
B. The Web method is **SQLUpdateSP()** with eight updated columns. The data type for student image is **byte()**, which is compatible with the data type used in the stored procedure. Also the returned data type is our base class **Result**.
C. The content of the query string is equal to the name of the stored procedure that will be built later in Section 9.5.5. Keep in mind that this name must be identical with the name of the stored procedure to be developed later.
D. Some local variables are declared first for this method, including an instance of our returned class **Result**, Connection and Command objects. The local variable **intUpdate** is used to hold the returned value from calling a system method **ExecuteNonQuery()** later.
E. First we pre-set a good running status of this Web method to the member data **SQLOK** to indicate that so far our Web method is running fine. A database connection is established by calling a user defined method **SQLConn()**.
F. If any error is encountered during the database connection process, the error information is stored into the member data **SQLError** and reported using a user defined subroutine **ReportError()**.
G. The Command object is initialized with associated data objects such as connection object, command text and command type. One point to be noted is that the command type must be set to the **StoredProcedure** since this method will call a stored procedure, not a data query, to perform the data updating. All input parameters are also assigned to the associated dynamic parameter in the **UPDATE** statement. A trick issue is the data type of the **GPA**, which must be **Char** since it can be converted to the **float** type by C# as the project runs.
H. The **ExecuteNonQuery()** method is executed to call the stored procedure to perform the data updating. An integer value is returned from this method and it is equal to the number of rows that have been successfully updated in our **Student** table.
I. A cleaning job is performed to release all objects used in this method.
J. If the returned value from calling of the **ExecuteNonQuery()** method is zero, which means that no any row has been updated in our **Student** table and that data updating is failed. An error message is sent to the member data **SQLError** and reported using a user defined method **ReportError()**.
K. Finally the instance **Result** that contains the running status of this Web method is returned to the calling procedure.

For the detailed codes of two user-defined methods, **SQLConn()** and **ReportError()**, refer to Figures 9.19 and 9.22 in Sections 9.3.7.2 and 9.3.7.4, respectively. For your convenience, we show those codes again in Figure 9.98.

```
WebServiceUpDt Project                    SQLUpdateSP()

A   using System.Configuration;
    using System.Data;
    using System.Data.SqlClient;
    using System.Web.Services;

    [WebMethod]
B   public SQLBase SQLUpdateSP(string StudentName, float GPA, int Credits, string Major, string SchoolYear,
                                string Email, byte[] sImage, string StudentID)
    {
C       string cmdString = "dbo.WebUpdateStudentSP";
D       SqlConnection sqlConnection = new SqlConnection();
        SQLBase Result = new SQLBase();
        SqlCommand sqlCommand = new SqlCommand();
        int intUpdate;
E       Result.SQLOK = true;
        sqlConnection = SQLConn();
F       if (sqlConnection == null)
        {
            Result.SQLError = "Database connection is failed";
            ReportError(Result);
            return null;
        }
G       sqlCommand.Connection = sqlConnection;
        sqlCommand.CommandType = CommandType.StoredProcedure;
        sqlCommand.CommandText = cmdString;
        sqlCommand.Parameters.Add("@sName", SqlDbType.VarChar).Value = StudentName;
        sqlCommand.Parameters.Add("@GPA", SqlDbType.Char).Value = GPA;
        sqlCommand.Parameters.Add("@Major", SqlDbType.Text).Value = Major;
        sqlCommand.Parameters.Add("@SchoolYear", SqlDbType.Text).Value = SchoolYear;
        sqlCommand.Parameters.Add("@Credits", SqlDbType.Int).Value = Credits;
        sqlCommand.Parameters.Add("@Email", SqlDbType.Text).Value = Email;
        sqlCommand.Parameters.Add("@sImage", SqlDbType.Image).Value = sImage;
        sqlCommand.Parameters.Add("@StudentID", SqlDbType.VarChar).Value = StudentID;
H       intUpdate = sqlCommand.ExecuteNonQuery();
I       sqlCommand.Dispose();
        sqlConnection.Close();
        sqlConnection.Dispose();
J       if (intUpdate == 0)
        {
            Result.SQLError = "Data updating is failed";
            ReportError(Result);
        }
K       return Result;
    }
```

FIGURE 9.97 The codes for the web method SQLUpdateSP().

The only modifications are to change the type of the argument passed into this method to **SQLBase** since we only need to check the status of this data updating action, and change the member data of the base class to **SQLOK**.

Go to **File | Save All** menu item to save these modifications.

Next let's build our Web method **SQLDeleteSP()** to call a stored procedure to delete a student record.

9.5.4 Create a Web Method to Call Stored Procedure to Delete Student Records

As we discussed in Section 7.1.1 in Chapter 7, to delete a record from a relational database, one needs to follow the operational steps listed below:

1) Delete records that are related to the parent table with the foreign keys from child tables.
2) Delete records that are defined as primary keys from the parent table.

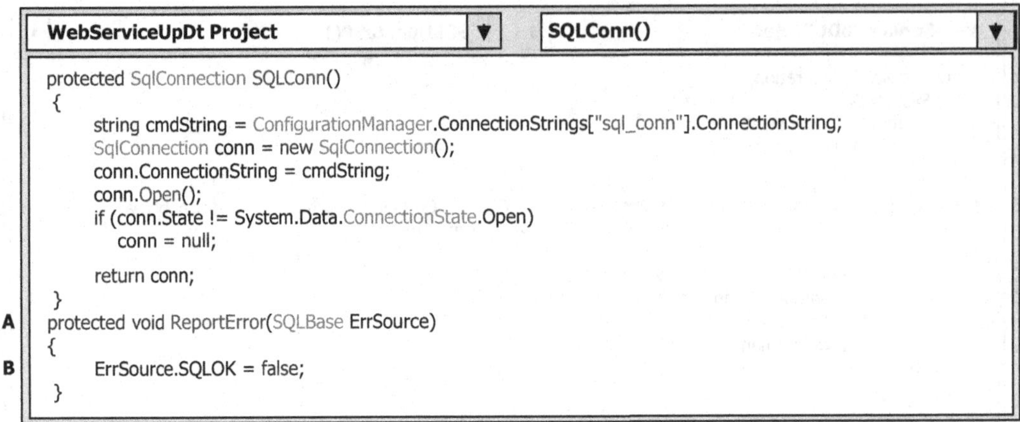

```
WebServiceUpDt Project                    SQLConn()

    protected SqlConnection SQLConn()
    {
        string cmdString = ConfigurationManager.ConnectionStrings["sql_conn"].ConnectionString;
        SqlConnection conn = new SqlConnection();
        conn.ConnectionString = cmdString;
        conn.Open();
        if (conn.State != System.Data.ConnectionState.Open)
           conn = null;

        return conn;
    }
A   protected void ReportError(SQLBase ErrSource)
    {
B       ErrSource.SQLOK = false;
    }
```

FIGURE 9.98 The detailed codes for two user defined methods.

In other words, to delete one record from the parent table, all records that are related to that record as foreign keys and located at different child tables must be deleted first. In our case, in order to delete a record using the **student_id** as the primary key from the **Student** table (parent table), one must first delete those records using the **student_id** as a foreign key from the **LogIn** and the **StudentCourse table** (child tables). Refer to Section 2.5 and Figure 2.12 in Chapter 2 to get a clear relationship description among different data tables in our sample database.

From this discussion, it can be found that to delete a student record from our sample database, two deleting queries need to be performed: the first query is used to delete the related records from the child tables, **LogIn** and **StudentCourse** tables, and the second query is used to delete the target record from the parent table or the **Student** table. However, because we selected the **Cascaded Delete** function when we built all tables in our sample database, we do not need to take care of those child tables and the database engine can handle those deleting actions for us automatically.

A point to be noted is that our dynamic input parameter to this deleting query is a student name, but we need a **student_id** to perform a deleting action. Thus, two queries are needed for this deleting function; first, we need to get a **student_id** based on the input parameter student name, and then perform a cascaded deleting to that student record based on the **student_id**.

To save the time and space as well as efficiency, we place these two queries into a stored procedure **WebDeleteStudentSP()** that will be developed in the following section. A single input parameter, **sName** (student name), is passed into this stored procedure. At this moment, we just assume that we have already developed that stored procedure and will use it in this Web method.

Open our main service page **WebServiceUpDt.asmx** and create this Web method **SQLDeleteSP()**, which is shown in Figure 9.99.

Let's take a closer look at this piece of codes to see how it works.

A. The name of this Web method is **SQLDeleteSP()** and the returned data type is our customer base class **SQLBase**.
B. The content of the query string is equal to the name of the stored procedure we will develop soon. The point is that the name used in this query string must be identical with the name used in our stored procedure later. Otherwise, a running error may be encountered since the stored procedure is identified by its name as the project runs.
C. An instance of our returned base class **SQLBase**, is created. This instance contains the running status of this Web method and will be returned to the calling procedure when this method is done. A local integer variable **intDelete** is declared and this variable is used to hold the returned value from calling of the system method **ExecuteNonQuery()** after this method runs.

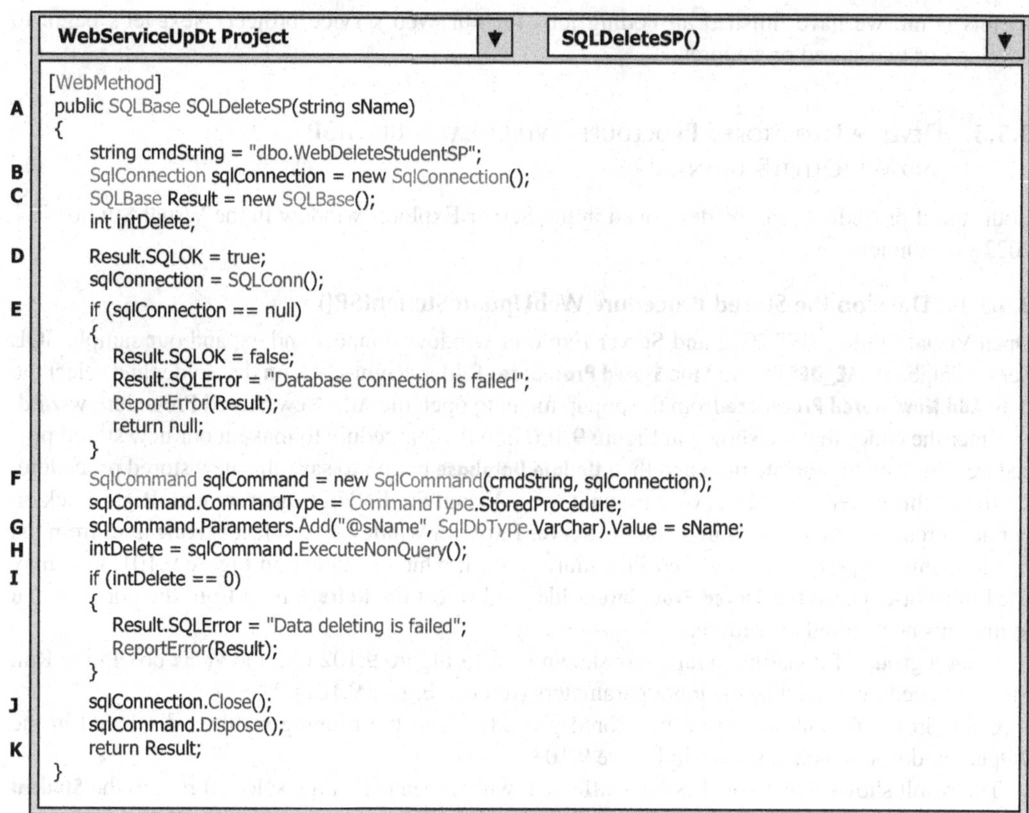

```
WebServiceUpDt Project                SQLDeleteSP()

  [WebMethod]
A public SQLBase SQLDeleteSP(string sName)
  {
      string cmdString = "dbo.WebDeleteStudentSP";
B     SqlConnection sqlConnection = new SqlConnection();
C     SQLBase Result = new SQLBase();
      int intDelete;

D     Result.SQLOK = true;
      sqlConnection = SQLConn();
E     if (sqlConnection == null)
      {
          Result.SQLOK = false;
          Result.SQLError = "Database connection is failed";
          ReportError(Result);
          return null;
      }
F     SqlCommand sqlCommand = new SqlCommand(cmdString, sqlConnection);
      sqlCommand.CommandType = CommandType.StoredProcedure;
G     sqlCommand.Parameters.Add("@sName", SqlDbType.VarChar).Value = sName;
H     intDelete = sqlCommand.ExecuteNonQuery();
I     if (intDelete == 0)
      {
          Result.SQLError = "Data deleting is failed";
          ReportError(Result);
      }
J     sqlConnection.Close();
      sqlCommand.Dispose();
K     return Result;
  }
```

FIGURE 9.99 The codes for the web method SQLDeleteSP().

D. First, we pre-set a good running status of this Web method to the member data **SQLOK** to indicate that so far our Web method is running fine.

E. If any error is encountered during the database connection process, the error information is stored into the member data **SQLError** and reported using the user-defined method **ReportError()**.

F. The Command object is created with a constructor that includes two arguments: Command string and Connection object. Then the Command object is initialized with associated data objects and properties such as Command Type. The point is that the Command Type property must be set to the value of **StoredProcedure** since this command object will call a stored procedure to perform this data deleting action later.

G. Also the dynamic parameter **@sName** is assigned with the actual **sName** that is an input parameter to this Web method.

H. The **ExecuteNonQuery()** method is executed to call our stored procedure to perform this data deleting action. This method returns an integer to indicate the running status of this method, and the returned value is assigned to the local integer variable **intDelete**.

I. The value returned from execution of the **ExecuteNonQuery()** method is equal to the number of rows that have been successfully deleted from the **Student** table. If this returned value is zero, which means that no any row has been deleted from the **Student** table, an error message is displayed and reported using the user-defined method **ReportError()**.

J. A cleaning job is performed to release all objects used in this method.

K. Finally, the instance containing the running status of this Web method is returned to the calling procedure.

At this point, we have finished all coding jobs for our Web service project. Next let's begin to develop our two stored procedures.

9.5.5 Develop Two Stored Procedures WebUpdateStudentSP and WebDeleteStudentSP

Both stored procedures can be developed in the Server Explorer window in the Visual Studio.NET 2022 environment.

9.5.5.1 Develop the Stored Procedure WebUpdateStudentSP()

Open Visual Studio.NET 2022 and Server Explorer window, connect and expand our sample SQL Server database **CSE_DEPT** to find the **Stored Procedures** folder. Right-click on that folder and select the item **Add New Stored Procedure** from the popup menu to open the Add New Stored Procedure wizard.

Enter the codes that are shown in Figure 9.100 into this procedure to make it our new stored procedure. Click on the **Update** item and then **Update Database** button to save this new stored procedure.

To test this stored procedure, we can run it in the Visual Studio.NET environment. Right-click on our new created stored procedure from the Server Explorer window and select **Execute** item from the popup menu to open the Run Stored Procedure wizard, which is shown in Figure 9.101. One may need to right-click on the **Stored Procedure** folder and select the **Refresh** item from the popup menu to find this new stored procedure.

Enter a group of updating parameters shown later in Figure 9.102 into the **Value** box in the Run Stored Procedure wizard as the input parameters (refer to Figure 9.101).

Click on the **OK** button to run this stored procedure and the running result is displayed in the **Output** windows, which is shown in Figure 9.103.

The result shows that 1 row has been affected, which means that the selected row in the **Student** table has been successfully updated. To confirm this data updating at this moment, we can open our sample database **CSE_DEPT** in the Server Explorer window and then expand to our **Student** table under the **Tables** folder, and finally open the **Student** data table by right-clicking on it and select the item **Show Table Data** from the popup menu to try to find this updated course record. As our **Student** table is fully opened, in the bottom line you can immediately find that this record has been updated according to the parameters we input when this procedure is executed (sometimes you need to refresh this table to see the updated result).

It is highly recommended to recover this updated record to the original one since we may use the same input parameters later to update this record again when we test our Web service project. So you can perform this record recovering in the opened **Student** table with the values shown in Figure 9.104. Refer to Sections 7.2.6 and 7.4.2.2 in Chapter 7 to do this recovery job.

```
CREATE PROCEDURE [dbo].[WebUpdateStudentSP]
    @sName VARCHAR(50),
    @GPA float,
    @Major text,
    @SchoolYear text,
    @Credits int,
    @Email text,
    @sImage image,
    @StudentID VARCHAR(50)
AS
    UPDATE Student SET student_name = @sName, gpa = @GPA, major = @Major,
                schoolYear = @SchoolYear, credits = @Credits, email = @Email, simage = @sImage
                WHERE student_id=@StudentID
RETURN 0
```

FIGURE 9.100 Detailed codes for the stored procedure WebUpdateStudentSP().

Execute Stored Procedure

The stored procedure [dbo].[WebUpdateStudentSP] requires the following parameters:

Name	Data Type	Out	Null	Default	Value
@sName	varchar(50)	No	☐	☐	Toney Black
@GPA	float	No	☐	☐	3.28
@Major	text	No	☐	☐	Information System Engineering
@SchoolYear	text	No	☐	☐	Sophomore
@Credits	int	No	☐	☐	82
@Email	text	No	☐	☐	tblack@college.edu
@sImage	image	No	☑	☐	
@StudentID	varchar(50)	No	☐	☐	T77896

OK Cancel

FIGURE 9.101 The input parameters to stored procedure WebUpdateStudentSP().

Parameter Name	Parameter Value
@sName	Toney Black
@GPA	3.28
@Major	Information System Engineering
@SchoolYear	Sophomore
@Credits	82
@Email	tblack@college.edu
@sImage	NULL
@StudentID	T77896

FIGURE 9.102 The input parameters to the stored procedure.

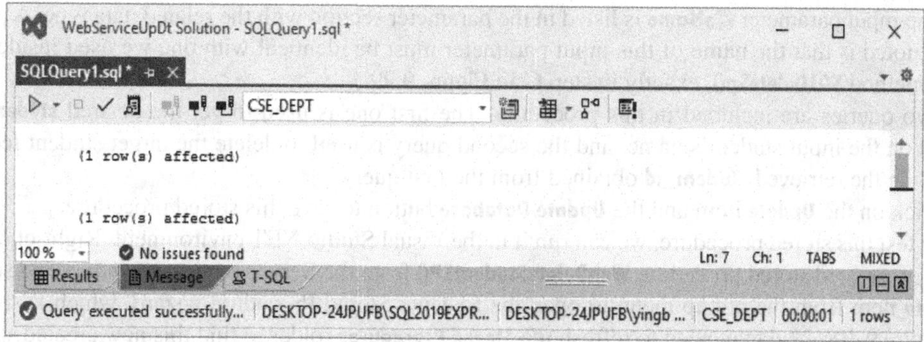

FIGURE 9.103 The running result of the stored procedure WebUpdateStudentSP().

An easy way to recover this student's record is to use one exercise project in homework on Chapter 7, use Exercise 4, **RTOUpdateDelete Project**. Let us suppose you did that exercise and completed the project. When running that project, directly perform an updating query for the student, **Tom Erica**, with the original record shown in Figure 9.104 without any other query, such as Select query.

Column Name	Column Value
student_id	T77896
Student_name	Tom Erica
gpa	3.95
credits	127
major	Computer Science
schoolYear	Senior
email	terica@college.edu
sImage	Erica.jpg

FIGURE 9.104 The recovered record for the original student.

```
CREATE PROCEDURE [dbo].[WebDeleteStudentSP]
     @sName VARCHAR(50)
AS
    DECLARE @sid VARCHAR(50)
    SET @sid = (SELECT student_id FROM Student WHERE student_name = @sName)
    DELETE FROM Student WHERE student_id = @sid
RETURN 0
```

FIGURE 9.105 The codes for the stored procedure WebDeleteCourseSP().

However, if you did not complete that project, an alternative way to do this recovery job is to update this student record to the original one when we test this project later by consuming this service project.

Next let's build the second stored procedure **WebDeleteStudentSP()**.

9.5.5.2 Develop the Stored Procedure WebDeleteStudentSP()

Open Visual Studio.NET 2022 and Server Explorer window, connect and expand our sample SQL Server database **CSE_DEPT** to find the **Stored Procedures** folder. Right-click on that folder and select the item **Add New Stored Procedure** from the popup menu to open the Add New Stored Procedure wizard.

Enter the codes that are shown in Figure 9.105 into this procedure to make it as our new stored procedure.

One input parameter **@sName** is listed in the parameter section with the related data type. A point to be noted is that the name of this input parameter must be identical with one we used inside our Web method **SQLDeleteSp()**, exactly in step **G** in Figure 9.99.

Two queries are included in this procedure. The first one is used to get the desired **student_id** based on the input student's name, and the second query is used to delete the target student record based on the retrieved **student_id** obtained from the first query.

Click on the **Update** item and the **Update Database** button to save this stored procedure.

To test this stored procedure, we can run it in the Visual Studio.NET environment. Right-click on our new created stored procedure **WebDeleteStudentSP()** from the Server Explorer window and select **Execute** item from the popup menu to open the Execute Stored Procedure wizard, which is shown in Figure 9.106. You may need to refresh the **Stored Procedures** folder to find this new created stored procedure.

If the updated student record, **Toney Black**, we did in the last section has not been recovered, enter that student's name into the **Value** box. Otherwise, enter the student name, **Tom Erica**, if that record has been recovered. Then click on the **OK** button to delete that record.

To confirm this deletion, open our sample database, our **Student** table, from the Server Explorer window. One can find that the student named **Toney Black** or **Tom Erica** has been deleted or removed from that table.

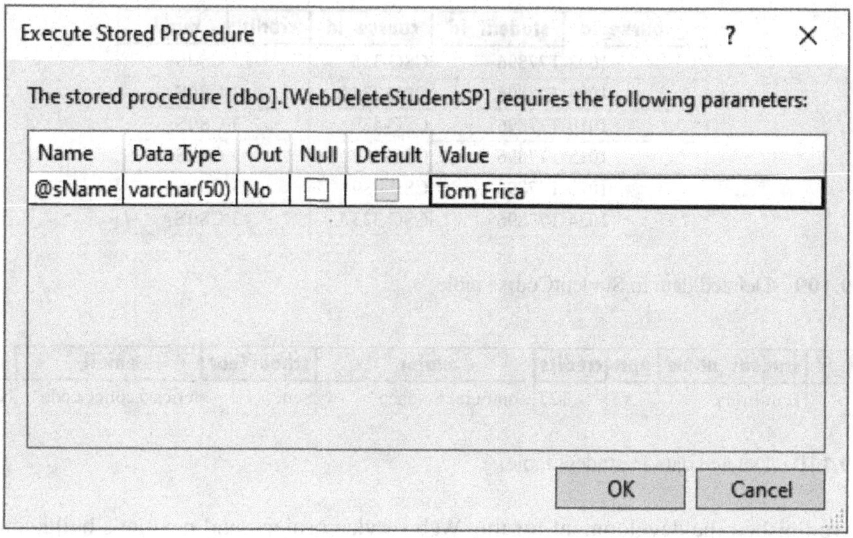

Execute Stored Procedure ? ×

The stored procedure [dbo].[WebDeleteStudentSP] requires the following parameters:

Name	Data Type	Out	Null	Default	Value
@sName	varchar(50)	No	☐	☐	Tom Erica

OK Cancel

FIGURE 9.106 The execute stored procedure wizard.

Table Name	Column Name	Column Value
LogIn Table	user_name	terica
	pass_word	excellent
	student_id	T77896
StudentCourse Table	s_course_id	1002
	s_course_id	1005
	s_course_id	1010
	s_course_id	1015
	s_course_id	1020
	s_course_id	1024

FIGURE 9.107 The deleted records for student Tom Erica in all tables.

Now if you try to open some other tables related to this deleted student, such as **LogIn** and **StudentCourse** tables, you can find that all records related to that student in those tables have also been deleted. These deleted records used **student_id** as a foreign key in those tables, and all of those deleted records are shown in Figure 9.107.

It is highly recommended to recover those deleted records from those tables since we will use the same input parameter later to delete this record again when we test our Web service project. One can use Server Explorer to open and recover those deleted records one by one based on data shown in Figures 9.108–9.110.

An important issue when doing this recovery job is the order of doing that recovery. One must first do recovery for the deleted student in the **Student** table shown in Figure 9.110 since it is a parent table, and then recover other deleted data in other tables since the **student_id** is a primary key in the **Student** table. For the student image column, **sImage**, just left it as **NULL** at this moment and we can handle that later when we test this service project by calling it from a consuming application.

user_name	pass_word	faculty_id	student_id
terica	excellent	NULL	T77896

FIGURE 9.108 Deleted data in LogIn table.

s_course_id	student_id	course_id	credit	major
1002	T77896	CSC-335	3	CS/IS
1005	T77896	CSC-234A	3	CS/IS
1010	T77896	CSC-439	3	CS/IS
1015	T77896	CSC-432	3	CS/IS
1020	T77896	CSE-439	3	CS/IS
1024	T77896	CSC-333A	3	CS/IS

FIGURE 9.109 Deleted data in StudentCourse table.

student_id	student_name	gpa	credits	major	schoolYear	email	simage
T77896	Tom Erica	3.95	127	Computer Science	Senior	terica@college.edu	NULL

FIGURE 9.110 Deleted data in student table.

We have finished the development for this Web service project, and next let's build some client projects to consume our Web service project to update and delete some student records from our sample database.

9.6 BUILD WINDOWS-BASED CLIENT PROJECT TO CONSUME THE WEB SERVICES

To save time and space, we do not need to create any new project and perform a full development process. Instead we can copy and modify an existing Windows-based project **SPUpdateDelete Project** we developed in Section 7.5 in Chapter 7. Copy that project from the folder **ClassDB Projects\Chapter 7** that is under the **Students** folder on the CRC Press ftp site (refer to Figure 1.2 in Chapter 1) and paste it into our new folder **C:\Chpater 9**.

Now let's perform the necessary modifications to this project to make it our new project. The modifications can be divided into two parts:

1) Add a new Web reference to our new client project.
2) Build the codes to two new buttons' click event methods in the code window.

First, let's perform the modifications to the first part.

9.6.1 Add a New Web Reference to Our Client Project

To consume or use the Web service **WebServiceUpDt Project** we developed in the last section, we need first to set up a Web reference to connect to that Web service with our client project together. Perform the following operations to add this Web reference:

1) Open our Web service project **WebServiceUpDt Project**, and click on the **IIS Express** button to run it.
2) Copy the URL from the **Address** bar in our running Web service project.
3) Then open our Windows-based client project **SPUpdateDelete Project**.
4) Right click on our client project **SPUpdateDelete Project** from the Solution Explorer window, and select the item **Add | Service Reference** from the popup menu to open the Add Service Reference wizard.
5) Click on the **Advanced** button located at the lower-left corner on that wizard to open the Service Reference Settings wizard.

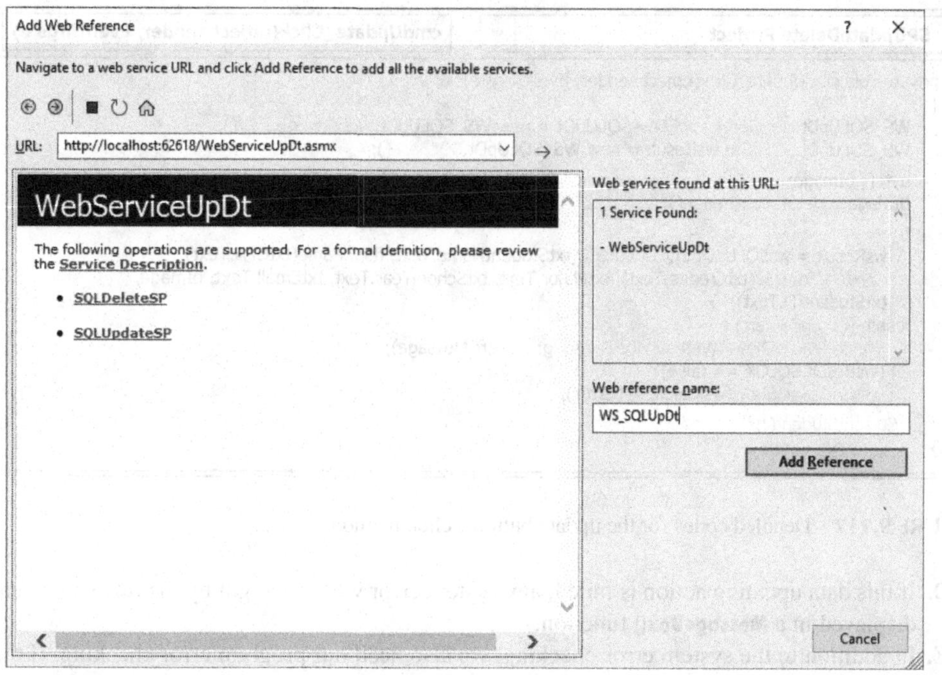

FIGURE 9.111 The opened add web reference wizard.

6) Click on the **Add Web Reference** button to open the Add Web Reference wizard, which is shown in Figure 9.111.
7) Paste that URL we copied from step 2 into the URL box and click on the **Arrow** button to enable the Visual Studio.NET to begin to search it.
8) When the Web service is found, the name of our Web service is displayed in the right pane, which is shown in Figure 9.111.
9) Alternately you can change the name for this Web reference from **localhost** to any meaningful name, such as **WS_SQLUpDt**, in our case. Click on the **Add Reference** button to add this Web service as a reference to our new client project.
10) Click on the **Close** button from our Web service built-in Web interface window to terminate our Web service project.

Next let's build and modify the codes in the related event methods and user defined methods to call our Web service to perform the desired data actions.

9.6.2 Build the Codes to the Update Button Click Method

Open this event procedure and add the codes shown in Figure 9.112 into this method. Let's take a closer look at this piece of codes to see how it works.

A. Two local reference objects, **wsSQLUpDt** and **wsResult**, are declared and they are used to access our Web service project via this reference.
B. An image object **bImage** is declared and this is a byte array used to hold the updated student image file. The user-defined method **getStudentImage()** is called to get the desired student's image to be updated in the sample database.
C. Our Web method **SQLUpdateSP()** is executed via our Web reference object **wsSQLUpDt** with seven pieces of updated student's information.

```
SPUpdateDelete Project                          cmdUpdate_Click(object sender, EventArgs e)

  private void cmdUpdate_Click(object sender, EventArgs e)
  {
A     WS_SQLUpDt.WebServiceUpDt wsSQLUpDt = new WS_SQLUpDt.WebServiceUpDt();
      WS_SQLUpDt.SQLBase wsResult = new WS_SQLUpDt.SQLBase();
B     byte[] bImage;
      bImage = getStudentImage();
C     try {
        wsResult = wsSQLUpDt.SQLUpdateSP(txtStudentName.Text, float.Parse(txtGPA.Text),
        Convert.ToInt32(txtCredits.Text), txtMajor.Text, txtSchoolYear.Text, txtEmail.Text, bImage,
        txtStudentID.Text); }
D      catch (Exception err) {
         MessageBox.Show("Web service is wrong: " + err.Message); }
E      if (wsResult.SQLOK == false)
         MessageBox.Show(wsResult.SQLError);
F      CurrentStudent();
  }
```

FIGURE 9.112 Detailed codes for the update button's click method.

D. If this data updating action is failed, any system error will be caught by the **catch** block and displayed in a **MessageBox()** function.
E. In addition to the system error checking, we also need our program error checking. If this data updating action is failed, the returned error code should be located in the **SQLError** member, and this error is displayed via an **MessageBox()** function.
F. Finally, the user-defined method **CurrentStudent()** is called to update the student's name and display it in the Student Name combobox control to enable us to perform confirmation for this data updating later if this data updating is successful.

Next let's handle the codes for the **Delete** button's Click method.

9.6.3 Build the Codes to the Delete Button Click Method

The function of this method is to call our Web method **SQLDeleteSP()** in our Web service project with a student's name to delete the selected student's record from our sample database.

Open this method and add the codes that are shown in Figure 9.113 into it. Let's have a closer look at this piece of codes to see how it works.

A. Two local reference objects, **wsSQLUpDt** and **wsResult**, are declared and they are used to access our Web service project via this reference.
B. Some local variables are declared first, which include a MessageBox buttons protocol object **vbButton** and a feedback variable **Answer**. The former is used to setup the button's format and the latter is used to hold the feedback value of calling the **MessageBox()** function.
C. The **MessageBox()** function is called with a warning message and two buttons, **Yes** and **No**, being displayed.
D. If the feedback value is **Yes**, which means that the user wants to delete this record, our Web method **SQLDeleteSP()** is called to perform this data deleting action via our Web service. A warning message would be displayed if any error is encountered during this data deleting action.
E. In addition to the system exception error checking, we also need to check our Web method to make sure that it is running fine. If a **false** is returned from our base class, exactly from the member data **SQLOK**, which means that something is wrong for executing of this Web method, a warning message is also displayed via the **MessageBox()** function.

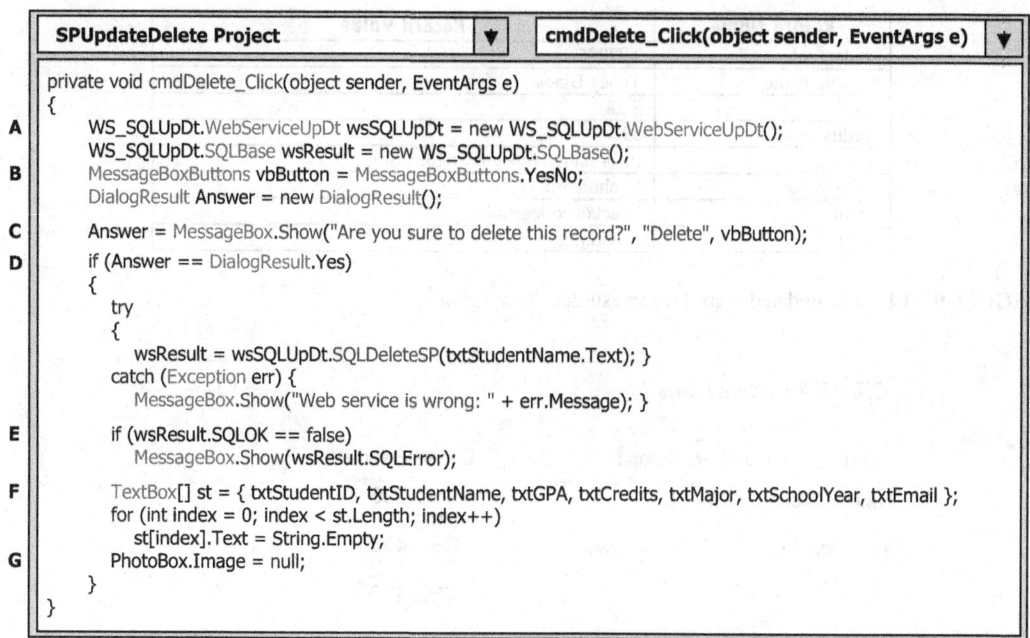

```
SPUpdateDelete Project                 cmdDelete_Click(object sender, EventArgs e)

  private void cmdDelete_Click(object sender, EventArgs e)
  {
A     WS_SQLUpDt.WebServiceUpDt wsSQLUpDt = new WS_SQLUpDt.WebServiceUpDt();
      WS_SQLUpDt.SQLBase wsResult = new WS_SQLUpDt.SQLBase();
B     MessageBoxButtons vbButton = MessageBoxButtons.YesNo;
      DialogResult Answer = new DialogResult();
C     Answer = MessageBox.Show("Are you sure to delete this record?", "Delete", vbButton);
D     if (Answer == DialogResult.Yes)
      {
         try
         {
            wsResult = wsSQLUpDt.SQLDeleteSP(txtStudentName.Text); }
         catch (Exception err) {
            MessageBox.Show("Web service is wrong: " + err.Message); }
E        if (wsResult.SQLOK == false)
            MessageBox.Show(wsResult.SQLError);
F        TextBox[] st = { txtStudentID, txtStudentName, txtGPA, txtCredits, txtMajor, txtSchoolYear, txtEmail };
         for (int index = 0; index < st.Length; index++)
            st[index].Text = String.Empty;
G        PhotoBox.Image = null;
      }
  }
```

FIGURE 9.113 The codes for the delete button's click method.

F. Finally, all seven pieces of deleted student's information stored in seven textboxes are cleaned up to indicate that the selected student record has been deleted.
G. The student image is also removed from the student image box by setting the **Image** property to null.

Go to **File | Save All** menu item to save those modifications and developments.

At this point, we have finished all coding developments to this client project and now it is the time for us to run this project to access our Web service to perform the data updating and deleting actions.

However, before we can run this project, make sure that our Web service project **WebServiceUpDt Project** is in the running status. This can be identified by a small white icon located in the status bar on the bottom of the screen. If you cannot find this icon, open our Web service project **WebServiceUpDt Project** and click on the **IIS Express** button to run it. Now click on the **Start** button from our client project to run it. Enter valid **user_name** and **pass_word** for the **LogIn** Form, and select **Student Information** to open the Student Form.

Let's update this student record by entering data shown in Figure 9.114 into related textbox and student image box **PhotoBox**. All students' image files are available in a folder **Images\Students** that is under the **Students** folder on the CRC Press ftp site (refer to Figure 1.2 in Chapter 1). One can copy those image files and save them into any local folder on your machine.

Click on the **Update** button to call the Web method **SQLUpdateSP()** in our Web service to update this student record. On the opened Find-File wizard, browse to the student image folder and select the student image file **David.jpg**. When this data updating action is completed, the updated student image is displayed with all seven pieces of updated information shown in related textboxes, as shown in Figure 9.115.

To confirm this data updating, go to the **Student Name** combobox. Now you cannot find the original student **Tom Erica** from that box, which means that the original student record has been updated to a new one. Scroll down that combobox and you can find our updated student's name **Toney Black** at the bottom.

Record Name	Record Value
student_id	T77896
student_name	Toney Black
gpa	3.28
credits	52
major	Information System Engineering
schoolYear	Sophomore
email	tblack@college.edu
sImage	David.jpg

FIGURE 9.114 The updated record for the student Tom Erica.

FIGURE 9.115 The running status of the student updating process.

Now let's select some other student's name from the **Student Name** combobox, and click on the **Select** button to get related information for that student. Then select the updated student's name **Toney Black** from the same combobox and click the **Select** button again to try to get the updated information for that student. You can find that all information related to that student has been updated and displayed in this form, as shown in Figure 9.115. Our data updating action is successful!

To test the deleting function, keep the current updated student **Toney Black** selected and click on the **Delete** button to try to delete this record from the **Student** table. Click on the **Yes** button to the popup MessageBox to confirm this deletion action. If this deletion action is successful, all pieces of information related to this student would be deleted from both our sample database and this Student Form window.

To confirm this data deleting action, click on the **Select** button to try to retrieve all pieces of information for the deleted student. Immediately a warning message is displayed to indicate that no matched student found.

Click on the **Back** and **Exit** buttons to terminate our client project. Our client project is very successful. However, the story is not finished. It is highly recommended that you recover that deleted student record for our **Student** table since we want to keep our database neat and complete. You can recover this record by using one of the following methods:

1) Using the Server Explorer window in Visual Studio.NET to open our sample database **CSE_DEPT** and our **Student** data table, and add the original record.
2) Using the Microsoft SQL Server Management Studio to open our sample database **CSE_DEPT** and our **Student** data table and add the original record.

Refer to Figures 9.108, 9.109 and 9.110 in Section 9.5.5.2 to complete this recovery job since all records related to the deleted student in all tables, including the **LogIn**, **Student** and **StudentCourse**, are also deleted. The recover order is: First recover the deleted record in the **Student** table since it is a parent table and the **student_id** is a primary key in that table, and then do recovery jobs for other tables.

To recover the student image in the **Student** table, one can just enter a **NULL** to that column and perform another updating action later by running this project. Alternatively, one can use a project **RTOInsert Project** or **RTOInsertSP Project**, which are Exercises 4 and 5 in the homework on Chapter 6, to insert that original record if you completed any of them. However, you must first delete the updated student record before you can insert the original record since they used the same **student_id**.

A complete Windows-based client project **SPUpdateDelete Project** can be found from the folder **ClassDB Projects\Chapter 9\SPUpdateDelete Solution** that is located on the CRC Press ftp site (refer to Figure 1.2 in Chapter 1).

9.7 BUILD WEB-BASED CLIENT PROJECT TO CONSUME THE WEB SERVICES

There is no significant difference between building a Windows-based and a Web-based client project to consume a Web service. To save the time and the space, we can create a new ASP.NET Web Application (.NET Framework) project, and then add and modify a **Student** page to consume our Web service project.

This section can be developed in the following sequences:

1) Create a brand-new ASP.NET Web Application (.NET Framework) project **WebClientSQLUpDt Project** and add an existing Web page **Student.aspx** from the folder **Web Forms** that is under the **Students** folder on the CRC Press ftp site (refer to Figure 1.2 in Chapter 1) into our new project.
2) Add a Web service reference to our new Web project.
3) Add and build codes in the related methods on the **Student.aspx.cs** file to call the associated Web method to perform our data updating and deleting. The code additions and modifications include the following sections:
   A. Build the codes inside **Back** button click method.
   B. Develop the codes for the **Update** button's click method.
   C. Develop the codes for the **Delete** button's click method.

Now let's start with the first step listed above.

9.7.1 Create a New ASP.NET Web Application Project and Add an Existing Web Page

Open Visual Studio.NET and go to the **File | New Project** menu item to create a new ASP.NET Web Application (.NET Framework) project. Enter **WebClientSQLUpDtProject** into the **Name** box and **C:\Chapter 9** into the **Location** box, click on the **Create** button, select the **Web Forms** and click on the **Create** button on the next page to create this project.

On the opened new project Solution Explorer window, right-click on our new project icon **WebClientSQLUpDtProject**, and select the item **Add | Existing Item** from the popup menu to open the Add Existing Item wizard. Browse to the folder **Web Forms** that is under the Students folder on the CRC Press ftp site (refer to Figure 1.2 in Chapter 1). Select the items **Student.aspx**, **Student.aspx.designer.cs** and **Student.aspx.cs** by checking them one by one, and click on the **Add** button to add these items into our new Web project.

Perform the following operations to make the **Student.aspx** page the main page:

1) Right-click on the **Student.aspx** page from the Solution Explorer window and select the item **Set As Start Page** from the popup menu to set it as a start page.
2) Go to **File | Save All** to save all changes.
3) Go to **Build | RebuildWebClientSQLUpDtProject** to build the entire project.

Next let's add our Web service project **WebServiceUpDt Project** as a reference to our Web client project.

9.7.2 Add a Web Service Reference and Modify the Web Form Window

Right-click on our new project icon from the Solution Explorer window and select the item **Add | Service Reference** from the popup menu. Then click on the **Advanced** button on the next wizard, and **AddWeb Reference** button on the next wizard. Then open our Web service project **WebServiceUpDt Project**, and click on the **IIS Express** button to run it.

As the project runs, copy the URL from the Address box and paste it into the URL box in our Add Web Reference wizard. Then click on the Arrow button to add this Web service as a reference to our client project. You can modify this Web reference name to any name you want. In this application, we prefer to change it to **WS_SQLUpDt**. Your finished Add Web reference wizard should match the one that is shown in Figure 9.116.

Click on the **Add Reference** button to finish this adding Web reference process. Now let's take care of building the codes in related methods in the **Student.aspx** page.

9.7.3 Build the Codes inside the Back Button Click Method

The function of this method is to terminate our Web client project when this **Back** button is clicked. Therefore, just open that method by double clicking on the **Back** button from the Designer View of the Student page and place one coding line as below:

```
Response.Write("<script>window.close()</script>");
```

Next let's take care of creating codes for the **Update** button click method.

9.7.4 Add the Codes to the Update Button Click Method

The coding job is to add the codes to the **Update** button's click method. Open this method by double-clicking on the **Update** button from the Designer View of the Student page, and enter the codes shown in Figure 9.117 into this method.

Let's take a closer look at this piece of codes to see how it works.

A. Some new instances related to our Web service and methods, including our Web proxy class, **wsSQLUpdate**, and base class, **wsResult**, are created and those instances are used to access the Web method **SQLUpdateSP()** we developed in our Web service **WebServiceUpDt Project**. The key point is that our current project' name **WebClientSQLUpDt_Project** must be

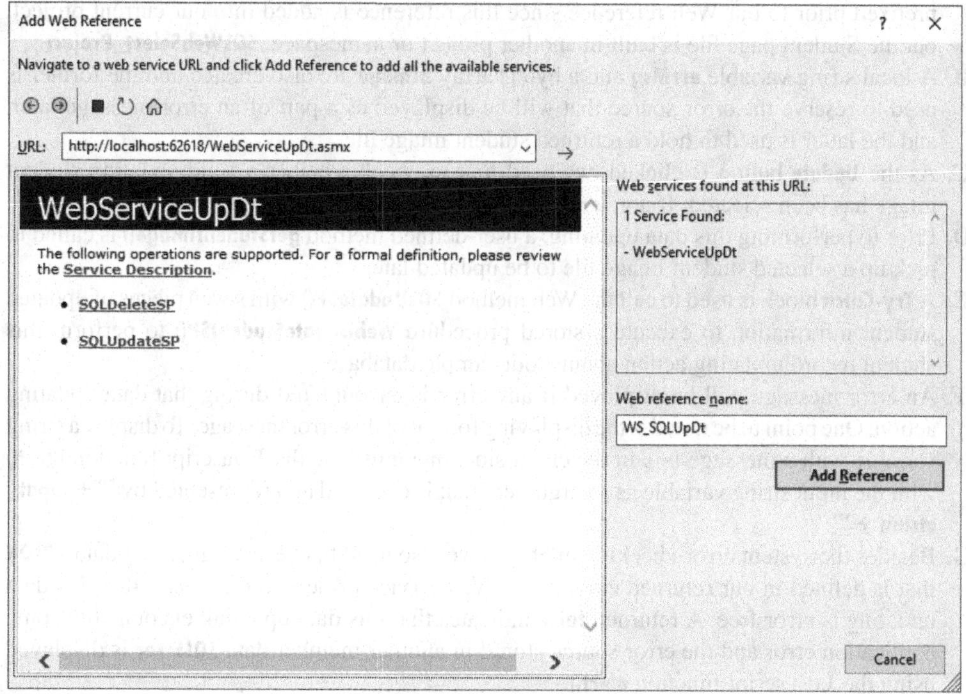

FIGURE 9.116 The finished add web reference wizard.

```
WebClientSQLUpDt Project                cmdUpdate_Click(object sender, EventArgs e)

  protected void cmdUpdate_Click(object sender, EventArgs e)
  {
A     WebClientSQLUpDt_Project.WS_SQLUpDt.WebServiceUpDt wsSQLUpdate;
      wsSQLUpdate = new WebClientSQLUpDt_Project.WS_SQLUpDt.WebServiceUpDt();
      WebClientSQLUpDt_Project.WS_SQLUpDt.SQLBase wsResult;
      wsResult = new WebClientSQLUpDt_Project.WS_SQLUpDt.SQLBase();
B     string errMsg;
      byte[] bImage;
C    if (!FileUploadImage.HasFile)
        Response.Write("<script>alert('Select an updating image using FileUpload!')</script>");
     else
     {
D      bImage = getStudentImage();
E      try
       {
          wsResult = wsSQLUpdate.SQLUpdateSP(txtStudentName.Text, float.Parse(txtGPA.Text),
          int.Parse(txtCredits.Text), txtMajor.Text, txtSchoolYear.Text, txtEmail.Text, bImage, txtStudentID.Text); }
F      catch (Exception err) {
          errMsg = "Web service is wrong: " + err.Message;
          Response.Write("<script>alert('" + errMsg + "')</script>"); }
G      if (wsResult.SQLOK == false)
          Response.Write("<script>alert('" + wsResult.SQLError + "')</script>");
       else
H         ComboName.Items.Add(txtStudentName.Text);
     }
  }
```

FIGURE 9.117 The codes for the update button click event procedure.

prefixed prior to our Web reference since this reference is added into our current project, but the Student page file is built in another project or namespace, **SQLWebSelect_Project**.

B. A local string variable **errMsg** and a byte[] array **bImage** are also created and the former is used to reserve the error source that will be displayed as a part of an error message later, and the latter is used to hold a returned student image file.

C. As the **Update** button is clicked, we need first to check whether a valid updating student image has been selected. If not, a message is displayed to remind the user.

D. Prior to performing this data updating, a user-defined method **getStudentImage()** is called to pick up a selected student image file to be updated later.

E. A **Try-Catch** block is used to call the Web method **SQLUpdateSP()** with seven pieces of updated student information to execute a stored procedure **WebUpdateStudentSP()** to perform this student record updating action against our sample database.

F. An error message will be displayed if any error is encountered during that data updating action. One point to be noted is the displaying format of this error message. To display a string variable with a message box in the client side, one must use the Javascript function **alert()** with the input string variable as an argument that is enclosed and represented by **'" + input_string + "'**.

G. Besides the system error-checking methods, we also need to check the member data **SQLOK** that is defined in our returned class in the Web service project to make sure that this data updating is error-free. A returned **false** indicates that this data updating encountered some application error and the error source stored in another member data **SQLError** is displayed using the Java script function **alert()**.

H. If this data updating is successful, the updated student's name is added into our Student Name combobox to enable users to verify this updating later.

The detailed codes for the user defined method **getStudentImage()** can be found from Figure 8.91 in Section 8.9.2.3 in Chapter 8. For your convenience, those codes are shown in Figure 9.118 again without any explanations.

In the next section, we will develop the codes for the **Delete** button's click method to perform the data deleting actions against our sample database.

9.7.5 Develop Codes for the Delete Button Click Method

Double-click on the **Delete** button from the Designer View of our client page window to open the **Delete** button click method, and enter the codes that are shown in Figure 9.119 into this method.

```
WebClientSQLUpDt Project        getStudentImage()

  private byte[] getStudentImage()
  {
A     int length;
B     string imgPath = Server.MapPath("~/StudentImage/");
C     if (!System.IO.Directory.Exists(imgPath))
         System.IO.Directory.CreateDirectory(imgPath);
D     FileUploadImage.SaveAs(imgPath + System.IO.Path.GetFileName(FileUploadImage.FileName));
E     PhotoBox.ImageUrl = "~/StudentImage/" + FileUploadImage.FileName;
F     length = FileUploadImage.PostedFile.ContentLength;
G     byte[] img = new byte[length];
      FileUploadImage.PostedFile.InputStream.Read(img, 0, length);
H     return img;
  }
```

FIGURE 9.118 Detailed codes for the user defined method getStudentImage().

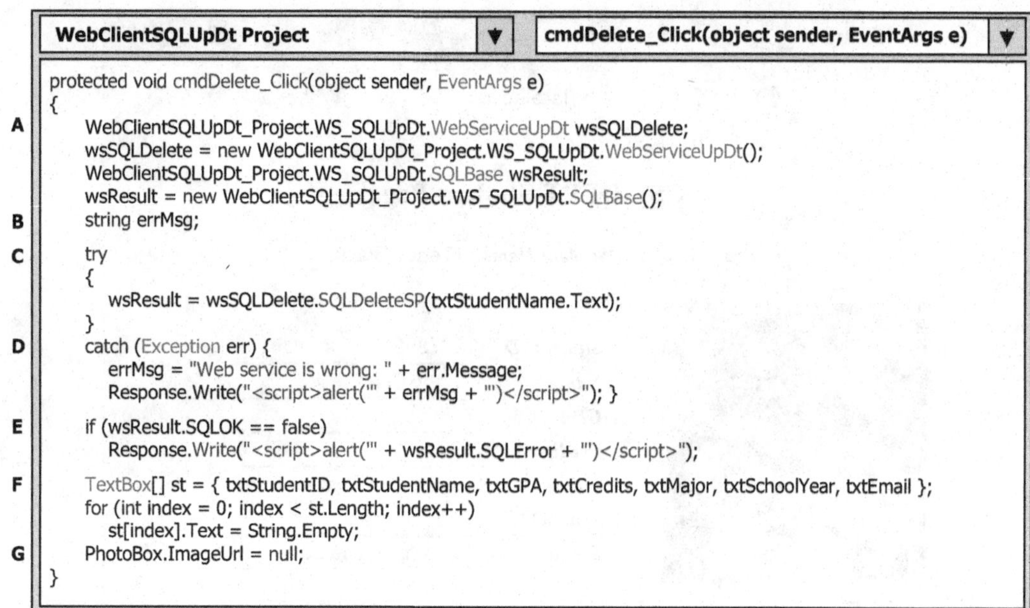

```
WebClientSQLUpDt Project        cmdDelete_Click(object sender, EventArgs e)

  protected void cmdDelete_Click(object sender, EventArgs e)
  {
A     WebClientSQLUpDt_Project.WS_SQLUpDt.WebServiceUpDt wsSQLDelete;
      wsSQLDelete = new WebClientSQLUpDt_Project.WS_SQLUpDt.WebServiceUpDt();
      WebClientSQLUpDt_Project.WS_SQLUpDt.SQLBase wsResult;
      wsResult = new WebClientSQLUpDt_Project.WS_SQLUpDt.SQLBase();
B     string errMsg;
C     try
      {
        wsResult = wsSQLDelete.SQLDeleteSP(txtStudentName.Text);
      }
D     catch (Exception err) {
        errMsg = "Web service is wrong: " + err.Message;
        Response.Write("<script>alert('" + errMsg + "')</script>"); }
E     if (wsResult.SQLOK == false)
        Response.Write("<script>alert('" + wsResult.SQLError + "')</script>");
F     TextBox[] st = { txtStudentID, txtStudentName, txtGPA, txtCredits, txtMajor, txtSchoolYear, txtEmail };
      for (int index = 0; index < st.Length; index++)
        st[index].Text = String.Empty;
G     PhotoBox.ImageUrl = null;
  }
```

FIGURE 9.119 The codes for the delete button click method.

Let's take a closer look at this piece of codes to see how it works.

A. Some new instances related to our Web service and methods, including our Web proxy class, **wsSQLDelete**, and base class, **wsResult**, are created and those instances are used to access the Web method **SQLDeleteSP()** we developed in our Web service **WebServiceUpDt Project**. The key point is that our current project's name **WebClientSQLUpDt_Project** must be prefixed prior to our Web reference since this reference is added into our current project, but the Student page file is built in another project or namespace, **SQLWebSelect_Project**.

B. A local string variable **errMsg** is also created and it is used to reserve the error source that will be displayed as a part of an error message later.

C. A **Try-Catch** block is used to call the Web method **SQLDeleteSP()** with one student's name, **txtName.Text**, that works as an identifier, to run a stored procedure **WebDeleteStudentSP()** to perform this deleting action against our sample database.

D. An error message will be displayed if any error is encountered during that data deleting action. One point to be noted is that the displaying format of this error message. To display a string variable in a message box in the client side, one must use the Javascript function **alert()** with the input string variable as an argument that is enclosed and represented by **"' + input_string + '"**.

E. Besides the system error-checking methods, we also need to check the member data **SQLOK** that is defined in our returned class in the Web service project to make sure that this data deleting is error-free. A returned **false** value of this member data indicates that this data deleting encountered some application error and the error source stored in another member data **SQLError** is displayed.

F. Finally, a cleaning job is performed to empty all pieces of information related to the deleted student from all textboxes.

G. The student image box is also cleaned up.

Go to **File | Save All** menu item to save these modifications and developments.

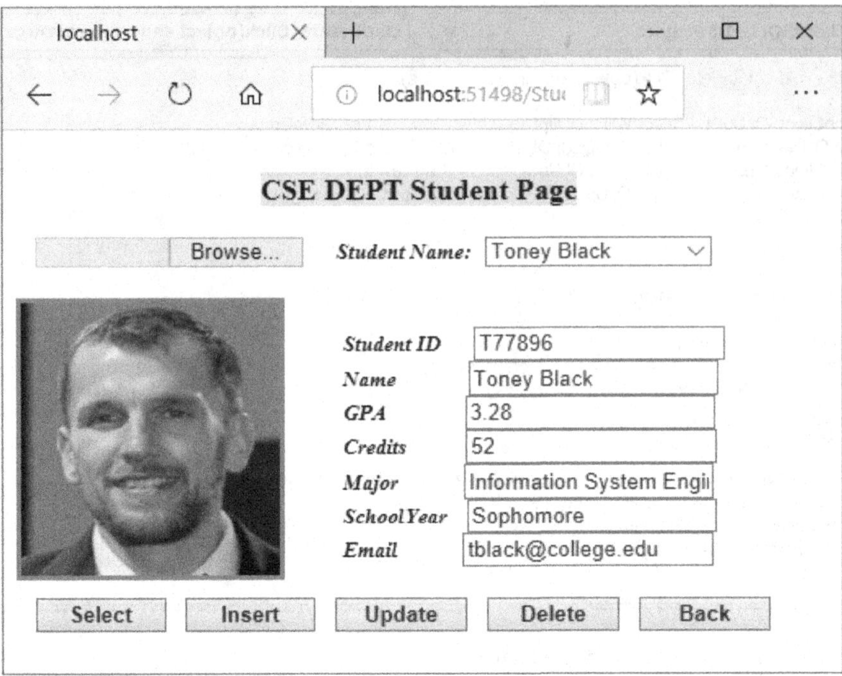

FIGURE 9.120 Running result of updating a student record.

Now we have completed all developments for the data updating and deleting actions in our client side. Before one can run this client project to access to our Web service to perform data actions for any student record, make sure that all student image files should have been stored in a local folder in your machine to enable you to select one from there as an updated student's image as the project runs. All student image files can be found from a folder **Images\Students** under the **Students** folder located on the CRC Press ftp site (refer to Figure 1.2 in Chapter 1). The reason for that is because we will use a virtual folder or path to save those student images for this Web client project to enable them to be found during the project runs.

Now let's run our projects to test the data updating function first.

First run our Web service project **WebServiceUpDt Project**, and then run our client project **WebClientSQLUpDt Project** by clicking on the **IIS Express** button. The running status of our client project is shown in Figure 9.120.

As we did before, we want to update a student record, **Tom Erica**, to a new one with a different or an updated student image. Thus, on the opened Student page, enter the following data items as an updated student record into the related textbox:

Student ID:	**T77896**
Student Name:	**Toney Black**
GPA:	**3.28**
Credits:	**52**
Major:	**Information System Engineering**
SchoolYear:	**Sophomore**
Email:	**tblack@college.edu**

Then go to the **FileUploadImage** control and click on the **Browse** button to browse to the virtual folder or path where all student image files are located, which is **StudentImage**, and select the updated student image file, **David.jpg**, and click on the **Open** button to select this image file. Now click on the **Update** button to perform this data updating action. The updating result is shown in Figure 9.120. Click on the **Back** button to stop our client project.

To confirm this updating action, open our sample database **CSE_DEPT** and the **Student** table via the Server Explorer window, and one can find that the student record with a **student_id** of **T77896** has been updated as the one shown in Figure 9.120.

Now let's test the data deleting actions.

Run our client project again and perform another updating action by entering the following data items into the related textbox, and selecting the image **Erica.jpg** and clicking on the **Update** button to recover the updated student back to the original one:

Student ID:	**T77896**
Student Name:	**Tom Erica**
GPA:	**3.95**
Credits:	**127**
Major:	**Computer Science**
SchoolYear:	**Senior**
Email:	**terica@college.edu**

Now click on the **Delete** button to call the Web method **SQLDeleteSP()** defined in our Web service to try to delete that student record from our sample database. One can find that all pieces of information related to the updated student have been removed from this Web page. Click on the **Back** button to stop our client project.

To confirm this data deleting action, open our sample database **CSE_DEPT** and the **Student** table via the Server Explorer window, and one can find that the student record with a **student_id** of **T77896** has been removed from that table.

Our client project is very successful.

However, the story is not finished. It is highly recommended to recover that deleted student record for our **Student** table since we want to keep our database neat and complete. You can recover this record by using one of the following methods:

1) Using the Server Explorer window in Visual Studio.NET to open our sample database **CSE_DEPT** and our **Student** data table, and add the original record.
2) Using the Microsoft SQL Server Management Studio to open our sample database **CSE_DEPT** and our **Student** data table and add the original record.

Refer to Figures 9.121–9.123 to complete this recovery job since all records related to the deleted student in all tables, including the **LogIn**, **Student** and **StudentCourse**, are also deleted. The recover

student_id	student_name	gpa	credits	major	schoolYear	email	simage
T77896	Tom Erica	3.95	127	Computer Science	Senior	terica@college.edu	Erica.jpg

FIGURE 9.121 Deleted data in student table.

user_name	pass_word	faculty_id	student_id
terica	excellent	NULL	T77896

FIGURE 9.122 Deleted data in LogIn table.

s_course_id	student_id	course_id	credit	major
1002	T77896	CSC-335	3	CS/IS
1005	T77896	CSC-234A	3	CS/IS
1010	T77896	CSC-439	3	CS/IS
1015	T77896	CSC-432	3	CS/IS
1020	T77896	CSE-439	3	CS/IS
1024	T77896	CSC-333A	3	CS/IS

FIGURE 9.123 Deleted data in StudentCourse table.

order is: First recover the deleted record in the **Student** table since it is a parent table and the **student_id** is a primary key in that table, and then do recovery jobs for other tables.

To recover the student record in the **Student** table, especially for the student image column in the **Student** table, one can use Server Explorer window and just enter a **NULL** to that column. One then performs another updating action by running this project one more time by selecting the image file **Erica.jpg** with the original data items. Then one can do recovery jobs for the other two child tables, **LogIn** and **StudentCourse**, by using the Server Explorer window.

A complete Web-based client project **WebClientSQLUpDt Project** can be found from a folder **ClassDB Projects\Chapter 9\WebClientSQLUpDt Solution** that is under the **Students** folder located on the CRC Press ftp site (refer to Figure 1.2 in Chapter 1).

At this point, we have finished the discussion about how to access and manipulate data against the SQL Server database via ASP.NET Web services.

9.8 CHAPTER SUMMARY

A detailed discussion and analysis about the structure and components of the Web services is provided in this chapter. Unlike the ASP.NET Web applications, in which the user needs to access the Web server through the client browser by sending requests to the server to obtain the desired information, the ASP.NET Web Services provide an automatic way to search, identify and return the desired information required by the user through a set of methods installed in the Web server, and those methods can be accessed by a computer program, not the user, via the Internet. Another important difference between the ASP.NET Web applications and ASP.NET Web services is that the latter do not provide any graphic user interfaces (GUIs) and users need to create those GUIs themselves to access the Web services via the Internet.

One of the most popular databases, SQL Server database, is discussed and used for three example Web service projects:

- **WebServiceSQLSelect**.
- **WebServiceSQLInsert**.
- **WebServiceSQLUpdateDelete**.

Each Web service contains different Web methods that can be used to access different databases and perform the desired data actions such as **Select**, **Insert**, **Update** and **Delete** via the Internet.

To consume those Web services, different Web based client projects are also developed in this chapter. Both Windows-based and Web-based client projects are discussed and built for each kind of Web service listed above. In total, nine projects, including the Web service projects and the associated Web service client projects, are developed in this chapter. All projects have been debugged and tested and can be run in any Windows-compatible operating systems such as Windows XP, Windows 7, and Windows 10.

HOMEWORK

I. True/False Selections

____1. Web services can be considered as a set of methods installed in a Web server and can be called by computer programs installed on the clients through the Internet.
____2. Web services do not require the use of browsers or HTML, and therefore Web services are sometimes called *application services*.
____3. XML is a text-based data storage language and it uses a series of tags to define and store data.
____4. SOAP is an XML-based communication protocol used for communications between different applications. Therefore, SOAP is a platform-dependent and language-dependent protocol.
____5. WSDL is an XML-based language for describing Web services and how to access them. In WSDL terminology, each Web service is defined as an abstract endpoint or a Port and each Web method is defined as an abstract operation.
____6. UDDI is an XML-based directory for businesses to list themselves on the Internet and the goal of this directory is to enable companies to find one another on the Web and make their systems interoperable for e-commerce.
____7. The main service page is the most important file in a Web service since all Visual Basic.NET codes related to build a Web service are located in this page and our major coding development will be concentrated on this page.
____8. The names and identifiers used in the SOAP message can be identical, in other words, those names and identifiers can be the same name and identifier used by any other message.
____9. A single Web service can contain multiple different Web methods.
____10. You do not need to deploy a Web service to the development server if you use that service locally in your computer, but you must deploy it to a production server if you want other users to access your Web service from the Internet.

II. Multiple Choices

1. A Web service is used to effectively ________ the target information required by computer programs.
   a. Find
   b. Find, identify and return
   c. Identify
   d. Return
2. Four fundamental components of a Web service are ________.
   a. IIS, Internet, Client and Server
   b. Endpoint, Port, Operation and types
   c. .asmx, we b.config, .asmx.vb and Web_Reference
   d. XML, SOAP, WSDL and UDDI
3. The XML is used to ________ the data to be transferred between applications.
   a. Tag
   b. Re-build
   c. Receive
   d. Interpreter
4. SOAP is used to __________ the data tagged in the XML format into the messages represented in the SOAP protocol.
   a. Organize
   b. Build
   c. Wrap and pack
   d. Send

5. WSDL is used to map a concrete network protocol and message format to an abstract endpoint, and ________ the Web services available in an WSDL document format.
   a. Illustrate
   b. Describe
   c. Provide
   d. Check
6. UDDI is used to ________ all Web services that are available to users and businesses.
   a. List
   b. Display
   c. Both a and b
   d. None of above
7. Unlike Web-based applications, a Web service project does not provide a ________.
   a. Start Page
   b. Configuration file
   c. Code-behind page
   d. Graphic User Interface
8. Each Web service must be located at a unique ________ in order to allow users to access it.
   a. Computer
   b. Server
   c. SOAP file in a server
   d. Namespace in a server
9. To consume a Web service by either a Windows-based or a Web-based client project, the prerequisite job is to add a _______ into the client project.
   a. Connection
   b. Web Reference
   c. Reference
   d. Proxy class
10. The running result of a Web service is represented by a(n) _______ format since each Web service does not provide a graphic user interface (GUI).
   a. XML
   b. HTTP
   c. HTML
   d. Java scripts

III. Exercises

1. Write a paragraph to answer and explain the following questions:
   a. What is ASP.NET Web service?
   b. What are main components of the ASP.NET Web service?
   c. How an ASP.NET Web service is executed?
2. Suppose we have a Web service project and the main service page contains the following statement:

```
<%@WebServiceLanguage="vb"CodeBehind="~/App_Code/testWeb.vb"Class="testWeb"%>
```

   Answer the following questions:
   a. What is the name of this Web service?
   b. What are the name and the location of the code-behind page of this Web service?
   c. Is the content of this page related to the WSDL file of this Web service?

3. Suppose we have developed a Web service named **WebServiceSelect Project** with a Web method **GetSQLStudent()** that has an input parameter **student_name** and returns seven pieces of student information, such as **student_id, gpa, credits, major, schoolYear, email** and **sImage**. Please list steps to develop a Windows-based client project to consume that Web service.
4. Add the Web method **GetSQLStudent()** in question 3 into our Web service project **WebServiceSelect Project** and develop the codes to that method to perform the data query for the Student via our sample SQL Server database **CSE_DEPT**. The project file can be found from the folder **ClassDB Projects | Chapter 9 | WebServiceSelect Solution** that is under the **Students** folder located at the CRC Press ftp site (refer to Figure 1.2 in Chapter 1). One needs to add a new returned class **SQLStudentResult.cs** to hold all columns retrieved from the **Student** table.
5. Develop a Windows-based client project to consume the Web service developed in question 4, exactly to consume the new Web method **GetSQLStudent()**.

   Hints: One can use project **WinClientSelect Project** that can be found from the folder **ClassDB Projects | Chapter 9 | WinClientSelect Solution** that is under the **Students** folder at the CRC Press ftp site (refer to Figure 1.2 in Chapter 1) and add a **Student Form** window that is located at the **Students | Windows Forms** folder at the CRC Press ftp site. You may need to build the codes for the **Select** button's click method on the **Student** Form window. Set that Student Form as the start form by setting the coding line as: **Application.Run(new SelectWizard_Project. StudentForm());** in the **Program.cs** file. One also needs to re-add service reference since a new method **GetSQLStudent()** has been added into the Web service project.

6. Similar to question 4, add another Web method **GetStudentCourse()** into our Web service project **WebServiceSelect Project** and develop the codes to that method to perform the course query for the selected student via our sample SQL Server database **CSE_DEPT**. The project file can be found from the folder **ClassDB Projects | Chapter 9 | WebServiceSelect Solution** that is under the **Students** folder at CRC Press ftp site (refer to Figure 1.2 in Chapter 1).

   One can use a joined query to perform this course query action inside that Web method (refer to Figure 9.56 in Section 9.4.2.3). That Web method should return a **DataSet** that contains all courses (**course_id**) for the queried student to the client project.

   Also consume that Web method in our client project **WinClientSelect Project** in the **Select** button's click method in the Student Form window. Refer to Figure 9.61 in Section 9.4.2.4 for the codes).

7. Develop a Web-based client project to consume the Web service developed in question 4, exactly to consume the new Web method **GetSQLStudent()**.

   Hints: Refer to project **WebClientSelect Project** which can be found from the folder **Class DB Projects | Chapter 9 | WebClientSelect Solution** that is under the **Students** folder located on the CRC Press ftp site category (refer to Figure 1.2 in Chapter 1). In fact, you need to add three pages, such as **Student.aspx**, **Student.aspx.cs** and **Student.aspx.designer.cs**. One can find those files from a folder **Web Forms** under the **Students** folder at the CRC Press ftp site (refer to Figure 1.2 in Chapter 1). Build the codes in the **Select** button click method in the Student Form in that project to complete this jo b. You may need to update the Web reference to use those new Web methods.

8. Develop and add a Web method **SQLUpdateCourseSP()** in our Web service project **WebServiceUpDt Project** to perform a course updating function. This method will call a stored procedure **dbo. UpdateCourse()** built in homework (Exercise 2) in Chapter 7 to do this course updating action. Test this Web method when it is done and confirm its correctness by checking the **Course** table in our sample database. The service project **WebServiceUpDt Project** can be found from

the folder **ClassDB Projects | Chapter 9** that is under the **Students** folder at the CRC Press ftp site (refer to Figure 1.2 in Chapter 1).

Hint: It is highly recommended to test this Web method in the Web service side to make sure that it is working fine.

9. Create and add new codes in the **Update** button's click method in the Course Form window located at the project **SPUpdateDelete Project** to consume the Web method **SQLUpdateCourseSP()** built in Exercise 8 above. Confirm this updating action by opening our sample database to check the **Course** table. The project **SPUpdateDelete Project** can be found from the folder **Class DB Projects | Chapter 9 | SPUpdateDelete Solution** that is under the **Students** folder on the CRC Press ftp site (refer to Figure 1.2 in Chapter 1). You may need to update the Web reference for this **Update** method.

   Hint: Refer to codes shown in Figure 9.112 in Section 9.6.2 to build the codes for that **Update** button click method.

10. Develop a Web-based project to consume the Web method **SQLUpdateCourseSP()** built in Exercise 8 above.

    Hint 1:One can use the **Update** button's click method in the **Course** page in a Web-based project **WebClientSQLUpDt Project** that can be found from the folder **Class DB Projects | Chapter 9 | WebClientSQLUpDt Solution** under the **Students** folder on the CRC Press ftp site (refer to Figure 1.2 in Chapter 1).

    Hint 2:One needs to add three pages that are related to the Course page, such as **Course.aspx**, **Course.aspx.cs** and **Course.aspx.designer.cs**, into this project. All of those pages can be found from a folder **Web Forms\Chapter 9** under the **Students** folder on the CRC Press ftp site (refer to Figure 1.2 in Chapter 1). You also need to develop some initialization codes to display all faculty members in the **Faculty Name** combobox control and place those codes in the **Page_Load()** method in the **Course** page. You also need to build codes for the **Back** button's click method to close the project. Set the **Course** page as the Start page to test this project.

    Hint 3:You may need to update the Web reference for this project to test it.

    When test this updating action, one needs to enter the updated course information to the related textbox with a selected **course_id.** To confirm this updating, one needs to open the **Course** table in the sample database via Server Explorer.

Index

Pages in *italics* refer to figures.

D

I

J

K

L

M

N

Printed in the United States
by Baker & Taylor Publisher Services